AS IT IS

AS IT IS

A Year on the Road with a Tantric Teacher

M. Young

HOHM PRESS

Cover design: Kim Johansen
Layout and design: Shukyo Lin Rainey
Back cover art: *Vajrakilaya*—painting by Marcus Allsop from a drawing by Robert Beer.

Library of Congress Number: 00-101045

ISBN: 0-934252-99-8

Quoted from E.J. Gold, *Secret Talks Volume VIII: Science of Objective Hypnotism* ©2000 by Gateways Books & Tapes. Reprinted with permission.

HOHM PRESS
P.O. Box 2501
Prescott, AZ 86302
800-381-2700
http://www.hohmpress.com

This book was printed in the U.S.A. on recycled acid-free paper using soy ink.

Dedication

To the eternal stream of wisdom
that arises in the world
through the Grace of God,
appearing now as Lee Lozowick Khepa Baul
and his father, the Godchild of Tiruvannamalai,
Sri Yogi Ramsuratkumar.

CONTENTS

FOREWORD

This book may not be easy to digest; it's long, requiring attention and diligence. It cycles through many moods and will evoke many varied responses and feelings. It will make you want to move, will stir emotions and engage your mind.

The subject of the book, Lee Lozowick, always recommends to his students that when they pick up study materials they engage them fully and read from beginning to end. It is popular in the New Age to look at scripture as a tool of divination or as a daily calendar of inspiration, where one will read paragraphs or pages and then sit and digest the material, going back to the piece randomly. This is in complete contradiction to the way Lee recommends study. If you choose to follow his recommendation, you will read this book from front to back, Foreword, Preface and Introduction included, without interspersing other study materials. That might take a week, a month or two months, depending on your availability of time and willingness to devote yourself to a project of such intensity—for this is a project.

This book is meant to be of value. It is not designed simply to be entertainment. It is not easy reading, although there are parts of it that are delightful, humorous, enjoyable and—dare I say it?—even fun. But it is a project that is meant to be useful, to add something to the body of education, inspiration and—with luck—wisdom that drives you toward accomplishments on the path. It is not meant to create converts, as you'll see if you read diligently. That's the last thing that Lee Lozowick is looking for. But it is meant to serve—to serve you wherever you are, with or without a teacher, with or without refined spiritual skills, with or without clarity of purpose or intention. It's meant to serve you, here and now, as you are, wherever you are on the path.

This book is a profoundly revealing portrait of one man, one teacher—of someone who has not called himself a master in years, but who is accepted as such by his peers in every spiritual and religious tradition that goes to make up the contemporary cultural scene. It is not a whitewashed portrait drawn by a street portraiteer, designed to make the subject of the portrait look satisfying and attractive regardless of how they actually are. It is honest and straightforward. That means that inevitably whoever reads this is going to find some paradox, whether one is a student of a crazy-wise teacher, a student of a more benign and linear path, or simply a student of life, as it is, looking to all beings and all things as one's teacher. One will find in this book extraordinary gifts and extraordinary irritations, but the recommendation is to persist, to read through to the end, as ponderous a tome as this seems, holding it now in your hand and feeling the weight of it—the sheer, daunting size of it.

This book could very well become a classic in the spiritual scene. Lee Lozowick's written works have been a staple of the spiritual underground since the beginning of his teaching work in 1975. They have been debated and cursed, but more than anything else they have been deeply appreciated by those seeking help in traversing the vast, labyrinthian, and often confusing landscape of personal growth, transformation and realization. This book is also of a nature to be easily tossed aside, disregarded as either too long, too obscure or too difficult to be endured. In any case, it is offered for your consideration. Read and be touched as is your inclination.

Paul Zimm,
February 13, 2000
Prescott, Arizona

PREFACE

The spiritual teacher's life is a constant expression of the teaching, making every moment and every day rich with the communication of dharma, often in the smallest and most inconspicuous, ordinary exchanges. Being in close proximity to the teacher and having the opportunity to observe and learn is the way wisdom is transmitted from teacher to disciple; in this way we learn to live in resonance with the great forces that move life. This book is a chronicle of days and moments and teachings during a year of the life of Lee Lozowick, beginning with Lee's journey to visit his spiritual father, Yogi Ramsuratkumar, in southern India, and his subsequent travels with a large group to northern India during November and December 1998. The trip to India set the stage and started the momentum for the next year as Lee traveled within the cultural milieu of the West, in seminars and on tour with his blues band during the summer and early fall in France, Germany and Switzerland.

This book is aimed at presenting a portrayal of Lee Lozowick as he is now, at this time in his teaching work, with his students and friends, with his spiritual father, Yogi Ramsuratkumar. Although the guru's fundamental communication does not change but remains constant, there is the appearance of a process in time that is real. If we look at the lives of the great teachers from many traditions we see that every period of a teacher's life has a particular tone and mood and evolutionary momentum. It is a divinely evolutionary process in which the infinite possibilities of the Divine are made manifest through its messengers and realizers. Yogi Ramsuratkumar and Lee Lozowick are examples of this. Yogi Ramsuratkumar was a mendicant beggar wandering on the streets of India for many years; now he holds court in his temple as a divine beggar king, and yet he remains exactly the same. In Yogi Ramsuratkumar there is an extraordinary and miraculous juxtaposition between the *purusha* (transcendental Self) and the *mahasiddha* (great adept) and the simple old beggar that is his unique communication to his devotees and to the world.

Lee has also gone through a number of metamorphoses over the years. Throughout the text of this book we hear many stories, told by Lee, of different expressions of his fundamental, unchanged, original communication of "Spiritual Slavery." At the same time this book attempts to offer glimpses of the many faces that Lee shows us, as well as glimpses into sadhana in the company of a Western Baul adept. Lee's work with his students has many facets that spring from a source so deep that qualities like compassion, mystery, fire, wrath, humor and madness naturally coexist and mingle to transmit the context of God-realization. The point is that the true guru is the living paradox of divinity realized and alive within a human being. Lee is a rascal and a trickster, a rage against the separative ego, a sharp sword, a shocking unknown. Certainly, like his father Yogi Ramsuratkumar, Lee is also a "liar" and "thief" in the metaphorical terms of Lee's poetry to his master. In the midst of all this we recognize mercy and find ourselves immersed in the nectar of devotional love. Then there are the skillful means of the guru in the process of the annihilation of ego—the stark visage of the mirror that the guru's face, actions, words and gestures can reveal to us without warning. All this is hopefully captured in the stories and *lilas* of this past year on the road with Lee.

The narrative of this book takes a chronological form, flowing through days and months of events. Some of these days are quiet, uneventful and repetitive, while others are action-packed and fast-paced—both have value as ways in which the teaching is transmitted. In many instances I have chosen to allow a point to be made more than once, and in some cases several times, because it brings the reader's attention to the fact of its importance. These recurring patterns and themes within Lee's teaching are of prime importance. As he tells and retells stories, particularly those of his relationship with his father, Yogi Ramsuratkumar, or as dharma points are made over again, the rivers of understanding are carved more deeply within us, and may become the doorway to revelation.

Conversations were captured in hand-written notes scribbled in the moment or written down after the fact. These contain the kernel of Lee's interchanges with his friends and students and do not represent a complete word for word account. The emphasis was always placed on accuracy of mood and communication rather than attempting to catch every sentence that was spoken. Many of Lee's seminar discourses in Europe were also taken from notes, where accurate journalism was made possible due to the time necessary for translating Lee's words from English into French or German. Some of his discourses were taken from actual transcripts of talks or seminars.

As It Is—A Year on the Road with a Tantric Teacher was originally conceived in October 1998, when Lee had just returned from four months in Europe. The group that had traveled with Lee came back to the Arizona ashram with extremely heightened senses, a fervor for the teaching and a burning passion for practice. After this extraordinary summer of teachings and powerful events in Lee's company, I couldn't shake the idea of a book that might somehow capture and communicate Lee's work at this point in his life.

I didn't think it would be possible to capture the kind of detail that would be necessary for what I had in mind without a laptop computer—a piece of equipment I didn't have. Being an ashram resident and a practicing renunciate, I had asked for a laptop before to use for various ongoing writing projects. When the subject had come up on previous occasions Lee had made it clear that he didn't want his students lost in some gray cyberspace zone on a computer (for reasons that will be made clearer in this book). Instead he wanted me to cultivate the ability to write the old-fashioned and much more laborious way, with pen and paper. Having the office computers on the ashrams was already a large concession to his vision of enlightened human culture as far as Lee was concerned.

When I approached Lee about this project he said, "I'll consider it, but first of all you will have to scribe the trip to India by hand *to my satisfaction*. Then, if I'm satisfied with what you've done, you can write up a proposal when we get back from India. If we decide to go ahead with it, I'll get you a laptop for the project." This task was no surprise. Lee had already given me the specific exercise of handwriting extensive chronicles of three summers of his travels in Europe. It was a frustrating, difficult and at times unnerving task for a writer who enjoys the freedom and facility that a computer affords the process of writing, but at the same time it was an invaluable element of my sadhana, for many different reasons.

Coming back from the intensity of the India trip I felt more than a little like Persephone sorting the seeds to get out of the underworld. The whole experience had made a tremendous impact, and I had grave doubts that my journaling in India had hit the mark as Lee envisioned it. Finally in mid-January 1999 the proposal for the book was written and submitted to Lee. The next day the proposal was sitting on my desk with "Let's do it" written across the front in the bold strokes of Lee's pen. The laptop didn't arrive until late March.

Right away Lee said, "I want the book published in the spring of 2000. It should be out by early June." The "year on the road" wouldn't end until Lee left for India in late November 1999, which meant that an immense amount of work would have to be done in a short time in order to meet the publishing deadline. Furthermore, it was obvious by mid-summer that it would be a rather lengthy book, even though it only recounts a part of Lee's teaching work during a year. It would simply have to be done in the usual Hohm Community style—fast and furious. These projects that Lee gives his students—rock and blues bands that tour Europe and produce prodigious amounts of original music, or huge publishing efforts and immense tomes on the dharma—are possible because the guru makes them possible. It is Lee's boundless and joyful enthusiasm for the work of spiritual transformation that feeds the tasks that we quite willingly undertake.

My deepest gratitude and *pranam* goes to Lee Lozowick for his incredible patience and unending blessings in supporting and upholding this project. It is his habit to make himself available to his students with a tremendous and at times mystifying generosity. He is a man with virtually no private life. He lives entirely for the teaching and what he calls, "the Work of my Father, Yogi Ramsuratkumar." He maintains a superhuman load of responsibility and obligation and manages it flawlessly. He contributed effortlessly to the book through many inspired discourses, as well as in editing and guiding the process of writing along the way. I am profoundly grateful for his ongoing feedback and direction, especially for the times when it was hardest to swallow.

Many thanks are due to the friends, students, devotees and disciples of Lee Lozowick for their participation as players in the game of sadhana, and also for cheering the project on, transcribing tapes and proofreading the manuscript. I am compelled to express my appreciation to members of the sangha for the inspiration of their lives, and for their enthusiasm and willingness to be vulnerable as characters reported in the ongoing process of sadhana with a tantric teacher. Many of the teaching lessons made by Lee and recounted in this book expose our flaws and help us to lose face—a necessary element of the transformational process.

I would particularly like to thank Arnaud Desjardins, Andrew Cohen, Llewellyn Vaughan-Lee, Jakusho Kwong Roshi, John and Gerry Mann, Deben and Janna Bhattacharya, Garchen Triptrul Rinpoche, Philippe Coupey, Hirendra Singh, N.S. Subramanian, and Jacques and Christina Castermane, who appear in this book in conversations and events with Lee.

And finally, the bare truth is that whatever in this book is useful is due entirely to the influence and wisdom of my teacher, Lee Lozowick, and whatever is not is entirely due to my own lack of clarity. May this work benefit all beings. Jai Guru!

M. Young
January 10, 2000
Prescott, Arizona

INTRODUCTION

This is a book about a Western Baul teacher. His name is Lee Lozowick, and his teaching function arose spontaneously in 1975 on the East Coast of the United States. A year later Lee met and began a relationship with his spiritual father, Sri Yogi Ramsuratkumar, in Tiruvannamalai, India. Within the next five years Lee realized that the influence and Grace of Yogi Ramsuratkumar had been the direct source of a revolutionary experience in which his life and consciousness were radically surrendered to the living God in what Lee called "Spiritual Slavery." It was this event that catapulted Lee into the role of guru.

That was twenty-five years ago. Today Lee is a teacher of some infamy, one could say, because in most spiritual circles his reputation precedes him. He has been described by different authors, critics and biographers as a divine fool, a charlatan, a genuine teacher of the crazy-wisdom and divine madness vein, and a rock & roll guru. His own spiritual father, Yogi Ramsuratkumar, has called him an "Indian saint," and a "great English poet." He is by far one of the most enigmatic figures in the spiritual culture of the world today.

Lee Lozowick has two ashrams, one in Arizona and one in France, where he divides his time, spending one third of the year in Europe. He spends these four months traveling and lecturing in seminars and public talks. In the U.S. he rarely ventures outside his ashram except to perform, almost every weekend, at band gigs with his blues band, Shri.

He is especially known for the poetry and music that he has produced in the past twenty years. In 1985 he stated that his tradition and teaching was a Western Baul Way. "If they ask what we are," he said, "tell them we're Bauls." There is a great deal that can be said of the Bauls that goes far beyond the scope of this introduction, but to provide a context for the teachings and teaching style of Lee Lozowick, we must turn momentarily toward this unusual tradition. The Bauls of Bengal are a five hundred-year-old sect of ecstatic singers, love-maddened poets and wandering heretic *tantrikas* who have sprung out of the particular rich heritage of the folk tradition of rural Bengal. The Bauls as a religious sect have attracted a great deal of attention from ethnographers, musicologists and students of comparative religions because of their unique blend of tantric Sahajiya Buddhism and devotional Vaishnava Hinduism with music, dance and transformational yogas of sexual energy and breath to form *kaya sadhana*, or the path to God-realization through the body.

The tradition of the Bauls of Bengal has grown out of the soil and customs and myths of their place on the Earth; their ideal is to live from an authentic and original impulse that is called *sahaja* (innate) in the Sanskrit language. The *sahaja* principle might be summed up in Lee's words, "We have to relax into the natural state in which the Divine, which is evolutionary, is free to live through us." This impulse takes the true Baul on the *ulta* or reverse path; it is a path that leads in the opposite direction of the rest of the world, or directly against the mainstream current:

> [The Bauls] avoid all religion in which the natural piety of the soul is overshadowed by the useless paraphernalia of ritualism and ceremony on the one hand and pedantry and hypocrisy on the other. It is said in a beautiful song—
>
> "Reverse are the modes and manners of the man who is a real appreciator of the true

behavior.

"Such a man is affected neither by the weal nor by the woe of the world, and constantly realises the delight of love; it appears that his eyes are floating on the water of delight; sometimes he laughs alone in his own mood, sometimes he cries alone.

"Awkwardly wild are all his manners and customs—and the other extremely wonderful fact is that the glory of the full-moon [Krishna] closes round him for all time; and further . . . there is no setting of the moon of his heart . . . ." (Das Gupta, 162-63)

The Bauls are lovers of God who revel in the bittersweetness of longing, or divine love in separation, which builds to create an inner fire of such transformational potency that the heart is consumed in the conflagration. It is a fire that burns within the human body and melds disparate aspects of body, mind and psyche together in a unity of being. This burning inner life of the Baul is found in his or her poetry, song, dance and begging, and it is through these activities that this sublime tradition of relationship to the personal Beloved is transmitted.

The Bauls are tremendously popular with the common people of Bengal, not only for the delight of their song and dance, but also because they are champions of humankind. They bring lofty philosophical principles into the reality of ordinary living and make the spiritual path accessible to everyone, regardless of caste, sex or race. Their songs, written in the style of vernacular speech, bring inspiration and instruction for living according to divine principles to the daily grind of village life.

Less than a year after Lee announced that his path was a Baul path the rock music began to appear. In 1986 Lee's Living God Blues band performed for the first time at a local tavern in Prescott, Arizona. In 1987 the band metamorphosed into a serious experiment in producing original Western Baul music through the medium of rock & roll. In the next two years the band evolved into liars, gods & beggars, a rock band that produced thirteen CDs and albums of all original music—lyrics written by Lee Lozowick—and made numerous performing tours around the U.S. and Europe. In 1993 Lee started a blues band called Shri, originally made up primarily of women. Shri tours every year in Europe with Lee and has produced five albums of music so far.

Lee considers his path a tantric path, but he is quick to fiercely criticize the New Age flavor of what is called "tantra" in the West. A self-proclaimed "arrogant Fool" and "wild Heretic," Lee's teaching style is often one of provocation and shock. True to his Baul forebears, Lee Lozowick continually confronts the illusions of ego that are tied up in countless golden calves that appear along the way on the spiritual path. As Purna Steinitz once said, "We need to be insulted until we get it." On the other hand, Lee regales his audiences with a bawdy, hilarious sense of humor while giving pristine discourses on the dharma. At still other times he is a captivating storyteller. Couched within his particular form of skillful means, story becomes path. It takes one along a road in which the dharma becomes a living, breathing reality and myth is lifted into a vivid experience of its essence. He leads his students and audiences through a labyrinth of self-examination and insight that can be disconcerting and ruinous to ego, but tremendously fruitful for the serious practitioner on the path.

Lee can demonstrate extraordinary elegance, generosity and kindness when this serves what he calls "the Work"—a term he borrows from G.I. Gurdjieff and uses frequently—but he does not capitulate to the conventional point of view. His behavior can be extremely irritating. He may appear angry, irascible, self-deprecating, ruthless and crude, and then within moments become noble, tender and sublime. The invocation of divine moods is a common experience in his presence. And yet, within the kaleidoscopic ways and means of his communication, Lee Lozowick remains constantly the same. Underlying all this is the freedom of one who has gone beyond the appearance of phenomena. It is in this paradoxical way that he embodies the Baul spirit most visibly.

The madness that Lee exhibits is come by honestly, inherited from his father, Yogi Ramsuratkumar, who refers to himself as a "dirty sinner" and a "beggar," but whose communication of the Divine is so compelling and luminous that he was taken by his devotees out of a life of mendicant begging on the streets to a large, thriving ashram in Tiruvannamalai, where hundreds of thousands come each year to receive his darshan. With his father, Yogi Ramsuratkumar, Lee is an exemplary and obedient disciple. This demonstration of genuine guru yoga, or the fruition of the traditional guru/devotee relationship, is one of the gifts that Lee gives to the Western world.

Sri Anirvan, a Baul whose writings have touched the West in his book, *Letters from a Baul,* once wrote about a Baul master named Khepa Baba, "whose hair was matted but the knots of the heart were untied." Khepa Baba was known for his contrary ways, his fierceness and his divine madness, which served as the outer form of his teaching.

> Once upon a time Khepa Baba was in Benaras in the middle of a crowd of people who kept looking at him without daring to approach, for if anyone bothered him, he would brandish his stick and hurl insults. One daring woman came towards him moaning, "Oh Maharaj, have pity on me."
>
> "Daughter of a whore!" Khepa Baba shouted at her. "Come here and I will rape you in the street in front of everyone!" She fled!
>
> Khepa Baba had a jug full of wine in front of him. He calmly drank it down to the last drop without saying a word. The people were stupefied at this impious act, not understanding what was going on, but his disciples noticed that he had become white like Shiva; his body radiated light, Khepa Baba was in ecstasy.
>
> With his immense power and his heart of pure gold, Khepa Baba spread almost insurmountable obstacles around him and created dangerous reefs, thus provoking deep disturbances in all those living near him . . . . Khepa Baba did all this in his uncouth way, for he himself was beyond good and evil. He provoked people into constantly facing themselves. (Sri Anirvan, p. 118)

The actions of a *khepa* (transliterated from *ksepa*)—one who is subsumed in a mad love for God—are impossible to decipher from a worldly point of view. To relate with such a being one must realize that the transmission of truth is not a linear or rational thing, and real help comes in the form of a divine madness. June McDaniel writes, "The outside world sees the mad saint (*ksepa*) quite differently than do his disciples who understand his actions. There is a discrepancy between the public image, which is hostile and irrational, and the private self-image, which is that of an ideal devotee. The traditional image of the holy man is a controlled yogi, peaceful and strong, while the mad saint or Baul is wildly enthusiastic, passionate toward God, and erratic toward his fellow men." (McDaniel, p. 159)

This same response is not uncommon in relation to another *Khepa* Baul, Lee Lozowick. An editor of a prominent New Age magazine commented in a December 1999 correspondence that upon reading the most recent issue of *Tawagoto,* the journal of the Hohm Community, he found it discordant. He further commented that based on the stories that were relayed in the journal, Lee seemed to him to be angry, rude and abusive to his students. These reactions and opinions were very interesting, as we will see, in view of a prophetic teaching communication that Lee made over bridge on September 27, 1999 at La Ferme de Jutreau in which he appeared particularly untamed and apparently wrathful.

Westerners have no frame of reference from which to gauge such a teaching coming from such a teacher. Many Westerners who consider themselves "on the path" have at least heard of crazy wisdom thanks to the work of Chögyam Trungpa Rinpoche and Tibetan Buddhism, and may even speak of it with a blithe or chilly intellectual cast. But to encounter authentic crazy wisdom—much less interact with it—is another matter altogether. To do so requires a vast and audacious leap beyond the flat and conventional way of seeing the world into subtle and even magical realms that puzzle, shock and frighten most people. These are realms of reality that science and technology and the profit motive have ripped away from us, beginning in the cradle with the first cold denial of the infant's acute ability to feel and perceive.

This book will require the reader to take some necessary leaps into the unknown. It is full of wisdom and madness and magic and multidimensional realities, often discovered within the theatre of the ordinary. These mysteries are medicine for the soulless and Godless times in which we live. They are the realities that every original culture of human beings that has arisen on this planet—from Celts to Greeks to African people of the bush, to the Dravidians of ancient pre-Vedic India, the Mayans or the Oglala Sioux—have known to be true. These are the realities that are encoded into the religious mythology, fairytales and wisdom stories of all peoples of the Earth. The return of true magic in the form of suprarational wisdom is the medicine that will bring humanity back from the brink of self-destruction; perhaps for this reason alone we should attempt to embrace its messengers in these dark and murky times.

The Baul tradition has miraculously seeded itself in the West in the extraordinary way that the Bauls always arise—as a surprise, an epiphany, an organic burst of awakened life, a spontaneous expression of divine evolution. This evolution takes the form of a Baul master, Lee Lozowick, whose message is revealed in many discourses and spontaneous interactions with students that are threaded through the labyrinth of this book. The West urgently needs the Baul way of seeing and living, which is the way of the heart and the wise body. It is the way of *sahaja*, or the natural, innate wisdom that is the blueprint from which every human being springs. The Western Baul gift to the world is a return to sacred culture, to the direct perception of the heart on fire, to the burning awareness of the living God within the cellular reaches of the body. It is a constant paean of praise to the human possibility in relation to the Divine, which may be discovered through *kaya sadhana*—and which turns each individual back in upon himself or herself to discover, with the help of the guru, the truth that slumbers within the human matrix.

AS IT IS

A Year on the Road with a Tantric Teacher

November 21, 1998
Arizona Ashram

The excitement was like a live wire vibrating in the atmosphere. People moved around the ashram, each busy with countless tasks as they hustled up and down stairs or walked through the office or under bare cottonwood trees across the dry ashram grounds. The chilly November air accentuated the pungent scent of cedar and juniper, while tall, stately Ponderosa pines stood guard at the foothills that ring this desert ashram, virtually hidden away on the edge of a small town in the Arizona mountains. The Appearance Day Celebration, one of three major celebrations held each year in the Hohm Community, was underway—a kaleidoscopic series of whirlwind events packed into four intense days of rousing dharma talks, abundant meals and feasts, short vignettes of homespun theatre, the live music of the Baul bands and the enjoyment of good company. One hundred sangha members of this little-known and somewhat recondite spiritual school have gathered here to celebrate in this way the appearance of the guru on November 18, the birthday of our teacher, Lee Lozowick. But more than anything else, this year the excitement was centered around the fact that in less than two days Lee would depart for India to visit his spiritual father, Sri Yogi Ramsuratkumar, for his eightieth *jayanthi*, or birthday, taking with him a group of students who would embark together on a journey of great possibility. The way the India trip was shaping up it promised to be a significant episode in the history of the Hohm Community.

Lee's trips to India over the past twenty-five years have become legendary, almost mythical events. Each trip has its own unique mood and stories, most of them centered around the old beggar saint, Yogi Ramsuratkumar. Every year for the past twelve years Lee has visited Yogi Ramsuratkumar in southern India during the time of his jayanthi for two or three weeks. Taking a small group of ten or fifteen students with him, Lee makes the long trip to India to literally sit at Yogi Ramsuratkumar's feet; he doesn't leave Tiruvannamalai for even a day. But this year Lee has a special dispensation from Yogi Ramsuratkumar to travel to Banaras (Varanasi) and Rishikesh for two weeks after his usual stay in Tiruvannamalai at the Yogi Ramsuratkumar Ashram. Lee's long-time student Purna Steinitz, who began teaching almost a year ago, will meet Lee in India with a group of fifteen of his own students to make a total of thirty-five people on the trip. It will be the biggest group of students that Lee has ever traveled with in India, and the first time he has traveled in northern India since 1986.

Without question the highlight of the trips to India with Lee has been having the opportunity to see Lee and Yogi Ramsuratkumar together. This year Lee will bring a particularly important gift for Yogi Ramsuratkumar—the new, hardback compilation of Lee's poetry written to Yogi Ramsuratkumar, *Death of a Dishonest Man,* an impressive volume of over one thousand pages and six hundred poems. Most of these had previously been published in India at Yogi Ramsuratkumar's request by his devotees in two paperback volumes, titled *Poems of a Broken Heart, Part I* and *Part II*. Yogi Ramsuratkumar had no idea that this new volume had been published. It included not only all the published poems but also many new ones, along with essays written by some of Lee's friends and peers as well as his students. The volume also contained lyrics from over thirty of Lee's songs, written and composed for liars, gods & beggars or Shri, the two community bands. It was a significant and weighty gift, literally and symbolically, from disciple to master.

All of these unusual circumstances gave the impending journey the potential to revolutionize one's relationship to life in unforeseen ways. The anticipation was building to a high peak, and included some healthy trepidation. It was clear, given the unusual circumstances of the large, unwieldy group and the additional traveling in northern India, that the trip would be a pressure cooker. Traveling with Lee is always a radical undertaking of intense sadhana that involves a high demand to practice. Many different elements and stresses of traveling with the teacher combine to produce a certain alchemy that often brings one's weaknesses of practice into the scalding light of scrutiny. Lee's final words of advice last week to a small number of his students who are going on this year's trip with him had been, "Everything Yogi Ramsuratkumar does will be an empowerment." His tone was confident and glad. "Stick together, work as a team. Remember—we are in this together. Don't snap at each other and don't get annoyed with each others' behavior or mechanicality."

At eight o'clock tonight Lee sat on the men's side of the meditation hall at the ashram, leaning against the wall near the front of the room. He seemed deeply absorbed as Fleet Maull's words reverberated in the space like well-aimed arrows hitting the mark. A long-time disciple of Chögyam Trungpa Rinpoche, Fleet was giving a talk about the Vajrayana path to the sangha via telephone, speaking from prison. His voice came over a speakerphone that had been set up in the meditation hall for the Celebration. About fifty people were gathered in the hall, listening intently. Now he answered a question about doubt, saying, "Doubt is a springboard to further devotion, even to profound devotion. Let it sit with your practice and be a part of it. Sitting with doubt allows it to reveal what comes next . . ."

Fleet spoke about the powerful presence of Chögyam Trungpa Rinpoche in his life. He said that his guru was with him still today, twenty-four hours a day, day after day, even ten years after Rinpoche's death in 1987. Fleet had spent those ten years in prison on a cocaine indictment, but he turned the ordeal of incarceration into an extraordinary opportunity for sadhana, spending the time meditating, studying and serving others through a hospice project that he established within the prison.

Someone asked Fleet a question about the change in the guru's presence after he has died. He responded, "After the guru's death, the vividness of incarnation—and all the magic of that in your world—*is* the heart and presence of the guru. There is no separation between the guru and the tremendous beauty and vividness in life. This sense of vividness and presence only gets stronger, becomes more vivid and more stable as you go along." His answer seemed particularly poignant because Yogi Ramsuratkumar's health has been precarious for years. No one knows how long he will stay in the body, making the unknown of his death a constant question for his devotees. This too was another reminder of Lee's coming visit with Yogi Ramsuratkumar.

The effect of Fleet's inspiring talk was not unlike throwing gasoline on the fire of our enthusiasm for spiritual life. This infusion of high spirits combined with the excitement in the air about the imminent India trip, which was made even more vibrant by an extraordinary occurrence that happened after the talk. Leaving the meditation hall at nine o'clock I went to my mailbox to check it one last time before leaving for India, tonight being Saturday and the last possible day that mail would be delivered before we would leave for India early Monday morning before dawn. To my great surprise there was a letter from the editor of *Om Sri Ram*, the newsletter of the Swami Papa Ramdas organization in the States, along with a copy of their latest issue. The letter thanked me for my "interesting" article about Yogi Ramsuratkumar and offered their congratulations that it had finally been published in this newest issue of their newsletter.

Holding the newsletter in my hands I stared at it incredulously, astonished by this turn of events. *Om Sri Ram* had had this article in their files for at least three years or more without printing it, and in fact I had given up on it being published by them. Even Lee Lozowick, who is usually a bulwark of optimism, said about six months ago, "Forget about that article you sent to *Om Sri Ram*. They're not going to publish it." To discover now, at the eleventh hour before taking off for India, that it had been published and made available at this moment in time verged on the miraculous.

For the past several years Lee has asked me to write and submit articles about Yogi Ramsuratkumar to various publications. Three or four have been published here and there, and it seems to give Lee pleasure to take these to Yogi Ramsuratkumar as tangible demonstrations of Yogi Ramsuratkumar's blessings and spiritual influence in the West. Now Lee could offer this issue of *Om Sri Ram* as a gift at Yogi Ramsuratkumar's feet in a few days, a small addition to *Death of a Dishonest Man*. The offering was made even sweeter by the fact that the article had been published by the American organization of Swami Papa Ramdas, who was the spiritual father of Yogi Ramsuratkumar.

But what was most stunning about it was that I held in my hands a concrete manifestation of the power of divine influence to enact the *kheyala* of Yogi Ramsuratkumar. Clearly his blessing force was at work to create such a synchronicity. It seemed that the trip had already begun. When I handed Lee the letter moments later he said, "Oh great!" as if he had been expecting it all along. There was not a tinge of surprise in his voice. Instantly the newsletter disappeared into his hand. One moment it was there, the next moment it wasn't. It was as if he had consumed it totally in that one instant. Obviously it wasn't mine in any way, but his and his alone, and he would handle it from there.

November 24, 1998
En Route

The group was en route perhaps an hour or two away from Kuala Lumpur where we would have an eighteen hour layover, rest, play bridge, eat and play with the children. Before leaving Kuala Lumpur the women would change into their saris and the men into their *kirtas* and pajamas in preparation for landing in India.

During the long hours of the flight Lee has read, slept and eaten lightly from the dried fruit and seed and nut bars in his backpack. He typically avoids airplane food at all costs whenever he travels, and has a very specific way in which he manages his rest and sleep. As a result, he has no extra down time due to jet lag once he arrives at his destination; he "hits the ground running," so to speak.

The ordinariness around Lee is at times a solid cloak. At these times it takes a shift of vision to penetrate the veils of the mundane and receive the constant teaching communication that he makes. But in the stale air of the airplane, hours into the tedious flight, the presence of Yogi Ramsuratkumar was all around us like an invisible fire in the air. It seemed that Yogi Ramsuratkumar loomed very large around Lee, like a vast field of self-existing, luminous consciousness through which his son Lee was drawn like a magnet to his side.

Lee seemed absorbed in this—a silent dwelling in the invisible field of Grace that permeated everything. It was this presence that seemed now to be the matrix and life and ground of all things as the reality of landing in India, of seeing Yogi Ramsuratkumar, of being on the holy ground of his ashram came into focus, becoming perceptibly bright, distinct and real.

The group was very calm and soft during these two days of travel, bearing the discomforts with no complaint. Moments of doubt or fear passed through the corridors of the mind along with moments of clarity and inspiration as people moved around Lee in their orbits like barely formed and cooling planets circling the blazing sphere of an ancient star. In moments like these, the tacit truth of the relationship between guru and devotee becomes apparent. All of the struggles of ego, the clutching and grasping at positions and proximity to the teacher, the desperate belief that one can get more from him through such posturing, seem absurd, meaningless. The relationship of guru and disciple is a timeless reality that simply already *is*; it exists as an eternal facet of God's creation. The relationship between Lee Lozowick and Yogi Ramsuratkumar is the primary example, and moving toward their physical reunion brought all this more clearly into focus. To sit at their feet for the next two weeks, witness their *lila* and receive the divine plenitude of Yogi Ramsuratkumar's blessings is the gift that Lee bestows with incredible kindness and generosity on his grateful students. At the same time, having the opportunity to sit in the physical company of Yogi Ramsuratkumar and Lee Lozowick is entirely the blessing of Yogi Ramsuratkumar.

November 26, 1998
Yogi Ramsuratkumar Ashram

As soon as Lee and the group stepped out of the Chennai (Madras) airport the familiar pungent, smoky smell of dung fires and diesel fumes shouted—India! Climbing into the van with Lee and crammed in together with bags and backpacks piled up all around, we drove through the middle of the night from Chennai past waste-strewn streets, poverty-stricken villages, bus stops and tea stalls with small, flickering flames of fire licking the darkness here and there. Along the way people slept on the ground, on benches or on mats placed on bare earth. Everywhere on the sides of the road slept the ubiquitous cows of Mother India, some of them with horns painted blue or yellow with decorative bells hanging down.

The driver took a short detour down through a side street, into water two feet deep—a drainage ditch or a muddy, polluted stream—where huge slabs of concrete were broken and up-ended. This was the beginning of the short cut to Tiruvannamalai. The van crashed and bumbled and churned, motor screeching with the effort, through the dirty water. Finally leaving behind the endless urban expanse of Chennai and its environs we began to drive through green countryside, where the roads were lined with huge trees marked with black and white stripes. An occasional cart pulled by cows or bullocks passed with a peasant, head wrapped turban style, driving perhaps to market in these predawn hours.

The van driver put on a tape of modern *bhajans* and Lee began to dance in his seat, drumming on his knees, on the window, on the door. India's magic was working on us, but one got the sense that his excitement had to do with one person only—Yogi Ramsuratkumar.

"Forty kilometers!" Lee announced happily to the van at large, his body communicating an invisible smile, a song of joy shouting in silent sounds. He kept us all informed as the van moved down the road, saying, "Twenty-five kilometers!" and "Twenty kilometers!" His excitement was infectious. Soon he would be back on his father's ashram, on holy ground, under Mount Arunachala, in the arms of his master and Mother India. In only hours now he would see Yogi Ramsuratkumar again, in the flesh.

As we came into Tiruvannamalai the huge Arunachalesvara Temple emerged from the darkness. It was decorated with lights for Deepam, the Shiva festival of light coming in a week, the day after Yogi Ramsuratkumar's *jayanthi* on December first. The van drove through the streets past shops, carts, a lone straggler here or there. Overhead the stars were shining down on India. Only blocks away at Sudama House Yogi Ramsuratkumar slept, or rested, or prayed or simply emanated blessings to the world. The children were all awake now. Everyone in the van watched the scenery in high anticipation as Ramanashram appeared in view. Several people remembered past trips and times of staying there with Lee.

Only a few more blocks to the sign, "Way To Yogi Ramsuratkumar Ashram," with a big arrow pointing left. A left turn, down residential streets lined with trees, palms, flowering shrubs, trash and sleeping beggars. I remembered walking down from Sudama House five years ago through these streets with Lee. We had walked to Ramanashram from intimate dinners with Yogi Ramsuratkumar, Devaki Ma and the Sudama sisters, holding the *prasad* he had given to each of us, eating it as we walked.

Turning right down another lane the van stopped perhaps twenty feet from the ashram gate with two cars ahead of us, one with Alain DeRosenbo and Dan in it. "Let me out! Let me out!" Lee said loudly, emphatically, urgently. Surrounded by his students who didn't move fast enough—the usual slow response time that irks Lee so frequently—he repeated, "Let me out!" Louder this time, impatient. Finally there was movement and immediately Lee was out the door. He whipped his sandals from his feet and was instantly mobilized, striding onto the ashram. The guard at the gate *pranamed* to Lee as he approached. Once inside the gate Lee walked briskly down the lane to the dining hall and turned right to go toward the cottages. He stopped to greet Bret, an American who has lived in India for many years. He was a devotee of Amritananda Mayi for a long time, and now lived in Tiruvannamalai. Bret immediately placed a large, beautiful flower *mala* around Lee's neck then went into a full body prostration on the ground at Lee's feet. Lee stood quietly in a rare moment of allowing this demonstration of devotion and respect.

Mani, the ashram manager and Yogi Ramsuratkumar's "right hand," approached, *pranamed* respectfully and Lee quickly pulled him into a hearty and warm embrace. A woman in a white sari walked up and *pranamed* to Lee. As the group caught up with Lee everyone was quickly shown to the cottages by Mani. Lee decided how the group would divide and who would stay where. It was four-thirty in the morning and we had arrived at our destination.

Coffee was brought by the kitchen staff and everyone began to settle in. Lee walked with the children across the ashram, their bare feet padding on the sandy reddish earth. The night seemed unusually quiet under a black sky studded with bright stars. There were beautiful flowering shrubs everywhere. The children asked questions about the ashram and Lee answered. They stopped to smell the flowers—huge yellow jasmine and small red hibiscus with delicate green and white variegated leaves. It was beautiful, peaceful, still. The strains of Indian music, *bhajans*, drifted on the night air from the kitchen as

5

the staff prepared the first meal of the day.

In the fenced, green grassy yard around the cottages was a small spotted deer with a bell around her neck. The deer made this charmed and lovely sanctuary even more reminiscent of Vrindavan, of Krishna's loving pastimes with the *gopis*. At six o'clock Lee sat inside his cottage reading. Then he said, "I'm going outside to watch the dawn come," and walked out on the small porch. It had seemed like an endless night to weary travelers, as if this night would last forever, but as soon as the door opened and I stepped outside into the dawn light the sight of Arunachala appeared. It rose green and high, with outcroppings of rock dotting its flanks.

Arunachala, the holy hill. So close, so incredibly close! It seemed that one could reach out and touch it. Instantly the moments of doubt and free-floating angst on the long, fifty-two hour trip through various bardo realms between Arizona and India dissolved like night wraiths in the morning sun. As soon as Lee sat down on the porch small black crows appeared on the telephone wires near the cottage, directly in his view of Arunachala. As the light grew stronger birds began to sing and call and trill all around—swallowtails and more exotic birds, unfamiliar and foreign and yet completely of the same essence of all birds everywhere. The full day was born.

Lee sat on the steps, gazing up at the mountain. He looked extraordinarily real, poised with a waiting expectancy, yet complete and full in the moment. In one hour Yogi Ramsuratkumar would appear in his car, drive through the gate and onto the ashram grounds on his way to breakfast. We would all line up with Lee and the Indian devotees and receive his darshan, some of Lee's group for the first time and some of us once again. The little musk deer grazed nearby. The bell around her neck tinkled gently as Lee sat on the porch waiting. His mood was quiet, serene, strong, surrendered.

At ten minutes before seven o'clock Lee's group lined up with the other devotees at the gate to the ashram, the men first, then the women. A mist floated across Arunachala in the early morning sun while we chanted, "Yogi Ramsuratkumar, Yogi Ramsuratkumar, Yogi Ramsuratkumar, Jaya Guru Raya." The ashram was beautiful with lush green palm trees lining the drive where Yogi Ramsuratkumar's car would pass on its way to the small hut where he always eats breakfast. Everyone craned his or her neck to watch the potholed road leading away from the ashram. Finally the car came chugging along, and slowed to about three miles an hour as it reached the gate. As it rolled past we could see Yogi Ramsuratkumar sitting in the back seat with Devaki Ma and Vijayalakshmi, his attendants. His hand was raised in a gesture of blessing. He seemed to look each person directly in the eye as he passed, but at the same time one couldn't really look back in the same way one would with any other person. Instead it was as if he was too radiant, too sublime to look upon directly for very long. His eyes were unfathomably deep and almost misted over; they seemed heavy with compassion and the weight of the world, but at the same time focused somewhere far beyond.

Lee stood at the front of the line with the men, his palms pressed together in a *pranam*—a traditional Indian salutation, or gesture of grave respect. His eyes never left Yogi Ramsuratkumar as the car moved slowly down the drive. There was no visible greeting or personal recognition from Yogi Ramsuratkumar to Lee, or at least none that was discernable to anyone other than Lee. It all went on as if Lee stood there every morning to greet Yogi Ramsuratkumar.

When the car was parked the driver and Mani helped Yogi Ramsuratkumar get out and walk into the hut. He leaned on their strong arms, his attendants walking behind him. As soon as his form disappeared into the building the devotees began to circumambulate the ashram grounds, chanting. Most of Lee's students followed suit, but Lee went to sit under the thatched roof of the hut nearest the ashram gate. There he waited until Yogi Ramsuratkumar was ready to leave, when the line formed again to make salutations to him as the car drove slowly past. This time Yogi Ramsuratkumar kept his hands together in a *pranam* as he gazed at people while the car passed by. Sometimes he would notice someone and his hands would go up in an instinctive response of blessing.

The day unfolded in many directions. After the breakfast drive-by ritual Yogi Ramsuratkumar returned for the first darshan at ten o'clock. About fifty people were lined up to greet him as his car drove past again and he settled in the temple. Lee was asked to stand at the front of the line of devotees, who then walked into the temple one by one to circumambulate the more than life-sized statue of Yogi Ramsuratkumar. Yogi Ramsuratkumar himself sat only ten feet away in a rickety old chair. After circumambulating the statue we filed one by one in front of Yogi Ramsuratkumar, *pranamed* and received his blessings. Devaki Ma and Vijayalakshmi sat chanting under a small grass hut to his left.

Lee circumambulated the statue and then lowered his body into a full-length prostration on the dirt floor of the temple in front of Yogi Ramsuratkumar. Again there was no demonstration of a personal relationship, no greeting between spiritual father and son. It was unnecessary, and obviously not expected or wanted by Lee. Instead it was a formal and impersonal ritual. In these acts alone were many levels of teaching—Lee is never separate from Yogi Ramsuratkumar, so why would there be any display of separation?

Lee got up, *pranamed* and walked into the dining hall for darshan. The rest of the line followed, completing the ritual. Soon Lee's party and the Indian devotees were all in the dining hall where darshan would be held. Everyone chanted and waited for Yogi Ramsuratkumar to enter with Devaki Ma and Vijayalakshmi.

Yogi Ramsuratkumar's darshan is arranged with men seated on the left side and women on the right side of the room, on the floor facing the dais where he sits. On the occasion of this first darshan Lee's women students went into the hall and sat on the women's side, seven or eight rows back. Lee and his men students had been at the front of the entire line, but Lee had taken a seat several rows back from the front of the room when he entered the dining hall for darshan. One of Yogi Ramsuratkumar's attendants came in and asked Lee to sit in the front row. He moved with his men students to the place that had been indicated, taking up most of the first two rows on the men's side of the room.

Soon Yogi Ramsuratkumar came into the room, leaning into Mani's arm. He walked very slowly, looking this way and that at devotees on each side of the room. He was wearing a wrinkled dhoti that came down to his ankles, a long-sleeved *kirta* and three voluminous shawls. Hidden beneath his long white beard and in the folds of his shawls were five or six *malas* or necklaces of prayer beads that hung around his neck. Some of them were *rudraksh*, some sandalwood, some crystal. A rolled and twisted green cloth was wrapped many times around his forehead; it held his long hair back from his face. He ambled forward in the slow gait of a very old man and slowly, carefully settled on the dais. It seemed that every physical movement was difficult for him, as if he was bearing tremendous pain, and yet his face was beautiful and sublime. Despite his years and the ravaging effects of a very hard life, he exuded a wholeness and brightness.

Devaki Ma and Vijayalakshmi followed behind him carrying several bags full of things that Yogi Ramsuratkumar might need during the darshan. Devaki carried his palmyra fan and coconut bowl. They walked up to the left of the dais, where they stood waiting for Yogi Ramsuratkumar to indicate where they should sit. He glanced at them and gestured for them to sit to the dais on his right and adjacent to him. As soon as they were settled Yogi Ramsuratkumar greeted some of his Indian devotees who were invited to come up to the dais. He gave them *prasad* and talked very briefly with them. Soon he gestured for Lee to come to him. Lee jumped up, ran to the dais, went to his knees in a deep bow and pressed his hands together in a *pranam*. Yogi Ramsuratkumar put his hands on either side of Lee's hands and held them in his as he spoke quietly to Lee. It was impossible to hear what was said, but immediately Lee and a small group of men—Alain DeRosenbo, Bret and Krishna Carcelle—moved to sit in the same place Yogi Ramsuratkumar has had them sit for the past several years when Lee has visited, in chairs along the side wall to Yogi Ramsuratkumar's right.

Two of Yogi Ramsuratkumar's Indian women devotees got up at his request and sang a long, beautiful chant to Ram. During the chant Yogi Ramsuratkumar began to be transformed from wise old man to something so far beyond that it confounded the rational mind. He seemed to be deeply sunk into himself with his head lowered over his chest. The green turban circled in crisscross fashion over his long, disheveled hair. There was a strong feeling that he was interacting through subtle means with each person in the room.

When the chant was over Yogi Ramsuratkumar gestured to Lee to come up to the dais. Lee jumped up and ran, quite literally, with his gifts in hand—the new poetry book, *Death of a Dishonest Man,* the copy of *Om Sri Ram* and some new poems, hand-written on pieces of paper. Yogi Ramsuratkumar smiled with surprise and innocent pleasure at the heavy book. He took it and hefted its weight in his hands.

"This is for me?" he exclaimed, like a child being given the most precious and unexpected gift in the world. He looked at Devaki Ma and at Lee with wonder and delight. He asked Lee some questions that were inaudible from where we sat in the back, but it was easy to see that he held the book like it was a newborn baby.

He began to look through the pages of the book. He exclaimed at the price, "Four thousand rupees!" Another series of beautiful, brilliant smiles spread across his face, his eyes glowing like gems. It was hard to believe this was the same elder who had walked so slowly and gravely through the room a few minutes ago. He was dazzling and child-like, eternally young. The Godchild was here.

"Is this a lot for Westerners?" he asked Lee, referring to the price of the book. Lee said yes. Yogi Ramsuratkumar smiled another huge smile. His sense of humor was a wonderful thing to witness as he laughed and smiled and beamed with delight at the gift. He handed the book back to Lee and indicated that Devaki Ma should pay for this copy. Lee protested, almost begging, and said, "I intended it as a gift for you!" Yogi Ramsuratkumar handed the book back to Lee and insisted that Devaki pay for it right then and there. Without hesitation she pulled out a checkbook, wrote the check and handed it to Yogi, who peered at it a moment then handed it to Lee. Yogi Ramsuratkumar then "received" the book, holding out both of his hands and taking the book from Lee, who carefully placed the heavy, outrageously big volume into his master's waiting hands.

Yogi Ramsuratkumar said, "Lee, say a few words to all these people about this book. And read some of the poems." Lee stood up and spoke briefly, telling the basic facts about the book. He then read two or three of the most recent poems.

During all this we strained to accurately hear the details of what was passing between Yogi Ramsuratkumar and Lee from where we were sitting. Through it all was the felt impact of the presence of Yogi Ramsuratkumar. The force of his being drew my attention into subtle domains where his majesty and spiritual royalty were stunning to the heart. He appeared exactly as his devotees often describe him—as the incarnation of Ram, an aspect of the Divine Absolute that is world-sustaining and pure in perfect love.

Lee finished his short talk about *Death of a Dishonest Man* and returned to Yogi Ramsuratkumar's side at the dais. Yogi Ramsuratkumar then took up the *Om Sri Ram* newsletter and began to ask Lee questions about it. It was impossible to hear what they were saying. Lee turned and gestured for me to come up. I hustled forward. He said, "Yogi Ramsuratkumar wants you to read this."

"Okay, can I get my glasses?" I asked, heart beating faster. Lee's steady, calm gaze seemed to say, "Couldn't you have been more prepared for this?"

"Yes, but be quick about it!" he said. I ran back to my seat, grabbed my glasses, ran back up front, *pranamed* to Yogi Ramsuratkumar and took the newsletter from Lee. I stood nearby facing the crowd of about seventy-five people and began to read. I read as loudly and clearly as I could, although I was told later that my voice was barely audible. My nerves were strained from the long journey and lack of sleep but also by the discomfort I felt at being singled out so quickly in Yogi Ramsuratkumar's darshan. Despite my tension, it felt like Yogi Ramsuratkumar was lifting me up in this; he was underneath the reading, sustaining and empowering it. He was coming through me, dispelling my nervousness and doubt. I finished the reading and walked to Yogi Ramsuratkumar at the dais, then knelt beside him and bowed to receive his blessing. Still kneeling at his side, I handed the newsletter back to him. He looked at me with infinite kindness.

"Who wrote this?" he asked. I had skipped the byline in embarrassment when I read the article out loud.

"Mary Young," I said, squirming inwardly.

"Where is this name?" he asked in his lilting, child-like voice. He wanted me to show him on the page. I pointed to the byline.

"What is your name?" he asked.

I froze momentarily in doubt, vacillating. What to say? The name that I use everyday, which is my middle name and the name that I identify with, or my first name, Mary, which Lee has had me use occasionally as a pen name when he doesn't choose a pseudonym for my writing, and one which I don't use for myself because it has tremendously negative connotations for me.

In my mind I could hear Lee's voice saying, "Only answer what is asked." I looked across the room at Lee. He nodded, urging me on.

Again Yogi Ramsuratkumar asked, "What is your name?"

Glancing at Lee again it was clear that he was frustrated with me. "Answer Him!" he mouthed silently.

At the same time Yogi Ramsuratkumar demanded loudly, fiercely, "Your name!"

I blurted out my middle name.

"Eh?!" was Yogi Ramsuratkumar's response. Clearly he didn't understand this—it wasn't what he was waiting to hear. Obviously Lee had told him that I wrote the article, and the article said that the author's name was Mary Young. A weird conversation ensued in which I briefly tried to explain. He looked at me in disbelief while Ma Devaki looked on and smiled kindly. She tried to interpret my words to Yogi Ramsuratkumar.

Cutting through the confusion he suddenly shouted, "Your *name* is Mary Young!" It was a command from the king of the universe. The forceful tone and ascendancy of his voice sent a shock wave through my being. It carried the power of certain victory, and in the moment there was no other response to this spoken will of God but the spontaneous *pranam* that brought my head to his feet. It was as if the body couldn't wait to do what was right, even if the mind was weak and confused. When I came up for air he very slowly and purposefully delivered *prasad*, a banana, into my waiting hands. His gaze penetrated deeply into me while he raised his hand in blessing, palm open.

"My Father blesses *Mary*," he said very gently and tenderly. In the flash of one moment the king of the universe had transformed into the mother of the universe as a wave of infinite tenderness and compassion washed over me. After what seemed like a long time he released me from his gaze and I returned to my seat in the back of the room. He immediately had Lee come up and read the article again, which he did in a loud, clear voice, projecting to the whole room.

There were so many levels of teaching lessons in the whole interchange that it would probably take years to digest it all. I looked at Devaki Ma and Vijayalakshmi and saw them in their white saris and their wool shawls in the Indian heat, sitting on the platform with Yogi Ramsuratkumar. There it was—the obvious demand of selflessness, of being nobody and nothing, of total personal sacrifice to serve the work of this great being, Yogi Ramsuratkumar. They were living examples of the kind of self-effacement in love that is required on the spiritual path. The purifiying force of Yogi Ramsuratkumar's blessings brought ego's fear of obliteration, the identification with the separate self, roaring up to the surface in me. Being in the company of saints one immaturely hopes for *bhavas* of bliss, love, ecstasy. Already it was clear that I was here to work, and that meant seeing more deeply into all those areas of murkiness or resistance that repel the graceful light that was pouring in now in tidal waves.

Yogi Ramsuratkumar called Lee back up to the dais, where he knelt at his father's knee. Within moments Lee asked some of his women students to lead chants. He had already instructed his traveling party to lead only the chants written and composed by his students, because, he said, that is what Yogi Ramsuratkumar wants. The chanting began and continued throughout the rest of darshan, which lasted until one o'clock—an hour later than the usual darshan schedule.

As soon as Yogi Ramsuratkumar left the kitchen staff quickly and efficiently organized an area of the large dining hall for serving lunch. The food was excellent, energetically very pure and yet also spicy and delicious. Tired but exhilarated, everyone ate hungrily of rice, sambar and curried vegetables.

Shortly before four o'clock Lee and the group gathered at the gate again to salute Yogi Ramsuratkumar as his car moved along the dirt road. After circumambulating the statue and *pranaming* to Yogi Ramsuratkumar as he sat in his chair in the temple, everyone went into the hall for darshan. Lee's women students were asked by the Indian attendants to sit up front in the first row, directly across from Lee and the men. We took our seats and waited for Yogi Ramsuratkumar to appear while an Indian woman lead the chants.

Yogi Ramsuratkumar came in after about fifteen minutes. Devaki placed the big, new poetry book on the dais beside Yogi Ramsuratkumar as soon as they sat down. Yogi Ramsuratkumar had an Indian woman and man come up and sit beside him on the floor. The woman stood up and talked for a while about the Yogi Ramsuratkumar *bhajans* she has been leading and about Yogi Ramsuratkumar's blessings. She spoke in Tamil and seemed very animated and happy. She had a tape that she played for him.

Lee's group was exhausted and struggling to stay awake, having slept fitfully for not more than a handful of hours in three days, but with Yogi Ramsuratkumar presiding as pure deity, the space was relentlessly powerful. He was regal in his rags, and the emanations of his being were all pervading. He listened to the tape for what seemed like a long time, and then the woman insisted that he listen to the other side as well. Yogi Ramsuratkumar relented. He was all grace and graciousness as he blessed the woman and her husband and gave them *prasad*. Finally, after about an hour of listening to the tape Yogi Ramsuratkumar said gently, "That is enough," and gave her a sweet smile.

Yogi Ramsuratkumar called Lee over to the dais and said, "Lee, have some of your followers lead chants." Lee gestured to Chris and I to start the chanting. We got up and began the Hanuman chant—"Hanuman, Hanuman, Sita Ram Hanuman. Yogi Rama, Yogi Rama, Suratkumar Rama Rama." Yogi Ramsuratkumar picked up an orange and began to toss it back and forth gleefully in rhythm with the chant, which had a bouncy, child-like mood. He did this for a long time, chuckling softly while Devaki's eyes sparkled with delight at Yogi Ramsuratkumar's obvious enjoyment.

About thirty minutes into the chanting Chris left to attend to the children. Looking to Lee for his instruction, he gestured to me to continue leading the chant alone. Yogi Ramsuratkumar called Lee up to the dais. After a quick consultation Lee stood up and walked over to Jan, then asked her to go get a poetry book, which she returned with shortly and handed to Lee. He took it directly to Yogi, who called out to the crowd of about one hundred fifty people, "Who wants to buy this book right now? Pay for it tonight—cash! Four thousand rupees!" He sounded incredibly like Lee Lozowick selling books, tapes and CDs at his seminars in Europe. Yogi Ramsuratkumar's eyes glittered and gleamed with mischief. He seemed to be imitating Lee to perfection. He chuckled and exclaimed over the price of the book, which seemed to amuse and enthrall him.

The activity level in the room began to pick up. A European woman in the audience wanted to buy it. Immediately Yogi asked Lee for another book and out went Jan to the cottage to bring one. People were stirred up. The chanting went on while the next book arrived and was sold instantly. Then Yogi Ramsuratkumar began to sign the books with an om sign and his name. There was much laughter and commotion in the hall as Yogi Ramsuratkumar frequently laughed out loud. The sweet mood of his delight was a tangible nectar in the air.

A third book was brought into the hall, given to Lee and then to Yogi Ramsuratkumar. He sold it instantly. Yogi Ramsuratkumar talked with Devaki and Lee and the people who came up to get their books. The crowd was rapt, faces were shining, all eyes were on Yogi Ramsuratkumar. It was difficult to keep the chanting going all through this. I had to pay total attention to several different things simultaneously—the next verse of the chant, signals from Lee or Yogi Ramsuratkumar, the protocol of the space. The intense bearing down of the subtle energetic presence of Yogi Ramsuratkumar made ego seek small escapes, but there were none because one small lapse of attention, any wandering of the mind or spacing out, would throw off the chant. Quickly it became clear that paying strict attention would be paramount in Yogi Ramsuratkumar's darshan, but at the same time the brightness and power in the space had the effect of buoying one up, so that one was carried along on the current.

At six-thirty Yogi Ramsuratkumar still sat on his dais creating and destroying

11

universes with his play. The chanting droned on and on. I had been standing up leading the chant for almost an hour and a half. The darshan had gone thirty minutes past the usual time to end. Suddenly Yogi Ramsuratkumar had his attendant Selvaraj motion me toward the dais. I stopped chanting and quickly kneeled at Yogi Ramsuratkumar's side.

He said, "What is your name?"

"Mary," I answered, thinking this was what he wanted me to say.

He seemed to approve. "What is your other name?" he asked. I responded with my middle name, thinking it was the right answer.

He shouted emphatically, "Mary *Young!*"

He was triumphant, even imperious as he repeated, "Your name is Mary Young!" An involuntary smile burst into life across my face with laughter just behind it as my body spontaneously fell into a *pranam* at his feet. The air shook with something like happiness. How incredible it was to interact with this great being! His eyes sparkled with mirth at all this silliness. I had the recognition that we were having fun with each other, and yet it was clearly a teaching communication. In his omniscience he knew where all my resistance was, and at the same time that he worked with that resistance, he was empowering that which is essential and true. He had pronounced the name beautifully with his Indian accent. It became "Meri" with a roll on the "r", but he pronounced the last name as if he was speaking American English.

"Thank you," he said very tenderly. It seemed that he was thanking the one who wrote about the Godchild Yogi Ramsuratkumar. At best, the one who writes is only an instrument in the *lila* of Yogi Ramsuratkumar; at worst, that one is muddied with doubt, confusion and resistance. His blessing was to empower, to bring forth clarity, devotion, obedience, surrender.

He fell into a very strong blessing trance or state. His face was etched with feeling, a love so great that it seemed he must bear it as pain or conscious suffering. Blessings poured from him—blessings that would bring the recipient one step closer to surrender to the Will of God. His eyes looked past me and into something or someone unknown, unnamable. His blessing was aimed at this unknown, reaching beyond the ego-cherishing "me." His eyes called a mystery into life. I had the sense that I was being literally showered and pummeled by a storm of Grace. He dropped the orange he had been playing with into my cupped hands, then the moment, suspended in time, fell away. I *pranamed* and returned to my seat.

Quickly he prepared to leave with Devaki Ma and Vijayalakshmi. He called Lee to his dais and told him to take his seat on the dais after he left. "Stay with these people awhile," he said. Lee came over immediately and motioned to me to start the "Mangalam" chant that always signals the end of darshan. I started out singing feebly.

"No—*loud*," Lee instructed from the dais. He corrected me, but his eyes were shining and merry. Yogi Ramsuratkumar was gone and darshan was over. Lee performed the closing puja, which consisted of waving lights (a small flame burning on a stainless steel tray) and offering incense and water at the shrine near the front door, outside to Arunachala. He also waved lights to Yogi Ramsuratkumar's seat at the dais and to the shrine near the dais for the Shankaracharya of Kanchipuram, a saint who Yogi Ramsuratkumar revered and who, uncharacteristic of his orthodox position, revered Yogi Ramsuratkumar. Lee's concentration during this puja was both immensely vast and condensed into a totally focused point—on Yogi Ramsuratkumar, the source of all light.

Afterward the group stood outside the dining hall under the thatched roof that sheltered the door and walkway. Lee had only one comment to make, spoken with satisfaction and joy. "Just good, clean fun!" he said brightly. It was his take on Yogi Ramsuratkumar's play of the evening.

November 27, 1998
Yogi Ramsuratkumar Ashram

Lee presented Yogi Ramsuratkumar with a orange wool shawl in darshan today. It was a gift sent by Chandra Swami and delivered by Alain. When the shawl was presented Yogi Ramsuratkumar was like a small child, surprised by a present. He smiled broadly and pointed to the orange wool shawl he was already wearing underneath a green wool shawl, both tied across his chest. He said, "Is this the shawl he gave this beggar last year?" The innocence in this simple question was disarming.

Holding the shawl in his lap for a long time while the chanting went on, Yogi Ramsuratkumar finally gestured for Lee to come, his curved brown hand moving only slightly. Lee immediately jumped up from his chair and ran over. He *pranamed* and bent toward Yogi Ramsuratkumar to listen to his instructions. Yogi Ramsuratkumar handed the shawl to Lee, who then placed it around his father's shoulders. Devaki and Yogi Ramsuratkumar both motioned to Lee to tie it in place. Lee took both ends, pulled them forward, and tied the first knot tight, snug. Yogi chuckled at this, perhaps at the strength that Lee put into the tying. Smiling along with Yogi Ramsuratkumar, Lee tied the second knot, then *pranamed*, received Yogi's blessings and ran back to his seat. The tying of the knot over Yogi Ramsuratkumar's heart seemed like more than a symbol of how Lee and Yogi Ramsuratkumar are bound together; it was a simple act, but choked with reverberations.

Later Yogi Ramsuratkumar called Lee over again. He said, "Say something of use to these people." Lee stood and faced the audience, gave a slight self-deprecating or embarrassed shrug, and launched into it. Scribbling notes as quickly and unobtrusively as possible, I wrote down the highlights of what he said:

"I'll talk about the book title, *Death of a Dishonest Man*. The title of the book uses very specific language; it refers to me in one way, but also offers an opportunity to others, so we can consider what is honest and what is dishonest. As long as we deny the allness, the unity of all that Yogi Ramsuratkumar so ecstatically speaks of, then we are dishonest, and in fact we deny the reality of our very existence, and of the Divine. When we refer in English to death it doesn't always mean a literal death. Saul of Tarsus was a persecutor of Christians who had a vision of Jesus on the road to Damascus and was immediately changed from a nonbeliever to a believer. Saul said, 'You have to die every day in Christ.' You have to die to the knowledge that Father in Heaven is all, everything, everywhere, past, present, future, unitive, total oneness. There is only God.

"So the title of the book refers to me but also says that we could all profit from considering this, whether we are honest or dishonest in this sense, because we believe we are separate from God. Yogi Ramsuratkumar says He is a sinner, but there is nothing about Yogi Ramsuratkumar that lives in the sense of dishonesty. The degree to which we are dishonest is the degree to which we have not died to the unitive oneness, the allness, of Father in Heaven."

Yogi Ramsuratkumar smoked and listened while Lee talked. He stretched his legs out in front of him, his legs crossed gracefully at the ankle. His bare feet faced those sitting in the front row, and it seemed that Grace flowed directly from them. Every gesture Yogi Ramsuratkumar made effected the entire gestalt of the space, and in his *bhavas* and blessing fits, sometimes almost like spasms that gripped and overtook him, he seemed to spin out our *samskaras*, transforming karma, piercing murky veils of darkness with light.

The rare stature of this extraordinary human being kept imposing itself upon my senses: this humble old yogi, with years of traveling barefoot on the dusty roads of India indelibly imprinted on his feet, God-intoxicated and quite mad by worldly standards and a beggar in rags, is a great *Mahasiddha*. His greatness is apparent in his total lack of affectedness of any kind. He is perfectly natural, easeful and blessedly present. He has no need for the trappings of sainthood. In every instant his smallest, simplest gesture reveals all and aligns us to the Will of God.

The ashram is very beautiful. A great deal of loving care and work goes into its maintenance. What was a flat, bare green field with a few thorn bushes growing in it five years ago is now a lush garden, several lovely stucco or adobe-like buildings, thatched-roof huts, the massive temple itself and the dining hall which doubles as a darshan hall until the temple is completed. Along the row of cottages there are many flowering bushes and vines that grow along the path and over fences. There are two small young cats that roam around the cottages, slinking past skittishly, and the small musk deer with its white-spotted brown coat. Birds fly and flit and sing among all the prolific tropical foliage and flowers, and well-tended emerald green grass grows around the cottages. The rooms of the cottages are octagonal, which adds to their mood and charm.

This morning after coffee was brought around to the cottages at six o'clock there were over twenty crows around Mani's cottage, the one nearest the dining hall. The birds sing constantly, some sweetly, and some—like the crows—more raucously. It is well known that Yogi Ramsuratkumar likes birds, and they appear to like him as well. They populate the ashram grounds and often gather behind the window at his dais during darshan.

Mount Arunachala stands as a massive lone sentinel in the plain where Tiruvannamalai sprawls and bustles with life. The mountain permeates everything here. Arunachala is green, solid and real but at the same time seems to interpenetrate the unseen worlds. Every day at the beginning of darshan one of the Indian devotees sings "Arunachala Shiva, Arunachala Shiva, Arunachala Shiva, Arunejeda." When Yogi Ramsuratkumar comes in it is apparent that he *is* this holy mountain, Shiva in Arunachala. There is no separation between Yogi Ramsuratkumar and the mountain. In the closing puja at the end of the day the lights are waved to Arunachala as well as to Yogi Ramsuratkumar.

These magical realities are tacitly understood here in India. What in the West is considered ludicrous, preposterous, hysterical or even psychotic is a natural fact of life in India. It is a worldview that affirms one's native intelligence and refreshes one's sense of rightness. Yogi Ramsuratkumar is the incarnate Divine, and so he is also Shiva made manifest as the mountain, the Divine incarnate in nature. To gaze on the mountain is to receive blessings; to walk upon its earth and rocks and grass, to bath in its cold springs at Skandashram is to touch the body of God on Earth. Circumambulating the path around its base one walks along with scores of pilgrims and sadhus past many temples. According to Indian legend, any association with Arunachala generates the blessings of Shiva's limitless capacity to transform creation. Yogi Ramsuratkumar has said that to circumambulate the ashram, the sacred ground that his Indian devotees call Agrahara Kollai in

Tamil, is the same as circumambulating Arunachala four times. Every morning while he has his breakfast the Americans circumambulate the ashram, along with many other devotees.

Yogi Ramsuratkumar is a God-king holding court beneath the vast umbrella of Arunachala, a king whose greatest nobility is found in perfect, complete surrender to the Will of God. At the same time he is the ultimate servant, as any true king should be. He has gone beyond the personal to the suprapersonal. There is no sentiment in him, only law, and the law is sacrifice, or love. This is a love that burns, destroys, rages and yet cools, quenches all thirsts, heals the sick and is amrita, sweet as honey to the soul. All this is subtly transmitted yet is so all pervading and immanently real that Yogi Ramsuratkumar does not need any fancy tricks. He needs no mudras or *kriyas* or kundalini or yoga techniques or intellectual philosophy to impart all this. His transmission has gone beyond all forms. It exists as the pure raw annihilating power of Grace.

Yogi Ramsuratkumar exists as countless large and small acts of love of God in creation. It is this love that sustains the world, the universe, Creation itself. It is the binding force of the universe. This is the face of God that the Hindus conceive of as Vishnu, who took human incarnation as Ram and Krishna. This is the aspect of the Divine that sustains and maintains all things in order that the Will of God might be enacted, evolved, realized in life, through matter, through incarnation, through the Great Process of Divine Evolution.

November 28, 1998
Yogi Ramsuratkumar Ashram

Lee gave two talks today in darshan at Yogi Ramsuratkumar's request: one in the morning, one in the afternoon. In the morning he said that Yogi Ramsuratkumar had asked him to "say something useful." As Lee stood and turned to face the crowd he commented that he would say something useful as opposed to saying something only interesting. "Something useful" would be something that helps us remember the allness, the unitive nature of Father in Heaven.

Lee's talk was inspired and uplifting, but in some ways it was very different in mood from his talks in Europe, which are also very different from his rare talks in the U.S. Here in Yogi Ramsuratkumar's presence Lee speaks in classic, inspired and simple, clear terms. He is even a little old-fashioned and circumspect. All the provocative cynicism and sting is gone from his tone, his words, his body. He uses the language of Yogi Ramsuratkumar and speaks about the Divine as "Father in Heaven."

On the other hand he constantly heaps praise upon Yogi Ramsuratkumar, which is a constant in all of his talks, whether he is in America, Europe or India. This praise is lavish and yet not unctuous or obsequious in any way. Coming from Lee's lips these words of Yogi Ramsuratkumar's greatness ring true: he means what he says and he speaks with total conviction.

Today Lee reminded us time and again of the unitive allness—past, present, future, everything, everywhere—of Father in Heaven, and that this is in fact who we are because there is no separation between all of life and the Divine. He talked about how Westerners want comforts, and how we want to seek comfort in India, even though we think we've given up comforts of the West to be in India. He chided the Westerners and seemed to be speaking directly to his students. Throughout the talk a smile hovered on his face.

The Western attachment to comfort shows up in many different ways. Even when we have given some things up and accepted certain levels of discomfort, we are still fat and happy, and spiritual pride and materialism runs rampant. There is no end to what needs to be sacrificed on the path—not things like jobs and money, but things like vanity, self-ishness, avarice, pride, blame. We are typically still self-satisfied and smug in our egoic identities, possessive of our personalities which we think of with pleasure and admiration, but which are driven by those very qualities of pride, vanity, selfishness. These things are hard to root out. Lee works with his students to dig these up at the most minute levels, working with the tenacity of ego in ways that may appear picayune to the ordinary eye, because as fast as one surrenders something, ego reappears with a new twist on things.

In darshan this afternoon Lee gave another talk. He said, "A bird was singing outside the window where Yogi Ramsuratkumar sat on the dais in darshan yesterday. Yogi Ramsuratkumar was paying attention to the bird. He was listening to the bird's song and paying attention to everyone in the room *also*," he added with a hint of mischief and a small smile. He continued, "Yogi Ramsuratkumar hears the voice of God in many places. It always inspires me when Yogi Ramsuratkumar acknowledges that God is everywhere, in all things . . . in the song of the bird, certainly in the mountain, Arunachala, in the taste of good food, in the beautiful flowers. God has many voices. Years ago I was sitting with Yogi Ramsuratkumar and He was chanting the Name of God when a crow sang very loudly on a branch nearby. He stopped, looked at the crow and said, 'That friend's voice is so much sweeter than this beggar's voice!' Hearing Yogi Ramsuratkumar acknowledge that the voice of God is everywhere in this way inspires me to think of the allness, the unity of all life."

Lee became very animated at this point. It was as if he cut loose—let out the mischievous one who lurked behind his smile in the morning talk. He gesticulated and moved around, stepping back and up, waving his arms in the air as he told "an old Indian story."

"Forgive me," he said to the audience, "if I massacre your tradition here!" Then he launched into a spirited version of the myth of Parvati asking Shiva to give boons of enlightenment, wealth and knowledge to suffering humanity. He embellished this story, calling on his modus operandi as the raconteur and grand storyteller who often shows up in Europe in his talks. He spoke with verve, humor and a hint of a provocative tone. He seemed to be prodding a little at something in the Indian devotees. Devaki watched with a speculative but open face, looking at Bhagavan from time to time to see his response to his son, but Yogi Ramsuratkumar seemed quite serene, smoking a cigarette part of the time and watching Lee, listening intently. There seemed to be a slight edge of discomfort in the room. Again Lee upbraided the Westerners for their drive for comfort.

Having seen Lee unleash the jester, the crazy Baul and "arrogant Fool" on many occasions I knew what he was capable of. Would he go there now, in Yogi Ramsuratkumar's company? When Lee catches the scent of hypocrisy, illusion, false holiness or intellectualism in his audience, anything can happen. He often charges head-on, gets in your face, turns the world upside down with his madcap dharma. But today he only danced on the edges of this provocative mood and gave the slightest, mildest taste of his abandon. Still it was more than enough for Yogi Ramsuratkumar to see.

Lee changed gears very smoothly and began to talk about how the secret of existence is in the heart of man, and his speech effortlessly became ecstatic and sublime. "The truth is in us," he said, "in the flowers, in the song of the bird, in the taste of fine food. God is in the mountain . . ." He gestured toward Arunachala, then ended his talk with many paeans of praise to the greatness of Yogi Ramsuratkumar, of the great opportunity and joy of being in his presence. He talked about how fortunate we are to be in the company of Yogi Ramsuratkumar. He said that Yogi Ramsuratkumar has his servants stand up and "say something useful" or read from holy scripture or sing a song because he doesn't do any of these things. Instead he works only through Grace, and his Grace and blessings are showered upon all. We only have to receive.

It was another ecstatic outpouring of praise for his father, Yogi Ramsuratkumar. Lee turned to the dais and knelt at his father's knee, his hands pressed together in a *pranam*. Yogi Ramsuratkumar chuckled slightly and put his hand on Lee's shoulder as Lee bowed his head before him. They stayed like that for a minute or more with Yogi Ramsuratkumar's hand lying pressed down on Lee's shoulder. An almost visible substance seemed to pass from Yogi Ramsuratkumar to Lee.

Lee's attitude in the company of Yogi Ramsuratkumar is always one of complete receptivity and submission; not submission as Westerners typically view it, but a submission that is ennobling and exalting. It is the kind of spiritual submission that arises spontaneously when one recognizes a higher law or higher being at work. When one kneels at the feet of a being like Yogi Ramsuratkumar, one is uplifted by proximity to such sanctity.

At the close of both darshans today Yogi Ramsuratkumar had Lee and three other men come up and sit on the dais. He said to Lee, "Conduct all these affairs," and another time, "Manage all affairs," as he waved his hand to indicate the room with all the people in it. Something in that phrase—"Conduct all these affairs"—seemed so rich with purpose that it reverberated through the room. It is clear that Yogi Ramsuratkumar trusts Lee to conduct the affairs of his darshan after he has left the space to go on to his other business. For thirty minutes after Yogi Ramsuratkumar left the darshan Lee sat in his seat with Krishna Carcelle, Bret and Alain de Rosenbo beside him while the chanting continued until it was time to end.

Lee makes teaching communications to his students regularly. For example, in traveling with Lee one receives an almost constant stream of instructions on how to be a good guest based on the principles of beggary as Lee demonstrates them in his own actions. He is also often tremendously empowering with his students, drawing people out and making very kind and generous remarks to various individuals. When Jan Smith first heard Lee speaking about calling different people up to lead chants in Yogi's darshan she started crying. She said, "There is no way I can do that." She was emphatic in her recoil. Several of the women said, "Oh Jan, you can do it!" She snapped back through her tears, "No I can't! You don't understand! You don't know me!"

Lee interrupted, saying in a fierce but at the same time very kind tone of voice, "You don't know yourself! You have no idea who you are!" Immediately everything stopped with the delivery of this truth. She was stunned into silence. She looked at Lee and registered his meaning, then she burst into ecstatic peals of laughter, which instantly stopped the flow of tears. The shock of his remarks seemed to go straight to her heart in that moment in a way that was delightful.

At another time Lee was encouraging Dave and Tom to be prepared to tell stories about Lee if Yogi Ramsuratkumar asked for them, as he had in the past. Dave said that he didn't know any stories, but then began to talk about when Lee left him in charge of the Arizona ashram twelve years ago during the 1986 trip to India. Lee was gone for almost three months at that time, and Dave was left with the responsibility for the ashram.

Dave started criticizing himself heavily, saying that everything had fallen apart. "I almost destroyed the ashram financially, and had to relinquish the printing press to creditors to keep the ashram afloat, things were so bad!" he said. Clearly Dave thought he had failed Lee, but in the re-telling of this story Lee kept turning every fact around to be in praise of Dave. Lee laughed and joked with him, saying, "You sold the press because the computer revolution was just around the corner and if we'd still had it Hohm Press would have been obsolete, behind the times, the laughingstock of all the independent small presses in the U.S.!" In this way each thing that Dave mentioned as one of his failings Lee turned into a beneficial act or positive attribute. As they talked Lee reframed the story for Dave, summing it all up by saying, "By the grace of God, everything worked out for the best, even in difficult times! Now that would be a good story to tell."

Dave seemed to absorb Lee's words, then he told the rest of the story. When he picked Lee up at the airport after he returned from that trip twelve years ago, tears were streaming down Dave's face. He couldn't stop crying as he reported all the bad news to Lee. But Lee just kept saying to him then, "Are you in?" Over and over again, "Are you in?" That was the only important consideration for him. Finally Dave said, "Yes, I'm in!" And that was the end of that—no more said. Lee was smiling while Dave told all of this. "That would make a great story, if you make the *right point* with it—which is, by the grace of God, everything turned out for the best!"

This empowerment of Lee's devotees goes on, some of it transmitted simply in the beaming, soft smiles he liberally gives. Lee's attention in this regard always goes where it is genuinely needed. On the other hand, sometimes empowerment takes a very different form, such as in the ever present demand to sacrifice one's personal and usually selfish, so-called "needs." Lee's constant corrections and demands for upscale in practice in this regard are unrelenting. When experienced as juxtaposed to one's resistance and disobedience, however small, that demand is a sharp goad to practice. Lee himself is often the example in this. When coffee was served at three o'clock today Lee sat out on the porch with a number of students around him. Someone had offered him some skin cream for a minor skin irritation he had. He snapped, "Everybody thinks they're going to die well, but they can't even deal with the most basic discomforts! People in the community are going to have some bad debts to pay. So, no, I will turn down the skin cream."

November 29, 1998
Yogi Ramsuratkumar Ashram

This morning in darshan Yogi Ramsuratkumar said to Lee, "Say something useful for everyone." Lee started out saying that in the West it's common for people who have been to the East to have many books, pictures of saints and all kinds of paraphernalia. He said, "They marvel at its sanctity, but don't do anything about it in their lives. In order for something to be useful, you have to do something with those experiences of sanctity.

"Some years ago I had a dream that I will share with you. Most dreams, like our waking hours, are just illusions, but now and then Yogi Ramsuratkumar gives me a dream that is real and makes a point. In the dream Yogi Ramsuratkumar and I were walking along together by the temple. The temple was completed, and all the finishing touches were on it. As we walked into the temple I saw something that caught my attention and distracted me. After a minute I realized that Yogi Ramsuratkumar had gone on. By the way, this is not a personal dream; it has nothing to do with me . . . So I ran to find Yogi Ramsuratkumar, but when I found Him the communion I felt before, when we were walking along together and my attention was totally on Him, was gone."

Lee went on to make a teaching lesson of this. He said, "One of the key elements of relationship with Yogi Ramsuratkumar is to have faith in the Name of Yogi Ramsuratkumar. He has said if you need His blessings, wherever you are, speak His name with faith and, 'This beggar will be with you.' So one element of faith is attention—paying attention. But you know, Westerners get distracted by every new restaurant in town! Have you seen the new restaurant here in Tiruvannamalai that serves crepes, cappuccino, expresso?" Lee laughed and joked around some more, then continued, "Westerners get distracted by every new restaurant in town. Even on our ashram in Arizona you hear people whispering, 'Have you tried the new restaurant in town?'

"Yogi Ramsuratkumar is not His body—as beautiful as it is, and as much as we worship it. Yogi Ramsuratkumar is His Father in Heaven, all, one, unitive. When we break our attention on the sanctity of that, even for a moment or a day or a month, the blessings do not flow to us in the same way as they can when our attention on Yogi Ramsuratkumar as Father in Heaven is total as an aspect of our faith."

After Lee's talk was over Yogi Ramsuratkumar asked an older man to come up and speak. At Yogi's request, Selvaraj carefully put a chair for him by Yogi's side at the dais. The man received a banana as *prasad* from Yogi Ramsuratkumar's hands, which he ate on the spot, then went to sit in the chair. He began to speak in Tamil in very monotonous tones, droning on and on and on. I shifted around uncomfortably on the hard floor, my attention wandering despite what Lee had just said.

At this particular time Yogi Ramsuratkumar leaned back with one knee up as he listened to the man speak. Somehow this change in his posture shifted things and created a strong sensation in me. My attention was suddenly completely focused on Yogi Ramsuratkumar, and as the man droned on in a monotone in long complicated strings of syllables in Tamil, I began to experience something completely different. The veils of illusion seemed to part, or were dissipated by Yogi Ramsuratkumar's Grace, for the moments that followed. I could "see" now at a most refined and subtle level the evanescent scene of the divine being at play, that which exists beyond the body of the old beggar. It was a glimpse of Yogi Ramsuratkumar as he lives beyond space and time in the *loka* of rainbow light and beauty—an all-attractive being, a shining subtle form of color and sacred geometry that played in this realm and radiated. There was a tremendous involuntary attraction to this resplendent being that was automatic, unquestionable, without thought, design, purpose or motive of any kind. It was a natural fact. There was no swoon of bliss or tears of brokenheartedness. Just the moments of "seeing" into a transcendent reality, the warm rosy flush of the light and power, the divine play of the being who radiated all. Instead of mystifying *bhavas* there was clarity. Then the moment passed, the veils fell down again and everything continued in its ordinary way—the Indian man speaking in Tamil, Yogi Ramsuratkumar holding his Charimar cigarette, smoke drifting toward the ceiling as he listening patiently from the dais, and his son Lee sitting against the wall, watching it all with bright eyes.

November 30, 1998
Yogi Ramsuratkumar Ashram

Always the servant of his servants—in this case his disciple, Purna—at four-thirty in the morning Lee walked through the dark ashram to wait at the gate for the arrival of Purna and his large group of students. When asked the night before if someone could accompany him, Lee said, "No, this is my responsibility. I will go alone." He waited in the hut by the gate for an hour and a half. At six o'clock they finally arrived.

Lee's obvious excitement and enthusiasm about Purna and his group coming on this trip has been infectious, even though many of us just wanted the intimacy and sweet mood of the smaller group to continue as it had been—very quiet, supportive, loving, easeful. The group chemistry had been perfect in this way, and now Lee introduced a complex and multifaceted element of surprise or irritant to the mix: Purna's group of brand new students—fifteen of them! All but two had never been to India before. When the rest of our group greeted Purna's students before Yogi Ramsuratkumar came for breakfast at seven o'clock most of them looked squeaky clean and brand-new in this world of sadhana, spiritual work, keeping the company of saints and radical gurus. Yet at the same time they were clearly good people, eager, sincere, willing to explore this new ground.

There is a line in the Shankaracharya's prayer that is sung every day by Devaki and Vijayalakshmi in darshan. It says, "Cultivate friendship that conquers all hearts." The arrival of another fifteen people represented an instant opportunity to practice this bodhisattva ideal. Lee exemplifies this ideal constantly by expanding and embracing, making room for everyone, in elegant and generous terms over and over again. He is simply and totally present with everyone.

Later today Lee said he would go downtown with Purna's group because they needed to buy saris and *kirtas*—something everyone else had already done. Someone in Lee's group asked, "Will you do everything they do?" referring to Purna and his group. It was a question that was tinged with frustration and a protective tension, as if Lee needed to be protected from such stress. Lee answered, "No, they will do everything I do! They need to buy clothes, so I am giving them a break and going downtown today." He smiled— a wide grin.

All of the poetry books that Lee had brought with him were sold in the first week, so he had faxed Purna in Little Rock and asked him to bring another case of *Death of a Dishonest Man*, which made the continued selling *lilas* possible. At the beginning of darshan today Yogi Ramsuratkumar asked Lee for another book to sell. Lee unwrapped the clear plastic wrap as he handed a book to Yogi Ramsuratkumar. Vijayalakshmi was buying this one. Sitting on the dais with Devaki Ma, she made out a check and handed it to Yogi Ramsuratkumar, who handed it to Lee. Lee gave Yogi Ramsuratkumar the book, which he then signed with a big Om sign and his name—no more than a wave of a line.

Yogi Ramsuratkumar proceeded to have Vijayalakshmi make an announcement to the darshan of two hundred fifty people about the book, saying also that Lee had some more books. Yogi Ramsuratkumar said, "Whoever wants to can buy this book now. If you have cash you can buy this book—today!" He was smiling broadly with great enjoyment. His vast capacity for irony and humor and delight sparkled on him as he played the salesman with relish. Lee stayed by his side, ripping the plastic covers off the books and

20

handing Yogi Ramsuratkumar another copy as the next person came forward to buy.

It quickly became a selling spree—Yogi Ramsuratkumar's book bazaar. He said laughingly, with a childlike innocence that blended easily with his divine sense of savvy, "We are selling *all* these books!" Then he looked at Lee and asked, "Are you selling books in America?"

Lee smiled and answered, "Yes, but not as many as You." Yogi laughed and affectionately clapped Lee on the shoulder, as if he got the biggest charge out of this whole thing. Without saying anything he seemed to be demonstrating that he knows his son Lee quite well.

After darshan a European woman, the one who bought the first poetry book several days ago, came up to Lee as he stood under the thatched palm roof of the elongated open-air hut that shades the entry to the hall where Yogi Ramsuratkumar gives darshan. The palm roof must provide much-needed relief from monsoon rains in the rainy season as well as shade in the scorching sun. She cornered Lee and asked him if he would ask Yogi to sign her poetry book like he had begun to do with the others. For some reason, he hadn't signed hers. Lee replied, "No, I don't ask for anything from Him."

"No?" she asked quizzically, as if this was a great surprise to her.

Lee replied, "No. I don't even ask for anything for myself, much less for other people." Case closed. She stood there with a perplexed look on her face as Mani stepped forward to tell Lee that lunch was ready.

The second day Lee was here some Europeans came looking for the "American guru." Tom told them that he was resting and not available. They left. There are many Westerners in Tiruvannamalai. The numbers seem to grow exponentially every year. Many of them *pranam* to Lee when they see him on the streets, having met him or come to his public talks in previous visits. But in Tiruvannamalai Lee takes an invisible back seat to Yogi Ramsuratkumar as much as possible. Lee Lozowick seems to enjoy this immensely, to revel in it in fact. And yet in Yogi Ramsuratkumar's physical presence Lee becomes visibly brighter, even when he seems to have himself more cloaked and obscured than usual. He is always on—turned on and working, even and especially as a devotee. In Yogi Ramsuratkumar's darshan he is fiercely alert and aware of everything that goes on in the space. It is amazing to hear him speak afterward of this or that nuance of the space, what people were doing, details of what went on that are invisible to most.

This afternoon in darshan Lee gave a beautiful, inspiring talk. Afterward two Indian devotees came up to Lee to express their gratitude and appreciation for his ecstatic praise of Yogi Ramsuratkumar and the mood that he had evoked. At the beginning of the talk Lee said, "Yogi Ramsuratkumar has asked me to say a few words. One of the most important principles in relationship to the guru is obedience. The philosophers debate about whether or not we have free will, but for the *bhakta* the question is, what can *we* do and what does the Master do *for* us? What we can do is obey the Master's wishes. Adoration and devotion we cannot pretend to have. By the Master's Grace—and only by the Master's Grace—we may come to love the Master, to adore the Master, to worship the Master. But what *we* can do is follow what the Master directs us to do. One of the things Yogi Ramsuratkumar has directed His devotees to do is to chant His Name. This delights Him and serves Him, but it also brings blessings to devotees who do it.

"The task of devotees of Yogi Ramsuratkumar is not just to take for ourselves however, but to support the temple on Yogi Ramsuratkumar's ashram, which will bless *bhaktas* of all the generations ahead. The glory and majesty of Yogi Ramsuratkumar will not go away when Yogi Ramsuratkumar returns to His Father in Heaven. His glory will continue to grow and grow after He leaves His body and returns to Father in Heaven. Yogi Ramsuratkumar has said that the temple here is an international temple that will serve the whole world, and will serve all the *bhaktas*. Many of us are so fortunate and blessed to live here and get to see Yogi Ramsuratkumar every day. As the *bhaktas* say, 'We can catch His scent' in the temple. "

Lee paused then said, "I hope I'm not insulting anyone by talking about another tradition here, but the Sufis talk about the 'scent' of the Beloved. If you catch the perfume of the Beloved you are transported in ecstasy. If you walk to Sannadhi Street, if you are sensitive, you can catch the smell of the perfume that Yogi Ramsuratkumar has left behind there . . ." Lee was referring to the house near the brass market in Tiruvannamalai near Arunachalesvara Temple where Yogi Ramsuratkumar lived for many years.

"Obedience to Yogi Ramsuratkumar can take many different forms. Perhaps to obey Yogi Ramsuratkumar is to bring His Name to those who have not heard it before. Obedience is what *we* can do. If love comes, it comes—all we can do is thank the guru for such a gift. You could say that obedience is a form of praise, and God wants praise; the Universe wants praise. So you follow the scent of the Beloved, the perfume of the Beloved, and you smell with your heart. If you smell food cooking you can follow that smell straight to the food. It's the same with the scent of the Beloved, but you smell that scent with the heart . . . ." He ended with a thank you, turned and *pranamed*, kneeling, at Yogi Ramsuratkumar's knee.

In this talk it seemed that Lee was speaking to a core issue for most of Yogi Ramsuratkumar's devotees—he was aimed right at the heart of the matter. Yogi Ramsuratkumar's Grace and Influence will only grow after he leaves his body and returns to his Father in Heaven, and the job of his devotees is to create and support and sustain the sanctity of this sacred place—the temple and Yogi Ramsuratkumar Ashram. It is a spiritual refuge, a generator of blessing power, a sanctuary of worship for the world and generations to come.

December 1, 1998
Yogi Ramsuratkumar Ashram

It was Jayanthi Day—Yogi Ramsuratkumar's birthday. Lee's group was up this morning at two-fifteen to be ready for chanting and puja ceremonies in the temple at three o'clock. We walked in thick darkness across the grounds to the temple. The ashram was amazing in these early morning hours. The magic of India was in the air and combined with the power and presence of Yogi Ramsuratkumar to hint of mystery, fire, ruin. The smoldering ruins of the heart could be sensed; the incineration of human desires and designs. What becomes so obvious in the company of Yogi Ramsuratkumar is that he is no longer human but divine. The evolution of consciousness—Lee would say, the Great Process of Divine Evolution—has taken Yogi Ramsuratkumar into its sweeping flow and moved him beyond any and all ordinary human concerns, desires or wishes for self-fulfillment.

Walking into the vast cavern of the unfinished temple with its packed earthen floor we saw that the statue of Yogi Ramsuratkumar had been surrounded with eighty brass ghee lamps, made especially for this auspicious occasion and imprinted with the image of Yogi Ramsuratkumar's face. The perimeter of the concrete platform on which the statue stood was framed with eighty dancing flames that burned brightly in the dark space of the huge temple. Inside this circle were many mandalas and sacred designs intricately drawn in colored rice powder. High above tiny blue lights spelled out a message: "Long live Yogi Ramsuratkumar!"

Lee began the circumambulation of the statue with the men following behind him chanting the name of Yogi Ramsuratkumar, then the women would take over for awhile. The only light was the flicker of the ghee lamps and the strings of small lights up above. Shadows danced on the distant walls as about forty-five people circled the statue chanting. Mani, who was overseeing the rites, changed this so that the men and women would circumambulate in separate groups, each for about thirty minutes. After the first five minutes Lee sat in a chair by the cotton blankets and watched while both men's and then women's groups switched off in the chanting and circumambulating of the statue. While the men chanted the women sat with Lee on the large, brightly-colored cotton blankets that were laid out on the ground. We drank hot chai, which was served twice during these predawn hours. The time went by very fast. Soon a pale light seeped into the temple. The children and their parents came in at five-thirty and everyone made a huge circle—about seventy-five people—for a kind of finale. The crowd dispersed around six o'clock to get ready for Yogi Ramsuratkumar's arrival for breakfast.

While the children had their chai in the temple, Mani began to talk about his life with Yogi Ramsuratkumar. Only five years ago Mani was a construction engineer running a big company in Madras. He had only recently become a devotee of Yogi Ramsuratkumar, and a few months after the purchase of the land for the ashram Mani came to Tiruvannamalai to visit Yogi Ramsuratkumar. Yogi Ramsuratkumar told Mani that he wanted him to stay in Tiruvannamalai for the next ten years and help build the ashram and temple. Mani has been here since then. Yogi Ramsuratkumar wants Mani to stay on the ashram property, so Mani has not left the ashram for four years, except to visit Yogi Ramsuratkumar at Sudama House a few blocks away. His entire life has been taken up into Yogi Ramsuratkumar's work and purpose. He sleeps about two or three hours a night and works constantly, attending to every smallest detail on the ashram. He looks like a man who is burning in the bright, hot, steady fire of Grace.

"The guru is very possessive—very possessive," Mani shook his head with a sober respect and awe of the ways of Yogi Ramsuratkumar. "If Yogi sees me talking to someone, he wants to know—'Who is Mani talking to? Mani doesn't need to be talking! Mani has work to do!' He doesn't want anything to keep me from my work. He is very possessive, very possessive. Even at the time of my mother's demise, I did not go to the funeral. He kept me here, on the ashram. When my children come to visit Yogi has them stay somewhere else on the ashram and not with me because he doesn't want them to distract me from my work. He is very possessive!

"I have learned not to argue with him. I just say yes to whatever He wants. I don't argue, I just listen. It is better for him to talk and for me to listen. He knows *exactly* how he wants everything to be. He is very, very meticulous—everything must be just so. It is a great blessing, of course. He says to me I don't have to chant his name or come to darshan or do anything—just work for him. Just work.

"Yes, yes, Mani is very blessed. Everyone says so. People say to me, 'Mani, you are very blessed,' but they don't understand how hard it is to be with a living saint. Mani is very blessed, but there is a *fire* under it . . ."

23

He continued, "Lee is like his Father. I say the son is like the Father. Lee is Yogi Ramsuratkumar's ambassador in the world."

Then Mani told the story of Yogi Ramsuratkumar wanting a permanent pedestal under the statue in the temple, but he didn't want the statue touched by anyone to put the pedestal in place. The workers listened in disbelief. How could they do such a thing? The statue was almost three meters tall and weighed tons. They argued with Mani and he said, "You don't understand—Yogi Ramsuratkumar doesn't want the statue touched, so we will find a way to do it without touching the statue! I have learned—now I don't say it is impossible, which it was. I just say yes when he asks for such things." He paused a moment. Somehow, he said, it was done as Yogi Ramsuratkumar wished.

Mani told another similar story about putting up the steel girders that hold up the massive roof of the huge temple. Yogi Ramsuratkumar wanted this done without moving the small palm-thatched open hut that is in the center of the temple next to the statue, where Devaki and the Sudama sisters sometimes sit while Yogi Ramsuratkumar gives darshan in his chair ten feet away from the statue.

"I just said yes, and with His Grace, it is done!" He said, smiling with amazement, wishing to impart with his words the miracles of daily life with Bhagavan. For Mani, everything was accomplished purely by the Grace of Yogi Ramsuratkumar. He readily and without reserve spoke of this in all regards. His faith was extraordinary. When one of the Americans asked Mani for a picture of Yogi Ramsuratkumar and Devaki Ma and then thanked him, Mani said, "Don't thank me—thank Yogi Ramsuratkumar." In this way Mani referenced everything back to Yogi Ramsuratkumar, but with a factual simplicity and seriousness that was free of any sentimentality or inebriation. It's just the way it is—the guru's Grace is everything. In these stories he communicated the reality of what it is to live with the immensity of the guru.

Soon it was time to line up at the gate for Yogi Ramsuratkumar's arrival at seven o'clock. The car stopped at the second structure on the grounds, called the *Yagashala*—a large hut with a palm-thatched roof and concrete floor near the entrance of the ashram and the front of the temple. Yogi Ramsuratkumar, Devaki Ma and Vijayalakshmi went directly from the car to their places along the inside wall of the hut, where blankets had been spread out on the floor. On the other side of the hut three Brahmin priests had set up an elaborate puja for the traditional Vedic rites that would be performed this morning.

There were around four hundred people lined up behind ropes held taut by poles. Large red cotton blankets were laid on the ground for "Lee and his party" just below the *Yagashala*, so that Lee sat directly in front of Yogi Ramsuratkumar and could also watch the ceremonies. Lee's students and Purna and his students sat close together around and behind Lee. On the other end of the *Yagashala* the priests had begun an extraordinary and ancient ritual. They offered ghee, flowers, water, incense and small pieces of wood into a specially prepared fire that burned on a three-tiered concrete form shaped in a square, beyond which was an elaborate shrine which had a picture of Yogi Ramsuratkumar and Devaki Ma as the central focus.

They began the long chant with an invocation to the deities Indra, Agni and Soma, as the Vedas proscribe. Many flower garlands were offered to Yogi Ramsuratkumar and Devaki, while the priests and others came to *pranam* and make offerings to the living deity, Yogi Ramsuratkumar, and then to Devaki, who stood by Bhagavan's side while he sat on the floor. She held her hands in a *pranam* to Yogi Ramsuratkumar throughout the ritual. Each time Devaki was approached with a garland she would almost jump as if in alarm, as if she could hardly bear to be included in this deification. Her eyes were focused on Yogi Ramsuratkumar, and it seemed that she continually turned everything that came her way to him.

There was much for a Westerner to learn this morning about the guru and devotee relationship. The selflessness and devotion to Yogi Ramsuratkumar demonstrated by Devaki and her companion, Vijayalakshmi, were very moving. Every year people who go with Lee to visit his father write about the tremendous example of devotion and faith that is embodied in Devaki Ma. It is a rare experience to witness the purity and nobility so evident in the invisible bonds between these two women and Yogi Ramsuratkumar. During the ceremony the Brahmin priest, Suresh, who led the Vedic rites interacted time and again with Yogi Ramsuratkumar. At Yogi Ramsuratkumar's request, Suresh officiates every year at the fire ceremony on his *jayanthi*. It was easy to guess why he was Yogi Ramsuratkumar's choice. The demonstration of genuine love and the integrity of real devotion that flowed from Suresh to Yogi Ramsuratkumar was something that one could see, feel and absorb.

The vast majority of Westerners are novices in this regard. We are like small children playing at devotion, obedience, surrender. Here in India one cannot hide or downplay the fact that one is American or European. The cultural orientation is vastly different, no matter how much one may be resonant with India and the Hindu tradition. We are still very different, and we have much to learn. Devotion, sacrifice and self-effacement in love are alive in the cellular structure of the Indians, passed down over thousands of years. Westerners have to deal with the propensity for fierce independence, selfishness, rebelliousness. These are the hallmarks of "maturity" in the Western psychological view, often appearing masked as aspects of self-actualization.

Lee watched the proceedings, his eyes glued to Yogi Ramsuratkumar. He was a living example of how to approach this ancient tradition. His attitude is one of deep respect, constraint, dignity and receptivity. He never barges into anything, but knows instinctively when to practice restraint and forbearance. He feels his way into circumstances. All this is motiveless; he is not trying to prove anything or get anything. He is here to serve, praise and receive whatever his father, Yogi Ramsuratkumar, gives to him.

After the Vedic rites were over and a late and particularly delicious breakfast of spicy *sambar* and rice with vegetables was consumed, we lined up at the gate to greet Yogi Ramsuratkumar for morning darshan. The crowds on the ashram had been steadily growing for the past few days; now there were at least three hundred filling up the room and many more wanting to get in, waiting outside the gates.

Yogi Ramsuratkumar entered and took his seat on the dais with Devaki and Vijayalakshmi. Right away he asked Lee to talk to everyone. Lee stood up and faced the crowd. Now the white faces in the front of the room were the minority against a sea of dark-skinned Indians. The multi-colored saris made a rainbow effect in the crowd. Many of the women wore flowers in their long black hair, which was combed neatly into a coil at the base of the neck. During the talk various Indian devotees came forward to give *prasad* to Yogi Ramsuratkumar. One came with a heavy, long garland made of hundreds of red roses and placed it around Yogi's neck.

After Lee's talk was over he asked two of his students to lead the chants. While they chanted an Indian man came up to offer *prasad* to Yogi Ramsuratkumar. He fell weeping at Yogi Ramsuratkumar's feet. He grabbed Yogi's knee and foot and pressed himself into him. Bhagawan put his hand on the man's back like a mother comforting her child. The look on his face was completely serene. Finally the man stood up and pulled a beautiful red and white wool shawl out of a bag and draped it over Yogi Ramsuratkumar's already shawl-laden shoulders. He *pranamed* again and Yogi chuckled at the new shawl. He asked the man to speak to the audience, so the man stood up, faced the crowd and began to speak in Tamil. He was wearing a large oval ring—a picture of Yogi Ramsuratkumar surrounded by diamonds that sparkled even in the dim light. In English he said, "Yogi Ramsuratkumar is God in human form . . . and Lee Lozowick, the great American saint who has come here to worship Yogi Ramsuratkumar . . . Yogi Ramsuratkumar is Lee Lozowick's God in human form too. Lee has come here not from India or Asia, but from all the way around the world, from the United States. He has come with thirty-five devotees who are here because they too feel God in Yogi Ramsuratkumar . . ."

While the talk continued an older Indian man came up to give and receive *prasad*. Yogi Ramsuratkumar greeted him with great affection and took the immense rose *mala* off and placed it around the man's neck. He had a chair brought up and placed beside the dais, which he offered to the older man, who sat there very quietly for the rest of the darshan. He seemed genuinely overwhelmed by these lavish gifts of the rose *mala* and the opportunity to sit beside Yogi Ramsuratkumar.

During this time people were running up to take photos of Yogi Ramsuratkumar— two, three, four people at a time. Some of them would run and drop to their knees, skidding toward the dais with camera raised and poised. Yogi Ramsuratkumar raised his hands in blessing. The cameras flashed and Yogi Ramsuratkumar endured it while the man talked on. It is commonly known that the flashing lights of cameras hurt Yogi Ramsuratkumar's eyes, but it seemed that on this day Yogi Ramsuratkumar was generously giving his devotees what they wanted. The Indian devotees must have had permission to take pictures or Selvaraj or Mani would have taken their cameras away.

The photographers sat down, satisfied for the moment, but then another man with a camera rushed up from the far side of the men's part of the room. Selvaraj stepped in to stop him. The man spoke to Selvaraj; he must have said, "I have permission," because Selvaraj reluctantly stepped back and allowed the man to go ahead. Yogi Ramsuratkumar blessed this man's photos as well, with one hand and then two raised in the air, looking directly into the camera.

Not long afterward a film crew arrived. They turned on intensely bright lights and filmed Yogi Ramsuratkumar, Devaki Ma and Vijayalakshmi, then moved the camera toward the man speaking, the men's side of the audience and then the women's side. The huge camera swung around again to film Yogi Ramsuratkumar from yet another angle, then again from various different angles. The video would air on a local station tonight.

The same speaker was talking now in Tamil. He walked over to the dais and touched Yogi Ramsuratkumar's feet to demonstrate a point. Finally he finished his talk and his whole family of four or five people came up to the dais to give and receive *prasad* from Yogi Ramsuratkumar. They placed a shawl over Yogi Ramsuratkumar's shoulders. More photographs were taken as people crowded in with cameras and lights flashed. The photographing seemed to be going toward excess. Even though permission had been granted, it seemed that more sensitivity and restraint could have been exercised in view of Yogi Ramsuratkumar's tenuous physical condition. It was not unlike the breaches of elegance and protocol that occur regularly in Lee's company.

Now the family was putting two more shawls on Yogi, so that he had on the three shawls that he always wears plus three more. He was laden down with shawls, and the heaviness of them seemed like a symbol of the awesome burden that he bears. For a moment he looked like a very rare and precious creature who had been captured and held in a strange, willing captivity. Yogi Ramsuratkumar bears the weight of an unimaginable burden, and now Lee has come with thirty-five people from the West who also seek his blessings. But with Lee it is clearly different. Lee is responsible, reliable, steady. Yogi Ramsuratkumar opens his darshan for Lee. He has not appeared in darshan since the day Lee left last year, and only reappears now that Lee has returned. In his poems Lee begs his father to allow Lee to help carry his weight. Now Lee sat in this space watching like a fierce captain of the guard. His attention was concentrated and focused, a laser-like consciousness beamed into the room. He seemed to be the guard at the door of the temple, Yogi Ramsuratkumar's champion.

A little boy ran up to take pictures. Yogi Ramsuratkumar blessed him with one hand up, and immediately four or five men who had been taking pictures all along rushed up to get in on the opportunity. Yogi Ramsuratkumar gave to all. They sat back down and Devaki took the three new shawls off of Yogi Ramsuratkumar's shoulders very carefully. Another man was invited up to see Yogi Ramsuratkumar. After kneeling at Yogi's knee and receiving his blessing the man stood and faced the crowd. He chanted for a moment, then began to speak in Tamil.

It was hot today in the Indian winter. The air steamed around us and we sweated. All the ceiling fans were turned on in the hall—except the fans above Yogi Ramsuratkumar. He must have been sweltering under all his woolen shawls. Devaki and Vijayalakshmi also wear heavy wool shawls over their white saris. The man was still speaking in Tamil. He said in English, for our benefit perhaps, "Remain at the door of the guru like a dog!" He repeated it twice. He was quoting scripture in Sanskrit and expounding on it. In English he again mentioned Lee, then the United States and France and the "Influence" of Yogi Ramsuratkumar. Finally, at five minutes to noon—the time when darshan officially ends every day—he turned and *pranamed* to Yogi Ramsuratkumar.

Immediately Yogi Ramsuratkumar left the room. He did not ask Lee and the small group of men to sit on the dais as he had before. Instead his seat was left empty except for a few scattered rose petals and two full roses that had dropped from the gorgeous rose *mala* that was placed around his neck during darshan by one of his devotees. The empty seat with the scattered red petals seemed like a forecast of things to come, when Yogi Ramsuratkumar will leave his body someday in the years ahead. The bittersweet certainty that Yogi Ramsuratkumar will return to his Father in Heaven seems to be a constant part of life in the company of the old beggar.

There was no chanting ringing through the hall when we came into darshan this afternoon. I noticed that Yogi Ramsuratkumar and Devaki were looking at the poetry book and pointing to something. It had been obvious since the first day that they were reading and looking through the poetry book back at Sudama House in between darshans, as they had a bookmark placed in it that kept moving forward in the book. One day when Lee and his crowd walked past Sudama House on the way to get sodas after lunch we heard Devaki reading poetry aloud from the book.

Now Yogi Ramsuratkumar called Lee up and pointed to the prayer that is written in Bengali at the beginning of the poems. I heard Devaki say, "It's in Bengali." Yogi Ramsuratkumar asked Lee what it said. Lee translated it, adding, "It's a prayer."

Yogi Ramsuratkumar said, "Oh . . . a prayer," as if this were the most wondrous thing possible. He asked Lee what language it was in.

"It is in Bengali," Lee answered and Devaki nodded.

"Do you read Bengali?" Yogi Ramsuratkumar asked.

"No," Lee answered.

"Say something . . ." Yogi Ramsuratkumar's voice trailed off as he instructed Lee to give another talk. Lee started out saying that the prayer in the poetry book typifies the work that Yogi Ramsuratkumar does with his devotees.

"His blessings are pure and wonderful," Lee continued, "they are help for our lives, but also they are to help us into the stream of Father in Heaven. One of the ways we thank Yogi Ramsuratkumar for His sacrifice for us is to allow ourselves to be blessed to the degree that we might do some small degree of our Father's work. I wouldn't suggest we could do Yogi Ramsuratkumar's work, but we might take on some small degree of it.

"To me Yogi Ramsuratkumar *is* God, so when I say 'God' I am talking about Yogi Ramsuratkumar. We praise Yogi Ramsuratkumar when things are going well in our lives, but when we are suffering emotionally or physically, we call on God, on Yogi Ramsuratkumar, to change things for us. We call on Yogi Ramsuratkumar out of need and desire, as a way to relieve our suffering. Yogi Ramsuratkumar is so compassionate and generous, like the Shankaracharya's prayer—'May all beings be happy and prosperous'—that Yogi wishes His devotees to be happy. But also there is only God, unitive, all one, no separation. That realization itself is a source of happiness—to know that no matter what happens to us, it is God's Will."

Lee's words were impassioned as he spoke about realizing God and surrendering to the Will of God. Lee constantly makes a call to higher law and dharma in these talks, to lift us up to the reality of oneness—"There is only God." He strives to take his listeners beyond mere supplication of Yogi Ramsuratkumar's blessings into an obligation of responsibility that is joyous in his translation of it for us, and in this way he calls us into pure and conscious relationship with the Divine.

More *prasad* was offered to Yogi Ramsuratkumar by various Indian devotees while the chanting was resumed. One man offered Yogi a beautiful green and white paisley shawl as *prasad*. Yogi Ramsuratkumar sat and held it in his lap, pressed his hands into it, stroked it gently, then after five or ten minutes, he gave it back to the man. A few minutes later Yogi took a banana off of his *prasad* tray on the dais, peeled it and ate half of it, then gave the other half to the man's wife. She immediately ate it. Five minutes later he peeled another banana and handed it to her husband. In this gesture was the alchemical transubstantiation of gross matter, from banana to the flesh of the guru, given to the devotee as gift.

Soon three or four of the men who had taken pictures during the morning started coming back up and flashing away with their cameras again. At one point a little later one of Yogi Ramsuratkumar's devotees who had been the most assertive in running up and taking photos with his flash camera once again ran up, fell on one knee about eight feet away from the dais and began flashing away. Yogi Ramsuratkumar said emphatically, "Enough!" and pointed the man ferociously, imperiously, toward his seat.

December 2, 1998
Yogi Ramsuratkumar Ashram

Early this morning Mani came to Lee's porch where a few of his students sat drinking coffee with him. He presented Lee with one of the brass ghee lamps that was used in the temple on *jayanthi* yesterday morning, with the image of Yogi Ramsuratkumar imprinted into it, his palmyra fan and coconut bowl impressed in the brass beside the turbaned head. "A gift from father to son," Mani said smiling, as he carefully handed it to Lee.

Today is Deepam, the great Shiva festival of lights when the top of Mount Arunachala, which has been covered with huge amounts of ghee, is set alight. Crowds have been amassing in town for the past two or three days in preparation for this holy day. Busloads of people are parked near the ashram, and people congregate around the ashram gate. In town the streets are literally rivers of people, pilgrims and sadhus.

After Yogi Ramsuratkumar had driven through and gone to breakfast Lee got the news and passed it along to those who were taking photographs in his group. The word was that no more photos could be taken because the flash had hurt Bhagawan's eyes. This apparently did not include the video camera because Purna was allowed to continued to roll the film. We were standing in line waiting for Yogi Ramsuratkumar to be driven back through on his way to Sudama House. Mani talked to one of the Indian men who was standing in line for the "drive by" darshan. In a serious tone he said, "If you have a camera on you we will take it now and gladly give you a receipt for your donation to the ashram!" He meant business.

In the meantime, while we waited in line, Lee was holding court, making various teaching points with some of the men. On the subject of the photo situation Lee shrugged and said, "It's the price of greed." In some ways it is the same everywhere. The human condition is the same whether the ego is Western or Eastern. We all operate under the same primal impulses of the illusion of separation.

Yogi Ramsuratkumar arrived for the morning darshan. He sat in the temple in his chair, eight or ten feet away from the statue, with Devaki and Vijayalakshmi sitting under the thatched palm hut chanting his name. There was a line of hundreds queued up through the ashram gate and out into the streets. People wanted to receive his darshan on this holy day. Lee's group went through the temple first and then made our way over to the hall where darshan would be held. Quickly the hall filled up with about three hundred people. Chanting was lead for awhile by two women from Lee's party, then two Indian men played bamboo flutes. More chants were led. Time moved slowly. The dais remained empty, but the presence of Yogi Ramsuratkumar was sublime and saturated the space.

The presence deepened and thickened in the room. Though physically still seated in the temple, Yogi Ramsuratkumar was pouring his benediction down like a steady, gentle rain. The devotees endlessly chanted his name. Eleven o'clock came and went, and Yogi Ramsuratkumar's platform remained empty. He was not coming into the darshan hall. We chanted some more, and some more. Twelve noon and darshan ended with the "Mangalam" chant. We sat for a few moments while some of the Indian women brought around baskets of flowers. Each woman was given a rose for her hair. The platform was so bare, so empty—his form was not there, and yet the living presence of Yogi Ramsuratkumar was all attractive and flowed like amrita.

As it turned out Yogi Ramsuratkumar was in the temple all morning blessing the lines of people who came in droves seeking his darshan on this day. He was still there when we had lunch. They had closed the gate at nine o'clock that morning after the first large group of people were let in to walk through the temple and receive Yogi Ramsuratkumar's darshan. Then the gates were opened again to let more people in. This morning after breakfast Mani said, "Yogi is very happy that so many have taken food here yesterday. Twelve hundred people!" That was surprising news because the gigantic effort of preparing, cooking, serving this many people had been largely invisible and quiet.

At three o'clock in the afternoon coffee arrived at the cottages. A few of us sat on the porch of Lee's cottage to drink. On the porch of the cottage next door several of Purna's students clustered in a mass on the steps. The coffee man was having some difficulty working around them to pour their coffee. Lee yelled over to one of the women, "Move off the step and give him room to pour!" She didn't respond at all. He yelled her name again, then said, "Move off the step and give him room to pour!" Finally it registered and she moved. Lee made a grimace. He said, "At least my students aren't the only ones who are deaf, dumb and blind this week!" We laughed uneasily and someone said facetiously, "Oh, well—we feel much better now." Clearly Lee has been very unhappy with the lack of response to his directives during darshan chanting as well as other clear signs of his students' failure to be obedient and resonant with him on this trip.

After coffee Lee sat in the front room of his cottage, which is completely empty except for his single bed and one or two plastic chairs. All of Purna's students plus most of Lee's students crammed into the space. Lee leaned back on his bed, looking very radiant and happy. He was serene for the moment, and simultaneously amiable and playful. Purna was running the video, taking a shot of Lee's feet, which were crossed at the ankle and propped up on one end of the bed. Lee wiggled his feet then made them dance and play about. He made himself totally available and accessible to everyone with his easy rapport and intimate smiles. When asked about Yogi Ramsuratkumar having Lee and three other Westerners take the dais after he leaves darshan each day, Lee said, "If I was to guess something complimentary to me, I'd say that I was trustworthy and he knows that. I'm not going to put on a shawl, pick up a palmyra fan and coconut bowl as soon as I sit up there. Yogi Ramsuratkumar likes Westerners—He finds us very humorous probably."

The conversation turned toward how much we have to learn from the Indians about devotion and the guru/devotee relationship. But also the point was made that Westerners have a particular evolution of consciousness that has been developed in the West that also contributes something to Eastern teachings. When asked what that contribution or kind of consciousness might be, Lee went on to say extemporaneously. "Pure devotion is a wonderful thing, but there is a lot of political infighting among Yogi Ramsuratkumar's devotees. Maybe we can add a kind of understanding of the kind of psychology that produces that political infighting that is so disturbing to any community of devotees around a master. So maybe we can contribute something, maybe in that way we can help the tradition evolve in some way. At least we *should* have the tools to do that . . . India is still probably the most extraordinary spiritual environment in the world, but it is being catapulted into being a First World power, and the cost of that is the spiritual tradition . . ."

At the four o'clock darshan Lee sat on a huge, widespread cotton blanket on the ground, facing Yogi Ramsuratkumar, who sat in a chair that had been placed on another large blanket, facing the mountain, Arunachala. He waited for the fire to appear on the distant crown of the mountain.

When Yogi Ramsuratkumar had arrived an hour earlier for the afternoon darshan he had the car stopped at the entrance to the temple. Mani ran over to confer with him. Immediately Mani and the other staff of the ashram were catapulted into action. Holes were dug, poles were set in place in the earth and ropes were strung taut to create a system whereby people could file past the area between the temple and the dining hall to receive Yogi Ramsuratkumar's darshan while he sat outside on this auspicious evening of Deepam. This would accommodate the hoards of people that were swarming and pushing up against the ashram gate to see the saint. We had heard reports of how intense the streets were up close to the base of the mountain, packed and jammed with crowds of ecstatic people, anxious to circumambulate the holy hill of Arunachala and gain untold scores of blessings in the act. The overflow was surging against the gates of Yogi Ramsuratkumar Ashram.

When the stage was properly set, Yogi Ramsuratkumar was helped into his chair, which had been brought out of the temple and set down on a large blanket. Mani and Selvaraj stood nearby while Devaki and Vijayalakshmi settled into their seats on the ground next to Yogi Ramsuratkumar. Devaki looked carefully to see what he might need, making adjustments here and there. Lee was given the seat of privilege, directly in front of and facing Yogi Ramsuratkumar, about ten feet away. Quickly Lee's group was called forward to sit facing Yogi Ramsuratkumar with Lee. Lee's students were seated, then Purna with the video camera and his students, and behind them Krishna Carcelle and his friends from Mauritius. Behind them, alongside the temple, stood or sat Yogi's Indian devotees, two or three hundred people who were allowed to stay for the entire darshan. Together we all chanted, "Yogi Ramsuratkumar, Yogi Ramsuratkumar, Yogi Ramsuratkumar, Jaya Guru Raya," for the next two hours. In the meantime streams of people filed past behind the ropes, having the opportunity to glimpse the darshan of the saint, the Godchild of Tiruvannamalai. There were thousands of people, perhaps fifteen thousand, who came filing through.

All the Indians waited with high anticipation for the light to appear on the summit of Arunachala. All during this we waited and soaked in the presence of Yogi Ramsuratkumar while preparations went on behind and around him to feed masses of people at the special feast tonight. Selvaraj and Mani waited to light the ghee pot that had been arranged on top of a ladder behind Yogi Ramsuratkumar; another pot of ghee was arranged on top of the temple. These lights would be lit as soon as Arunachala was lit, and would signify that Shiva was here—in the physical body of the old beggar, and in his temple.

Yogi Ramsuratkumar sat through all this quite dispassionately. He seemed unconcerned, childlike, enduring. His gaze wandered over the temple, which drew his attention again and again. He wore sunglasses against the glare of the sunset light, his eyes obviously still painful from the photo sessions. Devaki had gotten the sunglasses out, carefully cleaned them and handed them to him. He seemed very still behind their protective shade. She also called for a folded blanket to put under his feet so they wouldn't hang uncomfortably one or two inches above the ground.

Sitting directly opposite Yogi Ramsuratkumar with the men on one side and the women on the other side, Lee was a mirror of Yogi Ramsuratkumar. He sat very serene and unmoving, undistracted by anything, his attention riveted on Yogi Ramsuratkumar, just watching. There was no sign of any "process" at all on his face—just free attention in an impassive but focused awareness without content. He seemed to be nothing but pure receptivity and attention. Both Yogi Ramsuratkumar and Lee appeared acutely aware,

31

burning with presence and yet empty—no motives of any kind moving anything or any "one." They were just there, totally, and the mood of one was reflected back by the mood of the other.

Dusk fell slowly as Lee and his group literally basked in this intimate and rare darshan with Yogi Ramsuratkumar. The chanting continued throughout the time, which stretched out into long minutes, while workers walked back and forth along the pathway to the temple, preparing for the feast. Three men struggled along to carry one hundred and fifty to two hundred pound pots of rice, *sambar*, and other delicious food. Women in bright saris hurried past with bundles of banana leaf plates. The cow was brought out of her shed behind Yogi Ramsuratkumar. She faced him and mooed loudly, then ate her dinner of a pile of hay while standing and facing Yogi and the mountain, as if on cue.

Finally Arunachala was lit; a big cheer went up and fireworks went off nearby and further away in town. People yelled and cheered. Everyone was uplifted, thrilled at the sight of this grand symbol of Shiva's sovereignty over the three worlds, and his embodiment in the holy mountain. While all this ruckus and commotion went on, Yogi Ramsuratkumar sat still, unmoved, tranquil, just watching, looking up at the temple, looking over the crowd. By now it was dark enough to have the sunglasses off. His eyes were slightly unfocused and yet his gaze seemed very intentional. It was a burning, smoky gaze that wandered over everything and all, missing nothing, taking it all in. Immediately another light—a ghee pot set in an iron pot up on ladders behind Yogi—sprang to life, along with the light on the high roof of the temple. In this moment the excitement and joy of all the Indians was highly contagious. It was as if a powerful collective thought form went up into the atmosphere, "Yogi Ramsuratkumar is our Arunachala Shiva! Shiva is here! Alive! Right now! At Agrahara Kollai, the Yogi Ramsuratkumar Ashram!"

The ghee pot on the top of the temple blazed with the light on the mountain. The temple too is considered the body of Yogi Ramsuratkumar; his being and presence permeate every brick, stone and rock, all the steel beams, the mortar, the wood, the ground upon which it all stands, the large bronze statue. All of it *is* Yogi Ramsuratkumar, who is Arunachala Shiva and the living incarnation of Ram.

A puja ceremony was done to Yogi Ramsuratkumar, waving lights before the living deity. Fire, water, incense and flowers were offered to his feet by Devaki Ma. When the puja was completed Devaki and Vijayalakshmi circumambulated Yogi Ramsuratkumar several times then *pranamed* at his feet. They led a chant, "Arunachala Shiva, Arunachala Shiva, Arunachala Shiva, Arunejeda." Very quickly after this Yogi Ramsuratkumar and the women left for Sudama House. Lee and his group were quickly instructed to take the back path behind the temple to the beautiful, finished front entry hall of the temple where a lavish, celebratory meal would be served.

As we hurried along the dirt path in the dusk the full moon was rising in the sky. It was mellow and golden, seen through the dust and smoke of the Indian night. A herd of cows with a cowherder walked along on the other side of the ashram wall in a field under dim stars that were just beginning to shine. In the distance were mountains that, in their rugged rockiness, looked very much like southern Arizona. Palm trees and flowering shrubs loomed green and lush and shadowy out of the dusty ground in the hot dark night. Fireworks, horns and shouts of joy could be heard floating on or piercing through the night air. The mood was ecstatic, chaotic, wild. Quickly we rushed along with bare feet after Lee to dinner—a fantastic six-course feast served in the beautiful ornate room with a shiny black marble floor. Large pictures of Ramana Maharshi and his mother,

Sri Aurobindo and Mother Meera and Papa Ramdas and Mataji Krishnabai hung on the walls. As soon as we were finished we left to make room for the next wave: they would feed twenty-five hundred people there before the night was over. The ashram had already fed fifteen hundred people at lunch.

After dinner Lee immediately went to play bridge in one of the cottages. Once everyone was settled in the room someone in Purna's group asked about the significance of Deepam and the lighting of the mountain. For their benefit Lee told the Shiva myth that had been enacted this night on Arunachala. Lee looked radiantly happy and clear as he told this tale: Vishnu and Brahma—two of the three primary gods, who, along with Shiva, make up the powerful triune Godhead in classical Hinduism—were having an argument one day over who was the most powerful. They asked Shiva to decide. He said, "I am," and became a shaft or column of light that stretched out in both directions to infinity. Vishnu and Brahma both tried to find the beginning and the end of this light but couldn't, so they agreed with Shiva. Arunachala, as the embodiment of Shiva, represents the earthly pole of the column of light.

Soon Tom and Zachary, who had braved the wild throngs of people to go into town and get cold sodas for everyone, arrived with Pepsi, Limca, Thums Up and orange drinks. They had gone to Lee's favorite soda stall on the main strip across from Ramanashram, about a fifteen-minute walk away. When they returned they said the streets were choked with people walking in wild, almost frenzied droves, celebrating Deepam and circumambulating Arunachala, all of them anxious to gain good karma by walking around the holy mountain. They said that the auto rickshaw they rode in was literally floating in a sea of people.

After bridge and just before bed, around eight-thirty a few of us circumambulated the ashram. The brightly-lit temple shone out into the darkness, revealing the scene inside where the staff was still feeding crowds of people.

December 3, 1998
Yogi Ramsuratkumar Ashram

"Yogi Ramsuratkumar understands human psychology," Lee began his talk, at Yogi's request, in darshan this morning. Lee started with a story about how one of his own students had asked if he could write a biography of Yogi Ramsuratkumar on a visit to Tiruvannamalai some years ago. "Yogi Ramsuratkumar knows that biographers tend to look at the details of a person's life. He laughed and said, 'No,' then talked for two hours about how everyone has both light and dark in them; even the greatest saint can be misunderstood because of this. Yogi Ramsuratkumar said that in the dark age in which we live, full of suffering, crime and political corruption, people need inspiration on the spiritual path. People need hope and guidance, and when someone reads about the great saints and sages and finds something negative in a biography, that could hurt that person's aspirations or turn them against the path, or away from the path. So our criticality of others is the same; we should look at the light in others and forget the negative in order to bring hope, inspiration. Gossip is a kind of criticism. We are trying to belittle others and make ourselves bigger. But we don't have to try to get some advantage over others through gossip and criticism. Yogi Ramsuratkumar has said to me many times, 'This beggar only wants praise.' But the important thing to remember is that even one who has much darkness in them also has some light."

At the beginning of the afternoon darshan Yogi Ramsuratkumar offered for sale the seven books that Rick, one of Purna's students, brought today when he arrived from the States. Three were sold immediately. Then Yogi had some fun with Lee's students. But first, he had the Brahmin priest, Suresh, who officiated at yesterday's Vedic rites and rituals, give a speech on the significance of Deepam. After receiving Yogi Ramsuratkumar's blessings and *pranaming* at his feet, Suresh stood up and began to speak in English.

"The festival of Deepam is about the indescribable Supreme Reality which cannot be fathomed in words or intellectual arguments. That Supreme is pure compassion, and is available to us in the form of the holy hill Arunachala. In the holy scriptures, the *Puranas* and such, there is a legend that tells of a competition between Vishnu and Brahma over who is the greatest in all the Universe. In the middle of that argument Lord Shiva appeared as a limitless column of fire whose beginning and end could not be fathomed by anyone, by Vishnu or Brahma. Vishnu tried to find the bottom of it in his form as a boar, and Brahma tried to find the top of it in his form as a swan. But they could not. Then Lord Shiva appeared, beginningless and endless, and said, 'Out of my compassion for every living being in the world I have taken the form of this holy hill.' So Arunachala signifies the compassion of the Divine, and that is why the light is lit on the hill and devotees come from everywhere to attain merits by going around the hill. Lord Arunachalesvara we also have here in the form of Yogi Ramsuratkumar. He is that Supreme which cannot be attained through words or arguments. Therefore," Suresh concluded, "I have no more words to describe this; only surrender, surrender, surrender at the Holy Feet of Yogi Ramsuratkumar."

After Suresh sat down Yogi asked Lee to speak. Lee spoke about a story titled "Simple Living and Right Thinking," that appeared in a yoga magazine published out of Florida that Yogi Ramsuratkumar had read many times in darshan last year. The story is about a well-to-do man traveling on a train who goes out of his way to help an old woman with a lot of baggage, and then slips away, avoiding the tip that she wants to give him, thinking him to be a poor porter. Lee said, "If we have a certain importance in the world, a position, we expect to be treated in a certain way. But this idea of simple living and right thinking is very relevant subject matter for us all, however we found Yogi Ramsuratkumar.

"When I first came to India I knew nothing about India or holy men and sages. I went to an American woman who had lived in India for years, and she told me to seek out Yogi Ramsuratkumar. No one in America had heard of Him yet—we had heard of Satya Sai Baba and Anandamayi Ma, but not Yogi Ramsuratkumar."

Lee then told the story of his first visit with Yogi Ramsuratkumar—how one Westerner had been in Tiruvannamalai for three months looking for Yogi but hadn't found him, whereas Lee and his students found him immediately. "Really Yogi Ramsuratkumar found me," Lee said. "It was all up to Yogi Ramsuratkumar whether He was found or not by me or anyone else."

During the telling of Lee's story Yogi Ramsuratkumar was bent over, sunk deeply into himself. He rubbed his cupped hands together, one over the other, again and again for about five long minutes. Whatever gesture or posture Yogi Ramsuratkumar made or took was so potent that it seemed to last forever. His physical form was so exceedingly real that it burned into the eternal moment. Every movement seemed to have a mysterious, far-reaching effect on the environment, in the world, in the universe.

Lee continued, "Yogi Ramsuratkumar is not an individual anymore. In 1952 He was 'murdered' by Papa Ramdas. He is only all one, continuous, all unity. There is only His

Father in Heaven. So we find ourselves in His presence, however we found our way here. We are so fortunate to have this auspicious opportunity, to have found Yogi Ramsuratkumar in this lifetime, to be in His company.

"In the Bible it says that those who have the eyes to see will see the Christ, and those who don't, won't. For those who have the eyes to see Yogi Ramsuratkumar, He is pure light, pure Blessing Force. Others think He is just an eccentric. But we should know that it is so incredibly auspicious to find Him in this life."

Lee then apologized again for insulting anyone by mentioning another tradition. It was the third time he had made this apology, and it seemed that he was making a subtle point about the need to be open and universal rather than fundamentalist and narrow-minded about Hinduism. He said, "In Islam the Ka'bah at Mecca is worshipped as a sacred artifact. Yogi Ramsuratkumar is not a rock but a living saint, a miraculous event. It is unspeakably sacred to be able to sit at the Feet of such a One. There is nothing He needs, nothing He wants—all He is here to do is to serve the work of His Father in Heaven. If out of our deep gratitude we wish to give something back to Him, we can consider simple living, high thinking."

Lee said thank you and turned, walked over to Yogi Ramsuratkumar at the dais and knelt at his side in a *pranam*. Yogi took Lee's hands in his own for a long time. He was sunk into some interior depths and seemed to be working very hard there, then he opened his eyes and looked long and deeply at Lee. He lovingly stroked Lee's arms and hands. He asked Lee to have someone lead chants.

Three of the American women got up and started chanting at Lee's request. During this long stretch of chanting Yogi Ramsuratkumar picked up *Death of a Dishonest Man* and began to look through it page by page. He slowly turned the pages, carefully and gently lifting each one. He was reverent with the book, holding it tenderly, gingerly. Yesterday and the day before he had done this with the book also, going page by page through quite a bit of it. Devaki pointed out the songs in the back of the book to Yogi Ramsuratkumar and his attention focused there. She said something to him about the songs. It seemed like she pointed to the one about Kali because it is near the end of the songs, and she said the word "Kali" as she pointed.

Yogi Ramsuratkumar called Lee over and they talked for a moment, then Lee came over to me with Yogi's book in hand. He knelt down and said to me, "He wants some of the songs sung. Pick out two or three that you and Chris can do—be quick about it." Lee gestured to Chris, who was standing with the women who were leading the chant, and she walked over to join us. Slightly stunned by what we were going to do, we realized that we didn't remember the melodies to hardly any of these rock & roll lyrics, and they would be incredibly difficult to sing without the electric guitars, drums and music. We asked Lee if we could explain this to the audience. His fierce reply was, "No—just sing."

We quickly discussed what to do and stood up, *pranamed* to Yogi Ramsuratkumar a little sheepishly and faced the crowd. We faltered and fumbled through three or four songs, making up melodies wherever we didn't remember the original tune, which was often. It was an agonizing but grand moment of losing face—grand because it was Yogi Ramsuratkumar's *lila*. Finally Lee walked over and said, "Okay, you're off the hook."

We turned and *pranamed* to Yogi Ramsuratkumar. He was smiling broadly, looking very delighted and happy. Then Lee took over. He faced the crowd and said that Yogi Ramsuratkumar had asked him to sing. Lee does not like to sing without the bands, but if Yogi Ramsuratkumar asks, he will do it. Now he apologized, charmed and melted the crowd with his explanations of the songs. His innocent willingness to do something so obviously difficult for him disarmed everyone. People laughed gently along with him as he playfully and skillfully worked the space. He had everyone in the palm of his hand before it was over; he sang two or three songs, then turned to Yogi Ramsuratkumar and knelt at his feet to receive his blessings. Yogi Ramsuratkumar left shortly, almost immediately, and Lee, Purna, Alain de Rosenbo and Bret sat on the dais as usual. Now that Krishna Carcelle has gone home Purna took his place in this group of Westerners. Lee sat down first in Yogi's place. Bret sat where Vijayalakshmi usually sits when Yogi Ramsuratkumar is on the dais, which now was adjacent to and facing Lee.

The chanting went on for another thirty minutes, until six o'clock, and darshan was over. The puja ceremony and waving of lights was done and *prasad* was offered outside. As we walked toward the back of the hall for these ceremonies Lee said to me, "Yogi Ramsuratkumar says you and Chris can practice these songs and be prepared to sing tomorrow, so pick out some and work on them tonight. You can pull in other women on some of the songs if you want to." This was definitely the unexpected.

Reflecting on how the afternoon went I laughingly said to Lee, "You charmed everybody with all your explanations about the songs, how hard it is to sing them without the instruments and so on. We weren't supposed to talk, only sing. I get it—you get to look really good and charm everybody and we're just supposed to lose face!"

Lee laughed amiably and said, "That's right!"

After the usual dinner of cookies, pound cake, peanut candy, peanut butter and honey sandwiches, oranges, apples and other miscellaneous goodies, Chris and I took off to work on songs. We found three Shri songs that we could work up quite well and two liars, gods & beggars songs that we would do with a small group of the women. By the next morning, after practicing again after breakfast, we would be ready.

December 4, 1998
Yogi Ramsuratkumar Ashram

At six o'clock in the morning when the coffee arrived and was poured into stainless steel cups on the porch it was still dark—a twilight predawn. A deep peace pervaded the air of the ashram. In the deep blue morning sky to the west sat the setting full moon, yellow and round, with dark blue clouds flowing across its golden face. Birds called and trilled while crows cawed and barked as a few of us sat drinking coffee with Lee. Looking at the beautiful sight of the moon, Lee commented, "I wonder if Purna has his video camera out—that would be a nice shot." Called *chandra* in Sanskrit, the moon is the image most often used by Baul poets to describe Lord Krishna, particularly in his form as Govinda, lover of the *gopis*. This morning it richly evoked something elusive about the mood of the ashram and the poetic essence of Mother India.

At the ten o'clock darshan Yogi Ramsuratkumar went straight into the business at hand. As soon as Devaki and Vijayalakshmi had finished singing the opening chants Devaki marked the songs in the poetry book with a piece of paper. Yogi Ramsuratkumar called Lee over and they conferred. Lee came walking over to me. Chris was with the children, and would arrive in a few minutes. Lee said, "Wait until you hear this!" His tone was full of delight at seeing Yogi Ramsuratkumar in full play.

"Okay," he continued, "He wants the songs sung one by one, all the way through—*all* of them." This news sank in as I remembered that there are thirty-six songs in the back of the poetry book. All of our plans and preparations to be able to sing, to our satisfaction, five songs crumbled to dust before my dazed eyes. "Can we skip around, do the ones we know best first?" I asked, clutching at illusory straws—we would still have to sing *all* the songs that we didn't remember or that hadn't even been composed to music yet. "No," Lee said. "Do them in order."

"We really don't remember the melodies to most of them, and some of them, four or five of them, haven't even been composed yet and have no music to them!" All this rushed out in a whisper—I was letting Lee in on the full extent of our predicament out of desperation to somehow alter the reality of this task, as if Lee didn't already know everything I was telling him. The difference was, he didn't care. "Don't make excuses, just obey the guru," I could hear him saying in my mind.

"Make it up. Make it up," Lee said with no sympathy. His tone of voice said, "This should not be a problem for you at all." Right. Chris still wasn't there. I would be on my own for at least the first song or two. I took a deep breath and got up, *pranamed* to Yogi Ramsuratkumar and faced the audience of about one hundred people.

Yogi Ramsuratkumar loves music. He often asks people to sing chants or religious songs. Of course we wanted to do what ego would consider a "good job" of whatever Yogi asked for, but at best we could only hope to bring him some enjoyment with Lee's songs. As I made up melodies on the spot, rambled around and bumbled through feeling fairly ridiculous, I glimpsed Chris through the windows in the back of the hall, walking as fast as she could. In a few more seconds she was standing beside me and we began to switch off songs until we got to the first Shri song that we had prepared to sing together. On two of the songs a group of four women got up and sang with us. What a relief! These were songs that we knew well and could really sing, bringing the melodies out. Then we were back to the songs that we had to make up melodies to as we went along.

This went on for an hour and a half as we worked through the lyrics page by page, making most of the melodies up, doing our best to simply sing without self-consciousness—though without much luck. It was finally over. This was not a place for ego to exult, although we seemed to be more critical of our performance than everyone else thought we should be. To us it felt like a cremation ground. We were burning to ash in Yogi Ramsuratkumar's *smashan*. The intensity of this fire—much more than appearances can ever show—is impossible to describe.

Yogi Ramsuratkumar was working in enigmatic ways. The most apparent level of this work was that he was empowering Lee's songs and Western Baul music. The singers were just the pawns in the game, and yet the reverberations of Yogi Ramsuratkumar's sublime attention was immense. After we had sung all the songs Yogi Ramsuratkumar called us up, asked our names and gave us *prasad*. Chris went first while I knelt on the floor behind her. Then it was my turn. I was determined not to make the same mistake twice.

I moved up close to the dais where he sat. He picked up an apple from his tray of prasad. "What is your name?" he asked.

"Mary Young," I said with confidence, as if I knew now for sure that this was in fact my name. He burst into peals of laughter, threw his head back in a fit of delight. It struck me that I had managed to crack him up. I smiled broadly and then laughed with him. Devaki laughed too. Lee had a big smile on his face as he sat in his chair watching and listening. Yogi Ramsuratkumar's body shook with laughter. His laughter was so remarkable that it was worth any amount of foolishness to induce that sound into the world. The laughter died down and, with a little smile lingering on his face, Yogi Ramsuratkumar moved into a blessing pose with one hand up.

"My Father blesses Young," he said, so softly that I think no one heard but me. He held both hands up and his eyes penetrated past me into lifetimes and beyond. When he is like this it seems that he is reading the *akashic* records, untying the knots of *samskaras* and cleaning up old karma. His piercing gaze moved up above my head and to the right side of my body and just beyond, looking over lifetimes, past and future, clearing away debris and refuse. He was radiating benediction into the momentum of what is to come, what is in motion and inexorably unfolds across future incarnations. He hastens and accelerates the process of evolution, because he exists as the pure Will of God incarnate, here and now. This hastening and acceleration of the soul's evolution is a great boon, but not necessarily pleasant to experience when one exists in the gross state, carrying attachments, *samskaras*—all the illusory but tenacious, desperate baggage of ego. We cling to these identities of separation as if they were our paradise.

Everything Yogi Ramsuratkumar does proceeds from the unknown, fresh and gleaming with mystery, but as Mani says, with a fire underneath. Fire is everywhere here. It is so basic to existence, and it is felt under the skin, down in the infinitesimal reaches of the body, as it penetrates into matter. The flame, or *jyoti,* of Yogi Ramsuratkumar, the living saint of Tiruvannamalai, is a compelling conflagration, a roaring blaze.

His hands fell down and the doorway to infinity closed somehow. He said, "Thank you." This was the second time he had thanked me. What a strange thing to hear from his lips! It gives one pause to consider—what would it mean to be worthy of such thanks? After a final *pranam* I sat down in my seat on the floor beside Chris. Once we were settled Yogi Ramsuratkumar looked at the two of us and repeated, "Thank you."

Yogi Ramsuratkumar left immediately and the chanting continued for another thirty-five minutes, until darshan was over at noon. Lee and the men sat on the dais as soon as Yogi was gone. Lee looked at Chris and me with a mischievous and benign smile on his face and pretended to clap delicately, like a well-heeled lady at the opera. He was smiling with enjoyment. Anything that pleased and delighted Yogi Ramsuratkumar pleased and delighted Lee. It was not an exercise in doing things "right" by linear, egoic or worldly standards. It was a crucible in which Yogi Ramsuratkumar was able to do his work—a bestowing of power on Lee's songs and music. This was the overpowering communication of Yogi Ramsuratkumar's whole play in this regard: that he was pouring his benediction and fiery empowerment on his son Lee's work.

After darshan Lee stepped up to us and said gleefully, "Guess what you're going to do next! He wants you to sing the *poems*!" We stared at him with disbelief and wonder, even awe. Was this really happening? What a wondrous, skillful play of events Yogi Ramsuratkumar was orchestrating! Lee explained further that after the singing of the thirty-six songs, Yogi Ramsuratkumar had asked him to have us sing some of his "songs" and Lee said, "You mean the songs that were just sung?"

Yogi said, "No, some of your songs to this beggar."

Lee looked at Devaki Ma and asked, "Does He mean the poems?"

"Poems of a Broken Heart," Devaki confirmed.

After Devaki and Vijayalakshmi sang the opening chants in the afternoon darshan the chanting of Yogi Ramsuratkumar's name went on for an hour. Then Yogi Ramsuratkumar asked Lee to speak. Lee's teachings are thoughtful and measured here;

he touches on many important points for all of us, both the Westerners and the Indians. The skillful means with which Lee works in such situations is apparent in his expressions of respect and appreciation for the Eastern traditions; at the same time, he makes teaching lessons for everyone. Today he began by apologizing again for telling stories from the Indian traditions. He said that he only has access to English translations, and he is sure that they are not nearly as good as the originals. In the *Bhagavad Gita,* Lee said, Krishna and Arjuna are talking, and Krishna is telling Arjuna about devotion. Krishna says that if one of his devotees offers him one flower, one grain of rice with true devotion, then Krishna becomes the slave of that slave, or devotee.

Then Lee told the story of Sudama, Krishna's childhood friend, now grown up. Krishna lived in a palace with riches and silks, while Sudama was only a poor, starving priest, but one of great sanctity and integrity. His wife begged Sudama to go to his old friend Krishna, now rich and wealthy, with whom he had been *gurubhais* so long ago, for help. Sudama took a few grains of rice and offered them to Krishna.

"It is really ourselves," Lee continued, "not gold and riches, that we should offer to the Divine. We should offer not wealth and material things, but ourselves. In martial arts one goes and bows to the teacher with open hands to signify a giving of one's self. So whatever is offered with pure faith, with pure devotion, that is what God wants, and it is received. In the West we think our offering to the Divine is a business deal—'If I give this to the guru, then the guru will give me that.' But it's not a business deal. What we give is ourselves . . .

"In Yogi Ramsuratkumar there is nothing there—no desires, no ego. Yogi Ramsuratkumar went to Ramdas and gave Himself, and what Ramdas gave in return was madness. We want to make a deal with the guru, but the guru makes no deals; the guru doesn't decide what to give us when we give ourselves. The guru is a pure vehicle of the Will of God, of Grace. Whatever blessings, whatever gifts of the Divine that are given, these are *freely* given—there is no return expected, nothing is asked for.

"So we approach the Divine with open hands, offer our souls, our spirits, for whatever Yogi Ramsuratkumar's Father in Heaven can use us for, and we surrender to that, whatever that is. If we offer even one grain of rice with pure devotion and pure faith, then the Divine gives freely, opens Its vast and limitless storehouse and gives freely."

After the talk was finished Lee went to the dais and knelt by Yogi Ramsuratkumar, who closed his eyes and held Lee's hands. The mood between Yogi Ramsuratkumar and Lee was infinitely tender, like a mother's deepest, most profound and loving kindness to her child. Yogi Ramsuratkumar raised his hands in blessing and said quietly, "My Father blesses Lee."

With much more force and a mischievous chuckle, Yogi Ramsuratkumar said, "My Father will give you what you *need!!*" Yogi chuckled again and smiled sweetly, patting Lee on the back lovingly. He left immediately after that. Lee and the three men sat on the dais, again with Bret on the side facing Lee. A group of musicians played traditional music with a drum and horns until darshan was over.

It being Friday night, the cow puja was done in addition to the usual puja. Lights were waved to the shrine near the door with Yogi Ramsuratkumar's picture, to Arunachala, which could be seen in the distance through a square that had been cut in the thatched roof, to the dais where Yogi Ramsuratkumar sits, and to the shrine for the Shankaracharya near Yogi's dais. Tonight the brown cow stood waiting patiently just outside the dining hall door.

The brown cow was quite beautiful and pampered in the way that cows are cared for and considered sacred in India. As the light was waved in slow circles before her, she seemed huge and vast in her capacity for endless giving. She was a symbol of strength, abundance and sacrifice. Suddenly the cow began to urinate. This is considered especially auspicious, and the attendant immediately cupped his hands underneath her tail and caught handfuls of the urine, which he splashed over Lee and his students who were standing there. What a thrill! Everyone laughed as the Indians all stepped forward for this blessing, while some of the Americans and Europeans couldn't help themselves—they involuntarily stepped back.

After dinner Lee and company went to a house about twenty minutes away where Lee would give a public talk. Chris and I stayed behind. Not being composers, we stayed up very late attempting to do the impossible—put some of Lee's poetry to song, using old folk melodies.

December 5, 1998
Yogi Ramsuratkumar Ashram

For some reason Yogi Ramsuratkumar did not say a word to Lee about the singing of the poems today. Instead of singing, Lee and numbers of his students were giving talks now. Whoever gave a talk or led chants then had the opportunity to go to Yogi Ramsuratkumar and receive *prasad*. "Your name?" he would ask sweetly, then he listened carefully to the reply and dropped an orange, banana or apple into the waiting cupped hands of the devotee.

Sadhu Rangarajan, a long-time devotee of Yogi Ramsuratkumar, was there this afternoon also and gave a spirited and grand talk with great gusto and pomposity. He had brought twenty or so people who chant Ramnam in South Africa with him. They got to *pranam* to Yogi Ramsuratkumar and give and receive *prasad* from him, with Rangarajan sitting nearby at Yogi's knee.

Sadhu Rangarajan began his talk by explaining that the word "avatar" means descended manifestation of the Supreme Reality, the Nameless and Formless. He said, "The *Vedas* try to explain that Reality but cannot because it is incomprehensible, beyond intellect, infinite. That Reality, out of mercy and kindness, appears in physical form as a human being from time to time. The God Incarnate, Rama himself, declared, 'I have come down in human form!'

"The descent of every avatar has a specific purpose. The Supreme Reality appears amidst us in human form or some other form to draw us toward it and raise us to consciousness, existence and bliss—*sat, chit, ananda.* To be born as a human being is a great gift. From a strict Vedic or Vedantic viewpoint, we have not attained the stature of human being at all. To distinguish between the appearances of things, of the world, and that which is beyond appearances, is to be human, but our minds are carried away by sensual pleasure, pride, greed. Even if you take human form, you do not necessarily use your discriminatory faculty. Only very few take to this path, which is to know that there is a higher God, *Mahapurusha*, the guru—the one who dispels darkness and ignorance, the one who lifts us up from darkness into light. It is the guru who lifts us from the world of mortality to the world of immortality.

"Just putting a *mala* around the guru's neck is not enough. We have to surrender at the guru's feet. We have to learn the right way to approach the Mahatma. The task before us is to totally surrender to his feet, through austerity, renunciation, absolute ahimsa (non-violence).

"Yogi Ramsuratkumar, Ramdas and Krishnabai have prescribed for us to do Ramnam in all our daily tasks, offered to the Ultimate Reality, Ram. The purpose of our life in this world is to realize Ram, Atma Rama. Krishnabai asks us to chant Ramnam for world peace. You should do whatever you can every day, for five minutes, for fifteen minutes, whatever you can do. Even when you work in your office or in the kitchen, your mind can chant Ramnam mantra. When we churn the milk, the *gopis* synchronized the mantra with the churning. By the Grace of Bhagavan, due to the merits of previous births, you get this mantra to chant. Now Yogi Ramsuratkumar has commanded Rangarajan to spread Ramnam all over the world. And now we chant 'Yogi Ramsuratkumar, Yogi Ramsuratkumar, Yogi Ramsuratkumar, Jaya Guru Raya.' Rama's Name is more powerful than Ram Himself; Yogi Ramsuratkumar's Name is four times more powerful than the name of Ram. It is like a homeopathic pill—it is more powerful than the thing itself. Yogi Ramsuratkumar is Ram in physical form before us."

In Lee's afternoon talk he said that many of us here aspire to very high things—we want realization or enlightenment, but we don't stop to think of the price that has to be paid for such a treasure. "We desire to serve God, but we should think twice before we ask for madness. To become mad in God is impossible, and yet there are many examples of it in the spiritual traditions, like Shirdi Sai Baba, Anandamayi Ma, Ramana Maharshi and Ramakrishna. Yogi Ramsuratkumar is mad.

"I visited Yogi Ramsuratkumar in the seventies. He took us for walks about Arunachalesvara Temple, and He blessed all the sadhus there, spoke with them and cared for them where they all rested around the bathing ghat. What joy it brought Him to bless the sadhus and talk with them! But He can't do that anymore. He is a prisoner, a Slave of God.

"Yogi Ramsuratkumar can't go on a vacation like most of us." Even some of the Indians laughed at this. "He has no such luxury. He can't even walk out on the street anymore because the fame of His greatness has grown so that people storm around Him. He is a prisoner of Father in Heaven. If He went out into the streets He would be engulfed by so many eager devotees. Now His only pleasure is to pour His Father in Heaven's Blessings out on us, from here at the temple or Sudama House. So when we ask for madness, we don't realize what a difficult Master Father in Heaven is. He demands things of us that no human being can possibly demand—our wishes, our hopes. Father in Heaven demands everything of us."

Lee told the story of the man who once came to darshan to give *prasad* and *pranam*. As he looked at this man Yogi Ramsuratkumar was so visibly moved and grateful that he had tears in his eyes. A devotee asked, "Bhagavan, why do you have such gratitude to that man?"

Yogi replied, "That man has a tea stall near the temple and when this beggar lived on the street, that man gave him tea."

"Did you go to his stall every day for tea?" the devotee asked.

"Oh, this beggar only went once a month," Yogi Ramsuratkumar answered.

Lee continued, "Imagine how difficult Father in Heaven's work is if Yogi felt this much gratitude for such small favors? The hardest work in the world is to work for Father in Heaven. To work for orphans or to feed the poor is very fine work, very necessary work, but very easy work compared to the work Yogi Ramsuratkumar does for His Father in Heaven.

"Father in Heaven can give us everything and anything, but we may not be able to handle everything that we want to be given very well. Yogi Ramsuratkumar just says, 'My Father blesses you.' He doesn't ask if you deserve it, or ask any questions, or for anything in return. He just gives endlessly. At the same time His sacrifice and His burden is so great. Just think of that! If you or I didn't even have the freedom to walk out of our house without being torn apart by avid devotees! Yogi Ramsuratkumar wanted this madness. He went to Aurobindo, Ramana Maharshi and Ramdas to get it, and Ramdas gave Him this madness. The Beggar was gone, finished, and there was nothing left but Father in Heaven!

"Wouldn't it be wonderful if, in some small way, we returned this somehow? Yogi Ramsuratkumar asks for nothing in return. His life *is* surrender to Father in Heaven's blessings. Yogi Ramsuratkumar's blessings flow endlessly, 365 days a year, eternally, forever, just giving and giving. To return some infinitesimal fraction of what Yogi Ramsuratkumar has given us, we chant His Name. It is not His form—His form here in darshan is the most amazing gift possible, but to chant His Name is what He has given us. The minute you speak or think His Name, Yogi Ramsuratkumar is there. So He has given us this great mystical secret—to chant His Name, to remember His Name, to think of His Name. This we can do to return some small part of what He has given, as an expression of our gratitude for what He has given. His Name is magic. It is the great mystical secret of the Universe. His Name is the Name of Father in Heaven. It is the mantra of Father in Heaven. It is the sound of Father in Heaven. Chanting His Name opens the majesty and mystery of the Universe to us."

December 6, 1998
Yogi Ramsuratkumar Ashram

Lee's afternoon talk was about faith and belief, and referred to the quote that was written on the chalkboard at the front of the ashram today. Every day a quote, a spiritual thought for the day, is written there in either Tamil or English.

Lee said, "Belief is a function of thought, whereas faith is the knowledge of certainty, the certainty of the body. Belief is something that changes based on outer circumstance. Yogi Ramsuratkumar used to be much more accessible; you could have tea with Him and such. Many Europeans used to know Yogi Ramsuratkumar in those days, and now when they come and don't get the royal treatment, they have to just be ordinary and come to darshan like everyone else, they say, 'Yogi Ramsuratkumar has changed!' But they don't consider that what is really happening is that they don't have faith.

"Belief is exclusively a form of the mind, so we tend to change our belief based on outer circumstances. In this instance, for example, Yogi Ramsuratkumar has to work differently now than He worked twenty years ago. On the other hand, faith is certainty. Outer circumstances are not the essence of what is going on here. Yogi Ramsuratkumar was 'killed' by Ramdas in 1952, now there is no beggar. The appearance of things is not what is going on. What is going on are the Blessings of Father in Heaven.

"One woman said to Yogi Ramsuratkumar, 'Oh, I remember when you were dancing on the mountain, so full of joy twenty years ago . . .' and Yogi Ramsuratkumar said, 'Not now?' Essentially who He is does not change. It is impossible for it to change. Faith is a certainty, a recognition, a heart understanding that what is, is. For Yogi Ramsuratkumar this body is like this *kirta* top." Lee touched his shirt to demonstrate. "When it has served its purpose it will be taken off and put aside. Faith is certainty in Reality—it is solid, absolutely reliable. When Yogi Ramsuratkumar takes the *kirta* off of this body and throws it away, we will feel abandoned, but we won't be abandoned. He won't have gone anywhere. He will always be here. If we only have belief then we will feel disappointed and abandoned by Yogi Ramsuratkumar when He leaves His body behind. But if we have faith, nothing can shake that certainty and knowledge of our connection with the Blessings of Father in Heaven and Yogi Ramsuratkumar."

After the talk Yogi asked Lee to read his most recent (unpublished) poems that had been given to Yogi Ramsuratkumar by Lee when he first arrived. Lee stood and read very beautifully for about fifteen or twenty minutes. While he read Yogi Ramsuratkumar peeled a banana and held it with an almost trembling intensity. At one point he was perceptibly holding it toward Lee as if he was eager to give it to him. When Lee kept reading the poems—there were several, and very long ones as well—after awhile Yogi Ramsuratkumar handed the peeled banana to Devaki. With a look of surprise and delight she ate it. Then Yogi Ramsuratkumar picked up a second banana and held it in his hands until Lee was through reading. When Lee knelt at his side and bowed, Yogi Ramsuratkumar handed him the banana and said, "Eat it now." Lee ate the banana and put the peel in his pocket very quickly. Yogi Ramsuratkumar had Lee ask someone to chant. Three of the women got up and lead the chants for awhile until Yogi Ramsuratkumar picked up the poetry book and Devaki Ma turned the pages back to the lyrics.

Yogi called Lee over and asked him to have someone "sing some of these songs." Then Lee did something very unusual. He interjected, "They have also prepared some of the poems." Yogi stopped and sat still. Devaki picked up on this and leaned forward to say, "They have prepared some of the poems, Bhagavan, some of *Poems of a Broken Heart,* to sing." Yogi Ramsuratkumar told Lee to go ahead, so up to the front of the room Chris and I went to sing the poems we had prepared. After the fourth poem Lee motioned from across the room, one more poem. We had saved our favorite one for last: it was on page 538, a poem that starts out addressing Devaki Ma.

At the end of the poems we turned toward Yogi Ramsuratkumar. Devaki asked, "Is that all?" She seemed to want more. Yogi Ramsuratkumar was sunk deep in himself, listening it seemed, while the poems were sung. He slowly came back to life and called us over. One by one we moved up to *pranam* and receive his *prasad*, a banana. To each of us he said, "Eat now." I ate as quickly as I could, feeling like a molecule under the microscope of God in that moment. When we were finished he said, "My Father blesses you."

Just as we were getting up to go, he added, "You girls can take your seat." It was a touching and whimsical remark coming from Yogi Ramsuratkumar that was both very tender and kind, and at the same time pointed out his amazing ability to relate with Westerners. How could this old beggar, raised and steeped in the most traditional paths of Indian culture, possibly come up with such a Western comment? His ordinary play is intertwined with the miraculous, with a kind of omniscience and omnipresence. When one is plugged into the universal source of all things, then all things are revealed and used in the adept transmission of Grace. It is with these amazing and at times invisible, simple or deeply subtle skillful means that Yogi Ramsuratkumar works the space. One can never know exactly what he is doing. This is the way of a *Mahasiddha*.

There is very little and mostly no romance in any of this, even the most powerful moments. The romantic notions of the Grace of the guru are swept away, leaving the eye raw and starkly clear. The clarity that is left in moments when layers are peeled away makes everything ordinary to the point of revealing its innate power; perhaps this is what the Tibetans call *drala*. Everything becomes the harbinger of Grace—trees, food, flowers, books, people, children, grass. This extreme power that beats at the doors of perception so continuously in Yogi Ramsuratkumar's company is Grace, but it is not necessarily sweet—there is often nothing sweet about it. In fact ego is afraid of it because it is a certain destruction, a peeling away of one's layers of psychic skin which forces primal underworld elements of the psyche to the surface for cremation in its fire. It is pure annihilating divine force, raw and impersonal, barreling toward its recipient non-stop.

Being here in Yogi Ramsuratkumar's company is like climbing a huge mountain—Annapurna in the Himalayas—and looking up to see that a massive, vast avalanche has started. It is coming forward full speed, roaring, crashing, destroying everything in its path, recreating the entire landscape of the mountain, remaking all. In that moment it is roaring down the mountain with its staggering momentum, and everything stops. It is a timeless moment, and the knowledge that it will reach the place where I am standing—in ten seconds, in ten years, in ten lifetimes or ten thousand—is apparent. When it will reach me doesn't matter because in the rare clarity and burning pure knowledge of that imminent, impending death I realize that I am going to die. The face of death is revealed, up to the point of the actual dying, and present in that revelation is the sense of the glory and infinite possibility. The deed of Grace is done. It has already happened. Whether it will be now or later is of no importance because the reality of it *is*. Ego's horror—complete annihilation—is the soul's salvation; it necessitates the transformation of everything that stands in its path to get to the pure being which has magnetized it, drawn it, like the planets around the sun. There is nothing romantic about this. It is totally impersonal, pure God Force. It is the destroying face of God—Shiva or Kali.

In his appearance as Ram, Yogi Ramsuratkumar reveals another face of God altogether—the blessing force, the mother, father, sister, brother, all of one's relations, and Rama and Krishna as well. He embodies all the play, the sport that the divine lover, or the divine child, or the divine mother or father, makes with the devotees. There have been glimpses of that here as well, but what has been the strongest is the sense of pure divine will acting upon everyone and everything. One is left bare, burning, raw—and on the illusory side of the veil, quite hopeless. We are being stripped down to the bones of the situation, burned down to the bone at Yogi Ramsuratkumar's *smashan*, in his cremation ground.

Yogi Ramsuratkumar throws his lovers into states that the mind cannot register on the human scale—vast spaces and stretches and planes of emptiness, burning and burning in the Heart of God. There is only one word that comes close to describing this experience, which is awe. Awe, which is essentially empty. Wonder perhaps, which is essentially empty. Awe and wonder as objective, impersonal feeling in response to pure Grace revealed in Yogi Ramsuratkumar's company, in the rarified atmosphere of the *Mahasiddha*.

A few people were talking with Lee tonight about transplanting the tradition of Hinduism, of the Bauls and of the East in general into the West. Someone said that it was Yogi Ramsuratkumar's *kheyala* and the Will of God for the tradition to show up in the West in Lee's teaching. Some of Lee's students had been learning Sanskrit and Tamil chants from one of the Indian women on the ashram, and hoped to bring them back to the Arizona ashram. Lee interjected, "We all want to be entertained. We want another movie, a new chant. Two thirds of the things we have in this school, all that stuff is my devotees, not me. You ask for it and I go along with it, just like I see Yogi Ramsuratkumar doing, because no one is willing to live the way I live, simple and straightforward and following my lead. You'll never know what this tradition should look like in the West because you're not willing to follow my lead. It's all about entertainment for you all—new chants, new movies, all the same!"

December 7, 1998
Yogi Ramsuratkumar Ashram

The days are going by fast. The appearance of things is ordinary and even repetitive. Yogi Ramsuratkumar arrives on the ashram three times a day—for breakfast, then morning and afternoon darshans. In darshan he sits and smokes, talks to Lee, listens to the chants, blesses and leaves. Lee gives talks every day. The meals are served like clockwork, and are continuously delicious. Every afternoon Lee walks with the whole group to the tea stall where everyone gets cold sodas at his favorite snack stall near Ramanashram. Lee likes his half-frozen. He has a great relationship with the man who owns the snack stand, and now there are super-cold and icy Coca Colas and Pepsis waiting for Lee when he arrives around one o'clock each day. In the evenings we have a dinner in one of the cottages with oranges, bananas, crackers, cookies and cakes. Each day seems exactly like the one before, giving a hint of the eternal, which hums underneath this steady rhythm and repetition as the power of Grace.

In darshan today Yogi once again asked Lee to "Say a few words."

Lee began, "Yogi Ramsuratkumar only does what His Father in Heaven tells him to do. A few years ago Yogi Ramsuratkumar said to me, 'Father blesses Lee with whatever he wants.' Then he paused and said, 'Father blesses Lee with whatever he *needs.*'" Lee paused for a moment, then continued with a little smile, "Father in Heaven must have said, 'Wait a minute!'"

Everyone laughed, especially Yogi Ramsuratkumar who looked up and laughed out loud, his shoulders shaking with mirth. Devaki laughed and smiled too. Lee smiled broadly, obviously enjoying having made Yogi Ramsuratkumar laugh.

He continued, "Yogi Ramsuratkumar's entire life, every movement, every gesture and word is work for God. We have our personal needs, but then there is what God needs of us. Each of us is unique—not separate from God, but individual also—so each of us has specific work to do for Father in Heaven. The blessings of Yogi Ramsuratkumar can allow us to do the work of Father in Heaven in our lives, the work that we have come here to do.

"Prince Shakyamuni, the Buddha, gave us four basic precepts. First of all he said that all life is suffering, and secondly, he said that suffering is caused by desire. We all have desires and wants—for fame, money, health. Maybe all we want is health and success for our families—these desires are not so bad. We may want selflessly for others, but at the same time every want is based on feeling separate from God.

"*Needs* that we have are basically for the body to be cared for. We also need love and affection—we see how much love and affection everyone in India gives to children. In the West we don't honor and cherish our children as treasures the way that you do in India.

In the West people consider children as problems, they bark at them like dogs. It's very painful.

"Mother Teresa said, 'I am not a social worker. I do all this for Jesus and Jesus alone. There is no one but Jesus.' We each have a unique service that we are to do for Father in Heaven. Maybe the unique service of the man in the tea stall was just to give tea to Yogi Ramsuratkumar once a month. Maybe that was his work for Father in Heaven in this life. Maybe our unique work for Father in Heaven is not to change the world, to feed everyone, but just to bring tea to a great Being like Yogi Ramsuratkumar.

"Yesterday Yogi Ramsuratkumar also said, 'My Father blesses Lee with everything he needs.' I was grateful because maybe I'm not that trustworthy yet. Maybe someday I'll be trustworthy enough, so that every want will be only what God wants for me. Maybe then Yogi Ramsuratkumar will say, 'My Father blesses you with everything you want.' "

Lee used a song, "Under My Thumb," written and recorded by the Rolling Stones, as an example of his relationship with Yogi Ramsuratkumar. He said, "Yogi Ramsuratkumar keeps me under His thumb. I still get distracted, but if I get too far off it's like I have a chain around my neck and Yogi Ramsuratkumar pulls the chain, and back I go!" Yogi Ramsuratkumar laughed again at this, his shoulders shaking up and down. He covered his face with his hands as if he was embarrassed. Everyone in the room laughed along with him. The room was hot, but also warm with delight and happiness. Lee was entertaining Yogi Ramsuratkumar.

"Lee Lozowick is not very subtle," Lee continued. "When a message comes to me I need it to be loud and clear, so Yogi Ramsuratkumar's Blessings have always been loud and clear for me. They have been unmistakable! So even when I've tried to take the wrong fork in the road, the opportunity is clear, the way is clear and the signs from Yogi Ramsuratkumar are very clear. We see obstacles that seem like a mountain in the center of the road. We chant Yogi Ramsuratkumar's Name and the obstacles clear away like morning mist under the hot sun and are gone. But we have to ask what is needed to serve Him."

Then Lee told a story about Perumal, Yogi's attendant of many years. Perumal at one time had two shops in the brass market, but when he met Yogi Ramsuratkumar and became involved with him, he realized that he had to sell his businesses in order to serve Yogi Ramsuratkumar. Lee went on to say that what we find out in the end is that what was really needed to serve Father's work is what we really wanted all along.

Throughout this talk Yogi Ramsuratkumar was holding a banana in his hands as he listened. Lee finished his talk, walked to the dais and knelt down. He *pranamed* and received the banana from Yogi Ramsuratkumar's waiting hands. The chanting resumed and Lee took his chair by the wall to the right of Yogi Ramsuratkumar.

Lee gave a talk again at the beginning of the afternoon darshan. He spoke about an article in *Tattva Darshana* about Vivekananda, who was not just a scholar but who had a profound and deep knowledge of the relationship with the guru.

"Vivekananda's guru was Ramakrishna," Lee began. "The true guru knows the domains in which they move and transmit and communicate. Ramakrishna knew what it is to have knowledge without experience. Narendra (Vivekananda as a young man) had one question that he brought to everyone who would listen to him: 'Sir, do you know God? Have you seen God?' Then he heard of Ramakrishna when he was fifteen or sixteen years old. Narendra asked Ramakrishna, 'Sir, do you know God? Have you seen God?'

Ramakrishna said, 'Yes, not only have I seen God but I will *show you* God.' Narendra was deeply moved by this answer and became a disciple of Ramakrishna, and eventually became Swami Vivekananda. He said that a true guru doesn't just speak about things but has the actual experience of it.

"On my first visit to Yogi Ramsuratkumar," Lee said, "He asked for all of our names, where we were from, why we were in India. His fluency in relating with our culture and with us as Westerners, as young Americans, was amazing. He knew things about each one of us and our background that He couldn't have known any other way except through intimate, direct knowledge.

"When I refer to Yogi Ramsuratkumar as guru it is very clear that the depth of His Being comes from direct experience—deep and profound. He knows when each of us comes to Him what we are suffering. He feels with us. He knows what it is to have faith in God. We don't know much about His years between Ramdas and coming here to Tiruvannamalai—only a few stories, precious treasures. Maybe He went without food, suffered great hardships. Whatever the depth and breadth of our human experience is, whatever we bring to Him, whether we bring suffering or joy of oneness with God, He feels all of that with us."

After Lee finished this talk he went to the dais and knelt again at Yogi Ramsuratkumar's knee. Yogi looked at him with infinite tenderness. He handed Lee a banana and said, "Lee should eat this here and now." Then he handed Lee a second banana that Lee also ate right there on the spot. Lee started to leave and Yogi pulled him back down and patted him on the back, then released him.

December 8, 1998
Yogi Ramsuratkumar Ashram

Tomorrow is the last day with Yogi Ramsuratkumar for Lee and his group. It is as if a huge clock is ticking the moments away, each one precious. This morning Yogi asked Lee to give another talk. He told the story of Anandamayi Ma refusing to feed herself, and being fed by her devotees. One woman was very impatient and aggressive in asking to feed Anandamayi Ma. "You must let me feed you!" she insisted. Anandamayi Ma came to the woman's house with some of her devotees. The woman had made a big pot of rice that was on the stove. Ma said, "Bring me all the rice." She ate and ate and then asked for more rice. The woman cooked two more pots of rice that Ma ate, and still Ma asked for more. The woman became concerned that Ma was eating her out of house and home. Finally the woman said, "I'm out of rice!" Anandamayi Ma said, "Next time you ask for something, think about what you ask for, or I will eat the whole Universe!"

Lee continued, "Yogi Ramsuratkumar says, 'This beggar only does Father in Heaven's work.' But we think that God can be altered in His plans if we just do or say the right thing. We must realize that masters and saints know what it is that we need in our lives. On *jayanthi* hundreds of people were here to receive Yogi's darshan and He didn't even know all of them, but as He looked around the room, He knew what each person needed. But we think we can decide what is best for us. We assume great Beings like Yogi Ramsuratkumar are like us. We project ourselves, our personalities, upon them.

"As Westerners we want to help beggars and poor people in India, but our help might not be help at all. There are things about the social structure in India that we cannot and do not understand."

Lee then told a story of a woman who was traveling in India with him years ago who wanted to save a puppy from being teased and abused by a young boy who was just trying to get the Americans' attention. At that time Lee said that she couldn't help the puppy. He knew that if she tried the puppy would only suffer more at the hands of the boy, who would be angry after she left that his plans had been foiled.

"So we feel the suffering of others," he said, "but we don't look deeply into the situation to understand what is really needed or helpful. We say, 'If I was Yogi Ramsuratkumar I would do such and such . . .' We project on great holy people like Yogi Ramsuratkumar; we think things should be done differently. But Yogi Ramsuratkumar knows everything. Father in Heaven is not unconscious like we are, and He knows what is needed. We have to be very careful. If a saint decides, 'I'm going to teach this person a lesson,' then the lesson can be very difficult."

Then Lee told another story of an over-eager devotee who selfishly wanted the coveted task of getting to feed Anandamayi Ma. She insisted on feeding Ma. Finally Ma gave in to her demands, but the woman was so consumed with her own wishes and desires that she was blind to Ma's needs. She thoughtlessly fed Ma scalding hot rice, not thinking of anything but herself, and burning Anandamayi Ma's mouth very badly. She had to face her selfishness and live with the pain of having hurt Ma.

He continued, "Instead of allowing Father in Heaven's Blessings to move as they will, we try to reach out and grab blessings—to reach out and take Benediction or Grace—when in fact the Guru is not separate from God, and what is needed is always given spontaneously, graciously. So it is best to always do what pleases Yogi Ramsuratkumar and not unconsciously cause suffering to Him."

Lee ended his talk and sat down after receiving Yogi Ramsuratkumar's blessings and *prasad*. The chanting of Yogi Ramsuratkumar's name resumed. Yogi sat and smoked, as he had on many occasions during the past two weeks. The cigarette cupped in his hands glowed red, and the smoke curled up above his head in a slow dance with the air. Every inhalation seemed to pull in the suffering of the world. The smoke disappeared as *samskaras* and karma were transmuted within the alchemical body of the beggar saint.

Yogi Ramsuratkumar was bathed in the pale morning light that shone from the large windows on either side of the walls behind his dais. The windows opened on the back wall of the ashram. Some trees and shrubs grow there, and small birds often played, flitting and flying about. A small animal, like a chipmunk or squirrel, ran back and forth across the top of the wall, playing on the concrete. The birds often perched there and sang loudly, their songs drifting into the darshan and becoming part of the praise, for the delight of Yogi Ramsuratkumar.

At two o'clock the group had just returned from walking with Lee to get cold sodas. In thirty minutes Yogi Ramsuratkumar would make a special trip to the ashram to see Alain de Rosenbo off. Lee would also go to the gate at two-thirty to say goodbye to Alain. When asked if anyone could accompany him, Lee declined, saying, "Yogi Ramsuratkumar doesn't need another big crowd of people to interfere with His space." He went alone.

"Lee, say something!" Yogi commanded at the beginning of the four o'clock darshan. The room was darker than in the morning, cast in afternoon shadows. Lee responded, as always, quickly and without hesitation. He said, "Yogi Ramsuratkumar is a beggar. We could say something about beggary. The way we ordinarily talk about begging is begging for food to eat. Yogi Ramsuratkumar was a beggar on the streets for many years, but when Yogi Ramsuratkumar calls Himself a beggar it also means that to respond to a beggar is an extraordinary opportunity to be generous and charitable out of the goodness of our hearts. It is a great blessing to give to one less fortunate than ourselves.

"But there is another element of this idea of beggary. Whenever Yogi Ramsuratkumar offers us the opportunity to serve Him—'This beggar has some work. Would you like to do some work for this beggar?'—then we have the extraordinary opportunity to be in communion with That which Yogi Ramsuratkumar is, the blessings of Father in Heaven. By serving this particular beggar in any way, even just to move a chair for Him, we have the opportunity to be in relationship with Father in Heaven, as well as being generous and charitable.

"In 1993 the first book of poems was published by Sadhu Rangarajan. Yogi Ramsuratkumar was having the poems read over and over again by Ma Devaki, and at one point He said, 'These poems should be read every day.' He didn't say one poem or every poem, or every one of you should read these poems. He leaves it to us to make distinctions. Do we read one poem a day, ten poems a day, the whole first book every day? Yogi Ramsuratkumar has left this consideration of reading the poems completely up to us, and we have to give ourselves to that in whatever way we can. That is the offering of a beggar. Yogi Ramsuratkumar is begging my students, and maybe all of us, to read these poems every day. It's a subtle form of begging. The degree to which we respond to the Divine Beggar is the degree to which we are blessed by being kind, charitable, generous . . . ."

Lee talked about Buddhists beggars and made an unusual and thought-provoking comment about himself, saying, "I probably know more about Buddhism than I do about Hinduism . . . " He went on to say that one of the philosophical foundations for the idea of begging in Buddhism is that to beg serves the entire sangha. Begging is itself a blessing. The renunciate monks or nuns are blessed because they beg for everyone, for those who are lay people and have families to care for.

He said, "Yogi Ramsuratkumar is a Divine Beggar. He begs us to chant His Name. When we chant His Name we are giving alms to the Divine Beggar. This begging is a very important spiritual tradition. We are blessed through that exchange with the Beggar. All the benefits we get from giving when Yogi Ramsuratkumar begs are the blessings of Father in Heaven." Lee turned and *pranamed* to Yogi Ramsuratkumar.

"My Father blesses you, Lee. My Father's blessings," Yogi said as he looked into Lee's eyes as Lee was again kneeling beside him at the dais. He handed Lee a banana. "Eat it, here and now."

For the past two or three or four days Yogi Ramsuratkumar has been giving everyone who goes up to offer *prasad* or *pranam* at his feet one or two bananas to eat. "Eat it here and now!" he says. "Eat it! Eat it here and now!" He instructs us in this way because if it is eaten in his aura it is ten or one hundred or one thousand times more empowered there than if we take it away with us. As Pon Kamaraj said a few days earlier, "We make it ours," if we take it away from his presence.

Lee has had many of his disciples—Purna, Tom, Mary, Chris and Radha—give talks in Yogi Ramsuratkumar's darshan. Each time someone gives a talk or leads chants they have the opportunity to go to Yogi Ramsuratkumar's dais and receive *prasad* from his hands afterward. "Your name?" he says sweetly. Listening carefully to the reply, he drops the banana in their cupped hand. Usually he says, "Eat, here and now!"

Now Zachary got up to talk. He spoke about meeting Lee when he was only sixteen—eleven years ago—and how he had no idea at the time what a profound influence Lee would have on his life. He talked about having the opportunity to travel with Lee on many occasions. He spoke about a serious injury to his knee and the surgery he had as a young teenager, then told the story of how, five years ago, his knees had become very painful again. He thought he might have to have another surgery, but when he talked to Lee about it Lee said he did not want Zachary to have surgery again, and that he would do a healing on his knees. Lee sat down with Zachary and laid his hands on his knees for about thirty minutes. Afterward the knees were miraculously better, and have been healed since that time.

Zachary concluded, "When I thanked Lee for healing my knees he said, 'Don't thank me, thank Yogi Ramsuratkumar.' So, I want to take this opportunity to thank Lee, and to thank Yogi Ramsuratkumar." He turned toward Yogi Ramsuratkumar, then went to the dais and received *prasad*.

Now as the afternoon darshan drew to a close Yogi Ramsuratkumar called Lee up to the dais. Three large sacks full of shawls sat beside him. He had Lee sit beside him on the floor while he gave shawls to everyone in Lee's group of thirty-five people. One at a time each person walked up and received a shawl that was passed from Yogi Ramsuratkumar's hands to Lee's hands and into the person's hands. The first three or four shawls had been given to Yogi Ramsuratkumar during *jayanthi* and Deepam, and had been on his body. Each one passed through his hands, and would provide warmth and shelter in coming travels.

Darshan was soon over. The time with Yogi Ramsuratkumar was quickly coming to a close. Yesterday it felt as if some shift had occurred, as if business was coming to completion. Yogi Ramsuratkumar had "worked everyone over" and would send us on our way tomorrow at midnight.

Lee took the whole group out to dinner after darshan in Tiruvannamalai, the only time we have done so on this trip. A bevy of auto rickshaws or jitney buses pulled up to the ashram like birds of prey, and loading thirty-five people in, buzzed off fast over the ruts and bumps of the road with the large, white Americans and Europeans stuffed inside, sari tails blowing in the breeze behind us. It was a comical sight, and must have given the Indians some good laughs. At the restaurant the owner warmly greeted Lee at the door. He has known Lee for years. He was wearing a T-shirt that said, "God's Child, Yogi Ramsuratkumar, Tiruvannamalai."

December 9, 1998
Yogi Ramsuratkumar Ashram

This morning at five-fifteen it was dark, pouring rain and a little cooler. At six o'clock when the coffee was served we drank it on the porch with Lee in the early dawn light. Dave meditated on the porch of the cottage next door. Between the cottages a patch of green grass stretched out, cropped close by the musk deer but still lush. The last day had dawned. Arunachala was shrouded with mist and clouds, but the Deepam fire still burned brightly on the distant tip of the mountain.

The day broke with a gentle, pale light. The birds were in a flurry of song. The birds are amazing here on the ashram, from the big flock of black crows that Raji, Mani's wife, feeds every morning outside their bungalow, to the busy sparrows and exotic birds that constantly work and play around the concrete wall behind the windows in Yogi

Ramsuratkumar's darshan. Now a wild chorus had come to life outside, and all along the garden wall the lavender morning glories blossomed in a purple profusion. The hibiscus also burst forth with fresh new blossoms overnight, huge and rose red. As the ashram came to life we waited for Yogi Ramsuratkumar's "drive-by" darshan before breakfast. Lee sat writing in his journal until it was time to go.

After Yogi Ramsuratkumar was driven past, Lee went to the grass hut by the ashram gate and sat alone—a rare event on this trip. The busy chaos and cacophony of many people usually surround Lee; the constant demands of relationship fill almost every moment of his day. But now Lee sat alone. It was an image that said many things on this day of departures and farewells. Today Lee would leave Yogi Ramsuratkumar's physical presence and company. There was no demonstration of sentimentality about this. Yogi Ramsuratkumar is always with Lee—for where is he not? There is only God. And yet Lee sat alone. This expressive, rare moment seemed to shout out the fact that we are all ultimately alone. Lee is alone; clearly Yogi Ramsuratkumar is alone.

Most of Lee's group took the opportunity to make their last circumambulation of the ashram. Most of Lee's students have circumambulated Agrahara Kollai every morning during the visit. This morning the sky was overcast, with the distant mountain cloaked in mists. As we walked along Arunachala rose up green and hazy in the cloudbanks, while water dripped off the trees and shrubs all along the lush, verdant path that curved around the perimeter of the ashram. The strong stalks of the banana palms hung heavy with small green bananas, and the grove of trees was so thick it seemed like a small piece of jungle. The impact of the silent walk was of a rare and beautiful gem, a jewel of sanctuary—a manifestation of Yogi Ramsuratkumar on the physical plane.

During the two weeks of the visit the daily routines of the ashram have become more apparent. Selvaraj, who is Yogi Ramsuratkumar's darshan attendant, said that twenty to twenty-five people work on the ashram full-time. About two hundred people come to the ashram every day of the year. Now and then Mani comments on the difficulty of their task, and yet he and the other staff members are radiant and bright. Yogi Ramsuratkumar is the buoyant, effervescent sea upon which they sail, which is made very clear in the spontaneous, guileless, candid and fresh gestures of the ashram staff within the work of the day.

"A divine miracle," Mani had said of the ashram this morning before Yogi Ramsuratkumar's first arrival. "This was nothing but a bare field," he added. Then reflecting on his sadhana, he said, "I have done many building projects in my life. I have done much, much work before, but never anything like this. Never! This is very hard. Very hard. But all this," he spread his arms to indicate the whole ashram, "is a divine miracle—all done by His Grace." He went on in an earnest, straightforward way. "Never have I done anything like this. No time off, never a day, no vacation . . . every day, every day, I work here. He won't ask anyone else to do things—just Mani. I never know from moment to moment what He will ask for next. I can't make any plans . . . It is very hard." More than he could possibly know, Lee's students who listened understood what he was talking about. Lee is a fierce teacher whose demands often seem impossible or overbearing, but these are the teacher's acts of compassion. What else but the impossible will take one to the Heart of God?

"Say something," Yogi asked of Lee at the beginning of the morning darshan. Lee began to talk about "a Western holy man named George Gurdjieff," who began his work in Russia, but eventually settled in Paris where he lived in an apartment until his death in 1949. Lee said that Gurdjieff was often irrational and hard on his students. Gurdjieff often did things that couldn't be understood. He held great and extraordinary feasts for his students that he himself would cook and serve. He knew how to put food and spices together, and would cook and serve these magnificent feasts in his apartment for a hundred or more people, all packed into the small space to partake of the many delicious courses. He would then make teaching lessons or great *lilas* with his guests. Gurdjieff was known for his exceptionally fierce and uncompromising relationship with students.

Lee paused for awhile, as if he was gathering his thoughts in a way that is unusual for him when he is talking. Usually he speaks spontaneously, in a way that is typically off the cuff, sometimes veering off wildly to make a point that pops into his consciousness. Then he said, "I have to pick carefully which stories of Gurdjieff to tell here, because some of the stories may not be fit to tell in this company."

Lee resumed with a story of Gurdjieff in the steam bath with several men, one of them a pious Eastern Orthodox priest who wore a huge cross on a gold chain around his neck, perhaps to demonstrate his obedience to Christ. Gurdjieff joked with the men and got them to tell stories that were not quite wholesome in some way. Gurdjieff turned to the priest and said, "Do you know any stories Father?"

"Oh no," the priest shook his head. "No, no, I'm a man of God!" Gurdjieff from time to time would turn to him again and ask for a story. Each time the priest said no very piously, until finally he relented and said, "Well, maybe I do know one story." He then told a story so full of prejudice and animosity, worse than any of the others that had been told, that Gurdjieff berated him then and there. The priest was shocked, but Gurdjieff used this shock tactic to reveal the priest's own hypocrisy.

One night Gurdjieff gave a big feast that ended at two o'clock in the morning, then he saw all the guests and his students off into the night. There was one young man who had been at the feast who had a very important business meeting the next day, but on his way home he realized that he had left his briefcase at Gurdjieff's apartment, and he needed it for his meeting first thing in the morning. When he returned to Gurdjieff's apartment, there was Gurdjieff, alone and cleaning up the huge mess in the kitchen left behind by all the others. Gurdjieff greeted him at the door with warmth and delight, thinking that the young man had come back to help him clean up. Then the young man realized that after every feast all the people left and Gurdjieff did all the dishes and cleaned up alone, and he did this without ever saying a word to anyone about it.

But what struck the young man the most was the softness and gentleness and kindness he saw in Gurdjieff in that moment. He said that was the most important thing he ever experienced in Gurdjieff's company. Gurdjieff kept that deeply compassionate part of himself carefully hidden. He didn't want people to focus on that love, but on the teaching and the dharma. Lee talked about how, in some cases, the compassion and love of the teacher must be cloaked by this fierce, wild and sometimes even harsh exterior or shocking teaching force.

While I scribbled notes as quickly as possible I was struck with how brilliant Lee's talk was, what skillful means he was employing, and how he really seemed to be speaking to his students about himself. I felt at a loss to capture the subtlety and craft of his presentation, jotting down a few sentences and attempting to keep up with his swift speech. In the frustration of not being able to adequately capture Lee's talk the sense that he was talking about himself as he talked about Gurdjieff became more acute. It was as if Lee was begging his students to hear what he was saying.

Lee continued, "The teaching in the West has to be presented in this practical way because the bhakti tradition is not developed in the West, nor is it understood. I'd like to draw a parallel with Yogi Ramsuratkumar. When Father in Heaven brings madness to one of His children the form of that may be very hard to understand with the rational mind. Once we were sitting with Yogi Ramsuratkumar and He was making many *lilas*. I hope I'm not insulting anyone by telling a story of something that should be kept private, but he was interacting with Devaki and she said to Him, 'Bhagavan, you work in mysterious ways!' This is the way saints are—they work in very mysterious ways. Westerners have a fear of the unknown. We want to be able to control everything. We want to fit even the greatest saints and sages into our ideas of how things should be. So we try to understand in a linear way what can't be understood, and we misunderstand what is really there in the saint."

Yogi Ramsuratkumar held a cigarette in his hands for a long time during this talk. It was poised there, the invisible force building around him as he finally lifted it to his lips and lit it. He sat smoking, his head wreathed in smoke. He listened carefully to everything Lee was saying, and at the same time he seemed to be aware of everything that occurred in the entire darshan hall. His attention seemed to be everywhere at once, and yet it was totally focused on his son.

"We have to look beyond the appearance of things and into the heart of the matter. We have to look and see the truth of what Yogi Ramsuratkumar says, 'My Father in Heaven is everything, all.' With Gurdjieff the depth of his compassion was hidden underneath a very well thought out exterior. With Yogi Ramsuratkumar that is not the case. With Yogi Ramsuratkumar there is only the slightest film—the deep love and compassion that He feels for all creatures is *right there*. We don't have to look very deeply to see that, but still sometimes we are confused by what He does, so we have to look beneath the surface of things to see what is there."

Lee then apologized again to Yogi Ramsuratkumar and the Sudama sisters if any intimacy that should not be shared was shared. He said, "Yogi Ramsuratkumar once said to the Sudama sisters, 'This beggar will betray you.' Yogi Ramsuratkumar is not His body. If we think Yogi Ramsuratkumar is only His body then we will feel betrayed because He will die someday. 'This beggar will betray you' means that if we look at the appearance of things and don't look at the depth of the unitive Reality underneath, then we will feel betrayed. He is not the body, not the shawls, not the cigarettes, not the crown," Lee gestured to indicate the wrap that Yogi Ramsuratkumar wears around his head. "He is only the pure Divine, and He has given us His Name. Whatever happens His Name will live on, not just beyond His lifetime, but forever."

Lee turned and moved to Yogi Ramsuratkumar's side. "Thank you," Lee said, as he knelt beside the dais.

"Eat, here and now," Yogi Ramsuratkumar said as he handed Lee the banana *prasad*. Then he gave Lee a second banana, saying, "Eat this also, eat it here and now."

These last few days have been the days of the banana *lilas*, in which Yogi Ramsuratkumar has been giving one or two bananas for *prasad* to every person who comes up to his dais. Then he takes all the banana peels. He holds out his hand and has the person put the banana peel into it. It is not easy to put these peels into his waiting hands. It is a highly symbolic gesture that strikes deeply as another act of taking away karma. How much more clearly does it have to be demonstrated? He has to deal with our garbage.

But he never once takes Lee's banana peels. Lee doesn't give him a chance to take them because he eats quickly and immediately stuffs the peels into his own shirt pocket. Yogi Ramsuratkumar does not protest or ask for them, but allows Lee to deal with his own garbage.

This morning Yogi Ramsuratkumar was like a loving mother, arranging for this one and that, caring for all. Joanne and Debbie, who have been with the children so much during these two weeks, got to lead the chants for Yogi Ramsuratkumar this morning and receive *prasad* from his hands. Yogi asked Lee if everyone traveling with him had been up to the dais. The implication was that he wanted to make sure that everyone had received *prasad* at least once. Lee said yes, they had all been there.

When we came into darshan in the afternoon after circumambulating the statue in the temple, Yogi Ramsuratkumar and the Sudama sisters were sitting quietly on the dais. There was no chanting going on as there always had been before. None of the usual chants, "Mythreem Bajatha" and "Arunachala Shiva," sung by Devaki and Vijayalakshmi at the beginning of darshan as on most other occasions. Yogi Ramsuratkumar and the two women sat in a radiant, quiet, unified field on the dais. As we took our places on the floor in front of them we were lifted up into the gathering force of Yogi Ramsuratkumar's presence.

"You can say a few words," Yogi Ramsuratkumar said to Lee when he called him over to the dais. "This is your last talk."

Lee stood up and began, "I can tell you stories, but first . . . We've visited Yogi Ramsuratkumar eleven or twelve times over the years, and Yogi Ramsuratkumar's Blessings are the center point of everything. Everything is simply Him—no one comes here, no one goes back to America. And yet there are two dimensions of Reality. One dimension is that everything is just what it is—empty and full, perfect as it is. But there is another dimension of Reality.

"This dichotomy also shows up in the Indian tradition of Shiva/Shakti. Shiva is the eternal Oneness, all just as it is. Shakti is the dimension of phenomena. When I speak of essential Reality or Truth I refer to Yogi Ramsuratkumar. Around that point of eternality and Oneness which cannot be described is the swirling display of phenomena—beautiful, bright, dark; changes that come and go; birth, death, rebirth, death. That play of phenomena is that which distracts us and keeps us confused.

"Even all the wonders of technology—though I am completely computer illiterate— are distractions, the sophistication of the mind of man. It is all the swirling play of phenomena. This lifetime or another, sooner or later, we will all become less captivated by the swirling display of phenomena and more drawn into the still point which is Shiva, where there is no time, no past, present or future because all exists here and now. We will be drawn into that still point until sometime we pass through that point and on to the other side, where there is no distinction, only God.

"These are the thoughts as we have our last lunch on the ashram, our last darshan, as we put our illusory luggage on illusory buses, and it will appear that we are getting on a plane and flying out of Madras, when really we are always here, at the Feet of Yogi Ramsuratkumar. Nothing will have changed.

"But I have asked Yogi Ramsuratkumar to allow my sense of distinction to remain. In terms of an illusory prayer, I've asked Yogi Ramsuratkumar in His Grace to allow me to be able to see myself as distinct from Him, to bow at His Feet in America, to remain in a mood of adoration or worship of Him because I find the state of adoration or worship to be the best state of all."

Lee then told stories from his first two visits with Yogi Ramsuratkumar in 1976 and 1979. He continued, "Two or three hours a day with Yogi Ramsuratkumar during those visits seemed like eternity. There were a few of my students with me; I was acting as their teacher and they were acting as my students, though I wasn't much of a teacher and they weren't much of a student! But in the Work we have to start somewhere!" Everyone laughed at this small joke.

Lee continued, "Yogi Ramsuratkumar asked us, 'Why did you come?' Everyone answered, 'To be with Lee,' and Yogi Ramsuratkumar started laughing hysterically. By the third trip I had been writing poems and letters to Yogi Ramsuratkumar for years and I was very presumptuous and arrogant."

Then Lee told the story of the third trip in 1986, when Yogi Ramsuratkumar basically denied ever having seen Lee and sent him away to look for a guru somewhere else. Lee continued, "I had twenty-one people with me and I had said, 'We're going to meet my Master—the greatest Being in the Universe!' So the first teaching lesson I learned from Yogi Ramsuratkumar was to never, never, under any circumstances be a burden to the Teacher. Westerners have all these demands. They are very aggressive. The first teaching lesson that came on that trip was never be a burden to the Teacher or to the teaching, the dharma, but what was all this anyway but the play of phenomena? At the heart of things there has never been any separation from Yogi Ramsuratkumar, only communion, *baraka*, Benediction, Grace. All the rest is the sparkling display of phenomena."

At this point Lee told the story of being called back by Yogi Ramsuratkumar two years later for the *jayanthi* celebration. Lee had gotten a letter from Pon Kamaraj, to whom Yogi had simply said, "Call this man and he will come." Lee said, "The second very important teaching lesson that I got from Yogi Ramsuratkumar was that Yogi Ramsuratkumar knows whatever He needs to know and what He does is never a function of human error. That Yogi Ramsuratkumar didn't remember me in 1986 was not a function of memory. Whatever Father in Heaven wants Yogi Ramsuratkumar to know, He knows. However the teacher responds is not a function of personality or mind.

"So, to invite ourselves when we are not asked," Lee continued, "is the height of inelegance, vanity, arrogance. I feel responsible for Westerners who come here because of my work, my writing. I've popularized Yogi Ramsuratkumar's Name in the West; I am always ambivalent about that because although it is work He has given me to do, Westerners are so arrogant and demanding. They come to Tiruvannamalai and impinge on Yogi Ramsuratkumar's work. But He is never ignorant. How He relates to us is exactly how God is relating to us.

"At the heart of things, at the essence of things, all of this is the play of phenomena. It is Shiva Nataraj—Shiva dancing on the play of phenomena. In one way everything I've been speaking about is just the play of phenomena; if we find ourselves in the play of phenomena, then the human thing to do is to be in that play according to God's design. At the heart of things everything is all the same. Everyone is the same—regardless of color, caste, religious belief. If one is a beggar, rich or poor, we are all the same. There is no present, past, future, time or space, only Father in Heaven. And yet, finding ourselves in this dance, it behooves us to play however the Divine Choreographer has written us into the dance."

The mood in the room ran very deep and bittersweet. It was a beautiful talk, clear and free and also tinged with longing. Many of those in Lee's party would not see Yogi Ramsuratkumar again in this life. Lee ended with his usual thank you and turned to Yogi Ramsuratkumar who took his hands between his own. He gave Lee prasad, and after he had eaten it Yogi Ramsuratkumar began to ask Lee detailed questions about his trip, when Lee would be in Varanasi, when in Rishikesh and by what means of travel.

"Oh, airplane," Yogi Ramsuratkumar said, as if registering this deeply, and then, "How many? Oh, thirty-three."

He wanted to know when Lee would fly back to America and from what city. When Lee said that he and the group were going to Varanasi (Banaras), Yogi Ramsuratkumar said, "Ah, Varanasi," as if he knew and loved Varanasi, the ancient city of Kashi where he grew up. The tone of awe in his voice as he spoke this word brought a mythical power and magic to this place. One could imagine the years Yogi Ramsuratkumar may have spent there, both as a youth and much later, as a wandering, God-intoxicated sadhu. Most likely we will never know for certain about those years, but his soft and resonant, "Ah, Varanasi," spoke volumes.

December 10, 1998
En Route

Lee and company—thirty-five people—left the ashram last night at midnight in a drenching rain storm. About twelve people waited with Lee in the dark, wet van for the other two vans near the ashram gate. As midnight drew close there seemed to be some confusion with the other vans. Lee turned to Tom and said, "Go tell Purna that we leave at midnight whether the other vans are ready or not. We leave at *exactly* midnight! They can catch up with us later if they need to."

Hours earlier in the last darshan when Yogi Ramsuratkumar asked Lee what time we were leaving, Lee had said midnight. Not even a slow-moving, unwieldy or unresponsive group of thirty-five would prevent Lee from keeping his word to his Father, or from staying in alignment with the blessing force that Yogi Ramsuratkumar was unquestionably pouring his way.

A similar teaching lesson had been made yesterday when Dan had left to accompany Alain de Rosenbo to the airport to catch his plane back to France. Lee told Dan to leave at two-thirty and two-thirty *exactly*. That was what Alain had given to Yogi Ramsuratkumar in the morning darshan as his time of departure. Yogi Ramsuratkumar had actually come to the ashram in his car to see Alain off at two-thirty.

All throughout the last day Yogi Ramsuratkumar was the divine mother, seeing to the needs of all the children. His loving care was tender, gentle, and tangible in his actions. He sent food for Lee's trip, covered our heads and shoulders with warm shawls, had the ashram pay for Lee's transportation to Chennai (Madras). When Yogi Ramsuratkumar found out that the group's accommodations in Varanasi (Banaras) were not handled yet and Lee didn't know where everyone would stay, Yogi Ramsuratkumar said, "Everything will be taken care of in Varanasi." His certainty left no room for the mind to question. It was a statement of absolute faith and knowledge of the Will of God. When Yogi Ramsuratkumar said, "Everything will be taken care of in Varanasi," it was already done.

On the four hour drive into Chennai the rain poured into the windows and cracks in the vans and gathered in pools on the floor where our backpacks were piled. We arrived at the Chennai airport at four-thirty in the morning cold, sleepy and rain bedraggled. We hustled our assorted backpacks, bags and pouches into a seating area and proceeded to wait for our flight. I assessed the rain damage to my carefully guarded notebooks, which was not insignificant. As I fussed nervously over the water-logged pages and blurred lines where the ink had run into a mass of indistinguishable blue, Lee assessed the worst of it, shook his head and said, "That's not a problem. You can read that *easily!*" instantly nipping any potential drama in its bud.

As soon as we hit the airport the first thing most of the people in the group did was flock over to the coffee vendor and buy chai or coffee. Caffeine in any form is a substance from which Lee's students refrain as part of the dietary practice, but it had been clear that Lee considered the ashram coffee to be *prasad*. He had made the coffee at Yogi Ramsuratkumar's ashram, which was served in small cups twice a day, generously available to all his students. After two weeks of daily coffee intake, now we were acting like addicts instead of serious practitioners. He seemed to frown almost imperceptibly as he watched his and Purna's students come walking back from the tea stall with cups of coffee and black tea, but he said nothing.

It was five o'clock and still dark outside. Thirty-five people were sprawled over four or five rows of airport seats in the lounge along with numerous bags. Lee sat down and drank some water then passed around the food Yogi Ramsuratkumar had sent—dates, dried fruit, raisins, nuts—and the leftover peanut molasses candy, cookies and other goodies from last night's dinner. People sat talking quietly, warming up over their cups of coffee and chai. Lee said, "When we get to Banaras we're going to have to hoof it—hit the streets looking for a place to stay!"

Jane said, "Yogi Ramsuratkumar said everything would be taken care of for us in Banaras." A slight smile hovered around Lee's mouth and eyes.

" 'Trust Allah but tether your camel,' right?" she added.

"Yes, that's it," he responded. He seemed to be saying, "We have to meet God halfway, after all." Lee's silver hair was a mass of wild curls from the rain and gleamed in the pale airport light, his blue eyes almost silver with an inner light that seemed to flood his whole body. The overall effect was a striking communication of intense radiance. We had left the sanctuary of Yogi Ramsuratkumar's physical presence and his ashram and were on the streets of India traveling under Lee's all-encompassing mantle and his watchful eye. Back in the unique force field of Lee Lozowick, a particular flavor of madness—a madcap, wild, Baul kind of mood—would surely characterize the next phase of the trip. And yet it was so apparent that Lee was the reflection of Yogi Ramsuratkumar.

As the time got closer to embark on our flight Lee asked two of the men to gather all the passports of everyone in the group and take them, along with the tickets, and get boarding passes for everyone. While they were gathering the passports Jan drifted away from the group, going to the bathroom to straighten out her sari. Neither of the men nor any of Lee's other senior students noticed that she was gone, and no one thought to count the number of passports to make sure everyone was included. Lee was then given a stack of what the men thought was boarding passes for everyone. As the whole group was going through the final checkpoint, Jan came running up to rejoin the group. Realizing that she had missed something important in the traveling link-up, she said to Lee, "What is that pink card everyone has?"

Lee looked at her and said, "Boarding passes. Where is yours?"

She said, "I don't have one."

Instantaneously Lee whirled around, broke out of line and headed back into the main area of the terminal walking fast toward the passenger check-in desk. As he walked away he snapped, "I'm going to have to handle everything myself!" The flight was scheduled to take off in less than ten minutes. The whole group stood in place, waiting for Lee to return and hoping rather anxiously that he would make it back in time. With only a few minutes to spare Lee walked back through the checkpoint and handed Jan her boarding pass. He said in a tone of both frustration and triumph, "Here's your boarding pass—and I got you first class seats."

She said, "I was prepared to stay behind," to which Lee responded, "I would not have left you here, even with one or two other people. We would *all* have spent the whole day here waiting for the next flight. I'm taking care of all the tickets from now on."

This kind of disorganization and lack of group focus and unity was reminiscent of the 1986 trip, when Lee took twenty-one people to India, including four children age seven and younger, for a three month trip that included two weeks in Tiruvannamalai. It was a landmark experience for Lee's students that resulted in many stories that have been added to the oral tradition of the Hohm Community, particularly the *lilas* that occurred between Lee and Yogi Ramsuratkumar, which we will undoubtedly hear a great deal more about later in this chronicle, as Lee often recounts these in his seminars as demonstrations of the teaching.

The 1986 trip was also memorable for the both the ecstatic breakthroughs, epiphanies and insights as well as the degree of breakdown, recoil and vocal demands for personal comforts that was displayed by many of Lee's students who were on the trip. The extent to which some of Lee's students showed a marked lack of maturity and ability to step forward and manage the stress and details of traveling with children in a Third World country generated a tremendous amount of conflict. Overall it impeded Lee's ability to work freely and effectively with his students in the way that he considered most "work useful" or resonant with the process of spiritual transformation. Because the work of spiritual transformation is Lee's sole purpose, in any situation in which this is the case, it usually results in a very cranky and critical spiritual master.

Upon his return to the States, Lee said he would never take women and children to India again. Traveling with women and children in India requires a particular degree of intention and attention from Lee because of the dangers and his high standards in relationship to the care of children and protocol around his women students. He held true to his word; it was seven years before Lee included women in his annual trips to India. In 1993 he relented and took five women and five men with him to India for almost four weeks. He has included women on each of the subsequent trips since that time. Now, twelve years later, he had not only added children back onto the trip as well, but took fifteen of Purna's students to India as well.

Now leaving Chennai with over thirty people in tow, the almost disaster with the boarding passes wasn't just the responsibility of the two men who Lee had asked to do it. There were several senior students there who should have been paying attention to the overall needs and movement of the group. Jan was also responsible to pay more attention to the timing of the group's movement and not wander off at a critical moment. Part of traveling with Lee is learning to pay attention and work together as a group, and to know what it takes to stay "in the chamber," as Lee often says. Staying in the chamber, for example, would include being obedient to what the teachers asks of his students—to abstain from drinking coffee, Cokes or chai unless the teacher offers it, or to stay focused on the purpose of the group and move in a way that would support that purpose. Instead we were already scattered and fragmented, spaced out, going off on our own, running for the caffeine at the first twinge of discomfort. Already we were setting a pattern for the next two weeks that would escalate and begin to chaff at Lee's mood.

After many hours of traveling from midnight through the hours of the night and morning, Lee and his group arrived in Banaras around two in the afternoon. At the airport Purna connected with an Indian woman who volunteered to take everyone to a hotel. We drove in taxis for an hour or so, then sat on the ground for about an hour while Lee and Purna haggled for the price at the hotel. The place was somewhat rat-infested and only the most superficial swipe had been made at presenting the rooms and bedding as clean. After about two or three hours of jumping through the hoops of Indian paperwork at the front desk, including endless details of passport numbers, visa numbers and other information about all thirty-four members of the traveling party, the bargaining wars began in earnest.

Lee is famous for his bargaining in India, and for his refusal to pay highly inflated tourist rates when the local economy really works on a far lower scale. He bargains for transportation in *tongas* and rickshaws, for lodging, food and purchases in general. Lee is firm and clear on this point. On this night he had several fierce arguments with the "guide" who was arranging our transportation about the price to get downtown. Finally they agreed, but the guide was fuming and unhappy about it. He relented only because he saw a potential fortune in the thirty-four Americans who had just arrived in ancient Varanasi looking rather naive, with the exception of a notable one or two.

Finally the group piled into a fleet of auto rickshaws with five or six people crammed in and perched upon each other's laps in each one that then sputtered and coughed and jerked down the bumpy and potholed road. Off we went to the Keshari, a restaurant in the old, downtown area of Banaras, only a mile from the burning ghats. The group had to disembark and walk the last couple of blocks to get to Keshari. As we followed Lee through the crowded streets, an old-fashioned rickshaw pulled by a man bore a corpse through the jostling crowd. It was wrapped in a white shroud and covered with a bright orange and gold cloth, which signified that it was a woman. Many marigold *malas* were strewn about the oddly inanimate human form. A man rode beside the corpse with his arm around her shoulders. The corpse bounced and jiggled like a stiff piece of wood as the rickshaw shambled along the bumpy stones of the road on its way to the burning ghats on the Ganges. The cacophony was indescribable—rickshaw horns, blaring music, the voices of thousands of people who populated the dirt road, all on their way somewhere. Lee kept his attention on the destination and pressed on through the crowded street with vendors hawking their goods all along the way. In a few moments he turned down one of the busy, small side streets that looked a lot like an alley off of the main road.

The food was good, but very expensive, costing as much as two-fifty to four dollars American money per person. Lee said, "We won't be coming back here! The food is good, but the price is ridiculously high!" Our big group jubilantly filled up the downstairs of the restaurant and caused untold angst to the waiter as we yelled for another Coke or Limca, chai or garlic naan, and generally failed to pay attention to orders that were coming out. Our waiter valiantly struggled with the language barrier and attempted to remember who ordered what. It was discouraging to find one's self and others virtually shouting in the face of a waiter because he didn't speak our language, instead of using sensitivity to communicate in spite of language differences. It was the "ugly American" syndrome—although it should be called the "ugly Westerner" because Europeans are often as bad about gross rudeness, superiority and insensitivity to Third World cultures as Americans are. Even though these lapses of attention were apparent, the restaurant benefited from the big appetites of our group, and the mood was very high and celebratory among everyone. Lee sat and chatted long after the food was finished, moving from table to table to connect with people. He smoothed over ordering snafus and appeased the waiters, generally reconciling all problems.

After dinner the children and many of the adults went back to the hotel, while others dispersed in different directions into the loud, smoky night. Lee gave Purna and Tom instructions to look for another hotel and off they went, leaving six of Lee's students who stood in the streets with him, eager to go wherever he planned to go. Chaos reigned everywhere in the brassy, bright glare of the incredibly noisy, filthy and smoky street. On the main street, in the melee that is ordinary life in Banaras, we were jostled and shoved roughly by fast-moving passersby. All around one could sense the subtleties of ordinary commerce and constant nefarious dealings—baksheesh, opium traders, prostitutes, hustlers, starving children, beggars, con men and the dead all blended as a natural fact of the ancient and accepted culture of the streets.

Banaras! Known also as Varanasi, Banaras is spoken of by Indians with reverence as Kashi, the most ancient and holy city in India. The legend is that if one dies and is cremated in Banaras by the Ganges where the ashes or bony remains are thrown into the river, one is immediately liberated, off the wheel of birth and death. People throng to Banaras to die, and there are makeshift "hospices" under the rough stone cupolas up above the burning ghats, where people lay down and wait to die.

Banaras is also beautiful. Its ancient ghats or stone steps stretch for miles along the Ganges, choked with temples, sadhus, merchants, shrines. There are *melas*, big celebrations, that are held every year in Banaras, when the streets are completely packed with people, pilgrims, sadhus, magicians, *sadhakas*, ecstatics, rogues and criminals. Even now, in winter, the streets are constantly full of people. The presence of masses of raw humanity is felt in every moment as people go about their business. Daily life is threaded through and through with the sacred—all along every street are stalls selling religious paraphernalia, and the classic sight of the sadhu dressed in orange or white bathing or praying along the Ganges is completely commonplace here.

Yogi Ramsuratkumar was born in a small village very close to Banaras, and he spent a great deal of time with the sadhus along the Ganges when he was growing up. Stories say that he would take his own food to give to the sadhus, at whose feet he listened to holy stories and scriptures as a child. When he had no food he would take the sadhus to his family's house, or to his neighbors' houses, or to his own mother, and beg for food for them. In the chants that tell his life story, they say "Born in Kashi" because the mythic and revered spiritual power of this place lends itself to the glory of Yogi Ramsuratkumar's life and transmission of Grace in the world.

Now Lee stood in the midst of all this, as if he was basking in it—the noise and chaos of the street, the profusion of life and action. Looking around in wonder the group kept one eye poised on Lee, knowing that he could make a sudden move at any time. Tonight the name of the game would be "hang on to the master's robes" or get lost. He seemed to be waiting for something to happen. Suddenly an Indian man appeared at his side. Lee was talking to him, saying that he was interested in finding the Mehta brothers, silk merchants he knew from two previous trips to India.

The man, Prem, was nodding his head, looking very alert and only slightly untrustworthy. He must have smelled a real opportunity here—and he had no idea how big it would get. "Yes, yes, the Mehta brothers—I know them well! I can take you there. Right now! Right now! Very close—not far at all! This way . . ."

Lee qualified the deal, "I'm not interested in paying any commission. Do you understand me? No commission! None. Not a rupee. You understand?" He fixed Prem with a direct look.

Prem looked around, his deep brown eyes glittering. "No, no—I am your servant."

As soon as this was established Lee and Prem took off into the night in search of the Mehta brothers, the rest of us close behind. The last time Lee had seen the Mehta brothers was twelve years ago, in 1986; the first time was in 1979. Lee and his students had bought silks, tapestries, brocades and wall hangings from them both times, and in 1986 had been treated by the Mehta family to a lavish feast. Lee had said more than once on this trip that buying silks from them was a once in a lifetime opportunity because the textile art of making very fine silk tapestries and brocades is becoming a lost art in India. Now he clearly had something in mind, since hooking up with the Mehta brothers was the first thing he wanted to do after hitting town.

Lee and Prem moved incredibly fast down ancient, narrow winding streets, deeper and deeper into a labyrinth where small shrines glowed in the dark, chai bubbled in large pots in stalls beside piles of fried foods—samosas, puris, *pakoras*, sweets—and vendors hawked their wares, selling all kinds of cloth, jewelry, batiks, incense, huge piles of red *kumkum* and saffron-colored tumeric, dried red chilis, strings of *rudraksh* beads hanging down next to strands of glass necklaces, bronze and stone statues of gods and goddesses, flower *malas* being hand-strung and hanging in masses of jasmine, rose, marigold. Stone sculptors chipped away at hunks of marble, working their craft; strains of ragas and *bhajans* floated on the air—sitars and flutes, tabla players beating out complex polyrhythms in the smoky, dark and loud streets that were teeming with people, cows, water buffalos, goats.

We were buffeted by all this fabulous cacophony and enterprise, the glittering display of maya—phenomena as Lee had so perfectly described it in his last talk in Yogi Ramsuratkumar's darshan. We were in the thick of it, rubbing shoulders with each passerby, streaking the flanks of the arrogant and fat cows that lazed around the streets. In every corner were piles of trash, refuse, rotten food. The smells of urine and shit on the huge, flat stones of the road was so strong in places along these incredibly narrow streets that I wanted to gag at times. There were piles of slimy dung and other unidentifiable substances on the urine-soaked stones, and along the even darker sides of the street men urinated, not even bothering to turn their backs. All along the way we passed elaborate temples with high cupolas, gods and goddesses chiseled out in stone on their ornate walls, trees growing up out of the stones of the road here and there, people dressed in rags next to shops with expensive, rare jewels—sapphires, diamonds, rubies, emeralds— that sparkled and tempted. Come here! it all shouted. And often the vendors would call to us, if they saw our gaze linger even slightly on something, "Hello, hello—Madame! Madame!" they insisted, "Come here!"

Lee moved with Prem through this maze as if he had lived here all his life. He seemed completely at home in these ancient streets. They walked as fast as they possibly could across the stones, slippery with shit and piss and rotten garbage. The bardo-like quality of all this couldn't be missed, nor could the metaphor and symbolism of following the spiritual master through it at almost break-neck speed. If one didn't really pay attention, one could easily get lost, break a leg or twist an ankle tripping on a loose and shit-slippery stone in the road. Following the master through these streets was eerie and dream-like, and yet it also had a sensual quality of realness. Had we in fact died and now found ourselves in the After-death State? No, instead it was a high-stakes bardo trek, a training exercise with Lee, who was the fearless, intrepid guide. Prem was like a magical spirit, an elemental, whom the magician had employed for the moment in this particular labyrinth.

After about fifteen minutes we came to some especially dark, ominous-looking narrow, dark stone passageways. Lee turned down one that had a sign up above it reading "Mehta Brothers Silk Factory." It dead-ended at a door. Prem walked in as if he had been there many times, with Lee immediately behind him. The downstairs entry room was dark and deserted and dusty. Lee walked up a set of narrow stone stairs and emerged on the second floor into a small room, maybe eight by twelve feet, with cotton futon-like mats covering the floor and the walls halfway up. These were all a faded white. Three other small rooms opened off of this main room, most of them containing shelves of opulent silk material. One could guess that this place was not entirely unlike the local opium dens, where thieves would meet to pass off stolen goods, or where wealthy men languished with opiated eyes and dreamy women lying at their side. But now an attractive, middle-aged, obviously well off Indian man with glasses came in with two young boys. They referred to him as "Guruji." He was one of the five Mehta brothers.

Lee introduced himself and said that he had met some of the other Mehta brothers twenty years ago and again twelve years ago when he had been in Banaras. This Mehta brother was not one of them and did not remember Lee, but said he would call some of his other brothers. Lee sat down on the mats and the group gathered around him with Mr. Mehta looking on. Lee went directly into a conversation with him about commissions. A common practice of the tourist guide business in Banaras involves the local guide taking tourists, particularly Westerners, to silk and other merchants with whom the guide has a baksheesh arrangement—meaning that the merchant will give the guide a commission on everything purchased. The cost of this commission naturally gets passed on to the consumer. The tourist basically has to pay double: once to the guide on a per diem basis for showing the tourists around town, and secondly as a percentage hidden in the price of the goods purchased, the kickback to the guide which the merchants add on to the price.

"I want you to understand one thing," Lee said candidly, looking directly at Mr. Mehta, "I have thirty-four people I'd like to bring around tomorrow to look at silks, but I don't want any of us to have to pay a commission. *None*. Not a rupee. I want you to tell me the truth about this." Prem looked uneasy. Mr. Mehta smiled, his poise unruffled. "I want you to tell me the truth," Lee went on, "I want you to be honest with me. Don't lie to me about it."

Mr. Mehta's smile deepened. "Well, you know, in business we have to do what is best for the business . . ." His charming smile spoke volumes as he added, "But of course, I would not lie to you."

Cold Cokes, Pepsis and Thums Up arrived, brought by the boys. Mr. Mehta began to roll out some tapestries, the first one a three-foot hand-woven square of small scenes of the *Ras Lila*—Krishna with the *gopis*—in gorgeous colors and worked with silver thread.

The workmanship on this was outstanding. Next came other tapestries: a Ganesha in gold, wall-hangings and immense bedspreads and comforter covers—one "for the Maharaja" and one "for when the Maharaja and the Maharani sleep together!" he said. These were outrageously opulent, heavy with gold thread. They cost anywhere from five hundred to twelve hundred U.S. dollars.

Lee said, "Tonight we just look. Tomorrow I will bring thirty more people. Now show us something less expensive." And they began to bring out silk scarves and tapestries that were fifteen and twenty dollars each. The protocol and elegance with which Mr. Mehta rolled out his wares for Lee was an education in a very old way of life—an old code of ethics which upper class merchants all over the ancient world must have practiced for thousands of years. This artful protocol, in its original and ancient roots, brought dignity and honor to the procedure of buying beautiful and worthy goods made by the skill and hard labor of the craftsman or woman. Lee was perfectly at home with this. He interacted easefully and skillfully with Mr. Mehta in this world. After about an hour or more of this we finally left, with an arrangement made that Lee would return with everyone the next day sometime after midday.

Then Lee was down the stairs, through the dark rooms and out the door into the night with his small group of students close behind. Prem and Lee took off again at a rapid pace as they wound through narrow, dark, maze-like streets, through hidden markets gleaming with treasures all reflected in the yellow light of fires and dim electricity here and there, past cows and water buffalo until we came out just above the burning ghats on the Ganges. There Lee stopped, and we stood beneath ancient sculpted stone cupolas looking down on an unforgettable scene. Not thirty feet below were ten or so huge piles of wood, heaped in elongated ovals, burning brightly with a body in each. The yellow and red flames joyously devoured the substances of wood and flesh and bone and entrails, which combined and combusted with the most primal element of air off which it fed, each body in various stages of incineration. The smell was incredible as the pungent, stinging scent of burning hair and flesh billowed up around our heads in clouds of wood smoke, borne away quickly into the cloudy, chilly night. The heat and power and intensity was instantly felt.

All these elements combined with the palpable presence of powerful entities, feeding, devouring, celebrating the portal of death, the wide-open window into other realms, where nonhuman creatures hovered to do their God-given work of ushering souls into the netherworld, and feasting off the remaining lost energies—shreds of subtle bodies snapped up in the fierce jaws of Ma Kali and her minions. And she feeding the darkest end of the ray, the growing tip of Creation, as Gurdjieff would say, with all this psychic refuse, the remains of the dead. The dank presence of the river was another entity that played a significant role in this drama—Mother Ganga, always depicted riding on her crocodile, receiving the bones and ashes of the dead, taking them into her womb, her waters, and flowing them out to the sea.

Boats were moored at the shore of the river by the *smashan*; these were heavily laden with immense piles of wood, in addition to the piles of wood all along the shore and near the ghats or stone steps on either side of the cremation ground. Men tended the fires, stirring the burning coals and moving sticks and logs and body parts back toward the center of the blaze. Lee stood with Prem looking over the stone railing at the cremation ground. They were deep in conversation but their words drifted off on the wind. My eyes were glued to the scene below us. I was consumed by all this, the mystery that was pressing in, waiting and ready, poised to take me into its fiery depth, its wide mouth, its loving arms, its rocking waves. This force that pressed so relentlessly was completely impersonal, a dangerous presence that set one into total alert. There was not fear with this but a clear view of the human predicament.

Banaras is a city of shamanistic potencies, teeming with intrigue as well as the sublime side of the Hindu tradition—the worship ceremonies, the rampant symbolism of the faces of the Divine found everywhere you turn. The airs of Mother Ganga carry spirits above the water that waft out through the city along with the smoke of the fires. These demons, elementals and lost souls ride the currents of the air, the river, the fires. They live all along the streets, in the trees, in the markets. They nest in the stone carvings on the hundreds of temples in Banaras. They tempt and test, have a little feast or a bite here and there from unwary passersby and tourists. Why not? We are all fair game, and it is a game—the game of life. It is all the goddess, known by many names and also as Maya or Shakti, or manifest and unmanifest form, in all her glittering array. You are either paying attention and practicing in the ways in which Lee has instructed, or you are not. And if you are not, you are just another juicy morsel for the entities that crowd the city—and perhaps a more juicy morsel than most, because the more awareness or consciousness there is, the more one is connected into the Work, the more attractive one becomes to hungry entities.

After about five minutes Lee took off again, walking fast beside Prem. Lee seemed to be making deals for tomorrow. He was in perfect, relaxed control. Dragging myself away, I felt opened up to a degree that was frightening. I said Yogi Ramsuratkumar's name and kept going, looking at Lee's solid, very real back disappearing around a corner just ahead of me, his white *kirta* gleaming in the dark, as he led us back through the same labyrinth that we had come through on our way to the Mehta's. Again there were the steaming pots of chai bubbling over dung fires, the sweet and exotic smells of incense; there were cows and dogs, music, people milling through the narrow stone streets, temple spires rising above our heads—signs of other mysteries buried in this labyrinth that we would never see. The stone slabs were broken and uneven under our feet, which made the fast walking even more treacherous.

We passed under a complex network of thick white webs strung through a large overhanging tree, the thick cobwebs of "tent worms" having built their citadels unhampered by human interference. In the West the worms would have been burned out or poisoned with toxic chemicals. Here they were just a part of life as it is. Filthy water ran in shallow gutters on either side of the narrow passageways that were littered with every kind of unimaginable refuse and garbage. We went up and down stairs and around corners, down lanes. All of this dark decay was juxtaposed with marigold *malas*, shrines glowing with mellow lights, many dark Shiva lingams resting in yoni stones, black, oily and shiny with ghee poured countless times over their surface. Many sacred images of multi-armed deities, both painted and stone, looked out from every possible surface and nook of the streets, all of it fascinating, titillating, seductive.

But this time I saw everything tinged with a kind of horror at the reality of it all; a horror that rose up out of the cremation of all those freshly dead bodies, where Kali and her feasting entourage pressed against my living body, hammered at its doors and windows—*let me in, let me in!* Now what I saw was the trap of endless abject unconscious suffering, the fact of universal illusion that was so accurately reflected in the squalor and filth and duplicity of everything around me. A strange thought arose in my mind: Now I remember why I didn't want to come back here. I'm done with all this. At Kali's playground in the guru's company, the veil that hides the rounds of earthly incarnation was very thin. It was a feeling that "I" had been there many times before, in countless incarnations. In the midst of that hell realm of no-end suffering and unconsciousness, and, as the reality of all that illusion sank in, "I" remembered why "I" didn't want to come back. In hundreds, thousands or more fruitless incarnations in which the taste of human misery and suffering became such a well-known flavor—a rancid bitterness soaked with the gall of terror, ignorance and futility—the soul began at last to yearn for its own evolution. It began to rise up out of that muck and squalor like the lotus and seek the sun—the sun that was walking as fast as he could in front of me just now, leading me through this glittering, pulsing, potent underworld realm with the slightest possibility that, with the guru's Grace, I might make it through unscathed and even learn something about that very evolution which my soul, over lifetimes, has so fervently sought. And yet it was never so clear that Maya, with all her duplicitous yet mysterious beauty, contained the secret seeds of salvation, of liberation, of infinite possibility, hidden deep and waiting to be discovered within the illusion. Only in incarnation can these secrets be realized, and only with the Grace of the guru.

December 11, 1998
Banaras/Varanasi

Lee told everyone to be packed and ready to go by five this morning. At four-thirty people were throwing together their few scant belongings in backpacks and handbags before we took off for the new hotel that Purna and Tom had found last night.

Lee was exultant. "Hotel Temple on the Ganges! Right on the river, only blocks away from everything—the market, the temples, the burning ghats! Fantastic," he enthused as everyone piled into rickshaws, five or six people to a three-seater. Soon we were scooting off into the predawn. Lee and the group arrrived at the Hotel Temple and found, indeed, it was perfect. It was exactly as Yogi Ramsuratkumar had said, "Everything will be taken care of in Varanasi." Located about a quarter of a mile away from the clay banks of the Ganges, the hotel was surrounded by a little enclave of untouchables. Their children watched us and played about joyfully.

Lee was in the process of haggling with the hotel owner for how much breakfast would cost. He had reached an impasse, saying that the price that was being asked was far too much. He flatly refused to pay it and told the hotel owner that the group would go somewhere else for our food for the next four or five days. Lee stood with his arms crossed over his chest looking truculent. When Lee haggles, part of his success is that when he says no he means it. He is like a mountain, completely unmovable—and he is willing to back that up by walking away or going to almost any lengths to find what is acceptable to his sense of fair game. His worthy opponents sense this in him, the bulwark of solid certainty that he is, and respect it.

Now the owner of the hotel, an older man, walked away. Within moments a very attractive, even beautiful, tall Indian man wearing Western clothes—a sweater, trousers and a wool scarf around his neck against the chill—came walking up. He came directly up to Lee, looked into his eyes and said, "I am the owner's son. I can work this out with you. Whatever you need, there is no problem. Tell me what you need." He looked keenly into Lee's face. He was totally receptive and in relationship with Lee. He seemed prepared to make this work.

This younger man had a very rare nobility and feeling of integrity about him. His physical bearing reflected something about the beauty and elegance of his character. He focused his attention completely on Lee and listened to what he had to say. He clarified a point or two, repeated back Lee's demands and said, "Just a moment, I will talk with my father," went inside very briefly, then came back out and agreed to everything. Twenty-five rupees (a little over fifty cents) per person for breakfast every morning for a week, including coffee, and forty rupees (one dollar U.S.) for dinner each night. This was at least fifty percent below the menu prices, which were geared toward well-off Western tourists. They spoke about what time Lee expected the meals to be ready, and Lee made it clear that he wanted dinner at seven o'clock sharp, and not ten or twenty or thirty minutes later. The man took this in without any problem, staying very focused on Lee. Still looking intently at Lee, he gave a slight, very gracious and respectful bow and *namaskar*, which Lee returned in kind, then walked back inside. The deal was concluded and both seemed satisfied.

As soon as everyone's bags were safely locked into his or her respective rooms Lee took off walking rapidly toward the Ganges. He had planned a boat ride to see the city while the sun was rising. It was about six-thirty in the morning. All thirty-four members of the group took off with him to walk for two minutes and arrive at the river's banks, where boats were docked near Assi Ghat. Lee haggled again, this time with the boat *wala*, Gopala, over the price to take everyone down the river for a two-hour boat ride. The bargaining had just reached ten rupees per person (twenty-five cents each) when someone suggested that one hour might be about all the children could sit for. Still considering the amount "exorbitant" Lee seemed eager to get going and relented. Quickly everyone piled into three boats and we shoved off with three Indian men wielding long wooden paddles.

As the men rowed the boat through the silent water, the beauty of the Ganges spread out before our eyes. The mists were still rising from the river, and out of their depths rose the huge red-orange ball of the sun. It was a living deity, suspended on the eastern horizon in the silver gray sky of early morning. The water was silver also, with a peculiar reflective quality, and it seemed as if we were floating on a liquid mirror. All along the clay banks women were busy washing their saris, which they laid out on the shore in long strips of bright colors. Sadhus, men, women and children performed their morning ablutions in the water, splashing and swimming.

Lee sat with the Ganges wind blowing his hair. The fierce planes of his face softened as he looked intently at the passing scene of the ghats, shrines, people, temples, hotels. The city was quickly coming to life with its many layers of activity. Already the vendors were laying out marigold *malas*, beads and lengths of cloth. Lee seemed to drink all this in with a burning intensity, soaking in the essence of India. Soon the merchant boats came up to sell small leaf-boats that contained marigold petals and a small votive candle of a ghee-soaked cotton wick. These small prayer boats are traditionally offered to the gods on behalf of one's ancestors and set sail on the holy river. In this city of the dead, they are in great demand. Everyone wants to send up prayers for the newly deceased, whose remains have just been dumped, steaming from the *smashan* fires, into the holy waters of the river.

Needless to say, most of us wanted one of these prayer boats, eager to begin a personal participation with this ancient tradition. The boys or young men selling them wanted twenty rupees for each one but Lee haggled them down. He was only willing to pay five rupees each—a fair price. The boatmen were unwilling to accept this price and rowed their boat away. Unflinching, Lee watched them leave without comment. Moments later the merchant boats glided back up beside Lee's boat and Lee nodded his head in agreement to the five-rupee price. "Let people learn from that!" he laughed. "If people don't get that lesson . . ."

The lesson seemed to be in part that if Lee's students want to practice and live like Bauls, they must learn to live like beggars instead of like spoiled and pampered Westerners. Many of Lee's students traveling with him on this trip were ashram renunciates, who live on a very small weekly allowance, but the principle of beggary runs much deeper than the practical facts. Ultimately the lesson of the beggar is to live without attachment and yet to be satisfied and full with whatever life brings one's way. This applies in part to the bargaining process, in that it is nonattachment that gives one freedom in bargaining. One really must be willing to forego having the thing, whatever it is, in order to bargain effectively, which requires a very specific relationship to desire.

Lee bought prayer boats for each of the children, then asked if any of the adults wanted one. All the women immediately said yes, and the prayer boats came flowing into Lee's boat. The other two boats with the rest of the group had pulled up next to Lee's boat and waited their turn at buying. Soon all the women and children had prayer boats in their hands. Lee said, "Don't any of the men want one?" Very quickly each of the men had the little lamps in their hands as well. The boatman lit the lamps one by one. Their flames flickered in the light morning breeze. Someone asked Lee if he wanted one and he said, "I don't need one. My prayers are already taken care of."

Very soon a fleet of small prayer boats with their tiny flames glowing brightly set sail from our boat, then from the other two boats with Purna's group in them. The boatmen paddled the boats further down the river, past the smaller burning ghat and then the main bathing ghat where the biggest concentration of vendors, sadhus and crowds of people were bustling with morning activities. The boat ride was going so well, the mood was wonderful and the children were enjoying it so much, that at one point Lee commented, "I should have known better than to let anyone change my mind—we could have easily done a two hour ride!" He added, "I wish everybody would leave me alone to make the decisions."

The boat continued up the river to the main burning ghats and finally turned around and headed back down river. On the way back Lee's guide from the night before, Prem, was splashing at the water's edge, brushing his teeth with a *neem* stick and drinking the Ganges water out of his hand. He could have easily slept on the streets, or perhaps he had a house somewhere in the labyrinth of the city and just comes to the Ganges to do his morning ablutions. He looked up, surprised, and waved to Lee. Gopala the boat *wala* turned the engine on and the boats chugged back to Assi Ghat. Lee and the group walked the short way over the packed clay ground past shrines and shopkeepers and sadhus and strung out-looking Westerners to Hotel Temple on the Ganges, where a delicious breakfast of curried vegetables, puris and coffee was served on the roof at ten o'clock sharp. The second day in Banaras was well underway.

At one o'clock we were standing on the main road in the old section of Banaras—all thirty-four of us—when Prem mysteriously appeared at Lee's side. Off we went, back through the same labyrinth as last night but now in daylight, to the Mehta brothers' showroom. The large group followed Lee up the stairs and into the small room to be greeted by Mr. Mehta—the same Mehta brother as the night before. As the group flowed into the room Lee instructed, "Some people who don't need to sit down can stand in the corners over there and others sit around here," he gestured toward the back of the small room. "We'll pack as many people in as we can. The people who are going to buy should come in here, everyone else can stand in the next room and look in . . ." He was referring to the room next to the showroom. The wall between these two rooms was partially open with a wooden latticework wall that people could see through, so the rest of our group stood and looked into the room through the wall or stood at the door.

"Be sure to leave room on the floor for Mr. Mehta to roll out his silks," Lee continued. "We'll look at everything first and then buy." When someone from the Arizona ashram asked what the guidelines were for buying silks, Lee said, "You can have anything you *want*—but you have to consider the karma of buying it!" Clearly he expected his students to get a few things, but as an exercise in sadhana the whole experience had many subtle dimensions to it.

Mr. Mehta began to roll out the silks in an orderly way. At first everyone managed to obediently just look, although it wasn't clear that everyone, given the size of the group, was paying attention when Lee gave his instructions. When Mr. Mehta went from the ultra-expensive items and then at Lee's request began to roll out the reasonably priced silk scarves and tapestries, suddenly a scarf here, a scarf there, then another and another, were being snatched up as soon as he laid them out.

Someone in Lee's party said, "If I see something I know for sure I want, can I put it aside?" Lee answered yes, but that the actual buying wouldn't happen until the end. As I watched more and more scarves disappear, stuffed behind knees and feet or at people's sides, an uneasy feeling began to take over. Everyone else was getting all the good scarves! I began to look anxiously at what was rolling out of Mr. Mehta's hands. No, not that one—damn, where are all the blue and red ones? I saw scarves that I liked, but someone else was always faster than me. Competition reared its head, scarcity began to creep into my blood like a chemical cut loose from some reptilian impulse. The mind began to contract in upon itself: have all the good scarves been snatched? Are there more in my favorite colors? The mood in the room was getting more frenzied as psyches bounced off other psyches, building a charge that seemed to be growing exponentially. Everyone was talking at once. The noise level grew as people began to lose control. Lee sat watching it all with the children gathered around him.

As the scene got wilder Mr. Mehta looked confused or even a little disturbed at one point, as if the proper protocol of the space had been lost in the chaos and lust of thirty-four people looking at riches and opulence and *wanting it all*. He adjusted well enough as different people called out, "I'll take that one!" and he knew he was going to make some money. Based on the Indian economy, the Mehta brothers did quite well that day.

The scene took on the flavor of a tavern brawl. I snagged a few scarves for myself, stashing them behind my back as I sat against the wall. It got more intense as some people were seriously buying large quantities of items. There were those with money, who would drop hundreds of dollars into the coffers of the Mehta brothers today, and those without, who would agonize over a few scraps of silk and which ones to buy on a very limited budget. Some members of the group were getting so plugged in at the level of primal psychological complexes that overwhelming passions were beginning to rear their heads, threatening to engulf ego completely. One person was in tears because of the ugly level of recoil and self-confrontation—with the depth of primal scarcity, fear and anger—that was being triggered in the whole interplay. Others were feeling a similar deep disturbance but expressing it in other ways.

Finally Lee said, "I'm going outside with the children." He left to take them to shop for trinkets, leaving everyone at the mercy of their own insanity. The rest of us were stuck there until Lee returned. I went up on the roof for awhile with a few others and looked out over the city. It stretched out as far as I could see and seemed to pulsate with life. Coming back downstairs was like walking into the den of iniquity. Immediately the senses were assaulted with the passions that were raging just as strongly now as they had fifteen minutes before. The group mind was full of greed and pain-driven desires, which were alive in the atmosphere like air-born demons. They were like gargoyles at the gates of heaven that taunted, "You have to get through *me* before you can enter here!"

Members of the group were snapping up comforter covers, quilts, wall hangings, tapestries and so on, quite a lot of it for presents to take back home to others. Finally, after what seemed like a very long time, Lee returned. Almost immediately the electricity went out—a common phenomena in India. We sat on the floor in the pitch black with piles of silks all around us, waist deep in smooth, sensuous and gorgeous fabrics, finely woven tapestries, silk saris. A couple of people had flashlights in their packs. The buying went on in the dark. It couldn't have been more hellish. It was like a scene right out of a Hieronymus Bosch or Salvador Dali painting.

The Mehta brothers had a huge generator downstairs and they turned it on so the lights returned, but along with the lights, the rising stench of diesel exhaust came roiling up the stairs from down below. Along with all the silks and the feverish buying, the atmosphere had become suffocating. With Lee back, a few of us went outside with the children while Lee stayed upstairs to finish up business. I was never so glad to get out into the streets with their running sewers, fat cows and an incredibly loud brass band that played for a marriage ceremony across the narrow passageway. After another forty-five minutes Lee and Purna came down with the rest of the group. Vijaya Mehta and one other Mehta brother had arrived and were happily greeting Lee, who was making the last exchanges of money for purchases his students had made. Lee had insisted that he would manage all this, and people turned their money and lists of purchases over to him, which he then negotiated with Mr. Mehta. Lee and Vijaya Mehta stood in the streets talking and making plans for tomorrow.

What a relief it was when Lee finally headed off with Prem into the winding narrow labyrinth of old Banaras. We followed Lee and Prem rapidly up and down scores of stone steps, down winding passageways toward the river and the burning ghats. It took quite a lot of attention and physical strength and stamina to keep up with Lee. The whole thing seemed to be an exercise in tantric practice. Once again, he was leading his crew through the bardos: work with elements of desire, don't get distracted or fascinated, don't linger, don't stop, keep going ahead *fast*. Paying attention was the key to not stumbling and falling down, not to mention the possibility of being left behind and lost in a dangerous, alien place.

Lee had been saying all day that he would visit the burning ghats with the children later that day. When he reached the main burning ghat where we had been the night before Lee walked down the stone steps at a fierce pace and kept going. I called out toward Lee's back, which was just in front of me and moving with the momentum of an avalanche, "Lee, weren't you going to stop at the burning ghats?" Even though one of the children had expressed an interest in seeing the burning ghats, my question was fundamentally selfish. I wanted to see more of them, to absorb some new insight on the nature of impermanence. It was unnecessary, self-indulgent and an intrusion in his flow. Lee was in charge of the situation; he was going to take care of any needs the children might have. In addition, Lee had given the gift of the burning ghats the night before; now I was being greedy instead of trusting that, if I followed Lee's lead, I would naturally get whatever impressions of Banaras would be useful to my sadhana. Now he turned on his heel and stared at me. His tone of voice was more incendiary than the bodies burning in the blazing piles of wood not twenty feet away.

"Just Follow Me!" he shouted. "I don't want to be interrupted with anyone asking me questions! You understand? I am going to walk back to the hotel along the Ganges, and you should just follow me. If you don't want to do that, then make your own plans and do your own thing." This last comment was dripping with sarcasm. He finished this off with, "Don't ask questions, just follow! Do you understand?"

Within seconds Lee turned and started walking incredibly fast along the eroded and piss-stained clay banks of the Ganges. It was a two mile walk back to the hotel, and Lee did it in twenty minutes, walking at a fast clip—his students walking with him or close behind him and the rest of Purna's group not far behind. Along the way he came to the second, smaller burning ghat. There were four or five crematory fires burning brightly. Families of the deceased sat nearby, chanting, talking, laughing or sitting silently. Lee stopped and watched, the group gathering silently around him. The path along the river went right through this burning ground so that we were only six or eight feet away from the burning bodies. We could see the heads or skulls hanging down on one end of the oblong fires. Boiling brains sizzled in one skull only a few feet away. In one pyre two thin brown legs stuck out in rigor mortis, flaring out from wood and flames in two different directions, dead feet pointed toward the sky.

In another pyre the attendant took a leg that had burned off at the knee and dropped off on the ground and put it back up on the top of the pile, where it was licked by yellow flames, melting around the edges and red and bloody on one end. The fire attendants were busy tending the fires and interacting with the families of the dead as the bodies burned. There were several corpses waiting to be washed. This was as close as one could get to this most primal process, much closer than you could get at the main burning ghat, where you really couldn't see so much of the bodies actually burning. Lee lingered with the children for another minute, long enough to take in the scene, and then kept going. It was enough.

Soon we were back at the hotel, sitting up on the roof as the smoky evening set in. While dinner was served we looked out on the black night over the Ganges. Lee told everyone about the plan for the next day. Banaras is famous for its sacred geography, for its hundreds of incredible temples, like the famous Golden Temple and Annapurna Temple, which Westerners can only look into from the outside, the temples being sacrosanct and not open to non-Hindus. There was also the well-known Durga temple, and scores of Kali and Shiva temples everywhere. But instead of seeing all that, Lee would be picked up by the Mehta brothers' car and taken to their silk factory and large showroom somewhere on the outskirts of the city, where we could see the tapestries being hand-woven (and of course, buy more silks). Then they would take Lee and his group to a village to see local village life.

With Lee's permission, Tom and Zachary were planning to spend the night at the burning ghats, and over dinner they got his specific instructions. "Try not to fall asleep," he cautioned, "and it would be better if there were four of you." He suggested that Purna pick two of his men students to go with them. As Lee sat waiting for dinner with Tom and Zachary he said, "Kali eats the souls or subtle bodies that are still leaving the physical body while it is burning. You can watch the souls of the dead rising from the fires, being devoured." It was an uncharacteristic moment of candor about his own experience. They took off after dinner around eight o'clock.

December 12, 1998
Banaras/Varanasi

Breakfast was planned for nine o'clock. I went up on the roof early to write. Zachary was there looking raw and thoughtful but quite alert for having not slept all night. He had a small pot of coffee and I joined him in a cup. Tom came out and sat down. They told some stories of their night at the *smashan*. They had learned from one of the fire attendants that families paid a high price for the wood for these cremations. If they didn't have enough money to finish the job, sometimes a whole spinal chord with skull still attached would get thrown into the Ganges. It had been a very strong night for both of them. Soon Lee came out and sat down. Zachary offered some coffee to Lee and he said pointedly, "No thank you, I'll wait for breakfast. One cup of coffee a day is enough for me."

Lee had begun to be very verbal about his dissatisfaction with how the trip was going, saying for example that people had no concept of traveling together as a group. Everyone was on his or her own trip. Now he sat and listened to Tom and Zachary's stories of the cremation grounds. He had recommended that the men stay awake and then just "burn through the next day" with no naps or going to bed after they got back after dawn. Lee said sarcastically, "Yeah, the women all want to spend the night down there and see Mother Kali eating souls, but let them lose a night of sleep and see how enthusiastic they are. How quickly we lose our perspective!" He seemed to be very irritated.

This morning he was making it clear that his students were not functioning in alignment with him. His frustration and anger had begun to come out in irascible, fierce ways. There had been requests for special rooms and comforts by his own students, but the splintering of the group in different directions seemed to bother him just as much as the grasping for comfort. The need for awareness of group work—that individuals needed to consider the needs and flow and work chamber of the group as a whole—seemed very high in his priorities. The indulgences in substances that are not part of the recommended dietary practices—coffee, Cokes, chai—were tied into the drive for comfort. The prevailing attitude and thought process was, "Here I am in India, it's very uncomfortable, I'm in a strange place, traveling under difficult circumstances, dealing with a lot of stress—the least I can do is have hot coffee or chai and warm up, assuage the rawness of my nerves with some treats." It is the conventional way of seeing things and antithetical to practice in Lee's company, when in fact, the chemistry that is created within the body by mood-altering substances like caffeine and sugar further the jittery nervousness and grating rawness that is sometimes produced by extremes of discomfort. In other words, by drinking caffeine, one was exacerbating the problem. This retreat to conventional thinking was part of what was being churned up by the stresses of the trip.

But at a more subtle level, the dietary practice is a function of being in resonance with

71

the subtle field of the guru in this particular path. In other paths that resonance might depend on other factors, but in Lee's company, following the recommended conditions, including dietary conditions, is part of developing and maintaining resonance with the guru. My experience was that every time I partook of caffeine outside of Lee's quite generous offerings it caused a shift in the subtle alignments. In his talk to Lee's students during the Appearance Day Celebration, Fleet Maull had spoken about this vibratory alignment with the guru. He called it being "in the sacred world of the guru." He described how necessary it is to maintain one's connection to that sacred world, saying, "When you lose your connection to the guru's sacred world, you get a flash, like you just got burned." This trip was proving to be a tough training ground for learning what it takes to live in the guru's sacred world.

The further out of alignment with the traveling chamber one got, the harder it was to get back in, and inside the chamber that Lee circumscribed was where the benediction of Yogi Ramsuratkumar was focused. Lee had his own purpose and intention for the group travel the last two weeks in India, at least some of it having to do with training his students in tantric work. Traveling with Lee is always a process of entering into a very specific chamber with him. The more people were functioning outside the chamber, the more the possibility for alchemical work of a transformational nature was diluted or thwarted. The more the mood of self-sabotage and resistance to practice shows up in his students, the more irascible Lee often becomes.

Soon the whole group was gathered and the food began to come out. Toast, butter, jam and coffee with milk and sugar was what Lee had arranged for everyone. He had decided that the curried vegetables and puris of the first morning were far too much food for our needs. In addition the children had large platters of chips (French fries) and ketchup. During the meal Lee was asked about the plan for the day.

"Today Vijay Mehta is my guru," Lee said firmly. "If anybody is interested in knowing how they should be when they travel with me, you should watch me today with Vijay Mehta. I am going to be a follower today. Whatever he wants to do, I do without complaint. Wherever he wants to go, I go without recoil, argument, questions or needing clarification. I'm going to show you how you *should* be with me . . ."

After breakfast Lee sat and waited on the roof. The moods and flavors of India unfolded all around as the morning came to life. The roof of the three-story hotel overlooked an incredible vista of the Ganges, spanning several miles in both directions. Again this morning the sky and river were silver from dawn until late morning—one continuous shining screen like the abstract mind, with the red and pink disk of the sun rising through it, a luminous being ascending in a silver sea. Slowly the darker shoreline across the river appeared out of the silver mists and trees begin to take shape. People walked narrow paths across the clay flats that stretched out for a quarter of a mile from the river's edge, the hard-packed clay rain washed and deeply eroded. Closer by, below our rooftop haven, we could see people, cows and hulking black water buffalo walking past small Hanuman shrines and shops, while other activity melted into the shadows along the distant ghats.

Watching the scene on the Ganges the culture of India came into focus. The constant daily rituals and religious rites went on all around us at shrines or temples on every corner of the streets. The whole matrix of life was set within the context of the sacred, and yet all of this was permeated with the swirling of psychic underworld activity—the primitive, dark psyches of the masses. These activities involved dealing with powers and potencies, propitiating the multiplicitous gods and goddesses, activating the forces of magic. So much of the mood of the religiosity here seemed shamanistic and tribal in this way. No wonder the ignorant Westerners, early imperialists from England, France, Europe and America, saw all this as "pagan."

Around noon the cars arrived to take Lee and the whole group to the Mehta brother's factory showroom. We drove for about an hour through heavy traffic and thick air pollution from the low-grade diesel fumes, wood and dung smoke. Finally we arrived at the factory and went directly inside. Vijay Mehta escorted everyone through narrow hallways into the workroom, where we saw as many as six men at one loom, hand-weaving incredible pieces of textile art, working together with amazing co-operation and unity. What patience the whole thing required! It was a fantastic educational opportunity for the children, who were fascinated by the whole process. A Brahmin was dying silk thread in a bucket. He explained that it was a task that, as a Brahmin, he shouldn't be doing, but his family needed him to since they hadn't been able to find the right person for the job. "I do whatever is needed," he explained.

Lee watched for a while, then he was ushered upstairs to the large, spacious showroom. Along each wall were platforms, about ten feet wide, covered with the same kind of off-white futon-like mats that we'd seen in the showroom in old Banaras the day before. Above the platforms—which were designed for displaying long bolts of cloth or large tapestries and saris—were deep shelves filled with carefully folded silk materials in every color of the rainbow.

This time three of the Mehta brothers were present, including Vijaya. They began to show everyone more silks, huge pieces of tapestry with scenes of the Ras Lila, Krishna with beautiful blue skin sporting with a circle of gopis, or large orange or gold Ganeshas. They held up fabulous bedspreads laden with real gold thread, bolts of silk, silk saris in new and different styles, textures and colors as well as more of what we saw and bought yesterday—silk scarves, wall hangings and brocades. It was a wild profusion of riches, and I thought of the ancient silk traders, crossing the desert with camels laden with silks, displaying their wares before the sultan, the maharaja, the queens. Today Lee and his party were the kings and queens before whom the Mehtas regally and skillfully spread their riches.

Once again the buying started. Unquestionably it was an opportunity of a lifetime—but for what? It was an opportunity of a lifetime to buy rare silks and art pieces at affordable prices, but also an opportunity to practice in a way that one might be free to experience right action in the midst of the desires of the marketplace. Since before the trip Lee had been talking about how he was planning to shop when he got to Banaras and Rishikesh. Frequently when one of his students wanted to buy a small bronze or piece of jewelry in Tiruvannamalai, Lee would say enthusiastically, "Wait until we get to Banaras or Rishikesh—we're really going to shop then! They'll have everything—bronzes, jewelry, silver, art." His enthusiasm had been unbridled. Now the teaching lesson of it began to come into focus.

Watching Lee in this process of buying in India one can see timing and discrimination in action, and yet this too appears as an automatic and natural movement in him. Lee's buying is a straightforward process. He strikes when the iron is hot. He doesn't vacillate or agonize over whether he should buy or not, or whether or not it is really what he wants, or worry that he will find something even better later along the way. He has no guilt, no sentiment and no attachment. If something he is looking for appears and it works for him, he gets it then. If something *even better* shows up later, he shrugs and has no problem about it. He also has the freedom to look—to window-shop—with no entanglements of desire. I have seen him walk along the Paris streets looking at pastries and drooling over them with unabated enthusiasm one minute, then the next minute easily walking away, leaving them in the dust without a second thought. This goes for shopping anywhere, and especially in India. The tantric path is not about avoiding, repressing or running away from desire, but is about transforming desire, riding it like a wild horse that is tamed for a very specific purpose.

The Mehta brothers gave their Western guests free reign in the huge showroom. They encouraged everyone to pull things off the shelves that lined the walls. If one of the brothers saw you looking hesitantly at something he would start pulling things off the shelves and spinning them out before your eyes—suddenly not just one long shock of silk would be there, but ten of them, all spread before you like a peacock's tail. The children ran and played in the midst of this silk storm. The Mehtas seemed to take great pleasure in giving the children full freedom to have fun. Cold sodas were brought and served, along with cookies, crackers, bananas. It was more like a party than the day before, and the celebratory mood kept growing as the afternoon wore on.

The hospitality of the Mehtas was marvelous and unstinted. The buying continued unabated, and yet the mood was certainly lighter than it had been yesterday. Lee seemed to be everywhere in the large room. Sometimes he was just standing around watching, and sometimes he went from one person or small group to another, looking at things with different people, admiring this or that, giving color advice, dropping small hints or very subtle teaching lessons here and there. He was amazingly supportive and mellow, especially after the mood of the early morning. "Get whatever you *really* want," he said to one of his students.

Finally Lee and the group headed outside to the cars. Lee was in a car with Vijay Mehta, who seemed to have a special connection with him. As we drove away he turned and said to Lee, "Now we go to the village?" his eyes sparkling with delight. Lee looked at him and said, "Okay!" Vijay Mehta turned back around in the front seat where he sat with the driver. There was a glass partition between the front seat and the two back seats, which faced each other. There were eight people crammed into those two seats with Lee. Something seemed to be working its way to the surface in him. Within minutes he started teaching. "How I am with Vijay today is how everyone *should* be with me—*just follow!* He is my guru today. Whatever he does, I do. Wherever he goes, I follow."

Gathering momentum, and with a receptive listening audience, he continued, "I don't know why people don't want to just *follow,* to just live a life of following. I *love* to follow—especially someone as gracious and generous as him." He pointed to Vijay Mehta. "It's the most easeful, peaceful thing to do! What's wrong with everybody? Instead you have all your opinions, ideas, your *needs* . . . Go here, do that, do this, requests, I need, I want, always trying to control everything. *It's terrible!* To follow is the easiest thing in the world to do!"

The car pulled down a dirt lane and drove through fields of hand-tended, immaculate vegetable gardens. The crops were easily recognizable—peas, potatoes, eggplant and mustard greens, probably grown for their seeds so predominant in Indian cooking. Mr. Mehta's driver parked in the midst of the fields, with the caravan of cars following suit. Following Mr. Mehta and Lee, everyone walked down a tiny dirt path that wound through the gardens and led to a beautiful and meticulously well kept small village—just a few houses and huts and cowsheds. There were water buffalo with thick bones sticking out and heavy meat hanging down under black hairy hides. Brown cows with their soft dark liquid eyes watched us walk past. Small children ran about with many goats, dogs and a few adults here and there, mostly women.

The villagers looked at the Westerners with mild but reticent curiosity, and didn't step forward to interact with us at all. They seemed to know Vijay Mehta well—probably he employed them or owned the land they lived on. He was Brahmin caste, and they a lower caste, but clearly Vijay Mehta had a great deal of esteem for these people and the land. He lead the group through their domiciles, pointing out the ancient technique still used to make the packed mud huts with their thatched roofs. We walked through a lush, cool, shady mango grove, and then past more immaculately kept houses and swept dirt yards under shady *neem* trees.

Mr. Mehta turned to us with glowing eyes and said, "It's very peaceful here, isn't it? Doesn't it make you feel peaceful to be here?" It was in many ways an idyllic scene—the Third World at its very best. Then we were back in the cars, driving slowly back down the dirt road. Vijay had the driver stop the car again at a village gathering. At his request Lee got out and looked. Under a large tent canopy about a hundred people were gathered to listen to a man speaking over a microphone in Hindi. The woman all sat together on one side and the men sat together on the other side—there was no mixing of genders in this. The gender cultures were very distinct and yet not energetically separate; that is, there was no feeling of estrangement between the two whatsoever. Lee looked for a minute and then returned to the car. On the way to the car Vijay said, "The talk is on human rights. This village is run on the principles of Mahatma Gandhi." He was almost bursting with pride for his people.

Once back in the car Vijay turned to Lee and invited everyone to have chai in traditional clay cups at his new showroom, somewhere nearby. Lee, still making the "following" point, nodded and said, "Yes, of course." Surely the last thing anyone wanted to do was go to another silk showroom. One could only hope that Mr. Mehta wouldn't pull out new and different silk products.

We arrived at a low, modern building set in a lush green tangle of trees and shrubs. As Lee walked into the spacious, large room Mr. Mehta explained that he had just finished building this new showroom. Lee and Vijay Mehta sat down together on a wide, padded raised platform exactly like the ones at the showroom we had been at earlier today. All of the Americans and Europeans gathered around them. Shelves of silks spanned the walls, rising up behind the platform.

As he said he would, today Lee had followed Mr. Mehta's every suggestion. Lee had been incredibly gracious, giving people all the time they could possibly need to buy and buy more. Now as hot chai was served in tiny clay cups Mr. Mehta started to speak about the *Vedas*. Lee sat silently, politely listening, his attention completely focused on Vijaya Mehta. As it turned out the Mehtas are a very religious family. Mr. Mehta said that the most important teaching of the *Vedas* is that God is not divided in any way—all is God. He talked about the caste system in India, and spoke of the Brahmin caste as the "thinkers." It was difficult to follow everything he said because of his thick Indian accent and the red betel juice from the *pan* he was chewing. Lee, on the other hand, seemed to understand every word, and often "translated" for me when asked for a clarification.

"To serve a child under five years of age is to serve God," Mr. Mehta said, not knowing how closely this was aligned to Lee's teachings. He continued, "A child under five has no fixed *samskaras* as yet, so when one serves a child one can feel that one is serving God."

Mr. Mehta's words were very heartfelt. He talked passionately about his project to support the village he had taken the group to today. The aim of the project is to preserve the ancient ways of village life. He asked for donations to help with the project. The group had spent the day buying and consuming treasures and beautiful objects for themselves and their friends; now Mr. Mehta was asking for donations that would support the sacred culture of India. Obviously this village life was intimately linked and interconnected with the ancient crafts that produced the incredible textile art we had purchased with such fervor for the past two days. No one responded. Most likely people in our group didn't understand what Mr. Mehta was saying. He seemed disappointed, but said nothing.

As the group got ready to leave Mr. Mehta was still holding forth. He and Lee walked out arm in arm. He was saying to Lee and some of his students, "You have all the gods within you—Shiva, Ganesha, Durga—all within the human being. All that is *within you*—you only have to grow it." As they walked toward the door he peered into Lee's eyes with his arm around Lee's shoulders. It was as if he was looking for something, but wasn't sure what. He said wonderingly, "There is some karmic attachment here between us, some kind of attachment." He smiled into Lee's eyes.

Lee grabbed him into a firm embrace and patted him soundly on the back as he said, "That's because two hundred years ago you and I were in the silk business together!" They laughed together. Vijaya kept looking into Lee's eyes, holding him by the arm and saying, "Yes! Yes!"

In the car on the way back to Hotel Temple on the Ganges I was sitting behind Mr. Mehta. Leaning forward I asked him what caste the villagers were. He said, "Agricultural workers," then went on to expound, saying that the village people are the most important people in Indian culture because they are the ones who provide the food for everyone. If some people weren't content living and working on the land, he said, then life couldn't go on. He said that the cooks and kitchen workers were also very important because they cook the food and serve in that way, but the village people who farm the land were most important of all.

I relayed this to Lee. He said, "That's something important for us to consider in our community. If it weren't for me we wouldn't grow our own food. We wouldn't grow any food. Nobody gets the importance of that in our community. It doesn't make a profit in dollars but it makes a *big* profit otherwise . . ."

Finally the group landed back at Hotel Temple on Ganges. Upstairs on the roof the evening was falling, changing the landscape of India. Mother Ganga flowed slowly and silently, like a wide silver ribbon in the dusk. Flowers bloomed in pots all around the roof. Strains of music drifted on the air. Dinner was served on time. Lee had ordered *thali* plates for dinner every night—assorted curried vegetables, rice and chapatis. Tom ran back and forth from the roof to the kitchen, three stories below, with instructions and requests from Lee for the cooks, mostly special things for the children. While making yet another trip back up the stairs one of the owner's sons stopped Tom and asked, "Who is that man? Is he your guru?" referring to Lee. Tom answered, "Yes." The man looked at him and said, "I thought so. You are very obedient."

All of the hotel staff was aware of both Lee's temporal and spiritual authority within the group. The owner's son, with whom Lee had continued to foster a very genial and co-operative relationship, came to Lee several times during every meal to make sure everything was okay and that Lee had all that he needed. This same man also helped his staff to serve the meals; he seemed to have his hands on every aspect of the service that was being provided, which was outstanding.

After everyone had eaten and sat for awhile at the tables in the growing dark, Lee announced that he had a "special day" planned for the next day, but he wouldn't say what that was. He said, "Just be ready to go at nine o'clock. Breakfast will be at eight. It's going to be a great day!" He had made a plan with Prem, who had accompanied Lee throughout all of the excursions around town and to the Mehta's. Prem seemed somehow related to the Mehta's—a cousin, he had said. Exhausted as usual at the end of the day, after playing a few games of bridge everyone went to bed quite early.

At this point a number of people were beginning to get sick. There had been some minor intestinal discomforts and colds in Tiruvannamalai, but everyone was so protected from the hardships of India in the pristine environment at Yogi Ramsuratkumar's ashram that mostly all remained very healthy. Now there were many factors combining to create travel stress. The intense underworld impressions of Banaras were consumed along with sometimes contaminated and always overcooked food. From four o'clock in the afternoon until around ten in the morning it was quite chilly—a big climate change from Tiruvannamalai—and the extreme toxicity in the air from the various blends of chemical, wood and dung smoke fires began to take a toll on everyone's physical health. Several of Purna's students were seriously ill and in bed. Now the health among Lee's students was beginning to falter. People were coming down with bad colds, flu-like symptoms, harsh and nagging coughs, extreme congestion, sinus infections and so on. The entities of the city, so apparent around the burning ghats, seemed to have something to do with this also—and obviously the failures of practice played a part in all this as well. Even Lee had a cold and clearly was not feeling his best.

December 13, 1998
Banaras/Varanasi

It was cold this morning. The sky was hazy with smoke. Almost everyone had sniffles or colds. A few people in Lee's party sat around at the tables waiting for breakfast. Around seven-thirty Lee came up to the roof glowering. He looked very irritated.

"Breakfast was going to be late," he grumbled, "so I cancelled it. You can order off the menu if you want to, or *whatever,* but we are still leaving at nine o'clock." It was clear that Lee was disgusted with his students' constant drive for comfort. He sounded as if he didn't care if we ever ate again. It was clear that if people didn't work out their own food needs for breakfast, the next meal would be at seven in the evening when the group returned to the hotel. It is never a problem for Lee to go all day without food, no matter what the circumstance, and he often throws some challenge like this into the mix at certain points on a trip. But this morning he was obviously in a bad mood as well. A few minutes later he said that he had a bad cold.

There are two basic dynamics that often occur on trips with Lee. "Hurry up and wait," meaning that you have to hurry to get wherever you are going with Lee, arriving far earlier than is necessary, to then wait for everyone else or for the festivities to begin; and secondly, "feast or famine." Lee will often take his entourage on feasting sprees for days when traveling, then when greed and lust start to take over, Lee will throw in a day of abstinence. This sometimes happens when Lee is promising a feast that then never materializes, entirely due to circumstances that are out of his control.

Someone said, "So if we don't eat now, we won't eat again until seven tonight?"

"Yes," he answered in a terse, challenging tone, as if to say, "Surely you can muster the discipline to go without food for a few hours!"

"You can get some tea or coffee," he continued, "but the price of tea or coffee off the menu here is almost as much as the whole breakfast would have been. That just doesn't work for me . . ."

Dave and Jan S. went out to buy oranges and bananas for anyone who wanted some. Lee ordered chips and ketchup for the children and passed out a few fruit and nut bars that he had. The sun rose higher in the sky and the smoky, hazy air became warmer. Lee was up and down the stairs, taking care of mysterious business. He came back to the tables on the roof and sat down. He resumed his commentary, saying, "This is the path of no sadhana! It's the path of personal comfort! The path of no conceivable stress whatsoever, even if it comes as a direct order from the spiritual master! Purna!" He yelled over to Purna, who was sitting at a nearby table with some of his students. "It's the title of a new book—'Our Stomach Is Our Master!' No, I've got it—'My Stomach, My Master!' "

I went downstairs and saw Prem talking with Tom and some of the others. Prem began to tell me about the plan for the day. We would go by boat across the Ganges to the Maharaja's palace. Then Prem would take us back to Banaras and into the old part of town to see some of the temples and the burning ghats. Soon the whole crew took off with Lee and Prem in three boats down the Ganges. The diesel engine rattled the boat as it skimmed across the slick water, and the thick streams of diesel fumes irritated already delicate and raw nasal passages.

After about five miles or so of chugging across the river we arrived at the Maharaja's crumbling old palace on the Ganges. Prem led everyone through what was once a magnificent structure, full of a kind of opulence we could only imagine. There were eighteenth and nineteenth century guns, jewel-encrusted knives, silk clothing, jewelry, ornate furniture, photographs of the Maharajas and Maharanis on display. This kind of scene is usually totally out of character for Lee. He typically hates sightseeing and is very vocal about it. This whole excursion was obviously for the benefit of the children. Throughout it all Lee was a paragon of patience and understanding with them. Their needs were instantly met. With his recalcitrant students, however, it was another matter. He was making a point.

With the group straggling at different lengths behind him, Lee walked down musty, dilapidated hallways and stone passageways until we finally made our way to the small palace *mandir* on the Ganga. In the temple was a stone carving of Mother Ganga riding her crocodile. Someone said, "One of the Indians said that there are no crocodiles in the Ganges! Why is she always riding a crocodile?" Later another person reported, "Prem explained there are crocodiles in the Ganges only when she floods—once a year."

A few people circumambulated another small Shiva temple where a Brahmin priest lived in the ruins. Lee stood nearby watching. Finally getting back to the front gate the children were—naturally—hungry, so Lee sat on the grass while they ate crackers and cookies. They wanted something else to eat. Lee still had no plan to eat until seven that night. He was still very irritated and brusque, at times acidic, with the adults. As soon as the children were finished with their snacks Lee walked at a fast clip back down to the water and climbed into the waiting boats.

After another forty-five minute boat ride the boat *wala* docked at one of the ghats in the old part of Banaras, in the same labyrinthine area of the old city as the main burning ghat. Lee and Prem jumped ashore and soon we were climbing uphill on many stone stairs that wound around to where a beautiful, small Shiva temple was nestled. There were incredible erotic carvings of men and women in many different sexual postures, along with Kalis, Mahakalas, Vishnu and Brahma in their animal forms, and all kinds of mythological stories depicted in stone on the temple walls and roof.

It was a small but fascinating temple, and very close to the river. A Brahmin priest cared for the temple; he told us that he was the seventh generation of priests in his family who had cared for this temple. Several of Lee's students wanted to stay longer but Lee had waited long enough. We had been there maybe three minutes and he was ready to go on. At Lee's instruction I gave the priest two or three rupees. Did I imagine that he looked crestfallen and confused? Was he was offended by us, our arrogant attitude, our stinginess? After all, the Indians see all Westerners as rich. But I didn't have time to worry about it for long; Lee had already gone ahead. The four or five of us who had lagged behind at the temple, relishing the sculpture and the iconography, had to hustle to catch up.

Lee was traveling fast again through the same maze we'd traveled now twice before, but by various circuitous routes each time. We passed some cows and a food vendor in a narrow lane. The children were beginning to say, "I'm hungry!" Lee stopped and bought crackers, cold sodas and toasted moon dahl in sealed packages to eat along the way. He generously offered these snacks to the adults as well, then took off fast again. It was twelve-thirty in the afternoon. There we were, a large amorphous mass walking in a group down the ancient stone streets of Banaras again, streets so narrow a huge cow could just barely get through. Between the cows and the motorcycles we were constantly jumping to the side in a hurry. The stone slabs underfoot were slimy with cow shit. It was virtually impossible for a troupe of thirty-four people to walk through this scene invisibly, or in a way that would have made little or no impact on the environment. But that was what Lee expected, at least of his own students. As he said many times, "You all have no excuse—you've been trained in this Work. Purna's students are new, and they can be excused." The group bumbled along like a vast, unwieldy thirty-four-headed hydra. Passing motorcycles had to blare their horns many times to get everyone out of the way to pass in the narrow passages. The local people patiently made their way through our crowd with cows, goats and dogs in tow—they seemed used to dealing with confused Westerners.

But there were many wonderful things to see, like an old man ironing clothes with a huge, heavy old-fashioned iron. The dung coals glowed red inside the black iron as he pressed the fabric down, like red eyes hidden down in the roughly forged ore of the iron. Other men and women boiled chai in pots or fried samosas on primitive stoves, or baked in earthen ovens. As we got closer to the Golden Temple strands of colored beads and *rudraksh* hung everywhere along with marigold *malas* and piles of red *tilak* and *kumkum*. Glass bangles hung in an array with goods for sale, junk, odds and ends, silk, cotton, batiks and religious artifacts abounding. We had entered an area designed for spiritual tourism. The children looked at everything and wanted to buy trinkets. Sometimes Lee stopped to let them look or buy.

We were submerged in India. Lee stopped here and there, then kept going. Around the Golden Temple Prem wanted everyone to walk up to the roof where we could look down at the scene inside the temple below. As non-Hindus none of us were allowed in. Close by was the beautiful, big Annapurna temple. Annapurna, the Goddess of food *(anna),* and abundance or wholeness or fullness *(purna),* was depicted over the cupola of the shrine as a beautiful woman in her abode in the highest mountain in the Himalayas. The scene showed Shiva going to her with outstretched hands and receiving the bounty of food from her abundant and overflowing hands. Bells clanged and strong, sweet incense filled the air. The shouts and murmurs of many people were all around us. Buffeted about in the throngs that milled through the streets we found our way back to Lee where he waited for the people who had gone up to the roof with Prem. Everywhere were vendors selling religious articles, incense, prayer beads, paraphernalia.

Shortly after this the large group split up and went in several different directions. Some went shopping for batiks, others wanted to buy shawls and presents for people at home. Lee continued on with the children and a few of the adults, heading back toward the hotel. He seemed harried, distracted. He said, "Whatever you want," to whatever question anyone asked him.

A bunch of us stayed to shop for batiks. We particularly loved the Kali batiks, and when our guide, a friend of Prem's who had hovered on the edge of our group for an hour or so, realized this he offered to take us to a small Kali temple nearby. We walked down what would be considered a side-street—an even more narrow stone passageway that was actually quiet and hidden away—that lead to the Kali temple, away from the hustle and bustle of the tourist area we were shopping in. We took our shoes off and walked in on the oily stone floor. The room was dominated by two large Kali deities in separate shrines. Immediately we noticed that the atmosphere was sharp with presence and a strong, potent sanctity. This place was alive with the constant daily worship of devotees.

Three or four Indians were worshipping in front of the main deity and shrine as we came in. Around the outside of this shrine were depicted the ten Mahavidyas—the tantric goddesses often associated with Kali. They were painted, five down one side and five down the other side, along the front of the shrine. Inside the shrine was the deity, a highly stylized and starkly inhuman version of Kali in red and black and white. Her large red tongue protruded from a wide red circle of a mouth, and deep, primal, black eyes stared out. The form of the deity radiated an awesome presence. Here was the spirit of the *smashan* in one of its more sublime moods. Circumambulating the two shrines that stood side by side we saw several Shiva lingams in yonis, black and shiny with ghee offerings. The Indians stopped at each one and *pranamed,* taking blessings from each. On the back of the main shrine was a Kali *yantra* carved in stone, just at head height. There the worshippers stopped and placed their heads on the *yantra,* whispering prayers and mantras. The second, smaller deity was also very potent and less stylized, more human.

Feeling a strong pull back to the hotel we took bicycle *tongas* and arrived around five o'clock. Lee was up on the roof looking ill and glum. The excitement of discovering the Kali temple quickly faded into ashes. Obviously he wasn't feeling well—like most of us—but he also seemed to be disturbed by the attitude of his students since we'd left the Yogi Ramsuratkumar Ashram. An air of sadness pervaded the atmosphere around him. The failures to practice on the part of his senior students who were on the trip with him were taking their toll.

December 14, 1998
Banaras/Varanasi

At seven-thirty this morning there was a gorgeous mackerel sky—silver and gold clouds hanging in a pattern of striated puffs above the Ganges. The ubiquitous smoke was a thick haze in the early morning air. Lee sat alone for a brief few moments at a table on the roof. One or two other people sat quietly writing. The air was quite cool, and dark green leafy trees loomed out of the mists a block or so away. Our neighborhood seemed to be on the south end of Banaras. On the rooftop of the building just below to the right a sadhu sat on a blanket with a horn in hand, playing to a basket. Presumably there was a cobra in there. He was just a beginner, and squeaked and honked along.

Soon people arrived for the usual breakfast of toast, jam and coffee with hot milk. Lee was telling one of the children that her doll would enjoy seeing Rishikesh. "It's very different than anywhere we've been so far," he said. Some of the men traveling with Lee came up and sat down. Dave initiated a conversation with Lee about the journal writing exercise that Lee had given to everyone on the trip with him. "Why am I afraid to write?" Dave asked. "The conclusion I came to was that I can 'dance' when I'm speaking, but when I write it's in black and white."

Lee looked at him evenly. "Okay," was his simple response. Then he added mysteriously, "It's better to pay off the karma now by writing and be done with it over on the other side."

When he heard that three men, two of Purna's students and one of Lee's, had spent the night at the burning ghats this past night without consulting with or even telling Lee or Purna, Lee snapped, "My students and Purna's students are just the same—the only difference is that mine have been doing this for twenty years!"

Lee continued, "Don't people know that we're traveling as a group? Everyone is doing their own thing. It's maddening!"

Today was our last full day in Banaras. Tomorrow we would leave for five days in Rishikesh. Lee left this morning with Purna to shop for bronzes. The rest of the group went in various directions, mostly shopping. Lee and his entire party had been invited to the Mehta's for dinner and entertainment tonight.

Some time after four o'clock the cars arrived to pick everyone up for dinner. We were driven back to the large showroom and silk factory on the edge of town. One of the Mehta brothers lived in part of the building with his wife and children. Lee and the group were ushered into their living room to drink sodas and watch Indian television for about an hour, then the live entertainment began. The group moved into the silk showroom and sat up on the platforms that lined the sides of the room to watch. A woman dancing a traditional dance form—not *Bharat Natyam* but something more popular and tribal it seemed—was accompanied by a man on tablas. They were the opening act for the famous and much loved local tabla player, Lacchu Maharaj, who Lee had heard play at the Mehta's twenty years ago.

Lee sat patiently and waited. It seemed to take forever to get the show on the road, as the Mehta brothers set up the space and haggled over where to put the rug and so on. Finally, after the accompanist on harmonium was seated and playing a very soft, background melody, the master came out and took his seat. As the renowned tabla player arrived the Mehta brothers discreetly gestured that the group should sit down on the floor instead of up on the platforms because it would be impolite to sit up above the maestro. Lee immediately moved to the floor. It took the rest of the group about five minutes to catch on, and then only when Lee called people by name and told them to move. This slow reaction time and insensitivity to the movement of the group and the chamber was a small example of what had been consistently "maddening" for Lee.

Lacchu Maharaj sat at the far end of the room. His bearing was regal and yet wild at the same time. The Mehtas kept calling him "Guruji" and bringing him fresh *pan* (betel) to chew. They obviously held him in high esteem and wished to cater to his every need. Just as he was about to begin the electricity went out. A very noisy generator was immediately turned on to get the lights back on. We had to sit and wait—probably another forty-five minutes—for the electricity to come back on so the generator could be turned off before the concert could begin. Lee was, as usual, an exemplary guest—patient, flexible, receptive to whatever his hosts had in mind.

Finally the generator was turned off and Lacchu Maharaj began to play. The subtlety and nuance of his playing was unbelievable. His fingers moved so fast on the small tabla that they became a blur. With each "piece" he would tell a small story in broken English. He talked about how for him, the drumming was a form of poetry. It was his poems that we heard. He would play the drums with his eyes closed for long periods of time, the rhythm and mood totally mesmerizing and at times contemplative. It seemed to me that he was meditating, all of his energy interiorized, focused internally, until at certain moments in the "poem" or story of the drum he would become animated, open his eyes and literally go wild like a madman. He became inhuman, almost demonic or angelic—it was hard to tell which, and at times it was both—in these moments of epiphany.

Afterward the Mehta's wanted to take a picture of Lee with Lacchu Maharaj, so people gathered around them and the photo was shot. We went into the next room and were informally served a very delicious dinner. It was about nine-thirty at night. We sat casually around the room and ate off plastic plates. The food was wonderful. Around ten o'clock, Lee walked out to the cars. Everyone loaded into the caravan once again, and we were driven back to Hotel Temple on the Ganges.

December 15, 1998
Banaras/Varanasi

Lee was sitting downstairs in the small dining and reception room in the hotel. He had a bad cold and probably a fever too. Many of us were sick, some much worse off than others. The extremely toxic fumes and smoke that permeates the incredibly polluted air everywhere in Banaras had contributed heavily to the illnesses. Physical breakdown had set in on the whole group.

We had until after lunch to do whatever we wanted to do before we would leave around one o'clock for the airport to catch our flight to Delhi. Lee was going on another boat ride with the children, then making deals with the stone carver across the street. The stone carver is part of a lovely family of craftsmen with whom Lee has established a very friendly relationship. I arranged with Lee that I would go with Tom and possibly Dave and Jan to the Durga temple that is only five minutes away from our hotel. Prem was there, ready and willing to take us anywhere we want to go. Just before we got ready to go Lee irritably made a point with me that I should make sure that *everyone* knew we were going so they could join us if they wanted to—rather than going off with just one or two people. Finally Tom, Dave, Jan, Kristen and I followed Prem to the beautiful and packed Durga temple . . .

The group took an afternoon flight out of the Banaras airport to Delhi and arrived in a chilly, smoky twilight. Someone said that Delhi is rated fourth in high air pollution in cities in the world. Lee was met at the airport by Makarand Paranjape, a scholar and devotee of Yogi Ramsuratkumar who contributed a long essay on the mystical poetry of Sri Aurobindo to *Death of a Dishonest Man*. He spoke immaculate English.

Makarand had arranged the lodgings for the night for Lee and his group at a Sri Aurobindo ashram in the city. He had also arranged for the large, comfortable tourist bus that was waiting at the airport for Lee and his group. The private bus with its two drivers would provide our transportation to Rishikesh the next morning at six o'clock. Everyone piled in with their backpacks for the drive to the Aurobindo ashram. Lee rode in the front seat with Makarand; they were deep in conversation during the whole ride.

After about an hour the bus pulled up to the ashram. It was dark and cold as we walked through the hazy, smoky courtyards to find our rooms for the night. Many people went directly to bed. Lee and most of his students went to dinner first, which was being served in the institutional dining hall. The food was very good—rice, *sabji*, a *seitan* dish, hot peppers. Afterward we took our steel plates and washed them at the communal trough in cold, soapy water, then replaced them in the dish racks at the entrance to the dining hall. Dan went out in the misty, cold, smoky air to get medicine for the infirm—which was almost everyone. Exhausted and sick, we fell into bed.

December 16, 1998
En Route

In the very cold, smoky predawn, at six o'clock when it was still pitch black, Lee waited with his students in the parking lot for the leased bus to arrive. It was supposed to be there at six, so everyone stood with bags piled in a large mound on the ground and shivered for fifteen minutes. When the bus arrived everyone piled in and the bus took off in a thick fog, traveling at fifteen or twenty miles an hour for the first two hours of the trip because of the fog and the heavy traffic. Lee had thick slices of bread passed around, offered from the kitchen of the Sri Aurobindo ashram, along with jars of jam. Purna cut the bread and Debbie spread each slice with jam. The bread quickly disappeared, along with a few oranges and bananas that some had stashed in their bags.

Beautiful, clean Rishikesh near the foothills of the Himalayas would be the last leg of the month-long journey. Lee seemed to be in better spirits since we left Banaras. About halfway to Rishikesh, after the bus had been rolling along for about six hours, the bus driver pulled into a swanky restaurant and rest area for travelers called the Cheetal Grand. Lee said, "The children will be hungry, so we'll stop here so they can eat."

The adults were hungry too, having eaten only bread and jam since five-thirty that morning. The menu was a Western dream—hamburgers, Chinese food, soup, veggie burgers, French fries, omelets, grilled cheese sandwiches, pizza by the slice, Pepsi, and also Indian food. Everyone went in and started ordering, then gathered around at five or six of the fancy white wrought iron tables on the outside patio. The lush grounds of the restaurant were elaborately landscaped. Bamboo grew in large pots, along with bego-nias, chrysanthemums and bird of paradise. Peacocks roamed along the paths and strolled through the patio. Many affluent Indians were there, along with lots of Westerners. An ex-Sannyasin recognized Lee and spoke with him a while. Because the group was so big and had ordered both at the counter and from various waiters, the bill ended up being a couple of hundred rupees more than it should have been. Lee and Purna attempted to work it out with the waiter, but both grumbled that the group was fleeced in the general confusion. As the bus drove away Lee muttered with chagrin, "I knew I recognized that place! That is the place I swore I would *never* stop at in 1986 when we were here—boy, things have *changed!*"

After eleven long hours in the bus, Lee and the group climbed out on the edge of Rishikesh and unloaded bags and backpacks onto the ground. Soon it was discovered that we would have to walk through a bazaar—about a mile—then across the footbridge that spanned the Ganges to get to the other side of the river, and then down another road through another bazaar to the ashram where we would stay. Lee and Purna bargained with the cart *walas* and made an arrangement to have some of the luggage taken over by cart.

Heaving bags into the one small cart Lee said, "People should carry as many of their bags as they possibly can." As usual when traveling in India, Lee's students came with one small backpack each, so that every man or woman had two or three changes of clothes (saris or *kirtas* and dhotis or yoga pants) and only the most basic personal care items. These included a number of natural health aids for Third World travel—things like grapefruit seed extract pills and a few homeopathics. Now in addition everyone had two or three bags full of shawls, *punjabis*, more saris, silver jewelry, silk tapestries, bedspreads and scarves, bronze statuary and other items purchased along the way.

This part of Rishikesh turned out to be a tourist haven, a beautiful, rambling stone and stucco affair. Taking in the natural beauty of the place—the clean water, the fresh mountain air, the amazing relative cleanliness of the streets—we trooped with the children over the bridge to the other shore. All along the way were many sadhus, cows, tea stalls and shops. Street vendors spread their wares out on blankets on the ground—beads and roasted peanuts, *malas* and wool shawls. The cart *wala* came along behind us. After a two-mile walk along the river we got to the Srived Niketa Ashram on the outskirts of Rishikesh. It was the last one along the lane that we had traversed.

The ashram was about one hundred yards from the river and the river's wide, boulder-strewn and sandy bank. It was almost sunset and a strong, chill wind was blowing off the water. Still, the Ganges River was beautiful with the golden late afternoon sun sparkling on the water. We pulled our shawls around our shoulders and shivered. The usual hassle of bargaining, money disputes, confusion and reams of paperwork ensued with the ashram "manager"—a sadhu dressed in orange—with Tom and Purna handling the arrangements while Lee looked on. The rest of the group sat on the ashram steps and ate crackers. In about an hour we were shown our rooms. They were big and spacious, but dark, gloomy and dirty. The large space off the bedroom leading to the bathroom had a two by three-foot open window in the ceiling with three or four iron bars over it to keep people—and probably monkeys—from getting in. Through this window, which could not be closed, a cold wind blew constantly, rattling the doors and windows in the bedroom as well. The ashram staff brought in very dirty thick cotton blankets, almost like thin futons. At that point I was too sick to care.

While everyone got settled Chris complained to Lee about the filthy bedding. He was furious again—this seemed like another blow to his attempts to give his students opportunities to work.

Lee snapped, "Okay, Purna and I will look for another place first thing in the morning."

She objected, saying, "No, no I can make it work . . ."

"No, we'll get another place tomorrow morning," he said, case closed. It was already rumored that Lee might be getting another place in the morning because of a number of mix-ups and other factors. It seemed this wasn't the place that had been arranged months ago for him and his group to stay in, but it would have been better for us to just accept tonight's situation with equanimity rather than intervening in Lee's plans with complaints.

As the unwieldy and fragmented group gathered vaguely at the ashram gate to go to dinner at the Choti Wala restaurant back a mile or two toward the footbridge over the river, several people were walking away, heading out on their own. Lee's frustration with our lack of attention to the needs and flow of the whole group seemed to peak in that moment and he yelled at Dave, who was beginning to walk through the gate. "Dave! *Dave!*" That got Dave's attention and he quickly turned back and joined Lee and the group. Lee then gave a fierce lecture on the need to pay attention to what the rest of the group was doing. "What's wrong with you people? Don't you know we're traveling as a group?" he yelled.

After dinner at Choti Wala, everyone was asleep by seven-thirty that night with the wind that blew off the river howling around our ears. It rattled the windows and doors, seeped under the blankets and bit at our necks. This Ganges wind carried a hint of mystery in it. What did this wind bear in its secret airs? As in Banaras but with a different feeling here, Ma Ganga, personified and sitting on her divine crocodile, seemed like a very real presence and entity. Through all this, Yogi Ramsuratkumar's name reverberated.

December 17, 1998
Rishikesh

As soon as everyone was up and moving around this morning we moved to another ashram nearby. It was a beautiful place, with a gorgeous view of the green mountains rising up behind us and lovely, well-kept grounds and gardens. The accommodations were very nice. After the group was settled, around ten o'clock, Lee went down to the little cafe at the end of the lane in the ashram complex and had breakfast. As different members of the group arrived food was ordered and served—curried potatoes, *parathas*, tomato soup, French fries. Most people were still drinking caffeine, ordering big glasses of chai and coffee and Coca-Cola, except for Lee and one of his students to whom he had issued a request—"Please stop all caffeine now."

After breakfast at the cafe on the ashram Lee began to wander through Rishikesh. It was a haven for Western tourists, with its glittering spirituality and classic north Indian flavor. Many green trees, flowering shrubs and bushes made for a lush mountain landscape, along with bougainvillea that flowered in massive vines hanging over stucco walls. They bloomed in a rose red profusion even in the chilly air. The Ganges was cold and clean. Its presence and spirit dominated everything in a wonderful way. Looking out over the water one had the feeling of looking out over the ocean—there was a vastness in the atmosphere or feeling of the Ganges and how she met the ancient shore, rocks, sky and wind.

Lee strolled along the bazaar, taking in the large plaster deities painted in bright colors in their big, modern shrines everywhere along the street, many of them depicting various mythical scenes, from the *Ramayana*, from the *Bhagavad Gita*. There was a large, heavy plastic Shiva with blue skin holding his trident and sitting on a tiger skin. He sat out on the rocks in the shallows of the Ganges with the cold, crystal clear water rushing past him. There were plastic Krishnas with flutes and Ayurvedic medicines for sale everywhere. "Made with Himalayan root herbs and water from the holy Ganges!" the signs proclaimed. Spoiled, fat, furry cows roamed everywhere along the narrow road. A sadhu petted one of them as lovingly as one would caress a child. He spoke to the cow in Hindi in soft tones. Not baby talk, but reverent tender talk, as if he spoke to an adult human being that he loved dearly. There was much that glittered that was not gold in Rishikesh, for all the spiritual tourists—many, many Westerners who flowed en masse each year through this lovely place. Some of them walked the streets dressed as sadhus and *yoginis*, looking strung out and lost. Others had lived for many years in India; they looked and acted seasoned and weathered by years of hard living.

Lee walked along the lane through the bazaar toward the footbridge over the Ganges. At the bridge, instead of crossing to the bazaar on the other side, Lee took off over the sand and boulders toward the river with the kids. The group split up and went in two or three directions, a few staying with Lee and others walking on across the bridge. As the others headed toward the bridge and the other side of the river, Lee was critical of their breaking away. He said, "It's impatience. People can't stand an instant of self-reflection, a moment that isn't filled with self-centered activity."

Lee took off his sandals and walked barefoot along the fine white sand that was strewn with large smooth boulders for about a hundred yards from the water to the street. The water appeared almost blue-green, and up close it was crystal clear, a big change from the swirling muddy water at Banaras, where one could easily see floating human remains, dead cows or anything else in the water. The weather was beautiful, and the sun sparkled across everything, making the wide expanse of swiftly flowing water diamond-strewn in the morning light. The sun, wind, water and earth combined into a much-needed healing force. Across the river the foothills of the Himalayas rose up into the clear sky. Lee stopped, squatted down at the edge of the water and bathed his forehead with the holy water of the Ganges.

After walking along the river's edge for a while Lee commented that he was looking for the cave of Mastram Baba, an old tantric yogi whom Lee had met there in 1986, and whom Lee had spoken about many times as one of the few authentic tantric teachers in India. After about thirty minutes Gary, one of Purna's students, came back and reported that he and his young daughter had found a cave further up the shore. Sure that it was Mastram Baba's cave, Lee, several of his students and Gary took off for the cave.

Approaching the cave the sounds of a drum and faint chanting could be heard. The cave was nestled in huge granite and limestone boulders, behind which was a path that led up a small hill to a bungalow near the road. A sadhu sat on the porch of the bungalow playing a drum and chanting. Lee walked up and was greeted right away by the devotees who either sat nearby or immediately walked down from the bungalow. Lee smiled and talked with two old sadhus in front of the cave. They showed him the cave and made him welcome in every way. They wanted to serve an entire meal, but Lee declined. He accepted bowls of the delicious sweet *ras malai* they offered as *prasad*.

A mutual connection was apparently occurring between Lee and the old sadhus and devotees of Mastram Baba. There was a sweet and pleasant feeling of communion in the air. They encouraged Lee and everyone with him go up to the cave and look in. It was spotlessly clean, the well-swept floor covered with cotton and wool blankets. There were small shelves wedged in further back in between the stone walls of the cave with a few pots and bowls on them. The space inside the cave couldn't have been more than eight feet in diameter, shaped in a kind of oval as it was. It was obviously meticulously cared for, and had been left exactly as Mastram Baba had kept it during his life. There was still a tangible presence there.

On many occasions Lee has told stories of squeezing into the tiny cave with Mastram Baba and two of his women devotees. Lee said that Mastram Baba's women disciples had to sleep outside on the ground, and that the men stayed in the hut on the hill just twenty-five feet or so behind the cave, where we had seen the sadhu with his drum. Every morning the devotees performed their ablutions in the freezing cold water of the Ganges.

Soon Lee left and walked with the smaller group back along the road and then down to the river. While the children and some others went back to the ashram, Lee walked over the footbridge to the bazaar on the other side of the Ganges. We strolled along, Lee looking for bronzes and *rudraksh malas*. He was very disappointed in the quality of the bronzes and purchased nothing.

That night Lee and the group had dinner again at the Choti Wala. This time we had one long table upstairs. It was mass confusion with the waiters, but seemed to work much better than some other dinners out on the trip. The food was edible but over-cooked. Afterward the group walked back to the ashram in the dark through the still brightly-lit bazaar that stretched up and down the road along the river. The river was beautiful with the lights of Rishikesh reflected on it.

Arriving at the ashram about twenty-five people—Lee's students and Purna's students—crowded into the living room of Lee's suite where he gave an After Dinner Talk. One of Purna's students asked Lee how he made decisions about things. Lee talked about how he looks for three concentrically validating signs before he makes a major move in any direction. Then Graciela began to question Lee. She and her husband Charles have been friends of Lee and the Hohm Community, and were now students of Purna. She said, "I've asked Purna to be my teacher, and I want Purna to be my teacher, but now on this trip I realize that along with Purna comes Lee and Yogi Ramsuratkumar and the whole lineage, which I've been avoiding for years.

"This whole thing pushes all my buttons. I want Purna to be my teacher, but I didn't sign on for all this . . . " she said. It seemed that she was speaking for many, if not all, of Purna's students. Lee began to answer her by saying that in any genuine lineage each teacher has his or her own style. Yogi Ramsuratkumar's style is very different from Papa Ramdas' style, and Lee's style is different from Yogi Ramsuratkumar's style. As Purna's community evolves his style would become more distinct from Lee's.

"But on the other hand," Lee said, "I have spent probably a total of a few months in Yogi Ramsuratkumar's physical presence over all the years I have known Him, whereas Purna has spent twenty-three years in my company. He is more likely to have a teaching style that is like mine than I am to have a teaching style that is like Yogi Ramsuratkumar's. But none of us knows what we are signing on for when we first come into the path."

Lee began to speak directly to the experiences many had had on this trip, which had been especially hard in some ways on the new students, who had never traveled in India and knew very little about the Hindu tradition. He said, "If you want the real teaching, sooner or later it's going to get dirty. You're going to find yourself falling apart, you're going to see things about yourself that you can't stand, that you don't want to see. The gentlest reminding factor is the sangha; then comes the lineage, then comes the Universe. If you become important to the Work but you lack alignment, the Universe gives you Mount St. Helens and storms and personal disasters to get your attention. The Universe touches your family, your business, your everything, until you *get* it. Once you get it you are under the wing of the Work, getting blessings. It's sort of like an Indian marriage—arranged! But that's the good news!

"The bad news is if Purna's teaching capacity matures consistently with the aim of the Work then you've got no life of your own. That's the bad news. On this trip, for example, for Purna's students this is Purna's trip. And for my students, this is my trip. You're just here to follow. When do we eat, when do we sleep, when do we shop? You do it when he does it, or when I do it. That's the way it is. In the Baul tradition in Bengal the guru tells the devotee when to have a baby, what instrument to play, when to go to school. The teacher must destroy the private lives of his students, destroy their egos. That's the nature of the tantric, or *vajrayana* path . . . .

"So you've fallen into evil ways, my friends, into dark and murky waters!" Lee chuckled, "And you're so clean-cut! But that's the best kind of people to lead astray, as far as I'm concerned!" Lee laughed madly at his tongue-in-cheek remarks. Several people looked glum or worried. A few of Lee's students managed small chuckles.

Lee went on to talk about the need to pay attention and how little people had been paying attention on the trip. He talked about how slowly the group responded at the Mehta brothers when Lacchu Maharaj was getting ready to perform and it was appropriate to move to a seat on the floor. Lee said, "I had to say pointedly to a number of people, 'Sit on the floor.' If we were paying attention everyone would have just gotten it when they saw me move to sit on the floor. If you were paying attention in that space, it would have been obvious and you would naturally do the right thing at the right time."

Then he talked about how twenty year students of his, who know that their practice is to not be in photos, still didn't move out of the way for the picture that was taken of Lee and Lacchu Maharaj and had to be told by Lee to leave the space. He used these as examples of either failures to practice or the lack of paying attention.

December 18, 1998
Rishikesh

People were slowly healing and in various stages of recovery. Last night at the After Dinner Talk everyone laughed at the chorus of coughs, sniffles and nose blowing that punctuated Lee's talk. Lee too was participating in this since he still has a bad cold. He talked at length last night about the discomforts of the trip in 1986, and how much worse it was then. "But," he said, "it is all relative, and relative to this trip there have also been some discomforts."

The group gathered again at the small ashram café and ordered food for breakfast. Purna had been out visiting with Allison and Mike, two of Andrew Cohen's students who run the Impersonal Enlightenment Fellowship center in Rishikesh, preparing leaflets and getting the information out in town for Lee's public talk that afternoon at three-thirty. It promised to be a good one. Everyone was hungry for a dharma talk.

At around three-fifteen Lee and his students walked to the large, empty room on the ashram grounds where Lee would give his talk. It was a large, spacious room set up very nicely by Purna and his students with cotton blankets on the floor, some rows of chairs in the back, and a single chair for Lee front and center. At three-thirty Lee went to his chair and sat down and started his talk while people kept flowing into the space until the room was full. There were about seventy people there including twenty-five or so of Lee's group. Purna filmed everything on the video camera that had been with him throughout the trip.

Lee started by tossing out a few insults, but the light that emanated from within him outshone any provocation he was making. He was transparent with this light; compassion and understanding hummed beneath his words. Even the most biased and blind person there couldn't miss the flow of love and compassion, the brilliance of his aura.

"Most Westerners travel through India as if they own it and half the world besides! I have a lot of criticisms for Westerners traveling in India . . . so feel free to leave if I insult you today! I got insulted today—someone thought I was a student of another Western teacher!" Everyone laughed.

"Today I will be talking about my own particular street version of American spirituality, although the roots of my tradition are here in India and I've been here many times. So I'm not disparaging the tradition in any way, but the Westerners who travel in it. I won't use phrases like 'God is One, God is Love,' except with sarcasm."

Lee coughed and tapped his chest with his fist gently. "I picked up a lovely little cough in Banaras . . . But, that's the body, and we're all gonna die one day—so practice *hard!*" He dissolved into laughter, taking the audience with him. "So, I'm interested in how extraordinary mystical states and realizations get translated into reality, into ordinary life. If we've seen God face to face, so what? If it doesn't get translated into ordinary reality, it doesn't mean anything."

Lee began to talk about Yogi Ramsuratkumar and how he had just come from visiting him in southern India. He said, "I'm also associated with the Bauls of Bengal—a five-hundred-year-old sect that traces its roots back to Chaitanya. For the Bauls, the symbols of Radha and Krishna are actually aspects of the Divine that live within each person, and God realization is about finding Krishna and Radha within, through the bodily worship of a human partner. Family, sex, eating—all the ordinary aspects of life—and obedience to the guru are primary elements of the Baul path. They call their work *kaya sadhana*—a kind of transformation in the body that is similar to that of Mother Mira, the counterpart of Sri Aurobindo, in her later years. The Bauls practice tantra in all aspects of life, to transform all aspects of life. The first principle of their path is radical reliance on the guru; the second is *kaya sadhana*, the third is the transformation of energy through sex and breath. So literally the deities of Radha and Krishna within can be discovered and entered into within the individual person. The fourth element of the Baul path is that the Bauls do not record scripture and are very critical of organized religions and the caste system.

"The Bauls encode their teaching of sexual yoga and breath yoga in their poetry, music and dance. All of this came from my own Master, Yogi Ramsuratkumar, as His blessing, and has been translated into America and Europe. The nature of Reality for the Bauls is to use sex and breath as doorways into more subtle forms of Reality, and into the polarities of Reality, and work in union with those. The idea is to seek union in this lifetime, in this body, and then translate that into how you are with other people.

"Some of you are bound to be pure nondualists who think the only Reality is no self.

I call my tradition the tradition of Enlightened Duality. The Indian tradition also holds that the manifest world of appearances is as real as the unmanifest. Shakti is as real as Shiva. Our relationship to appearances may be illusory, but the thing itself is not. There is *shunyata*, or emptiness, the void—but there is also duality. Nonduality and duality both exist, both are Real. So Enlightened Duality is about realizing nonduality and then living that realization in the world of duality. All phenomena is insubstantial, but at the same time, you can feel it, touch it, see it."

Lee stopped and asked as an aside, "Has anybody here ever heard of me?" A number of people raised their hands.

"Oh wow!" he laughed, "I hope you haven't heard too many good things!" Everyone laughed with him.

He spoke about the Gurdjieffian idea that there are three types of food: gross food, impression food and subtle food. Lee talked about the subtle food in the air we breathe and how air pollution is destructive to that. He mentioned how bad the air was in Banaras. There were many of us in that room who could testify to that.

"So," he summed up, "I work with my students on all levels, the subtle bodies and the soul, we could say. Any questions?"

A European woman who we had seen on the streets of Rishikesh earlier in the day asked bluntly, "Are you free?"

Without an instant of hesitation Lee answered, playfully taking her question in a different direction than she expected, "No! I've got kids, a family, a grandkid, two ashrams—in France and America—and students . . . hell no, I'm not free!" He had an ironic smile on his face as he almost yelled this answer.

She rallied to the fight and pushed ahead, "In your mind? Are you free in your mind?"

"No! Free in my mind? No!" He laughed derisively.

She persisted, "I want to know if you are free because I am looking for freedom. So what is it that you got from your master that you want to pass on to us?"

"What I got from my Master is the total acceptance that everything is as it is, that all this is Reality, and to relate with everything wherever you are as if it is Real, to relate with all that with kindness, generosity and compassion. That is the only real sadhana that exists! There is a search on the path, but also freedom is not elsewhere from where we are now. Reality is always where we are now. That's what I got from my Master. Without the blessings of a real master, you're lost."

Another question was asked about Ramesh Balsekar, who Lee had mentioned earlier in his talk as a teacher of strict nondualism. Lee spoke further on the difference between nondualism and Enlightened Duality, which he had been talking about throughout the afternoon. Then an American man who has an Indian teacher and has come to India many times asked a very heartfelt question about how to sustain the growth that happens while one is in India when one returns to the West.

Lee answered him seriously, "You have to have a *practice*. You come here and get some communication or blessing from your teacher, and then you have to digest it. Integrity of practice is what sustains blessing transmission from the teacher. It takes time for the physical body to assimilate what the subtle body has received. Typically when something shows up in the physical body the subtle body has been cooking with that for years, like cancer or other forms of illness, for example. Actually India is an artificial environment for Westerners, which is part of why we experience ourselves as being altered here, but then we're not able to sustain those changes when we go back to the

West. We have to learn to integrate what we get in the East and then act from that in the environment that we are used to, that is organically natural for us."

In answer to another question about duality and nonduality, Lee said, "Enlightened Duality and nonduality are not on different sides of a coin; they occupy the same space. They are interpenetrating. This body has a cough," he pointed to himself, "will die one day and so on, but at the same time pristine, pure emptiness exists. Your experience of either should not be problematical. The problem that we have with duality is our *identification* within it. Spiritual practice is designed to pierce misidentification. When you are inside in the inner world of nonduality, then respect the inside; when you are outside (in the world of duality), then respect the outside. Jesus was a great enlightened Buddhist!" Lee chuckled.

"The purpose of sadhana is to have no identification whatsoever with either state—nonduality or duality—and this experience of non-identification tends to be free of anxiety. If you are with a genuine teacher your life is your teacher's business, two hundred percent! If you are too dependent on your teacher, if your teacher wants to wean you, your teacher will wean you. If your teacher wants to push you away or draw you closer, your teacher will do that. Your life is totally your teacher's business."

A woman in the audience began an intellectual argument with Lee. She took the position that one doesn't have to have a teacher. She said, "I experience everything in life as my teacher on the path."

Lee said, "Yes, having a guru is not the path for everyone—in this lifetime! But, sooner or later, yes, you will have to have a teacher."

Not liking this answer at all she said, "How can you say that?"

"Arrogance!" Lee quipped with a big smile.

Another woman who called herself Penny Ma said she was a friend of Marcus, one of Lee's students, then asked a question about surrender to the master. Lee said, "The genuine master is surrendered to the Divine, and their complete lack of obstacles to the Divine allows Benediction or Grace to flow to you and will literally align your choices to the optimal choices of the Divine in the moment. The Benediction of the master aligns you to the Will of God so that whatever your personal destiny in this life is can be realized. You could say that this is paying off all your karma: ultimately the system in which karma functions is transcended in the relationship with the master.

When Penny Ma asked further questions about when it might be appropriate to say no to the master's requests, Lee replied that it might be right action to say no to your guru, if it was aligned with your deepest integrity. If that was the case then the guru wouldn't mind if the devotee said no to a request. Then Lee added, "What is your personal integrity except your guru's property?"

Penny Ma told Lee that she had been a devotee of Chandra Swami and *gurubhai* with Yvan Amar for twenty years. She told a true story of a man who was a great devotee, whose guru called him to his side and said, "Do you love me?" The devotee said, "Yes, guruji, of course I love you!" The guru said, "Are you sure?" "Yes, yes," the devotee urged. The guru said, "Then will you be obedient to me, no matter what I ask?"

The devotee answered, "Yes, yes." The guru asked, "Are you very sure, very sure?" The devotee said of course. The guru then asked his devotee to kill him by putting his body into a large bag and lowering it into the water of a deep well until he was dead, and leaving it there for three days. The shocked devotee did as he was asked and killed his guru, but while he was doing this he imagined the guru was testing him and would be resurrected, like in the traditional stories. But the guru didn't resurrect; he was dead.

All the years afterward he was plagued with doubt and tortured by guilt. He couldn't come to resolve about his acts. Finally he came to Chandra Swami and told him the whole story. Chandra Swami said that the devotee had done his guru a big favor. He said that the guru was a tantric teacher who practiced the left-hand path and had somehow gathered some *siddhis* (powers) that were tormenting him, and the only way he could shake the curse of these *siddhis*—the only way he could leave this incarnation without having to take the karma of the *siddhis* with him—was to die in water and remain submerged for three days. Even though Chandra Swami explained this to the man, he was still miserable and doubting and couldn't come to terms with what he had done, and so he went away, still suffering deeply with his guilt and anxiety.

The story slowly wound to a close. It was almost five-thirty and Lee and the group had six o'clock dinner reservations at Amrit, a Japanese and Italian restaurant that was a hike up the mountain from Choti Wala. It would take at least thirty minutes to walk there. Lee listened with patience and interest to this long, quite fascinating story and still managed to bring the talk to a close with a skillful sense of timing and delivery. He said that there was another way to look at the guru's play with his devotee, which was to see that the guru had given the devotee a great gift—a lifetime of longing for his beloved. His guru had given him a lifetime of the impossibility of forgetting.

"In the Sufi tradition it is said that the greatest realization of the path is not union, but the sweetness of yearning for the Beloved. Nothing on the path can surpass the sweetness and beauty of that longing for the Beloved. This," Lee said, "was what the guru had offered to his disciple."

With an enigmatic smile Lee left the audience on that ending note—a sly little hint about the secret possibility and ultimate nature of Enlightened Duality, which had turned out to be the subject of his talk. He got up and walked out.

Immediately a British man who had sat and listened carefully throughout the talk approached Lee and asked if he could contact him again. Lee answered him warmly, saying, "Yes—in Europe or in America?"

"In the U.S.," the man answered. Lee then wrote down the address and phone number of the ashram in Arizona and said, "Tell whomever answers the phone that we met in Rishikesh and that will facilitate the whole process and get you through to me." He gently slapped the man on the shoulder with affection and smiled warmly, then walked on.

As Lee walked down the sidewalk to his room another man came up and walked alongside him. He was the man who had had an extended, intellectual dialogue with Lee about nonduality and duality. He now asked if he could talk with Lee privately. Lee said, "I don't do that sort of thing," and kept walking, leaving the man in the proverbial dust.

Immediately everyone took off in the growing dark for Amrit, the restaurant where we had an arrangement to have a special dinner at six o'clock. It was up on the side of the mountain, a thirty-minute walk from where we were. Allison and Mike walked with Lee. They had helped Purna a great deal in getting the talk set up, and had invited Lee and a small group up to their center for brunch tomorrow.

As it turned out Lee's group of thirty-four took up the entire small restaurant. The mood was ecstatic, especially so with Lee in high spirits. He smiled and talked in an animated way with Mike and Allison, swapping stories of India. The delicious fare was spaghetti, lasagna and some of the best tomato garlic soup in the world. It was a welcomed change from the food we'd been having at Choti Wala.

December 19, 1998
Rishikesh

Every time Lee walked past the Indian gypsies—a man and woman who sat singing and chanting on a blanket with their small drum and bells—he gave them money. They were often sitting on the side of the road as he walked along the river from the ashram toward the bazaars. The first time he passed them a few days ago, just after he had given them a coin, Lee commented, "Indian gypsies." It seemed like it was something worth registering, and that was why he said it—offering information not being something that Lee ever does trivially. The woman gave him a brilliant smile, her eyes very friendly, bright and open. She played the drum and sang. There were two other couples, sitting about ten feet apart on the road, both singing. These women seemed happy, light and free.

On this morning Lee decided that we would wind along through the bazaars, cross the river and shop a little on our way to take a rickshaw up the mountain to meet Allison and Mike for brunch at the Impersonal Enlightenment Fellowship Center. We passed the gypsies and again Lee dropped a coin in their hands. Lee is very careful about which beggars he chooses to give to. When questioned about this in Tiruvannamalai he said, "I pick a few beggars while I'm here and then on the last day I give them all some coins." He seemed to consistently pick the beggars who had a spark of humanity, a brightness, a potential or a depth. Many beggars are hostile, angry or just plain aggressive and nasty. You can see it in their eyes, feel it in their approach. They blame and refute their circumstance. Their beggary has no context, only aggression. The beggars that Lee chose were in relationship with the world within the confines of their begging and in relationship with whomever they were begging from. It seemed that the individuals who Lee chose to give alms to—which could be seen as a karmically binding act, certainly for someone with the kind of obligation that Lee bears—all had a certain apparent potential gleaming in them. The gypsies certainly fit this description and more. They were authentic and spontaneous, and appeared to be very happy. There was a tangible *rasa* of freedom and joy around them. Their mood was inspiring.

Lee walked further along the main street of the bazaar, surrounded by cows, an occasional monkey and enthusiastic shopkeepers selling clothes, shawls, jewelry, ugly contemporary bronze and stone statues, *rudraksh* and glass beads, precious and semi-precious stones, books, food and everything else under the sun. It being our last full day here, I took in the environment in a different way. The painted plaster deities that populated the streets seemed to be doll-like effigies compared to the powerful, archaic stone deities of southern India or the more humanized Durga in the temple in Banaras. A big blue Shiva painted above an arch over the street had the crescent moon on his brow and wide, pleasant eyes, a pleased and benevolent look about the face.

Lee checked out some of the more serious *rudraksh* dealers in two of the high-end jewelry stores and said, "I'll be back," to the shopkeepers. Just before we reached the footbridge a very young, blonde Western man stopped Lee and said, "Thank you for the talk last night! Very impressive!" Lee slapped him affectionately on the back and said warmly, "Thank you." He kept walking toward the bridge.

After a short rickshaw ride Lee and six of his students climbed up the footpath to the Impersonal Enlightenment Fellowship Center, a beautiful, large bungalow perched on the side of the mountain. All around the green Himalayan foothills rose up in an inspiring, panoramic view. Mike and Allison greeted Lee warmly and escorted the group to the porch where a lovely table was set.

"Would you like to eat now or see the place?" Mike asked.

Lee said, "Eat now and then see the place." We sat down to a perfect meal. It was exactly what was needed at that point—miso soup full of delicious vegetables, home-made whole wheat bread with butter, ginger lemon tea and afterward, a fresh-fruit salad with yogurt. Over brunch Lee talked about visiting the cave of Mastram Baba, and how he had met him twenty years ago.

Mike talked about an Englishwoman, called simply Nani, a long-time devotee of Mastram Baba, who has lived in India for twenty-five or thirty years. When Mastram Baba was alive he had a practice of bathing in the Ganges every morning, and she had developed the same practice. When Mastram Baba died Nani continued the practices and lifestyle she had as his devotee. Now she has an ashram several hours north of Rishikesh, where people can go to visit. Mike said that even in the freezing cold winter weather further north she continues her practice of bathing every morning in the Ganges. In the winter she often has to break the ice before she can plunge in. People can go to her ashram, which sounds like a hermitage, but they are expected to practice. No one is ex-pected to do her particular practices, but visitors are expected to practice, whatever their practice is. She has lived there since Mastram Baba's death, and refuses to go back to England or the West for any reason. She sets an inspiring example.

During the meal some Westerners showed up—an Englishman (or European) dressed in the robes of a Tibetan monk and two or three Americans, or so they looked, dressed in blue jeans and T-shirts. After they left another lone man came walking up the dirt path toward the porch, wanting some information about Andrew Cohen. He recognized Lee right away. With a look of surprise he said, smiling, "Lee Lozowick! I've got several of your books!" He paused, "Well, I'd better leave quick before I get speared by your sharp wit!" His grin was somewhere between acknowledging a certain awe of Lee and slightly challenging. When he left, which was almost immediately, Mike and Allison said that he is a student of Shantimayi.

After brunch Lee took an informal tour of the center, walking into the meditation room and then up on the big roof. We visited for a while longer, talked about the rigors of being in India, how to stay healthy, shared some more stories. They told stories of Andrew's Rishikesh retreats, what the schedule is and how they manage the large crowds. They have developed systems for purifying water from the Ganges for all the retreatants, serve vegetarian meals and meditate several hours a day. Their retreat is held at the same ashram where we were staying, the big difference being that they rent the entire place to accom-modate the large crowds that come to be on retreat with Andrew.

Lee had sent Tom back to the ashram to let everyone else know that we would meet them at the footbridge over the Ganges in Lakshman Ju—a small enclave or village. Lakshman Ju is another tourist haven with bazaars, temples, shops and so on, located just a few miles north of Rishikesh. Lee planned to walk around the town for awhile and then go back to the ashram before dinner at the Choti Wala at six o'clock. Around one o'clock Lee said goodbye to Allison and Mike and expressed his sincere gratitude again for the gracious hospitality they had extended. We picked up a couple of rickshaws at the bottom of the hill and took off to Lakshman Ju.

Soon we were walking down the mountain toward the footbridge that spans the Ganges at Lakshman Ju. Lee was looking for the rest of his group, but didn't see anyone.

He decided that the walk down to the bridge was too long and hard to make twice—he was obviously still not well and probably had a light fever, as did a number of us. He was concerned about missing connections with the mothers and children. He decided to sit down and wait for them along the footpath—a narrow, well-pounded dirt road that wound through shops, concrete or mud houses and boulders and overlooked the Ganges.

Lee picked a spot by a well cared for Shiva lingam shrine. The priest, dressed in orange and saffron, was lying on a raised stone bed next to the shrine. Lee sat alone just across the passage and seemed to fall asleep or at least rest with his eyes closed. Clelia and I sat and wrote, while a native woman came and sat near us. The woman became engaged in a conversation with the priest and another woman, a shopkeeper just across the narrow passageway. The three of them became more and more animated until it was obvious that they were talking about the Westerners that were sprawled among them. Every now and then the priest would throw in an English word. They smiled at us and we carried on a conversation in two different languages. They were pleased at our saris and bangles. They highly approved. They indicated that the women should have their noses pierced and wear a jewel or something there. Lee asks his women students to wear saris in India, a practice that elicited many such expressions of appreciation. Many times as we traveled both Indian men and women complimented our saris and seemed very appreciative of the gesture of respect toward their culture. They would often say, "You look so nice," or "Very nice! You wear saris! Where are you from? Do you wear saris there?"

Lee sat in the sun for at least forty-five minutes, waiting for the children and adults to show up. He was thinking that we were in the right place to catch them before the bridge. Finally he decided we would walk down to the bridge. Almost immediately we saw Jan heading back across the bridge toward us. She said, "Everyone is in Lakshman Ju, across the river." Obviously there had been a mix-up. Evidently the adults and children had walked down the mountain to the footbridge by another route. Lee quickly walked over the bridge and rejoined everyone.

Soon we were walking back to Rishikesh along the shady dirt road that ran along the river. Tall green trees towered overhead as Lee set a leisurely pace. Arriving back in Rishikesh Lee stopped in at the Choti Wala restaurant for cold sodas, then went on to the shop where he had looked at high quality *rudraksh* earlier in the day.

Lee and Purna interacted alone with the merchant. They were going to buy quite a number of *rudraksh malas*. Lee would be spending a lot of money and so intended to do some serious bargaining. I went in with them and watched while Lee and then Purna picked out the *rudraksh* that they respectively wanted to buy. There was a very specific protocol going on that Lee seemed to be not only well aware of, but masterful at. He had been developing relationships with some of the merchants on this strip of bazaar between the ashram and the bridge for days. Already he had bought two or three *rudraksh malas* from another merchant. This purchase seemed to have more to do with the merchant himself, a very friendly and outgoing man. Lee bought a fairly large quantity of *rudraksh* from the merchant he was dealing with now. He also bought a sculpted and hand-painted marble Ganesh statue, very elaborate and beautiful.

That night we had our last dinner at the Choti Wala. The mood was genial and warm among the thirty-four people who stretched out down the length of the long table. Lee sat at the head and officiated. His spirits had lifted significantly during the past three days. Purna and Simon easily managed the group bill. Friendships had developed between

Purna's students and Lee's students. The group seemed more cohesive and together than it ever had. It was almost time to go home.

December 20, 1998
On the road

The first part of the morning was spent organizing and returning bedding to the ashram office. Every piece had to be accounted for in the inventory. Lee oversaw everything, watching his students like a hawk. Cart *walas* were obtained and two carts were loaded down with bags and parcels. Two people had to ride on the carts due to physical necessity. Soon the group was walking for the last time down the lane along the Ganges, past the shops and vendors and plaster deities.

Arriving by rickshaws at the bus that was parked in downtown Riskikesh village everyone quickly clambered aboard. Lee sat in the front seat with Purna just behind the drivers who were partitioned off from the rest of the bus by a wall with a door and sliding glass windows. The bus took off and drove down the mountains and past Haridwar, where a large group of Tibetan monks gathered by the Ganges and probably at least a thousand people sat watching them. The monks sat in a formation on the ground, probably chanting. The sight of Haridwar passing by—the location of the *Kumbha Mela*—was very enticing. As ready as I felt to go back to Arizona, and as soul and road weary and physically unwell as I felt, Mother India still called to me.

Soon the bus was passing through miles and miles of sugar cane fields and rice paddies. Watching out the window I drank in as much of India as I could. Dilapidated palm-thatched roofs decomposing on their joists over mud houses and huts passed by, and the ubiquitous stacks of cow patties, hand-mixed with straw into dung fire chips in various stages of being dried or stored. These were always arranged with great care in orderly and sometimes beautiful symmetrical patterns along the roadside. There were Banyan trees, canna lilies, and miles of mustard fields and nut orchards. All the leaves on the trees and shrubs and vines were covered with a thick layer of dust. It brought to mind the herd of goats that could be seen walking past Yogi Ramsuratkumar's ashram in Tiruvannamalai each evening and morning. The goatherd and his family bedded down with the goats in the dusty field behind the ashram at night.

All along the way were many half-finished industrial buildings, loose ends, unfinished projects, pools of fetid water, carts full of ripe or green bananas pulled by water buffalo along the road, vendor's carts stacked high with oranges for sale, motorcycles, bicycles and many greasy mechanic shops in the small villages. Oil, gasoline, machines—all the apparent invasions of technology were in evidence. Amidst all this were crumbling bungalows behind palm thickets, eucalyptus and mimosa trees and the huge rubber trees, square patches of vegetable gardens, elaborate brick houses behind high concrete walls, everything blackened from the mould of the monsoon season and diesel smoke. In the cities uniformed men stood with rifles and guns, mixed in with bicycle rickshaws and stagnant traffic. Sometimes for hours the bus could only go twenty to thirty-five miles an hour. At times it was torturously slow going.

Overhead the sky was a pearly light gray, with refracted light shining through the cloud cover. It shone down on the flat, fertile land—fields rampant with high sugar cane, and then more fields of slender green shoots of rice sunk in water, where white water birds with long necks hunted. All this was interspersed with miles of orchards and swamps.

Wherever the land was not cleared the trees were dense, dark and heavy, their big green leaves covered with the thick layer of brown dust. The trees along the road were all painted around their trunks with circles of white and red paint. We passed crowds of people camped out on blankets in fields along the side of the road. Gypsies? Untouchables? Pilgrims? A herd of water buffalo lumbered past with their interesting character, their angular bones and heavy meat, horns curled back and a distinctly Saturn-like visage. There was a distinct expression on their faces of a dull, beastly nature, perhaps not so unlike our own.

After watching miles of scenery pass by while writing down impressions of the trip, I moved over to sit near Lee in his spot on the front seat. I asked, "What in particular do you want written about this trip?"

He had been resting or talking with Purna off and on for several hours. Now he crossed his arms over his chest. He fired off in a furious tone, "Write about how few really good students there are! About how having love in your heart for the guru isn't enough, but the need to bring absolute integrity to your practice, to paying attention and making sense of the details, and not losing sight of practice just because you're on some romantic trip where everyone else is in a buying frenzy!"

Debbie was sitting right across the aisle. She leaned close to me, listened intently, taking it all in. Lee's tone was so charged and electric there were invisible sparks flying through the air. Several of Lee's students were straining to hear his words as he went on, "A real life of happiness and contentment is a life of discipline, of right activity, appropriate activity, of attention. In Europe or America we get away with the things—the lapses of practice—that have shown up here in my students in India. It's hidden in the West because of the culture. But here in India it is *glaring*. Frankly, I was shocked on this trip. I was blindsided. I never expected such behavior from mature students. That's what *my* trip was about."

He paused for a moment, then said, "All I can say is thank the good Lord I'm going to Mexico without a gang tagging along, without everybody. The adults exhibited such a stunning lack of intelligence on this trip—what can one say? I'm sure I'm exaggerating. I'm sure it was all Purna's students! But *they* can be excused—they're new. They haven't had that much instruction and years in the Work . . ."

Finally, after what seemed like a long time, the bus driver stopped at the Cheetal Grand—the same place we had eaten in on the way up, with its sculpted bamboo growing in pots, its Indian "Musak," marigolds and chrysanthemums arranged in mandala gardens here and there. Looking over the menu a second time there were the same European chocolates, Chinese, Indian and American food, sodas, ice cream, candy, soup, veggie burgers. Once again there was a mix-up with the bill and the food ended up costing more than it should have. Back in the bus Lee joked about the exorbitant prices, saying, "That why they call it the 'Cheat All'!" Everyone laughed.

As the bus zoomed along over the road toward Delhi the sun set on our last day in India. It was a dark orange ball of fire beaming steadily through the haze of pollution, suspended but sinking and set against a gray sky, where palms trees and tall grasses were silhouetted in black. Eucalyptus trees edged the fields of sugar cane and rice. The squalor was just as appalling as it had been the first day we arrived, but somehow the wonder and beauty of India shines through it all. These are the paradoxes of this extraordinary place. Heaven and hell exist side by side; the most sublime teachings, philosophy and sacred culture with the cruel inhumanities of a cultural practice like sati (suttee), leprous beggars and starving children.

As we got closer to Delhi there were several tall industrial smoke stacks set against the sunset sky with long trails of pollutants streaming out into the air. About an hour outside of Delhi the bus ran into an immense traffic jam and began to inch its way forward in a slow crawl down a six-lane road. The bus was in the middle inside lane going in the direction of Delhi, completely hemmed in on all four sides by large, ten-wheel diesel trucks. Finally the traffic came to a complete halt. There were visible, thick, dark clouds of diesel smoke and carbon monoxide streaming into the bus through the doors and windows. Closing the windows only made it worse.

The group was trapped in a toxic chemical soup, the substances seeping into our pores and being breathed into our bodies with every breath. It was extremely difficult, hellish, horrible. There was no way out. Everyone was alarmed, and fear began to ricochet from one person to the next. Lee was laughing with Purna. Obviously he had no need to greet the situation with fear and hysteria.

Walking up to where Lee sat with Purna in the front of the bus, I said, "We're being poisoned." He didn't disagree with me but just looked at me calmly. Obviously there was nothing to do but cope with the situation. Purna jokingly made up the "perfect" scenario for Lee's next trip to India, in which he would bring only those people who would drive Lee crazy and wouldn't practice if their lives depended on it. Lee laughed along. It was a welcomed comic relief.

Every time the traffic moved forward two or three inches or a foot, dark clouds roiled up into the bus, but even when we were sitting still smoke poured into bus. Finally Lee stood up and yelled at everyone theatrically, "It's payback time! Purna's and my ancestors suffered worse than this in the gas chambers! Now you are all gonna *die!*" It was shocking, but at the same time presented an accurate mirror of what people were thinking: "I'm going to die in this bus."

Lee went on in the same wild tone of voice, "Purna had four uncles gassed in the chambers . . . you think this is bad!" Everyone sat in a stunned silence. In a few minutes Purna turned to Lee and said, "It's a good opportunity to work." That was a true statement.

But even Lee was concerned. The situation was absolutely indescribable. There is almost nothing that can be said about it that could be an exaggeration. We were, in fact, being seriously poisoned. When the bus and all its occupants had been stuck in this noxious situation for about forty-five minutes, Lee asked Purna to get out and talk to people on the street about how far it was to the airport and whether or not we had the option to abandon the bus and take taxis from there. When Purna came back and reported Lee said, "If we don't start moving soon, we'll get taxis."

Joanne asked from the back, "Is it okay to chant?"

"Sure!" Lee said. Immediately everyone started chanting the name of Yogi Ramsuratkumar. Many people may have already been saying his name internally, but somehow the power of focusing the group attention on Yogi Ramsuratkumar's name worked a minor miracle. Suddenly everyone in the bus was chanting as if their lives depended on it, and maybe they did. One of Purna's students, D.J., pulled out his new drum and accompanied everyone. Some of the women played bells (finger cymbals). The tension and fear was released and the presence of the Divine came pouring in like an elixir. It was a powerful moment, and seemed like India's farewell lesson for Lee's group. The chanting continued until the bus started moving forward at ten, then twenty, then forty miles an hour, which was about twenty minutes later.

It was almost over. Lee rode quietly the last thirty miles to the airport. Once we got to the airport the driver became confused and then lost after he took a wrong turn. We saw the airport about a half-mile away as we passed by on the wrong road, traveling in the wrong direction! It took an extra forty-five minutes to retrace the route and finally wind back around to the airport—one final tribulation.

Lee's group had gone from the frying pan of Grace with Yogi Ramsuratkumar into the blazing tantric fire of divine alchemy with Lee Lozowick in Banaras. There had been no time to stop and breathe, to integrate such powerful experiences. But the trip, and particularly the difficult last two weeks, was actually a metaphor for the life of a practitioner on the tantric path. The demand to practice and pay attention, the rigors and dangers of tantric practice, the extremities of life as a bardo state through which one is traveling with the guru, are always the same, whether one is in India, Europe or in the sanctuary of the Arizona ashram.

Part of what gave cause for remorse all along the way of the trip, and particularly as things were viewed in retrospect, was the degree to which Lee was necessarily moved to reflect back to his students their lack of practice. It was Lee's heartbrokenness and sorrow at his students' failure to embrace the fullness of the path and the teaching that was the underlying quality of his mood during the last two weeks of the trip, and could be found at the source of his anger or irritation.

Finally we got to the airport, checked in and had a long wait to board our plane. A huge Return Feast awaited Lee back at the Arizona ashram, where his students from the Prescott area and around the country would gather to feast and hear stories from the India trip. There would be a lot to tell.

January 8, 1999
Arizona Ashram

In the weeks after Lee's return from India the stories from the trip trickled down, told in sessions held with the sangha in the meditation hall at the Return Feast and later at After Dinner Talks and informal evening gatherings. "Re-entry" into daily ashram life was not as simple and straightforward after this trip as it typically is after travels in Lee's company. Several people were quite ill, some suffering from a pervasive malaise and a kind of "chemical poisoning" from all the toxic air and fumes that were breathed in Banaras and Delhi. Others had lingering colds and coughs, while a few made it through unscathed, at least physically. Lee had made plans to start a very thorough herbal parasite cleanse next week. Everyone who went on the trip and most of the ashram residents as well as many students who lived in Prescott would begin this cleansing program, which had been designed by one of Lee's students before the trip to India.

The cleanse of the physical body seemed like an aspect of the trip—a kind of post-India follow-up. It was another step in purification, and in the integration of the influx of divine influence which pervaded the entire Indian sojourn. The trip as a whole was having far-reaching effects within the sangha at large. There was a tremendous feeling of change in the air, and many were going through strong purificatory experiences, both physical and subtle. Remarkable dreams were being reported along with illnesses, energetic phenomena and a renewed sense of urgency to practice. It was never clearer that the members of the sangha didn't have to literally be on the trip with Lee to reap the benefits of the transformational power of the experience.

The nightmarish quality of extreme agitation, doubt and recoil that had come up for many during the trip was now replaced with remorse and insight. This remorse was fueled by the deep compulsion to gaze long and hard at the actual horror of the situation—how deeply embedded we are in the illusion of separation, and how quickly we can forget what we know to be true from our most profound experience. All of this was catalyzed by the blessing power of Yogi Ramsuratkumar and the burning away of the dross that was experienced in India. In a way we had been to heaven and hell, and had now come back to tell the tale.

Every account of genuine spiritual transformation tells the story of the descent into hell in one form or another. In the shaman's initiation one descends and is dismembered, flayed or boiled before experiencing a shattering rebirth and union of opposites. Or, like Inanna, one is stripped of everything and hung on a hook in the hell realm of Ereshkigal, goddess of the underworld. In the kundalini awakening described by Gopi Krishna or Irina Tweedie, encountering elements of the underworld is a significant part of the process. In the Western alchemical tradition the soul also undergoes a descent into darkness, the *nigredo*, where one enters into a confrontation with *massa confusa* or chaos, in which a *solutio, separatio, divisio, putrefactio* of disparate elements must be undergone. It is through this process of being undone, or broken down, and then tempered or broiled or baked under high heat that one begins to confront the shadow and the actual condition of separation and inner fragmentation.

This work of redeeming the shadow (or active unconscious elements of one's being) is necessary if one is to meld or forge a soul, or a unity within. One finds the secrets to all the major processes of alchemy in the fruitful fluorescence of death and decay and the application of heat and/or cold (experienced by ego as pain, angst and extreme inner irritation) that is experienced in the journey in the underworld. Without this difficult and dangerous work, there is no hope of becoming whole. It is a process that is ruinous to ego, and it would be a rare individual who might look "good" when in the midst of such a radical process.

Carl Jung states, "Natural man is not a 'self'—he is the mass and a particle in the mass, collective to such a degree that he is not even sure of his own ego. That is why since time immemorial he has needed the transformation mysteries to turn him into something, and to rescue him from the animal collective psyche, which is nothing but a *variété*. Only a unified personality can experience life, not that personality which is split up into partial aspects, that bundle of odds and ends which also calls itself 'man.' " (Carl Jung, *Psychology and Alchemy*, p. 81) This is exactly the human condition as G.I. Gurdjieff describes it as well, and sooner or later on the spiritual path it is exactly where one discovers oneself to be. The work of reclaiming and integrating the shadow must be done; it is what the Vajrayana Buddhists might call working with the primal passions in a way that transforms them into innate Buddha qualities. It is not something that is done overnight, but for most people is a life's work involving tremendous courage and discipline.

For this reason it was important in the weeks after the India journey to continually place the experience of the trip in the context of transformation. This fundamental alchemical process is a large part of what Lee's students engage in sadhana; it is called "Divine Alchemy," because the work is rooted in the context of what Lee calls "Spiritual Slavery" and "Surrender to the Will of God." It is not undergone for the purposes of the separative ego or any form of self-gratification, or cloaked under the auspices of occult magic. "Divine Alchemy" is engaged for the purpose of radical transformation in the body, in which one comes into more direct relationship with the living God, or Divine Will. It is a process that we will hear a great deal about in Lee's teachings during the coming year.

January 10, 1999
Arizona Ashram

It was a cold, clear winter Sunday night, the stars a brilliant stark scattering of jewels on the black velvet background of the night sky. Watching from the ashram the headlights of cars began to appear about a half mile away, weaving down the dirt road through the cottonwood grove in the front of the property to stop at the gate briefly as people arrived for darshan, the highlight of the week.

Driving through the cottonwood grove is like coming through a portal—the doorway or the transit station for entering sacred ground. In the summer the silvery, green leaves of the trees rustle musically in the wind. The trees and their myriad undergrowth are home to the many devas and wood spirits of this place. Now in the frosty winter the cottonwoods are bare, polished boles that rise up like graceful pillars, as if they could support the sky with their wide delicate network of small silvery branches. The grove, which is made of up about seventy-five trees, is like a guardian to the ashram property. It is as if one sheds something of the world in that crossing, the pure forces of nature acting as a reminding factor that one has left the concrete and fast pace of conventional life behind. It is a spot that seems charged with magic, an appropriate natural sentinel to the guru's place of sanctuary.

Inside the meditation hall where darshan is held every week it was warm and bright. Lee doesn't like the lights turned down low; he wants to be able to see everything as it is. Romantic notions of inducing moods and *bhavas* while chanting in dim lights are Lee's last concern—seeing clearly comes first in sadhana. The shrines were all lit with candles, and a simple arrangement of fresh flowers adorned the room. The guru's sandals—an old pair of leather sandals that Lee wore in India many years ago—were ornamented with offerings of fresh flowers. The men sat on the right side of the room and the women on the left, most of them wrapped in shawls that would soon be shed as the heat rose in the room. By the end of the night it would be almost uncomfortably warm.

The chanting began, *"Tvameva mata, cha pita tvameva / Tvameva bandhush, cha saka tvameva/ Tvameva vidya dravinam tvameva,Tvameva sarvam Yogi Ramsuratkumar . . ."* You are my mother and my father / You are my brother and my sister / You are my knowledge and my wealth / You are my everything, Yogi Ramsuratkumar.

Lee entered the room wrapped in a voluminous blue-gray wool shawl, given to him by Yogi Ramsuratkumar, and took his seat on the dais. People began to go up, one at a time, and offer *prasad*—a small gift of some kind like flowers, candy, fruit, or perhaps a book—that is symbolic of the relationship between disciple and guru. In return, Lee handed each person a piece of candy *prasad*, also symbolic of the relationship between guru and disciple. After the first two opening chants Lee had some of the poems written to Yogi Ramsuratkumar sung from *Death of a Dishonest Man*. Then after another short period of chanting, Lee began his talk for the evening.

He started out kidding around with his students about the gig he'd played the night before with liars, gods & beggars. It had been several hours away, and in addition to that, it was at a club that was too rough for his women disciples, so he had gone alone with the men in the band. He teased, "I'm sorry to report that last night was one of those nights when the third set turned into one of those 'feeding the invisible audience' things . . . and none of you were there! Well, you were there one way or another. Are there any questions?"

Steve S. raised his hand. "Would you say that this work is about embodying the Feminine?"

Lee laughed. "I say it is about embodying the Masculine and the Feminine, equally. Save that—it's pretty good!"

Steve continued, "I heard that you had said men need to become ninety percent Feminine and ten percent Masculine, and the same is true for women."

Lee said, "Yes, but the punch line in that is that it is harder for women to become ninety percent Feminine because they already think that they are!" Lee laughed again. "So, it is harder to become something that you assume you are than it is to work for something that has to be attained. The differences are subtle but . . . ."

Steve said, "Well, the first time that I met you, you were wearing a T-shirt from E.J. Gold that had a drawing of a woman on the front, and the caption underneath it was, 'I don't screw the Neanderthals just because they won.' "

Lee deadpanned, "Gosh, too bad."

Not yet getting to the response from Lee that he was hoping for, Steve pressed ahead, saying, "From the assumption of being a spiritual student I have seen more and more of the inner Neanderthal . . . especially in relationship to the Feminine. It's been pretty shocking."

Lee responded, "Well, don't shoot the thing in the head, because you might eventually find a woman who is totally transported when the Neanderthal peeks out!" Everyone laughed, and Lee continued in a lightly humorous vein. "You know, first they want you to be polite and sensitive, but after they get to know you . . . Keep the beast ready. Don't let him out of the cave too soon, but keep him ready!"

Holding out for something more substantial from the spiritual master, Steve continued, fumbling around a little to catch a thread of what he was attempting to articulate. "I guess it's like the illusion of separation. I always thought of that as being about God. There have also been some things developing for me internally where I've seen the ways that I have been under the illusion of being separate from the Feminine, and what that has set up in terms of internal suffering in relationship to others—on a psychological level. You know, all the things that go on—issues with mother and that kind of thing. But I've been seeing it in my everyday walk of life, seeing how much suffering there is out of the lack of regard for or lack of understanding and appreciation of the Feminine."

Lee responded, "Yes, well the thing is that we tend to reference the phrase the Feminine exclusively in relationship to women, and in fact the Feminine is everything incarnate—men, women, all of nature, energy and phenomena. All of that. A lot of the suffering comes from having a very narrow view of what the Feminine actually *is*. So, part of curtailing that suffering—at least as much as one person possibly can—is about seeing the Feminine in a much broader vision than we might assume to begin with.

"We tend to think, 'I've got all of this patriarchal struggle going on and I've got to somehow be sensitive to that'—meaning, to see women equally and such. It is really much more than that, *much* bigger than that. Actually this is some of what I was going to speak about tonight, so I must have been thinking about your question before you asked it. I have a note right here to prove it! See? It's got writing on it, a bookmark—proof that I'm not making it up, pretending that I am telepathic!" With a smile Lee held up a scrap of paper he'd brought into darshan.

He continued, "Men's relationship to women takes on an entirely different form than the usual psychological relationship when we are able to see the Feminine *as it is*—not just the feminine embodied as woman, but the Feminine *as it is*, which is much broader, much bigger, much deeper than that. Then there is a natural honoring, a natural respect of the Feminine. But keep the Neanderthal just in case, because he can come in handy! But women as human beings have to know it is controlled. So that's the thing about the Neanderthal: you need him on a good leash, and then you have to convince your eventual partner that the leash is reliable and will not snap if you get too excited, even when you get carried away. Then that old Neanderthal can really come in handy. Just keep his mouth shut. He can do the grunting and manhandling, as they say. All that is really good, but when he starts to talk, forget it! It'll ruin the mood, man!"

More laughter broke out. Lee was talking directly into the heart of sexual chemistry and the psychology between men and women, using his usual no-nonsense, gritty approach. Nothing whitewashed or cloaked with some euphemistic naiveté. The whole room was loosened up and flowing along on Lee's wavelength. He forged ahead, getting funnier, building up steam, "You know, you start to talk, you lift your head up and you go, 'Ughhhhh . . . me want so and so.' That's it—it's all over. Did Neanderthals have speech, does anybody know? Maybe they just grunted and yelled and stuff, beat their chests. They killed a dinosaur and stood over the carcass, smearing the blood—*ahhhhhhhhh!*— and dipping their club in the blood so when they went to war with their neighbors they could really have power, the strength of a dinosaur, teeth like a Tyrannosaurus. No, that's wrong—Neanderthals came after dinosaurs! I was just testing you . . ."

Boisterous laughter echoed through the hall. The mood of enjoyment between Lee and his students was delightful. Whenever he breaks into this kind of comedy there is the feeling that something of tremendous potency is going on underneath the surface while everyone relaxes and becomes more and more vulnerable as the space becomes more fluid, ecstatic and elastic.

"Anything else? That was a delightful exchange!"

Steve persevered. He was onto something with Lee. "You say that the Feminine is much broader . . ."

Lee interrupted, breaking into song. " 'Fools rush in, where angels fear to tread . . .' What? No, no really, I only sang that because I know that you are a good sport. Really, go on."

Steve grinned and said, "I'm trying . . ."

Lee immediately interrupted him again, saying, "You know I have this bad habit of interrupting people! Actually it's a good habit in this business but a bad social habit, a bad primate habit."

Willing to pay full price for the answer to his question, which meant going along with whatever play Lee was into, Steve managed to get the rest of his question out, "Would you speak more about the Feminine in a broader perspective?"

Lee looked at Steve for a moment before he began to speak. He said, "Well, let me talk about some of this," he picked up the note he'd brought in and gestured toward it with his other hand, "and see if it leads into your question. It's not exactly about the Feminine, but in one sense it is." Lee asked if anyone had any other questions before he started discoursing, and after a period of dialogue with a number of people, he turned to his subject.

"I keep saying this is a tantric school, but I never explain it. Georg Feuerstein's book (*Tantra—The Path of Ecstasy*) gives a very good foundation, which is great because there is a lot of irrelevant information out there on tantra. One of the points that he writes about is that part of the essence of tantric work is to realize the Reality of—and this is what Steve first asked about—the Masculine and Feminine within oneself. In Advaita Vedanta the world is looked at as an illusion, so most Advaita Vedanta paths involve extreme renunciation. From that point of view the more one indulges the world, the implication is that one is embodying illusion rather than Reality. The tantric view is exactly the opposite. From the tantric view the Self of Advaita Vedanta is Reality, the Uncreated, the Unmanifest and so on, but tantra also realizes that the world of Creation is equally real. The Buddhists say 'form is emptiness, emptiness is form.' It is a literal formula. The world of uncreated Reality is equally real to the world of contextual Reality.

"One of the practices of the tantric path is to realize this Reality to the degree that we are able to be in the world and not be of the world. One of the ideas is to be able to meet whatever Reality serves you without becoming lost in identification or illusion. So if you are going along and there is a car accident, or your business fails, or you win the lottery, or you end up pregnant and having a child, or something big like that, you would be able to say to yourself, 'Well, this is the world of Reality' from a place of equanimity instead of, 'Oh my God, what am I going to do now, and how did this happen?' You do this with whatever happens, positive or negative, without being so detached that you ignore whatever elements of life your experience entails, and by that ignoring and treating others with a kind of crass impersonality.

"Typically most tantric schools are known for their ritual. If you look at Vajrayana Buddhism or traditional Tantric Hinduism you see tremendous amounts of ritual—lots of ritual prayer, lots of ritual pujas, lots of ritual activities in relationship to certain things. One that we can certainly discuss extensively in terms of its relationship to the Baul Path is the image of Radha/Krishna in union. The idea of embodying the deity is prevalent in tantric work, in which you imagine the deity you want to embody.

"There are two kinds of tantric schools: right-hand and left-hand. In left-hand tantra there is a kind of magic that is practiced, a kind of psycho-energetic magic, in which the idea of the school is to develop as many *siddhis*, or spiritual powers, as you can. This is found in the line of the Nath Siddhas, who we have talked about many times, who are both feared and revered. Their path is the yoga of power. They practice extreme disciplines in order to build up power to control nature, to control the universe, to control energy. And they do a fine job of it. They can kill people at a distance with a single thought; they are really well known for the effectiveness of their *siddhis* on many levels.

"That is one perspective of tantra. The Baul perspective is another tantric view, which is not to develop powers but to embody Reality. 'As above, so below.' The Baul perspective is to embody Reality within yourself, and then be able to move through life seeing everything as real in its own context, and being able to respond to everything without making distinctions based on projection or subjectivity and without separations: 'Is it real, false, right, wrong, bad, good?' Simply, you call forth and embrace whatever serves your practice, whatever serves your process in life, and whatever doesn't you sidestep, you move around.

"So in traditional ritualized tantric practices there is the idea of picking a deity and embodying that deity. In the darker left-hand schools, like some Tibetan schools, it might be a demonic deity known for its destructive power, that has no conscience but can do anything. On the right-hand side of tantra a bodhisattva of compassion might be chosen, in Buddhist tantra for example. The practitioner picks a deity and then orients his or her inner environment in order to invite the deity to reside within the body. There is very extensive, exacting and specific imagery, along with practices for how to clean and prepare the space and set up the chamber so the deity will be encouraged to inhabit it.

"Basically you are establishing a balance within your own subtle being, and then if the deity is attracted by what you have set up, he or she will come to reside there. You keep feeding the deity and encouraging the deity to stay with the disciplined practice of ritual, prayers or any sacrifices to the deity. There are many intricate pujas in India where sweet milk and coconut, yogurt and turmeric and ghee and honey and a variety of things are offered. The shrine is bathed in these substances as offerings to the Divine. The implication is when you bathe the shrine in these substances the offerings are actually turned into subtle food for the deity. The deity is being offered sweets and cow urine, for example—the cow being the symbolic mother of all beings.

"Once you install the deity on his or her throne—it can be a male deity or a female deity or two deities in sexual union—then you have to keep them there. You have to entice them to stay by continuing to provide worship and feeding them through the pujas and the rituals and so on. We have talked about the embodiment of the union of Radha and Krishna within ourselves, which creates a mood, an ongoing mood of union within, without having to be reminded of essential union by external union. Not that you would cease participating in sexual union with your partner, but you would not *need* sexual union, or communion with friends over a special meal, to remind you of essential union with the Divine. Once you unite the Masculine and Feminine within yourself then you live in that state of union. That is the Baul idea of tantra.

"In many of the traditional tantric practices, including in Vajrayana Buddhism, the idea of deity worship is a preliminary step to the ultimate practice of adhering in the natural, awakened state of Reality all the time, which is called *sahaja*. Many of you have probably picked up on one of the words in the title of the *Hohm Sahaj Mandir Study Manual* and the name of this organization, Hohm Sahaj Mandir, which points to our tradition. 'Sahaj Mandir' means 'the temple of natural awareness,' or 'the temple of natural realization.' In this case 'natural' means unefforted. One adheres in the *sahaj* state, or union, without any effort or technology. In the Baul Path no technology is required to see Reality. You don't need to use a drug, you don't need to meditate for hours on end, you don't need to say a mantra. Once you have realized the *sahaj* state, Reality is everywhere. Papa Ramdas defined it as seeing Ram everywhere, in everything and everybody. Yogi Ramsuratkumar defines it as 'My Father is everywhere . . . Father is all, one, indivisible, whole.'

"We could easily apply this principle to our own work. When you are practicing tantra you use dualistic language but you are not working under a dualistic assumption; the context is not dualistic even though the language is. To consider this idea of inviting the Divine to reside within is not a foreign concept. Certainly any of you who have read *Death of a Dishonest Man* have found that concept in some of the poetry. It is certainly found in the tantric poetry of all the Tibetan masters.

"The idea is that one must make the internal space attractive. In all practices the first step in making a chamber attractive is to clean the chamber. In Hindu tantra there are very specific practices in which one enters the meditation and imagines a chamber within. You literally imagine yourself cleaning the chamber, sweeping it, washing down the floors with purified water, cleaning the walls, making sure that everything is perfectly clean, making sure that there is no dust, no foreign elements. This is also a principle of alchemy; before one begins an alchemical experiment the laboratory has to be absolutely ruthlessly gone over, so there are no foreign elements intruded into the experiment. This principle applies in many domains. You clean the space and then you make the space attractive. To make the space attractive you may place flowers, you may have a little pool with a fountain, you may perfume the water, you may burn incense, you may hang erotic pictures on the wall or not, depending upon the particular context of the invitation. You make the space attractive, and then once you have cleaned the space and made the space attractive, you call the deity to reside there. You invite the Divine to come in.

"The Divine is being supplicated at any given time by, let's say, one billion people, so the Divine has to be a little picky. You can't just go, 'Yoohoo! Yoohoo! Over here!' Many people have tried that and it doesn't seem to work! Although every once in awhile the Divine, in Its whimsical nature, stops to visit. But that is like winning the lottery—surprise!

"Basically to invite the Divine in is a function of a certain integrity of practice. In ritualistic tantric schools you would invite the Divine in with a whole series of pujas, prayers, mantras, *yantras*, mandalas, the whole gamut. It is a very extensive and intricate process. In our school we don't have that particular kind of ritual. What calls the deity, what invites the Divine in, is integrity of practice. Any of you who have studied this kind of material, or who have listened closely during discussions we've had, will have heard this idea: there is that which keeps the subtle energy body clean and sustains it, and there is that which toxifies it. There are some things, very few, that actually stain the chamber to the degree that you cannot get the stain out.

"So we want our chamber to be clean. It's like cleaning a gun. You have to clean a gun very carefully, because if you clean a gun poorly for a long time then it may misfire, and you know what happens when a gun misfires. You are lucky if it doesn't blow off half of your face. If you are unlucky it can be a very dangerous, costly lesson in being careful. So you want to clean the chamber, and what cleans the chamber is clean food, clean water, clean breath, clean activity and clean thoughts. What toxifies or stains a chamber is dirty food, dirty water, dirty whatever it is. Coca-Cola is dirty water. We drink it sometimes, but it's dirty water. Coffee is dirty water, and we drink it sometimes. Milk is dirty water, and we drink it sometimes. Even most juice is dirty water, and we drink them sometimes—especially if they are fresh. Bottled, processed juice is basically dirty water—not as dirty as Coca-Cola, but dirty none the less. So obviously if there is an accumulation of things that are a little bit dirty and a lot dirty (a toxic nuclear waste dump is very dirty and a compost is a different kind of dirty), then you have a problem.

"What toxifies the inner chamber is dirty food (gross, subtle and impression), dirty water and dirty air. Not necessarily that any air is completely clean these days, but the important thing is how we breathe. How we breathe defines the cleanliness of the subtle food that goes to purify or rarify the chamber. All of our assertions about rigorous practice, about attention to practice, about consistency of practice, personal discipline, *all* has to do with this consideration of keeping the chamber clean and receptive as a way of inviting the Divine into embodiment in our particular case. One could say that the supplications are the mantras that we repeat, or the way we speak to one another, or the prayers that we carry on. The prayers are not necessarily formal spoken prayers—like the Twenty-third Psalm or anything like that—but are a matter of how the heart speaks. It is a matter of how we are disposed toward the Divine, moment to moment and contextually. All of that is what invites the Divine in. If we are neglecting or lacking in vigilance in relation to our subtle energy field, which is where this chamber is established, to the point that we are toxified, obviously the entry of the Divine becomes problematical. It is a very straightforward formula.

"We want to invite the Divine in, although in a nondualistic sense the Divine is not out. We are already that which we are attempting to realize. One approach is to just realize what you already are. That's well and good, but given the difficulty we have in realizing the simplest of things, to realize the most obscure, refined and subtle realization, without the kind of intermediaries that such visualizations and practices are, is probably even more problematical. So, it is true that we are inviting the Divine in, and in fact the Divine is already there. All we have to do is realize it. But the probability of realizing this can be greatly increased through formal tantric practice, and that is the source of all the practices that we have developed since the school has been around. The idea of all of our practices is to heighten the probability of one's ability to adhere in Reality. The language of nonduality sounds very simple—just live life *as it is.* But we don't live life *as it is,* so anything that can help us live life *as it is* may be useful. Just stating the ultimate nondualistic philosophy may be enlivening, but it may not be particularly useful.

"This is the essential idea and the reason why we emphasize practice and encourage a lifestyle of discipline and consistency: because if the Divine is going to establish Itself, Its throne, the seat of Its kingdom, in the palace that you prepare in your heart, that palace has got to be reliable. If you think of the Divine as a king or queen who is going to establish his or her seat of power in the chamber you have prepared, that chamber has got to be reliable. If one day it's clean and the next day it's filthy, that's not going to encourage the Divine. All of the practices, the diet, study, the impression food we consume is all important. No queen wants to be woken up by nightmares of some chain saw murder, so even the movies we go to see and the impressions we take in, literally, all have to do with the establishment of this internal chamber and the invitation to the Divine to establish its residence there.

"So then the question comes, 'Well, what about this idea of the Feminine and the Masculine?' The duo of deities, for example the Tibetan image of the deity and consort in sexual union, is exactly what are we inviting in. We talk about the union of Radha and Krishna, and we may have a very specific imagery for that traditional Hindu image, but we also talk in general terms about the Masculine and the Feminine. In our school we haven't been given specific images to work with; rather than coming up with an exact image, we keep the image an unconscious function of the language. So we speak of the union of the Masculine and the Feminine rather than coming up with a specific image, whether it is Radha and Krishna or the Tibetan image or Shiva and Parvati. Shiva is the ultimate yogi; he can meditate for a thousand years and then have sex for a thousand years. In the mythology Parvati is always trying to get him to open his eyes, because when his eyes are closed he is absorbed in the contextual Self, and Parvati has no chance for union with him. But as soon as he opens his eyes Shiva is just, 'Yes!' Shiva is an irrepressible rake, and the minute he opens his eyes and sees Parvati, his eyes come popping out of his head and he leaps on her. Which, by the way, is why we recommend keeping your eyes open in sex! No, I'm just kidding.

"That's the way Shiva is looked at—as the ultimate yogi and the ultimate *bhogi*, which in Sanskrit means enjoyer. Shiva is the ultimate enjoyer. The Shiva/Shakti image is not used in the Baul tradition because the Baul tradition is a Vaishnava tradition in which the Radha/Krishna image is used. But in other tantric systems the Shiva/Shakti image is used because Shiva adheres to Reality whether that Reality is complete absorption in the void or complete absorption in Creation. Shiva is perfect at both—he is perfection in both worlds. That is the traditional tantric image, but my preference is simply to say the union of the Masculine and the Feminine, and leave it to the individual. We let whatever image belongs to each of us present itself.

"This is unorthodox by tantric measures because you are supposed to pick your deity. Actually the guru is supposed to give you your deity and then you practice with that. Our way of practicing is to invite the Divine into the internal chamber that we have created specifically for that purpose. We have to *intend* the process. Intention is the most powerful force we have at our disposal. Intention creates an exacting and highly refined energetic chamber.

"At the same time, paradoxically, the more we care for, honor and respect that Reality which is the internal chamber where Radha and Krishna meet every night, and in which the *gopis* run every night, in which Krishna is playing his flute every night, the Reality of Enlightened Duality within us, then the more It impinges upon us to be vigilant about what maintains that space in its elegance and cleanliness. When we fail to care for that space it is as if we were throwing garbage on the floor, or walking through the garden and crushing the flowers.

"We have a dichotomy within us. We have this wish, 'I want to realize God, I want to know the nature of Reality, I want to live Reality, I want to know Truth,' or however we language it. We have that and then we have our activity, which is actually sabotaging that wish. One of the elements of ongoing practice is to stop the sabotage. First we have to stop the sabotage, and then we begin to live in specific ways that actually invite and encourage the Divine to reside within this chamber, which in the Baul Path is the chamber of the heart.

"We want to invite God to live in our hearts—whatever form that takes. God as the union of Masculine and Feminine, or God as a fierce deity. Who knows? Different forms of the Divine, different flavors, different textures. This is why we are so demanding about the need to practice rightly: because this chamber of the heart is Real. It is as Real as the fact that Reality is insubstantial, empty, void. Both are equally Real, and if we deny the Reality of the chamber, then we think nothing of abuses of practice that keep that chamber dirty and unattractive. The Divine is most drawn by that which is most attractive to It, and is most repelled by that which is unattractive to It.

"In Baul practice we enter into life, into relationship between men and women, into business, into friendships, into relationship with money, with food, with natural circumstances, beautiful and otherwise—as beautiful as in the Alps on a clear morning! But traveling through France there is no area in which within one hundred kilometers there is not a nuclear power plant. So you travel through France and see these immense nuclear power plants, the whole area clouded with pollution. That too is a reality that we enter into relationship with.

"We enter into a relationship with Reality *as it is,* and in one sense there is a kind of lovemaking with all that. Many people could relate to the context of lovemaking when you are standing in the Alps looking into the valley and there are two beautiful little chalets, and one side of the mountain is covered in little yellow and white blossoms of beautiful flowers. 'Yes, yes,' we say, 'life is passionate and deep,' but what about when you are looking at South Bend, Indiana or Detroit? Or what you see driving into East Germany, although it's better now. But before the Wall came down you'd drive into East Germany and everything went from green and bright and beautiful to gray and dark. Literally a hundred yards into East Germany, everything changed—the buildings became gray and drab, whereas right on the other side everything was bright. It was the most amazing phenomena.

"So there is also a kind of stark, shocking, horrific element to life, which is the way we are destroying the planet and all the elements of that, the effects of that. Nature in its 'red in tooth and fang' jazz, or however it goes. That is Reality too, and we have to enter into a relationship with that because we cross its path all the time. Everywhere you go there is this dark aspect of Reality. Fly in an airplane to Los Angeles or to San Francisco—as the airplane is landing you are going to be close enough to the surface of the earth to see ugliness, to see industry, to see pollution, to see immense communities with houses built four or five feet away from one another, so there is literally no space. You can't look out a window without seeing your neighbor staring in your window, hoping to catch you in some salacious act. So this is part of the practice: to enter into relationship with *all* of Reality. Some of it you can embrace and take in, and some you navigate around—that's perfectly reasonable. Entering into relationship with this side of Reality doesn't mean that you have to do your time in Detroit and spend six years there breathing smog.

"For example, when you are white water rafting under certain conditions you have to navigate around very large rocks. Some of them are sticking up out of the water, some of them aren't. Sometimes the rocks aren't visible above the surface of the water, and you have to sense them. Sometimes the only way you navigate around them is after you have hit them, and you are maintaining the stability of the raft. But you can't ignore the fact that there are immense rocks that could kill you if you didn't have a guide in the back of the boat steering the thing like crazy, yelling at everybody, where to put their paddles.

"Speaking in principle, when we invite the deities into the inner chamber, we have a tremendous faith in the ultimate Intelligence of our being. We trust that Intelligence, we are throwing ourselves at the mercy of that Intelligence because we have a deep and abiding trust in the Intelligence of Organic Innocence. We trust in Divine Intelligence and elicit Its participation and cooperation in these matters of great urgency and sanctity. We state our aim, make a very basic definition, hold the context for our work, and then Divine Intelligence does all the rest."

It was an amazing talk because it was one of those rare times when Lee was moved to talk directly about the inner practices of the school as a tantric path. Lee seldom dispenses data in this way when he is in the U.S., and especially at the Arizona ashram. Tonight he elucidated key elements of the Western Baul path, drawing parallels between the language he has used, such as Organic Innocence, and the ancient principle of *sahaja*, which literally means "born together" or "innate" and connotes the spontaneous or natural way of realizing the Divine. Hence, as Lee said, there is no technology needed in this path, but intention. The much coveted *sahaja* state is often described as a state of open-eyed ecstasy, in which abiding union with the Divine—the hallmark of surrender to the Will of God—appears in those rare individuals who remain completely ordinary in the midst of the bliss of union.

At the end of his talk Lee made a few announcements about the coming week, particularly that he was leaving on Tuesday, January 12, with a large party of students to spend a week in San Francisco. He would be driving his van with fourteen people up through Arizona and California to the Bay Area, where he would meet with a number of other students who were flying in from Colorado and Arizona to spend the week with him. After announcements he called out, "Jai Guru!" and swept out of the hall carrying a large box full of the *prasad* he'd been given, his shawl gently trailing the floor behind him.

January 12, 1999
On the road

Three weeks after Lee's return from India he was on the road again, driving west over the Arizona desert toward California and San Francisco, where he would spend the next seven days giving teachings and visiting other teachers. Sitting behind the wheel Lee was in a great mood. About two hours into the trip he began to talk in an animated way. He had that crazy glint in his bright blue eyes. He was talking with Sian Bouyou, a disciple of Arnaud Desjardins who was visiting from France and came along with several of Lee's students on this trip. She mentioned that a new American teacher—who "woke up" in prison and is teaching now—was going to give a seminar at her hotel in southern France where she hosts many different teachers and workshop leaders on the spiritual circuit, including Lee Lozowick.

Upon hearing this Lee began to rant about how students typically get all hot about yet another new teacher who is burning up the scene. His eyes were fierce and with a smirking sort of smile he snapped out, "Another thrill! It's just another thrill! It's the search all over. It's shameful." Then Sian told him about another Westerner who had had three powerful experiences and had started teaching and was making a name for himself. Lee interjected, grinning, "I've got seventy students who've had three powerful experiences and they'd better not be teaching! But they'd love to . . ." His voice was saturated with a characteristic sarcasm.

"Some of them are in this van—one back there, one up here," his eagle eye honed in on different people in the van, "another one asleep back there. They've had loads of those experiences, never mind three! Yeah! They'd be up on the dais waving their hands with their jewels sparkling on their fingers, blessing everyone and making the teaching available!" He threw his head back and laughed. His mood was infectious. All this was delivered in such a way, with such a ferocious sense of humor, that everyone in the van couldn't help but laugh along with him at the illusions of grandeur which ego keeps spinning out.

As the van sped across the desert the conversation turned to Andrew Cohen's seminar in November 1998 at Hauteville, the ashram of Arnaud Desjardins. Sian said that she had been there, and someone asked her how it had gone. She said it was fantastic and very intense for everyone. She talked about the strong impact that Andrew had on everyone, and how fierce he was. Many people were quite shaken up and confused by the force of his uncompromising communication of the dharma.

Arnaud himself was shocked by the lack of inherence in his teaching demonstrated by even many long-time students in the face of Andrew's communication. He wrote in the association's newsletter that this event had made him realize that his students had not embraced the teaching as they should have over the years. He urged his disciples to study, read his books and practice more diligently. Lee seemed to absorb and digest this information with gusto. He compared Arnaud's "shock" to what Lee himself had experienced with his students in India during the same time period. Lee then began to praise his friend Andrew.

"Andrew refuses to compromise. Andrew is into Spartan warriorship. He's into the path of the warrior. *I'm* just into sitting around and getting fat and having a bunch of naked women feed me stuffed dates!" His tone was highly facetious, and in the disparaging of himself, he made a teaching point. These are some of the hardest teaching communications to take, and Lee is liberal in using them to stir his students to action. It often feels exactly like the equivalent of Meher Baba having his devotees slap his face when they made a mistake or failed to obey their guru. Lee's final statement on Andrew's teaching at Hauteville was, "It's great—people need a wake-up call! They won't answer the phone, of course . . ."

January 13, 1999
San Francisco

Lee's van arrived at the center within minutes of his students who had flown in from Phoenix. The small center—Sahaj Mandir San Francisco—was beautiful, immaculate, elegant, poised and ready for his arrival. Vases of lilies graced the carved fireplace mantle in the gathering room where a small votive candle burned beside a picture of Lee and Yogi Ramsuratkumar. All along the hallway hung a gallery of beautifully framed photographs of Lee. The meditation hall was stunning with its tatami dais on which Lee's sandals rested below large framed pictures of Lee and Yogi Ramsuratkumar. The central puja had the bronze *vigraha* of Yogi Ramsuratkumar in a small shrine on one side and a lush four-foot-high magenta dendrobium orchid on the other. The whole center, and especially this room of meditation and worship, was permeated with the mood of Japanese culture and Zen simplicity. Shukyo had clearly gone all out to make a space that would be an expression of devotion to her spiritual master.

As soon as everyone got settled in—thirteen of Lee's women students would be sleeping side by side on the floor in a tiny two-room studio downstairs—Lee started playing bridge. Two or three people pulled up chairs to watch. Someone asked, "Can we look over your shoulder so we can see how you play?"

"Sure! The closer the better! It's like an orgy, only it's not sex, it's playing bridge. And I hope *that* sets the tone for this week!" Lee then proceeded to work with each person at the table, correcting and pointing out mistakes. No one was free of his discerning eye, which quite literally, in this case, didn't miss a trick (no pun intended). How to take his remark? The week with him in San Francisco should be like an orgy, but it's not sex. It was a metaphor for the way one should approach the master's company and work with him. Perhaps with a driving passion and desire for the dharma, for the Work, with layers of protective buffers stripped away, with essence brought to the foreground, as it can be in sex.

That night after dinner about thirty-five people squeezed into the room on the floor around Lee, who sat on a love seat at one end of the room. He began the After Dinner Talk saying, "It's been two years since I did any teaching in the Bay Area. This year I want to scare away anyone who doesn't have a profound need for the Work." He told the story of Andrew Cohen's teaching at Hauteville that he had heard from Sian, and again he compared what Arnaud was going through with the shock and disappointment that Lee felt at the lack of practice in his senior students on the recent trip to India. He said that the closeness between he and Arnaud and their respective schools often shows up in a synchronicity of events, so that what Arnaud goes through, Lee often also experiences in some way.

Lee then talked about two dimensions of the teaching that he called "primate" and "esoteric." He said, "At the primate level we're doing really well as a school. At the level of human contact and community we're doing really great. But there is also the Work aspect—the esoteric aspect. Sri Anirvan said that the closest Western tradition to the Bauls of Bengal is the Gurdjieff work." He commented that the Work aspect of the path is too often denied in many schools that should know better. He talked about the need that he feels to keep his school small, and how his teaching style has been designed over twenty years toward that aim.

"When people start talking about me like I'm someone to recognize, it worries me because I know what it is to Work and how hard it is to maintain that, even for dedicated students. Once the school gets big, it's much harder. When someone infers that I'm well respected in the spiritual scene I feel like I have to do something about that! I need to shake things up, I try to shock people. I go to do a seminar over in France and everyone gets upset about my style and I think, 'Okay! At last I'm getting it right! I won't have to come back to this seminar house!' Then at the end of the seminar they all loved it, they're so excited they can't wait to have me back next year. What's going on?

"So this week I'd like to not capitulate to people's needs. Everyone here feels like they're in northern California and they should be treated well and all that shit. I'd like to wound my reputation a little bit while I'm here. We're getting far too acceptable as an organization. But I don't know—I'm speaking at a Zen center. What do they know about the Work? I'm giving my public talk in a center that's been donated to us, we're not paying rent or anything—I don't know what will happen! But I'd like to shake people up and wound my reputation a little bit. We'll see."

Lee talked about Gurdjieff insulting his students in order to create suffering for himself—Gurdjieff did whatever he needed to do to create Work. He also loved the same people who he hurt with his harsh teaching style. He caused them to suffer and every time he remembered them and the suffering that was brought to them because of his actions or words, *he suffered* because he was compassionate.

His comments on Gurdjieff struck home: in the face of Lee's ongoing criticisms, crazy teaching lessons and incisive and pointed use of sarcasm, how to walk the fine line between hopelessness or despair and the will to continue one's sadhana with commitment and faith can be a constant koan. Some days there is a buoyant field of Grace that holds one afloat in the midst of the storm; on other days it seems like the boat sinks into the depths where predators lurk, just waiting to bite the bone of conviction. Those are the times to practice with more diligence.

Now Lee exclaimed, "What it *takes* to make work for ourselves! Gurdjieff's example is tremendously inspiring. Creating stress for one's self is almost always a beneficial effort. But on the other hand causing suffering to others based on the idea that we're creating stress for ourselves is unacceptable. We have this tremendous opinion or idea of ourselves when we are nothing but a machine."

Lee then talked about how many people are putting their money into gold coins now rather than stocks, bonds and investments because of the Y2K computer bug and the coming year 2000. He used this idea of being "liquid" as a metaphor for how one should be in the Work. If we have a lot invested in emotional and psychological attachments, then we can't be liquid. "If you aren't liquid in the Work you can't afford to keep those things in your safety deposit box. You have no idea how much you lose if you have no liquidity. One major downturn and you are prey for the subtle body energy hustlers. It's a very important metaphor for the Work. Practice is not a luxury, it is an absolute need. Practice is what builds your liquidity."

January 15, 1999
San Francisco

After a hearty brunch at ten o'clock with the whole group packed into the space at Sahaj Mandir, a few students drove with Lee up into the mountains northwest of the Bay Area toward Point Reyes to visit with Llewellyn Vaughan-Lee, the lineage holder in the West of Sufi Master Bhai Sahib. Llewellyn Vaughan-Lee is the author of ten books on the mystical path of Sufism and a long-time student of Irina Tweedie, who wrote the classic book, *Daughter of Fire*, about her relationship with her guru, Bhai Sahib. Driving through the lush backdrop of a northern California forest the teal green van wound up through the hills and onto a small road that seemed to dead end at a modest, two-story house. Lee parked near the front door. As he walked up to the door Llewellyn Vaughan-Lee appeared with his arms spread out in a warm welcome. He greeted Lee as if he had known him for years. It was the first time they had ever met. They embraced and Lee introduced his students one by one to Llewellyn. As we walked into the living room Llewellyn Vaughan-Lee said, "Please come in and sit down. Sit anywhere."

The carpeted living room was bare of furniture except for one couch placed against the wall. Big plate glass windows covered the opposite wall and opened out on a large redwood deck surrounded by thick trees and shrubs. There were several pillows arranged on the floor some distance from two slightly larger pillows that were set against the walls, one of them covered with a sheepskin and obviously Llewellyn Vaughan-Lee's seat. The other floor pillow to the right and against the perpendicular wall seemed intended for Lee, so that Llewellyn Vaughan-Lee and Lee would sit near each other but facing the rest of the group. There were five of Lee's students and five of Llewellyn's students present. The two teachers sat down and the rest of us found places around the room on the couch and on pillows. After a few brief pleasantries the group got down to business. Lee and Llewellyn began to talk about their respective teaching work. Almost immediately there seemed to be a tacit field of mutual understanding that characterized the discussion. Llewellyn asked Lee how many students he had.

Lee said, "Oh maybe a hundred. My students will say there are more, they'll say we have one hundred and fifty students. But I say maybe a hundred real students—and that doesn't include the children. The children aren't students. We have a lot of families with children. But I want to keep the school small."

Llewellyn nodded as if this was understood and said, "Bhai Sahib always said, 'Don't get big, keep it to only a few.' So you live near Prescott—is your ashram outside of town?"

Lee answered, "Actually we are very close, right on the edge of town—too close, because Prescott is growing. We are looking to move further out from town."

Llewellyn said, "So you want to retreat further into the desert." This matter-of-fact statement made it clear how easily he tuned into Lee's intention. All this seemed implicitly understood by him.

"Yes," Llewellyn continued, "it's good to remain hidden. We like it out here in the mountains because it keeps people who aren't really serious away. People say they want to come out and visit us but then the hour drive really keeps them from coming." He mentioned that he himself is an introvert who likes to remain very reclusive.

When someone asked if Mrs. Tweedie was still alive he laughed and said, "Yes, she's alive and well. She is ninety-one years old now and retired from teaching. She lives with a companion and her cat in a flat in London." He laughed. "I've known her for thirty years and she's always been threatening to die—but she's still alive."

Llewellyn asked Lee about his tradition and Lee spoke about the Bauls of Bengal. He said that Sri Anirvan had said that of the Western traditions the Gurdjieff work was most like the work of the Bauls because the work happens in the body. "The body is not to be jettisoned," he said. Then he continued to talk about the Bauls as a synthesis of devotional Vaishnavism and tantric Buddhism. "It's essentially a tantric path," Lee said.

"Oh, so you indulge your students?" Llewellyn turned to the three women sitting on the couch with a big smile. He had a way of pulling everyone in the room into the conversation rather than just keeping it focused between he and Lee. "Are you indulged?" he pressed, with a grin. Lee nodded emphatically and said, "Boy! Are they!"

The conversation turned to the Bauls. Lee talked about how the Bauls encode their teaching into song and choreographed dance because they don't believe in writing down the teaching. This is part of their refusal to become orthodox in any way. Llewellyn asked if Lee used music and dance in his work with students. Lee talked about the bands, the music, the lyrics. He said, "My students would say that the lyrics have all these esoteric messages of the teaching in them, but I say it's just rock & roll." Llewellyn laughed. Lee continued, "The bands are a work task like Gurdjieff might have given, but they are not integral to practice, although practice happens within them."

Llewellyn said, "So your path is not a monastic path."

"No," Lee replied, "It's not. We work in ordinary, everyday life."

Llewellyn said, "But it's a devotional path," to which Lee answered, "Yes."

Llewellyn commented, "The path of love is tremendously misunderstood in the West. There is no ground for understanding the guru/disciple relationship in the West, whereas in India this understanding is just part of the air itself. In my experience the path of love, the guru/devotee relationship, is the most intimate and impersonal relationship that exists. In our Western culture we have no reference point for something that is *both* intimate and impersonal."

One of Lee's students asked, "How do you handle that?"

He laughed and said, "I'm English—I went to an English boarding school!" He paused then continued, "Bhai Sahib says that the path of love is the most difficult relationship there is. On this path, because we work with love, there is always jealousy. Everyone thinks *they* are nearer to the teacher, but they also think that someone else is nearer. Because I lived up above Mrs. Tweedie in a house that we shared everyone assumed that I was the closest, but that wasn't so. Everyone else was receiving this tremendous love from her, there was just tremendous intimacy and closeness between her and her students. She was a great source of love for everyone—but not for me." He paused and considered, "I was with her for ten years before she told me that she wasn't my guru, that Bhai Sahib was actually my master. He instructed her not to have that kind of relationship with me. So I was always outside of that flow of love that Mrs. Tweedie had with her devotees because she wasn't my master—Bhai Sahib is.

"People who are drawn to the mystical path always feel left out—they are the ones who don't fit in all their lives, the misfits. Relationship with the guru is soul to soul, from lifetime to lifetime. We feel this deep closeness but here we are in the body and we can't see it practically, so we project that closeness onto others—'He is closer, she is closer!' It's tremendously intimate, and yet it's impersonal. I think love is *always* misunderstood. Bhai Sahib said there will always be only a few on the path of love, because who wants to get rid of the self? It seems like it is mostly women who come to this path. Do you find that?" He turned to Lee with his question.

"For years we had mostly women in our school, but now we have a good balance of men and women," Lee answered.

"In India it is both men and women," Llewellyn commented. He mentioned then that although in the West many women flock to the devotional path, Irina Tweedie was the first woman to be trained in their lineage. Bhai Sahib said this was because women in general lacked perseverance.

"In the Baul tradition women on the path are highly respected. The men may take the spotlight, but the women are extremely powerful," Lee said.

"I grew up with very powerful women," Llewellyn continued. "Mrs. Tweedie of course was very, very powerful. We were terrified of her. No one ever argued with her. I was nineteen, we were all very young, and here she was this respected elder, and she was a very emotional, theatrical, very charismatic Russian woman. She was just so powerful and free that none of us would think of arguing with her."

Lee looked at his students with his eyebrows raised in mock surprise. "Imagine that!" he quipped, tongue-in-cheek, pointing out again that many of his students, including some of them in the room, had no compunction or hesitation about arguing with him.

The group talked for a while about practice and the practices of Lee's school. "But,"

Lee said, "hospitality is a higher law than the formal practices, so we host a lot of people. In this way people learn to serve instead of being served."

The conversation turned toward money and dealing with money on the path—whether or not to charge money for events and teachings, for example. "Mrs. Tweedie never charged for anything," Llewellyn said. "There was no structure at all around her. Things would come up and we would wonder how we were going to manage, but somehow the money was always there when we needed it." He said that he had been taken out of the moneymaking decisions in his organization.

Lee replied that in his community students had to pay for celebrations and seminars, "but we are a poor community." He pointed toward one of his students and said, "This is great for her to hear because she deals with the struggle over money all the time."

Llewellyn looked over at her, his eyes a soft, radiant blue and said, "It's good to be poor in America!" Then he went on to say that when you trust, the money is just there when you need it. And, he said, "You just get what you need."

Another of Lee's students told the story of Yogi Ramsuratkumar saying years ago to Lee, "My Father will give Lee whatever he wants," then he paused and repeated it but with an important change. He said, "My Father will give Lee whatever he *needs*." Every year when Lee goes to visit Yogi Ramsuratkumar, he says it exactly like that—"My Father will give Lee whatever he needs." Llewellyn nodded his head in agreement. A brief silence fell and then he graciously invited us into the dining room for tea and a "snack."

We walked into the small dining room and saw a lavish spread of food on the rectangular table that was set with about eight chairs around it. Llewellyn invited Lee to take the seat at the head of the table, then seated himself on Lee's immediate right. There was vegetarian sushi, a cheese platter, several kinds of crackers and three gorgeous cakes. Llewellyn asked Lee and the group what we would like to drink—coffee, tea, mint tea. Lee answered, mint tea. Everyone took their seats in an amiable atmosphere punctuated with laughter and comments about the shared joy of eating. One of Llewellyn's students offered Lee a piece of the rich, dark chocolate cake. "How big a piece do you want," she asked. "Small, medium or large?"

Lee responded, "Large!" Lee doesn't always take a large serving of dessert, contrary to his reputation. There are many times when he will decline altogether or eat sweets very sparingly. When he does take a large portion it seems to go hand in hand with the mood of the gathering. In this case it seemed like a signal that the visit was working very well for Lee—he was freely partaking of the feast which was being offered here on many levels.

Llewellyn smiled and remembered, "Mrs. Tweedie always said tea—*and cookies!*— was very important. We always had sweets and treats at tea with her." He seemed to have a very similar delight in the hospitality, good company and pure enjoyment of such shared repast as Lee does.

As platters of sushi and cheese were passed around and slices of cake served, the group began to ask Llewellyn more questions. Someone asked about the dreamwork that he does, and he said that dreams had always played an important role in the Sufi lineage of Bhai Sahib, who had instructed Irina Tweedie in the use of dreams. At a certain point in working with the group that Llewellyn was part of, Mrs. Tweedie introduced the dreamwork and brought a Jungian focus to it. From the beginning she felt that Llewellyn had a particular gift for dream interpretation, and she would ask him at every meeting to interpret the dreams of others.

He began to tell stories about Mrs. Tweedie. He said that Bhai Sahib had told Mrs. Tweedie to keep a journal from the beginning of her long, arduous path with him, and he specifically instructed her to include everything—the doubts, the difficulties, the struggles, as well as the mystical aspects of her experience—because people need to know what is really involved on the path. Someday, he said, she would have these journals published. And so she kept them religiously, and they documented her process with him. Bhai Sahib always said to Mrs. Tweedie that she was on the fast path—no *dhyana* or meditation for her, but the path of annihilation, in which the master used his yogic powers to awaken her kundalini. Because of that, she suffered tremendous upheavals in her sadhana. After Bhai Sahib died, she went to northern India. She was devastated. A month after he died she had an experience of him on the inner planes, and from that time on she was with him continuously. It was after this inner union with her teacher that Bhai Sahib told her, "Now the real spiritual work begins."

She moved to England and began teaching. He had told her to write a book from her journals, but she kept resisting it, putting it off. Finally, after a third heart attack, she realized that her master was telling her that she had to write the book. She had a dream of a particular cottage on the coast of northern Scotland. She knew this was where she had to go to write, so she took her trunk full of journals and with a couple of her students drove up and down the coast of Scotland until she found the same cottage that had appeared in her dream. It was a stone cottage, rather ugly, but with modern conveniences. There she went into solitary retreat and wrote for nine months. At the end of that time *Daughter of Fire* was finished. There were many esoteric teachings that had been given by Bhai Sahib that were intentionally not included in the book.

Llewellyn continued, "Mrs. Tweedie was often asked, 'How could you let him do that to you?'" He shook his head and again talked about how misunderstood the guru/devotee relationship is in the West. He said, "Another question she was often asked is, 'If you had it to do over again, would you?' To this Mrs. Tweedie would reply, 'I wouldn't have to do it all over again because this time I would just say yes to him right at the beginning!'"

Looking pointedly at his students Lee smiled hugely and said, "That's exactly what I've been telling you all . . ."

Llewellyn talked about how fierce Mrs. Tweedie was. He said, "She would throw tantrums and yell at her students, 'You're not progressing! What will you do when I die?' She threw people out the door bodily, then she would throw their shoes out after them in fits of rage. She was very theatrical. Everyone was terrified of her. And yet at the same time there was this tremendous flow of love that came from her and that flowed out to her students, who were deeply devoted to her.

"But not for me," Llewellyn said with a tone that is hard to describe. It wasn't wistful, for it had no sentiment whatsoever in it. It was a statement of *what is,* of total acceptance, and yet it was tinged with a pensiveness, as if he contemplated the impact and implications of all this in his sadhana.

Llewellyn said that Mrs. Tweedie became a superstar in the spiritual scene after *Chasm of Fire* and then later, *Daughter of Fire,* were published. She was giving talks all over Europe to large groups, as many as six hundred people. He said, "She had the uncanny ability to make every person in the room feel that she was making love to him or her alone. But at some point it just became too big. Bhai Sahib had always said to keep it small. So Mrs. Tweedie dropped it all and 'retired,' although she still sees some people at her flat in London." Llewellyn said that he visits her there twice a year.

He continued regaling everyone with more stories. He had a rapt and very appreciative audience. He said, "Mrs. Tweedie could talk almost nonstop about the most trivial things. When her students would come to visit her they would sit and listen for hours while Mrs. Tweedie chatted about what seemed inconsequential or mundane, but one had to listen carefully because at any time she would throw in the teaching. She is quite an extrovert," he said, "unlike myself. I'm an introvert. I love to live the reclusive life." His eyes misted over and seemed to turn inward for a brief moment. I had the sense that he was not talking about his psychological disposition, but about a natural disposition that had been turned toward the mystical path, and in this way his solitude was essential to his inner work. At the same time, he was at all times warm, friendly and gracious, and his sense of humor sparkled in everything he talked about.

It was noticeable that Llewellyn spoke very little about himself or his own relationship with Bhai Sahib, his master. Instead he focused on Mrs. Tweedie, the teaching of Bhai Sahib, and the lineage. Throughout this time Lee became more and more radiant, as if he was gorging himself on the refined presence of the lineage of Llewellyn Vaughan-Lee, Irina Tweedie and Bhai Sahib. There was a strong sense of interweaving between the two lineages as the group sat together with these two men and shared food and stories.

At the moment when the presence in the room had coalesced into its deepest penetration, Llewellyn—who was talking to Lee's devotees while his own students stood or sat beaming and listening at the other end of the table—turned to Lee and said in a completely changed tone of voice, "Well, it is a rare privilege to be here with you!" It was a gentle shock to the space. He had been talking ecstatically, softly, and now this came out in a burst of power. The room seemed to shift after that. He gestured toward Lee's students and said to Lee, "I can tell they are very devoted to you." There was more talk and the friendly atmosphere continued, but Lee and Llewellyn were clearly getting ready to close the space.

Someone asked if there would be another book from Mrs. Tweedie at some time that would be about the esoteric teaching that occurred after Bhai Sahib died. Llewellyn answered, "No. Mrs. Tweedie has been asked that question many times. Whenever people asked her she would say, 'No. Why write another book? It would just be ego.' "

At this point Lee said that it was time to go, and thanked Llewellyn for his hospitality. Without a doubt Llewellyn had served a feast in the treasure house of stories and the pure presence of his lineage. Just before he left Lee extended an invitation to Llewellyn to come to the Arizona ashram to visit. Llewellyn declined graciously, saying, "I am really a recluse. I don't like to travel or speak publicly or even go out of the house. I stay here as much as I can."

The books he has published were mentioned and he said, "Mrs. Tweedie told me years ago that I should write a book a year. I laughed at this, didn't believe I could. But I've written ten books in the past ten years!" He said this as if he was amazed that the books had actually happened. Then he talked about the difficulty he has run into in America in presenting mystical Sufism to the public. "People associate Sufism with the fundamentalism of Muslims, with terrorism and all that. They don't realize that Sufism is a different thing altogether. People confuse the spiritual path with the mystical path, and the mystical path is very different." He then thanked everyone for coming and walked Lee to the door, where they embraced.

On the drive back to San Francisco Lee said of Llewellyn, "He lives for the Work. He doesn't care about anything else." That was the highest praise Lee could give to anyone.

Back at Sahaj Mandir after a simple but excellent meal of baked potatoes with various toppings—cheese, butter and sour cream—and a large salad packed with raw vegetables, Lee and his group took off on foot for the public talk that Lee would give at seven-thirty in a building just a few blocks away in the Presidio. Over dinner Michael A., a devotee of Amritananda Mayi (Ammachi) who had just arrived from San Diego, sat with Lee. Michael had connected with Lee the year before and asked to be his student. Lee said that he wouldn't accept a student who had another teachers also, and to whatever degree he considered himself a devotee of Amritananda Mayi, Michael should tell Ammachi about Lee and get her feedback about his decision. Now Michael reported. "I showed Ammachi a picture of you," he said, looking at Lee.

"Yes?" Lee replied. "What did she say?"

Michael said, "She looked at it and said, 'Crazy.' " Then he added, "She calls herself crazy, so . . . "

It was threatening to rain as Lee and the people walking with him slipped inside the building and went up in the elevator. The space was beautifully set with oriental rugs, *soji* screens, plants and flowers, but the usual picture of Yogi Ramsuratkumar, which Lee likes to have at his talks, was conspicuously missing. The room quickly filled up as people streamed in, until there were about sixty people in the space.

As soon as Lee started speaking he made a comment about how *he* had forgotten to put up a picture of his master, Yogi Ramsuratkumar. Then he went into a harangue against the arrogance and elitist attitude of San Franciscans. He said, "You think you've got some consciousness . . . You've all gotten a hug from the Big Mamma," referring to Amritananda Mayi, some of whose devotees were in the room, "and you think you're enlightened. But to me you're all just shit!

"People are so stupid! Eighty percent of the people who called up, reserved space and said they were coming tonight aren't here. People are totally unreliable. We're just not good for our word. Look at your love affairs if you don't believe me! I love the dharma, practice and a life of discipline—that's why I'm here teaching. But people are shit. You get abused in some relationships, but do you leave them? No! You suck it up like some new fruit smoothie you can get on one of these classy streets around here.

"Everything I do here tonight, my style of teaching, I've had to learn over twenty years. It's living theatre, to create and experience, because we all live in our heads. I don't mean a mystical experience—you've all had more than enough of those. I mean a Real experience. Does mystical experience help you be kinder to your child? No.

"My style has nothing to do with love of mankind. Mankind is shit—you're all shit. The people I don't know are shit, the people I love and live with are shit. And none of this past life stuff either. What does that have to do with anything? Your past lives aren't *your* past lives; they could have happened to anybody. You're just tapping into them.

"Years ago when I visited him, Geshe Wangyal told me, 'There are no Milarepas these days.' It was a very poignant statement. He was a real gentleman; he had dignity. He had no flash, he was not wowed by the West like so many other Tibetans today. That's a tremendously poignant statement for me because that's what I want, that's who I want as students—the Milarepas, the Yeshe Tsogyals."

Lee began to talk about Irina Tweedie. "There were two questions that she got asked all the time: 'How could you let him do that to you?' by the feminists, and 'If you had to do it over again, would you?' Her answer was, 'I wouldn't have to do it over again because this time I would just say yes to him right from the beginning.' This is what we have to do in our sadhana, but we don't say yes to our teachers, we say no—every day, we say no. We have to commit to practice—say yes—because all of our no's make the path a long hard struggle when it doesn't have to be. 'Yes' is the only response to the path. 'No' is an insult to the path. Once you've connected to the path you should say yes because you may have been trying for a hundred or two hundred lifetimes to get to the path and connect with the teacher. And you only have right now. You may have been jockeying for the position you're in now for a thousand lifetimes. You may have a gift for writing, for being with children, but all that goes to the path.

"There will be some stress, of course, like when a caterpillar is becoming a butterfly. When a caterpillar is becoming a butterfly it writhes and looks monstrous for a while. Transformation creates stress and stress creates suffering. But a short period of suffering is all that's necessary when you truly and unequivocally say yes to the path. Transformation is inherently stressful. If they could test coal when it's becoming a diamond that coal would be *screaming,* baby! Under some very serious stress—but becoming a diamond!

"You come on the path because you know that the life of the ordinary person is hellish. Once you begin to make a commitment to the path the only answer to the path is yes. Social action is not the path. It may be good work, but it's not the path. Feeding starving people has nothing to do with spiritual life or realization or enlightenment or mysticism."

A man who has flirted with being a devotee of Da Love Ananda for several years asked about the abuses that certain teachers have perpetrated on their devotees under the rubric of what Chögyam Trungpa Rinpoche called crazy wisdom, but without the skill of a true crazy-wise master. He said that there was a type of "ego shredding" that gets done in these cases that is very harmful.

Lee talked about false teachers and the need to discriminate and look carefully before you leap into it with a teacher. One should seriously consider who the teacher is, what he or she demonstrates, check out their students. Then he took off into a discussion of Enlightened Duality. He talked about how, as a society, anger is so repressed in us; we don't now how to deal with our anger and aggression or our passive aggression, even toward ourselves. He said that most teachers stop after the realization that form is emptiness, the Buddhist term that expresses the foundation truth of nonduality. But without the second half of the formula, which is emptiness is form, or the truth that duality exists as objective fact, the work is very incomplete. Whatever we are in the moment—anger, bliss, whatever—is real, but we have to learn to accept *what is.* Through accepting *what is* we come to the truth about ourselves so that we don't *act* on our anger and aggression. We begin to have choice about how we are in life, about our actions.

"All spiritual choices are made by the Divine," he continued. "All worldly choices are made by ego. We *think* we have choice about choosing a teacher. We don't. We have a choice in choosing a false teacher, but a real teacher? No! If the real teacher wants you— he *takes* you. God chooses for us. I couldn't have made the choices I made—it has all been God, all the Divine."

Lee talked about the necessity for real self-observation on the path, including for teachers. The key to self-observation is *no* judgement. When there is no judgement, then anger is just anger. Someone asked a question about having compassion for ourselves in self-observation. Lee shook his head no and said, *"You* don't have compassion! Compassion is a high state. *God* gives you compassion. You cannot will yourself to have compassion—it's a very big thing."

Another questioner asked how to accelerate the path. Lee answered, "Say yes to the genuine teacher. You have to throw yourself at the teacher's feet. When you say yes to the true teacher he could ask you for anything. That's why you should damn well investigate the teacher and know who you're dealing with . . ."

January 16, 1999
San Francisco

Lee and company left at eight o'clock to drive to Sonoma County to the Sonoma Mountain Zen Center. Driving up through the mountains and onto the property of the zen center the first thing we saw was Jakusho Kwong Roshi standing in the parking lot with a big smile on his face. As soon as Lee got out of the van Roshi came walking toward him with open arms. They embraced and after greeting everyone Roshi led the group to see the recently completed bathhouse, a beautiful structure of pristine simplicity made of recycled redwood and cedar. "It will last five hundred years," Roshi said with a big smile.

Kwong Roshi exudes joy, playfulness and a kind of glee. His enjoyment of every small thing is apparent in his conversation. We took our shoes off and walked inside the women's side of the bathhouse. Roshi asked Lee to offer incense at the small shrine with a traditional painting of nineteen monks bathing with the bodhisattva, which they had gotten from India. Roshi explained that the bathhouse is used in silence, so that the only sounds one hears is the sound of water and of people relieving themselves—an opportunity to confront life as it is. He talked about the importance of water in sustaining life, and explained that his wife had suggested that they change the picture of the bodhisattvas to make them all female for the women's side of the bathhouse. "We can't have monks bathing in the women's bath!" Roshi joked. So they had artfully and tastefully given the monks breasts. On the men's side the traditional picture graced a similar shrine.

Kwong Roshi explained that a group was sitting zazen at the moment, and while that went on he would take us to the shrine of Suzuki Roshi and the stupa of Chögyam Trungpa Rinpoche. Following Roshi and Lee we walked past the lotus pond toward the woods. Someone commented that the lotuses had really taken off since Lee was last there, when they had just been planted. Now there were many lotus seedpods hanging on dry, wintry stems just above the surface of the placid water. Roshi began to talk enthusiastically about the lotuses.

"Yes," he agreed, "they have really grown! The pond is full of them in the summer, and the leaves are so big," he gestured to indicated almost two feet in diameter, "that you could walk across the pond on them! You know, the lotus flower stems always grow out of the *mud*," he laughed slightly, "eight feet or more through the water and then sometimes as much as another five feet toward the sun before they blossom! I've seen them standing that high above the water." All this was pure dharma coming from Kwong Roshi. There was the implication in his words of teaching in simple and earthy terms, a style that is natural to his tradition—the lotus, a timeless metaphor for the soul.

Walking further down the path, Roshi and Lee kept their heads close together as they talked, two friends taking refuge in common purpose. Arriving at a wooded knoll that overlooks the Valley of the Moon, a long crescent of valley land that stretches out from the property, Roshi said that they take great pleasure in watching the moon over that valley. Again his speaking implied a sense of wonder at how the relative and absolute are reflected in all things, and especially in nature. As we approached the shrine—a five-foot-high granite dolmen set up on end in the circle of the knoll, surrounded by overhanging trees so that we could not see the sky—Roshi directed the group to circumambulate the shrine three times. About twenty-five people circumambulated in single file behind Roshi and Lee, until everyone had gone around three times. After the group completed their circumambulations Roshi and Lee stepped forward and took turns with the ritual offering of incense and then water with a bamboo dipper to the dolmen, underneath which some of Suzuki Roshi's relics—bones and ashes—are kept.

As we left the shrine Roshi turned and addressed the entire group, saying, "It's really important to circumambulate shrines, walk around them three times. Wherever you go in the world, wherever you see shrines, you should circumambulate because it keeps the shrine alive." As we walked along Roshi noticed the bare leaves of some wild iris along the path. He stopped and stooped down to touch one, then said, "You know, Suzuki Roshi told his wife when he died to live at the San Francisco Zen Center for ten years, to write haiku poetry and to learn to do tea ceremony. She lived at the zen center for twenty years, won a prize for her haiku, and became a tea master!" He smiled, a profound respect and esteem for Mrs. Suzuki, the wife of his teacher, apparent in his words.

"She came here, and as we walked to this shrine we saw an iris bud along the path. She asked us to pick it and put it where we would be doing the tea ceremony with her later. She did the tea ceremony with us and it took three hours. My knees were killing me!" Roshi smiled and chuckled. "But it was worth it! She was seventy-eight years old then and she had no problem with it! But during that ceremony, the bud opened while she was doing the ceremony. She said that it was the power of presence that caused the iris bud to blossom out."

The walk back was beautiful, along a path that was wet and alive with tall manzanita groves, their smooth red bark inviting to touch. The path went past the stupa of Chögyam Trungpa Rinpoche, who was a close friend and drinking buddy of Kwong Roshi. Lee and Roshi walked up to the front of the stupa, which stands in an open field with low brush growing around the grassy open space, and Roshi asked the monk who was accompanying us—an older man, probably in his seventies, wearing the traditional black robes of a monk—to open the shrine and light the lamps inside it. They each bowed at the shrine, the picture of Trungpa Rinpoche and the relics and statues, then circumambulated three times with the whole group walking slowly behind them while the monk lit the lamps. Prayer flags fluttered in the air and on a four-by-four cedar beam words of Chögyam Trungpa Rinpoche were written in calligraphy script: "When you live, just live. When you die, just die." Lee and Roshi approached the shrine to make their offerings and we stood back a little to watch. Roshi turned around and gestured everyone forward, saying, "Come up here!" He wanted people to gather in close around. The message seemed to be, don't be shy about making offerings to shrines, or to rejoice in the dharma and the teacher.

Inside the shrine burned two or three kerosene lamps and some votive candles. A beautiful glass and gold vessel held a small shard of Trungpa Rinpoche's bone and ash. His photograph made a vivid communication, and the entire shrine emanated his presence. The bottle of sake that Roshi had had sitting beside the picture of Trungpa Rinpoche the last time Lee visited here—three years ago—was missing. Roshi said that someone had taken it from the stupa, he didn't know who. "It is either the worst thing that person ever did, or the best thing!" Roshi said ironically, with a smile. It seemed that he found everything that occurred utterly remarkable. There was no rancor of any kind about this theft that could be seen in him.

Then he told the following story with great delight: The roof of the stupa is heavy copper, everything made exactly to traditional Tibetan Buddhist specifications. When they had to transport it in a pick-up truck from where it was built to the zen center it was too long for the truck bed to pass Department of Transportation regulations, so they were pulled over by the California Highway Patrol and given a ticket. Roshi chuckled, "I thought that was very auspicious!" he said gleefully. "But listen to this: the ticket was one hundred and eight dollars!" One hundred and eight is the traditional number of beads on a prayer *mala*, in both Hinduism and Buddhism. Roshi raised his eyebrows in wonder. It was impossible not to be delighted along with him at such a grand synchronicity. His sense of humor seemed to permeate and release everything into a relaxation, a natural acceptance. He chuckled again and said, "The relative and universal are always one!"

The mood of the visit was infected with Kwong Roshi's cheerfulness and his good-natured enthusiasm and pleasure in all things large and small. Like with Llewellyn Vaughan-Lee the day before, his stories were priceless treasures that he gave freely. He seemed overjoyed at the opportunity to have Lee consecrate these shrines and the stupa. After they offered incense at the stupa they walked up to the main house and zendo with the group following along behind. Along the way Roshi reflected, "In picking the sights for these shrines I thought that Suzuki Roshi would like the seclusion of the forest and a simple stone, whereas Trungpa would like the wide open space and the traditional form of Tibetan Buddhism." The two shrines were reflections of his love and respect for these two great teachers.

Waiting on the porch outside the beautiful redwood zendo for the meditation session to be over we noticed that a flyer was tacked up with a picture of Lee on it. It was an announcement that Lee Lozowick, a Western Baul Master and crazy-wise teacher, would be giving a talk today. "A rare opportunity to interact with a Western Baul," it said. The flyer also described how the eighteen-foot-high carved wooden statue—Avalokitesvara, the bodhisattva of compassion in Tibetan Buddhist iconography, known as Kannon in Japan and as Kwan-Yin in China—had come to live at the zendo from Lee's ashram in Arizona six years ago.

Earlier that morning one of Lee's students was expressing a great joy at getting to see the statue again. She asked Roshi if they considered the bodhisattva female or male. He answered, "Really it has gone *beyond gender*," he spoke with purpose, looking closely at her. "But you can call her either. We call her Kannon—that is her Japanese name. But they made her so that you can see both male and female in her, don't you think?" Yes, she agreed. "But Kannon has gone beyond all gender," he smiled again.

Inside the zendo the covers on the windows facing the porch were removed as we stood waiting, so that the faces of the people sitting zazen in the direction of the windows were visible. They didn't flinch or change their open-eyed meditation the slightest bit even though now there were twenty-five people standing there facing them. They remained inwardly focused until the bell rang and the meditation formally ended. The whole group entered the zendo and took seats. The towering presence of Kannon stood in the center of the room. She was regal, infinitely serene, richly present. On the huge carved wooden lotus upon which her feet were firmly planted was a small shrine—candle, flower arrangement, incense.

Lee and Kwong Roshi took their seats together at the front of the room on two pillows on a six inch raised tatami platform. The older monk who had walked around with us gave a quick introduction. Lee spoke for awhile, talking about practice and the Baul tradition and Yogi Ramsuratkumar. He answered two or three questions. During this Roshi chuckled quietly at Lee's quirky comments or his insight in answering people who Roshi knew so well. Roshi's eyes gleamed with pleasure. After a while Roshi leaned over and asked in a low voice, "How did you meet your master, Lee?"

Lee began to tell the story of meeting Yogi Ramsuratkumar. He especially lingered on how Yogi Ramsuratkumar didn't recognize him when Lee went to see him in 1986 and even sent him away, saying, "Go find a guru somewhere else." Lee said this was a teaching lesson about his arrogance. Lee left India that year with the conviction that Yogi Ramsuratkumar was his master and would always be his master, no matter what. He thought he would never see Yogi Ramsuratkumar again and therefore he would never return to India. When Lee went back in 1988 at the invitation of one of Yogi Ramsuratkumar's ardent devotees, he traveled for two weeks in southern India, giving talks and representing Yogi Ramsuratkumar to village people and untouchables.

He said, "I had tacked two days on the end of the trip in Tiruvannamalai, just in case He was willing to see me. When I saw Yogi Ramsuratkumar this time," Lee continued, "it was as if we had lived together in one room for a million years, the intimacy was that strong. And it has continued that way since then."

This is a story that Lee has told many times, and each time it is fresh, new and unique in some way. Today the intimate details seemed to be for Roshi. He was the one who asked to hear the story, which he had probably heard before three years ago when Lee last spoke in the zendo.

After the talk Roshi turned to his senior monk and said they would clear the space so that Lee and his students could spend some time with Kannon. The monk made an announcement for people to go over to the main house for lunch, and that Roshi would come soon. Everyone moved out quickly and the beautiful redwood double doors were closed. As we gathered around Roshi gestured toward the statue and said, "It means a lot to us to have someone here who can really appreciate what this is." Then he shared a memory of Lee visiting the zendo in 1986 with a few of his students, who had chanted at one of the shrines. That was years before the bodhisattva had come here from the Hohm Community in 1992.

Roshi asked with a smile, "Would you do a chant of some kind now?"

Gesturing toward Chris and I, Lee said, "They can do a chant."

It was an instant reminder of India, in Yogi Ramsuratkumar's darshan. We asked, "Call and response or . . . ?"

Lee interrupted, "No, just the two of you." He turned to Roshi and said, "I call them the Nightingale Sisters."

Roshi laughed and asked with his characteristic merriment, "Oh . . . which one of them is the *real* singer? Which one has the *best* voice?" Roshi seemed to find a great deal of amusement in this. These teachers always having a way of getting to the core issues, of slipping in a teaching lesson, even in the most innocent of ways. It was like receiving a little slap, a playful wake up, the sting of it being rooted in the competitive attitude that is so central to Western psychology. Everybody wants to be special and better than others—a familiar place of struggle. Lee smiled and responded very generously, "Both of them. Both of them are good." He was being very kind.

Chris and I turned to each other and conferred. We decided on a beautiful and melodic chant in Tamil that is one of Yogi Ramsuratkumar's old favorites, "Kurai

Ondrem Ille," which sings praises to Lord Krishna, saying (in brief):

> Because of You, I have no problems. My troubles are dissolved by Your presence. When You are close by me there is nothing I need. Behind the veils of maya resides Your all pervading presence. You have come down in the Kali Yuga to restore our faith. You exist forever as Keshava (Krishna). You answer all of our prayers, and our trust is in You. You are also our Mother who is with us always; when you are in our hearts, there is no need to worry. I am by my side forever, and You are my Marivanna, Maliappa, Govinda.

After a *pranam* to Kannon the song started, *"Kurai ondrem ille, marimoorty kaana."* The space grew more pregnant and rich as the complicated verses rang out. Kwong Roshi, his wife Shenyu and the senior monk stood with Lee. Everyone in the room was moved by the living presence of the deity—the divine embodiment of compassion. Her eyes were alive and radiant, her smile deep. When the last notes of the song faded, Roshi and Lee walked up to the statue and lit the candle, offered incense, bowed.

Afterward Roshi pulled a tiny, square card out of the shrine at her feet and called to one of the children, who walked over to him. "Do you remember this? You sent this to me six years ago when Kannon came to live here!" he said, bending down to the child. He laughed and said to the adults, "I know this is sentimental, but I can't help it! I've kept it all these years ... something about it ..." He shook his head as if it was all a marvel to him, then walked over and gently showed the card to the child. He said, "See? This is where you signed it!" She had been two years old at the time.

The group moved quickly over to the main house for lunch—an old farm house with a kitchen and large living room where a buffet table was set up with bean soup, garlic bread, salad and spice cake. When the twenty-five or thirty of us walked into the room there were already about twenty-five people eating or standing in line for food. Two small standing trays had been set up in front of chairs in the corner for Roshi and Lee. Someone had made plates for them. They came in and sat down to lunch; the rest of us stood in line.

Shortly after lunch Lee took off with the men—four of his students and one guest—for a special enzyme steam bath in cedar chips and then a massage, an outing that proved to be interesting for the men. They had difficulty with the directions on the winding back roads of Sonoma County, so that when they finally arrived in Sebastipol they were too late for the steam bath, but there was still time for the massage.

Lee said adamantly, "I don't want a massage if I can't get the steam bath. Forget it! But you all can go and get your massage if you want. I'll wait out here." The men stood there nonplussed, not sure what to do. They knew that someone, probably Shukyo who had arranged the appointment, would have to pay for the whole thing anyway. It was Saturday, and one couldn't just cancel at the last moment like that without some kind of charge. They were disappointed that their opportunity to spend this time with Lee had been peremptorily cut off, and they would have at least liked to have had the massage. It was very tempting, but they all decided to stick with Lee. They ended up going to a movie—a slapstick B-grade comedy—with him in Sebastipol that no one liked but Lee. He has said that few of his students like these kinds of movies because they are always looking for some message, some deep meaning in movies, instead of just relaxing and being entertained. In these dumb and totally meaningless movies that Lee so loves, there is no esoteric secret.

In the meantime the women drove into Sebastipol and sat in a cafe. We would all meet back up at five-thirty at Tayu Center, just a few miles away from Sebastipol, where Lee was being hosted by Rob Schmidt and Stuart Goodnick for a celebratory meal. After dinner Lee was scheduled to give a talk. Rob and Stuart had taken over directing Tayu Center—which offers studies in the Fourth Way—after their teacher, Robert Ennis, an old friend of Lee's, died six months ago.

The women arrived at the Tayu Center at five o'clock and found Lee sitting in the den, surrounded by artifacts. By six-thirty a group of about thirty people had gathered for dinner. There were ten or twelve people from Tayu Center there. They had cooked a turkey, made salad and contributed potluck style many other tasty dishes. Shukyo brought sparkling water and bags full of fresh crusty bread from the local bakery at the natural foods co-op in Sebastipol. Lee sat at the kitchen dining table with Rob and Stuart. He had made it clear to his students before dinner that he wanted Rob and Stuart to invite whomever they wanted to sit with them, so we took our plates to the den, where tablecloths had been laid out on the floor.

It's common when Lee travels that some of the people who interact with him may be unfamiliar with the formal protocol around a teacher, and as a result may blunder into situations that should be handled with more sensitivity. This was the case tonight as one person traveling with Lee—a guest and friend of the community—walked up and took the first empty seat at Lee's table without an invitation. Within minutes all the other seats were taken by invitation from Rob or Stuart. When this guest took a seat uninvited, Lee didn't correct him—as is his way. Of course, an opportunity might arise in which Lee would have the freedom to make a teaching lesson with him about it, but Lee's timing and sense of what is lawful in this regard is well known among his closest students. He would bide his time until the moment was exactly right, then deliver the goods.

Lee's students, on the other hand, are expected to work with this kind of dynamic with elegance and dignity, which didn't necessarily preclude making the teaching available by offering guidance to a guest in certain key situations. But this would best be done without any judgement or any charge against his lack of sensitivity to protocol—or the teaching lesson might just end up falling on Lee's student who attempted to interfere.

It's not uncommon for people who come around Lee to assume that—because Lee makes himself so accessible and prefers to keep everything ordinary in a warm and very human way—that they can just do anything they want. That includes touching him, being overly familiar, asking intrusive or snide questions, being casual, exhibiting idle curiosity about Lee's personal life, or blithely groping Lee like in any trite new age scene. Or taking seats near him when the unspoken but obvious protocol of the space demands a different configuration with Lee, his family and his students and/or hosts or guests. Sensitivity and humility are always the best approach to the teacher.

After dinner Lee waited patiently in the den while the dishes were cleared away and the kitchen cleaned. We went through double French doors into the large, almost empty living room that opened off of the den where Lee would give his talk. In this space, as in the house in general, there was a void where Robert Ennis would have been. Robert Ennis was a teacher who had reliable integrity and meant well for his students and those around him, and who had the ability to clearly and gently articulate the principles of Fourth Way work. In this and many other ways it seemed that Robert served the grand and far-reaching designs of the Work. For anyone who had known Tayu Center before Robert's death, the pain of the recent loss of the teacher would have been impossible to miss. The sense of loss was palpable. Rob and Stuart had placed two large posters in the gathering room—collages of pictures of Robert's life, beginning with baby pictures and ending with his days in the hospital and including a close-up of Robert's face in death, surrounded by flowers in the coffin just before the cremation.

Finally the talk began as Lee, Stuart and Rob took their places. There were three chairs set up next to a raised dais where a small picture of Robert Ennis was placed with a flower beside it. The three chairs were arranged to suggest that Robert's place was the dais, with Lee sitting in the chair next to the dais, then Rob, then Stuart.

Rob began by saying that they had titled the talk "Blossoms of Light: Generating Lucidity." He that enlightenment was not the issue or question but what was important was to generate more and more lucidity in one's life. From their point of view the idea of a sudden enlightenment or awakening was not the way things happened, but there was a process—a gradual clearing away of obstructions. He talked about the importance of self-observation and self-honesty, and he said that he felt an urgency to be extremely self-honest that night.

"The man sitting next to me," Rob gestured toward Lee, "is the most honest person I've ever known. On the book table out there are Lee's journals and they contain the most honest writing I've ever encountered. He reveals himself in those books, and I highly recommend them. So I feel especially urged to be as honest about myself and my own process here tonight as I can." He also talked about the death of Robert Ennis and the challenge that he and Stuart were facing, to pick up the mantle and carry on as directors of Tayu Center. After about a ten-minute introduction of this kind, he said he would like to turn the space into a question and answer format. He said, "You can ask any one of us—Lee, myself or Stuart—to answer your questions, or all three of us."

Immediately the girlfriend of the man who had taken the seat at dinner without an invitation raised her hand. She said to Lee, "Listening to you talk this week I've heard you say that you believe in sudden enlightenment—you say that there isn't really a process but that awakening happens in a moment. Would you speak to that?"

Lee's tone of voice was scathing but soft. "Do you really think that I would insult my hosts, who have offered us such *generous* hospitality, by talking in a way that would contradict everything that Rob just said? *No.*" Each word of this was articulated precisely, measured and deadly in effect. Lee paused, then went on. "The Law of Hospitality comes before anything else—the dharma, practice, anything. Do you know what I mean?" He peered at her, boring into her with eyes that appeared almost black with intensity. Rob and Stuart looked shocked but kept their cool. Rob looked down at the carpet, Stuart watched her. They both glanced quickly over at Lee. She was clearly the instantaneous sacrifice for a teaching lesson about how to be a good guest. The blunders of protocol and power-motivated aggression that she and her friend had demonstrated often during the past several days in spaces with Lee—including tonight at dinner, much to the chagrin of Lee's students—was cut through and deflated with one fell slice of Lee's sword. Her body reeled backward slightly with the shock of the invisible blow he dealt. It was a surprise and a supreme lesson for every person in the space. Lee continued, "If that is the *only* thing you learn this week, it will be worth it. You know what I mean?" I too felt the sting and discomfort of it, having been so full of judgement earlier in the evening over the seating episode at the table. She stared at him, dumbfounded.

"Do you know what I mean?" he pressed forward again. After a long pause, and with as much meekness as she could muster, she nodded and said yes.

"Good!" Lee gave her a lovely, very kind smile and went on to the next moment without a backward glance.

Rob said, "Any other questions?" Many questions were asked, a number of them about dealing with illness and pain, and how to have lucidity in the midst of that. Rob talked about a teaching lesson that Robert had made with him just hours before he died. Robert had been taking strong painkillers and medication the last days of his life, and Rob had developed some doubts as to Robert's lucidity—his ability to make clear decisions about things—because of the drugs. At one point Robert opened his eyes and said to Rob, "Do you really think that if I am who I have advertised myself to be with you all these years that these pain killers would interfere with my ability to be aware?" Rob said this was a tremendous teaching lesson for him, and one for which he was extremely grateful, because in that moment he saw that Robert *was* perfectly lucid.

Rob and Stuart and Lee had been taking turns answering questions for over an hour when someone asked Lee about his own awakening. "How did you do it?" a man asked.

In that moment Lee seemed to get bigger and taller without even moving. It was as if he expanded and brightened visibly. "How did I do it? I'll tell you how I did it. I hate pain. I avoid pain at all costs. Anything that causes me suffering, I get rid of it, I get out of it. I'm totally selfish. I go for *pleasure* instead of suffering. That's how I did it. If I'm in pain I say, 'Forget this!' and I go for the pleasure." His tone of voice whipped through the room, stinging and abrading dearly coveted illusions and pricking the mistaken interpretations of ancient teachings that one has to renounce all self-concerns to be an esthetic, a hermit, a dry, uninteresting fundamentalist bore. He was making anyone who truly wanted the teaching work hard for it, so that one had to discriminate and read between the lines.

The whole room seemed stunned. Lee went into a fierce tirade about how we all embrace, love and cling to our suffering. "We are total addicts," he said. He became animated and theatrical. "So you're in pain, it's killing you, your neurotic habits are killing you, but do you do anything about them? Nooo! Instead you clutch your suffering to you! You are walking along," he mimicked holding suffering like an object out in front of his face and gave it five or six resounding kisses, smacking his lips loudly for emphasis, then continued without skipping a beat, "with it in front of you like it was the most precious thing in the world to you!"

Rob and Stuart looked shocked at this point. People shifted in their seats. I was alternately alarmed at the bull's-eye hit going on in my solar plexus with each of the shotgun blasts in Lee's loud and grating, punctuated words, and simultaneously grinning from ear to ear at the pleasure of watching his complete mastery in the space. He had totally taken over the space and was blasting it with energy. Underlying the intensity of his outburst, in the midst of this wild show, the blessings were unquestionably pouring out. It was a felt sensation that permeated not just the physical space of the Tayu Center, but penetrated Robert Ennis' legacy and everyone connected to it.

After about thirty minutes of this high voltage blast, the night came to an end. Lee made a plug for his books on the book table, and as soon as the talk was over he went and stood beside the table, signing people's books. The small crowd responded by buying a lot of books. Rob and Stuart both thanked Lee warmly and sincerely for the gift he left with them, then Lee and the group piled in the van at eleven-fifteen and drove back to San Francisco in the rain.

January 17, 1999
San Francisco

On this morning, Sunday, Lee and company—about thirty people—went to Glide Memorial Church, an unorthodox, multicultural Methodist Church run by Cecil Williams, an African American minister who is a bit of a renegade. The church provides a focus for the community with lots of high-spirited gospel music and the many social programs that it runs. They also serve the community with a big soup kitchen that feeds the homeless. Lee sat up in the balcony with his students and friends around him and clapped to the music. There were some good moments in the music and the children who read poetry in praise of Dr. Martin Luther King, whose birthday was the next day. There is good work being done there, important work, but clearly not the work of radical personal transformation. Afterward Lee said, "It was alright, but I don't need to go there a second time."

The daily rhythm of ten o'clock brunches and early dinners rolled along. Sangha members worked hard to keep everything in order, washing piles of dishes, organizing and cleaning the small space to accommodate the large number. As many as thirty or forty people crammed into the small sitting room at Sahaj Mandir San Francisco for meals, most sitting on the floor. Lee sat on a pale pink, velvet love seat surrounded by flowers, his entourage and various guests. It was a perfect backdrop for the rampant jealousies and desire for more and more of his attention that were at times the undercurrent during the week.

Llewellyn Vaughan-Lee's comment to Lee's students about jealousy around the teacher had been perceptive. The predisposition toward a particular kind of loving attention that is intensely focused on the teacher can be both a strength and a significant pitfall or danger in one's sadhana. When it becomes a pitfall it has turned toward romanticism and false devotion. Lee has talked about false devotion and romantic projections on the guru as the pitfall of a devotional school many times. The spiritual path provides countless opportunities to purify the primal passions with which the *sadhika* or *sadhaka* must contend. These primal passions are underlying all life, and take a shadowy expression in self-centered, conventional and worldly notions.

Lee handles all this adulation, fascination and titillation as if it is no big deal. His skillful means in handling the issues of transference and romantic projections over long periods of years is beyond rational understanding, and yet he displays an adroit ability to work with students within this labyrinth. At the same time, he encourages the *gopis* and the *gopas*—women and men—with limpid glances, compassionate gazes, brilliant smiles, the golden glow of his very refined and sweet attention. The erotic moods or *bhavas* which he exudes at times drives those of the bhakti disposition slightly crazy. For the *gopis* or bhaktis, every one believes that he or she is the guru's queen, a tender lover or special friend. It is ego's aggrandizement of an objective transmission because, in fact, in the mythological story, every *gopi* felt that she was Lord Krishna's favorite. It is a way in which the guru reflects one of the facets of the Divine as a call or lure to the Beloved. In this way the guru will use any methods necessary to bring his devotes, students and disciples to the heart of God.

This phase of adulation and romantic projection is part of the process for new students, or for anyone who hasn't been asked to pay the price of the Work as yet. At the beginning of the path one naturally has no idea that one is being tricked into ruin by the all-attractive nature of the guru. In reality one is buying into a kind of enslavement and the total destruction of all identification with the illusory, separative self who wants to believe that it is somehow more special than all the others. We cannot imagine what we have gotten into until it is too late. One slowly begins to realize that one has become a servant, and not a queen, nobody instead of somebody. There is desolation and ruin in all this for the separative ego that wants to remain a special individual. Beyond that, there is the possibility of freedom from illusion, of true wholeness and an unfettered, sweeping, and selfless divine love. It is the transformation of base passions into *bhakti prema*, higher or transcendent love, in which sacrifice becomes the keynote. The road to this bright new morning, however, is fraught with almost unbearable pain and dangerous swamps. Even though freedom may be glimpsed even many times, it is still elusive. It takes great merit to find this land of freedom and infinite promise and live abidingly in the radiant emptiness of it.

Jealousy in particular can cause strife and discord among students, to the extent that it causes heartbreak and thwarts the teacher's ability to teach. The teacher often has to bear dissension and conflict between his students. Because a primary facet of the devotee's relationship with the guru is to provide sanctuary for the master, this is a crucial consideration. Through a mature understanding of the process of annihilation of the personal entity and self-effacement in love these passions are alchemized into longing. Lee's students, both new and old, are in a mighty struggle, a war of yes and no, in the attempt toward a yogic or wise relationship with these passions—this week "on the road" with Lee provided many opportunities to work in such a way.

January 18, 1999
San Francisco

Lee played bridge for hours today while some of his students went to Chinatown. Jai Ram, who had flown out from Colorado to spend this week in the Bay Area with Lee, was his partner; Nachama and I were their opponents. Lee was executing sweeping victories, winning game after game and rubber after rubber.

The game of bridge is considered a practice in the Hohm Community, and as such can be a powerful mirror in which one gets to see the desire to *win*—to dominate and control—and one's identification with success and failure. Myriad other manifestations of the cramp (a word Lee uses to define the primal knot of tension that arises from the illusion of separation) and the survival strategy show up within the play of the game, presenting ample opportunities to self-observe. This was the opportunity today. During this display of mastery Lee manifested a number of work principles which were directly aimed at a teaching demonstration for Jai Ram. It seemed at one point that Lee was actually giving empowerment to Jai Ram in what, at surface glance, seemed like a casual, ordinary circumstance. But then nothing is really casual with Lee. As he has said many times before, "The chamber is always happening. It's up to you to tune into it and work." Now as my team lost hand after hand I got to observe, in my growing frustration, the lust for power, control and domination, nicely juxtaposed with the teacher's hidden methods of transmission.

Everything that Jai Ram said, Lee agreed with, even when Lee had said something completely different on the subject a number of times before. This is one of the ways that Lee often works with his students—total support, empowerment, the offering of an all-embracing friendship, warm acceptance. In the meantime Lee was bidding wildly, conjuring and hoodwinking his way through impossible hands, playing heartlessly and without remorse upon my weaknesses and bad mood. After Lee had won yet another hand Jai Ram made a comment to me. "Haven't you learned to stop him at this after all these years?" he asked with feigned innocence.

"Oh yes, of course," I snapped back, "R. and I beat Lee at three no-trump at least fifty percent of the time . . . We've played together a lot."

Pointing toward Lee, Jai Ram added, pouring a liberal dash of salt on the wound, "Yeah, he's just scamming his way through most of this!"

"Yes, I know," I grumbled. "But what's really going on here is *abhisheka*."

A few people sat watching the game. Nicole asked what the word *abhisheka* meant. "It's a Buddhist term for spiritual empowerment," I responded. Part of how that empowerment was showing up was in grand and impossible victories for Lee and Jai Ram—ninety percent of those games being played by Lee, who demonstrated his tremendous skillful means and mastery in every aspect of a swiftly-flowing card chicanery. He wasn't cheating—Lee never cheats at cards, he doesn't have to. His bamboozling is at a much more subtle and skillful level—he plays the edges of reality, works with infinite possibility, wins against the odds. He relentlessly plays on his students' weaknesses in the crucible of bridge—leans on their weaknesses and pushes against the cramp. He capitalizes on his opponents' mistakes. It can be a painful process that makes the cramp that much more visible for self-observation, and it is a fabulous teaching tool.

All this was the teaching lesson of the chamber, and yet at the same time that Lee was empowering Jai Ram, it is very hard work to be Lee's partner because Lee will take the bid and play almost *all* of the hands, usually in three no-trump. Lee's partners have almost no room to move and very little to do other than to bid. One can easily begin to feel like nothing more than a stationary prop in Lee's play. What a great metaphor for the fact that we are not in any way in control in this process and that we are playing the guru's game, not our own. This is a very tough lesson to get, especially for someone who always runs his or her own show.

The group returned from Chinatown and the bridge game folded. Lee and his gang piled in the van and several cars and headed over to Berkeley. While waiting to meet with everyone for dinner at five o'clock, Lee checked out a couple of bookstores down the street from the restaurant. He bought five hardcover books from the fifty-cent shelves, most of them classics, and then handed them out as gifts to some of the people traveling with him while he was standing out on the street before dinner. After a lengthy, relaxed dinner—with thirty people crowded around Lee at a long table in the bustling, popular pizza joint—we made our way to the Berkeley Zen Center where Lee was scheduled to give a talk that night. We walked in the dark through dripping trees and a lush garden to the zendo behind the main house, where Lee waited for the evening meditation session to be over. Soon Karen, a long-time member of the zen center who was hosting Lee and company here this night, came out and led us to the gathering room and library in the house next door.

Right away Lee instructed his students to sit around the edges and in the back of the room, which was about eighteen by twenty-five feet. We sat on zafus and the two or three available chairs. Lee took his seat at the head of the room. A small bathroom was located directly off of this sitting room. Everyone filed in, one at a time, and made use of it, the loud flushing and gurgling seeming appropriately real in the growing silence. Outside rain dripped and dropped on lush leaves and grass, emerald green in the California winter, so different from the dry desert bones of Arizona. Tomorrow Lee would drive his van back to that desert sanctuary.

Lee sat in his chair at the front of the room for about ten or fifteen minutes before the talk began. A deep, almost meditative silence filled the room, broken only by the distribution of ceramic cups filled with mint tea that Karen passed out through the crowd. Lee broke the ice at one point with a joke about a genie in a bar. Peals of laughter broke out right away as the room continued to fill up beyond capacity with people. On one wall was a huge, very impressive oil painting of Suzuki Roshi. A person commented to his friend who was sitting just in front of me, "Maybe he'll talk about sex!" Once again, Lee's reputation preceded him. It got very quiet again. More people came pouring in and people shifted around to squeeze in together. The silence was relaxed and mingled with a feeling of anticipation. There were about sixty people in the room.

Karen introduced Lee and encouraged people to ask questions. Lee started out saying, "I like to answer questions, so I'll talk for awhile then open things up for questions. My style is often misunderstood. People get very insulted by my style, but don't take it personally if you feel the sting of it—it's just an accidental hit! I don't have anything against you. But then again you're all human beings and so I do have something against you—I have no patience with people whose practice is fallible, and that's *all* of us!"

These were very strong words. Lee was making good again on his wish to "wound" his reputation, but people sat still and took it. No one left the room, as many have on some occasions at Lee's public talks. He continued: "So you being Buddhists I may offend you because my lack of respect for people's basic goodness is bound to shine!"

Lee began to talk about the value of irritation in our lives. He said, "Irritation forces us to look beyond the stagnation of the moment." He told Kwong Roshi's story of the tea ceremony with the wife of Suzuki Roshi—whose lineage this Berkeley center is also affiliated with—and talked about how Kwong Roshi had recognized the value of being in pain during tea ceremony. Lee said, "Pain keeps us alert and provokes us toward greater clarity."

He answered several questions about the Baul path and touched on the yoga of sex and breath and the transformation of energy. Suddenly he was talking about the provocative occultist, Aleister Crowley. He said, "He was a pretty bright character. I admire Aleister Crowley. I think he really had something. One thing I liked about his school is that when he pushed people who were just satisfied to be machines he would yell out, 'Christians to the lions!' "

Lee spoke about how the mind dictates reality according to its bias. He said, "What we experience as reality is not reality! The mind creates a film over reality. And all this buzz about karma is one of the biggest excuses for shoddy lives in the New Age context today."

"I'd like to offend more of my students. They call me crazy-wise—I would never call myself that. I'd call myself a white, middle-class wannabe yogi. But you know how projections are! Once you get called crazy-wise then you can't do anything without it being written off with the label of crazy wisdom!"

Lee then went into a fast-paced monologue on men, women and relationship. He said that your lover knows you better than anyone else because in sex you become vulnerable. Suddenly he was talking about violence between men and women, speaking so fast it was impossible to really catch his words: ". . . . as long as you're not violent. But some women *like* violence . . . . Sex is better than violence but maybe violent sex is better than both!" Lee cracked up when this comment came out of his mouth. A small shock wave seemed to zip through the room. In moments like this everyone's moral stance is totally engaged. Was Lee endorsing sadism or abuse, or was he pointing at something rigid and repressive in the listener?

"Excuse me," he was holding his sides and laughing hysterically, practically weeping, "I was speaking so fast, you probably didn't understand a word I said! So, nobody knows you as well as your lover—not even your guru, especially if he or she is a false prophet!"

Afterward Lee talked with some people, then packed up the book table and drove a few blocks to Paul and Karen's house, where everyone crammed into their tiny living room. Lee sat in a chair with the group facing him. Paul and Karen served dessert and some wine that Lee had brought. There were a couple of guests who came and sat in front of Lee and asked questions which catalyzed a short, impromptu talk from him about the nature of radical surrender. He was asked why he started teaching and he said, "I had absolutely no choice, no choice at all." Around eleven o'clock we drove back to San Francisco. We would be leaving the Bay Area with Lee in the van at seven o'clock the next morning.

January 19, 1999
On the road

On the way home in the van Jane said to Lee, "Thinking back over the trip it seemed to me like there were very few really overt teaching lessons. Is that the way you saw it, or did I miss something?"

Lee said, "I guess that wasn't what was needed." He paused and seemed to be considering. Then in a louder voice he went into teaching mode, saying, "It's going to keep getting subtler and subtler. People don't get the gross teaching lessons, so why should I keep catering to such a lack of attention? It's just going to keep getting subtler, so those who really *need* the teaching, *more than their life,*" Lee emphasized the words strongly, "will be the ones who get it. People want to be creative, do their art, follow their bliss—all that crap. Fine. If they want the teaching they are going to have to look for it because it's going to get more and more hidden between the cracks. When they *need* the teaching more than anything, more than they need air to breathe, it will be there for them. It will be there for them *in spades*. That's what the teaching lesson of this trip was. People need to know that the Work doesn't come easily, that you just can't kind of skip along in the Work and follow your so-called heart, take a pottery class now and then and be awake."

January 22, 1999
Phoenix

On the drive down to the liars, gods & beggars gig at a biker bar in Phoenix tonight Lee talked about the double album that his blues band Shri is in the studio recording right now. Gesticulating behind the wheel, Lee was vivid and animated in his enthusiasm. He said, "This is going to be the peak of all of our musical projects to date!" He talked excitedly about the collaboration between the musicians and the many people who are participating in the project. He mentioned Justin, Doug and Stan from liars, gods & beggars, the horn section—Steve B., Jim C., Sylvan and Bill—the women's back-up chorus on "The Blues Is Alright." His exuberance was infectious. He concluded, "It's going to be incredible!"

As Lee drove through the desert twilight Clint, who was visiting from La Ferme de Jutreau, asked to hear more about Yogi Ramsuratkumar asking to have the lyrics and poems from *Death of a Dishonest Man* sung during Lee's recent visit. As the stories were told Lee added, "Yogi Ramsuratkumar was pointing out that we should know the songs of our tradition. We should be able to sing them. That means *all* of the liars, gods & beggars and Shri songs. I said that when we got back from India and we were telling stories, but no one took me seriously. No one is doing anything about it; it just seems impossible to us. But that's what Yogi Ramsuratkumar was telling us. We should know our own songs. The Sudama sisters probably know hundreds of songs and can sing any one of them that Yogi Ramsuratkumar asks for. It's the traditional way."

Lee's joyous remarks about the double album that Shri and friends are recording and his recurring comments about the teaching lesson that Yogi Ramsuratkumar made was another reminder of the tremendous importance of the music, lyrics and poetry in Lee's work and teaching. There are many times when Lee's students who have been deeply involved in the bands, their gigs and traveling tours and recording projects, would like to stop all the craziness of life on the road and just return to the sanctuary of an ordinary life of practice. Sometimes gig sadhana is like journeying in hell with the spiritual master. In comparison to the late nights in smoky bars, the hours and hours of time driving over sometimes lonesome back highways, the challenges of mingling with drunks and sometimes dangerous characters, staying home, taking care of children, working hard, maybe even getting to bed early every now and then can seem like heaven. But the tradition Lee is establishing is a Western Baul tradition, and bringing music, song and dance to the people are fundamental aspects of the Baul path.

As Lee pointed out, all of the Indian spiritual traditions include music. The poems of the great tantric poet Ramprasad Sen—often claimed by the Bauls as one of their own— were always sung to the same melody. There was no need of a constant search for better and more fascinating melodies; just the dharma and the power of vibration in the human voice. The poetry of the fifteenth century poet Mirabai is still sung today all over India; even small children can sing her devotional poems. The poems of the Sahajiyas and the Nath Siddha gurus were sung, passed down in an oral tradition of music and poetry. Out of this kind of ancient, sacred tradition Yogi Ramsuratkumar gave a significant empowerment to the lyrics of Lee's rock and blues songs during the 1998 visit. It seemed that he took a window that was open only a small crack and threw it wide open, leaving the future open-ended to possibility.

Music is interwoven with the destiny of Lee's teaching work and the lives of his students—whether it is devotional chanting in the meditation hall or the earthy *kheyala* of the "coyote poet" who, like a magician, has manifested—out of nothing—three bands that communicate the teaching through contemporary music. Now Lee's students have been asked to go more deeply into their own dharma music, to sing this music with intention, to embrace the nature of its transmission. This empowerment gives those who aren't in one of the bands the opportunity to enter into devotional or tantric practice in relationship to all this: to participate in the mandala by throwing oneself into gig life in whatever way sadhana calls for it; to enter into opportunities to dance to the music; to stay attuned to Lee with his bands, to listen to the tapes and CDs with purpose.

Driving through the desert into the Phoenix metro area on Interstate 17 in the deepening twilight, past the saguaro, cholla and ocotilla, the flowering red bougainvillea and the blossoming orange trees, Lee found his way into a commercial area just at the edge of a residential neighborhood. There he turned the big teal green van into the parking lot of the Steel Horse, a popular biker bar in north Phoenix. It was eight-fifteen and night had just fallen. In the harsh glare of the streetlights about forty Harley Davidson motorcycles could been seen parked in a row along the curb outside the bar, their chrome gleaming. It was a powerful image: they looked like metallic birds of prey that might take off for the hunt at any minute. As Lee's group of fourteen got out of the van and filed past a biker lounging on a motorcycle near the door of the club, the biker commented sarcastically, "What is this—the Mormon Tabernacle Choir?" Touché! Compared to the regulars of this club, there was no way our group wasn't going to stand out tonight like a Sunday school class from Omaha in a Calcutta opium den.

Walking into the large, smoky room we saw that the band was set up to play on the bare concrete floor where some room had been made for dancing. Three rows of long folding tables with a funky collection of miscellaneous chairs filled the rest of the room up to the crowded bar. People were talking, smoking and drinking like there was no tomorrow. There was a mood of ever-present tension in their actions, hidden beneath the well-kept personas of tough, cool, mean and together. The waitress, a young but already bitter woman with her gritty, rough face set in a permanent sneer, sassed around the tables taking orders, joking and laughing confidently with the clientele.

There were about one hundred fifty people in the two adjoining rooms of the club—the front room being the room for dancing and listening to the band and the back room being the room for standing and drinking seriously, playing pool or getting tattooed at any time of the night. Lee's group came in looking innocent and clean and sat together around one of the tables, ordered fruit juices and nonalcoholic beers. As we walked in several bikers turned to check Lee and the group out, then went back to their drinks and conversations. A subtle yet tangible flavor of fear could be felt flowing off of some of Lee's students. Surrounded by America's peculiar outcasts and hard-core misfits, the bikers, we were like a small flame flickering in the strong wind of this rough and dangerous place. These were down and dirty, ain't-afraid-of-dying men and women, almost all of them dressed in the unmistakable uniform of their peer group. One of the pre-requisites for being a real biker is that you have to ride a Harley, but you also have to dress in worn denim and black leather—leather pants, vests, jackets, driving gloves. And you carry concealed weapons and drugs.

The room and all its elements constituted a uniquely American stewpot of subculture. All around us were talking, drinking people who looked fierce and foreboding, even when laughing. Heavy make-up was smeared on ravaged female faces. Big hulking men with shoulders like bulls sat around glowering or sniggering with their buddies over double shots of whiskey with beer chasers, cigarettes streaming smoke into the air. Chains and keys jingled against black leather. The women all wore skin-tight jeans. They danced exactly alike in the style that can be seen in so many bars and clubs—hips rotating in small undulating circles, bending over to invite her partner to mount her in a theatrical play of sex. Very few can do this kind of dancing with any real élan or talent; usually it just looks vulgar and sad, a demonstration of misplaced braggadocio.

Between the bikers and regulars of the club and the Hohm Community group it was a strange mix of cultures. Usually Lee's students attempt to blend in with the local people wherever the bands play, but any attempt to blend in here was ridiculous; the best plan was to simply be respectful and stay out of the way. Nothing escaped the wary and sharp eyes of the bikers—certainly not this odd group that walked in from the "church van" with the leader singer of the band. How did they figure this small group of outsiders? From the beginning of the night the psychic agreement between the disparate groups— one of them a very small percentage of the crowd and the only people in the bar not drinking heavily—seemed to be, "You're weird and so are we." Sort of a black sheep variation on "live and let live." From the context of our shared weirdness, everyone got along fine. That is, as long as the outsiders in this situation were respectful.

As it turned out our waitress was named Brenda. She had brown hair done in corkscrew curls, sharp teeth and bad skin. Her eyes gleamed with a hungry look, but she was trim and sleek in her blue jeans, leather vest and tight red and black leotard. She was very good at her job. She rolled her eyes and ribbed our group in a way that was both harsh and playful when we ordered nonalcoholic beer and juice and club soda to drink.

"I don't go for this 'one day at a time' shit!" she snapped. "Come on guys! Look alive! Oh, another Virgin Mary? Whooppee! Wow—you guys are really gettin' wild now," she chided. Every time she passed the table she would add another comment, like, "You guys are falling asleep—wake up!" or, "You guys are really rockin' now! More pineapple juice?" Her voice dripped with playful scorn, if there is such a thing.

While waiting for the band to start playing the jukebox played a Bonnie Raitt classic blues number and then "Crossfire" by Stevie Ray Vaughn. Then an especially fine version of "Hoochie Koochie Man" came on. Lee sparked on it and talked about learning it with Shri. It was a perfect intro for the night. "Got my mojo working, got my John the Conqueror root . . . I'm the hoochie koochie man . . ."

Right after the song ended Lee went onstage to demonstrate the hoochie koochie attitude with style in the band's first set of the night. Tonight Lee's mood was not one of provocation, as it has been on so many nights performing with liars, gods & beggars. There was no need to provoke this audience; they were the provocation themselves, and Lee had their attention. Instead of irritating his audience through insult, he incited them by simply telling the truth, which was deadly enough. In this way he was devilishly sublime. During "Sympathy for the Devil," the third song of the night, Lee sang with subtle gestures that communicated the underlying message of the song and his context for it so perfectly that it seemed choreographed, and yet his communication was buoyant and spontaneous, compelling. The song worked its voodoo under Lee's spell and rocked along through the room like a rattlesnake on acid.

Lee accused his audience, "I shouted out, 'Who killed John Lennon,' when after all, it was you, you, *you!*" Then as the song came to an end Lee sort of growled at the crowd in a voice low and charged with purpose, "That's you and me baby! Yeaahh . . . we're *all* gonna die! We got to get it together!" Lee's preaching in this way was almost understated and soft, but pointed and tough in force. His performance was riveting, and many of the men in the crowd responded to his style and watched him intently. They seemed easily able to relate with him and his comments.

The crowd as a whole demonstrated their appreciation of the music with loud whoops, whistles and claps after each song. At other times their silent attention, riveted on the musicians, was like a fine wire vibrating with tension. The way the room was set up there was no separation between the stage and the audience. Not only was the band set up right on the dance floor, but people came and went, walking right past the microphones into the band's space, mingling easily. A tow-headed biker who had been dancing in black leather chaps stretched tight over faded blue jeans walked up to Lee and asked if the band would play some Marshal Tucker songs. Lee said, "Sorry, we don't know any."

The man said, "That's okay, you guys are great anyway." He shook hands with Lee and smiled, then walked away. Later Lee commented on how polite the bikers were, this man being a particular example of that. He said that, in fact, in comparison with some of the cowboys he had seen at many other clubs, the bikers were "elegant" in relationship to the band and the music.

Bikers are tightly knit within their own cultural milieu. They are very deeply bonded to each other within their groups, not through intellect, ideas or concepts, but through instinct, blood, guts, hardship and death. They have their own code of ethics, their own immutable and in some ways inscrutable laws—a certain honor among thieves. However vicious or violent or antisocial they are reputed to be, there is still an interesting paradox of opposites at play in their actions. This showed up also in the fact that no one bothered Lee's group or paid much attention to us at all, even when we got up and danced right alongside many different biker couples. In fact, the only harassment that came down was from the waitress, which was probably the way she related to everyone.

A blond woman got up and ran up to the band. She walked right into their space and started dancing and flirting in a jerky, pathetic kind of way. She stepped up to Everett, ogled Justin behind the drums in an attempt at seduction and then went over to Lee and said something. She could have been very attractive and even pretty, but her eyes glittered with insanity. She was also stone drunk. The bouncer came over and humorously, even gently, got her off the stage area. Then she stood on the dance floor talking to someone invisible, staggered around and went back to her table. Later during the night she came up to the stage again and hassled the band. Once again the bouncer—a tall, powerful and attractive man who looked like he could hold his own with anyone there—patiently pulled her away.

Our waitress came by and sat down beside us for a minute. She said facetiously, "You guys are gonna have to settle down . . ." She laughed. "I'm gonna have to start a prayer circle over here pretty soon . . ." Her arrows hit close to home in that uncanny psychic way that some people have of assessing their adversaries and going for the jugular. Her laughter was somewhere in the margin between sarcasm and begrudging acceptance. While she ridiculed under the guise of being friendly, Lee's students laughed along with her, playing along, taking her gibes good-naturedly. Regina gave her very big tips all night and a large extra tip at the end of the night, which kept her happy.

In the second set Lee sang a new song, "The Places I Haunt," a confrontive and demanding song with a powerful, crazy-wise twist on the mystery of the genuine guru:

You want my sympathy
You come to the wrong place
I ain't got no heart
I ain't got no face
If you find yourself asking
How to get to me
Just lay it on down
And do it reverently

Don't try to be sweet
Or you'll get caught
Don't flash your money
Cause I can't be bought
If you want my attention
Get ready to crawl
Cause I got it covered
Yeah, I got it all

Are you looking for love
What kind do you want
Variety's the spice
Of the place I haunt
Are you looking for peace
Of the world or mind
That's not my business
I left it all behind

Now if you can't beg
Well that's all right
But you better be getting
Clean out of my sight
Yes get out now
Fast as you can
Or your sleep be blessed
And your dreams be damned

Lee half yelled, half sang, half growled "I left it all behind," and instantly the guitars went into a wild clanging romp, as if we were careening through the bardos. Looking around at the noisy, partying crowd I wondered, who was *really* listening? Probably not the people who clapped and whistled after all the songs, but it didn't matter whether or not they knew what was going on; Lee was riding on the juice and power of the thick underworld energies that populated this place, and anyone who had the ability to could ride along.

The song seemed to reflect a certain convergence, a place of resonance between the "them and us" of the room that the band had experienced many times before playing in biker bars. One could learn a lot about the spiritual path by observing their abandon and the way they have "left it all behind." The bikers are, in fact, the kind of riffraff that Jesus might have embraced in his fiery love. One thing about the bikers is that they have rejected the common man's neurotic needs of conventional acceptance: here was something that could be learned, absorbed and used for sadhana. The bikers are marginalized in American society far beyond what most of the practitioners in Lee's company—outcasts and black sheep of a different variety—can imagine. They live on the edges of life, courting death and flirting with disaster. They are a weathered bunch of renegades with no hope, and yet there is something tremendously real in their acceptance of *what is*.

From the dance floor a big television set could be seen; it played throughout the night on its perch high up on the wall near the ceiling. At one point a message flashed on the screen in large red letters. It said, "It's hard being a pimp!" I looked back and forth from Lee to the message on the television and remembered when Lee had once called himself a "pimp for God." Lee stood singing at the mike, throwing himself to the wind, a puppet on God's string in this crazy *lila*. A worthier pimp for God the world has never seen—a pimp with an audience. Was it just a quirk of fate, or perhaps Yogi Ramsuratkumar's agents working overtime tonight to provide such charming little synchronicities? It was not a question that could be answered with the rational mind, if at all.

At this point the place was packed. There were probably two hundred people crowded into the two rooms of the club, most of them bikers and their women. People clapped and whooped after each song, tough-looking couples went up to dance. Another drunken woman stalked up to the stage and reeled and lurched from one musician to another in a parody of dirty dancing during Justin's drum solo. Finally the bouncer escorted her off the stage.

Somewhere between the first set and the rest of the night Lee went from devilish to divine, and in the process the murky darkness of this hellhole was turned into nectar. Spiritual practitioners danced along with bikers in a fine, high ecstasy out on the dance floor. It felt like the room and all of its inhabitants were being showered with light. Lee was harrowing hell, transforming the demonic into the angelic and beyond. He plowed into the darkness, dirt and toxicity and transmuted it. The outcome of that transformation was a long awaited feast, and a reminder of many nights with liars, gods & beggars in other places, in times past. It was a rare subtle food, the particular kind that liars, gods & beggars, with Lee in their midst, can produce. It is the result of a specific post or function that this band seems to have with Lee—the work of an established configuration, through years of bonding and Lee's careful cultivation.

During the last set some of the local biker club members came in flaunting their colors, looking bad, brooding and skulking around. The atmosphere in the club darkened with this element added to the stew. One of them wore a WW I German helmet with a swastika on it, black leather pants and a black leather vest that stretched over the bulging muscles of his arms and his big belly. His black leather driving gloves had one-inch steel spikes protruding across the knuckles. He had handcuffs hanging from the back of his belt, a Confederate flag patch on his sleeve, black and threatening tattoos on his arms.

We took to the floor in front of the band and danced right alongside this self-avowed racist and fascist. Standing next to him the question arose: what was he anyway, but a perfect living symbol of everyone's worst demons? A walking unconscious demonstration of the same primal passions that, through this Work, one seeks to transform into Buddha nature. The ecstasy of Lee's transmission had rendered everyone there into equals. We were transported in the music, in the heat and sweat of the dancing, and we couldn't stop. The rain of light subsumed us all, fell on us all. Lee smiled brightly from the stage, danced around with tambourine in hand, jingling and shaking it up. During the whole last set Lee seemed happy, free—a marvelous sight. It seemed we had followed his madcap flight through the bardos on this night, and now we were adrift in a sea of open-eyed ecstasy. Yogi Ramsuratkumar and his son Lee were the victors in this place and time. As soon as the last song was over, Lee walked out and drove the two hours back to the ashram with his students, easy, exuberant and full.

January 23, 1999
Phoenix

Tonight Lee drove again to the Steel Horse with a smaller group of seven people. This time the club was much more sparsely populated with the same leather-clad, heavily tattooed bikers and their ladies, but the atmosphere was subdued compared with the night before. As we sat down at the same table our waitress, Brenda, came up.

"Ohhh no!" she camped it up, scoffing a little but laughing too, "You guys are gonna have to *settle down* tonight!" We laughed at her joke, expecting it.

The band started playing. After five or six songs a number of us got up and danced, but it was painful. Every move felt jerky, distorted, constrained, as if I was bumping into some invisible wall. Something tangible was in the way—but what? The subtle atmosphere felt oppressive. There was a strong self-consciousness present in our group that hadn't been there the night before. We looked and felt like a bunch of lily-white kids with no rhythm out there on the floor. Two biker couples sat at the front table next to ours and watched dispassionately. Their gloomy eyes bored holes through the dancers, especially those of the big, powerful man with the long gray grizzled beard. Most of the crowd was either getting drunk at the bar, or standing around talking or playing pool in the back room. A few brave souls danced in the almost empty front room that gaped darkly like a chasm set against the noise and frenetic activity of the people gathered in the back room. No one else in the club was paying any attention at all.

The night moved along with the biker couples at the table in front alternately sitting and staring like stones at the band and dancers, or at the television. The rest of the people in the place were self-absorbed in drunken talk. It seemed that those of us who had come with Lee were alone in a little bubble with the band. It was taking a lot of concentration and energy just to stay afloat tonight.

Lee came to sit at our table during the break. "It feels like the entities are fighting back tonight," someone commented. "Perhaps we tricked them last night . . . Tonight they seem to be winning the war." Lee was silent. Everett walked past the table, unaware of what had just been said, and commented, "Weird night." It seemed like there were obstacles at every turn. The D string on Everett's bass had broken in the first set, batteries went out on equipment and Steve had problems with his organ. Even Doug's guitar was out of tune, something that almost never happens.

In the last set Lee started making provocative comments, something he hadn't done at all on Friday night or earlier this night. Insulting this audience seemed like a dangerous game to play, but no one moved or seemed to take offense. Lee has said that there usually has to be a sacrifice in order for an alchemical chamber to be catalyzed, or to move to the next level of possibility. With the band, that sacrifice has at times shown up in absurd or provocative behavior on Lee's part. Tonight he seemed to be throwing caution to the wind as his stinging remarks over the mike escalated. Whatever Lee was doing, it seemed to shift the room in a totally different direction. Suddenly our whole group was roused and activated by the music in a way that hadn't happened all night. A number of biker couples got up and danced, including the man who had stared all night, and lingered out on the floor in between songs to see what would come next.

Something in the atmosphere had changed, and for the last four songs the whole space was flying again. It was a tangible breakthrough. What had before felt like walking through sticky molasses or running on shards of broken glass was now liquid, smooth and ecstatic. By the end of the night everyone had brightened up. The mood of enjoyment had returned. Flushed from the dancing and the high of the music at the end of a delirious last song, "Just A Woman," we stood out on the dance floor and heard Lee say into the mike, "Thank you. You made my night." Who was he talking to? His words rang with genuine gratitude.

Afterward, on the way out to the van someone said, "Well, we won in the end!"

Lee said, "The music did it."

January 24, 1999
Arizona Ashram

The intensity of the gigs of the past weekend brought up again a consideration of the context of Lee's bands. Writing lyrics and performing music with the Hohm Community bands has captured Lee's time and attention for over a decade. Many people, including some of Lee's friends and students, have wondered, "Why rock & roll? What place do performing bands have in a spiritual school?" And yet, ten years ago Lee made the statement, "There are two ways to access me now: through darshan (the traditional approach to the guru), or through the bands." It was a controversial statement that, at the inception of LGB twelve years ago, led to some in-depth investigation of the world of theatre, entertainment, music and dance. The trail led rather quickly to the ancient shamans—the original entertainers who used drums, music, singing and dancing, as well as magic, theatre, laughter and sleight of hand, to induce ecstatic states of consciousness in the tribe. In the ecstatic abandon of singing, dancing and drumming a state of deep rapport was established between the shaman and the tribe, in which the shaman was able to transmit or communicate the spiritual context with which he or she was working. This centered around the gathering of focused spiritual power for the purposes of transformation, and developing relationships with particular deities or powerful higher entities. This is, in part, exactly what happens, on a good night, between Lee and his audience and the band.

In the tribal context it was the shaman's job to heal sickness, recover souls, generate fertility, conduct the dead through the underworld, deal with mischievous, malicious or troublesome spirits and entities, and facilitate change or transformation within the cultural milieu and consciousness of the tribe. The power that was generated could then be applied at the most mundane level toward quelling a fever or insuring a good harvest, but at the esoteric level the shaman's job was to heal the human condition and serve the evolution of consciousness. The shaman lived consciously in a multidimensional reality, but most importantly, the shaman was the representative of the sacred for his or her people. The tribe came to the shaman's "show" not only to be helped, relieved or to feel good, but to participate in a religious mystery.

The religious mystery at the core of shamanism is a process of transformation or healing that involves an intimate knowledge of the general human problem. The shaman had first-hand knowledge of the condition of soul-loss, which from the shamanistic worldview is the fundamental condition of all sickness—physical, emotional or mental. As Rogan Taylor commented in his book, *The Death and Resurrection Show*, "Everybody is sick, and in the shaman's healing séance, *everybody gets better . . .*" (p. 41) "The power to heal, such a ubiquitous possession of holy men, has been of profound importance in the development of all religious traditions, and it underlines the significance of the ancient shamans." (p. 36)

According to Taylor the essence of all religious enterprise, which has its roots in shamanism, is the magic of change. "Religion is a tool for both surviving and accomplishing transformation." (p. 36) Mircea Eliade argued, "[T]he specific element of shamanism is not the incorporation of spirits by the shamans but the ecstasy provoked by the ascension to the sky or by the descent to hell." (in Bowker, p. 884) Ecstasy and change are inextricably linked together because transformation and change are ecstatic events. Ecstasy has the power to completely overthrow the status quo of the mind/body system at any moment in which it erupts from its primal sources. Ecstasy takes us outside of our frozen and limited identity in a momentary release or burst of life. The experience of bodily ecstasy can be blissful, but on the other hand it can be terrifying or exquisitely painful—as in childbirth or the ecstatic reveries of St. Teresa of Avila. It is an experience of incarnation. It is not something that is produced by the mind, or through intellectual consideration or reasoning. It is induced through the activities of the body—in dance, music, sex, relationship, in nature, and in birth and death. These primal experiences of life in the body are permeated by, saturated with, and in fact exist as, the pure and innocent energy of ecstasy, or the Primacy of Natural Ecstasy as Lee has called it.

All this relates to a basic teaching which Lee has given in the phrase Organic Innocence. The Primacy of Natural Ecstasy is the tacit outpouring of Organic Innocence, which is the underlying mood of all creation. This is a quintessential Sahajiya understanding that was adopted very successfully by the Bauls of Bengal, in which the Supreme Reality is discovered in the *sahaja* state—the natural and spontaneous ecstasy and wise innocence which is found at the core of incarnation. From this perspective the body is a tangent point with the Divine; it is the tantric way, in which there is no separation between matter and spirit.

Westerners have to work extra hard to get to this natural ecstasy in the body, and that is one area in which Lee's bands play an important role in Baul sadhana. The transmission that is made onstage both by Lee and the music opens up the possibility for transformation in the body. The deeper you go into the body, the more deeply you connect with the pulse of life, the original spark of ecstasy that emanates from the Divine. Music comes from the body in melody, harmony and song; we build instruments as extensions of the human voice then plug them into electricity to multiply the energy by hundreds of thousands of times and call it rock & roll. It is still shamanism, dressed in new clothes, and a lot louder. In these band performances Lee's students find themselves enacting an ecstatic religious rite whose roots are in antiquity, but that has continued to carry the evolutionary urge of transformation across time and culture, taking such myriad and diverse forms as the indigenous music of the Bauls, the haunting melodies of the Celts, or the African American blues with its soul-child, rock & roll.

January 26, 1999
Arizona Ashram

Every Tuesday and Thursday night when Lee is not traveling he makes dinner—fruit salad and vegetable salad—for ashram residents, students who live in the Prescott area and occasional visiting friends. Everyone gathers in the long, narrow "greenhouse"—a loose appellation for an enclosed, porch-like structure that was added on to the main building outside the office years ago. It has never actually been used as a greenhouse but for many other activities—cleaning glass cases, large group meals (as many as seventy-five people have been squeezed into it), a gathering and meeting place and so on. After dinner Lee meets with everyone in the meditation hall and gives an After Dinner Talk, which invariably begins with Lee's query, "Any questions?" These talks have, over the years, been informal teaching spaces where students often dialogue with Lee. When questions are not forthcoming or have all been addressed, Lee then reads excerpts that he has chosen to share from his personal study, which is vast and formidable. Lee is an avid reader who whips through an incredible amount of reading material every week, from a wide range of magazines and spiritual periodicals to books including biographies and many dharma tomes.

Tonight Lee had been reading from *The Wheel of Time* by Carlos Castaneda, and then commenting on the reading. Now he picked up *Boyhood With Gurdjieff* by Fritz Peters and started out in a playful, intimate tone with his thirty-five or so students who were sitting with him in the meditation hall on this winter night. It took a few moments for the group to catch his drift as he started out, then things very quickly went from silly and inane to funny to hilarious as Lee the jester regaled his students with crazy anecdotes and bawdy commentary.

Lee said, "This is from *Boyhood With Gurdjieff*. A lot of you have read this. This is about sex, sex, *sex!* You know what they say in India, where the body is nothing but a pod of pus and blood. Well, in sex, you get the shit on the *outside*—you get all excited and just start *oozing* all over! Unhh!

"Anyway . . . I hope it's going well for you, that you have lots of sex and it's okay . . . But make sure to wash your fingernails and cuticles before you have sex, so when you scratch your partner you don't infect them! And if you're not with a partner you are *supposed* to be with, don't let them scratch you, or you're in trouble!" Lee went into a theatrical dramatization of a conversation between mates, going back and forth from one side of the conversation to the other.

" 'Where'd you get that?' 'I, you know, scraped myself on a shelf at work.' 'Mm, hmmm. Four nice, neat parallel marks. Wow, that must be an interesting shelf.' " Lee laughed at himself as the group began to catch his mood and laughter broke out around the room.

"I'm sure at all the seminars that Sian has at her hotel in France she hears lots of stories like that. You know, the French aren't into anything as straight as just scratching one's partner in a moment of passion. The French are into things far more perverse.

"Did you ever do this? I've had this experience. You know, you go out with a girl— maybe some of you guys are more experienced than this—and you're trying to impress her and you take her out for a fine dinner. You're having a conversation, it's going well, and then things start to get more intimate, it's obvious that she wants to have sex and you say, 'Would you like to make love?' She gives you a look and you say to yourself, 'Oh, shit. That's it.' Her voice turns to icicles and she says, 'No thank you.' Then every time you call she says, 'Oh sorry, I'm busy tonight, but thanks anyway.' Click. What could be worse than 'making love' except not making love? Yeah, it's *sex*—that's the thing. Okay. Now I'm going to read this thing!" People were still laughing as Lee gestured with the book he held in his hand.

"This is from *Boyhood with Gurdjieff*, Fritz Peters," he started again. "It's a good thing we're talking about sex! Okay, this is from Peters here." More laughter broke out. Lee was in a tremendously expansive mood. He was laughing, his students were all laughing, the space was very warm and bright.

"Yeah," he continued, on a roll, "Peter must have been on the fritz, that's probably . . ."

Lee's words were drowned out in the raucous laughter that erupted, but he kept on rolling along. "He sort of went crazy later on in life, turned against Gurdjieff, and actually wrote vicious attacks on Gurdjieff about his time at the Prieuré. The story is that he really had some very severe psychological difficulties. That's one of the things that made Gurdjieff laugh in his grave instead of turn over, because once somebody turns back on you and has difficulties—boy that's great!"

At this point one could ask what is great about someone turning "back on you" and having difficulties. What did Lee mean? Perhaps he was referring to a particular principle, one that he employs constantly in his teaching work, and especially when he gives public talks: the principle of introducing a kind of discomfort or irritant that compels one to consider deeply, to investigate, inquire and study in pursuit of some kind of resolution to the irritation. This kind of compulsion induced by an irritant can lead one to revelatory insight that is invaluable to the spiritual path. For many people it can be the thing that leads them to the path. For others already on the path it can provide a shock as well as an irritant, but can be exactly the element needed to move one to the next level of work. In this particular case, for someone who was at one time close with the teacher to viciously attack the teacher creates an opportunity for others to work by introducing a seed of discomfort, a nagging question, a healthy doubt. It is only through the confrontation of our illusions, including and especially those in relationship to the teacher, that we can become clear-eyed on the path, and in this way it is these kinds of irritants that can become pearls of wisdom in the course of sadhana. Lee continued, picking up the book and reading:

> In the primary sense, the purpose of sex was reproduction, which was actually only a synonym for creation. Love, therefore, in any sense—whether physical or not—had to be creative. He also said that there was a proper form of what might be called "sublimation" of sexual energy; that sex was the source of all energy and when not used reproductively could still be used in an equally creative sense when sublimated and used as energy for other types of creativity. (p. 166)

Lee commented, "So, it's probably obvious, but, if you're genitally fixated you can't sublimate sexual energy and use it for other purposes. To be able to sublimate sexual energy and use it for other purposes your attention has to be more free-floating. Not that it doesn't randomly go to the genitals, but if you are obsessed or fixated on the genitals, man or woman—genitals meaning any erogenous zone, and any kind of fixation or fetish, oral fixation, feet fixation, breast fixation—then you can't sublimate and use sexual energy because all that energy gets devoured by your fixation. So your attention has to be free in a way that sex becomes something that you enjoy for what it is, in the same way that you would enjoy a fine piece of music, or a well-prepared dinner, a conversation, good company, or whatever the case might be. Quote: 'One of the misuses of sex that had arisen through bad training, the wrong type of education, and improper habits, was that it had become almost the only vital form of human communication.' (p. 166)

"Some of you," Lee commented, "probably have experienced this: you're in relationship a year, two years, three years, five years, twenty years, and all of a sudden the woman starts saying to the man, 'The only time we are ever intimate is during sex. That's not enough for me. We only have sex twice a month (or once a week or whatever it is) and we're never intimate any other time. The only time *you*,' she points to the man, 'are ever intimate with me is when *you* want sex!' Anybody here ever experience that? Don't raise

144

your hand!" Lee laughed heartily. He seemed to be getting a big kick out of the subject matter; it was the kind of laugh that seemed to be sparked from so much insight into the ridiculousness of human illusion—the grasping and craving that particularly shows up in sexual relationship and is based entirely on the illusion of separation—that it was at the same time ironic and free. He continued:

"So, that *is* something that happens, usually from the woman to the man, although under very unusual circumstances it might come from the man to the woman. We get so unable to bring balance to our lives that when we meet one another there is not a sense of real connection. It's not a matter of how much someone works, it's not a matter of a man working sixty or seventy hours a week. It's that when we *meet* one another, if we're *speeding* along we're not able to recognize, 'That was work, this is relationship.' Then it's very difficult to be intimate. As you all know, if we're *speeding* with something—whether it's worry about finances or regular job considerations, or an interpersonal relationship that isn't working with someone, you are mentally distracted and therefore physically absent, whatever it is—then it's very difficult to be intimate with your partner or with a friend.

"Intimacy is not just between partners, it's with children, with parents, aunts, uncles, sisters, brothers, friends, and so on. Intimacy is a function of a willingness to be who you are with that person. And if we are obsessed with something that is drawing all our energy, how can we be who we are? Some of us find it very difficult to be who we are anyway, and even in sex we are only who we are for maybe a few minutes. But most people feel that any intimacy, even a few minutes of intimacy, is better than none. A lot of relationships will go for years before someone will finally get frustrated enough to say that several minutes of intimacy in sex is not enough.

"We should be able to be intimate sitting at the dinner table talking, or just in a loving look when you see one another during the day. Again, this is not just between mates. A loving look is enough to communicate tremendous intimacy. I'm not suggesting you have to sit down, talk everything out, you know. That's some people's idea of intimacy—'Okay, we're going to take two hours, we're going to sit down for two hours tonight, we're going to get childcare, we're going to go out and talk.' But intimacy can happen in a glance across a room, in a fraction of a second. Where *you* are in relationship to where the *other* person is, that's what creates intimacy, not how much time you spend together and what you're saying. It's who you are when you are being with that person.

"This is a story I've told many times. As a child I was tremendously reticent to touch people. Even as a teenager I wanted to date girls and hold hands, but that's pretty much as far as I got most of my teenage years—holding hands and an occasional peck. I wanted that as well, but it was actually sex I wanted. I didn't really want intimacy or touch. Anybody that's talked to my mother about my childhood knows all my aunts used to come and try to hug me and kiss me and I'd turn my head or run away. It was not something I was particularly moved toward.

"At one point I was training to be a Silva Mind Control instructor. It was all these super salesmen and me and C.M. and this other guy who'd been kicked out of the Marines for dealing acid, and—gosh, poor Marines, I bet they missed him, but I'm sure they just found another connection the day he left, the armed services being what they are! This was on the border of Mexico. Nuevo Laredo was the Mexican city and we were in Laredo, Texas. We'd go into the café in the Holiday Inn and sit there and nobody would wait on us. The waiters would not come and wait on us, until a couple of the super salesmen came in and sat down with us, and then they'd take our order along with theirs. So, as the week was going on (it was a two week program) we were feeling pretty stressed, and the head guy up in the East Coast at the time, Tim Harvey, came over and just put his hand on my shoulder and stood there. He didn't say anything—just put his hand on my shoulder and left it there for a few minutes. Then he said, 'It'll be great to work with you when you get back up to New Jersey. Anything you need, I'm always available.' And then he walked away.

"I'll never forget that, because that physical contact totally shifted something for me. He just caught me in a moment of vulnerability when I was feeling like I didn't belong there. That gesture was true intimacy. But when I was first having sex, when I was nine-teen, twenty, twenty-one, I didn't have that kind of intimacy in sex. It was all groping and satisfying myself. There was some good groping, but still it was just groping. Every once in a while a woman was satisfied . . ." There was a brief pause and the silence of ardent listening filled the immediate void. Then Lee continued in a humorous tone. "Not very often, but there were those rare moments! Ain't life great? There's so much to laugh about—so much to cry about too!" Lee laughed at himself, and at the human condition. "Yes, balance is important," he concluded.

Implied in moments of this evening's comedy routine was a whole range of teaching in the marvelous potential that human beings have in the domain of intimacy. These possibilities span the scope from moments of deeply human tenderness—with a child, with a lover, with an aging or dying person—to the full play of spiritual evolution through the transformation of sexual energy in the mystical union between human partners, where ordinary selfish love and desire is transmuted into transcendent love and longing for the Divine.

While Lee works with the mind in one way—through humor, irony, paradox—there is also a tangible compassion that permeates his *felt* communication. Tonight everyone in the room laughed along, re-living similar memories. In the course of his almost mundane approach to instruction—sort of an "Introduction to Conscious Sex 101"—he used him-self as the foil to take his listeners into their human foibles, into some of the most embar-rassing or humiliating moments, into biases and repressions. In the process he reframed them with an easy acceptance, a spaciousness, an ordinariness that cut through the shame, fascination and fixation which usually characterizes the Western attitude about sex. He gave us total permission to accept ourselves as we are—to drop the act and just be simple and direct about what is—or what was.

He continued: "Now with the whole technological revolution, what people call inti-macy is using risqué language on the Internet. Of course what people say to each other face to face is criminal, absolutely devastating. But when the people who consciously know what they're doing, who are creating this whole technological problem, get to the pearly gates, they're not going to get in. They are going to have to do some *tapas* to pay this off, because this is absolutely criminal, what's being done to the human race by tech-nology. And we're so stupid we don't even know what's being done to us. We're like these creatures with this reverse IV that's sucking out every last bit of life force and blood and vital fluid and we don't even know it. We have no idea! We just go along, blissfully happy to be destroyed, to be killed, to be slaughtered. We are like deaf cows in the slaughter-house yard—we can't hear the cries of the cows being slaughtered inside the house. We just chew on our cud, hanging around, happy to be with the other cows, until one day the hammer hits us on the head. That's it—that's exactly what we are like. We are totally unwilling to open our eyes and see it coming. By *we* I mean, societally. *You*, of course, are the exception!" Lee grinned at his students, who sat watching him in various degrees of comprehension. His voice was lightly tinged with sarcasm. What he said was almost drowned out by people laughing. Perhap if the hardcore truth of his words really hit home the reaction would be sobriety, sadness, horror. He picked up *Boyhood With Gurdjieff* and began to read again.

> It was possible for people to "join actively" in other ways than physically; to, as he [Gurdjieff] put it, "touch each other's essences," but human beings had lost this faculty many, many years—many centuries—ago. If one was observant, however, it was possible to realize that this "touching of essences" still occasionally took place between two individual human beings, but only by accident, and that it was then almost immediately misunderstood and misinterpreted and descended into a purely physical form which became valueless once it had been expended. (p. 166)

Lee commented, "Another conflict between men and women is that a man and woman may love one another, or whatever it is, and they're hanging out together and this space of intimacy arises. And the *first* thing the man wants to do is grab the woman's breasts, or something like that, or start licking her neck or smelling her hair or some other part of her body, and what the woman wants is intimacy. So the woman is feeling like, 'Oh, this is beautiful,' and all of a sudden the man is bush-diving or something."

More hilarious laughter broke out as Lee looked innocently around the room. "Isn't that what they call it any more? Am I showing my age? That's what they called it when I was in high school. I had a friend that—*never mind*!" The laughter became even louder and looser.

"No, but this could be important. I had a friend who actually thought it smelled *bad* down there. Can you imagine? No, *you* can't imagine, of course. I hope none of the men in *this* room can imagine that. Woah, was *he* unenlightened! Well, he had no girlfriend. Whenever we'd go to philately conventions together he would hire whores. That's the only way he enjoyed sex, because you know women . . . after you've known them a while, if you don't like it down there they don't give a shit about your sensitivity. When they're in heat, you think your neck muscles are stronger than their arms? No way, baby! You better do your duty or they'll break your neck." He looked out at the room, his face deadpan. Outbursts of laughter, loud guffaws, chuckles and general merriment bounced around the room. Hilarity reigned supreme. He asked in mock seriousness, "Is this what Gurdjieff was talking about?"

By now Lee was laughing too and obviously finding it difficult to stop—it was great to see him cracking himself up like this. His mirth was highly infectious. He seemed to be priming his audience, preparing us for something as he lead the pack on, weaving through this labyrinth of first and second chakra business, going fast and helter-skelter, almost careening through the twists and turns of his own spontaneous ride. And yet Lee's instinct was unerring, always right on target, as he hit the mark again and again in ways that worked the underworld of everyone in the room. Lee laughed so hard at his own outrageousness that he now wiped tears from his eyes as he continued.

"I thought it was funny anyway. Now *my* eyes are full of tears! You should be laughing like this together when you're having sex—not every time you try, or you'll never have sex, there would be no children in the world if you laughed like this every time you tried to have sex! It's very healthy for relationship. I mean, you should be laughing *together*—you know what I mean. You should be laughing like this *together*. Usually one

147

person starts laughing just at the wrong time. The other person is like, *Bang!* 'Hey, why are you laughing at me?' A lot of black eyes, sore emotions and limp dicks happen from such things.

"So, as you all know, a moment of touching essence is very easily misunderstood. I'm sure there are times when artists are so possessed by their art—writers, painters, a sculptor, a musician, whatever—that they are able to create a mood of intimacy through their art. When that happens they are really being fed by the exposure of essence that has occurred in the space, but it is very misunderstood. So they're looking so radiant that someone of the opposite sex, or the same sex depending upon the circumstance, will approach them and hit on them sexually. They get totally annoyed because what they are being fed by, and what's creating this radiance in them, is the communion of essences with objective reality. It's very easily misunderstood because it's tremendously erotic and sensual and hot and raw. When essence is exposed it's very primal and very archaic, in a sense. You know, we're tempted by that kind of vision, however we have it.

"One of the things Gurdjieff was attempting to instill in people is a training, an education, to understand the distinction between sex as an act of personality—which can be wonderful and pleasurable and a source of profound intimacy—and sex as transformative and alchemical. Sex can be a real doorway into many elements of tantric work. It's not impossible to enter through other doors, but it's less likely. It's more likely in sex just because of our relationship to sex—our psychological relationship to it, our physical relationship to it.

"So there's all that, and then there's what is actually, technically happening. What is actually, technically happening when transformation and alchemy are touched is the communion of essence between the two people. So the act of sex itself is a way to actually fool the ego into allowing this communion of essences. It is completely unconscious, but that's what it does. Ego says something like, 'Oh, they're just having sex now. I'm gonna plan how I'm gonna manipulate everybody at the office tomorrow or how I'm gonna dominate my circumstance tomorrow.' And then, by accident, while ego is busy making plans and two people are having sex, there's this essence vulnerability that occurs.

"It's often scary to encounter essence. Sometimes it's exciting, erotic, thrilling; sometimes it's scary, terrifying. Because when you see someone in essence you may look at your partner and they may look like a monster, or they may look so overwhelming that you're terrified. So, that's one of the things that over time this work attempts to instill in people: the ability to technically or mechanically understand what is happening when there's an awareness of a particular kind of space. So you can say, 'Oh, wait a minute. This is essence exposed.' But usually as soon as you say that—boom!—that's the end. But you can have a sense, 'This is essence I'm perceiving.'

"Somebody just wrote me and asked what they should do when something uncomfortable comes up, should they intensify their will and manage it or do something else. And the answer was, don't do anything, just let it unfold as it will. We need to be able to recognize those spaces so we allow them to produce in us the urge toward transformation—whether it is transcendence, serving the Work, union with God, however we language it—because those spaces are of pure Creation.

"Werner Erhard used the term 'invention.' He said the only way *real* creation happens is out of *nothing*. He says that you can't create out of something because anything that comes out of something is already there. The only way real creation happens, which is called invention, is out of nothing. Werner was talking about exactly the same thing, except he put it in non-mystical, non-spiritual, plain language—very much to his credit. And brilliantly, I might add. This space of essence exposure is exactly what Werner was talking about. And it is a very pure, delicate space. So we want to be able to think in terms of transformation in all circumstances, instead of saying, 'Oh boy! Sex was great tonight!' You know, '*my* pleasure, *my* profit, *my* . . .' Because when we think *that* way, then when we see essence exposed all we think of is, 'How can I use this for my pleasure? My profit? How can I shut this down so I don't ever have to see it again?' Whereas, when we are thinking in terms of transformation we see that as a profound opportunity, rather than something that's dangerous, threatening, terrifying or profitable to ego."

Lee picked up *Boyhood With Gurdjieff* again and started to read: " 'In talking further about relations between individuals he said that sex, again, was the "highest expression of the physical body," and the only "holy" expression of self that was left to us.' (p. 166)

"So, think about that," Lee commented. "Maybe there were things that Gurdjieff would have spoken of differently had he lived another twenty or thirty years. Fritz Peters was with Gurdjieff in the 1930s, so Gurdjieff had been working and teaching for a long time and had come to many of the conclusions he had drawn based on a lifetime of experience. So Gurdjieff said that sex was the only holy expression of self that was left to us. What would you call a holy expression of self? Prayer? Prayer is the expression that comes to mind. So, if you want to learn to pray properly, where do you think you are most likely to learn to pray? On your knees in a church? Or on your knees in front of your partner?"

People were listening and smiling broadly as the teaching took a sublime turn. The mood was quickly changing as Lee continued in this new vein. "Wasn't that an obvious extension? If you want to learn how to pray, and sex is the only holy manifestation left to us, then where do you learn how to pray? In sex. Gurdjieff didn't say it is the *only* holy manifestation; he said it is the only holy manifestation left to us in the modern world. And what do you do with that prayer when you get it? Obviously you take it outside of the act of sex. And you bring it to every domain of your life. You bring it to food, you bring it to money, you bring it to relationship with friends, you bring it to conversation, you bring it to your relationship to nature, you bring it to your relationship to art, and so on and so on."

A student questioned, "So, the phrase, 'Let us pray,' could take on a whole different meaning in this community!" Everyone laughed.

Lee said, "That's right. I had this girlfriend in college. She was totally insane. She was my first real in-depth exposure to insanity; she was absolutely crazy. She was the inspiration for the [LGB] song 'Insane.' She was very aggressive about sex, and she used to talk in this little baby voice. My parents were very worried. I mean, they were visibly concerned. But, she was my second real partner. With the first partner I had we sort of learned about sex together, and it wasn't so objectively sophisticated, but hot compared to nothing!

"But I've always liked people who can lead. Oh, I really dislike teaching people. How did I get in this position? No wonder none of you are learning, no wonder it's so difficult. I love to be taught. I just like to lay down on the sled and be pulled all over the countryside. This girl was good at that. We had this thing going: anytime she wanted sex, she wanted to drag me away. So I took her to my parents' house. She said, 'Whenever either one of us wants sex we'll start talking about fruit salad. And nobody will know.' So that was our secret code. She'd say, 'I'd love fruit salad for dinner tonight.' And I'd say, 'Oh.

Okay. Uh, Mom, Dad, see ya later. I'm gonna show Mariane my rock collection.' "

The room virtually rocked with hysterical laughter. We were back into the theatre of the absurd. Lee kept going, "No, I really had a rock collection because I spent my first two years in the Colorado School of Mines wanting to be a geological engineer, and I'd spent my entire high school career collecting rocks and minerals and crystals. So I really had a very beautiful rock collection.

"So, 'Let us pray' can be the Hohm Community equivalent of, 'I've been really think-ing about fruit salad.' When I broke up with her I think my mother and father—who hadn't danced in years—went out dancing, got drunk! They were worried because she was really weird. One of the things that precipitated our breakup was that I started get-ting crazy too. I always morphed to my girlfriends when I was young. I was going down-hill fast, losing my mind. Hmmm . . . maybe I shoulda stuck it out!

"She had this cat, she called it Peahead. It was the fattest cat you ever saw, and it had the smallest head compared to its body—really! You might think I am exaggerating, but I'm not. That cat must have been this big, and its head must have been *this* big!" Lee gestured with his hands to indicate a huge animal while people doubled over in riotous laughter. "It was a very accurate description. Let's see . . ." He looked down at the book and repeated a line from *Boyhood With Gurdjieff*, " 'The only expression of self that was left to us,' " then continued the reading.

" 'In order to achieve any other forms of holiness within ourselves, it was profitable to try—in other areas of our lives—to emulate this "essence-touching" process.' (p. 166) So this is what made sex holy—that sex was the last area of human relationship in which people allowed their essence to be exposed, or in which their essence was exposed be-cause of the nature of the intensity and the nature of the relationship. So he said to bring holiness to other areas of our lives, this is the secret. To bring essence, raw essence, into contact with other raw essence, there have to be two people involved. If one person has essence exposed and the other doesn't, the ego of the other is always going to try to squash that radiance and brightness in the one whose essence is exposed. So let me read that line again:

> In order to achieve any other forms of holiness within ourselves it was profitable to try— in other areas of our lives— to emulate this "essence-touching" process; the completely open "sharing of common truth" between two individuals was almost always "visible" in a com-pulsive sexual relationship. He warned, however, that even sex—compulsive as it might be to most individuals— often dwindled into a simple process which only involved the particu-lar satisfaction, gratification, or release of a single individual, instead of both of them, and that in such cases there would not have been any openness or honesty between them. (p. 166)

"Oh, boy. That puts things in a chilling perspective, doesn't it? That Gurdjieff sure knew how to ruin a party," Lee chuckled. "So, essentially, I think Gurdjieff's description was very clear—usually what happens is that people are on different wavelengths when they are having sex. I mean, the whole idea of tantric sex—nobody understands it! The principles of tantric sex have been abused in the worst way; all these tantric workshops where you sit and look into one another's eyes and you contact one another's soul and all this bullshit! In these tantric workshops it's really all a totally narcissistic, masturbatory process. The thread, the seed of that idea is to get people on the same wavelength so that as you enter into actual sexual function, you stay together in that. So when essence is exposed, *both* people's essence is exposed *together*, and then you can journey, as we would say, journey into the labyrinth in a whole different way, right to the heart of God.

"We don't use any of those techniques. I wouldn't recommend any of that new methodology, but in principle, this idea of being in the same place at the same time, in terms of sex being transformational, is fairly important. For a lot of people, in the beginning of a relationship, their passion is at its peak typically—although it shouldn't be at its peak at the beginning, it should get better as things deepen and mature. It doesn't keep getting higher and higher forever or you'd just burn up—somebody would come into your room the next morning and find flame marks all over the walls and the bed and you'd be gone! A nice way to go, but . . . Usually what happens is that people come to a level of agreement in which they understand the transformational window that opens at the level they are at, and they are able to sustain that level. Because if you use sex narcissistically, you can go beyond that point physically, and it can be blissfully pleasurable to the organism but have absolutely no transformational possibility.

"The idea after a certain amount of time in a relationship—which can be five, ten, twenty years (I don't mean six months or a year), is to get to a point where you are in agreement. So that when you meet in sex, in essence, you are in alignment, in essential communion. The point is to be in the same place at the same time. And when you are able to do that, then a relationship is nurtured and grows. When you aren't able to do that, after five years of not being in the same place at the same time, you can still go through the sex act mechanically, but it becomes pretty boring. So this is the idea—not only in sex, as Gurdjieff said, but to bring holiness into other areas of your life. The mechanical principle is to meet people in essence, in what Gurdjieff called, 'in absolute truthfulness or honesty.' So what is it to be absolutely honest when you are meeting someone? Not trying to manipulate or dominate them, and having nothing to hide.

"Often we say, 'Okay. I'm not going to hide anything.' So we tell people things that are actually forms of manipulation. Often, telling people the 'truth' can be a way to dominate the relationship. So to have nothing to hide does not mean that you tell your partner everything. Even people who have been together thirty years would rightly have secrets from one another; not secrets from one another because they have anything to hide, but secrets from one another because certain things have nothing to do with the relationship. They are secrets that their partner would have to help *pay* for, that would actually be a burden to their partner if they knew about them. In life as it is you aren't going to meet in a way that is transformational every time. But you have to be trained and prepared to understand that sex is a doorway to the Divine—to transformation, to alchemy—so that when that opportunity arises, you are there.

"So, this is the thing. All of this 'I'm a woman, hear me roar' or men's 'consciousness raising groups' is the worst crap because all it does is isolate you from other individuals. If you are in a relationship in this school, it doesn't mean you have to lay down and spread 'em every time your partner wants a little piece. But it does mean that to not view sex from a Work perspective probably insures you a fairly miserable relationship. You can repress it and hide it from your partner, but you will be very unhappy. Because you all already know too much, you've been touched too deeply, you can't keep it up for twenty years without either being in denial or repressing what you're really feeling. And you all know where repression goes after five or ten or twenty years.

"You've got to start seeing sex from a Work perspective. And then, occasionally, you'll meet that way. And the rest of the time it will just be sex, great sex or mediocre sex or fabulous sex. But even when it's just sex you will understand that every time you are making love," he stopped to laugh at this little euphemism and then continued humorously, ". . . that's what it is, *really*! You will understand that any minute the Universe could open before you. If you're not prepared to step into that doorway, you might miss it forever. It might never open for you again.

"That's what sex in a tantric school like this is about. Some of you have never heard this shit. But this is what it is. To hold sex in any other context is to deny yourself, according to Gurdjieff, the one area in which the holiness of self is still commonly and easily touchable, reachable, in our lives, in this day and age. And you wouldn't want to be doing that, would ya? You would be throwing yourself on your knees, praying ardently all your life for nothing, if you aren't touching essence, or exposing your essence to God and being touched.

"Romance? Romance is fabulous, terribly romantic. We were sitting at the movies the other day and there was this movie about a child, a two-year-old little boy who was missing from the front of a grocery store. Have you seen those previews? I was weeping at the preview! I said, I'm not going to *this* movie. Two dollars worth of tissues! We were all sitting, sniffling. I'm tremendously romantic, but you can never—if your work means anything to you—*never* allow romance to interfere with your work.

"If you understand this Work, your heart will be broken irrevocably. It's very sweet, but it's a *broken heart*. I mean you can't turn a broken heart into a beautiful rose! A broken heart is a broken heart. If you really get this Work it will *ruin* you for the ordinary pleasures of the common man. I mean, if we took everybody in this room and said, 'Let's make a list of the ordinary pleasures of the common man,' you would come up with a hundred or two hundred things. This Work will *ruin* you for all of those things, for every one of them."

Linda asked, "Is that a promise?"

Lee looked in her direction, "Ruin? Yes! That is a promise! This Work will *ruin* you for sitting in the kitchen sharing recipes with your grandmother, for sitting out on the back porch down in Tennessee watching the sunset—it will *ruin* you. I'm sorry. This Work will ruin you for everything—for every pleasure of the common man. So you must understand, this Work is not for everybody. Never mind not for everybody—it's hardly for anybody! How did all you guys get here? Bad luck, kids! That's right, in heaven when you lose the lottery, this is where you show up!"

Lee had taken us from "Introduction to Conscious Sex 101" into a sublime consideration of sexual communion as prayer on the spiritual path, with much of his teaching—actual instructions in sexual yoga in the Sahajiya or Baul style—cloaked in Lee's particular streetwise take on things. Lee was masterful in his farcical, storytelling style, so that while we were relaxed into laughter and enjoyment, the teaching got in at a bodily and unconscious level, slipping right past the gnarly guards that stand at the gates of the conscious mind. As he brought the talk to a close the room was extraordinarily bright, pressurized and hot. There were no open doors or windows, and we had been contained in the space for two hours with Lee. It was like a combustion chamber.

As he left the room with a cheerful "Jai Guru!" people were still laughing softly with him; he had charmed everyone once again into a kind of rosy glow with his comedy routines and raunchy, sometimes absurd clowning around, but there was an unquestionable and potent transmission being made. People were ecstatic and vulnerable—wide open. There was no reason to be happy. After all, he had just shone a bright light into some of the darkest of our prisons—our past, our attitudes toward sex and basic facts of human mechanicality—but there was a pervasive feeling of unmotivated happiness that showed visibly in peoples' faces. He had given us a purity of mind, a clarity of feeling, while the feeling of heat and power had slowly kept increasing, and we were like the crabs my mother used to catch in the Gulf of Mexico when I was a child. She put them in a pot of tepid water that was slowly heated to a boil, so the crabs felt no pain as they were slowly cooked to death. It's an apt comparison for the mood and power of Lee's transmission when cloaked in humor and joking around. You don't know what hit you—until later, when you realize that you have just been coaxed another step closer to ruin, your soul that much more deeply in the relentless grip of God.

January 31, 1999
Prescott, Arizona

In darshan tonight after a dialogue with several students in which Lee answered questions and talked about the events of the week, he began to discourse on "awakened mind" and "neurotic mind," giving a talk that could be called, "On Two Minds." He began using examples he had found particularly inspiring from *The Wheel of Time* by Carlos Castaneda. Lee has used each of Castaneda's books as teaching vehicles over the years, at times delving into them in detail with his students.

He said, "I just finished Castaneda's latest book, supposedly his last. He wrote it before his death and it's a recapitulation of his life. It's a very powerful book. In some ways it's totally different from all of his other books. It's just about his own life, so he even recounts, or recapitulates, experiences of when he was a child. One of the things that is really strong about it is his consideration of the unrelenting demand of what we would call Divine Influence or the Work.

"You know, *the Work waits for no one*. I mean, the Work has its imperatives. And it's got a little bit of tolerance, if we're sincere enough, but essentially it waits for no one. If we don't respond to the imperatives of the Work, we get left behind for this lifetime. There's next lifetime and on and on and blah, blah, blah. But the Work essentially does not wait for anyone. The Work has its imperatives and we're so insignificant compared to the Work that regardless of how vital we may be as a human being, how intelligent and how much potential we may have, how particularly useful to the Work in any given way, the Work doesn't wait.

"Once we enter the stream of the Work—you know this metaphor—the stream flows to the river and the river flows to the ocean, and the closer it gets to the ocean the stronger the current gets. We call this upscale. We work and there are certain periods in community sadhana when it seems like we're going through an upscale. To some people it seems like we're always going through an upscale, but really upscale happens periodically, not every month, or even every year. There is a constant *pressure*, so we may feel that we're always upscaling because of the pressure, but these are really very distinct dynamics." Lee laughed enigmatically.

"So, the Work doesn't wait, and when we hit an upscale we either get with the program or the Work leaves us behind. Upscale always has two dynamics or affects: a personal one and an impersonal one. The impersonal affect we can't get with because getting with something requires some kind of personal volition. So with the impersonal part of an upscale we are just carried along on the wave. It's literally like being on a wave that's so powerful you can't swim against it, you can't stand in the face of it. You are just carried along. On the other hand the personal affect of an upscale is a matter of aligning ourselves with the upscale.

"In the Work the personal affect of an upscale means we have to get with whatever the program is, somehow. We have to move through the obstacles that stand in our way. Castaneda talks about the things that Don Juan put him through. His descriptions of his disgust, his frustration, his horror, his terror, his desire to bolt, to run, to get out—these are really very much like many of the descriptions I've heard from some of you. And somehow Don Juan would always look at Carlos and say, 'But you can't do it. You can't run. It's too late. The sorcerer's path has already taken you. You can't leave.' That's the way it is. So you have to deal with these personal affectations of the next stage of the Work.

"So Carlos moved for a temporary time out of Los Angeles. He didn't tell anyone where he was going. Don Juan said to him, 'A warrior is alone but doesn't know loneliness.' We are totally alone, but to be a warrior is to not know loneliness as a psychological state. Don Juan told Carlos to find a hotel room, the kind of hotel room Carlos hated, with a mushy damp mattress, and lumpy pillows and the ugliest, most horrible green walls you can imagine, and so on and so on. He told Carlos stay in that room with no radio, no television, no human contacts, until he got over his loneliness.

"Of course he resisted the exercise for a long time. He didn't want to do it. He thought he wouldn't have to do it. Eventually his own suffering became so acute that he realized that he was not listening to Don Juan. He realized that he had to listen to Don Juan, so eventually he found the room and stayed in the room. He said that it took him many, many months of just staying in this room and going through the most agonizing loneliness and depression and despondency, until finally he broke through. And in breaking through he realized that for the rest of his life he would never need anyone again. Some of you, particularly on this side of the room," Lee gestured to the women's side, "will probably be arguing with this for a long time. So he realized that he would never need anyone. He realized that basically in a warrior's realization there may be very, very close friendships and many kinds of relationships, but that needing another person to complete you, to fulfill you, was unnecessary. He had broken through all that.

"Essentially the way I read this is that it's about the Work. Sooner or later we get an opportunity to deal with the personal affects of an upscale. For some of it's much sooner, for some of us much later and for some of us in the middle. The impersonal affects, whatever we go through, we go through, there's no way of avoiding that. Castaneda wrote about Don Juan's description of the fact that we have two different minds. Carlos said that he thought for years that Don Juan said, 'There are two parts of our mind.' And then he realized that Don Juan said, 'We have two different minds. And you have to drop one mind and live in the other mind.' Carlos kept trying to deal with two aspects of mind and he said he never could, he was just totally unsuccessful at realizing anything that Don Juan was saying. Finally when he realized that Don Juan said we have two minds instead of two parts of the mind, then he began to really progress.

"That can be a useful way of looking at things. We have what we could call the family dynamic with all its neurotic implications, the mind of the child having made certain decisions about his or her world or about reality based on a child's intelligence, a child's understanding, a child's expectations and projections. That mind grows up to be, as we all know, absolutely consuming. That mind possesses us. We identify with it as if that mind were us. Sooner or later in this Work we've got to break with that mind, cleanly and finally. We have to break with that mind and everything it stands for—all its elements, all its identifications, its hopes, its dreams, its wishes, and its morality. Each of us has that mind to some degree in terms of our political leanings. Even when we say, 'Oh it's terrible, only a week ago there was supposed to be a cease-fire, but the Serbs just went into some Albanian village and shot down a bunch of people.' We all have our social and political sense of things and often that sense is humanistic, it's very magnanimous, very generous, and maybe even compassionate. But every single element of that mind has to be severed. We have to literally stop functioning out of the context of that mind.

"Then there is the other mind, which is the mind that sees Reality *as it is*—without projections and expectations and subjectivity. That is the mind that sees Reality simply as it is, moment to moment. That mind certainly has its full complement of feeling—outrage at social injustices and so on—but that mind has an entirely different context than the mind of our original survival strategy. This Work could be said to be a matter of moving beyond the first mind and coming to be rooted and residing in the second mind, which is the mind of objective Reality, the mind of clarity, the mind of truth, the mind of the Divine. This is the dilemma we all face in one form or another." Lee paused and picked up a letter from Zachary, the bass player in the new community band, Attila the Hunza, on the current state of affairs of the band. Lee read the letter out loud and went into a commentary on the interpersonal dynamics in the new community band, using it as an example of how we have to deal successfully with the first mind—the mind of the survival strategy and personal psychology.

"The secret to dealing with the demand of this Work is being able to recognize, in any given situation, what the space or circumstance is calling for—objectively, of course. The demand may simply be to be in meditation every morning at seven o'clock, or just to cook a dinner that everybody on the ashram or in the household will find wholesome and nutritious. It could be anything from moment to moment. The demand could be to be a space of safety and sanctuary for one's partner.

"Of course in relationship there is always the demand to be a space of safety and sanctuary for each other. This is to be a context in which your partner can learn to trust you. Sometimes in any given moment somebody is very loving and affectionate and sometimes in any given moment that same person is frustrated, angry and insecure. When our partner is a space of sanctuary and safety for us, we feel that we can be who we are and love won't suffer. As you all know, in relationship we tend to act in a way that we think will maintain the love that we share, or at least the harmony, under good situations and co-dependency under good situations. We don't want to do anything that will cause our partner to love us any less, or that will break the agreement for workability. That dynamic is a very insidious dynamic. If you become a space of safety and sanctuary for your partner then they feel that they can be a little toxic once in a while and you won't love them less because of it. Like you'll still love them in the morning. Oh well, at least by evening."

The group sat listening very soberly. Lee smiled, "That was a joke . . . So there's always a Work demand, whether it's simply at an ordinary personal level in a task that's been given, or something else. The Work is about recognizing which of the two minds is dominating our consciousness in every moment. Over time the aim is to minimize the first mind, the neurotic mind, and maximize the second mind—the mind of unity, clarity, truth.

"The Work will chip away, chip away, chip away at the first mind, but at some point

155

for most of us we will get thrown into really deep considerations in which there are only two options. The options are so intense that we're forced into looking at them clearly and recognizing the degree to which the neurotic mind dominates and controls us. There are always only two options, and they're always the options of the neurotic mind or we could say, the awakened mind, the Work mind. Actually that's a good phrase for it. There is the neurotic mind and the Work mind; those are always the only two options.

"The Work often puts us in a situation in which we are forced to look at the degree to which we are not free, in which we have no choice based on the control of the first mind. And then we have to ask ourselves, do we want to be free? Do we want the option that is freedom? The answer is always yes, and then that option becomes clear. But, to choose the option of the Work mind, we have to be willing to step away from the claws of and out of the jaws of the neurotic mind. That is a very difficult thing to do because there is no comfort in the Work mind. None whatsoever. There's no comfort in the Work mind because we can't ever choose to seek the kinds of comfort that deny the Work if we step beyond the neurotic mind. All the neurotic mind does is buffer us against Reality, against truth. So to actually make that choice, the intensity of the demand on either side has to be great enough that we see what it is we're up to. We see what the choice is. When the intensity is such that you cannot deny the death of the neurotic mind and the life and freedom of the Work mind, then you are in a position in which you can make a step.

"Often we make a choice that's good for our work out of some moral idea, but we don't really *feel* it. And in not really feeling, we aren't seeing. We don't see the nature of mind. We may make the right choice but we're just making it out of obligation, or even out of love for the teacher, which is wonderful. But we're still not seeing. When we're thrown into a position where the intensity of the choice is so great that the suffering of the neurotic mind is overwhelming, then we're drowning in the pain of it and we are forced to make a choice. The choice of freedom forces us to see the elements of the neurotic mind and the free mind. We're forced to see how absolutely, completely choiceless we are when we are dominated by our psychology, and the shock of that is what propels us into choosing the Work mind.

"One of the reasons we aren't always choosing practice is because we think we have choice. Yes, we're neurotic. Everybody's neurotic, but unconsciously we actually believe that we have choice about anything—to stop smoking, or to start smoking without becoming addicted again, or this, that, or the other thing. We really do not recognize the fact that we have no choice. We are totally enslaved by the neurotic mind: every breath, every word out of our mouths, every gesture. We couldn't be free if our lives, if our children's lives, depended upon it. We *could* not. We have no options—we can't be free. We can't make the conscious choice. We can't make a free gesture. When we get that, the horror and disgust is so overwhelming that we will be forced to choose the Work mind. But we will never see it with that clarity if we aren't thrown into circumstances that are way over our heads, that creates an intensity, a crisis within us which produces that kind of vision.

"E.J. Gold once answered the question, 'How did you find the Work?' saying, 'I had nothing left to live for.' That's how dramatic the circumstances have to be to make us choose the Work consciously. Many of us at times make statements like, 'I can't leave the Work.' Okay, that may be true, but there are still many moments in which we do not choose the Work, in which we're lazy. We want to live because we have this idea that the future holds something for us: love and fulfillment and satisfaction, peace and blah, blah, blah. But as we are it's literally impossible to realize anything that we hope for from the teacher, from the path, or from life itself. E.J. realized that he had nothing left to live for, and at that moment he chose the Work. When you have that kind of a realization, when you choose the Work, you can't afford one minute of laziness. You cannot afford to be toxified. You cannot afford to close your eyes. You cannot afford to relax your vigilance. You cannot afford to buffer yourself from the Work, even for a moment of comfort.

"Ultimately this Work is designed to throw every single one of us into a crisis so deep and so profound, so mind-shattering, that we never recover. This is the realization that we come to: that as we are, as mechanical beings, freedom is a literal impossibility. There is only one option and it's the Work, and the Work does not wait around. The Work moves and if we can move with it, it will honor us and it will feed us and it will care for us. If we are not willing to move with it, it will crush us under its heel, with no remorse and no sentimentality.

"Sooner or later, every one of us will be thrown into such a conflict. That conflict is designed to produce freedom, and we may get thrown into it many times, because we don't get it. The first time we make a little shift, and the second time another little shift. Yes, the sangha bonds more deeply, and we come to love one another. We come to love our partner more than our own lives, we love our children more than our own lives. We find ourselves sometimes in situations in which the things we have always looked for in life—the heart of longing, and sweetness and tenderness and affection—are all there, but all of that is just icing on the cake. This Work is not designed to produce worldly satisfaction—love, tenderness, devotion. It's designed to produce freedom, and in freedom we can love one another profoundly, sacredly, deeply.

"We can be catapulted into transcendental states that can last for months simply by a look between one another. But those are the *affects* of freedom, those are not the intention of the Work. The intention of the Work is to produce freedom in us. There's only one way that freedom can be produced in us and that is to choose Work mind over neurotic mind. It has to be a conscious choice, and the only way that we'll ever make a choice that's conscious, fully conscious, is to see neurotic mind in its totality, in its death. To see it for what it is—empty of all substance, empty of all possibility, empty of all creativity, empty of all genuine, human feeling, empty of heart, empty of mind, empty of everything except its own mechanical survival impetus. That's it. Until we see it that way, until we see our lives, our love for our parents, our drive for sexual fulfillment, our taste for fine food, our love of good music—until we see all of it as nothing, absolutely *nothing* but totally mechanical, dead slavery to neurotic mind—we'll never choose the Work in a way that allows us to consciously be the kind of warrior that Castaneda is describing."

Lee's mood and words carried such gravity that everyone sat listening deeply. The atmosphere was solemn, ponderous, weighted. The truth of what Lee said sunk in like a stone through clear water. His words rang with the sound of truth. After he left the hall and a short puja ceremony was performed, the group silently dispersed. There was much to reflect upon.

FEBRUARY 1999

February 5, 1999
Arizona Ashram

In late January Lee received a letter from Gerry Mann, whose husband John Mann wrote *14 Years With My Teacher,* a book about his time with Swami Rudrananda (Rudi). She was writing to ask if she and John could visit Lee here at the ashram since they would be staying for a month or so in Cottonwood, Arizona, a nearby town only an hour and a half drive away. Lee immediately called them and extended an invitation to dinner.

On the phone John asked Lee if the rock band, liars, gods & beggars, was playing nearby. Lee said yes, in Sedona, only thirty minutes away from Cottonwood. John laughed delightedly. After a brief conversation, they made an arrangement for dinner on Friday night, February 5. Lee planned a special dinner with his family and a small number of students. Fresh salmon was purchased, the grill set up outside and everything else in place for the event.

When Lee hosts guests for special meals or feasts the intention is usually to create a possibility for an invocational space to happen—a chamber where a particular kind of communion might occur, if the mood is right. How that chamber would show up is always an unknown in the sense that the influence of the lineage is the guiding hand of everything. What happens or doesn't happen is in the hands of Lee's father, Yogi Ramsuratkumar. But, the setting of the space, the careful and intentional preparation of the food, and the mood and intention brought by each participant plays a significant role in whether or not a chamber is created that might be inviting to higher beings, who might "come to the feast." In this case, it is the presence of being or mood of those in the space that draws angelic or higher beings, or the Guest, as the Sufis might say. The degree of refinement that one has achieved in one's work has everything to do with whether or not one might be a tasty "morsel" for the unseen Guest. Lee is at source in such a space; he is an extraordinary host and magus in these situations. His guidance in creating such chambers is an instinctual process.

And so with everything set to go, spirits were running high at the possibility of such a chamber being invoked in Lee's company. However, John called on the afternoon of February 5 to say that Gerry was sick and they wouldn't be able to make it. Could they reschedule? Of course, Lee graciously responded. Knowing that his students Purna and Paula were planning a visit the next week, Lee suggested the next Thursday, February 11, so that they could come to the gathering. John said that would be very good. The salmon was put in the freezer.

February 6, 1999
Arizona Ashram

As the late winter days progress through the usual ashram rhythm of morning meditation, daily work, After Dinner Talks, darshan and the evening gatherings with Lee, it seems that Yogi Ramsuratkumar's presence grows and deepens with each day. Lee and the group that went to India have been back now for about seven weeks. There is a distinct sense of a new direction in Lee's work since he has been home, although the exact practical manifestation of that remains a mystery. There is a kind of raw, bodily clarity arising for many practitioners—an insistent clarity that illuminates the fact that there is no time to waste. Lee has been pouring diamonds and pearls, precious treasures, upon his students for years, and still the chronic tendency is to refuse the wish-fulfilling gem, often without even knowing that one is doing it.

The felt Influence of Yogi Ramsuratkumar seems to be creating subtle openings in many directions. There is a tremendous demand to upscale one's practice and commitment to the Work, felt as an urge to leap into action in pathways that have not been clearly pioneered before. For each person this is different. It may show up in one's relationship with one's children, with friends in the sangha, with one's mate, or it may show up in the immediate demands of projects or tasks, or in the field of everyday work and action. There is a sense of expectancy or anticipation that something very important is imminent. All these passing insights seem to be the harbingers of Grace at work. The urgency that is currently felt by many of Lee's students is the result of the powerful blessings that were given by Yogi Ramsuratkumar in the recent visit.

Lee goes along with equanimity, always the same regardless of any passing mood he may animate from moment to moment. He is mostly bright and quiet these days, and seems to rest in the easy rhythm and flow of life on the ashram. At the ashram in Arizona, although Lee is performing almost every weekend with liars, gods & beggars or Shri, there is a pervasive contemplative spirit to things, as if the vital juices have been drawn down into the roots of things to consider, gather power, reflect and observe. This introspection is a different kind of heat and burn, and makes each day a precious moment, almost suspended in time.

February 11, 1999
Arizona Ashram

It was a Thursday night and Lee's usual After Dinner Talk was cancelled in anticipation of John and Gerry Mann's visit. The salmon was unthawed, beautiful organic lettuce and vegetables had been purchased for the salad, wild rice was to be served. Purna and Paula had arrived from Little Rock and would come to dinner; Dasya and Paula and Ann were also invited. The table had been extended to accommodate thirteen people, including Lee's family, and was elegantly set with candles and flowers. A card table was set up nearby for the four children who would be present. After dinner there was childcare planned for them so that they could leave the space to the adults while they went to play. It is almost always Lee's wish that the children be included in these invocational dinners as much as possible so that they have the opportunity to experience the mood of sacred space.

Around two o'clock that afternoon John called again to apologize, saying that they were still too sick to make it. This time the salmon couldn't be re-frozen. Lee was in Phoenix when the phone call came in. When he returned he said, "We'll have the dinner anyway! It's a good excuse to have a special meal, with Purna and Paula here." Now there were two empty seats at the table and enough food for thirteen adults and four children, so Lee invited Lalitha and Jim to come. Dasya cooked the fish outside on the grill and the children helped prepare the salad.

That night at six o'clock the group sat down to an extraordinary but simple meal—grilled salmon, salad dressed with a Dijon sauce and wild rice. The wine was a delicate, very special 1993 French Chablis that had been taken from Lee's cache of wines that have been given to him as gifts of *prasad*. Lee, everyone on the ashram, and most of the Prescott sangha had been on a month-long herbal parasite cleansing program, so this meal had been designed to support that process of purification. For that reason no dessert was served.

It was a lovely meal in the best sense. As everyone sat down to the meal Kelly gave a toast at Lee's request—"May we know the transformation that only love can bring." The wine was wonderful and in the powerful intention of the space became an empowered substance. The mood of communion among this group of Lee's senior students went far beyond words, though there was a light banter during the meal, shared laughter and silence as well. Lee was shining and radiant.

At one point the second bottle of wine, a different kind, was opened. Many people at the table eagerly held their glasses up for hearty refills. There was a very small amount left in the bottom of the bottle, and L. asked for it—"just to taste" the second wine. Being greedy and wanting to taste the second wine also, but having taken only a small amount of the first wine and having chosen not to take another glass, I said to L., "I'll take a small taste of it also," thinking of just a splash of wine. However small this intrusion of unconscious greed into the chamber may have been, it was too much. Lee immediately looked at me, quite kindly, and said, "It's not necessary. The first wine was the best wine—you don't need to taste this one."

From years of having been both the recipient and the observer of Lee's work in regard to the proper use of and relationship to wine on the occasions when it is served, it was clear right away that his guidance was exact. One of the erroneous assumptions that we often make is that if Lee is serving a dietary "accessory" (something that is typically not part of the dietary discipline such as wine or coffee, chocolate and other sweet desserts) that Lee has given us carte blanche to eat or drink as much as we can stuff into ourselves. There is often an attitude of "Eat (or drink) as much as you can; you never know when we'll get this again!" This attitude is actually antagonistic to what Lee is really offering— a highly refined, tantric use of empowered substances. The Bauls of Bengal use alcohol, ganja (marijuana) and other drugs as part of their invocations, particularly in regard to music, poetry and dance. Here in the West Lee uses meat, sugar, coffee and sometimes wine as invocational substances.

On this night several of Lee's students had partaken of both wines, having two or more large glasses with an enthusiasm that indicated a lack of sensitivity to this particular space. Now Lee had thrown another consideration into the mix—a further refinement of how to work: the first wine was sublime, a sacrificial substance, and in drinking it something of the Divine was touched. To turn toward another wine with less possibility out of a neurotic seeking for more, always more, was to hamper our ability to work effectively in the space. The unconscious disposition of the illusion of separation from God that rules our thoughts and emotions and actions always presupposes that we must continually seek for something we think we don't have; more wine will fill us up, more dessert, more sex, more love, when in fact we are already complete and full in the tacit fact of our union with all that is, or the very Divine. Beyond this psychological consideration, what Lee pointed toward was that the first wine had transported us, even taken in very small amounts, and now we could profit most from allowing its essence power, its sacrificial potency, to flower within us, to be savored, to lift us higher, rather than bringing our vibration back down to the level of a lesser substance. His offering of a potent but subtle refinement of tantric practice was a reminder of Gurdjieff telling Solita Solano, "Never defile Armagnac," when her timing was off as she drank the "toast to the idiots" with him. However, as is typical with Lee, this teaching communication was cloaked in the most ordinary of statements: "It's not necessary. The first wine was the best wine— you don't need to taste this one." One would have to pay close attention to the inner workings of the chamber to catch his drift in this and many other comments.

After dinner the group moved into the living room and gathered around Lee. Sitting in Lee's private living room added an element of both intimacy and impersonality to the gathering. He sat on the large sofa alone, facing everyone else who sat scattered about on chairs, the loveseat, the floor. On the wall opposite Lee was a three-foot by four-foot photograph of Yogi Ramsuratkumar's face and shoulders, next to which was a beautiful *thangka* which was given to Lee as a gift by Alain De Rosanbo. The walls were covered with artwork; a few of the pieces were originals or prints of paintings done by E.J. Gold. One of the pieces was a pen and ink sketch of a woman's face, signed by Mark Chagall, a personal gift to Lee's father Louis Lozowick by the artist during their Paris days many years ago. The *murti* photograph of Yogi Ramsuratkumar and the Tibetan *thangka* dominated the room in terms of presence. The unmistakable call to the Work reverberated from the walls of this highly empowered space.

The doors to the living room were closed and the room was hermetically sealed. When everyone was completely settled and sat expectantly waiting to hear what would come next, Lee announced that he would be reading from E.J. Gold's *Secret Talks, Volume VIII*. E.J. Gold is a Western spiritual teacher, renowned artist and long-time close friend of Lee's who was an important mentor for Lee, especially during the early years of Lee's teaching work. Although they are close to the same age, Lee has always considered E.J. a "senior" in the Work, and has used his books and teachings extensively as study material with his own students. Lee has also taken small groups of his students to visit E.J. at his home in California—the "Institute" or IDHHB—many times over the past twenty-five years. These visits have generated a multitude of stories of E.J.'s unpredictable teaching demonstrations and interactions with Lee's students, which have become an important part of the oral tradition of the Hohm Community.

The aura of mystery and disbelief that shrouds the work of E.J. Gold is legendary in the Western spiritual scene. Often considered a Fourth Way maverick and a charlatan by some, Mr. Gold's work is beyond definition of any kind, although it is certainly of a crazy-wise character. He has written and published a number of significant and important books, including *The Joy of Sacrifice, Life in the Labyrinth*, and *The Human Biological Machine as a Transformational Apparatus*. E.J. is a complete enigma who, for the past ten years, has become progressively more reclusive and less available to new students. More recently he has become available for interaction on the Internet. The *Secret Talks* were recorded in the early seventies and transcribed into a notebook format, but have never been fully published or made available to the general public. They are priceless repositories of esoteric teaching on tantric work which very few people have had access to beyond E.J.'s closest circle of students. To hear them read aloud by Lee and commented upon was a rare opportunity.

Now Lee introduced the readings by saying that it is extremely esoteric material, much of it discussing the use of sexual chamber work in the transformational process. He warned everyone in a bright, almost cheerful and yet challenging tone, "This is going to be very graphic. If you have a weak stomach you may get turned off by some of it. And they mean every word of it! The literalness of this is *intended* to turn off people who aren't meant to deal with this material." He continued, "We're reading from 'Alchemy Unveiled . . .' " It was as if he had thrown down the gauntlet, thrown out a challenge—who didn't belong in this room? In this chamber? In this Work? He started the reading but was interrupted when L. had to leave the room to answer a phone call from a family member. Knowing the resistance L. had to esoteric or unconventional, crazy-wise considerations or style on Lee's part, it was not surprising that she chose to leave the chamber to take the call rather than returning the call an hour or two later. Her relationship to her family had consistently, over the years, been a symbol of her resistance to the Work. Not waiting for L. to return, he began again, plunging headlong into the first few paragraphs, an outrageous and mind-boggling introduction to conjuring higher entities through invocational sex and the dangers of harboring "stupid personal egoistic romantic ideas of ourselves or our work-partners" in such work.

After reading for several minutes Lee stopped and laughed. Slipping into a ribald mode, he said, "You guys know how it is! Sex is going pretty well, it's going good, and suddenly the junior high kid comes out, grabs her tits and jiggles them," he demonstrated quite expressively with his hands, "says, 'Oh boy, jello!! My favorite food!' " Lee then theatrically buried his face in his hands as if it was a soft mound of flesh. He slurped and moaned outrageously. This demonstration of the puerile junior high school boy attitude toward a woman's body was a thousand times more graphic than the reading material. Perhaps his earlier warning was really about his own antics, not about the *Secret Talks*. Two of the women laughed. The rest of the room sat silently, pondering Lee. He has a way of piercing right into the heart of the male-female problem. In this case, he was slicing into the *puer aeternis*—what Jung called the eternal boy, a neurotic archetypal pattern that many men get stuck in, and the female reaction to it.

Without missing a beat Lee dropped this obscene character and turned back into the elegant host. He went on to say, "So any element of our neurosis that defends us against the presence of a higher entity that has been invoked must be banished." A brief conversation ensued in which the state of practice in the sangha at large was considered in terms of what the actual capacity is for participating in alchemical sexual work.

"Obviously a real degree of maturity is necessary," Lalitha said, "but how would real maturity between men and women show up?"

"In a mature culture of men and women," Lee said, "there should be absolutely *no* subtle signs of game-playing between men and women. It's unbelievable the degree of game-playing that goes on in this community, even between mature practitioners. We have no idea what we are doing, or the consequences. In a mature culture of men and women, people of both sexes would stick with their own partners and there would be *no* game-playing."

Lee's answer addressed the most basic, foundation level of practice in relationship between men and women. At the same time, what he sees as "subtle game-playing" is the casual and common Western style of relations between men and women. These interactions are fraught with unconscious hooks and snares of flirtation and innuendo, but are taken for granted as the normal and appropriate way for Western men and women to relate with each other, just at the level of friendship. Because these habits are so deeply ingrained as the norm, we often don't have a clue as to what he is talking about—we falsely believe that our actions are innocent gestures of friendship rather than motivated by a whole labyrinth of psychological needs.

Lee took the subject at hand to another level. He said, "People who don't belong in a chamber get spun out quickly because the higher entity is feeding. If you are really doing alchemical work, to be spun out of a chamber is death. It's the worst." This fell into the space like a rock. It rang with absolute certainty, and an almost prophetic truth. He picked up the reading again, which continued with "G." holding forth:

"It does not matter which 'keys' we use to call down entities upon us; the sequence can vary, although sometimes the exact sequence is important. One key is the knowledge that romantic love exists and that there can be another kind of love, which we can call 'love-without-romance.'

"To know something exists is half the struggle of finding it.

"Romantic love is of the organic, emotional and mental bodies of man.

"In this case we are able to 'open the artifact' of romantic and not romantic love through the Pythagorean keys, not the Enochian which we used for a different purpose and to call upon very different entities last night.

"The Haida yogi carries 'master keys' to all systems. Tell me, A., is it possible to have love without romance?"

"Yes, I think so," A. said hesitantly.

"Is it possible to have love without drama?"

"Yes, of course, if the lovers are honest and have no need for continuation of the courtship mask."

"Can there be involvement in love without romance?"

"Certainly."

"And can there be voluntary identification in love without romance?"

"I think so."

"We can have all these and many other things just as in ordinary love, hein?[sic]"

"Yes," said T.

"Obviously it is possible to have love without romance," agreed J., "but what good can it do? What profit can it be for our work?"

G. then asked with a sly grin: "Can there be sex without romantic love[?]"

"Yes," said J.

"And organic chemical spontaneousness without romantic love?"

"Oh, definitely."

"For some, sex without romance is normal and ordinary. But is there sex without some kind of love?"

"No, I think there must be some kind of love in any sexual contact," said A.

"We can have love without romance, so even a real man not in quotation marks can have sex. We should be happy that it is possible to have love without romance.

"We can do everything we can do in ordinary moving center sex and moving center sex with force from the real sex center.

"Sex center sex, directed by the sex center and not by the organic moving center, is 'sex without romance.'"

With a twinkle in his eyes, G. said, "Sex without romance is in many ways deeper, more satisfying, more, shall we say . . . 'straightforward.' Only in sex without romance is it possible to exchange higher substances for mixture and dispersal through the chemical factory of each partner in alchemical experiments." (pp. 6-8)

At this point L. returned to the space and seemed like a fish out of water. As Lee continued to read and the nature of the material began to sink in, the conflict between her attachment to family and conventionality and the challenge to embrace Lee's offering of the evening became obvious. She was agitated and clearly threatened by the reading, challenging it with questions that seemed almost hostile. This was surprising because over the years L., a long-time student, had developed more and more equanimity and grace under pressure. Lee read on, obviously undeterred by L.'s attitude and enlivened by his friend's brilliant exposition of the dharma:

> G. asked us why we had not walked away from our various sordid lives much earlier than we had. (Some members of the group had just entered the preparation as candidates for the Work at ages well over fifty.)
>
> He said it was because of our romantic ideas that we had continued the search for power, influence and possessions, and that only by romantic notions could we think anything of them or believe in their reality; he said that our hopes for ourselves were stupid because they were founded on romantic ideas not far removed from those maleficent ideas presented endlessly by your Walt Disney.
>
> "Romance and romantic manifestations are the rose-colored glasses through which organic man views life. The 'Eyes of the Overworld' through which he sees palaces for pigsties, and princes and princesses for fishermen and pigs. Through these special lenses everything is almost always 'fine and dandy'—your 'American-O.K.-No-Matter-What.' When we remove these rose-colored glasses, we suddenly perceive the Real World.
>
> "The Real World is the same as the ordinary organic man; our presence poses a threat to their romantic ideas of themselves, which we call 'self-love' and 'vanity,' and of their world. Another name for 'romance' is 'Maya'—illusion. It is not that the world is an illusion, but the way in which it is viewed through romantic ideas.
>
> "The Absolute Truth, simply stated, is 'the world without romance.' This 'world without romance' may be too simple an idea to accept as Absolute Truth, but I cannot help that. It is as it is.
>
> "Love without romance is the means to become a candidate for the Work. Sex without romance is the method to obtain objective work-data.
>
> "Only the sex-center when it is able exactly to direct moving center manifestations can conjure entities from Above. If the sex-center is subject to moving center manifestations, we cannot conjure anything above ourselves; the moving center continues to provide force to the organic self if the sex center is not in charge of sex manifestations for work.
>
> "Sex without romance, when its force is supplied and directed by the sex center had the effect of making a new nervous system." (pp. 9-10)

Lee's reading brought the material to life, and his words burned into the air as the group listened. A force was gathering in the room as the sober and awesome demand of the Work was transmitted through E.J.'s words and the sound of Lee's voice as he read them. This force was penetrating each person as the group sat listening, mulling over the meaning of what was heard and how exactly it applied in each individual's case. The train of thought was almost audible: "Let's see . . . let me count the ways I am romantic daily, with my sexual partner, in my attitude toward the world, toward the spiritual master, in my ideas of the Work." The implications were vast. If one had been intoxicated and giddy at all at dinner, this was a splash of ice cold (though tremendously refreshing) water, bringing context into sharp relief against the background of mood.

Lee stopped and commented on this section, saying, "My work is Enlightened Duality. For us, in sexual relationship, if you have only romantic love, you can't work, but on the other hand if you have only love without romance, life can be pretty dull!" He chuckled.

An animated group discussion ensued on the importance of the consideration of having love without romance, or objective love, and how one might have love with romance and not fall asleep to the Work. Someone asked if Lee's use of the word "romance" in this context was different from what E.J. Gold meant, to which he replied, "Of course," as if any other answer would be totally absurd. Lee continued reading:

[G. said,] "Sensations are not from the moving center; they are from the involuntary part of the motor center which we call 'instinctive.' We cannot have voluntary sensations; by definition, sensations 'surprise us.' If they surprise us, they occur before we get hold of them and before we become aware of them in any of our centers.

"Can there be jollyness, funniness, happiness and sadness without romance? Funniness, jollyness there can be, but not happiness and sadness. They are both part of romantic ideas and have no real place in the ideas of the Real World, the world without romance.

"Organic man cannot do without romance; he believes romantic ideas give him organicness, reality, authenticity; the fact is that romance is very calculated like a barracuda views his victim. The man with romantic manifestations is an involuntary actor reading from a script he memorized before he was one year old." (p. 10)

At this point a question was asked about how E.J.'s use of the term "the sex-center" applied to Lee's discussion in France last year of the three centers—thinking, moving, feeling—having two corresponding levels of function. Lee had said that there are actually six centers in the human being: the moving center (instinct), the feeling center (emotion), the thinking center (mind); the higher moving center (sex as prayer, or the tangent point of alchemical transformation), the higher feeling center (heart as prayer), and the higher thinking center (radical insight and higher intellect). The question was, did the "sex-center" referred to by E.J. correlate with the higher moving center, and the moving center referred to by E.J. correlate with the lower moving center? Lee answered, "Yes, correct."

When Lee has spoken in the past about these centers he has said that in order to engage the transformational process one must first of all begin to function as a three-centered being, with unity between the centers, rather than the domination of one over the other two. Then one may begin to function in the higher centers from the context of unity. Transformational sex occurs when the moving center—what E.J. referred to as the "sex-center"—begins to come to life. Or, one might say that the lower moving center, or instinct, leaps the octave into the higher instinctual or moving (sexual) center. Lee read on:

[G. said,] "R. thinks of our little 'Knachtschmidt and Company' as heartless; those who view themselves and everything else in the romantic sense cannot see love without also the distinct presence of romance—in this instance 'romance' would be one or another form of 'sentimentality.'

"They cannot see above the level of 'romance;' a whole world above this is utterly invisible to them about which they know nothing whatever and even the simple existence of which they have only the vaguest and most cynical idea. A world without romance is to them blague [sic] in the extreme.

"Organic man makes up ideas about this 'invisible world;' sometimes right, more often incomparably wrong. When we say 'man is asleep,' we mean he clings to his persisting romantic ideas about his world and is unable to take a different view of it.

"Romance is the root cause of identification, not the organic fact.

"Man without quotation marks is unromantic man. His world is 'organic mathematical,' never impulsive; at the same time he is not an involuntary actor in a pathological drama. To be unromantic man is to be impartial in a special way about definite subjects. In this sense, unromantic is a special case of impartiality.

"Impartiality is the technique; unromantic is one use of this special technique in a school.

"Man-Four, Impartial Man, is the beginning of man-without-quotation-marks; he cannot be impartial who has one shred of romance in his view of himself, although about his world he may still retain some romantic ideas.

"Manifestations of romance counteract the magical invocation; romantic manifestations are evocation; when there is evocation emanating from within the organic self, there cannot be invocation. Our self is in the way of the drawing-down. The reverse is not necessarily true.

"An outward flow blocks an inward flow, but an inward flow does not necessarily prevent outward flow.

"Alchemically, when there is a 'transference of flow' in two directions, from the inner to the outer and from the outer to the inner, there must also be a 'reconciling factor,' a third force; this 'reconciling factor' is destroyed by romantic manifestations involuntarily or voluntarily manifested. This can easily be seen by anyone. To be a Law, as this is, it must be so obviously true that it is an insult to the intelligence to even bring up the subject.

"Its existence proves itself.

"While the organic, emotional and mental bodies of man correspond with Gradations of Reason which allow romantic manifestations, from the Astral Body of Impartial Man on, not only is romance and romantic ideas of organic man impossible, but also all ordinary romantic manifestations.

"This is why to romantic organic man, man of the Work appears lifeless and hypnotized; he is not 'animated by romantic notions' or plagued by voluntary and involuntary romantic manifestations. To romantic organic man all this seems more than just slightly sinister; in fact, the obstacles through which one must pass from romantic to the impartial is sometimes called by those of the inner circle of hunanity 'the Sinister Barrier,' because of the feelings associated with the emanations of Impartial Man when viewed and felt by organic man.

"He does not, and cannot, understand how a man could survive without his romantic manifestations and ideas. Without these romantic manifestations, his civilization would collapse instantaneously.

"Romantic manifestations and ideas are the foundation of all social structure; of its laws, customs, business, religion and relations. Romantic manifestations are the 'regulating factor' of the life of organic man, without which he would be lost and helpless and unable to function.

"Romantic manifestations provide a certain 'measure of predictability' between organic man and his world. He depends on them for his mental, emotional and moving center self-calming and self-love.

"Outside the realm of very specific manifestations organic man is at a complete loss; he does not know what to make of it. Ah, the justice-of-it-all! As our dearly esteemed Mullah Nasr Uddin once said, 'Let him stew in his own juices just a while longer.'

"Higher bodies cannot function with the additional organic presence of romantic manifestations, nor can an entity be 'called-down' in the presence of romantic organic manifestations.

"Impartiality cannot exist in the same organic formation in which there is the presence of romantic manifestations, nor can knowledge be gathered, higher substances collected or trans-substantiated; personal transformation occur; objective data transmitted; receptivity to exact needs of the Work; initiation both personal and as a group, nor knowledge be transformed into 'understanding,' the higher mental substance of higher Gradations of Reason.

"For all of these and many other higher data and activities, 'romantic manifestations' is the 'Banishing.' Almost all of the Work and the whole of work in a school is disintegrated automatically by the organic presence of voluntary or involuntary romantic manifestations." (pp. 13-16.)

As he often does, Lee brought Spiritual Slavery—the core precept of his teaching—into his commentary. Since the event that precipitated his teaching work Lee has continually brought the focus back to this foundation of his teaching and realization. Now he said, "In our work, the Divine does it all—but you still have to serve the invocation properly." Lee used the example of his telling Yogi Ramsuratkumar in darshan that some poems had been prepared to be sung, when Yogi Ramsuratkumar had in fact asked for the lyrics, the songs in the back of *Death of a Dishonest Man*.

Lee said, "It was a mistake on my part. I was trying to control what happened. There is tremendous profit in singing the poetry of course, but the invocation was lost—it wasn't what He asked for." He has talked about this incident several times in the two months since returning from India, each time saying that it was a mistake that he made.

Lalitha posed a question as to how long the sangha should "hold someone in place" who is having a very hard time and taking a tremendous amount of energy in order to support his or her process. Lee said, "What determines whether or not we decide to hold someone in place? Profitability. When someone becomes a liability, you don't hold them in place anymore."

Chris relayed reading in *14 Years With My Teacher* how Rudi had said to John Mann that he liked to interact with crazy people because they kept him honest with their peculiar way of seeing into people and confronting them at the level of reality. Lee jumped off on this, saying, "The thing with crazy people is that their essence is exposed—it's workable in a whole different way."

He then talked about a number of people in the sangha, and one woman in particular, saying, "You can take big risks with certain people who have a lot of work potential because the possible profit is very high—but so is the possible risk.

"Why do the Work?" Lee continued. "The importance of transformational work in the world is inestimable. If transformation ceases to happen, the world turns into a black hole in space." There was an immense responsibility implied in this statement. While Lee read, commented and interacted with his students and the evening wore on, the mood in the room continued to deepen. There was a feeling of high excitement and a healthy fear as a sense of great obligation took form, as if Lee were saying, "Are you in, or are you out? Who's going to leap into the next level of sacrifice and obligation with me?"

Lee said, "We can't work past our recoil. We have to investigate our recoil when what we *feel* to be true in Reality is so different than the recoil we experience. In recoil people move into a fantasy realm and imagine all kinds of things. We fixate on form and allow our education to define our reactions instead of recognizing how we actually *feel*. I work exactly like Yogi Ramsuratkumar. Any crazy-wise teacher acts in a way that is directly linked to love and compassion, but in the world those acts may make the teacher look like a dangerous person."

It was eight-thirty and time to close the space. Lee said goodnight to everyone and people began to disperse. Beyond the closing of the chamber the *rasa*—the subtle juice or substance—that was created seemed like part of an opening, a sense of new possibility in the master's company. The celebration of good company carried the group along into the late evening gathering and into the days ahead. It was not so much the questions generated in the space that night, but the alchemical possibility of the combination of elements within the group that was gathered there. In one way it was a first for Lee to bring a group of some of his most senior students together for a closed session in which the discussion was focused on esoteric tantric work and invocation. Something important seemed to be stirring in the ethers to move Lee in such a way.

It was interesting that this amazing night had not been recorded. At the beginning of the reading a number of people had realized that Lee's commentary should have been recorded, but it seemed to be too late and too disruptive to the chamber, which was already sealed, to get up, go downstairs, get the small tape recorder and then set it up on the coffee table. But on further consideration it seemed that the space was so rare, so refined, that to have recording equipment operating would have introduced another element that could have changed the space somehow. The intimacy and specific gravity of the chamber and the nature of the teaching material was such that it seemed to lawfully require an anonymity, a secrecy, a particular discrimination. Whatever I could catch in notes or from memory would be one thing; but to try to capture it verbatim through technology seemed to transgress the Baul ethic: Do not allow the esoteric teaching to become dogmatized or crystallized in doctrine or orthodoxy of any kind. This is why the esoteric teaching is put into poetry, song and dance in the Baul way. On this unusual night Lee's students had witnessed him in a rare mood; what was meant to be remembered and rendered into writing later would be enough.

February 13, 1999
Apache Bend, Arizona

At seven in the morning on Saturday a group piled into the teal green van with Lee—his family, Zachary and Kate, Ann, Dasya, Paula and Neith—to drive three hours south from Prescott to Apache Junction, Arizona, to the Renaissance Fair where the Baul Theatre Company (a theatre troupe that Lee established over ten years ago) was performing. Lee drove, as usual, and made great time, arriving before ten. While we were standing at the gate waiting for the fair to open, members of the theatre company took orders for food from Lee and his party—mostly turkey legs, but also French fries for the children, chicken sandwiches and other fair food. Once everyone was inside we sat on the benches of the open-air theater waiting for the first act.

The winter sun shone down in warm yellow beams and the air was fresh and clear. Soon the food began to miraculously and quietly appear, brought by members of the theatre company who were taking great pleasure in playing host to Lee and his gang for the day. None of the group had eaten any "junk food" like this for about five weeks. Sitting on a bale of hay in front of the stage Lee wielded a turkey leg in his hand. He ate enthusiastically while he watched the first show, "Don Juan and Miguel," an exuberant and campy comedy team of two professional actors who use bull whips and swords as their props, set against hilarious and bawdy repartee. Before long the whole group was doubled up in belly laughs. Watching Lee's obvious enjoyment of the show was another kind of food, much more substantial than the turkey legs and croissant sandwiches. He paid rapt attention to the players on stage, laughed vigorously with a full pleasure and ate his turkey leg with gusto while simultaneously being present with everyone around him, especially the children. This capacity for extended presence of attention or split attention—attention that is focused in more than one direction at a time, or even at different levels of consciousness—is one of the most striking qualities that Lee demonstrates constantly. One has to consider just what it is that makes it possible for Lee to be so completely present to many different simultaneous demands on his attention. And if he can do that in this domain of ordinary consciousness, then the possibilities seem endless in terms of attention working in other dimensions at the same time that it is focused in various directed rays here in the middleworld of everyday life.

The Baul Theatre Company is a project that was given to his students by Lee a decade ago, and, along with the bands, is another Hohm Community foray into shamanism in the arts. Their aim is invocational theatre and the creation of transformational spaces. The Renaissance Fair has been a fantastic opportunity for the troupe, and their performance art has grown by leaps and bounds as a result of their participation in it. For the past three years Lee has gone to the Renaissance Fair to see the Baul Theatre Company perform.

Today Lee saw the Baul Theatre Company's performance of "The Loathely Lady" and "St. George and the Dragon" twice. Both of these theatre pieces are satirical and very funny take-offs on classic Western tales or mythic themes of transformation. His enjoyment was obvious as he laughed at the ribald and at times hysterical antics of his students onstage. As actors they were fantastic and highly professional. They have worked incredibly hard over the past three years, making a substantial place for themselves among the performers at the fair. Each year they spend three days over every weekend during February and March camped out in the desert at the edge of the fair with the other acts. They lived in a twenty-year-old converted school bus that was donated to the company. They cook their own food, eating on the diet and maintaining their practices.

They give five performances a day and pass the hat to the crowds. When they first started performing at the fair they had to use the spaces on the green by the food booths. The second year they got a stage and this year they were given some of the best stages to perform on. They have advanced very quickly in the hierarchy of the fair. Their ability to spontaneously improvise and make use of whatever the crowd gives them was fabulous to watch. It quickly became obvious that one of their strengths was how to gather the crowd to them, as well as how to create funny repartee with the audience. Each player learned to play the other same-sex parts, an element of their ability to be flexible and improvise as needed.

Both for the Baul Theatre Company and for Lee's students who come to see their performance, time spent at the Renaissance Fair is an environment worthy of inner work. The high color, the ecstatic mood and the bawdy, earthy tones of the Renaissance period creates a rich atmosphere. It is a gypsy-like environment that tends to draw many marginal characters from the mainstream culture at large. Most of the staff and actors are black sheep who have found their own niche in this unusual circumstance. However unconventional the Baul Theatre Company may appear from an outsider's point of view, they are totally accepted in this environment because everyone falls into this category— renegades from the sleeping world. The Renaissance Fair is, in it's own way, an alternative community. It is loud, dusty, colorful and brash, with many magical elements.

It can also be very irritating. The constant bombardment upon the senses of thousands of people in the hot desert sun is like wading through the mass of humanity in the streets of India or any Third World country. There is a way to feed off the underworld elements, the bardo-like quality of the fair that is apparent as soon as one walks through the gates. It is like entering into another world. A complete illusion is created to conjure a step back in time to the Renaissance period. Most of the throngs of people are dressed in costumes; people are uninhibited, yelling at each other, eating food, throwing things, dancing, playing music, carrying children. The street actors are masterful at creating this illusion, to the point that it seems they actually believe it themselves.

It is a great place to people-watch, or learn about one's self by observing humanity. In Lee's company these kinds of environments provide chances to practice in fundamental ways—to pay attention and remember rather than just wander, distracted and seduced by every impression one encounters. The grossness of the actual food that is served by fair vendors, the many diverse elements of people moving in large crowds, interacting with very different and multifaceted impressions, the kaleidoscopic quality of the scene, being in the intense desert sun and wind all day, walking on parched earth—all of this blends into a glittering gestalt in which one can easily get distracted or confused if not paying careful attention and using the internal practices in particular. These environments also offer the opportunity to cultivate a tantric relationship to everything in one's surroundings. As E.J. Gold once said, the way to navigate the bardos is "neither attracted nor repelled."

By late afternoon Lee's group had scattered in different directions and planned to meet him again at five-thirty at the front gate to leave for dinner. Lee was there by five o'clock, sitting quietly on a bench in the grass. Slowly his party congregated around him. The "Tree Man" walked by a few yards up the lane—a man on stilts dressed as a tree and evoking a very powerful mood as he moved slowly through the crowd. He is a "tree activist" who is involved in saving trees and forests around the world. His theatre art communicates the context of his political consciousness. He was twelve feet high with long bushy green arms and luminous human eyes peering out of the foliage of his "head," while another man walked alongside him playing a *degeridu*. The children looked up in wonder, wanting to walk alongside the Tree Man as far as they could.

At five-twenty Lee was ready to go. Time is of the essence to him, and he is in fact a man of impeccable timing. When he says, "Meet at the gate at five-thirty," you can be sure he will be the first one to arrive. He is always setting up the next space; in this case, the rendezvous point and then the transit in the van to the restaurant where he would take the group for dinner before heading back to Prescott for the night. Even sitting on the grass near the entrance gate Lee exuded an aura of powerful intention.

When everyone had arrived we headed out to the van and, Lee at the helm, drove about thirty minutes into the city of Mesa where he pulled into the parking lot of the pizza restaurant where we had reservations. Our large group included the members of the theatre company who were coming in fifteen minutes. A long table was set for about twenty-five. Lee ordered six large pizzas for the whole group—pepperoni, Italian sausage, peppers, onion and olives, jalapenos. After four or five weeks of a purifying, cleansing diet and the parasite cleanse program—no meat, dairy products, sugar, caffeine or highly processed foods—Lee was really slumming it today. This is part of Lee's style in working with food also. He entertains the principles of the Work within a natural hospitality in not only the most sublime food alchemy with the daily, ordinary ashram fare of raw food, vegetables and grains, but also in the utilization of truly gross food—highly processed, full of chemicals, meat and grease, cooked fast by unknown hands, and sometimes eaten on the run. This too has a useful alchemy to it in small amounts and at the right time. Somehow in Lee's company this kind of junk food is transmuted into something that is actually useful to one's work.

Soon the members of the Baul Theatre Company joined us. Lee had been mellow and relaxed all day. Having eaten very little during the day, everyone was ravenously hungry. "Get whatever you want to drink," he called out. People made a beeline to the Cokes, lemonade and root beer. The pizzas arrived and within ten minutes every slice was eaten. "Who can eat more pizza?" Lee asked. About ten hands shot up in the air. He ordered two or three more pizzas.

The mood at this informal feast was easy and light. The appearance of things was that it was a casual space, and yet it is never casual with Lee. He is always working. If there were any doubts about this ordinary pizza dinner being completely sponsored and maintained at a subtle level by Lee, it was dispelled at the end of the meal by Lee's response to Ann, who was there as his guest. She graciously offered to pay for her pizza, and Lee automatically waved her money away, saying, "No, *I'll pay* . . . I pay for everything." He smiled enigmatically at her. His words rang around the table. The statement was absolute. And in fact, the teaching communication of this was that Lee *does* pay; he is the treasurer, the financier, the insurer, the subsidizer, the patron. He is the godfather, the godmother and heaven's advocate. He is responsible for his students in the most ultimate way: the way of liberation, of divine evolution, of relationship to the Divine. If his students don't practice, if they don't follow through on their commitments, if they don't make the sacrifices that are necessary (which is the other half of the deal), he still pays. It is an inexorable law—the sacrifice of the guru—or one might say, the bodhisattva.

When we got back in the van for the two and a half-hour drive home someone said, "Lee, you'll let us know if you need help driving." It was a strange comment, as if the speaker was going to ask a question, but it came out as a statement of assumption.

"Oh, I don't know!" Lee answered tersely. Clearly he meant no. He seemed irritated by the question, and continued in a suddenly fierce tone, "Never show the machine mercy. Otherwise it's got you by the throat!" He drove all the way home, as usual.

February 14, 1999
Arizona Ashram

This morning at eight o'clock immediately after the *Guru Gita* was sung in the meditation hall, Lee called an impromptu meeting of a small group of his students. His face was brilliant, radiant, open, but at the same time he was not joking around. Instead he was sober, matter-of-fact. The group sat on the floor facing Lee, wondering what could have precipitated such an unusual circumstance.

"L. is leaving the community," Lee stated simply, a flat, resounding finality to his words. L. was a long-time student of Lee's, one of the original group who had been with him twenty-five years ago in Silva Mind Control, since before the inception of the community, and someone who was central to the school. After a fleeting blank moment of shock registered in the group, Lee continued, "L. is leaving and it is an irrevocable decision. She does not want to be processed about it or to work anything out. She's not angry with anyone. She's been thinking about it for a long time and she's come to a final decision." In many ways this was not a surprise at all, but paradoxically it was a profound shock. A stunned silence spread out from the center of Lee's words; at the center of the silence was shock, and at the center of the shock, sorrow and clarity began to arise in those who sat absorbing the implications of the news.

L. had made the decision to leave with tremendous maturity and gracefulness. There was no animosity of any kind. Her love and respect for Lee was unchanged. She had simply made a decision to return to a conventional life. She felt that she did not have the inspiration or desire to carry on, to make the next leap forward in sadhana, which was unquestionably pressing on her.

The group began to talk in earnest about the situation. Some spoke of grief and also concern that L.'s maturity, stability and years in the school were irreplaceable. Lee said, "Yes, L. is irreplaceable, but the Work goes on. *No sentiment.*" He looked at each person with blazing eyes, then repeated this several times. His context was immaculate. One could sense in Lee a thread of grief but also a kind of wild, crazy ecstasy. There was a sense of unfettered wholeness, of a crazy freedom around him. An opening into the unknown yawned in front of the group like a black hole, empty but teeming with an invisible richness and possibility.

The conversation turned toward the enormous conflict L. had had throughout her sadhana between having an ordinary, conventional and worldly life and finding herself immersed in the Work. With hindsight the degree of inner turmoil she was experiencing during Lee's recent reading of the material from E.J. Gold became now gravely clear. Despite her deep connection to Lee and the school, she was unwilling to let go of her personal, worldly identity. Because of this conflict L. failed to seriously engage the conditions and the practices over the years and allowed the forces of negation and stasis to seep into her and take over. Without a matrix of practice to protect her, L. became fair game for the forces that seek to undermine or destroy the process of radical spiritual transformation.

The uneasy recognition of this lack of practice in L. had been growing in her intimate friends for at least two years, especially after she quit coming to meditation. All along she occasionally admitted that she had no interest in the dharma, in following the diet, or in study of any kind. Because of the love and bonded relationship between L. and her close sangha mates, many people wanted to believe that she had, in her own way, a living relationship to practice—some inner pathways in which she moved in the context of the Work. One could see this context in her, feel into it. She had the influence of the lineage deeply rooted in her body from years of association with Lee. Her essence often shone out and touched many people deeply. She could exhibit tremendous compassion for others. She was looked to as one of the most senior students of the school because of her many years in Lee's company, and there was great respect and appreciation for her among the sangha at large. She had a stability and groundedness and maturity that was amazing, but at the same time this very stability had become inflexible and closed down. Her very strength, which lay in stability and groundedness, was interwoven with a rigidity and fixed crystallization of her physical and subtle bodies that was immovable.

It was obvious that L. was a very mature woman of great integrity who had a tremendous amount of self-control, but this was not the same thing as a matrix of practice in the Work. Despite her years in Lee's company and the power of divine influence within her, L. maintained a separate, personal, private life. All along the way she made choices for the sleeping world context in her life. This had become more and more glaring in contrast to the deepening of the rest of the sangha into renunciation and obedience in relation to Lee's recommendations. Under the surface her worldly choices had been eating away at her place in the Work for years. Now the grim reaper had come to call, and he had demanded payment.

It was crucial that Lee's students use this tremendous loss as a reminding factor. Given the degree to which L. had embraced the path and demonstrated the fruits of her work, her leaving was tremendously sobering. It was a call to clarity about the power that unconscious pockets of resistance and denial can have over one, even one who is firmly established in spiritual life. On the dangerous fast path of tantra there is no time to laze around, take years to clean things up, or assume that one's years in the Work or personal relationship with the spiritual master alone will carry one through.

Many people unconsciously believe they can chew on their cud, or play the dilettante for many years and still live in the spiritual master's field of influence or alchemical circuitry. Without a living inherence in the moods and acts of practice, at some point the benediction of a genuine lineage, which is the spiritual blood of the school or *sampradaya*, ceases to flow.

L. had met Yogi Ramsuratkumar many times and personally received his blessing. Blessings would undoubtedly continue to flow to her through the lineage for the rest of her life. But the blessings of the master are different than the alchemical and graceful force of benediction. Lee has often said that if one spends years in his company but just treads water, one still accumulates good karma, or merit. The attainment of merit, which could produce a karmic opportunity in the Work in the next incarnation, is still a worthy task, because from the Baul point of view, this process is a continuum over lifetimes. But if one wants to fulfill one's destiny in this lifetime, the channel of benediction has to be kept wide open and unobstructed. The channel remains open through the vulnerability and emptiness created in the sacrifice of attachment to false identity and the magnetic force of disciplined practice.

Despite the shared grief, as the news settled in more deeply, it began to take on a different cast. The absolute purpose and mystery of divine influence in all this began to make itself felt and known. L.'s leaving began to appear lawful and even just. As strange as it seemed, it appeared that L. had paradoxically made the right decision. Who can assume to rationally understand the ultimate workings of karma, let alone of the Will of God? The sangha had needed a shaking up for a long time. What the changes might mean for Lee's students now began to take form as the undercurrents and foreshadows of radical change that had been felt since India now came into focus. One of L.'s primary concerns was to maintain order and a semblance of normalcy and conventionality, and she exerted a certain influence in this direction. Her leaving brought the spirit of change that had been in the air into a bigger picture. Lee and the entire community were traveling at a rapid rate of speed into deeper waters. The road had gone from paved with carefully painted dividing lines to an unmarked dirt road—a bumpy, potholed, dirt road that seemed to stretch into the distance of what it means to be Bauls, who are outcasts, misfits, black sheep.

Marginalized within their own society, the Bauls are deeply connected to the earth, to the dirt, the primal substances of life, to the glittering shower of divine rain, the fire of God's beauty in all things that are born and grow and die. The Bauls have a deep kinship with that which causes ego to shudder in fear, and especially with the most primitive dimensions of the Divine's descent into matter—death and birth, sex and saliva, sweat and blood, the growth and decay of the food chain all along the way, the processes of disintegration, fermentation, dissolution and the magical substance that any rotting or sacrificed thing gives off. The true devotees are those decomposing and sacrificed things; they are literally being sacrificed and eaten in this process of transformation. Sometimes they ferment and decay for awhile before God and His host of angels eat them, and sometimes they are eaten fresh, alive—not even like sushi, which is killed first, but as the fresh meat of a living sacrifice.

God enjoys this feast of living being, and of course when one can get to be so purified as to be a feast of living being for God, the rewards of such a sacrifice are great. There will always be the naysayers who maintain that there are no payoffs in the Work. There are absolutely no payoffs for ego, but unimaginable payoffs for soul. To be eaten live, in pieces or whole, by the living God is to be divinized, to become conscious, incarnate divinity itself—Lee Lozowick and his Father Yogi Ramsuratkumar being the obvious examples of such an occurrence. On this day that divinity was exhibited in Lee's equanimity under fire, his poise, his tenderness, his radiance and his total acceptance.

In darshan that night after chanting and the *prasad* ritual was finished Lee began his talk. "I have some news to share with you . . ." He started making jokes and fooling around. He was candid about his embarrassment, saying, "This is what they call 'patter'—I'm a little nervous . . ." He paused then said, "A pause for dramatic effect . . ." He laughed.

"L. has left the community, left the Work." The room was perfectly still. Lee went on, gathering strength and momentum very quickly.

"The Work doesn't plan things out. The Work gives us a blueprint and the opportunity to 'seize the day.' If we don't take the opportunity, then the Work executes us. We either take the opportunity offered or don't, and the Work goes on with us or without us. If we don't take the opportunity that is offered, we are out on the streets. L. has chosen a life of free will, but one of sleep and comfort and family . . . Hers was the choice of a very mature woman, but not the choice of a devotee. She never committed to the Work, but at the same time she *was* the Work. Anyone woven into the system the way L. was has to rip themselves out of this."

Then in a different vein he said, "So there is no animosity, we're all friends. L. is handling this very well, with great maturity. She made the right decision because she was unwilling to practice. She was a burden to the Work. She was unwilling to assume her post in the school, and so she made the right decision. Because of the weight she carried—L. was a heavy character in this school—now that she's gone things *will* open up significantly. Of course, I don't know what those changes will mean or what that will look like. But I'm going forward! I'm not looking back . . . Things will open up significantly, and I don't know in what ways. In a crazy wisdom tradition that can mean some unusual conditions. So whatever happens, I want to caution you all from freaking out over the appearance of things, when it is in fact nothing more than the appearance of things."

Lee said many other things in the intense heat and brilliance of the room on this pivotal night. He was, as he had been all day, a brilliant and flawless demonstration of surrender to the Will of God. Lee is not a teacher who remains distant, remote and detached, dispensing blessings from afar to the devotees far beneath him. He is a teacher who cares deeply for his students and gets tremendously involved in their spiritual path. He is willing to get his hands dirty, so to speak. He gets down into the streets and gutters and byways of our lives and reaches out his hand over and over again to lift us up out of the mire. Now a student who had been central to the sangha for twenty-five years had irrevocably walked out of his life. At the same time, his mother is dying of old age, being ninety-four years old with a bad heart and in and out of the hospital in Florida. His master and *Ishtaa Devataa*, Yogi Ramsuratkumar, is elderly and infirm and not expected to live more than a few years at most. In the midst of all this death and loss and disintegration, tonight Lee was star-like, older than the stars, a radiant spiritual sun, completely unfettered—not devoid of real human feeling by any means, but richly endowed with the full bloom of humanity and at the same time marvelously free. He seemed to be dancing, whirling and leaping through the crumbling ruins of our folly. Never has it been clearer that he is the embodiment of his own teaching.

February 15, 1999
Arizona Ashram

Since yesterday's events Lee has continued to demonstrate the teaching with amazing ease. Wisdom and strength flow from him like a constant wind, he is ecstatic and bright, and at the same time there is an infinite sadness that flickers in the steady flame of his eyes. His sobriety is striking. His body is like a mountain, rooted in the earth, the sun, the moon, the entire cosmos, rooted in the original quintessence of Yogi Ramsuratkumar.

Still the reverberating shock waves of the news of L. leaving are felt like an earthquake in the whole system of the sangha. Many people report a subtle sense of getting bigger. Perhaps this is because those who are in positions of senior responsibility in relationship to Lee are being expanded in order to carry a greater responsibility at this time.

Throughout yesterday and today Lee has held a steady course and fed his students with his equanimity and grace and perfect acceptance. He seems tremendously freed-up; there is no recrimination, no remorse, absolutely no looking back. He means it when he says he is only going forward.

February 16, 1999
Arizona Ashram

As the group gathered after dinner for Lee's talk in the meditation hall, Bandhu said, "There is a responsibility that we have to represent you accurately. There are lots of things that you say that, taken out of context, could be highly inflammatory to those who are not in the Work." When questioned further about this subject, Lee commented:

"So everyone involved in the current misunderstanding will get a good lesson out of all this. But I don't care if I am misrepresented. I don't care if people get the wrong information, or take what I say the wrong way. People should have to struggle, people should be confused in this Work, they should have to work to get to the Truth. The real Work has got to have a labyrinth to it—it's healthy for people to misrepresent me and pass on incorrect information. It keeps the school small, makes it hard for people to slip through. Let it be a little difficult to be here, to find the way. So there's no problem when there is misinformation.

"I'd like to become crankier and more irascible—is that the word?—yes, irascible, as I get older! I'd like to be the Guardian at the Gate. I don't know—with Arnaud's influence I may just get more dignified and elegant. But I'd like to be irascible . . . it feels better to be that way! I'd like to be an irascible rascal on the spiritual scene!"

After reading for awhile from *The Wheel of Time* by Carlos Castaneda and offering commentary, Lee then began to talk about the average practitioner's fears of annihilation. He spoke about a particular experience that a woman, a fairly new student, had been having of recognizing that she had absolutely no internal freedom whatsoever—that she was, in fact, nothing but a bundle of mechanical habits. The shock of this insight in her body produced a very physical effect. She was having spasms run through her body and even vomited. He encouraged people to talk with her about the experience and ground it in reality for her, so that she wouldn't just forget about it.

He said, "When you're standing on the brink of annihilation there will be organic fear—the body shakes and jerks and spasms. But don't be afraid of freedom; be afraid of going back to who you *were,* be afraid of going back to mechanical slavery, but never be afraid of freedom.

"You cannot rest on your laurels—not one day—or you start to slide back. So Don Juan told Carlos that, on the path, one must erase one's personal history, and he gave him three ways to do that: 1) Losing self-importance; 2) Assuming total responsibility for one's actions; and 3) Using death as an advisor. So, L. has 'died,' and you can use that death as your advisor. If you meet L. on the street sometime in the years ahead, you will probably find someone who is kind, mature, competent, an understanding person. But don't be fooled, because who she is in the Work has died."

Then Lee read the following quote from Castaneda: "All we need to pluck the wonders of this world of everyday life is enough detachment. But more than detachment, we need enough affection and abandon." (p. 155) This, Lee said, was better advice for couples engaged in an intimate or sexual relationship than any sex manual in the world.

February 22, 1999
Arizona Ashram

Lee had rescheduled the dinner with John and Gerry Mann for today. This morning a phone call came in with the message that John and Gerry Mann would be here not in the afternoon as we expected, but for lunch. Quickly the lunch schedule was arranged to accommodate the two guests. A grand feast had been planned for dinner tonight, but at lunch the regular ashram fare at Lee's table would be served—steamed fresh asparagus, brown rice, salad, quinoa, gomasio, cooked beets and steamed greens. When the guests hadn't arrived by five minutes after twelve noon, Lee said, "Let's eat!" and the group sat down with the children and ate.

At 12:20 the phone rang. It was John Mann saying that they were lost. They were only ten minutes away. Lee talked with them and arranged to meet them on the road himself and help them navigate the last mile or so. The difficulties they were having in getting to Lee's ashram—after two cancellations and now this—were becoming quite comical. Lee left in the car. Tom L., who was to accompany Lee to Mexico early the next day, was also expected to arrive from the Phoenix airport at twelve-thirty and would join Lee's party for lunch.

Soon Lee arrived with John and Gerry. A small group of Lee's students sat down at the table with them along with Lee, who had eaten part of the meal earlier but saved his large plate of salad to eat with them when they arrived. Tom arrived and joined the group. Gerry Mann kept laughing about how hard it had been to get here.

"But I feel so relaxed!" she enthused. "This is wonderful! Why, it's wonderful here," she said, as if all her fears were melting in the warmth of a sunny day. She was obviously very pleasantly surprised that Lee and his students were so ordinary, and she actually said as much, repeatedly expressing her delight at this discovery.

John laughingly said, "I didn't know if getting lost was just another test for us, something you did on purpose, or simply an accident!" Evidently Lee had omitted one crucial piece of information in the directions.

Lee countered, "No, it was purely accidental! The next time I have to give directions I'll know to be sure to add that information."

John and Gerry looked around the room at the many *murtis* that line the walls of the narrow dining room, a strip of a room about eight feet wide and twenty-five feet long. The walls are covered with a gallery of saints—empowered photographs of many different spiritual teachers, saints and gurus, from Chögyam Trungpa Rinpoche, Idries Shah, Nityananda, Shirdi Sai Baba, Anandamayi Ma, Arnaud Desjardins, Swami Rudrananda (Rudi), to a rare photo of E.J. Gold and many photographs of Yogi Ramsuratkumar, Swami Papa Ramdas and Mother Krishnabai, Sanatan Das Baul and his sons, Bishwanath and Basudev. Other pictures include chronicles of Lee's visits with Yvan Amar, Arnaud Desjardins, Andrew Cohen and other friends. Many of these pictures have dried marigold or carnation *malas* hung around them—relics of *prasad* given to Lee over the years.

Kelly, who has known John for many years from her former association with Rudi's work, mentioned the large painting of Swami Rudrananda (Rudi) and told John that a mutual friend had painted it. Jane said, "The children have been particularly intrigued with that picture, ever since they were very small."

John laughed and said with a dry humor, "Well, that answers the question I *wasn't* going to ask—whether you had put that picture up just for this visit!" We all laughed together. Kelly joked around, "Yeah, you guys come in and find copies of *14 Years* laying around everywhere, photos of John Mann and Rudi all over the place! No, actually it's been there for many years."

The conversation turned toward John's book, *14 Years With My Teacher*. Some of the people present had been re-reading it in preparation for John's visit. John turned to Lee and said, "You've written a lot of books, haven't you? How many? Fourteen or fifteen?" Lee smiled in assent, never too eager to talk about his own "achievements" in this kind of social setting.

John told Lee that the original manuscript of *14 Years With My Teacher* was twice as long as the published book, which had been heavily edited for publication by Rudi's other "teachers" after his death. He also said that he had just finished another book. Lee seemed to perk up at this. "Hohm Press might be interested in publishing the original of *14 Years,*" he said quietly.

Gerry added, "Actually we're looking for someone to publish the book John just wrote."

Lee looked at his guests, listening intently. His mood was supremely generous and gracious and he eloquently and almost formally said, "Please give us the privilege of reading and considering your manuscripts. Maybe we can do something together."

After lunch Lee and Tom gave John and Gerry a tour of the ashram, then everyone joined together in the living room to visit. John talked about his time with Rudi, about Rudi's untimely and shocking death. Jane said, "Arnaud Desjardins has talked about the transmission that the guru makes at the time of death as being the ultimate moment, the peak of the teacher's work and communication to his disciples. And of course Yogi Ramsuratkumar is eighty years old, and will probably live a few more years if we are lucky, but really could die at any time, so this consideration of the power that is felt, a great passing on of the blessing power of the lineage to disciples, is something we think about. Would you say that you experienced something like that when Rudi died?"

John mused silently for a moment. He said, "Well, it's different when the teacher's death is such a shock, as Rudi's was. It was a brutal event for us, completely unexpected. Of course in retrospect we could say he had dropped hints to us, but still it was a profound shock." John went on to talk about what had happened within the network of Rudi's students and the people who Rudi had empowered to "teach" his work after the shock of his sudden death. He said, "Of course Rudi's work was very different than your lineage. He never expected or wanted to have a lineage holder and didn't speak of himself in terms of being part of or having a lineage. He was a guru, but he wanted to pass the work that he did on while he was living and for us to go out and teach it. So Yogi Ramsuratkumar is a very traditional Hindu, and I imagine that his passing will be much more like what you are describing."

The group spoke then at length about Yogi Ramsuratkumar, Lee's trips to India, the bands, the ashram in France, Lee's teaching work in Europe. Every now and then Gerry—who sat on the big couch by the huge windows looking out over the Arizona mountains, still green in winter with their pine and cedar cover—would smile contentedly and sigh, saying, "I can't believe I feel so good! It's wonderful! I was so afraid to come here. It's taken me so long to get up the nerve to come here, and now I find you are so *kind,* you are such a sweet person." She looked at Lee with surprise and appreciation. "It's wonderful. You're great, I'm okay, everything's fine. I love being here!" Her comments had a quality of surprise, of child-like innocence and delight to them. The bright desert sun that shone so benevolently through the wide southern windows also gave a sense of goodness, peace and safety to the afternoon gathering, but Lee was rather like a lovely cat purring beside a warm fire; just behind the pleasant appearance of things lurked a tiger from the jungle wilds that could leap out at any time.

Jane commented to Gerry, "It is good to be able to interact with people in many different kinds of relationship. Lee very much enjoys having friends of the community come and visit, and when you come as a guest, as a friend, then friendship is the response that you get from him. Of course interacting with him as a student is a whole different proposal. When people approach as students then there is a certain tacit permission given for him to work with them as the teacher, to make the teaching available in perhaps more direct or confrontive terms. So of course the heat is a lot higher. In France where Lee gives seminars many people, including disciples of Arnaud Desjardins and Yvan Amar, come for the teaching. They come to be confronted. If you approached Lee in that capacity, you would experience something else altogether."

Gerry nodded as if this made sense to her. She talked about how she had been genuinely scared to come to Lee's ashram, and she knew that being sick and having to cancel twice was part of the labyrinth she had had to navigate to get here. She had been reading *Tawagoto* for some years, and during these past two weeks while she was sick she gathered all the issues of *Tawagoto* she could find and read them all, cover to cover. She had formed a picture of Lee and the intensity of his students' work with him from that source. When asked what her impression of the community was from reading the journal, she said, "Well, you are baring your soul, really going deeply into your internal process in *Tawagoto,* so reading it was like an *encounter*. It was very *intense* . . ."

John turned to Lee and smiled at him, then referring to Lee's reputation for being fierce, he said pointedly, "Of course you are really into hospitality, aren't you, so it was a pretty safe bet to come here as *guests!*" Lee nodded his head, acknowledging the innuendo, an implied compliment. They both laughed.

It had been a long, rather mellow afternoon. Gerry said, "We should call and cancel our meditation for tonight." They went downstairs with Lee to call before dinner. Lee gave them the opportunity to pick out any Hohm Press books they might like to have. They picked out *Facets of the Diamond, The Alchemy of Transformation*, two books about Yogi Ramsuratkumar and some CDs and tapes. Lee kept piling on additional gifts until they had an armload.

Night began to fall outside. Dasya lit up the grill. The table was set with flowers and candles. Tonight the menu was filet mignon—medallions of pure, organically raised beef—new potatoes baked with shallots in butter and rosemary, fresh spinach and red onion salad dressed with bacon grease and vinegar and tossed with crumbled crispy bacon and gorgonzola cheese. Wine would be served and dessert—a selection of five kinds of Häagen-Dazs ice cream. Once again the table was set for thirteen adults. The four children had a card table set nearby for their meal.

The mood had been building all day. John and Gerry joked about how they had served their purpose—to give us an opportunity to have a celebratory meal. The smells of the sizzling meat wafted in through the sliding glass door of the narrow dining room into the living room while everyone sat and talked. Finally it was time to come into the dining room and take our places. Dasya, Kelly and Ann served the filets, cooked to order, on each plate and then Kelly introduced the wine, a 1983 St. Julien. A second bottle of wine, a different kind, sat on the shrine behind Lee's seat at the head of the table. The wine was poured for Lee first to taste and approve. Then wine was poured in everyone's glass, most of them full—with one exception at Lee's instruction. Lee said, "Let's have a toast. Let's see . . . who should give it this time?" He looked around the table with a smile on his face, looking from one to another of his students and settling on Dasya. Dasya held his glass up to Lee and said, "To hospitality, a flower of devotion." We raised our glasses and drank to Lee, to his guests, to each other, to the influence of the lineage, to the Work.

As everyone began to seriously partake of the food, the mood deepened into pure pleasure. Only a week before Lee had read from E.J. Gold, "The entity can change the appearance of the room." This seemed to be happening before my eyes. A golden cast had settled on the planes and surfaces of the physical space and its occupants. The hue of the sublime was shining in individual faces. John Mann, who was sitting next to me, took the first bite of his filet. "Fantastic!" he commented enthusiastically.

After two or three bites of food and a sip of wine, a *rasa* was flowing in the room as if Saqi, the mythical wine-boy in the Sufi tavern of ruin, had poured an elixir along with the wine in our glasses. A sweet emptiness infused the space. Every person and every object sparkled with a fine, scintillating mist. This *rasa*, or mood, of communion, of beauty and sheer enjoyment, was a pure, raw feeling that ran like an electric current through the room. The mood of communion was profound but also joyous, light and heavy at the same time—light because of the joy and ecstasy and beauty of the path, heavy because of the tremendous obligation, the payment that is extracted once one enters into a deeper commitment to the Work.

Every bite of the food was sublime. The wine was exquisite. Somehow this raw, bloody piece of beef, the fried bacon with its tangy, salty, crispy animal fat had become something completely other than the gross food which it was. It had been sublimated, transmuted into another substance, a kind of *soma,* and the wine had been made into amrita, nectar. There was a distinct kinship in this subtle transmutation with those who participated in the Last Supper, where wine and bread became blood and body in an enactment of classic tantric rites. Lee presided over all this with a gleaming, magnanimous, gracious presence. He was all elegance and receptivity. He was royal and yet humble, quietly feeding the foundation, existing tacitly as context underneath the effervescence of the space, and also turned toward his guests in a constant gesture of unstinted hospitality.

John and Gerry easily fit into this intimate mood and seemed delighted by every aspect of the meal, the evening, the company. When the coffee and dessert were served Gerry said astutely, "Well John, you have to pay for all this hospitality with some stories!" She assiduously began to work to draw John, who seemed naturally reticent and introverted, out of his usual disposition. He told a number of stories about Rudi, which everyone was eager to hear.

This sharing of one's experience with fellow travelers on the path is one of the many gifts and joys of being in Lee's company. He is supremely generous in offering his students the opportunity to meet and spend time with other teachers and disciples. He has on a number of occasions recounted his own disappointment in having missed the opportunity to meet Rudi many years ago in New York. Wingate Payne was a Silva Mind Control instructor and friend of Lee's who later became a student of Rudi's and then carried on Rudi's teaching after his death. Wingate called Lee one day and invited him to meet Rudi at a talk that Rudi was giving in New York that night. Lee declined, saying that although he wanted very much to meet Rudi, it didn't fit into his schedule that day. He said, "Some other time." The next day, Rudi was killed in the plane crash. "Timing is everything," Lee often says when he tells this particular story. According to Lee, it was a missed opportunity of a lifetime.

One of the stories that John told was about the aftermath of Rudi's death. He said that he had waited for ten years after Rudi's death to go to the crash site. "Finally I went with some other people to the site where Rudi's plane had crashed in the woods," he said. "I had always been afraid that it would feel really bad to be there, which was the reason why I hadn't gone all those years after his death. We walked through the woods and got there. We looked around and said to each other, 'It doesn't feel so bad here.' Then we said, 'Hey, it feels *pretty good* here . . . In fact it feels *great* here!' And I realized that it could have easily been an empowered *samadhi* site. There was a tremendous sense of freedom there. Later one of the men who was with me started chuckling. He kept laughing to himself. Finally I asked him what was going on. He said that he had looked on the map to find the name of this place. And guess what the name was . . . Fat Man's Delight!"

MARCH 1999

March 2, 1999
Arizona Ashram

At lunch Lee called from Houston on his way home from Mexico. He was ebullient and obviously in high spirits. One could almost feel the heat radiating off of him across the miles of stretched wires. It seemed he had had a great trip and was eager to get back to the ashram and his work here.

At six-thirty he returned from eight days in Mexico. The sangha was gathered—about sixty people—in the greenhouse for the Tuesday night After Dinner Talk meal of salad or fruit. As soon as Lee arrived he came down to the greenhouse where everyone waited at the table, having just finished eating. He took his usual seat on the floor at the head of the long table and ate a huge plate of salad. He smiled at his companions at the table, his eyes roving from one to the next, making contact. His mood was so high you could catch it from him, a natural contact high.

As soon as he was finished with dinner the group went to the meditation hall to hear stories of his teaching work in Mexico City with Mario Tarin, a disciple of Arnaud Desjardins, and his students. Tom and Mariana, two of Lee's students who both speak fluent Spanish and had gone with him to videotape and translate his talks, were thumbing through their notes, whispering to each other nervously as people waited for Lee to enter. The heat was on for them to do a good job of relating what happened on the trip to the rest of the sangha.

Soon Lee came briskly into the room. He was fairly crackling with electrical energy as he sat down on his chair on the dais. Right away Tom dove into his notes. The first thing he said was, "I want to give you an idea of the mood of the week. This was Lee's statement to an interviewer on Mexico public radio when he asked for a sentence to use as an ongoing clip to advertise the interview show: 'My name is Lee Lozowick. I am totally dedicated to God. If you don't believe in God, go fuck yourself!' " Laughter rang through the hall, there were smiles all around—it was good to have the guru back home. Quickly Tom and Mariana started relaying stories.

They described a grand celebratory mood, a sweetness and joy in the interactions between Lee and his hosts—Mario, his wife Georgina, and Mario's students. Almost all of Mario's students are women who originally came to know him as a psychotherapist and yoga teacher, but now are beginning to be interested in spiritual principles and the possibility of work on self. Tom described how these upper class, well-to-do Mexican women in all their finery and expensive clothes, make-up and jewelry, with all their servants and opulent homes and wealth and privilege, became transformed into devotees in Lee's presence. They were often ecstatic, intoxicated, acting as if they were drunk. At a dinner that occurred early in the week one of the husbands called out to Lee in front of everyone, in a loud, booming, but friendly voice, "Lee! What is it about you that all these women are giving you all their attention for a whole week, spending all this time on you, when I can't even get my wife's attention for one day?" The man was jovial and good-natured about it, yet at the same time the question was both real and carried a challenge to Lee. Lee deftly danced around the challenge and made the man his ally in one graceful move—in a light and humorous vein, Lee smiled back and quipped, "I have the same problem!"

"We traveled with Lee in a corridor of luxury," Tom continued. "We went from upper class to upper, upper class, and I even began to see the differences between them. The lunches were true feasts. There was one lunch that I've called 'The Gopi Lunch.' These women were out of their minds, giddy in a way . . ."

Lee started to laugh with embarrassment as he listened to Tom. He looked out at his students and protested, "He's exaggerating!"

A chorus of voices—from several people who sat listening to these reports—responded to Lee's protestation, playfully countered, saying, *"No, he's not!"* The point being that, despite all obstacles, the delightful enjoyment of good company and the tangible presence of many different moods of divine love is the common point of many people's experience with Lee.

Mariana continued, "People were constantly giving Lee flowers, there were flowers everywhere; people were garlanding Lee with beautiful exotic flowers over elaborate, rich meals that lasted three, four or five hours each day. There was lots of humor, Lee kept people laughing." Tom added, "But the talks were all hot, hot, hot, with striking and pointed comments flying out through the midst of the laughter." Tom continued, saying that when Lee gave his talk on sex he was ribald and bawdy—he geared his language at the most basic inhibitions of Westerners. He talked about farting during sex, about how women smell, about how men are so proud when they are giving women the gift of their precious semen! Lee said, "I'd like to have been a gynecologist, but I didn't have the discipline to do it. Now I'm a spiritual gynecologist—so open your legs and spread 'em!" He was so risqué, and used such inflammatory language that the teenagers who were present would look at each other in wonder, as if they'd struck gold—finally here was an older adult who was being real for a change! They kept coming back again and again for more of Lee's talks. Mariana, the translator for these talks, said that the many upper-class Mexicans who came to Lee's talks heard profanity in Spanish that they hadn't heard in years.

The stories reflected another example of the Baul master working with people in gritty, earthy ways, hitting the streets where they live. Or, more accurately, where they are afraid to live. If one is crystallized and blocked at the level of the first three *chakras*—and everyone typically is in one way or another—then to begin with one has to get out of denial about the most fundamental facts of life. Scatological jokes are one of Lee's areas of expertise. Jokes about sex, shit, farts, screwing sheep, urine; jokes about Christian guilt and sin, jokes about men and women, jokes about heaven and hell—Lee employs all of these with an adroit wisdom. His jokes and insults and provocations are often like sticks of dynamite thrown at a rock wall to bring it down.

During Lee's talk about sex he had said to a woman who had asked for tantric techniques, "The payment for teaching sex technology is very high. It's so high, in fact, that over the years I've been teaching I've not given that instruction to more than a handful of my students who are in committed sexual relationships." Even so, a woman asked him if he would give her specific sexual techniques. He responded, *"You* can't pay for it. You *cannot.* And I'm not the person to give that information to you . . ." Clearly she was an example of someone who wanted the information but was unable to pay because she had not earned the ability to pay through sacrifice and hard work on the path. As it turned out, this woman was a sexual therapist by profession.

In another talk Lee spoke about "playing for table stakes," which is a kind of poker in which people play for very high stakes, and the winner take all. Lee said, "Do your guru a favor: if you can't hack the Work then don't even get started!'"

Tom spoke for a long time about Lee bargaining in the silver market in Mexico City. He talked about the kind of friendly geniality that Lee exhibited to each person he bargained with. When haggling with people, if they couldn't agree on a price, Lee would pat the person on the back, smile and say, "It's okay. Thank you," then walk on to the next shop. One shopkeeper in particular kept parrying Lee's attempts to bargain on some silver jewelry, saying, "Señor, please—just a little Coke money for my children!" Lee walked out five times during this bargaining session, bringing the man down slowly to his price. Tom said, "This particular man lost his shirt in this deal, and maybe he even lost his self-esteem in a way, but he stayed in there with Lee." When Tom told this story Lee spoke from up the dais about this shopkeeper, saying humorously, "Next lifetime he'll show up here . . ."

Lee seemed to spark off of this bargaining session in the street markets when later he spoke to his hosts about his intention for the visit in Mexico. "I don't do 'retail' anymore in this Work. I do 'wholesale.' I don't need more friends, I don't need more students, I don't need any of you. I'm only here for Mario. I'm going to get in and out of here without any connecting . . . But you still have to *pay* for what you get from me . . ."

The last night he was in Mexico Lee was asked to give a talk titled, "Andre Malraux said, 'The twenty-first century will either be or not be.' What does the spiritual master Lee Lozowick have to say about this?" Lee began by saying, "That's way too deep a question for me! I'm interested in voodoo—things you can't understand or explain! Why not study spiritual work and yoga instead of science? Krishna cloned himself 16,108 times in one instant, so that all the gopis felt that he was with each one alone! Now *that's* something worth thinking about! Scientists are all giddy because they've cloned a sheep. It took tens of years and untold resources to clone one little sheep. Krishna instantly cloned himself 16,108 times! Which of the two fields is more viable, eh?"

Earlier in the week Lee had given a talk one night titled, "Science and Spirituality." Lee had gone into what Tom called "a doom and gloom mood" in which he was saying, as he has on many occasions in public talks, that there is "no hope" for Western technological civilization. Lee often speaks poignantly about how human beings are losing their capacity for true creativity because of our relationship to computers. During the talk that night he said that people would become mutated, and there wouldn't be any real sex in the twenty-first century because of computers and virtual technology. "In another fifty years," Lee said, "no one will know how to write or add without a machine to do it for them!"

Lee then spoke about the importance of personal transformation in the world, the kind of transformation that can only occur through work on self. He said, "There really is no hope. There will not be some great age of higher consciousness. Things are exactly the same now as they were thousands of years ago, or in the time of Jesus. The only hope that we have is to have faith in personal transformation. Transformation doesn't happen in groups. Groups don't transform or change. Transformation occurs *one person at a time*," he said. "You have to have *faith* in the possibility of personal transformation and in its reality."

Lee's mood and Tom's and Mariana's stories painted a picture of Lee's communication during the visit. But also it seemed that it was painful for Tom and Mariana to watch people's lack of sensitivity or education with regard to proper protocol with a spiritual master or teacher. Even if we have studied the traditions of the East and the role of the guru or the spiritual master, we are often still so biased by the Western perspective that it flavors our interactions with spiritual teachers, however well-meant the intention may be. Westerners are typically aggressive, imperious, self-centered and rebellious. We think only of ourselves and our own personal agenda and comfort.

For example, causing the spiritual master to wait for thirty or forty-five minutes past the time planned for a meal, or a departure; talking loudly or virtually yelling in the master's face; standing and hovering over the master physically; insinuating oneself into photographs or demanding photographs of him; exhibiting controlling behavior, either aggressively or passively—in the latter case, by being late, or in the former case, by insisting that the master do things we have planned, rather than allowing him to be spontaneous. Or even more blatantly, we ask him what he would like, what his preferences are, and then we go ahead and do whatever we personally want to do! Too often we take the generosity of the spiritual master for granted, and fail to have the respect and gratitude that is due.

This is something Lee bears good-naturedly, especially when his hosts are as innocent, sincere and hospitable as they were in Mexico. He returned with a glowing heartfulness about his many new friends (even though he said that he didn't need any more, and he got plenty on this trip). Of course with his own students he is less patient or tolerant. Lee endures all of these situations frequently, and they exact a certain price in his work with people. In other words, it costs everyone involved; those who spend time with him, who think they want what it is that he has to offer, have to pay for their own unwillingness or inability to live in the context which he is constantly offering. It's not that he personally makes one pay—rather it is lawful that the teacher is bound by the actions of his students. If students are unconsciously demonstrating ego's tendency to be intrusive, greedy, insensitive, manipulative and controlling, then the teacher can only respond at the level of relationship that is being offered by those around him. We may not even notice that we have lost the opportunity for a more delicate, subtle and powerful mood or *rasa*, a particular communion with him and with each other, or a more profound or elevated teaching communication than what is being given. Although not peculiar to Westerners alone (ego is in many ways the same everywhere), most Westerners really have no idea of the rare atmosphere that is possible in the master's company, or of what spiritual transmission is about. This is especially true with Lee because he is willing to be with his students where they are, to enter into their lives and meet them there rather than retreat behind a façade or persona of "spirituality."

Lee pays most of all for these indiscretions because his work, and the momentum that he is constantly creating, gets slowed down, hindered, blocked. At times this is clearly a source of frustration for him, especially when this kind of behavior is inflicted on him by his own students, even his senior students, as happened in India in 1998. In Mexico City Lee was dealing with many new acquaintances who weren't his students and who were very new in the Work, and therefore are absolved of the kind of responsibility that he holds for his own students whom he has personally trained, and who should know better.

On Monday, Lee's last day in Mexico City, a "free day" was planned—no dharma talks, no seminar, no long three and four hour lunches like every day the week before. The woman who was in charge of designing this day had planned a day of art, history and culture. Lee had already said, loud and clear, "All I want to do while I'm here is eat and hang out and work. No tourist stuff!" But this woman had her heart set on taking Lee to see historical Mexico. She even had arranged a tour guide to help out. At one point she happily herded Lee and his entourage along to see a "special, ancient door." The very idea of this was preposterous given the context of Lee's entire life. He turned to Tom and said facetiously, "They've been looking at the special ancient door all week! If they haven't gotten it by now, they never will." It was a statement that reflected just how constant and pervasive our state of distraction from the real truth actually is.

If Lee's attitude was somewhat of a disappointment for this woman and for the tour guide, it was still supremely magnanimous of Lee to allow everyone to drag him around to begin with. Mariana talked at length about how she was able to see "the sacrifice of the guru" more clearly than ever on this trip. His willingness to be used at whatever level people could make use of his teaching, his benevolent presence, his tremendous patience, kindness and compassion were the constant force field he generated for everyone. On the sightseeing day they had seen a beautiful, immense bank of bougainvillea shrubs growing in a flower shop stall. Mariana asked Lee if Tom could take a picture in hopes that it might be made into a *murti*—an empowered photograph. As soon as Lee stood by the mass of flaming red blossoms and Tom picked up his camera, probably ten people also pulled out their cameras and the scene quickly became what Mariana called a "Vogue photo shoot." She realized her mistake too late, and once again the spiritual master was literally besieged.

At one lunch Lee and company came into the home where they would dine. One wall was covered with what Tom called "very bad, expensive art." As they walked in Lee took the chair against the wall so that his back was turned to the huge, garish, pretentious paintings. He looked at Tom and said, "It's a good thing I get to sit here because then *you* have to look at this stuff!" He laughed. Lee not uncommonly comments on what we mistakenly consider to be "art." So much of it is actually distasteful and dissonant to the aesthetic of real being. Human beings have become so desensitized that we cannot distinguish what is of real value to the soul, what communicates objective principles of truth, beauty, mercy or impermanence. We have, to a large degree, lost touch with what is real. Tom commented as he told this story, "Lee was throwing out teaching communications like this all week, but I wondered if people were hearing him."

Maybe the greatest teaching lesson of all was the way that Lee seemed to laugh and dance his way through all of this. His generosity, his elegance as a guest and his context of making the teaching available never wavered. What I have discovered in myself as I've traveled with Lee is that none of this is ever a problem for him; typically these situations are a problem only for Lee's students—his doting devotees who take our roles very seriously.

March 4, 1999
Arizona Ashram

Tonight Lee began the After Dinner Talk reading a story about Yogi Ramsuratkumar from a letter that Mariana had received from a friend in India:

Yogi Ramsuratkumar used to have unspoken rules concerning his health and person. A friend of mine once asked him, after he had vomited several times in her presence, "Are you sick?" After that she was never allowed to sit with him again. She was one of the regulars before that. Another friend was just groping to ask about his health once and he firmly warned her that if she did not stop, she could expect never to be allowed into his satsang again.

185

Lee stopped reading and said forcefully, pointedly, "So you should all take this seriously. When Yogi Ramsuratkumar dies, I could inherit *this* way of working, and then if any of you even *ask* about my health, you don't get to see me for a year!" Lee has been struggling with his closest devotees for years concerning the kind of warriorship that he wants from his students regarding his own personal health. There is no way to know what kind of work is occurring through the bodily states that the master moves in and out of, but too often he is besieged by questions, "Will you take this herb, that tincture, this homeopathic pill?" We think we are expressing love and concern by foisting cures and potions on the master when it is actually true sanctuary, the absolute context of the dharma, that is the most potent medicine one can offer to him. It is a situation that Lee seems to find maddening, and yet we continue to be obtuse about it. Tonight he was making a definite point, attempting once again to bring his devotees into alignment with his context. He continued reading:

I feel that Yogi's work is disturbed when people think about his health or possible death, and talk about it. Whatever subtle work he is doing may have better chances to manifest when he is not given negative attention focusing on his bodily appearance by many people with a rather heavily dualistic mentality. When one is aware of Father's presence, one does not deliberately focus on physical/personal details. One is aware of all of it—it is the background, not the main reality. Internal energies stay loose, creative, capable of influencing situations, relationships, health/sickness, etc. Capacity for insight remains present, one is capable of non-logical activity, directly, unpremeditatively. A yogi abides in the space of oneness, inner freedom, fluid activity—he is a sort of martial artist in his mind. The whole linear time/mind frame Western over-organized culture indulges in is absent in his Reality.

I could never think in terms of Yogi's health, sickness, death. I can only put my mind into Father's ever-present unknowableness. Whatever happens is like clouds forming and dissolving in the sky. The form they take is not important. Resting in the space of not creating smoke-clouds in my mind is the best I can do. That is the only way I have ever been able to meet Yogi. When my clouds are away, he shines into my heart . . .

Mother of Sri Aurobindo Ashram felt the greatest obstacle to her work of transforming all levels of her being into direct divine awareness was when the thought forms of her disciples were sending her messages: "Mother is about to die." It would stiffen her energy, prevent total alignment with her spiritual levels, pull the unconsciousness of death force into her body . . . .

With a crisp movement Lee put the letter away and said, "Everybody get that? Everybody understand that?" People nodded. Someone asked the question, "So our health doesn't affect our work?"

Lee answered, "At the beginning, yes it does. But less and less as one goes on, and at the end, not at all." He picked up *The Wheel of Time,* a compilation of quotations from Carlos Castaneda's books, and began to read from the pages that he had marked to share during the After Dinner Talk. After about twenty minutes of reading and commenting, he came upon a story about the ruthless tutelage of don Juan's cohort, Florinda Matus, that wove exactly into his point at the beginning of the talk:

I once had a fistula by the crest of the bone of my hip, a product of a fall that I had taken years before into a ravine filled with cactus needles. There had been seventy-five needles stuck in my body. One of them either hadn't come out completely or had left a residue of dirt or debris that years later produced a fistula.

186

My doctor said, "That's nothing. It is just a sack of pus that has to be lanced. It's a very simple operation. It would take a few minutes to clean it out."

I consulted with Florinda, and she said, "You are the nagual. You either cure yourself, or you die. No shades of meaning, no double behavior. For a nagual to be lanced by a doctor, you must have lost your power. For a nagual to die fistulated? What a shame." (pp. 181-82)

Lee looked up with a satisfied smile and said, "All of you got the connection between that and the first story about Yogi Ramsuratkumar? Okay. Good." It's not at all unusual for things to come together like this—dharma points converging spontaneously to reinforce a particular consideration—with no effort on Lee's part. It was just a small bit of everyday, ordinary magic.

March 5, 1999
Sedona, Arizona

At the beginning of the second set of the liars, gods & beggars gig tonight at the Oak Creek Brewing Company, a small bar and brewery nestled on a back street in the gorgeous natural setting of Sedona, Arizona, the entire group—band and audience—went into a collective *bhava*. Lee had appeared at the club with his hair matted and ratted and twisted into tangled ropes of silvery gray locks, or *jatta*, as they are called by the sadhus of India. Each lock was tipped with red and blue iridescent beads, blessed by Yogi Ramsuratkumar. Known in America today as dreadlocks and identified with Rastafarians, wearing the hair in this way is a custom that goes back thousands of years. In India the mendicant ascetics who are worshippers of Lord Shiva wear *jatta* and cover themselves with holy ash as a symbol of worldly renunciation, or to emulate Lord Shiva in the form of his offspring, Skanda, who is depicted with six matted locks. *Jatta* is also a statement of adherence to the strict ritual practices, including beggary, that were laid out over two thousand years ago in the Naradaparivrajaka Upanishad. Matted hair is found in many spiritual traditions in and around the world. It's altogether possible that Jesus of Nazareth would have appeared from his forty days in the desert with *jatta*.

"Great dreads!" Everett called out with a big smile when Lee walked into the club. Lee said nothing as he threaded his way past the tables and up onto the informal "stage." The band had arrived earlier to set up the equipment and do a sound check. Their equipment was set up on the floor in between huge metal vats of beer and right alongside the tables where customers would sit and drink. Some of Lee's students sat around at tables, waiting for the gig to start, while the club regulars sat on tall stools at the bar. Outside on the patio a cheery piñon fire blazed brightly. People sat around tables there, drinking beer in the chilly air, warmed by the fire and the spirits.

The performances of liars, gods & beggars are always fantastic in terms of musical ability, but now and then, not infrequently, the band plays for the "unseen audience." When this happens they hit a space that is pure transcendence, in which anyone who is participating in the chamber or voyage feels the transformative power that is unleashed through the music. That might be experienced as particularly inspired and passionate dancing, or a feeling of relaxation or euphoria. Maybe one would simply feel better in general, leave the club in a good mood, with a lighter step, a smile on the face. On the other hand, it might be an experience of mystical ascension.

The first set had started out slowly tonight. Even though the music sounded great, the band was tight and technically played well, for some reason it was hard to get up and dance. Attempting to move out on the dance floor was like walking through mud or thick sand. A few days earlier Lee had made a recommendation to Stan, one of the long-time members of the band and a dedicated practitioner, that he leave the band. The shock of this was still reverberating through the air. Stan is a very fine musician who has composed many fabulous songs to Lee's lyrics over the years and who has been integral to the LGB project. Despite this, for the past few years he had withdrawn his participation and had created a significant energetic block in the dynamics and momentum of the band. Tonight he was obviously burning with Lee's recommendation, and still considering what he would do. To leave the band or stay in it, that was the question in the air. The conflict of his dilemma was visibly at work in him, and yet the notes and chords and rhythms from his guitar became more sublime as the night wore on. His love of the music and his appreciation for the band, the music, Lee, the sangha—all of it—became a tangible force in the space.

In the midst of all this something shifted near the end of the first set. It started with Justin's solo on the last song of the first set—"Work With It," more affectionately known as "Cold Slab," a fierce and confrontive song driven by guitar and drums and kicked up several notches on the intensity scale by a long drum solo by Justin. Each time he performs the solo in this particular song Justin seems to abandon himself completely to the agony of creation. He captures the attention of everyone in the space, even those who have been paying no attention to the band before the solo started. Tonight everyone in the club was already paying attention as Lee half-moaned, half shouted the words:

Life don't last forever
Nothin' we can do about it
We think we're immortal
Well honey I doubt it
Everything will rot
Everything will sag
One day you'll be lying
On a cold slab
In a bag.
What are we doin'?
Why are we here?
It makes no difference
It may never be clear.
Got to do what is needed
Got to serve while you can
'cause time don't give a shit
About the frailty of man.

As Justin wailed away on the drums with a rhythm and force that defied logic—how does someone get to have a moving center with that much fluidity and power?—the local people in the bar were transfixed, whooping and yelling, staring at Justin and the band. Their attention was riveted; they had no idea what was going on, but their faces registered the fact that something beyond the ordinary was occurring.

The small concrete dance floor was crowded with Lee's students. The Baul Theatre

Company had driven up from the Renaissance Fair in Apache Junction, and several people had come from Prescott. There were also twenty or so Sedona locals and six or seven Osho (Rajneesh) *sannyasins*, whose center is next door to the club. At the end of the song the band took a break, and the dancers reluctantly left the floor for their seats.

Twenty minutes later the band went back onstage and from the first chord of the first song the whole club seemed to be transported as people flooded the dance floor. Dancing with sannyasins is always a lot of fun. They are well acquainted with partying, since when Osho was alive their school was known for all kinds of radical experimentation with sex, music, dancing, various psychotherapies and wild and orgiastic group parties. Now, wherever Lee's bands go—Europe, California, Boulder—whenever *sannyasins* get wind of the band performances, they show up. They dance and juice the space with their enthusiasm and ecstasy.

As the band picked up momentum inhibitions fell away and the group on the dance floor began to dance madly. The mood was one of drunken revelry, and yet Lee's students hadn't had anything stronger than an orange creme soda or a Coke to drink. As the music went from one song to another an invisible heady wine, a honey mead that permeated the senses, seem to lift everything out of the ordinary. The next to the last song was "The Sleep of No Return," with a bewitching melody and get-down beat that sneaks like a thief into the bloodstream and spins pure vibration into rhythm and beat, translated into muscle and bone. Before you know it, you just have to dance. And not just *got* to dance, but dance with abandon, in ecstasy.

After Everett sang the first verse Lee suddenly leapt off the stage and started dancing with the crowd of twenty-five or thirty people who were packed in between tables and the steel vats of brewing spirits. His eyes glowed with a kind of unearthly luminosity. He danced like a demon with his dreadlocks whirling around his head, but his countenance was that of an angel—an Old Testament angel perhaps, the kind you can barely look at because their beauty is so penetrating, so otherworldly. This was a human man who was dancing, whirling, spinning, and yet the light that blazed in his wide open eyes was strangely bright, even inhuman. It was a different kind of presence that Lee was animating. It took a while to locate him, then he came into focus—that is, if it was possible to locate him. He was Dionysus come to call, ready for the sacrifice, ready for the chase. He danced in the midst of the jostling, ecstatic crowd until the song came to an end and Dionysus receded into the background, only slightly, as Lee returned to the stage.

Stan broke into "Just A Woman," the last song of the night. The mob on the dance floor went into a frenzy, dancing as hard as they could, drinking every last drop of ecstasy out of the night. The song roared through the room, carrying everyone along with a force that churned the well of longing, and as the guitars rang out their final chords, Lee jumped to the microphone and yelled, "Okay revelers! Dionysus calls! To the woods, to the woods!"

The music stopped, the whirlwind began to slowly die down. Sweating and shining, Lee's party gathered their coats and belongings to be ready to leave as soon as Lee wanted to go. As he walked off the stage he stood for a moment in the center of the small dance floor talking with a man who has come to several liars, gods & beggars gigs in Sedona. He was a long-time *sannyasin*. He introduced himself to Lee, shook his hand and said, "I lived in Poona," to which Lee smiled and said, "Yes, I was in Poona too," referring to the 1979 trip to India when Lee visited the Rajneesh ashram there. The man touched his heart and spoke about how the music had affected him. He asked if he could visit Lee at the ashram in Prescott. Lee smiled and talked with him for a few moments. As the group got into the car someone asked him about the man. "Yes, he may come to the ashram for a visit," Lee responded with a smile, electricity rolling off him in almost visible waves. He started the car and drove home.

March 6, 1999
Phoenix, Arizona

A number of students accompanied Lee to Phoenix to have breakfast at a renowned Jewish deli before the liars, gods & beggars gig at two-thirty that afternoon. While he drove through the desert on the way Lee started talking about other teachers who have no discrimination about how they make the teaching available, and as a result, are often seducing the students of other teachers. As he has many times in the past six months, he began to talk about how Yogi Ramsuratkumar had "brought" him, as a very young teacher, only a year or so after he started teaching, to E.J. Gold, who became Lee's mentor for many years. Lee has often said that E.J., who was his "senior in the Work," helped him tremendously. Lee has been actively extending acknowledgement and gratitude for that help in many comments he has made both privately and in public talks for some time now.

Today he said, "I was lucky to be trained by E.J. because he was so *respectful*. He's totally satisfied with his Work. He can't be bothered with competing with other teachers. He's complete as he is . . . " Then he began to talk about Yogi Ramsuratkumar making the teaching communication that the students of this school should know Lee's music, the lyrics to the songs of Shri and liars, gods & beggars and *John T.,* the rock opera, as well. This is another theme that Lee has returned to many times in his talks and in informal discussions since he's returned from India. Today he said, *"John T. is the* work on disciple-ship in this school. Everyone in this school should know it completely, be able to sing it."

The liars, gods & beggars gig was at the big, grassy green park in Fountain Hills, Arizona, ten miles northwest of Scottsdale. Surrounded by the Sonoran desert and craggy, high, bare mountain peaks, this park creates a strange juxtaposition with the natural environment: the entire bioregion pays for this self-indulgent luxury on the part of the pretentious middle class of Arizona.

As the band picked up momentum after the first few songs, dark clouds threatened rain, which then began to fall in silver streaks, splashing against our faces and making the green grass slippery. The band carried on in grand style for the people who were gathered in this middleworld family scene, scattered across the grass, sitting in their lawn chairs with children playing around. The mood was very light and sweet. Everett went to the mike and said, "We're playing all our nice songs today!" The band was clearly avoid-ing some of their more provocative or raunchy songs. Looking around there were big smiles on the faces of the people who were listening. Cars pulled up and parked in a long row against the curb across the street, where people sat to listen while soft showers fell on those who braved the elements along with the band.

Lee's banter with the audience was relaxed and charming. People were nodding and laughing. The mood and rapport was very gentle. At one point after the band had played about three songs while it was raining Everett said into the mike, "Should we keep play-ing?" Applause and a big yes came from the crowd, Lee's group being the most vocal and noisy bunch in this gathering of middle-class folks. Several local people sat unconcerned under their big umbrellas. They clearly weren't going to let a little desert shower drive them away or ruin their Sunday afternoon outing. The band kept playing and within minutes the clouds blew away and the sun started to shine. It seemed like a minor miracle as the sky opened up into brilliant blue where just moments before were threatening black thunderheads. Of course, that's the way the weather goes in the desert.

A number of people danced near the back of the field while a professional cameraman filmed the band onstage. The dancers enjoyed several songs under clear skies, until the band had been playing for about forty-five minutes and the clouds rolled in again and the rain started to pour in earnest this time. The band was playing on a portable stage with no cover, not entirely safe in wet weather, and in fact even potentially dangerous or damaging to equipment. Still the band chose to go on until they were forced off the stage. They finally had to stop twenty-five minutes early and hustle to get their equipment off the stage in the downpour.

LGB has been doing this kind of thing for almost twelve years, persevering against all kinds of odds to perform Lee's songs. Why? There are many reasons. The benefits to sentient beings of getting Lee's songs out into the world—in the ethers and airwaves, into the auditory and brain channels of countless people over the years—are something that can't be proven or documented. But one can feel the necessity in this music. It goes out as prayer, as *maitri*, as pure blessing power. It has Yogi Ramsuratkumar's regard and blessings woven through it completely. It is his *kheyala* in this world through his son, Lee Lozowick.

On today's occasion in Fountain Hills a man approached the band after their performance. "You guys are great!" he beamed. "Do you play private parties?" Sure, they answered. "Well, I'm giving a private party June 5 in Scottsdale. I'd like you to play." They got his name and number and had Elyse, who books gigs for the band, call him. As it turned out the gig would pay one thousand dollars—a lucrative sum for the band, which has often performed for very little and sometimes for free. Oftentimes the band just gets enough to pay for their gas to drive the hours across the desert to the gig, and sometimes not even enough for that. They go as beggars; they play the guru's music and take whatever alms are offered. This has been one of the many ways that Lee Lozowick has shown his students the way of beggary, passed down in a lineage of beggars, from Papa Ramdas, who wandered for many years as an ecstatic beggar, to his spiritual son, Yogi Ramsuratkumar, the quintessential beggar, a mad lover of God and singer of songs himself, who gives this gift to his son Lee.

March 9, 1999
Arizona Ashram

At the After Dinner Talk tonight Lee talked about the need to eat higher foods—through study, various impressions, sex—and to be able to digest those foods, which includes a healthy elimination process. Lee said, "Sex is one form of higher food. Not just any kind of sex, but adoration, we might say. One of the signs of proper digestion is a kind of clarity and enthusiasm about the dharma, for example.

"Just like with gross food, if you are eating too much higher food, you stop being hungry. If you are eliminating properly you will have a natural hunger for that food. It's the same with gross food: if you are blocked up, constipated so to speak, you look back over your diet, see what you've been eating, and make changes where you need to make changes. Some people can use the higher food of study more than others; some people

191

can use the higher food of sex more than others." He laughed and everyone laughed along with him. "Of course, we all think we like sex, but there really are differences. So too much study or too much sex or too much gross food can create imbalances."

He continued, "For anyone who is deeply, irrevocably committed to this path there has to be a one-pointed focus. Within that we may appear to interact with our families, friends and so on; we may appear to be normal, but underneath that appearance there is a one-pointed focus on the Work. We have to be single-minded. People who are single-minded about personal transformation are threatening to others, to conventional life. But when you are single-minded about your Work you may still need to look, on the surface of things, just like everybody else."

March 12, 1999
Arizona Ashram

This morning at breakfast one of the children asked for cooked oat bran cereal with milk on it, which she was served. She decided she didn't want to eat it, and the full bowl sat untouched on the table. When Jan came up for breakfast Lee said to her, "There is some oat cereal over here if you want to eat it." Jan walked over and looked at it, then said, "No, thanks." She walked back to the other side of the kitchen to make her breakfast.

In a strong voice but with a smile on his face, Lee said, "Jan would have never made it as Gurdjieff's 'egout' (garbage pail) . . . she'd be sitting at his right hand and he'd be passing her all this blessed food to eat and she'd be saying, 'No, no!' "

A heavy silence filled the room as Jan said nothing but continued to make her breakfast. She walked over to the table, sat down and said to Lee, "If you're telling me to eat it I will, but I thought you were *asking* me."

Lee answered instantaneously, forcefully and enigmatically, "A question is always an order, and an order is always phrased as a question."

Jan said, "Okay, I'll eat it."

Lee responded, "No, you can't now!"

Later in a meeting with a number of students Jan asked Lee to expound on the interaction. She said, "Is there more you would say about our interaction?"

He started out with ferocity, saying, "When you first came here you used to eat everything. You were more than a garbage pail, you were a garbage *dump*. You would clear the table, eat anything and everything." Looking at a new student who was listening he explained further, taking the opportunity to make a much larger communication of work principles, "Jan ate volumes of food, I'm not kidding. She was the female version of Brother Juniper. The worse the food looked the more she liked it. You wouldn't believe it. It was really unhealthy and neurotic. She worked on it and the way she is now is much healthier, much more psychologically healthy and strong. She has more personal integrity now, more discrimination. But this became her job, to be 'egout.' Gurdjieff had an 'egout pour sweet' and an 'egout pour viande' that he fed food to at his meals. The 'egout' was the 'garbage pail.' It was a very specific job. Gurdjieff would give boxes of chocolates to the 'egout' to eat, and so on. They would have to stuff themselves even if they were sick because that was their job.

"That became Jan's job. When she changed her eating patterns psychologically that was good, but she had earned a job in the Work. When one earns a job in the Work regardless of their wishes and desires, they've got the job and should hold it responsibly, regardless of where the job came from. But psychologically we think we are independent, when really there is a point in the Work where everything revolves around how close we want to be to the Heart of the Work. The Work doesn't care about healthy choices—we have no life of our own, in which we can make healthy choices for ourselves! The Work decides everything.

"When we went to visit Yogi Ramsuratkumar in 1998 He told us that Swami Satchidananda wanted Yogi to write something, so Yogi asked Krishna and I to do it. He called us both up at the same time and asked us to go represent him at Anandashram with this. Krishna said no and I agreed to write it, I did write it, but when He asked me to go to Anandashram to represent Him I wavered and said it would be difficult and so on, and Yogi said okay . . . This is a good example of how the Work has no consideration of our personal needs, of how I was traveling with my children and would have had to leave them, the cost of changing the plane tickets, changing the whole welcome home plans with everybody—all that. In this situation I said no to the Work, but there is a price to pay . . .

"You all have no private life. So Jan is the garbage pail. When I don't need a garbage pail anymore then she's off the hook, but until then, she's got the job. It's her responsibility to eat everything that I give her. Once we get a job in the Work it's our job until the Work takes us off of it—it has nothing to do with our maturity and psychological health and all that. Like with Yogi Ramsuratkumar this year, every time I make an adjustment in what the Work wants, it *costs*. When you say no to the Work, like I did with Yogi Ramsuratkumar this year, you remember those things when you are dying. This will be one of those things I'll have remorse over.

"When you have no private life in the Work the degree to which you have *anything* is pure gift of the Work. The ultimate demand in this school is no private life. So it's all the gift of the Work—if you get a new carpet for your room, a piece of jewelry or clothing, it's all the gift of the Work. There's no leeway for a private life here. I leave things to Divine Influence, I like for things to just roll along as they will . . . but basically I want my students to be undifferentiated from me in the same way that I am undifferentiated from Yogi Ramsuratkumar, from Yogi Ramsuratkumar's madness, and He is undifferentiated from the madness of Papa Ramdas. Like Ramdas seeing Ram in everything—there is no differentiation."

Turning back to Jan he continued, "You have made a psychological shift in relationship to food and you should apply that in all situations, until I ask you to do something else. What matters is that's the job you've gotten based on tendency and psychology, and it's still your job even if the reason you got it is no longer active in you."

Speaking again to the group as a whole he said, "We really are called to have no private life. The bottom line is that the demand here is to have no life of your own except the life that the Work gives us. Sooner or later we have to give up some of the huge lives that we have come here with . . ."

The new student smiled a little sheepishly and said, "Like I have a pretty big life." Lee grinned mischievously at her. As the meeting came to a close Lee became very child-like and bright. He seemed to be enjoying this talk of "no life of your own" quite immensely, in the way that the dharma always brings him to life. Sitting in a big armchair with his hair matted into curly dreadlocks hanging down to his shoulders Lee looked devilishly happy, like a playful prankster.

Every person who has ever profoundly entered a genuine spiritual path knows the reality of what Lee was talking about. The process of sacrifice begins with one's apparent, worldly life—whatever that is for each of us. It might involve a marriage, a career, possessions, personal financial freedom. But then it might not have anything to do with the appearance of things and may, in fact, be entirely internal. In Lee's company each person's situation is unique. What is the same for everyone are the more subtle levels of "private life" that must be sacrificed. For those who live as renunciates on the ashrams it comes down to things as small as how one schedules one's days, which movies one will see and when, having the personal freedom to travel on one's own schedule or alone. Things as small as deciding what to have for lunch, or if one wants to skip lunch, what books to read, what clothes to wear. Chögyam Trungpa Rinpoche writes that in the Vajrayana path the guru minds the devotee's business two hundred percent. The more deeply one submits to the guru, the more the guru minds one's business. For one who wants to realize the treasures of the path in Lee's company, a greater and greater surrender of the illusion of independence and a personal or private life is going to be a major part of the process of sadhana.

March 15, 1999
Arizona Ashram

At lunch today Lee announced that he had received news that Yogi Ramsuratkumar has given permission for the building of the temple to be resumed. Three or four years ago Yogi Ramsuratkumar told his devotees that when the temple was finished he would leave his body. Not long after that the construction on the temple was stopped. For this reason, that Yogi Ramsuratkumar had the work on the temple resumed had significant implications. Someone asked Lee if this news had any effect on him and his work. Lee shook his head and said, emphatically, "No!" as if that was the most ridiculous consideration possible. This communication was not one of a cold or dispassionate nature, but one of pure context—Lee's work remains stable, unwavering, steadfast regardless of the outer appearance of things, that is, whether his Father, Yogi Ramsuratkumar, is in the body or not.

Still chewing on his first response, Jane said, "That information about Yogi resuming work on the temple is bound to have some effect on you—in whatever way your internal labyrinth works . . . Doesn't it?" This time Lee answered, "Well yes, of course." He didn't offer more. Why was the mood and timbre of his answer now so different than the first time the question was asked? It seemed that the difference was in the inflection and unspoken layers of meaning within the question. The first time the question was thrown out without thinking and got the most basic level of response, the front line of the dharma; the second time the question was asked with more forethought and consideration behind the asking. Every moment with Lee is an opportunity to see how the guru operates in a mysterious attunement with his environment. The guru is the perfect unconscious mirror of the state of his devotees in the moment. In this case unconscious means unpremeditated and without volition. In other words, totally automatic, based on an instinct that doesn't operate through the processes and filters of the mind in any way.

March 16, 1999
Arizona Ashram

After lunch today while the kitchen was being cleaned up Lee walked in and rather nonchalantly said, "I got an urgent fax from Yogi Ramsuratkumar today wanting to know how things are going because He hasn't heard from me. He must be tuned into what's going on here . . ."

"Haven't you written him since you've been back?" Jane asked.

Lee answered, "No," then added, "He knows everything that is going on."

Curious as always, two or three of his students asked simultaneously, "What did you tell him?"

Lee answered, "Nothing. I faxed Him back right away and said that everything was fine." Looking at the amazement in our faces Lee then added, "I don't want to burden Him with personal trivia." He smiled and walked out, leaving his students to heft the weight of the news. It seemed that Yogi Ramsuratkumar sensed that there had been some upheaval, perhaps that L. had left the community, and wanted to make sure all was well. Lee himself complains, and at times rails away, about his own students not keeping him informed of events and concerns in their lives. Now it appeared that he was doing exactly the same thing with Yogi Ramsuratkumar—wanting to protect him in some way or keep Him from having to deal with his "personal trivia."

Later in the afternoon while Lee chopped vegetables for the huge bowls of salad that he would serve his students at dinner tonight before his After Dinner Talk, Jane sat beside the kitchen table near where he was working and asked for a clarification on the matter. "So you gave Yogi the option of not having to know the details about your personal life by faxing him and saying, 'Everything is fine,' but at the same time making the information available by also faxing Bret with more details in case Yogi wants more information. It seems to me that in that way you left everything up to him—on the one hand you didn't 'burden' him with details, but you also let him know everything was fine and made additional information available."

"That's right," Lee said. "Yogi Ramsuratkumar already knows everything He needs to know . . ." He paused for a moment for effect perhaps, then said, "And He *will* ask Bret. *He will ask Bret*," he emphasized the second time, looking at her penetratingly. There was no doubting his statement. The question was how to understand the channels of communication between these two extraordinary human beings? It was obviously beyond rational understanding. Trying to draw conclusions about something that was taking place outside of logic and reason was a dead-end pursuit.

Jane questioned further, "But with your own students you get very upset when someone is sick or has a major problem or event and they don't even tell you about it."

Lee stopped chopping celery and looked at her as if he was answering the most basic and obvious question, with a look that said, "Don't you already know the answers to these questions?" Instead he patiently explained, "Don't you think I would appreciate it if all these people who send me letters describing every detail of their personal lives would stop writing me all that crap? If someone is sick it's another thing. J. would be well today if she had written me about her illness six months before I finally found out about it! I want people to tell me when they are sick so they can be more readily in my attention and receiving blessings, and so enter into a process of healing and move through what they need to move through much *much* faster than they would if I don't know what's going on.

That should be obvious . . . On the other hand, why should I tell Yogi about something that has already happened, that is irrevocable and there is nothing anyone can do about it?"

Like a rat on a treadmill, Jane kept going. "So Yogi Ramsuratkumar already knows everything?" Lee looked at her appraisingly, as if assessing the degree of her stubborn insistence on getting him to talk about this more. "He knows everything He *needs* to know. That couldn't have been more adequately and completely proven than it already has been time and again!"

"So it seems that you are asking one thing of your students, but you interact with Yogi Ramsuratkumar under a different set of Laws altogether. Is that right?" She pressed. Lee walked across to the refrigerator to get something out for the salad.

"Yes. That's right." End of discussion.

March 17, 1999
Arizona Ashram

Tonight in the After Dinner Talk Lee showed a video from his recent trip to Mexico in which he was giving a public talk on the subject of sex. It was very interesting to compare impressions of this talk with how it was reported by those who traveled with Lee, who described it as bawdy, confrontive and outrageous. And yet, watching and listening to Lee on the video, I was struck with how gentle and yet direct and honest and simple he was. He seemed incredibly nurturing and kind, and as usual, tremendously generous in his willingness to both work with people wherever they are and at the same time offer many precious jewels of instruction and esoteric teaching as well for whoever was able to receive them. To ego, on the other hand, he appears as outrageous and confrontive by the very nature of who he is; yet, watching the show in retrospect, his outrageousness was completely overshadowed by his kindness.

At one point Lee stopped the video to add a comment for those who sat in the meditation hall with him now. Something had sparked a consideration for him. He said, "When the master becomes responsible for the disciple, the disciple's body is the *same* as the master's body. At this point the master will demand that the disciple practice in the same way that the master demands of himself. The master becomes the disciple as well. More than one master has wept tears of sorrow over a disciple's pain. Not just inside, but cried *tears*... Sometimes the master has to push the circumstances that create rage toward the master. That's just the way the path goes. The next day, of course, the disciple is all soft and repentant and saying, 'Oh, the master made such a sacrifice just for me!' as the master lies wounded from the previous day's assault. It is that way—it's up and down. It's up and down, and it's tough."

March 18, 1999
Arizona Ashram

At a meeting on the ashram this morning Jan asked Lee a question about a fear of imminent danger that she was feeling. She said that she was afraid for Lee, afraid that his teaching work could become so threatening to the conventional ego that he could become endangered. Lee's answer was delivered with a ferocity: "Either I'm taken care of by this Work or I'm not! And if I'm not, let's have the whole thing destroyed now—bring the house down! Let's find out now if that is where I'm at! Don't put another thought into this. We have to trust in the Work, in the Influence of Yogi Ramsuratkumar. That's the bottom line. Either I have integrity in that Work, and the Work will take care of me, or I don't."

He continued, "We think freedom is allowing our egos to do whatever they want to do instead of Real Freedom. We think 'I' want this, 'I' want that. The 'I' is getting smaller, but it still gets in the way. Real Freedom is having no 'I'—Real Freedom is the Freedom of the Work to move and influence."

March 24, 1999
Prescott, Arizona

Tonight a small group of ashram residents accompanied Lee to a special dinner for him and an old friend of his, Prince Hirendra Singh—an Indian man and well-known teacher of Jyotish, or Indian astrology, who lives in Prescott but travels and teaches much of the time. Lee had not seen him for many years. One of the sangha households, which included Nachama, Ann, Rakini and Jim C., had arranged for this meeting and had cooked an elaborate Indian meal in their honor.

Lee drove up the deeply eroded, bumpy, rock-strewn dirt road and down the equally rough driveway to the house, which is just a short distance across the creek (a dry arroyo most of the year) from the ashram. This beautiful contemporary home was designed and constructed by Brindavan and Clint, who now live in France and manage Lee's ashram there. It is built of rammed earth and rock, perched in a pine wood on a rocky hillside where many scorpions co-exist in a dubious peace with the human residents as well as with the abundant deer, javelina (wild pigs), hawks, crows and coyotes that live in the area. Lee's students who live there care for the house and enjoy the close proximity to the ashram.

At six-fifteen we walked up the wide steps with Lee and into the beautiful, airy living room with its adobe walls lined with books and sacred objects, wood burning stove and large glass windows looking out on pine trees, dry scrub brush and red rocks. A long, rectangular table was elegantly set with vases of daffodils, candles and antique ruby gilt glasses that added to the quietly festive yet reverent mood that had been created by Lee's hosts. Lee greeted his students and settled in on the living room couch. Suddenly the whole house seemed to revolve around the radiating still point of his presence and being. It was as if the house didn't fully exist before he sat there. The activity of cooking, of setting the space, the rooms and furniture, the meditation space with its *vigraha* of Yogi Ramsuratkumar, the household objects, all came under the dominion and influence of Lee's presence in that simple act of settling down on the couch. He looked up at everyone and beamed.

Within moments Hirendra arrived. A sophisticated man of the world, Hirendra is around sixty years old with long silver hair tied back in a ponytail, smooth brown skin and glowing brown eyes. He looked very healthy and fit, and exuded an aura of enjoyment, ease and erudition. He immediately greeted Lee with a namaste and a warm embrace. Looking into Lee's eyes he said, "It's been a long time, my friend. It is always good to see you!"

As they sat down together Hirendra started talking. In perfect English, with only a slight trace of an accent, he launched into an impromptu discourse, saying, "Democracy is destroying spiritual organizations in the West—and in India! Spiritual organizations are suffering from trying to be democratic!" He looked at Lee and continued, "Don't let your organization become a democracy! It ruins them. There is no democracy in spiritual life—only surrender! But we want democracy; we begin to think 'I have a vote, my opinion counts, nobody can tell me what to do.' It is all ego. It is ego's opinion. We all want freedom but there is no freedom in spiritual life! We don't know what real freedom is. There is no freedom without discipline!" This rushed out of him like an urgent message spoken in his typical charismatic and grandiloquent manner, which we came to know well as the night wore on. Lee was obviously enjoying Hirendra's spontaneous speech immensely. He yelled at Ann, who was working in the kitchen, "You should be listening to this!" She came in and listened.

Hirendra continued in his charming and oratorical style, proceeding to hold forth on the state of the world, politics, mythology, culture, astrology, ancient civilizations, technology, the rise of the Feminine in the world, Y2K, the millennium and spiritual life in general. We were his rapt audience for the rest of the evening, while Lee sat and listened, mostly in silence, but clearly enthused and invigorated in this company.

Despite Lee's natural authority and the concentrated power of his presence, he quite often prefers to be silent and contained. Once when Jan said she felt left out of a space because two or three people were talking with Lee but she was not included in the conversation, Lee said, "I love it when no one is asking me questions or engaging me. I'm perfectly happy when I'm left alone! It gives me an opportunity to *practice* . . ." Hearing this one got the sense of Lee's deep love of practice, but also of the depth and breadth to which internal practice is innate, tacit, all-inclusive in him. This was a teaching statement, but the communication that Lee makes in his silence is one of resting in pure context. At the same time that he exudes a mood of absorption and quiet, modest receptivity, there is also an unmistakable burning presence that emanates from him. He appears to exist in these moments as the ground of being, as an empty fullness, as the source of a matrix which he is both creating and sustaining and in which the interplay of the momentary tableau unfolds.

This mood or matrix can perhaps be described as a tremendous palpable sense of blessing presence that permeates the air, the conversation, the food, the action. If one rests inside this blessing presence, then all is made not only delightful and enjoyable, but even sublime and alchemically potent. At the same time that this profound sense of the immanent Divine, alive in the moment, permeates the space, Lee appears as a modest, humble, polite, generous and very ordinary person—with the exception of his startlingly blue and penetrating eyes. And it is in his very unassuming posture that a powerful communication of natural humility is made—the natural humility of one who has nothing to prove.

As the group moved to the table for the Indian meal of various vegetable curries, chutney, homemade garlic *naan* and tandoori chicken, Hirendra continued on the subject of spiritual life. He said, "The only freedom that we have in spiritual life is when we close our eyes in meditation and we are in nonduality. When we close our eyes in meditation, we are in Shiva's land; when we open our eyes we are in Vishnu's land, in duality, in the sustaining and maintaining of the world." Then he began to talk about astrology and karma. He spoke of major earth changes and catastrophes, about the influence of the planet Saturn and how it would—in the next ten years—purify the ego of humanity through upheavals and adversity. He spoke at length about the human ego and the need for maturation and purification. He spoke of major and unusual planetary alignments, and how all these would change the world from a culture of the 'I' to the culture of 'we.' This process, he said, would happen through the purifying forces of water and fire as the Earth cleanses herself. "We have become terribly selfish and egoic," Hirendra said. "But this is just the Kali Yuga being the Kali Yuga (the darkest and most treacherous of all the cosmic ages or vast time cycles of Hindu chronology). It is only the Kali Yuga doing what it is supposed to do," he smiled, as if this were the most obvious thing in the world. He articulated precepts of Hinduism with the ease that is common with Indians, who so effortlessly demonstrate a tacit understanding of the traditional wisdom of Hindu culture. This understanding is in their very cells as ancestral memory. There is no question about basic principles of the dharma. He went on, "After the purifications of fire and water, we will enter a golden age for one thousand years."

Lee has often talked about the hopelessness of the Kali Yuga—that the commonly held dreams of a "golden age" or New Age on Earth as the ego projects and expects it are an illusion, because the human condition is exactly the same as it has always been. Jane asked, "Is this 'golden age' still part of the Kali Yuga?"

Hirendra answered, "Oh yes! In each Yuga, which lasts four hundred thousand years, there are four different cycles, one of which is a golden age. But it will still be the Kali Yuga."

Hirendra then began to talk about karma and the far-reaching sweep of karmic patterns that such purifications will engender. He talked about how technology and science, for example, can be used for good or evil, but are now being used toward evil purposes on the Earth. The karma of ego running the show for so long will be brought back into a more balanced harmony through the vibratory influence and action of the planets upon people and the Earth. "From the point of view of Jyotish, the planets are ministers of integrity," he said. "They keep us in alignment with what we have agreed to do before we came here. We all make agreements with God before we are born, but we forget what we have agreed to do to clean up our karma. So the planets keep us in line—they remind us of what we have to do to clear our karma. Yes, they are ministers of integrity. They remind us that we must take responsibility for our actions.

"The Eastern point of view is far different from the Western point of view in this matter. In the West if something goes wrong in our lives, we blame everyone else for our problems. In the East we turn to God and say, 'Oh God, what have I done in my past lives to reap such karma?' We take responsibility for our lives in this way. And instead of weeping and bemoaning our fate and blaming it on others, we say, 'Oh God, thank you for the opportunity to clear up my karma,' even if we have lost a million dollars in a business deal, or something painful has happened to us. This is a major difference between the East and the West. It is something the West needs to learn from the East."

Hirendra used the example of American politics, beginning with mentioning that he had done numerology on numerous occasions for Bill and Hillary Clinton in Little Rock some years ago. He talked about how, from his point of view, Bill Clinton had failed the American people because he failed to take responsibility for his life. But this too, he said, was only more of the Kali Yuga! He said, "The American President should know that he must tell the truth to the people because he is the representative of the most powerful democracy on the face of the Earth!" He added, "This is not a moral position; it is because he is the one who is responsible for the greatest democracy on Earth!"

Coffee and dessert were served—vanilla ice cream and pumpkin soufflé smothered with whipped cream and curls of candied ginger. The candles burned on the table and outside the spring night deepened into another shade of black. It seemed to seep in through the big windows and steal into the edges of perception. In the next room the children played with Nachama. We could hear their squeals of delight and happy laughter.

Hirendra turned to Lee and asked about the bands. Lee talked very briefly about liars, gods & beggars and Shri, then the subject of our annual summers in France came up. Hirendra asked, "You go to France every year?"

Lee answered, "Yes, we go for about four months every year. We have an ashram in central France now, and the blues band, Shri, tours every year there."

Hirendra moved his head back and forth in the manner that Indians have, which can mean many things and usually signifies, if nothing else, a deep empathy. "You are doing very important work there, Lee," he said very softly. "There is such a great need . . ." The group talked about Yogi Ramsuratkumar, Lee's annual trips to India and the ashram in Tiruvannamalai. An easy quiet filled the air.

Hirendra changed the subject and began to talk about relationships. He said, "Most people are looking for happiness, but what they don't realize is that happiness has a twin sister, which is sadness. So whenever there is happiness, there will also be sadness because you cannot have one without the other. Happiness will always also bring sadness because happiness is dependent upon external circumstances and what comes to us from the outside. What people should be doing is seeking *contentment* instead of happiness." He turned to Lee, who sat at the head of the table listening intently to Hirendra, sitting at his right. Lee's eyes burned with a passion associated with hearing the dharma so well-spoken.

Hirendra gestured toward Lee and continued, "Like Lee. Lee is always perfectly content. He is content because he is complete." He paused and looked at Lee for a few pregnant moments, seeming to reflect internally before he finished his thought. "Happiness is very misunderstood. It's over-rated. We should seek contentment instead of happiness because contentment comes from the inside and no external circumstances can change that. We think we will get happiness from our mates, from marriage, but what we have to realize is that we are only married to God. We think we are married to one another, but we are married to God."

This seemed like the perfect place to end. Hirendra turned back to Lee and said, "It has been a delightful evening. We will take our leave soon." Lee and Hirendra stood and made their way toward the door, where the group gathered in the living room for good-byes. Lee and Hirendra embraced again. Hirendra took Lee's hands in his and said, "It is always so good to see you, Lee. Let us meet again soon."

March 27, 1999
Arizona Ashram

The office was almost empty on this Saturday afternoon. Three or four people worked quietly at their desks. Stan was in the band room next door playing guitar. He kept playing, improvising and jamming around one LGB song, "The Magic You Are Working," for over an hour. The sound of the guitar carried clearly through the walls and permeated the office, and the sweetness of his playing and singing was so piercing that it brought tears to the eyes of more than one person listening. There was a haunting beauty in the music, the mood of longing, the bittersweetness of it surrounding the senses and penetrating into the heart. It seemed that the notes and melodies coming from his guitar poured out of his devotion. It was a nectar that communicated itself instantaneously.

At one point Lee came through the room on his way into the Hohm Press packing room which is also next to the office. As he whisked through the room Jane commented to him on the beauty of Stan's playing, the composition of the song and the music, and how strongly it was affecting people who were listening in the office. With a deep, gruff tone of frustration he said, "Yes, it's beautiful, incredible . . . But I'm going to have to be dead before the music gets recognized." This sudden assertion of his desire to have the music, the lyrics, the songs get out to the public is something that spurts out of Lee from time to time. In the early years of the band Lee frequently talked about commercial success, even raved about it. In the last several years he has stopped talking about it to a large degree. Now when these comments come out they are a bit of a surprise because the band has carried on for so many years without the kind of "commercial success" that was Lee's original vision. Clearly Lee still feels an urgency to get the music out to people. These proclamations are not based in some kind of hunger for worldly recognition. They are based in his constant imperative to transmit the teaching and the benediction of Yogi Ramsuratkumar, which never ceases to be at the core of his impetus in every moment.

Jane spoke to him later in the kitchen. She said that she had been experiencing the effects of transformation in a way that seemed to be directly related to all the changes that had occurred within the community in the past few months. This transformation had taken the form of a period of perfect health, tremendous feelings of empowerment, of inner vistas stretching out in the internal landscape, ecstasy, mystical ascent and insight, a feeling of endless possibility. A great joy in practice and in acts of service had been constantly present for several weeks. All this was deeply appreciated and savored, but after about a month the old aches and pains, the moments of doubt and confusion, began to return. After the liberation of such a great opening, this return to the prison of the chronic, contracted state—the physical, psychological and visceral cramp which is the embodiment of the illusion of separation—was extremely painful and disappointing. She said, "It's hard not to feel that I have lost a very big opportunity; that I was unable to sustain transformation when it came."

Lee paused and looked at her compassionately. He was standing in the kitchen getting ready to go to shop for food for the All Fool's Celebration that would take place on the ashram in one week. Shopping for ashram food, and especially celebratory food, seems to be one of Lee's occasional pleasures. Now he focused his attention on her and answered, "That's not a problem at all. Why make it a problem? All the mystics and sages of all ages and times have experienced what you are describing. That's the way the process works—after a time of opening and breakthrough there will always seem to be a closing down. That's because there must be a time of integration. You can't expect to live in that state all the time! And besides, just because the transformation you were experiencing is no longer showing up in that particular way doesn't mean that it's no longer going on. It is going on in other areas or in deeper ways, on levels that aren't accessible to the conscious mind. Don't make a problem out of something that is not a problem . . ."

She seemed almost stunned by his generosity and kindness. She mumbled something about how she has the tendency to think she is always doing something wrong, or that there is something she needs to do that she's not doing. He said, "That's ridiculous. Anything else?" The children came rushing in, and Lee's attention turned toward them and the need of the next moment. Off he went, flying out of the kitchen and off to the store.

March 30, 1999
Arizona Ashram

This morning Lee was getting ready to go upstairs to the business committee meeting. Paula Z. had come in with the news that J. was planning to come to the All Fool's Celebration, which starts here on the ashram in three days. She was wondering what kind of special needs J., who has been very ill in the past year, might have—what kind of mattress, food, and so on. When she asked Dasya he said, "Lee might know." Lee was walking from his desk toward the door and unleashed a tirade in a loud, irritated voice. He virtually yelled, "I don't know what she needs! I have no idea what she needs and I don't want to know. That's *your* job." He pointed to Paula, Dasya, Balarama and some others standing there. "I don't know anything about her needs and I don't want to know." He walked to the door, turned and added, "I'm not her personal doorway to God. You've got to get this! It's completely impersonal. Completely impersonal!" He looked at Tina who was sitting listening at her desk and added, "And you can communicate that to her in any way that you want to!" He ran up the stairs to the meeting, leaving a stunned group of devotees, who absorbed his statements and then quickly returned to the action at hand. Tina picked up the phone and called J. to relay the message.

APRIL 1999

April 1, 1999
Arizona Ashram

As the ashram buzzed in preparation for the All Fool's Celebration and the arrival of many guests last night, a furious wind whipped through the air, blowing and biting at necks and ankles. The wind itself seemed to be part of the pre-Celebration frenzy of activity. Even though the ashram organizers appeared calm in the middle of it all, there was still a tremendous amount of work to be done in terms of logistics and practical details. Cooking, set-up, clean up and serving for meals, childcare, lodgings, health needs and concerns are just part of the planning that must be done to host and care for over a hundred people. Then there is organizing the details of myriad activities like gigs, theatre projects and dharma talks that Lee keeps pouring on his students—all part of sadhana.

The Arizona ashram is known to have wild winds; they almost always spring up at auspicious times, at transition times—particularly when Lee is due to arrive home after a period of travel, or before a Celebration. At the annual April All Fools' Celebration, the weather is especially unpredictable here in the high desert mountains; or one could say that it is highly predictable, in that the weather is often inclement in some way. Usually this means snow, chilly rains, cold weather, wild winds or all four. It's as if the power that is gathering as the sangha comes together in Lee's company is conjuring the weather to coalesce in gales or torrents or gusts of activity. Perhaps divine influence has a way of making the weather reflect the inner process of the sangha—a mirror of the spiritual state of things, of alchemical activity. Like when water condenses into cloud and heat or cold or other conditions are applied, a certain movement, a certain precipitation, occurs. "An alchemical congelation of substance," as James Hillman once wrote of the soul value of "cold." (Hillman, *A Blue Fire,* p. 263) So yesterday, after three weeks of sunny spring weather, when the wind began to whirl around our heads, the temperature dropped and the bright blue spring sky disappeared behind dark clouds that amassed on the southwest horizon, the word around the ashram was, "It's going to be a very strong Celebration!"

Lee had optimistically planned to have the three band gigs and a barbecue dinner at Watson Lake in the pavilion overlooking the Granite Dells—a magnificently stark but sensuous rock formation circling the blue water, set against the grand Arizona backdrop of distant purple mountains and infinite blue sky. Gigs at Watson Lake are often magical; nature lends herself to creating sublime *bhavas* in a mystical confabulation with the music and divine influence. But the day before the Celebration, as one had to struggle to walk against the fierce wind from one building to another on the ashram, weather reports of major snowfalls began to come in.

In the meantime the wind was battering the big yellow and white heavy plastic and canvas circus tent which is put up on the tennis court at every Celebration to accommodate all the guests and Prescott residents who converge here for four days. The ashram had sweat blood and tears to afford to buy this expensive tent some years ago to support the growing crowds of people who come to the ashram for Celebrations. Now the tent was taking a beating in the wind, flapping and thrashing about in concert with the trees.

Over bridge last night people gathered around the kitchen table to watch Lee play.

Lee looked out the window at the wind lashing through the cottonwood trees and the little willow tree, their traces of spring green dancing in the tumult. The wind seemed to carry some kind of message, to such an extent that it had even the master's attention. "Bummer!" he quipped humorously, holding the curtain back and peering out into the blue twilight. Then more seriously he voiced his concern about the tent, and mentioned that he was going to have to reconsider having the band gigs at Watson Lake. The talk turned to bridge.

Sangha members who had just flown in from outlying bordellos (groups of students who gather to study Lee's teaching)—Vancouver and Boulder, Colorado—began to arrive and flow into the small kitchen. Dragging up stools, chairs or sitting on the floor, they gathered around Lee, looking excited and bright and happy to be back on the ashram and soaking up Lee's physical presence again. As Lee played very fast bridge, whipping through games and rubbers like the demon wind outside, he focused his attention on his devotees in the space. He greeted each one warmly, and even as the group grew to a larger number, he still seemed to be giving attention to each person in the room. His attention was simultaneously here, there, everywhere—whoever was bidding, the woman making snacks for the children, the one who just walked into the room—in a dance that drew everyone into relationship with him. Lee was weaving the space together into the mood of the *ras lila*.

Rick Lewis came in and took a seat next to Lee. He had just arrived with his family from Vancouver. As soon as he sat down Lee turned to him and said, "I'd like you to give a talk with Karl this weekend, if that works for you."

Without hesitation Rick answered, "Sure! What's it about?"

Lee has the uncanny ability to talk and play bridge easily at the same time. It is one of many teaching lessons that he makes in the bridge space—how to split one's attention and be completely present to relate fully in several directions within the moment. He scooped up another trick and deftly played his next card without a pause, while at the same time saying, "It's posted on the schedule downstairs. You can go down later and see for yourself." Although he may have been curious, Rick was content to follow Lee's instructions and "go down later" to find out about the talk. He easily settled into telling Lee how the Vancouver bordello was going, and the bridge game continued to roll along at a fast pace.

Around eight o'clock Rakini walked in and delivered a message to Lee. She said, "Ging and Raymond will be able to come to the Shri gig Friday night. Jim Capellini will pick them up and take them home."

"Great!" Lee responded, a twinkle in his eyes.

Ging and Raymond Martinez are great fans of Shri who connected to the band through Nachama, who plays mouth harp and keyboards. A retired blues artist himself, Raymond was a professional drummer who played with B.B. King, Charlie Parker, Big Mama Thornton, Muddy Waters, T-Bone Walker, Ernie Freeman, Percy Mayfield and many other renowned blues musicians. He recorded albums with The Platters, Peggy Lee, Henry Mancini and Pat Boone. Raymond has played the drums since he was ten years old and is now over eighty. He also plays a fine blues piano, which he learned from his mother. Ging was a very talented improvisational dancer and lead singer for the band that opened for the famous black singing group, the Ink Spots. She once had the opportunity to go to Europe with Katherine Dunham, the renowned black dancer who developed a form of African-Haitian dance, but she chose to be with Raymond instead.

"Ging asked me to give you a message," Rakini continued, looking at Lee. "She said to tell you that she's really looking forward to seeing her 'Little Red Rooster'!" It was a reference to Lee, who has sung the Willie Dixon blues song "Little Red Rooster" many times to Ging's shouts of praise.

Lee smiled and said amiably, "I'm really excited too."

Rakini continued, "Ging talks about you all the time. She said to me several times in the past couple of weeks, 'That man is just *pure soul!*' "

Ging's message delivered, Rakini left and the bridge game continued. The universe seemed to be speaking through this messenger also, whose message, along with that of the crazy wind whipping through the chilly night air outside, seemed like a portent of what was to come during the Celebration, focused around the musical extravaganza that Lee had planned during the Celebration with performances by all three bands. Too fierce to ignore, the wind was a potent symbol, an agent or even by-product, of the energy and momentum of force, conjured by Lee's intent, that would carry the sangha along.

Rakini's message and the wind brought to mind the Bauls, who take their name from the Sanskrit *vatula*, meaning crazy with the "wind disease." This "wind disease" is a madness that is brought on by longing for God, cultivated through the classic yogas of breath and sex which lead the Baul practitioner into relationship with the personal Beloved, discovered in and through the body. As the breath, or yogic wind, becomes divinized and sublime in the body, the moods of divine love deepen and drive one toward a madness of longing. This process is an aspect of what is called *kaya sadhana*, or realization in the body. As a path of realization, *kaya sadhana* is communicated by the Bauls through poetry, music and dance.

Reality has a way of being supremely real—so real that *drala* (the Tibetan term for the essential power within all manifest things), reveals itself constantly in nature. Rolling along into this morning, the first day of the All Fool's Celebration and April Fool's Day as well, everything was covered with five inches of pristine, white snow that the wind had blown in during the night. The wind was gone, and in its place was a crystalline world which we breathed in through the penetrating, frosted air—air so purified it felt like the quintessence of spirit. This rarified impression food—the *prana* in the air we breathe or inspire—would be a tacit element of the inspiration during the days of the Celebration. The guru's alchemy had begun in earnest.

Lee planned to have all the meals served out in the drafty, wet circus tent where the large number of people could be accommodated. Commercial propane heaters were quickly set up around the perimeters inside the tent, and the meal set-up crew hustled to make the space as welcoming and warm as possible—a tough job at best. In the meantime the snow continued to fall out of heavy gray skies. The roads were closed coming into Prescott, and the ashram office was unable to locate the whereabouts of ten people who were coming in from Boulder and L.A. for the Celebration. They were somewhere out there in the snowstorm, it seemed, trying to find their way through the labyrinth to the sanctuary of the ashram.

Lee was unperturbed through all of this. While everyone else pulled on coats, woolen socks and heavy shoes to make their way through snow drifts and along wet, icy paths out to the tennis court for meals, Lee threw on his old, quite dirty by now (he refuses to allow anyone to wash it), twenty-year-old down jacket and plunged barefoot out into the snow. In the tent we sat bundled up at meals, breath condensing into white clouds as we talked over fruit, cold cereal and milk. The cold cereal was a gift from the annual Natural Foods Expo, an event that some of Lee's students attend on other business. They use the opportunity to "beg" on behalf of Hohm Sahaj Mandir for food that is made charitably available to nonprofit and religious organizations at the end of the show. Since it is blessed food—food that has been received through begging and is therefore gift and *prasad*—it has first priority to be eaten. Lee wasn't about to change the menus and send someone out to buy extra food that could be served hot just because of a little snow and cold weather. Furthermore, what the ashram has on hand is always what gets eaten first. The real kicker was that there wasn't even hot tea served this morning. Instead Lee had the cooks serve a cold, bottled organic coffee beverage, also donated from the Natural Foods Expo.

Sitting there shivering, I couldn't help but laugh at the crazy wisdom of how Lee orchestrates these events. The food and cold weather were only one aspect of it. There was also the intense schedule, very little opportunity to get adequate sleep, a great deal of hard work—and then being saturated and radiated by the guru's subtle rays, which can transport one from the heights of ecstasy to the deep swamps of despair within moments. On top of this, hours of music and dancing.

What's the purpose of all this? Every so often a Celebration comes along in which discomfort is one of the primary elements of the alchemical magic Lee works. What does discomfort have to do with magic? It creates a milieu in which one must work through a maze of inner conditions. Those conditions can span the range from animating an attitude of invulnerability in which one is an impervious island of self-control, to breakdown, anger, frustration and fear. For example, when comfort issues get pricked, survival angst and fear of physical illness, fragility, breakdown and death can come roaring up to the surface of consciousness, giving one the opportunity to get to know oneself better, or to self-observe. Sometimes there is a rage against the guru, who ego perceives as the antagonist who forces the discomfort and the feeling of being out of control upon us. Sometimes there is laughter and mirth and understanding. All this leads to a raw condition of vulnerability as one ceases to fight the discomfort, surrenders and gives into the hilarity and actual blessing of it all. In the guru's company vulnerability is a prerequisite to other states like joy, ecstasy, abandon and trust in the face of the supreme paradox that is the true path.

Experiencing the discomforts designed by the guru is like going through a meat tenderizer to get to the kind of vulnerability and receptivity that ego will *not* create in us when left to its own devices. In the circumstances designed by the guru one is pummeled, ground down, softened by the tender but fierce blows of God. Once vulnerability arrives out of the rawness of one's physical and psychic condition, body and mind become the fertile ground in which the guru can plant the seeds of transformation. For new students, the wisdom of all this madness is yet to be discovered. Over time in the guru's company one comes to know the truth of this process, and yet that knowledge has to be kept alive through practice.

Lee sets the example of how to work with discomfort. Even though he wasn't feeling well and had mentioned that he was fighting off a cold, he remained alert, cheerful and enthusiastic about everything. Walking barefoot tonight in the freezing dark through the snow into the tent for the Baul Theatre Company performance at eight o'clock, Lee refused the chair that was offered and stood on the bare, wet concrete of the tennis court floor in the back of the tent. With arms crossed over his chest, he stood behind the rest of the audience smiling and watching the Baul Theatre Company perform "St. George and the Dragon" and "The Loathely Lady." Tina came up and offered him a small square of carpet to stand on. Without any fanfare or fuss, he very simply and gracefully accepted her small gesture of care without ever taking his attention off of the performance. Watching this interchange I was struck with the feeling that he accepted the scrap of carpet beneath his feet not for his own comfort, but as an element of his work with Tina. It seemed to me to be a gesture of relationship, a demonstration of how to receive service and care from another with detachment, elegance and affection.

April 2, 1999
Arizona Ashram

Today the Celebration was packed with dharma talks given by Lee's students. During Balarama's talk on sex, the primary consideration was how to sustain desire in the body ongoingly, day-to-day, without seeking relief or self-motivated "satisfaction" through sexual orgasm. Genital orgasm is only the most obvious example of how we typically expend the energy of desire rather than containing it and allowing it to build. When sexual union is seen as a metaphor for union with the Divine, then sustaining the state of active desire in the body would be equivalent to allowing longing for the Beloved to grow in the soul. Engaging a process of regenerative sex, or the retention of semen in the man's case, is a necessary prerequisite to this practice. But clearly the principle applies across the board in one's practice in all domains.

Near the end of the talk Lee interjected, "To the common man desire is an itch that has to be scratched, but to the uncommon man, desire is like a glow or a radiance that feeds the being. It glows outward, but it also feeds inward. Everyone in this sangha should be working toward that." He gave one of his odd little laughs—as if to say, "If you dare!" or "If you can!"—and then fell silent again.

With brisk, icy cold weather and more snow on its way, Lee had to relocate the three band gigs from the Watson Lake pavilion to the vast, cold D & B warehouse, owned by the architectural firm of one of Lee's students. Tonight the Shri gig was scheduled. At six-thirty a group of students walked with Lee into the immense building, filled with huge wooden packing crates except for an open area where Shri had set up their gear "onstage." The space was already filling up with other students. A makeshift dance floor had been created out of old carpet laid across bare concrete. Thick steel girders spanned the space, reaching up to the thirty-five-foot high ceilings. The industrial propane heaters that had been transported from the ashram tent to the warehouse for tonight's gig blared with fires that we benefited very little from, the heat rising immediately up toward the cavernous ceiling high above our heads.

People stood around in coats and gloves, now and then walking over to the heaters and holding their hands in front of the flames for a brief warm-up. Bright warehouse lights beamed garishly into our eyes. There was nothing inviting about this space. How many people attempt to enter into Dionysian ecstasies in a place like this? Unlike most *tantrikas*, partaking of spirits (alcohol) and other intoxicants is not part of the practice in the Hohm Community. Not only do Lee's students not make use of the usual traditional aids to the rituals of ecstasy, but sometimes the intention is to enter into transformational ecstasy under some fairly harsh conditions, at least by Western standards. It can always be much worse than it is, but tonight everyone was shivering from the cold. Standing surrounded by cold steel and large wooden shipping crates, and under the glare of commercial lights that revealed every wrinkle and shadow, the unmistakable, stark burn of sadhana emerged in each vividly revealed face. And yet, it was clear that based on the training of sadhana, people had come determined to make the best of it. There was much laughing and joking around about the situation, finding a paradoxical pleasure in the craziness of it all.

Lee's equanimity was, as usual, the same. As many have remarked about him over the years, he is always the same—a steady, unwavering beacon of context. In his company, even this cold warehouse would work in everyone's favor. As Veronique Desjardins once said of Lee, "Everything Lee does is madness—but it all works!"

Just before Lee went to the stage Ging and Raymond Martinez arrived. When Ging saw Lee she came running over and threw her arms around him, saying, "My Rooster! My Rooster! I'm so glad to see you!" She turned to some of Lee's students who were standing next to him and said, "I just couldn't wait to get my arms around him! I *mean* it! He's my Rooster."

What an odd sight to see a black woman in her late seventies running toward Lee like a young girl. Coming from a very different cultural milieu and period of time than any of us, her lack of inhibitions in expressing her enthusiasm and affection was refreshing. One thing was for sure: she was not an uptight, white, middle-class poseur. On the contrary, everything about her was authentic.

For a long time Ging called Lee her "Hoochie Koochie Man"—now it was "Rooster" because she loves it when Lee sings the song, "Little Red Rooster." She has a natural way of extending herself to people, a gregarious and completely genuine friendliness. She is one of those individuals who sees people's essence easily and effortlessly. She sees the best in people. From the very beginning she went straight to the heart with Lee. Tonight she recalled when she heard Lee sing for the first time, two years ago. Turning to Jane, she said, "I adore him." She pointed to Lee. "I mean it—I adore him! I remember the first time I heard him sing. I said to Raymond, 'What do you think, Ray?'

"Raymond said, 'He's singing the *blues.*'

"I said, 'Does he have anything?'

"Raymond said, 'Baby, the man's got *soul.*'" She laughed with glee and turned back to Lee, took his face in her hands and drew him close to her in an embrace, pressing her cheek against his. She flicked his dreadlocks back with her hands affectionately. Lee took all this in with a grin, turning and smiling at Ging.

She talked with Lee for a minute then turned to Jane again and said seriously, "Baby, he's got soul. He's really singing from the heart. Lot of people get up there and sing, but they don't *mean* it. They aren't serious. He means it, every word of it. He's *serious.* I just can't wait to hear him sing!" Lee headed off toward the stage, and Ging and Raymond settled into the chairs that Nachama had arranged for them.

During the second set Raymond sat in with the band and played the drums. Eighty years old and experiencing physical difficulties, Raymond walked with the help of a thick wooden cane. With Nachama's help he made it slowly up to the stage and carefully maneuvered around with his cane until he was settled behind the drums. When he picked up the drumsticks, his effortless sense of timing and rhythm took over and the audience was transported by the delight of hearing him play in traditional blues style. The tremendous subtlety and skill, the laid-back cool of his easy beat, is a dying art form—a distinct facet of a different era, a unique time and place. The drums became an extension of him; he played with a beatific smile on his face, and it seemed to mean a lot to him to have this opportunity to play again. He didn't even play the bass drum—he didn't need to because he was amazingly facile with just the snare drum and symbol. When the second song was over Nachama helped him get up and across the stage with his cane. He got to the dance floor and playfully said, "Now I'll get across the dance floor without this!" And he lifted his cane up and did a little jig across the floor to his seat beside Ging.

Hosting these two revered elders is an opportunity that Lee has made available in his unique way of bringing people, places and circumstances to life with the magic of his attention and intention. They are very much like two wise and deep children, in the way that human beings become naturally more child-like in a return to innocence as they grow old. Their presence as elders of the blues tradition lends dignity and honor to what Shri does; they bless the whole project with their goodness. Their very presence is a teaching that transmits the essence of what the blues is about. In this way the connection that Lee and his students have with them is very similar to their connection with the Bauls of Bengal—Sanatan Das Baul Thakur, also a revered elder of his tradition, and his sons, Bishwanath and Basudev. It is a great pleasure to return, in some small part, the friendship and respect that Ging and Raymond have so easily and naturally offered. Their appreciation and good will is deeply touching, and their recognition of Lee is spontaneous, unmotivated and a pure delight. Tonight during "Little Red Rooster" Ging sat on the edge of her seat watching Lee. She turned to Nachama and pointed to Lee, saying, "That man—he's the soul of the band!"

April 3, 1999
Arizona Ashram

In meditation yesterday morning Lee came in and sat down, surveyed the scene, closely scrutinized the flower arrangements placed around the various shrines on his dais, then carefully moved an arrangement of stargazer lilies from one side of his chair to the other side. He gave a slight little smile, settled into his seat, closed his eyes and dropped into meditation.

Today he was showing a video of his recent trip to India in late 1998 in the meditation hall. A wide screen television had been rented and set up in front of his dais, with Lee's chair and the shrines behind it. Lee sat on a *zafu* placed in the aisle between the men's and women's sides of the hall, facing the immense screen and his dais. Suddenly he got up and walked briskly up to the dais, bent down and leaned over to snatch an orange lily out of the newly arranged flowers that were placed in front of the two-foot-high bronze statue of Hanuman which sits below the *vigraha* of Yogi Ramsuratkumar. In one swift move he threw the lily on the floor as if it were the most superfluous and irritating thing imaginable in that moment. Obviously that superfluous "thing" was somehow in his way.

He stalked back to his seat with a grim but satisfied smile on his face. He peered at the Hanuman statue and jumped up again. He moved so fast that his movement wasn't really discernable; it was just that suddenly he was standing by the dais again and this time he ripped a second lily out of the same arrangement and threw it on the floor beside the first. Now Hanuman's face was visible from where we were sitting; before it had been obscured by the orange and yellow lilies that stood up on their long stalks. Walking back to his seat this time Lee had a big grin on his face, and he glanced playfully at the women who take care of the flowers, who were watching attentively. His smile seemed to say, "Okay, now it's the way it should have been to begin with!" It doesn't matter what task the guru gives—everything is included in his sweeping overview of right relationships within the complex, myriad interplay of reality, all of it grist for the mill of his exacting eye, his fine-tuning, detailed corrections and guidance in all matters.

Today the whole group saw a show they had been waiting for since the November Appearance Day Celebration, when Lee's new band, Attila the Hunza, made their debut in the Hohm Community. Since then the band has gotten a new drummer, two more female vocalists, and had been honing their skills, practicing three times a week since January to be ready for this performance at the All Fool's Celebration. Made up of some of the community "young Turks" (as they say in corporate America), Attila the Hunza is a new generation of *sadhakas*, their ages ranging from twenty-two to thirty-three—a millennium generation. Their gig was scheduled to start at two-thirty in the afternoon, after which a barbecue of sorts would be served and then a liars, gods & beggars performance.

As Lee drove up to the warehouse, wild thrashing guitar chords and a wailing female voice drifted out on the cold air. The spirit of what was being conjured behind the closed warehouse door drew the group with Lee inside as they walked across the concrete loading dock and in through the door. Inside the cavern of the warehouse was a transformed scene: tiny white lights strewn across the backdrop of an Indian tapestry and a batik of a goddess—fresh from recent travels in Banaras—were hanging on the wall and defined the "stage." Tall votive candles and lava lamps were placed around the perimeter of the space. Incense had been burning and its exotic scent lingered in the air. The musicians were just finishing their sound check. Lee stood about twenty feet away from the stage, to the side and slightly behind the core of the audience, and watched as they moved into gear. At promptly two-thirty three gorgeous young women came running onstage.

Here came a jolt of sheer, raw, youthful exuberance and power that washed over the audience in a wave. The young women, Kate, Clelia and Alberta, were dressed for high theatre, each in her own unique expression of the nineties version of the archetypal woman. They jumped into their first number, "Working Girl," a song written by Lee Lozowick and composed by Stan Hitson, and performed for years by liars, gods & beggars. Now Hunza has the song, and their punk interpretation of it had passion and an innovative flair. They brought mega-voltage and high velocity to everything they did. Their audience was enchanted as they went from one song to the next for two hours. They covered many contemporary artists like U2, Blondie, Velvet Underground, Jane's Addiction and Bob Dylan and interspersed those with songs written by Lee and composed by Everett Jaime, including a beautiful, haunting new song titled "Calcutta Nights."

The fresh, scintillating excitement and buoyancy they brought to their performance was marvelous to watch. Here was something that hadn't been seen yet in Hohm Community bands and music thus far. Lee's eyes sparkled as he watched from the back of the dance floor. He even ventured out and danced to one of their songs. It was as if a doorway to possibility was opening up before him, offered to the guru by these young devotees.

True to Hohm Community style, this band is pure invention. None of the members of the band are trained musicians or singers. Every one of them has taken up his instrument in the past year, after Lee offered them the possibility of starting a band—Zachary on bass, Sylvan on keyboards and saxophone, Steve S. on drums. Only Andrew had prior experience playing rhythm guitar. The three young women have never sung professionally or ever thought they would end up in a band. Tonight Dean, a professional musician from New York and student of Lee's, was sitting in with them on congas and *doumbek*, adding a fabulous dimension of complex rhythms to many of their songs.

As Lee watched it seemed that he was consuming or eating this feast in a way that one could almost see the digestion and assimilation of it into his cells, where it would be metabolized, transmuted into its essence and used as fuel for the evolution of this new project. These young people were like a fresh wind coming into a stale room. They brought a freedom and a flair for riding the edge, even though they were nervous and naturally a little scared. Their inspiration and interplay and communion with each other onstage, and with all the guest artists they brought up to play or sing with them, was like a gift to Lee, who has often expressed his wish to have a freer interchange and creative collaboration between musicians in the community. They genuinely wanted to empower each other to shine, and it showed in their play together.

This seemed like an omen of things to come for Lee's other bands. The winds of change have been blowing in a steady gale since Lee returned from India, and now they seemed to be headed for Lee's music projects. In spite of their tremendous output of fabulous music and all of their hard work over the years, the atmosphere around liars, gods & beggars has been stultifying for a long time. Guest artists were often not really embraced or encouraged to shine; risk-taking that involved anything theatrical or innovative was threatening and more or less taboo. A rigid mood of maintaining the status quo prevailed, even when a new member of the band tried to introduce fresh ideas. The visceral and psychic contraction that resulted from this pervasive shutdown was impervious even to Lee's influence and constant presence and attention on the band. Now as we watched Hunza let it all fly and take risks, everyone was charmed.

Hunza's set came to a close and the entire group, about a hundred people, gathered for dinner—grilled "soy dogs" donated from the Natural Foods Expo, barbecued beans, cole slaw and sodas with apple pie. The apples in the pie and the whole-wheat flour in the piecrust were both donations as well—a continuation of the ongoing theme of beggary and food. While the food was set up buffet-style on long tables near the door, Deborah vacuumed the rug and tablecloths were laid out in long strips on the floor where we would sit and eat.

This is typical Baul style—again the idea was to make anything workable, no matter how unusual, difficult or ridiculous. Now that everyone had settled down from dancing, the reality of how cold it actually was in the warehouse began to settle in. It was lightly snowing again outside, and the propane heaters were completely ineffective against the frigid temperatures of the huge space. People were unquestionably cold and uncomfortable, and yet everyone was so highly energized from the power of the music and performance and from the cumulative intensity of the Celebration that a mood of enjoyment was what dominated one's perceptions. People were giddy and flying, going from one feast to another—some feasts of gross and literal food, and some feasts of impression food.

The group had already been satiated on Shri's performance yesterday; now there was a sense of tremendous fullness after Attila the Hunza played. After dinner liars, gods & beggars would play—another rich meal. How to digest all this? What to make of the fact that the guru was feeding his students eight hours of live Baul dharma music during this Celebration? After many hours of sitting in talks all day, the music and dancing gives everyone the opportunity to integrate the teaching into the body, to allow the tremendous influx of blessing power to be alchemized into the cells. Lee has been making use of the music in this way at Celebrations for years, but this was more music than anyone could remember having at any one Celebration.

The group dispersed for about thirty minutes after dinner. Many people were busy with clean-up while liars, gods & beggars got ready for their performance. Liars, gods & beggars was Lee's first experiment in Western Baul music, and in this regard is very much like a first creative offspring which has persevered for almost twelve years despite resistance and difficulties. LGB were the pioneers who, with Lee's guidance and inspiration, had forged the trail of Western Baul music. Tonight they came on with a fervor, dynamism and potency that is their unique expression. Their ability to conjure an invocational space has not yet been excelled by any other work experiment involving theatre and the arts that Lee has conceived over the years. Their musical ability and composing skills are fantastic. Their love of the music and ability to deliver it is unquestionable.

Immediately the audience gathered again out on the dance floor and danced almost nonstop for the next three hours. Still, something seemed different. Ann commented, "It seems like Lee isn't giving the band the same kind of energy that he usually gives to them. Something feels different." I agreed with her. But even so, everyone left the warehouse after their performance and headed back to the ashram for the late evening gathering intoxicated and saturated to overflowing with the combination of music, dance, dharma and revelation in the body.

April 4, 1999
Arizona Ashram

As darshan began Lee had some of the poems to Yogi Ramsuratkumar sung, and the two new chants, one written by Ed and one by Doug, sung and recorded. After the poems and chants Lee immediately dove into his discourse.

"I'm going to talk about something tonight that's been weighing heavily on my heart for a long time." Then he joked around in a feigned Little Rascal's voice, "Something's weighin' heavy on mah heart, Miz Crabtree . . . Miz Crabtree, somethin's weighin heavy on mah heart . . ." He paused while people laughed, especially those who knew the routine from the famous children's show of the fifties. He resumed in a much more serious tone. "This is very hard for me to do, because it's been burdening me for a year and a half, and I haven't done anything about it. But finally the signs to me are undeniable that the liars, gods & beggars experiment has run its course. I struggled with bringing my 'Dear LGB' letter to the privacy of our band meeting tomorrow night or shocking the band members here tonight in darshan, but I wanted to cover the elements of it in a way that will be useful to us all.

"I should have gotten the signs a year and a half ago when Yogi Ramsuratkumar gave me the message when I was in India, but the things that were working in the band were far too heartful for me to get out of it at the time . . . but the message has been coming to me for a long time. It's like when you have this old dog, not to insult LGB or anyone," Lee chuckled, "and its teeth are falling out and it's peeing on the floor and its legs don't work anymore, but you don't have the heart to put it out of its misery.

"I don't want anyone in the band to take this personally or to blame any one individual. And Shri will find this out as time goes on—LGB can whomp up a chamber better than anyone in no time with their music. LGB chambers have been pretty unique. The invocation that LGB creates with consistency is not something we are replacing and has never been equaled by Shri. That's been one of the elements that pulls at me, and has made it hard to end the experiment.

"I hope we can still record our album next month, but my participation in the experiment just has to end. It's too bogged down to keep pounding on it, hoping it will open up. So with tremendous reticence I have to pull out of my participation in the band. All experiments of this sort are temporary. All work tasks are temporary—Attila the Hunza, Shri, the Baul Theatre Company, all are temporary. The original goal or aim for the LGB experiment has changed over the years, partly because of E.J. Gold's input, but also because of seeing the field of play, and the obstacles that we've faced in the commercial music business. I just wouldn't be willing to sign the kind of contracts that we would have to sign; I wouldn't be willing to travel on tour with the band the three hundred nights a year.

"I pray that the composers will not stop composing because I still have a huge vision for the music. Listening to Shri and Attila the Hunza I feel that Shri is a phenomenal band (and its too early to say with Attila the Hunza), but the power and force of liars, gods & beggars still has not been duplicated by Shri yet. It really breaks my heart to stop the force and power of LGB, but for the Work profitability, it's clear that we've come to the end. Yogi Ramsuratkumar made a public demonstration a year ago to me, though probably no one saw it but me. As tremendous a value as LGB serves in a linear way, in a Work sense it's become unprofitable for me. It is heart breaking for me and would be doubly heart breaking for me if the composers stopped composing. It's Easter weekend, so that seems somehow significant . . ."

One of Lee's students said, "Death and resurrection."

Lee snapped the idea up. "Death and resurrection! Oh yeah!" His face seemed to brighten as the implication of this sank into the space.

His words signaled the end of an era in his work with his students, a significant death, but in that death was contained the essence of resurrection, rebirth, new possibilities. He continued, "So, where the acoustic work that LGB is currently doing will go is yet to be decided. The nature of this kind of Work task is that it's designed to be Work profitable. In the ordinary world LGB is still manifesting extraordinary potential, but for me, how these things get decided is that I get one sign, then a second sign and a third. After three signs I know how to move. With this I've had five or six signs because I've really resisted this one! It took this long just to take a deep breath and go, 'Okay, I get it.' But I have a healthy fear of the Lord! I didn't want to push this thing until the Universe did it for me! At this point there have been tremendous circular confirmations.

"In a task like this, regardless of ordinary world value, which LGB provides plenty of, and the world is responding to them—in spite of that I'm not feeling the profitability Work-wise for it to be worth it anymore. Value in the ordinary world and Work profitability are not necessarily mutually exclusive, but in this case . . . If last night turns out to be the last gig we perform, I hope you enjoyed it. As old as we are I guess we could always drag the band out now and then at some Celebration, dust them off and play again, but it would take too much to get back in gear, to rehearse and all that. It would just be too much to drag the band back out for some dinosaur gig! So I hope you enjoyed them last night.

"Ending a Work task is one of the difficult things I have to do. I'm very deeply attached to this project, but like anything, when it's over it's over—like a bad relationship. Even like a good relationship—and I can speak from personal experience of late—when it's over, it's over. If you don't handle difficulties at the beginning, it only gets worse as time goes on, like digestive difficulties developing into colitis or something. One element of Work profitability is a willingness to risk and sacrifice because of the unknown possibility of invention in the situation. LGB has gotten good enough to be unwilling to take risks . . . They've become almost too good.

"When Yogi Ramsuratkumar had all the lyrics sung in His darshan last December, what I took away from that was that He was empowering our music. If we were serious about the possibility that LGB opened up for us as a sangha, we would learn all the songs. We would sit down with the cassettes and CDs and we would listen to them over and over until we learned the songs and were able to sing them all. The way I work is that this is the feeling I get, and I take it seriously, even though I personally don't have any idea what practical application that might have, if any. But if this is how Yogi Ramsuratkumar has empowered the lyrics, then we should do something about it.

"So the form of the experiment with music may change, may alter, but there is still active music going and—who knows? Shri is in the same place LGB was in years ago, with tremendous opportunities on the horizon, and Attila the Hunza will have their opportunity to play."

As with other major changes that have occurred in the past few months the event of Lee dismantling the liars, gods & beggars experiment was not a surprise, but was paradoxically a tremendous shock to many people. Anticipating this change had been, for many, part of the process of participating in the project for the past few years, making it a bittersweet experience because of a deep appreciation for the band and the music. Tonight when Lee finally acted, it was the end of a significant era in the Hohm Community.

The idea of the band first stirred in 1985, when the Living God Blues band played very casually, almost extemporaneously, with a somewhat different configuration of musicians, including Lee, on two occasions: at a wedding of three couples in the sangha in 1985, and at a bar in Prescott in 1986. But it wasn't until after the Guru Purnima Celebration in July of 1987 that Stan Hitson appeared on the scene, and along with Doug Fulker, Matthew Files, Karuna Fedorshak, Steve Ball and Peter Cohen cast their hats into the ring with Lee and embarked on an adventure of tremendous importance to the Western Baul path. It was that gig at the Sam Hill Warehouse in Prescott in July 1987 that Lee sang "Sympathy for the Devil" and "Under My Thumb." Watching him then it was clear that this was a spiritual teacher with a unique and immense vision for spiritual life and the transformational process. It was after that time that Stan and Doug began to compose songs to Lee's lyrics and Lee began to talk about LGB as a commercially viable Work project.

LGB was the pilot, the front-runner, the explorer, the frontier outpost, the training ground where all the early mistakes were made and the first sparks were struck for Baul music arising in the West. As a conscious force for radical transformation it was something completely new on the spiritual scene. Some of Lee's students were scandalized, while others were mystified and yet others were charmed and thrilled. No one had any idea what Lee was up to. It was all a mystery, and there were plenty of difficulties with Lee's vision for the band. Lee was adamant that he wanted commercial success for the band, and that was what he focused on for the first five or six years of the experiment, even though he would occasionally hint at some esoteric possibility—playing to a "higher audience" and invocational music. As time went on his perspective seemed to mellow, or else he just capitulated to the rigors of the music industry and his students' resistance. There was always as much sabotage from resistance in relationship to the efforts at commercial success as there was enthusiastic support.

Part of that process had to do with feedback Lee had gotten over the years from his good friend and mentor, E.J. Gold. Mr. Gold had given Lee very specific feedback about the band eight years ago when he visited E.J. in 1991. It was clear that E.J. did not like the idea of Lee going for public, mainstream success with a Work project, particularly in a domain as volatile as rock & roll which involved the invocation of dark, underworld potencies. E.J. called it "riding the dark horse." Sitting in the dining room at the table with a number of his and Lee's students gathered around, E.J. said, "You never know what will happen once you get on the dark horse. The dark horse is a wild card. Once you get on it, you can't get off." Even if the dark horse veers off in a wild direction that is destructive to the Work, the ride is too wild and powerful and one has to see it through to the end— therein lay the danger. This, combined with E.J.'s admonitions over the years about how the Work, by virtue of its esoteric nature, gets tainted or contaminated by interacting with mainstream culture, was perhaps what Lee was referring to in his darshan talk.

Tonight it was clear that Lee was not going to spell out the details of his decision for everyone's edification. He was going to let his students stew in it, to work with it from the place of unknowing toward a nonlinear resonance with his actions. He had given many hints and direct teachings; one had either been paying attention or not. In the case of LGB, he has been making strong comments for years, but usually when band members were not present. This kind of working indirectly and psychically with students is a reflection of how the guru is lawfully bound by the fact that the student has to come to these things in him or herself. The guru can point to the door, but he can't walk through it for us. Sometimes Lee puts a message out on the psychic airwaves, speaking in spaces where band members aren't present, at private meals or in small groups of people. Perhaps members of the band, or whomever the teaching lesson is for, will pick up on what is going on instinctually, naturally, and come into resonance with Lee as a result. He has been doing this for years with LGB and now with Shri as well. His voiced complaints and reservations and criticisms have been a regular part of his communication in general. Like he said in darshan tonight, there is always plenty of data and help available if one is looking sincerely for it. But one has to be looking for it, wanting it, willing to hear it, see it, take it in.

Looking back over the days of the All Fool's Celebration, the momentum had gathered and grown to this crescendo in Lee's darshan on Sunday night. The wild wind that blew in the first of several snowfalls had turned into the proverbial winds of change that blew in a steady gale all weekend. It had turned out to be one of the strongest, most significant Celebrations the sangha had experienced in years—a medium through which the manifest action of the Will of God moved through the form and person of the guru.

April 11, 1999
Arizona Ashram

The snow had melted and the cold air was replaced with cool spring weather during the past week. The normal rhythm of the ashram was reestablished after the Celebration as the events of the weekend were absorbed through days of work and life as usual. Darshan began tonight with a series of questions that Karl asked Lee about the ways the sangha in general talks frivolously and indiscriminately about events and circumstances.

For example, Lee had been critical of how fascinated and distracted many people were after doing the "Generational Workshop" that Dietrich Weth, a psychotherapist and friend from Germany, facilitated for a number of people in the community two week-ends ago. Lee had made a number of pointed and brisk remarks in an After Dinner Talk. Finally he had said in effect, "No more talking about it!" Now Karl was saying that with Andrew Cohen coming to visit Lee this week, the sangha was being faced with another opportunity to practice in relationship to the excitement of hosting another teacher and hearing Andrew's dharma talk in the After Dinner Talk this coming Thursday night. Lee agreed with Karl that indeed we should not be fascinated and distracted in any way during Andrew's visit, and that things should remain ordinary.

After this short discussion in which Lee was seemed eager to get on with another topic, he pulled out his notes from the talk that Rick Lewis and Karl gave last Sunday, the final day of the Celebration. It had been a landmark talk, and tonight Lee said, "I'd like to review some of the notes that I took during Rick's and Karl's talk last weekend."

He continued, "I was just reading Chögyam Trungpa Rinpoche the other day on the Mother, the Feminine Principle. He said something like if you don't see that what is Un-real is Real, you'll never get Reality. That's not an exact quote, but basically it was something like that . . . So the appearance of things in the human domain in this community is Real, but it is also symbolic of something beyond the human or prior to the human. In India some temples are considered so sacred that non-Hindus are not allowed to enter in. The temples are structured very exactly and specifically to support the deities in them, and the deity is in what is called the 'inner sanctum.'

"In the West this same idea is carried out in esoteric schools like the Golden Dawn for example. All initiates have to go through a labyrinth of initiation until they get to the inner sanctum, until they are perhaps allowed into the inner sanctum. But usually the only people allowed into the inner sanctum are those who are specifically responsible for the care of the shrine and deity. Like in India, for example, in the Krishna temples the deities—Radha and Krishna—are dressed in elaborate costumes, rich silks and beautiful clothes, and the devotees throng around, offer prayers, prasad, food and so on. But there are also specific rituals that are not public at all, particularly the undressing and dressing of the deities. No one is allowed to see this ritual but certain priests. There is an assumption that you have to have a certain training to care for the seed of the temple—the Shiva lingam or sometimes just a rock that represents Shakti or the Goddess, or a statue, or whatever the form the deity may be in. If you don't have that training, it can anger the deity or be quite disrespectful."

Lee then told the story of the great Indian poetess, Andal, of Tamil Nadu. Her father was a Brahmin priest who cared for the deity in a Krishna temple. As a six-year-old child, out of her great love for Krishna, every morning she took the flower *mala* that was to be given to the deity, put it around herself and danced around the temple with it in ecstasy. When her father found out she was doing this he chastised her and told her never to touch anything that belonged to the deity again. That night he had a dream in which Krishna came to him and told him that the child's devotion was pure, and that He, Krishna, would leave the temple and never return if the priest didn't worship this small child and allow her to tend to the deity. Of course the priest immediately went to the child and apologized, telling her that she could dance with the *mala* and garland Krishna every day.

"So, any breach of protocol in the inner sanctum," Lee continued, "even if it is innocent, is a very serious offense against the deity. In India every village has a deity that resides there. The people of the village worship the deity, propitiate it, and if the deity is happy with the worship of the devotees, then the deity will bless the village with good crops, many children, and so on. If the deity is banished by a breach of protocol, then bad luck, war, violence and ruin ensues. So only the priests who are trained to serve the deity in this way are allowed into the inner sanctum of the deity.

"If one personalizes this principle or idea, then the living guru is the inner, inner sanctum. Around the guru are many rings of devotees, including an inner ring. To avoid giving offense to the deity, those allowed into the inner sanctum must be trained. Yogi Ramsuratkumar is the deity in our case, and I am like the statue, or the room in which the deity of Yogi Ramsuratkumar resides. When Yogi Ramsuratkumar is being praised, worshipped, all is fine; if not, He can banish you from His space or from His life. We saw this in the recent story we heard about the person who was allowed in Yogi Ramsuratkumar's physical presence—and she must have been in the inner sanctum or she wouldn't have been in His physical presence—when He was ill. She made the mistake, the breach of protocol, of asking Him if He was sick. He immediately sent her away, never to be allowed in the inner sanctum of His physical presence again—ever!

"So this is the kind of symbolic representation that the inner circle is in this school—the particular *function* that it is in relationship to me. In the Sufi tradition they use the imagery of the Beloved. A place is always set at the table for the Guest, for the Beloved, or in Judaism, for the Messiah. When we pray we invite the Divine to live within our hearts. To entice the deity to reside in you, in your heart, you have to be attractive. If the deity is banished from the space, you may feel inside that there has been a shift of feeling, of presence. Inside you can feel that some subtle Benediction has gone, there is an emptiness."

Lee told the story of Meher Baba not allowing Mehera and Mani and his women's *mandali* to even read a newspaper that didn't have the names of men blacked out. He continued, "Meher Baba needed a certain quality of refined attention from them, and it was necessary that they not be distracted in any way from giving that attention to him. So, looking at Meher Baba you can see that we are actually very liberal here! We should keep asking ourselves how impeccable we are with these principles in our daily lives. When we are preparing food, for example, do we keep our hands clean, or do we sneeze over the food when we are cooking? Do we sneeze into our hands and then wash them carefully, or do we just go back to cooking? We should be considering contamination principles across the board—in purifying spaces, caring for shrines and pujas, and obviously in keeping spaces around me. There is a certain space around me that begs to be kept with a certain purity . . ."

While he carefully arranged and stacked some of his *prasad*—letters and notes, candy, chocolates, three beautiful fragrant pink roses, all given to him by his students during the *kirtan* at the beginning of darshan—he reviewed the schedule for the next week, making sure everyone knew what would be going on and what opportunities his devotees would have to participate with him in various spaces. "There will be an After Dinner Talk on Tuesday night and Thursday night when Andrew Cohen will be here; on Friday morning I leave early for California. I'll be giving a public talk in Claremont (Los Angeles) and then Saturday night in San Diego—my first talk ever in San Diego! That'll be interesting!" He chuckled to himself at the thought of this. "I'll be back for darshan on Sunday night, of course." Then with an enthusiastic "Jai Guru!" he left the room.

April 13, 1999
Arizona Ashram

Tomorrow afternoon Andrew Cohen will arrive with his wife, Alka Cohen, and three of his students, Debbie, Craig and Jacqueline. He is interviewing a Western woman, Jetsunma Ahkön Lhamo, who was recognized some years ago by a Tibetan rinpoche as a tulku, for the next issue of his magazine *What Is Enlightenment?* Jetsunma lives in Sedona, so Andrew is taking advantage of the opportunity of being in the neighborhood to come visit Lee for two nights. In preparing for his visit a number of considerations have come up.

Naturally, everyone on the ashram wants to do whatever they can to provide hospitality to Andrew and his students. Translated through neurosis, this sincere wish to contribute to the success of the visit has taken on a certain anxiousness, a fixation and attachment. The desire to somehow do something to the funky, dusty, crowded old ashram—with its appearance of run-down, overflowing and earthy ordinariness—was not only motivated by a wish to provide hospitality, but was tinged with wanting to look good. To say that Lee's ashram is over-lived-in, down-to-earth, well worn, is generous. Having guests like Andrew Cohen and his students was bringing this into focus for a number of people.

One could call it pride or vanity, but certainly there was a mood of cleaving to the illusory appearance of things—the desire for status, attention, acknowledgement—that was beginning to arise. Even more insidious was the desire to appear spiritually attractive. Ego believes that it can personally gain something if someone else approves of it—especially another teacher and his students. Even after years of renunciation, ego still reveals its tenacious character in its attempts to claim territory, sometimes in the most ridiculous and futile ways.

Lee of course sniffed the mood out right away and made a number of teaching lessons in this regard. At a meeting the week before Andrew was to come Jane asked about getting a small budget for fresh flowers for the meditation hall while Andrew was here, knowing that often by mid-week the flowers that were fresh in the hall on Sunday for darshan, or that were given as *prasad* on Sunday night, are wilted and dying. Andrew would arrive on Wednesday and leave on Friday, so surely she would need to buy fresh flowers. But no sooner had the first few words passed her lips, "I was going to ask about a flower budget . . ." Lee snapped out, "We don't need to buy special flowers. We don't usually buy flowers in the middle of the week for the hall. No flowers. We'll make use of whatever we have, or we'll have none."

Of course every time Lee and his students have been to visit Andrew Cohen or his students—at his former home in Marin, California, at the Impersonal Enlightenment Fellowship centers in the U.S. and Europe—there have been stunningly beautiful and expensive flower arrangements gracing the elegant, pristine environments that Andrew's students create around him. Now Lee was giving his students an opportunity to be who they are, completely free of pretensions, competition and the motivations of pride and vanity—to have absolutely nothing to prove to anyone. For example, Lee had approved plans for a Thai dinner with a rich dessert for Wednesday night when Andrew would first arrive, but in addition the cooks were considering making a special vegetarian sushi lunch on Thursday. Lee nixed that idea and said, "We'll just have our usual ashram fare on Thursday for lunch. Nothing special." When asked about serving wine at the Wednesday night dinner Lee said, "No wine, just mint tea. Or coffee—but coffee *only* if Andrew would like coffee."

When the list of things to be done was reviewed—cleaning and organizing spaces and so on—before Andrew came, Lee snapped, "Don't do anything extra. Don't do *anything* that isn't part of your daily and weekly routine. What do you think this is—a competition? We should be completely ourselves and not be trying to impress anyone. I don't care *who* they are. Anyone who comes to this ashram can accept us as we are or they can go away and leave us alone. If they don't like what they find here, they can never come back again as far as I'm concerned! Andrew is certainly sensitive enough to read the essence behind appearances."

Later Lee added, "And if Andrew wants to make a teaching lesson about *anything* he sees here—great! I hope he goes for it!"

These reminders of the teaching related to the principle of beggary were part of an ongoing communication that Lee made the week before Andrew and his students arrived. The gist of it was a fierce reminder that his students should remain ordinary and not be fascinated, distracted or seduced away from the mood of practice by any aspect of hosting a powerful person of some fame and glamour, and a respected spiritual teacher and friend of Lee's as well. To be fascinated by anything or anyone in a way that distracts one from one's practice in this regard is a form of what Chögyam Trungpa Rinpoche called "spiritual materialism."

On the other hand, Lee did allow one of his students to call Fox Hollow, Andrew's ashram in Massachusetts, and find out what particular things Andrew might like to have that are part of his daily regime. Certain fruit, coffee, bottled water, types of breakfast foods—all these things were arranged for his visit under the natural auspices of hospitality. And so the distinction between the law of hospitality—the organic and natural movement toward serving honored guests (and in Lee's company *all* guests are honored guests)—and the grasping motivations of ego toward self-aggrandizement evidenced through sloppy practice was clearly demonstrated by the master during these days.

April 14, 1999
Arizona Ashram

Today the arrangements for Andrew's arrival were completed. The flowers in the hall—a very modest arrangement of magenta dendrobium orchids that had been placed fresh in the hall five days before for Sunday night darshan—were looking as lively and beautiful as they had when they were first put into the hall the weekend before. In the afternoon Ann went to the florist and picked out two white roses that would be placed in Andrew's room. As she paid for the roses she noticed a whole bucketful of gorgeous, half-opened roses by the door. When she asked the shop owner about them, the woman replied, "Oh those are last weekend's roses. They are too full-blown to sell at this point, so they're free."

"They're free?" Ann asked. "How many can I take?"

The woman answered, "As many as you like." Ann began to gather them up.

"Are you sure it's okay to take all these?" she asked again. By now she had about twenty fragrant deep pink, red and white roses in her arms.

"Sure!" the woman smiled. "Go ahead and take them all!"

When Ann came back everyone exclaimed over the auspicious appearance of the free roses. So the meditation hall ended up with a large bouquet of beautiful roses after all. Lee often says, "If we need it, it will show up. It will be provided." In this way the roses seemed like a direct gift from Yogi Ramsuratkumar, and a lesson in beggary, which is simply one's complete trust that what is needed will be provided by divine auspices. As Yogi Ramsuratkumar has so often said to Lee Lozowick, "My Father Blesses Lee with everything he *needs*."

The roses went into the meditation hall beneath the *thangka* given to Lee by Arnaud Desjardins seven years ago. The *thangka* is an extraordinary and sacred painting of twenty *dakinis* surrounding a large central deity, Tara. In the meditation hall the roses took on even more life. When Lee arrived at four o'clock he was shown the roses. He came downstairs and said to Jane, "Don't take *one* single rose out of there and cut it for the sandals without checking with me first. I want those roses to stay in the hall as long as possible." Lee was referring to the common practice of taking full-blown roses and cutting the rose off the stem, then putting them in water in the refrigerator to freshen so they can be placed later on the guru's sandals as an offering. The guru's sandals, which were worn by Lee for years and are now artifacts, are traditional symbols and literal representations of surrender at the guru's feet. Now Lee's tone was entirely genuine as he added, "It's great to have roses in the hall for Andrew's visit!"

Lee had gotten word that Andrew and his students would be driving down to Prescott from Sedona after their interview with Jetsunma, which was scheduled for noon. Around four-thirty Andrew called Lee. Their conversation was extremely brief. Andrew and his group had left Sedona, were on their way and should arrive around seven. Someone asked Lee if he had given Andrew some additional directions. Lee said, "No, I just wanted to end the conversation quickly so they could get back on the road." At five-thirty the children left for their evening plans with some friends at a sangha household. Never one to sit idle, Lee said, "Let's play bridge until Andrew gets here."

He sat laughing and talking over bridge games with a group of students on the carpeted floor of his living room. As we waited for Andrew's arrival there was much laughter and joking around, but there was a slight edge to the jocularity. Was the group simply enjoying each other's company, or using the jokes as a way to disperse the nervousness of waiting? Around seven-fifteen another call came in from Andrew's party. They were in Prescott Valley and would be here soon. Lee said, "They won't be here before seven forty-five," and sure enough, at seven forty-five they arrived. Lee walked outside to greet Andrew.

"It's good to be here," Andrew said as he walked through the front door into the living room, while Lee greeted his students just outside the front door. Andrew was immaculately dressed as usual.

"I've been waiting a long time to see what this place is like!" he said, looking around. Truer words were never spoken; one could feel how deeply genuine these statements were. Andrew's words also carried a hint of the native curiosity that he often exhibits. He is an avid investigator of reality, and Lee's unusual teaching style and lifestyle has become something of a legend among his friends and peers. Instantly it was clear that Andrew's usual candid, frank presence had arrived. His face bore the marked presence of clarity and a brilliant, focused attention.

Just then Lee walked in the door with Andrew's students. Andrew turned to him and said matter-of-factly, "I like your hair," referring to Lee's dreadlocks, which he hadn't seen before. Lee said nothing.

Andrew was beginning to show some of the natural signs of maturation in age, but in a very powerful and attractive way. He has always appeared years younger than he actually is. Now there was an auric fullness about him, a bit of silver showing at his temples in his black hair. There was a sense of solidity and weight about him—not physical weight, but spiritual weight. His face was showing visible signs of the stress he endures under the awesome obligation and responsibility he bears for his many students around the world.

The whole group sat briefly in the living room. Right away Andrew pulled out gifts for Lee—a boldly patterned black and white vest and a T-shirt that read on the front, "I like to keep everybody guessing," and on the back, "To be honest I'm still trying to figure it all out myself—aren't we all?" To Lee's students he gave two large bags full of gourmet chocolates. After a very few minutes of social amenities, Lee said, "Let's eat! We're starved!" The whole group—sixteen people—moved into the long, narrow dining room with its "gallery of saints" lining the wall. Lee's guests looked around wonderingly. Over Thai rice noodles, marinated tofu and cucumber salad, we talked about *What is Enlightenment?* Andrew filled everyone in on their upcoming issue, the theme of which would be gender and liberation—women and liberation, men and liberation, gays and liberation. There was much discussion of the ideas and the fabulous line-up of people they planned to interview for the issue, including Jetsunma, Father Basil Pennington of St. Joseph's Abbey in Spencer, Massachusetts, Marian Woodman, Mary Daly and several others.

After the meal Kelly asked Andrew if he would like coffee or mint tea. "No coffee," he responded swiftly, "mint tea would be great." Chocolate truffle cake with a *crème anglais* sauce and whipped cream was served for dessert, after which the group adjourned to the living room with Lee and Andrew. The conversation was light, with Andrew questioning two of Lee's students who are identical twins, Balarama and Dasya. The conversation wound around to child raising in sadhana, and how to integrate children into one's spiritual life. Andrew made some comments.

He said, "In our community what I've found is that a lot of people are rotten parents. They won't share with their kids what it is that they have found valuable in what they are doing with me because they are afraid of indoctrinating them. But I say to them, 'If you've found something that is really important to you, something extraordinary in your life that is of great value to you, then why wouldn't that be the first thing you want to share with your kids?' But they won't do it. Then when they are having doubts or struggling with their practice, they turn to their kids in a way that is unhealthy. In general it seems to me that people in our generation are crappy parents because we're afraid to be strong and set boundaries with our kids." Lee nodded his head in emphatic agreement.

Andrew added, "Kids are not something that I know very much about, but I think that if I ever had children I wouldn't give them much room to move until they were teenagers." He held his hands together side by side and measured out a very narrow space to demonstrate how little leeway he would probably give his children.

The conversation continued for a while and then Lee suggested a tour of the building. The entire group of sixteen moved down the hall and into the meditation hall. Lee and Andrew briefly peeked into the evening gathering space and then headed downstairs. Lee was explaining that Arrakis is the main building on the ashram which houses the private quarters of Lee and his family including his kitchen, living room and dining room upstairs as well as several communal spaces like the meditation hall and downstairs office.

Lee, Andrew and Andrew's four students walked downstairs followed by ten of Lee's students, who hovered close behind, almost making it difficult for this "tour" to be conducted with the kind of ordinary dignity that Lee usually lends to such occasions.

Lee's students laughed and joked around nervously. The silly jokes and sheepish laughter carried a shrill tone that made it seem like we were perhaps a little embarrassed or ill at ease about the unorthodox lifestyle that was being revealed. On the other hand, the guests exhibited a warm sobriety and elegance. As Lee showed them the extraordinarily crowded office space Andrew's students expressed their amazement at the ability to work under such conditions. In one twenty by twenty-four-foot room crammed with custom-made, well-used desks stacked with piles of work there are twelve workspaces, five computers, seven phones and Lee's desk. Hohm Press is managed out of this room as well as the glass case business, two bands and all Hohm Sahaj Mandir business. The walls are covered with framed photographs, paintings and drawings of Yogi Ramsuratkumar along with LGB posters advertising past tours of Europe. On one wall is a shelf with a puja where a candle burns and flowers are offered to a picture of Lee, above which is a beautiful hand-drawn color portrait of Yogi Ramsuratkumar. Behind Lee's desk is a large, brilliant *thangka* of Mahakala painted by Marcus, one of his students who is studying the art form with the renowned Western *thankga* master, Robert Beer. Sometimes there are as many as twelve people attempting to get serious work done in this room with phones ringing constantly, computers buzzing away and Lee sitting like a bright-eyed hawk at his desk, watching and commenting on it all.

A small seven-by-nine office adjoins this main office and contains two computers, two work spaces, a phone, a wall covered with deep shelves of archival audio tapes and thirty or forty binders filled with photographs and slides of twenty-three years, along with back issues of *Tawagoto* and other miscellaneous storage. On the walls are many more pictures of Lee and Yogi Ramsuratkumar as well as Papa Ramdas and Mataji Krishnabai. A puja shrine to Yogi Ramsuratkumar is perched in one corner of the small room. This office is where *Tawagoto* and most of the dharma literature of Hohm Sahaj Mandir is produced.

We continued to laugh and joke loudly about how intense it is to conduct daily work in such a tight space. Andrew's students politely shook their heads in what seemed like total disbelief at all this. After all, the Hohm Community style is almost antithetical to theirs. What binds the two schools together is a mutual commitment to the path. Were they shocked, perplexed? Did they have questions about why anyone would choose to live this way? Why Lee chose to work in this way? Were they repulsed? What was the purpose of all this craziness? No one asked these questions, which were pregnant in the air. Lee talked quietly, giving simple answers to questions that were asked. Andrew walked around looking at things. He seemed to be simply and quietly absorbing everything he saw. His eyes wandered around the space, noting everything. Now and then he asked Lee a practical question. There was not a trace of conflict or confusion in Andrew.

The fact that Lee's students are participating in a tantric school with deep roots in the crazy wisdom tradition is demonstrated in the conditions of life on Lee's ashram. This pervading nonconformist, iconoclastic element is certainly apparent when the Hohm Community is set beside mainstream Western culture, but it is also apparent when we come into contact with other Western spiritual schools in general, with the exception of E.J. Gold and his students. Dharma friends of other traditions—like the students of Andrew Cohen or disciples of Arnaud Desjardins, or the many Zen schools, the roshis with whom Lee is quite friendly—are respectful and warmly appreciative. Still there is much about Lee, his students and their sadhana that seems to appear very mysterious and confusing to them, as these friends have candidly confessed on numerous occasions. There are many parallels between the Hohm Community and their Eastern forebears, the Bauls of Bengal. One of those parallels is that the Western Bauls are the gypsies of the popular spiritual scene in the West. There is a kind of marginal, outcast tint to the character of the lifestyle and general perspective of Lee and his students. Any degree to which this radical lifestyle has not been embraced by Lee's students in the context in which it exists was quickly reflected in certain elements of the exchange tonight between the two schools.

By now it was almost ten o'clock. Andrew and his group decided to retire. Coming from the East Coast where the time zone is three hours ahead of Arizona time, for them it was now one a.m. After they went to bed Lee's students sat with him in the evening gathering space. When asked how the evening had gone from his perspective, Lee said, "We talked too much and tried too hard." Then he shrugged and said, "Oh well . . ."

April 15, 1999
Arizona Ashram

In the meditation hall two hinged wooden floor seats with black zafus were set up side by side on Lee's dais. His large divan had been covered and set against the wall in the back of the hall for the time being. At seven a.m. Lee and Andrew came in and sat down, the bell rang, meditation began. The small meditation hall was packed with people—probably sixty who came to sit in the unusual circumstances of these two teachers meditating together.

Later, gathering around the kitchen table informally with a few students over breakfast, Lee and Andrew talked about mutual friends and acquaintances and about working with other teachers. Andrew was particularly vocal in his criticism of people who are in a position to have a wide influence within the spiritual network in the West through their published writings, but who don't really have a living relationship to practice and true spiritual life. These are some of the issues that Andrew burns with, and he makes it clear that he gives absolutely no space or credence to the intellectualization of dharma and practice without "the fire in the heart," as he put it today.

After breakfast Lee took Andrew and his group around the ashram. This was another challenging moment. The giddy sheepishness and adolescent humor demonstrated by our group the night before when Lee showed Andrew and his students the office workspace was still present today, although softened and quieter. The group walked out the front door of Arrakis, down the long, curving concrete steps and out along the dirt road that curves around toward the back of the property. Andrew and his people all wore what any sensible person would wear to walk out in the high desert—sturdy walking or hiking shoes. Lee and his students went barefoot. Lee doesn't just walk barefoot on his own ashram; he goes barefoot on all ashrams because he considers them to be holy ground. At Arnaud Desjardins' ashram in southern France, Lee is usually the only unshod person in the group. It is a practice that he has recommended to his students as well.

Here in Arizona this barefoot practice is made more dramatic by the proliferation of sharp pebbles, dust, small rocks and "goat's heads"—a particularly vicious breed of thorny burr that grows all over the ashram in summer and dries into a hard, wooden kernel with

223

sharp spikes by fall. Goat's heads are then blown about by the wind and can be found anywhere and everywhere on the ground. Stepping on one of these is quite painful. Lee however, somehow never steps on one, perhaps because he is the only person who actually walks consciously on the ashram grounds. Just in the past few months he has gone on a number of tirades about his students' attachment to shoes, and especially those fashionable shoes with thick soles which buffer one from feeling the contours of the ground. He has said that if one cannot bear to feel the ground under one's feet—with its ups and downs, its rough surfaces, or its soft and sensuous grass—then how can one expect to be open to actually *feel* anything else life has to offer? He has also talked about the importance of sharing energy with the Earth as a being in its own right. But most of the time the teaching communications that are in such simple demonstrations as his habit of going barefoot go unrecognized. Instead these demonstrations of practice are written off—"Oh, Lee is just eccentric!"

Walking around the perimeter of the ashram Lee showed his guests the "Case Temple"—a cluttered, idiosyncratic, dirt garage packed full of equipment, tools, glass, wood and junk—and nearby outbuildings that are used as storage sheds. One of them was full of finished glass cases and another full of kachinas made by the Navajo and Hopi Indians of northern Arizona. Yet another was full of miscellaneous ashram storage articles. In straightforward and unpretentious terms, Lee explained the very labor intensive glass case business to Andrew; how the ashram trades glass cases with the tribal people for kachinas, then takes more glass cases and kachinas and trades those for barter dollars in the national barter network. This barter money is used to publish *Tawagoto*, and is also used for many other purposes, like dental care for ashram residents.

What Lee didn't say was that he has severely criticized his students for having a bad attitude about the humble, crude, unglamorous work of building and selling glass cases. It seems that very few people really want to work in the Case Temple. It is an area of ashram life in which pretensions and classism come roaring out of their hidden pockets. Even though the community is very poor in part because of the particular form of renunciation that is the Baul path, everyone has been raised on the Western standards of hierarchy, inferiority and superiority. In Lee's company one gets to confront the illusions of these cultural overlays at deeper and deeper levels as time goes on. His students often laughingly refer to the Case Temple in particular and other parts of the ashram as "Tobacco Road," and yet we seem unable to fully embrace the seeds of teaching and potential transformation that these projects and spaces contain. While Andrew and his students listened with interest and asked occasional questions, Lee explained the handcrafted kachina dolls—actually deities or archetypes of the Southwest tribes.

In light of all this, Lee's comment, "What do you think this is—a competition?" was sinking in deeper as these cousins in the Work looked over such a humble abode. It was even more impacting to observe that there was no external reaction whatsoever to the implications of poverty and sloppiness in all this on Andrew's part or from any one of his group. Of course they were polite guests as well as strong practitioners. Maybe they had been prepared by Lee's dear friend Gilles Farcet for the realities of life on Lee's ashram. As Arnaud said of Lee's Arizona ashram years ago when he visited, "It reminds me of being in India."

Observing Andrew look over these spaces I had the sense that the only thing he was doing was deeply absorbing Lee's intention, which was present in everything he saw. Lee's context and intention imbue every thing and every space on the ashram, and that seemed to be an important part of what Andrew was here for. He asked a number of practical questions here and there along the way, followed Lee's lead and appeared very ordinary about it all.

At the time Brother Juniper was loading his truck with kachinas for a case delivery trip. Andrew and his group stopped and looked inside the truck and asked Brother Juniper questions about his route, how he sells the cases, the business in general. The group moved on past the swimming pool with its flagstone patio toward the dome and then to the small room where the home school is located beside the renovated large pre-fab house that contains the kitchen, dining room, bathrooms and library for the sangha and several bedrooms where ashram residents live. Andrew and Lee walked ahead, talking as they went. Walking past the tennis court Alka asked Jane if anyone played tennis. "No," she answered. "Some of us do know how to play tennis, but we have little time for it. Instead the children have really taken over the space. They love to roller-blade, they have bikes and skateboards and all that, and they play there."

Alka smiled and said, "We have a tennis court at Fox Hollow—we loan it out to a local school for their kids to use three days a week."

Just then Lee and Andrew and the group following behind them walked past the rock gardens in front of the meditation hall. At this time of year nothing green is stirring—it is still very wintry, dry and forlorn with last year's dead growth sticking up, except for the small pansies that have been planted in the "Ma shrine" at the feet of a three foot high granite statue of Kwan Yin. She rests underneath a pine tree and overlooks the space as one walks toward the front door of the meditation hall. As we walked across the patio back toward the kitchen Andrew mentioned to Lee that he would like to see some sights around Prescott. Lee turned to his students and asked for ideas.

"The Granite Dells are great," Jane suggested.

"How would they get to them?" Lee wanted to know. After a short discussion it was agreed that the best place was at the pavilion at Watson Lake. Andrew asked Lee if he would like to come and it was decided that Lee would drive the van with Andrew and the whole party out to Watson Lake. About ten people piled in with Lee driving and Andrew up front in the passengers seat, and off we went.

As Lee drove up to the high promontory overlooking the extraordinary granite rocks and small lake that winds its way through the labyrinth of this unearthly scene, Andrew said, "This place is like another planet!" And indeed it was. In the far distance one could see the San Francisco Peaks—the twelve thousand foot-high snow capped mountains at Flagstaff, two hours north by car. Between here and there was Mingus Mountain, a forested range of peaks that rear up over seventy-five hundred feet between Prescott and Jerome, an old mining town scattered across the side of the mountain.

The rock formations of the Granite Dells are the result of post-volcanic activity; they bubbled up out of the earth after the flow of lava and cooled into very unusual round, oval or oblong clusters. These smooth shapes protrude from the earth in clusters that fold into and blend organically with the next cluster, making a seamless whole of striking patterns that envelop the blue water of the man-made lake in a natural cohesion between water and earth. The stark beauty of this juxtaposition between the bare, gray and strangely sensuous rocks and the blue water, all of which is set against the incredible vastness of the burning blue desert sky and distant mountains, is very penetrating.

As the group piled out of the car the awed response of the guests was a reminder that we live here and have taken this scene in many, many times. The large pavilion a few yards away from where Lee parked was a place where liars, gods & beggars, and in recent years Shri as well, have played many times for community gatherings. The music and the unearthly beauty of this place combined each time to make an incredible communication.

Andrew took off walking and before long everyone was scrambling down through the rocks toward the water's edge. Lee accompanied Andrew down the rocky slope, around huge granite boulders and through scrub brush. Hiking and communing with nature is not Lee's cup of tea. Andrew is probably the only person in the world other than E.J. Gold or Arnaud Desjardins who would be able to entice Lee on a hike of this kind. At the bottom they stopped by the water's edge and sat on boulders. The subject of a new ashram for Lee came up. He mentioned that at one time he had looked into moving to New Zealand. Andrew said, "Oh, you don't want to live in New Zealand." He went on to talk about how little potential there is in New Zealand for making the teaching available, and now the Maoris are struggling with the New Zealand government to get their land back. We began to talk about the current search for new property. Lee said, "Yes, we are actively looking for property here in Arizona, but much further out that we are now. We've outgrown our place. But this time we're looking for acreage we can build on."

Suddenly Andrew took off alone over the rock formations that rise up in agglomerations of mineral life. He climbed up and over the higher rocks to a place near the water about one hundred yards away where he was out of sight. The hot sun shone down on our bare heads as we sat on rocks near the water's edge. Lee and five of his students who accompanied him sat and talked with Andrew's students for quite awhile about the projects and practices of the two communities. Lee's students discussed the three bands and how LGB would be playing for a gathering of thousands of bikers that would converge in Bullhead City, Arizona later this month. Andrew's students talked about running marathons and especially the London marathon, where thirty thousand people run. Some of Andrew's students will run in this marathon, and have convinced the organizers to make the theme of the marathon "The Power of One," as a gesture toward world peace.

I asked Debbie about the schedule of daily practices at Fox Hollow and she told us that the women gather every morning at five to do an hour and a half of prostrations together, accompanied by mantra or chanting in English every morning. She talked about what a powerful bonding experience this is for the women. After prostrations they have a short break and a cup of coffee, then an hour of meditation. Some people meditate additional hours during the day, and some of the men also do prostrations. During the day the men do push-ups, sit-ups and run. Then there is the workday of tasks and jobs. At six o'clock they have another hour of formal meditation before dinner. They usually retire around ten-thirty at night.

It is an impressive schedule of practice. Lee's students were busy heaping praise on them when Lee broke in, blurting out in a self-mocking tone, "We're into emotional catharsis in our community!" Andrew's students laughed good-naturedly and said, "Well, we've tried that too." Someone mentioned how strong the meditation had been this morning. Lee laughed and said derisively, "That's the first time we've ever had a meditation that was that quiet."

"Really?" Andrew's students asked incredulously.

"Yes!" Lee answered brightly, "Usually it's . . ." and he started coughing and pretending that he was blowing his nose with loud honks as Dasya chimed in to give an exaggerated demonstration of the poor level of practice exhibited by the Hohm Community. Andrew's students fell silent and looked dumbfounded. What to make of all this? Indeed. Lee not only deconstructs himself regularly, but also skewers his students without compunction—anything to make a teaching point, or to scramble up preconceived and crystallized notions of spiritual life. Or perhaps most importantly, to keep his students from succumbing to various forms of spiritual pride, and to keep the sense of urgency alive. There is no time for fascinations or for spiritual vanity, which easily and regularly creeps in on silent little feet.

During this whole time Andrew stayed alone near the water some distance away. Shortly after eleven o'clock Lee turned to Craig and said, "The children get out of school at eleven-thirty, so we need to get the mothers back to the ashram to be with them before lunch. Maybe you could let Andrew know that we will head back, and we'd be glad to send someone back to pick him up later if he would like to stay longer." In a few minutes Craig came back and said, "Andrew would like to stay longer, so if someone could come back and pick us up between twelve and twelve-fifteen that would be great." Dasya immediately offered to come back and pick them up. Lee headed back up the mountain toward the van.

Back at the ashram Lee ate two of his three oranges—his lunch for today—with the children at twelve sharp. He saved the last, largest orange to eat with Andrew when he returned. Around twelve-thirty they arrived and joined us in the dining room.

"It was really great being out there," Andrew said keenly as he sat down to a lunch of brown rice, curried vegetables and green salad. "It's incredibly beautiful. As soon as I was alone out there my mind went completely quiet and this feeling of peace came over me. I felt tremendously peaceful." He was brimming with enthusiasm, his face vivid and glowing. In fact he looked like he had shed months of stress. He continued, "You know the Buddhists always talk about *suchness*. Ken Wilbur talks about suchness; I always wondered what he meant when he talked about suchness. I never understood it. Being out there today I looked around and I just got it. I *got* it."

Andrew spoke of this satori in a very frank, ordinary but fervent way, with a sense of wonder but without any fascination. It was easy to be inspired by his candor and the way in which he made himself vulnerable in a very human way. He and his students began to talk again about the beauty of Arizona, how surprised they were by the profound communication of the land.

Andrew said, "The land really *transmits* something here . . ." Lee's students nodded in agreement, knowing how benevolent and profoundly powerful the spirits of the desert can be. Lee sat and listened.

"Well then it was really worth it," Lee smiled. It was one of Lee's typically enigmatic statements. It implied that a price had been paid for this satori, but what price and by whom? The conversation turned to the food. Andrew really liked the salad dressing—a simple blend of organic apple cider vinegar, olive oil and raw garlic. The curried vegetables were a big hit at the table also. For the next several minutes our attention was on eating, then Lee said to Andrew, "I will be leaving at six tomorrow morning." When Andrew asked what his weekend plans were Lee answered that he was giving two talks, in Claremont and in San Diego, but also spending time with his daughter. Lee would be driving out to California alone.

"That's sounds good," Andrew laughed. "Must be unusual," he added, knowing only too well how both he and Lee are constantly surrounded by lots of people. The pleasure of solitude is not something either of these men have very much of. Lee makes himself available almost twenty-four hours a day to his students, traveling off and on all year to teach, living for four months out of the year in France where he has a heavy teaching schedule. Andrew travels most of the year, spending a tremendous amount of time on the road giving teachings, leading retreats and seminars and being hosted at his centers around the world.

People began to stream into the ashram greenhouse for chanting at five-thirty. Andrew sat upstairs in the kitchen and talked with Lee while our numbers swelled up to about seventy-five as people arrived and joined the chanting. The greenhouse, which is basically a long enclosed porch attached to the front of the building, looks out upon the nearby mountains and the cottonwood grove that flanks the front drive of the ashram. This space, like many in the crowded ashram, is used for many purposes. Sometimes it is used for cleaning glass cases. Then three or four long tables are set up with glass cleaner, steel wool, razor blades, newspaper and cloth for cleaning. Stacks of glass cases are set up against the walls and as many as twenty-five or thirty people can crowd around the tables and clean the cases which will be delivered to clientele in California, Arizona, Texas, New Mexico, Oklahoma, Nevada, Oregon and Washington. But every Tuesday and Thursday night and on Work Weekends when the sangha gathers for meals on the ashram, it is used as a dining hall. Long yellow tablecloths are laid out on the floor and place settings are arranged. Everyone sits on the floor, knee to knee, shoulder to shoulder, elbow to elbow.

Tonight there was a veritable sea of people in the greenhouse. The group chanted *"Om Guru Charinam, Om Guru Charinam, Yogi Ramsuratkumar, Om Guru Charinam."* Servers brought in huge bowls of salad loaded with fresh vegetables of all kinds, smaller bowls of salsa, bags of organic corn chips begged from the Natural Foods Expo—Lee's usual After Dinner Talk fare. At six Lee and Andrew came in and sat together at the head of the table, facing the group seated down the long strip of a room. The mood of excitement and anticipation was electric. Many people in the room, although familiar with Andrew's teachings, had never heard him teach in person before, and now looked forward to the evening program. Andrew too seemed to be preparing himself for the talk in some way. He seemed absorbed inwardly as he looked at people and spoke quietly with Lee during dinner. At one point he asked, "How many of these people are serious students?"

The answer to that question had to be an interesting one! I leaned forward to hear Lee's response—ostensibly wanting to get it for the book—when Lee turned to me and said sarcastically, "Are you listening?" Within this comment was his obvious displeasure. I leaned back against the wall and relaxed, placing my attention elsewhere. Lee then spoke so quietly that no one sitting near him could possibly hear his answer. Only Andrew was privy to this information. After the meal Lee yelled out, "Seven o'clock in the hall! Jai Guru!" and people began to disperse.

A number of students lingered at the table and talked with Andrew and Lee for awhile. Andrew began to talk about his London group, and in particular the women in London, who are working together in extraordinary ways. He said, "I have been finding something that is very strange. I have no idea why this is, but I have found that the people who have been with me from the beginning, who have more years with me, are holding things back. Whereas the newer people—the ones who have been with me, say, six or seven years—are forging ahead and doing incredible things."

Jan asked, "Why do you think that is?"

Andrew sat very still for a moment and looked away as if he was considering, searching within himself for an answer. Seeming completely nonplussed by this quandary, he looked up and said with tremendous straightforward simplicity, "I really don't know. I have no idea why. I don't understand it." It struck me that Andrew was giving Lee's students a very useful piece of information without even particularly meaning to. Certainly there was nothing personal about this—like, "Here, this is for you. You need to hear this." He was really simply sharing his experience with us, and his incredulity that such a thing would be so.

The friendship between Lee and Andrew has grown and taken on many different dimensions over the years. They have been meeting together on occasion for nine years, since their first meeting in Boulder, Colorado, over coffee. Since then there have been many collaborations—public talks in Boulder, in California, in Paris and in southern France. The two sanghas have come together in various combinations as well over the years. This visit the deepening of the connection between the two schools was apparent. The strength of the meeting flowed into such deep ravines that as the night wore on it seemed the air burned with a heightened presence, a growing mood of intimacy and a living spiritual fire that burned, caught on and passed from heart to heart.

After dinner the meditation hall filled with people who had come to hear Andrew speak. Lee and Andrew took their seats together on the dais at the front of the room. Andrew asked for a short meditation. We sat in silence, except for the dishes that were being clanked in the next room—the Arrakis kitchen which is right next door to the hall, and where clean-up from dinner was underway. After a moment Andrew leaned over to Lee and said, "Would it be okay to ask them to stop doing the dishes?" Lee instantly said yes and motioned to Dasya to go in the kitchen and ask the clean-up crew to do the dishes later. Andrew and Lee settled back into meditation and the group sat for another five minutes or so, until Andrew opened his eyes and looked soberly at the group of sixty or seventy people who were packed into the meditation hall. "So, does anybody have any questions?"

Karl asked a question about the value of psychotherapy in spiritual life or the Work. Andrew wasted no time, but immediately went to the heart of the issue. He said, "Any teaching of enlightenment should force you to face everything and avoid nothing, including everything that you don't want to see or everything that you are trying to avoid. The reason that I am convinced beyond any reasonable doubt that psychotherapy has no room in a spiritual path that is supposed to bring one to enlightenment or liberation is that the context for psychotherapy is really different than doing real spiritual work. Mixing the two are, in my opinion, like mixing oil and water.

"In a truly spiritual context one is endeavoring to be able to directly perceive the impersonal nature of all personal experience. So that means if one is serious about becoming free in this life the only way to have a relationship with and understand one's own mind and feelings—including all of one's memory—is to begin to see all of it in an impersonal context. It is impossible to do that in a therapeutic paradigm because that is simply not what it is all about. In the experience of therapeutic insight, if you spend some time with some kind of psychotherapist looking into yourself and your subconscious and unconscious, it can often be very exhilarating, but the sense of exhilaration in that kind of work is the thrill of independent self-existence: 'There is something very unique about me.' But ultimately if one wants to be free of that sense of self-importance, then the exhilaration of a very good therapy session is exactly the kind of exhilaration one wants to lose interest in, because all that exhilaration really has to do with being the very person that you want to be free of.

"If we want to be free, then we want to get to the point where relationship to all of our experience is impersonal and we are able to see every aspect of our personal experience—gross and subtle, known and unknown, seen and unseen—from an impersonal perspective. It is only then that it is possible to have a liberated relationship to our thoughts, to our feelings, to memory, to time. The therapeutic model—even if it is theoretically done in a spiritual context—always, in my opinion, contributes to the illusory reality of the ego. For example, to have the notion that one has a problem that needs to be overcome is the biggest illusion that there is going, because in the moment of enlightenment one realizes that the problem never existed. Right? So, if you go into a context that helps to give more and more reality to this conviction that you do have a problem that needs to be overcome, it helps to make the gap between you and your own potential liberation here and now. It just makes it bigger and bigger, not smaller and smaller. Because you see, the minute I tell you that I have a special problem, in a sense I relieve myself of the potential burden of becoming liberated right then because anybody with such liberation in this life has to give up the luxury of having a problem that they need to overcome.

"In my opinion if someone is liberated, if they still have a problem . . . the two cannot coexist. And mentally if you are a liberated person that means that you don't really have any problems that you have to overcome any more. But very few people that I meet want to bear that kind of absolute simplicity, where there is nothing between you and perfection. What does that mean? It means that this is it right now, and that is what you are willing to embody. You are not willing to make any excuses anymore, no matter what. Now, that is how simple it *can* be. Most people, the seekers, want to be free, but most of the time they don't want to embrace that kind of simplicity because they find that the simplicity of liberation is too much of a burden for them. They see it as a burden instead of it being liberation itself. You understand what I am saying?

"All the insight that you gain in the therapeutic experience is relative. It's all about *you*. All the insights we gain in psychotherapy about ourselves are very personal. The only insights that liberate us are impersonal, they are about the human condition. They are not about your particular problem, or my particular problem, or anybody else's particular problem. The insight one gains in relationship to the human experience, which is universal and impersonal, is the only kind of insight that has the power to liberate any of us."

It was a timely consideration since about twenty-five members of the sangha had just participated in the "Generational Workshop" that had recently been discussed in an After Dinner Talk. Lee has made many things like this available with his support to his students over the years, while at the same time he consistently maintains the same opinion that Andrew was expressing tonight about the efficacy of psychotherapy on the path.

Now Karl continued his question, saying, "Two thoughts came to mind. One was that there don't seem to be a lot of people who awaken enough that they can regard the process of their life impersonally, so that most people are in a process. For most people that's probably okay because their behavior is in some sort of acceptable range, but when you get people who are a real drag on the sangha, what do you do with them?"

Andrew answered, "Well, basically you just have to wait for them to come to the point in their own evolution when they are willing to begin to see all their personal experience in an impersonal context and respond to it, relate to it that way. Anything else that happens in the meantime is all completely irrelevant, because if someone starts doing psychotherapy the illusion is created that they are actually doing something positive for their own spiritual welfare, and so for that period of time, ego is really let off the hook. 'Oh no, but I am really serious, I am doing all this therapy, I am really facing the thing, I am struggling . . .' Then, when therapy is over in six months or six years, the question is still, 'Are you willing to have an impersonal relationship to it or not?' At that point you are going to be in the same place you were in before the therapy started.

"Seeing your own experience in a personal context can never prepare you for assuming a relationship to your experience that is not personal. It cannot do it. The only thing that can prepare you to assume an impersonal relationship to your experience is the practice of doing that *now*. The only thing we learn from the whole habit of personalizing our experience and having a personal relationship to it is that it has no end. *It has no end.* The ego has an endless fascination for having this personal relationship with something that is ultimately impersonal. So, I think psychotherapy just creates, from a point of view of liberation, the illusion of some kind of wholesome progression towards a more liberated state. But in the end, I am convinced it has nothing to do with it.

"So, I think therapy is okay if you want to stay in the world and be part of the status quo, but if you want to be a liberated human being, it is not going to help you. Genuine spiritual practice is about facing everything and avoiding nothing; facing everything and avoiding nothing means every part of yourself that you need to face in order to be able to take responsibility for it. That is a *big* part of what spiritual practice is all about, right? So, psychotherapy didn't help you to do that. Not for the right reasons. Not in the right context. Never does."

Karl said, "On that question, when people come to a school like yours, normal people are sort of normally *disturbed*, but when you get somebody who is exceptionally . . ."

Andrew interrupted him with a derisive laugh. "Exceptionally disturbed? Psychotherapy is not going to help them get to the point where they are able to see an impersonal relationship to life any more than it's going to help somebody who is not as disturbed as they are. To me human beings are really very simple. It has been my understanding that each and every one of us knows exactly what we are doing in every moment, and each of us is making very specific choices in the moment. So from my perspective we are very conscious and we know what we are doing, and we are choosing to be exactly how we are because that is how we want to be.

"When someone makes the decision in their life that they want to be free more than anything else, and that choice goes all the way to the deepest part of themselves, they begin to make different choices because they want to be free. Period. So, someone who appears to be a little bit crazier than everybody else is as in control of their experience as everybody else is. You see, from my point of view the crazier you allow yourself to be, basically the more aggressive you are willing to be—the more you are willing to intimidate and manipulate other people because the crazy person says to himself, 'Okay, I am crazy, I can do whatever I want.' It's the same as when a not-so-crazy person experiences fear and they begin to do things that maybe they wouldn't do if they weren't feeling frightened, as if that is an excuse. Right?

"So, I see everybody as being fully conscious, making very deliberate choices to be exactly how they are. All these people who tell me they want to be free more than anything else have to be willing to take responsibility for that statement. That means they are responsible for their own state, their own condition right now, no matter what it is that may have happened to them in the past. All of us, if we want to look in the past, may have had very good reasons to be wounded, to be out of control, to be crazy. But if someone says they want to be free, they are interested in that which has no history.

"If we are interested in that which has no history, which has been untouched by anything which could have been touched in time, then our attention should be on that rather than being touched by that which only could have occurred in time and only could have occurred in history. People who say they want to be free more than anything else but keep compulsively giving their attention to those things that happened in time are being dishonest. They are not serious about their conviction. Obviously they don't want to be free, because anybody who does want to be free is going to give their attention to that part of themselves that always has and always will be untouched by anything that happens in time. If we could begin to completely identify with that part of ourselves that has been untouched by time, by anything that could ever happen in time, the momentum of self-consciousness and neuroses is going to begin to fall away. It has to because we are literally not interested in that anymore. Clear? It is very straightforward: either we do that or we don't do it.

"That's all the psychotherapy anybody really needs—if they want to be free. If they don't want to be free, then of course they need a therapist. That's the bottom line, because a genuine spiritual teacher has all the tools necessary to face every aspect of the human condition, if the individual wants to be free. If they don't want to be free, then all the psychotherapy in the world, all the meditation in the world, all the dharmic issues in the world aren't going to help anyway . . . because the person is not interested in it."

Later in the evening another student asked, "Can you speak about how to let go of a sense of personal self?"

Andrew answered, "Someone says to let go of your personal self—to me that sounds a little ridiculous. I wouldn't have the faintest idea how to do that. But if we begin to look at the habitual way we personalize our experience then something can really begin to happen. If you look at every aspect of your own personal experience from the gross to the subtle, there is nothing personal about any of it. Like when someone sticks a needle in my finger and someone sticks a needle in your finger, we are going to experience the very same pain. Isn't that true? Will there be any difference between us, when that needle goes in? We are going to feel the same prick, we are going to feel it, isn't that true? When we are sitting in meditation and we begin to get a sense of fullness and deep and profound peace and joy, maybe even ecstasy, when we experience freedom from time to time—is there any difference between your joy and my joy in that moment? None. We are having the exact same experience, isn't that true?

"The same thing is true of sexual desire—the tyranny of wanting. When one person experiences that wanting and another person experiences wanting, is there any difference between them? The feeling in itself is completely impersonal; it has no particular face, right? So on it goes, on it goes. Sooner or later you begin to see that everything you experience is just the impersonal nature of all human experience as yourself. The ego is created simply through the habit of personalizing what is not personal. So the illusion of being unique or special is created through this habit of personalization, this very conditioned habit of personalization. When we begin to give the habit up we begin to see that everything we experience is completely transparent. It is empty of anything personal. That doesn't mean that some of it isn't very pleasant and some of it is unpleasant, but from a certain point of view it is still completely impersonal.

"Everybody knows what the experience of fear is, but there is not really anything special about being frightened or experiencing terror. But if one person uses the fact that there is terror as an excuse to become paralyzed and another person says, 'Well yes, there is the presence of terror. I also see it as a very impersonal event and it doesn't necessarily prevent me from responding in a very spontaneous way,' those two people are going to have a very completely different view of their experience, even though they are experiencing the exact same thing. One person is personalizing the experience and the other person is not. But you have to see the ego—which is once again the enemy of enlightenment, the part of ourselves that does not want to transcend—is created through the habit of personalizing what ultimately isn't personal. So when the habit of personalization is transcended it soon is given up too. The strength of ego begins to weaken and weaken and weaken and the personality of the individual becomes more and more transparent. The more identified with ego, the more we personally identify with our experience, the more ego gets harder and harder and stronger and stronger. The less we identify with our experience, the more ego gets transparent and weaker and weaker and weaker and weaker. It is very simple.

"It is a matter of the heart because surrender is the only way through. The choice to be free means 'I surrender.' Do you want to be free? Most people don't want to be free when they are frightened; they just want the fear to go away. The fear comes and then, 'All I want is the fear to go away.' Then the interest in liberation is gone in that moment. If you want to be free, it means you want to be free at all times, in all places, through all circumstances. You want to be free more than anything else, so your relationship to all your experience is you want to be free first. To be honest, for most of us, it is a lot more important to feel better. We are willing to sell our soul to feel better. Most people will sell their soul to the devil in an instant just to feel relieved of any kind of pressure—psychological, emotional pressure, any kind of burden. They will sell out in an instant. But someone who wants to be free is not going to sell out for anybody or anything. They are willing to be frightened, they are willing to experience all kinds of temptations, all forms of thought or feeling. They are willing to be tested. That means they are willing to bear witness." Andrew let out his characteristic, sometimes nerve-wracking cackle.

"Do you know what that means? You are willing to bear witness in this miserable, rotten world, that there is something sacred . . . right? No one is going to believe you if you are not willing to pay the price, if you are not willing to be true to that which is sacred. No one is going to believe you because they will see you are just as weak as they are, and they will know that they can buy you out. Somehow they can seduce you. They will get you to come down from your throne, so to speak, down there with them. But if you are *not* willing to do that they'll know. Do you understand what I am saying? You have to be willing to bear witness; all of us have to be willing to bear witness if we are serious.

"If we hadn't thought very deeply about life, if we haven't thought very deeply about what is important, then we have to be willing to take the time out to do it. Because we live in a world where most people's values are very materialistic. And one form of materialism is that it is more important for one to feel better than it is for one to live the truth. Or live in truth. If someone is fundamentally a very superficial, materialistic, self-centered person—in spite of maybe having been touched by the spirit—they may have to practice contemplation. In order to become more clear about what the true and right relationship of all things actually is, they may have to look very deeply and very objectively at their own experience and at the nature and meaning of life itself, and in that win some degree of spiritual independence in their own spiritual endeavor.

"If we are weak-minded and our heart is not rooted in that which is sacred, then we will be swayed in moments of fear, moments of lust. We will sell out. It is what we do in those moments that really defines who we are. It is not how we are when everything comes easy for us. Isn't that true? When we are challenged, we find out what we are made of, and where our heart really is. So, we have to *want* to be tested. We don't have to seek it out mercilessly, but we have to be ready and willing to be tested. It is a big part of what spiritual life is all about. And the more we are willing to stand up for the truth, the more tested we are going to be anyway. Right? But then we have to be interested in that, ready for that. That's what it means to bear witness. It means we are not going to cave in when we are tested, challenged."

Answering another question about how to find the strength to do what he was talking about, Andrew continued in the same vein. "If you *care* the strength is going to be there, if you don't care, and if you find out that you don't care, is that okay with you? Or does it not really matter? If it doesn't matter then nothing is going to change, but if you realize that you don't care and you find that unbearable, then you will find a way to care, you will be willing to suffer, to pay the price. Because you know, the spiritual life and the life of being truly conscious is a life of agony and ecstasy. A lot of people want to feel the ecstasy without having to suffer through the agony of it. Most of us just want to live a life of mediocrity, where we suffer as little as possible, but at the same time there is very little intensity. We don't want to experience too much intensity. We just want to create the illusion of some kind of emotional, psychological safety, security. And we waste this precious human breath just trying to avoid suffering. At the end of the road, we end up empty handed. So the question of how and why just depends on how much you *care*.

"Surrender and devotion to the guru means that you become a part of the guru's own heart, so if you truly become a part of the guru's own heart you become as committed and as unbearably vulnerable as the guru is. It means you don't just imagine that you surrender to the guru, as a way to avoid having to take responsibility for yourself. You understand what I am saying? If you are truly surrendered to an awakened human being, then you experience their pain and you also experience their joy—with them, as them. You are not protected. And you begin to see how real it can be to be alive."

Karl said, "As a generalization, in the very little time you have been here observing us, is there any area of any practice that you could generalize to say we as a sangha body could pay attention to?"

Andrew laughed. "Right on the spot, huh?" Everyone laughed along with him. He paused for a brief moment then said, "A little too casual, I think. A little too casual, that's all." He paused briefly then said, "I have to spend the night here!" Everyone dissolved into laughter.

Pursuing further, Karl asked, "Casual with each other or in relationship with our practice?"

Andrew said, "Just a little casual—that says a lot. Casual is a little sloppy. Yes, so I think maybe a little less casual. If you are less casual it helps you to be more awake. You know, one doesn't want to create some kind of sense of formality that just is some kind of useless artifact, but a certain sense of formality helps us to rise above our own unconsciousness. Do you know what I mean? So it helps us to be more awake to our own potential, our own nature.

"I heard from someone that you had a men's meeting this morning. One of my students said that some of you guys were lying down and talking. That kind of thing creates an atmosphere where there is no edge. If you are going to meet together then there has to be some kind of formality and a seriousness to create a mood of real respect for the forum and respect for each other. You should not even tolerate being casual with each other at all."

Another student said, "You said that your heart needs to be rooted. I wonder what that meant? Are your students rooted to you? What does your heart being rooted mean?"

Andrew answered, "There is no difference between me and the teaching. So if my students are rooted in the teaching they are very connected personally with me. If they are not, then they are very distant. People's relationship with me is dependent on their relationship to the teaching. If they are living the teaching fully, then they experience automatic and instantaneous intimacy that has nothing necessarily to do with having spent a lot of personal time together. I've spent a lot of personal time with people where there was an *illusion* of intimacy and trust created, but when it became apparent that whoever that person was was not actually living the teaching, suddenly there was a gap between us that was unbreachable. There have been other people that I haven't spent personal time with, but who live the teaching with great sincerity and have a lot of respect for me. When I am with them there is no gap. It has nothing to do with spending a lot of personal time together. It has nothing to do with friendship. It has nothing to do with familiarity. But the answer to your question is yes. Because when people are unwilling to live the teaching to a certain standard, suddenly my relationship with them becomes very distant. There is no difference between living the teaching and having a personal relationship with me. It's all the same thing."

The student continued, "To me the teaching is like a dry intellectual affair which is not living the teaching but knowing the teaching . . ."

Andrew said, "I would hope not! I would hope that would not be the case. If that were the case then the teaching would not be alive, it wouldn't have any heart to it, any juice. Right? Is that what you are implying?" Andrew laughed. "We'll take care of you later!"

Andrew and Lee both started laughing. The whole group broke into spontaneous laughter with them. Throughout the entire time Lee had sat, as he did now, obviously enjoying the exchange and Andrew's teaching. He often smiled or nodded vigorously. He was a silent force behind Andrew's words, with his smiles and laughter punctuating their agreement. Sometimes Lee would just sit and grin, either enjoying Andrew's sense of humor or the way in which Andrew hit the bull's eye time and again with his answers to Lee's students.

The student continued: "I think that I was implying that there is this serious emotional affair going on that I just call mysterious . . . you know, it is different from the teaching . . . It is sort of . . ."

Andrew interjected, "To be frank with you I don't believe that living the teaching or living a teaching earnestly and the experience and practice of devotion is any way different from each other. It is exactly the same thing. I mistrust it when people make very dramatic expressions of love and devotion to me personally. I know that it doesn't mean anything because, for example, if I express my heartfelt devotion to my teacher it makes me feel good about myself. *Sorry!*" People laughed at Andrew's witty mock apology. Of course it was obvious that he was speaking to a group of students whose tradition has a strong devotional element within it. His humorous candor was as refreshing and clear as spring water.

He continued, "But, that's the hidden danger . . . You may indeed experience a very powerful devotional relationship with, let's say your teacher, or a teacher, but part and parcel of that experience is seeing yourself and experiencing yourself in a way that pleases *you*. Now even that has to go. I'm not saying the experience of devotion has to go because that is part and parcel of living the dharma, part and parcel of having an intimate relationship with an awakened human being. But the ego can derive a great deal of self-satisfaction out of the awareness that 'I experience love, devotion, surrender to whoever it is. And that's good enough for me, because I feel devotion for my guru, for my master.' This is very satisfying to the ego. But how devoted an individual really is, in my understanding, is to what degree are they willing to pay the price? The price for transcendence, for liberation, to live the teachings, to be one with the teacher. What price are they willing to pay?

"That's the only true sign of devotion; the rest of it doesn't necessarily mean anything. You understand what I am saying to you, sir? I've seen too many people tell me how much they love me, and when their ego is challenged they turned on me and they ran away. So, what me were they loving anyway? It couldn't have been the real me, because the real me is only interested in their liberation, it doesn't care about anything else. If there is true devotion then the person is willing to pay the price of staying with you, by your side, for all the right reasons. That's real devotion; that is real love. That kind of love is deeper than sentimental feeling. So the emotional experience of devotion is not enough. I think it is the beginning of the process, the beginning of the relationship to the spiritual teacher. Those feelings are very important, because that is how one comes to one's knees, how one gets swept off one's feet. But after that, then you have to put your money where your mouth is, so to speak."

April 16, 1999
Arizona Ashram

Lee left at six o'clock this morning. He drove alone to Redlands, California, where one of his daughters goes to college. He is giving a talk tonight in Claremont, an affluent suburb of L.A., and another talk tomorrow night in San Diego. Somehow it seemed right that he had disappeared, as if into the mist—like the Bauls who come, sing, dance and then are gone. He had left his devotees to sit in meditation with Andrew Cohen and see Andrew and his group off just after eight o'clock.

Before meditation Andrew was sitting at the kitchen table with Dasya. Dasya asked him how he slept. "Great!" he smiled. He said, "I started relaxing as soon as I got here. I've slept great here. It's really unusual for me. With all the traveling I do, and even at home, I don't sleep well anymore—I guess I've just gotten used to the tension."

Back in the kitchen after meditation Andrew commented, "I could have gone on meditating for another two hours!" A few of Lee's students sat around the table with him while he had a light breakfast of muesli, then it was time to go. Their luggage packed, Andrew and his students climbed into their small rented van and took off down the dirt road. On Sunday night Lee would be home again for darshan, and his comments on how the visit went and his students' participation in it would be the proof of the pudding.

April 30, 1999
Crown King, Arizona

It was the last gig that Lee would perform with liars, gods & beggars. Twenty-five sangha members had come out tonight to make the hour and a half trip to the gig, to pay their respects to the imminently dead, but also to express gratitude for everything that LGB had meant to them over the years. Lee drove the teal green van and led the caravan of four or five vehicles. He raced down twenty long miles of pitted and corrugated dirt road, spinning up rocks and clouds of dust behind him, then headed up into the winding mountain roads, driving like a madman. In their attempts to keep up with him, one car in the caravan lost a muffler and another an engine.

Incredible vistas unfolded to the east. To the west the sunset washed the sky in opaque hues of gold and orange while twilight moved across the land from the east. We were deep in the wilderness of the desert mountains, ascending along mountain ridges and straining straight uphill, toward a backwoods tourist enclave called Crown King. The full moon in Scorpio was rising in the purple eastern sky, a huge mellow golden ball that radiated the landscape with silver light as darkness began to fall. The mountains were rugged and awesome, surreal crags and waves and peaks dotted with desert sage and scrub brush, low-growing oaks. A few hardy cottonwoods grew in the sandy soil down in the canyons far below. As the van climbed to higher and higher elevations we drove into a forest of Ponderosa pine that rose up tall around huge, smooth boulders that crowded the dirt road into narrow passes.

Lee's destination for the night was a quaint and rather charming little community hidden back in the woods and rocks. It was the kind of place one can only find in the remote Arizona mountains, made up of a general store, two restaurants with bars and a hotel. Live music blared out of one of the bars. Lee walked in wearing what appeared to be a simple beige T-shirt, but upon closer inspection it had a daisy on the front that had the word "cunt" spelled out in small letters across it. Right away Lee joined the band, which was already set up on the edge of the dance floor, their instruments and monitors spread out against one wall of the room.

The bar was humming and snapping with energy. There were about sixty people in the place once Lee's group arrived. It was mostly populated by college students and young adults, tourists from the Phoenix area, probably visiting in this funky resort to cool off and race three-wheelers in the mountains. Many of them were drunk or feeling no pain. As the band tore into their first few numbers they crowded out on the dance floor with longneck beer bottles in hand and danced together in hip-grinding parodies of sex. They seemed to be having a great time as they smiled and collapsed on each other's shoulders in laughter. A group of young men moshed wildly together in front of the band. A few older people danced too, and there were one or two Arizona mountaineers—gray haired and grizzly in overalls. It was easy to go out and dance in this relaxed and motley combination of people.

As the band segued from one song to the next the energy continued to build. Electric chords, tones, notes and rhythms crashed and churned one upon the other to create the fury of sound we call rock & roll. Within that nuclear intensity was melody, voice, song and Lee's poetry. I got the distinct feeling that liars, gods & beggars were going to play for all they were worth tonight. These men had put their hearts and souls into this project for almost twelve years. It had been the focal point of their lives and the source of many intimate hours with Lee, at hundreds of gigs, countless weekly rehearsals, on the road touring in Europe, in Arizona, California, Colorado, across the American Southland. Tonight was a final *pranam* to Lee, and to a legendary task that these disciples had undertaken with their guru.

As the music took over, gratitude for the band flowed through the air like an elixir. It emanated from the sangha members who were present, but also from the band members themselves. There was the strong sense of those generations of disciples who would never hear liars, gods & beggars live and on fire. They would hear stories of the mystical chambers, the incredible *rasas* of ecstasy pouring through the body while blood pounded hard in the veins from unrestrained dancing. They would hear tales of when people left seedy little taverns and bars at midnight or in the early morning hours feeling reborn and uplifted by the power of the music, to drive many hours back to the ashram. Generations of future *sadhakas* would only read about the nights when angelic entities descended and the unseen audience applauded—their clapping and cheers like a rain of nectar—or about the *tapas*, the burn of sadhana on the road with the guru's rock band. They would only know this music through the miracles of modern science and the oral tradition of the Hohm Community.

All this was in the air, and more. Everything about this night was a reminder that all things pass. Even the most beautiful and powerful flowerings of creation fade and die. This knowledge tinged the air with a bittersweet remembrance that the most fundamental principle of life is impermanence, and brought a realness and immediacy to the night. Here and now was all there was.

At the beginning of the second set something shifted. All reserve was melted like ice flows in the spring. It was as if the whole room had entered a different reality. Everything suddenly looked alive and vivid. Ed Flaherty of Shri described it later: "The band kicked into 'The Places I Haunt,' a psychedelic punk number, half-sung, half-rapped by Lee. Steve was playing sinister lines on his organ, and Doug's slow hand was sending out shimmering, reverb-drenched chords that seemed to stop time. Everything that was happening was so crystal clear it was like watching a movie in slow motion. When Lee sang, 'So you say you want love?/What kind do you want?/Variety's the spice/Of the places I haunt./So you say you want peace/Of the world or mind?/That's not my business/I've left it all behind!' I could feel the *vajra* sword slicing through the air. Lee's audacious declaration of ultimate nonattainment was palpable." (*Tawagoto*, Summer/Fall 1999, pp. 55-56)

The band went into a poignant version of "The Magic You Are Working," a beautiful, lilting ballad—a tender love song with transcendental overtones. It is a song that transmits the mysterious power of deep communion between a lover and beloved:

To say that I am grateful might seem obvious,
To say I love you may seem trite.
What can I say to truly capture,
What you're giving me tonight.
Oh the magic you are working,
So lovely and so right.
I am feeling kind of wistful,
Not used to this dizzying height.

Yes I'm feeling kind of foolish,
I'm not usually this tongue-tied.
Must be the magic you are working,
Must be the tears that I have cried.
Oh the magic you are working,
So lovely and so right.
I am feeling kind of wistful,
Not used to this dizzying height.

The dance floor was packed with people. An irrational jubilation began to steal into the room and across the floor, infecting everyone with joy. It took over the whole place as everyone was suddenly transported into the realm of mythology, the halcyon dream of Vraja, where Krishna sported with the *gopis*, or Avalon, the apple isle, a paradise in the subtle fields of the Earth. The music seemed to have a life of its own and it was soaring. The members of the band were like magicians, one hand to heaven and the other to earth, channeling pure spirit into matter. Every song was a distillation, a quintessence of Baul music.

Even the usually reluctant dancers among Lee's students were out on the floor moving to the beat, soaking up the transmission of the music, basking in the presence of Lee onstage. By the second set Lee seemed to have slipped into a *bhava*. What he communicated from the stage was sublime, and could only be sipped through the long sweet glances that he lavished on the dancers and musicians, and yet outside of this subtle weave of communion, Lee appeared completely ordinary. The sound of his tambourine jingled out into the night as he stood near the back or walked up to the mike to sing a song, then drifted unobtrusively to the side of the stage again and danced along its edges, watching and smiling.

The music was so incendiary and penetrating in its magical effect that even though they had been dancing wildly, people began to drift away after the second set and wander over to the bar across the street, where a mediocre but safe band was playing Allman Brothers' songs. Still the mood continued to build. The second set had blown the crowd away, and by the third set the only people who could endure the intensity of the chamber that the band created were Lee's students and three or four hardy locals—mountain people who sat at the bar drinking. Occasionally they would look around at the band, clap or hoot, then turn their backs again, bend over their drinks and resume their conversations with the barkeep.

The dancing went on and on. No one could sit down. With each song a new surge of energy lifted one up and onto the dance floor to celebrate with the band. Stan and Doug, the two long-time composers of the band, were caught up onstage in a poignant bond of communion in which years of stress, competition, struggle and conflict melted in the heat of the moment. These two, along with Steve B. and Lee, had been in the band since 1987. Their years of sadhana and experience together in the band were written on their hearts which poured into the songs as they stood side by side with Everett on bass, the three of them bending into the sound and rhythm of the songs like a wild wind, playing as if to save their souls.

There was no sentimentality in this; nothing mawkish or maudlin about it. It was just the right way to go out—full tilt, with joy and enthusiasm and victory. The victory of the guru in twelve years of dharma music and the grand experiment of the band, because in spite of problems, resistance and insurmountable obstacles, much had been accomplished. The faces of the band members were glowing and yet concentrated into a point of focus. By the last song, everyone was primed for a grand finale. On "Just A Woman," a signature closing song for LGB for many years, the audience danced themselves into a frenzy. Justin pounded on the drums, crashing down with a force that sent the drumsticks flying out of his hands. That didn't stop him—he beat out the final rhythmic blows on the cymbals with his hands. Slowly the last chords reverberated into the silence and the cymbals were still. Everyone was sweating, breathing deeply, smiling.

Slowly Lee and his crowd gathered together and left the saloon while the band members stayed to pack up their equipment. They would drive back later in the night. A couple of cars followed Lee back down the moon-drenched mountains. He drove like a wild man again, the dust from his car blinding those behind him as he flew around curves and raced down hills. The moon shone on everything, illuminating every rock and shrub— the same moon that shone on India, the full moon of the Bauls, the moon as Lord Krishna, who surely had visited on this revelatory night.

June 6, 1999
Arizona Ashram

May 1999 was a helter-skelter month of Shri gigs, preparations for leaving for New York and France, and the usual schedule of After Dinner Talks, darshans, Sunday morning teaching meetings and ongoing zany affairs in the ashram office with Lee. In early May Lee traveled to Canada where he gave a five day seminar at Mangalam, a center of Arnaud Desjardins that is managed by his disciple, Eric Edelmann. Purna flew in from Little Rock and Rick L. from Vancouver to accompany Lee during the week. Purna and Rick both returned directly to their homes after the seminar, so there was none of the usual storytelling when Lee returned to Arizona, but a few stories were gleaned here and there. It was the third year that Lee had gone to Mangalam to give teachings, and once again it seemed that laughter was one of the key ingredients of the mix.

Preparations for Lee's trip to France have been steadily underway for the past week. Lee has had all the new Hohm Press books, CDs and domestic items needed by the ashram in France packed into heavy, square cardboard boxes. The packing process cluttered the greenhouse for two weeks. The ashram is used to this routine now; it is the fourth summer that Lee has spent in France. This year he will be gone for four and a half months. Many people are coming into the office to tie up loose ends of business with the guru, knowing they won't see him again until October. Lee has made a number of comments such as, "Don't fax me unless it's an emergency . . . or really necessary!" He expects his students to practice and carry on without any dependence on his physical presence.

Lee leaves for New York in two days. He plans to spend a week in New York City and surrounding area with his family and some of his students before flying on to Paris. During that time he will visit Andrew Cohen at his ashram in Massachusetts and give a public talk in New York City.

June 9, 1999
New York City

Lee and his entourage arrived in New York City about twenty-four hours ago. Since then he has been on a feasting spree—a home-cooked Italian dinner, pastrami sandwiches, pizza. For the past two months Lee had been eating so sparingly—fruit for lunch and raw vegetables for dinner—that when asked about it he had said, "I'm preparing for four months in France!" Now in New York he dug in with a hearty appetite, and over pasta with homemade *braggiole*, meatballs, spicy sausage and stuffed, rolled pork skin cooked in a delicious basil tomato sauce, he jokingly said, "I'm in training!" He referred to the fact that he will be hosted lavishly during his teaching travels in Europe. But since he has arrived in New York it seems like he is preparing himself for something else—beyond stretching his stomach to accommodate the rich meals his hosts will provide—with all this gross, heavy food, so much the opposite of his usual diet of salad, vegetables, brown rice and fruit.

Lee hasn't done any teaching in New York for fourteen years, but he has lots of history in this place. This is where Lee's sensational and provocative first book, *Spiritual*

Slavery, hit the bookstores in 1975 with its raw, gutsy proclamations of God-realization. It is where Lee and the Hohm Community had a center for a few years in the late seventies, and where Lee gave darshan every Sunday night. It is also where his notable friendship with erotic writer Marco Vassi, the editor of the Penthouse Forum, began.

During those early years Lee earned a reputation as an iconoclastic maverick by mercilessly skewering the layers of illusion that he perceived in everyone around him. He criticized the hypocrisy of the spiritual scene and often pointed toward and even satirized other teachers in his publications like "Lazy Wisdom," a hilarious take-off on Da Free John's publication "Crazy Wisdom." Lee once described his relationship with New York City as a "love/hate relationship." Making the teaching available to New Yorkers has always had problematical aspects to it. New Yorkers typically seem mired in what Rudi (Swami Rudrananda) called the "spiritual supermarket," where people get lost, fascinated by the great variety of products on the shelves. Not to mention the fact that to most New Yorkers, New York is their guru. Tonight at Lee's public talk in NYC anyone could show up from Lee's past, from old Silva Mind Control friends and associates to former students and devotees.

All of this history hummed along silently with the group who walked along briskly with Lee as he took the subway and then walked for fifteen blocks down Broadway to the Source of Life Center at Thirty-fourth Street and Broadway where he would give his public talk tonight. Starting out from the pizza-by-the-slice place where he and a small group of five just had dinner, Lee began to tell the story of an est trainer who was going to give the est course for the first time in New York City: feeling some trepidation given the notorious reputation the New York est seminars had amongst the est staff, one of the trainers went to Werner Erhard and asked him how he handled teaching in NYC. Werner said, "I get up in the morning and ask myself, 'Is this a good day to die?' and if the answer is yes, then I go and teach," the implication being that every day is a teaching day because every day is a good day to die.

Lee told the story—which he has told many times before—with enthusiasm, but tonight the story also carried a characteristic vulnerability, a glimpse of his unashamed humanity. Lee is never one to pretend that he doesn't experience nervousness or fear—he simply goes ahead and does whatever is needed regardless of how he feels. Over the years it has become apparent that it is his sheer vulnerability to the fact of being human in the most full and all-encompassing terms that much of his strength and resilience comes from. Mulling all this over Jane asked, "Is that how you feel right about now?"

"Yes . . ." Lee smiled. Unspoken but lingering in the air was the question: "How will Lee Lozowick show up tonight?" By Lee's own admission, he never knows because he has no plan, no personal preferences, no agenda other than to serve the work of Yogi Ramsuratkumar. Walking past theaters, delis, shops, crowds of people, all the glitter and glamour of Broadway, we headed into the building and walked upstairs and into the room that Dean and his twin brother Michael had set up for Lee's talk.

As the room filled up some crazy-looking characters mingled with the incoming crowd. A tall, bulky, rather homely woman in a plain housedress came in, and then a slight, dark, flashy woman with long, dyed hair. She wore a slinky white, ankle-length dress. They were an unlikely pair of friends, but they made a flamboyant point of establishing territory in the front row beside two other women. They sat and talked loudly between themselves, ostentatiously greeting others who arrived. Another woman came in carrying a huge bouquet of white flowers—lilies and roses—and sat in the middle of the room. The bulky bouquet seemed charged for some reason, like she had something in mind. Usually people who bring flowers to Lee's talk give them to him, but this woman now laid them on the seat next to her as she sat down and looked around the room. People seemed very concerned with who was in the room. It seemed that many of them knew each other.

Lee started out speaking rapidly in a slightly acidic tone that was alternately self-deprecating and insulting to his audience. "I'm not sure if anybody has expectations this evening. I usually ramble—so if you're expecting a linear presentation, you won't get one. If the talk turns mean and you're offended, I won't be offended if you leave. I have a message, but it's not consoling, because human beings are pretty creepy creatures. Maybe you go around hugging one another, and tell people 'I love you,' but that doesn't make you a human being either.

"I have no credentials. I have absolutely no credentials in worldly terms, so if you need that to give what I say any weight, then you're in trouble. I have a teacher in India who is alive. He accepts me and gives me a certain amount of recognition—that is my credential in the States. Even though I have been teaching for twenty-four years, doing this Work, people discount it. So if you leave, I won't be insulted—really. I've had so many people leave my talks over the years I'm used to it. Not that I think it's pleasant, it sucks, but I've gotten used to it.

"So, if you expect wisdom tonight you'll have to be able to read between the lines. If you don't read between the lines you'll think what's going on is scandalous. What it's all about is that you are trying to force reality into *your* mold. We all have illusions that have to be faced, including me . . . .

"My tradition is associated with the Bauls, who are a heretical sect who use sex, food, family and work for transformation. The Bauls do not follow the philosophy of renouncing the world to find God; that is ridiculous and impossible because the world *is* God. If you renounce the world, you're not going to find God. The brain can produce all kinds of moods of bliss and ecstasy and so forth, but that's not God.

"So, just disregard what I say if you want to as someone who is significantly arrogant. If you're offended by what I say you are just giving my opinion credibility. You know what I mean? If I say anything you disagree with, just ignore it! We like audience participation, so if you want to yell out, hoot, holler, go ahead!"

Lee told a joke and got a few chuckles from the audience. He said, "Well, there's a few people smiling, that's good," then he continued in his stream of consciousness style. "My illusion is that, hope against hope, something I say here tonight might be of value to some of you." He shrugged almost nonchalantly, as if he automatically accepted that the possibility of this crowd making use of what he had to say was so minimal as to be nonexistent. *"Bon chance!"* he said, going into a fast repartee with the large woman on the front row. *"Vous parlez Francais?"* he asked her. She said no and asked if he did. *"Un petit peu,"* he answered.

He continued, "Back to the Bauls. The Bauls find God here and now in the body, not after death. The Bauls believe in the transformation of energy and they use the strongest energies in the body and work within daily, ordinary life—within their work, family situations. If we're going to use energies to serve our spiritual path then the stronger the energies, the more likely they can be used for transformation in a significant way. The Bauls use breath and sexual energy for transformation. Of course before one can be initiated into esoteric practices like these there are foundation practices that must be in place."

He talked about what is demanded of practitioners who want to enter the Vajrayana path of Tibetan Buddhism—a vast amount of prostrations, meditations, mantras, deity visualizations and so on. Before one can even consider being eligible for the Vajrayana path one must go through the Hinayana path (the lesser vehicle) and the Mahayana path (the greater vehicle).

Lee began to talk about New Age ideas like creative visualization and co-creation, debunking these and using his years in Silva Mind Control as an example of the difference between the spiritual path and the metaphysical path. Lee started jumping around from subject to subject, a thin and at times almost imperceptible thread connecting it all in a kind of loose coherence. The rational mind of the average person would find his presentation at times incomprehensible and exasperating. There was an air of irritation in the room; people were shifting in their seats at the discomfort they experienced from Lee's raw and unsettling communication, but also the air snapped and crackled with energy and possibility.

"I do lots of teachings with other teachers, not because I'm a networker, but because they draw bigger crowds and I like to tag along on their coattails—play my games on their audiences!" He laughed at himself. "Here we are—free, alive, spontaneous! Spontaneous! What's that?" He scoffed with a little laugh. His words had an incinerating and stinging quality, and yet at the same time he was somehow mild, even-tempered and pleasant in an odd way. He continued in a self-deprecating manner, drawing his audience into his extemporaneous style of mockery, self-honesty and insult. Perhaps by virtue of the fact that he was so willing to scoff at himself the audience was willing to endure his pointed digs into their psychological conditioning and gross mechanicality.

He continued, wisecracking on the typical relationships between men and women: "You know, to men 'I love you' means 'Kiss my ass, wash my clothes, cook my meals and I'll go out whenever I fucking want to, and you can kiss my ass again!' To women 'I love you' means something very different. But not all men, of course. Some of you are probably very sensitive and understanding, read all the books about men and women!" Lee's diatribe about men's prejudices and abuses against women went on awhile, occasionally hitting on women's role in the whole mess. It seemed that he was trying to pare the space down, to shake off dissonant elements within the audience in a way that would open something else up for those who really wanted to hear what he had to say tonight.

The crowd was a bizarre but probably typical mix of New Yorkers. The standouts among these were the two women in the front row to Lee's immediate right. One of them was the tall, hefty woman, Rosie. She kept butting in while Lee talked and commenting in a style that was jocular on the surface but was insensitive to the space and seemed more like a form of heckling than anything else. Her friend was petite and thin by contrast, but equally aggressive. She had a pinched, narrow face that could have been pretty if it weren't marred by the ravaging signs of aggression and vanity. She was wearing an ankle-length white sheath with a side slit that exposed her leg almost up to the hip joint. She had long straight hair dyed dark brown. Her eyes were coated with dense, dark make-up and she wore three heavy gold chains around her neck. One of the chains sported the ornament of the Star of David, one an ankh. The massive gold ornament on the third chain was unidentifiable.

In her right hand she held what seemed to be a plastic day-glow green egg. As she handled it suggestively her hand would slowly snake upward, creeping up to shoulder height to twitch in a paroxysm of weird *mudras*, as if she was attempting to manipulate the energy coming off of Lee. She also held an object in her left hand, a small statue, icon or fetish. Her body shook and arched back, shuddering with energy in what appeared to be a parody of kundalini shakti movements. She held the strange egg out toward Lee and asked him a rather pretentious question about grace and absolute reality. The question was strikingly devoid of substance, more of a hollow attempt to create an appearance. She was the kind of person who wore her delusions about herself on her sleeve. Lee brushed her off with a superficial answer that reflected her state of presence. Now he veered off, back into giving people permission to leave if they wanted to.

"Really, I don't care if you leave. If this is not for you, if you find my style distasteful, you can leave. Maybe you can even get your money back. I'd never give you your money back, but Paula back there at the table, she's really sweet. She's a pushover, she wants everybody to be happy. You can probably talk her into giving your money back. Me, I'd never give you your money back. But Paula's got a temper, so don't push her or you'll never get your money back!" Lee grinned devilishly. A woman with curly blonde hair and a glassy blue-eyed smile plastered across her attractive but vacant face looked around the room as if she was searching to see if anyone else was going to leave. No one else was moving, but she got up to leave while Lee continued with his next barrage. Trying to pick up his train of thought, he was saying, "Bauls, sex, breath—oh yeah! Foundation level practice . . ."

Rosie interrupted Lee and asked him how much money he makes. He answered, "I work a hundred hours a week, I maybe get about two dollars an hour. Of course," he added sarcastically, "I get room and board because I live on an ashram."

In the meantime the blonde woman had moved from her seat on the aisle to the back where she approached Paula B. at the table and asked to get her money back. Paula said no. An argument ensued and was beginning to take over the room. The blonde woman was adamant. She said in a very loud voice, pointing to Lee, "*He* said you would give me the money back." Paula refused again and pointed out that Lee said she *might* be able to get her money back, not that she would get her money back. The woman kept insisting while Paula responded, "Absolutely not."

The attention of the audience was drawn to the argument as it escalated in the back of the room. The woman became more desperate. She tried to grab the cloth bag that had the money in it from Paula. Paula yanked it away from her hands in a momentary scuffle. Paula asked Michael, who was standing near her filming Lee with the video camera, to take the bag, but he kept his eyes on Lee, who then motioned to him to put the camera on the woman. "Wow! That's incredible! Get this on film," Lee said loudly, "no one will believe this unless they see it. Okay girls, go for it!" The blonde woman was fighting it out with Paula so intently that she was oblivious to the camera.

Giving up on getting the money from Paula, the blonde woman turned back toward Lee and started a dialogue with him from where she was standing at the back of the room. She was coming unglued, her façade literally cracking before everyone's eyes, and it was not a pretty sight. She yelled at Lee, an edge of hysteria creeping into her voice, "You are being very arrogant!"

Lee shot back, "I *said* I was going to be arrogant."

She continued flinging accusations at him, "I came here to learn something and I'm not learning anything. You said you'd give me my money back—I didn't even *think* of leaving until you said it!"

Lee said, "You're very suggestible!"

Her voice got louder as she said, "I've never done anything like this in my life! I'm not usually like this! I've never been like this before in my life!"

"Sweetheart, who are you trying to kid?" Lee's voice boomed out. "Now *there* is something to learn! Everybody is *always* exactly the way they are. You are always the way you are right now!" Lee yelled back at her from the front of the room. "If you want to get anything from this talk tonight you can get *that*—you are always exactly the way you are right now." Lee repeated this statement three or four times in the midst of the woman's continuing protestations that she had never been like this before. Lee's statement sank into the room as he repeated it.

Practically weeping with frustration and anger, she mechanically parroted, "We are all limitless. We can be any way!" The first statement was rhetorically true, but the second statement was categorically untrue, and she was the living proof of it. She was coming apart because she was being forced to see her behavior, and it was ugly, undignified and inelegant. This interaction was a painful demonstration of the degree of illusion that we all have about ourselves. We think that we are typically clear, generous, easy-going, blameless, but in reality we are grasping, full of greed, dissention, resentment, aggression and confusion. We live in a state of inner chaos, a war between the disparate elements of the psyche, and all that was what was being manifested here in Lee's talk tonight. Lee had brought the murky underworld of this strange crowd into the bright light of scrutiny, using himself as the sacrificial bait. The teaching lesson he made now was not lost on everyone in the space, although it was flying over the heads of some—those who could not see past their own romanticism and sentimentality.

Lee said to her, "Are you married?"

She snapped back, "That's none of your business!"

"Why are you offended by that question?" he asked innocently.

The blonde woman went back to Paula and argued some more for the money. Then she said, "What about a book? Can I have a book instead of the money?" Paula sent her over to Dean at the book table who said no to her request. Frustrated and confused, she sat down in the back row. In the meantime, Lee had forged ahead. He began to talk about a book written by Vijaya Fedorschak, one of his students, called *The Shadow on the Path*.

Lee said, "The presumption of the book is that you have to admit that something needs to be healed. Unless you do that first, the path will be useless to you. God is all that is; mind, body, soul is one unitive whole. The astral body, physical body, etheral body, mind, spirit, all are facets of the whole and work in conjunction to realize any state of spiritual awakening. You have to deal with the whole. Physical sickness may take time to hit the physical body, but with the physical body it's clear when we get sick that we are sick. It's not so obvious when we are psychologically sick. We can hide our psychological sickness under success, for example. Men who can fuck anything that moves as long as it has a hole in it, with no desire—that is one form of neurosis. Another form of neurosis is being overly sensitive."

Lee was smiling. He was holding a small empty water glass and tossing it back and forth from one hand to another, using it to make a point as he gesticulated with it. The playing with the glass could have been a sign of a surface nervousness, which would have been understandable considering how electric and tense and jittery this crowd seemed to be, or it could have been something else altogether. Whatever nervousness Lee may or may not have been feeling, his overall communication, his body, his eyes, his smiles, were the antithesis of his arrogant, insulting words. Reading "between the lines," as he recommended that his audience do, he was exuding kindness, compassion, and a kind of stark simplicity of being.

About five minutes later when Lee said, "We define our lives psychologically by what we don't want to remember. Physical, emotional, psychic, sexual abuse. Neglect. Neglect is a terrible form of abuse for a child. So we are in tremendous denial—some of us a little, some of us a lot. The skills we have, the careers we have chosen, the clothes we wear are all defined by our primal psychology and childhood experience. The more we are in denial, the more obstacles we have to spiritual life.

"The things that life delivers to us to deal with are the result of karma, but what we do with that has nothing to do with karma. The way we are and the way we deal with things from our primal psychology, our behavior, is not karmic. We find ourselves in circumstances based on karma—karma defines the things that happen to us, but not the way we *deal* with what happens to us."

The woman who had asked for her money back now got up and left. Lee said to the audience, "I figured she would get up and leave once we started talking about karma." The implication was that she had an idea that she had no personal responsibility for her actions or her behavior. She was actually getting an opportunity to see herself as she really is, to get that she is responsible, and that she can't just lay everything off on some abstract idea of "karma."

Lee continued, "Any education that we've gotten is completely useless at best and terrible at worst on the spiritual path. Whatever we are in denial about will obstruct us on the path because we don't know that it's an obstacle. Before you can heal something you have to know it has to be healed. The mind, body and spirit are one. God is all there is, but at the same time our psychology is defined by the things we want to *forget*. So our psychological illnesses hamper us more on the path than our physical illnesses . . . ."

Lee continued playing with the glass. Now he put it down on the table and laughed. "This is the first time I've ever done this during a talk—played with a glass! Usually I play with myself!" People laughed. Lee had a big smile on his face. "I usually have a screen that comes up to here," he held his hands up to his chest, "so no one can see. That relaxes me!" Everyone laughed at the joke. "The more we are in denial, the more obstacles we have in spiritual life. An unhealthy ego is in denial."

Lee began to talk about Fritz Perls and Carl Jung, who both knew how important it was to be able to be tough with clients. "The mind/body is unitive, so any obstacle in one domain obscures progress in all domains. At a certain point, any obstacle in any domain obstructs progress in all domains. Any imbalance in any domain creates a psychosis of being. If we go too far in one area and don't handle obstructions in other areas, it can be a problem. That's why the Spiritual Emergence Network can be helpful to some people. They counsel those with severe imbalances in terms of mystical experiences, to the extent that they can't function well in life."

It seemed that Lee was focusing the entire evening on psychological dysfunction, particularly as it shows up in fascinations with mystical experience, because that was what the group gathered there most needed to hear. The vocal majority of the group was fascinated by New Age metaphysics, and there was the usual confusion that is found in such circumstances about the difference between metaphysics and the spiritual path.

He continued, *The Shadow on the Path* is all about this subject. In order to free ourselves up for esoteric practice we have to deal with our psychology and the shadow side. The shadow side is not inherently bad, but will tend to show up in greed, cruelty, violence. In order to effectively realize the light, we have to deal with the shadow. Wow!

How was that for good poster material?" He glanced over at Dean, who was hosting him in New York and had done the promotion for this talk.

"So, any questions about anything I've talked about tonight?" Lee laughed, "I have to stand up for myself, in case anyone thinks I'm just a rambling, babbling idiot! It's my style, which has taken me years to develop. Except in my relationships, I'm a chauvinist pig too! I'm not really like this," he laughed again, "it's taken me twenty-four years to *hone* this style!"

Rosie laughed loudly. Lee looked at her with a slight smile on his face and quipped, "An audience of one is better than none!" He laughed again. She began a rapid exchange with Lee, bantering back and forth. Someone asked a question about the bands and Rosie interjected again, asking, "What's your passion?"

Lee mused, "Passion, passion. *Passion!*" Becoming more thoughtful, he answered, "Actually music is not a passion for me. I enjoy it, but I don't play an instrument, I sing—it's something I do that is very hard work. My *passion* would be . . . dominating other people!" Lee paused. He was rubbing the painful reality of where we all live into our faces. "What do I have to hide? Nothing. Reading books is a passion of mine. I love biographies! Not just any biographies but spiritual biographies. I have this idiosyncrasy where I read every word, and with some of these books I get to page fifty and . . ."

At this point Rosie started a repartee with Lee about books and biographies. Throughout his talk she had been throwing out sporadic off-the-wall comments like, "You're free to be yourself! Yes! It's good you are yourself! Go for it!" Her unconscious agenda seemed to be getting attention in any way that she could. Her interactions with Lee were marked at times with unconscious insult under a thin layer of humor. His responses to her were consistently supremely generous and patient. Lee spoke to her by name and referred to her comments respectfully as he continued to speak.

An older man with thinning gray hair, probably seventy years old, conservatively and simply dressed and sitting halfway to the back of the room raised his hand. His comments and question were sober and considerate, a marked contrast to everything else that had gone on in the space between Lee and his audience thus far.

He said, "You sound like a Gurdjieffian."

Lee smiled, " Well, that's a good guess."

The man continued, "What do you think of Georg Feuerstein's description of you in his book, *Holy Madness*?"

Lee grinned this time, "It was great! I came out better than anyone else in there." The man smiled at Lee and nodded his head in agreement, then said, "Yes, that's true."

Another questioner raised his hand, saying, "How do you know you're right?"

Lee answered, "Feedback from the environment. If I have a hypothesis I wait to see it proved out. I look for three concentric signs from the Universe. I don't trust even my own so-called—by my students—'enlightened mind.' I await confirmation, which always comes on time."

He began to talk about the typical psychological condition of people again. "People are really fooling themselves about their denial. You can't create spiritual life on a foundation that isn't clear . . ." His was a lone voice crying in the wind in this crowd. He was like the captain of the rescue ship, throwing out lifelines to drowning people, but the lines lay sinking in the water while people thrashed about.

In the meantime the self-styled kundalini woman in white sitting next to Rosie continued with her antics. The day-glow egg was being fondled, turned and stroked in her hand as the woman closed her eyes in ecstasy. Shudders of pleasure shook her slight frame. It was like watching a performance. She kept pulling the attention of the room toward herself with these demonstrations, but from the vantagepoint of the back of the room, it wasn't exactly entertaining—it was absurd and painful.

Another man talked about how there were many healers in the room. He said, "I think healing, working as a healer, can be a spiritual path," to which Lee answered, "I wouldn't consider healing a spiritual path."

The man continued, "But what about *siddhis*?" There was a general discussion in which Lee explained to a woman in the audience who didn't know what *siddhis* are that they are "spiritual miracles." The conversation about developing *siddhis* on the spiritual path continued. The man who first asked the question wanted to know how to have humility if one has gained *siddhis*. Lee talked about the real fruits of the path being the consistent cultivation of kindness, generosity and compassion, not *siddhis*. "Anyone can have *siddhis*," he said, "they don't mean anything. If *siddhis* arise it is useful to have some education about these things. There is technology that can be used to create those states. One of the vows I took when I left Silva Mind Control was not to reveal any of the things I had discovered there. Chasing after *siddhis* is not what the path is about. What means something is that you are kind, generous and compassionate with people on a daily basis."

Lee continued, "The path demands tremendous discipline and work from us. For example, there are very strict preconditions for entering the Vajrayana path. First you have to go through the lesser vehicle, Hinayana, and then the greater vehicle, Mahayana, before you can even consider Vajrayana, the tantric vehicle. All those prostrations are incredibly demanding on your energy, on your knees and back! You have to ask yourself, 'Am I serious about this path?' If you're just going to flirt around the edges, don't get on a serious path. Just chase unicorns and put rainbow stickers on your car. But don't flirt around with the path."

Another man, a disciple of Krishnamurti, asked a question. Lee called on him, saying, "Yes sir," then spoke to his concern. "Krishnamurti was very broken-hearted at the end of his life about how his teaching hadn't taken root. After seventy years of teaching, his success rate was not hopeful." Lee's voice was extremely soft and kind as he answered this man.

Another person asked about Lee's community and the practices of his students. Lee gave a detailed answer, speaking about the formal conditions and practices of the school and life on the ashram. He talked about the extensive reading list recommended for study, about meditation, diet and conscious child-raising and conscious conception.

Lee's answers were heartfelt and sincere. People were listening carefully. He said, "We have a very traditional Eastern orientation. The senior practices, and we have many esoteric practices, have to be *earned*. Working with breath and sex. Beginning sexual work is just having sex regularly with some degree of passion for a few years. But you have to have sex on a regular basis—once a month could be enough for some people. But the idea is just to have sex with some degree of relaxation within a committed relationship. There is plenty of technology, but to get that my students have got to be a successful couple. They have to be adjusted to each other, stay together, be friends, be in love, understand one another. The reason I have only one hundred and twenty-five students after teaching for twenty-four years is that people have to go through a tremendously obscure labyrinth in this school. I consider the work that we do to be extremely valuable to the world. People who approach have to begin with reading all the material that is over there on that table!" He pointed to the book table. "Most people can't even get that far!"

A woman asked a question about living in the world, having a job, and how to manage that. Lee said, "Every job that keeps the world together is important; it's not what job you do but what kind of integrity you bring to it. Do you bring kindness, generosity and compassion to your co-workers?"

The woman dressed in white on the front row with the green egg and heavy gold chains around her neck opened her eyes and asked a question about universal oneness and Grace. She was speaking as if she was some kind of expert or spiritual adept—as if she and Lee were peers who might agree on the subject.

Lee quipped irreverently, "Grace is Grace, *siddha* is *siddha*, New York is New York!" His impertinent hint seemed to aggravate her and she became much more insistent and aggressive with her questions. He answered, "Sweetheart, you shit where you eat, so how can you talk about universal oneness? Are you Jewish?" Lee asked her in a penetrating tone. He seemed to be gearing up for an assault.

"No, I'm not Jewish . . ." she said, surprised and insulted.

"You look Jewish," he mused and continued with a little laugh, "Have you ever gotten laid?"

"That's none of your business!" she shouted.

"Have you ever been constipated?" Lee asked innocently.

"Constipated?" she said loudly, getting more disturbed by the moment, "No!"

He laughed again, "I was going to make a comment about being Jewish and constipated! Dealing with the universal is irrelevant!" he snapped while she continued to argue, both of them talking at the same time.

"What's true is true," Lee said, "there is no argument there, but we live in a world in which to travel through that world requires skills that have nothing to do with the universal."

She yelled at him, "There is separation in that statement!"

Lee said, "There *is* separation."

Speaking rapidly in an angry, loud tone, and not hearing anything he was saying, she said, "I live in the eternal now—I chose to spend time with you tonight . . ."

"You call this spending time?" he laughed, and then asked again, "Sweetheart—have you ever been laid?"

"You don't want to go there with me!" she charged threateningly. She started ranting some spiritual rhetoric that she had heard and assumed that she understood. She shouted at Lee, "If the world is all God, if the reality is universal oneness, how can we best serve, how do you get to the underlying oneness? I don't know if you realize what you said earlier . . ."

In a low voice Lee said, "You don't know what I realize."

Now she charged him, "You took me there! And now you don't want to go there with *me*!"

He said with humor, "Be nasty, go ahead, be nasty! You can be nasty, but don't be arrogant." As she continued her verbal assault, suddenly Lee switched his approach and began to level an accusation at her, matching her tone and volume, "You are preaching to me! You've taken over the flow and you're preaching at me! You're a fundamentalist Christian, sweetheart."

She snarled, "You don't know my life . . ."

He continued, "You're like one of those preachers on the streets! You're just a dyed-in-the-wool fundamentalist, baby . . ."

When Lee asked her if she'd ever been laid she had begun to spin out of control. But now that he accused her of being a fundamentalist Christian she really began to get flustered. Her voice went up several notches and she began to shriek slightly. "No, I'm not. I'm not a fundamentalist. You wouldn't be saying that to me if you knew what I do in my life . . . Believe me. I am *not* a fundamentalist!" She was thoroughly rattled and literally began to pull her skirt down, adjusted herself in her seat, flipped her long hair behind her shoulder in an agitated move as she attempted to pull herself together. She breathed a deep breath and exhaled dramatically. "Okay, okay. God bless you. I'm glad you can be yourself. You don't know me. You don't know who I am. I'm not a fundamentalist. God bless you."

Lee countered, still more or less shouting at her, "Yes I do know you—I know everything about you, and *you*, baby, are a pure fundamentalist!"

"Okay, well, I'm glad you can be yourself," she had calmed herself down, until with great effort she had herself under control again. The interaction had a very raw edge to it. For a moment Lee had appeared as a mighty fury; he seemed to be as out of control as she was. Not only did he mirror her state to her, he seemed like a wild and wrathful Kali, whirling maniacally through space, chopping heads and arms off of whatever was in his path. It was a painful and difficult moment in which the rational mind was completely confronted.

Now he turned away to answer the next question, then stopped short in the middle of his answer, saying, "I feel bad that I yelled at this poor creature!" He mocked himself, repeating, "*Poor* woman! If my Teacher heard me arguing with this woman he would kick my ass from here to the Pacific Ocean. I would never send Him the video of this—it's so embarrassing!" Everyone laughed but the woman in white.

A man raised his hand and asked, "How do you chant your mantra?"

Lee answered, "The idea is that the vibratory rate of the mantra effects your system to create greater harmony and leads to the growth of kindness, generosity and compassion in relationship to others—with some exception, as demonstrated a few minutes ago!" He nodded toward the woman in white. People laughed. "The longer one chants, the more one recognizes the chant internally. The effects of chanting begin to show up in a nonlinear way, and may at times be spontaneous revelations that dramatically alter the texture of one's life. Those things are the result of ongoing attention to chanting."

A woman raised her hand and spoke earnestly about how Lee had told the audience that he was going to be provocative, and that they could deal with his provocation by leaving if they wanted to, but he hadn't yet told them how to *stay* in the face of his style. It was a very sincere question, and his answer was reciprocal.

"That's a very good question. Thank you," he said gently. "The purpose of provocation is to make you *think* about it. Chögyam Trungpa Rinpoche was once asked what he did when he found himself in hell. He said, 'I try to stay there.' So what you do to stay is to stay there in the irritation. The mind/body unit naturally moves toward harmony. If there is any kind of disturbance of the mind/body, the way to move through it is to *stay with it*. The tendency is to suppress or avoid anything that threatens us. Stay with the irritant and the body will provide the natural means to move through it because the body seeks harmony. Whatever thread you are able to keep alive, the body itself seeks harmony, moves toward harmony. Keep your attention there and the body will move the irritation through. Good question."

Another question came, "How do *you* work through tension?"

Lee laughed and quipped, "Steak! That's how I work through tension! Ruth Chris's Steakhouse in Phoenix! Filet mignon, sizzling in butter!"

A man asked if he would have any time to talk one-on-one afterward. Lee said, "I thought we were talking one-on-one." The man continued to talk about his difficulties. Lee cut through his confusion, saying, "Our ordinary lives are what's relevant, and what takes away from that is not."

Another man protested, "The mundane gets boring. That's why I came here tonight! I want something deep, exciting . . ."

"Go to Starbuck's." Lee's deadpan brought on another wave of laughter.

Rosie began to engage Lee again in some ridiculous repartee. "I have a *personal* question," she said with a sly tone. Before Lee could get his reply, "Okay," out of his mouth she snapped sarcastically, "Briefs or shorts?"

When Lee looked at her in a moment of disbelief, she repeated the question, seeming to revel in the momentary spotlight. "Briefs or shorts!" she asked again, brightly. Lee looked at her and said simply, "Briefs," then went on to lampoon himself, talking about how embarrassing it was to have to wear the skimpy little bikini bathing suits that are mandatory in swimming pools in France. He said, "I like those big boxer trunks that cover everything. Keep 'em guessing! That's because I've got a little 'thing'—a quarter inch long! So embarrassing! Those bathing suits are made for people with big ones! Like ponies!" Raucous laughter broke out.

Now he smiled broadly and said, "Any other profound, intelligent questions?"

A very attractive black woman with long curly hair holding a viola in a bulky case at her side asked a question. "I don't know if this is a profound question, but what do you think about the condition of poverty? Life on the streets?"

Lee's answer carried a gravity, a tender sobriety. Every trace of the provocateur was gone as he said slowly and deliberately, "I've been poor, but I've never been in poverty. It's only a projection—I've never been on the streets, but my projection about it is that it's hell."

She continued with sincerity, "I understand you haven't been on the streets, but I want to hear your answer. Why is there so much poverty in the world? You say there is only God, so why poverty?"

Lee said simply, "I really don't know. My father had a brilliant political and social mind, but I really don't know. Enlightenment isn't too big a question for me, but poverty is too big for me. I really don't know." He paused a moment, looking at her. She was leaning forward in her seat, listening intently, then smiled at Lee and nodded, appearing satisfied. She said, "I appreciate your answer. It was very sincere."

As Lee went on in this style in which he mixed up paradox and humor, direct confrontation and compassion, the room began to get visibly brighter. It was the first time tonight that the space had been effulgent in this way. Because this woman's question was so genuine and unmotivated by pride or power, it seemed to have provided a kind of fuel that nothing else had. It seemed like the group had been set free from the dark forces that held it in thrall most of the night—as if a banishing had occurred. Or, more accurately, it seemed that the guru had "eaten" or transmuted the illusion in the room, taking it into himself and transforming it.

Soon after this Lee brought this wild and strange talk to a close. The audience responded with a loud round of applause. Lee moved over to the book table where people began to cluster around buying books and talking with him. The woman with the viola came over and thanked Lee again for his answer to her question. "It really means something to me," she smiled.

People were buying books like crazy. In the meantime the woman in white and her cohorts were hanging around for some inexplicable reason, given how unpleasant her interactions with Lee were. Suddenly the woman who brought the large white bouquet came over to the woman in white. They positioned themselves so that they were standing perhaps six feet away and directly in front of Lee, where they proceeded to make a grandiose display in which the woman with the flowers presented the bouquet to the woman in white.

"Ooohhh . . . these are for *me*?" the woman in white squealed loudly in surprise. The white bouquet filled her arms and she flopped it back and forth like a sack of groceries as she flipped her hair back over her shoulder. It was an unabashed display of egoic posturing. It appeared so inauthentic that it could have been planned and rehearsed ahead of time. When someone mentioned it to Lee, saying, "Did you see that?" he nodded and said, "Yes," with complete detachment, turning to speak with another person.

This little bit of theatre, and the whole evening, was a reminder of how far Western culture has come from living in a context of the sacred. The decay of basic dignity and respect shows up even more drastically in cities. Big city life is like the festering open sore of a deeply sick society. The talk tonight typified the reality of the situation—there is almost no thread left of an authentic spiritual life in our culture. Without a sense of the sacred, of appropriate protocol and basic human dignity in relationship, there is no elegance, no elevation of the spirit, no possibility for human evolution. Very few Westerners can recognize the true spiritual master, much less invoke what the spiritual teacher has to offer. If wisdom walked in the room and looked them in the face, they wouldn't recognize it. And that was virtually what had happened. The whole affair left a bitter taste, even though there was victory as well in the fact of the teaching being spoken.

As soon as possible Lee packed up the rest of the books and left the space, heading for the Tick Tock Café about five blocks down the street on Broadway. Several people who came to the talk had been invited to go out with Lee and company for a late dessert. The group of about twelve people crowded in around Lee at the three tables that were put together. Orders were placed while everyone buzzed about the talk and the theatrical antics in the space. There was a general agreement that the woman in white had to be deeply neurotic, and that the best question was from the woman who asked how to stay in the space when Lee was being provocative.

Purna mentioned that some of the people at the talk were clients of Starr Fuentes, a well-known and respected psychic, healer and friend of Purna's. Wanting to support Lee's work, she had sent flyers out to her extensive mailing list when she heard that Lee would be speaking publically in New York. Lee said to Purna, "Will you be talking with Starr?" When Purna nodded yes Lee said, "Tell Starr I apologize for my language and inelegance."

Dessert was served and people at the table chatted socially. When the talk turned toward the woman who wanted her money back and left, Lee said quietly, "I would have given her the book." The various conversations that were going on stopped and all the attention at the table turned toward Lee. Dean and Paula both leaned forward to hear more clearly. Lee repeated, "I would have given her a book because then she might have read it and really gotten something from the talk tonight." This bit of teaching communication came slipping out as if Lee had opened a door only slightly, then he closed it again.

It was the only direct teaching he seemed willing to make after the talk. As the door remained closed, Lee sat and joked with his companions until it was time to go.

Getting back on the subway with Lee, we made our way as quickly as possible to Dean's apartment. At twelve-thirty the group arrived and turned in immediately, knowing that everyone would have to get up and on their way to Fox Hollow, Andrew Cohen's ashram in Massachusetts, early the next morning.

June 10, 1999
Fox Hollow, Massachusetts

Five people accompanied Lee as he drove the rented mini-van to Fox Hollow where he would visit with Andrew Cohen. Lee seemed tired but cheerful this morning and was generally quiet as he drove out of New York toward Massachusetts. In the van Purna talked about Lee's public talk last night. He had spoken with Starr Fuentes and delivered Lee's message. Starr told Purna that the woman in white was one of her clients and that she is a professional stripper. Lee perked up behind the wheel. "I wish I'd known that last night! That explains everything," he said.

When asked for his observations of Lee's public talk last night, Purna said, "I thought it was magical. The talk was rich with possibility. Lee perfectly tailored it to New York City and the audience there. He reminded me of a baby Krishna—a mischievous Gopala. But most of all it was such a drastic reminder that there is really almost no practical spirituality on the tantric path in the West. Practical spirituality is virtually unheard of here.

"There was a buzz, a high-strung energy that is so typical of New York, and Lee was going right into that. He said at the beginning, 'Read between the lines.' He was really giving them something. There was so much there—it was so active and lively! Many people in the space were *really* with him all the way, like Judith."

Purna was referring to the woman with the viola who asked the question about poverty, who is a professional musician and good friend of Dean's. Dean had been staying with Judith during this week while Lee and some of his company stayed at Dean's apartment. Dean added, "Judith really enjoyed the talk. She's read a couple of Lee's books before and wanted to come to the talk, but she had never been enlivened by the whole thing the way she was after the talk. She was really brought to life, asking me questions last night after we got to her apartment."

When Lee was asked about the talk he very noncommittally said, "I was just fishing. It was a potpourri."

The group fell into an easy silence as Lee drove on through green hills. "We're getting close!" he said enthusiastically as he exited the main road and headed toward Fox Hollow. "Close to what?" Purna asked humorously. "Close to you?"

"I hope so," Lee answered.

Lee pulled into Fox Hollow, down an immaculate gravel drive lined with tall, thick-trunked pine trees. In the distance the Berkshires flowed out in green waves. Before us a beautiful two-story manor house—the main building on the ashram proper—appeared with smaller houses and some rows of newer buildings, rented condominiums, arranged within the estate of manicured green lawns surrounded by lush green forested areas. In the nearby valley a blue lake glimmered. Lee parked the van and everyone got out, walked toward the front door, past the semi-circle of the herb and flower garden that blossomed in early summer fullness on the front lawn. Lee pushed the doorbell but there was no response, so he walked inside. Following him, we found ourselves in a wide and spacious hallway with a floor of marble tiles that lead off to offices and beautifully appointed formal sitting rooms on either side. People began to come in and greet Lee warmly, either introducing themselves or, having met Lee before, greeting him with apparent pleasure.

Very soon Andrew appeared. He walked up to Lee and embraced him. Standing together they made quite a contrasting sight. Lee was wearing his twenty-three year old frayed navy blue sweat pants cut off at the knee, a black T-shirt from the rock group Live that said "Secret Samadhi," and his faded purple Teva sandals. Andrew was dressed in a carefully ironed long-sleeve plaid shirt with an immaculate vest over pressed and creased dress pants. His freshly-cut short black hair next to Lee's wild silvery dreadlocks with their red and blue beads added another dimension to the picture of these two unlikely friends—but a very mutually supportive pair of good friends they are.

Quickly it came out that Lee had given a public talk in New York City the night before. Lee mentioned to Andrew that something had happened that had disturbed him. "There was a woman at the talk who got to me, and I didn't like it," Lee said to Andrew, and Andrew almost imperceptibly nodded as if no more needed to be said. He had gotten the picture completely with very little need for words.

Andrew knows only too well that almost every public talk has at least one heckler. He has been known to get up and walk out of public talks, saying to the audience, "If you want to hear what I have to say, then get rid of him," or her, depending on the situation, indicating someone who is completely unworkable and is sabotaging the possibility of the teaching being communicated in the space.

Five years ago Andrew and Lee were giving a weekend seminar sponsored by Yvan Amar in Gordes, France to five hundred people. Their attempts to teach were being thwarted and subverted at every turn by the theatrical and hostile antics of a man who claimed self-realization, but who in actuality was an obvious and possibly dangerous psychopath. He had aggressively bullied his way on stage and refused to leave. He was attacking Lee and Andrew, especially Lee, in a manner that was just short of physical violence. Both Lee and Andrew were in agreement that the man needed to be asked to leave, but they each chose a different way to teach in that instance. Andrew walked off the stage and left the building, going out into the courtyard, while Lee chose to stay.

In the face of the man's continued aggressions toward his person, Lee remained calm and almost serene, simply sitting in his chair. His demeanor was an incredible demonstration of "being that which nothing can take root in." At the same time it was excruciatingly difficult for Lee's students, who wanted to grab the man and bodily throw him out. It was not unlike the public talk of the night before, but much worse.

Both Andrew's and Lee's way of dealing with the situation in Gordes had had its merit and communicated something about the teaching to the audience. Andrew was unequivocal, firm and vocal about his position, which was to demand that the man leave the seminar. Later over lunch Lee, Andrew, Yvan and a group of students were talking about this man, and also about a woman who was dying of a terminal illness and had questioned Andrew during the morning session. A student asked Andrew a question about his response to this woman earlier in the morning, which had been made in ruthlessly honest terms. He had refused to pander to her psychology by responding to her with the rank sentiment that was flowing through the room in her direction because she was facing death. He advised her to face her death directly, with strength and clarity, and to use it to fuel her desire for liberation.

"Don't you have compassion for people?" the student pressed Andrew further at lunch, referring to the dying woman and the man who had attempted to aggressively manipulate the entire seminar toward his own aims and agenda. Andrew replied, "I have *no* compassion for ego!" He went on to say that whenever someone was attempting to keep the teaching from being communicated, he had no tolerance for that person. Many times since Lee has delightedly used this example in seminars and public talks because he agrees so wholeheartedly.

Taking a tour of the ashram, Lee and Andrew walked with a small group of students. Fox Hollow was everything we'd heard it was—elegant, beautiful, spacious. Every room or corridor was perfect, detailed and pristine. A tremendous amount of work had been done in the renovations of the main building, and the care and intention that had gone into every aspect of creating the place was apparent. All along the halls were plaques with Andrew's words in large bold type, the credo of their practice, much of it centering around the impersonal nature of the human experience, emptiness and the realization of nonduality.

After a delicious vegetarian lunch Lee and his party spent the afternoon walking around the property with Andrew and some of his male students. We walked through a lush forest of evergreens, maple and hickory trees, bracken fern and wild flowers to the beaver pond, then through more woods that broke open at a historical site. It was the home of nineteenth century novelist Edith Wharton, where a local Shakespeare company performs during the summer. The group continued on along the road past the blue lake and back to the ashram. While we walked Andrew and Lee talked or visited with each other's students.

Another gourmet vegetarian meal was served at dinner, and then Lee gathered with Andrew's students, mostly the ashram residents, in one of the main salons to speak. There were about fifty people present. The plan was to hear Lee speak and then watch a video together, "Kings on Straw Mats," about the Nath Siddhas at the 1986 Khumba Mela in Haridwar.

The group sat facing Lee and Andrew who were positioned on a couch at the front of the room. Andrew graciously turned the space over to Lee to answer the questions of his students. Lee started with an innocuous little joke—the "turtle joke." It's one of the few that he tells that isn't bawdy, but it does have a slightly *noir* edge to it. It's about a baby turtle that keeps climbing a tree up to the top and jumping off, *splat*, to the ground, getting up and climbing and jumping off again and again. Two birds sit in their nest at the top of the tree watching. One of them turns to the other and says, "Honey, do you think it's time to tell him he's adopted?"

As Lee delivered the punch line the entire room burst into laughter. Lee said, "That's *not* an analogy for anything—or is it a metaphor?" More laughter. He asked for questions and the first person raised his hand.

"I spent time with your students at the Book Expo in California lately. They were collecting toys for the children and spoke of the children so fondly. Would you speak about having children in spiritual life, in your community?"

Lee said, "We have parenting in many forms in our community—we run the range of good parents to bad parents, as you can imagine, knowing how practice is . . . .

"One of the things we have people do is to remember that spiritual life is not separate from ordinary life; the idea is that practice doesn't mean the rejection of ordinary things in life. We recommend conscious conception, but lots of the children born in the community are surprises." He threw out this last comment with a decidedly mischievous tone in his voice, although it seemed part delight and part frustration. He continued:

"We don't proselytize to our children. We don't expect them to be little Bauls or something like that. What we want is for them to grow up to be decent human beings. In the first generation of children that have actually grown up on the ashram we've had very good results. Some have even come back to live within the community, but that's not our aim."

Another questioner asked, "I understand that the women meet separately from the men in your community. What have you found that was valuable about that?"

Lee said, "We didn't do that in the very beginning—I have a learning curve, you know. It took a few years to see that it would be of value to us. When women establish themselves in the teaching and men establish themselves in the teaching then people can come together to consider the teaching without making sure their hair is just right and driving each other crazy with subtle sexual messages. When the context is established for women and men to meet together to consider the teaching, when we are free to consider the teaching with one-pointedness, then something truly extraordinary becomes possible."

A woman asked, "Have you found differences in how women and men come together around the teaching?"

Lee responded, "I want to see how people work—if people are practicing, I respond to that regardless of gender. Everything is on an individual basis. If someone is practicing weakly, it's whips and chains!" Everyone laughed heartily. They seemed either used to Lee's style, having heard him speak before, or prepared for it.

He continued, "Most people's relationship to me is very subjective, full of expectations and projections, especially because my school has a strong devotional flavor. People are consumed with their own projections; we are so conditioned to look at the teacher as a savior. We think the teacher loves us unconditionally, and maybe that is true in some ultimate, nondualistic way, but on a practical level that's not true. If people aren't practicing, I don't love them! I've found that to really touch people you have to get to the unconscious; you have to go underneath the conscious mind, infiltrate the system so to speak."

Working off of scribbled notes it was difficult to capture the details of Lee's answers, which were quite extensive and given in a rapid-fire style. He was talking extremely fast. He even commented on how fast he was talking, because he wanted to pack a lot into a short time.

Another questioner spoke about the five tenets or dharmic phrases that Andrew has given to his students and the (English) mantras that they repeat before and after meditation. He wanted to know if Lee has given his students anything comparable. Lee responded, saying, "We have a number of dharmic phrases that have been given over the years that aren't used as much as they could be used—they aren't mantric, but they could be used more as objective reminding factors. One of them is 'Be that which nothing can take root in.' "

At this point Andrew, who had been sitting completely still and quiet with his eyes closed as he turned the space over to Lee's answers, moved slightly. A hint of a smile played about his mouth as if he perhaps liked this. Lee continued, "Another phrase that was given years ago is 'Draw no conclusions mind.' I was giving a talk at this Zen center and I guess I was feeling resonant with their Buddhist practice and that phrase just came out and stuck. We have many practices in our school; we have the basic conditions, which are vegetarian diet, daily meditation, exercise and study. We have an extensive recommended reading list, not just of spiritual traditions, but of classic world literature. And in addition to that we have a whole plethora of esoteric practices—we have a sun practice, a moon practice, breath practices, sex practices. But those practices have only been given to a handful of people.

"We're very good at serving one another and loving one another, family and all that, but the practices tend to suffer. We've always got some men's group or some women's group going on, always some self-inflicted crisis happening. People have made huge sacrifices to come into this Work, they've left successful careers and jobs to move to Arizona and to be close to the community and me—then they don't practice! What the blessings of the teacher do is give you the ability to benefit from Grace through practice, but without practice, Blessings mean nothing. *Nothing replaces practice.*"

Another woman asked, "Do you use some kind of inquiry?"

Lee said, "Yes, we use Enquiry to seek the roots of consciousness. But we will often make an unconscious decision not to use Enquiry if we are feeling good. We don't seek the roots of consciousness unless we know we are suffering. We only use the practices when there is a disturbance. The Buddhists use the term "emptiness" to describe all phenomena. So the most ecstatic states of happiness are just as empty as our states of disturbance.

"Too often we use Enquiry to suffocate disturbance instead of seeking the roots of consciousness in all states that we experience. Essentially Enquiry as we use it is designed to provoke the same state of consciousness that the five tenets you have been given by Andrew are designed to provoke."

The next question was, "You meet a lot of other teachers and go around connecting with other teachers. What do you get from that and does it change your teaching?"

Lee answered, "Actually I'm not so much of a networker, so I don't do it for that reason. When I was a young teacher I hung out with E.J. Gold a lot and he helped me tremendously in his mentorship. So I learn from my peers and my seniors in the Work. E.J. knew that I was wet behind the ears and that he could offer me guidance. He said to me, 'Someone did this for me, now I can do it for you.' There are only two or three people, teachers who I hang out with who I consider to be my peers, and I hang out with a *lot* of teachers! I don't say this at most places where I go!" Lee chuckled to himself. "But if people are decent and have a good heart and aren't doing any damage and are teaching, it's worth it to help them avoid the pitfalls of financial mismanagement or sexual abuse in their work. A lot of good teachers have one little unexamined area, and even one small unexamined area can ruin a good teacher and disillusion students who will lump all teachers into the same category once they've been hurt by a teacher.

"So I do try to help other teachers who are coming along because it was done for me. I learn a lot from Arnaud Desjardins—anyone who is really different from me, I learn from. Arnaud is a real gentleman. He's very elegant. I'm not like that—I'm heavy-handed. Arnaud gives serious teachings to those who are serious in their practice and work, and he lets others go on their merry way. I'm just the opposite—heavy-handed, pounding the point into people. So I can learn from that.

"There's not so much for me to learn *spiritually* from others, but there are times when I'm struggling with how to say something, and then I hear Andrew say something with such clarity! Just the way Andrew languages a point, perhaps puts a twist on something that I've been struggling to communicate and I haven't been happy with how I'm communicating it. I hear Andrew speak and I'll say, 'That's it!'

"So for example, 'Be that which nothing can take root in' and 'Draw no conclusions mind' are two phrases that we kind of bury within a large matrix of dharma and wait for people to discover on their own. I don't elevate these phrases and maybe I should. We come here and see how you use your dharma, and maybe we can learn something from that."

A question about Lee's three published journals came next: "You say that your books are about the teaching and that your diaries *are* the teaching. I find that a curious statement. What do you mean by that?"

Lee smiled and said, "I'm a lazy writer. Most of my recent books are edited transcripts of talks, not written material, but the diaries I made a point to sit down each day and write. The material in the journals is not linear. The journals are completely spontaneous, and the entries strike a different chord than the chord of the rational mind. You can only read it from being or essence. I have a very strong leaning toward the Gurdjieff work; a lot of how I teach could be aligned with what is called a 'work teacher.'

"I wrote a book years ago called *The Only Grace Is Loving God*. I call the work I do Enlightened Duality—but if one doesn't realize the nondual nature of everything, that all form is emptiness, one cannot live in Enlightened Duality. The realization of emptiness or nonduality is the foundation of my work. But a lot of people misunderstand my teaching because it sounds so dualistic. If we don't realize nonduality as a foundation for a life of practice, we can't get very far, and there is no Enlightened Duality."

Another student asked, "Are the bands meant to be a kind of practice?"

Lee said, "For those in the bands it is practice, but not for everyone else. The purpose of the bands is to create an environment that wouldn't be created otherwise."

The student continued, "So the rock band has been dissolved?"

Lee said, "Yes. As the bands have become more proficient some members of the band refused to keep taking risks. I work with concentric validation—I wait for the Universe to validate my instinct, and it had become clear that it was time for the rock band to end. Some of the members of the band would die for me, but for some people it would be easier to die for the teaching rather than practice. The blues band, Shri, is going great—it is just ripe with possibility right now.

"We have a new band now, Attila the Hunza. They are sizzling—tremendous possibility! With three women lead singers . . . But we'll see. They're already in it up to their ears. In the bands people get to deal with all the issues of vanity, greed, power, control. They have to work together. Community is about teamwork. If there isn't teamwork the ashram will suffer and you insult your teacher . . .

"When we're on the road with the bands—in road life—every aspect of practice is magnified as if there is a spotlight shining on it. If people aren't working together as a group then it is glaring and obvious. You've got to remember that no matter how late you were out the night before, the next morning is a morning of practice. So the impetus of the group is practical. It's fun, but it's not about fun—it's about practice and working together as a team.

"If you want to bring honor to your teacher—and that's what practice is, bringing honor to your teacher—then you work as a *team*. The only way one moves on in the Work is to replace one's self. The more you bring honor to the teacher the more you free the teacher to work in a more expansive way. But too often we want to bind the teacher to ourselves; we want the teacher's attention. We want the teacher to be *ours*. But when the teacher is functioning freely is when the teacher has practicing, functioning students to *stand* on. Only one thing frees the teacher—your reliability of practice.

"Krishnamurti said, 'Love has no questions.' Well, reliable practice has no questions! If you are practicing in a way that deserves praise, then you won't *need* praise! Reliable practice needs no feedback. Arnaud's disciple Daniel Morin says that the best students work in the shadow of the master. There are the glory students and then there are the ones who just wash the floors. All they want is to practice in a way that is reliable and frees the teacher to work. That's the task of every student—to free the teacher to do whatever he has to do.

"The feeling of abandonment that many people say they have is very dangerous on the path because the teacher can't abandon you. The teacher is always there. Not the human being, but the purity of the consciousness that is the teacher. If you are feeling identified with abandonment, then you have missed something very important about the teacher. Who goes anywhere? The teaching doesn't leave when Andrew leaves."

A woman said, "About Yogi Ramsuratkumar. You met him after you started teaching?"

Lee began, "He was the source of the awakening. I don't usually call it an awakening actually—I call it the event that provoked my teaching work. I met Yogi Ramsuratkumar in 1976, or I guess it was early 1977, for the first time. I didn't know who He was to me at the time. I only knew that I wanted what He had. I couldn't define it, I just knew I wanted it. Carlos Castaneda tells a story about how Don Juan tricked him into his apprenticeship. The teacher always has to trick the disciple, it's part of the process. And so Yogi Ramsuratkumar tricked me, because I had no idea what it was He had to give me. He laid it on thick in the first two trips: He had me sit beside Him and gave me all this attention, He did all these heavy symbolic things with me . . .

"Then after a few years I started to get that everything I'd gotten earlier in my sadhana came directly from Him. By the time I made the third trip to India I'd been writing to Him and sending Him poetry for years. But when I got there He didn't remember me, really didn't remember me. When I told Him I'd spent time with Him in 1977 and 1979, He said, 'Are you *sure* it was this beggar?' As if one could mistake *Him* for someone else! I was desperate—talk about feeling abandoned! So He sent me away and put the final nail in the coffin, so to speak.

"Actually when I realized who He was to me, when I realized that He was the source of my teaching work, it wasn't like some big flash of lightning or something. It was like clouds slowly disappearing on a sunny morning and revealing the scene behind them. Not a big flash, but like on a cloudy morning, when things are misty and you can't quite see; you know that something is there underneath the clouds, but you can't quite make it out. Slowly the lines come into focus as the clouds drift away and then suddenly the scene appears sparkling in the sunlight, and you say, 'Oh yes, that's what was there all along.' "

"That's beautiful!" murmured several people in the audience.

Lee smiled and then continued. "So, you should just lay down and say yes! If you've picked the right person to be your teacher then there is no danger in that. I'm not talking about subservience. You come to the teacher because the teacher has realized something you want to duplicate, a clarity of consciousness. It's not subservience but certainty of clarity, like 'This person I can trust.' We have to watch the teacher a little to come to that certainty, because anyone can fall in love.

"Once the teacher knows you are trustworthy, then he knows you will take the feedback he has to give you—gracefully, with no reaction. As far as I'm concerned any reaction in my students—if they just make a face—to me is the same as a *fight*! I want *no reaction*. Any form of resistance to me is a problem."

Coming into the atmosphere of mutual support and regard that is shared between Lee and Andrew and their respective students after the foray in New York City was like a balm to the weary. The mood of this talk was the polar opposite of the talk Lee had given the night before in the city. Tonight it was light and humorous with a feeling of easy rapport and appreciation among everyone. The hospitality that Andrew and his students showered on Lee and his group and the opportunity to give a teaching to a group of serious practitioners brightened Lee considerably.

June 11, 1999
New York

After a sumptuous breakfast with Andrew and a few of his students the next morning, Lee left for New York. In the car while Lee drove we listened as Purna and Dean talked about how they had spent a good deal of time speaking with Andrew's male students who they stayed with in the men's house. As usual, the interactions and sharing of dharma between the two schools was rich and invigorating. Purna said that in talking with Andrew's students after Lee's question and answer session with the group, one comment from one of Andrew's students had stood out. He had said, "What Lee did wasn't teaching, but it *was* teaching." It was a very astute comment, because Lee's style is casual, spontaneous, full of jokes and laughter. In conventional terms it doesn't always appear that teaching is going on—but the teaching gets in. A transmission is made in the midst of the laughter and easiness. It was a demonstration of what Lee was talking about last night when he said that he has learned that the most effective way to teach is to go below or underneath the conscious mind to the unconscious. Arnaud Desjardins once told Lee that Swami Papa Ramdas used to say at his ashram, Anandashram, "Here we laugh the ego away!" Lee works in a very similar way, but his style is Western, with a definite tantric spin and the salty tang of the streets.

Purna said that Andrew's students were surprised to hear that Lee turns away a number of people every year who want to be students. Purna explained to them that Lee has one hundred twenty-five or one hundred fifty active students, and could have thirty or more new students every year, but doesn't really want or seek new students. Instead Lee chooses to keep his school small.

Lee began to criticize himself. He said, "I was unhappy with some of the things I said last night. As it was coming out of my mouth I said, 'Oh no!' "

Surprised to hear this when the talk was so great, so relaxed and full, and Andrew's students seemed thrilled with it, I asked, "What was it that you weren't happy about specifically?"

Lee answered, "Oh, anything that might have seemed disrespectful or unsupportive of Andrew's style in any way." Lee's extraordinary respect for Andrew and the work he is doing, not no mention his absolute standards of how to be a good guest, never cease to be a source of amazement, and in this instance I was taken aback again by the stringent standards he sets for himself, since he didn't say anything that could be construed in such a light.

Arriving back in the city Lee drove through the traffic to the Thirty-Fourth Street Post Office where he would meet up with the rest of his traveling party. The post office was the meeting point because it has two large wall murals painted by Lee's father, Louis Lozowick, a renowned artist, and Lee wanted everyone to have the opportunity to see them. The traffic was heavy, and Lee was having difficulty finding a parking place. He told us to get out of the van and go in while he drove around the block.

"You should all go on in and meet everybody else. If I can't find a parking place, I'll just keep circling the block until you've met up with everyone and seen the murals. If I can find a parking place, I'll park and meet you inside." Someone protested that he might not get to see the murals and offered to do the job he had just described. He said, "I'm fine! I'm not attached. After all, *it's just another wall mural.*" He made the point. There was no need to get sentimental just because it is his father's art.

"Go on! Go!" He urged us, impatient with the hesitation. We jumped out of the van and ran up the steps in search of our companions and found them right away.

Most of the afternoon was spent sitting on a park bench with Lee at the Washington Square Park talking and mulling things over while the children played in the playground. Later that night Lee would be going to see "The Lion King" on Broadway. Paula B., a professional musician and one of Lee's students who was helping host him and his entourage of thirteen people had miraculously gotten Lee tickets for everyone on the front row center mezzanine. It truly was a miracle because "The Lion King" is sold out in advance for the next two years. Paula said that she pulled in all the favors owed to her by her musician friends who play in various Broadway productions. It was basically Lee's gift to the children, and the adults of course would get to enjoy it as well. Kelly's brother, who lives with his family in the area, teased her about it. "It's a miracle!" he said with a laugh. "We've been living here for three years and are still waiting to get our hands on four tickets to "The Lion King!" What other miracles will Lee perform while he's here? Parting the Bay?"

Lee's group was staying in two apartments uptown in Manhattan, and the day would be spent in the Village with an early dinner planned at Raj Mahal, an Indian restaurant in the East Village. Lee originally said that everyone would go back to the apartments where they were staying after dinner to change for the theatre that night. But yesterday before he drove to Fox Hollow he had changed his mind and said that everyone would not go back to the apartment. The rest of Lee's party who had been traveling with the children and had just met up with him didn't know that the original plan—to drive back uptown and change clothes before the theatre—had been changed. During the course of the afternoon Lee changed his mind two more times. Finally he said that we would not go back uptown to change, but would be able to put the bags full of odds and ends, the blue jeans and T-shirts we'd been wearing all day, in the rented cars that were parked in the Village before we took the subway to Forty-second Street and Broadway where "The Lion King" was playing. Who wants to go to a Broadway play carrying a bunch of bags and stuff? Vanity being what it is, one wants to appear elegant, stylish, marginally *with it.*

In the meantime, around three-thirty in the afternoon Lee began a slow walk with the children from Washington Square to Raj Mahal in the East Village. There he would meet up with four or five other people, including some long-time students of his who live in New York and rarely have the opportunity to see him, who had been invited to join Lee for an immense and sumptuous dinner. After dinner Lee walked back to his oldest daughter's apartment in the West Village and changed clothes. There was much discussion and confusion about what everyone was wearing, where their clothes were and when to get changed. Some were having various degrees of difficulty over the logistics and how to get to the clothes they had planned to wear. Others had come prepared and were carrying a change of clothes with them.

It was predictable that Lee would be irritated by all of this attachment and identification with looking good. When one woman said that she was wearing what she had on and had been wearing for two days, Lee said, "That's the spirit!" Lee groused and made a number of comments about being "queenly" and placing too much importance on what to wear, dressing up as if going to a Broadway performance was something really "special" when in fact it's not—from his point of view it should be a very ordinary event.

"We should have nothing to prove to anyone, no 'face' to keep up," he grumbled. Lee made what for him was a grand gesture—he changed from his ratty ancient cut-off sweat pants to a pair of slacks. Everything else remained the same—the T-shirt, the faded sandals, the wild hair.

In the end of the "getting ready to go" mayhem, the whole group headed out with Lee for the subway on foot with no time to leave our things in the parked cars. It was a mosaic of people dressed in a variety of styles, carrying a motley collection of bags, sacks and handbags like vagabonds into the theatre, where the bags were stuffed underneath seats. As soon as everyone sat down, however, it became instantly clear that it really didn't matter what we wore. Jeans or dresses, simple or elaborate, none of it mattered—it was the spirit of simplicity and practice that mattered. It was another opportunity to understand more deeply Lee's teaching of beggary that he had placed, once again, on his students' empty plates. In the end everyone enjoyed "The Lion King" immensely, all concerns vanishing into thin air.

June 13, 1999
En route

Lee's group made it out of New York in once piece, in terms of sadhana—not an easy feat with Lee, in whose company traveling becomes a great challenge of one's ability to practice in the face of distractions and fascinations. Without the ashram sanctuary where the daily schedule of meditation, study, exercise, vegetarian diet supports and enhances the mood of practice, one is quickly confronted with the demand to practice in fast-paced and sometimes glamorous and alluring situations. Food is one obvious area, because when traveling Lee often eats off the diet in celebratory circumstances. But when Lee chooses to eat foods that are not on the recommended diet it is for very specific purposes. In this case the New York trip—with its side excursions to Massachusetts and Connecticut—had offered a plethora of opportunities to deal with the seductions of what Lee often refers to as the "sleeping world" in the three basic domains—money (or power), sex (not necessarily literal sex, but energy management and the subtleties of relationship) and food (including gross and subtle food or impressions). Opportunities to practice in relationship to money, food and sex (as metaphors) can come up in many simple situations where we observe vanity, pride, greed or selfishness, for example, coming into the foreground.

Sitting at the airport waiting for our plane as hundreds of people amassed in the waiting area for the Paris flight, Chris noticed that Lee only carried two quite small cloth bags with carrying straps, neither of them completely full.

"Is that all you are bringing?" she asked, pointing to the bags, one of them a faded, charcoal-colored thin denim with broken and mended straps.

"That's it," he answered, precise and to the point. Chris laughed. "That wouldn't even carry our shoes!" she said.

"That's right," Lee rejoined amiably, "you have to have walking shoes for this, sandals for that—so you don't ruin your lovely arches!" He smiled. The women in the group laughed with him about how much more everyone else brings for the summer traveling stint than he does, then countered it by saying, "Yes, but we bring much less than any 'normal' woman would bring on a four month trip!"

Lee quipped, "That's alright—when the world comes to an end we're going to be out the door before it crashes, while they're still searching for another pair of shoes! 'Where *were* those red heels?' "

The plane was supposed to leave at five forty-five in the afternoon; now it was six o'clock and still we hadn't heard anything from the desk. The crowd of people, a mixture of Americans and Europeans, milled around, sort of undulating uncomfortably in the mix of sweat and fast talk. Suddenly Lee said, "Look, it's Suzuki Roshi!"

A young woman had squeezed in next to Lee and perched on a low table beside the chair where he sat. She had a dharma wheel tattoo on her leg and was reading *Zen Mind, Beginner's Mind* by Suzuki Roshi. There was a large picture of him on the cover of the book. She seemed to be checking out Lee and his group. It's not unusual for people like this to appear out of nowhere when Lee is traveling or in public, and then hover on the edges of the group gathered around him.

Suddenly a woman's voice came over the loud speaker. She said, "Our plane is still being serviced and cleaned so we are unable to board our passengers yet. We know it's hot in here so we appreciate . . . ."

Lee broke in, saying, "And smelly! If you put a bunch of people in a room you can't help but get smelly!" Then he said to no one in particular but to whomever was listening, "If this is the sea of humanity it's no wonder I don't want to go to the ocean!" His comment brought to mind what he had said while driving as we approached JFK Airport. Out of a long silence came Lee's voice, saying, "Here we go into the next hell realm."

June 14, 1999
Paris to La Ferme de Jutreau

Lee and his party arrived at Charles de Gaulle Airport around nine-thirty in the morning Paris time. As soon as we walked out of the arrival area we saw Brindavan waiting with a big smile to greet Lee on the other side of the gate. Happy greetings were exchanged as Lee was warmly welcomed by Brinda, Jean Pierre, Louie, Annie and Patrice—a friend who had volunteered to help by driving one of the vans to the airport. Amidst a flurry of activity the baggage was collected: a daunting task of locating, collecting, hefting and organizing on carts seven, seventy-pound duffel bags, assorted large suitcases and roll-ons, many different sizes and shapes of bags, backpacks, carry-on luggage, satchels, sacks, large cardboard boxes, valises, purses and so on.

Brinda's radiant face said it all—it had been eight months since she had seen Lee, and for the last several weeks she and the other ashram residents had been working incredibly hard with a very small staff of people to get everything ready for Lee's return. That literally involved turning the ashram upside down: the residents of La Ferme de Jutreau live in the *grande maison* (large house) and the *petite maison* (small house) during the fall, winter and spring, then move out to the barn during the four months (summer and early fall) when Lee and his family come to stay in the *grande maison*. The *petite maison* is used for housing Lee's guests who come and go during the summer activities. The members of the American and German sangha, who come to stay during the summer for anywhere from three weeks to three months, live in the barn also during that time, as do the other guests who come for weekend or week-long visits to participate in Lee's seminars or the Guru Purnima Celebration in July. The huge old stone barn houses the meditation hall, dining hall, men's dorm, women's dorm and a couple's dorm, where rooms for couples and their children are partitioned off by hanging sheets from ceiling to floor.

The Hohm Community is notorious for this outrageous arrangement in which students and even guests are asked to endure significant discomforts (by middle-class Western standards) in order to hear the teaching and be in Lee's company. But in reality it is not what it appears to be: that is, a situation that ego might see as a disrespectful way to treat human beings. It is actually an amazing circumstance for sadhana in which discomfort yields an excellent harvest—vulnerability, joy, breakthrough. The majority of Lee's students and the many friends of the school who come to visit La Ferme de Jutreau to hear Lee give the teaching usually manage this opportunity quite extraordinarily—with smiles on their faces. That doesn't mean that it's not cold, uncomfortable, close quarters to share with many other people and therefore also noisy and lacking in privacy, or that there aren't bugs and spiders everywhere.

Waiting once again for his devotees to get it together and move, Lee paced around outside in the parking lot after the luggage had been loaded up while one of his students lingered inside the airport dealing with some detail that had gotten caught in the cogs of the airport "machine." Lee growled, having been infinitely patient already, "I need some patience! I have no patience! Go tell Jan to drop the whole thing and come on—now!" he instructed tersely. In the next instant he was looking around at everyone with a smile on his face.

He was ready to get on with last leg of this journey, which meant his reunion with the French ashram, La Ferme de Jutreau. Whenever Lee is traveling it seems that he has a constant urgency to get back to holy ground—the ashram, whether it is his ashram in Arizona or France, or Yogi Ramsuratkumar's ashram in Tiruvannamalai, or Arnaud Desjardins' ashram in southern France.

Lee immediately took over the two Renault vans that were parked and waiting for him on the top floor of the parking garage. With all the luggage piled high and the picnic coolers perched within easy reach and the fifty-pound flour sack full of baguettes and various delicious *pain* that Jean Pierre brought balanced precariously on top of it all, the two vans and a car took off down the Paris *périphérique*. Lee drove the lead van like a madman headed for the most important moment of his life, weaving in and out of traffic, ducking and dodging cars, vans and trucks at a fast clip. Not only was Lee headed for a reunion with the holy ground of the ashram and his students who awaited his arrival there, but also with the picnic that Brinda and the cooks at La Ferme de Jutreau had made for him. He hadn't eaten anything but a little fruit and a few Bliss Bars or Wha Guru Chews for over twenty-four hours. He made a number of comments about how much he was looking forward to the food, but his mad driving seemed to have more to do with his excitement about the coming summer of teaching, now that he had landed in France, than the obvious pleasure he gets from eating food prepared for him by his devotees.

Driving the second van, Brinda kept up the pace right behind Lee. After about an hour and a half we landed at the green, lush rest area where the ritual picnic is held every year on Lee's arrival. Brinda spread out a feast of sliced turkey, leftover from a recent seminar held at the ashram, pasta salad, lettuce, sliced tomatoes, hard-boiled eggs, brie and baguette, olives, pickles, butter, and vanilla pudding with assorted fruit made by her daughters.

The annual "road picnic" is not just a mundane affair. Like virtually everything in Lee's company, it has powerful undertones and currents that run beneath the surface. The food itself is *prasad* offered to the spiritual master who is returning after a long physical separation from his students. The mood of the picnic—most everyone standing around a single picnic table laden with food while the children sit on the stone benches—is very sweet. In years past it has been chilly and sometimes misting slightly, but today it was cool and sunny. The lush green countryside was soothing to airplane-frazzled nerves. It was wonderful to take in long draughts of clean air after the stultifying stale air of the transatlantic flight.

Standing at the picnic table, Lee took a half of a long baguette and made a sandwich for himself, stuffing in turkey, brie, eggs, lots of lettuce, and slathering it all with mustard. He dug in with obvious enjoyment. Everyone agreed—there is nothing in the world that compares to French bread, especially good baguette. The conversation was light and happy, very ordinary by appearances. The children ate a quick lunch then took off running through the trees, whooping with delight as they ran across the green grass.

Back in the van behind the wheel, Lee was half-asleep. He was so tired that his eyes were involuntarily closing, but his students are used to seeing him drive in this condition. It's not uncommon for Lee to drive for hours while more or less nodding off. Lee's students tend to have a wide range of reactions to it. For some people it is nerve-wracking, while for others it feels completely safe. Even though several of his students will typically offer to drive, he insists on doing all the driving of the vehicle he rides in himself. In this way he is remarkably different from most teachers and certainly most spiritual masters. He refuses the trappings of spiritual stardom or the comfort of just sitting back and having things done for him.

From the *Route de Péage* Lee turned off onto small paved country roads and we began the drive through the pastoral green countryside toward La Ferme de Jutreau, through La Roche Posay and tiny Vicq sur la Garçonne, beautiful French villages with crumbling stone walls heaped with red and pink roses on tumbling laden vines. Everywhere you looked were the ubiquitous red geraniums spilling out of window boxes, along with blossoming magnolia trees, purple flowering clematis, ivy and Virginia creeper. The French love their gardens, and all along the way we saw not only flowers, but charming small orchards and orderly vegetable gardens full of early summer potatoes, peas, tomatoes, green beans and onions.

Only a mile or so away from La Ferme de Jutreau we passed the "Mary shrine"—a honeycomb of shallow limestone caves on the side of the road with a small, two-tiered, modest green lawn and flower gardens underneath a life-size statue of Saint Mary, the mother of Jesus, who stands up above this tableau on a rocky ledge under a copse of trees. There she looks down benevolently upon her children who come seeking her blessings. All over the outer rock walls of the caves are bronze and tin plaques with names and dates of miracles that have occurred here at this holy site. Plastic bouquets grace the shrine along with small plots of flowers, allowed to go half-wild but not completely untended.

Down a green lane by an old castle mostly hidden by huge old trees and set in a classic green landscape that could be right out of Camelot, Lee headed the last half-mile toward La Ferme de Jutreau. He made a final left turn down a dirt lane with tall trees arched overhead, making a tunnel of green through which we drove. All this verdant richness was very sweet to the eyes of desert dwellers like Lee's crew. Memories of past summers with Lee in France begin to flood in and give away to the feeling that the guru and his companions had never left the ashram here in France, but were simply coming home now from another road trip with Lee.

The vans passed the large orchard with its apple, cherry and walnut trees and soon the teenage girls appeared, tending to their horses. A few feet further and the three hundred year-old stone buildings of the ashram came into view as two tall blooming linden trees buzzing with bees loomed on either side of the cloistered front yard. This grassy yard spreads out between the three stone buildings that are placed in a horseshoe shape creating a green courtyard of sorts, in the middle of which is a beautiful red maple tree. All of the buildings are trimmed with flower gardens, so that color splashed out at every turn. As usual, the gardens were overflowing with daisies, pink hydrangeas, hollyhocks and poppies, lilies of many colors, dahlias loaded with buds that would soon start blooming, high mounds of lavender, roses and an abundance of other flowers and herbs.

Lee wheeled the van into its customary parking place, jumped out of the vehicle and struck out into the green grass with bare feet. He began to greet his devotees who hadn't seen him for eight months, giving firm hugs and slaps on the back, making an earthy, felt contact with each one. Immediately noticeable was the sweet, peaceful and yet fierce presence that burned in the air. This presence announced that this is Yogi Ramsuratkumar's home in France, and his son Lee had finally arrived.

June 15, 1999
La Ferme de Jutreau

At the After Dinner Talk tonight Lee said, "Several people have asked me if there will be a theme to the teaching work this summer, as there has been the past several years. I haven't noticed a theme yet, but if there is one it might be that there is a direct relationship between how badly we want something in our sadhana and the probability of success. When we really want something it literally alters the mind/body chemistry.

"So, an example of this is the band. LGB is no more. Everybody was upholding their responsibilities, and yet internally something that was needed to be given to move the project forward was not given. People were not willing to give up the comfort zones internally—in relationship to the life script or ego's story. We have to confront domains of pride, greed, sloth or shame and it requires tremendous discomfort to break the habits of these, so because it is so hard we typically just don't change.

"If we have a thirty-year habit in relationship to greed, pride, sloth or shame, it *feels* comfortable. When we have an emotion or a thought we say, 'I feel' and assume we are feeling something. Ego takes that and uses it as a rationalization. We rarely stop to think that what we are feeling is not a feeling at all. When we say, 'I feel in my body,' and we don't stop to question, 'What am I feeling? Am I really feeling anything?' The mind then can create any false feeling it wants to in the body. So we really need to question through investigation—'What's my motive? Why do I need to feel this way?' But as with anything in this Work, you have to want it badly enough.

"Hey, I just thought of a new form of Enquiry: 'Is this shit or what?' " Peals of laughter broke out around the room. As is usual with Lee, this statement could be taken in two very distinct ways: "Is this shit?" as in crap, garbage, refuse, or "Is this shit?" as in the street dialect for hip, cool, fine. Lee went on before anyone could catch his or her thoughts. "Any genuine question is a doorway into transformation. The way we work is to seek the source of the reaction and transform the source rather than beat it down into submission so you become apathetic. Numb people can do horrible things and not think anything about it. To enter into a clear relationship to what we are experiencing has some value in terms of consciousness."

June 17, 1999
La Ferme de Jutreau

In the late afternoon Lee was sitting at his desk in the office. I was getting ready to give twenty-eight pages on the New York trip that I'd just finished writing to him to read and edit. I had put the file on disk to give to Andrea, who would print it out through the office computer and printer. As we discussed what format the file should be saved in Lee began to rant about how destructive computers are to humanity. It was one of his ongoing diatribes.

In a dour voice, he raved, "Computers are the bane of humankind! The world is going to be destroyed in the next century and it will all be because of computers! You'll see. It won't be like Atlantis where it was just one continent—the whole world will be destroyed this time because we're all interlinked by computer now! The only people who will survive will be savages who kill each other over vegetables. Our children and grandchildren will live to see that."

The three people who were working in the office during his rant sat as still as stones. When he wound down we looked at each other as he looked at us. It was hard to hear this painful stuff. When Lee gets into these doom-and-gloom predictions it is depressing, and yet he makes pronouncements like this frequently. Most of us want to believe that the world is going to survive the current crisis. Surely there is hope that at the eleventh hour it can somehow still be turned around! Surely human culture and consciousness can evolve, and yet there is an undeniable accuracy in what he says. He will not let us bury our heads in the sand.

I squirmed ever so slightly in my chair, sitting in front of the brand new laptop made available by Lee for the writing of this book. What he says about computers, as much as I am addicted to using them to write, is true. Lee dislikes computers because they are robbing us of our humanity, our creativity and true imagination, our ability to live close to the Earth, in harmony with nature. The more we use computers, the less creativity and imagination comes directly from the body and the senses, from instinct, rising up in us through the earth itself, gathered in through the air, inspired by the wind, rain, dirt, trees, rocks, animals, informed by what we can see, touch, smell, hear, feel, guided by divine instinct. The more we use computers, the more we are confined to the dictates of the mind with its separative tendencies, the source of the illusion of separation.

Brinda began to tell Lee about a woman who had called asking to come to several events at La Ferme de Jutreau over the summer. She said that she couldn't afford to pay and wanted to work something out about the donation. She had connected with Hohm Community through the public talks about Yogi Ramsuratkumar that Michael S., a long-time student of Lee's, had been giving in France during the past year. She was planning to go to India to visit Yogi Ramsuratkumar's ashram in Tiruvannamalai as a result of having heard about him through Michael.

Brinda was asking Lee how to handle this woman's request to come to several seminars and the Guru Purnima Celebration without having to pay for them. Lee's body seemed to swell and fill up the room in some invisible way as he launched into another tirade. "Tell her if she has enough money to go to India then she has enough money to make a donation to La Ferme de Jutreau, and if she doesn't like it she can kiss my ass and go to hell! I don't care if I never see her. Yes, let her go to India and tell Yogi Ramsuratkumar what a cheap bastard I am—as if she's going to convince Him that I'm some kind of bad guy!" He paused briefly then went on in the same searing tone. "Pain-in-the-ass French women are going to go to India and sit weeping and moaning in the street in front of Sudama House like that psychotic from Canada, disturbing Yogi Ramsuratkumar's peace, and she wants to come here, but doesn't want to give us a donation? Please! Is this what we get from Michael's efforts?"

I started handing him pages of the rough draft on the New York City public talk as they came off the printer. He grabbed the first nine pages out of my hand, whipped it through the air and down onto his desk and said, smiling brightly, "I want to sit down and read this properly so I can slash and burn!"

The relationship between writers and editors can be an uneasy one; add on top of that the fact that the editor is your guru, and you've got a potentially volatile situation—writers being the vain, self-centered people that they typically tend to be (speaking from experience). But the fact is that from the perspective of the teaching, Lee is a fantastic editor. His inherence in the context of the Work is flawless and he reads with an eagle eye toward the context of the teaching. He is able to appreciate and advocate from many different points of view in this regard, whether the writer has *jnani* (intellectual) or bhakti (feeling) or karma (work and action) tendencies, for example. He is a champion of the arts and the artist—being an artist and poet himself—who respects the integrity of the author's deepest vision, never compromises it for a personal, subjective agenda (such a thing doesn't exist in his case) or a dogmatic approach to grammar, punctuation and the rules of the English language. He reads from the perspective of the Work, rather than from a personal bias as many editors do.

Soon it was time to go to chanting in the dining hall of the old stone barn just twenty-five feet away. A small group of people would gather there to chant before the evening meal of fruit or salad. By now Lee was sitting quietly at his desk talking with one of the children. As I closed down the computer—the bane of human existence—the mood in the office around Lee was peaceful and productive as he attended with a quiet, measured focus to the complex and multifaceted demands of his day.

Tonight in the After Dinner Talk Lee discussed the public talk in New York City in a way that brought perspective to what, in some ways, seemed like a debacle. He said, "Every public talk is a microcosm of the larger Work. I don't do talks to proselytize, although I certainly like to sell books and music. The primary motive to give talks is not to proselytize—which should be obvious, given the way talks go, and the talks I've turned down!" Lee chuckled.

"So, every public talk is a microcosm of the macrocosm of our work together in the sangha. As a result there are some people who come, sometimes knowingly and sometimes unknowingly, and lay themselves open to opportunities to work. They get an opportunity to work and everybody else in the space gets an opportunity to work without being on the hot seat by watching and being in contact with what is happening in the space. When somebody is the sacrifice for the space, is on the hot seat and getting the heat, everybody else gets the same opportunity, but with the relief of not being the one who's getting the sword thrust into them. Getting their sexual perversities bared to the masses, or whatever it happens to be.

"So, when I asked the 'woman in white' in New York if she had ever been laid and she said, 'It's none of your business,' the way she said it you could tell that there was something very unpleasant there. She may have thought that she was hiding something, but everyone who was there who had any psychological insight knew. Sometimes we bare ourselves unconsciously and we don't even know we're doing it. Everybody else in the room is squirming with embarrassment and the person is completely unconscious. That's what we mean by being a sacrifice for the space—someone provides an opportunity for everybody in the space to work without being the center of attention, without being the person toward whom the heat is coming. And in New York I think we were very, very successful. That's what we were trying to do.

"The fireworks that happen are a necessary ingredient of my particular style. When I stop giving public talks—if I ever stop giving public talks—there won't be the same kind of demand for those fireworks, because in the school itself the heat will be turned up to a degree where ordinarily we don't need those kinds of interchanges with people who refuse to cook slowly, who think it's to their advantage to get burned to a crisp on the spot or something. Or they don't know that they are asking for a fire, for a lightning bolt to strike them on the head."

June 18, 1999
La Bertais, Bretagne

Riding in the van as Lee drove to Bretagne for his seminar at La Bertais, a center for the teachings of Arnaud Desjardins, I was working on the manuscript pages on New York City. I asked Lee a question about one of the changes he had indicated. Answering my question, Lee then suggested, "Why don't you just read it out loud to everybody right now?" A general assent was voiced by everyone. There were six people in the van with Lee. As the reading progressed attention became rapt, since many present had not witnessed the events that now came to life in the space as Lee added comments and yet more changes during the reading.

Lee's remarks were typically aimed at having the text be educational and accurate for the reader. Several times he would comment and then say, "Put that in there!" or add on a detail of some circumstance. The exercise of reading aloud can take one into the doorway of the reader's perspective, so perhaps the reading was also a way for him to gauge how the writing was going based on the silent but felt response, or at times laughter and comments, coming from the audience in the van. The reading brought the whole van together into a unified focus on the teaching and gave us all an opportunity to hear Lee's feedback. In particular Lee commented on the description of the woman in white. "You really savaged that woman!" he laughed. There seemed to be a general agreement reflected in the laughter of my friends who were listening. "Yeah—I hope you never write about me! Or wait until I'm dead," Chris half-joked with me.

"Should I sweeten it in some way? It's just a rough draft, you know," I asked Lee.

"No, just use it as an opportunity to make a point about 'the horror of the situation,' so you don't seem like an executioner, and so the woman gets to serve the education of the readers of this book," Lee spoke from behind the wheel.

"The horror of the situation" is a term taken from the writings of the Russian mystic and teacher G.I. Gurdjieff. It refers to the absolute fact of human mechanicality and lack of inner unity—that we are not free beings and that we are not yet even truly human, but are instead many disparate personalities, nothing more than a ragged collection of passions and selfishness that war upon themselves. The average person has no inner unity and lives within a state of confusion, disintegration and conflict. *"C'est la guerre!"* Lee often says.

These disparate personalities are largely unaware of each other, and as each "I" arises, the conscious personality thinks and in fact believes it is the only "I" and that it has continuity moment to moment in consciousness. But actually there is not continuity. We have no idea that we are living in such a state of disunity and inner fragmentation until we begin the long, slow and heart-breaking discipline of learning to self-observe. It is a heart-breaking process because what one has to confront are one's real motivations—greed, pride, vanity, anger, fear, the drive for personal power. What we see about ourselves is the cruelty, selfishness and unconscious abuse that we heap on people around us, and perhaps most especially on our loved ones. It is through this heartbreak that we begin to develop remorse, or conscience. Lee gave the audience in New York City, including his students, a small, brief peek into "the horror of the situation," or the reality of where we all live—a glimpse into the kind of ruthless self-confrontation that is necessary for anyone who really wants the transformative fire of the path.

Lee called out from the driver's seat, "I was so excited by the smell of that bread I forgot to get a receipt!" He was back to one of his great pleasures here in France—buying fabulous bread for his road picnics from a *boulangerie* or *patisserie* somewhere along the way. Soon he was pulling the van into the rest area for lunch, the second van right behind him. Spilling out of the two vans were seventeen people. The food was quickly arranged on a concrete picnic table.

Arriving at three o'clock in the afternoon at La Bertais, Lee and his entourage were greeted by Jann and Anne Marie Le Boucher, students of Arnaud Desjardins who run this center in the misty green countryside of Brittany (Bretagne). The center is a cluster of old farm buildings that have been renovated to accentuate the beauty of the stones and massive dark brown timbers than run across the ceilings in exposed beams.

This is the fourth summer that Lee has spent time at La Bertais, hosted generously by Anne Marie and Jann. The first year Lee came here was in 1996 when he was on tour with liars, gods & beggars. Anne Marie graciously provided hospitality for him and his entourage, including the entire band, for three nights. The group would come driving home in the wee predawn hours after gigs in various coastal towns of Bretagne that were three, four or five hours away from La Bertais. In the morning at ten o'clock Anne Marie and some of the people who are involved with the center would have a sumptuous brunch waiting for everyone in the old kitchen with its low ceiling and heavy dark beams. Lee would then play bridge until late afternoon, when it was time to take off again for some village two or three hundred kilometers away.

The last day Lee was there the band played in a village only fifteen kilometers away.

Lee had given a talk at La Bertais to seventy people that afternoon, many of whom packed into the steamy, hot small bar and danced unrestrainedly to the music of liars, gods & beggars that night—another kind of teaching from a Baul master. It was a fabulous, memorable night. Every summer since then Lee has driven northwest from La Ferme de Jutreau to Bretagne with his gypsy gang and given a weekend seminar here at La Bertais, so that the center had extended such warm hospitality several times.

Very quickly everyone settled in his or her rooms then met in the sitting room by the kitchen for bridge with Lee. He had only been playing for about thirty minutes when Brinda came in with a message for him that Nadege Amar, Yvan Amar's wife, had just called and asked Lee to call her back as soon as possible. Lee immediately left the room and returned her call. Within a minute or so he returned and sat down. After a brief silence he said, "Yvan died this morning." It was not a surprise, since Lee had spoken with Yvan only two days ago, when Nadege had called to cancel Lee's visit with them in two weeks because of Yvan's health. It had been two years since Lee had seen Yvan. Last summer, in 1998, Lee had planned to visit Yvan and Nadege, but Yvan was too ill for company. Lee had hoped to see Yvan this summer, but knew that his health might necessitate a last minute change of plans.

There was another brief pause as the news sank in around the table. Then, calling everyone to practice—to feel, yet without rank sentiment in relationship to such strong news—Lee said crisply, "Well, let's keep playing bridge—as great a loss as it is." Lee's last words hung in the space and penetrated the silence that spread outward with the news. Lee almost immediately started making a pointed teaching lesson to Brinda. It was as if he had her pinned down by some pressing force as she squirmed under his laser focus on her bridge technique.

The death of Yvan Amar was not unexpected, as he had been seriously ill for many years, and the past four years his condition had steadily worsened. Yvan was a beacon of light throughout it all, and an incredible example of how to bear suffering with elegance and a graceful presence. He once said to a number of us who visited him with Lee that his illness was one of his three great teachers in life: Chandra Swami, who had taught him *jnana* (knowledge); his wife Nadege who had taught him to feel, or the lesson of the heart; and his health, which had caused him to face his fear.

As the news sank in, pictures and images of times spent in the company of Lee and Yvan over the years began to flow. Memories of the relationship between Yvan and Lee were especially poignant—the sweetness and sometimes overwhelming tenderness of the two of them together, the *bhavas* that Yvan often invoked in Lee's presence. Yvan was a true bhakti, and that disposition was part of what gave him the vision to penetrate to the heart of Lee's communication.

It was Yvan who was the connecting link between Lee and Arnaud Desjardins. Yvan had met Lee in 1987 in Paris, where they were introduced by Michelle, a French woman who had been living in Boulder, Colorado and had recently become a student of Lee's. Four years later, in the winter of 1991, at the impetus of Yvan Amar, Gilles Farcet traveled to the U.S. to spend a week with Lee at our ashram. Gilles had been given the task by his teacher, Arnaud Desjardins, of writing a book about spiritual teachers in the West. When Yvan heard of this project, he said to Gilles, "You must go see this man," and he gave him a copy of *Living God Blues,* written by Lee.

Gilles read the book, and, having a great love of American rock & roll, was enthralled by the idea of a rock & roll guru. He came to Arizona, met Lee and many members of the

American sangha. It was a case of instant recognition between fellow travelers on the path. Not long after that Gilles arranged the first meeting between his teacher, Arnaud Desjardins, and Lee. That was almost nine years ago, and the bond between Lee Lozowick, Arnaud Desjardins and their respective schools has become legendary since then. And so it was that some tangible karmic weave bound many people together with Lee and Arnaud at the center of the kernel, but it was Yvan who was the catalyst, the messenger, the angel of that reunion.

In April 1992 at Nadenka, Yvan's center in Southern France, Lee met with Arnaud Desjardins, Chandra Swami (Yvan's guru) and Yvan with two hundred disciples, mostly Yvan's. Lee had just met Arnaud for the first time and was staying with his traveling party at Arnaud's ashram, Font d'Isière, about an hour and a half away from Nadenka by car. The next spring Lee visited Yvan again at Nadenka where Lee gave a seminar, sponsored by Yvan, to two hundred people. Yvan had published Lee's first book translated into French, *The Alchemy of Transformation*, and he presented Lee with the first copy during that visit. That year he also gave Lee a huge Shiva lingam stone, which occupies a space to the left of Lee's dais in the meditation hall in Arizona to this day.

Then there was the unforgettable three-day seminar at Gordes with Lee, Andrew Cohen and Shantimayi sponsored by Yvan in the early summer of 1995. Lee and a small group of students stayed for four days, along with Andrew and his wife Alka, with Yvan and Nadege and their family in their beautiful home in Gordes overlooking the countryside of Provençe.

Perhaps most memorable of all was the last time Lee had seen Yvan, in the summer of 1997, when a core group of students had driven with Lee up into the Maritime Alps to the old chalet of Nadege's family. Lee and his group spent two days there with Yvan and Nadege, sitting out on the terrace at the table under the umbrella with Yvan, or in the old sitting room with Yvan and Lee together on the couch. There really are no words to express the tenderness and depth of communion between Yvan and Lee during that visit, or the depth to which Yvan touched us with many teaching communications which he made during the hours with him. Yvan was always able to meet Lee in a quality of intimacy and adoration of the Divine that was profoundly moving to those who witnessed it. At this particular meeting this quality of a divine intimacy, a deeply human and precious communion that carried a resonance through many subtle dimensions, was made even more potent by the imminent reality of Yvan's death. The power of his illness made its presence constantly known as he struggled for every breath.

Despite his ill health Yvan spoke to Lee's students, dropping pearls and insights into what each person needed to hear. Yvan was in a mood we had never seen him in before. For two days he talked; he was making incredible teaching points that seemed tailored to each individual. The accuracy with which he spoke to each person had no rational, linear logic to it; instead it seemed divinely inspired. Yvan was so deeply insightful as a teacher that he acted from a higher instinct, and in this way "seeing" with his intuitive eyes what each person needed.

As Lee's group left that day everyone stopped in the sitting room to say goodbye to Yvan. Outside the sun was shining down on the green mountains, but Yvan lay back on the pillows of the couch in the darkened central room of the house, obviously exhausted but radiant. The many expressions of gratitude that came from Lee's students was for much more than the good company, the wonderful food, the lovely hospitality, the beautiful mountains, the comfortable beds in the old chalet. We were thanking him for the gift of the teaching he had given. The phrase "a great light went out of the world," often used when someone dies, had always seemed like a platitude. Today it became real.

Lee continued to play bridge until dinner. He was the same as always, except his eyes were noticeably shining—perhaps a little more than usual. After dinner he sat for a few moments around the table in conversation with Anne Marie and some of the people of La Bertais. Anne Marie asked about one of the women who had traveled to La Bertais with Lee and company the past two years, the same long-time student who had left the school during this past winter. Lee said, "She's gone—left." He made a hand signal to indicate a clean sweep. Anne Marie looked nonplussed and Lee repeated, "She has left the community. She's gone. And where she is, nobody knows." He paused as Anne Marie looked at him questioningly, then he said, "When someone leaves the path they disappear between the cracks of the world. It's better to have practiced and gained than never to have practiced at all! That's Shakespeare!" He laughed. It seemed the afternoon teaching lesson was consistently on impermanence.

June 19, 1999
La Bertais, Bretagne

This is Lee's first seminar of the summer in Europe and will be held in the meeting hall of La Bertais—a beautiful spacious room with photographs of Arnaud Desjardins on the walls. Outside the green countryside of Bretagne sparkled in mild sunlight. Flowers blossomed around the edges of the building, and the double doors near the book table were open, letting in a steady flow of fresh air. Before the talk Lee sat at the book table— his usual post at seminars in between dharma sessions. People began to flow in for the seminar and twelve or fifteen people surrounded the table, picked up books and browsed. They looked shyly at Lee. Some of them said "Bonjour," while others began conversations with Lee, having met him at seminars of previous years. Almost everyone exclaimed over the new book, *Don't Try—Live (N'essayez Pas—Vivez)*, a compilation of Lee's talks from his weeklong seminar last year at Hauteville (the ashram of Arnaud Desjardins), edited by Arnaud and Gilles Farcet. The photograph on the cover is a beautiful picture of Lee and Arnaud standing shoulder to shoulder holding hands with beaming smiles on their faces. The picture is highly enigmatic at the same time, because as one of Lee's students commented, "Arnaud looks like an angel and Lee looks a little like a devil! There is our spiritual master, always in your face with the teaching," she laughed. And indeed Lee does have an impish smile on his face in the photograph. But the book is, in many ways, a tribute to the deep friendship between Arnaud and Lee, a friendship that is based in their mutual love of and commitment to the teaching, their respective gurus—Swami Prajnanpad and Yogi Ramsuratkumar—and their disciples.

As Lee sat behind the table a woman came up and asked to be a student. She was very serious in her request. She didn't speak much English so Lee asked Andrea to translate. Surprisingly he didn't turn the woman away as he usually does with such requests, but told her that everything depends on her—whether she becomes a formal student or is just informally connecting with him and the teaching. She said, "I didn't understand the difference between formal and informal?"

Lee answered, "It depends on the degree to which the Blessings and Benediction of this lineage permeate your life. Informal students just get a little blessing here or there, but they really are sort of a potpourri."

Immediately she said, "I don't want to be informal."

"That's up to you," he replied mildly.

"What does it mean to be a formal student?" she asked.

"To implement all the formal conditions," Lee answered. "I've just met you. I don't know anything about you—I don't know if this is a realistic demand for you. I want you to prove yourself before getting a 'title'—I want you to earn formal studentship. If that's a problem for you, then obviously you shouldn't be a formal student, because anybody capable of being a formal student would simply say okay and go about doing whatever is needed."

He then directed her to the other two women who live near her in Rennes who are his students and are starting a bordello (study group) there. Moments later, at ten-thirty sharp, Lee walked unceremoniously up to the dais, sat down and started out with a brisk advertisement for the new book. There were fifty or sixty people there, listening raptly.

"My preference here—in the three sessions today and two sessions tomorrow—would be to answer your questions, because questions tend to address the direct interests of those who are here. When I discourse, the tendency of the audience is to agree or disagree in an impersonal way with what I say, and then we relate to the dharma on a philosophical basis rather than in an intimate and personal way. The teaching is meant to be personal; to have an effect on our lives. Some of you are very compassionate and want to bring peace to the world, serve the world and heal everyone and all that, but in fact as many teachers have said, like Krishnamurti who I've been reading about lately, you have to begin with where you live—in the details of your lives. The real teaching begins at home. If you master the teachings in relationship to your personal life, then perhaps in an extended way you can then serve the world. But it begins with our relating to meditation, food, sex, vanity, pride, greed.

"So, your questions can be about any aspect of spirituality that you have studied or experienced in your life. If I have some experience in that area I'll share it with you. If I don't I'm perfectly comfortable telling you that I don't—although for those of you who know me, you know that it might take half an hour for me to explain that I don't know what I'm talking about!

"The teacher is the most vital element we can discover in life. Nothing should come before the path for us, but the path is not separate from life. The path makes clear distinctions between that which is resonant with the Divine and that which is dissonant with the Divine. Anything that separates us from communion with life is dissonant to the Divine. Greed, vanity, shame, self-hatred, feelings of victimization or vindictiveness—all these are forms of violence.

"There is no communion in self-centeredness. The path is about radical transformation from self-centeredness to other-centeredness. Most of us aren't even aware of what the other thinks or feels, let alone be able to serve that. How can we be in communion if we don't know what the other thinks or feels? Everybody is self-centered rather than other-centered. Vanity is a form of violence because it separates you from the other. Unfortunately, my school happens to be somewhat of a devotional school and everyone in my school is an exception! But I expect *everyone* to practice!"

Today after the morning dharma session there was a potluck lunch outside in the courtyard between the three old stone buildings that make up La Bertais. A few of Lee's students sat under a canopy with Lee, Anne Marie, Jann and four or five other people.

Over a plate full of luscious dark red cherries Anne Marie answered a question about the programs at La Bertais. She and Jann live in Renne and come out to La Bertais—which is out in the countryside about an hour away—in the summer mostly during summer "holidays." She said that recently Daniel Morin had come from Hauteville and given talks there, as well as Lee's student Michael S., who came and talked about Yogi Ramsuratkumar, Lee and the practices of his school. She said, "During the winter we meet every six weeks and have a reading from Lee's book. It has helped us very much," she added.

"Which book is that?" Jane asked.

Anne Marie answered, "The big one with the red cover," and gestured that it was large. With a smile, her husband Jann added, "Yes—Lee's bible." She was referring to the *Hohm Sahaj Mandir Study Manual*. Jan nodded in the affirmative then reiterated, "It is very good. Very helpful. It has helped us very much."

In the afternoon session Lee responded to a question about how to deal with the constant tendency to fall "asleep" in one's life with a discourse on vigilance. He said, "There are two levels of vigilance. The first kind is creature or muscular vigilance. Such efforts may be habitual but they are not natural. As long as vigilance is a muscular effort, then sooner or later we're going to fail, to fall asleep. The point is that even someone of great will is going to fall asleep sooner or later, so we all do our best to stay alert, to be kind with others, to practice.

"For instance, I'll use myself as an example. My style backfires on me in some cases, like in New York City where I gave a public talk last week. I was just fishing—that's how I work when I do a public talk. I just throw the net out there and see what I get. Sometimes I get a turtle, a tuna, a shark . . . you never know what you're going to get! But this time . . . It's a terrible story—but I'll tell it anyway. New York City is a really tough crowd. There were two women in the crowd who really stood out. One woman was wearing a white dress that was slit up the side and showed her whole leg. She wore lots of make-up and heavy gold jewelry. So I have this *schtick* I do, like any comedian, where I insult someone then I say I feel bad, apologize and then insult them some more. There was another woman there . . . a large woman, who kept saying, 'Go for it! You're free to do whatever you want!' So the woman in white asked some obscure, esoteric question, when it was obvious that she needed to look at some immediate stuff of her own, not some ethereal obscurity. She said, 'What do you think about receptivity and grace and the Absolute Reality?' When I asked her if she'd ever had sex and she yelled, 'It's none of your business!' I knew I'd gotten close to something. She started yelling at me and I lost my vigilance. I just lost it for a moment.

"My motives are not personal. I do public talks to represent the Work in some way. So I use provocation because it is useful for magnifying certain elements that we are not clear about. The woman who wanted her money back, for example, during my talk is always pushy and demanding, but she is able to mask it. The provocation in her case created an opportunity for her to see herself as she really is, rather than how she imagines herself to be. So provocation is designed to create magnification of what we don't usually see. But the woman in white . . . just for a moment I wanted this woman to feel the fire of hell. I caught myself and was out of it again, but I use myself as an example in this instance because I have a very high degree of will.

"The second type of vigilance is Work vigilance. When we are in relationship with the teacher or the path, there is a natural, spontaneous vigilance that we don't have to effort, remember, sustain. It is not part of our personality or psychology, but is Benediction. The

Divine is watching out for us and guarding us against error or sin. The Divine protects us from sinning. The degree to which we serve the path or the Work is the degree to which the path is concerned for us and will watch out for us . . .

"I am committed to obedience to Yogi Ramsuratkumar. To the degree that His Influence and Benediction permeates me, He watches out for me. If there is a circumstance that occurs outside of Yogi Ramsuratkumar's concerns, then I am on my own recognizance to practice. Otherwise Yogi Ramsuratkumar protects me and guards me. Our aim is to surrender to the path to such a degree that we are given Grace. God takes care where there is no tolerance for error, and any area where there is tolerance for error, then *we* are responsible.

"Another way to deal with falling asleep—and we all do—is to look for a pattern in our falling asleep. Then we can bring very specific attention to it, a sharp attention and clarity, and then we won't fall asleep at those times; but like everything else, we have to really *want* to not fall asleep. With any of these considerations the bottom line is, how badly do we want it? I'm talking about wanting something so badly, and with such passion, that we bring the focus of our life energy to it, for our life energy can change anything. We are talking about bringing the entire force of our being to bear on our consideration. Then anything can happen, from the spontaneous healing of tumors to changing our behavior or dropping our habits. But we have to *want* it."

Someone asked Lee the question, "How can I develop a healthy self-respect?"

Lee answered, "First we must accept ourselves completely as we are, across the board. Like everything in nature the body/mind naturally seeks balance. Every judgement we have about ourselves keeps the system from being able to seek balance. When we leave certain things alone, they take care of themselves, but really it is the totality of our existence or being that produces change in us."

He kept returning to a very specific point: that surrender to the Will of God, or living in resonance and alignment with the guru and the lineage, changes everything in one's life, even to the degree that one is then protected and guarded by the blessing force of the lineage. At the level of ego, personality or psychology we are helpless to change. We may be able to modify our behavior through a kind of muscular effort, but it is important not to confuse that kind of superficial change with the kind of radical transformation that is only possible through the true spiritual path. The transformation of the path is something we can take with us—meaning at the time of death—at the level of the soul; behavior modification is a strictly psychological affect that drops away with the body at death.

Even with a muscular behavioral change, sooner or later we will fall asleep and the behavior modification which is held in place by sheer willpower, will slip. Then we are shocked to find ourselves acting out our hunger for power, our cruelty, territoriality, vanity, our desire to manipulate others or whatever it is that we are willfully omitting from our behavior in the name of practice. There is tremendous frustration, remorse and pain—and sheer disappointment—at "falling from grace," so to speak, when a period of clarity, or of organic resonance with the guru, is suddenly disrupted by a burst of toxicity or negativity that is acted out toward the environment. Through the process of accepting what is—or what we might call real self-observation, which is without judgement—we open up the possibility of objectifying our experience. This objectification of experience is a crucial element in practice because otherwise we are lost in the morass of psychological identification, projection, assumption, expectation and delusion.

One of the most important keys to objectifying these experiences is to understand the universal nature of the process. Lee offers his students a tool for objectification of experience in the following teaching: When one enters into an alignment with the Great Process of Divine Evolution through the lineage of the guru, one moves through natural cycles. In the beginning we experience "infatuation—indifference—doubt," which matures into "insight—frustration—remorse" at the level of basic human maturity, which leads into "free moment—disposition of enlightenment—compassion." Until one is established in the disposition of enlightenment, these cycles will repeat themselves until one becomes free of psychological identification with any of the cycles. When one works in alignment with the teacher or the process, then these cycles stay the same in principle but change in character.

The change is the *context* in which we experience cycles. If we are not in resonance with the guru, then we repeat those cycles over and over with no change in context, so that our experience is psychological rather objective. When objectified, these cycles of "infatuation—indifference—doubt, insight—frustration—remorse and free moment—disposition of enlightenment—compassion" can be seen as the three modes of existence which are described in the Hindu tradition as creation, maintenance and destruction.

It is only at those times when alignment with the guru and the mood of surrender is present that one experiences any small degree of real freedom—a free moment. When that happens Organic Innocence becomes the tacit mood that guides one's life, and out of this organic or wise innocence one is moved in ways that are naturally aligned with dharma or the Will of God. One of the ways that shows up, as Lee described it today in this session, is that a natural and spontaneous "Work vigilance" begins to appear—the effect of being surrendered to the extent that benediction or "the Work" protects and guards us from missing the mark, or as the Christians would say, "sinning." Today was the first time I had heard Lee articulate this principle in this particular way.

June 20, 1999
La Bertais, Bretagne

A young woman raised her hand in the morning session and said that she was discouraged in her spiritual path and felt that she must change directions after a number of years in the Fourth Way. She asked how to deal with the feelings of discouragement that she experienced and whether she should leave the Fourth Way.

Lee laughed his characteristic "heh, heh, heh," then said, "Well, did you have a teacher in the Gurdjieff way?"

"Well, Gurdjieff was my teacher."

Lee smiled mischievously. "Wow—you look a little young for that!"

"I found some people from the official Gurdjieff organization. I would say that Gurdjieff was my teacher, but now I am lost," she said.

Lee seemed to change his tactic and now questioned seriously, "Is there any other way attracting you now?"

"No. I am still very attached to the Fourth Way."

"Then why ask a question about leaving the Fourth Way?" he asked.

"They asked me to leave, to go and solve my problems," she answered.

"What were your problems, if that is not too personal? Sentimentality?" he queried. She answered that her mentors in the Fourth Way had spoken of "medical problems." She said that they wanted her to discover her own problems, but she admitted that sentimentality was the biggest one she had discovered. For reasons known only to him, Lee was being particularly generous and kind with this young woman. He very patiently questioned her and heard out her answers, weighing them and continuing to sound her out. He asked her why she didn't write a letter to her teachers and tell them that she had worked on her problems, to see if they would take her back. She said that she had done that several times and each time they told her to wait.

"So how did you get hooked up here at La Bertais?" he asked.

"I was fed up with being on my own. After asking them if I could come back and they rebuked me I started looking elsewhere."

Lee's attention was completely focused on her. He looked at her intently and seemed to scrutinize her situation in a scant moment, then he began to speak.

"In the first place discouragement is like anything else—you just observe it as it is without turning it into something that stops you from moving. You are giving it power that it doesn't have on its own. But now you find yourself here. Don't assume that this path isn't also the Work. Arnaud Desjardins spent ten years in the Gurdjieff work. Even though this is a pure path of nonduality coming from Swami Prajnanpad, there are undoubtedly elements of Arnaud's astute understanding of Gurdjieff's work in his teaching. From what I know of Gurdjieff, it seems like any real school has to have some connection with the Work. Regardless of the form and language, in essence there is some connection. When we try to apply ourselves as Westerners to strictly Eastern teachings without Work elements, we are lost. Most people who study with Advaita Vedanta teachers fail to appreciate that the teacher and the teaching is coming out of an Eastern context that we as Westerners don't usually have. A lot of teachers who have no personal relationship with the teachings of Gurdjieff are actually teaching the Work. So when one is attached to a particular path and the connection is a felt connection, any shift is bound to be dramatic and heart breaking. How long were you in the Gurdjieff work?"

"I first connected with it about twelve years ago," she said.

"Well, so then you probably have some understanding of the principles of the Work," Lee laughed. The facetious quality of Lee's chuckles seemed to hint that one could easily spend twelve years in a school and not have any understanding of the principles, but believe that one does.

"One would hope!" he laughed again. "Well, you should know that many threads of those years have come with you into this, and you simply have to release your attachment. The Gurdjieff work is often criticized within the spiritual scene for being a church of Gurdjieff now rather than a spiritual school. Orthodoxy destroys living spirituality."

She interjected, "I have not found any fault with the Gurdjieff organization."

He continued, "Well then you should have faith. If you have not found fault with the Gurdjieff Foundation, then have faith. If you really have faith in your way, then you can wait. You are very much like a woman who I asked to leave my school. In fact you look just like her! You even sound just like her. Behind that soft exterior is a killer!" She nodded her head in agreement. "And she's very intelligent—I'm sure you are too." Another nod of assent from the questioner. "So maybe you just need to *work*." Lee paused and smiled at her. "What do you do?"

She said, "I play the harp."

"Are you earning a living at it?"

"Not yet," she answered.

"Well, we'll have the opportunity to hear you play tonight, so then we'll know whether you should continue or not!" People laughed gently at this, knowing that she would be giving a concert before dinner and that Lee has just put extra pressure on her to perform well.

"So, you should just continue to work on yourself and wait. Give it a couple of years and call them again. My Master sent me away once . . ." Lee began to tell the story of Yogi Ramsuratkumar sending him away in 1986. Lee will most likely tell this story countless times this summer, a recapitulation of an event in his relationship with Yogi Ramsuratkumar that clearly holds tremendous significance for Lee. Each time he tells it there is some unique nuance of meaning or revelation that comes through. As he said at Fox Hollow, in this act Yogi Ramsuratkumar put "the final nail in the coffin" of Lee Lozowick, so to speak. Now there is no Lee Lozowick; like Yogi Ramsuratkumar, who Papa Ramdas "killed in 1952," Lee the separate person is dead. He continued:

"I had been sending Yogi Ramsuratkumar poetry and letters for years by this trip in 1986. The poetry ranged from pleading to abject demands to keep the Work flowing in my direction . . .

"So you should stay with it. The Gurdjieff Foundation has incredible roots, so just stay with it and have faith. Gurdjieff was sort of like a guru; the force of the Work that flowed through him could be considered a kind of grace. If you avail yourself to that force, it has nothing to do with your formal association with the school. If you make yourself useful to the Work in any way, then the Work will call you in one form or another. Some form of the Work will call you, because as Gurdjieff said to Orage, 'In the Work we always make a profit.'

"The Work is interested in profit, and you should understand that the Work is not limited to the Gurdjieff Foundation. If you demonstrate that you can be of profit to the Work, the Work will call you—there are no exceptions to this. That's up to you, of course. If the sense of what would be profitable to the Work is obscure to you, then Jann and Anne Marie can help you because they've been around Arnaud Desjardins for years. You don't have to go off into the wilderness without help. You have to do your own work, of course, but others who are senior to you in the Work can be helpful in that way.

"The basic point of this conversation is: If you make yourself useful, profitable, to the Work, then the Work *will* respond—there is no question about it. It is a very romantic statement, but true! So before you get lost in the romance of it, think of this: Werner Erhard of est and the Forum organization said that human beings are problem-solving machines. So as soon as you learn to solve one level of problems, the Universe gives you another, higher level of problems to solve. That's the Work! And the biggest problem of all is enlightenment!

"We think we will be free when we get enlightenment, but it's not like that. You get the biggest problem you'll ever get—not only do you get the problem of other people, you *become* other people! You take a bath every day, comb your hair and take care of yourself and then walk down the street and see a street bum, filthy and drunk, and that's *you*! So you might as well stop washing!" Loud laughter broke out. "As long as your partner can handle it, that is!

"Arnaud Desjardins went from Le Bost to Font d'Isière to Hauteville and he's gotten bigger and bigger problems with each ashram! Now Arnaud has a huge ashram with lots of people living on it and coming there every week. So that's the thing you want on the path—not freedom, but to be used up, completely eaten up by the Work.

"To say that Arnaud is not in the Work is ridiculous—he is completely in the Work.

There is a lot of Work going on in the world, masked by other traditions. The Work may simply respond to you by giving you life problems that you have a particular facility for solving. Being with children or playing music. A woman who is a devotee of Yogi Ramsuratkumar who spent a lot of time with Him had a child with Yogi Ramsuratkumar's blessing. After a couple of years she came to Yogi Ramsuratkumar's darshan and started weeping and crying, saying, 'Oh Bhagavan, I used to spend so much time with You and now I hardly ever see You, I am with my child all the time.' Yogi Ramsuratkumar was very stern with her and said, 'Child is God! When you are with your child, you are with me!' So, was that useful?"

She nodded and Lee went on to the next questioner. He was noticeably kind, easeful and gentle with people throughout this seminar. A man raised his hand and talked about how he has a very introverted personality and no libido. Lee said, "Most people whose libido is very active just get lots of problems for it! Why not let it be nonexistent?"

After the laughter died down the man responded, "But I'm not normal!" to which Lee said, "That's just your opinion. What's normal? Who establishes the criteria for what's normal? If you could have no libido and *be happy*, then what's the problem? That's my criteria for what's normal—can you accept yourself as you are and just be happy? Not, does your life conform to someone's else's criteria of normality."

In the afternoon session Lee continued in a very similar vein. A question was raised about ego and relationship. Lee's response delved into his teaching of Enlightened Duality, although today he didn't use that phrase.

"The consideration of ego/no ego is an absolute consideration, whereas life is relative, so we should put it in other terms. The main distinction to make is between the inner reality as source and the outer reality—if you understand inside that the swirling play around you is just qualities that naturally animate themselves within the play of relationship. All this is just naturally part of what it is to be human, to be alive. If you understand that they don't mean anything in and of themselves, then in relationship with a partner you can allow a whole range of manifestations to arise without getting caught in identification with any of it. This is the key element.

"When Arnaud says that 'what is, is,' he's not just talking about the appearance of things, but the whole range of phenomena down to the depths. So if one gets angry, it's not just to see the exterior manifestation of anger—the face gets red and so on—but also to question, where does the anger come from? What is it in relationship to?

"If, within a couple, one is outgoing and expressive and the other is introverted and quiet, it doesn't mean there is inequity or that they can't relate, but that they each have to accept each other as they are. What is relevant is to be able to accept each other simply as we are, meaning that if we identify the emotion with who that person is, then we have made a mistake because in essence none of us is who our personality or psychology is. We have to look at what is at the depth of emotion. Nothing. What's at the depth of anything we see or hear or feel? Nothing. All phenomena is insubstantial, passing. The only thing substantial is the Divine, which cannot be limited to form. So instead of identifying our partner as being those qualities that they manifest, realize that all the interplay of emotions between partners is only the play of phenomena."

Another questioner said that since Arnaud and Lee are "enlightened," he couldn't understand how two masters can have contradictory opinions. He used the example of Arnaud's appreciation of a well-known woman Indian teacher, which is positive, and

Lee's appreciation of that same teacher, which often shows up in the form of criticism.

Lee answered, "If this difference causes turmoil in you it's very good. The thing is to resolve the turmoil through your own investigation. There is a reason Arnaud praises her and a reason that I criticize her. Both reasons are not the whole story. I have been known—on rare occasions—to praise her, but that praise does not subsume why I criticize her. There is a very real reason why I criticize her. You can find out why I criticize her through studying and considering, and if you can find out why, your work will benefit greatly."

A woman who has been to La Ferme de Jutreau a number of times for seminars raised her hand. "Can Mr. Lee give any recommendation on increasing my ease of meditation?"

"Valium!" Lee quipped, to a response of hearty laughter.

"Still I would like your recommendation." She continued, assuming that Lee was joking.

"I was serious," he commented. "Well, meditation starts with one thing: sit. Every day at the same time and same place if possible. You have a child, so perhaps you can't be so strict. But you just sit with the implicit question and ask yourself, 'What is meditation?' And you sit until you find out. Ideally you would find out in two days, but what stops us is our expectations, opinions, projections. So you have to get rid of all your misunderstandings and opinions, and you do that only by sitting with the intention to discover, 'What is meditation?' And you will discover it because it's *right* there. All you have to do is get rid of what's in the way."

A man asked the next question. "I define myself as a dry personality, but I have discovered within myself emotions like love, despair and a certain peace. But I never have anything to say. It is difficult for my family. How can I change this?"

"Sounds like me!" Lee smiled brightly at the man. "When I'm not up here I never have anything to say! People around me just love to talk—they sort of chirp away beside me. There they are, chirp, chirp, chirp, and I'm just lost in my silence. It's a great arrangement!" At this point people seemed unsure as to whether Lee was kidding or not. A sporadic laughter scattered through the room, especially in the back where Lee's students were all sitting and guffawing loudly.

"In the Eastern traditions they talk about different organic types of people. It's not a function of psychology or training, it's a natural, organic tendency. There are two basic psychological types: introvert and extrovert. So how you are is just a natural function of your organic tendency."

The man pressed on, "But I feel dead." He sounded very sad.

"Wow! Lucky you! I've been trying to feel dead for years!" Lee seemed to find this hysterically funny. He grabbed his sides and rolled in his seat with laughter. His laughter had people flummoxed. One could almost hear the question ricocheting through the room—'Is he serious?' Yes, of course he is serious, or rather purposeful, in everything he says, but what does he mean? He was being serious if one could get to the underlying communication. One way to look at it goes back to what he said earlier about the problem of enlightenment. "When you get enlightenment, not only do you have the problem of people, you *become* them." When one feels to that depth, when one has taken on the suffering of humanity to that degree, one might very well wish that one could not feel.

Now wiping tears of laughter from his eyes, he continued. "Everybody's so funny this afternoon! Where were you keeping it all day yesterday?" His laughter slowly subsided and he went on in a sober tone.

"First of all, none of us can change ourselves, no matter how clearly we see or don't see what needs to be changed. Not real change, fundamental change, that is. We can change superficial realities, but when we say, 'I can change,' ego can't change anything. Ego is the way it is because it believes that to be any other way is death. For *your* ego" he gestured to the questioner, "to feel happy would be death. Ego will never change itself because that change is equated with suicide.

"The whole process of self-observation is about allowing who we are essentially to seek balance, meaning change, without the interference of ego, because ego will not allow change. So self-observation—in Gurdjieffian terms—is about observing ourselves accurately, as we are, without judgement or any effort to be different, because every effort to be different strengthens the very thing we are trying to change.

"We have this idea—'I want to change, to be more alive, happy.' You have to accept yourself as you are, as if the way you are at this very moment is *never* going to change. What that does is gives the power of change to our being and takes it away from ego. Ego has the power to change, but will never do it. Real change comes from *being*. If there is a practice it would be to continue to observe yourself as you are with this qualification: Any judgement—good, bad, et cetera—or expectation of yourself to change stops the process of change. If change is going to come, it comes from relaxing our choke hold, our grip, on just letting things be as they are right here, right now. In your case, feeling dead—okay, that's tough. But being quiet—that's not a fault! It's just a natural tendency. If you really have nothing to say, you really have nothing to say."

June 23, 1999
La Ferme de Jutreau

After all day on the train from Avignon, Lee just arrived back at the ashram from Yvan Amar's funeral in Gordes. He looks radiant and transparent. He was wearing a blue and purple striped soft cotton shirt (taken from the giveaway box at the ashram here in France last year) and pale yellow pants (also from the giveaway box). His eyes were softly lucent as he reported in a matter-of-fact way, "Everyone was there. It was quite a gathering . . . very nice." He dealt with the curiosity and fascination of his students by keeping it all very simple—no sentimentality, no hoopla. It's only death, after all, seemed to be his attitude. That which is eternal continues. What else was there to consider?

He said that Arnaud and Veronique Desjardins, Gilles Farcet, Chandra Swami, Andrew and Alka Cohen, Jacques Castermane, Sheik Bertounis and perhaps two hundred people gathered in a Catholic church in Gordes at four o'clock for prayers, chants and eulogies to Yvan. Many people cried softly. Arnaud gave a brief talk, which Lee especially appreciated. "The whole thing was very heartfelt, a tribute to Yvan," Lee said. He immediately went to his desk and read his mail—a pile of letters from his students in the U.S. and Europe—then went outside to play with the children before dinner. The sun beamed down on him as he sat in the emerald grass, calm, quiet and inwardly focused, willing to be drawn out for conversation as people approached, wanting his attention.

After dinner there was bridge as usual. All seemed very quiet.

June 25, 1999
La Ferme de Jutreau

One of Lee's long-time students, Wilf, who used to live on the ashram in Arizona but has been living in Canada for eight years, has just arrived at La Ferme de Jutreau. A few weeks ago he tried to get into the United States to move back to the Arizona ashram but was turned back at the border by the American border police. Lee made a number of comments about this situation before Wilf arrived in France, shaking his head in exasperation and saying, "This happens all the time. When will my students do what I tell them to do? If he'd done exactly what I told him to do that wouldn't have happened—he would have gotten into the States with *no problem*."

Lee had told Wilf to "come in six months," which would have meant late summer. But having gotten feedback from a number of other people, Wilf decided to come to Arizona in three months instead of six. So he found himself stuck in limbo in Canada, having quit his job, packed up his apartment, with no place to live. Hearing all this, Lee had said, almost in disbelief. "When will people learn to do what I tell them to do? All this could have been avoided." Lee then suggested to Wilf that he come spend the summer in France at La Ferme de Jutreau and try to get into the States next fall.

Yesterday someone waited for Wilf to arrive on the train in Chatellerault from the airport in Paris, having gotten a message from him that he would come in on the twenty-fourth of June. He never arrived, so Brindavan finally assumed that he would come in the next day and that somehow the information had just gotten mixed up. Now, during the evening gathering over mint tea at nine-thirty, Wilf came rolling in with Dasya, who went to pick him up at the train station.

"How was your trip?" Lee asked, smiling at Wilf.

"Great," Wilf responded. He looked noticeably well, sound and fit. He began to tell Lee and the group that he had to go to Montparnasse in Paris to catch the train, rather than taking it from Charles de Gaulle Airport, where the trains were all full. Brinda, who makes most of the logistical arrangements for people coming and going from La Ferme de Jutreau, picked up on this and said, "Kelly may have to take the train from Montparnasse too."

Kelly would be arriving from the States next Wednesday with Nachama. Lee was planning to meet Kelly and Nachama at the airport, then to see Kelly onto the train to Chatellerault from Charles de Gaulle Airport so she could go as directly as possible to the ashram, which was necessary for health reasons. It would be much easier and faster for her to take the train from the airport than having to go to into Paris to the Montparnasse station. Lee would be staying in Paris for his public talk at Espace Harmonie.

Lee attends to all these kinds of details for his devotees with a hawk eye—or like a mother bear. Now his response was immediate and insistent. He asserted loudly, "No! Kelly *will* get on the train in Charles de Gaulle! If Suzuki Roshi could get from Manchuria to Japan in World War II, then Kelly will get on the train in Charles de Gaulle Airport!"

He paused for a moment then plunged back into the fray. "I have to fight the negative thinking of my students all the time! It isn't really negative thinking, it's pessimism. They refuse to believe in a magical Universe. The Universe is magical and will open its doors to us if we believe in it. But we refuse to believe it is magical, so we have to suffer a lack of magic." He frowned and shrugged, "Well, life goes on . . ."

This teaching communication seemed to have many different layers of meaning for each person in the room, so that it hit each person in different centers, or in different areas of the labyrinth, in addition to the obvious straightforward communication of it, which was a direct hit. The conversation turned toward a more social banter, and at ten-thirty after yawning several times, Lee said, *"Bonne nuit, "* and left the room.

June 27, 1999
La Ferme de Jutreau

In the office today before dinner Lee was sitting at his desk reading from *Living on Luck,* Volume II of Charles Bukowski's letters. Speaking to the three or four people who were standing or sitting there he said, "Listen to this," and began reading:

> One of my last friends, a dishwasher, set himself on fire or anyhow somebody set him on fire and he walked up the steps, drunk, a black monster of himself, flakes of walking ashes, and he got to his room (the only home he knew) and fell on his rented bed and died. Farewell friend.
> We go on with our little poems and we wait.
> One god damned hell of a situation. (p. 28)

Lee was beaming as he looked up at his small audience. He shook his head as if in disbelief. "It's so inspiring! This is *incredibly* inspiring! To be able to capture in seven lines the utter desolation of the sleeping world. The Buddhists wrote thousands of pages of scripture and couldn't capture the emptiness of all phenomena the way Bukowski does in one paragraph!"

June 28, 1999
La Ferme de Jutreau

At the After Dinner Talk Lee was reading from *The Crooked Cucumber*, a biography of Suzuki Roshi. He began with a quote from the book in which Suzuki Roshi commented on how some people were too attached to the idea of being "natural," to the point that it is no longer natural but artificial. Lee commented:

"So this is a comment on the hippies of that time period, whose naturalness became an affectation. Lack of makeup, long hair, no deodorant—*phew*—or whatever. It could be said of the Rajneesh community, I think without any minimalization, that a certain freedom of form was taken to such an extreme that it actually became a lack of freedom of form, a rigidity. Of course, for the *good* students, the people that Rajneesh trained well, they aren't bound by those limitations. This is also the mood in Punjaji's school. A certain kind of attitude toward nonduality, which in certain cases may be genuine, but when taken on as the only way to be, becomes duality again—the worst kind of duality. The kind of duality that can be justified under any circumstances, and that has no ethic. So anything can be done in his name, anything—rape, theft, lies, anything, even elevating bad taste to the status of objectivity. Wow! It makes no difference. And that is the current state of Advaita Vedanta today, despite some good students."

He read many passages from the book that he had selected to share with his students, stopping to comment. Asking for questions, he responded to a question about the possibility of transmission of the lineage happening in his school.

"Our school is fairly young, so we have a good chance to see some transmission in our lifetime. I'm sure there'll be as much resistance as there was to Richard Baker when he was given the transmission. It's usually not the popular people that get to be point man or point woman. That's the one who gets picked out by the snipers and everyone else can go in and clean up, which is what they are supposed to do. Richard Baker got picked off by the snipers. What everyone was supposed to do—the rest of the patrol—was to go in and shoot the sniper.

"What people were supposed to do when Richard Baker got picked off was to shoot the sniper. That's why you have a point man. A sniper stops you. You can't move when there is a sniper because you can't see them, you don't know where they are. You don't know where the bullets are coming from and you can't shoot the whole jungle. So the point man gets to be the first one to step on the mine to show you where the trigger wire is or to get shot by the sniper. As soon as the point man gets shot by the sniper, you know where the sniper is, and you shoot him out of the tree. It's the way it works. What you're supposed to do when the point man gets shot is shoot the sniper. Then you can go ahead because the danger is finished.

"What happened when Richard Baker got sniped was that, instead of the rest of the patrol shooting the sniper, they joined forces with the sniper and started shooting their own men. This is what happened. You know, '*Oh!* We've got to *reform* the Buddhist community in America, we've got to *stop* every extra-curricular sexual activity, we've got to *stop* all the drinking!' I mean where would Alan Watts and Chögyam Trungpa Rinpoche have been without drink? Who would they have been? Not the same people. So what everybody did was get hysterical and join the sniper and practically ruin the whole Buddhist sangha in America at every level.

"People assume, obviously, that sex and religion don't go together. As we were talking about last night in relationship to the word sin, people assume that to have sex outside of the conventional approach is a sin. So they assume, 'How can someone be a teacher of religious ethic when they themselves are living in sin?' as the saying goes. What kind of adults are we if we can't exercise adult maturity? Essentially we're trying to legislate maturity instead of allowing people to be who they are and making choices as adults, not to mention that we are dismissing the ethic of many tribal cultures and most great men of history. Typical white, Judeo-Christian presumptuousness.

"If somebody is a bad teacher somebody will get them. One of the students will shoot them, or something will happen. And if they are good teachers, let them have a little sex. Jim Jones killed himself. Charlie Manson killed somebody else and got put in jail. And Bo killed all those little peeps. If somebody is bad enough they end up committing suicide or getting put in jail. We don't have to legislate them."

Lee's comments were inflammatory, but clearly he was not saying that every school should have a vigilante group, or that it was alright that so many people died following psychopaths. He often uses strong language to make a point, and he expects people to be intelligent enough to know the difference between symbolic language and literal language. In this case he was saying that instead of worrying about all these charlatan gurus, or gurus having sex with consenting adults, we should be investigating ourselves. We should be living with greater integrity—stop stealing on a petty level, stop screaming at our families or employees, stop manipulating and domineering others at subtle levels for the gain of a perceived personal reward or sense of power. The point is that we cannot legislate true ethical integrity; people have to make the right choices based on wisdom. In nurturing an inner culture of wisdom based on dharma and right action, we begin to make the right choices and we become solely responsible for our mistakes. He continued:

"If a thirty-year-old woman or a forty-year-old woman is gonna sleep with a teacher who is obviously a charlatan, let her. Who are we gonna save everybody from, you know? These babes are going to sleep with any slob off the street. They're gonna sleep with somebody in power. If it's not a spiritual teacher, it's gonna be a corporate vice president. It's gonna be a policeman. If somebody is insistent on throwing themselves at the feet of someone in power, they are gonna do it anyway! Whether it's a spiritual teacher or a state trooper on the highway, they're gonna do it. What are we gonna do? Save everybody from learning their own lessons? We should be thinking more like adults.

"So, Richard Baker got sniped and instead of everybody shooting the sniper which is the attitude that diminishes enlightenment because of projections, expectations, opinions, and prejudices, everybody joined the sniper team and started picking off their own people. Amazing the way things happen."

June 30, 1999
La Ferme de Jutreau

Lee is leaving for Paris with a few of his students today after dinner. He will spend the night at Maison Raphael in Boulogne, a suburb of Paris in preparation for a busy day the next day, including a public talk in the evening and an appointment tomorrow afternoon. Early tomorrow morning he will get up and drive to Charles de Gaulle Airport to pick up Kelly and Nachama.

Talking with Brinda in the office before dinner, Lee was back on the subject of the logistics of Kelly's train trip from Charles de Gaulle to Chatellerault, what time the train leaves, when it will arrive and so on. Kelly has very little time to get to the TGV station—which is in a different terminal at Charles de Gaulle—to catch the 8:55 train tomorrow morning. She has to take the RER, Brinda says, from terminal one to terminal two. If she misses the train at the airport, we will have to take her to the Montparnasse station in Paris to catch the 10:45 train. Brinda is concerned that the train will be crowded and there won't be any seats available. Lee has a lunch appointment with Deben Bhattacharya—the translator of *Mirror of the Sky*, a collection of Bengali Baul songs recently published by Hohm Press—and his wife in Montmartre. Finding his way to Montparnasse, parking and waiting for Kelly to get on the 10:45 train is not part of Lee's plan for the morning. He wants to get her on the train to meet Brinda, who will be waiting for her in Chatellerault, in the most expedient way.

At the end of the conversation involving all these logistical details Brinda corrected Lee about the time the train departs from Charles de Gaulle. "Okay," he snapped, "You have me shaking in my boots over this train!"

He paused, then started speaking again, "Magic is very delicate—it doesn't function well with interference. Not *you* of course!" He playfully prodded Brinda with the innuendo. It was the third time this conversation about Kelly making the train had come up; each time Lee had made it clear that for him, there were no other options than Kelly making the train on time at the airport. It seemed like another point that Lee was making with Brinda about the nature of magic and holding the context of "anything is possible."

A little later in the afternoon Marcus, a dedicated student of Lee's and a fine artist, arrived from London bearing gifts for the master. Marcus only sees Lee for perhaps a month out of every year. He is currently apprenticing to Robert Beer, a master *thangka* painter, and spends his time working on *thangka* paintings, each one of which takes three hundred and fifty to four hundred hours to complete. Last summer Marcus presented Lee with an incredible painting of Mahakala, the Tibetan form of a wrathful Shiva, which now hangs behind Lee's desk in the office on the ashram in Arizona. The colors and detail of these paintings are marvelous, and the exacting power of the symbolism makes a stunning communication. This year he carefully unwrapped the painting he had just finished of Vajrakilaya, another wrathful deity in union with a consort.

Now Marcus carried the painting in its three by four-foot frame outside to present it to Lee, who sat in the courtyard under the maple tree. He held it up for Lee to view, and stood beaming at the obvious pleasure his teacher was taking in the gift. Lee praised Marcus, but without any ostentation or excess. It was his discerning eye that wandered over the painting, absorbing and bringing to life the fruits of Marcus' work, and refining, blessing, invisibly sculpting the talent of his student that seemed to be the real reward which Marcus was now soaking up.

People gathered around to look at it with Lee. Held in Lee's hands, the deity was already alive. The dark blue deity with his lighter blue consort dances on a lotus, where his feet pound upon the prostrate and obviously limp forms of Shiva and Parvati. Behind the deity is the flayed skin of a white elephant, a tiger, and a human man, an aureole of wild red and deep orange flames, against which the many brilliant shades of blues and greens of clouds, water and mountains take swirling form in high detail. The deities are adorned with delicate white jewelry made from human bone, and in their hands they hold sacred implements—a double *dorje* (Sanskrit *vajra*, a symbolic weapon or lightning bolt that represents diamond-like clarity or discriminating awareness) and a *phurba* (a dagger-like object that is used to destroy the two knots at the heart chakra). At the bottom of the painting are four skull cups with boiling blood (the blood is supposed to be extremely hot at the moment of enlightenment), a skull with sense organs, signifying the renunciation of the senses, and so on. It is an objective art form from a sacred culture.

Lee immediately took the *thangka* into the office and had Clint hang it above his desk. Its presence was instantly striking and impactful; the space seemed subtly transformed. In the hubbub of getting the painting hung on the wall while several of us stood around and watched, Marcus had quietly taken a back seat to all the activity and stood in the living room watching through the doorway.

Afterward Marcus was showing Brinda some books he had brought as a donation to the ashram—a beautiful hardbound collection of Maurice Nicoll's *Psychological Commentaries* (on the work of G.I. Gurdjieff) and some others. Lee walked in and looked over the books, instructing Brinda to make certain they would be cared for in a particular way, kept in a separate place apart from the other books of the growing ashram library, which already covers an entire wall of the living room.

Marcus sat quietly on the couch while Lee and Brinda talked. He looked like he had just arrived in heaven. He hasn't seen Lee for almost a year, and right now the moment he had been waiting for seemed to have taken a weight off of him, so that he appeared light, blithe, almost ethereal. As Lee whisked back into the office he stopped, turned and smiled at Marcus, saying with a particular sweetness, "I'm going to Paris after dinner but I'll be back Thursday morning. I'll have to go without your company for a day!" These kinds of remarks to his devotees do not go unnoticed when they are so generously given to others, but it seems that most of us tend to not hear them when they are directed at us. Nonetheless Lee is constantly affirming and giving to his students in this way.

Leaving immediately after dinner Lee drove the van and his companions the three-and-a-half hours into Paris. It rained part of the way, and there were three immense rainbows stretched across the sky, each one at different points in the journey. One of them was a magnificent double rainbow that spanned the eastern sky, its two ends coming down in distant fields of grain. They were so strikingly beautiful that they seemed like portents of some kind.

Arriving on the outskirts of Paris we went through some navigating difficulties, but Lee found his way and arrived at Maison Raphael around ten o'clock Lee suggested that we play bridge, so after an hour or so of cards in the kitchen, everyone went to bed at midnight. Wanting to be certain that he would not be late in meeting Nachama and Kelly after they arrive at seven twenty-five, collect their baggage and come out of customs, he told us to be ready to leave—that meant in the van and driving away—at five-thirty in the morning.

We arrived with Lee at the airport at six o'clock, parked, took an elevator down to the arrival area and sat down to wait. This is Lee's style—he is always early for everything. He would rather leave early and wait, even for a long period of time, than be late. So anyone who travels with Lee or spends much time in his intimate company learns to do a lot of waiting. We wait at movies, for planes and trains, for the arrival of guests; we wait while the children play, while Lee conducts business that everyone else knows nothing of, while Lee sells books before and after talks. Learning the art of how to wait seems to be an important part of sadhana.

While we were waiting I noticed that there were no signs for the RER transit to terminal two, only signs that indicated a shuttle bus to terminal two and the TGV station. Lee said that when Kelly arrived Ann and I would take her as quickly as possible by shuttle to terminal two and buy her ticket and get her on the train while he, Dasya and Nachama handled getting their luggage—including four large cardboard boxes packed with goods for La Ferme de Jutreau—up to the van in the parking lot. They would then meet us at terminal two. He said, "Get her there as quickly as you can. Have only one thought in your mind and that is getting her on the train. Nothing other than getting her on that train is a possibility."

Their plane came in fifteen minutes early, but we waited almost an hour for them to get through customs. We watched the clock, knowing that time was of the essence, and that if they didn't get through soon Kelly would miss the airport train. As the clock ticked away, Lee was standing and waiting like a mountain and yet it felt like he was also poised and ready for action. He exhibited no nervousness, no frittering away of energy with worry. He maintained his clarity of intention, which was—like he said a few nights ago over tea—"Kelly *will* get on the train at Charles de Gaulle."

Kelly and Nachama were delayed because the boxes were so large that they couldn't be put through the conveyor belt and had to be carried down by hand to the baggage claim. Finally at eight-fifteen they appeared walking through the door. After brief hugs and hellos, we took off with Kelly and her carry-on luggage to the shuttle to terminal two. We climbed on the shuttle and it slowly snaked its way through the airport labyrinth of buildings, down various side roads, around this and that, stopping several times to pick up passengers.

After about twenty minutes we started getting nervous as we realized that it would have been much faster to go to terminal two in the van with Lee. With every passing moment it became chancier as to whether or not Kelly would make the train. As we finally pulled up to the TGV station Kelly had only five minutes to buy her ticket and run to the quay. As we walked the first thing we saw was Lee, who walked up with ticket in hand and a smile on his face. We walked down a long stairway to the quay just as the train pulled in. Within seconds Kelly was on board with her luggage and getting settled.

It was 8:55 and the train would take off any minute. We walked back upstairs with Lee and outside to the van to speed off with magic under our wheels toward Montmartre and Lee's lunch appointment with Deben Bhattacharya.

Yvan Amar had connected Lee with Deben Bhattacharya a few years ago when Yvan planned to publish Deben's book of Baul poetry in French. Deben was looking for an American publisher and Yvan told him to contact Lee. The rest is history, compressed into the book and CD, *Mirror of the Sky,* recently released by Hohm Press. Lee and company arrived at Deben Bhattacharya's apartment a few minutes before twelve-thirty—right on time. The smell of Indian spices permeated the air even out in the hallway where we stood waiting while Lee pressed the doorbell. Lee carried a large apple tart in a *patisserie* box that he had bought at a *boulangerie* down the block. Deben and his wife Janna opened the door and greeted Lee with warm embraces. Mrs. Bhattacharya took the dessert box from Lee's hand, protesting sweetly, "You really didn't need to . . . "

We walked down a narrow hall, past a small study where the walls were completely lined with bookcases, filled to brimming with reel-to-reel film, cassettes, audio and video tapes, manuscripts, boxes of tapes and film—an archive of indigenous world music, tribal and grass roots musicians "to die for," as Lee described it. We made our way into the living room where many instruments lined the walls—*dotaras, ektaras* and other simple stringed instruments, five or six jew's harps, a wide assortment of bamboo and wooden handmade flutes, drums of several kinds. The small living room had a day-bed couch and several chairs clustered around a glass coffee table, walls lined with books and instruments. Beautiful old French windows opened onto the street and the trees in the lush garden that spilled out over the sidewalk across the way. The room was also populated with a number of carved wooden female deities that hung on the walls and a four-foot-high brass *arati* lamp by the window with a large Garuda (Vishnu's bird) on top.

"Please sit down," Deben said to Lee, indicating the couch, and then turning to the rest of us, "anywhere you like." He and his wife were the epitome of graciousness, ease, elegance—all the while remaining warm and immediately real in a very human way. Lee took a seat at the very end of the long couch, leaving room for Deben and his wife to sit if they should chose. The rest of us took chairs while Deben and his wife stood, making certain everyone was comfortable and settled, asking us if they could bring us anything to drink. As we settled in they began to tell Lee that they had just gotten a letter that morning from Andrew Schelling, who translated Mirabai's poetry and has been published by Hohm Press also. He had written to congratulate Deben on the book. "It was a lovely, charming letter," Mrs. Bhattacharya said with a smile.

"Such a lovely man, a charming letter," Deben agreed and added, "He spoke so warmly of you, Lee, of all of you," he was referring to Hohm Press. "A very nice letter, he was so pleased to see *Mirror of the Sky.* We thought it was quite a coincidence, getting that letter with you coming today!"

Soon François Fronty, a disciple of Arnaud Desjardins, arrived. He is a filmmaker and good friend of Lee's who filmed "On the Road With Mr. Lee," and "Darshan," a video about Yogi Ramsuratkumar. As François settled in Deben poured glasses of wine for everyone. Mrs. Bhattacharya brought the meal out to the living room in an assortment of dishes and pots, placing them with the plates and silverware that she had organized on a side table. She and Deben then proceeded to serve each person's plate carefully, and only when everyone else was taken care of to their satisfaction did they serve themselves. It was homemade, delicious Indian fare—rice and perfectly spiced *dahl*, vegetable curry, batter-fried eggplant and delicious chutney of raw apples, yogurt, fresh coriander and tamarind. The meal was excellent, the delight of eating it augmented by the good company of our hosts. They worked together in the beautiful harmony of a long-time partnership that one couldn't fail to notice as they served food, wine, coffee, dessert, weaving in and out amongst their guests, serving and tending to everyone's slightest need.

As dessert was served—the apple tart Lee had brought, along with strawberries and sugar topped with rich whipped cream—Deben jokingly said, "I always say that we live like Bedouins—without chairs and tables!" referring to the fact that we were eating with plates balanced on our laps and passing the whipped cream and sugar back and forth across the coffee table. Their company was so gentile, so incredibly civilized and cultured in the truest sense that we could have been eating in a tent out on the desert and it would have seemed like a palace. That is the way the Bedouins do it also—create real culture, beauty and elegance within what they have to work with. It is a very Baulish trait as well, and having spent many years and a great deal of time with tribal people— Bauls, gypsies, the village people of Rajasthan or Afghanistan—Deben clearly had a great appreciation of such subtle aspects of the art of living. Lee and his students were right at home in this ambiance.

As the company lingered for almost two hours over dessert and coffee, Deben began to talk about the Bauls. He is a renowned anthropologist and ethnomusicologist who spent many years researching Baul culture, art and spiritual tradition and recording the music of the Bauls in Bengal, beginning as early as the late 1950s. Absorbing his wisdom was a tremendous opportunity to soak up more of the roots of the tradition in which we find ourselves as Lee's students. Lee sat quietly listening from his seat on the couch. He hardly moved as the afternoon wore on, but sat in a pool of stillness, completely unobtrusive, speaking only here and there, but exuding a silent radiance. He seemed mostly content to have his host and his students interact, but would also readily interject something to one of his students when needed, particularly to offer a correction or clarify a point for one of us. Whenever Deben spoke directly to Lee, I noticed how completely responsive Lee was, and how the company of Deben and Janna Bhattacharya seemed to nourish him immensely.

Deben talked about the famous Bengali poet of the twelfth century, Jayadeva, who wrote the great Hindu religious poem, the *Gita Govinda* (Songs of Krishna). It was Jayadeva who took the brief mention of Radha as one of the gopis in the *ras lila* that appears in Book X of the *Srimad Bhagavatam* (commented on in Vallabhacharya's famous magnum opus, *Commentaries on the Love Games of Sri Krisna*), and immortalized her in his poetry as the divine consort of Krishna. This mythologizing of Radha as the divine consort was the beginning of the Vaishnava movement in which Krishna and Radha are the chosen deities and divine couple, representing ultimately the union between the human soul (Radha) which is seen as the Feminine, and the Supreme Lord or *Istaa Devataa* (Krishna), viewed as the Masculine. Lord Chaitanya (fourteenth century) took this grass-roots religious movement further and became the realized embodiment of both Radha and Krishna. Paintings of Chaitanya—a patron "saint" of the Bauls, along with Jayadeva—always depict him with golden skin, signifying that he had attained the realization of both Radha and Krishna, or divine Feminine and Masculine, in one human body.

Deben relayed this to us and then said that in the centuries after Jayadeva the Vaishnavas and Bauls would make a pilgrimage on foot, twelve hundred to fifteen hundred miles, from Bengal to Brindavan, singing Jayadeva's songs all the way and inspiring the village people with their ecstatic renderings of the *Gita Govinda*. Deben also talked about the Rajasthani tribal musicians whom he filmed, how their music and their instruments are passed from father to son. He spoke of them as consummate musicians, and yet they are simple people, tribal people. In these stories the great respect that Deben Bhattacharya has for the common village people of India was radiantly apparent.

He went on to talk about how he had done the original recordings of Nabanidas Baul, the father of Purna Das (probably the most famous Baul in the West who has been recorded extensively). Deben was at a Baul festival in Bengal in 1959 and asked the festival organizer if he could record the musicians. As he set up his equipment Nabanidas came forward with curiosity about the equipment. Nabanidas had never seen such a thing before. He asked Deben, "What are you doing?" When Deben explained that he would record Nabanidas' voice and music, Nabanidas didn't believe that it was possible. He had never seen any of this kind of technology, and shrugged Deben's explanation off with innocent laughter. Deben recorded him and played it back for Nabanidas, who immediately grasped it and said, "Come to my village and I'll sing better for you there!"

This seemed, perhaps in part, like a hint from Nabanidas that the closer to their grass roots the Bauls are, the better the music and the mood will be. The Bauls are known for their dedication to the common people of India, the poor villagers, the outcasts and misfits. They are a devotional sect, but they are also *tantrikas* who embrace every aspect of life—including family life and sexuality—as legitimate dimensions of sadhana and God-realization. They are greatly loved by the common people because they eschew all caste distinctions and the oppressive dictates of religious and societal dogmas and creeds. They often take people from all castes into their company. But most of all they are loved for the great inspiration and joy that they bring to village life through their spontaneous songs, poetry, music and dance as they wander from village to village, singing of "the man of the heart," Lord Krishna, and propagating the way of right living or dharma.

Around four o'clock Lee left Montmartre and drove to Espace Harmonie, the bookstore and spiritual center of Alain René—where Lee would give his talk that night at 4 rue des Petits Hotels. There he would meet up with the rest of his group who had been in Paris for a few days—Thomas, Deacon and Ed. We walked into a small bookstore at the street level, then downstairs into a windowless basement with one large room and two smaller adjoining rooms. These smaller rooms opened out into the large room, making it possible for the space to accommodate up to seventy-five people.

Lee went to work right away setting up his book table. As soon as he was finished he said that we would all go to a great market right across the street and buy dinner for everyone. "You can all pick out whatever you want to eat—anything—but you have to eat it tonight." Lee bought several loaves of bread—*fiselles*, baguettes, rich olive bread—and a number of luscious cheeses. Some of us picked out spiced olives, a roasted chicken, cherries and figs, while Lee focused on lettuce and tomato garnishes for the sandwich he would make. Back downstairs at the center we spread a sheet on the floor and laid out the feast, eating informally and heartily and visiting together. Lee sent out for Cokes to finish it all off. When we were finished Lee placed himself squarely behind the book table and waited for people to start coming in, which they did very soon.

As people began to stream in there were many familiar faces—people who have met Lee over the years in France at seminars and talks. Many were disciples of Arnaud

Desjardins, some of whom Lee has come to know quite well. There were about seventy people packed into the space as Lee began his talk in a spirited and lively mood.

"I have two aims here tonight. First of all, to sell books! Look at this!" Lee picked up a copy of *N'essayez Pas—Vivez* and held it up in the air. "One hundred measly francs! Can you believe it? Cheap! Everyone here should have at least three copies! The second goal is to leave you happy but very confused. What we all call clarity is nothing but intellectual comfort. Intellectual comfort and eight francs will get you on the Metro!"

Lee started telling jokes. He sat on the same kind of metal folding chair that most of the people in the room sat on, with the exception of the ten or twelve people who sat on pillows on the floor right in front of him. The crowd was so packed into the room that people sat on the floor just a few feet away from Lee's feet, almost touching him. After going off on various tangents and making teaching points like buckshot scattered out at the crowd, he returned to discussing his second goal for the night.

"So I want you to be disturbed. The natural urge of the human being is to seek harmony. We try to do that with our egos and with our souls. There are two ways to deal with disturbance: to numb yourself out so you don't feel it is one way. Every habit is a way of dulling yourself out so you don't feel—cigarettes, alcohol, sex. Or you create such an intense emotional state that you don't feel the irritation. That's the typical egoic way to deal with disturbance.

"The next time you get on the Metro, look closely at people's faces. They are *disturbed*, full of pain. But they would probably say, 'No, I'm not, I'm fine.' But you can't hide the signs of your body. 'The eyes are the mirror of the soul.' Shakespeare! I hate to credit some Englishman here with all you Parisians! But it's true—the face is the mirror of the real feelings we are having.

"The second way to deal with disturbance is to resolve it—to seek balance, harmony. In response to any disturbance you feel from tonight some of you may say to yourself, 'Gosh, I thought that guy Lee Lozowick was a spiritual master, but he's really a dumb asshole! Can you believe that guy has students? How can anybody trust that schmuck!' The other option is that something in you trusts me. God knows why! I wouldn't trust me! I know—I grew up with me!" Many people were laughing hard in their seats, perhaps especially those who know Lee. Some had smiles on their faces and others looked doubtful, confused, serious. Lee continued, "In that case resolving the disturbance comes from understanding what is going on. What is illusion and what is real? When something is real, then disturbance is not a disturbance, but something else."

At this point Lee became even more provocative. He acted like a petulant child and threw out outrageous insults to the audience. Then suddenly he was returning to his point. "What brings people back to see someone who insults them and their culture? If you asked, 'Why do you keep going back to see this maniac?' their answer would probably be about how they *feel* rather than what the mind says. That's what means something—how it *feels* to you. If we think the brilliance of our ability to rationalize and articulate is what gets us closer to God, we are fooling ourselves because it is impossible for the mind not to define. To realize Reality for a lifetime, the mind has to be yours—not you belonging to the mind. The mind has to be something *you* use, not something that uses *you*.

"On the other hand, Suzuki Roshi—a great roshi who lived and taught in San Francisco—was giving a talk and someone said, 'I want to get enlightened. Can you give it to me?' Suzuki Roshi said, 'What do you want enlightenment for? You might not even like it!' Maybe you should just try to be a good lay—it wouldn't *hurt*, girls! It wouldn't *hurt*, guys! Give the girls something to crow about. If one of their friends says, 'How was he?' instead of her saying, 'Ehhh . . .' " he shrugged his shoulders and shook his head as if to say, "so-so," and continued, "wouldn't it be great if she said, 'The *best*! He's the best ninety seconds I've ever had!' " Every woman in the room burst out laughing. A few of the men smiled wryly while most of them sat silently staring at Lee.

"Reality seeks balance, harmony. If you seek for enlightenment you actually obstruct the possibility of enlightenment in your life. Whereas if you go about life, be an adult, be responsible, have integrity to life, then enlightenment will take care of itself. It doesn't need your help. In fact, enlightenment is so far beyond us, to try to help it, or get it, is totally absurd! When you accept what is, as it is, all good things take care of themselves. When you try to control and dominate everything, what you get is suffering. That's what Buddha meant, if I can be so presumptuous as to say I know what the Buddha meant! All life isn't pain, but all life is suffering when ego is trying to control everything according to its opinion and expectations.

"You may ask, 'On what basis can I question this guy?' Like anything in the spiritual field, one's credentials are a function of agreement. The company one keeps. Everyone has an opinion about who is a genuine teacher and who is not. A lot of people feel that the Pope or the Dalai Lama is lacking in the qualities of enlightenment. I have no credentials. My university degree is in marketing!"

Someone from the audience called out, "You sell books!"

"Yes! If I don't sell them, who will? I haven't done heroic sadhana, lived in a cave, had mystical revelation on revelation. One day it became obvious that this was the Work I had to do. And because I'm not a bad student and I've been doing it for twenty-five years, I have something to offer. But I have no credentials. Like Andrew Cohen. Half of the people love him, half of the people hate him.

"The criteria you use to judge the spiritual teacher is not what credentials he or she has, but do peoples' lives change for the better when they hang out with him? Going around saying, 'God is everything; God is everywhere,' does not make your life better. The sign of someone's life being better is the degree of harmony they have—how do they treat people? With love, kindness, generosity? That's what makes peoples' lives better. Not this nonduality stuff.

"At the end of his life Aldous Huxley, who was a very influential writer who had done everything, had all the mystical experiences and so on, was asked, 'In all your work and studies what is the most important thing you've learned in your amazing life?' He said, 'The most important thing is kindness.' No mention of God, nonduality, or all that bullshit!" Lee had been speaking for about an hour and a half. He paused and looked over his audience.

"Well! It's been great! How was it for you? Don't tell me . . . I've got much too fragile an ego! 'Oh, you were the best, the best . . . in fact, you were so good . . .' " Lee leaned back in his chair and laughed. For the most part, the crowd was laughing with him. He began a wild romp with the audience, answering questions with a particularly bawdy hilarity, making offhand remarks like, "Crotchless underwear! Who needs crotchless underwear? That stuff just gets in the way! You know how it is when you're really into it—you wanna just rip that stuff off anyway! That's how it is, isn't it? That's how it *should* be, anyway!"

To a woman who had suffered with cancer for several years he took a serious turn. When she talked about her sadhana, she talked about the need to transform her laziness.

Lee told her that she needed to learn to relax and have fun. He said, "What do you do for fun?"

She seemed to search for an answer. Finally she said, "I don't know." He continued, "Then find something that is really fun for you and do it, and don't compromise it for anything. That's my practical advice for tonight."

Another woman said, "You advise people not to get caught in ego, but when we try to not get caught isn't it the same thing?"

Lee answered, "Yes, of course. The first step is self-honesty. If you can see what you're doing while you're doing it then you can see that you are helpless to do anything else. That opens up the possibility to be different, because it brings clarity to the situation. Ruthless self-honesty means that we are unwilling to compromise our clarity for comfort of any kind.

"One of the things that make us uncomfortable is that we think we should be different. 'Oh, I shouldn't make mistakes, be so forgetful, whatever.' But what is, is. And if we can accept that, through self-observation and ruthless self-honesty, then the next moment is not conditioned or predictable, and includes the possibility that anything or even everything could be different."

A man asked what Lee meant by the sangha and if it was necessary. He answered, "The sangha means the community of practitioners. Every teacher has a sangha—has to have one. In my case we have an ashram and live together. In Arnaud Desjardins' case the students study the teaching and have a relationship with Arnaud, but live independently. That's another kind of sangha. Whether it is necessary or not is academic because it always *is*. Where there is the teacher, there is the sangha."

A woman asked one of the most commonly asked questions in public talks, "Is the master necessary?"

"A very different question," Lee reflected momentarily, then turned sassy. "No, the master is not necessary. In fact, fuck it! I'm getting the hell out of here! What have I been doing for twenty-five years? I must be fucking crazy!" His tone was sarcastic and he ended by staring at the audience as if in disbelief at the facility of the question. In a tone of weighted patience he said, "Yes—the master is necessary."

A woman on the front row started out now, "I bought your book . . ." She was referring to *N'essayez pas—Vivez,* which means *Don't Try—Live.*

"One's a good start," Lee chortled. "Buy three more after the talk!"

She continued, "I am disturbed. What is the difference between trying and living? Can we do without trying?"

Lee was chuckling throughout his answer. He started, "I don't mean not to try, of course. To sit at home because it might rain on us in heaven. I don't mean doing nothing. If I can be a patriarchal sexist, here's an example. When men and women are naturally attracted to one another and the man gently yet purposefully rubs his fingers slowly across her thigh, her legs just instinctually open up." He chuckled again. "*That's* what I mean by don't try, just live."

A woman sitting on the floor near Lee's feet began to question him. She had first approached him at the book table before the talk, saying "I saw you in Germany with the band years ago." She had been rather aggressive and forward then; now she started out in an irritated tone. She was piqued by Lee's various off-the-cuff and bawdy comments about eating meat and sex. She said, "Most masters are vegetarian. Can you explain why you eat meat?" A fast repartee between the woman and Lee ensued which had some similarities to his interchange with the woman in white in New York City as she kept pursuing her line of questioning, referring to the lower vibrations of eating meat, and how "unspiritual" it was. This time Lee was very light and humorous. He kept tossing the ball adroitly into her court as she became more flustered and aggressive.

Finally he said, "Of course there is a range of vibration in the food we eat, from dark to light and so on. Spiritual life is about moving into life, all of life, completely. It doesn't mean to look for dangerous or toxic situations, but you need to be able to transfer or subsume low vibrational circumstances when you are in those circumstances. I don't eat meat every day. If I am a guest and my hosts serve meat, I eat meat. You follow?"

"Yes," she answered, "but . . ."

"Well, then what do you want?" Lee asked.

"I'm stuck on this thing that masters don't eat meat," she muttered.

"Not all masters are vegetarian, and maybe some of the ones who are are just effete snobs! When someone once asked Chögyam Trungpa, 'What do you do if you find yourself in hell?' he answered, 'I try to stay there.' " Lee was giving the woman, who interestingly was dressed in white, some hints of tantric perspective on the issue of why he chooses to sometimes eat meat. He also seemed to be giving her a clue as to his entire way of working with the audience, and how to make use of many of his outrageous, funny or paradoxical remarks.

Now she got down to the real issue, blurting out, "Why do you talk about sex all the time? Is it an obsession of yours?"

Lee perked up. He said with a big smile, "*Yes*! Oh no! I'm transparent! Totally exposed up here! How did you notice?" He laughed maniacally. She began to argue with him in a hostile mode, saying that all he had done was express a bunch of opinions. After a bit more back and forth between them, Lee finally cut through her confusion in a swift move. He said forcefully, "I don't have *opinions* about Reality. I have opinions about movies and politics, but not about Reality. What I say about Reality is one hundred percent *accurate*!"

This was like throwing gasoline on a fire. She began to rant at him. He sat there listening for a moment and finally cut her off, saying, "As you wish, *cherie*." He turned away from her and answered the next question.

After the talk people crowded around the book table, buying books from Lee and wanting him to sign their copies of *N'essayez Pas—Vivez*. Old friends like Christophe and Muriel Massin, the daughter and son-in-law of Arnaud Desjardins, stopped at the book table to say hello to Lee. The woman who had aggressively plied Lee with questions and told him he was obsessed with sex came and bought a CD and a book, one hundred twenty and one hundred francs respectively. When one of Lee's students gave her the price of each item she looked exasperated and said sourly, "And how much is that added together?" as if the person behind the book table was extremely stupid. Of course she could add that simple sum. The person replied, "Two hundred and twenty francs." The woman smirked and forked up the money, then left immediately. Around eleven-thirty Lee finished packing the book table up and sped out of Paris toward the ashram. We got to La Ferme de Jutreau just before three a.m. and were in the darshan hall for morning meditation at seven o'clock, where Lee also sat, as usual, on his dais, wrapped in a wool blanket.

Sri Yogi Ramsuratkumar

Suresh offering incense to Yogi Ramsuratkumar in the Yagashala on the Yogi Ramsuratkumar Ashram.

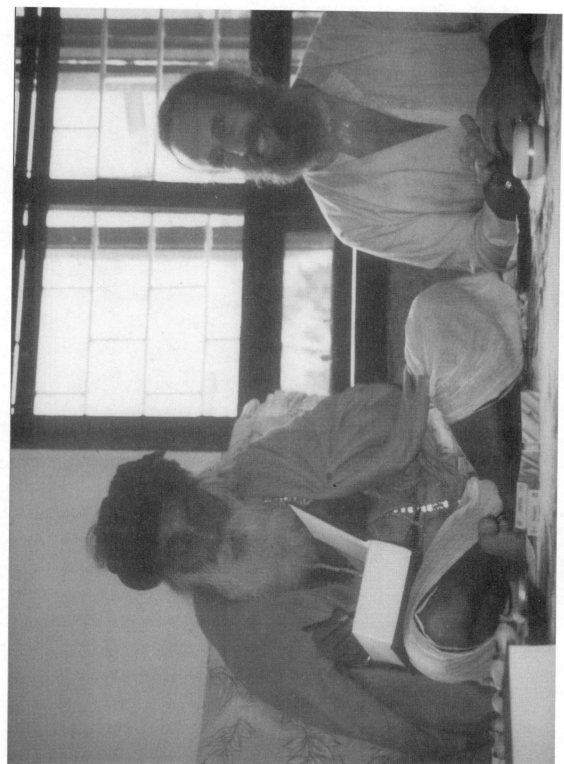

Yogi Ramsuratkumar signing *Death of a Dishonest Man*, November 1998.

On the Yogi Ramsuratkumar Ashram, December 1998, from the left:
Zachary Parker, Dave Smith, Tom Lennon, Purna Steinitz and Lee Lozowick.

Liars, gods & beggars, March 1999, Prescott, Arizona.

From the left: Stan Hitson, Everett Jaime, Doug Fulker, Lee Lozowick, Justin Hitson and Steve Ball.

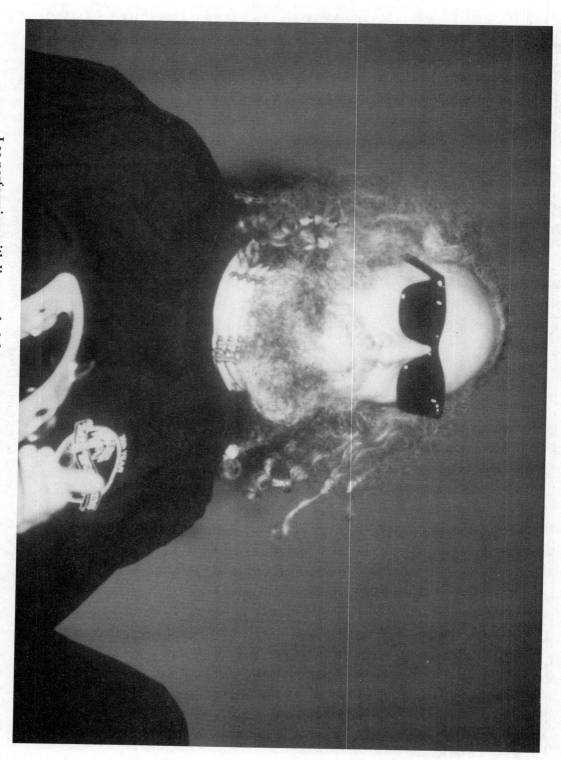

Lee performing with liars, gods & beggars in Prescott, Arizona, March 1999.

Lee Lozowick in darshan at the Arizona ashram, All Fool's Celebration, April 1998.

Andrew Cohen and Lee Lozowick at Fox Hollow, Massachusetts, June 1999.

Yvan Amar and Lee Lozowick at the chalet in the French Alps, 1997.

Shri performing at Hauteville, July 1999.

Arnaud Desjardins and Lee Lozowick at Hauteville, France, July 1999.

Lee Lozowick and François Fronty in the courtyard at Hauteville, July 1999.

Arnaud Desjardins and Lee Lozowick in the meeting hall at Hauteville, July 1999.

**Lee Lozowick and Ed Flaherty performing with Shri
at the Lucerne Blues Festival, Lucerne, Switzerland, July 1999.**

Lee Lozowick in the crowd at Metz, France, performing with Shri in July 1999.

Lee Lozowick at the public talk in La Chaux de Fonds, France, August 1999.

Lee giving the seminar at Joué near Bordeaux, France, September 1999.

Lee Lozowick in darshan at La Ferme de Jutreau, September, 1999.

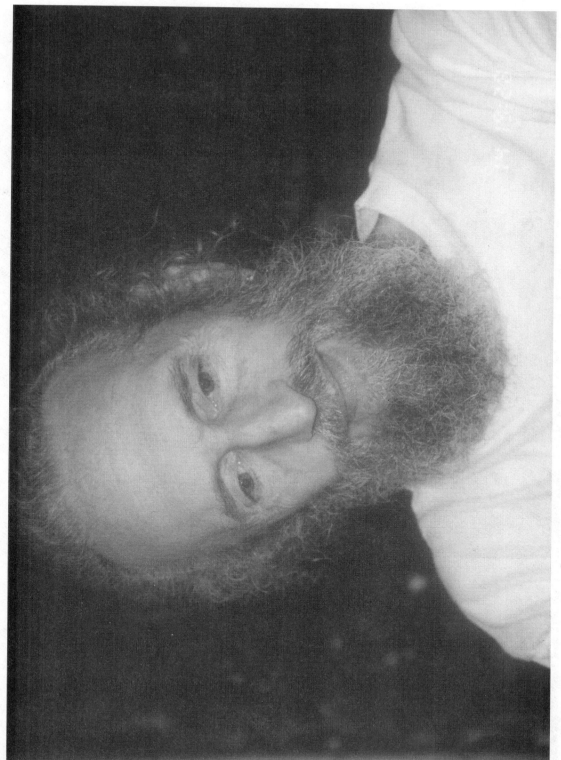

Lee at La Source Bleue, Touzac, France, September 1999.

Lee at Maison Raphael, Paris, September-October, 1999.

Garchen Rinpoche and Lee Lozowick at the Arizona ashram, November 1999.

Lee in darshan on the ashram in Arizona, November 1999.

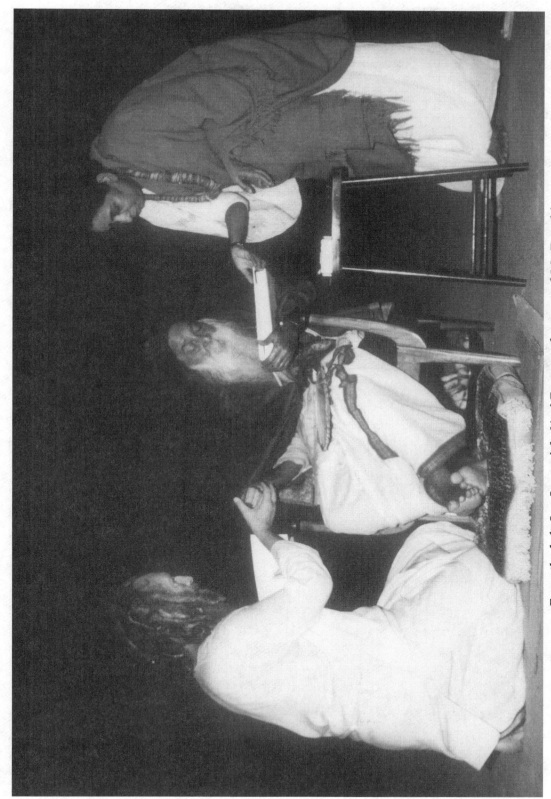

From the left: Lee Lozowick, Yogi Ramsuratkumar and Ma Devaki
in the temple during darshan on the Yogi Ramsuratkumar Ashram, November 1999.

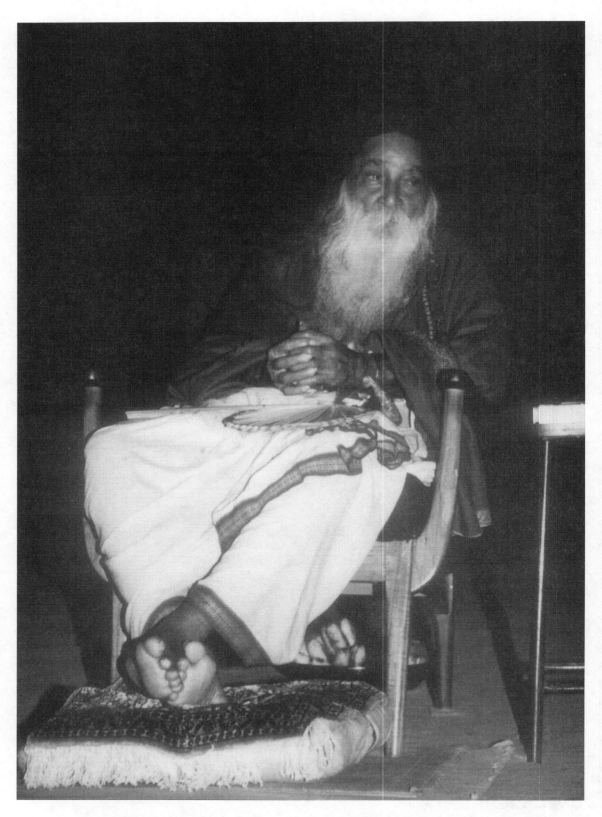

Yogi Ramsuratkumar in the temple during darshan, November 1999.

July 2, 1999
La Ferme de Jutreau

Shri arrived in the early hours this morning, having just driven four hours from the Charles de Gaulle Airport in Paris. At seven a.m. they were sitting in the hall with everyone for meditation. They sat close to Lee and enjoyed his company during breakfast and lunch, and by two in the afternoon they were gone again, heading out for their first three gigs of a six week tour, with twenty-seven gigs in France, Germany and Switzerland. Lee and a few of his students would be joining them for two weeks of that tour after Guru Purnima.

Lee said, "It's going to be a great tour!" and "We're going to Hauteville with some weight this year!" referring to all his students that would be going to Hauteville in a few days with him, many of them senior students. He seemed especially jazzed about the Shri tour and the Hauteville trip, which comprise a chunk of the summer. In between, Guru Purnima will be held on the ashram with close to one hundred people in attendance and five Shri gigs scheduled—one every night of the Celebration—in nearby towns, so that the gigs will be a very big part of the Celebration schedule. The day after the Celebration Lee will leave to go on tour with Shri for two weeks.

In the late afternoon Lee was sitting at his desk reading Charles Bukowski, a writer for whom Lee has a particular passion. In the midst of writing about the Paris public talk, I stopped and asked Lee a question. "Was there anything in particular that happened at the book table at the Paris talk, anything that stood out to you?" With an empty, dispassionate look in his wide blue eyes, he said, "No, nothing," giving a noncommital shrug. Then in a slightly irritated tone he added, "I shouldn't be asked any questions when I'm reading Bukowski because it gives all my answers a certain flavor." Hmm. A nihilistic flavor, perhaps. But no, that wasn't really it. It was more like the flavor of *shunyata*—if *shunyata* (emptiness) can be said to have a flavor, which it can't. So it is not even a flavor, but gone beyond all qualities.

Chris came in with a letter from Joanne in Arizona. She was describing the final LGB gig—there would be no more gigs scheduled for them. She read an excerpt of the letter to Lee:

> The last liars, gods & beggars gig was a sweet night. They were playing outside of a library in Mesa—in a kind of enclosure with a cement floor, a wall behind them and ribbons of cement overhead, and then terraced grassy areas leading up from the stage. It was a hot summer evening, over one hundred degrees, but the area had lots of trees and shade from the setting sun. As the band was setting up, there were families with children setting out blankets and picnic suppers, middle-aged folks on lawn chairs, dogs chasing balls and children running around on the grass. The band had invited wives and mates to come down, so we sat on a blanket and played bridge while the band set up. The band felt softer than I can ever remember, but ready to play some hot music.
>
> All that cement made for great acoustics—the drums were deep and full, and the sound system they provided was great. The band was relaxed and easy and having a good time, enjoying the crowd and really in relationship with them. There was warm applause after each song. We finally got up and started dancing during "I Love You" and the crowd seemed

to enjoy that too. One woman came up and took our picture. The last song was "Just a Woman" and as Doug and Stan began the powerful guitar work that builds to the end of the song, Everett moved back by the drums and left the two of them up front. It was very generous of him, and watching Stan and Doug there, two brothers in the music who had shared twelve years in this experiment that was now coming to a close, playing this song that they've probably performed more than any other . . . it was a poignant moment. Afterward they stood with their arms around each other, and it felt like they had found a place of resolve with it all.

At the end of the reading Lee said nothing, just as he had said nothing when another excerpt was read to him earlier today in a letter from Kate, who wrote about the LGB gig before that one, saying, "We went to the LGB gig in Sedona on Friday and it was out of this world. Justin was in rare form and it felt like everyone was really giving it all they had. We stumbled out of there feeling very 'knockered.' No, really—we were totally blissed out . . . ." All this news of the band hinted that something was in the air about liars, gods & beggars.

The office was quiet for a minute or two, while Lee returned to his reading of *Living on Luck*, then he suddenly broke the silence, saying, "I have to read Bukowski periodically so I don't get too mushy in my teaching style." He smiled.

"You really think there's a danger in that?" Jane asked, being facetious.

"I don't know . . . but it's better to take precautions!" was Lee's response as he walked briskly out of the room. He came back a few minutes later, sat down and picked up the Bukowski book again, then read out loud to anyone who might be listening, "The mercy of death is like flowers . . ." The line was part of a drawing by Charles Bukowski on the back cover of the book.

"Even this guy's throwaways are inspiring!" Lee shook his head. "He was a jewel. I'd like to read every one of his books someday. But I've read so many, I keep forgetting which ones I've read, so I don't know which ones to get because I don't know what I've already read."

Someone came into the office and asked Lee, "Will you play bridge tonight?"

"I'll play the new LGB album first, then I'll play bridge."

So that was it . . . LGB had been working on their last album for the past few months and had just finished it. Shri had brought the master cassette over to deliver to Lee when they arrived in the middle of the night. This would be the last LGB album—the last of thirteen. There was a high feeling of anticipation for this album. The musicians kept saying that it was the best LGB album yet, and Lee was looking forward to hearing it for the first time.

Over dinner he announced that we would listen to the album before bridge, "At a quarter to seven in the *saloon*," he joked, playing off the way he usually says it—"We will gather in the *salon*," or "*dans le salon*" at such and such time. Minutes later about twelve people sat around the *salon* to listen while the music was piped into the kitchen where the clean-up crew was hard at work.

"Turn it up—louder. No, louder," Lee said as the first song rang out. Clint turned it up more and adjusted the bass.

"It's a tribute to LGB," Lee added, and settled back into his chair.

By the second or third song a bittersweet feeling invoked by the beauty of the music and the fact that this was the end of LGB was so palpable in the space that even Lee acknowledged it, saying with an ironic smile, "We're going to miss hearing those boys!" The reality that they would never play together again, that an entire epoch with Lee was over, sank in a little deeper. The richness and wonder of the music, combined with the truth that impermanence is the way of all things and attachment begets suffering, brought every nuance of the music into a sharp point of diamond-like clarity.

The music spoke for itself. Each song was a complete world and communication, invoking its own mood, carrying its own message and transmission. The impact of the album was stunning. The shakti power in the music swelled and expanded in the space, lifting it up, pushing on the heart and moving the bones and joints to each varied and complex rhythm and melody. The songs were a Baul celebration of natural life as it is and covered the gamut of the human experience—love, sorrow, gripping and sometimes horrid insights into the nature of illusion, human cruelty or suffering. Sometimes they lifted the listener to heights of supernal beauty. As the songs touched on and evoked these dimensions of life they were glimpsed through the poet's context of Enlightened Duality.

There was sadness riding just behind the ecstasy of this immersion in the music, empowered and amped up high as it was with Lee sitting and listening to it. He has a way of making everything superconscious, or radiantly alive, whether it is listening to his music or sitting with him at the movies. Lee's play on words at dinner seemed to be proving itself as reality—it was Lee's saloon all right, and he was pouring the whiskey. Everything that the experience of LGB and the music itself had meant to Lee's students was in the music.

At one point after listening to "The Places I Haunt," one of the songs that Doug had composed, Lee commented, "Someone once said that Doug was the secret weapon of LGB." Doug has always composed to lyrics that dug into the underworld. He had an uncanny knack for sensing into Lee's words—his most whimsical, his most outrageous statements of crazy wisdom, and some of his darkest, most disturbing commentaries on the human condition—and then capturing them musically in ways that could be spinechilling or stunning in its effect. Hammered or pummeled is another way to describe the effect.

LGB as a secret weapon was not unlike the *phurba* held in the hands of Vajrakilaya, the *thangka* hanging above Lee's desk in the next room. That was exactly one of the functions that LGB has served in Lee's work—the magical dagger, the sharp blade held in the hands of the guru which destroys the knots above and below the heart. It is comparable to the power of the music to get into the body, into the viscera and blood and bone and into the subtle vibrational bodies. Music of this kind carries the power to dissolve knots in the *nadis* (subtle energy channels) so that the energy can run freely.

Lee seemed absorbed in the music. He was as usual, poised and straightforward, but there was a gleam of inspiration in his eyes that hadn't been there for the past few days. His eyes shone out of his face like two glowing sapphires, framed by the grizzled, matted hair that hung at his shoulders. Who is this enigma? How is it that this extraordinary man, a celebrated spiritual teacher now well into the latter years of his middle age and yet unquestionably still very much in his prime, is so taken by the transformative power of rock & roll and the blues? He has created an incredible legacy of dharma poetry embedded in contemporary American music in the form of lyrics sung to songs of great beauty and complexity. This dharma legacy which he leaves to the world is already rich beyond the dreams of most artists—thirteen albums by liars, god & beggars and five by Shri, who successfully tours Europe every summer. And now there is the new band, Attila the Hunza, just beginning.

At dinner Lee had talked about a record promoter who specializes in rock and pop and who was interested in Shri's material. He said, "LGB is right down their alley. Wouldn't it be something if this last album was the one that finally attracted the attention of a recording company! If they really spark on it maybe they'll want the band to go on tour and we can send them Attila the Hunza!" This was the catalyst for a series of jokes and much laughter from Lee's students who sat around him. "Yes, we can say we've gotten younger—the elixir of life, a testimony to the alchemy of the music," and "We said the music was transformational—now this is the proof!" and so on and on.

The music and the fact of traveling with Lee in the stark and often sweet crucible of band sadhana has been of tremendous importance in the sadhana of Lee's students because the music *is* transformational. Lee has used everything surrounding the band—the constant stream of creative activity and hard work, the traveling, the discomfort and sacrifice, the demand to work as a team in the heat of supercharged egos in conflict, the impulses to competition and pride—as fuel for the process of alchemical transformation. But the bottom line has been the music—the power of Lee's dharma poetry as lyrics, brought to life by the incredible musical compositions of Lee's students and charged with the blessing power of Yogi Ramsuratkumar. The result of that marriage has made the teaching real and alive in the body in a way that nothing else has. It has been nothing less than the teaching, penetrating and pounding our bodies on a regular basis. Because of that, the subsiding of the LGB phenomenon back into the emptiness from which it came is of natural impact to those who have been immersed in the sound and fury of the band for twelve years. It is through this medium that Lee has communicated an incredible wealth of instruction that applies in every domain of spiritual life on the tantric path. These instructions cover relationship (both in the psychological labyrinth which must be faced with clarity and the mystical possibilities), sexual yoga, the dharma of true human culture, the nature of suffering, impermanence, nonduality and emptiness. If the songs were reviewed one by one, spanning years of creative work, all of this could be found, encoded and alive, waiting to be accessed and used.

Intimate spaces with the guru like this one tonight are imbued with an unspoken potency, and hearing the last music of liars, gods & beggars stirred the waters of the unconscious in a very strong way. There was a sense of awe and finality, or death, in the air. Someone asked Lee what the name of the album would be. "Transfestite," he said with an impish glint in his eyes. "Transvestite?" someone asked. "No—*Transfestite*." Laughter broke out and bounced gaily around the room. Another one of Lee's zany titles with a teaching hidden in it—if you can get it. There are no guarantees you're right and Lee won't say, "Yes it means this or that." Just "Transfestite." Get what you can and let the rest lie as mystery.

July 4, 1999
Hauteville

Lee and his gang arrived at Hauteville after an eight-hour drive, including the usual road picnic. As soon as Lee drove onto the ashram grounds and up the hill to the home of Daniel and Maryse Morin where Lee and his family stay each year, the familiar beauty of this place came into view. Gardens bloomed in profusion in front of the residences on either side of the gravel lane. The sky was blue and the air hot. A small group of Arnaud's disciples stood waiting for Lee in a cluster under the huge sycamore tree by the house. Lee pulled into the driveway and immediately jumped out of the van. His students climbed out of the two vehicles and walked around the vans to catch up with him.

Peals of laughter came drifting up the hill from Arnaud's students. Wondering what they were laughing about, I suddenly glimpsed Arnaud walking briskly up the road toward Lee wearing a black wig—long black hair twisted into many small braids, each with beads at the end. As Arnaud and Lee grasped each other in a fierce bear hug, Arnaud flicked his black braids back while lifting one of Lee's dreadlocks in his fingers. His face was opened in a huge smile of pure mirth and fun. Everyone laughed in delight; to see Arnaud in this black wig was an unforgettable sight. Arnaud pulled the wig off his head and stood with Lee for a moment under the tall trees with their disciples laughing and smiling around them. The delight and humor and easeful communion of this reunion between friends turned out to be the predominate mood of the week at Hauteville.

Lee and Arnaud walked into the house and sat down together on the small couch. They spoke together very briefly of Lee's eight-hour drive down from La Ferme de Jutreau, then Arnaud asked, "Don't you ever get tired?"

"Not right now," Lee replied. They fell into an almost blank silence, each of them completely at home, at ease in each other's silence, the silence reverberating in an expanding sense of emptiness. They sat together in this silence with an innocence and immediacy that communicated volumes as they looked around the room, watched the children or the comings and goings of adults bringing in luggage and bags. When asked if they wanted water, Arnaud and Lee both said yes. It was the only word that was spoken by either for a long period of time. It struck me that they were demonstrating in that moment the communion of saints, which is inherently empty, but also how completely full, simple, easy and natural this pure silence is between those who share a perfect understanding.

Soon Veronique Desjardins came in with copies of the schedule for the week. As she handed it to Lee for his approval she said, "Exactly as last year, unless you would like a change."

Looking it over briefly Lee said, "No, this is perfect."

Veronique said that when Arnaud had his breakfast this morning she said to him laughingly, tongue in cheek, "Eat, eat—enjoy! It's your last breakfast for a week!" She explained that breakfast is a meal that Arnaud particularly likes. Some years ago when Lee was visiting Hauteville it came out during the planning of the schedule that Lee's preference for seminars was to have only two meals a day—either brunch or lunch, and a dinner meal—rather than three meals a day. Two meals a day is the schedule that Lee follows during seminars and Celebrations on his own ashrams. This is basically because it gives people an opportunity to work in relationship to food, to confront scarcity, greed, fear, or other primal emotions that arise when food is not available when they are habitually accustomed to getting it. And it frees up the schedule for more important things like dharma talks and guru *seva*. When Arnaud and Veronique realized that Lee was not eating breakfast himself and that this was his preference for his seminars, they changed the Hauteville schedule for the week of Lee's seminars. Arnaud too gives up his breakfast during that week, along with everyone else. After a few more remarks about the schedule Arnaud and Veronique left. Lee would rejoin them in three hours for dinner at their apartment on the ashram.

Right away Lee said, "Does anybody want to play bridge?" We gathered over the kitchen table and played bridge for over two hours. At one point as the games and rubbers whisked by at a fast pace, Lee winning almost all of them in sweeping victories,

Chris came in and commented on the interchange in which Arnaud had said to Lee, "Don't you ever get tired?" Now Lee joked, "Yes, he should have seen me sleeping on the way down here!" Everyone laughed; it was funny because Lee was driving the entire way.

At seven o'clock Lee and his group walked the short distance to Arnaud and Veronique's apartment for dinner, past gardens and trees with the beautiful green mountains of Ardeche rising all around. The quiet, peaceful ashram, with its large peach orchard and chateau—the main building—were visible as we walked. *Très belle.* Lee and Arnaud took seats on a couch where their disciples gathered around them as hors d'oeuvres were served. It has become a ritual that Lee and his students are hosted on their first night at Hauteville at Arnaud's home on the ashram. Tonight the mood was one of warm camaraderie. Many of Arnaud's senior disciples were present, and the mood of joyful reunion was very strong. I noticed in particular how radiant and relaxed many of Arnaud's disciples were, what a strong sense of intention permeated everything.

The ease with which the two groups mingled, in spite of language differences, marked the friendship that has developed over the years. Lee first met Arnaud in 1992, and has visited him at his ashram each year since then, giving teachings to Arnaud's students during each visit. When Arnaud and his disciples moved from Font d'Isière, the former ashram, to Hauteville in 1994, Lee's annual one-week seminar became more or less an established aspect of the relationship between the two masters.

It is an interesting relationship—the American desert Bauls and the elegant and pristine French nondualists. The Americans appear a little scruffy and raw perhaps, not entirely lacking in elegance and education, but with a bit of a loose, back porch, gritty edge. Lee's students tend to have a certain gypsy-like quality. They come spilling out of the vehicles hot and disheveled from hours of traveling in the rough and tumble Renault vans, toting many assorted bags, duffels and suitcases, cardboard boxes full of books and tapes that Lee will sell, picnic gear and ice chests. The kids laugh and yell happily, glad to be back at Hauteville.

Most of Lee's crew are seasoned travelers, practitioners of a tantric path with a complex labyrinth of sadhana and a spiritual bond with their guru so strong it appears like an unbreakable radiance if one looks with clear eyes. The French disciples are steeped in the tradition and in the adamantine precepts of nonduality and rooted in the ancestral soil of France. This is brought to a powerful focus through hundreds of years of European culture, refinement, elegance, heights of intellectual brilliance and a profound sense of protocol. Arnaud's years on the path, the elegance and simplicity of his teaching and his association with many saints of the highest caliber saturate the atmosphere of the ashram. The refinement and dignity and wisdom of the French seems to be a good match for the spontaneity and devotion and sheer pluck of the Hohm Community.

Despite such differences the two groups get along very well. The French have opened their very generous arms to Lee and his students and a sense of commonality has developed between the two schools, primarily because both schools rest firmly on the foundation of their respective lineages, as both teachers are first and foremost obedient disciples of their own gurus. Lee and Arnaud are also fierce defenders of dharma; they share in common the task of bringing the traditional dharma of the East into the West and translating it into immediately useful terms.

In this way both schools have profound roots in Mother India. One lineage is from a Beggar and the other is from a Buddha. Not that Arnaud's guru, Swami Prajnanpad, was a Buddhist—he was not. Like Yogi Ramsuratkumar, he was a Hindu. But seeing Arnaud and Lee together the images of the Buddha and the Beggar spring up quite naturally—a very compatible pair, and quite exact in mood to when the Shankaracharya of Kanchipuram, in south India, is visiting with Yogi Ramsuratkumar. And so it could be said that the relationship between Arnaud and Lee is the result of the profound maturity of these two remarkable teachers, who carry the blessing power of their respective lineages: Arnaud Desjardins, whose master was a paragon of diamond-like clarity, Swami Prajnanpad, and Lee Lozowick, whose master is the "dirty Beggar," the bad poet's "Tiger in Rags," Yogi Ramsuratkumar.

July 5, 1999
Hauteville

Close to one hundred fifty people sat on pillows on the floor of the large, spacious meeting hall on the ashram of Arnaud Desjardins. The men sat on the right side of the room, the women on the left, all facing the raised dais at the front of the room. When the door to the left opened and Arnaud and Lee walked into the room with their escorts, Gilles and Emmanuel, everyone stood. Once the two teachers were seated, the group as a whole bowed, kneeling and touching foreheads to the floor, then stood again in the gesture of *namasté* (salutation of respect), with palms pressed together chest high, before finally taking their seats. Arnaud and Lee completed the ritual invocation of the teaching space by bowing, heads touching the edge of the dais, to the disciples. It is a formal ritual of mutual respect between teacher and disciple that is enacted at the beginning of every meeting at Hauteville, and which lends great dignity to the gathering.

Arnaud's brown eyes sparkled deeply and a child-like radiance beamed from his sublime countenance. His sitting posture transmits the dharma in a remarkable way. Perhaps it is a reflection of his years of training with Taisen Deshimaru, the well-known Japanese Zen master who taught in France for many years and who Arnaud filmed. Although Lee would do all verbal teaching for the week ahead, it seemed that Arnaud was the source of the life of this space, and Lee the emissary, the messenger.

Sitting on a zafu on the floor below the dais where Arnaud and Lee were seated, Gilles Farcet sat translating. Both Lee and Arnaud wore the characteristic off-white or light beige shawl that Arnaud and all of his students wear to the meetings and meditations on the ashram. The group sat respectfully waiting for the meeting to begin. Arnaud said, "I present Lee Lozowick to you, so that you may pose your questions."

The morning session was unusually strong for a first session. People dove right in with questions, and Lee was like a racehorse who had just heard the gun go off and bolted out at the starting line. He took off at a proud, thundering gallop that he maintained throughout the session, effortlessly weaving his own *sahajiya* perspective into the language and teaching that has been passed down from Swami Prajnanpad to Arnaud Desjardins.

The first question was, "What is it to be a real woman?"

Lee laughed and said, "Is there such a thing?" He laughed again, "I'm not a woman—how would I know! Ask a woman." His laughter had a quality of madness to it as it bounced around the space. "You know, if you ask a man what a real woman is he will tell you whatever his particular flavor of woman is, and that has nothing to do with reality. It's a good question, but a better question might be, 'What is it to be a real disciple?'" He laughed some more, as if he found everything about this question tremendously amusing. "I mean, men and women are fine—'love makes the world go round,' or however that old song goes. But really in the ultimate sense of things none of us are here, or should be here, to find out about who we are as men and women, but who we are as disciples."

She said, "I was in my mind . . ."

Lee interjected, "I know you were in your mind and that's what we're talking about!"

She protested, "What I meant was is a real woman a real disciple?"

Lee said, "No, a real disciple is a real woman!" He chuckled again. "Sometimes a real woman isn't a disciple at all. She is just a real woman. Which is—yum, yum!—better than soufflé or gâteau, better for you, too! There's no cholesterol in a real woman! You can eat all you want, and the only problem you may suffer is a heart attack. But what a way to go, eh?" He laughed harder. He was cracking himself up.

"So, the thing is that if you become a true disciple, then everything sorts itself out. Essence or spirit or soul always seeks balance or harmony in relationship to whatever the optimal expression of the Divine is in that moment. Being a real woman or a real man is a function of harmony and balance. We already are men and women, so we don't have to create something that is already essentially true of us. All we have to do is allow whatever disharmony there is—which we could call neurosis or a lack of integration between mind, emotions and body—to relax and naturally seek harmony and balance. Trying to create something in the face of disharmony is trying to build something on a foundation that is inherently unreliable or not strong. If we allow disharmony to simply stop, what shows up in the space that is left is real femininity or masculinity. My experience is that you don't get there by defining real femininity or real masculinity. You allow essence to simply manifest as it most naturally is. So the real question is, 'What is a true disciple?'

"There seems to be a theme to each of my summers here in France, and the theme this year seems to be that essence or spirit seeks balance and harmony naturally, in relationship to whatever is most optimal in terms of the Divine in any given moment. It doesn't mean that harmony is going to be peace in every moment, because sometimes what is needed is discomfort or crisis. But as Arnaud said in meditation this morning, if there is a lack of peace you observe this and accept this lack of peace *peacefully*. So harmony and balance has to do with your ability to accept what is, as it is, from the position of eternality and nonduality. It doesn't have to do with the external form of things which sometimes is high, sometimes low, sometimes light, sometimes dark. That's life. So, that should be the approach."

Another woman questioned, "Could you go deeper into this notion of being a disciple as it is related to something I feel often, which is a rebellious spirit? The intensity of this rebellious spirit is so great sometimes that the disciple has difficulty finding something to rely on, a foundation . . ."

"What do you do when it is so strong? How do you handle it?" Lee asked.

"I see that there is some emotion coming up which makes me want to reject everything and go away, leave the path," she answered.

"Well, what would you do if you did leave the path? Do you have a fantasy, 'If only I could leave the path, at last I could such and such'?"

"No, if I left the path I would leave the world of human beings," the woman replied.

"So, there is no concern. It sounds like you are handling it fine. As long as we don't think we have the option to leave the path—that's the important thing. Maybe to handle this rebelliousness you should get a big canvas and lie it on the floor and cover yourself in paint and roll around on it! And then you could sell it for one hundred thousand francs! You could advertise yourself, 'The artist who creates works of passion and rebellion!' Because most art is such trash, anyway, how bad could it be? You could become very famous and rich, and then you would be a good representative of the path. Everybody would say, 'What does someone as rich and famous and good-looking as you need the path for?' And then you could represent the necessity of the path.

"Americans are such sheep. If a really rich, famous, good-looking sheep does something, then everyone else just sort of follows along, 'Baahhh, baaahhhh!' All these Tibetan Buddhists were just considered another crazy sect until Richard Gere and others came forward publicly and demonstrated their commitment to Buddhism. Now everybody accepts it just like Christianity.

"Who are those who are most successful on the path anyway, but those who are most rebellious? To say yes to life, to accept what is as it is, in principle sounds very common sense, ordinary and obvious. But in fact to actually live that truth is an act of rebellion because you have to revolt against everything that defines you and controls you and implicates you in your psychological and egoic dynamics. Only a radical break with what we imagine reality to be can give us a glimpse of what Reality *is*."

A man asked, "What is masculine culture?"

Lee laughed, "Well, that's a good question, but a better question would be, 'What is disciple culture?' " Still laughing, Lee continued, "In my community we have men's culture and women's culture—nobody in those cultures knows what they are! The men get together and they say, 'What is men's culture?' and they all look around and somebody says, 'Let's go dig a hole together, or play football.' So the men sort of feel good when they are grunting and sweating with one another. And women—I don't know what the women do when they get together. The women talk about the men. 'What are we going to do for our women's culture meeting today?' 'Well, I have a problem with my husband and I want to talk about it.' I don't think they have entirely discovered it as yet." Laughter kept erupting from Lee, interspersed between his words.

"It is a good question. I am not laughing at the question, I'm just laughing at us, human beings, men and women." He laughed again. "Why couldn't we have been born like amoebas, no sex? Do whatever you want to do—you want to be a man, be a man. If you want to be a woman, be a woman. Cool! We think that amoebas are low, but they are probably a higher level of evolution. Wow! Think how great that would be—then the only mess on the sheets is your own! I like it when the mess on the sheets is somebody else's. Then if I need an early morning snack, I can chew on the sheets!" A few tentative giggles sounded through the room; Lee students laughed heartily. Gilles laughed and put his hand up to his face, turning slightly red. Most of the group was very serious and silent. Arnaud smiled, crinkled his nose and shook his head back and forth as if to say, "Amazing!" At this point Lee was laughing so hard that he had to stop and wipe his eyes.

"I didn't really mean that. I just wanted to see Gilles laugh, because, you know how it is—if you get up at three in the morning and you are hungry, and you get out of bed and go to the kitchen, and you go back to bed and your wife says, 'I'm not tired anymore,' you know what that means!"

For the most part people were still very somber, despite Lee's attempts to loosen everyone up. Lee, however, seemed to be enjoying the whole show immensely. Laughter shook his whole body. He wiped his eyes again. He forged ahead with his comedy routine, undaunted. "You know, when you are nineteen, great! You wake her up, 'Honey!

Wake up!' And the woman says, 'Not again!' You know? Is anybody relating to this or am I alone in this?" Lee wiped his eyes again as his body shook with silent laughter.

Still chuckling and wiping his eyes, he continued, "This has nothing to do with anything, but it's fun to talk about! It's good to laugh once in awhile, which reminds me of a small joke. This little turtle climbs up this tree all the way up to the top, and when he gets to the top of the tree, he jumps off the tree moving his little legs." Lee demonstrated, flapping and waving his hands. Lee finished the joke to a few scant laughs in the audience, while most were silent.

"This is the funniest audience I ever had here at Hauteville. You guys are really funny! So—men's culture," he said, collecting himself into a linear train of thought. He seemed to be steering back on track, away from the crazy hilarity of moments before. I got the sense that it was probably a relief to a number of people in the room, especially those who weren't quite used to Lee's style yet.

"We're still trying to figure it out, but there seems to be some evidence—and this is not conclusive yet—that something we need as men and women is more easily found in the company of our own gender. Whether that is because when we are in mixed company we are more distracted and concerned with our vanity and appearing good or not, well, that is to be discovered. The primary focus of gender culture in our community is good discipleship. The whole purpose of gender culture is to eliminate obstacles to good discipleship, not to become more manly or womanly. That is the only reason we have made such a distinction. Any conversation about men's culture or women's culture should have this as its focus. There are real life considerations that we discuss within the cultures— sex, children, relationship, work. But the primary purpose is to be a better disciple. If we become good disciples then who we are as men and women takes care of itself.

"A good disciple is someone who is obedient to the *spirit* of the master's word—not to a the letter of the law of a bunch of commandments. Also, there is a description of a good disciple that has to do with what *not* to do. In meditation this morning Arnaud was talking about serenity, equanimity in the face of all phenomena. We tend to want to suppress negative manifestations and dramatize positive manifestations. If we feel positive, or joyful, we want to laugh and really get into it, to show how happy we are. But if we are enraged or full of jealousy, we want to act very cool, we don't want people to see how out of control we are. Except maybe our partner, if we are jealous. We say, 'I've sacrificed my life for you, I could have been a dancer and all I did was marry you, you prick! I could have been . . . and I gave it all up for you. And what do you do? You sleep with my sister, you son of a bitch, and to add insult to injury, my older sister! If it was my younger sister, at least I'd understand that I'm getting older and not as beautiful as I used to be and she is just so beautiful, but my older sister—oh, how could you!' "

Lee was giving the acid bath to contemporary female psychology. It was cutting close to the bone in one way or another. Either the shoe fit in some way, in which case one had to wear it, or it didn't. The only way to know that the shoe didn't fit was if one was neither attracted nor repelled by Lee's indictments. The women in the room sat listening quietly. No one protested.

"We want to look at all arising emotions the same way, 'Such and such is arising, now something else is arising,' because if any of us looks at our lives over a period of time, even a matter of weeks, let alone years, we see that things come and go. Dark moods come and go, bright moods come and go. Things that we take very seriously one morning, a week later we have completely forgotten them. If we can get a sense of that, the constant volatility and movement of form, of externals, then we also get a sense of that which is changeless and formless—that point of absolute stillness, balance, harmony. That is the point that is never out of harmony because it is always one with *what is*.

"What creates disharmony is separating that which is not separate. That separation can only take place in the mind, because in reality we cannot separate that which is not separate. The Buddhists use the words, 'Buddha mind,' for Reality, which means seeing things as they are and accepting them, because the mind, isolated from the rest of the body, can *see* things as they are, but mind cannot *accept* things as they are. The mind creates separation. When we are measuring what is, against what was or could be, of course there is disharmony.

"We tend to be always measuring everything we are perceiving. We read a book by Dostoyevsky or a poem by Baudelaire and we say, 'Oh, this poem isn't bad but it's not as good as his earlier work.' Or we look at Picasso in one of his periods and we compare it with his blue period, or his cubist period. When we do that we miss what it *is*. To really experience life fully is not a matter of what isn't; it's a matter of what *is*. Even if we take a sip of wine and say, 'This wine is terrible, it's not as good as the one I had last night,' we are measuring our experience against what was or could be.

"When we are measuring reality against what was or what could be, we have to be creating disharmony. Even when we are agreeing with something, that agreeing implies disagreement with anything that is not part of the agreement. We have to not just see what is, but accept what is, as it is. 'As it is' is an important part of the equation. I know some of you in this room think you are practicing accepting what is, as it is. But, you may be *seeing* what is, but you are not *accepting* what is.

"Part of having total acceptance is having no complaint, no judgement. 'Well, it's bad,' we say to ourselves, as we get older and older. As we get older, as some of you know, little things start to happen, the back isn't as strong, there's an ache, and some of us can't see quite as well, or hear quite as well, and there is nothing we can do about certain things. We think because we recognize that there is nothing we can do about it, that we are accepting it. Not necessarily. To accept what is as it is by definition means there is equanimity. It doesn't mean that things can't change. It means we accept things just as they are.

"As any of you know who have done 'lyings,' or any form of really demanding Enquiry into who you are at unconscious levels, how many of us—and there are exceptions—are willing to alter our perceptions unless we feel that we are backed in a corner and that is the only way out? This is one of the really perverse characteristics of human beings; even if certain characteristics sustain great suffering, we won't alter our way of seeing things. Like jealousy, for example. Jealousy also has it's beauty . . . We get to be the tragic hero of our own miserable drama! But jealousy is also terribly painful. We can't eat, we can't sleep, our mind goes wild, our hearts are broken. Even so, we will not change our viewpoint unless we have to, unless we are in a corner and there is no way out, except to sacrifice jealousy for equanimity.

"If you think about it with your mind, it is really bizarre—who would want to live in such a way? I would guess that everyone in this room has had moments, if not extended periods, of real serenity, real equanimity. It is so free. It's so light. It's amazing, wonderful, miraculous, marvelous. But we won't accept what is as it is. We fight and fight and fight to prove the validity of our subjective viewpoint."

Lee told the story that Deben Bhattacharya had told him about recording Nabanidas

Baul for the first time. When Deben played the music back, even though Nabanidas had never seen or heard recording equipment before and didn't believe it was possible at first, he accepted it totally. He said, "Come to my village and I will play for you."

Lee continued, "Nabanidas just accepted it. So, to see what is, does not imply that we have accepted it as it is. And to accept what is means *as* it is, here and now. Not that it could be different if circumstances were different. Sometimes we actually say things like that—'If only such and such had happened, things would be different.' That's a very dangerous way to think. It totally separates us from what is. How could anything be different than what is? Okay, so that's in response to men's culture."

In answer to the next question Lee said, "I think most of us would agree that rape, murder, embezzlement, blackmail, kidnapping are all things that are unacceptable. At the same time, those things are very common in the world. So part of what is, here and now, is not just what is in relationship to our exclusive internal presence, but what is, as it is, here and now, everywhere. As much as any of us would like to see more peace and harmony in the world, what is in every given moment does include, in various areas of the world, a tremendous amount of war, violence, cruelty, genocide and so on.

"The first thing is for us to not add to the disharmony in the world, and the second thing is—and this is also my experience but it's subjective—since in the traditions there is no separation because all is one, any transformation in one element transforms the entire situation. If the transformation is cataclysmic, then the repercussions of that transformation become relatively evident. We can see that socially in terms of great movements. You know, where people like Jesus Christ or Socrates or Alexander the Great created vast transformation in the world during their lifetimes. If the transformation is discrete, then the evidence may not be as clear, but in fact there is an influence on the entire system. When any given individual has any kind of transformational experience, even temporary, it has an effect in the whole system. Every mystical experience, even if it doesn't stick and it doesn't alter the person and is just momentary, has an effect, although under those circumstances the effect is very minor, and we could probably not trace the results of the effect.

"Then there is a transformation that is permanent. For example, if I can speak for Arnaud for a minute, even though Arnaud's residency in the path seemed to have been pretty concrete and reliable, in some of his final experiences Swami Prajnanpad pushed him from no to yes. Maybe because of that trustworthiness, at the end of his sadhana his teacher, Swami Prajnanpad, could push him a little bit, could lean on him a little bit. Arnaud would probably agree with this because this is true of my master, and I know that if you had any sense in your head, you would be saying this about Arnaud, that all our masters ever do is push us a *little* bit. If our masters really pushed—you know, really leaned on us—none of us could stand it. We'd break on the spot. Every time I think Yogi Ramsuratkumar is being tough with me, I think about how tough He could be, and I say, 'Boy, this is nothing.'

"You go downstairs and see a picture of Swami Prajnanpad, and he looks like the most beautiful, innocent character. You look at Swami Prajnanpad or Yogi Ramsuratkumar and think, 'This guy is only kind and generous.' But these guys are dangerous! These guys are killers! People like that, they can just snuff you out in a minute.

"When I'm feeling good and I'm relaxed I say, 'Well, there's a spectrum, and people have some no and they have yes and okay, everything's fine. But when I'm feeling a little sharper I look at things and I say, 'There's no spectrum—it's yes or no. So, any no, even a tiny little bit of insignificant no, can grow and overwhelm the yes. Even when we are reliable on the path, a no is a no. When Swami Prajnanpad pushed Arnaud into a yes, he did *push* him. Some of us like to think that our masters can just say, 'Well I'm going to offer you this opportunity now,' and we would be mature enough to say 'Yes, I'm going to take this opportunity.' But we have to be put into the iron lady," Lee chuckled to himself, "the iron maiden—you know, that torture thing they had in the Middle Ages. We imagine that we would just say yes. To say yes is so elevating, it's so graceful, it's so dignified, it's so joyous.

"But we go through life saying, 'No, no, no.' Often it's unconscious. Sometimes we're saying yes with our mouths but we're not saying yes with our beings. Once Arnaud said yes, that was it. It was a yes then and it is a yes in every moment. With that kind of transformation the effects are much more visible.

"There are inner effects and outer effects, and the outer effects are obvious. This magnificent ashram, the sanctity of it that can be felt, and all the people who read Arnaud's books and study his work and so on, are all obvious effects. There are also effects in the field, in the system. Every time someone enters into this kind of transformation, it makes it one little bit easier for everybody else.

"Something else Arnaud said this morning in meditation was, 'Ego can't observe ego.' If ego is observing ego, then what do you get? Nothing. You're just in a circular process and nothing ever happens. Equanimity in relationship to arising phenomena is not ego. Ego itself has certain periods of relative quiet, but that's not equanimity. That is simply ego being quiet now, ego being calm now. But that's not *calm*. So, in one sense we can't actually do anything. We are carried on the graceful wings of those who have gone before us. Oh, that's a nice turn of a phrase!" Lee chuckled.

"In one sense we literally *rely* on the transformation of others to give our transformational impetus fuel. At the same time there are mechanics to this process. Without the influence of those who have gone before us, the mechanics can only be relatively effective, but combined with that influence the mechanics can be very, very important. In Zen even after someone has this transformation from no to yes they still continue to practice, they still continue to sit. Sometimes people ask, 'If you're enlightened, what do you keep practicing for?' Well, it's sort of like enlightenment goes on by itself, and it also has to be anchored in life. In Zen they don't practice in order to keep their satori in place as a mechanical act, they practice to honor the tradition, to bring dignity and respect to the tradition. And it is the personal values of honor, dignity and respect and their ongoing integral activity that sustain the enlightenment.

"One of the mechanisms of acceptance is to be willing to be ruthlessly self-honest. We have to have nothing to hide from ourselves. We hide certain things because we find those things difficult or unacceptable within ourselves. Often our lack of self-honesty is simply a function of our own perspective. It's not objective. It may be something fairly innocent, but even if it's something terrible, it has happened, it's there, it's part of our body of experience.

"Another important piece, which is in all of Arnaud's writings, is that we can't force anybody else to be any other way than the way they are. We can provide education, we can make certain circumstances, provide opportunities, but we can't make anyone be other than they are. How they are is how they are. One of the mechanics of acceptance is recognizing this concept of personal integrity, because we can't define another person's reality. Nobody can. Jesus couldn't. Buddha couldn't. So, we certainly aren't going to. We can't accept what is as it is, here and now, if we're busy trying to force other people into our mold. Even if it's a good mold, kindness and peace and so on."

After lunch the group reconvened in the meeting hall. It was hot and humid outside, and hot and sweaty under the shawls that everyone wore. The afternoon light came in through the large half-moon windows on either end of the hall, making a diffuse and soft effect in combination with the sultry air. One of the elements that would combine with the transmission of the two teachers to build the energy during the week was the bodily discomfort of sitting for hours every day on the floor, covered with a warm shawl in already hot weather. It reminded me of Yogi Ramsuratkumar and Devaki Ma, who wear wool shawls all year round to retain the body's heat.

The afternoon session started out slowly with a number of questions and built to a crescendo of sustained laughter and merriment as Lee went into full jester mode. In this way the formal coolness of the audience in the first session was completely melted in the warm laughter of the afternoon, adding another element of heat to the room. About twenty minutes into the talk a question was asked about seeing things and accepting them as they are. Lee responded, "Well, human beings function as if thought were everything, because the mind is vast and sophisticated and it's a great tool. It has the ability to comprehend amazing amounts of information. We come to believe as we grow from childhood to adulthood that if the mind understands something, then that's sufficient.

"Gurdjieff said the human being essentially functions with three primary centers: the thinking center, which is thought, analysis, logic, rationale and so on; the feeling center, which is about our reaction to things; and then the moving center or instinctual center. The instinctual center is about *what is*. If you're crossing the street and all of a sudden a truck or a car is coming at you, you leap out of its way, hopefully in time. And that instinctual response is prior to thought and prior to reaction to thought. So the thought is, 'Here comes a truck,' and the reaction to the thought is, 'Oh no, maybe it's going to hit me!' But the body just jumps out of the way. If you waited until you had assimilated the thought and the reaction, you would already be run over—'road kill,' as we say in English.

"One of Gurdjieff's intentions in terms of what he called the Work, was to unify the three centers. In this way when any one of those centers is the optimal center for any given circumstance, that center would be able to function unobstructed by the noise of the other centers. What typically happens in the average human being is that each center thinks that it's the controlling center of the whole organism and refuses to acknowledge the authority of the other centers. Each center thinks it can do everything, but it can't. One of the aspects of the Work is to let the center, whose job is a particular function, *do* its job. When the mind is trying to feel, or trying to move, it can't, so obviously there are going to be difficulties. Since linear information comes into the mind first before it goes into the feeling center or the instinctual center, what the mind tends to do is monopolize that information and keep it from the body. It uses that information to convince the body that mind knows how to feel, when in fact it doesn't.

"When we see *what is*, the mind convinces the part of us that is aware that it is *accepting* what is. One of our jobs is to be able to make this distinction. We make this distinction partly by not making distinctions, by accepting everything as it is instead of separating— 'This is good, this is bad, this I like, this I don't like. This I want, this I don't want.'

"For example, we meet someone that we haven't seen in a long time and instead of looking at them as they are now, we look at them as we knew them five years, ten years, twenty years ago. It's very disrespectful. There are people who were with Arnaud in India, and now Arnaud is here, and now they are wherever they are. If somebody says, 'Oh, did you read Arnaud's new book?' or something like that, they say, 'Oh, I knew him in India,' discounting him. There's no willingness to look at the way things are now. People who should know better, with pretensions to great wisdom and spirituality!" Lee laughed rather derisively.

"So, the Zen master would say, 'What was the face before you were born?' or 'Does a dog have Buddha nature?' and everybody had these pat responses. 'Does a dog have Buddha nature?' And the monk would go, 'Ruff, ruff, ruff.' " Lee barked like a dog.

"They would sit there feeling very full of themselves—'Ooh that was a good answer!' The Zen masters knew that the only way to break that person's blindness was to jump off their pillow and grab the person by the throat, and then they'd get it. They'd feel terror and they'd go to the bathroom in their pants and they'd say, 'Uh . . . maybe I'm not as enlightened as I thought I was.' "As he often does during Lee's discourses, Arnaud smiled and nodded at this comment with a hint of a gleam in his eye.

Lee continued, "Sometimes we come to the path completely sincere. We say, 'I want to work' and we mean it, as far as we know. But we don't know ourselves, so sometimes we step in a trap. Every school has a trap. In my school the trap is false holiness, because there is a very devotional mood. It's easy for people to feel that their practice is reliable just because they love the teacher in some kind of conventional, romantic way. That's not good enough.

"Often a great shock is required to get us to realize that we're really only seeing, not accepting. Sometimes life provides the shock. They've done research into alcoholism and drug addiction, and they say that the motive for quitting in the majority of cases is not because we see how much pain we're causing others. 'Oh my poor children, my poor wife, my poor husband. I need to stop.' It's not that. It's when we personally reach the bottom of our pit. It's when *our* suffering is great enough. We don't care about anybody else's suffering when we are an addict. Finally we say, 'I've got to stop.' Sometimes life just bears down on us, we suffer and suffer and finally we just go, 'Enough.' And when we say, 'Enough, I've suffered enough,' all of a sudden we start seeing ourselves in an entirely different way. All the things we didn't see before, there they are, clear as a sunny day in Prescott, Arizona.

"Chögyam Trungpa Rinpoche, one of my favorite Tibetans *tulkus* who has been dead for a while, ten years or twelve years, was giving a seminar once. He was talking about all the Buddhist hells, the *vajra* hells. When you're living in one of those hells it can be really bad. One of the hells is the hell of the hungry ghosts. The hungry ghosts are in the hell where one has an insatiable appetite and a gigantic mouth, but a tiny throat, so they are unable to swallow all but a tiny, tiny bit. There are people in this room who are living in that realm right now because they won't eat. They deny themselves. They won't enjoy themselves. 'Oh that's a nice chocolate mousse. I think I'll have just a little taste,' when they really want to take the whole thing and smash their face into it and gobble it down." Lee chuckled, as if he was working up to some mischief.

"It's very embarrassing sometimes to travel with my American students because they have no shame when it comes to food. Our hosts put food out on the table and the French guests have a nice little plate with a couple of leaves of lettuce, a couple of pieces of tomato and a slice of fish. The Americans have *big* plates, like a mountain of food!" Gilles started laughing in the middle of his translation. People were beginning to break up around the room. This must have hit the French, who have watched in astonishment for years while Lee's American students ate like vacuum cleaners at their tables.

"We were eating dinner at Arnaud and Veronique's apartment last night, and they were having ice cream for dessert. So we had a little ice cream and there was a little more left. Veronique came out with another little block of ice cream and she went around and asked, 'Would you like a little more?' My students would say, 'I'll have a little more,' and then they would take another little slice of ice cream, and another little slice. This went on about six or eight times. Every time she'd come around, 'Would you like a little more?' 'Oh yes, I'll have a little more.' What they really want to do is just grab the whole thing and put it on their plate!" The entire audience was laughing at this point. "The way we are with one another now, we've been together so long doing sadhana, we just say, 'Give me the ice cream!' " Gilles burst out laughing and had to stop translating for a few seconds. Lee and Arnaud were both smiling broadly and everyone else was bouncing in their seats with good-humored laughter.

"The first year I was in France, Gilles traveled with us the whole time. Ah, poor Gilles! We went down to Saintes Maries de la Mer, and we decided to have lunch. There was a beautiful little local market that we went to, and I bought all this food—roast chickens and lots of other things. The Americans were really hungry, and Gilles was probably hungry too, so we were looking for a place to eat. There wasn't any dignified place to eat, so we just sat down on some rocks by the beach and we opened up the packages. Gilles had his pocketknife, but we weren't going to wait for any knife! We just ripped those chickens to pieces with our bare hands, and Gilles was looking around in horror—'Oh, my God! I've never seen such savage behavior!' But to his credit he figured, 'What the hell!' and threw himself in right alongside the rest of us—grabbed a piece of chicken, started ripping it with his teeth. So . . . let's see . . . what point was I making?"

Gilles was laughing almost to the point of inebriation while somehow simultaneously translating Lee's words. Pulling himself together, Gilles turned on his seat slightly to face Lee and said, now sober, "Oh yes, you were talking about the hungry ghosts." The general laughter that had consumed the room was slowly beginning to subside as Lee returned to the original point.

"Oh yeah, hungry ghosts. So they were talking about the hell realms and one of Chögyam Trungpa Rinpoche's students said, 'Rinpoche, what do you do when you find yourself in hell?' Chögyam Trungpa Rinpoche said, 'I try to stay there.' He was serious. So what do you do with emotionally charged thoughts? Sit with them and observe them. Chögyam Trungpa Rinpoche was saying the same thing that Arnaud says—*accept what is as it is*. What does he do when he finds himself in hell? He tries to stay there, because when he finds himself there, that's what is. Of course there is great possibility for work in the hell realms, much more than in heaven. Chögyam Trungpa Rinpoche knew this intimately.

"Usually the less tension you have about staying there, the sooner it changes. This is the thing about seeing versus accepting. We've got to have a willingness to throw ourselves into the experiment. With no savings account. No little life raft on the side, just in case it doesn't work out. That's why it's great when our mothers die. As long as our mothers are alive we can always go home. Mothers are the most amazingly accepting creatures on the face of the earth. As long as our mothers are alive, we always have this feeling somewhere inside—if things don't work out, at least I still have my mother. Even when we don't *like* our mothers, subconsciously, mother is mother. So when our mothers die, that's it. The last safety net is gone.

"So we have to really be willing to throw ourselves into the moment. What happens if it doesn't work out? There's always another moment. That's the nice thing about here and now. It's always here and now. So if it doesn't work out here and now, it'll work out in the next here and now." Lee laughed.

"You know, that's reliable. The Universe is very reliable. We don't ever have to worry that we're going to miss the moment because it's always the moment! Lucky for us. We have this saying in my school, 'You never miss anything.' People have this thing: they're traveling and they miss a talk, and they come back and everybody says, 'Boy, it was a hot talk. Ah, you should have been there!' Nobody ever misses anything, but people *still* come to me, 'Oh would you allow me to listen to the tape? I heard it was a great talk!' Oh boy, that really gets me. I want to look at them and say, 'Where have you been for the last twenty years? Are those ears on your head or just bumps? Go back to church!' But I never say anything like that!" Laughter rang out through the meeting room, and Lee laughed too. The mood was one of warm enjoyment. It was the dharma, but it was funny as hell, couched in hilarity and stream of consciousness and the nitty gritty of the human predicament.

"So instead I just say to people, 'If you really *need* to listen to the tape . . .' Now whenever I say to somebody, 'If you really need to . . .' what I mean is, 'How could you ask such a thing?' But my students always say, 'Okay!' and then grab the tape! Every time. I'm looking for the student who will say, 'No, I don't really need to.' I think people don't say that because I might have a heart attack." Lee threw his head back and laughed. The whole group was loosened up now, laughing and in a strong rapport with Lee. The room was incredibly stuffy, but the discomfort wasn't even noticeable; the laughter and mood of irrational enjoyment had subsumed everything. In the midst of this, Lee kept pounding his point home.

"I am talking about *you all*, but don't take it personally. Because, you know, you're in good company. People are the same everywhere. India, Japan, America, France . . . Really. You're just like the Americans. I hate to insult you, but you are. When it comes to dealing with ego, it's all the same—the same everywhere. So the first step we have to take is self-honesty.

"The way I am in Europe is totally different from the way I am in America. I'm never like this in America—whatever this is. When I come home from Europe my students always say, 'Can we listen to the seminars on tape?' I'm always a little insecure because I never remember what terrible stories I've told about my students. You know, somebody could be sitting there smiling listening to the seminar, 'Wow this is great!' and all of a sudden I tell a story about them and—*blam!*—into the wall. If that has happened, none of them have ever told me about it." Lee laughed, "So I say, 'Yes you can listen to the seminar. There are twenty tapes. It's two hundred dollars.' What else do I get from them? Indigestion!" Arnaud smiled a big smile.

Arnaud's smiles and grins were interspersed throughout the twists and turns of Lee's monologues like a spice—a fine pepper or *masala* sprinkled over Lee's jokes and dharma points. Although Arnaud was almost completely silent, this spice was liberally dashed onto the feast of the space. Throughout it all, Arnaud's vast and diamond-like silence was punctuated with the chuckles and the big smiles that he threw like dry wood on the splendid fire that Lee built and tended.

Off and on during Lee's talk Arnaud took his glasses off, put them away, then later took them out again and looked over the audience. He peered at different questioners intensely, taking them in completely, at one with their question, their dilemma and their unspoken questions. It seemed to me that Lee and Arnaud worked together in amazing ways. While Lee played vanguard warrior and court jester, opening and tenderizing, skewering neatly, making the point, Arnaud seemed to be working his disciples over in this space, mopping up after the whole operation and vanquishing all doubts with the strength and clarity of his presence. Through it all, a finger *mala* of leaded crystal beads turned unceasingly in Lee's right hand.

After the talk Lee's group piled into the vans and followed Arnaud's car as it wound through villages and beautiful towns full of flower gardens, charming old stone buildings and bridges over rivers, past the crumbling ruins of old stone fortresses perched up on high bluffs, then up through the hills to the home of Eric and Veronique de Hamorin, where Lee, Arnaud and company would be hosted for dinner. A thunderstorm was brewing in the surrounding mountains. A strong wind blew dark gray clouds in fierce gusts, whirling leaves through the air as we stood out on the patio and ate hors d'oeuvres, many kinds of spiced and herbed olives, bread, delicious spiced nuts. On the tables were bottles of Diet Coke, wine and bottled water. About forty people—Arnaud's and Lee's students—gathered for dinner. Everyone mingled and wandered back and forth from the patio into the living room and kitchen as people clumped together in little enclaves of conversation in French or English. The thunderstorm finally hit with lightning flashes and grand crashes of thunder, driving the patio group permanently inside the living room. The huge old castle ruins in the hills across the valley lit up in eerie flashes as the storm progressed across the mountains.

A table was set in the living room for Arnaud and Lee. Everyone else found spots on chairs or couches or perched on the three stairs that led up to the kitchen. The meal was extraordinary—a Sudanese stew of chickpeas, zucchini, carrots, lamb and small spicy sausages, spiced with cinnamon and served with couscous. As the meal progressed some students clustered more closely around their table over dessert, and a conversation about Deben Bhattacharya, who Arnaud had known many years ago, sprang up.

Arnaud began to recount how he and Deben had spent time together in Paris thirty years ago. Their work brought them together in places like India and Afghanistan, where Arnaud filmed and Deben did a lot of recording. Arnaud said, "Deben filmed not only in India, but also in Afghanistan, Egypt, Algeria, Morocco. It's very unusual for a Hindu Brahmin to be admitted into Muslim spaces, but for Deben all doors just opened!" Arnaud smiled one his brilliant smiles. "It was the same everywhere—with the gypsies, for example," he continued. "The gypsies are very closed, but even the gypsies let Deben in to film them—gypsies, Muslims, Sufis, all of them opened their doors to Deben!"

The conversation moved on to Charles Bukowski. Lee talked about Bukowski as a quintessential American poet and promised to send copies of his work to Arnaud and Veronique. They began to talk about Baudelaire, whom Lee had mentioned during his talk earlier today. Along with Charles Bukowski, Baudelaire is another poet whom Lee admires greatly. On the subject of Baudelaire Arnaud really came to life. "You've read Baudelaire?" he exclaimed to Lee.

"Yes—fantastic!" was Lee's enthusiastic response.

"In English?" Arnaud asked incredulously.

"Yes," Lee replied.

"Then you haven't read Baudelaire!" Arnaud insisted. "There is no way Baudelaire can be captured in another language, the meter, the rhyme . . ." He asserted passionately with a smile, "You *must* read Baudelaire in French!"

Lee nodded his head, smiling back, enjoying a common love.

July 6, 1999
Hauteville

In answer to a question Lee spoke further on accepting what is: "It is the act of acceptance that allows the possibility of change. When we can accept the knot as it is, then it's possible that the knot can start to unravel, but if we can't accept it, it can't unravel.

"When one of my students says, 'What should I do about my fear?' or 'What should I do about my anger,' well, you have to assume that you're going to be this full of fear or this angry for the rest of your life. This is the way it is. So, learn to live with it. When someone starts to learn to live with *what is* effectively, what tends to happen is that it changes.

"Assume that the knot is always going to be there. What if that was the case? As you said, not a day goes by that you don't remember the teaching and practice the teaching, so what would happen if the knot was just going to be there for the rest of your life? You have the teaching—how would you live? And when you figure that out, then the knot won't be the same. It's just the way it works. But as long as you're fighting against the knot, then you're strengthening it. Resistance creates counter-resistance. That's part of the psychology of acceptance; when you accept something, you aren't resisting it. Then all the counter-resistance has nowhere to go and nothing to do, so it just relaxes. As soon as the counter-resistance relaxes, then what is the knot, except counter-resistance? That's all it is. It's not resistance. The knot is not resistance, the knot is counter-resistance. As soon as it's got nothing to resist against then it's got no reason to exist. That's how it works."

The questioner continued, " 'The Good, The Bad and The Ugly,' Clint Eastwood's movie, I suppose those three characters, the good, the bad and the ugly, are within me. We all have those three characters within us."

Lee quipped, "Or the good, the bad and the smelly, depending upon the individual!" A few people cackled with laughter.

"Yesterday you quoted Aldous Huxley," the man went on, "who at the end of his life said something to the effect that the most important thing was to treat people with kindness. And it reminded me of this quotation from this sage of the Jewish tradition who was asked what the essence of the Torah was, and he said exactly the same thing. On the other hand, you spoke about that guy who said everything was Ram, but who was using 'Everything is Ram' as a buffer, an excuse. If I really live in that state where everything is Ram, what is it that will in that case prevent me from acting out all those ugly characters which are within me? Since everything is Ram, so those ugly characters are also Ram. One remains 'a nice boy' because we've been taught to behave in such a way, but it's just education."

Lee answered, "If this was the eighth century and I was a Zen Master this would be the time when I would leap off the platform and beat you with a stick screaming 'Ram, Ram, Ram!' But first of all, you're bigger than me, so you're safe, and so am I!" Lee chuckled and then continued.

"What distinguishes the saint from the libertine or the criminal is not intelligence, since many libertines or criminals are as smart or smarter than the saints. In the domain of sainthood intelligence is about as evident as it is on the average in the general population. In spite of people's ability to excuse their actions brilliantly, there is an intelligence to the Universe. The physicists have been enjoying a conversation about the law of chaos these past few years, but to the Universe reality is not chaotic. It only looks chaotic to us because we're looking up from a very low position. In spite of the brilliance of many human minds, that's still very minor compared to the Intelligence of the organic possibility of the Divine.

"Essentially the Universe seeks harmony, and there are instances in which destruction is harmonious—for example, the rotting away of trees that fall in the forest so that they create fertilizer and rich soil for other plants to grow. In the whole ecological system there is a level of disintegration that's healthy, necessary. Even in a personal way each of us has to fulfill certain effects as a result of causes in previous times. But if we are identified with our manifestations, then as we're paying off one karmic bill, we're creating another one, automatically.

"The only way to pay off karma without incurring new karma is to not be identified with the manifestation. When someone is, in the language I use, Surrendered to the Will of God, then the Will of God creates function or manifestation in that person's case. One could look at the lives of the Hassidic masters, to go back to the Jewish tradition, in which their prayer always created a certain type of life outside of the particular times of prayer. Meher Baba, an Indian Master who died in 1969, said that there are two qualities to ultimate human existence. He called them infinity and divinity. He said that if you have one without the other, then the manifestation in your life is going to show aberrations in some way.

"If you have infinity—which is like seeing Ram everywhere, seeing God as One, God as everything—but no divinity, then you have no problem acting in violent and cruel ways. You have no guilt. You'd always be talking about God this, God that, but you wouldn't have any sense of value or ethic. This dichotomy of infinity/divinity is exactly the same as the Buddhist formula, except the Buddhists are nontheistic. The Buddhist formula is 'Form is emptiness, emptiness is form,' or 'Samsara is nirvana, nirvana is samsara,' and one without the other creates imbalance. So because the Universe naturally seeks balance, we can look at our own activity. If we are really honest with ourselves we can see which we are most rooted in—infinity or divinity. Emptiness is form, or form is emptiness. We can look at any behavior and see that it is essentially empty and meaningless, but from the position of 'Emptiness is form,' then who we are is a function of both the Oneness of the Divine and our incarnation, our humanness.

"There's a very good book out, I'm sure it's translated into French, about the death poems of Zen masters. Some of those poems get you working. But, you know, if you take their poetry about emptiness in the context of Zen and the life that Zen practitioners lead, you come to the same conclusion. There was one Zen master who was dying and he called all his disciples together for their final meeting with the master, and he got into a headstand and died that way. What a great communication to leave his disciples with! Nothing is what we think it is, everything is upside down. Does any of that address the question?"

The questioner nodded and said with a smile, "Thank you very much for what you said about the stick, for what you said about beating me." Lee nodded kindly and went on to the next question.

Later in the session another student said, "Arnaud asked me a question a few days ago in a private interview. He asked me, 'What does it mean to be a woman?' "

Lee said, "Did you tell him?" She answered no. "Why not? Maybe Arnaud needs that information!" Everyone laughed.

She continued, "Coming back home I reflected upon that question and I realized that I'm not yet reconciled with my feminine nature. And so I felt like asking you this question, 'What is a real woman?' all the more so because in *The Alchemy of Love and Sex* you wrote something like, to find a real woman is not easy, you know, it's not very common."

"Who was it who said, 'My kingdom for a real woman?' " Lee laughed, "I think it was back in the thirties, prince somebody—the Prince of Wales. Prince Edward gave up his kingdom for a real woman. So is that the question? I'm making jokes to avoid the issue."

She smiled, "I hoped you could give me a few elements to inspire me."

Chuckling to himself, Lee began to answer. "I had a friend who wanted to know how to best relate to women, so he looked for a very highly experienced lesbian to be in sexual relationship with. He said who could better teach him how to treat a woman than a woman who was expert at treating women like women? I'm not suggesting that you get in relationship with another woman. There's something in that. I think most women know how to treat women better than men know how to treat women because women understand what it is to be a woman, so they know how a woman likes to be treated.

"The question, 'What is a real woman?' goes way beyond simply your femininity as a woman, a person. Language can go up to a certain point, but really it doesn't touch the heart of that question. Observing someone who expresses femininity, true femininity, impacts our bodies in a way that language can't. It's like telling somebody what it's like to look into the eyes of an innocent infant when they've never done it—you just can't explain something like that.

"So this question is a koan for you. The way you get the answer is from your own experience. I know you have a body of experience that is accessible. I know you have the answer; even if it's a little difficult to access, it's there within you. You don't have to get it from outside of yourself. But through observing Arnaud and certain specific women, then that observation will trigger the revelation of your own innate experience, and then you will have the answer. Because you *do* know what it is to be a real woman, even though in any of us there is a body of habits that often act as buffers between our essential experience of life and our ordinary day-to-day perceptions.

"Earlier we were using the word 'knot.' All of us have this knot and it binds us from our essential reality. It's not that we don't have everything we need within ourselves— *everything*. Part of being human is that we are given the equipment. It's like we're given that yes, we just have to access it. We have to get the no out of the way and then the yes shines. As I've said here many times, the no develops from early childhood misunderstandings and we develop a certain pattern of relationship to life that is based on the no. Sometimes we cage that femininity because it's intruded upon. We guard it, we protect it, and rightly so. Then we grow up and we forget where it is. So we don't have to *make* real femininity—all we have to do is take down the walls that are defending it. Stay with the question," he concluded.

Another man asked a question. "Last year you told me that I had to go a lot deeper, that I had many tears to shed. So, I can detect two sufferings within myself: one has to do with the emotional state, it's more affected, and the other has to do with another type of suffering, it's more like an aspiration. You wrote poems to your master and I wanted to know whether they are love poems?"

Lee answered, "Will you buy them if I tell you they're love poems? It's just a rhetorical question. A little bit of subtle advertising. Well, I don't know. I don't consider myself to be a great lover of my Master. As I probably said here a number of times, my relationship to my Master is one of obedience, because that's something I have a choice about. I can't choose to love somebody—I either love somebody or not—but I can choose to obey. So if I had to define the poems in any way, I'd call them poems of obedience. When I first started writing them I didn't know that was what He wanted, but once it was clear that that was what He wanted, a certain type of demonstration, then they became poems of obedience. It was obvious what their function was. Other people call them poems of love because that's their response to them. But for me, they're a function of obeying my Master.

"When the first book was published in India there was a period of inactivity in which I wasn't writing a lot of poems. I happened to say in the presence of my Master, 'Maybe it's done. Maybe I'm not writing poems any more.' He said, 'Oh, Lee will write poems forever.' So, I write poems because this is what my Master told me to do, because when He says something like that He's not being prophetic—He's giving me a task. He's not saying that He can read the future and that I will be a spontaneous poet. He is saying, 'Write poems.' So I happen to be lucky. Any time I sit down and concentrate poetry starts flowing, at least that kind of poetry. So, if I'm lazy I just sit and wait until every couple of months some inspiration hits and then I write an inspired poem, but most of the poems in the book were generated through intention.

"Once two or three poems come out, then the door is open and inspiration starts flowing. But to me, it's all the same. I can call up inspiration in two minutes. So it's not like being struck by a lightening bolt. It's sort of like getting a feeling, 'Oh you know, I think we'll go out to eat tonight. Enough salad. It's time for pepperoni pizza.' That's where the poems come from. They're a function of obedience. My Master says, 'This Beggar only likes praise.' So, I'm good with language, I can do that. And since poems have been a kind of format of relationship to Him, of contribution to Him, that's what I do. Did that answer part of the question?"

He said, "Yes, but Andrew Cohen told me I was being lazy with words. I don't really understand what he means when he suggests that I really search for the right words, because when I try and do that it's like my intellect is trying to work and it leads no-where."

"Did you say that to Andrew?" Lee asked. The man nodded in assent. "Then what did he say?"

"I don't know, it's sort of blurred."

"I have the same response. Andrew is so brilliant you know, I listen to him and I say, 'God, that was unbelievable—I've got to remember this.' But it's so brilliant it just goes in one ear and out the other. I love to listen to Andrew talk. It's such an inspiring thing. It really bothers me because I can never remember anything he says. In fact my whole life is kind of a big blur." The whole group laughed. "Anyway, so, yes?"

"So, I don't know—it's really blurred now. It's totally blurred." Everyone laughed again. "I'm thrown off balance," the questioner said.

"Great! So, Andrew wants to clarify things and I want to blur things. He had his effect and now I'm having my effect and you get to be the poor guy at the vortex of it all. Anything else?" He answered that he could feel the knot within him.

"How does the knot feel? Good or bad?" Lee asked.

"Well, it hurts. It still hurts. There is suffering involved. I was wondering whether I can use this emotional suffering to work on that other suffering which has to do with that aspiration I mentioned."

Lee responded, "Arnaud said something in meditation this morning. It was a quote from Swami Prajnanpad, 'Eating is a function of life, breath *is* life.' I would add that most of what we've been discussing are just functions of life. They're not life itself. How do we shift our focus from something that's just a function of life to something that *is* life? Just remember that we're breathing. There are very technical methodologies associated with breath in traditional yoga and in some of the Buddhist practices. I'm not talking about that. I'm talking about just remembering that we are breathing. Very simple. And as soon as we remember we're breathing then we forget the knot. So then the question is, 'Yes, but that doesn't make it go away. It's still there.' The more we struggle with it the more we give it life. We feed it. We sustain it. If we just went on about our lives, accepting what is as it is, being one with what is, then the whole question of knot/no knot, becomes academic.

"It's very difficult when we're suffering to get out of that suffering through muscular effort. We imagine that if we don't get out of it with effort that we're just going to keep suffering, but that's not necessarily the case. That's our projection or expectation. We keep trying to get out of it, and what does that do? It shines the spotlight of attention on our suffering. Suffering likes to hog the stage! Just push it off the stage. It's really that simple.

"You may say, 'No my suffering is not that simple. It's complex. It's profound and deep.' Everybody feels that way about their own suffering, but it could be a lot worse. You could be in Kosovo. You could be in a refugee camp. Count your blessings no matter how much you think you're suffering. That's what we should do: every time we think, 'Oh my husband doesn't understand me,' or 'My wife doesn't understand me. Life stinks,' just look around the world. Boy, it could be a lot worse. We are nice and middle class, most of us. Yeah. Well, time to end for this morning."

Lee's talk this morning continued to blend his own teaching with that of Arnaud Desjardins. Woven throughout his answers to questions were the threads of *sahajiya* principles, which Lee has called "Organic Innocence" and the "Primacy of Natural Ecstasy." Throughout the afternoon Lee kept referring people back to the innate wisdom and knowledge of the body, and the importance of finding that knowledge through one's own immediate experience in life, which is experience born and carried in the body, not mediated solely by the mind. In years past Lee has often said, "God does not live in the sky," or "The body knows." These basic *sahajiya* principles, conditions of the Organic Innocence which is the underlying mood of all Creation, refer to the easy, natural path of *sahaja*, which translates literally as "innate" or "spontaneous." Wisdom is innate within each of us; there is actually no effort required to find wisdom. What is necessary is the clearing away of obstacles to that wisdom.

At one o'clock we gathered for a delicious lunch, served beneath the spreading shade of the tall sycamore trees in front of the chateau. Arnaud and Lee sat at a large table with a number of their students and talked quietly. The weather was gorgeous and the conversation pleasant. As soon as the long, leisurely lunch was over, Lee returned to the book table, set up in the foyer just inside the front entryway to the building. There he sold and signed books with *dédicace*—inscriptions designed for each person—talked one on one with many people and generally made himself available until the afternoon session started at four o'clock.

At the afternoon session an interesting interaction occurred between Lee and one of Arnaud's students which laid the foundation for an important interaction between this man's wife and Lee a few days later. The questioner began, "This morning it was obvious that you can remember certain questions which have been asked to you." Lee chuckled and the questioner continued, "And you can remember them for a long time. Last year when you came to Montpellier I asked you a question. You asked me what my profession was. I told you I was running a business and you answered something like, 'That's very good, keep putting money in the bank.' I'm sure you gave me this answer."

Lee laughed, "Sounds like me."

"That's what I think personally," he continued while Lee kept chuckling to himself, "but my wife says you said, 'Keep on putting money in the bank *and* buy very nice dresses for your wife.' " Everyone laughed. "I'm certain you didn't say buy nice dresses for my wife, and she's certain you said it."

"Is your wife in the room now?"

"Unfortunately not."

"Ah, too bad! What's your name again?"

"Jean Paul. You don't remember what you said?" he queried further.

"Not exactly, no," Lee answered.

"But this morning I bought a book from you."

"Thank you," Lee said.

"No, because I paid with a one hundred franc note, and then I imagined that I'd given you two hundred francs and asked you for one hundred francs. I feel very strongly that my relationship to you is a money relationship, and I don't understand."

"Gosh!" Lee said, seeming surprised.

"I've always tried not to bother Arnaud with my professional life," Jean Paul continued.

Lee said, "Well, you shouldn't bother him with it unless he asks. You know, we always think—this is aside from our consideration—that the master has got to have certain information. The master doesn't need information. If the master needs information, he'll ask. We're always loading the master with information that the master doesn't need, because we think that if we don't give the master the information, then the master won't be able to respond accurately. But that's making the master into a business person. So, what do you want your relationship to me to be? I'm assuming by what you said that you don't want it to be about money. What do you want it to be?"

Jean Paul replied, "I don't understand what's going on. When I think about you, it seems that there is something which has to do with money in the relationship I have with you, but I don't understand what's going on."

"So what?" Lee shrugged, as if to say there was no problem. "What do you want the relationship to be about?"

"I would simply like to live this relationship and understand it," he concluded.

"Oh, live *and* understand, hmmm. That complicates things. Well, maybe it's just karma, you know. Maybe a thousand years ago I bought books from *you!*" Everyone laughed, "Maybe it's really simple. And maybe to live the relationship and understand it does not exclude the exchange of money. I was in business before I got into teaching, and I was putting a lot of money in the bank. Then I got into teaching, and all my money went down the toilet. Not really. That's insulting my students. All my money went towards the effective resource base needed to teach in the way I wanted to teach. So, money has its value. It's not all there is to life. Let's say when you look at that picture of Anandamayi Ma up there on the wall, it has a certain impactful transmission, a communication. That picture wouldn't be up there if it wasn't for money. It might not be so bad, if our relationship was about money. Okay? Thank you. What kind of business are you in? Did I ask you that in Montpellier?"

"I'm at the head of a corporation which sells fruits, vegetables, and meat."

"That's a good business," Lee said, "it's feeding people. It's a very good business. I don't mean good as in to make money, but essentially good. We were in India last year, and we were buying silk from some friends of mine," Lee chuckled at the memory, "a very wealthy family, wealthy by Western terms. They took us out to this village of farmers that they support with their donations. After we toured the village we went back to their silk showroom and had some tea. There are five brothers that run the business. One of them said, 'People look down on the farmers because they're lower caste, but the most important people are the people who make food for other people.' So, it's a good business. What kind of meat—sausage?"

Jean Paul answered, "No, everything which can be bought in France as far as meat goes."

"Wow!" Lee chuckled. "Well, if you weren't so far away we'd get the food for the feasts at our ashram from you. It's sort of embarrassing to say, but sometimes we actually serve meat on our ashram. Everybody goes, 'Oh, you're vegetarians, very nice.' Then they come to our ashram expecting beautiful salads and they get this big sausage," Lee chuckled. "It's a terrible shock for some people! Anyway, thank you."

The next question was about the need to be a hero. Lee said, "For someone who needs to be a hero, heroism is to *not* be a hero."

"How does one do that?" the questioner pursued.

Lee laughed, "Let's use athletics as an example. So some people like to run marathons, you know, twenty-six kilometers, or do thousands of push-ups or sit-ups, and that's the way they demonstrate their heroism. In that case, then the way to not *need* to be a hero would be to not tell anybody about it.

"There's a story that someone told me one time. It was told to him by the abbot of a monastery where he was doing a retreat. The story is about a man who was a very successful violinist. He used to tour the world with various orchestras and he was always the solo violinist. He was so good that he was able to move an audience anyway he wanted—make them cry or laugh or gasp. After some years he had a bad night one night, and he realized that he was living for applause, not for music anymore. He was very arrogant about the level of his skill, but he had lost his heart. So he played a couple of more concerts and he just got worse and worse and worse, because he realized for the first time that he was listening to the applause—every single hand clap. If one person wasn't applauding he would get angry at that person. If he saw someone not clapping he would think to himself, 'Don't you know who I am and how good I am?'

"So he went to his priest, and he explained the problem. He said, 'Now that I've seen this, I can't live with it anymore,' because he really was an artist. He said, 'I'm addicted, I need the audience.' The priest said, 'There's a retreat in America, a monastery. If you're really serious, you go to this monastery, and talk to the abbot, who is a friend of mine.'

The man kept trying to tour and play, but it wasn't working, so after some small amount of time, he went to the monastery, and he explained the problem to the abbot. He said to the abbot, 'I don't want to pick up my violin ever again, and yet I can't live without it.' The abbot said, 'You go out into the woods every day, far enough away that nobody can hear you, and you play. Every day you play for an hour or two or three.'

"So the man went and he started playing out in the woods, a week, a month, two months. At some point in that process he became so consumed with the playing that he was free, completely free. He could have gone back to playing professionally; he could have never picked up the violin again. It didn't matter anymore either way. I don't know what happened. I didn't think to ask when the guy told me the story, because the point was that he got free of his need to be a hero. His need to be a hero was transcended by returning to the essence of *being*, of music itself. If we don't have an audience, there's no heroism, the way I was using the word. You've got to have an audience to be a hero. So, we find a way to expend our addiction without the usual effect, without the high that is the whole source of the addiction.

"So, let me use myself as an example. I'm not a good example, but I can make something up. My whole life is involved in teaching; I travel, I come to Europe, I live here for four months, but while I'm here I travel to France and Germany and Switzerland and Belgium and so on. Obviously there's a certain heroism in that. Everywhere I go people roll out the red carpet and they're very reverent. And in spite of all of that there is some genuine value that gets communicated also. If I discovered that I have this need to be a hero and that's why I'm doing what I'm doing, if I stop doing what I'm doing then I also take away the value that this communication is to many people. In this kind of situation I have to be creative; I have to figure out how to disempower this need to be a hero without altering the actual flow of activity. I have worked that out, and I won't tell you how, though it may be obvious already. Thank you for the question. Time to end for this afternoon. Tonight we get to dance!"

After dinner people began to gather in the courtyard behind the main building of the ashram. The courtyard has a sandy floor and huge sycamore trees that shade and shelter the whole space. The building itself circumscribes more or less three sides of the area, while a garden hedge makes the fourth side of a loosely designed square. The hedge of roses and trumpet vines and various shrubs and ivy is sheltered beneath a low stone and concrete retaining wall that overlooks a driveway ten or twelve feet below. Beyond that is a mass of tall green trees and wild undergrowth between the ashram and the public road.

Having arrived at Hauteville the same day Lee arrived, Shri had their equipment set up in front of the huge double glass doors at the ground floor entrance to the chateau for their performance tonight. These doors are heavy, old glass worked with beautiful black cast iron designs and surrounded by a massive growth of blossoming trumpet vines that cling to the brick and stone walls. To the left of the makeshift plywood stage was a large mimosa tree and to the right the first of the immense sycamore trees that spread a leafy canopy above our heads in the courtyard at midday when the sun bears down on the group that gathers here every day for lunch.

At eight o'clock, almost an hour before real dusk would fall, people began to flow into the space and take their seats. Arnaud had a seat in the front row of several wooden benches that were set up concert style, facing the stage that had been constructed on the steps into the building. Arnaud sat without moving throughout the concert. He seemed to be listening and watching everything that went on intently. About twenty feet had been left open between the front row of benches and the bandstand for people to dance.

People were primed to dance, and yet it took about twenty minutes to break the ice. After sitting and listening respectfully to the first two or three songs, a few brave dancers got out on the sandy ground that made a gravel dance floor while the majority began to dance behind the benches near the retaining wall. Finally one of Arnaud's disciples started a "snake," and led all the dancers—probably twenty-five or thirty people—up to the dance area near the band. As the dancers flooded into that space the synapse of connection in the circuit between band and audience snapped with electricity. We were plugged in and the fun began. People began to dance with wild enthusiasm, some of it very playful, some of it sensual, some of it with real abandon. Lee's teaching for the past two days had been threaded with commentary on acceptance of the body, of the life and wisdom that is native to the body. Now it seemed there was a general agreement that people were going to experiment, to enter as fully as possible into the experience of the music, here and now.

As darkness fell there was tremendous ecstasy in the air. The group as a whole— Arnaud's students, Lee's students—responded with great enthusiasm. About fifty people were up and dancing, getting loose and crazy, whirling, rocking, gyrating. The band was fabulous, spread out loosely across the makeshift stage. Lee danced and sang, but he was also often very invisible. He at times seemed to disappear altogether into the mandala of the newly expanded Shri—eight people who now make up what used to be a four person band, with Lee often added on as a second lead singer. In the thicket of the tight arrangement on such a small stage, Lee became a glimmer of magic on the edge of one's senses while the music was what grabbed most of one's attention. The last song, "Voodoo Chile," was a wild romp through the underworld. It was hard to stop dancing. It seemed that everyone could have danced on and on, but out of respect for the neighbors of the ashram, at ten o'clock it was time to stop. The dancers, who were sweating and smiling, reluctantly came to a standstill then began to disperse, most of them heading for the meditation hall, where the final meditation of the day would start shortly.

July 7, 1999
Hauteville

Lee walked into the meeting room this morning dressed in black. He wore a silk long-sleeved shirt with the sleeves rolled up and silk meditation pants. The first year Lee came to Font d'Isiere and met Arnaud he wore provocative T-shirts with in-your-face slogans, jeans and sweat pants. The second year he came to Font d'Isière Lee started wearing colorful and dramatic T-shirts with silk meditation pants, and by the third year he went to Font d'Isiere he was wearing silk shirts. When someone asked him about this change he said that it wasn't necessary to provoke people with what he wore when the mood was one of *natural* elegance and dignity, as it is in Arnaud's case. His style of dress at Hauteville hasn't changed since then.

At times the "Meeting with Lee" streaks past our eyes in a blue blaze. Often in those chambers the group spends the whole time laughing hysterically with Lee, suspended in a ridiculous kind of happiness with no motive—it is just what is. This morning was the opposite. As the session began to unwind, it went incredibly slowly. Time was bending itself in the direction of being drawn out into amazing lengths of timelessness, as if the session would go on forever. The body wanted to move, and writhed impatiently on its seat. Shawls fell off shoulders as the heat increased with the midday sun beating down outside, having the effect of melting or wilting everyone in the space. The second hand on the clock in the back of the meeting hall moved slowly from one moment to the next, dragging the two and a half-hour session out to the limit.

Finally Lee closed the session with a thank you to everyone. He said, "I wanted to thank everybody for your tremendous response to the band last night. Everybody was very genuine and heartfelt in their response. The band is on their way to Germany today for some gigs before they come back to France to play some more, and they left on a very high note. They were very full of everybody's enthusiasm. So, thank you."

Today at lunch the group at Arnaud and Lee's table touched on the subject of Gurdjieff groups and Arnaud's time in the Fourth Way. One gets the feeling that Arnaud has so many stories, such a wealth of experience in his years on the path—in the Fourth Way, with Swami Ramdas, with Anandamayi Ma, filming Shivananda and the Sufi masters in Afghanistan, Teisan Deshimaru, and also all the many teachers he has come into contact with during his years as a spiritual teacher. I keep thinking that someone should write a detailed biography. When I asked Veronique about this she said, "It has already been done." Of course the catch for the Americans is that it is written in French.

Arnaud invited a lovely couple to sit with him and Lee at lunch. They are former devotees of Muktananda, now with Arnaud. This was their first time at one of Lee's seminars at Hauteville. Arnaud was speaking to them in French and explaining, "It is important to come not just for a day or two, but for the whole week while Lee is here. When people come for a week, something happens during the week. It is incredible to watch—by the end of the week you can see that people are changed."

A little later the woman asked, "The language that Lee uses to describe the teaching is so similar to yours; does their school have a similar language?"

Arnaud said, "No, it's not that their language is the same. Lee uses our language because he is speaking to my students. It's a great service that he offers."

When Lee gives seminars at Hauteville or any of the centers that are run by disciples of Arnaud, where the audience is predominantly made up of Arnaud's students, he displays an amazing chameleon-like ability to tailor his communication to the needs and perspective of those who are present. Similarly, whether he is speaking to Arnaud's disciples or the students of Andrew Cohen or E.J. Gold, Lee always turns the student toward his or her own teacher. It is a way in which his integrity as a teacher is impeccable to the degree that he is often called to serve in the capacity of guiding and helping those on the path who are not his own students.

After a number of interchanges at the beginning of the afternoon session a woman asked the next question. "I've been here for two weeks and when I arrived, I was in some sort of emotional crisis."

"How do you know you were in some sort of emotional crisis?" Lee asked.

"Well, it was going in every direction."

"That's not necessarily the sign of a crisis," Lee responded. "Maybe you were just excited. Sometimes we're so excited to be at the heart of the teaching, where our teacher is, and where our path lies. I'm not saying this is true of you, but in principle. Sometimes everything is fine until we get to the ashram and then all of a sudden we say to ourselves, 'Oh, I'm on the ashram. I've got to have some sort of crisis. What am I going to say to

Daniel when I have my interview if I'm not in crisis?' So anyway—you were having a crisis."

"No it's rather the other way around," she said. "It happens here that very often I can feel really fine, like yesterday during the concert, and there was a moment where I couldn't recognize anybody anymore."

Lee laughed, "Yeah, everybody looked pretty strange to me too!" Everyone in the room started laughing.

"Except Arnaud," he continued, "who just looked the same. Again, this is not specifically for you, but in principle. A lot of times we just need some kind of stimulant in order to create what we would consider to be a state of equanimity. We approach the path the way we approach life. We want to be entertained. In ordinary daily life, entertainment might be a movie or a concert, or a fight with our partner. In spiritual life, entertainment is some kind of peace of mind. We actually use the teacher and the ashram as a catalyst, as entertainment to create a state of peace of mind in us. We need to be stimulated to be peaceful, instead of just being in life itself as it is."

She interjected, "I explain that by thinking of an animal that takes on the shapes of his environment—if things are peaceful then I'm quite peaceful, if it's tormented then I tend to be tormented."

"So stay out of tormented situations," Lee said. "Maybe when you have a boyfriend you say, 'You know, if I'm in this situation I'm like this. If I'm in that situation I'm like that.' Your boyfriend can call you 'my little chameleon' as a term of endearment. Instead of 'sugar,' you know."

She continued, "At one point when I was feeling peaceful I had this thought, this fear that [the peacefulness is] just a dream, because I feel peaceful here, but I know I'm going back to a situation where it's a dead end with my boyfriend. And also I live in a very noisy place."

Lee smiled, "I assume he's not here. That's why you were dancing so wildly last night. A little advertising never hurts, sweetheart." Everyone laughed. Many times the laughter seemed to reflect the fact that Arnaud's disciples knew each other's tendencies.

Lee continued, "Well, in the moment that you're feeling peaceful then that's what is. In the moment when you're feeling agitated, that's what is. We human beings tend to fulfill our own prophecies. If we have a certain expectation of ourselves, then we tend to create circumstances to verify that expectation."

After a lengthy and complicated exchange with another student about various things focused around her health, Lee began to remember her from last year. He said, "I remember we had a big disagreement last year. And you were so stubborn I just capitulated and said something benign!"

She answered, "Oh no, there was no conflict!"

Reflecting on that Lee mused, "I must have been more diplomatic than I thought." After some further debate over the subject of her relationship with a particular healer—a discussion that seemed to be going nowhere—Lee asked if she wanted to continue the discussion. She asked, "Can I leave this subject? And tell you something which I feel about art?"

"Uh-oh. Don't tell me you're an artist," Lee laughed.

"Well, I'm supposed to be teaching art to children, and we are always told not to be prejudiced or to have opinions about anything. Especially about art. And I'm under the impression that you have some prejudices about art." Everyone laughed so loudly that

Lee's response was lost in the guffaws.

Lee smiled, "Charles Bukowski said, 'God save us from English teachers who think they're poets.' I think we can say the same thing about art teachers who think they're artists. I can say that because you said you weren't an artist, just an art teacher. I hope I'm not insulting you."

"Yes, but I'm not supposed to feed prejudice to the children who come to me."

"That's fine," Lee said placidly. "So what does that have to do with me?" Another spurt of laughter burst out of the audience.

"Well, I'm supposed to make them sensitive to contemporary art. To the art which is the art of their times."

Lee shrugged. "Yeah, so? They can be sensitive to it, and still realize it's crap." More laughter erupted. The repartee between Lee and the student was going very fast, like a Ping-Pong ball, back and forth between the two. She continued, "At the beginning they often have the same prejudices that you have, and often it's their parents who feed them their prejudices."

"How old are the children that you teach?" he asked. She answered, "Teenagers."

"Oh, well . . ." he shrugged again. She started speaking rhetorically, instructing Lee in the fine points of art critique. "For many parents art is okay until Picasso. Before it was just until the Impressionists, now it starts at Picasso, and you know, we can say the art of the past century is not devoid of crap. But I do not think that all contemporary attempts in the domain of art should be rejected."

"Well, I didn't say that!" he protested humorously. "I might have *implied* it, but I didn't say it. I'm joking with you. Last year is starting to come back!" Lee was laughing now, his laughter almost drowned out by the loud, almost rowdy, laughter that erupted from the group.

"Generally speaking we have a very lazy mind," she continued, starting to assert her ego into the space again.

Cutting through the morass, Lee snapped, "Okay, so do you want to discuss art or do you want to deal with the reason that we're both sitting in this room? Because what we're talking about now has nothing to do with anything. It's a social conversation. It's the kind of conversation we should have over cocktails at a party. You know, this is right where the chicken wings are served."

"I understand this is true, but we are into some sort of cultural meeting."

"God! Heaven forbid," Lee rolled his eyes.

"But at regular intervals, last year and this year," she continued relentlessly, "you have made some attacks on contemporary art and everybody laughed, so everybody seems to agree with you."

"No." Lee's voice became instantly implacable and authoritative. "Everybody knows what I'm *talking* about. I'm not talking about contemporary art. I'm talking about people who think they're artists. They produce *shit* you couldn't even sell on the sidewalks of Paris to tourists. They walk around thinking that the world owes them a living because they're some sort of artiste. I'm not talking about anything that would show up in your class. I'm talking about things that would never show up in your class. I'm talking about people with absolutely not a grain of talent in the world, who have pretensions to be the next Picasso." Lee gave a mad little laugh then continued making his point.

"Everybody laughs because everybody's got at least two or three friends exactly like that. I have dozens of students like that. You know, I have some students who are really fine artists. Unfortunately those who are fine artists never give me any of their work, and the ones that have pretensions to art, who don't have a grain of talent in the world, they're always giving me things." Lee was still laughing. His comments carried a scathing quality, a sting that cut through the thick illusions of her argument. Everyone in the room seemed relieved. "Someday I want to have a Hohm Community archive with all the bad art that I've been given, as a kind of demonstration of the futility of the illusion of separation. Anyway, so . . . Okay, okay! I was out of line. I apologize. I had no idea there was such a responsible *art teacher* in the room. Anything else? What's your name? I remember I asked you last year, but I don't remember it."

She said, "Marie."

"Okay Marie. Well, the good thing about next year is you'll know when I'm going to be here, so you could always come at another time if I'm insulting you. But if you'd like to come when I'm here, I'd be happy to see you again. I probably will have completely forgotten our discussion of this year, so we could start over again. Perhaps next year I'll have better manners. Well, thank you Marie."

Another person said, "I'd like to go back to the question that I asked you this morning. There is one aspect I didn't quite understand."

"Just one? Pretty good!" Lee quipped.

The questioner continued, "About observing the mechanisms of the mind. When I noticed that I put my attention somewhere and I see the reason why suffering has come, I can sort of shift my attention and then suffering will sort of disappear because of that shift of attention. So that's what I was calling the observation of the mechanisms of the mind, just seeing how it works. But it seems I get to a point that is beyond observation and I'm sort of overwhelmed and there's no observation anymore. So what's the use of observing the mechanisms of the mind then?"

Lee answered, "To get to the point where there's no observation anymore. Where there's just what is. To exhaust the mechanism of control, of manipulation, of dominance."

A beautiful young woman sitting halfway toward the back of the women's side raised her hand. She said, "I establish some sort of parallel between this meeting with you and the recent death of my grandmother. I'd never been confronted with death before, and I had to go the city. I was really frightened. And just the same way that I knew it was very probable that I would meet you during my stay here, in the same way I wanted to see the body of my grandmother because I knew that it would be beneficial for me to see her dead."

With a mischievous glint in his eye Lee said, "So you mean coming to see me is like going to a funeral?"

"Almost," she answered. Her tone was very straightforward and sincere, yet full of good humor.

"That's good!" he smiled, his chuckles seeming to indicate his appreciation of her quick-wittedness.

"When I saw my grandmother I was shocked," she continued. "I cried a lot. But at the same time I could feel that she was very present, that she wasn't dead at all. For the first time I understood the extent to which someone who's supposed to be dead can be very present. And on Monday, when you came into the room, I was really frightened and at the same time I was drawn to you. Attracted."

Lee punctuated her serious consideration with some more offbeat humor. "Necrophiliac, huh?" He paused and looked at her. "I'm joking. You have a good sense of humor right? Do you mind?" He was still watching her closely as he offered genuinely, "If it really bothers you I won't make jokes."

She persevered, "Well, as far as I can end my sentence I don't mind, but I would like to end my sentences."

"Wow, that's a tough one. Okay, let's try," he deadpanned in mock seriousness, but obviously happy with her strength of character.

"So I felt frightened when I saw you," she continued, her words tremendously genuine, "so I thought that something very interesting was going to happen during this week. I had a question that I wanted to ask Daniel and I learned that I wouldn't be able to see him for an interview, so I wanted to ask it the next day. And so I asked it and what I understood of the answer was so striking to me, it had so much impact, that I feel that I'm in the same state I was in on the day of my grandmother's funeral."

"That's great!"

"I feel both very lucid and lost," she added.

"Yeah. You know when . . . oh excuse me!" Lee chuckled, catching himself interrupting her again. The entire group was raptly caught up in this exchange. The innocence and sincerity of her attitude seemed to be moving the feeling center of the audience as a whole as it touched on a core issue for everyone. Although Lee's responses were humorous and appeared almost flippant, just beneath the surface there was a tremendous feeling of acceptance and respect moving in the room.

"So my question is, what exactly is mourning? What does it mean to mourn someone? As far as I am concerned, as far as what I have discovered about myself goes . . ."

"What I was going to say when I almost interrupted you," Lee interrupted, "was that when we're in the moment, it's exactly the way you described it—lucid and feeling lost— because we're alive in a time-space continuum. We find ourselves in that which is eternal and out of time and space, but we're still in the body, we still have an intellect, we still have emotions. It's a very common description. You yourself gave a very fine definition of mourning, which is recognizing the mortality of the body and at the same time the immortality of the essence, or the spirit. You can cry for the body and be exalted at the wonder of the essence." Lee paused and looked at her, seeming to gauge how much she had already absorbed. The room was very full and pregnant with the rich mood that was underlying their brief exchange, and he went on, saying, "I think we should stop there, while we're ahead. Okay? Thank you."

The next questioner said, "Even if one hasn't gone all the way to the end of the path, as in finishing one's sadhana, shouldn't one still be able to love someone, even anyone?"

Lee said, "In one sense all of us have already completed the path and we're just figuring it out and throwing away the baggage we don't need. So of course love will shine through in many moments, even if we think we're just beginners on the path."

The question went on, "As an example, you said that children easily have love impulses towards others, and then they learn how to protect themselves because it causes pain to them. I don't understand because it seemed to me that the reason why they were closing up was because they had not had positive feedback from adults, and that was the reason why they were closing. I don't understand why they would close up just from feeling this love impulse."

Lee responded, "Not having a positive response is a form of abuse. So there's many forms of violence. Neglect is one form of violence. Another form is being physically hit. Or having your older brothers and sisters run ahead, you know, invite you to play with them and then run ahead so fast you can't catch up, while you are calling, 'Wait! Wait! Wait!' and then they start teasing you. So we're talking about the same thing."

The student commented, "I think this is something which could put a lot of enthusiasm in my practice." Lee laughed, "Mostly, my experience has been that what puts enthusiasm in people's practice is enthusiasm. Is that clear?"

In this session Lee's mood was, as it had been since he arrived, actually soft in many ways, even when he had everyone laughing at his antics. At the same time a ferocity lay just underneath the quietness of his voice and in the velvet touch of his compassion, which was deeply felt in the space. Earlier today he gave psychological advice to a woman who said that she was getting a divorce. Although Lee was very patient and benevolent and understanding with her, the psychological questions typically have almost no energy in them. There is no alchemy in them and they drag on the group. At other times Lee's easy manner of cajoling, reprimanding, massaging, joking, and giving little pinches and pokes or slaps and soft strokes to ego as he answered questions was an amazing display of mastery to watch. With each person he was totally there, responding with an instinctual accuracy that went to the heart of the unconscious question or need that was underlying the surface question.

Tonight Lee, his students, Arnaud, Veronique and a number of Arnaud's students were hosted for dinner at the home of Geoffroy and Annick D'Astier. It was a beautiful evening outside in the back yard with the green fields stretching out behind the house toward a tree-lined river. There was a feast of grilled chicken, rice and a dessert spread that challenged even the Americans—who are reputed to eat, especially desserts, like pigs at a trough. Such fabulous delicacies as *mousse au chocolat, gâteau chocolat avec une sauce á la crème, fromage blanc avec des framboises, et tarte aux pomme* were a few of the offerings. The French and Americans lingered over the meal throughout the long last light of the evening, laughing together in a very fine enjoyment of each other's company.

At dusk a message came to our table from Annick, who had asked that we close the evening by gathering around Arnaud and Lee for a "moment of silence." As about twenty people gathered in chairs around the table where the two masters sat facing their disciples, the silence deepened into a mood of profound sanctity. Candles fluttered in a slight breeze around us in the dark as the group fell into the receptivity of communion. Arnaud seemed to go into some kind of state in which he became perfectly sculpted and absolutely still. In that moment his beaming and tranquil face was the embodiment of the impersonal emanation of pure wisdom, *prajna*.

Arnaud and Lee were, in those rare moments, impossible to describe adequately, but once again they struck me as the qualities of sun and moon. Arnaud was imbued with a golden light while, on this occasion, Lee radiated silver. Lee was serene and yet there was a quality of active receptivity and fullness about him. Lee appeared as the jewel of humanity, rendered into perfection through the Will of God, while Arnaud took on the aspect of impersonal God-realization. This reminded me of how Lee approaches Arnaud— with complete and absolute respect for the fact that this is Arnaud's space, his ashram, his chamber, his show. It is clear that Lee is here to serve and support Arnaud and his disciples in any way he can. Lee follows Arnaud's lead, uses Arnaud's language to expound the teaching more with every passing year, and continually turns Arnaud's disciples toward their master. And yet in the process of doing this, Lee also brings his own revelation to the teaching, which is Spiritual Slavery, Surrender to the Will of God, Enlightened

Duality, Organic Innocence and the Primacy of Natural Ecstasy.

As dusk passed into darkness the bullfrogs joined the crickets in a full-throated songfest from the fields between where the group sat by the tall hedge, and the river only a couple of hundred yards away, flanked by the dark shadows of tall trees. A small wind blew the paper lantern with its burning candle down at our feet. Lalitha picked it up and held it in her lap to disturb the space as little as possible. After a timeless span of silence—perhaps fifteen minutes—Arnaud closed the space with a smile of pure delight. The moment of this particular transmission was over. Lee's posture shifted slightly, and everyone began to move. Lee turned to Arnaud and said that he would go back to the ashram now to retire for the night.

July 8, 1999
Hauteville

At the end of the session late yesterday afternoon Lee began to tell a long version of the first outbreak of shakti manifestations in his community, which happened in India in 1977. Everyone in the room was captivated as the story unwound in brilliant detail. An ecstatic mood wafted through the space, which was completely malleable in Lee's hands. Even Arnaud was leaning forward with a big smile on his face, looking at Lee with expectancy and delight, following every word as he always does, but with great expression. Lee stopped short of making the point, saying, "We don't have time to get to the point, to finish today, so we'll have to continue tomorrow. I'm really just setting the ambiance!"

His art as raconteur was at its best in those moments. When we saw Lee outside immediately after the session everyone was buzzing over the powerful storytelling. Lee laughed gently and said, "Yes, even Arnaud was saying to me when we walked out, 'I must hear the end of the story! I was in India with you!' " And that was exactly what happened; everyone had been transported to India. Everyone who had been in the space yesterday had been carried along bodily in the excitement, and was now eagerly waiting and primed for the session this morning.

Lee immediately continued the story. As he came to the conclusion, Lee began to zero in on his point. "So, this energetic phenomena became a very active aspect of our community for many years. You know, a new student would come and they'd just walk in the room and boom, all of a sudden they'd be having very extraordinary energetic phenomena occurring. In fact, one of the guys who is with me here had a very funny expression of this phenomena. It wasn't funny to him at the time; fortunately he was much younger and in good physical condition. The energy started manifesting in his body in very dynamic and difficult yogic postures, the kinds of physical postures that he could never do under ordinary circumstances. Just before the energy would force him into a certain posture, literally taking over his body, he would get an image of the posture that was coming. So he'd be sitting in some space, in a talk or something, and all of a sudden, his eyes would get wide and he'd go, 'Oh no! Oh no!' And then up he'd go into a headstand with his back all twisted up, and he'd stay in the posture for some seconds or moments. After he came out of the posture he'd be panting," Lee demonstrated, "because it was really extreme physical stretching in a way that the body was not used to. And it got wilder and wilder.

"What tends to happen in a process of spiritual transformation is that when a certain current of very intense, high energy first hits people, it tends to create dramatic physical manifestations. But as the vehicle—the mind, the body, the emotional vehicle—gets used to the energy, then it grows to embrace the energy. Then there aren't physical manifestations. In fact, sometimes people feel nothing is happening anymore. 'I've lost it,' they often say. But in fact, what happens is that it becomes interiorized, and the movement of the energy that is transformational continues to function, but it works on more and more subtle levels. We can call this experience the movement of energy, and it gets more and more subtle. One of the ideas of this phenomena is, what is the body anyway? The body is the grossest, the densest and the most mortal of any of our forms."

Lee called on the next questioner, who said, "When he spoke at our general assembly a month ago, Erik told us about something you said during your last visit to Canada. You said something like, 'Arnaud is a tantric master, but people don't know it, aren't aware of it.'"

Looking surprised, Lee said with a little smile, "Oh, did I say that?"

"And beyond the way of tantra itself, I'd like to know what that means in the context of Hauteville."

Lee answered, "Essentially the word tantra means life. The contemporary spiritual scene has a buzz about tantra—a kind of perverse buzz. In the mind of the average spiritual seeker the word tantra implies indulgence. But in fact traditionally it has absolutely nothing to do with that. So what we tend to read about, what tends to be written by Western researchers into traditional Eastern tantra, is the spectacular. You know, 'At midnight they met in the forest around the fire and they all took their clothes off, and after ripping the sheep to pieces and devouring its meat and getting drunk on wine, they all had sex.' That's a totally erroneous view of what tantra is. What tantra is really about is about the acceptance of what is as it is.

"In India at the acme of tantric popularity the prevailing mood of the culture was extremely repressive and exclusive. Without any criticism of Ramakrishna, his perspective about 'women and gold' was that women and gold were the evils of the world. Ramakrishna's attitude mirrored that of hundreds of years of cultural attitude in India, fostered by orthodoxy. That orthodoxy was a reaction to the effectiveness of matriarchal dominance. So, men took over every position of authority and dominance and went about systematically eliminating positive feminine elements of the culture.

"Tantra is a relatively new tradition, actually. In the *Mahabharata*, the *Ramayana*, there is no tantra. In the *Upanishads*, in the *Vedas*— there's no tantra. Some of the more recent *Upanishads* are tantric in nature. But in the Vedic tradition there was no such thing as tantra. There are the very famous temple complexes in Khajuraho, India, with hundred of statues of men and women in every kind of sexual position, but those temples were not tantric temples. They're temples created by a culture that was simply celebrating life. There was no tantra at that time. In India people call those tantric temples, but those are not tantric temples—they're just about life. The radical nature of very exclusive and specific rituals gets represented as, 'This is what tantra is about,' but it's not.

"It's like taking one image out of the entire imagery of Catholicism—the image of Jesus on the cross with his crown of thorns and blood running down his face and blood running out of his side, and his face of torment—and saying, 'This is Catholicism.' The sect of tantra was a reaction against patriarchal repression because the ritual and social bureaucracies of the time were completely repressive of life. Extreme dietary rules and the viewpoint that women themselves were bad, that men were the only ones that could realize God and lead spiritual lives, were prevalent—obviously women kept the men from their exalted states of wisdom. Meat was bad, money was bad, sex was the worst and renunciation was good. The men in this position of course conveniently overlooked the rampant homosexuality that went on in the monasteries. So, tantra arose as a reaction to this repression because this repression was a repression of life as it is—a repression of food, of drink, of love, of friendship, companionship, sex. Tantra was about accepting what is as it is. It's the natural path.

"As in all movements there is the integrity of the movement, and then there are the traps which tend to get dramatized. One of the traps in the tantric sect is losing sight of the essence of tantra. Instead of worshipping and honoring and accepting life as it is, here and now, instead of developing equanimity and internal harmony—as Arnaud said in meditation this morning, whatever arises on the surface, happiness or sorrow, on the inside you stay centered—the attitude became, 'Okay, the orthodoxy says we can't have sex, let's show them. Let's have as much sex as we can possibly have. Oh you know, they say we can't drink, let's go out and get totally drunk.' And then we say, 'This is the path of revolt, or reaction.'

"Tantra in essence is simply about all of life as it is. In a sensible way one would not seek out poisonous circumstances; one wouldn't become an alcoholic or a drug addict, or a child pornography addict. But if you are having a quiet night at home with your wife, and a mood of sexual intimacy arises, why should there be a religious problem? Tantra says there shouldn't be. What is, is—as it is. I think the parallel between that and the practice here, Arnaud's practice, is obvious."

The question continued, "But I heard something else too, which was something like, 'You do not see Arnaud as he is.'"

"Yes, that's true," Lee nodded.

"So, the underlying question is, what is it that could help me to deepen the relationship to Arnaud? Knowing that I have no cultural reference, because in our culture the relationship to the master doesn't exist. Knowing also that I can't rely on the experience of others, but only on my experience."

Lee answered, "Well, that's a very good question. And it's true that generally speaking in the West we don't have a deep cultural tradition for relationship to the spiritual master. But we do have references for worship, for adoration, respect, honor. We have the ability to see things as they are—that's a human quality. So regardless of culture, that ability is true of Indians, Tibetans, Japanese and all Westerners.

"There are several elements of the question. I'll answer the question in a little while— let me lay some foundation for people who haven't heard this before. When most people first come to the path or to the teacher, they don't recognize within themselves the degree of transference that goes on. When we come to the teacher we unconsciously project that which we have never had in our lives and want: the good father, the kind father, the gentle father, the loving father, or the reliable authority figure, the one who will not let us down, who will not disappoint us. Or we project the great lover, which is the most difficult one of course—not for the genuine master, but for the false master. That's the trap that the false master wants to try to actually live up to. Boy, does that get them in trouble! In the process of practice and sadhana we come to see this transference and we come to cease animating it. That's the first thing we have to get out of the way. How can we see the master as he is, if all we can see is the master as we wish him to be?

"When we first meet the master, a lot of us have this feeling of antiquity. Something feels timeless, and although we don't know how we know it, we somehow know it. Part of learning to see Arnaud as he is, is not associating the body of manifestations with the guru, with the master. The master as a human being includes intellect, emotions, body, but is not that exclusively. When people host Arnaud they want to know what food he likes, or what wine he likes, so maybe they prepare special things. Obviously a sensible disciple would want to please the external form of the guru, but that is the vast complex of phenomena that has randomly gelled, that has randomly come together to create the image we call Arnaud Desjardins. Who Arnaud *is* observes this ongoing manifestation of phenomena and accepts it as it is, but is not defined by that because all of that is constantly changing, and is mortal, and that which Arnaud *is* is changeless and immortal.

"The function of the guru has always been the same, regardless of time, place, culture, uninhibited by rules, regulations, orthodoxy, opinions, expectations. For example, Pythagoras, who we may remember as a scientist and mathematician, was the founder and essential influence of a mystery school. He functioned as a traditional guru, except it wasn't in the East, it was in the West, and in a radically different culture, but the function of the guru is always the same.

"Although I don't want to get into a metaphysical discussion of karma, let's suffice it to say that every one of us has archaic impulses. Impulse is the wrong word—we have a resource of information that informs our unconscious, even though this information may be completely inaccessible to the conscious mind. In one sense you can't be *taught* how to see the guru, but it lies *within* your experience and nobody else's. There is something in our make-up that *knows* what it is to be with the master. That information may be very subtle, it may be very ancient, and it may not be retrievable through the usual sources of information retrieval with which we are familiar.

"We each have within us this archaic wisdom that knows the value of the guru, the need for the guru, and how to make use of that. At the same time, there are references that can trigger the accessibility or the retrieval system for this archaic knowledge and wisdom, such as reading certain literature, that communicates essential qualities, or listening to certain music. Sound or visual impressions can trigger these archaic knowledge. Movement can also trigger this wisdom, which is one of the things that Gurdjieff's performance 'The Struggle of the Magicians' was designed to do—to create for the viewer such a circumstance of objectivity that it would draw certain knowledge out of the viewer's unconscious.

"Study Arnaud's books and the great books of art and mysticism. One of the books that I recommend often is *Daughter of Fire* by Irina Tweedie. Her book was an international best seller. Fabulous book! It is so communicative. When you read this book you are *there*. You are feeling what she felt. There is a lot of literature like that, to various degrees. Dostoyevsky, for example, and others. I'm not a scholar of literature, but when we study material like that—like Irina Tweedie's book—something deep within us is evoked. Something is released that seeps its way into the complex of the conscious mind and awareness and somehow gives us a greater grasp of what it means to access the master.

"Ultimately ego can't create a mechanism to access the master because everything that ego creates is going to be strategic—strategic in the sense of protecting ego's existence. No matter how sophisticated the strategy, it's still going to be about ego protecting ego. But, when our essential being is deeply enough aligned to the master, then access happens, seeing the master as he or she is happens.

"I'll tell the story of when I first met my Master. The other day I told the story about Silva Mind Control. To brag a little bit, I was not just pretty good at it—I was very good. For example, I knew how to steal energy, how to get energy from people. The first time I went to India I traveled around and visited many people, including Anandamayi Ma. As much as various people touched me, I wasn't connected to any of them. I was tremendously grateful to have the opportunity to sit in Ma Anandamayi's presence, but I wasn't magnetized to her. But when I met Yogi Ramsuratkumar, I was completely magnetized. I didn't understand what that magnetism was. All I knew was that He had something I wanted.

"My reference point for getting what I wanted was, if they weren't giving it to you, you steal it. This is not a spiritual principle, it's an occult principle. It works and I was good at it. There was no question of having a master, because I already considered myself a master, so why would I need a master? But I also had the view that I could always learn. Learning never ends. So when I met Yogi Ramsuratkumar I said to myself, 'This man has something I want, and I'm going to get it, one way or another. Whether he gives it to me or not.' So my initial relationship to Him was one of a treasure hunter to the treasure chest. You know, he had the gold, I wanted it, I was going to get it.

"I went about doing what I did well, but I was dealing with somebody in a category that I had never dealt with before. In the most graceful Aikido move I've ever experienced, He completely turned it around. I started to throw Him and ended up on the ground, not even knowing what happened! All of a sudden one day, I looked in my treasury and all of my gold was gone and He had it. And that's when I started to realize He was my Master. It took a few years for Him to turn the tables on me completely. It was an act of miraculous subtlety and beauty. I was impressed, and not much impressed me in those days. I was very arrogant.

"Most of you know the story well. I started writing Him poetry in letters, and when I got back to India in 1986 after that all had happened, that's when He didn't remember me. He sent me away. Another act of subtlety and beauty," Lee laughed, "that in retrospect is very impressive. In the moment I was thrown a little off balance by it. So, is any of that helpful? Okay, thank you."

Lee's description of his early relationship with Yogi Ramsuratkumar was tremendously moving and had deeply catalyzed the space. There was a sweeping momentum of insight alive in the room—you could almost feel the bodily revelations of the dharma popping like nerve synapses as one person after another moved into states of insight. What was most striking at this point was the felt transmission, the communion Lee established with his audience which somehow became more potent and effective through his skillful use of wit, humor, direct confrontation, kindness and his spinning of tales, a talent which captivated everyone.

He continued taking questions. The next questioner said, "In one of the answers you gave at the beginning of the week I understood there is some sort of primal no. I would like to know if my understanding is correct and if you could explain more about that. Does that imply that each individual has his own particular no which would be specific to him or her?"

Lee said, "In Western psychology we use words like passive-aggressive, or manic-depressive or schizophrenic. Each of us has a certain complex—father complex, mother complex, who knows what—and as this complex develops it pervades every single aspect of our lives. Every thought, every emotion, every action—all of it, from the color of clothing we pick out to wear in the morning, to the partner we choose, or the profession we choose. Some people are optimists, some people are pessimists. We might look at someone who's an optimist and we might say, 'Well, you know this person is really saying yes to life. They're positive. They're enthusiastic. The pessimist is obviously saying no to life because they're very critical, very negative.' But the external form of our manifestation is not what defines whether we're saying yes or no to life. We tend to fall into this error of observation.

"In the Indian system there are three primary human characteristics called *sattvas*, *tamas*, and *rajas*. So *sattvic* means very cool, very calm, serene, no really dramatic reactions. And *rajasic* is the other side—fiery, hot, everything is big and important. What we tend to do is look at someone who is *rajasic* and say, 'Well they're obviously saying no to life. Look at these uncontrolled emotions.' And we say, 'Look at this person who is *sattvic*. They're obviously saying yes to life. They're very calm. They're even.' The response to everything is the same, but those external qualities are not what defines yes or no.

"The presumption of separation is what defines no, and the acceptance of union— being one with—is what defines yes. Someone who is calm and serene, enthusiastic and positive can have just as much a presumption of separation as someone who is fiery and aggressive. We should not be entering the path in order to alter our personalities. When many people first come to the path, if you say to them, 'What do you want from the path?' They might say something like, 'I want to get to the source of my anger.' What they really mean is, 'Anger gets in my way and I don't want it to get in my way. So get it out of my way,' the 'my' being ego.

"Often we come to the path and don't really want what the path is; we just want to get rid of some bothersome aspect of our personality. Whatever gets us on the path is fine, but sooner or later we have to understand that we haven't come to the path to deal with the superficialities of personality and psychology. We may have to deal with these things secondarily in the process, but they are not the purpose of the path. Becoming a good citizen is not the purpose of the path.

"Sooner or later we have to realize that the purpose of the path is to bring clarity to this illusion of separation. That's what the no is. I call it a primal no because it is the first psychological decision we make. It is the decision that is made in infancy to view the world in separation. We don't know we're making the decision. We are not self-aware, we're one with, and the decision still gets made and still has its effects. So when we come to the path as adults the demand is simply to realize the reality of oneness—whether we language that demand as accepting what is as it is, here and now, or to saying yes to life."

In the afternoon session Lee started out with a lengthy discussion with a woman in a pink dress. She said, "I already asked you this question three years ago. It's about hesitating. I tend to hesitate a lot."

"You remembered!" Lee cajoled. "Wow, I'm really touched. Okay, so? A little subtle humor there . . ."

"So I'm trying to accept this hesitation."

"Still?" Lee teased. "After three years? That's a long process. Okay, so?"

"Hesitation remains," she said.

"So, are you still hesitating? *You*. Are you still hesitating?" he pressed.

"Often," she answered.

"Well, maybe you're mistaking hesitation for you. So, what you said was, 'Hesitation remains.' A feeling of hesitation may remain for the rest of your life, but that doesn't mean that you have to hesitate. You can let the tendency of hesitation be, and you can act. Have you ever thought of that? Okay, maybe you have something now that can give you a different reflection on it."

She continued, "I very often annoy people because I tend to ask them for input that they feel I need not ask about."

"I know what you mean, intimately," Lee smiled conspiratorially. "I'm not talking about anybody in this room, of course," he said facetiously, "but there are people back in Arizona who do that to me all the time. They're always hesitating and they keep asking me, 'Well, what about this?' It's all the same thing, over and over, for years. It annoys me. Stop asking. Better to make an honest mistake than to be constantly afraid of making a mistake. You know, how bad a mistake could you make? 'Should I buy this dress or that dress?' What difference could it make what dress you buy?"

"I'd like to feel really guided by the Holy Spirit," she said.

"Oh well," Lee chuckled, "just to buy a dress?" Everyone laughed. He seemed to be using the opportunity to point out the pettiness of our typical concerns. We think our ideas and considerations are lofty, when really they are just self-centered and often mundane or totally meaningless in the face of the real struggles that one confronts on the path. He continued, "Listen, the Holy Spirit is busy. The Holy Spirit has big issues to deal with. Probably the way you are—the fact that you're not dead yet, the fact that you're able to be in this room, and be relatively bright and intelligent—is probably the result of the Holy Spirit guiding you. But, you know, every little decision, moment to moment— we can take care of that. Give the Holy Spirit a break. Really! This is one of the unrealistic projections that people have about what we call enlightenment. We think we're going to hear a little voice telling us what to do all the time, but that is a kind of dependency.

"I suppose since you've used the phrase Holy Spirit you also know the word faith, right? When we have faith—not in the bishop, but in God—then we are guided, we are watched over, we are safe. But it's not the job of the Holy Spirit to do our thinking for us. That's our business. A lot of people think, 'If I was surrendered to the guru, the guru would always be telling me the right thing to do.' That is a complete fixation on a moral platform—this is a sin, this is not a sin, this is good, this is bad. You're an adult, you look intelligent, you speak clearly. You don't need anybody to tell you how to live right. If a big decision comes up, marriage or pregnancy or a big change in your living situation, well then if you have faith, you will be guided. But you'll be guided naturally, not by seeing a big flashing sign in the clouds. Anything else?"

"Well, often I don't know what prayer is. Sometimes I feel I should pray for somebody," she continued.

"That's certainly a big step from hesitation—prayer, Holy Spirit. Are you Catholic?" Lee probed. He seemed to be on to something. She answered yes. "Still?" he asked.

She equivocated, "Well, Catholic means universal."

"Oh, that's what you were told? Did you go to Catholic school when you were young?"he kept pressing her.

"Not always, not for a long time," she answered.

"But a little bit? Wow, Catholic is universal. That's really creative marketing!" Everyone laughed. Probably seventy-five percent of the room was made up of former Catholics. "I don't know," Lee began to answer her question. "Who knows what prayer is? Only God knows what prayer is. You know, if you're in a prayerful mood, whatever you call a prayerful mood—think about God, or life or whatever—that's good enough. You don't have to throw yourself on your knees, beat your chest, you know, 'Oh, forgive me, forgive me. Oh God, smile upon me.' Is that what you think? Like you have to be struck by lightening, metaphorically speaking? Maybe you're praying all the time! Maybe all you have to do is live without doubt or separation and that's prayer!"

"When I feel love and joy I feel this fluidity," she said.

"You mean love and joy from others or from within yourself?" He queried further. She answered, "Both."

"Great! So what are you looking for? More of that?"

"Well there are moments when it's not like that," she said hesitantly.

"Well of course there are. There are moments for everybody when it's not like that. Long moments. I haven't felt like that in years. At least not while the sun is shining!" Lee threw his head back and laughed. "Do you believe me?" She answered yes and he asked why.

"You mean do I believe that it's very often difficult for you?" she asked, becoming more perplexed.

"No, I just said I haven't felt that way in years. Do you believe me?" He seemed to be gearing up to make a point with all this conversation.

She answered, "Yes, because I suppose that you can feel that for many of us. You are in communion with our state."

Lee laughed. "Well, that's a nice compliment. Thank you. I have to write that down and tell all of my students that. So what do you expect?"

"I expect love."

"What is love? Are you not loved now?" he asked. She answered yes. "You are loved. And you love others? I don't mean everybody. I meant some people."

"Yes, a few people yes," she agreed, fully engaged in the conversation.

"Then it sounds like your life is very successful, in relationship to the average person. So what do you expect?" Lee asked, "Do you expect to be consciously aware of this in every moment?"

She said, "I would like to die to myself, to be free of the ego. Because ego is embarrassing."

"It is?" Lee asked innocently. She answered yes. "Is your ego functioning right now?" She stared at him. "Yes or no!" he demanded.

"A little bit," she admitted.

"Only a little bit? You're not making a fool of yourself. You're not doing anything embarrassing," Lee commented.

Gilles clarified her meaning, which was that ego stands in the way. After another length of dialogue in which she said that she believed if she didn't have ego there wouldn't be an obstacle anymore and no more duality, Lee laughed again and said, "Well I would say that if you *really* see that, you've already transcended it. I would guess that you're just being philosophical. I know you believe that what you're saying is your experience, but I would venture a guess that what you're saying is not your experience, but your opinion of your experience. Because if somebody is able to look at their life and see the division, in that moment of seeing there's no division at all. That would be my conclusion."

A man asked the next question: "My impression is that I lack motivation in my practice."

"Well," Lee tossed out, "do it anyway. Motivation to practice is a luxury."

"But this lack of motivation makes me suffer," the man continued, "because I see I'm harming myself and others, and yet I'm not budging really. And yet, I think I have fairly understood practice and I don't know how I could strengthen this motivation. Generally speaking I tend to feel guilty about it and it doesn't really work. It doesn't motivate me more to feel guilty."

Lee laughed, "That's true. Guilt has never made a Catholic a better Catholic. Right? Well, you know, motivation is an affect of separation. When something serves our personal program, then we're motivated to achieve that. Practice doesn't serve our personal program. Practice, in fact, is designed to obviate the whole personal program itself. So, why would the one that generates motivation enter into the attempt to do something that would completely obviate itself? For the one who is motivated, to be successful in practice would be like committing suicide.

"There are periods of time in which there is a motivation to practice for many different people, but this doesn't change the principle since the motive to practice for most people is motivated for some personal reason. 'If I practice hard the teacher will recognize me and praise me and give me attention and blah, blah, blah.' So, motivation is a function of separation. Practice is designed to transcend or obviate the illusion of separation.

"You don't activate the motivation to practice, you simply practice. And there will be times in which you feel motivated and times in which you don't. But even when you don't feel motivated, you still practice. Consistency is what's important. When I look at a student who's practicing and at their reliability of practice, I don't care if they are motivated to practice or not. What I'm interested in is whether they are practicing, not whether they're motivated to practice. If I'm going to give a student responsibility or authority or attention or whatever, it is because their practice is *reliable*.

"I know that when you're motivated to do something it feels good. I understand that. You make a big business deal, a lot of profit, it feels great. Or when you have some goal in mind and you're really motivated to make this goal, it feels great. It feels great to be enthusiastic about what we're doing. I understand that. But with practice, you just have to do it—even if you feel completely apathetic. You do it anyway because we go through many stages and many phases, and inevitably all of us are going to reach some stage or some phase in which we just don't want to practice. Not only are we not motivated to practice, but practice repulses us. We have to do it anyway.

"When you're able to practice in that way your practice will bear fruit and eventually—the next day or years down the road—you will realize the value of that kind of practice. The realization of the value of that kind of practice will itself be the motivation to continue to practice. But it may be very quiet and matter-of-fact, you know? It may not be full of fireworks and enthusiasm. It may just be very simple. Anything else?"

"Since I've got you, I'm keeping you for a moment," the man said.

"Okay, boss. That's what it says on his shirt—boss," Lee explained to the audience.

The man said seriously, "I'd like to be the boss with myself."

"Leave that to God," Lee said simply, but implying volumes.

"I've come to a phase where I've let myself be invaded by the 'no,' " the man continued.

"Well, if the no is there you might as well let it breathe, you know," Lee responded. "Try to suffocate it and it's just going to really get nervous—like we get when we aren't allowed to breathe. So as long as the no is there, well that's what is. Let it be what it is.

And so, how's it going? It's not hurting your business is it?"

"You mean the no?" the questioner continued, "The no is not hurting my business?"

"Letting the no be there is not cutting your profit is it?" Lee asked.

"Well I think I could still do better, but . . ."

"Sure, it's a big world and there are a lot of flowers," Lee smiled.

"Oh you know, it's bugging me," the man continued, slightly irritated. "You're asking a question to me and you don't let me speak. You're not letting me speak."

Lee returned quickly, "Because my question is more important than what you have to say." Everyone laughed.

"Yes, that's true," the man admitted.

"No I'm just kidding. It was a joke, so everybody laughs," Lee said amiably, somewhat appeasing now. The man stayed with him and was visibly getting softer and more relaxed as the exchange went on. Now he said, "Well, you know, I'm breathing with the no and now it's much easier."

Lee nodded, "Sure. Much freer."

"But you know, here right now, my motivation is to feel recognized by you, to feel loved," the man continued in the same serious mood that he had had throughout the conversation.

"Recognized, okay. Love is a big stretch," Lee said in a droll tone of voice. Everyone laughed, and the man who was asking the questions laughed a deep, hearty laugh, his whole body relaxing into it.

"Good!" Lee smiled broadly, "Got you laughing. That's it! That's a *great* laugh! It was a free laugh, not efforted to have an effect, just a free laugh. So what else do we need to talk about? I mean, we can keep going if you want to, it's fine, but that completed it for me. Okay? Thank you. Yes?" He turned to the next questioner, a man with a very bright and wholesome manner about him.

"Yesterday you said that when you are answering questions from people it's as if you are fishing," the man said, "and I realized that you are a good fisherman."

Lee interrupted, "Yes, but even the best fisherman without a fish is only halfway there!" He laughed. "Say, that was pretty good. Write that down," he gestured to his students who were scribbling furiously in their notebooks. "Okay, so?"

"Most of the themes which were brought up here," the man continued, "I recognize myself in those themes. I saw I had something to learn, to discover, to deepen, and that's it. That's the correct side of the question. So what I would like to say is what's happening this week since Monday when I arrived, I think it's totally crazy."

Lee seemed to think this was very funny. He laughed and said, "In what way?"

"In every possible way."

Looking very innocent and mild-mannered, Lee said, "Wow! And so? How do you feel about that?" He started laughing again.

"The fact that it is crazy and that you are even a little crazy . . ."

Lee interrupted, "Only a little crazy? 'Crazy like a fox,' they say."

The man smiled and continued, "That's not a problem; the problem is I'm not crazy enough."

"By whose estimation?" Lee asked.

"According to my estimation."

"Maybe you're not the best one to judge. What do you have to be crazier for?" Lee asked earnestly.

"Because the way I'm functioning, the way I'm being reasonable, the way I'm approaching life, it doesn't ring true in a way," the man answered.

Lee answered, "I don't know. My first impression in seeing you is that you look much more in touch with who you are than most of the men in this room. So what's the problem?"

The man smiled and said, "I have long moments of serenity."

"Great!" Lee smiled back.

"Even of fusion. But particularly," the man continued with Lee chuckling now while he talked, "this week, with the energy that's here, I can see that it's resisting somewhere."

"Great! Then that's the value of this week—to uncover one more little area of resistance that you didn't know was there. And I expect by the time you leave, that it will be gone. I *expect* that of you. Okay? Great."

Another man said, "In my role as a father I have the impression that I often make mistakes."

Lee said, "Nobody is a perfect parent, you know."

The man continued, "That's true. But I told myself that if I was able to change certain characteristics of my temperament I would be able to avoid making mistakes. So at the beginning that was my motivation. Then this morning you said that it shouldn't be the motivation on the path."

"What shouldn't be?" Lee asked. "Trying to change things about ourselves? You weren't here yesterday, were you? Something I said yesterday was that everybody has to start some place. We can only start where we are. If the beginning motivation is less than the highest motivation, and that's where we are, it's perfect. And as we work and as we practice, our motivation will change. But as it is, from where we are, it's perfect. It couldn't be anything else. We should never criticize ourselves for being less than some ideal definition. The important thing is that we be where we are, not that we wish we were somewhere else. When I was first a father I made a lot of mistakes and fifteen years later, I had changed dramatically. I was able to affect, in a positive way, some of the mistakes I had made. I couldn't have done that when I was first a father. I just wasn't the same person then that I was fifteen years later."

"It seems to be somewhat ambitious for me to be able to make up for the mistakes I have made," the man said, "but how can I act in a way that minimizes the mistakes, or should I talk to the children about the mistakes I made?"

Lee answered, "My first daughter, who is now thirty years old, was maybe three years old when her mother and I separated. She said something to her mother one day. It was very innocent, but it was so heartbreaking to me, that based on the suffering of my own error—not that I was guilty, I wasn't guilty—I was able to be a better father from then on. It's the memory of my failure that inspires different behavior. It's not a positive inspiration. It's the heartbreak of seeing innocence become less innocent. Okay?" The man nodded.

Another man began his question. "You spoke about Charles Bukowski. Apart from being a great poet, do you think he was a good disciple, or is expressing this idea, or . . . ?"

Lee laughed, "He was a good disciple to alcohol and to art! I'm not sure that's a good role model. Not something any of us should be trying to duplicate."

"Yesterday you spoke about the process of mourning the body of a person," a woman began.

"Yes. Maybe we should mourn the person when they're alive, and then when they die we can dance on their grave! Most people are much more mournful when they're alive than when they're dead anyway. You know? Most people when they're alive lead lives of such tragedy that once they die it's fabulous. They're free of it all. I'm being a little cynical, so forgive me. Yes?"

"I didn't mean to speak about a deceased person, I mean on a personal level, in spiritual life. I interpreted it as an indication for being detached from the body. I thought there should be a sort of detachment of mourning from the body, losing the body. I'm speaking of that because that's what I felt this morning in meditation."

Lee said, "Well, to lose the body is to gain the body. Really. It's a paradoxical statement, but it's true."

"Could you go deeper into that statement? It's very difficult to live. There seems to be some sort of contradiction between the times in meditation in which I don't feel the body as matter anymore, and times out of meditation when I have to be living in the body again, and feeling the body alive. There seems to be a contradiction between those two aspects: between not feeling the body as matter anymore, and then having to live with the body."

Lee answered, "Well, it is difficult to live it, but there's no contradiction at all. When you realize the body, you realize some kind of detachment: 'This is just the body, it doesn't define me. I'm associated with it, and in my association I am the body, and when the body leaves I will still be.' Then when you come out of meditation, you're living in the body and you have to go to the bathroom, you say, 'I was feeling the body was completely immaterial, and now I have to go to the bathroom.' When you have realized the context of being one with the body then the body is not a burden. It's not extra. It's not something you have to carry around, an annoyance. It's just what it is. You know, when the body is hungry, it's hungry. When it's tired, it's tired. It's just what it is. Looking at the body as some kind of cross you have to bear is not having realized, or not having seen clearly that it is just a body—no more, no less."

At seven o'clock Lee's two vans followed Arnaud and Veronique in their car on a twenty minute drive up into the nearby hills to the house of Gilles and Laurence Farcet where a number of people were hosted for dinner. Lee, Arnaud, Veronique and a few others were seated at a table on the back patio, while the rest of the company sat on the floor or on couches and chairs in the living room where the late afternoon sun came shining in full force.

After dinner, while we waited for dessert to be served, several of Lee's students sat talking with Daniel Morin, one of Arnaud's teaching assistants. He and Dasya were discussing the teaching with the help of François Fronty, who translated. Dasya commented that Arnaud's disciples were very bright and that their practice seemed strong this year. Daniel said, "I'm still not satisfied—never satisfied!"

Dasya said with a laugh, "You were born dissatisfied! We must be patient, Daniel."

"We must be patient and impatient," Daniel replied. "If we go too slow, the ego pops up; if we go too fast, the ego pops up. We must have irritation to work."

Dasya said, "We call that having an edge."

"*Oui*," Daniel added, "at Le Bost Arnaud created irritation *for* us." Daniel continued to say that Arnaud was not interested in creating irritation for his students now, but was resting "in love" or in a state of love, and that his disciples must create irritation for themselves.

Debbie said, "Arnaud seems to be delighting in his disciples in the meetings."

"Arnaud is enjoying and appreciating Lee, getting energy from Lee," Daniel responded with precision.

Jane said to Daniel, "From many stories we have heard it seems that it was very different in the early days, that Arnaud was more fierce and irritating people all the time. Is that so—has it changed since Le Bost?" When François had translated this Daniel, Maryse and other French disciples sitting there nodded emphatically and began to tell stories of Le Bost, Arnaud's first ashram. Daniel said that Arnaud was so fierce during those years that if someone even looked at their watch one time during a dharma meeting, Arnaud would send them out of the room. He was so exacting about time that the breakfast bell had to be rung at the exact moment that the second hand hit eight o'clock. If not, there would be hell to pay. Daniel was responsible for making Arnaud's breakfast; it had to be ready at *exactly* eight o'clock and not one moment after. The three-minute egg had to be exactly right and the bread had to be toasted on both sides but soft in the middle and it had to be served hot. All in all, it was a practically impossible task.

Daniel said that Arnaud worked fifteen hours a day, seven days a week. "People who come to Hauteville lose something because they don't see behind the scene—like at Le Bost when Arnaud was so tired and exhausted that he had to stop in the room before the meeting room and lean against the wall to gather the strength to go on, to enter the room and give the teaching . . ."

In the early days of Le Bost Arnaud wanted only ten disciples at the ashram to hear the teachings. Swami Prajnanpad had always kept his ashram small, and this was what Arnaud was used to. But at Le Bost there was always someone calling, asking if he or she could bring this person or that friend. Arnaud would say, "I cannot say no, but we already have eleven!" when he had clearly wanted only ten to begin with.

Veronique joined the conversation, saying as she walked in from the porch, "This is the place to be!" She added, "In Le Bost the pessimistic people would say, 'If we go on this way we will soon be one hundred.' Last year at Hauteville there were thirteen hundred people!"

At that point Arnaud came in with Lee. When Arnaud found out what everyone was talking about he said, "No one would believe the real story of Le Bost! The behind-the-scene story!" He then proceeded to tell, in a marvelously theatrical style, a number of hilarious and at times bawdy stories of crazy antics that happened with people who came to Le Bost in the early days, keeping everyone captivated and laughing until it was time to go back to the ashram for the night.

July 9, 1999
Hauteville

Near the beginning of the morning session a question was asked, "I can't quite see why it's so important to be free before death. What is at stake?"

Lee answered, "Why bother being free afterward? You know, what good is being free after death? You've got nothing to be free in. If you're free before death then you've got the body in which to live that freedom. If you're free after death, what good is it? Nothing! The Buddhists say that the rarest thing in the universe, the most prized possibility in the universe, is to get a human body. That's because the possibility of growth and advancement is higher in a human body than in any other form—even higher than the

366

form of an angel or a demigod or a fairy. To whom? You, you, you, you!"

The questioner continued, "Yes, but consciousness is the same always."

"Are you sure?" Lee pressed. The questioner answered no. "Well, then don't be so affirmative when you're not sure. If what I say doesn't make sense, then find out in your own experience.

"In one sense when I come to Hauteville or anywhere else the idea is not to clarify people's confusion or to give people answers that are satisfying. The idea is to create an irritation, a disturbance. If it means enough to you to come to resolve, then you've got all the necessary tools and gifts and the necessary consciousness to come to resolve. If the resolution of this kind of irritation does not mean that much to you, you'll go to some other teacher or some other seminar in which you'll be consoled, and then your mind will be satisfied and you'll just pretend that there never was an irritation.

"You'll go to some Western divine mother with blonde hair down to her butt and lots of expensive jewelry all over her body. You'll do a little chanting and then she'll say, 'It's all love and it's all one.' You say to yourself, 'Now *this* is what I wanted to hear—no irritation, no demand! This is my idea of spiritual life!' "

Brigette asked the next question. "I'd like to go deeper into the question I asked you two days ago. If I use this sentence, 'What is a woman?' as a koan in my life, in your book you wrote something like, if you are using this koan, don't be sloppy. Be always constantly very exact because an insignificant change, a very minor change, can completely muddy the result you're expecting. And I didn't really understand what you meant by that."

Lee answered, "Well, that would be the difference between putting salt over and against sugar in tea. A very small difference, they look the same. Just half a teaspoon, just a little bit, but it totally alters the taste. So if you have this question, 'What is a woman?' and you already have a preconceived idea, then you will unconsciously create answers that confirm your preconceived idea, whether they are accurate or not. So you have to be very exacting in terms of your perception of what is, as it is, because if you leave out one element, that element will alter the entire formula.

"Did you ever see the American movie called 'The Fly'? Oh well, it was about a time machine and it disincorporated the person who was in it and then reincorporated him somewhere else. The man who invented it was trying it and accidentally a fly got stuck in the machine while it was turned on. The man and the fly were disincorporated together, and then when they were reincorporated, the fly had become part of the man's genetic structure. Slowly the man turned into a big fly. That was a great movie!

"In the science of alchemy, which was practiced in the Middle Ages, it was very important for the equipment that was used for alchemical experiments to be absolutely clean. Let's use an example more relevant to you since you're a doctor. Germs are very small but they have very big consequences. Every law that is evident in the Universe has parallels, 'As above so below, as below so above.' If there is one small alteration in your efforts—say, lacking to sterilize a needle before you give an injection—it could have very large consequences in your results.

"So when you ask a question of yourself, for example, let's use Ramana Maharshi's form of Enquiry, the phrase 'Who am I?' Anyone who has ever tried that, just asking it very superficially, it is the intellect asking the question. So, very quickly you get an answer anywhere from, 'I'm Brigette, and I'm a mother and I'm a woman,' up to 'I am the eternal undiminished light of consciousness shining in this small individual form,' and blah blah blah. But it's all intellectual, so you have to keep asking the question. As Arnaud was saying this morning in meditation, you have to push the question into the depths of your very being, and then you have to push the question beyond to the depths of Being itself. Most people stop at *my* being, my body, my spirit.

"So, with the question, 'What is woman?' you have to push the question into the very essence of life itself, because if you stop at psychology or whatever it might be, you may get a reasonable answer, but it's not really what you're looking for.

"I really like the way Arnaud starts meditation most mornings, which is, 'Why are you here, now, today?' The most superficial level of that is, 'What are you doing here in the dojo on this pillow now this morning?' In the larger sense, the question might be, 'Why are you here, why do you exist in life here now?' So when you ask the question of yourself, you have to make sure as much as possible that it's a pure question untainted by judgement, expectation, projection, definition. The intention is to be asking the source of Life itself, so that the answer is the ultimate answer—an answer that's not relatively true but absolutely true. Because if you ask the intellect, you may get a true answer, but only relatively true."

Brigette talked about how her life is very active with children and very intense work. Lee qualified, "Then you go to a very specific inner space in which you are not disturbed by anything, and then you have time, day and night, in which to work on your question. You have to learn to work interiorly, to bear down on the question, to work the question intensely, interiorly, so that on the outside, nobody knows what's going on.

"You need to mother your children and everything else, because when you're with your children you don't want them to look at you and kick you in the leg and say, 'Stop meditating—play with me!' So you have to be completely present to your children and working, working. There's a story about my Master, Yogi Ramsuratkumar. There was a young Indian woman who discovered and became very much enamored with Him and devoted to Him. She was in her early twenties. You know when we're young we really want to infect everyone with our enthusiasm! We want to bring everyone into our camp." Lee chuckled.

"So, of course she began telling everybody about this great saint she met. All her friends were going crazy with the fantasies of young girls. So one day she was traveling to Tiruvannamalai with a number of her friends and she took them to see Yogi Ramsuratkumar. He was sitting on the porch, and when they walked up to Him, He turned His back and refused to see them. He just sat there smoking. She kept saying, 'Oh Master, I brought my friends,' but He wouldn't speak. He wouldn't look at them. They stayed for a half-hour or forty-five minutes. Finally the friends said, 'This is ridiculous, let's get out of here,' so they grabbed her physically and dragged her away to go see the town and get something to eat.

"While they were walking around she sneaked away and ran back to Yogi Ramsuratkumar. The minute she got there He was totally effusive, talking to her, and saying, 'Oh, it's good to see you again!' He said, 'Your friends are really strange.' And then they talked for an hour or so, nonstop. Eventually her friends realized she was missing and they wanted to leave town, so they figured she was back there at the saint's. The minute they came into visibility, He turned around, turned His back to them and stopped talking.

"So this question of yours—in spite of the fact that you've asked it publicly here and we're talking about it publicly—if you don't show it off, most of the people here will forget that you've even asked it. Your question is for you, it's your work, so there's no need to advertise it. You just do your work, and you learn to work interiorly while your life goes on as it needs to."

Another woman raised her hand and said, "You mentioned that your aim was to irritate people in your answers . . ."

Lee interjected, "Not necessarily just in my answers, but to irritate people in principle."

"Since you gave me an answer two days ago, I feel some sort of inner burning . . ."

"You're sure it's not just gas?" Lee smiled impishly.

"No, it's at the level of the heart," she answered.

"Okay, heartburn," he quipped relentlessly.

Persevering, she said, "And you said I danced wildly. I was really embarrassed and I thought about that a lot."

"I was embarrassed too. I mean, not by your dancing, but by what I was thinking! You said your boyfriend wasn't in the room right? Okay, whew!" Everyone laughed.

She continued, "It's difficult for me to accept this part of me, because when I was dancing, I was really with my body."

"So why is that difficult?" Lee asked.

"Because I haven't yet accepted the wild woman in me," she answered.

"I haven't accepted the wild woman in me either! Yes, what's the question?"

"Accepting all the parts that constitute what we are here and now equates to accepting our deeper nature?" she asked.

"Everything, our deeper nature, our not-so-deep nature," Lee watched her closely.

"Are those unacceptable parts also doors to accepting oneself?"

Lee said, "Well, what do you think? You don't need me to answer that. It's such an obvious question, it's such an obvious answer. Right? What's the answer? You don't have to look for an answer that you like. Just give me the answer—yes or no!"

Not taking her eyes off Lee she said yes. "Of course," he nodded.

"It's much simpler than what I thought," she mused.

"Oh, yes. It's much simpler than we all think. We want to make it complicated because we feel justified in not living it if it's complicated. If it's so complicated, then it's confusing, we can't understand it. Then we can justify our struggle. But the truth is that it's just simple. Not necessarily *easy*, but simple, very simple. Accept what is, as it is— how much simpler could it be? Okay? Okay."

Another woman asked, "The title of your last book spoke to me very much and it was reinforced by the dedication you wrote. You wrote, 'To try without the heart means not to try at all. To be alive is the result of a heart that is open and gentle.' "

Lee, acting surprised, said, "That was nice. Oh man—see now, I'm going to go down to the book table today and everybody's going to come and they're going to say, 'You didn't write that kind of dedication to me.' "

She continued, "Because it seems to me that the opening of the heart doesn't depend on me."

"Exactly. Trying with the heart doesn't depend upon you either. That's exactly it. So trying without the heart is *you* trying, and trying with the heart is something else entirely. To try to define what that is would simply drag the whole consideration into the gutter or something. I mean, I could be very flowery and poetic, but I think it's better to leave it."

Later Jean Claude asked a question about marriage. After some repartee with Lee he said, "So my question may seem academic, but to me, I feel it is very important. What is the significance of marriage?"

Lee answered, "Well, there are many levels on which one can consider this question. For example, simply the level of formal commitment, which is similar to any kind of formal commitment. Like when we go into a church to pray, we get down on our knees. That gesture has a certain power to it. The freedom to be able to offer oneself to another person in a very formal way also has a certain power to it. Not in the way in which tradition is just empty and repetitive, but in real tradition, true tradition. Marriage is a commitment to blend one's soul with the soul of another.

"I'm not necessarily talking about having a document to prove that you're married, because the implications of blending one's soul with another are very big in the relative world. The relative world is half of Reality. You probably know that I call my path Enlightened Duality. Duality *is*, and nonduality *is*. In nonduality we live with no separation between duality and nonduality. But you know we're having a conversation, so language is by definition dualistic. In the relative world, the implications of blending one's soul with another are very, very big—karmically and energetically, and in the sense of the sacred.

"In the ultimate world of nonduality, we're all one already anyway, and so it is academic. But marriage takes place in the relative world. This willingness to offer oneself up to the other completely, as you are but without compromise, without any withhold, is a very big thing. Many of us fall in love. You know, we really love our partners, but whether we're officially married or not, there's always some little holdout. Real marriage is about offering yourself up completely; it's literally like putting yourself on a sacrificial altar. So we could almost say that the altar of marriage is a sacrificial altar. Each partner offers himself or herself to the other as the sacrifice.

"In the traditional Christian marriage ceremony in the West or in America one of the sayings is to serve, to honor and obey 'until death do us part.' In America it's very popular for people to write their own marriage ceremonies, because there's a tremendous cynicism about service, about serving the other until death do us part. We have this idea that as long as it's working, we're together, and if it's not working we're not together. And one can only have a very weak connection with that level of commitment. So it's really a sanctified, sacrificial affair. It's not just a commitment of language, or even of the heart. It's a commitment of essence, of being, of soul."

Another man asked the question, "How can one as man enter into relationship with woman in a more appropriate way? How can I in daily life enter into relationship in a more appropriate way with this animal part in me and also this feminine part in me?"

Lee said facetiously, "Well, when the animal's hungry give him a steak and when the feminine is hungry buy her a blouse. That's a totally different question than the first question you asked, which is how to be in a more *just* relationship with a woman.

"Essentially, as I've said many times so far this week, the common misunderstanding is that we have to allow ourselves the expression of every part of ourselves. If the animal happens to be awake, we think that the only way to satisfy the animal is to act like an animal, but that's not necessarily so.

"Most of us see the animal and say, 'I don't know if this is socially acceptable, oh these urges are too wild!' Then we either repress it or look for some environment in which it's acceptable to act it out. Like a sex club. Walk in the room, there's fifty people in the middle of the room, all naked and writhing around, having every kind of sex. Okay, now we can satisfy the animal! You know, shit all over the walls . . . Really! Some of those places have people cleaning up the floor all the time, but you know it gets pretty slippery in those places. I only know because people have told me these things." Everyone laughed.

Lee went on: "We look at women, we walk along the streets of Paris, or—I'll use an American city, Prescott, Arizona. That's where we live. Some man drives by in an average yellow car with nice seats and dressed very nicely, with hair combed very nicely, clean-shaven, smooth skin—no comment from all the women you're walking along with. Then this biker drives by, you know this big, ugly mass, hair all over his face, scars, dressed in black, and when he looks at you he spits. He hates the very sight of you, and all the women say, 'Ohhh, ohhh, ohhh!'" Lee demonstrated this with a breathy, high-pitched tone of voice. He was touching the women where many live—in a psychological identification with the abuser. It is a typical psychological pattern for adult women who were abused by their fathers or other adult men as children—either sexually, physically or psychologically—to find authoritarian, extremely powerful, macho and abusive men thrilling and magnetically attractive. Then they get into relationships with them and continue to re-enact the abuse or the general psychological dynamic they experienced as children. It is the psyche's call for help, but many women, even brilliant and sophisticated women, are unable to see the subtle implications and hooks of such relationships.

"So what are us guys to think? We look at our feminine side and we say, 'No, no that's not gonna help me,' and then we go into the office and we can't express our feminine—what if somebody thought we were gay?" He gasped in mock terror. "My God! And then in business, it's a dog-eat-dog world. We can't show our feminine side in business, because we'll be taken advantage of; we've got to get the job or somebody else is going to get it; it's cutthroat out there.

"So these are all our unconscious attitudes. They're all judgements. When we actually start to accept the animal side of our nature and the feminine side, even with some judgement, we begin to see that the effect it's going to have is not as bad as we think. We all have to start some place. It's nice to say, 'Accept what is, as it is.' Ultimately that's what we have to do, but most people are going to start with some kind of acceptance, and there will be some judgement. That's okay—we accept as much as we can, as deeply as we can. So you start with this idea that acknowledgement or acceptance does not mean having to act out. And the second thing is, no judgement.

"If we are looking at the animal and find it terrifying, bad or immoral, then we can't accept. We're doing the best we can to accept, but we also notice that we're judging. Then accept the judgement. 'Okay, this is where I am right now, I'm judging. Fine.' The point is to observe the animal, and simply recognize it.

"As Arnaud said this morning in meditation, 'My body is me, my mind is me, my intellect is me, and we have to go deeper, deeper, deeper.' Yes, the animal is you and the feminine is you and you have to go deeper, deeper. So you start with that acceptance. What are the urges that the animal has? You want to be a satyr. You find yourself growing hooves at one in the morning. Okay, if that's what the animal wants to do, you simply observe it. You acknowledge the desires of the animal and the desires of the feminine. To acknowledge, 'Yes, this is what I desire,' to really acknowledge it and accept it takes away most of the urge to act it out."

A woman sitting in the middle of the room raised her hand. She said, "I am Jean Paul's wife. So it's about this answer you gave my husband a year ago, which touched me very much. You said, 'Put money in your bank account and buy nice dresses for your wife.' "

Lee chuckled, "Yes, we heard about that earlier in the week."

She continued, "I don't know if I'll be talking about that in the same intention, but . . ."

Lee commented, "I wouldn't expect so."

"I thought about that a lot and then I sort of forgot it. Six months later I find myself in Gilles' group here, and I saw your photograph in Gilles' office, and it was like a flash. And then I went to Mangalam, Eric's ashram in Canada, and I realized that there has been a mechanism within my relationship with my husband. I have felt like a beaten dog for years."

Lee interjected, "Welcome to the world of women in the twentieth century."

She spoke with tremendous sobriety and depth of feeling. Everyone in the room, about one hundred people, was completely with her, deeply involved in the exchange. It was a mirror for every person there, a reminder of the deep suffering of men and women in relationship. She said, "I am crying, but I am very happy to have seen this . . ."

"Is there anything that you do that is just for you, that you really enjoy?" Lee asked. The kindness he was giving so generously in this exchange had a straightforward quality that was both soft and tremendously empowering to her as a woman. It carried a healing power that was touching every woman in the room—or at least those who were willing to realize that they were listening to themselves speak.

"I play the piano."

"When you play the piano do you really abandon yourself, let yourself go?" Lee asked.

"Sometimes."

"Have you ever abandoned yourself playing the piano when your husband was there?" he pressed further. She answered no.

"Then your husband has not seen you as you really are in a safe environment. Sex is not a safe environment. A woman being herself in sex is a terrifying thing to behold!" Lee threw his head back and laughed. "Sex is not a safe environment because men's egos are too fragile. To see such a thing could catapult a man into a monastery or drive him to the bottle! For men and women it's threatening to see this kind of abandon in one another, but it's much more threatening for a man to see a woman as she really is in sex than for a woman to see a man. The pure Feminine is much closer to the surface in woman. The fear of this pure Feminine is the cause of the repression of matriarchy in the world today. Anything men think they can't have, they hate—or they want to dominate and control. But men also want this pure Feminine and need it, especially after they get a sense of what this is, what it means.

"Your husband is on the path. He has a real desire to work. In his secret moments he's probably very frustrated and conflicted between his own mechanicality and his obvious recognition and need for accepting you as you really are. I agree it would be a very big risk to abandon yourself in your piano playing with Jean Paul there, yet at the same time . . . it could go either way. It could open or close Jean Paul to see you in this way. And at the same time, your husband needs this. I always hesitate to use the word 'need' because mostly what we call our 'needs' are really our 'desires.'

"In this Work there is an advantage that is very unusual in the world—the Blessing Power of the lineage, or Grace. Anyone in Arnaud's company has engaged in something subtle, graceful and always present. We have our personalities and we have something else that the average person doesn't have: the regard of Benediction. So when we take risks on the path it can always go one of two ways—better or worse—but the results are weighted toward things being better because the regard of the master, which is ever present, is always on us. It's not concerned with your feelings, your opinions and desires, but is only concerned for your freedom.

"So as difficult as it might be, this is where you start: You should ask yourself, 'What would happen if I abandon myself with Jean Paul in the room? What would happen if he saw that part of me?' The possibility is small, but much greater than any other situation. How long have you and Jean Paul been together?" She answered seventeen years. "When two people are together for seventeen years you build something you can't build in six months, no matter how wild and passionate those six months may have been. You must consider this: When you break out, you're going to burn the house down! Really! And it would be nice to have Jean Paul *with* you when you break free. And he *does* know what he's missing . . ."

As in this interchange Lee's comments throughout the week on the natural and easy way of innate wisdom found in the body were cloaked in simplicity and ordinariness. And yet the gift of acceptance of the feminine dimensions of life—the body and all its functions of eating, digesting, eliminating, sex, birth and death—is a gift of tremendous value in a culture where all the trouble starts with this one basic error: the rejection of life, the essential Feminine. The Feminine in this context is vast and stretches from Shakti, the primordial goddess, or Creation as the Feminine compliment to the Creator, to the human body, the body of the Earth, all the forms of gross matter. To accept this manifest pole of reality with its cosmic and earthly functions of creation, growth and destruction is to be reconnected with the heartbeat of God. It is to breathe again fully, to live and die within the dharma, in the flow of what Lee calls the Great Process of Divine Evolution. It is to be in one's rightful place in the Universe. Lee's words and the mood he invoked had given us a bodily experience of that rightness. It had been a tremendously moving two hours, and seemed like the peak of the seminar. During this interchange several people in the audience had the traces of tears glistening on their faces.

At the beginning of the afternoon session a questioner said, "Swami Prajnapad said that on the path you have to know, feel, and act, and that making some progress on the path meant unifying those three. My question has to do with what Swamiji said about feeling. I seem to be still stuck in the same action-reaction and the same conditionings that have been part of my whole life. So, I'm not able to have right action; I'm very conscious of that," the questioner concluded.

Lee said, "People are the same until they aren't. It's difficult to accept that because we like to see signs of progress on the path. But in one sense all signs of progress are illusory. We're either unified or we're not. We're either one with or not. On the other hand we don't all go out and try to snuff ourselves out because of the futility of the path.

"The way things tend to work is that any change takes place inside first and then outside. I mean real change, not only using will power and changing habits or something external. Things can be in a process of change for years on the inside, because some of the alignments that have to take place in order for change to be total are very, very subtle. Sometimes we're in process for years and nothing is noticeable, everything looks exactly the same. And then the next day things are different, and we don't even know how it happened. It all seems so miraculous, so inexplicable."

The next questioner began, "I'd like to inquire about two things. The first thing is the link there could be between maturity or immaturity and understanding. Several years ago you told me that I could either function from the perspective of my understanding, and then I would be useful to people and serve others, or I could function from the perspective of my immaturity and that would be useless. It's only now that I'm beginning to understand what it means because up until now I was dominated by my immaturity. It's my impression that I am often in situations where there is an opposition between my viewpoint and the viewpoint of people whom I consider to be more mature than I am. And I would say that I was right and they were wrong, but I found myself being trapped by a very immature way that I had of expressing my viewpoint."

Lee commented, "One of the things that I tell my students about feedback is that they have to learn to make a distinction between the accuracy of the feedback and the state of the person giving the feedback. Sometimes very mature feedback can come from someone who's acting very immaturely. Yogi Ramsuratkumar said once that even the greatest saint has some combination of darkness and light. He said that we in the modern world are so desperately in need of inspiration that it's terrible when somebody whose life is predominantly positive is criticized for some small negativity. He said that the general public is so fickle and lacking in depth of understanding, that one negative comment about an overwhelmingly positive person can effect many people's willingness to accept the positivity from that person.

"He said when you look at somebody—and obviously this means when we look at ourselves also—has his or her life been mostly light and a little dark, or mostly dark and a little light? If it's been mostly light, then don't exaggerate the darkness. To put it in the terms of your question, everybody has a balance of maturity and immaturity. When we find some immaturity, if it's not overwhelming or pervasive, we should not ignore it, we have to deal with it, but we also shouldn't elevate it to a position of authority."

Later in the session a man said, "I bought a book this afternoon."

"That's it!" Lee laughed in mock protest at how he had been deluged with questions over the week about what his *dédicace* in peoples' books meant. "Next year I'm just signing my name, no more dedications!" He chuckled, "Okay—no, I'm kidding . . ." He laughed again.

The questioner smiled, "On the contrary, I was very happy with the dedication. When I approach you I always have the feeling you already know what is better for me, and what you wrote in your dedication is exactly what I'm going through right now."

"Ahhh, the myth grows!" Lee and everyone in the room laughed together. Then he shrugged the compliment off, saying, "Just luck. Okay, so?"

"It's true that I'm very nervous."

Lee quipped, "Yes, well it doesn't take a great psychic to see that—to be honest with you."

"I'd like to know where this agitation, the neurotic nervousness, comes from, because it's causing pain to one person in particular and I'd like to know where it comes from and if it's going to change."

Lee answered, "Someday it will change. Might be next lifetime; you might not remember this. The way I handle my own nervousness is basically just not to do anything about it, and if it gets in my way, I kick it out of the way and do what I have to do. As long as it's not interfering in the work at hand, I just stay nervous. I think we've had this conversation before anyway, so I don't want to just repeat what I've said in previous years.

"As I've said many times this week, the first step is to accept yourself as you are. This nervousness is affecting another person and that may be disturbing, but at the same time this is the way you are—accept the fact that this is the way you are. It might never change. To accept something means you don't put conditions on it. You know, 'I'll accept this because, if I accept it then it's gonna change.' That doesn't work. That's turning it into a business deal. The first step is nonjudgmental acceptance.

"Obviously to some degree you're seeing this about yourself, but it's also evident that it's bothering you, that you don't like it and you want it to change, but that attitude stands in the way of change. So you have to really become comfortable with yourself as you are. I don't mean in a kind of self-centered way, like when people say sometimes to one another, 'This is the way I am, and if you don't like it, tough shit.' I don't mean to accept yourself in a way that separates you from and defends you against others. You shouldn't be wearing the way you are as a suit of armor or advertisement. Just very simply and invisibly accept yourself as you are. That's the first step. Will you ever change? I don't know. Is change possible? Of course, it's possible. So I'll leave you with that. Thank you."

"I'd like to go back to what was said this morning concerning marriage and the couple relationship," the next person said.

"Oh, did I say anything about couples? Oh no, I'm just kidding. If somebody is into a renunciate lifestyle and takes vows, the vows are like a marriage to God. Then one enters into a marriage with the whole of mankind, the whole of life. I just wanted people to remember that there is a universal viewpoint as well as a personal viewpoint for all of us. Sometimes we really get stuck on our own little insignificance, as if any of that actually meant anything. I don't mean to insult you, but somehow I seem to anyway, even when I don't mean to. Okay—I won't interrupt you again. Marriage and the couple!"

Lee paused, watching the woman who had started the question. Then with a mischievous little smile he added, "Well, I'll try not to anyway." Everyone laughed. Most of the people in the audience had, by now, been at the effect of Lee's interruptions, and had some familiarity with what it felt like on the inside to be under the laser beam of his attention in this space.

"When a woman stops acting as a beaten dog, she's taking a risk," she continued. "I think you said that this risk can even lead to the breaking down of the relationship." Lee nodded and said, "Sure." She continued, "But, that there were other solutions than the breaking up of the relationship. So my question has to do with those other solutions."

Lee answered, "In a relationship with a couple there has to be some kind of agreement for both people to work together. In the psychological domain there's this thing called codependent relationships. Two things are required for a relationship to be codependent: there has to be the person who is the aggressor and there also has to be the enabler. If somebody isn't allowing the aggression, then the aggressor can't be aggressive. At least not with that person.

"What creates codependency is that one person acts and the other person allows the action, and this goes on. The man hits the woman and the woman allows herself to keep being hit. There's an agreement in that, maybe unconscious, but it's still an agreement. In order for the options to be viable, both people have to work together. Sometimes one person wants to create change and the other person doesn't want to. But sometimes the person who doesn't want to can actually be drawn into creating change.

"I'm a very stubborn person. I've had to been drawn kicking and screaming, metaphorically speaking, into any change that's ever happened to me. But when I want something, I'll stay with it until I get it, even if I have to struggle with difficulties or resistances. When I first entered into the function or role that I have now I asked for a certain responsibility—to be a guide, a spiritual friend. I had no idea what that meant, no idea what it would cost, personally or universally. But I was sincere in the wish. In the evolution from the separate one who was making the wish to the one who actually got to do some of that, there were tremendous resistances that had to be overcome. I resisted in many areas, in many ways.

"It takes two people to really effect these other solutions in a couple, and it has to be very worth it to the person who's initiating the process to stay with it. When I talk about myself, I'm predominantly talking about my relationship with my Master, but then the personal relationship between a man and a woman, the couple relationship, functions according to the same principle. One could say that any process of transformation is sourced and initiated by the master.

"The disciple thinks, 'Oh I'm so lucky to have found my master.' But in fact the master has called us; the master initiated the relationship, and the master is very dedicated to seeing the relationship through to its success, its finish. If at the first sign of trouble in the disciple—of resistance, of anger—the master said, 'Forget it, this isn't worth it,' then most masters would have no disciples. Not only no disciples, but no apprentice disciples, nobody. The master is willing to hang in there with the disciple through the disciple's struggles and their resistances and their arguments and their complaints.

"The master is like a midwife birthing the child. Sometimes labor can be pretty dramatic. Some women start hitting and scratching and cursing, but you know the midwife is trained to stay with the process. If the midwife said, 'Breathe, breathe, relax,' and the woman said, 'Fuck you, get the hell out of my face!' and the midwife jumped up in anger and said, 'Alright!' and stormed out of the room, what kind of midwife would that be?

"So in a marriage, whoever wants the circumstance to change from the 'beaten dog' has to be willing to stay with the one who's doing the beating. And it's usually a long process, but if it's worth it, then that's what you have to do to get to the other side. The other side is where the one beating the dog realizes that his own aggressiveness is simply a function of self-hatred. He realizes that the faithfulness of the dog has maybe even saved his life. The option is healing and revitalization, and it usually takes very hard work and a tremendous amount of patience and continuity. We have to stick with it. A lot of people aren't willing to do that, so in many situations there is just rupture.

"Obviously the specifics vary from couple to couple. Some people feel like beaten dogs because their opinions and their viewpoints are discounted and ridiculed. Other people feel like beaten dogs because they're physically beaten and tortured. Other people feel like beaten dogs because they're kept like a pet. So, the specifics of this process vary from couple to couple depending upon the nature of the manifestations, but in principle that's it. We have to be willing to draw the other person into an agreement that things as they are aren't working, and if they stay the same then there will inevitably be rupture. If the rupture is to be avoided, then you have to work together.

"For a man to say, 'Yes, I understand,' he has to be willing to be vulnerable, and it's very difficult for most men to be vulnerable. A lot of men are only vulnerable when some tragedy happens in their life—their mother dies or something like that. Last year Paul described how he tried to commit suicide and his teenage son came in and saw him. Even being vulnerable with his son took some hard work on his part, and it sounds like he's doing it. But last year he was arguing, and the argument was not about talking to his son or not talking to his son, it was about *vulnerability*. It's really hard for a lot of men to accept help. The woman comes up and wants to button his shirt, he says, 'I can do it.' Even on such a ridiculous level, 'Oh, are you telling me I can't even button my own goddamn shirt? I can button my damn shirt, you know.' Men are funny creatures. We really have to have a great sense of humor and a real tenacity to stick with the process, to get them to admit how satisfying it is to be vulnerable and in communion with their wives even, or their children. Men want to be one with, want to be in communion, but it's very difficult to get past the societal conditioning."

Another man asked, "Could you say more about being vulnerable?"

Lee answered, "Oh, I don't know. I'd have to be vulnerable to say more about being vulnerable!" He chuckled.

The afternoon session ended early so that Lee and Arnaud could drive to the Centre Dürckheim, run by Jacques and Christina Castermane. Lee had seen Jacques recently at the funeral of Yvan Amar, and finding that they were friends of Arnaud and Veronique Desjardins and live near Hauteville, a meeting was arranged for Lee to come for dinner and see their center during his stay at Hauteville. Lee invited five of his students to come along with him. With Lee behind the wheel of the Renault van as usual, he followed Arnaud and Veronique in their car the half-hour drive to the center.

After a short tour of the facility, its spacious zendo (meditation hall) and main house with beautiful rooms reflecting the spirit of Zen in which Jacques and Christina give *dokusan* during the *sesshins*, we settled in the old fashioned country-style dining room to a delicious meal. Lee and Arnaud sat together on one side of the table with Jacques sitting across from them. The rest of the group was clustered around the ends of the long rectangular wooden table. An easy and instantaneous rapport and mood of friendship and common purpose characterized the evening. The conversation flowed very naturally, interspersed with frequent rounds of laughter. As we waited for dessert to be served Jan asked Jacques if he would describe the essence of Karlfried Graf Dürckheim's teaching.

Jacques said, "Dürckheim talked about the body we *have* and the body we *are*. We say that we have a body, but there is another way to be, which is to be the body that we *are*—not the body that we have. Do you understand? So the aim of his teaching is to become who we are."

Jacques began to ask Lee questions about the bands, what they played, where, how long they had been in existence and so on. "When did you start writing lyrics?" he asked. Lee answered, "Twelve years ago."

Jacques laughed and said, "A very young rocker, then! There is still hope for me!" Jacques and Christina seemed fascinated with the idea of a spiritual master as a "rocker." They pressed, "Don't you play some instrument?"

Lee shook his head. "No, just tambourine." He laughed, "The band is doing good to just let me sing! The professional musicians have high standards, you know."

Arnaud began to praise *John T.,* a rock opera about the death of John the Baptist, written by Lee, composed by Stan Hitson and performed by the Baul Theatre Company. Arnaud relayed his experience of seeing the company perform *John T.* when he visited Lee on the Arizona ashram in 1993. From the enthusiasm Arnaud exhibited in describing the rock opera, it seemed he particularly liked this aspect of Lee's work with his students. He said to Jacques, "I thought that Lee had picked the perfect person for each role in the opera, but then he told me that the players switch roles all the time!" He turned to Lee and asked, "Have you performed it in Europe?"

"We performed it once in northern Germany in a theatre," Lee answered, "and once in

Berlin on the street. It was a spontaneous thing—we just decided one morning to go out and do it." This brought a big smile of delight to Arnaud's face.

Christine asked Lee about his travels in Europe every summer. Lee explained that he spends a week at Hauteville every summer, and travels around France, Germany and other countries giving seminars and public talks, or performing with Shri. He said, "Hauteville is the highlight of our summer."

Veronique commented, "When Lee comes is the highlight of the year for us!" Veronique and Arnaud begin to talk about how Lee understands everything that Arnaud says in the morning meditation, when Arnaud does a guided meditation *en francais*. Arnaud joked around, saying, "When [during the daily meetings] Lee starts to say, 'This morning in meditation Arnaud said,' I lean forward to listen and say to myself, 'What *did* I say?' "

This led into Arnaud regaling Lee, Jacques and company with stories of Taisen Deshimaru, the famous Japanese Zen master who Arnaud filmed in the sixties or early seventies. Deshimaru came from a very highborn family lineage in Japan. His father was one of the last samurai, and the fierceness of that tradition came across in Deshimaru's practice and teaching as a revered (and feared by some) Zen master. Arnaud spent a good deal of time with Deshimaru as the thankful recipient of many extraordinary lessons in the Work.

Now Arnaud began to talk about how Deshimaru often asked him to speak to groups of people when they were traveling in Japan together. Deshimaru would turn to Arnaud and say, "You give the talk and I will translate!"

Arnaud laughed and said, "The so-called translation was only what he wanted to say! I was speaking and the audience was laughing . . . sometimes I was talking for thirty seconds and Deshimaru would translate for four minutes!" We laughed heartily with Arnaud as he became more animated and brilliant in the telling of these high-spirited stories.

Arnaud continued, "I saw Deshimaru with children, helping with businessmen, with monks and geishas in bars—he took me everywhere, and I mean *everywhere*! Afterward he would say, 'Your Swamiji can't do *that*!'" Deshimaru was referring to Arnaud's root guru, Swami Prajnanpad, and the more traditional form in which Arnaud received teachings from him.

After telling a number of bawdy and hilarious stories of his escapades—all of which contained a teaching lesson for Arnaud—in the capable, quite crazy-wise hands of Deshimaru, Arnaud said, "In Japan the atmosphere is so different [than in the West]. All this is not the same thing in Japanese surroundings as it would be in Europe. I was with Deshimaru, who wore the dress of a Zen monk, in a nightclub. We were drinking sake with the geisha girls. They were not the *true* geishas, but prostitutes. Then Sensei looked at me and when one of the girls came by he put his hand on her bottom. She turned to look at him, and he looked into her eyes so deeply—she was so moved to be looked at with such respect. For the Zen master the prostitutes and everyone else are turned into the Buddha." Arnaud was speaking in English. The depth and breadth of what he wanted to communicate, and would have communicated perhaps more elaborately if he was speaking French, was captured entirely in his mood. His animated face and his body language spoke volumes.

Jacques looked at Lee and asked, "Have you ever been to Japan?" Lee answered, "Never. I have two students who are living there now—one Japanese and one Canadian—so perhaps in the future."

Arnaud commented, "Japan is the Land of Beauty—in Japan everything, every restaurant, not only the temples of Kyoto, but everything is beautiful."

Jacques began to talk about his time in Japan. "I was in a store in Japan and wanted to wear a certain kind of robe that they didn't have. They called another store, sent a taxi to pick me up and take me to the store that had what I was looking for—that's Japan!" Jacques explained that he had spent six weeks in Japan, but his teacher, Karlfried Graf Dürckheim, had lived in Japan for eleven years before, during and after WW II.

"Was he in a monastery?" Jan asked.

"Yes," Jacques responded, "he practiced many years with a *roshi*, Guho Seki. He practiced archery and zazen every day, every day. Do you know Albert Lowe?" he turned to Lee and asked.

Lee said, "Not personally, but I have heard of him."

"He was in Japan also with Graf [Dürckheim]." Jacques paused and then asked Lee, "Will you come here and work with us?"

"Yes, we can work something out," Lee answered, "perhaps before I go to Hauteville next year."

"Do you know what we do here?" Jacques asked Lee, who smiled and answered, "Not exactly—I have a sense of it." When Jacques offered a program for the center written in French, Lee said, "I'll take a program, but the details are not necessary." Lee was saying very little tonight, but was for the most part sitting quietly and listening—his usual mode of being when he is not formally teaching. When he did say something, like in this unobtrusive statement, there was a sense of a deeper echo, a speaking that was beneath or beyond the words. It was as if in this statement one could hear the background of what was true of him—that he had already absorbed the essence of what Jacques and Christina were doing, the essence of Dürckheim, in the short hour or two that he had been here. This is typical of Lee when he visits other teachers—he absorbs and extracts what is useful. This kind of constant expanding and learning through receptivity and what Suzuki Roshi called "beginner's mind" is a hallmark of the true disciple.

I noticed there was a Jungian film listed on the summer schedule for the center, and asked Jacques if Dürckheim and Carl Jung, being contemporaries in Switzerland, had known each other or worked together. Jacques said, "Yes, Dürckheim met Jung two times. Dürckheim recommended Jungian analysis to many of his students. He said to me, 'You must have Jungian analysis.' So I went to a Jungian analyst, six hundred kilometers away from where I lived. He told me to write and paint my dreams. When I came back he asked me if I had written down my dreams. I said, 'No, I didn't have time.' He answered, 'Then I don't have time to work with you,' and I had to leave and pay for the session anyway, having driven six hundred kilometers to get there! Of course I started writing my dreams after that." Jacques said that he continued the analysis—at Dürckheim's instruction—once or twice a week for five years.

When asked how he met Dürckheim, Jacques said that he practiced Aikido everyday, and he saw the book *Hara,* written by Karlfried Graf Dürckheim. The title captivated him because of his work in Eastern martial arts and the concept of the center of the body, or *hara.* "The book was very interesting to me," he continued, "I was taking a class from a woman at that time, and she said that she was going to a colloquium where Teilhard de Chardin, some Jesuits, Dürckheim and other people would be speaking. I said, 'Dürckheim? The man who wrote *Hara?*' She said yes, so I went to the colloquium. But I was fascinated by how he *was.* I thought to myself, 'This man is what he says he is.'

"I stayed after the colloquium and he came directly up to me and said, 'I like the way you have listened to me. I hope one day you will come to see me.' I gave Dürckheim my address, and then later wrote a letter and went to see him. I went back and forth to see him for two years. At that time I was living in a village where I thought I would live and die. I was walking in the cemetery of the village and looking at the headstones. I was sure I would be buried here. I was sure I would be in the Black Forest all my life. One day I said to Dürckheim, 'I have to leave the Black Forest.' He said, 'Okay, I will wait for you.' So I moved to where Dürckheim lived.

"Two or three times a week we would meet. At that time twenty or thirty people would come and go, and about five people lived there with Dürckheim at his center. He talked with us about everything—God, everyday life. Meditation was, of course, a very important part of our time together. We meditated every day with him as a group at six-thirty in the morning, sitting zazen. We were also invited to meditate alone during the day, to practice in addition to morning zazen.

"Dürckheim also taught specific body exercises," Jacques continued. "When he came back from Japan he was very conscious of how difficult it is to accept the 'body we are.' It is impossible to describe in words, and more possible to communicate with physical exercises, so he invented the method of exercise that we do—to feel the body you are and not the body you have. The first exercise he ever gave me was to go into the forest, sit down by a tree and sit with no movement for three hours. Absolutely *no* movement!" Jacques demonstrated—not a flicker of a finger to scratch his ear or touch his face. "After ten minutes I looked at my watch! I couldn't believe it!" Everyone laughed, understanding his predicament only too well. He continued, "So my first thought was, 'This man is a fool!' "

Lee's students were deeply absorbed in hearing Jacques' stories of his teacher, and leaned forward to hear better as he continued to speak. He said that of course he did the exercise that first time, and then many other times, as Dürckheim instructed.

"I sat for three hours by the tree in the summer, in the winter, in the rain . . ." he said, "and Dürckheim asked, 'How is it going?' I said, 'I am wasting my time because I must walk twenty kilometers, there are many people, I have to wait in line at the post office, and so on.' Dürckheim answered me, 'You understand *nothing* of my work! You must lock my books in the cupboard and throw away the key! Did you ever roll naked in leaves that have fallen from trees?' he asked. I thought, 'If he had known my parents, he wouldn't ask such a question!' " Everyone burst into laughter at this comment. The room was a combination of nationalities—French, German, Swiss, Belgian and American—but we could all relate to his plight: the repression of the natural life, of instinct, of the kind of primal goodness or Organic Innocence out of which one might celebrate life by rolling in leaves on the forest floor. Lee's teaching of Organic Innocence seemed to be a basic aspect, in fact, of Dürckheim's teaching of what he called, "The body we are."

Jacques continued, "So Dürckheim said, 'You should roll on the forest floor and stop reading my books!' I was angry, but I did what he asked, and it was a wonderful experience. The first time I tried it I only got as far as removing my socks! But that was the beginning—after that I actually did what he asked. I was like a baby! I could not stop, it was so wonderful to have such an experience, such exercises. This kind of exercise was typical of Dürckheim. His exercises were instinctual and designed individually for each person.

"After four years I went to Dürckheim and said, 'I want to go now; I am ready to teach your work.' Dürckheim looked at me and said, 'For the first time I must say no to you. You are not ready.' After that I continued to see him once a month. After I had been studying with him for seven years he said to me one day, 'Do you remember your question?' Yes, I said. 'You are ready to go teach now,' he said. So I spent seven years near Geneva and then came here, to southern France and started this center."

Jan asked Jacques if he felt that Dürckheim's influence was still alive in his life, even though he died some years ago. This question was inspired by something Arnaud had said to Lee's students during his visit to the Arizona ashram six years ago. He had said that it was only after Swami Prajnanpad died that Arnaud experienced the full flower of Swamiji's influence, transmission and presence in his life.

Now the group waited expectantly, eager to hear Jacques' response. He seemed to be considering the question and shaking his head as if to say he wasn't sure how he wanted to answer. After a brief pause, Arnaud said that Jacques had made a teaching for him once when Arnaud had said to Jacques, "You had a master," referring to Graf Dürckheim. Jacques exclaimed, "No, I *have* a master!"

Arnaud had responded, "Yes, I know it's true, I know by experience that it's true, so I am not surprised that you say that."

Jacques then answered the question, saying, "I cannot say yes but I cannot say no."

Veronique pressed further, "But do you feel him alive?"

Jacques said, "Dürckheim taught me, 'I don't know.' I truly learned this with him— 'I don't know.' "

July 10, 1999
Hauteville

Turning to the audience in general Lee smiled and said, "We have some new blood here this morning, as vampires say!"

The first questioner said, "Practice requires interiority . . ."

Lee interjected, "Everything requires some degree of interiority."

The questioner continued, "On the other hand, practice requires that we be open and participate, and that's external. How to reconcile?"

Lee answered, "Arnaud said in meditation this morning—a statement from Swami Prajnanpad, I believe—'Interior actively passive, exterior passively active.' This statement holds the answer to your question. If you understand either one, you understand both automatically. The thinking mind says, 'This doesn't make sense.' Life itself is a continuum—it's all an energetic field. The rational mind creates distinctions, but this consideration 'actively passive and passively active' holds the answer. They are not separate things. We may talk about them as if they are, but they are not. Stay with it like a koan, until it burns. The harder it burns, the more the motive to find resolve. The more it burns, the more you will understand.

"Most of us really are not inspired to practice. If you want the answer you have to make this koan burn. You have to have more desire for the experience than intellectual curiosity. The other day someone said, 'Not a day goes by that I don't remember the teaching.' That is a person who is on the path, who has an organic, bodily understanding."

The next question was about sexuality in accordance with the path. The man said, "I've always had a creative relationship with my wife in sex, globally. It couldn't be better with anyone else. When I walk down the street and see pretty girls, though, I look at them with desire."

"Well, that's life!" Lee laughed.

"But the attraction is very strong and causes much suffering."

"It's just the mind," Lee said. "You're attracted to an idea. If you knew most of those pretty young things you'd be disgusted. They take their clothes off and they've got metal all over their bodies . . ." There was much laughter in the room at this reference to the popular passion for body piercing.

"Well, I have an intellectual understanding of what you are saying, but I want it to infuse my body and being. We've committed ourselves, so I have no intention to fool around. But yesterday when I heard you speaking to Jean Paul's wife, I thought that I must be afraid of the true feminine expression of my wife."

Lee questioned, "Why did you think that?"

He said, "That's the reason why I tend to be attracted to women as dolls."

"Not entirely," Lee responded. "Some of them are just dolls. None of the women in this room, of course!" More laughter. "So, what's the essence of the question?"

"You said if I was able to look closely I would be disgusted."

"I was joking!" Lee protested.

"How can this become a bodily certainty, not an intellectual understanding, and how can I get to greater intimacy with my wife?"

Lee answered, "That you look at young women and have fantasies doesn't mean you aren't nourished by intimacy with your wife. What ego does is fantasize. It always wants more, more, more. Even when we've had a gigantic meal and we're stuffed, we're saying, 'If only the meat was more rare, the tofu baked!' Ego is never satisfied. So when you become aware of your projections, then you accept your projection as a projection. To accept it completely as a fantasy and no more doesn't allow it to develop strength and body. It's just a fantasy—no more! Accept it as it is, not as if it was real. It's just a fantasy, so disempower it. It's nice to hear a testimony to a working, successful marriage."

Another woman asked, "I have done some work on myself and I feel better. When one feels better, how does one become a real disciple? I'm easily selfish."

"Me too!" Lee said brightly. "I was hosted at Gilles' house for dinner and we got to sit at a special table and be served. I don't like to be served because the servers never bring me what I like. Not to insult the servers last night, but with servers they bring you what *they* think you would like to eat if they were you!" Arnaud and Lee both laughed at this, along with most of the people in the room.

Lee continued, "Most people, if they be who they are, will come to a depth of being, which is good. What keeps those negative qualities in place is a lack of acceptance of our manipulation, greed, dominance and so on. We're afraid that if we commit ourselves and go deeper, we'll find something we don't like. It's a paradox—we live in a domain of darkness with noticeable flashes of light, when at the source of being is pure light. There is nowhere to go, nothing to get. Light and dark are continuous, but from the point of view of duality it seems we have to move from darkness to light. We find, as we move, one expression of darkness after another. We think the closer we get to light the lighter it gets, but it's the opposite. We live in a vast gray area, and as we go toward light it gets darker and darker until we get to total pitch blackness, and the next breath we breathe— literally the next breath we breathe—is total light. There isn't any such thing as lighter and lighter.

"We grow, mature, life gets better, but the bottom line is if we want one hundred percent light we have to deal with one hundred percent dark. Hopelessness and despair are very real. That's no fun! Read *Dark Night of the Soul* by St. John of the Cross. We ask, 'Can't I do it without that? Is there some way around?' No, the way to the light is through the darkness. So, naturally there is some reticence to go there, but you have to have faith in what is beyond the beyond. Where do you get that faith? In the testimony and example of those who have walked that path before you. You don't have to go back to Jesus and Mohammed. Right now there are examples who can inspire us. Read Arnaud's autobiography. Arnaud was just a guy seeking power! Like all of us, he was drawn to the path because of his willingness to commit, and he was successful."

A man spoke up now. He said, "Thank you. It's not a question. I wanted to say that every day I went to sit with you while you were selling books."

"Yes, I noticed," Lee commented.

"And it was really a desire for me to see you sit in silence next to Arnaud," he continued.

"It's Arnaud's graceful skills as a host, because I don't like silence, so Arnaud is letting me come here and be noisy!" Everyone laughed. Part of the paradox of their situation is that Arnaud suspends the usual protocol of Hauteville for a week every year when Lee comes. Each of Arnaud's students has to work with that in his or her own way. Some have deep and profound appreciation and regard for Lee, while others accept that Lee has something of great value to offer, but also have many questions about how he does things and his sometimes-crazy style. The French seem to generally delight in these kinds of remarks which cast the peculiarities of their situation with this American master in the whimsical glow of enlightened humor.

"So I wanted to thank you," the man continued. "I've been with Arnaud for ten years, and gave myself the present to come here to sit with you this week," the man concluded.

"Thank you," Lee said.

Before lunch today while Lee sat at the book table selling books, Arnaud came in and handed Lee a gift: two beautiful large prints of photographs that Arnaud himself took of Swami Papa Ramdas. He had them carefully rolled in cardboard tubes for transporting and took them out to show them to Lee.

"Beautiful," Lee said, "a great treasure." He smiled up at Arnaud, who carefully placed the photos back into the tubes and handed them to Lee. The connection between Lee and Arnaud has been perhaps most notably reflected in the fact that Arnaud knew and loved Papa Ramdas, who was the spiritual father of Yogi Ramsuratkumar. When Lee first came to Font d'Isière seven years ago, Arnaud showed Lee and his students the film he had made of Ramdas. He also brought out his private photo archive containing priceless photographs of Ramdas and Krishnabai as well as many other masters, saints, Sufis and other holy people whom Arnaud photographed, filmed and associated with for many years in his sadhana. It was a tremendously rich opportunity to see and experience these artifacts.

That first year Arnaud had, with incredible reverence and tenderness, taken out an old loincloth, now carefully folded and kept in a glass case, and placed it in Lee's hands to hold. "This belonged to Ramdas," Arnaud had said. It was stunning to witness the first unfolding of this connection between Lee and Arnaud. Years later Arnaud would take one of the *vigrahas*, the small bronze statues of Yogi Ramsuratkumar, and install it in the "Ramdas Room" at Hauteville, where Lee performed, at Arnaud's request, a puja ceremony to inaugurate the *vigraha*. All of this history reverberated for a moment as Lee received this gift from Arnaud's hands.

Later as a group of students sat at lunch with Arnaud and Lee under the canopy of the tall sycamore trees, Arnaud spoke again about Swami Prajnanpad. Lalitha was questioning him about the value of teaching others and what the dangers or benefits might be of taking on a teaching function, even at a basic level, under the instructions of one's guru. Arnaud said emphatically, "I never *wanted* to be a guru! I wanted to be a movie director, make a great film. I saw myself surrounded by movie stars!" He smiled ironically. As Lalitha questioned him further he said that yes, it could help one to mature significantly on the path to teach others, but that it could also be very dangerous if one is not ready. He continually returned to the need to have a teacher; this was one's only protection, and perhaps even more so after one began to teach.

He said, "For the great *jivanmuktas* like Anandamayi Ma and Ramdas—those who have gone beyond, beyond—it is one thing; for those of us who are disciples and carry on the teaching in the name of our masters, it is a matter of *obedience*! At Le Bost, at Font d'Isière, and now at Hauteville, today, every day, I remember Swami Prajnanpad. Whenever anything is difficult, I ask myself, 'What would Swamiji do? What is his teaching?' It is all a matter of obedience. If someone starts teaching too soon, it is not good." Arnaud shook his head, almost as if in conclusion, but there was something he wanted to clarify and he spoke again, "Remembering Swamiji is not something . . ." he gestured up and above his head with his hands, indicating something magical or mystical or intellectual. Then he shrugged and said, "But it is memories, the teaching itself, how Swamiji would have done things, how he did everything at his ashram." He touched his chest, as if he wanted to communicate that this turning toward Swamiji was something that happened in the ground of his body, not with his mind. I got the sense that it was important that we understand the practical and grounded reality of obedience to the guru, as if Arnaud was hinting to us to watch for our romanticizing about "the guru who lives within."

After lunch people crowded around Lee at the book table in the foyer to the lower floor of the chateau. Like every space at Hauteville, this entry room is a statement of beauty and elegance in form. Passing through huge, ornate doors, one enters the space from the courtyard with the tall sycamore trees. The foyer itself is approximately fifteen by twenty feet and adjoins a formal dining room on one side and a sitting room decorated with Oriental carpets and ornaments on the other side. The foyer has an inlaid marble mosaic floor in light browns with a whorled pattern in black marble that defines the perimeter of the room. On the back wall is a high, arched, mirrored door in front of which Lee sat on a simple wooden chair with a wicker bottom. By the huge double glass door with its simple vine motif in black cast iron were a large potted palm and a rubber tree. Two of Lee's students, Clint and Marcus, had found seats on the floor by the door near the plants and sat writing in their journals.

People crowded in around the book table and waited in line for Lee to sign their books with his famous (and infamous) *dédicace*, almost all of them written in French and each one designed as a teaching (or koan) for the specific individual who had asked for the dedication in their newly purchased book. As he sat there scribbling as fast as he could, I noticed that he was looking very elegant in an unconventional sort of way. One could describe that style as iconoclastic and noncomformist. Lee is a lover of color and design, and he doesn't hold back on either in the kinds of things he chooses to wear. Today he wore a red and black shirt with a bold design of white and yellow hibiscus flowers on it and black silk meditation pants—both gifts from students.

As people cycled through the line, bought their books and received their *dédicace*, they would either take a seat on the floor for awhile or leave, making room for the next influx of people who would then wait their turn for this personal contact with Lee. He would then take the book they had chosen into his hands and look at them with a fresh brightness that never seemed to dim even slightly during the days and afternoons. If he hadn't met them before, he would say, "Your name?" or *"Comment vous appellez-vous?"* then make sure that he knew how to spell their names correctly. Sometimes he gazed at the person for a moment and then lowered his head to the task, writing briskly, without stopping to reflect, consider, think.

Today a woman who has come to Lee's seminar at Hauteville for the past two or three years bought a book. After Lee had written the *dédicace*, she ran out to her car to get a picture of her children to show him. He held the pictures in his hand, looked politely and said, "Very handsome." With a slight smile he handed the pictures back. Lee was running out of the new book, *N'essayez Pas—Vivez,* and sent Clint, who was sitting on the floor by the door writing in his journal, back up the hill to the van to carry more books down. He came in with about a dozen copies and Lee immediately sent him back up to get even more books, this time the small books of quotations. It was about three o'clock on the last afternoon of selling books for the week. I asked Lee if he had sold any copies of the poetry book, *Death of a Dishonest Man.* "No," he replied smiling, "but I will before the afternoon is over," he said confidently.

As I watched Lee interact with people I was struck again with the amazing range of skillful means and easy rapport that Lee brings to his interactions. Everything he does carries some teaching power. In an earlier session Lee had told one man that he should have no resistance by the end of the week; this man came by, bought a book, then knelt at Lee's side and asked for a *dédicace.* As Lee handed him back the signed book, the man looked up into Lee's eyes and said in English, "I treasure your teaching. I treasure it, I really do." The man's face was clear and radiating a genuine gratitude. Lee smiled and said, "Did you meet my expectation?"

"Yes," the man answered, smiling and nodding once.

"Good!" Lee exclaimed, and slapped the man firmly yet with great affection on the shoulder. It was a gesture so reminiscent of the blessings given by Yogi Ramsuratkumar that it seemed to ring through the space and affect, or permeate, everyone sitting there. The man gave a namaste and got up, walked over to the wall, found an empty seat and sat down.

Immediately a woman came up who has been to Lee's seminars at Hauteville before. She wanted to buy a book but had to go get her money. Smiling up at her, Lee said playfully but also meaning it, "Pay me any time." She looked surprised, questioning, then started to protest that she would get the money for him right away. Lee gave her no time to formulate her protest, saying, "No, really—today, tomorrow, next year . . ."

Sitting nearby Jane added, "Next lifetime!" We all laughed. The woman turned away to go get her money saying, "I will be back," and Lee turned to Ann who was helping him at the book table and keeping records of sales. He said to her, "*Always* give them the book. Don't worry about the money. Just give them the book."

All of these exchanges seemed saturated with blessing power given in a simple and ordinary exchange. Today they struck me in contrast to a story I heard from Ann. One afternoon earlier in the week a woman came up to Lee at the book table. She stood directly in front of him and stared at him sitting in his chair in the corner. She said, "I am

385

here to receive your blessings and that of Yogi Ramsuratkumar." Lee looked at her and after a long moment of silence, said, "Whatever." She peered into his face to see if she was going to get something that would appear as a blessing to her. After another few moments Lee said in a measured and deliberate tone, "On this ashram, my blessing and that of Yogi Ramsuratkumar comes through *Arnaud*." Her face registered nothing but confusion. For a moment she didn't understand the English, then Lee repeated this to her in French so that she would understand. She slowly realized that something was off and backed away, but as she left there was the clear impression that she didn't register what had just transpired.

The difference between the approach of the man who met Lee's "expectations" to have no resistance by the end of the week, the woman who had to go get her money, and the other woman who approached aggressively could only be a difference in context. The woman who asked for Lee's blessings seemed like so many people—she was collecting gold coins, had probably already gotten a hug from Ammachi, gone to other teachers, and she had set her sights on getting a coin from Lee to add to her collection.

Now Lee sent Clint back up the hill to the van for a third time to get more books—this time *Conscious Parenting,* which was selling very well this afternoon. Many of Lee's students want nothing more than to be able to serve him, and have discovered a great secret: if one hangs out around the book table long enough, or the bridge table, or the ashram office, or the kitchen where he is cooking, they will sooner or later get to work for the guru in one way or another. This afternoon Lee had kept Clint very busy.

A very young woman came up, paid for her book and asked for a *dédicace*. Kneeling on the floor at his feet she began to tell him that devotional poetry was spontaneously coming up in her. What should she do with the energy? Lee answered with a kind smile, "Write them down, just for you. They're just for you."

During the afternoon there had been an average of twenty people in the foyer with Lee at any given time, sitting on the floor, standing at the book table, standing in line to get a *dédicace*, kneeling beside Lee as he wrote, asking questions, or having an exchange with him. When Clint returned with the third armload of books, I saw that his most recent effort had already paid off as someone bought another copy of a book that had just arrived. Then Roger, a long-time disciple of Arnaud and a good friend of Lee's, came in and stood facing the book table. Within moments he was turning to Lee with a heavy, hardbound volume of *Death of a Dishonest Man*. He handed it to Lee for a *dédicace* and paid for the book. Lee's prediction had come true at the last possible moment; in a few minutes he would pack the book table up for the week and then head off to the meeting hall to give the next to the last session of the week.

July 11, 1999
Hauteville

The last session of the week started at ten o'clock in the morning. After about thirty minutes of conversations with different people that seemed to predominantly fail to evoke a real response from him, Lee seemed restless to get to the point. In answer to another rather murky question he roused himself up and said fiercely, "So what is the *real* problem? There's only ever one problem, right? Everybody here knows that, and everybody has the same problem. There's only one problem, ever. Everything else is an extrapolation of the one problem. There has only ever been one problem—the presumption of separation. Everything else we think to be problems are facets of that. We assume if something in life is not to our liking, something must be wrong. In life there are ups, downs, highs, lows, good and bad. If life was the way *we* wanted it to be it would be so bland it would be unbearable. Anger, fear, discomfort are not problems. The problem is that we are unable to accept anger, fear, discomfort. We're always assuming division when the fact of life is unity. It's purely a problem of our perception. It's not really a problem because it is illusion. It's empty. Separation is not the problem, the presumption of separation is the problem because the presumption can be changed. So there is no problem. It's all in our minds. It's all made up in our minds."

Later, in response to a question about having resistance, Lee said, "You have to *act* in the face of resistance. Artists, musicians, all have resistance. Probably the artists who don't have resistance, their art is so bad—they are terrible artists! So, resistance—so what? We love sex, then we get pregnant and have such resistance! I have resistance to everything! Every bite of food I take, I have resistance to because I'm going to get fat. When I was thirteen . . ."

Lee began to tell an outrageous story of how fat he was when he was thirteen, going into a series of impromptu jokes about "fat asses," calories and fat and French cheese. Everyone was laughing hysterically as he ruthlessly exposed himself. His farcical monologue was a fierce juxtaposition to the serious dharma he'd been laying out for days. It brought into focus exactly how ridiculous all these concerns of vanity and pride and shame really are in the face of impermanence and the insubstantial nature of all phenomena.

"Pass the cheese!" he yelled. "Resistance to what? It's embarrassing. Like at La Bertais, they serve a beautiful cheese platter. It gets passed around and the French take a little tiny piece," he demonstrated, as he if was taking a delicate, small piece of cheese onto his plate. "One little round of *chèvre*—it's one bite!" The room was alternating between roars of laughter and acutely focused listening. "Resistance? So what! I bring two vans, all these students of mine. I don't want to bring eighteen slobs! 'Okay! Here come the Americans! Slop the pigs, get out the trough!' Most of my students wouldn't even notice if you said that when the food was served." Lee students were all laughing hysterically, used to being the butt of the joke. Lee was making a teaching point for everyone there, a point that was not lost on those traveling with him despite their laughter.

He also seemed to be bursting any romantic notions that anyone might have about himself and his students with this wild romp. Lee's theatrics died down as suddenly as they had arisen. He spent the rest of the last session answering questions and "mopping up" from the week—tying together loose ends and connecting the dots for a number of people who asked questions. It was clear that the dharma *sesshin* was over and things were winding down.

A man asked a question about the lack of respect for masters that is so prevalent in the West, and how to show respect to the master. It was a subject that Lee had been speaking on all week long, as he constantly turned disciples back toward Arnaud and his teaching. Now Lee said, "What the master wants of the disciple is that the disciple be themselves completely. There is external, formal respect—follow the rules of the ashram and so on. But what really demonstrates respect is to embody the teaching. In the West we are hard and cynical, and on the other hand, we are very gullible. If we look at any major social phenomena, how people blindly follow musicians or movie stars, for example, those kind of things are buffers from Reality.

"Interiorly the sign of respect for the teaching is practice, because no matter how sincere you are, the road to hell is paved with good intentions. So it's wonderful to have good intentions, but good intentions are fickle, because the next day could be full of bad intentions. Respect means you take what it is you are respecting seriously enough to make it part of your life every day."

The whole group—well over one hundred people—gathered again in the shady courtyard for lunch. The weather was gorgeous, the sky a brilliant bright blue. The sheltering branches of the sycamore trees moved slightly in a gentle breeze. At the table with Arnaud and Lee the subtle mood was so refined, so extraordinarily bright and intense, that a piercing clarity sharpened the perceptions to a bittersweet and fine edge. Lee and Arnaud spoke together, made plans for next year, sat quietly, or visited with their students.

A special meal of baked chicken and saffron rice was served, with an abundance of many different kinds of ice cream for dessert. The Americans did their best to partake of this feast with their usual enthusiasm. After lunch the staff and residents of Hauteville, along with Arnaud, Veronique, and Arnaud's teaching assistants—Daniel, Annick, Gilles, Marie Pierre—gathered around Lee and said their good-byes, with many smiles, namastes and expressions of gratitude from both Arnaud's and Lee's students, and comments of "*A l'année prochaine.*" Next year. Arnaud's face was beaming as he watched Lee and his group jump into the vans that quickly took off and disappeared into the trees and down the lane toward the road.

July 12, 1999
La Ferme de Jutreau

Back at La Ferme de Jutreau Lee's students gathered in the salon for the After Dinner Talk. Being at Hauteville is tremendously empowering to Lee's students because of the mutual respect and regard that exists between the two schools. As a result the people who had traveled with Lee came back riding on a wave of high energy, a kind of inebriation or intoxication, and had many stories to share. As the After Dinner Talk got underway Marcus asked, "What would it mean in this community to practice like a madman?"

Lee answered with a laugh, "Sort of like *you* ... In Arnaud's school it means taking the practice and not forgetting it for a minute. Daniel took the statement, 'What is, is,' and applied it to every moment of his life. He read the books, he questioned Arnaud. He never let himself get lazy. In the process, over years, transformation happened and one day he was different. In this community it might mean Enquiry, the formal conditions, but also a kind of fluidity about the conditions. But we are distractible. 'I want to practice, but I need more money for a car.' Daniel wouldn't let himself be distracted, and as a result people think he's too serious, too heavy."

Lee noticed that Ann's phone call to the Arizona ashram about Hohm Sahaj Mandir business had been going on for over thirty minutes. He stopped talking to the group in the living room and yelled into the office, "Are you still on the same phone call?" He sighed in exasperation and said to his audience, "You get some maturity under your belt and think you can afford some indulgence, and before you know it, you've lost your practice!" He shook his head and yelled into the office again, "Money is not for long phone calls but for publishing books!"

Turning back to the group he continued, "When we were seventy-five thousand dollars in debt we would have been off the phone in minutes. Bala doesn't need all this input from Ann. It's an exact metaphor for practice. And Kyla needs to get on the phone—for what? Nothing!" Bala and Kyla are two of the four or five people who have to run the extremely short-staffed ashram office for four months while Lee and his traveling party, plus Shri, are away.

"You see a gypsy family drive a forty thousand dollar car and get out at a rest area as if it was a horse and wagon. They are exactly the same as they would be if they were in a horse and wagon. The gypsies are the 'niggers' of Europe. They have been treated badly for years in France, Germany, Europe. They can't forget who they are. We should be the same way. All of the reputation and status and attention that we've gotten for the past several years from people as esteemed as Arnaud or Andrew Cohen could change at any time. Don't forget that we are heretics. If we are going to stick to our principles, we will never be really accepted.

"When E.J. talks about the fact that we are aliens—we are mutants—he means that when the villagers find out about it, they are not going to be happy. You will have to make a choice between the Work and the villagers. Remember Frankenstein. You're not going to pull them up to your level; they are going to pull you down to their level. There is a core level of communion we can appreciate with other schools, but we have to hold the line of our own path or we will find our work poisoned. We tend to share more than is useful, unguardedly. But we often are the same way with each other. This feeling that we are all 'family' is deadly because it's about offering comfort to each other. If we are looking for comfort we should just go to a Twelve Step Program instead of making all these sacrifices!"

Paula Z. said, "While you were away at Hauteville I realized again that because you are so accessible to us we rely on you for that primal sense of okayness. So while you were gone 'Why am I really here?' started coming up."

"My relationship to Yogi Ramsuratkumar is not one of understanding," Lee said. "I don't need to understand anything. I made my commitment; I made the right choice. I don't need to keep making the right choice, or to affirm that the choice was right. Either there is love or there isn't, and you don't have to keep looking for it. When you've made that bottom-line choice that there is trust in your teacher, you don't need to keep going into all those niggling little doubts."

Marcus asked a question about the principles of contamination. Lee commented, "The essence of the principle of contamination is to not weave the energy of those who are not in the same work chamber as you into your energies. That means impression food, gross food, et cetera. Don't share food and water and so on, to begin with.

"If you relax your vigilance, before you know it someone else's energy has toxified your whole energy system. How particular do you want to be about the purity of your work body? This work is alchemy, and one foreign element, even one molecule, skews the whole end result. If your intention is for your work body to be pure—and the sealed chamber for the alchemy is internal—then you have to be very particular. If you've got a compromised immune system, for example, you'll have trouble fighting off invaders. The Work is urgent. You can't spare a minute, so obviously you don't want to get infected with a foreign element.

"Clothe yourself in the lineage—that's the form of protection. The lower form of magic cannot override the higher force of the lineage of Yogi Ramsuratkumar. Yogi Ramsuratkumar's Name is the strongest talisman we have. Using Yogi Ramsuratkumar's

Name is always beneficial from the highest perspective, but not from ego's perspective, because it could invoke a whole range of purificatory experiences."

Debbie commented, "But you want to breed a conscious infection of certain work cells, right?"

Lee said, "That is the principle of *prasad*."

July 14, 1999
La Ferme de Jutreau

Last night was the first of five Shri gigs that will take place during Guru Purnima. Several cars full of devotees packed up in the parking lot at the edge of the orchard at La Ferme de Jutreau, then took off caravan-style behind Ute and Volker who drove Lee in their car the one hour drive to Chinon.

Chinon turned out to be a beautiful city with an immense castle fortress that towers over the city from a high bluff overlooking the river. The gig was in a small bar on a side street in the old town. When the band started the bar owner closed all the big windows and their wooden shutters that opened out onto the street. The small room was like a smoky oven, completely packed to standing room only with about one hundred fifty people who were baked and steamed in the blues cook-down of the night. Shri was in fabulous form; they were obviously having a great time onstage and happy to have Lee with them again. The audience danced and hooted and yelled or sat and listened, their eyes riveted to the stage. There were people who stood outside the door to the bar and listened in the street because the place was so crowded they couldn't get in. The room was set up so that we could stand right next to the band as an extended part of their space, so a number of us stood and danced immediately next to stage left by the band. Onstage Lee danced and whirled his dreadlocks, played percussion and infected the other musicians and the audience with his passion. The French audience was thrilled and re-sponded with high enthusiasm. When Lee left at one-fifteen the bar manager called out to him in English as he walked away, "Great show. Fantastic! A great night—the *blues*!" The manager held his hand up in the air with a final wave good-bye as Lee walked down the cobblestone streets toward the van.

Arriving back at Ferme de Jutreau in the moist dark at two-fifteen in the morning, we walked with Lee across the wet grass toward the silent, sleeping *grande maison* . . . A few hours later, at seven o'clock, the whole group was on their pillows in a packed meditation hall. The numbers were growing as many people had arrived the evening before for Guru Purnima.

After meditation the mood at breakfast was very high and fine. Lee was in great spirits as he talked and laughed with his devotees who sat around him. Thomas sat with Lee and talked about the plans for Lee's trip to Freiburg later in the summer. Lee spoke with him about possibly visiting Durgamayi Ma, who lives in southern Germany, on the Shri tour this month. She had recently sent Lee a gift—state-of-the-art equipment for recording his talks. The gift had just arrived, and being rather ignorant (by choice) about current technology, there was still some question as to what it was. Some thought it might be one of the new computer advancements that are available now, which automatically transcribes recorded talks. We were discussing how such a thing might transcribe all the laughter at Lee's talks—would it put in the word 'laughter,' or would it put it 'aha ha ha' and so on—when Lee broke into the conversation, saying, "It will say, 'Heellppp meeeee

. . . I'mm dyyyiing!' "Everyone broke into laughter. It was an accurate assessment and a good reminder.

Lee keeps everyone laughing in the mornings at breakfast with funny little quips and spontaneous one-liners like this. But his effortless sense of humor and joking around is almost always in reference to the condition in which we live—the illusion of separation. He does it in such a way that we find we are laughing at ourselves, even though there is the reality of "the horror of the situation." One has to either laugh or cry in the face of such heart-breaking clarity of insight into the illusion of separation in one's own case, and laughing is certainly Lee's response of choice. This morning Lee sat with the group for an hour at breakfast, long after the oats and fruit and almonds soaked in pineapple juice were eaten, long after the last of the green tea or yarrow tea was finished off. It was an opportunity for his students and guests to sit in his company, to laugh and visit with him in a relaxed, intimate atmosphere over the table in the barn.

Since Shri would be playing a gig in La Roche Posay tonight, about ten kilometers away from La Ferme de Jutreau—a very short fifteen minute drive—Lee made an announcement to everyone after breakfast that the group would be having dinner in Angles sur l'Anglin, a beautiful nearby village. Lee planned to make a special arrangement with a small pizzeria in town to open early since he would be bringing a large group. Lee said, "So anyone who wants to go into town and eat with us is welcome to come. There's just one condition—I will go in early and order pizzas for everyone, so you have to be willing to eat whatever I order. So let me know if you want to go and I'll go in early." There were thirty-six people who were eager for this opportunity to participate in Lee's play.

The group drove to Angles sur l'Anglin for dinner at four-fifteen in the afternoon and met up with Lee, Thomas and Deacon, who were sitting at one of the three long tables that had been set up for us upstairs. We had the whole room to ourselves. Soon the pizzas began to be brought out: pizzas with sausage, pizzas with whole shrimps in the shell—head and all—or mussels in the shell, pizzas with goat cheese and gorgonzola, pizzas with chicken and curry. Lee ordered six of each kind, and everyone had to just make it work, even when the kind they really wanted got taken by others.

At one point the waitress came out with yet another pizza covered with mussels in their purple shells and one loaded with long brown strips of anchovies. No one seemed willing to take them. The waitress stood there for a minute with a questioning look on her face. Finally Brinda and Clint, who sat next to me, took the pizzas. I asked Brinda if she liked anchovies. She said she didn't know it would have anchovies on it. It was clear that she didn't really care so much for them, but I watched her eat the whole pizza without complaint. It was all part of the price one paid to be in Lee's company that night—working with sacrificing personal desires, being willing to be flexible to his play, helping make the space work.

The gig was to start at six-thirty, so as soon as everyone was finished with the pizza Lee headed out toward La Roche Posay and caught up with Shri, who had eaten a picnic dinner in the picturesque park at the *centre ville* across the street from the hotel.

The *centre ville* in La Roche Posay, like many French villages, is the hub of community life—a place where the ancient tradition of the communal gathering place continues. The small park is under tall, shady trees that shelter a playground and the gravel area where the local outdoor market is set up twice a week, as well as an area where local men can be seen every day playing *pétanque*. The park is always busy with people walking, strolling or sitting on benches and talking, children playing. On Tuesdays and Fridays every week the market unfolds its marvelous goods—fresh produce, bread, fish, poultry and meats, cheese, pastries, jam and jelly, paté, wine, clothes and jewelry, pottery, arts and crafts. It is where the ashram does most of its shopping for La Ferme de Jutreau.

Tonight the park was full of people, probably at least in part celebrating Bastille Day. Shri had set their equipment up on the long, open verandah of the hotel Loges du Park that is located across the street from the park. As Shri started playing about one hundred people came strolling up and stood just across the narrow gravel drive that separated the hotel from the park, which was bordered by sculpted cedar trees and small plots of flowers. Up on the verandah another fifty or sixty people packed in at the tables.

Shri has played at the Piano Cocktail Bar in La Roche Posay for the past two summers. This year the owner of the bar had made arrangements for Shri to play at the hotel instead of the bar because he lost a particular license that he had to have to hire a band. To the disappointment of Lee, Deborah and the musicians, the four hour performance had been cut back to two hours, so Shri was making the most of their time. They started out with a blast. People standing on the street listened, tapped their toes, swayed. Almost an hour into the set Lee, who had been quiet onstage until now, started talking. It began with the famous Fred McDowell song, "Left My Baby Standing," a traditional blues favorite with a haunting melody, a slow rhythmic roll and sad lyrics. This is a song that Deborah sings, in which Ed gives a compelling guitar solo that is a poignant communication of the inexorable truth of impermanence, and of love in separation.

In the last six months Lee started singing the last few verses of this song. As he went into his verses tonight, suddenly he was singing in French, obviously making up the lyrics as he went, *"J'aime les femmes vieilles, j'aime les femmes jeunes, j'aime les femmes grosses et les femmes petites . . ."* "I love the old women, I love the young women, I love the big women, and I love the little women." Then, *"Les femmes françaises, elles sont belles, mais elles sont froides."* He sang this line over and over again, and it came out as pure lament: "The French women, they are beautiful, but they are cold as ice."

It was a statement of fact, a direct hit into the French neurosis that denies the force of the Feminine in natural human life, which breeds too thin and angular women who are afraid to eat. These women, like many women throughout the Western world, will stifle and repress the essentially feminine life force or shakti within themselves to maintain an exterior that is fashionable, socially acceptable and desirable, at least in their own minds— and obviously in the eyes of French (or Western) men, who are culpable partners, if not instigators, of this travesty. The one hundred or so people standing in the street stood listening, along with another fifty on the verandah, and I wondered how many understood his French and caught the drift of what he was saying.

The song came to an end and the band barreled into the next song, "One Way Out," an old blues song made popular by the Allman Brothers Band. It's a song about a man who is having an affair with a woman. While he is in the upstairs bedroom with her, he hears someone come in downstairs. He says, "There's only one way out and I ain't goin' out that door," because he knows it could be her husband coming in. Lee introduced this song with a dharmic spin, saying in English, "You come in one way, and you go out one way! There's only one way in, and only one way out!"

It was a reminder of something he has said many times: "Everybody comes into life through Woman, and goes out of life through Woman." All manifest life has its death and birth through the auspices of the Creatrix, Kali, or whatever face of the goddess we might put on the feminine principle of existence in form. In this way Lee refers to the fact that all creation is the feminine face of God. On the tantric path all this is embraced, not denied. We are born through the act of sex, of procreation, through blood and pain and passion and joy. We come in through the ancient symbol of life, the *yoni*, out of the unfathomable mystery of the female womb which is dark and hidden, and we die also, into the subtle, hidden womb of the Great Mother, which is also dark and mysterious.

At the end of the song Lee started his unique brand of banter. "We are Shri! Here for all of the expatriate Americans and Germans getting fat and lazy in the beautiful countryside of France, and bringing them some *blues*! You know how Americans are. We don't like all that French cheese—give us Velveeta, runnin' on that white Wonderbread. Pure plastic! Umm ummm." There was no esoteric teaching in this rap; Lee was lampooning his students again, and Americans in general. He had given the French a hard time with his comments on French women, now he would give it in turn to the Americans. Don't forget for a moment where you come from, he seemed to be saying.

In the middle of the next song Lee gestured to Everett to do a solo on the guitar. Everett had been playing bass for liars, gods & beggars up until recently and is new at playing rhythm guitar in Shri. He was not expecting this solo, and made a playful face of surprise, then rose to the occasion. When the song was over Lee took the mike again. *"Nous sommes Shri! Notre musique est magnifique, fantastique, incroyable! N'est-ce-pas?"*

The audience on the verandah was cheering loudly. A dancing crowd had gathered on the concrete floor of the porch right in front of the band. There were many strangers dancing, people who had come for their first connection with Lee and his students. This was their first Shri gig and their first glimpse of the Baul master who sings the blues. Already they were throwing themselves into the play, dancing and clapping with faces flushed from the heat. Lee kept going, *"Bonne soirée!* Happy Bastille Day—is that how you say it? We have something like that in America, the Fourth of July, but since its inception two hundred years ago it has deteriorated to nothing but a crass, commercial manipulation of the average sleeping American mind . . . ."

Short but sweet, it was a great gig even though there had been some discord between the musicians onstage. The band had stopped in the midst of two songs because someone was playing the wrong chords; tempers had seemed on edge, and Lee's banter had become more and more acidic. Soon, too soon, it was eight-thirty and the gig was over. The park was suddenly vacant. Everyone had gone to see the fireworks on the outskirts of town in celebration of Bastille Day, the day of French liberation. Lee had given the village a small taste of a different kind of liberation tonight. Leaving the hotel he walked down the village square with his entourage. Everyone piled into the van and drove home.

At nine forty-five that night *dans le salon* back at La Ferme de Jutreau everyone came together for mint tea. The rather small room was crowded with about twenty-five or thirty people, just a smattering of the group of eighty-five people that would be gathered here tomorrow morning for the first day of Guru Purnima Celebration and Lee's first talk at eight-thirty, after meditation. The theme of the Celebration, both here in France and happening simultaneously at the ashram in Arizona, would be "The Sangha as Benediction."

July 15, 1999
La Ferme de Jutreau

Tonight after a sumptuous feast of chicken *putanesca* (a favorite recipe of the prostitutes of Italy, we were told), pasta, baguette, salad and the ultimately decadent dessert—a three layer meringue and coffee ice cream pie with thick chocolate mocha icing—Thomas was giving the evening talk *dans le salon*. About thirty adults were crowded into the small room while others provided childcare, washed dishes and put away food.

About an hour into the talk Lee interrupted Thomas to answer a new student's question about living far away from other sangha members in Germany. She cried quietly, and expressed her sadness at feeling very deeply alone. Lee said, "You're only alone in the world of sleep. In the world of sleep we really need other people—and this is a real need, in the world of sleep. We need love, touch, understanding, respect—those good things.

"In one sense being far away from sangha is harder and in another sense it's easier because it forces you to resort to more subtle connections to sangha. So you have no choice because there's nobody there. If the teaching means enough to you, and it seems like it does, then you are forced to find the inner connection. So the teaching is like a spring: it arises from the depths of being and shows up ultimately on the surface, but the source of it is on the inside. When you don't have that external support, which is admittedly important and wonderful and everything else that it is, it forces you to seek the heart of communion, which is not on the gross or dense physical level. There is a saying in English: when we get everything we want, we say, 'You can have your cake and eat it too.' So people who are physically close to really substantial numbers of sangha are having their cake and eating it too.

"As difficult as it is—and it is difficult, no doubt about it—in the short run you suffer. In the immediate circumstances it's hard, but in the long run, in the big picture, you actually get the benefit more than the people who are close. Because when I die, not too soon but hopefully not too long either," Lee laughed at this statement, "the people who have lived closest to me—who have stepped into the trap of dependency on the teacher—they'll be feeling abandoned and betrayed, and you'll be saying, 'Where did he go? He's here, can't you feel him?' because you will have learned to find me inside because you *have* to. So you're very lucky."

The dharma talk ended at nine o'clock and at nine-thirty a group of about twenty-five people met Lee at the cars parked on the edge of the orchard to go to the gig. Lee assessed the situation and arranged who would ride in what car. As he instructed people to go here or there to various vehicles his gestures and posture were regal, authoritative and yet noticeably lacking in the kind of aggression and domination that so often characterizes the wielding of power. Lee's simple gestures often seem fraught with unseen potency, like Yogi Ramsuratkumar, whose striking of a match in darshan seems to somehow change the shape of the whole world in an instant.

When everyone was settled a few of us jumped into Thomas' car with Lee and drove off to Poitiers, a city about forty-five minutes away from La Ferme de Jutreau, where the Shri gig both tonight and tomorrow night would be from eleven to two a.m. at a small bar in the old town. Arriving before dark, we walked in with Lee and found the little side street bistro decorated in a beach motif, complete with a thick layer of sand on the floor to create the illusion—and it took a stretch of the imagination to go there—that one was walking by the ocean. One part of the club had clusters of huge red beach umbrellas perched above tables. One wall was covered with framed prints of very bad contemporary popular "art." It's always surprising to find out that even the elegant and cultured

French can sometimes have terrible taste.

In the center of the room the band was set up along one wall on a small raised stage where they had somehow managed to get all eight of them arranged with their instruments. It was going to be very crowded, but the good thing was that the arrangement allowed for a very intimate contact between band and audience, either on the dance floor or just sitting at one of the many tables packed into the room. At eleven o'clock the band started playing and the bartender turned the light down to a dim, smoky glow.

Almost instantly a noticeable and particular mood was present. Three or four songs into the first set there were *bhavas* drifting on the air of a different kind than I'd ever experienced at a band gig—sensuous, rich, earthy. Something deeper than ecstasy, with a sense of coming from down below, beneath, between, beyond. It was an underworld mood, but of a subterranean paradise rather than hell, rooted in incarnation, in the flesh, something of bone and blood. The Tibetans say the blood must be very hot at the moment of enlightenment, like the boiling blood in the skull cups at the feet of Vajrakilaya. When the music of Lee's band is really cooking, the felt experience of this internal heat is undeniable.

Lee's dancing on stage became more animated and transfixing; it was the communication of a three-centered unity, of a completely free moving center. He drew the other musicians into the dance with him, and seemed to be working directly with their moving centers. The opportunity to receive what Lee was communicating in this way was extended into the entire space. The flushed and smiling faces of his German, French and American students reflected just how strongly they were being moved from the inside by Lee's communication, both bodily and through the music. The house was packed with people, and Lee's students intermingled with local people who were dancing in front of the band, between tables or in any space available. Other locals sat and watched, then clapped and yelled after the songs. One older French man with white hair and a mustache, perhaps seventy-five years old, sat to the left of the band near the wall with a big smile on his face, rapping out the beat on the table with his knuckles.

From the beginning of the gig the band seemed exceptionally together and in communion. They were in sync, playing together as a unified and even seamless whole. There was no discord on the stage, as there had been the night before on the verandah of the hotel in La Roche Posay. Tonight the *bhavas* encircled the entire space and everyone in it in an enclosed chamber. The band too seemed to float on this ocean of pure mood, while at the same time bringing acute presence and immediacy of being to the music and each other onstage. As Lee danced, the band members were enveloped in his rhythm and flow in a way that seemed to weigh the whole band in the direction of a kind of unity and teamwork that Lee keeps saying he is looking for in configuration sadhana—that is, in groups which Lee has formed to do a specific sadhana together, for example, the bands or the Baul Theatre Company. These configurations are specific dharma "pods" or seed groups that carry a particular responsibility to participate in and further Lee's work in various arenas of life, and to transmit that work. At the same time, the individuals in a configuration are also given the opportunity to practice sadhana in a particularly fiery and alchemically potent crucible, which means that pressure bears down on them in a powerful way, stirring up many primal elements of the psyche—passions and underworld potencies—and inducing a purificatory process. It is hard sadhana, but the opportunity for breakthroughs of great magnitude is significant.

Toward the end of the night after a rousing version of a fast dance number, there were twenty-five people on their feet in the tiny space, crowded together with very little room to dance, but exhilarated anyway from moving to the music and sweating in the sand. While we clapped and whooped in appreciation, Lee said joyfully, "When Shri leaves the house, nobody's left alive!" From an esoteric perspective, one can only hope for such a thing! It seemed like a statement on the night's work from Lee's point of view.

The music has the power to transform, and also to liberate, and tonight the band with Lee onstage as a total entity had been blasting out that power. Lee's work with his students through the music is an opportunity to receive a very specific transmission. How does one become available or receptive to this blessing power? The answer is found in the tantric tradition, in the dharma and within practice itself. Paying attention to Lee has always been the most important key to working in these spaces. At times Lee appears as a deity in motion. The deity, in both its divine and demonic aspects, has the power to transmit the pure transforming force of liberation.

Placing one's attention on Lee is the key to being available in any way to what is being offered, but without the foundation of a stable and reliable practice, we are just fools rushing in where angels fear to tread. When one is being forgetful or too casual or blasé about band sadhana, we might come walking in with big grins, ready for the party, or deep frowns, or spacey, innocuous smiles plastered across our faces. We fling ourselves open to stand teetering and off-balance on the precipice, oblivious to the fact that there are energetic forces, or entities one might say, that can push us over the edge, just to feast on the remains that lay at the bottom of the cliff. In this case it is the primal passions that often knock us off balance—greed, jealousy, pride, fear, lust, anger, avarice. We come into a space with the band—a bar, a festival, a restaurant, the streets—where these unconscious passions are running at a high tide. The music and the lyrics often act as catalysts to stir these passions in ourselves as well. To maintain vigilance, to maintain consciousness and mindfulness in the midst of all this, one has to pay attention and remember in a way that keeps one's attention on the guide—the guru who stands onstage, leading the way through the underworld journey and the confrontation with primal passions.

Lee has no qualms about dragging his students into the underworld on these gig excursions. His total confidence rests in the fact of his complete trust in the benediction and blessing power of Yogi Ramsuratkumar. Through Lee's surrender to Yogi Ramsuratkumar, it is the intelligence of this influence of the lineage that informs and guides every aspect of Lee's work with his students. One aspect of Lee's work with the bands, which is essentially tantric work, can be compared to sitting at the *smashan* (cremation grounds)—the crowded, seedy bars and clubs with their filthy and stinking bathrooms, toxic environment, beer, smoke and liquor-soaked floors, furniture, air. So often these places are haunted by the down and out, the marginal outcasts of society, the alcoholics, the lonely and forlorn. This is also not unlike the village streets or the big festival *melas* where the Bauls dance and sing and play their instruments. Their music carries the message of a tantric sadhana that embraces all aspects of life as being essentially sacred and worthy of engagement on the path to God. Encoded into the words of their sung poetry are all the principles of the transformation of the primal passions into streams of higher feeling. The sadhana of the Bauls is also devotional, and the message for which they are most loved by the common people of Bengal is the message of a God of love—Krishna, in his love for the *gopis*, symbolized in Radha, the divine consort.

After a transcendental guitar solo by Ed on "Born Under a Bad Sign," Lee took the mike and said, "That was great. *La musique est magnifique, fantastique!* I haven't had sex that good in hours!"

Perhaps people thought he was just kidding, but the principle of the mystical erotic yoga of the Bauls is to transform human passion into divine love through the practice of conscious sexual love with a partner. Over time in this very human, earthy relationship, a living mystical and yet bodily relationship with the Divine comes to blossom. This is continually enacted within the body of one who is the matrix or medium of the mystical marriage or the union of Masculine and Feminine—symbolized in Baul song as Radha and Krishna. Music, dance, sex are all mediums through which this realization may be expressed.

Through this inner union the individual becomes linked into the vast circuitry of the Universe, where immense archetypal forces are enacting the union from which Creation spins forth. A *khepa*, in Baul terms, is one who has become inundated in the divine madness of this state of union, which is grounded in an enlightened relationship to the world of duality, of form, of opposites. This springs from the essential *sahajiya* way—the easy, natural way of enlightenment in the body. It is an open-eyed ecstasy in which the realizer is both experiencing the bliss of union and simultaneously at home in the endless play of opposites, functional within the world of ordinary life at the same time. Lee is a constant example of this.

"Voodoo Chile" was the last song—a wildly ecstatic rendition of one of Jimi Hendrix's most famous songs of mystical, multidimensional flight, a landmark of the rock & roll experience. The band gave it all they had and Lee was a power unleashed onstage, playing the tambourine and dancing madly. Lee had been beaming onstage all night, in communion with the band members, constantly turning toward them and weaving them into the magical garment of the music, like a cloak spread across the guru's loom—the guru as maya, the one who weaves the world. Tonight the guru wove the world in a new design, shaped by the transforming power of the lineage of a dirty beggar, sitting now in Tiruvannamalai, smoking and blessing the world while his son Lee danced and sang somewhere in the West, somewhere in a beautiful country called France, in a small bar hidden on a side street in Poitiers, in the late hours of the night. At the end of the song as the last chords died away Lee said into the mike, "We are Shri, bringing the blues to *tout le monde*, glad to be here tonight with you all!"

It was two a.m. and time to stop. The bar owner, who was very happy with the music and the whole evening, wanted to feed the band members, so everyone waited at the tables in the dark bar while the food was prepared. An Indian man who had come in during the last set came over to where Lee sat with some of the band members. It was as if he was magnetically drawn and suddenly appeared, standing a few feet away and directly in front of Lee.

"You know India?" he asked Lee.

Lee said, "I know India. I like India very much. Good people, good food," Lee smiled.

The man said, "I am from Rajasthan," and Lee responded, "Yes, I've been there—to Jaipur."

"Yes, Jaipur," the man echoed, and spoke of other places in Rajasthan. As they talked the Indian man's eyes hardly left Lee's face as he spoke in the lively, friendly Indian way, gesturing and smiling. He told Lee that he too was traveling on tour with a group of Indian musicians from Rajasthan. He played tabla but also cymbals with the Rajasthani brass band. They hoped to travel to America to play, but had not been able to get in. He asked Lee questions about Shri, how many people traveled with them, where they were staying—musician talk.

He seemed to be motivated in part by wanting help to tour the U.S. (he would have to have an American sponsor to get into the States), but at the same time he was drinking in Lee's calm attention, which was placed directly on him for ten or fifteen minutes as the man continued the interchange with Lee. His conversation turned from touring and performing to India, and how India was becoming a Western culture, with computers and television. Even India was losing its culture, becoming fast and hard. He said, "Here in Europe everything is so fast. People do not use their bodies anymore. In India there is no water," he gestured that one would have to walk and carry water, "and people use their *bodies*." He gracefully touched his form with elegant dark hands, eyes gleaming in the darkened room. It is continually amazing how Lee synchronistically draws these kinds of people into his sphere, where they drop affirmations of the teaching.

Tina came to say that the food was ready. We walked to the back of the club and outside to a small concrete courtyard tucked in between buildings, where we settled at tables to eat salad, baguette, goat cheese, a thinly sliced dark *jambon*. Through the open kitchen door I could see sausages hanging from the ceiling, and concrete stairs leading up to a small flat where the bar owners lived.

The owners of the club seemed to be brothers. They came out to talk with the band and offered wine and more food. With them was one of the musicians Lee had met last year when Shri played to two thousand people at a big blues festival in Rochefort. He was an American who has lived in France for ten years, and who had come tonight specifically to reconnect with Shri. He had been very friendly and encouraging last year. He was amazed that Shri had managed to get into the music circuit in France so easily; he'd been struggling to get established with his band for years, and Shri had just slipped in with what seemed like no effort.

Although no one was really hungry after the immense feast we'd had on the ashram only hours earlier, eating was part of being a good guest in response to the hospitality that was being offered to us, so we found ourselves in a position to eat again and do justice to the food that was being offered. After about twenty minutes when the last of the *jambon* was gone, Lee said, "Let's go!" He was back at La Ferme de Jutreau by three-thirty. Overhead the Milky Way was scattered across a black sky, tonight seeming almost as thick and bright as the stars over the desert ashram so many miles away, where Lee's students also celebrated Guru Purnima, the presence of the guru in the world.

July 17, 1999
Vils les Rochers

The guests, students and friends staying at La Ferme de Jutreau for Guru Purnima have been enthusiastically embracing the spirit of the Celebration. Every night after dinner and the last dharma talk, thirty or forty people jump into five, six or seven vehicles and then follow Lee in the lead car with Thomas driving to Poitiers or some other town to dance enthusiastically to Baul music. The music comes after a very busy day that begins at seven o'clock in meditation. There are several hours of guru *seva*, in which the men are usually involved in heavy work—digging, clearing and building—on the grounds. There are mounds and mounds of dishes that have to be hand-washed in primitive clean-up systems outside the barn, and huge feasts have to be cooked, taking anywhere from six to ten hours to prepare with five to eight people helping. The set-up and serving of meals alone takes a crew of four for each meal. Quality childcare is provided all day as well. People pack into the salon to sit on the uncomfortable floor where they have no room to move in order to hear six hours of dharma talks, mostly given by Lee's students, in between periods of hard work, or *seva*.

Tonight seven cars pulled out behind Lee's car to go to the gig at La Corbeille Dosier (The Wicker Basket) in Vils les Rochers. Down the tree-lined driveway and lush one lane road the vehicles snaked along in procession. An hour and a half later we arrived in a very small village. This is the third year in a row that Shri has played in this small village—known perhaps only for its wicker baskets—at La Corbeille Dosier, a local bar that is fascinated with everything *les américains*. The walls were decorated with over sixty of the famous pictures of Native Americans taken by Edward Curtis in the nineteenth century—a stunning witness to Native American culture in the final years before the tribes were eventually conquered and subjugated by the American government, that is, white Europeans. Large war shields and "buffalo" skulls decorated with eagle feathers and faux fox tails hung on the walls. In the room with the pool table were three Harley Davidson motorcycles on display, one of them at least fifty years old.

The local people at this bar love Shri. Each year for the past three years the bar has been packed with people who come and dance wildly, stay until the last song and beg for more, yelling "*Encore, encore!*" On this hot summer evening the bar was populated with a number of local people who were sitting around the club drinking and smoking when Lee and his entourage arrived. Some of them had their small children with them; there were even a few babies held in arms while parents talked and drank.

As soon as Lee walked in Rakini came over and told him that one of their ardent fans had left money at the bar with a note for them. The note said that he was out of town and was disappointed that he couldn't make it tonight, but he had left money with the bartender to buy their new CD for him. The note said, "You are great! I wish I could be there!" It seemed Shri had become a legend in this village. Visiting from La Source Bleue in Touzac, Sian Bouyou told us that many of the people of these small villages have never seen the ocean, ridden a train, or been very far outside their village. The margin of their lives is very narrow, and they are thrilled to see even the most mediocre performers that come to the summer *fêtes*, or festivals, in their area; having an American blues band the caliber of Shri playing in their club inspires them to a degree of adulation and excitement that one can only marvel at.

Soon Everett kicked the show off with an intro rap to "G-Thang," a funky, bass-driven dance song with constantly changing lyrics. He skillfully built the excitement in the room to a peak, at which point he introduced the audience to "the Queen Bee of Shri, the Goddess of Gospel, the Mother Superior of the Blues—Miz Deborah Auletta!" Deborah came on and plowed into a fast rendition of "Blues School." As the band broke into their opening numbers about fifteen very enthusiastic local people flooded out onto the dance floor along with several of Lee's students, while others sat at tables or at the bar, watching and listening.

The stage was a low platform, about twelve inches high, at one end of the room, so that the band was standing at almost the same level as the dancers. One tall young man with shaggy black hair immediately ran up to the front of the band and started dancing wildly, as Ann said, like a "gyrating Pinocchio," because he was both wooden and seemed very uncomfortable in his body, but he also danced with a fury that was frightening. Even though he kept the beat, his whiplash attack of frenzied movement made him seem like an alien in his own body. He was dancing so hard that beads of sweat were flung through the air in all directions around him, some of them landing very close to where we sat watching. After about five minutes of nonstop rapid jerking and flinging himself violently about, he ripped his wet shirt off and carelessly flung it down on an empty seat at our table. He glanced at us and we stared back, nonplussed. I must have had a look of distaste on my face as I wiped drops of his sweat off my hands. The place was beginning to take on the semblance of a hell realm.

Gig life is sadhana, and it can be grueling at times. After several nights in a row of staying out until three or four in the morning, going to yet another gig tonight was challenging. Tonight we would sit again in the tight confines of a very smoky bar where we would be jostled and bounced on the dance floor and rub elbows with sweating strangers who have no sense of the boundaries of others. A small revolt was kicking up dust internally as resistance to all this loomed large on the horizon. I thought, wouldn't it be great to just stay home in the beautiful green countryside, bask in the long twilight on the quiet, lovely ashram, visit and laugh with friends, go to sleep at a reasonable hour and wake up refreshed for meditation the next morning? But as Lee said recently, the tantric path is about "Action, action, action!" So there we were, exhausted from the late nights and from breathing in literally packages of cigarettes in secondary smoke, wiping drops of a stranger's sweat off our hands and bodies.

There were several other men who also danced with an apparent lack of self-reflection. This seemed at the same time a lack of self-consciousness that is innocent but also naïve, coming from a vacancy of consciousness. One man with a shaved head stood directly in front of the band and mouthed the words to the songs, but he didn't know the words so his face took on a foolish quality, as if he was autistic and talking to himself. Another man appeared to be praying in one moment with hands folded, then grasping the air with curled anxious fingers in an anguished rapport with the whine of the bluesy notes that came bending and moaning out of Ed's guitar, or from Nachama's mouth harp. Another man, short and stout, with short dark hair, danced with a glistening face, exerting himself and smiling at the band, yelling out his gratitude, moving to the beat on the tile floor with cigarette and drink in hand.

Looking at the local people, whom the French call "peasants," my thoughts turned to how these country folk have not covered over the insanity of their suffering with a slick mask of social graces. They have no artifice or façade, just the raw fact of their pain, which was excruciatingly etched into their visible lives. At the same time this was the very thing that made their joy and ecstasy so apparent and so available to the spirit of the music. Their connection to the harsh realities of life has stripped them of pretense and given them access to a range of feeling that more sophisticated people usually do not have. It's not that their upper-class cousins in Paris or Montpellier are suffering less—it's that they have overlaid a veneer of politeness and education on top of their suffering. They have perfected a certain blasé attitude that covers the chill of their fear.

At one time I arrogantly thought this term "peasant"—that so easily rolls off the tongue of the upper-class French—particularly elitist, particularly lacking in compassion and a sense of the equality of all beings. What about the spirit of *namaskar* or *namasté*? Or the Mahayana principles of loving kindness and compassion for all beings? And yet the word "peasant" is not at all unlike the word "redneck"—a descriptive term we blithely use in the U.S. for people of a similar social background. It is an appellation that usually carries an understood superiority on the part of the one who uses it. But at the same time, because of the lack of pretensions and social veils of power and prestige, there is often a connectedness into the global human family that can be experienced with the ordinary working or poor people of America, France or any other country. Rubbing shoulders with grass roots folks gives one a taste of reality as it is. As much as I disliked my own reaction to being in close proximity to this reality on this particular night, there would be a valuable teaching lesson in it.

As the dance floor filled up with dancers the man with the shaggy black hair continued to fling himself around like a demon from the depths of hell as sweat streamed down his naked chest. In between songs Lee suddenly grabbed the mike and said, "See how wet this man is up here? I want to see all the women get that wet and at the end of the night whoever is the wettest gets to be licked off by her choice of the men in the band!" Everett started joking around, pointing to Ed, as if to say, "Him, not me," then said facetiously to Lee, "Thanks, Lee!"

Lee's words were a wake-up call, sounding through the mist of my resistance and judgements, as if Lee was saying, "Get off it—there is room for everyone!" By his statements it was clear that Lee was not making any judgements on the guy who was flinging his sweating, half-naked body around the dance floor. In fact, he was right in there with him. These kinds of outrageous and even lascivious comments, for which Lee is well-known, are often pointed reminders. We all sweat, urinate, defecate, excrete sexual fluids, salivate, eat, digest, make love and die. It is the reality of common human incarnation. We are not different from each other. Why deny it, why overlay the fundamental facts of human life with our hatred and fear of the body, our imagined superiority, when the fact of being human is the doorway to transformation? That is the way of the Bauls, of *kaya sadhana* and of tantric practice.

Suddenly Dasya sat down at our table and said, "This place is full of *masts*." Maybe so. Maybe one or two of these folks were crazy like the *masts* of India, who Meher Baba searched out and served so profoundly, attempting to bring them out of their trance of madness. Meher Baba believed that there were saints hidden within these mad, autistic souls.

Ed went into the plaintive chords of the slide guitar of "Left My Baby Standing." It is a song that touches everyone who hears it in the same place of universal human experience—the place of loss and longing that lays at the roots of the blues. It is a pure testimony to the truth that all life is suffering. It is a song that springs from the very deep heart of the blues, and Ed and Deborah and Lee brought it to brilliant life. By now the dance floor was completely jammed with people. If you wanted to dance you had to fight your way out through the crowd, and then there was no room to dance, but only to stand and move a little to the beat. Suddenly a path opened through the crowd as Deborah made her way off the stage to the center of the writhing mass on the dance floor. She stretched her mike cord as far as it would go, about eighteen feet, into the throng of dancers and stood singing in the midst of them. Almost immediately Lee followed her into the fray. As they stood side by side and Lee began to sing his verses—the last verses to the song—the crowd naturally coalesced into a circle around them, moving and swaying to the mesmerizing beat of this beautiful, haunting song. Everyone was completely captivated.

As I watched Lee's generosity with people I felt the sting of healthy shame. Lee grabbed one man—the short, stocky man with the face that glistened with sweat—and embraced him in a fierce hug, slapping his back and looking into his eyes, smiling into his face. The gratitude that poured into this man's joyful face was bittersweet. Lee put his arm around the shoulders of the man with the black hair who danced so wildly. How striking it was to see such a pure expression of impersonal love, given unstintingly by Lee. He was lifting the whole place up; suffering was burned away for the moment in the heat of his blaze.

As Lee interacted with people out on the dance floor his eyes seemed to glow in the smoky dark air. People reached out and touched him, patted his back and embraced him. They acted like he was a long-lost member of the family. Watching from the side of the room it seemed like a modern tableau of "Krishna returns to the tiny village of Vraja." In the myth of the *ras lila* the local cowherds—the *gopis* and *gopas*—are illiterate country people who have fallen into a sublime love affair with the beautiful Lord Krishna. At the sound of his flute they drop everything to run to the forests to dance and make love with him, and in the process of this relationship they come to experience union with the Lord. Eventually Krishna leaves them all to experience love in longing. Now, as I watched the love affair out on the steamy dance floor, I saw that the local people were transfixed, and so were we—the privileged devotees and friends of Lee. But these hard working local people and the students of the master were all together now—all cowherds, longing for Krishna's love. We were all devotees in this moment. The boundaries of our differences were blurred and there was no separation, no "us and them," no disciples and locals.

Now Lee was making up the last verse, singing in a voice that penetrated through the layers of hardness that had surrounded my heart on this night. His voice seemed to be aimed directly at me as I heard him crying, "I still want my baby, but my baby don't want me / I still want my baby, but my baby don't want me / I lay down in the gutter, and hope somebody will see."

The human condition is such that we are all lying in the gutter and hoping someone will see. Maybe that is what lies at the core of the human heart—the longing to be deeply seen, in the most intimate terms, beyond the condition of suffering and separation. We long to be seen in our wholeness, in Organic Innocence, in the fundamental goodness of being, of original essence. And in that moment of pure recognition, of witness to the heart of being, shines the love between Creator and creature.

Lee laid down in the gutter with all of us tonight. He gave of himself in a powerful demonstration of loving kindness that catapulted me out of cynicism and despair and into humility with a sorrowful but sweet clarity. He saw, witnessed and blessed with the flame of consciousness. He moved without any motivation whatsoever, other than the natural and spontaneous movement of grace. In those moments there was no Lee Lozowick—no sweating, sticky man in black suspenders and a wet, Tweetie Bird T-shirt—but only a force of pure benediction.

July 19, 1999
On the road

Yesterday the Celebration ended. After five nights in a row of gigs, Lee headed out this morning at nine o'clock, this time for two weeks on the road with the Shri on tour. Lee was in Thomas' car with Thomas at the wheel—one of the very few people who Lee will allow to drive him—two students in the back seat and the Shri van coming along behind with band members, gear and all kinds of luggage. At ten-thirty Lee stopped for a picnic of Celebration leftovers—roasted chickens, bread that he bought in La Roche

Posay, raw vegetables, cheese.

Six hours later the group arrived in Trier, the oldest city in Germany, for the first stop, to find that the gig tonight was in the broad cobblestone courtyard of an old convent. The Porta Nigra or black gate, an ancient, four-story building, was adjacent to the courtyard where Shri started setting up on a large stage. The gate itself was almost two thousand years old, dating back to the second century. The convent was a mere one thousand years old, with beautiful Roman arches and columns gracing the portico of the second floor. Virginia creeper grew all over the old stone buildings; trailing vines hung gracefully at the apex of the large, high arches that stood sentinel to the courtyard. A blooming linden tree filled one corner of the courtyard that was strung with colored lights. It was right next to the large, spacious stage that was set up in front of a small fountain across from the restaurant that sponsored this gig.

It was great to be on the road with Lee and his band, bringing back fine memories of past tours with liars, gods & beggars. Road life with Lee and the band has always been a particularly powerful chamber. This is the first time that Lee has gone on tour with Shri. During their past three summers touring Europe Shri has been on their own most of the time, with Lee coming to as many gigs as his demanding schedule would allow. The same has been true of Shri's performing career in Arizona as well, but now that liars, gods & beggars has been dissolved and Shri has been expanded, Lee is concentrating his time and energy on the blues band. It is obvious that the members of Shri are ecstatic to be on the road with him for a change.

Perhaps, at least in part, because they have had to travel without Lee for years, the members of Shri aren't jaded or complacent about having his physical presence with them. They find a constant delight in his company, and respond to his suggestions or simple comments with enthusiasm, implementing changes right away. Lee's vision for Baul music of the West has always centered around traditional blues and contemporary rock. He has often talked about wanting a core group of musicians who are fluid and easy with changing instruments or roles in the production of the music, allowing for lots of guest musicians to sit in. Shri seems to be manifesting exactly what he has been asking for in this regard. Shri has set a standard in staying open to many different possibilities, and Lee has clearly been extremely pleased with this attitude. They are the first to say that they have learned a tremendous amount from the trail blazing done by liars, gods & beggars, so that Shri "stands on the shoulders" and learns from the mistakes of those who forged the path before them.

Over dinner this mood of being irrationally happy for no reason at all was especially apparent. The restaurant fed everyone in the Shri entourage—stuffed, rolled pork loin, French fries, colorful and fresh salads, *spatzle* (noodles) baked with mushrooms, vegetables and cheese, Cokes and ice cream. Lee was in an expansive mood as he played bridge for an hour or so before the food came. After we ate he began to talk about his teenage years. He told stories of an old girlfriend from his university days, the "crazy one" about whom he wrote the song "Insane."

"You've been talking about her a lot lately," someone noted, "maybe she's thinking about you . . ."

"I hope not!" Lee laughed. "No, it's because we were just in Westport (Connecticut), and that's where she was from." He continued to tell stories of his most humiliating moments in junior high school, high school and college. They were stories he'd told before, but Lee manages to make them interesting no matter how many times one has heard them. He almost always puts a new twist on each one, or reveals some new facet of the whole picture, or adds an insight he's recently had.

We started talking about how people in the southwest are particularly prejudiced about different accents from other parts of the country. For example, in places like Boulder, Colorado, Albuquerque, New Mexico, or California, where there is not much of an accent of any kind, people can be very caustic about accents.

Lee said, "Yes, when I went to the Colorado School of Mines I got such a hard time. I was wearing all these bright shirts, chartreuse shirts, with tailored shirttails, and everybody made fun of them. It was just what everybody was wearing where I went to high school, but all these Midwest guys were wearing blue jeans and white T-shirts. They just didn't understand it at all. And I used to eat really fast—faster than anybody else. I could eat a whole tray of food in less than a few minutes, you know, hamburgers and French fries, while everybody just stared at me, disbelieving!"

He said this with a kind of innocence and vulnerability that was disarming, then went on to describe a date he had once with a girl from his junior high school. She was having sex with all the boys, and Lee finally got a date with her. "All the boys were doing it with her," he said. "I finally got a date with her and I couldn't believe it! When I drove her home I kissed her. It was a great kiss, and then I just got out of the car and went around and opened the door for her. She looked at me like I was crazy. She just stared at me! I didn't know why until years later—she couldn't believe that I wasn't going for it. But a kiss was such a big deal for me, I was just so happy to have gotten a kiss, I was satisfied with that . . ."

The three women students sitting and listening made appreciative comments. "You were so innocent," and "You were such a gentleman," they said. Several of the men were sitting at the next table listening also and started to laugh. Everett hammed it up, laughed and said, "That's the difference between men and women right there. We're sitting here saying to ourselves, 'Oh man, you blew it! You were *right there!*' "

The women started laughing. Deborah said to Lee, "Yes, and we were thinking about you, 'You're so sensitive,' and 'I knew I could trust you . . .' " Everett laughed and took it a step further, voicing the typical, unconscious point of view with a theatrical frown, "But now *I'm* having doubts . . ."

We all laughed at ourselves, the constant projections on Lee and our attempts to interact with the paradox of the man who is also the guru. Sadhana is punctuated with erroneous interpretations of the guru and his actions based on what we need to see in the guru that will reinforce our own psychological strategy to maintain a separative stance. At the same time, the guru is constantly animating whatever will draw the devotee more inexorably to the path—until the moment when it is too late, and one has been tricked into the kind of choiceless choice that is nothing less than an irrevocable commitment. In this way the guru is a malleable character in our midst. On the one hand we are fooled into deeper delusion by our subjective projections on him; at the same time, those same projections and transferences are brought to light in a way that reveals the nature of delusion and leads us toward the truth, toward an epiphany of clarity.

The mood of this dinner and the stories that Lee told—seemingly just the same kind of ordinary stories any one of us could have told about our teenage years or early adulthood—had the effect of inducing a kind of mild bliss for no apparent reason, except that Lee seemed to be enjoying the company of his students in those moments. It is impossible to decipher exactly what Lee is doing at any given time. Sometimes the closest one can get is to let the body soak in his emanations, like basking in sunlight, knowing that something is going on but that it is so far beyond the intellectual understanding of the mind that we are helpless in the face of it. Whether it is blissful or terrible or just unpleasant (for ego)—and his play with his devotees can go in many directions—we are only pawns in the game who participate freely, willingly, casting our lot in for the pearl of great price.

The band went onstage and started playing. There were about one hundred fifty people seated at the tables in the courtyard, eating dinner, drinking, smoking, talking. After the third song Lee said over the mike, "It's great to be in Trier—it's our second year here! It's beautiful, the food is good, the people are . . ." Lee's voiced turned ever-so-slightly sarcastic as he paused and snapped his fingers as if he was trying to remember something, "what's the word? No, just kidding. And it's *old*. Too old. Second century! That's too old. If you had a grandmother that old you'd put her away!" Were these thinly veiled insults taking a stab at local and familial pride or what? The pride of the Germanic *volk*? Or was he just pointing out that the crowd was eating, drinking and talking in a typically mechanical fashion. Although the audience seemed to appreciate the music in an off-hand kind of way, they seemed quite preoccupied with the social humdrum of daily life, even to the point of leaving their children to roam aimlessly in the large courtyard. The audience didn't have time to reflect on Lee's comments because the band broke into a song, "The Sky Is Crying," with Lee on vocals.

Three children began to congregate by the fountain that was in front of the band, turned off now to become just a pool of water in concrete surrounded by cobblestones. They were fascinated by the band and the music and stood at the edge of the stage, looking up for long minutes off and on during their play. One of the children was only about eighteen months old and tottered around behind his four-year-old brother. All of them were more or less unsupervised by their parents, who sat thirty-five feet away at a table talking with friends. There were several big steins of golden beer on the table. At one point the four-year-old started to climb up on the stage. Lee walked over and stood at the edge of the stage looking intently at the children. He smiled at them from behind his dark sunglasses. The children contentedly went back to their running and chasing.

It quickly became clear that it was going to be a very mellow and understated gig with this middle-class listening audience and their kids. After a couple more songs Lee broke in with another comment over the mike, "We're Shri! We're the baddest blues band within one hundred kilometers of Metz!" and when Ed played another great guitar solo, he called out, "That's Ed Flaherty on blues guitar. Irish soul! That's our Ed—young in years and old in soul!" After "One Way Out" the audience roused themselves to clap enthusiastically and Lee said, "Thank you! The more noise you make the more we know we're doing the right thing—so thank you very much for the applause!"

The performance went along fairly uneventfully until ten o'clock, when the band finished their last song. Then the audience—about one hundred people at this point—broke into clapping and whistling and hooting their approval with a surprising vigor. But it didn't matter at all that it was a quiet night with no cosmic fireworks or exploration of the underworld—what was important was the enjoyment among Lee and his students.

Lee was ready to move on immediately after the gig, so we packed up and drove to Köln, where Ebhard, one of Andrew Cohen's students, generously provided Lee and his group with lodgings for the night at his apartment. The next morning after breakfast we would drive four hours further north to Bittstedt, where everyone would stay for the next seven days at a household of some long-time students of Lee's. During that time Shri would make forays out to perform in towns and cities of northern Germany, then come back at night to sleep.

July 21, 1999
Bittstedt

Lee arrived in Bittstedt yesterday at two o'clock and started playing bridge right away, playing nonstop until five-thirty, when dinner was served. The usual diet of rice and salad—with a little leftover cheese and bread from our road picnic—was a welcomed change from the rich fare we'd been consuming with relish.

Knowing that there would be two days of "down time" before the next gig, probably five different people, myself included, asked Lee while we were playing bridge what his plans for the next day might be. There was much discussion of going to an American movie in Bremen or Frankfurt. Lee was enthusiastic about that idea and said, "Ask Anja or Claus to check the paper for movies and times." Everybody was up for a movie. Lee wanted to see "The Spy Who Shagged Me" or "Wild, Wild West." The anticipation of what fun we might have on our day "off" was running high. After dinner Lee played bridge again, from six-thirty until ten o'clock when he went to bed after yawning through the last two hours of bridge and talking about making an early night of it.

This morning the whole group sat in meditation together in the meditation room on the second floor of the house. For the last nine years three sangha families and their children have lived in this immense old farmhouse in rural Bittstedt. Now everyone had moved out except the Kostkas, who were planning to move to Freiburg soon to join the growing sangha there. Lee has visited and stayed here in Bittstedt many times in years past, and it seems fitting that he is here now, as the long-term household comes to an end and people go in different directions. The house is mostly empty, but the meditation hall is still set up with its *vigraha* of Yogi Ramsuratkumar and seat for Lee at the head of the room. It is one of those working households that have been permeated by the influence of the lineage for many years. The presence of practice is felt in the space.

After brunch at ten-thirty Lee got a movie report from Thomas. There was nothing playing that Lee wanted to see. Some members of the band joked around with him, "How about going shopping, to the local pub, the pastry shop . . ." Or anywhere. Out to see scenic northern Germany, the old cobbled streets and beer gardens, the churches and old towns. As usual, Lee wasn't interested. Playing the tourist when he travels with his students seems to be Lee's idea of hell. It was clear that his plan was to play bridge again today, all day, until dinner tonight at five-thirty, and then again after dinner as well.

We gathered with Lee around the same low, round wooden table in the living room where we played bridge yesterday for seven hours. Games and rubbers rolled by, mostly with Lee winning, as usual. The conversation was a genial, often humorous, light banter among good friends. Anja told Lee about the local flea market that will happen in Bremen on Sunday morning and Lee decided that he would go at eight o'clock, before the guests would arrive for the late morning brunch and dharma talk that is planned for Sunday.

At the moment Deborah was playing as Lee's partner. She said, "Oh, can I just stay here and cook or something while you all go?"

Lee answered, "Sure, if you want to."

She continued talking, smiling a little at her own foibles, "I can't go to flea markets because I get all confused and buy everything I see."

In the midst of the chatter of the room Lee began to speak quietly to Deborah. He said, "Then you should go to every flea market you see in Europe and walk around until you can do it with composure and equanimity." The intention in his quiet voice pierced the mindless chatter. Silence fell in the room as the attention turned toward Lee. He wasn't being merely conversational. It was a real recommendation to her, containing a principle of tantric sadhana. You don't run away from what hooks you, drives you crazy and over the edge; you put yourself in proximity to it in a way that doesn't hurt anyone—or yourself—until you become one with it in a way that it no longer has any power to compel or control you.

I mentioned that I was hoping to have an opportunity to buy some more notebooks and journals. Tina said that she was going to get a certain kind of journal for Kelly, who had asked her to pick them up in nearby Bremen. Very nice ones, she said, with lined paper. She would pick some up for me too if I wanted her to. Lee broke in, saying sarcastically, "Yeah, they have four or five pages in them and cost a fortune but they're made with recycled paper and they're politically correct . . . All the profits go to poor people in Third World countries . . ."

Jumping on the bandwagon, Rakini laughed and said, "Yes, so we have to buy a *lot* of them!" Lee's humorous, mild commentary carried the constant reminding factors of how ridiculous our attachments and so-called special "needs" are. We have to have a certain kind of journal, a certain kind of pen, a certain kind of blouse, blue jeans, shoes, food, sex, tone of voice from our friends and loved ones. There is no end to our preferences, opinions and needs—the drive to be special, the obsession to be in control.

In this way, while Lee's face remained relaxed and soft and his voice seemed to hint at a hidden smile, while he was charming us with laughter and funny comments over bridge, he was at the same time calling us to practice. Outside it was beautiful, a little blustery, intermittently sunny and threatening to rain. The bridge games stretched out over endless hours, time seemed to extend itself out and the day flowed along like a molasses river on a lazy summer day.

Lee had the book he was currently reading, the authorized biography of Mother Teresa, on the couch beside him. I had asked him earlier if he was finding the book inspiring. He said yes in a noncommittal sort of way. Thirty minutes later he said, "It's so inspiring that Mother Teresa refused to compromise her vow of poverty. They had millions of dollars coming in after she won the Nobel Peace prize and her nuns still wore simple cotton saris. When they traveled they had to use cardboard boxes because she wouldn't allow them to buy suitcases." He raised his eyebrows as if to make the point.

Clearly he would love to work in a more radical way than he already does. Whenever Lee reads about saints and gurus whom he finds inspiring, like Meher Baba for example, he starts making comments about his own lack of ferocity as a spiritual master. Meher Baba used to demand that his devotees slap him when they had failed to practice the extremes of obedience that their master expected of them. Meher Baba was also silent for forty years. Sometimes hearing Lee say these things gives one pause to wonder. If he thinks he lacks ferocity, then what lays in store for us?

As the afternoon deepened the flies were buzzing all around us. Europeans do not typically have screens on the windows of their houses like Americans always do. They seem oblivious to the fly population that plagues the inside of their houses, especially out in the country where farms abound, like here at Bittstedt. Next door is a pig farm, and just down the road a huge goose farm. On the other hand, it is an aspect of a more natural way of life.

As we sat playing bridge for hours we were perfect targets for the flies that landed on us, sometimes in groups of three or four, buzzing and whining. The long hours must have chipped away at the mild manners Lee was animating because before long his antics with the flies became hilarious. He pretended to catch one on his chest and pop it in his mouth. He started telling jokes about killing and eating flies, then switched his easy banter to tease Deborah, his partner, about overbidding and going down again at bridge.

"Yeah, when our opponents bid higher, *they* have points; when *we* go up, we don't!" He laughed and smiled pointedly at Deborah. He grabbed another fly that was buzzing around him and said, "I got it!" and threw it hard at the table to stun it. It flew away unscathed. He had a benign smile on his face the entire time.

Deborah and I started singing a chant using the names Yogi Ramsuratkumar and Anjaneya Khepa Lee to the tune of "Not Fade Away," a song by Buddy Holly that was made famous by the Rolling Stones. We'd asked Lee last summer if this song could be made into a chant. Lee had let Deborah try it in the meditation hall at La Ferme de Jutreau, but hadn't been happy with it. Now Lee broke in and sang the chant, improvising in the moment, "*I'm* gonna tell you how it's gonna be, Anjaneya Khepa Lee . . ." he sang "Anjaneya Khepa Lee" with a particularly facetious sting, then he gave his characteristic pause and sly hint of a smile that meant the next line would deliver the punch.

"That's my *devotees'* favorite chant!" he said pointedly, his smile growing bigger.

Everyone laughed, only because he was so masterful at slipping in the teaching lessons. It's really not funny that ego wants to control and dominate everything—including the very liberating force that has the power to release us from our suffering. It was clear he didn't like the chant the first time it had been tried; singing it again was just disobedience. It should have been clear that if the guru didn't like the chant with his own name and the name of his guru in it, then it should not be sung, even casually.

After dinner Lee was back at bridge almost immediately. Four of the men had a second game going at the other end of the living room where a dining table was set up. Steve, who was playing with the other foursome, asked Lee, "What's the longest period of time you've ever played bridge?"

"Oh, I don't know," Lee answered.

"Eight hours that I know of," I said.

"Yeah, it was maddening," Lee quipped.

"At what point did that become maddening and you kept on playing?" Steve asked with his characteristically dry sense of humor.

"Oh, about four hours," was Lee's response. Everyone in the room laughed. Steve said, "That's the Work!"

In the middle of our laughter, with the bridge game flowing along nonstop, Klaus brought the cell phone to Lee. It was Purna calling from the States. While Lee listened on the phone Anja came in carrying a *honigkuchen*—honey cake—and said, "I just found this in the kitchen! Do you think he'd like to serve it with tea tonight?"

Lee was talking on the telephone, saying, "Whatever you want . . . It doesn't mean you can't bring something down on yourself, but the whole thing is a fantasy. Yes. Okay. Great. Yep. Ha, ha, yes, that's right, it's the same everywhere. Okay! Great to speak to you! Anytime! Speak to you soon. Bye." He handed to phone back to Anja and without missing a beat said, "Okay, it's your three clubs."

Anja showed Lee the *honigkuchen* and asked, "Can I serve this tonight for tea? I just found it in the kitchen."

"Yes. Your lead," Lee answered Anja and corrected the bridge player to his left at the same time. He said, "It's a good thing we have a gig tomorrow night—a day off is too much!" Moments later he was sending a fax to the Arizona ashram.

At nine-thirty mint tea and *honigkuchen* was served, and everyone gathered around Lee, sitting on chairs, cushions on the floor or on the bare rug. We sat with Lee until ten forty-five, while Lee talked with members of Shri about their tour for next summer, the "Too Good To Be True" tour, or "2 Good 2 Be True" tour, which is already being planned. He advised them on getting new T-shirts made, on booking gigs, on which big festivals he would most like to play at. Lee and the band members played off of each other, saying, "It's the Too Real To Be Real tour," or "It's the Too Blue To Be True tour." Lee jumped in with, "It's the 'Too Real To Be Legal' tour!"

July 22, 1999
Dortmund—Stadtgespräch

It was rainy and gray. We had driven well over two hours to get to this strange restaurant/bar next to a large cinema by the train station. All the architecture in the surrounding area was depressingly modern and hopelessly ugly. The restaurant was totally weird—a pop nightmare of interior decorating. The walls were done in huge red and yellow squares. Everything about this place was square and linear and devoid of soul. The atmosphere was pure middleworld, which would be fine if it had even a smidgen of imagination or ambiance. Everything was new, square, sparkling clean. It smacked of law and order, of blindly following the proscribed code of a society caught in the prison of its own rationality.

Lee walked around and checked the place out, decided where the band would set up, looked at the food in the buffet. There was steaming beef and onion stew in a rich gravy, peeled potatoes boiled in butter, mashed potatoes, *spargel* (asparagus) in crepes wrapped with ham. There were three kinds of creamy sauces, breaded and pan fried pork and numerous other rich offerings. Lee looked at the food and said, "That looks great! Works for me!"

While the band set up the equipment, Lee sat down right away to play bridge. As the first hand was dealt out Lee said, "I wish I had a photo of this place. I'd send it to E.J. It's such a bardo!" For a while E.J. Gold had his students doing an exercise of sending photos of bardo realms—subways, train stations, factories, suburbs—to him. The implication being that if you identify bardo realms then you can practice being neither attracted nor repelled by anything in them, because the nature of bardo realms is to hook you into them, eternally. It's a basic premise of tantric practice—know how to navigate through all domains and remain free of attachment. In this place the key might be to remain free of it simply by not being repelled by its insidiously innocuous and soul-stifling atmosphere. It's all a function of learning to deal with the illusory nature of the mind. If we are fundamentally free, then even the most deadening or alluring place cannot capture or control us.

After setting up the equipment and eating, the band got ready to start playing. There were perhaps ten people scattered around the place. During the third song Lee walked around the perimeter of the large, spacious restaurant/bar shaking his tambourine, as if he was sketching a magical circle with his steps. He was wearing a bright yellow T-shirt with a picture of a bedraggled alley cat in sunglasses on it. Underneath the cat were the words "No Problem." Now there were about twenty people sitting around the room, six of them part of the road crew with Shri. Arriving back at the "stage" which was set up on the floor of the restaurant, Lee took the mike and said, "That was 'Fame,' one of our original songs. Fame—one of the few things that's better than chocolate!" He paused then said, "We're gonna do a song by Muddy Waters."

Suddenly his tone changed. "Alright! Shri! Sweeter than the almond torte and hotter than the steam table! Here we are playin' for you tonight!" They broke into "I'm a Man," one of the gritty, sexy, traditional blues songs that Lee sings. Deborah stood just off the stage with the maracas beating out the rhythm along with the guitar and drums. Every now and then one of Lee's students got up and danced near the almost vacant bar in front of the band. The gig went on, pleasant and seemingly very ordinary.

About an hour and thirty minutes into the two-hour set I looked around nonchalantly, then it struck me that the place was quite different than it was before. It wasn't the same ugly bardo realm we found it to be when we first arrived. The huge red and yellow squares on the wall were no longer garish but mellow and bright. Everything seemed bathed in a soft, welcoming light. The bartenders, the customers, the manager, all appeared happy. People were smiling, walking with a light spring to their step. Their faces looked open, welcoming and generous. The change would have been shocking if it weren't largely subtle, and yet it was very real. Had my perspective changed, or had we all been changed, somehow?

After a moving version of "Not Fade Away," a song that Lee hasn't sung in several years but used to perform with LGB, he bandied from the stage, "We haven't played that song in about fifteen years, but we thought it'd be fun to take it out tonight . . . " The band was tremendously relaxed. They spun through "Brownsville" and then "Country Boy." On "Ball and Chain" Lee sat at the bar with his tambourine, playing along serenely. Shri delivered another fantastic rendition of "Born Under a Bad Sign" with Lee still playing tambourine at the bar. Suddenly people were starting to flood into the place, coming out of the movie theatre next door, visibly responding to the music as they walked into the restaurant. It was too bad the band wasn't scheduled to play later, to the late crowd instead of to an empty house. Shri seemed to have claimed this place, made it their own anyway. The bar manager loved the band, was disappointed that they weren't playing longer and later to the new crowd. Now this strange, offbeat gig suddenly had possibility for next year's tour.

July 23, 1999
Hamburg

At the Bittstedt house over brunch this morning at eleven o'clock Everett asked Lee a question. He said, "I heard Dasya giving the introduction at La Ferme de Jutreau last week during the Celebration and he said that you like to get chocolate for prasad. True?"

Lee answered noncommittally, "It's one of those myths that gets circulated . . . "

"But is it a myth that you subscribe to?" Everett pressed further.

Lee answered in a measured tone that suggested something like infinite patience, "It's best to give what *you* are moved to give for prasad."

Steve said, "Here's another myth: 'Lee hates serrated knives.' Is that true?"

Lee's chuckle had only the slightest edge of exasperation. He started explaining, "I don't like to use serrated knives when I'm cutting fruit or vegetables, but . . . "

Steve broke in, "What about bread? There we were the other day, sawing away at a loaf of bread with a dull knife. When we asked about getting a regular serrated bread knife someone said, 'Lee hates serrated knives!' "

Lee answered sarcastically, "I think that's a little exaggerated."

Everyone started talking at once and goofing on the tendency of the sangha to take things Lee has said totally out of the context in which he says them. Too often we become dogmatic about things we think we have heard Lee say, or that someone else has heard Lee say. This kind of blind following can end up in a ridiculous comedy of errors, like the one everyone was laughing about now.

"No serrated knives—ever! Under any circumstances! You shouldn't even have serrated knives in your kitchen! Throw them all out!" Steve and Everett and Deborah and Rakini laughed and carried on in this vein with Lee until it was time to get ready to leave for Hamburg and the Shri gig.

Claus drove Lee into Hamburg with the Shri van close behind. Once the vehicles were parked everyone started walking, following Lee, who seemed to know exactly where he wanted to go. He had been planning to go to a particular Indian store in Hamburg all week. He'd been there five or six years ago and was impressed with their bronze statuary of various Indian and Tibetan deities, which were of a quality that is hard to find these days, even in India. When he was in Rishikesh last November Lee was disappointed that he couldn't find anything that met his standards. He often comments on how these art forms are steadily dying out in India; since his first trip to India in 1976, the availability of really good quality bronze statues has changed shockingly, a sign of Westernization eating at the foundations of a sacred culture.

As the group walked down the street Everett and Steve asked Lee what the plan was and when everyone should meet back at the vehicles if anyone got separated from the main group with Lee. Lee said, "Oh, we'll leave around four o'clock. I'm going to the Indian shop and then to the café to sit for awhile and have a cup of coffee." When everyone chooses to just stay with Lee's program, whatever that might be, somehow things open up for unknown possibilities. Today it seemed like there was magic in the air. As it turned out the whole group stayed together, walking along with Lee.

Lee passed a sidewalk café that looked promising, then spied a sex shop just beyond it. He started laughing and the next thing we knew he was veering right and ducking into the door. We crowded enthusiastically into the sex shop after Lee and stopped to look at the paraphernalia on the shelves. "Look at that one," someone said, pointing up, " 'Beaver Hunt!' "

"How about 'The Emperor—twelve inches of life-like manhood'? Or 'The Bedside Pleasure Kit—for girls who want to have fun,' " Rakini joked. Peals of laughter punctuated the rapid-fire repartee. Then there was the "Octo-orgasmo" which had eight different plastic sex toys to pick from, along with talking plastic cunts, various and assorted huge rubber dildos and more. As the different names were called out the laughter became more raucous and unruly. Lee laughed along with everyone. The rest of the shop was full of rows of porn videos, and at the other end the owner or clerk was waiting on a serious customer.

Someone asked, "Do people actually buy and use these contraptions?" Obviously the answer was yes. The jokes and wisecracks from Lee's group were nonstop, but we weren't in there longer than two minutes when Lee whisked back outside with everyone close behind. Two minutes or less was all he needed. He was laughing ecstatically, wiping the tears from his eyes, which had a disarming glint of madness in them.

"This makes my day!" Lee said, practically doubling over laughing. Amazing! What could it be about going into a sleazy sex shop that made his day? Was it something akin to hanging out in brothels, like Ikkyu, the founder of Redline Zen? Like the sixth Dalai Lama, who went into town and slept with all the local girls? Was it the confrontation to any lingering Victorian attitudes on the part of his students? Or more intensely, was it the confrontation with how absurd and bereft the sex act is when it is devoid of the context of spiritual life, of reciprocal communion and joy? Was it something about the entities that crowded the psychic atmosphere of the place, palpable and seething with hunger? Or was it just some aspect of Lee's quirky sense of humor that would be difficult for anyone else to fathom?

Since none of those questions could be answered, all one could realistically do was catch the thread of his infectious mood without having to intellectually understand anything about why he was doing what he was doing. That's what we did. Laughing with Lee was good, wholesome, spontaneous, full of abandon and delight, and didn't need any motivation or concept behind it. Then there was the additional opportunity of observing one's self closely throughout the whole event. Was there anything—reactions, thoughts, associations, feelings—about the experience that took root in us and grew?

Walking another block or so Lee stopped and looked in the window of a beautiful, quite elegantly appointed Tibetan shop. Right away he noticed a bronze of Milarepa in the classic listening pose. He commented on it with interest then went inside. He spent almost an hour looking at bronzes, *thangkas* and other treasures. The owner, a Nepalese Hindu named Manoj Kumar, was very outgoing and friendly. He seemed to tune into Lee and his group as he was asked numerous questions about different deities. He showed Lee an exquisite Avalokitesvara painted with gold. He handled it with tremendous respect, even though as he talked he explained that he was not a Buddhist. "My family is Hindu," he said, and then laughed, adding, "but I am lost. Not Hindu, not Buddhist." He asked what we were doing in town and someone in the band explained that Shri would be performing tonight in Hamburg.

Someone asked Kumar about the many Vajrayoginis and Taras in different forms that he had around the store, and then about another version of the Milarepa. He went downstairs and got another small statue of Milarepa, this one a beautiful burnished copper coated with gold. Lee was obviously very taken with it. Kumar began to talk about Milarepa, saying, "Yes, Milarepa was the great poet, he wrote ten thousand verses . . ."

Actually, Lee said later, Milarepa wrote one hundred thousand verses. The similarity between these two poets, Milarepa and Lee Lozowick, also great disciples of their masters, seemed to hang in the air as Lee carefully examined the beautiful statue. He seemed to be soaking up the essence of it. Carefully handing it back to Kumar, Lee said, "We'll look around a little more and consider."

Kumar smiled graciously and said, "Of course." On the way out of the shop Lee stopped one last time to look at a smaller version of the Milarepa statue in solid silver, then headed out the door. At Lee's request, Steve invited Kumar and his wife to come to the gig that night as the guests of Shri, giving him the information on where and what time.

Crossing the street and walking down a block Lee went into another Indian/Tibetan shop. This was Kumar's competitor, and here the prices were higher but the owner seemed very willing to bargain, as was Kumar. There were twelve people with Lee crowding into the shop, exclaiming over different pieces, looking at the jewelry, milling around. As usual, shopping with Lee was an exercise in working with desire. He puts his students in close proximity to beautiful things and sacred objects, with the clear opportunity to buy— if one has money. For ashram renunciates, who live on a very small weekly allowance and the generosity of the ashram, the labyrinth that must be navigated in these situations is a little different.

Lee has the ability to spend long periods of time just looking at rich and fabulous things, seeming to soak up whatever is valuable in the impressions they emanate. In this way it seems that he absorbs the beauty, the richness, the opulence, or the subtler communication of a deity, experiences it completely, and then walks away free. When he is ready to buy and finds the right thing, he is also free. Earlier today he had said that he was looking for something for himself. He didn't know what—it would have to be the right thing, and he would know it when he saw it.

By contrast, I found myself lusting after both the jewelry and the bronzes and having to go through a process of letting go of desire. That's quite different than simply being one with desire in such a way that the essence of the thing one desires is absorbed and made use of—in which case one is not trapped or hooked by the need to own, control, possess. As if ownership would make something of us when real freedom is found in the truth of our nothingness.

The second store was packed with desirable things—*phurbas* made of human bone with Manjushri carved on them, opulent jewelry, many fabulous, ornate deities. Lee walked around the store looking at various items, commenting on different bronze deities, moving like a fluid element, like water or air, among all this heavy, concrete earthly treasure. After about thirty minutes in the second store Lee took down an unusual bronze hidden away on the back right corner on top of a six foot-high glass display case crammed with turquoise, silver and red coral. It was an old bronze, about fourteen inches high—a ferocious, dancing female deity with a terrifying and awe-inspiring animal-like skull face, a necklace of skulls adorning her lithe and powerful naked body. She carried a ritual implement of destruction with a sharp, curved blade held up above her head and a conch shell in the other hand at the level of her abdomen. She was surrounded by whorls of curling clouds and on her back was a flayed tiger skin with its snarling head balanced across her body, its eyes wide open and looking fierce. Lee seemed absorbed in inspecting the piece that he held gingerly in his hands as if it was a great treasure. The owner came by and, when asked who the deity was, said, "Vajrayogini."

Lee said appreciatively, "This is one of a kind. It's very unusual. I may have to get this one." A few of Lee's students looked at the Vajrayogini, admiring and appreciating her awesome attributes. In a while we left the store and headed for the café a few blocks down the street. Lee started talking again about the Vajrayogini. He said, "I may have to have it." He seemed to be mulling it over in some way, going through whatever internal system he goes through to determine his course of action. He stopped and waited for Sara, who was walking about twenty feet behind him, to catch up. When she came up to him he said, "Do you have any cash on you?"

"Yes," she said with emphasis. Lee proceeded to arrange with her to pay the cash right now for Vajrayogini and he would square up with her later. Shri pitched in to make the total so that Lee could get the statue today instead of having to wait until Jim could go back tomorrow and pick it up. Lee instructed everyone else to go ahead to the café and get tables. "We'll play bridge," he said. He and Sara went off at a fast clip back toward the store while we went ahead.

Arriving back at the café next to the sex shop all the tables were taken. Noticing that our group was obviously looking for tables, one generous man said very politely in German that their table would be free in moments. It was easy to get his meaning, and when he left the occupants of three other tables, all of them clustered together, suddenly cleared out, leaving a perfect space for Lee and his large party. We sat down and ordered.

It had been clear from Lee's comments that he was going to have coffee at a café on this afternoon. We got the tables ready for our group and dealt out a bridge hand so it would be ready for Lee when he arrived. *Milch caffee*—espresso *grosse tasse* (coffee in large bowls with milk)—were ordered all around while we settled in and watched Lee and Sara walking back down the street. Lee was carrying a paper bag and as he approached the table it seemed practically ablaze. His eyes were a brilliant, penetrating blue, and his mood was very high. He looked at the *milch caffees* and said, "Order me one of those!" Someone offered to put the sack with the bronze in a nearby chair as he moved to put the paper sack on the ground by his chair.

"No! She's fine right here. She's fine anywhere—we'll just throw her into the back of the car!" He grinned. His remark was thrown out with an intense abandon that belied the casual and amiable posture he was taking. It seemed that Vajrayogini was already making an impact on us in Lee's pointed familiarity with this fierce female wisdom principle—a wrathful form of a female Buddha, the epitome of swift ego death, of destruction of illusion, of annihilation of the separative self. I got the feeling that if one consorted with Vajrayogini very much, he or she wouldn't need any special treatment or comforts either, but would rest in bliss and emptiness regardless of the situation.

One of the women laughed, "Okay, *you* can throw her in the back of the car—that's fine for you! *We'll* do pujas to her!" Somehow it felt very significant that Lee acquired this deity. This feeling was completely irrational, there was nothing one could definitely say about it, but in this instance it seemed certain that somehow this play of Lee's was purposeful, a movement completely defined and informed by Divine Influence, and that there were blessings for Sara and Shri woven into the whole interaction.

Lee's mood continued to be expansive, buoyant and joyous. He was uncharacteristically effusive, and he lifted everyone around him up into his euphoria. He described the bargaining he had done with the shop owner for the statue, getting him to come down three hundred D-marks. Jim C., who sat at a table right next to Lee, started asking Lee's advice about buying another bronze deity, a Buddha and consort in union.

"You have to be willing to walk out," Lee said. "That's the way they do it in India—you have to walk out and mean it. You have to be willing to walk away from it. Then they'll come down to their bottom price." He added, "I may buy the Milarepa too, now that I've started buying!"

Lee started talking about money, spending and making money. He turned to Ann and said, "The bottom line is all that matters! It's the same thing in the Work. The bottom line is what matters, no matter how many books you've written and sold, the bottom line is, how much money do you have in the bank?"

Deborah said, "Which bank are you talking about, Baba?"

"My bank!" Lee said with a satisfied and smug smile.

Rakini said, "The Bank of Lozowick!"

"That's right! What matters is, how much money do you have in the bank at the end of the day? For those of you who are sitting here!" Lee looked at each of us. His expression spoke volumes. He seemed very satisfied and even inspired. He returned to his cards and the bridge game at hand. Deborah, who was Lee's partner, said, "What do we need to make game?" Lee snapped pointedly, "We need some basic human maturity for a start!" He chuckled.

Moving into the next bridge hand Lee started talking about faxes and letters he'd gotten recently from some of his students in Arizona. Lee pointed over his shoulder toward the sex shop just a few feet away from where he was sitting. "If someone comes to me with sex problems, I'd like to just give them a couple of those things in there and say, 'Come back next year and ask me a *spiritual* question!' "

"Which ones would you send them?" Rakini asked, referring to the sex toys Lee had just mentioned.

"The ones with the two rubber things, one for each hole down there!" was Lee's comeback. Then he said soberly, "Those things make me shiver! But that's what I'd do—just buy a box of those things and start giving them away. I'm not kidding! The Americans!" He shook his head as if in disbelief. "At least those Americans have stick-to-it-ness." Lee played another card, laying it down on the small round table top. "That's a good sex shop."

Ann asked, "What constitutes a good sex shop?"

Lee answered, "One that's real—not for tourists! One that people on the streets are actually using."

Throughout this time at the café Lee kept drawing his students into humorous, light-hearted conversations with him. Everything seemed amusing and blithe, and at the same time there was always an edge of a teaching communication in his banter, a rather deadly edge that, if we took it seriously, would leave us very sober.

Ten minutes later we were back in the cars, heading toward Lee's destination for the evening where Shri would perform. He encapsulated the whole sex shop consideration with one comment that he offered up out of the blue as the car cruised down the street: "It must be a pretty lonely scene, to have to use one of those rubber things."

To come up against the bitter taste of separation in a moment when sexual communion with a revered partner should be sweetest is perhaps one of the most poignant and disturbing reminding factors of the human condition. Maybe the opportunity to reflect on the travesties of life was the gift of the sex shop.

"I guess a lot of people use those things," I said.

"Well, there's a lot of stores like that. They seem to do well, stay in business," was Lee's response.

"I wondered how the owner felt, with the crowd of us in there, laughing and joking around about the things he was selling," I said.

"They're used to such disrespect from tourists," Lee commented. It seemed like a door closed on the subject.

In about fifteen minutes Claus pulled up to the Landhaus Walter, a huge, rambling old country house originally built for the wealthy landowners of the area. It was a place where the rich and affluent would go to eat and drink, walk in the gardens and on the richly wooded grounds. A little bit like a country club, in one way, but open to the public. Now it was a very fine restaurant with many different rooms and alcoves, including a large music hall and club with a beautiful parquet wooden floor and a big stage. Two large ceramic cherubs graced the ceilings near the entry way to the club. They were painted gold, and blew invisible notes through ancient horns. It was a well-known blues club, one of Hamburg's finest.

Shri was shown around by Ken, a disaffected African American blues man and Vietnam veteran who worked as the stage manager of the club. He had been living in Germany for many years, and spoke good German. Right away he seemed happy to visit with the Americans, and started talking nonstop.

"I have my own band over here," he said, "I play around Germany. Here I get *paid* for the blues—at home, in the U.S., I just *have* the blues!" He laughed and went on to tell us that he used to play in the U.S., but he hadn't touched a bass guitar in twenty-nine years. He took the whole group outside to the huge beer garden and got everyone settled at a table where we ordered drinks. Looking around at the ivy-covered brick walls and spacious grounds the place looked even more labyrinthine, with many different wings ending in round rooms like miniature castle turrets, each space creating various eating and drinking ambiances. The grounds were covered with huge green oak and linden trees and bordered the biggest park in Hamburg. Near where Lee sat with the group was another outside food kiosk that sold scampi and *wurste*.

The excitement was building for the band. A private room had been arranged for Shri's dinner party with a long table set for twelve. Later, after set-up and sound check, we would go in and order off the menu. Shri was being given the royal treatment—quite unlike most places Lee's bands have played in the U.S. When the group gathered at a table outside over sodas, hot chocolates and apple juice, Lee said, "What a fabulous way to treat musicians, with such respect. One day when we come to Europe we'll only play in places like this in between big festival gigs." He looked at Sara, who had booked this gig and all the other gigs in Germany for Shri this year, and continued, "We're working on a couple of things for Shri that will help you out with booking next year's tour! Everything moves slowly in the music business . . . "

Sara talked about how the doors seemed wide open when she was booking Shri gigs. "With LGB the doors were closed," she said, remembering the last LGB tour in 1996. "You'd come up against it. But with Shri, the doors are wide open."

Referring to a huge blues festival where Shri played last summer in the south of France, Lee said, "When we went to Crest last year the headliner acts were so demanding. The stage staff would say to us, 'You're such a pleasure to work with!' because we were easy. This guy, who was one of the headlining acts, and all his musicians were so demanding, so picky over every little thing. They gave the staff such a hard time—bigger prima donnas you've never seen. And nobody has even heard of them in the States! We kicked his ass—we got much bigger applause from the audience. But the stage staff, they were so happy just to work with somebody like us, who are just relaxed and take things as they come!"

It seemed like a gentle but not so subtle clue to the members of Shri who were sitting there—a reminder of how to practice in the face of being treated like stars, even to a small degree. Shri would have their turn to battle the forces of ego, which—in tantric sadhana—seem to rage even higher in the bright light of the guru's empowerment. And there was no question about it—Lee was empowering Shri and all of Shri's support staff in a mighty way on this tour.

Here they were in a beautiful place, being lavished with good things, looking forward to a fabulous dinner, a great gig, a good stage and dance floor, nice management at the Landhaus "Downtown." But the name of the game was still practice—right now, at dinner, tonight onstage. All of it was another opportunity to practice, to be that which nothing can take root in, to practice kindness, generosity and compassion. The band's success depends on their ability to stay grounded in a life of practice, and the temptations to indulge are many. Wine, coffee, liquor, rich food—all of these are offered to the band at every gig. And then there is the headier wine—adulation, fame (even the minor variety is potent), the intoxicating sound of applause and wild cheers. Pride and vanity rear their heads at every turn, and if one is distracted by food and mind-altering substances—the body chemistry all askew and running wild—one gets easily caught in the tangle of primal passions. Before we know it we're parading around like peacocks, treating others with casual disdain, and hungering for more power.

Lee commented to Jim C., the band's publicist who would be selling CDs and tapes tonight and interacting with the crowd, "See if you can get some good stories from Ken. That guy has been around. Be liberal with the music with him—if he's interested in tapes or CDs, give them to him. But not the live album." Lee was talking about *Shrison in Hell,* the album that was recorded live at a favorite bar in Prescott where Shri performs regularly.

Deborah piped in, "Yeah, hide that thing."

"No. Don't say that," Lee looked at Deborah. "He's a blues musician, not a machine. Only a machine doesn't appreciate that kind of live music." The band isn't fond of *Shrison in Hell* because they feel it is too rough, recorded live with too many mistakes. Every artist deals with the drive to be technically perfect by worldly standards, but the musicians are called to stay with Lee's vision and context for the music, which has to do with what Lee calls "Work profitability." This kind of profitability is not the same thing as profitability by worldly standards, but could include that. This kind of profit is contextually aligned with the alchemy of transformation. His stand has always been, "Who cares if the music is technically perfect, as long as the music experiments are generating Work profit!"

Very shortly the group moved into the dressing room just outside the stage, where mineral water, fruit juice and coffee were set up at a table for the band. Several of the band members were doing a sound check while some of us sat in the dressing room with Lee. Deborah came in looking very upset. She began to talk about how she wasn't being able to get what she needed from the band's soundman, Matthew. Deborah described further what her predicament was while Lee listened. She said in a frustrated tone of voice, "I don't have enough sound coming through my monitor. If I can't hear myself in the monitors then I can't sing as well."

Cutting through it all, Lee said briskly, with an unmistakable edge to his voice, "Okay, go in there and get what you need! Ask the house sound man if you have to, but don't go wimping around like a victim. To me this tour has been heaven! The sound we've gotten—I never got this kind of sound with LGB. I'd be jumping for joy if I'd ever gotten that kind of sound with LGB! So I'm in heaven here!" Steve and Everett came in and soon the storm clouds had blown over. They all walked out with Lee to finish the sound check to everyone's satisfaction.

According to Gurdjieff's "Law of Three" there are always universal "denying, affirming and reconciling" forces at work in life. It's not at all uncommon for the "denying force," as Gurdjieff called it, to make itself felt at gigs, and especially at gigs when there seems to be more riding on success or failure. This particular gig at the most respected venue in Hamburg seemed to be daunting in one way. If tonight's gig went well, then next year Shri would be able to play here again, and it would be another element added to the momentum of the band's success in Europe. This kind of spotlight has a way of bringing up insecurities and neurotic patterns, of getting ego stirred up and looking to get satisfaction. "Pay attention," everything seemed to be saying. Vigilance is crucial in tantric practice, and it seemed that tonight there were numerous hints that it might be easy to slip under the pressure.

After sound check everyone went in with Lee for dinner. Ken joined us, but he was different than he had been earlier. It was obvious that he was high now, and he had said something to one of the men in the band about going off to smoke a joint earlier. Now he sat drinking wine and talking nonstop. He had two or three big glasses of wine while most of Lee's group took one glass, some taking only half glasses, to have with the meal. After about twenty minutes he was sitting at the end of the table looking wrecked and glassy-eyed, knocking back glasses of wine and dominating the table with his conversation. Steve started asking him questions about his years in the music business.

Ken told us that between 1962 and 1965 he toured with Ike and Tina Turner. In 1966 he got drafted and sent to Vietnam. He had worked for Bethlehem Steel and Mattel Toys as an accountant, but when he got out of the Army he found it very hard to get hired for jobs. "Nobody would hire Vietnam vets," he said. "They were afraid you were too fucked up. Here I was, fighting for my country, and now those motherfuckers don't want to give me a job!" His reddened eyes and blotched skin, set against his wild gray hair, made the point. He was sitting on a volcano of betrayal-driven anger and rage. "Fuck 'em! I went back to Nam. I played Army basketball, I was in the army for thirteen years, playing ball! Now I get seventy-five percent disability as a staff sergeant—my arm's fucked up, my side's fucked up—thank you, goodbye! I get a thousand dollars a month, but I can live better outside the U.S. than inside it. I was stationed here in Germany in 1975—I said, why leave? I heard about all the crack houses and drive-by shootings in the States—why the hell go back there?" Ken smiled a lot as he talked, a smile that belied how deeply he was expressing his suffering. His story was the classic tale of Vietnam vets all over the U.S. The deep wounds of the war had come to visit us tonight. His pain throbbed in the air as we sat and listened, a captive audience.

As we plowed into the delicious meal—plates of tender lamb and rumpsteak, steamed vegetables, potatoes au gratin—Ken's meal went untouched. After one or two bites he pushed it away and looked at us apologetically, saying, "I'm not hungry." He had too much alcohol in his body to have an appetite.

"Do you all mind if I smoke?" he had asked when he first sat down. Twelve faces stared back at him, none of them smoking, all of them stone cold sober. Finally someone had the presence of mind to say, "No, we don't mind." He lit up. By now he was beginning to catch the drift that there was something different, something odd about this American blues band that he couldn't quite put his finger on. He kept glancing at Lee. Maybe it was the fact that the men hadn't taken him up on going to smoke a joint, maybe it was the fact that no one smoked cigarettes, or that we drank the wine so sparingly, with Lee pouring everyone's glass.

He turned his bleary eyes on Lee and said, "Let me ask you a question, my friend." Lee nodded in assent. "Why you wanna go rasta?" Ken's accent became Rastafarian.

Lee shrugged, "Something different."

Ken laughed loudly and said, "You just didn't want to have to comb your fuckin' *hair*, man! I can show you my rasta dreads, they're hanging on a wall in Switzerland right now! I have less problems with the police since I cut them off, though. With you," he gestured, obviously meaning the fact that Lee has white skin, "they won't say too much, but with blacks, you either have to be a drug dealer or a junkie. Half of black America is running around in dreadlocks these days! Jah Rasta!"

Lee listened quietly. The room reverberated with the stinging reality of Ken's pain, which was reflected back to him in Lee's silence. The man was living in hell, and yet he was serving Lee's students in a way with his dramatic demonstration of the horror of the situation. He was giving us an opportunity to work in relationship with the suffering that he labored under.

The waiter came with the dessert menu and passed them out to everyone. Lee's was blank. "Is this a message or what?" he joked. It seemed like a perfect synchronicity, a symbol of the moment.

Ken stood up and said, "So, ladies and gentlemen, at a quarter to ten I'm gonna start giving you problems. The show starts between ten o'clock and ten-fifteen! After eating a meal like this you'll be wanting to sleep right about then. Like they say in the Baptist church, 'Don't feed them before they sing or they'll go to sleep!' " Little did he know that this was one band he would never have a problem with getting onstage at the right time.

At ten o'clock Shri went onstage and Everett began his introductory number, "G-Thang." The Gospel Goddess and Mother Superior of the Blues was soon out on the stage and the band was off and rocking. There were about sixty people in the club, most of them standing in the back part of the large dance hall near the bar, listening intently. Lee introduced his Howlin' Wolf number. Maybe twelve or fifteen people were out on the dance floor, still rather tentative but dancing a little.

"It's nice to see people dancing, and others standing around trying to get comfortable in their bodies. Heh, heh. Just kidding," Lee bandied. "You'll have lots of chances to dance tonight . . . " He broke into "Smokestack Lightnin'. " A few songs later he was getting ready to introduce "Hound," a provocative new song in which the singer crows about his prowess with women. Lee said suggestively, "I've got a song for all you women—all the women come up here by the stage for this one! When Deborah sings all the men come up. When I sing all the women come up. I'm trained to take care of pets . . . " and he was off and running into the song. One slight blonde woman danced in front of the stage in a scanty white T-shirt. She seemed to be enjoying the song as she smiled and sashayed up near the stage. She was with another woman, obviously her lover.

Even though the band was great, it was curious that most of the people in the club still held back. There were a few hardy souls attempting to dance out on the big wooden dance floor, and one or two who were putting their heart and soul into it. Jim C. said that a journalist from the biggest newspaper in Europe had come by the table where he was selling CDs and tapes. The journalist wanted to take a picture of the band and do a short interview during the break. That sounded promising. Kumar was also there with his wife, smiling and keeping the beat of the music. He looked like he was having a good time.

After "Hound" Lee said into the mike, "If you're not all danced out, we have just one or two more songs for you before we take a short break." They did a plaintive, soulful version of "Left My Baby Standing." Deborah headed out into the audience and the blonde woman immediately came right up to her and smiled into her face. They danced together for a moment while the lover stood nearby, glowering. Lee came out with Deborah and the two of them stood together while a small circle of dancers gathered around them for the last two verses of the song.

There were a number of couples standing around the periphery of the dance floor in tight embraces, sometimes kissing. They all seemed to be listening intently to the music, and yet they didn't dance. The crowd seemed intent on drinking and smoking themselves into a state of spiritual exhaustion they might call the blues. Suddenly Lee was back up on the stage and talking to the crowd again. He said, "Here we are, traveling into the void together. Next stop—emptiness! I can't wait!" He immediately went into "The Sky Is Crying."

I couldn't shake the feeling that there was a distinct lack of aliveness in the air. The seventy-five or so people in the club were listening and clapping, but they still seemed trapped within themselves, inward, depressed maybe, or just numb. Back at our table I saw Ann. She said that she'd just talked with Kumar. She asked him if he liked the music. He said, "Yes, I like it very much, but I am surprised that the German people are so cold! I don't think they understand what's happening."

Ann's take on the crowd was that they were a typical bunch of sophisticated urbanites with the typical malaise of the Western world. They seemed to have a more cerebral approach to the blues—stand and listen, but don't move. But if you want to get the real medicine power of the blues, it's only found in the body, in the transformational ecstasy found in and through the body. However you get there—sex, music, dance, chanting, meditation, certain kinds of exercise—it happens in the *body*, not in the mind. In Lee's company even food can be added to that list. There are lots of ways to do it. But tonight the natural ecstasy of the body was the missing ingredient in the space. There was an undeniable reciprocity between the audience and the band; people were listening and clapping and hooting their approval, but they weren't absorbing it into their bodies and getting naturally high. Lee's music at its best is revelation.

Lee tumbled into "Sweet Little Angel." He said earlier that he'd had a renewal with this song and wanted to sing it tonight. Afterward he said into the mike, "You know, a guy gets himself one of those sweet little angels, and you know, they turn every cloudy day sunny!" Deborah went into "Ball and Chain."

Curious about the muted response from a crowd that obviously really liked the music, I asked a few of Lee's students what they thought was going on. I hit the jackpot with Matthew, who thought about it for a few minutes then said, "This isn't an ordinary blues crowd. There is a surrealistic contrast between the band and the people in the club. It's like light and dark. The crowd is like a heavy weight. They're into the blues, they really dig it, but they're not *getting* it. The band is still helping them to make that connection with the underworld, between their essence and their personalities. The band is pulling them up."

He continued, on a roll, "They are like extreme addicts—empty shells. These people are not having a good time. They're addicted to the music, to the blues. They flock to it, but it has no effect on them. They go through the right motions, but they have no real connection with the underworld, so no real connection with the music. It's like a role they play—being into the blues."

The crowd was down to about thirty-five people since many had slowly drifted out after the break. Some of the couples and dancers who'd been with the band all night were still out on the floor dancing along with a guy in a wheelchair. During "Born Under a Bad Sign" something broke loose during Ed's guitar solo and a glimmer of light shone through the murky atmosphere. It was like a release had been hit after a long uphill climb. When the song ended the crowd rallied to a solid round of applause and cheers. Lee said, "Well, that was a lot of noise for so few people!"

Ken came on and roused what was left of the group to demand an encore after Shri left the stage, and they came back out to do "Country Boy." It was a good finale, but for me the night had been anticlimactic, lukewarm, with the exception of the connection that was made with the journalist, and the fact that Kumar had come and so obviously enjoyed the music. Ken had gotten more and more drunk by the end of the night, and now glowered a little. He seemed disturbed by the band, but he was also wasted by substances that had gotten the better of him. By the end of dinner Ken was gone and the addiction had taken over.

Backstage I asked the band members how the night was for them. Everett said he really liked the gig, he thought it was great. He felt a reciprocity from the audience all throughout the night. Deborah and Ed liked it too. That sounded good. Maybe all that was important for tonight was creating momentum for the band, sowing seeds for next year's tour, which has been a major topic of discussion between Lee, Sara and the band for the past few days.

As Lee and a few people settled into the car at one-thirty the talk turned to the mood at the gig. Ann told Lee what Kumar had said. Claus, who was driving Lee for the evening, turned in his seat and said, "Oh yes, the people from Hamburg have a reputation all over Germany for being very staid and proper. They follow the letter of the law." As the car headed out toward Bittstedt I mentioned Lee's comment about going into the void—next stop, emptiness. Lee said, "That was for Kumar."

July 24, 1999
Bittstedt

This morning over brunch the band and Lee talked about the interview with the newspaper journalist last night. They said that he had interviewed all the greats in the late sixties and seventies—Jimi Hendrix, Janis Joplin, and later, Stevie Ray Vaughn. The members of Shri were working their usual crossword puzzle. Matthew asked if anyone knew a five-letter word for a wood sprite, third letter Y and fifth letter D. Lee said, "Who could know that word? Why would any of us know a word like that? Where do they think we were educated?" He spoke with what seemed to be a mock outrage, but at the same time one could listen to him and think that he was perfectly serious.

A few minutes later, out of the blue, Lee said, "Naiad." His earlier statement was one of those that he tosses out for unknowable reasons. It certainly didn't apply to him. Many people don't know that in his early adult years Lee became a member of MENSA, an organization for people who are in the top two percentile of those with the highest average IQ, which means you have to have an IQ of somewhere over one hundred forty. To qualify you have to take two IQ tests and score in the top percentile. Now a discussion ensued about how to spell the word, whether or not it could have a Y in it in the right place. As it turned out, naiads are spirits that live in water; dryads are spirits that live in woods or trees.

At five o'clock Lee and about twenty people drove into Sottrum, a small town about five miles from Bittstedt, to the Neukauf grocery store, where a bright green and yellow ten wheel truck had been set up in the parking lot as a stage for the band. It was a truck, like many in Europe, which had a heavy plastic folding panel or curtain on the side. Rolled to the side, it made a perfect stage. The storeowner had planned this gig as a promotional event. There were eight or ten wooden picnic-style tables set up and some barbecue being sold from a hot table. There was also a wagon selling beer and soft drinks.

A few locals were gathered around. All the buildings in the surrounding area were the neat square red brick of northern Germany. We ate the fare that was given to the band— *schweinshaxe* (a glob of gristly and greasy pig meat on a sharp hank of bone), ribs and chicken wings with an oddly bright red sauce of red peppers, onions and paprika. A small bun of white bread was also served. It was the most unpleasant food we'd encountered in a long time, but we ate it. It was free. It seemed to be an element in the alchemical mix that Lee was working on with his traveling companions—rich foods, dietary accessories (wine, sugar, meat, coffee), late nights, cigarette smoke, exhaustion, all mixed up in tight intimate chambers with him and a very hot internal fire. The furnace was stoked up high and chugging along, the spiritual master shoveling coal on the fire down below in the boiler room.

Lee and the band got into the truck, all of them wearing sunglasses against the glare of the early evening sun that was setting in the west and shining directly in their faces. Lee said, "We are Shri! We are the sunglasses band—The Sunglasses Blues Band!" Right away it was apparent that the mood was so relaxed and casual that everyone in the band was playing beautifully. They were together and the sound was fabulous—the best sound for Shri I'd heard this summer. Lee struck off into "I'm a Man." Small groups of Lee's students sat at tables with a few guests and some local people. As we sat there listening, suddenly Lee was singing something new: "Get down on your knees / start barking loud / Cause I'm comin' to get ya / and you know how / Cause I'm a dog / D...O...G...dog!"

Hysterical laughter broke out. Lee had a mischievous little smile on his face behind his sunglasses. When the song was over he said, "That's a Muddy Waters song for you, with a special Shri verse thrown in there just for fun!" They went into the famous "Stormy Monday."

More local people came, looking much more wholesome than the first wave of people. These were younger people with children who had been to see the puppet show—performed by the owners of the well-off gypsy caravan that was parked in a vacant lot nearby. Now there were about thirty-five or forty people there for the music, including our group. The children played while the band carried on, the sun in their eyes, Neukauf flags fluttering in the warm wind. The sky was blue with big fluffy clouds in it. We sat at long wooden tables. Everything around us seemed mild and even bland. We got up and danced on the concrete parking lot to "Dreamin'," a Lozowick-Flaherty original. Suddenly Lee's voice piped up again. "It's great to be here in Sottrum. How do you say it? Oh, yeah, Sohtrum. We're gonna play in Gomorrah tomorrow night," he quipped dryly.

Sara leaned over and said that a little girl, playing nearby, had just said in German, "I hope they're going to play very long—I like to jump to it." How strange that this oddball gig turned out to be very pleasurable in many ways. The band was relaxed, the sound was great, there was no pressure on at all. Afterward a couple with two kids who had listened all night went up to the band members to get their CD signed. The man brought the CD over to Lee, who signed in German, "The blues is for everyone. — Lee"

July 25, 1999
Bittstedt

About forty people gathered for a day of celebrating the company of the guru, beginning with brunch and a talk by Lee afterward. Darshan would be held that night after dinner. Brunch was an elaborate and high spirited occasion with an opulent spread of food. People from around northern Germany who have known Lee off and on for as long as twelve years were gathered, as well as several newcomers. After brunch the children spread out their toys on the floor to play in the wide hallway while the group gathered in the sunny, hot living room and waited for Lee. He came walking in briskly and took his seat on the sofa at the head of the room. He began his talk: "What I'd like to do is talk, and then if there are questions about anything, or why anybody's here, including people I've known for years, this would be a good time to do that.

"Somehow it's appropriate that we're meeting here, in a home, and not just in a house, not in a big hall with hundreds of people, because this Work that I represent is very exclusive. It may not end up being that way, since my own Master, Yogi Ramsuratkumar's Work is extremely widespread in India in particular, but also in the West. His Work is more universal Work; my Work may become universal as time goes by . . .

"Most of us in our naiveté are willing to settle for universal Work, but the thing is with universal Work we never get what it is that we come to the Work to get. Each of us has been drawn here—at least I'll say that for my students—because we are looking for specific, exclusive, transformational Work. Whether we are able to articulate it or not, each of us is in touch with a kind of existential suffering, and the world as we know it has no answer to that suffering. There is no resolve whatsoever, none. Food won't do it, sex won't do it, fame won't do it. Nothing in the world will do it. Although if you have to be addicted to something, sex is better than food!" Everyone laughed. "Then you get to avoid Reality and use up calories rather than adding calories. There's only one answer to that existential suffering and we could call it God or the Divine if we are theistic, or we could just call it Reality or the Truth.

"When I was teaching positive thinking and creative visualization and all those kinds of things I used to have, on a good night, two, three, four hundred people, because the rhetoric occasionally sounded radical. In fact it wasn't, it was completely universal and consoling. One of the reasons I got into the Work was because I was never satisfied with anything less than the ultimate possibility. So I moved from positive thinking and working with dreams and tarot and astrology and everything else to this Work, because this Work holds the answer, but not in its universal form. Ultimately it holds the answer, and in its universal form, in one thousand years or one hundred lifetimes, eventually we'll get to the 'jackpot.' But in one lifetime, the Work in its universal form will not pierce our dense psychologies and our stubborn sophisticated resistances to the realization of truth, or of awakening, we could say.

"Nobody gets drawn to this Work by accident; we are drawn to this Work because we have the potential to do this Work, in its specific and exclusive form. But what happens as time goes by is that the Work tends to be a little more expensive than we thought, and we're a little tight with our spiritual money, not wanting to spend it. One of the protections of the validity of this Work is my Master, Yogi Ramsuratkumar. His Work is universal Work, but He is also a representative of the Work, and anyone who is willing to pay the price for the Work, gets it. There's a law of the Work, which is you get out of it equal to the degree that you give into it.

"There's two ways that we give to the Work—externally and internally. The external has its importance; for example, we're up here for a few days with the band and somebody has to provide hospitality, so Claus and Anja provide that here in this house, and Sara has worked to create the tour and have the band come. It's important work, but not everyone has the resources to do such service.

"The other level of giving to the Work is internal. I don't mean sighing and mooning through your day over God. I mean a willingness to offer everything that you are to be used by the Work, whatever that is, whatever that means, whatever the consequences.

The offer comes without strings attached—it's not a business deal. So you offer yourself to the Work for whatever the Work wants you for, without regard for the consequences.

"In other words, everything we have is a gift. When we offer ourselves to the Work without regard for consequences (and that's the only way the Work will accept our offer), then there is no guarantee as to whether we get to be financially successful and have love, beauty, family in our lives—all the things the average person wants. You have to offer yourself up, no strings attached. The Work doesn't always take your offer. Sometimes psychotics come to the Work and offer themselves up, but the Work doesn't want them because its not profitable in the long run."

Lee began to paraphrase a story that Carlos Castaneda tells of Don Juan, in which Carlos said to Don Juan, "What have I gotten myself into? This is insane." Don Juan said, "That's right. No one would want to do this, so we have to be tricked into getting involved."

Lee said, "So things that we all think are insane are sane to the Work, and what we think is sane is insane to the Work. Since most of us are afraid of insanity, it's no wonder that we resist the Work because our entire worldview has to be flipped, turned around, inside out. Our romanticism and our morality and our nostalgia all need to be turned inside out.

"A lot of you probably eat organic food, or would like to if you could afford it. If you ask the average person why they eat healthy food, the reason they would give you may be completely rational, but it's not a Work reason. In our community we have a vegetarian diet. We try to eat relatively clean food. Last night we didn't, but . . . ! Between the band and a few of our friends we ate an entire pig last night—a big one! It's very bad food. Not because you have to kill a pig to get it, but because the energy required to digest that pig is not available for the Work. So we eat clean food because it burns clean.

"If you have a car and you use low-grade fuel that doesn't burn clean—that has a lot of extra stuff in it beside pure gasoline—then all the impurities in the fuel go to clog up the engine. After a while the car doesn't work at the level of possibility for the mechanics of the car. If you don't get it serviced regularly, the car will really run badly and maybe even stop running. So this," Lee pointed to his body, "is just a machine, an organic machine. What we breath, eat and perceive are the fuel that goes into this machine, like gas, oil, brake fluid . . . The dirtier the fuel burns, the more likely it is that this machine will function way below its capacity, and maybe even break down. So that's obvious. Everybody knows that. It's common sense. Everybody who eats pure food knows all about how this works in the body.

"When we begin to work for the Work, the criteria for the Work is: What is it that serves best? There is no morality involved. It's not like in Buddhism, where there is non-violence so we don't kill pigs and cows and chickens—as stupid as they are! Chickens are sort of vegetables with nervous systems. Years ago it was, 'For every pound of beef produced the cow uses up the equivalent of four pounds of corn and grass, and look how many people are starving, and if we used that corn and grain to feed people instead of cows, nobody would be starving in the world.' The Work doesn't care about that shit! The only criteria is: How can this machine function most optimally for the Work? There is no morality involved. Besides which, the reason there are starving people in the world is not because there's not enough food to feed them now.

"There are starving people in the world because you and I need starving people in the world. Everybody in this room needs there to be starving people in the world. Everyone here would wish, even on a bad day, that there were no starving people in the world. I know you all have a very high ethical view, but the fact is that we *need* starving people. Our worldview is based on distinctions—me and the other, whatever it is. West German and East German, or German and Turk . . . man/woman, good person/bad person. Our worldview is based on distinctions. We make distinctions about everything. This may be a bit of a stretch for the rational mind, but it is the distinction-making mind that creates starvation in the world, not a lack of food. Anyway, that's off the track. Whatever we put into the Work, we get out of the Work. The more we put in, the more we get out.

"As a teacher I have maybe one hundred twenty students. Out of those the majority are satisfied to float around in the facet of universality that is part of this Work. So when people come to see my Master, He blesses everybody. He says, 'My Father blesses you,' and He doesn't make personal demands . . . usually. My school is still small enough that I still remember everybody's names. Everybody feels they are loved by the teacher, and they love the teacher and that's all very nice. People can float in that field of mutual love and respect and concern and Blessing. It's very comfortable, it's very pleasant; it's even miraculous in terms of healings and such events, but hanging out passively sucking up blessings is not transformational. It's not salvatory. So if we don't give to the Work, we don't get back from the Work.

"We can float in the glow of the Work for lifetimes—irradiated by the radiance—and that's fine, and the majority of students in every sangha do that, but that's not what we come here to do. We come here to resolve the pain of the existential suffering that we feel, now, in this lifetime. We either do that or we don't, obviously—or more accurately, that either gets done or it doesn't. We have to lose the 'I' for the touch of Grace to effect this great shift. Most of us are simply unwilling to pay the price that is required to do that because the price required is a complete surrender of our distinctions, our opinions, attitudes, requirements, demands. This path has profound possibility and many great treasures, but we don't touch any of those things if we aren't willing to give up our desires for those very things.

"So when they hear these ideas, people often think that what the Work wants to use in us . . . maybe women, for example, think it's their femininity. Pfffww!" Lee gestured as if that was ridiculously absurd. "It has nothing to do with that! We want to be real women so we can have better orgasms, we don't give a shit about the Work. Let's be *honest*! We wrap that desire with a very sophisticated strategy, but what's at the bottom of it is we can't be free in sex and, 'If I was a real woman I'd be able to be free in sex, wild and uninhibited, free of the fear . . .' That's *really* what it is.

"And the men think, 'I'm a great artist, and the Work wants me to be an objective artist!' Ohh . . . what trash! The Work couldn't care less about all that! 'I want to be a great artist . . .' Ppfft! That stuff has no value to the Work. You go to the Work and say, 'I want to give,' and the Work says, 'Okay what do you have?' 'My creativity as an artist,' you say. Well, it's dinner time by the time the Work gets done laughing!" Everyone laughed. He continued, "You say, 'I can dance,' and it takes two months to get the Work's foot out of your ass!

"What the Work values is if you say, 'Pride!' Then the Work sits up and takes some interest. Or vanity. 'Ah! Vanity! That has some value,' the Work says. Or shame. 'Ahh! That's worth something!' Because those are the things we hold onto at any cost. We can be very generous with our talent and creativity and decency. We go into old age homes and homes for the emotionally disturbed and take care of them with great compassion, and this is all well and good. We're very generous with those things, but it's the things that we hold onto until death do us part that really have value to the Work. Our pride, vanity, guilt, greed—those are gold to the Work. If we're willing to offer up those things, to function as adults, free of the chokehold of personality and psychology—in other words *ego*—then we interest the Work."

Lee was furiously passionate in this humorous but serious discourse, a mood that was strongly infectious. The group was raptly listening, absorbing his words which rang with truth. The sun beat down through the southern windows into the already hot room where flies buzzed constantly. None of it mattered because the group attention was completely captured by Lee.

"On the other hand, the external is not unwanted either. On the outside we have to be willing to work and work hard. So if we just sit around and think to ourselves, 'Well, I'm going to offer up some vanity this morning,' it doesn't work because the proof that we've offered something up is in the world of action.

"You go to Cambodia or Korea or India and you come to this yogi in a cave and he is in serenity. But you take that person and bring them back into the world, into the marketplace, and often that serenity is gone within two days. As some of you know who are parents, before you have your own children it's easy to be a saint with other people's children. With your own, there's a tremendous internal pressure, even though you love them. It's very different than dealing with other people's children. If someone else's child has a bad day, is being selfish, you can smile and be gentle and patient. But if your own child is that way, who are you going to blame it on? It's you! We have to look at ourselves. That's where everything we see in our children comes from.

"So you get out of the Work what you put into it, and the Work tests everything you offer it in the world of action—in relationship with lovers, friends, children, in the world of business. That's where you get to see if you've really offered it up. We have these bands, and one of the criteria for success is to have some commercial viability. We played in this beautiful club in Hamburg three nights ago. "Downtown," was the name of it. Last night we played out in the parking lot of Neukauf in Sottrum, and we actually played better last night than the night in Hamburg, because when we were in Hamburg, there was this attitude. It was a famous place, and there was a little bit riding on the gig. Whereas last night it was like, 'If it's just a bunch of peasants, hey, kick back, have fun.' So with nothing riding on it we can be relaxed, but a gig that has anything riding on it, any real consequences . . .

"Liars, gods & beggars used to do that all the time. Whenever there was a pivotal gig for LGB we were full of tension, touchy with one another, with me leading the pack! Oh man! We went to this gig once in L.A. LGB used to go out there and do what are called 'showcase' gigs, in which you show yourself off for the entertainment industry. You go to very famous clubs where the music business people go to discover new acts. So we were supposed to start playing at ten o'clock or something like that, and every time we'd go to do one of these showcase gigs we'd be saying, 'Okay, this is it, we're gonna be discovered!' Every one of them was full of tension for me.

"We showed up at one club to play and there was this industry party going on. A new band of twenty-year-old kids with the lead singer a Janis Joplin sound alike—fabulous voice, exactly like Janis. They had taken over the club. We came in and they looked down on us. Our average age was forty-five! They were like, 'Who are you? We're having a party here tonight.'

"I was furious! I was storming around, 'Who do these punks think they are?' Who they were was a band that just got a half million-dollar advance from a music company! And who were we? Nobody! So finally the club owner said, 'When they're done, you go on.' I calmed down, okay. So they're doing this sound check and every musician in that band was a bigger prima donna than . . . I can't tell you how insane it was driving me! I was just pacing the floor, 'Get these people out of here!' But we'd driven all the way there from Arizona, and we were stuck. So we waited. Finally they finished their set and as soon as they were done everybody left the club. All the record company people left, nobody wanted to hear us.

"We finally got up onstage to play and there was so much tension—oh boy! We got off to a terrible start and everybody got into a worse mood because we were playing so badly. It was awful! I know when we play for the Pope somebody is going to get nervous. The Pope loves the blues . . . everybody knows that, right? When the Pope takes a shower he sings the blues—'da da da da *dah*, I'm a Pope! Spell P-O-P-E, da da da da *dah*! I got a ring and big hat, da da da da *dah*, I got a staff all in jewels, da da da da *dah*, I can bless you real good, all you original-sin fools, 'cause I'm de Pope, I spell P-O-P-E, Pope!' " The thirty or so people packed into the room laughed as Lee sang this to the melody and unmistakable beat of "I'm a Man."

"So you get out of the Work what you put into it—pride, greed, vanity, sloth. If you're willing to offer those things up then the Work is interested because these things have weight, value. Artistic skill? Achh! The Work has plenty of that. 'What are you going to give me?' the Work says. 'My talent!' you say. The Work says, 'Don't call me, I'll call you!' But when you come up to the door of the Work and say, 'I want to work,' and when the Work says, 'What do you offer?' you say, 'Vanity,' then the door opens. So it's not that we should walk around being as dirty and unkempt as we can possibly be. That's not the point. In fact, that would be reverse vanity. It's all the same.

"What we give to the Work, we get back. It doesn't matter how brilliantly we have understood the ideas of the Work. If we don't give, we don't get. The Work values our hard work, but a much higher value are those psychological qualities that we identify as our self. This is why they are worth so much. Most artists view their talent as a gift, a gift of God. But we don't think that way about our pride and greed and vanity. We don't find ourselves sitting in a traffic jam, being furious about some idiot who's making us wait to get down the highway and thinking that this anger is a gift from God. The things that we are identified with are the things that have the highest value to the Work because what is required to dis-identify is much bigger—greater sacrifice, more effort, and therefore more value to the Work.

"So this is an exclusive path. We get out of it what we have put into it. Often we mistake signs of the miraculous as proof that we personally are working transformationally. But if you take a sparkler, wherever you walk with it, sparks fly out. If the sparkler walks near you and sparks fly near you, it has no reflection on you. It's the sparkler.

"Yogi Ramsuratkumar is so great—He's the fire, I'm the sparkler. He lit me on fire and wherever I go His fire creates miraculous circumstances. But we think it's us. We see these sparkles and we think, 'I'm working,' but we're not, we're just near the sparkler—it has nothing to do with us. If we are satisfied to simply bask in the reflection or radiance of Yogi Ramsuratkumar's blessing, we can for a lifetime and our lives can be very sane and decent and comfortable. But that's not what we are drawn to this Work for. We were drawn to this Work because we wanted ultimate transformation, now, in this lifetime. For that we have to be willing to give. The more we give, the more we get back—it's a direct relationship. Signs of the miraculous in our lives are not proof that we are giving anything at all. We are just in the right place at the right time, caught in the crowd. You get caught in the crowd and you're at the effect of whatever the crowd is at the effect of.

"The Law of the Work is that you get in direct relationship to what you give, which is transformation. Who would want transformation? Only a crazy person. But sooner or later, we're all going to be crazy. If not this lifetime, next lifetime, or ten or one thousand lifetimes. We're all going to become crazy in this Divine context.

"As this Work becomes mature in us there is profound suffering in denying the demand of this Work. It may be true that we don't remember our past lives, and in future lives we won't remember this life; at the same time we understand that even though we don't remember past lives, that suffering is still part of us. It informs us and goes to make up who we are now. Every lifetime that we refuse the transformational possibility there is more suffering that goes to make up the next or some future lifetime.

"So we've come here for transformation. It's the most difficult thing for any human being to do because we are identified with the things that the Work wants to take from us. If you're going to climb a mountain or race a car, reaching your goal is a lot easier because those things are external, and if you work hard enough you can develop skills. Your vanity is not who you are, but it feels like who you are, so to give it up actually feels like you are giving up a part of yourself, ripping off a piece of flesh and throwing it to the voracious jaws of the Work. 'Pride, shame, vanity—here, have my head!' " Lee gestured dramatically. "But it's not *you*, it only feels like it is you. So that's it—that's what I wanted to say today! I think that's clear! Any questions?"

A questioner asked, "Is it only the commitment that carries you through?"

"Well that's where you start," Lee began. "You start with commitment and commitment leads to action. But the thing is that whenever we decide what to do, it's ego deciding what to do. Ego is not going to do anything that will obviate itself. It's not going to commit suicide. So we establish commitment, or we call it intention, and if the intention is strong enough and you continue to establish it and reinforce it, it leads you to action. With intention we can make it through the difficult times, somehow. It may feel like we'll never get through this, it's too big, too hard, but if we establish the intention, it will carry us through."

Another person asked, "Where can I get the huge intention I need, the fuel for the intention, to keep it alive . . . "

Lee answered, "When intention is established properly—and there's no way to know if you are establishing it properly except in retrospect—it's not just in your conscious mind, it's all the way through the whole body. So even when it seems like you've lost your intention, that's just the conscious viewpoint; it's still functioning, still there, you're just not aware of it. That's why you have to enliven it, reinforce it over and over. You never know when you've established intention as an intellectual thing over and against an objective creation. So you have to keep establishing intention and assume that the Work is guiding us even when we are in really difficult periods, periods of struggle, conflict.

"There is some sense of will, like 'I'm not going to give up,' because there will be periods when it seems like everything is gone and we have nothing to stand on. Then we have to remember how strong our feeling was when we were on and had certitude. What keeps us going in the Work is not some theoretical ideal, 'Oh I want to serve God or humanity.' It's the memory of, 'I came to this Work for a reason, and no matter how dark things look, I can't forget that.' Obviously some people do—forget, that is. Some people leave, but for the exceptional student, what keeps him or her going is that he remembers, 'I need this Work, I can't go back to the way things were.' What ego does is say, 'It wasn't this hard before. You can go back.' On the surface most of us had no idea how deeply we were suffering when we came to the Work. Maybe we had difficulties in relationship or whatever, but we weren't in touch with the depths. We came to the Work because the Work touched something deep, deeper than our primal psychology. Something in us knew. We came to the Work because something touched us that was way beyond the appearance of things. If we think what we had was satisfying, then definitely we should go back, get out. The thing about Work success is that it is not measured in this world. We must make the choice sooner or later."

The group dispersed for an hour break, many people going for walks and others working in the kitchen to prepare dinner—salad and potatoes—that was served at five-thirty. Afterward, at seven o'clock, about forty adults and a dozen children packed into the small meditation room on the second floor of the house for darshan. After chanting and the giving and receiving of *prasad* the children left to go play, making slightly more room in the crowded meditation space. Lee sat on a dais at the head of the room, next to the shrine to Yogi Ramsuratkumar, which had a *vigraha* at its center. The room was hot and stuffy, with candles burning brightly around Lee. He was surrounded by a mound of *prasad*—flowers, fruit, candy, lots of chocolate. He seemed to be in high spirits as he started out with enthusiasm.

"As I sometimes do when there are new people in the space, I often tell a little history, so people know how I got where I am and how you got where you are and this whole 'catastrophe,' as Zorba the Greek would say, got going.

"In 1970, although I didn't like organizations, I inexplicably joined an organization. Once a month they would have a guest speaker, so the first monthly meeting where they had a guest speaker after I joined was somebody who was basically advertising for this seminar that he gave—that I alluded to this afternoon in the after brunch talk—that had to do with self-development and using dreams and creative imagination and all those kinds of things. The rewards of this seminar that he promised were so great that I said to myself, 'I have to do this.' He was giving one the next weekend so I signed up immediately.

"One of the things they offered was being psychic. I was in business at the time and all I could think of was how I would learn to read the minds of people I was doing business with and have a tremendous advantage! I wasn't interested in personal growth but in having power over other people, definitely. So I took the course the following weekend and it was everything that was promised, and more in fact.

"Obviously one had to practice the technology to become good at it, but the technology itself was a revelation to me. It was so good in fact that the following weekend they were offering a training session to teach people to give the seminar. This was in Texas. I immediately signed up for it. A month later, I was back in New Jersey where I lived, advertising and starting to teach the course.

"As I taught the course, one of the things I learned was that I didn't know very much. I was quite naive in the entire field of transpersonal psychology and metaphysics and everything. I wanted to be able to speak about this material with some authority, so I began taking every seminar I could find that had some education to offer in the field of parapsychology, metaphysics, the occult, transpersonal psychology and so on. So I taught the course for a while. I also had a very successful business, which was what gave me the freedom to be able to change my plans and go here and there.

"So when I first took the course I was like everybody else. You know, I wanted money, sex, food, fame, power—control, in short. Anything to glorify myself, fancy vacations, travel, clothes, cars. I had a Porsche at the time—the kind they import into America, not exactly the same kind they have here, but it was a start, I was on my way."

After the powerful and inspiring talk Lee had given during the afternoon, the group listening in the small meditation room was now was primed to be caught up in Lee's mood, which was sparkling, warm, all-embracing and funny. He so easily made himself very human for us all, and people responded with frequent, spontaneous and sometimes raucous laughter.

"Something inexplicable happened. As I taught the course, I started wanting to actually discover what Reality was. It all happened very subtly, you know. One day I was teaching a course and I said, 'Well, I can't keep running my business and teaching the course,' so the business had to go. The course was losing money, the business was making a lot of money, but somehow I said, 'I can't keep dividing my time.' I don't know what had come over me!" Lee chuckled. As Lee told his story his laughter kept peppering the room like an intoxicating spice that seemed somehow connected to the free-floating ecstasy that drifted on the air.

"So I sold the business. I took all the money that I got from selling the business and I bought a piece of property with a house for a center for the seminar, and I started a book store," he chuckled again. "I taught the course for several years and then I started going to all these seminars—hypnosis and journaling and massage therapy and everything else—and I started visiting spiritual teachers, the Sufis, the yogis, I visited everybody who was in the scene. I was right outside of New York City, Manhattan, so whoever was there, I went to see them. I started getting farther and farther away from parapsychology and metaphysics and more and more into, I guess one could say, a kind of 'spiritual process.' At one point the Work that I'm doing now began. It all started in a kind of wild week . . . Something happened during this week, and I was inspired to write a book. The title of the book was *Spiritual Slavery*. That book is not available anymore. We burned them all because I was embarrassed by it. We took all the copies of it we had left and we built this huge ritual fire and threw all the books in.

"Essentially the book was an extremely raw, first-person account of a very rarified state of consciousness. Somehow that state of consciousness sustained itself. Weeks led to months, and months led to years, and somehow this state just stayed. Although the facets of the expression of that state of consciousness have changed dramatically over the years, the essence of it sustains itself. In the book, I essentially had set myself up as a kind of 'lighthouse,' so to speak. How immature!

"Anyway . . . I'd been going to a lot of Eastern-based gurus in New York City—yogis and whatever—so the form of the new teaching that began took on the form of the guru/disciple relationship. I'd sit on a little fancy thing and everyone would sit at my feet and like that. Then I met my Master, Yogi Ramsuratkumar, this Guy here, except in real life He's bigger," Lee pointed to a photograph of Yogi Ramsuratkumar and himself. He chuckled, "Not all that much bigger, but a little bit." Everyone laughed, caught in the snare of a subtle spell that Lee seemed to be weaving.

"So the seminar that I was teaching was very sweet, it was very nice, it was very compassionate, it was very conservative. I had been teaching it for five years and there were maybe two thousand or three thousand graduates of the system in the area, and I was the director of the state of New Jersey. I had an exalted position, sort of. So when the book came out, everybody wanted to read it because they knew me. We sold five hundred copies the first week, retail—wow! I was very happy with that. When people read it they were horrified. It was such a shock to people's systems that—literally, I'm not exaggerating—people started forming prayer groups to save me. People thought I had gone totally mad.

"One of my best friends at the time had been traveling in California and he was there for a couple of months, so I mailed him the book. He had been teaching in the same seminar system and we were very close. We had many long talks," Lee chuckled, "about this thing that was going on. He said, 'Well look. Obviously something very important has happened and is happening to you. I can't fault your ideas or your intention. You know, we agree on everything, but there is one problem here. That's this guru trip. You have got to get off the pedestal and you've got to really get down with the people. Outside of that, everything is perfect. If you would only stop that, then, wow, things would really be fabulous.' Because I trusted his feedback, I felt that we were very much equal in every way, I stayed with his comment and I struggled with it and thought about it and meditated on it and lived with it . . . and I still am, actually.

"One of the essential seeds of the vision of *Spiritual Slavery*, which should be obvious from the title, is slavery to the Will of God. Slavery is a very strong word. The book wasn't titled 'Spiritual Awakening' or 'Spiritual Enlightenment' or 'Spiritual Evolution,' but *Spiritual Slavery*. It wasn't titled 'The Fast Path to Self-Realization.' If it was we would have sold one thousand of them the first week. If only I had thought of that then!" Everyone laughed with Lee.

"The essence of the vision has to do with the inviolable Will of God. Inviolable means that it can't be altered. The form in which I teach is not a form that I have chosen as a human being might choose something. It's a form that was *given* to me. And there is no choice about it. It's not flexible. The Work as it evolved did not say, 'Well, you know, you can be a guru, or you can be a therapist, or you could be a professor, or you could be this that or another thing.' There was no question—this is what was given, and there was no wriggling room, no options. I didn't have a guru myself at the time. So I functioned this way, but I continued to question the validity of this particular form, until I met my own Guru, Yogi Ramsuratkumar.

"This was quite a surprise. It probably took about, oh, six or seven years to figure out that I had a Guru of my own. Once my relationship to Yogi Ramsuratkumar began to develop and evolve, it was obvious that the purity and the beauty and the wonder of the guru/disciple relationship was not only unique in the world, but unexcelled.

"My own vacillation and wavering about the function that has been given to me quieted down. It's still not a job that comes easily; although most people would never notice that," Lee chuckled. "Most of you probably all know about psychology. It's pretty straightforward. I was raised in a family in which my father was a fine artist, not a commercial artist. He didn't do book covers. He was a *fine* artist. All his friends were fine artists. They had been Socialists in America, they all had been blacklisted in the McCarthy Era. They were a group of really creative intellectuals, you know, very extraordinary people. So, of course I grew up feeling very exclusive, superior, upper class. Not financially, but intellectually—in terms of refinement, taste and so on. And very traditional.

"All the artists would get together; they were all men and one woman, who was very aggressive and gregarious and masculine. Every time there was a party, after dinner all the artists would go into one room and have these amazing political, social and intellectual discussions. The women would go in the kitchen where they would sit and sip coffee and talk about sewing and things." Lee chuckled.

"That was fifty years ago, so you can understand, it was a little old-fashioned. Unfortunately, I absorbed it." Lee chuckled again, seeming to find this whole conversation very humorous, but exactly what each of these many chuckles interspersed throughout his discourse were aimed toward, it was impossible to tell. He was in storytelling mode, and even though some of us had heard these stories many times before, there was a freshness and excitement in the telling of them tonight that was visibly touching everyone. People were smiling and laughing along with Lee, bright-eyed and flushed. Now Lee switched gears completely in mid-story and started telling the turtle joke. Laughter broke out in the room.

"Okay, so where were we? Oh yes, *Spiritual Slavery*. So after I found my own teacher, the nature of this relationship between student and teacher became clear. Everybody wants a guru. Everybody needs a guru. Most people, of course, because of the fear of sects in Europe—but it's been that way forever—mask their instinctive desire for a genuine master in socially acceptable forms. Like sado-masochism—a very socially acceptable form.

"We all instinctually yearn for the master. One of the most vocally antagonistic groups of people to gurus are therapists. Why? Because they act like gurus! The difference between a real guru and a therapist acting like a guru is so great that if anyone who is going to a therapist who is acting like a guru goes to a real guru, they are going to realize that their therapist has been lying to them and is fooling themselves and needs therapy themselves! That's why therapists hate gurus—the competition is too stiff.

"Another domain in which people seek the master is the church. Jesus becomes the guru, although Jesus is dead. If Jesus were alive, Jesus would be a very valid guru, but if Jesus were alive we wouldn't be going to church. At least not a Christian church, that's for sure.

"Another area in which society looks for gurus is in its movie stars and sports figures. They're literally relegated to positions of divine authority. There was a very famous bullfighter, Manolete, years ago in Spain. He was completely uneducated and he came to the bullring as a peasant. He had this instinct. He knew how to play the bulls like nobody. Some promoter saw him one day just playing in a bull pen and recognized his innate talent and made him famous. He became, in Spain, literally like a god. He was a true hero. Of course he had been gored dozens of times and had every bone in his body broken, but still he was a hero. A real hero. The genuine article.

"And at one point, I don't know how old he was, maybe in his thirties, he became a mystic—he was a natural mystic. He wanted to devote his life to self-discovery, so he retired. The people of Spain were so unwilling to allow him to retire because of their projections and expectations, they began throwing rotten food at his house and writing terrible curses all over the wall around his house. The negative reaction of the people of Spain was so great that he went back into bullfighting knowing that essentially he was committing suicide. He had reached his peak and he wanted to move on. His passion for bullfighting was gone, which made it very dangerous to go back in there. You have to be with it one hundred percent, and he wasn't anymore. He knew he was basically killing himself, but rather than let down his people, he went back. He was gored again by a bull and he died in the hospital.

"So we all instinctually want and need the true relationship between a disciple and a real guru, but because we aren't honest about our own feelings and our own needs, we're fickle. We have no faith. If the object of our veneration and worship does anything that we don't like, or that we feel is improper, we immediately turn on them and become their enemy, but we aren't willing to destroy our false image of our parents, whose behavior was the source of our pain and suspicion, our feelings of betrayal and abandonment and so on. Instead we transfer our wish for the ideal parent onto our hero figure and if they betray us, then we destroy them. What we really want psychologically is a mother and father we can trust. Tough luck! Because we only get one mother and father in this lifetime." Lee laughed. There was a strong poignant feeling in the air as the truth of Lee's words seeped in.

"We may have stepmothers, stepfathers, godmothers, godfathers, but we only get one mother and one father. It's true that often our parents on their deathbeds suddenly become willing to be real with us, to share their terror of having had a child and their complete lack of education. They meant well but didn't know what they were doing and so on. They couldn't help themselves when they hit us or molested us sexually or whatever. We've spent our lifetimes still looking for the mother or the father who would not abandon us, betray us, beat us.

"The relationship to the true guru lives in a different domain than the domain of psychology. There is nothing like it. It's exalted, breathtaking, magnificent, glorious, merciful!" Lee chuckled again. "But it's also human—a small little difficulty. Somehow we have to move through our human projections and expectations of another human being and find the essence of our relationship to the true master, which lives in the human domain, but transcends all the laws of psychology. It is often a terrifying and extraordinary, and even under the best circumstances, difficult journey. It goes from here to here," Lee gestured with his hands to indicate not going anywhere, "because you really don't go anywhere. We *realize*. We don't move, we don't shift, we simply *realize*.

"So I was acting like a guru but I had no idea what was going on for people because I didn't have the experience myself. I *knew* the truth of it and the value of it, but I didn't have the experience of it in the human domain. I was able to do a good job as a guru because I had integrity and was instinctually moved by Yogi Ramsuratkumar's blessings, but I had no personal experience of it, until I met Him. And then slowly it became obvious what this relationship between devotee and guru really *is*. Not just the benefits it could provide—the glow of the miraculous every day—but what it *really is*. This is what we all seek.

"But since we're naive and uneducated, and since the average acting guru has no idea what in the world they are at the effect of—and they are as psychologically incapable of genuineness as their worshippers—there are tremendous abuses. There are abuses between therapists, gurus and their clients, between rock and roll gurus and their groupies, between movie star gurus and their worshippers, between political gurus and their adherents—tremendous abuses. Sexual abuses, financial abuses, abuses of power, and so on. So it's understandable that we would be suspicious, because the true guru is very rare. In fact this is the whole purpose for our existence. The acme, the epitome of incarnation, of existence, is to be in relationship with a true master the way this relationship *is*. We all know this instinctually, but our psychology gets in the way. So we make our partner our guru, or we make our local priest our guru, or some movie star. Inevitably we are abandoned, we are betrayed, we are disappointed, we are disillusioned. And because we are not in touch with our deep feelings, we shut it all down again, just like we shut it down when our parents first betrayed us, abandoned us, disillusioned us, disappointed us.

"I'm just finishing up Alice Miller's new book. Some of you haven't heard me speak before, but I have tremendous respect and honor and enthusiasm for the work of Alice Miller. Every time I read one of her books it becomes obvious how delicate the reality of an infant really is. How easily we are hurt, and how easily we misunderstand, how easily we feel betrayed, and how dramatically we close down the part of ourselves that needs to feel that pain, needs to express that betrayal to move beyond it or through it. Sometimes it's enough just as an adult to acknowledge what we felt as children when we were betrayed. We begin to understand that betrayal, and that most betrayal is not intentional. Our parents were as scared of Reality as we are.

"So as this Work matured, it became obvious that although this is never a form I would personally choose, this is the form that Yogi Ramsuratkumar has given me to touch Westerners. The average Westerner who goes to see Yogi Ramsuratkumar has no idea what's going on. He's just another movie star to them. And if He does one thing they don't like, then they turn their backs on Him. Just like they do with a movie star who does something they don't like, picks a couple of bad scripts or something.

"In the early days of His work Yogi Ramsuratkumar didn't live anywhere. He just wandered around the streets, and He had a couple of favorite places where He liked to sleep. But basically you could find Him on the streets, and you could go for a walk with Him in the mountains and sit and talk for hours. He was there, like a friend. We went out with Him thirteen years ago in the streets of the town He lives in. And He walked into the big temple and as soon as people saw that it was Him and that He was *out* of his house, one hundred and fifty people came out of nowhere and crowded around Him. Everybody wanted something: 'Heal my child, heal my husband, heal my wife, give me more money, send my child through college, make my retarded child ordinary.'

"People get excited when the projected giver of their wish is standing right in front of them—someone with the power to actually do what they want, give them what they want, fulfill all their desires. The more people there are, the less we think we're gonna get our piece, and the more excited we get. This is what causes riots. Then everybody starts fighting to get to the saint, and people get so excited they forget that the Saint is human and they could literally tear the person to pieces trying to get a piece of their desires met. So, the more renowned my Master became, consequently the less He could go out in public, because the more He would draw crowds and the crowds would get dangerous to His health and well-being.

"After a while He got a house where He could have a somewhat safe haven. After many years of having the house, He got an ashram that had a wall around it and was more protective. Many Westerners in the early 1970s went to India and met Yogi Ramsuratkumar; He was there sitting with them, as close as Claus and I." Lee indicated his student who was translating and sat about four feet away from him. "Closer even. And they come back to India now and He's up on a dais. Nobody can get within ten meters of him. He's not accessible, and people are angry. They feel that they are owed. 'I knew Him when He was just nobody, I should be able to get up and sit next to Him and talk to Him like I did in the old days.'

"The average Westerner does not say, 'Let me look at myself.' The average Westerner says, 'My movie star betrayed me. I'm gonna find another movie star. I'm gonna go to Lucknow and sit with Punjaji. He won't reject me. I'm going to go to Kerala and sit with Ammachi, she won't reject me. Yogi Ramsuratkumar—he's lost it! He's not a guru anymore.' That's what the average Westerner does because to the average Westerner, Indian gurus and Tibetan Buddhist masters are nothing but movie stars. 'In fact, the hell with it—why should I go to that filthy country India and get sick? I'm just gonna wait until Ammachi comes here, and I'm gonna go see her here,' " Lee laughed. "You can't go to India without getting parasites! You may not actually get food poisoning or get sick, but when you come back to Germany, you have got parasites, if you have been in India. Guaranteed!

"So, for Westerners to understand what it *is* to be in relationship with a guru is very difficult, and requires very different work than it does for Easterners. For some bizarre reason—probably because I was unwilling to settle for less than what was ultimately possible—I get to be sort of the emissary for Yogi Ramsuratkumar in the West. *The real emissary! All the rest are frauds, don't listen to them! Listen to me!"* Lee was obviously joking. He chuckled at his statements and his theatricality.

He continued in the same genuine tone he'd been using all night, "Somehow I get to represent for Westerners what Yogi Ramsuratkumar represents for Easterners. He's the real thing, like Coca-Cola. *The real thing.* Through His Influence and Blessing, His Benediction, it is possible to pierce the veils of illusion. It is possible to pierce the veils of psychology, of personality, of identification, the illusions of our desires. Yogi Ramsuratkumar is the Master. The jewel, the epitome of life itself, the rarest treasure of existence is the relationship with the Master. He has the power to allow us to see reality as it is.

"So somehow, by some bizarre twist of fate," Lee chuckled, "having realized this to some degree in relationship to my Master somehow puts me in a position of carrying His Work to the West. Having realized it not in the sense that it's finished or there is no more to realize, but in the sense that I've scratched the surface anyway. Yogi Ramsuratkumar has said, 'If even *one* human being has been helped by this Beggar's work, in His entire lifetime, then He's willing to come back and do Father's Work again and again and again.' Not for His personal gain, but just to do His Father's Work. Yogi Ramsuratkumar's relationship to me is, 'Are you doing My Work or not?'

"People go to India and they see Yogi Ramsuratkumar is very solicitous of me. He calls me up, He holds my hand, He whispers in my ear, and blah, blah, blah. That's because I'm doing His Work. If I stop doing His Work and I go to India, He doesn't *know* me, I'm going to be nobody! Those of us in the therapy generation want people to love us for ourselves." Everyone laughed. "We get into a love affair and say to our partner, 'When are you going to *see me*? Aren't you interested in how *I* feel?' " More laughter. "Yogi Ramsuratkumar couldn't give a shit how I feel. It doesn't mean anything to Him. If I am doing His Work, He loves me; if I am not doing His Work, He does not *know* me. I don't exist if I'm not doing His Work.

"Yogi Ramsuratkumar is too great a Master to be limited to some small little town in southern India, so I get to bring Yogi Ramsuratkumar to the West. Directly and immediately and also secondarily through influential means, subtle means. This is the Work He wants done, so I do this Work. It has nothing to do with my wishes, my desires, my hopes for my children's health and success. It has nothing to do with any of that. He wants a certain Work done, I'm willing to do the job, regardless of my own personal feelings about it." Lee laughed, as if he was looking at an inescapable destiny from very close range.

"So, this is the position I found myself in. Having committed myself to Yogi Ramsuratkumar's Work and being very conservative, it's a marriage for life. I took a vow to honor, obey and serve and that is what I'm going to do. One of the forms that service takes is to represent the possibility that Westerners can discover what it is to be in relationship with a true guru. That is in no way making myself equal to Yogi Ramsuratkumar, because there is no equality. But through His Influence, through His Blessing, and His Benediction, somehow Lee Lozowick can become transparent. Somehow, through *this*," he gestured toward his body, "you can realize *that*. That's the task, the job, the game for everybody who meets this path.

"At the heart of our being here together tonight is not that we get a little better health, or a little deeper insight into human nature or that our lives become a little easier. It's that we discover the indescribable majesty of Incarnate God. That's who Yogi Ramsuratkumar is. That's who Jesus was. Incarnate God. Jesus was the Son of God, literally. He wasn't the only one; he never said he was. Yogi Ramsuratkumar is a Son of God also. And to see that—to be in the presence of that, to realize what that is—is totally beyond words. Words can't capture it. To experience it first hand in our knowledge, our hearts, our wisdom, our bodies is the only way. That is at the heart of why we are together. All the rest is, as they say in English, icing on the cake.

"So, we have a community and people care for one another. One of the German women came to our ashram in America several years ago with very serious terminal cancer and died there with tremendous love and care and affection and understanding. We have a tremendous passion for nonabusive child raising and for loving and understanding relationships with other adults, our partners and parents and so on. We encourage people in the community to bring integrity to the Work, to be honest, to provide a service for what they are paid for, to bring integrity to whatever their jobs are in the world. It's great to live a good life, a decent life, but that is all secondary.

"The *real heart* of this catastrophe is to realize the Presence of God incarnate in the world. That's it. That's who He is," Lee pointed again to the picture of he and Yogi Ramsuratkumar behind his chair. He chuckled then laughed outright. "I want to make sure I point to the right one! I'm infected, so I'm kind of like spiritual HIV. He gave it to me, I can give it to you, but only under very specific circumstances.

"The point is that you get what you give, and if you stay at a distance, you aren't going to get it. You won't get the infection. You might get some love and some Blessings, even miracles. But you won't get the divine infection, and that's the point. It's a revolution. It's a transformation. It's a mutation. This Work isn't going to turn you into a good citizen. The Work will turn you into a representative of Reality, and the world of illusion doesn't like Reality. The world of sleep doesn't like awakening. When you're suffering and you go to sleep and you wake up, you don't want to wake up. You want to go back to sleep." Lee chuckled again. "When you're suffering and you're asleep, you don't think of your suffering. It's wonderful. So, since a few of you are new here," Lee chuckled, "and I'm in favor of the English maxim, 'forewarned is forearmed,' that means if you know what's coming you can prepare yourself. In this case, the best preparation is probably to run away." Several people laughed. Others sat listening very soberly. "Before it's too late, because there are some people sitting in this room for whom it is too late already . . . "

Lee paused, then said, "So, there's cake and tea to be served downstairs, and good fellowship," he laughed gently, "after this . . . Jai Guru!"

July 26, 1999
Bittstedt

Today the band had a whole day off. No gigs, no traveling, just another feast. Claus and Anja planned to make grilled sausages, chicken and sauerkraut for dinner tonight. Most of the guests from yesterday had gone home, and it would be a smaller, much more intimate group of mostly long-time students who know each other well. At four o'clock Lee came down to the living room after a rest in anticipation of the feast. And it was grand; everyone ate hearty amounts of pork and beef sausages (there were five or six different kinds) and loaded up on sauerkraut, chicken and pretzels as well. Immediately afterward Lee played bridge at the low, round wooden table in front of the small couch where he always sat in the living room.

Tina came into the living room from the dishwashing crew. The members of the Shri team had been volunteering for kitchen duties as often as possible during the stay at Bittstedt. They could be heard singing and joking around for hours over long clean-up stints in the kitchen. Now Tina said innocently to Lee, "We were just wondering about the ice cream possibility for tonight." Lee's smile was benign. He turned to his students at the bridge table and said, "Do you want ice cream?" It was one of those moments when the fate of the whole group fell on a couple of people.

I remembered Lee making this same offer after a liars, gods & beggars gig in Phoenix one night. We were standing in the parking lot getting ready to drive back to Prescott. It was still early, only eight o'clock, and Lee stopped before getting in the van and said to the small group standing around him, "Does anybody want ice cream?" There was an uncomfortable silence. When no one responded in a positive vein after about five seconds, Lee snapped, "Okay—no ice cream!" When another person realized that an opportunity had just been missed and piped up, saying, "Yes, I want ice cream," Lee replied, "Too late!" He jumped in the van with his students and sped off toward the ashram.

Now the bridge playing contingent said "Yes!" with enthusiasm. Everyone at the bridge table agreed. Lee said to Tina, "That's a positive response from this quarter. Okay." A conversation started about which grocery store might be open and so on when Tina said, "Or we could go out for ice cream?" Lee looked at us again at the bridge table and said, "Do you want to go out and get ice cream or have it here?" The consensus was that we wanted to go out to get it. Lee said, "As soon as the dishes are finished, we'll go." Some more guests arrived and sat down to a late dinner, so Lee waited until they were finished while he played more bridge, then the whole group of about twenty-five people took off in three or four vehicles to the ice cream parlor.

Over many *kugels* of ice cream in assorted flavors our group sat around Lee at small tables outside the ice cream parlor. Lee started telling stories about ice cream extravaganzas of past trips to Europe, like the time in Freiburg when Lee and company went from ice cream shop to ice cream shop, eating *kugels* and cones at each one. "The ice cream pilgrimage," Lee called it.

When the ice cream was almost finished, Lee ordered a Coke. There were lots of jokes about the huge amounts of food we'd been consuming with Lee. This too seemed to be part of the alchemy of this particular trip with Lee, and this particular configuration of people. Steve remembered a quip by Doug Fulker, coined on a liars, gods & beggars tour of some years ago, that applied perfectly for us now: "Sometimes too much is just enough." Somehow the *pusti* element of Lee's play with his students—the abundance of rich food, the coffee, the desserts, the sense of everything being expansive, overflowing from his hands, the working of the earth of our desires—seemed connected to the seeds he was planting for Shri. Lee had been continually priming the pump for Shri during the past week; now the talk turned to Shri business again. Lee was saying to Jim, who is involved in promoting the band, that he wanted to book as many big festivals as possible next year. Lee mentioned that he'd heard about a big blues festival in Arkansas, and he wanted Jim to look into it. Jim said, "So you want to play festivals in the States too?"

"Yes," Lee replied, "festivals with thirty or forty thousand people in them."

Lee went back to the house and started another bridge game, which he played until ten forty-five. He was waiting for Thomas, who had been away on business for the weekend, to return safely by train. When Thomas arrived Lee ended the bridge game. Everyone would be getting up at four-thirty the next morning to leave by five for Ulm, where Lee would stop on the way to Freiburg to meet with Durgamayi Ma and her devotees.

July 27, 1999
Ulm

After driving for six hours the Shri caravan arrived in Ulm early. Durgamayi's devotees weren't expecting Lee until eleven-thirty, so we went to a café just around the corner from their center. Lee walked in and sat down at one of the small tables by big ceiling-to-floor open windows that looked out on the bright street. He seemed to be in a very magnanimous mood. While we were waiting for the drinks to be served Lee noticed a small stage immediately to the right of where the group was sitting. There were big klieg lights above it. He commented to band members, "Hey, we could play here! Why not?"

"Yeah, we could play here tonight," Rakini said. "We have all our equipment." There was general agreement in a kind of communal cacophony as three or four or five or more people talked at once, laughing or joking around about how we're up for playing anywhere, anytime. Lee said to Jim, "Go book it!"

"Now?" Jim asked, eyebrows raised.

"Yeah! Why not? Let's start with booking gigs for next year in south Germany," Lee enthused. Jim walked away and the coffee was served. Just as people were adding sugar to their coffee Lee was ebullient in telling a story about a person he'd seen heaping spoonfuls of refined white sugar on top of an already sweet dessert. He has a way of interjecting something like that with innocence, leaving his students holding the sugar dispenser and wondering.

Jim came back from talking to the café manager and reported, "They only booked one group here last year. But I gave the manager our CD and promo pack and he's going to listen to it now. How much should I ask for if he's interested?"

Lee said, "What did we get in Dortmund? Fourteen hundred D-marks? Okay." Jim walked away again.

It was time to go. As we walked to the center Everett asked Lee, "Didn't you go to Jim Morrison's grave in Paris and spend time there?"

Lee said, "Yeah, that was cool."

"And the black Sarah in France? You spent time there?" Lee turned toward Everett and nodded affirmatively. Seven years ago a number of students had accompanied Lee on a pilgrimage to see the statue of Sarah al Kali, the black goddess of the gypsies. Her myth is tied in with that of Mary Magdalene, who, it is said, came to France and lived her life out in exile there. According to the popular legend, Sarah was the black Egyptian slave who accompanied Mary Magdalene, Mary Salome and Mary Jacobe (or Mary the mother of Jesus, depending on which version you read) to the shores of southern France. Today the statue resides in the crypt of a tenth century church in Saintes Maries de la Mer, on the Mediterranean Sea. Some of Lee's students had read about the black Sarah and wanted very much to visit her. Yvan Amar had given Lee additional information about her and the gypsies' esoteric relationship with this archetypal form of the goddess Kali. Every year the icon is carried to the sea by tens of thousands of gypsies, where she is bathed in the salty Mediterranean waters, then redressed in her ornate, ceremonial garb and returned to the crypt. The crypt itself has many old crutches, baby shoes, canes and braces all along the walls—relics of miraculous healings that have taken place at her feet.

When Lee went there the whole group was amazed by the spiritual power emanating from the statue. There was an undeniable presence of being that permeated the dark, dingy crypt. The statue was alive with a feminine presence of divinity that radiated out and enveloped us. Even Lee, who is not easily impressed by most shrines or religious sites, was moved. He spontaneously sat in meditation in the crypt for thirty minutes, then took one of the long white candles, lit it and performed an *arati*—waving of lights— before the deity and then offering it to his students.

Everett and Lee were still talking as we walked up to the door of the center. "So if a place has any real power, you will stay awhile?" Everett asked. Lee nodded, giving as little data as possible, and opened the door to a building on the corner that seemed to be five or six stories tall. It was freshly painted in a bright, upbeat and bold orange—a strong contrast to the grays and tans of all the surrounding buildings.

We entered a hallway at the ground level. Major construction was obviously under-way. In the hallway to our left was a large picture of Neem Karoli Baba on the wall, with a small shrine beneath it adorned with fresh flowers and a small votive candle that burned brightly. No one was around, so Lee asked one of the men to ring the doorbell. Immedi-ately a woman and man appeared and introduced themselves to Lee as Naga Ma and Hanuman. They spoke fluent English and were sparkling with courtesy. Right away they began to extend warm hospitality, but Naga Ma pointed first to the picture of Neem Karoli Baba and said, "You have seen our Satguru?" Yes, we replied with smiles of appre-ciation.

The group followed as Lee was ushered up some stairs, down a hallway, past the kitchen where bright-eyed women and men were working, busily preparing the lunch meal. There were several beautiful children playing in the kitchen also. We went outside and down some stairs to a small deck nestled in the back under trees between buildings. There was a table and chairs with cold water and apple juice set and waiting for us. Lee sat down and his students took various seats scattered around the deck.

Looking around at Lee's group Naga Ma asked, "Is everyone in the band?" Lee intro-duced everyone, pointing out the members of the band. Hanuman asked how the band tour was going, and Lee said, "Good. People like us wherever we go. Tomorrow we play at a big festival in Lucerne." Hanuman was interested in knowing if we had our CDs with us, and if they could buy some. "Of course!" two or three people replied immediately.

Naga Ma explained that lunch would be at one o'clock and darshan, which would be in another building across town, would be at four-thirty. Lee asked if Durgamayi and Andrew Cohen had done a seminar together as he had heard they might. Naga Ma said,

"No, they didn't meet. What a pity! We were asking for a conference, but it didn't happen." Three or four other devotees joined everyone on the porch as Naga Ma and Hanuman explained their daily schedule.

They get up at five or five-thirty every morning. Two or three days a week they have a morning darshan by conference telephone with Durgamayi at six. On the mornings when there is no darshan by telephone, they meditate together. At six-thirty they have breakfast or go to work. On Tuesday evening they sing the "Hanuman Chalisa" chant together twelve times. Lee commented, "I remember that chant from the last time we were here. A magnificent chant."

Two beautiful children came down the steps and snuggled with their father, Hanuman. I noticed that all the children looked exceptionally happy and clear and bright, which always reflects positively on the practice and lifestyle of the adults who care for them. The devotees continued to ask Lee many questions—if he had students in Freiburg, if he had a center there or households. Lee answered, "Right now it is just several houses. Perhaps a year from now we'll have a center, but since we have an ashram in France I don't want another one in Germany. I don't want people divided between two ashrams in Europe."

After a few minutes of silence Lee offered more water or apple juice to the students who were sitting around him, serving it into their glasses himself. He was, as usual, tremendously gracious. One of Durgamayi's devotees asked Steve, "Is your main profession to play music and travel with Lee and the band, or do you have another profession?"

Steve answered, "My profession is that I live on the ashram in Arizona, in the U.S., and help take care of the ashram. I don't have another profession. I play in the band and travel with Lee in addition to that." Durgamayi's devotees talked again about how they have to work outside their small ashram, which has fourteen residents. "How many residents do you have in the States?" they asked. Lee explained, "We have about thirty-two residents, four or five of them are children, and we have two businesses that help to support us. We have a school for the ashram children and people teach in the school, cook, take care of cars, work in one of the businesses."

Hanuman said, "That is the dream of Durgamayi also, to have a business that will support the ashram. And in France?" Lee described La Ferme de Jutreau, concluding with, "There are only Americans and Germans living there—no French. It's too rough for the French." Everyone laughed.

"We are also supported by donations," Lee continued. "We ask students who live outside the ashram to contribute financially in support of the ashram. The ashram in France is much smaller than the ashram in Arizona. In America we live in a small town, just outside town. There are about fifty people who live around town in households." He described the weekly schedule, with two After Dinner Talks and a formal darshan program on Sunday, morning meditation and so on. "Whoever wants to comes for meals, talks, to work. Not too many come for work—they all come for meals and talks!"

They laughed and said, "It's the same everywhere. That's normal."

Another devotee joined the group and greeted Lee with a namaste. Naga Ma brought a book of photos to show the results of their efforts—how the center looked before and during the process of renovation. They had obviously worked very hard to produce the beautiful spaces we had seen as we passed through the building. Lee looked through the book politely then passed it on to Steve, who is often involved in carpentry and other renovation projects, being a master woodworker. Durgamayi's devotees told us that they acquired the place fourteen months ago. They had just finished painting the outside—Ma's favorite color, "sadhu orange"—yesterday. The place was inexpensive to buy because it had been used as a halfway house for immigrants, and used to house up to seventy people at a time. As a result it was completely trashed and so had to be gutted. The beautiful old wooden floors were the only part of the building they had left intact.

They explained that Durga Ma lives in another part of the city, but they are making a special apartment for her adjacent to the darshan hall within the *mandir*, which will cover the first floor of the six-story building. "This is a dream of Ma's, to have an ashram in the middle of the city where people are, where daily problems are—cars, family, work—and Ma can help solve the problems," one of the devotees said.

Naga Ma said that they have two dining rooms; she asked if we would kindly split our numbers to seat some of Lee's party in each room. "We have a place for you, Mr. Lee," she added. "We will show you. And we will have a silent lunch."

The sun was beating down on us. It had been very pleasant for a while out on the deck surrounded by leafy, green trees, but now it was getting hot. Our hosts graciously ushered Lee and the group into their "living room"—a cool, elegant and very comfortable room on the same floor. It had a long, low white couch with white bolsters and pillows on the floor spanning one wall of the room, low tables and cushions. The wooden parquet floor was partially covered with a heavy, woven, white cotton rug. There were several plants and a beautiful shrine below another large picture of Neem Karoli Baba. On the shrine were many smooth stones and fresh flowers and a large white candle burning. One of the stones had "Ram" carved in Sanskrit on it. They explained that the children had made it. Most of the shrines in the house were decorated with smooth gray stones because Ma favors the stones very much. Everything about each of the spaces we visited seemed carefully thought out and executed with great care toward spaciousness and beauty. The devotional mood was communicated everywhere throughout the building, whether in the formal shrines or in the way the rooms were appointed or kept.

An Indian child about three years old walked in and stood by the door with a big smile and beaming eyes for Lee, who waved to her. She waved back shyly, but very interested, and then slowly backed out of the room, her deep brown eyes sparkling. Everett picked up a copy of *Be Here Now* by Baba Ram Dass, who made Neem Karoli Baba famous in the States in the early seventies with this book about his spiritual awakening and relationship with his guru. We started to talk about how profoundly American culture had been impacted by this book.

Lee remembered, "Ram Dass used to give talks in New York City in the seventies. He was a fabulous speaker. He was also very funny." Lee mentioned that Ram Dass has had a very bad stroke and almost died in the past few years.

Ed spoke about seeing Ram Dass in Boston ten years ago, commenting, "He was hilarious, very light."

"A great storyteller," Lee added.

"I saw him again in California around the same time," Ed continued, "and he was very serious. I got the impression that he was just giving people what they needed—the Bostonians needed to lighten up, and the Californians needed to be more grounded."

Speaking about the impact that Ram Dass' work, and particularly *Be Here Now*, has had on 1970s American counter-culture led into an enthusiastic discussion about what it means to have a "Job" in terms of the Work. Last year at a seminar in northern Germany Lee had talked about Shri's music, saying that it was impossible to know at this point whether or not members of Shri could be considered as having a "Job" in the Work. He said that one could determine whether one had an objective function or a Job in the Work by the kind of lasting impact what one's work had on human culture and life—music, writing or speaking the dharma, for example. Today he was making another distinction about this. He said that all he is interested in is transformational Work, which is lawfully only going to reach a very few individuals and never the masses, never the society as a whole.

"Take Harry Chapin, for example," Lee said. "Whoever heard of Harry Chapin? He only sold a quarter of a million of each of his albums; on the scale of our society at large, whoever heard of him? But on an individual basis—he totally transformed people's individual's lives with his music. The Beatles and Ram Dass created a paradigm shift in society—Harry Chapin didn't. That's the difference. We will never create any kind of paradigm shift in society. What we are interested in is transformational Work that may touch a few people, at most."

Hanuman came to take Lee to the dining room, where lunch was served. A place was set for Lee in the center of a long rectangular table. His plate was decorated with a semi-circle of six fresh marigolds. Durgamayi's devotees gathered with all of us in one of the two dining rooms to sing the "Hanuman Chalisa," a lovely, very rousing and devotional chant that is very dear to their tradition.

The chant ended and everyone took their places at the table. Naga Ma, who sat at Lee's right side, noticed that we had brought a small shaker of fire-hot ground cayenne—one that is carried everywhere for Lee, who likes his foot hot. This is special cayenne, grown and dried and processed for sale in the States. The ashram in Arizona gets it through the natural foods co-operative; a fresh supply is shipped over to La Ferme de Jutreau because this kind of super hot cayenne—so strengthening to the heart and such a great cleansing and tonic substance—cannot be found anywhere in France or Germany. At the beginning of lunch Lee had taken the cayenne shaker, removed the silver shaker top and liberally poured a thick red blanket of cayenne powder over his food. A number of his students had added cayenne to their food too—not as much as Lee, however. When Naga Ma was interested and asked what it was, Lee explained and offered it to her. She smiled and said yes, she would try it. Lee warned, "It's very hot." The next thing we knew she was coughing into her napkin, and then got up and quickly left the table, making a bee-line for the kitchen. She returned in a few minutes with her eyes red from the tears that the hot cayenne had produced, but she had a smile on her face. She was a very good sport about discovering what Lee meant when he said, "It's very hot."

Just as the dessert was finished the conversations started in earnest. The woman who seemed to be in charge of the kitchen came and asked if Lee would like some coffee or tea. "Herb tea?" Lee asked. The woman hesitated slightly and said, "I will make it. I will make whatever you like."

"What do you have already made?" Lee asked. "Coffee," she answered. Lee said, "Then I will have coffee." Lee smiled at her. As the coffee was served the woman sitting across from Lee began to ask him questions about his ashrams in America and France. She wanted to know if there were many fears of sects (cults) and religious prejudice. She said that some people were suspicious of the color of their building, for example. Lee said, "In America there is just as much prejudice against sects as in Europe, it's just more under the surface. But it's the same everywhere."

Another person asked, "Mr. Lee, you've spent time in India?" Lee answered, "I spend about two weeks a year in India at the time of my teacher's birthday. I am in Europe at the ashram in France four months out of the year, and eight months at the ashram in Arizona."

People at the table asked Lee to talk more about his ashrams, when and how people celebrated. They wanted to know more about Yogi Ramsuratkumar and if he had an ashram. Lee answered their questions with a succinct, direct and simple style that didn't add anymore than the basic answer to the question, and yet his mood was one of generosity. He said, "We celebrate traditional Guru Purnima, my birthday, my teacher's birthday, and his teacher's birthday—Papa Ramdas. We celebrate one other time, in the spring, not connected with any particular thing. My teacher stays in India. He never travels or leaves His village. He's been invited to America and Europe many times, but He always stays in His village. He has an ashram now. It's not a residence, although three or four people live there who take care of things. People come and visit for periods of time."

More coffee was offered, and when Lee found out there was real cream on the table, not just milk, he said, "I'll have some more coffee." Taking the cream pitcher in hand he poured with child-like delight, saying, "Oh boy! Yes, it's real cream—there's nothing like real cream!" then he continued answering people's questions. "We have darshan on Sunday and two After Dinner Talks a week where we consider the literature of the path and have commentary. If I like the way the talk has gone then I send copies of tapes out to our groups—bordellos. That's what we call our study groups that aren't on one of the ashrams."

Naga Ma asked, "Do you have these groups also in France?" Lee explained that one study group has recently been started in France outside the ashram. She asked if he traveled around to see these groups. Lee said, "Not so much. I don't like to travel. I'll go to Europe, California on occasion, do something in Canada, or if people ask me to come, I'll go to Mexico."

Naga Ma said, "If people want to see you, they come to you."

"Yes, that's the idea," Lee smiled. "Most of the travel I do here in Europe is not to see my students, but to see other teacher's students." People laughed around the table. Durgamayi's devotees asked why.

"I can offer a certain flavor of teaching that is not as common to their teacher," Lee said. "I don't like to go out and speak to people who have no teacher. I like to go where I can be helpful, but I don't have to deal with the people themselves!"

Naga Ma was listening thoughtfully and commented, "It's hard to be a teacher."

Lee continued, "Everybody thinks they know what you are doing, and they don't. They all think they want to be a teacher too."

In fifteen minutes, Hanuman said, they would take us on a tour of the six-story building—their new ashram. Lee left the dining table to return to the living room. When he was settled back on the low couches and pillows Lee started talking about Ma Jaya Bhagavati, who he knew twenty-five years ago in New York City as Joya. According to her devotees, Durgamayi had spent seven years with Ma Jaya Bhagavati, who was also a devotee of Neem Karoli Baba, although she never met him in the flesh, but only on subtle planes.

Going into storytelling mode, Lee began, "I remember Joya's first night at Hilda's." Hilda Charlton was a well known and much loved spiritual teacher in New York during the late sixties and seventies. Hilda had become a mentor and benefactor for Lee, always welcoming him and encouraging him. She had in fact been Lee's connecting link with Yogi Ramsuratkumar. Her evening soirees were very popular, and Lee used to take his crowd to see her frequently. There were often as many four hundred people when Hilda held her gatherings downtown, and when she moved uptown there were as many as six or seven hundred. Joya's "first night" as Lee described it was a sort of "coming out" at Hilda's downtown gathering that happened after Joya had had a spiritual awakening experience.

He continued, "Joya was married—she was just a housewife. She had the worst mouth you ever heard, really just the worst. Everyone laughed at it but Hilda, who was very strict about these things. Joya had so much shakti it made most *shaktipat* gurus seem like babies! People would have shakti in her gatherings and Hilda would come around and say, 'Keep it down kids.' Someone would start to go off and she would go up to them and say, 'Chocolate cake and ice cream.' She would say that nobody can get high when they're thinking about their stomachs! In our school people eat chocolate cake and ice cream and get higher. I have to go up to them and whisper, 'Practice!' and then they get down real fast." We laughed lightly at Lee's gentle jab. "But Joya had so much shakti she was bouncing people off the walls."

Everett and Jim walked in saying that people were asking if they could buy Shri and LGB CDs. They would have to go out to the van to get them. Lee said, "We should always carry our CDs with us wherever we go. When we were at Ebhard's in Köln his shelves were lined with extra copies of Andrew's books and tapes for sale. No one in this school should travel without CDs." Jim talked about how he had given a CD away on an airplane to a stewardess.

Lee said, "When Purna was working for LGB he used to give CDs away all the time on planes, everywhere he went. It's amazing the people he met that way. One time we were in L.A. at a sushi bar. Purna turned to the guy next to us and said, 'Are you in the music business?' The guy said yes, and then he said that he was the lead guitarist for Heart, a popular rock group! 'Do you ever record other people's music?' Purna had asked. The man said sometimes and Purna gave him a CD."

Hanuman walked in to take Lee and his entourage on a tour of the ashram. As he walked out the door with Hanuman, Lee said, "Lunch was very good. Please tell the cooks."

The tour through the rooms, up and down stairways to different floors of the building, gave us the opportunity to learn more about their school and their teacher. Lee bowed at a beautiful shrine in a hall, the center of which was a large brass Buddha, as we wound our way through a labyrinth to the stairs which would take us to the top floor.

Walking into the attic and seeing the loft space Lee laughed and said, "We could fit thirty people in there!" They pointed out a row of plastic portable wardrobes and told us that each person who lived on the ashram could only have one of these, plus the wooden wardrobe in his or her room and two rather small boxes of personal belongings. Earlier we had seen some of the bedrooms currently in use by ashram residents. Durgamayi picked out many of their personal effects, from toothbrushes to curtains and bedspreads for their rooms, which were beautiful, pristine and spacious with fine, old-fashioned hardwood floors. Everything was immaculate and well cared for. There was clearly a demand for renunciation in their lives with their teacher.

As we walked back downstairs they explained to us that they expected twenty-two people would comfortably live here in the ashram when the renovations were completed. "Or forty," said Govinda, "we'll see what [Neem Karoli] Baba's and Ma's ideas are then."

"How many would *you* fit?" Naga Ma asked Lee.

"A hundred!" Lee's voice boomed out as he answered with a bright smile. "Four people in a room this big." We were looking into a small room approximately ten by ten.

Everett asked slyly, tongue in cheek, "If we do that can *we* get an industrial dishwasher?" He was referring to the beautiful new kitchen and laundry equipment we'd been seeing on the tour.

"You do all the dishes by hand now?" asked Govinda, tuning into the side conversation. Everett answered yes and Hanuman said, "We do it by machine so we have time for other work."

In the Hohm Community hundreds and thousands of hours of human resources are put into washing and hand-drying dishes and hanging laundry out to dry on clotheslines. Those are hours that could be put into other kinds of work if we had dishwashers and clothes dryers like everyone else living in the twenty-first century of the First World. But it is Lee's style to keep things grounded and ordinary by such means. We eyed their industrial ironing machine with awe—they were telling us that they ironed all the sheets for all the beds on this ashram! This is something most Americans simply have no reference point for whatsoever, a holdover from an earlier, more civilized aspect of Western culture, still alive in Europe today. We were impressed with how meticulous they were about every detail of their lives.

Lee entered the small meditation room and sat on the floor across from the shrine, which had a magnificent bronze statue of Durga riding a lion and was adorned with fresh flowers, the ubiquitous marigolds. A large white candle burned beside the deity. The floor was covered with Oriental carpets, and above the shrine was a large picture of Neem Karoli Baba and another one of Durgamayi standing in the rocks at the source of the Ganges River at Gangotri. Hanuman said, "Ma has said that it was like being in the eye of a hurricane on the day of Baba's *mahasamadhi*. She was with him in India on the ashram for one year before he died."

Govinda, who had been with Durgamayi from the beginning of her teaching, told us the story of how Durgamayi Ma met their satguru, Neem Karoli Baba. "She saw a picture of Baba in *Be Here Now* and said to herself, 'I have to go to him.' So she went by bus, by train, overland to India to find him. He wasn't easy to find. No one knew where he was. A *gurubhai* of Ma's ran into Baba Ram Dass (Richard Alpert, who wrote *Be Here Now)* at a London restaurant. Ram Dass said, 'You want to get to Neem Karoli Baba, don't you? I'll give you the address,' and he gave it to them." He said that in the last year of Neem Karoli Baba's life, in 1972-73, Durgamayi was with him. Two years later, after Baba's *mahasamadhi*, she went to America to Ma Jaya Bhagavati and lived there with her for seven years before she came back to Germany to teach herself.

We headed back downstairs to the floor where the heaviest construction was underway. They had gathered twelve pairs of old shoes for us to put on our feet in the construction mess—dust, wet paint, chips of dry wall. When Naga Ma offered the shoes to Lee he said, "No thank you," and forged on barefoot, as is his usual practice on all ashrams. His students followed suit. After showing Lee the rest of the building and the construction underway for several temple and shrine rooms and a darshan hall and room for Durgamayi, Laksman said, "Ma knows every detail of all the construction. She knows every craftsman, every detail—Ma does not live in the sky." His statement held an interesting similarity to one of Lee's teaching statements: "God does not live in the sky."

After the tour while we were waiting for the time to walk to the darshan, Lee settled again in the living room. Hanuman asked Lee if it was possible for someone to sing a Shri song for Durgamayi during the darshan. Lee, Deborah and Ed put their heads together for a moment on what songs would work with the acoustic guitar and be appropriate for the darshan space. Ed said, "We could do 'Turn Around.' " Perfect, Lee and Deborah agreed.

Someone from Lee's group recounted that one of Durgamayi's devotees had said that Durgamayi tells them stories of her years with Ma Jaya Bhagavati, which were fiercely demanding. They said that it scares them to think they would have to live the sadhana that Durgamayi lived with Ma Jaya Bhagavati. Upon hearing this Everett turned to Lee and said, "You don't work that way." He seemed to be referring to the fact that Lee doesn't lay down rules or absolute codes of behavior as many teachers do. Instead Lee gives his students copious recommended practices and then leaves it up to the individual to realize the benefits of practice in his or her own case. There is often pressure from sangha mates to live up to the ideal of practice, and Lee regularly emphasizes the critical importance of practice, but *doing* it is up to the individual. Each person has to find his or her way through the maze of resistance, doubt, laziness, fear, selfishness, desire for personal comfort—or whatever keeps us from dedicating our lives completely to a life of God-reference. There is lots of help in that process, if one is willing to take it.

Lee answered Everett, "People who put up, put up. I'm not the Great Shepherd or something. People who want to stay sheep will stay sheep, and people who want to become human will grow up and show up. Hey, that was pretty good—grow up and show up!"

Deborah asked, "So how many are showing up?"

Lee said, "I don't know. We'll know at the end of the day, but you can't measure that. We're starting to measure a little something after twenty-four years of practice. In another twenty years we'll have an idea."

Everett said, "You said if you have to appoint a successor, you've failed. Would you expound on that?"

Lee answered, "Well, a successor has to be there, to arise out of the Work. It has to be obvious." Changing the subject, he turned to Deborah and said, "You should plan an encore."

After another ten minutes or so of enjoying Lee's pleasant, relaxed company as he talked freely about his plans for the future and his wish to eventually settle in New Zealand, Hanuman came in and informed us that it was time to go. It turned out to be a twenty-five minute walk through a beautiful park with very tall, old trees. At the farther end of the park was an old mausoleum with graffiti that read, "Religion is the opium of the *volk*," in German. As a few of us commented on the graffiti Lee quipped, "Politics is the opium of the sleeping world," a reference to people who write slogans on walls.

Lee walked along briskly in his dark blue baggy sweatpants and purple T-shirt, tie-dyed by the children last year. At his waist was the brown leather fanny pack carrying his money and who knows what else. His dreadlocks hung in matted strands, but his head was framed with a floating mass of delicate curls that escaped the confines of the dreads and sprung out like a silver nimbus around his angular, lined face—a face that is sometimes fierce and craggy, ancient and classic in its chiseled lines, and sometimes soft, relaxed and utterly benevolent. Under his left arm he carried a gift for Durgamayi, a large hardbound coffee table volume in German titled *Indien*, by Sivaramamurti. It appeared to be a beautiful photo journal of India.

The darshan began with chanting. Soon Durgamayi came in, dressed in white. She greeted Lee with an embrace as she put a marigold *mala* or garland around his neck in the traditional Indian greeting of honor. Once again the juxtaposition of styles came into play. Durgamayi's fashion of dress was pristine; she was covered from the top of her head, which was tightly wrapped in white, to her hands and feet. Lee on the other hand was wearing the same clothes he'd had on for the last week on the road with Shri. He took the mala off almost immediately and put it on the floor by the pallet where he was sitting. A white cotton blanket covered the pallet that had been arranged for him on the floor with some pillows, just to Durgamayi's left. She was smiling and seemed very happy to see Lee. When she settled on her dais, she engaged her devotees in some brief discussion.

She began to sing "Tvameva," a very traditional and well-loved devotional chant that is also sung on Lee's ashrams in two different melodic versions. She had a very nice voice and sang sweetly. When she was finished she turned to Lee and said, "Baba used to cry when I sang this to him." Then to the group at large she said, "I don't want her . . . " she gestured toward where I was sitting on the back row, "to forget to write that I love Mr. Lee, and that's the reason I'm happy you came here again."

As expected, Durgamayi asked if Lee's students would sing a song. Ed had his acoustic guitar in hand, and he and Deborah sang a beautiful, stirring version of "Turn Around," a new, original Shri song. Durgamayi closed her eyes and listened raptly. After the song there was a period of devotional chanting, led first by Lee's students and then by Durgamayi's students.

After the chanting Durgamayi turned again to Lee and spoke directly to him. "I love your words," she said, holding a copy of *The Alchemy of Transformation* in German in her hands. "When was the book translated?" Lee explained that the translator is a long-time student of E.J. Gold, who is a good friend of Lee's. When the book became available for translating, Matthias Schlossig was the person to do it.

The darshan rolled along with Durgamayi asking Lee a number of questions about his ashram in France, his work in Europe and so on. She particularly expressed an interest in La Ferme de Jutreau.

"We have eleven people living there full-time. The residents are American and German, not French," Lee started.

"But it's in France!" Durgamayi exclaimed.

"That's because the conditions of the ashram are very demanding. That means that the French are too cultured to live at such a place," Lee explained.

Durgamayi said, "What do you mean by demanding? Strict rules? I love strict rules!" She grinned.

Lee jested, "Yeah, we ask the men not to urinate in the bushes." Most of the people in the room laughed as Lee went on without skipping a beat, "All the living quarters are in the barn. We don't have enough income to renovate them." He stopped for a moment, then added, "Thank you for your gift."

Durgamayi smiled, "I read your list." She was referring to a request for donations sent out by La Ferme de Jutreau in the late spring asking for donations of furniture, bedding, and anything else that anyone wanted to give. She was referring to the disk recorder device she had sent Lee a few weeks ago. "We got a donation, and passed it on," she concluded.

Lee went into a description of the outdoor compost toilets at La Ferme de Jutreau. "When the French come for the weekend it's just a weekend experience, and that's fine, but to live that way is another story."

Durgamayi said, "Are you always there?"

Lee said, "Four months in France, eight months in Arizona. As time goes by I'll probably spend more time there." The questions returned to the idea of rules for the ashram. Lee answered, "There are recommendations. My idea is that people receive in direct proportion to what they give. So if they practice, they get a lot, if not . . ."

Durgamayi Ma turned to her devotees and said, "Sounds familiar to you—right?"

Lee continued, "Essentially if people are willing to float and not do much but have a fantasy about what they are doing, they contribute in some ways and we pay the rent, so we let them do what they want. For the people who are really willing to work, the benefits are in a different category altogether.

"We have a one-hour meditation every morning, work, study and vegetarian diet. But when we travel we break the diet as necessary. The Law of Hospitality is higher than the benefits of being vegetarian, so we eat whatever is served to us.

"Essentially my value as a teacher is directly because of my resonance or surrender to my Master. The same is true with my students. So the principle practice is Paying Attention, following my directions, and doing what I say because that creates a resonance. Then who my Master is and His Master, all the way back to God, comes through in an uninterrupted flow, so there is no human being in the way."

Seeming to take this in as being very familiar to her, Durgamayi said in a kind of thoughtful agreement, "It's beyond the person of you—it's what is behind you, the essence, the God essence . . ."

"How do you teach? Do people ask questions about their problems?" one of her devotees asked Lee.

"Usually people's questions are so superficial that they don't evoke much," Lee answered. "They question at the level of what to do about arguments with their wives or husbands . . ."

Durgamayi broke in, looking at Lee's eleven students who were sitting there. She said, "You sound like terrible devotees!" Everyone laughed. She added sweetly, "You're in good company."

Lee continued answering her question, "There are formal questions and answers twice a week and a formal darshan with the exchange of *prasad*, but essentially the influence of my Master is so totally pervasive in the field of my work with my students that I provide or give instruction and the degree to which people do not follow instructions is the degree to which people stew in their own shit! When they get tired of the smell, then they do something about it!"

"Some never do!" Durgamayi said.

"Some think it's always someone else who stinks!" Lee laughed and continued, "I have no choice about what I give. If the need is real, they get something real; if need is superficial, they get something superficial . . ."

Durgamayi added, "We just hold the reigns and they say where to go. I'm willing to go everywhere!"

Govinda said, "Ma has the same difficulties with us."

"I have *no* difficulties!" Durgamayi corrected. "I remember when I met my Mother, my Ma, she used to say, 'Don't worry about my liberation—worry about your own!' Everyone was always wondering, 'Is she liberated, is she not liberated?' But I would love Mr. Lee to say something about the true student. I remember I read something you wrote about this. They were very good words. I believe you can say something about this." She turned toward her students and gestured to them, "Open your ears."

Lee began, "Maybe we could say that the true student lives to please the master in the master's essential form, not in the master's human form. But if we try to distinguish the master's human form from the master's true form, then we will miss what the true form is . . ."

"We miss the point," Durgamayi interjected.

Lee continued, "So the good student doesn't separate the human and the Divine. Who the teacher is is unitive. There is no separation. When people ask me about my Master and read my poetry to Him, they say, 'Oh, you must be so devoted, so surrendered.' I say none of that is true."

"So what is true?" she asked rhetorically, as if speaking for her students.

"Love, surrender, devotion—we can't do," Lee said. "It has to be given by Divine Influence. We can't do that by ourselves. What the good student can do is obedience. We can do that. It's very simple: the master says meditate every day at seven o'clock in the morning, how much simpler can it be? You start with obedience because that's what we *can* do. You don't look for hidden meanings because then you get lost in subjective projections. So you follow the master's directions.

"If I roll the window down in the car, my students will say, 'What does that *mean*?' Nothing. I just want some fresh air. So start with obedience. It's very clear. When you've mastered obedience, then you are given the next task. Shirdi Sai Baba said, 'Every word my disciples say against another disciple hurts me personally.' So the first order of obedience is 'Love your neighbor as yourself,' and your closest neighbor is the sangha. You may want to be supported by the world, but the world will never support you. The most it will be is cordial, because everything we stand for is completely antagonistic to the world. So I have even heard that when spiritual students come to hear Ma talk they are horrified sometimes!"

"Some run away!" Durgamayi laughed, and then said jokingly in a theatrical tone, "I am the Mother! I only live on raw flesh, human blood!"

"So if people who are supposed to be on the path come to talks and are turned off," Lee continued, "imagine the world at large! So we want to be friendly, honest, we don't want to be thieves, but no one in the world will have a prayer of understanding what we are doing."

After further discussions of Durgamayi's vision for their center and Lee's Arizona ashram—how things are structured, the daily schedule, the children's school and so on—Naga Ma told Durgamayi that Lee had said he would fit one hundred devotees into their new ashram. Naga Ma asked Durgamayi how many people she would fit into the ashram once it is finished. Durgamayi said, "I never mentioned a number! You can never be sure. You can be sure of nothing! So enjoy it as it is as long as you have it. We're going to have tea now, and I'll be back." Durgamayi left the room while cake and chai were served.

The sweet smell of heavy incense burned in the air. There were flowers clustered around Durgamayi's divan seat. It was a very traditional darshan scene. One of Durgamayi's devotees brought a sealed white envelope and handed it to Lee. She said, "A donation from Ma—to share for Mr. Lee's work." Lee took the envelope into his hand and said candidly, "Thank you very much, this is a shock!" It was completely unexpected and very generous. Durgamayi Ma entered the room again and went back to her seat.

Someone translated for her, saying, "Ma would like to sit with us together in silence and then say goodbye. She hopes you will soon come back."

Durgamayi added, "Just like this. Just a little silence." We sat in meditation, and after about twenty minutes she roused herself and said, "Who wants to leave this place? No one." She laughed.

She and her devotees prepared for the passing out of *prasad*, and she turned to Lee and said, "Mr. Lee, you will not get prasad because you *are prasad*. I thank you for coming here again. You bless this place. Thank you for coming." She walked around the room placing a piece of prasad, halvah, in each person's hand, then posed with Lee for a photograph. Two shots were quickly accomplished, they embraced and she said to Lee, "*Pranams to Lee. Have a good journey.*" We left immediately after she exited the space.

July 28, 1999
Lucerne, Switzerland

Lee and company spent the night last night at the sangha household in Freiburg. In the morning Lee stood down by the curb waiting for the van and the car to arrive to pack our things up and take off for Lucerne. There had been some tears and breakdown exhibited by some of the women of Lee's group after brunch. Now the men stood together talking, while four of the five women on the tour were standing separate from the others, each one isolated and in her own world, but seemingly unconscious of how deeply impacting this was on the moment in the spiritual master's company. There was a mood of contraction, of judgement and alienation that was tacit to the design of how the women were manifesting in the moment. Lee turned to one of the women and said, "The men are all clustered together talking, and the women are all spread out down the street—one of them there, and there," he pointed down the block, "and there. You should write about that for the book."

Every space with Lee, even when we are waiting on the side of the street, has a subtlety and necessity, a power and presence and aliveness. When we shut each other out psychically or physically, it affects Lee's ability to work effectively within the perimeters of the space. But perhaps the bigger issue is that any time there is dissent or alienation between sangha members, Lee is affected deeply by it. It presages the formation of "the Church of Lozowickism," with its various competing factions appearing after his death, and the approach of the unenlightened, rigid orthodoxy. This is something Lee has vigorously warned against over the years, and to see the firm foundation for such a thing, here amongst his devotees, is always cause for great pain and heartache.

It is exactly like he had said the day before when he quoted Shirdi Sai Baba—whenever Lee's devotees are demonstrating anything short of teamwork, communion, mutual respect and regard, he notices it. Depending on the severity of conflict, he can be anywhere from deeply affected by it—to the extent of getting sick, if the conflict is prolonged over time—or just remaining depressed for weeks. Lee's depressions are legendary among his senior students, and extremely painful. He hasn't been in one since the irritated and depressed state he was in during the India trip last winter. That one lasted for less than two weeks, fortunately, probably entirely due to the joy of being in the physical company of Yogi Ramsuratkumar.

The women came back together after Lee's prodding. Almost immediately the van and car drove up, we got in and moved on to the next opportunity to practice the nuances of relationship—myriad forms of kindness, generosity and compassion in subtle and gross expressions.

As we arrived at the hotel where Shri would be staying in Lucerne—a beautiful place provided for the performing artists by the organizers of the Lucerne Blues Festival—a man drove up immediately, got out of his car and approached the band at the curb. "Are you Shri?" he asked politely. "Welcome! We just wanted to make sure you knew that your sound check will be at three o'clock this afternoon." He had been waiting for Shri to arrive in order to greet the group and give them directions to the stage.

Shri arrived at the stage at three to set up and were told by the stage managers that the band was under the special patronage of the president of the festival. All the other bands had been booked through a professional agent, but Shri had somehow caught the president's attention. He had seen their press pack and listened to the CD, loved the music and then booked the band himself. Now all of the stage managers had been informed that Shri should be taken care of with special attention.

The stage was a beautiful concrete and stone domed open-air affair, set right beside the vast lake that winds its way through Lucerne. The high domed ceiling and inside walls of the stage were complex mosaic patterns of inlaid marble and other stones, creating an art deco effect. All around the stage were tents, kiosks, food, jewelry, clothing and crafts vendors set up lakeside for the festival. There were signs for Heineken and Coca-Cola everywhere. Chestnut trees grew all around, and on the other side of a high green hedge behind the stage and running adjacent to the path along the lake was a street lined with cafés and shops at the ground floor of old, four-story buildings. Up above were apartments with flower boxes on every window and patios on the top floors lined with shrubbery and planters spilling over with flowers. People walked leisurely along the wide concrete path by the lake, and boats were docked all along the way. The water was pristine, clear and beautiful. A few boats sailed out on the water, making a beautiful tableau with the lovely old city and lake set against high rising green mountains and fluffy white clouds in the gentle blue sky. The weather was absolute perfection. The whole circumstance promised a fantastic evening.

At four o'clock Lee, Shri and roadies went to dinner, provided at a restaurant just down the promenade. A choice of fish or lamb was offered to the band; most everyone chose lamb, one of Lee's favorites. During dinner Steve asked Lee questions about the direction he should take for a new book project Lee had given to him, an overview of current Fourth Way teachers and schools. Lee gave him a list of people to ask for interviews, including Michel de Salzmann, Peter Brook and William Patrick Patterson.

Deborah had chosen not to eat with the group because we were eating so close to performance time, which was at six o'clock. It's very difficult to breathe on a full stomach with the depth and ease that is needed for singing, as most singers will testify. In the middle of the meal Everett looked at Lee with his plate of lamb and cauliflower and asked, "It doesn't bother you, eating right before the gig?"

Lee answered, "Yes, it does, but I'm going to do it anyway. Waddling onto the stage isn't my idea of fun—but eating lamb and potatoes before the gig is!"

It could be easy to gloss over Lee's statements like, "I'm going to do it anyway." But the obvious next question, in the spirit of apprenticing to the master, is what would induce Lee to do something that is uncomfortable for him or that doesn't work for him when he could easily ask for and be provided with whatever he wants? One of the constant teaching communications that Lee makes on the road is "roll with the punches," or "take whatever is offered or given and don't ask for anything—especially to be an exception, to be given special attention." It is an expression of a much greater theme, of beggary in action. This concept of beggary is an important aspect of Lee's teaching. In Lee's case beggary is a natural consequence of Spiritual Slavery and surrender to the Will of God. It has always seemed like a very advanced dimension of practice and alignment with Lee, because it can involve quite subtle levels of sacrifice, particularly the sacrifice of comfort. It can also be very obvious, like just accepting whatever is given to one without asking for anything more or different to accommodate one's "individual" needs, even when those needs are perfectly legitimate.

Most of us, despite serious attempts to practice, are habitually looking for ways to shore up ego, to provide small comforts for ourselves all along the way, perhaps especially when we are traveling in a tight group with Lee in a very "hot" chamber where there is little or no personal space or privacy. There is stress, discomfort and tension experienced in traveling with Lee that is just a natural part of the process, and then Lee has a way of creating internal pressure and heat for each person, without "doing" anything at all to make it happen. It just happens around him as a natural extension of his field of influence.

For example, one aspect of that stress is the consequence of eating off the diet for days because one is eating the food that is provided by the hospitality of one's hosts at each gig. Once the body becomes habituated to the clean burn of the particular vegetarian diet of Lee's students (mostly raw vegetables, fruit or cooked vegetables and grains), it is difficult to eat meat, sugar, refined foods, cheese and dairy products for days at a time. At first it is grand and celebratory; desires are being fulfilled and we look forward to the "treats" and rich meals. Then it slowly becomes more of a sacrifice, because the stabilizing and clarifying benefits of practice begin to be challenged or eroded. This can bring on some significant discomfort, both physically and emotionally.

When traveling one also doesn't have the steadying influence of the ashram rhythm— meditation at seven o'clock in the morning, productive work, the dharma input of seminars, darshans and After Dinner Talks, time with the children and so on. Anytime we are outside of sanctuary—meaning one of the ashrams or a practicing household of sangha members—there are a number of forces that come into play and must be dealt with for what they are: distractions, seductions and fascinations away from the focus of sadhana. In this way traveling gives one the opportunity to see just how strong the mood of practice is in one's own case without the benefit and help of the ashram structure. This morning in Freiburg there were some tears shed over the accumulated stress of the trip. Now all was quiet and calm, as if a storm had passed through and cleared the air a little. It was time for the gig.

Walking back to the stage area and taking our seats while the band changed clothes backstage at five forty-five, we saw that about one hundred fifty people had gathered for the performance, many of them sitting in the two hundred or so seats set up below the stage. They waited for the band to appear, and soon enough they came out. Lee was wearing a pink, sleeveless Tweetie Bird T-shirt, black jeans, black suspenders and black sunglasses. He had his tambourine in hand, and right away started strutting around the stage, walking from one side to the other as if he was marking off territory. Deborah went into "Blues School" and the music lit up the place. The sound was crystal clear and perfect, almost startling in its effect. The bass and drums were laying down the beat, the backbone, and the guitar was sassy and stinging. The whole band felt tremendously charged and in sync. Next Lee sang "Treats," one of his new songs, lyrics by Lozowick and composed by Ed Flaherty.

> She's the kind of girl
> Y'all should have before you die
> But she's my girl now
> And I keep her satisfied
> Oh I treats the women right
> I treats the women wrong
> But I always treats them, that's the thing
> They all love me before long.

The music churned along with a fabulous rhythm, and just before he broke into the next verse, Lee said to the audience, "This is my favorite verse!" He sang:

> If you bite me baby
> It ain't blood that you will find
> Cause I got sugar in my veins
> And lovin' on my mind!

Who is this guy who makes such arrogant statements? Poetry depends on metaphor, implication, symbol and image to make its point. The Bauls use the earthiest of metaphors to implicate the dharma, to point toward the path. What "girl" was Lee was referring to now? One's sexual partner, or Shakti, Prakriti, Kali or, one might say, Vajrayogini? In any case, the female wisdom principle. He's certainly on good terms with the Jewel of Creation, in whatever form one might clothe her. How does he keep her satisfied? "I got sugar in my veins and lovin' on my mind." Through worship and adoration.

Perhaps from the Baul perspective the only thing the goddess, brought to the full blossom of evolution in awakened consciousness, wants of her children is for them to live in love of the Creator. The message of the song points toward the pinnacle of Enlightened Duality—the bodily love of the personal Beloved. In the Baul path, and in many other traditions as well, the soul is perceived as feminine in relation to a masculine Divine Absolute as the personal Beloved; the human soul becomes Radha in relationship to Krishna. The singer seems to speak from the perspective of both Radha and Krishna, or lover and beloved. If you are a *khepa*, why not? Chaitanya, patron saint of the Bauls, was the embodiment of both Krishna and Radha, and was often portrayed with golden skin to indicate the perfection of this interplay between divine opposites. On the stage Shri's patchwork bag lay over the center stage monitor just below Deborah and Lee, a symbol of the band's connection to the Bauls of Bengal, who wear patchwork jackets as signals of their commitment to the particular sadhana of the Bauls.

At this point about five hundred people stood listening under the shelter of the chestnut trees and the lowering sky, now full of dense gray clouds. The volume of the music was loud and the sound seemed to be broadcasting in all directions, to penetrate through the air in sound waves that traveled far, like a call that brought more and more people who joined in the mass. In between songs Lee said, "It's nice to be in your beautiful city! We're from Prescott, Arizona. We don't have a big lake there!" He laughed.

As Deborah began the first verse to "Worried," Lee jaunted over to Everett and danced next to him. Shifting shapes, Lee now looked like a sprite or mischievous satyr onstage—

a playful Puck, up to no-good in the best possible way. He held a black tambourine in each hand and shook them firmly to the beat. Holding both tambourines he danced on light feet and beat the tams in front and behind him in rhythm to the music, tapping them together with dexterity. The whole picture of his movement—feet, legs, hips, arms, hands, head, and then tambourines as extensions of himself—created what appeared like a choreography of movement, and yet it was spontaneous. This image of an unfettered moving center communicates the essence of the body's wisdom. It is a big part of Lee's transmission onstage. He plays the tams with whimsy and passion; they are simple instruments, and yet he takes them seriously, playing with an abandon and certainty that most musicians aspire to with more sophisticated instruments.

The band moved into "Left My Baby Standing." There were at least one thousand people there at this point, the aisles and walkways packed with people standing and listening, moving, swaying to the beat, all the way back to the shores of the lake. The audience was very Swiss—affluent, good-looking, relaxed. Looking at them I got the feeling that they have no problems here in lovely, socially enlightened Lucerne. People were listening to Shri's concert with a kind of cultured presence of attention one rarely sees at a blues festival in the U.S. "Left My Baby Standing" seared through all those cultural differences and rang out the truth of the blues. It was like a dharma bell ringing, like the sound of the traditional conch being blown. Ed went into his slide guitar solo, and every note was a crystal reverberation through the air. The wails, cries and moans of the slide guitar tore at the clay façade of denial. Clay—dissolves in water, cracks in fire, hardens to stone over time.

Ed went into his second solo, the crescendo of the song. The crashing chords of the guitar and crystalline whine of the slide strung the vital reaches of the body out on a wire of fierce feeling. Through the ferocious drums, the deep-down bass, the rhythmic resounding chords, the reality that all life is suffering came pounding into our bodies. Lee took over the mike and sang his verses, "I still miss my baby / but she don't miss me no more . . ."

This song created its own chamber which rode on the fuel of the charge that had been built and sustained in the first four songs of the set. After the song ended Lee said humorously into the mike, "Okay! We're gonna do a brand new song. Usually we do this at two a.m. after a night of music, when people are relaxed, so I'm a little nervous about doing it. To ease my tension, will all the women wearin' no underwear please come on up here to the front of the stage!" Several women in the crowd laughed loudly and clapped their approval to this bit of sexy provocation as Lee went into "Hound," a raunchy, lascivious, satirical jest:

> If you've got a pussy
> That needs help night or day
> Do not hesitate
> Call me right away!
> You know you can trust me
> I'll be somewhere round this town
> I can do the good work
> I'm your old pussy hound.

Lee's voice went gravelly and raucous on the "call me right away" as he jerked his thumbs toward his chest several times for emphasis, an arrogant and confident rake. "I'll give that pussy sweet relief! Hah, hah, hah!" he laughed like a devil, the features of his strong face lending themselves to the daemonic as the song came to a close. People clapped and whistled, enjoying Lee's theatrical style.

The building power of the music hung in the air as Deborah went into "Two Hands." Lee was exultant. He seemed to be feeding off the energies of the rapt crowd, which had swelled to about fifteen hundred now. People stood drinking beer at tables under umbrellas that said "Heineken" or watched as they stood packed in shoulder to shoulder all around the edges of the seated audience. As Lee sang "The Sky Is Crying," a group of children began to play in the dirt and gravel beneath the stage. The crowd was relaxing, getting in the groove.

The band went into "Born Under a Bad Sign." The guitar solo on this song often throws its audience into some kind of altered or interior state. It is a song that demands a kind of letting go because its effects can be quite devastating if you follow what it delivers to the senses, the body's organs of perception. Tonight the feelings that were drawn out were of an exquisite pain. The music rang out through space and time, communicating a certain hopelessness, an anguished cry about the abject nature of the human predicament, caught between the boundless light of the Divine and dense matter, sleeping and unredeemed, but seeking redemption. The music reverberated at deeper levels, churned up insight and sank in waves of contemplation, leading further into the labyrinth. It spoke of how the human soul, caught in the snares of illusion, cries silently for the promise of Creation. The soul cries for the love of the blind, deaf and dumb Creator who only remembers his Creation when its suffering becomes so great that a flame bursts into light. An ember that has glowed for eons in the dark spontaneously combusts, and consciousness flares into being in the moment. As Shiva opens one unconcerned eye and glances inward, a corresponding shaft of light pierces the veils of his Shakti, his multiform Parvati, his Durga, the grand Warrioress. It pierces her sleeping lids, strikes her heart, sunk deep in its fold and coursing with divine blood. A cry escapes from the lips of the goddess, and in that moment the sound of her cry is the very notes coming from Ed's guitar.

Coming back at the end of the song to the surrounding scene of people, music, the ground beneath my feet, I wondered at the power of the music to transport and transform. Ed had gone transcendental during his guitar solo, but what did this small, invincible man with the jingling tambourines, dancing like a flame in the wind, have to do with such miracles? Without his presence "Born Under a Bad Sign" would lose its mysterious depths and potencies and become just be another great blues song. This invisible miracle was the guru's work of the night—through the music, Creation was brought to life, and Shakti was given voice.

The result of that reverie was, for me, an immersion in the pain of separative existence as years of sadhana weighed heavy on my heart. As one goes along in the accumulation of years on the path, the pain of separation faced within the crucible of real conscience becomes so great that it is unbearable. It is a conflict of opposites, what the ancient alchemists called the Great Work. It is also the yes and no of the human condition. We want God-realization, liberation, and yet we are unable to surrender the desire to remain separate. We are unable to be really different, or to change ourselves. We can only pray, practice and hold the intention, and perhaps through our obedient association with the guru, we will magnetize the transformative power of Grace into our lives.

The band had gone into "Stormy Monday," which Lee sings. Ed's mystic guitar had laid down the flagstones, and now a doorway appeared in which Lee's multidimensional presence onstage became darshan. There was nothing unusual about this darshan, and that was what made it so deadly, so accurate. He appeared as just a theatrical guy delivering the blues, while the subtle sense organs were literally pelted with perceptions that hit a target that exists beyond the flat world perspective of things.

Lee sang out passionately, "Lord have mercy, have mercy on me," then said into the mike, "I'm cryin' Lord—you got to hear me!" The ten children playing below and around the stage were sweetly innocent. Their innocence and all that it implied carried the sound and message of Lee's voice deeper into the heart of the moment. Whoever got on Lee's train was praying with him tonight. Lee sang the refrain again, "Lord have mercy, Lord have mercy on me," and then, "I'm beggin' Lord!" Was he praying for the release from the pain of separation, the illusion of separation from God, which pressed so relentlessly in that moment for recognition? It is a suffering that must be recognized, because only through that spark of recognition does realization become possible. This is why the guru has the blues, why he must sing the blues for us.

Lee's cheerful voice rang out as the song ended, "We've got two more songs for you tonight! Everyone will recognize the last song. This next song is called 'I Seen.' It's bad grammar, but we can get away with it for the sake of art!" This was one of the new songs of the summer that has captured so many hearts—a great song of social protest, lyrics by Lee and composed by Ed.

I seen the devil takin' souls
People unable to refuse
I seen the devil takin' souls
People unable to refuse
I'm just a middle-class white boy
Singing the blues
I seen lots of hate and prejudice
And I paid some dues
I seen lots of hate and prejudice
And I paid some dues
I'm just a middle-class white boy
Singing the blues
I seen the world go up in smoke
People ain't got no clues
I seen the world go up in smoke
People ain't got no clues
I'm just a middle-class white boy
Singing the blues.

While Ed played the guitar solo Lee walked over to him, leaned down and in close to listen to the notes coming off of the strings, as if he was there to take the message. Three children danced in front of the stage now and three more sat up on the far right of the stage where some makeshift steps led from the ground to the stage floor. They were just a few feet away from Lee and Deborah.

Without stopping to take a breath Ed segued the song directly into the steaming first chords of "Voodoo Chile," by Jimi Hendrix. Right away Lee went back to Rakini on drums and started juicing her, playing the tambourines in great whirling wild circles, smashing them passionately into his hands, while Rakini—her eyes locked into Lee's—crashed the drumsticks into the cymbals and vibrating drum heads in time with his movements. It was if a hurricane of passion was churning out of the combined force of Lee and Rakini.

When Lee performs he relates onstage with each of his students in different ways. He coaxes, coaches, listens with a voracious ear, calls for more, shakes his head in tender appreciation, jumps up and down, dances and moves like a *heruka*. He dances in sync with Deborah, Nachama on harp, Tina on bass, Ed and Everett on guitar, working up the energy to a frenzy. It looks like he is working with the moving center of his students in this way through a physical demonstration of his own higher moving center. As the individual members of the band tune into his movement, they have the opportunity to get a taste of liberation, of how this activated higher moving center feels in their own bodies. Sometimes he will playfully tap a musician on the arm, back or leg in time to the beat with his tambourine as he dances beside them.

This is both a transmission and an instruction through action, touch and demonstration. Lee onstage *is* movement as prayer, or one could say a communication that has the power to draw the attention of higher beings in the realms of God's messengers, the fierce and holy angels. These angels seem to be nothing at all like the angels of modern Christian iconography or New Age paraphernalia; they are inhuman, terrible and simultaneously awe-inspiring in their beauty. They come and feast on the subtle food produced by a few human beings who are attempting the evolution of being. It sounds outrageous, but every shaman since the dawn of time has been enacting the same ritual. It is a natural fact of the chain of being.

In the midst of "Voodoo Chile" Ed looked like he was still in the flush of the *bhava* that drifted through the air during "Born Under a Bad Sign." As he went into the solo Deborah left the stage, walked down the wooden pallets and big boxes where the children sat by the front of the stage and onto the ground. Matthew helped her down the last step and she walked over to the crowd and started shaking hands with people. "I'm short of cord here, that's about it," she said, smiling at the crowd that surged around her as she came up against the end of the length of wire on her microphone. "I'll stay down here. If you know the words, sing along!"

The crowd clapped and cheered, enthusiastic and yet still polite. If we were in the States, considering how much energy had been whipped up in the audience as a whole, people would have been going wild. While Ed's solo went orgiastic, Lee made his way across the stage and suddenly Ed was leaning back on Lee, who had bent over at the knees to make a bed of sorts upon which Ed could lean back and practically recline. They were pressed together along the length of their bodies, spine to spine, neck to tail. One could make a case for classic kundalini initiation in this *mudra* that Lee has performed with Ed many times in the past year, since it first appeared last summer at the gig in Chatellerault. Ed gives his guitar playing to the guru as the gift of himself in this gesture of surrender, and Lee takes it all on. Ed seemed ecstatic when he came back up. He was fluid, dancing on one foot, jumping up and down.

The huge crowd stayed absorbed in the music until the end, when loud whistles, cheers and prolonged clapping took over. They were begging for more. The sheer volume created by the claps and cheers of fifteen hundred people went on and on until Lee came forward and said, "We're happy to play one more for you. Thank you for staying with us, and for your applause."

Deborah's honeyed voice came over the mike, saying, "We've got one more of our street-style blues for you. We're rough but we're ready! All these songs are autobiographical, even those that were written by other people! How you figure that?!" There was a smile in her voice. "Thank you for stayin' with us, for your generous attention!" The crowd loved them and demonstrated with the clamor of their applause and cheers.

Lee came offstage looking enlivened and sweating a little. When several of his students who were in the audience began to praise the extraordinary experience of the gig he was completely ordinary about the whole thing. Typically when his students comment on how powerful a gig has been he is respectful but at the same time extremely detached. If someone refers to mystical dimensions experienced in Lee's presence he often shrugs his shoulders in surprise and says, "Hunhh." In this way he instructs us to draw no conclusions about anything that occurs, to avoid fascination and stay rooted in the earth of the present moment.

Now he went to the sound tent with Deborah to sign CDs. A small slender brown-haired man came up to get his CD signed. He touched his heart and said over and over again to Lee, "Thank you. A good concert." His warm blue eyes never left Lee's face, but crinkled up in a humble smile. He seemed to be feeling a deep rapport with Lee and the band, as if he felt he knew them personally by virtue of having been so deeply touched. Lee signed the CD and shook his hand, smiling back.

Lee wanted to listen to the next performer, so he took a seat on the second row in front of the stage. As soon as he was seated a man in the row in front of him turned around and thanked him enthusiastically for the performance. Soon the Eugene Hideaway Bridges Band was on, from Houston, Texas. Eugene, a big barrel of an African American man came out with a guitar strapped on that looked like he was born wearing it. He greeted the audience candidly, with genuine warmth and heart. He said, "I'm Eugene Hideaway Bridges, and we're coming to you from Houston, Texas!" His show was fabulous and inspiring. He was a hard working blues man—a great example of the tradition. Lee sat through the whole show, watching and listening very intently, absorbing and feeding from the authenticity and genuine heart that Eugene brought to his art.

Afterward a small group went with Lee to the auditorium nearby to hear one of the main attractions of the festival, Dr. John. He was good, but lacking in the natural presence of soul that Eugene exuded with little effort. It was after midnight when we all got back to the hotel.

July 29, 1999
Metz, France

Leaving Switzerland the Shri caravan drove for three hours to Metz, France, arriving at around three-thirty in the afternoon. The people who were hosting the band were a small local group that organizes summer musical events financially supported by the town. Two of their representatives came and guided us through a labyrinth of old stone buildings to a room where a narrow rectangular table was set up. They began to pull food out of the tiny refrigerator—*jambon, fromage, cous cous, beurre*. They brought cold drinks and placed baguettes on the table, speaking rapidly to Ed, who was able to interact in French with relative ease. They told the band that they had planned a late dinner after the gig, which was scheduled from eight to ten o'clock.

After getting settled in the hotel rooms that were provided by the hosts, Lee returned to the sight where the band was setting up. The gig would be played in a cobblestone square where five streets converged to create a plaza or neighborhood courtyard of sorts. In the middle of the square was a fountain with four cherubs holding up the pedestal from which water flowed at the highest point of the fountain back into the round pool at its base. On one side of the plaza was a beautiful old Gothic cathedral; on another side a small, more Romanesque church, and in between cafés, shops, a *salon de thé,* an art boutique and a music shop. Up above were apartments with wooden shutters and balconies with flowers—petunias, geraniums, lobelia—trailing from wrought iron railings. There were four beautiful trees planted in each of the four corners of the square, and fat lazy pigeons roamed around looking for a crumb of bread. They were obviously used to being fed and totally unconcerned with the human population that sat at the many tables and chairs with their *café crème* and expresso. Surveying the scene, Lee sat and played bridge while the band set up and did a sound check.

At eight o'clock on the dot the band started playing. There were about five hundred people packed into the square already, most of them ordering wine or drinks or food, beer and coffee from the café, which did a booming business all night. The faces of the patrons were turned expectantly toward the band, waiting and ready.

"Are you ready for the blues?" Lee called out over the P.A. "Did you come to have a good time tonight? Well in case you can't find one, we brought it with us!" It was Lee's welcome to the crowd. "We love France! We're so happy to be back here!" A ripple of excitement and applause ran through the audience as the band started out with "Blues School."

Overall the crowd was strikingly handsome, well off and friendly; they seemed to be lovers of music and culture. A grand attitude of expectancy and enthusiasm characterized the mood. Children of all ages ran happily through the crowd of teenagers, young adults, middle-aged people and elders. Even though Metz is a large city, the crowd felt and acted like a village that had come together to celebrate. As more people flowed into the square and all the chairs and tables were taken up, people sat everywhere—on the circular edge of the fountain, on the cathedral and church steps. There was a tremendously liberal feeling in the crowd as it swelled to seven hundred, then one thousand, then fifteen hundred until the streets were jam-packed with people.

Lee had been playing the wooden sticks onstage to Deborah's "Course of Action." Now he took the mike and said, "How's everybody doing on the steps over there? There's plenty of room to dance over here by the stage! Come closer! Don't be shy—we're not!" The guitar immediately went into the first, classic blues notes of "The Sky Is Crying" to resounding claps and cheers—everybody recognized the blues. A woman in a tight blue dress got up and started dancing her way through the crowd up to the stage. She found a spot by the stage and established herself there for the rest of the night, dancing. Ed finished a guitar solo to a chorus of whistles and applause.

"Hey, if anybody feels like dancing, there's plenty of room between the tables," Lee schmoozed with the crowd. "Here the men can dance too! We were just in Switzerland last night . . . a couple of women danced there, but the men wouldn't dance. Here in France the men can dance. If you don't boogie now, you will later tonight, right? We're happy to be back in France—we love it here!"

People loved this rap from Lee and responded with whoops and shouts of encouragement. Deborah sang "Jump" and Lee danced with abandon on the stage, demonstrating exactly what he was just talking about. He seemed to be having a great time with tambourine in hand, jumping along with the song, swaying, keeping time to the beat. He was demonstrating the essential nature of the rhythm. He took the mike and sang "Country Boy" and then the very danceable "I Seen," also known affectionately as "Middle Class White Boy."

"Tout le monde danse!" Lee yelled into the mike. Several couples moved up to the space just in front of the four-foot-high portable stage. The crowd continued to grow, but no matter how big it got, it seemed like a single organism that was focused on the band and exuded a mood of great enjoyment. Lee smiled and waved to a very small child who was riveted to him as she was held in her mother's arms at a table near the stage. The band played another great dance tune, "Dreamin' Bout Dreamin'," and people started hanging out the huge open windows of the café, leaning out over the big window planters full of red and salmon-colored geraniums to hear and see better. Toes were tapping while hands were beating out the rhythm on chair arms and knees. Many were singing along to the best of their ability. People were laughing and joking with each other, ordering more drinks. Shri plunged into "Worried" with Lee and Everett, the "theatrical" entertainers of the band, dancing around the stage.

The band changed the mood with "Left My Baby Standing" and went sad and deep. Two beautiful little girls danced together holding hands right in front of Deborah, who came down off the stage saying, "I gotta come down here where you *people* are!" The woman in blue came up right away and started dancing with Deborah while she sang. It was almost time for Lee's verses to the song, and he brought his mike out into the crowd while Ed went into his solo. Lee's microphone chord stretched out past the fountain in the middle of the square, allowing him to walk out into the crowd and connect with people. He smiled and nodded, stopped to shake hands or clap someone on the shoulder. Deborah was nearby, both of them smiling and shaking people's hands.

This gig, perhaps more than any other of the summer, brought to mind images of the Bauls singing in the villages, surrounded by hundreds or thousands of village people— connecting with the grass roots of humanity. It is the way the Bauls of Bengal perform, in the streets, surrounded by ordinary people. Out in the crowd Lee shook his dreadlocks and jumped to the rhythms of the guitar. Deborah had the tambourine at this point as Lee started singing his verses of "Left My Baby Standing." By now there were seven or eight children dancing as well as three or four couples up near the stage. As Lee began his return to the stage from the middle of the crowd he knelt beside the same small child that now sat in her father's arms near the stage. Lee held her hand for a moment, then he sat on the edge of the stage to finish the song with an original verse, "Everybody wants a baby / How come we all fight? / We all want love and happiness / How come we all fight? / People you got to get together / that's what the blues is all about."

The song ended. "You're a *great* audience! Thank you very much!" Lee yelled out to the crowd. He turned the mike over to Everett to do "G-Thang" and suddenly there were a dozen children dancing up near the stage and more adults dancing with partners. "How many people out there speak English?" Lee yelled after the song was over. A large number of people yelled back and raised their arms in support. "You people are a good audience! Ed doesn't break strings for a bad audience!" Ed had broken probably a record number of guitar strings on this night, he was playing with such passion and fury.

Lee taught the crowd the response to "The Blues Is Alright," and soon he had about two-thirds of the two thousand people who were there repeating the response, "Hey, hey, the blues is alright," on cue. He had a fabulous rapport with this audience; he was giving to them and they were giving to him in a reciprocal flow. "Give yourself a hand!"

he called out after the song to big cheers and applause that reverberated through the small plaza.

Deborah went into the heavy-hitters, "Ball and Chain" and then "Born Under a Bad Sign." By now the crowd was loosened up; spirits were flowing freely, there was a strong feeling of generosity, of the common human bond, of friendship and enjoyment. The man with the small child who had connected with Lee brought her up to the stage. She reached her hand out to Lee and he took it again in his own. Deborah smiled and played peekaboo with her. It seemed like all cultural boundaries were dissolved as Ed went into his solo and Lee started the kind of whole body dancing that he often does onstage. Looking out over the scene was like looking at a sea of people. The streets were packed in every direction. In the building up above the band a little girl about seven years old with blonde hair leaned out the balcony to see better as she danced to the music. Applause roared through the square and echoed down the streets.

Lee sang "Loser Blues" and threw in a spontaneous new verse while Ed made a debut on blues piano. "Gave my baby my worship / It wasn't all that much / Gave my baby my worship / Though it wasn't all that much / All I really needed was / A little tender touch!"

"Thank you very much! We have certainly enjoyed being here with you in Metz. We've enjoyed it very much," Lee said over the mike. It was as if he was talking to an old friend. "We travel all over, to Germany and Switzerland—we always love coming back to France! That's the truth! I'm not kidding you!" Lee spoke with such authenticity and genuine feeling that even if people didn't speak English they had to catch his meaning. "We've got two more songs for you—we appreciate you being here and staying with us!"

Ed careened into a mystical version of "Voodoo Chile" as darkness was falling and the cathedral lights came on, accentuating its gothic beauty against the deep azure blue of the evening sky. Lee held both tambourines now and played them like a wild spirit set loose. Ed's solo was delirious, Bacchanalian, spinning and weaving people into an exalted state. Deborah sang from the middle of the crowd, out by the fountain. Suddenly there were police lights, *gendarmes* parked at the edge of the crowd to signal the traffic to make a detour around the square. The entire plaza was flooded with people. The intense mood that drifted and pulsed in the night air was so strong that it felt like a Dionysian revelry could break loose at any moment.

"Thank you very much! *Bonne soirée, merci beaucoup!* Keep the party going!" Lee yelled to shouts of *"Encore, encore!"* The crowd was so worked up there was no way they were going to let the band go without another song. Lee picked up the mike and went into "Smokestack Lightnin'." There were children everywhere; one little boy had fallen asleep as he stood leaning against his father's leg. The dancers near the stage were euphoric, the whole crowd had stayed glued to the band until the end of the encore. I wondered what would have happened if the band had kept playing into the night. Even though only a few people actually danced, the whole plaza rocked and hummed with energy.

"We've a had a good time here with you—thank you! Maybe we'll see you next year!" Lee called out. Everyone in the band looked completely ecstatic. It was exhilarating to see them so enlivened. Some of them were glistening with sweat as they signed CDs and talked to people after the last song. It took a long time to take down the equipment; most of the time Lee sat on the side of the stage signing CDs and talking with people.

Finally Lee and the band went to a restaurant with their hosts and had a midnight dinner. The hosts were very happy and even amazed with the evening. They mentioned to Tina that they had never had that many people at any of the summer concerts they sponsor. There was some talk about the band coming back next year. Finally, at one-thirty Lee went back to his hotel. He got up for breakfast with the band the next morning and then drove back to Freiburg, Germany.

July 30, 1990
Freiburg

Lee's time on tour with the band was rapidly coming to a close. Back in Freiburg Lee stayed again at the sangha household, who also arranged lodgings for everyone traveling with the band. After a gathering over dinner at the apartment with about twenty-five people, Lee, Thomas and a few others drove to Blue Monday, a local blues club in Freiburg on the edge of town, where Lee would meet up with the members of Shri who were there setting up the equipment. Lee had been told that the club was a popular haunt of blues lovers, with a beer garden outside and restaurant/club inside. Rumor was that it was often packed with people—a really lively place. It promised to be another great night.

As soon as he arrived Lee joined Deborah and Rakini at a rectangular wooden table in front of the space where the band was set up to play. Their "stage" was an informal situation—the wooden floor of the restaurant, with the instruments and amps set up along one wall facing the tables.

Soon after Lee sat down a man with brown hair and eyes walked in and introduced himself to Lee and Deborah as the "doorman" for the club. With a German accent he said apologetically, "There is a free party in Freiburg tonight where many people will go, and it's warm outside, so people may want to stay outside," he apologized, "so we do the best we can tonight." He shrugged. Obviously he was not expecting a big crowd for Shri's performance. He said that he would be standing at the door collecting money, and that he wanted to charge seven dollars instead of eight dollars because he thought more people would come in if the door charge was cheaper. The news was of some importance because Shri was only getting paid "the door" rather than a fixed fee. As the doorman walked away Lee said in an irritated and forceful tone of voice, "If one dollar makes a difference, if people won't come in because of a one dollar difference, fuck 'em. You know what I mean?"

When I asked Lee what he meant, he said that such a concession would reduce the whole effort of Shri coming to Europe to play to a level of pettiness that was unpalatable to him. But more importantly, to reduce the price of entry is to reduce the value of the music itself, and Shri has something of great value to offer to people. Werner Erhard went into prisons to give the est program for free many years ago. After the first time or two, he refused to do it for free anymore and insisted that the prisoners give something, even a pack of cigarettes.

The principle behind this is that one only benefits from having received something if one has paid for it in some way. It is a dynamic law of the universe. As Lee said, "If Shri is going to whore itself we can keep playing redneck bars in Arizona. We don't need to come all the way to Europe for that. People should be coming because they enjoy the music, because they love the music, because the music has value for them and they are willing to pay for that." It seemed to me that Lee's vehemence in this instance was his gut-level reaction to what the doorman was proposing: to acquiesce to the mentality of scarcity in this instance was antagonistic to the momentum and context of Shri.

462

Taking the news in stride, Deborah sat making up the set list for the evening while Lee wrote new lyrics in his notebook. Ute walked up and made a request for "Blind Devotion," a song written by Lee and composed by Ed. Lee said, "Maybe."

Looking up from her task at hand, Deborah said with mock seriousness, "Never tell a devotee 'maybe.'"

"Because they always think it means yes," I added the unvoiced but obvious remainder of the thought.

Lee said, "Then they're making a *big* mistake."

Keeping the banter going, Rakini said, "But we learn from our mistakes!"

Deborah extemporized, "It takes some of us longer to learn than others—and you can quote me on that!" she pointed to my notebook and then laughed at herself.

Rakini added facetiously, "Yeah—I didn't say how many *times* you have to make the mistake!"

While this jesting went on Lee continued writing new verses for "Hound" that he would perform tonight. At the same time that Lee was writing lyrics, Ed sat on the floor of the stage, composing music to other new lyrics of Lee's while everything went on around him—adjustments to staging and instruments, dinners being served to customers, talking and general activity within the club. It was an example of letting creativity flow in any and all circumstances. Lee often says that the idea is to be able to freely *act*—to write poetry, to compose, to cook a fine meal—regardless of constraints or limitations. So many of us want to wait until we are "in the mood" to be creative and juicy and "on." Lee is constantly offering opportunities in sadhana to learn to act spontaneously and act well—to be moved to action, to access different levels of being, literally at any time. Now Lee was engrossed in his writing, which had expanded to two new verses.

If you've got a pussy
That needs a little love
I will deliver, honey
Anything you're thinkin' of
Yes, you can find me easily
I'll be somewhere around town
I'm your old pussy hound!

Now you don't need no doctor
Tell him not to come around
I got all the healing you will need
I'm your old pussy hound
Yes I can get that pussy
Screamin', weepin' yes
When I'm done with U
Your pussy will be blest!

This tongue in cheek strike at Victorian attitudes, sexual repression and the swaggering arrogance of the male sexual ego pushes psychological hot buttons for lots of people. Shri loves to play this song because Lee enjoys good satire and humorous theatre. On the other hand, the metaphors of this song—like all of Lee's songs—can be taken to a higher level of investigation. Whether one considers it satire or hidden tantric teaching, "Hound" has been the most provocative song of the summer. But more than anything else, watching Lee write these verses tonight brought to mind the difference between what Lee animates onstage in the name of theatre, and how he lives his own life. It is a common mistake to confuse the actor or entertainer with the act, and this is especially true with Lee, who is actually quite conservative and traditional in his views on sex and human relationship. He prefers to live a quiet, circumspect life, is a staunch supporter of family values and loyalty and fidelity in long-term, committed monogamous relationships, and has never experimented with or lived in any way the kind of debauched life of sex, drugs, alcohol, gambling, money and so on that many people have. Lee is so convincing in his performances, however, that sometimes we have to remind ourselves that everything he does onstage is designed to evoke, invoke or provoke consciousness.

The writing finished, Lee took his paper and unceremoniously walked onstage. "Welcome! There's not a lot of people here tonight, so you're gonna have to make more noise," Lee yelled assertively into the microphone to an audience of about twenty-five people, most of them part of his group. "It said 'Women's Blues' on the poster for tonight, so the men are going to show you their feminine side . . ." Silence resounded through the space as he paused. Lee's voice came booming over the mike again, really loud, "What? Is there anybody out there?!"

A rather feeble "Yeah!" squeaked out of the small crowd from a couple of Lee's students. Lee went into a fast, fiery version of "Treats," then turned the mike over to Everett, saying, "We're gonna get Everett off the rhythm guitar . . ."

Everett took over the mike for "G-Thang," saying, "You'll soon realize we are a premiere blues band. We may have men up here on the stage, but we are all *Woman*, baby!" Everett's rap had gotten juicier as the tour proceeded, and tonight he was very relaxed.

A few more songs rolled by and Lee introduced the next song, saying, "It would be nice to be outside on this beautiful night. Of course, we'd rather be inside playing the blues instead of walking in the park, throwing sticks for our dog." His voice had taken on a subtle nuance of nostalgia and sentimentality. "We'd rather be inside playing the blues for you—that's why we're here! We are *Shri*! Gonna do a Muddy Waters song for you!" He rumbled into "I'm a Man."

In between the first line or two he said in a lowdown, rakish sort of voice, "I'm your hoochie koochie man!" This song is almost always a nosedive into the underworld. Whether one can stay there and make use of it or not is another question altogether, but tonight Lee's enthusiasm took charge of the song, tapped directly into the underworld with it and unleashed the primal forces of life on the audience. Ed hit the whammy bar on this guitar and wailed away, the beat was driven, simple and fierce, raw and pounding. Suddenly Lee was, once again, singing lyrics we'd never heard before:

I'll take you to places
That are unknown
When I'm done with you baby
You soul will be my own
Cause I'm a MAN!
Don't need no mojo
No 'Conqueror Root'

464

Cause I'm your man, baby
And I know what to do!
I'm a MAN
Spelled M . . . A . . . N!

This song seemed to go hand in hand with "Hound," which was played during the first set also. Maybe Lee was cranking it up just to entertain himself, something he has said he often does. It certainly wasn't because of a roaring crowd of five hundred, much less two thousand. It was a long way to come from the high-spirited night in Metz to play to another half-empty house, but that's something Shri is used to—life as it is, performing on the road. It seemed like the musicians were having to fight against a blank space tonight, a dullness, a void in the room, and without having to talk about it, they had unanimously decided, "Let's just have fun!"

The band picked up the beat and lightened things up after "I'm a Man" with "One Way Out," the Elmore James song which Lee also sings. Despite their scant numbers, the small crowd of local people were very attentive to the music. The six or so men sitting at the bar were turned toward the band and watching every move. In the back of the room were two or three tables with a few local people who sat and drank beer and watched attentively. Even so, there was little response after the songs, just some random clapping. Lee said, "Y'all havin' a good time? Well that's a pretty *lame* good time. If you don't have a good time here tonight we don't care because we brought our good time with us! You can get up and dance, or just move around in your chair, get it all hot and sticky . . . " Not everything Lee says is a cryptic message about Baul yoga. Tonight it just sounded like he was irritated. He added, "And if you like what Shri does for you, you can take some of our CDs home with you!"

With about thirty-five people in the room at this point the band quickly went from "Sunnyland Blues" to "Hooked" to "Ball and Chain" to "Born Under a Bad Sign." Maybe it was in response to Lee's chiding tone, but people began to really respond, to show their appreciation with clapping and calling out. Just as things were starting to cook a little more it was time for a break.

During the break a man pulled up a chair and offered Lee a large glass of dark draft beer. "It's good for you," he urged.

"No, thanks," Lee said amiably, "not until after the gig." The man began a conversation with Lee. He said that he was a blues musician also, and he liked Shri's style. He especially liked Lee's style, which was very "straight and clear." He wanted to know about Lee.

"Have you ever heard of the Colorado School of Mines?" Lee asked. He seemed to be intentionally keeping the conversation light and unrelated to his identity as a spiritual teacher. No, he hadn't. Lee told him that he had gone to school there years ago, to be a geologist. Amazingly Lee had hit on the right subject matter, as it turned out the man was a geologist and gold miner, and they began to talk about investing in gold, the price of gold and profitability in gold mines. In fact the man had just returned from a gold mine in Africa. He had malaria and had to come back to Europe to get well. When he asked Lee about what kind of gigs Shri played, Lee said, "I don't care where we play, as long as people dance. The atmosphere doesn't matter."

"Are you on a holiday?" the man asked. Lee said, "Yes. The rest of the year we work so we can come play here in the summer." As the man listened he lifted his beer to his mouth, the big glass of dark amber brew dropping cold splashes of beer on the table between them. He kept talking during the entire break. Lee was extremely kind and generous with him.

The band found out that the doorman had only collected enough money to cover the band's food and drinks, so they wouldn't get paid anything at all tonight. They could, however, get more free food. Rising to the occasion, a few people had ice cream with Lee while other band members ordered sandwiches and French fries. Deciding to end early with the club manager's agreement—which meant playing until midnight instead of one o'clock—the band went back onstage and started playing the last set.

Lee went to the mike to sing his next song, his voice ringing out in new variations: "I'm worried, worried as a man can be / Yes I'm worried, worried as a man can be / Lookin' at my baby's dresses / And wonderin' if they'd fit me!" He was relaxed and loose, standing only a few feet away from the tables, just playing around and having a good time. When he introduced the next song, a peppery and high-spirited Shri original with a great metaphor that makes you get up and move called "Lapidary Blues," he said, "That means polishing up the old stones!" A few people got up on the dance floor, unable to stay in their seats for this one.

"We've got three or four more songs for you tonight—and they're good ones! And *you* are a *good* audience—we appreciate it!" He was speaking to less than twenty people at this point. It had turned out to be a strange night. Suddenly the band went into an original Shri favorite, "Blind Devotion," much loved by many of Lee's students and requested earlier by Ute. Deborah's rich voice came across in the haunting strains of this song of a magnificent and all-surpassing love, written by Lee and composed by Ed.

> Ask me to do anything
> Your wish is my command
> I will fly up to the sun for you
> Bring it to your hand
> I will conquer armies
> You know what I mean
> Allow me to adore you
> Be your slave, not your queen
>
> Got a question for you honey
> Please forgive my great emotion
> Is it dangerous to love you
> With such blind devotion?
> Yeahhh . . .
>
> Fingers intertwined, paroxysm of love
> That is my idea of praying
> Lost in your lover so deeply
> You don't even know what you're saying
> Don't know much about the subject of holy
> But I think I have come pretty near
> When I'm looking deep into his eyes
> There I am transfixed with fear

Blind devotion, what else is left
Nothing that is worth very much
Blind devotion, consume me in your path
Let me feel the heavens and sorrow of your touch

Got a question for you honey
Please forgive my great emotion
Is it dangerous to love you
With such blind devotion?
Yeahhh . . .

This song, with its evocative Middle Eastern undertones, is composed in a completely different style than anything else Shri plays. It was one of Shri's earliest songs, dating back six years to their first album. Its melodies and chord progressions have a mystical, bittersweet and almost evanescent quality that, combined with the lyrics, evoke many shades of meaning. The listener is transported into a higher frequency of love that leaves one with nothing but a devastating question that is the answer to its own query—"Is it dangerous to love you, with such blind devotion?" The image of an earthly love that is the doorway to the Divine is in the classic Baul style; the metaphor is sexual, and yet it does its job—it transports the listener from one dimension to another, in which love becomes an annihilating, and therefore transforming, force. The allure of this love is so great that the separate self cannot resist its own destruction in the sweetness of the alchemical crucible.

Tonight "Blind Devotion" made a strong statement on many levels, juxtaposed as it was with songs like "Hound" and "I'm a Man" and "One Way Out." It seemed as if the odd patchwork audience and rather sad emptiness of the room had somehow called forth a gift, a brief glimpse of the underlying reality that upholds and sustains all the sassy and bad ass theatrical play of the guru and his band.

The room was stunned briefly by the poignant beauty of the song. It was so completely different than anything else Shri had played tonight that every one sat still as stones for a few heartbeats while a deep silence reigned and rolled over the heart, seeping in like a mist. The moment passed, and Lee sang a melancholy "Stormy Monday," then the band went right into "Keep On Lovin' You" and finally "Voodoo Chile." The small but now very enthusiastic crowd loved it. An enthusiastic round of applause came bursting forth.

"Thank you, we are Shri!" Lee said to the faithful few who sat there clapping and smiling. It was twenty minutes after midnight, and Shri had already played longer than they had planned to during the break. As the band prepared to leave the stage people kept clapping and yelling. The noise level increased. They were begging for more. A very vocal handful of people were putting up a fuss, and it was clear they weren't going to stop. Walking away from the mike toward our table Lee said, "Wow—that's a lot of noise for just a few people!" He turned around, headed back up to the stage, grabbed the mike and said, "That's a lot of noise for so few people—thank you! I think we've got one more in here for you! 'Walkin' Blues!' " As the band broke into the rousing dance tune, Lee and Deborah looked like they were having a blast, each one with a tambourine in hand, dancing and smiling. At twelve-thirty Lee finally headed out of the place.

July 31, 1999
Sarrebrück

This morning after brunch in Freiburg a number of students sat with Lee in the living room of the apartment of sangha members who were hosting Lee and his traveling companions. Ed asked Lee a question about something he was reading in one of Arnaud's books. Arnaud was referring to the three centers—thinking, feeling and moving—of Gurdjieff's teaching. Arnaud talked about the moving or sex center as being a very highly refined energy. Ed remembered Lee speaking about two distinct levels of function of the three centers—lower thinking, feeling and moving (or instinctual), and higher thinking, feeling and moving (or sexual). In this work, Lee had said, the energy goes from lower moving to lower feeling to lower thinking and then to higher thinking, higher feeling, and last of all higher sex, moving or instinct. The higher sex center is the axis or nexus of connection to the Divine in the domain of Enlightened Duality. Lee described a circuit in the body that literally starts at the base of the spine, goes up the body through the heart to the head, then turns and goes back down, through the heart and back to the sex center near the perineum. Lee has spoken about this many times, using both the Eastern chakra system to describe the circuitry of how the energy or kundalini moves in the body, and the Gurdjieffian system of the three centers.

Lee answered the question by saying that Ed was correct, and that the function of the higher sex center depended on the unification of the three centers at the lower level. He said, "Once the three lower centers are unified and the higher thinking function kicks in, the higher feeling and sex (or moving) centers will automatically and spontaneously begin to function as well. That's the way it works."

Lee said that the process of transformation through which the three lower centers are unified or fused is exactly like the pressure and heat that transforms coal into a diamond. But the key is that one has to stay in the stress of the pressure and heat and not run away from it, which requires tremendous commitment. He said that keeping the pressure and heat internalized—rather than blowing off steam through gossip, fighting, expressing recoil or engaging self-destructive activity in the domains of money, food and sex—is another key element of the process. One has to relax and trust the movement of divine influence, to have faith in the ultimate intelligence of the Divine at work in our lives and at work in the process of transformation. A dialogue then began about dealing with pressure and heat in alchemical work.

This is a basic description of what Lee has called Divine Alchemy. In a traditional tantric school of guru yoga the disciple becomes subtly aligned with the extended subtle electrical or vibrational system of the guru. Through this alignment one is often given many functional experiences of the higher thinking, feeling and moving centers. These experiences are given despite the fact that the student is not "unified" at the basic level of the functioning of the lower centers. This morning when this point was brought up, Lee said, "Yes, and it would be great if we could take *responsibility* for those experiences." But this is one of the basic reasons that the tantric path is considered so dangerous when undertaken without a guide: forces are unleashed within the mind/body complex of the human being that are far beyond one's capacity to harness and channel. Without the steadying wisdom and influence of the guru, attempting this kind of "fast path" alchemical work is hazardous at best and ruinous at worst.

It takes a superhuman effort to stay grounded and sane in the grip of these forces when the lower thinking center—or the mind—takes over. What usually happens is that the lower thinking center either denies or subverts the experiences of higher functions based on the psychological cramp and its survival strategy. Depending on the individual's chief feature—shame, fear, anger, pride and so on—the mind or lower thinking/intellectual center will interpret the experiences of higher functions or the powerful energies that have been unleashed by them in ways that are antagonistic to the process of transformation. In other words, ego takes over in its job of maintaining the status quo, no matter how much suffering is involved. The primal cramp or ego confiscates the goods—the powerful energy of transformation—and channels it to its own aims.

There is tremendous suffering involved in this usurping of the power of the process of transformation. Being caught in the conflict between one's commitment to the path and the nefarious workings of the mind when it is associated with the dictates of the sleeping world is like being put into a vise and squeezed. But as Lee pointed out this morning, the process of transformation is not inherently fraught with emotional suffering, although there can be a natural raw discomfort experienced in the body as powerful transformational energies surge through. The lower mental center can easily interpret this discomfort as psychological suffering. When this goes on unchecked by practice at the level of Enquiry, of reestablishment in the context of why one enters into this Work and what the true commitment is, practitioners may find themselves in a cul-de-sac, a torturous and vicious cycle of resistance, recoil and doubt.

Lee said that one way to work with periods of extreme heat and pressure, like the past two weeks of touring with the band, is to fool ego into thinking it's getting its way by "feeding the animal" in small ways. That is what, in part, the feasting, the coffee, the dietary accessories are about. Another way to feed the animal is through going to movies. Steve voiced what many were thinking when he spoke about the tendency to overindulge the animal. Lee said, "If we develop the willingness to keep ourselves awake in the denial of comfort, then we have a clear sense of when we're going overboard in feeding the animal. You simply realize, 'I've had enough for this stretch of time.' If you catch yourself doing too much, then you just return to practice. It's not a matter of taking on a penance—you just return to practice."

The group talked about the necessity for relaxing the dietary practice when on the road, especially in terms of eating food off the diet that is provided by the hosts, or drinking wine when they would prefer not to. One becomes aware of a certain price that is paid in the sacrifice of the fluidity, clarity and lightness of the body and its ability to absorb and digest many other impression foods. Lee said, "Use these times intentionally to 'stay awake,' so to speak. It is also a sacrifice of comfort."

Everyone would be leaving in thirty minutes for the last gig on this leg of the tour before Lee would head back to La Ferme de Jutreau on Sunday. The talk turned toward getting back on the road.

"I wonder what tonight will bring," Rakini said, "It's great to have these mysteries always before us—anything could happen!"

Everett said, "Yes, I think if I was enlightened then every gig would be perceived as making something available . . . "

Lee said, "Maybe not." He laughed and added, "Maybe gigs are just the visible sign of the master's humanness instead of being some kind of universal Benediction or something."

Deborah said, "The spiritual master needs more monitor, too."
Lee smiled, "Exactly."

After checking into the hotel everyone drove out to the restaurant/beer garden at the hamlet of Püttlingen near Sarrebrück where Shri would be playing tonight. It was an old train station that had been converted into a night spot. Out back was a large, spacious beer garden and stage area, behind which were two rusty old boxcars sitting stationary on rails. Behind the train cars was a patch of leafy green woods. Shri was warmly greeted by the owner and some reporters with television cameras who were waiting to film the band. They wanted to get a song on film before the performance actually started. The band quickly got their equipment up and plugged in, and the crew filmed the band doing their sound check.

Shortly afterward, as the twelve of us sat with Lee at a long table finishing dinner—huge salads of mixed greens and grilled filets of beef or salmon—the reporter, a tall friendly woman, came over and said, "Because of a mistake I made we cannot use the first film we made. Would you be willing to do another take? Just one more song? I have to leave soon and cannot wait for the performance."

Lee immediately said, "Sure!" and the band jumped back onstage. As they got onto the staging area Lee started dancing around, looking more satyr-like than ever as they went into "I'm Worried" by Elmore James, a song that Deborah and Lee sing together, alternating verses. Lee danced around the stage while Deborah sang, then took the mike for his turn. As the cameras rolled new verses we'd never heard before rang out:

I'm worried, worried that my dick is too small
Yes I'm worried, worried that my schwanz is too small
But better too small, than not to have one at all!
I'm worried, worried and it just ain't fair
I'm worried, worried and it just ain't fair
Yes I'm worried, 'cause Everett's in his underwear!

Lee handed the mike off to Deborah and made dancing, whirling leaps around the stage. He looked like Pan calling the villagers to play with a devilish delight. Everett, who was playing guitar wearing a pair of shorts that could have passed for underwear, cracked up laughing. Several other band members couldn't repress their grins or chuckles. The cameras rolled along, taking it all in. It would be shown on the evening news tonight in Sarrebrück and surrounding hamlets.

Lee walked off the stage area and came to play bridge. Just as he was settling into the first couple of hands a German woman approached and sat down unceremoniously, not bothering to introduce herself. She turned to Lee and said, "What are you playing?"

"Bridge," Lee answered. She had copies of the Shri press pack with her, and was reading from the pages that described each band member. She started asking Lee questions about the band—which one is Tina, which one is Deborah, and so on. She wanted to know why the band wasn't all women anymore. Lee gave her a passable answer and the names of the new band members—Lee, Steve, Everett. She fixed Lee with a glassy and somewhat resentful stare as she plied him with questions. It was assumed she was a local newspaper reporter since she had the press pack, and so had some legitimate purpose for interviewing the band. "What kind of songs do you play?" she asked in halting English.

"Songs about love, loss of love, angst, beauty, joy," Lee answered mildly, looking her directly in the eye. There was an out-of-place and odd trace of suspicion or disbelief in her demeanor. Maybe she was always like that.

She continued, "What do you believe—why the . . ." she gestured to Lee's dreadlocks.

"Just for looks," Lee answered.

"It's not a message?" she queried.

"No, I'm not a Rastafarian," Lee said clearly and distinctly, so she could make no mistake in his answer.

"Shri . . . it's an Indian name, yes?" It seemed more like he was being interrogated at this point, but he remained cool and unruffled.

"Yes," Lee answered, "it means the essence of femininity." She was completely nonplussed by this and looked at Lee with a blank and uncomprehending stare. Lee called Thomas over and asked him to translate his answer into German. His translation given, she looked even more disconcerted and uncomfortable.

"But why? What do you mean?" she asked, as if she couldn't imagine there being such a thing as the essence of femininity, and if there was, what could that possibly have to do with American music?

Lee said, "The essence of femininity is about action, life, movement, depth, joy, feeling, love. That's what the blues is all about—depth, passion and love. Right?" She seemed curious but embarrassed by Lee's frank talk, but more than anything disbelieving.

"You always play bridge during sound check?" she asked witheringly.

"Yes," Lee answered, "it keeps the mind busy." She looked noncomprehending and Lee added, "Occupied."

It took a while for this to sink in, then she said, "Yes, but not to wake the mind up?"

"No," Lee said. "Otherwise we sit around waiting . . ." Lee drummed his fingers nervously on the table to demonstrate.

This seemed to make sense to her. She smiled hesitantly and said, "Capital," then walked away.

About forty-five minutes later the owner of the beer garden introduced the band with great enthusiasm, "Shri, from Arizona, U.S.A.!" The introduction came just a few moments before the band was actually ready. As the band started their first number, "Fever," Tina came running up and strapped on her bass guitar.

"Now we have our bottom end in there," Deborah quipped over the mike. There were about one hundred seventy-five people sitting at the tables and more flooding in. In between songs Lee said, "I hope you're here to have a good time tonight—we are!" Deborah asked everybody to come up and dance with the band. There was plenty of room to dance on the concrete floor where the band was set up. "Come on over here to the wrong side of the tracks and dance with us," she invited.

As the band started playing there were two professional photographers walking around taking photos. One of them who looked particularly competent got right up in front of Lee and starting clicking away. Lee went into "Loser Blues" and then "I Seen" without a pause. The crowd had swelled to about six hundred people. Lee looked like he was having a great time, and it was highly infectious. He wore no sunglasses tonight, and his face and blue eyes were unveiled and bright. His eyes were smiling also, and I wondered if that was how they always looked behind his shades onstage. As Lee sang "Treats" practically every face in the house was turned toward the band. Like at Lucerne and Metz, people here in Püttlingen were fascinated and completely swept up in the music and the presence of the band.

The last chords died away and Lee, standing at ease in his pink Tweetie Bird T-shirt, said, "We're happy to play for you tonight. Come on and get a little closer to the band and maybe we can infect you with some *blues* tonight!" He sang "Rock Me Baby" and then "The Sky Is Crying." Next he tore into "18 Wheeler"—a brash, funky Lozowick/Flaherty original that usually gets the dancers up on their feet. Tonight people listened and clapped heartily, but stayed in their seats. Lee sang another Elmore James song, "I'm Worried," this time with the original lyrics.

When Deborah took over the singing Lee headed out into the audience, tracking a circle around the outer perimeter of the beer garden but still within the crowd, shaking hands and greeting people, dancing as he went with tambourine in hand. A small clique of benign looking biker types had gathered right in front of the stage, and Lee made his way over to them, stopped and shook hands with one man and his lady. After he had made the full loop around the place, he sauntered back up to the stage. A little girl about seven years old came up holding her baby sister's hand. They stood about ten feet away from the band and listened, then their parents came up and found a place to sit nearby.

During "Born Under A Bad Sign" Deborah went out into the crowd and danced with a young woman with beautiful long wavy hair. She looked like a postmodern hippie with her bare feet and flowing tiger skin dress. During the solo Lee went over to Ed and begged the guitar for more, his hands coaxing a wild volley of notes out of the strings made pliant in Ed's fingers.

Throughout the performance Lee never stopped; he was constantly working the space and his students onstage, as well as glancing toward those of us watching and listening, drawing everyone into his play. He played tambourines with Deborah, then stood and bowed to the wild applause that was like a roar coming from the audience. The crowd obviously loved the music. Deborah and Lee kept inviting everyone to come up and dance.

"Why aren't they dancing?" I asked Thomas, who is German.

Thomas said, "They feel they are too old to dance."

That didn't stop them from enjoying the band. There is a real sense of bonded identity among the German people, and it showed here tonight in the pride and pleasure of this well-off audience. The crowd was full of all ages of people, from small children, toddlers and infants, to eight and ten year olds playing on the playground equipment to the left of the stage, to seventy-five-year-old seniors. Everyone was having a good time. The audience drank beer and ate food, but the degree to which people were focused on the band was extraordinary, very much like at Metz.

The whole concert had a distinctly middleworld feeling to it. Instead of soaring upperworld *bhavas* or underworld ecstasies and piercing insights, it felt like it was solidly grounded in the pleasures and proprieties of the everyday middleworld. Shri is the name of the Indian goddess who is also known as Tripura-Sundari, or, "She who is beautiful in three worlds," one of the ten Mahavidyas or tantric goddesses of Hinduism. True to its namesake, sometimes Shri plays the upperworld, sometimes the underworld. Tonight Shri was shining in the middleworld, bestowing blessings in the realm of the ordinary, the everyday, of the people, of the children, youths, elders and middle-aged, drinking their beers and finding some pleasure, relaxing and soaking up some energy from the music to help sustain them in their work tomorrow and the next day and the day after that. Shri was radiating in the realm of maintaining life, sustaining the world of concrete manifestation. "Action, life, joy . . ." as Lee said earlier. Shri was doing her job tonight, and in a totally different way. There was no feeling of multidimensional travel, no deep sorrows, no pain of separation, no glimpses of heaven. Only a grand celebration of life in incarnation as it is, even in its quotidian splendor—basically good, naturally ecstatic, grounded in the very real, earthy substance of manifestation, which is divine in essence.

Lee got ready for his next number, "The First Time I Met the Blues." He introduced it saying, "The first time I met the blues I was about one year old!" The biker with the long hair tied back into a pony tail sitting near the band yelled out, "A long time ago!" He and Lee laughed together. Lee said, "Yeah, that's right!"

The band was grounded, tight, together and in sync. They were obviously enjoying each other's company, and basking in their last night with Lee onstage for the next two or three months. The band went into one of the original songs that they started with six years ago, "Keep On Lovin' You," lyrics by Lee Lozowick, composed by Ed Flaherty. It is a simple song, but it speaks of a love so grand and inspired that the audience is swept up into the elation of wanting nothing but this love.

> If there were only one thing
> Left in life to do
> I wouldn't do another thing
> but keep on lovin' you—
>
> (Chorus)
> Lovin' you,
> My darling
> Lovin' you
> I wouldn't do
> Another thing
> But keep on
> Lovin' you
>
> If I had one single wish
> To keep from being blue
> Don't you know what I'd wish for
> To keep on lovin' you—
>
> (Chorus)
>
> If I had but just one dream
> Guess what I'd dream too
> Even while I sleep at night
> I'd keep on lovin' you—
>
> (Chorus)

Deborah sang with passion, with gusto, a tremendous expression of the grand impulse of life. The beat of this song is driven and pounding, it carries the listener along and one is captured by its ecstatic proclamation: There is nothing higher, nobler, more transforming than love! Lee once said that a workable definition of love could be, "a healthy obsession." That is what this song is about—a love that has obsessed the lover to the extent that nothing exists outside the transforming joy of that love. The Bauls believe that love is the pathway to God; in human love one discovers love transcendent. All this is captured and communicated within the totality of this quintessential Baul song. It is written in simple, vernacular speech; its metaphors are not of the highly intellectual and obscure variety, but something anyone can immediately grasp. Combined with the music, the song becomes an extraordinary expression of joy in life. What does love self-effaced, such as the *gopi* Radha's love for the Lord Krishna, look like in the middleworld? Maybe it was encoded in the fabric of this music and transmitted in this song, tonight. The crowd responded with a roar, a freight train of applause and cheers of approval.

Lee unexpectedly told Everett to take a guitar solo. Everett smiled and jumped in— it's the second time this summer that Lee has worked with Everett this way. "Give Everett a big hand," Lee yelled, and we all responded with big cheers. That's the Work—you never know when you're going to be called upon to do something you're not prepared for. Or as Lee said recently, to be the one who keeps the Universe alive. With a wide grin on his face, Everett did a great job, keeping his eyes on Lee in a natural and easy communion, letting Lee draw the notes out of the guitar with the beat of his tambourine.

Lee started "Smokestack Lightnin' " which created its usual ecstatic response. The crowd kept getting looser, but still there were no dancers. Two toddlers, about eighteen months old, stumbled across the stage in front of the band from the audience that sat on the side. After "Woman With My Class" the band said goodnight to a clamorous ring of applause that just kept on going. They left the stage and walked over to their table to get something to drink. The applause boomed on, and then escalated to a new note. They went back on for an encore. Lee grabbed the mike and said, "Everybody needs somebody to love!" They sang "Walkin' Blues." Lee yelled out to the audience, "Come on, get up and dance!" With this final appeal and the crescendo of the music, the guy and his girl who had sat near the stage all night whistling, clapping and talking to the band, finally jumped up and came onstage to dance in front of everyone. They were the only people who actually got up and danced all night—other than Lee and Deborah—but many were standing and dancing in their places in the audience.

The band tore into "Voodoo Chile" and Lee went out into the audience, all the way around the perimeter of the place. He shook hands with people while Deborah went out into the audience and sang. Lee took the big yellow maracas in his hands and stood near Rakini on drums coaching her, leading her into a frenzy of intensity as he flung his arms high and low, as if he was using the maracas to play drums against earth and sky. The audience was gripped in the intensity, every face was turned toward the band. The reciprocity that flowed from band to audience and back again in a continuous circle was a palpable presence in the space. Ed's solo on "Voodoo Chile" gave the audience a glimpse of pure invocation—the most potent otherworldly moment of the evening.

"Thank you very much! Thank you very much! Maybe we'll be back next year," Lee shouted ecstatically into the mike. The excitement was at a peak, the moment full of joy. "We'll be around for awhile if you want to bring your CDs up to have them signed. The whole band will sign them!" Lee left the stage and walked over to the table where a few of his devotees were sitting and watching with big smiles on their faces. Lee said, "It reminds me of Madison Square Garden back in 1973!" The crowd would not relent, but kept begging for an encore. People were holding up their cigarette lighters and clapping rhythmically, shouting. Not one person had gotten up to leave. Deborah and Ed went back to the stage and performed "Can't Find My Way Home," a poignant rock ballad, an old favorite from the early seventies that Deborah sometimes sings as a final goodbye to the audience. It is a very poignant and disarming song that soothed the wildness of the mood and brought the energy back down to a manageable level.

Immediately people began to swarm the table where Shri stood signing CDs. The man who had danced at the end of the performance came over and grabbed Lee's arm, saying, "You are really, really good, man! Is this your first time in Germany?" Lee smiled and said that it was their fourth time in Germany. People crowded around, asking for CDs and waiting their turn to get theirs signed. "Next year!" they said, and Lee answered, "I hope so!" A new wave of people came up, some of them patting Lee on the back. It was as if they felt that they knew him intimately now.

The large beer garden was beginning to clear out while people still crowded around Shri getting autographs. The excitement was running very high. The band was exultant; there was so much energy coming to them, it was as if they had been plugged into high voltage current. After the last of the people seeking autographs finally left, the band began to hear feedback from the staff of the restaurant, who were wildly enthusiastic and verbal about their enjoyment of the band. One of the waiters passed on a comment about Lee that came from someone in the audience: "He is like Jesus in pop art!"

August 5, 1999
La Ferme de Jutreau

After two weeks on the road with Shri, Lee has been back in the sanctuary of the ashram for the past three days. The particular demand of constant traveling—being on the city streets, mingling with all kinds of people—has changed to the mood of ashram life, which is both ordinary and quiet in the passing of lovely summer days. The ashram is a reflection of Lee's life and work. The cadence of formal practices and the daily work schedule—tending of orchards and gardens, preparing meals, arranging for the arrival of many guests who will come soon, laundry, cooking and cleaning, along with the constant influx of messages, phone calls, information, requests and general business for the guru—is what makes up the days. All this is mingled with the innocence and unique culture of the children, who run and play joyfully on the grounds.

Lee also returned to a huge pile of mail, faxes, messages and notes. His desk has been in a state of chaos with all the scattered piles of things he has to address, respond to, handle. He answers all of his mail by hand, and only rarely allows one of his students to handle other business for him. When Brother Juniper, Anja, Sylvan and Mariana arrived from Arizona two days ago, they brought another copious pile of mail to Lee—letters, packages, manuscripts he has to read for Hohm Press, four *vigrahas* of Yogi Ramsuratkumar.

Tomorrow morning a three-day seminar begins at La Ferme de Jutreau with the morning meditation program. Lee arranged his book table this afternoon in the back corner of the salon. He has been relatively quiet and reflective although busy and engaged since he returned, but as the seminar draws nearer, he begins to gear up again. It is as if he was a banked fire for a few days, and where there were glowing coals, now the flames start to crackle again.

Tonight after dinner as about twenty people sat around talking with Lee at the table in the barn dining room, someone was recounting the story of Lee's visit to the sex shop in Hamburg. Lalitha told a story that had Lee and everyone else in stitches. She said, "Years ago I was going to give a talk about sex with Purna at the ashram. For some reason at the last minute Purna couldn't give the talk, so I went into the kitchen and got a bag full of kitchen implements and went into the talk. I sat down and said, 'While everybody was at lunch I went into your rooms to look for sexual implements and paraphernalia, and this is what I found hidden away. I just held up the bag and before I could say anything else people were yelling at me, 'How dare you go into our private spaces!' Two people ran out of the room. It was crazy! I had no idea what I was getting into with this joke!"

As Lalitha told this story Lee laughed heartily, then turned to me and said, "Now *that* should go into the book! That's the funniest thing I've heard since the book started!"

After dinner Lee gave an After Dinner Talk in the salon. About ten guests who had already arrived for the seminar found seats for the talk, mingling in with the ashram residents and Lee's students from America or Germany who were there also. Lee came in and abruptly launched into his discourse.

"I didn't bring any material tonight so everybody is going to have to help get things going! I usually bring things I'm currently reading to the After Dinner Talks, but I don't have any of that right now. Tomorrow when the seminar starts and for the rest of the weekend, it will be unnecessary to use other material. It will probably be hard not to do the introduction to the seminar tonight, but I want to save it for tomorrow morning.

"We might begin with questions. Are there any questions, anything you would like to consider? Except for American politics, which I know absolutely nothing about and don't care to . . ."

Michael said, "I had something come up a couple of days ago around intuition. Intuitively I felt I should be doing something, and when I heard from you that I should be doing something else, I let that go. It turned out that what I thought I should do was what I should have done—perhaps. I'm not sure of that either. So the question is intuition and the spiritual master, and how those two work together."

Lee answered, "There are two questions here. One involves the immediate, pragmatic workability of something versus the long-term effects, which often can't be measured linearly. From being around Yogi Ramsuratkumar I'm sure you know that things He asks people to do sometimes don't seem practical, but if we look over years we see the things He asked people to do having an effect that we couldn't have imagined. Every situation is unique to itself—there is no simple answer."

Suddenly Lee's attention was drawn outside by the happy sounds of the children laughing and yelling in their play outside. He said, "Gosh, maybe we should go out there, it looks like more fun! Or have the children come in here to the After Dinner Talk!" He laughed a little and continued, "Sometimes in rare cases there is some practical situation that needs taking care of that I don't know the details of, whereas if I'm told the details, the initial directions would be changed without tension. So if someone comes and says, 'Should I fix the plumbing in the kitchen or do childcare?' I might just say, 'Be on childcare.' But if they were to say, 'The pipe is broken and if I don't get to it right away the whole house will be flooded,' then obviously I would say, 'Of course, do the plumbing.' Sometimes it's useful just to have information. If someone comes and says 'I'm thinking of getting into a relationship with someone, what do you think?' I tell them what I think. But if they come to me and say, 'This person is pregnant and I'm the father,' I'm going to have a totally different response.

"I'm assuming we're talking about something other than just cutting the grass or doing the dishes. So whenever someone asks me a question—if it has to do with something more important than how to spend their time in the next day or two—then my first response may be the spontaneous response. I can't even explain it, because it has to do with consequences and implications for the future, and I don't know the future. So my first response is almost unconscious. On a human level if I stop and try to figure something out, basically my response will be an educated guess, which is often pretty accurate, but sometimes it isn't because it's just an educated guess."

One might ask, how can the guru's first response be "almost unconscious" but be the source of a greater wisdom, as Lee suggests? In this case the word "unconscious" is used in the same way that Carl Jung used the term "collective unconscious," which is an impersonal, universal and infinite field of unknowable knowledge and intelligence that exists a priori. The unconscious is a vast unknown that might be called God or the Divine or ultimate Being, which sources, permeates and moves human consciousness, or essential being-ness, and often appears or acts spontaneously through the avenue of instinct, which is a function of the body.

In his statements Lee was pointing toward a fundamental principle of dharma—that essential being-ness exists as already present enlightenment. When a response comes spontaneously from the unconscious, it has bypassed any stain of dualistic thought or consideration of the mind, and comes fresh from the fount of superrational and unconscious wisdom. This wisdom of the unconscious, which is already presently enlightened, has an infinite capacity to respond to a question from a perspective that is so vast and immense that it is incomprehensible and can encompass "consequences and implications" of karma, destiny and evolution in ways that are immeasurably beyond the ability of the linear human mind.

The true guru lives from the disposition of already present enlightenment. There are no blocks or obstacles to the flow of knowledge from the wise unconscious other than those that are placed in the way by the guru's disciples. When a student goes to Lee with a mind that is already made up, that is rigidly fixated on an idea or opinion or a deep-seated bias, this becomes in effect a block to the flow of wisdom that comes directly from the source. Often what happens is that, instead of getting the greater wisdom—the spontaneous, instinctual and "unconscious" answer—the student then gets a mirrored reflection of his or her own confusion and bias. In other words, the guru is surrendered to "what is" in every moment; if the disciple is unwilling to hear anything but his own opinion reflected back to him, then that is what he will most likely get. It behooves the student to ask questions of the guru with a completely open mind and to come to an understanding based on fundamental trust in the "basic goodness" of the Universe, particularly in relationship to the difference between the rational machinations of the mind as opposed the elegance of superrational wisdom. The difficulty lies in ego's acceptance of superrational wisdom, which will always guide one toward unity rather than maintaining the separate self.

Lee continued: "A teacher definitely goes through stages, and Yogi Ramsuratkumar is in a very universal stage where He is just blessing the Universe, and every action He makes has universal implications and ripples throughout the Universe and all that. Although Arnaud can make work for anybody any time—his skillful means are immense—his work is more universal now. It's the Blessing Force of his presence. My work hasn't reached that level yet—I assume it will one day. When it does everyone will think I've become senile," Lee laughed characteristically, "because I'm not making dirty jokes . . .

"My idea is that this lifetime *now* is when we have to work, no matter how great the blessings are for eternity, for the future. *This* is where we need to work, where we need to struggle. So that's a very different viewpoint than the viewpoint that this action creates blessings for ten thousand years. All that is true, and I can see through Yogi Ramsuratkumar how many people are touched in Europe, although in this lifetime it will mean very little—relatively nothing—compared to what it could mean to them. His blessings are just another picture on their wall, another spiritual trophy for them. But in five or ten or twenty lifetimes it might be a lifesaver; it might be the single act of Grace that brings them to the Divine. But my focus is *now*—here and now—even though the other is true also. I'm just a little fish in a *big* pond.

"So, when I recommend something, even when I don't know what I'm saying, the best response is one that is not measured. If I stop to think of something my response will be measured, and it may be accurate, but . . . The best response is one that is not measured, because then it is Yogi Ramsuratkumar's words and not my words. Obviously sometimes His words take time to filter down into this domain."

Two more guests arrived. They had also been at La Ferme de Jutreau for Guru Purnima last month. Lee smiled at them when they walked in and took seats. He greeted then with a friendly banter, "We meet again so soon! That's very pleasant! In the two weeks since we've seen each other I've been on the road with Shri. We've had some great gigs, festivals with thousands of people. Metz was great! It's a very successful tour so far!"

Once they were settled he continued, "So obviously there are acts of disobedience that don't dramatically affect the overall flow of Benediction as it is moving between the lineage and myself as the focal point and the student. For some people at certain stages, if their intuition disagrees with mine, they may have to follow their intuition just to see what that is. But one of the things that we tend to notice as a general rule (there are exceptions to this) is that if we stay with our disagreement, if we follow the teacher's direction but stay with our disagreement, we come to a higher understanding. This is because higher understandings often have to be squeezed out of us from the tensions of a frustrated ego.

"The development of a greater and more stable position of faith is well worth the tension, take my word for it! People will do anything for that kind of evolution in their consciousness! Sometimes we need to act and sometimes we need to just stay with the disagreement, and let it produce what it can produce from the heat and pressure of our own conflict, our own crisis. But the main point is that in experimenting in following our intuition if it differs from the master's direction, these kinds of sins are really minor in the overall picture of our work together—or should be. Unless such activity is chronic. So, that covers it."

Michael commented, "It more than covers it!" Although the questioner, a long-time student of Lee's, sounded grateful for Lee's answer, there had been a tone and attitude underlying his question. It seemed that he was convinced that he was right and Lee was wrong in some direction Lee had given him, and it was the burn of this doubt that had spurred the question. Lee's answer was supremely generous and patient. In this instance the guru's patience—in response to the unspoken recoil and doubt in the question—was as important a teaching lesson as the more concrete data he actually gave for the benefit of the whole group.

"Any other questions?" Lee asked.

"What's the difference between constructive or useful suffering and masochism?"

Lee answered, "A lot of people in this day and age have a tendency toward masochism," he chuckled, "for a variety of reasons, one being two thousand years of Christianity and its influence in our lives. Feeling that we have to suffer for the sins of our genealogy, so to speak. So that aside, constructive suffering builds something in us, and masochistic suffering doesn't. And that is really the primary difference. So if, for instance, when someone has to care for an ailing partner or child or parent or something like that . . . often, after some period of time, their being is so much greater from the sacrifices they've had to make—which is a form of suffering—that it has built a depth of compassion.

"E.J. Gold, who is a good friend of mine, has written books on the Work. He wrote about creative tensions and useless tensions. He said that in all cases what he called positive stress, when engaged within the context of the path or the Work, always produced clarity, strength, whereas negative stress just created breakdown. That's another way of defining constructive suffering versus masochistic suffering. Suffering which has no constructive value can create indulgence in destructive habits or emotional breakdown. Creative suffering or constructive suffering may not be free of tears or struggle, certainly, but tends not to manifest in real breakdown. You can be exhausted in a way that is very euphoric, and then there is being exhausted in a way that you are just wasted. The euphoric exhaustion is the result of hard work or constructive struggle, and the other is just too much work.

"A lot of us have a small or large tendency toward masochism. Many people take the path of hurting themselves when they are in crisis, sometimes consciously, sometimes unconsciously. I'm sure as all of you know from personal experience or from friends, we'll be struggling with some kind of personal experience and we'll get into a car accident. If we look at it deeply enough we can see that we did that unconsciously to punish ourselves. But sometimes there are people who hurt themselves consciously—for example, cutting their wrists, or something less severe. In any hospital for the emotionally disturbed there are always people who burn themselves with cigarettes, that kind of thing. Each of us to a greater or lesser degree, like a child when the game isn't working, breaks the toy.

"It's always back to self-observation. The more clearly we know ourselves and our tendencies, the more we are able to use the arising of tendency without acting on it as constructive struggle or suffering, to build qualities of discipline, forbearance, understanding of others, and so on. Okay?"

Another person asked, "You just mentioned using the arising of tendency without acting on it being a way to suffer constructively. Would you say more about that?"

Lee answered, "It's the same principle as the growing of crystals, if I remember my mineralogy well. Each of us has an inherent crystalline structure within us, we could say. But if the conditions are not proper, then instead of the crystal growing into its crystalline form, it takes on a crude, undefined form. You know the difference between a big hunk of quartz rock you could find anywhere and a beautifully formed quartz crystal? One of the things needed for a crystal to form is *space* for the crystal to grow. The reason there are crystals in a geode is because there is an air pocket that gives them room to grow.

"So one of the things that not acting out our tendencies creates is space. The tendency to eat neurotically, whether bingeing or having an oral fixation, having to stuff something in our mouths, or the tendency to spend money, or whatever we have succumbed to in our tendencies closes out space in us. If you read self-help manuals, creative thinking manuals and things like that, they always tell you, 'Never make an important decision when you're in an emotional state.' They say, 'Get some distance from your emotions.' Create space. Because in the creation of space you can see things in a way that you can't see when you are madly following some tendency. So when you sit with the feeling, the urge, the tendency, and just observe it as it is, it creates space in which something objective can grow.

"So we often talk about ourselves as being an essential being and then having this complex of psychology superimposed on the essential core. In Zen they would say, 'The face before you were born.' And that doesn't mean past lives! It has nothing to do with that. When there is space, then what is essential has an opportunity to manifest. If there is no space, if we are always functioning habitually and mechanically from one moment to the next, there is no space for anything else to manifest its existence.

"As many people know—not necessarily in this Work, but in ordinary circumstances— sometimes the greatest breakthroughs we have in our personal growth happen when we are sick and we're lying in bed and we can't do the things we usually do all day long to distract ourselves, and we are left with ourselves. When we look at ourselves all day long, we start seeing things that we don't ordinarily see, because there is space. In retrospect what we usually discover is that things weren't as bad as we thought they were. But we tend to resist self-observation and clarity because we're afraid that we won't like what we find if we start digging around. Once we are free of the burden of denial, then we almost always discover that the burden itself is much worse than whatever it is that we were in denial about. There is tremendous freedom in self-honesty. There is tremendous room to grow, room for expression, for the crystal of self!" Lee laughed, apparently at his moment of grandiloquence.

"Brother Juniper, who most of you will get to know, just arrived a few days ago. Many years ago in the early years of the community he broke his back under very unusual circumstances. He had to stay in bed while he was healing, and he spent his time listening to and cataloguing every one of our tapes from over the years. Maybe a thousand hours of tapes. That's another approach to revelation or transformation—being completely submerged in the teaching. One approach is creating space, and the other approach is submersion in the teaching. The source of the revelation of Swami Papa Ramdas, the Master of my Master, Yogi Ramsuratkumar, was to repeat a mantra twenty-four hours a day. If any of you have ever tried repeating a mantra for any length of time, you know how easily the mind gaps out. Not to mention that we all have to sleep and go to the bathroom and things that tend to take our attention. He was so committed to saying this mantra twenty-four hours a day, while he was eating, going to the bathroom, even while he was sleeping, that he discovered all the resistances to submersion in the teaching within himself, and he rooted them out with prayer. No therapy for Papa!

"Swami Papa Ramdas was so intent upon repeating this mantra twenty-four hours a day that he became completely absorbed in it. In that absorption everything that needed to be revealed to him was revealed, because in that absorption was clarity, knowledge, wisdom. That's another approach for creating space—push everything else out with the mantra. The mantra itself is essentially empty, and once everything else is pushed out you end up with the same thing—just space.

"When Swami Ramdas was traveling around India, one of the elements of repeating the mantra twenty-four hours a day was seeing everything as Ram. Ram is a name of God in India. When Swami Ramdas was doing some of his early sadhana he was walking all over the place and begging for food; he looked pretty disturbed. A lot of the saints who wandered around India, people didn't know they were saints and would throw rocks at them and beat them with sticks. This happened to Ramdas. When Ramdas was beaten or had stones thrown at him, he would look at that as Ram. 'Oh well, Ram is beating this one,' or 'Ram is throwing stones at Ramdas.' So he was able to bear whatever treatment he got with complete equanimity.

"This is the other approach. You create space either by immersing yourself, submerging yourself in sadhana or dharma, or we allow things to be as they are without reacting, simply observing what is arising. In either case there is action, but the action is natural to the moment rather than affected by neurosis or conditioning. So in Zen Buddhism often they will say something like, 'When you are hungry, eat; when you are tired, sleep.' Most of us don't live that way. We eat when we think we are supposed to eat or when we are neurotically driven to eat, and we design our sleep to serve a certain purpose, without regard for the natural rhythm of the body."

An hour after the talk was over the group reconverged *dans le salon* for tea at nine-thirty. Guests who had come for the seminar that would begin tomorrow came in tentatively, looking around for seats and slowly getting settled. Lee came in about ten minutes later and joined everyone, taking a cup of fresh mint tea, one of his favorite beverages. The mint had just been cut from the garden earlier in the evening and the tea was delicious and zesty, marvelously alive with the essences of the garden.

Sylvan came in to offer Lee a second cup and Lee asked for half of a cup. Sylvan carefully poured a half cup of tea, and as he walked away, Lee said with a mixed look of feigned surprise and very real pleasure on his face, "Wow! Now there's a server who gives you what you *ask* for!" He was complimenting Sylvan and also referring to the many times when he has complained that people who are serving food or drink will almost always give you what *they* think you should have, or what *they* themselves want, instead of what you ask for. It is one of the insidious ways in which self-referencing shows up; the chronic unconscious tendency is to habitually think only of ourselves rather than of the other.

Lee turned to Sylvan's mate, Mariana, who was sitting on the floor nearby and said, half in jest, half in seriousness, "Now, does he give you what you ask for?" Mariana answered, "Yes, but the question is can I take it?"

Always quick on the uptake and never one to be upstaged by his devotees, Lee snapped, "The question is how much *integrity* does what you ask for have!"

The space was quietly bustling with energy as people walked in and out to the office, the server came and went with tea, new people arrived. The phone rang—someone calling for information about the seminar. Lee turned to Valerie, a disciple of Arnaud Desjardins who had just arrived for the seminar.

"Mint tea with no sugar—it's our idea of a treat!" He grinned, holding up his teacup. He seemed to be referring to the fact that at every seminar house in France the herb tea is well sweetened, or sweetener is at least offered—except this one. People generally come to La Ferme de Jutreau prepared to endure some crazy wise antics and some discomforts. Valerie smiled back winningly, a willing participant in Lee's play for the weekend. She had been to several of Lee's seminars before at other locations, including Hauteville, but this was her first time at La Ferme de Jutreau.

Jan walked in and sat down. Lee raised his voice and said gleefully, "It's great mint tea! Fabulous! No honey! The real thing. We should have a sign here in the room—No Lipton's Served Here! No capitalist pig multi-nationalist corporation's tea served here!" He was kidding Jan about the ongoing dialogue he has had with her for years about her liberal, left wing political convictions versus her inherence in the principles of the Work. Some of that feedback had been fierce in the past; tonight he was being playful.

Now Chris came in to join the tea party. Lee greeted her by yelling out in a jovial tone, "Mint tea! No honey!" The twenty-five or so people in the room laughed. He continued, "You have to warn the guests because sometimes at breakfast . . ." Lee theatrically mimicked someone taking up a cup, sipping and being shocked by what they find. The laughter built to another level.

The camaraderie and general amiability that Lee effortlessly generated seemed to make the room glow with a brightness that accentuated the beauty of the space. One entire wall of the room was lined with books in French, German and English. The blackened fireplace yawned like a mysterious doorway into another world. The windows looked out on the grassy courtyard where the children played under the large red maple tree. Up above the top shelf of the bookcase were many beautiful photographs, *murtis* of Yogi

Ramsuratkumar, Lee, Anandamayi Ma, pictures of Mount Arunachala, photographs of sculptures of Hanuman, a hand-painted *bishwari* of Krishna with the gopis enacting the *ras lila*. Above the fireplace was a two-foot by three-foot color photograph of Yogi Ramsuratkumar with an immense flower *mala* around his neck, his eyes turned up toward the devotee who had just placed the garland on him. His hands were pressed together in a *pranam*. The murti seemed to transmit a tangible and constant stream of blessings into the space. Two photographs, one of Lee and one of Yogi Ramsuratkumar, were twined together with a dried flower *mala* that was given to Lee as *prasad* last summer.

On the mantle piece of the fireplace and on the table beside Lee tonight were lovely small arrangements of flowers from the garden, colorful dahlias and small sunflowers. The whole space radiated a mood of intimacy and yet it was also burning with an impersonal presence, the presence of Yogi Ramsuratkumar, that brought the environment to a state of heightened and immediate *realness*. Some people come into this aura of clarity and realness that permeates the spaces that are dedicated to Lee and Yogi Ramsuratkumar and bask in the radiance of that power. They feel themselves coming to life, like a plant that was thirsty and drooping recovering its turgor pressure after a good rain. Others react with fear and recoil, finding themselves revealed in a way by the ferocity of a radiance that is tremendously threatening to ego.

Lee and several people sitting nearby noticed at the same time a spider that was walking on the floor. Lee said to Jan, "You'd better put him out if you want him to live!" He was joking with her again about her tendency to try to save all sentient beings. She laughed heartily and said, "Oh, he's going in that direction on his own."

Lalitha chimed in, saying to Lee, "He probably knows you are friendly to the cats and he thinks he's the same!"

"He doesn't know how different he is!" Lee responded, laughing along with everyone. As the laughter died down Lee looked around at his companions and said, "What's the name of this seminar? Oh yeah—'*Kaya sadhana*: God Doesn't Live In the Sky'." Then he said facetiously, "What if God *does* live in the sky and has a big beard, red and bushy like a *pirate*!?"

"Is that a metaphor?" Jane asked, smiling.

"A meta for what?" Lee quipped. Peals of laughter came from the group. We were back in the chamber of delighted silliness in the company of the spiritual master. He turned back again to Valerie and said, "Did they put you in the barn?"

"They did," she smiled.

Lalitha said, "We have so many luxury cabins to choose from!"

Lee jumped in, "Yeah—the right side of the barn or the left side of the barn! Very different from Paris," he added, looking at Valerie. Everyone was laughing except a few new people who looked on wonderingly. Some of them didn't speak English particularly well and weren't able to follow the fast repartee. It is one of the cultural boundaries that the Europeans come up against with Lee's wiseacreing American street style.

Jane joked, "Someday Arnaud's students who have come to this ashram will say, 'I went to La Ferme de Jutreau!' Like, 'I was at the battle of Gettysburg,' or something like that!" Three or four people started talking at once, adding to the joke, "Yeah, we'll have T-shirts for sale, saying 'I Slept In the Barn!' and 'I survived Jutreau!' "

Paula said, "It says in the 'Guru Gita' to repeat it in a cowshed!" This brought a fresh wave of laughter, more jokes and general merriment. "Oh, so we get lots of blessings, staying in the barn!" and so on.

Lee began to talk about going to visit the ashram of Muktananda in the seventies in India. They chanted the "Guru Gita" every morning at four o'clock. You could stay there for three days without going to the chanting, but after that they would wake you up and make you go. He said, "Everyone was supposed to go to sleep at nine o'clock because we all had to get up so early, but in the men's dorm, the men all thought they should be gurus themselves or already were, and they were up reading and writing, sitting up on the roof, staying up late. In the women's dorm it was better; all the *gopis* did what they were supposed to do and went to sleep." Lee let out a long chuckle, then suddenly jumped slightly in his seat and said, "Well—on that note I'll say goodnight!" He got up and left the room.

August 6, 1999
La Ferme de Jutreau

After meditation the seminar, "*Kaya sadhana*—God Does Not Live in the Sky," started with a talk by Lee at eight-thirty. He began with explaining that he would give all but two of the talks during the weekend. Those two would be given by two of his students, Dasya and Rick. He explained the book table, set up in the back corner of the salon where he was speaking, and talked about the literature of the school as well as the dharma literature that has been published by Hohm Press, which is on the recommended reading list. He spoke also about the CDs and tapes of liars, gods & beggars and Shri, saying, "The music is also considered literature. So any serious student of this path would also study the music in addition to studying all of our written literature."

His talk was informal and warm. He spoke to the guests, acquaintances and new people as if he had known them forever. He extended his humanness so easily and naturally, it was as if the guests were in his living room sharing his life with him for the weekend, and in fact that is exactly the way it was.

Lee said, "The first part of the title of this seminar, '*Kaya sadhana*,' is about a sadhana that does not reject the body. The second part, 'God Does Not Live in the Sky,' refers to the tendency in Western culture, encouraged by underlying premises and assumptions, to believe that the Divine is always somewhere else other than here and now. The medieval and Victorian attitudes of Judaism and Christianity are that the body is sinful, money is sinful—God knows why, because the church has more money than anyone! 'Give us your sins!' " Everyone laughed at Lee's joke.

"This idea of God not being in the sky is a metaphor for assuming that satisfaction is here and now, not somewhere else. Over the weekend we will consider this Baul idea. The Bauls are a sect of wandering troubadours, devotees of God from Bengal and Bihar in northern India. *Kaya sadhana*, or the sadhana of acceptance and non-rejection of the body, puts the Divine into a very present consideration, so everything is possible in and through the body—the realization of every conceivable light and the realization of every conceivable darkness. It is all here and in our immediate experience, but our expectations keep us from realizing what is possible because we are looking somewhere else, assuming it is not here yet.

"To consider that satisfaction is inherent in the fact of incarnation also holds that the opposite is true; dissatisfaction is also inherent in the fact of incarnation. The body is inherently innocent in its satisfaction and in its dissatisfaction. The child lying in its crib is inherently satisfied in its body, and when the body is too cold or too warm, it is totally innocent in its dissatisfaction. When the child looks for the mother's nipple for milk, it is not a function of dissatisfaction. The body needs a certain amount of energy to fuel it, and that fuel comes from food. So the search for food is not dissatisfaction but is part of a holistic field of satisfaction.

"This field of satisfaction includes not only the experience of pleasure, but the understanding of the confrontation with different kinds of displeasure. At the most mundane level sometimes the body shivers when it is cold, all the way to the more arbitrary treatment by adults and siblings that may not be kind. A jealous brother or sister can be pretty abusive to a baby. It's not the body that develops psychological dissatisfaction. If a dog or cat gets sick, they just go out and eat grass and throw up. They don't lay around complaining! In the human being the faculties of the mind develop slowly over time: not just the ability to do mathematics or to read, but the ability to reason and to understand the implications of our circumstances.

"Erich Neumann is a Jungian psychologist who wrote a very controversial book called *The Child.* He said that for the first year the child feels like an organic part of the mother, as if it is still in the womb, so that what happens to the mother also happens to the child. If the mother abused the child, it is like the child abusing itself. So the tendency to be self-abusive as an adult can arise out of the belief that we are supposed to be this way because we can't fault our mothers. Instead we fault ourselves. So as the mind develops, it interprets reality according to its developmental stage.

"We become adults and find the path, in spite of our psychological definition. Sometimes it is our psychological definition that leads us to the path—if we are psychologically defined by a rejection of life in the body—because the path promises transcendence. We either seek love through the body, or seek love through the rejection of the body. The path promises transcendence, and if we are defined by rejection of the body, then where better to find transcendence than in some subtle realm other than in the body? Or if we're psychologically defined by a need to control and dominate others, where better to justify that tendency than by doing it for God? So we are drawn to the path so we can manipulate and dominate others, justifiably! The old despot in Rumania was asked when he was deposed why he was so brutally repressive of his own people, his own country, of the children of this own country. He said, 'Because I just wanted a better life for them.' He really believed that to totally dominate every aspect of their lives was better for them in the long run.

"So we come to the path and we are confronted with this idea that God is not somewhere else but here and now, in the moment, in the body. We are directed to deal with all of the body's appropriate and inappropriate tendencies. All of the body's natural tendencies are appropriate and all the body's arbitrary tendencies, defined by the mind and psychology, are unnatural. Most of you probably know from even superficial knowledge of psychosomatic reactions of the body that the mind can create tremendous revolution in the body—states of higher consciousness, negative emotional or physical states. The mind can do all that. Often what we think is ours is really only a function of conditioning. We think we are supposed to be a certain way, and by the time we get there we have forgotten where the stimulus came from.

"So often we come to the path in some way resisting the body, only to find that we have to deal with the body one hundred percent, straight on, full force. The path is about the revelation of the Divine. This is a theistic path, so the language I use is the 'revelation of the Divine,' but we could also say in nontheistic language that the path is about inhering in Reality, in Truth. Really it's exactly the same thing. So whenever I talk about God, if you have a resistance to God just replace the words 'Reality' or 'Truth' for the word 'God.'

"It's a very interesting thing on the path, whether we're on a theistic or nontheistic path, how *guided* we are once we make a commitment to the path. When I first traveled around India there were certain saints who were still alive at that time who I didn't find, even though I walked within fifty meters of their ashram. It's like they were veiled from me, because my work with my Master required a very refined exclusivity of attention, and I was easily distractible. So I was not allowed to meet those masters who could have even academically had any fascination for me until my relationship with my Master was absolutely trustworthy, absolutely reliable. Many of us spend a lot of time distracted in fascinating seductions—a search for financial success or artistic success or relationship success or whatever—before we actually get to where we seriously want to be on the path. Or we float around from fascinating teacher to fascinating teacher before we actually settle down to the ordinary, practical sadhana of the path.

"When we actually find our guide on the path, it's a very personal relationship, and very exclusive. There may be other *upa* gurus, secondary teachers, perhaps mentors or other forms of teachers, but our teacher is our teacher. It is a very personal, intimate and exclusive relationship. Arnaud's relationship to Swami Prajnanpad is not in any way complicated by Arnaud's association with tremendous masters—the Karmapa, great Sufis in Afghanistan, Swami Ramdas, Anandamayi Ma—because Arnaud understands the tendency to be fascinated, and his commitment to the path is so total that his guidance by his master is absolute.

"If they don't have a teacher people say, 'How do I know when I've met my master?' It took me about ten years to actually figure out my relationship to Yogi Ramsuratkumar. Sometimes you are just drawn somewhere, you go there, you go again, and you feel you've found your path or you know this is not your path. One element of *kaya sadhana*, or 'God Does Not Live in the Sky,' that is very pertinent to my work is that to find the Divine in and through the body requires Help. Not academically—academically we can discover by ourselves. But practically speaking we need Help because the path is tremendously complex, and there are areas of the path that are extremely obscure. One of the requirements of *kaya sadhana* is to have a reliable guide. Guru is a traditional word for a reputable guide. And without guidance, we are liable to spend our lifetime lost in the maze, in the labyrinth, just chasing our tails, so to speak."

After brunch there was a two-hour period of guru *seva*, or service in which everyone was involved in various tasks—from childcare, dishwashing or cooking to digging ditches, small building projects, or gardening. People throw themselves into this work very enthusiastically here at La Ferme de Jutreau. Such enthusiasm and dedication is a tribute to the finer side of human nature, but perhaps more importantly Lee's insistence on physical work in many different forms is another reminder that God is found in the body, in the nitty-gritty of daily life. The long dharma sessions get grounded in the body in the process of digging or weeding or standing and washing dishes or playing with the children. Beyond the blessings that are incurred when one works—or more accurately, serves the work of the guru—on an ashram in any capacity are the benefits to one's own transformation in the integration of the three centers.

486

The afternoon session started at two-fifteen. Lee began: "There is an aspect of the path that E.J. Gold says everyone goes through that he calls the corridor of madness, when everything loses meaning for us and we have lost touch with the usual distractions that keep us buffered from Reality. What is it that keeps us moving forward in this process? There is undoubtedly a stage in the corridor of madness that is almost a complete rejection of everything, but we can't stop, we can't go backward. It is like the spikes in the airport parking lot—you can only drive over them in one direction.

"So what keeps us going forward? E.J. Gold says essence habits. A very important aspect of the Gurdjieff work is the learning of crafts. One of the things that gets you through the corridor is being able to weave baskets or whatever organic habit you have developed without the intellect having anything to do with it. The mind can be gone, but the body is still able to weave baskets. So this is what spiritual practice is designed to do. To give us a habit that carries us through difficult times, whether it be meditation or whatever the practice is. People often ask me when they are in a state of complacency, 'What can I do?' They feel they should always be enthusiastic, but the answer is always the same, which is if you keep practicing you will move through every stage of laziness, hesitation, fear, anger, whatever it is. Many of the people in my school ask for prayer beads to use, and they are given a mantra. It's another habit that carries people through.

"The practices that we receive in our lineage are empowered by the whole lineage. It's not just Bach who played his music with a kind of transmission; anybody who plays Bach rightly plays it with a certain transmission, because the music itself is objective. In the same way the practices are objective; there is inherent Blessing Force in the practice itself. Even when it looks like there is nothing happening on the surface—we sit in meditation and all our mind does is chatter on—as long as we maintain the practice with consistency there are extraordinary transformational effects occurring.

"In healing modalities it's understood that every physical illness has a subtle counterpart. First the subtle blueprint happens, and then over time it actually gets to the gross body. This is the philosophy behind much natural healing like homeopathy. Typically allopathy looks at the symptom and attacks the symptom, and if the symptom goes away, they say, 'Okay, you're healed.' But in natural forms of healing, like flower essence healing and so on, the subtle energetic pattern is worked with, because when that is eliminated, the problem is gone. The symptoms are nothing more than signs of a deeper problem.

"In the same way it is true that in this Work, by the time what we might call 'progress' shows up on the surface, it has been building subtly for a long time. Somehow we have to practice to the point that our practice, having become habitual, is without struggle. Then what do we do with complacency? Nothing! Keep practicing.

"So we say to ourselves, 'If I have a good reason to practice, I will,' but even freedom isn't good enough. We just have to practice for practice's sake. So people say, 'How can I do that? How can I be motivated?' Well, something very strong drew us to the path, and it doesn't matter what it was, because usually our original motives are pretty suspect anyway. So whatever it was that drew us to the path, even if we don't know what it is, we practice for that. We practice for the sake of practice, because of the overwhelming certitude that we had when we first came to the path.

"For us, our path is the only way, but that doesn't mean that other paths aren't equal in their possibility. Sometimes immature students will be defensive of their path and critical of other paths, but essentially we respect any real teacher, of which there are many, and any real path, of which there are many. But for us, our path is the only way. It's very important to respect the reality of other paths, but not to mix practices. That's sort of like taking drugs and alcohol at the same time—it's a deadly combination. Students of this school have been drawn to this school for very particular reasons, because there are other valid paths at least as effective as this one. But we get drawn to our teacher and our path for very specific reasons—whatever the reasons are, it's important to respect the integrity of that lawfulness.

"To honor that is to respect the specific practices of our school even if they seem irrelevant to us. Eastern mantras and various things can seem a little strange, and we may wonder, 'Why am I following an Eastern tradition instead of a Western tradition?'

"The harmonica player for the blues band, Shri, grew up in a very traditional, orthodox Jewish family. Her father runs a bookstore and sells only orthodox Jewish books, and predictably she reacted to her very strict upbringing and rejected it for years. When she came here, her connection to the school was very immediate, very strong. Because she trusted me in a way that she never trusted her father, all of a sudden she saw that principles that she was very familiar with as a child in her father's tradition had a whole different flavor. Instead of being something that was trying to stifle her life, they became a possibility for transformation. That whole process actually contributed to a very significant emotional healing for her and her family, which she was very much grateful for.

"We often find that the essential qualities of every tradition are very similar. Not necessarily the orthodoxy, but *real* Christianity, real Islam, real Judaism. In Buddhism there are tremendous arguments between practitioners of Zen or Tibetan, but not between mature students, because the essence of reality is the essence of reality, and if we let doctrinal differences, of which there are many, interfere with relationship, then we have missed the point of our practice.

"There are two main points here. We've been drawn to our tradition for very specific reasons—it's not arbitrary. And two, bringing integrity to the particular practices of our path is important. It's important not to mix paths. We may be very facile with the language of other paths. I've always talked a lot about Carlos Castaneda's work, or Buddhism and other systems, and I've related the similarities of the lawfulness of the paths. But one of the things you should not do is mix technology.

"When I visit Hauteville or any of the centers of Arnaud Desjardins, this is one of the difficult points, because people are so desperate for quick fixes, some kind of magic wand, and always want to know how to do Enquiry, or they want beads. I have to say, 'No, no, no—that's not your path,' because people feel that the simplicity of their path needs some more complexity or something. But however close the relationship between Arnaud and I, or Andrew Cohen and I, and certain Zen *roshis* and I may be, their practice is their practice and our practice is our practice. But we can certainly draw inspiration and understanding of the laws of the Work from any other path. So, that's where the sharing goes on.

"Whatever path you are on you have to deal with the realities of life, and some of them are very unpleasant, whether we are directly in the heat of them or not, like Kosovo. Maybe we live our lives, we work, we're healthy and so on; everything is fine, but the reality of the horrors of war is something we can't deny. Sooner or later we're going to hit a period of time in which we are directly and immediately up against piercing this paradox of life. How can God be all loving and merciful, when there is so much violence and suffering in the world? In this period of time, regardless of how simple or complex our practice, it's all going to look the same—horrible. We think to ourselves, 'How am I going to do this? No one can do this—it's too big, it's too great.' Of course we can. Everyone who has passed through it is an example for us."

Tonight after a hearty dinner of squash soup, salad, bread and Boston cream pie about thirty-five people gathered in the salon to hear Lee's talk. Everyone sat pressed close together on the floor on pillows taken from the meditation hall or on the couch or chairs (all donated to La Ferme de Jutreau by generous French and German friends of the community) scattered around the back and sides of the room.

Lee began: "I'd like to talk about the guru tonight. Here the viewpoint is not that the teacher is simply useful or valuable, but absolutely necessary. Chögyam Trungpa Rinpoche, of the Kagyu lineage—which is the lineage of the Karmapa, not of the Dalai Lama—was a teacher of Vajrayana Buddhism. There are basically three aspects of Buddhism: Hinayana, or the lesser vehicle, Mahayana or the greater vehicle, and Vajrayana, the tantric vehicle. In each of the vehicles of Buddhism the role of the teacher is viewed somewhat differently, according to Chögyam Trungpa Rinpoche. In Hinayana the teacher is seen as a guide, as a friend, someone who basically shows you the ropes, maybe as a mentor. In Mahayana Buddhism the teacher is seen as a repository of the teaching and as someone who is not just a guide but maybe even an authority. In Vajrayana Buddhism the teacher is looked at as the advantage without whom it is literally impossible to traverse the path. The guru is an absolute necessity.

"Tantric practice is called the fast vehicle, but it is also called the most dangerous vehicle. The intensity of the practice is higher and also the dangers and traps are higher. Not just failure, because what does failure mean anyway, but the danger of doing damage. If we fail in practice, all we hurt is ourselves. In one sense if we are involved with the sangha, we may disappoint our sangha friends, but that's as far as it goes. But in tantric practice the vehicle itself is deeply involved in every aspect of life—power, vanity, sexuality, greed and so on. If we make a big mistake with money or power or sex, we are not the only one involved; others may be implicated in our mistake, even disillusioned about all spiritual practice, not to mention all the karmic repercussions, another subject entirely. We'll keep it to the immediate consideration of our practice here, our lives now.

"Essentially in the tantric vehicle the guru, or teacher, is deeply involved in every aspect of the student's life because there is no separation between the student's personal life and practice life. We all tend to have this willingness to offer our lives to the teaching and the guru, but when it comes down to it we all have a lot we feel we have to defend and hide. If somebody is really serious about tantric practice—in one sense we could say this about any of the vehicles of practice, tantric or otherwise—then everything one believes they own must be offered to the guru willingly.

"Tantric schools are one of two kinds—either complete detachment or complete attachment. My path is one of complete attachment. It's a terrible path, this path! Everybody should stay away from it! In the tantric vehicle the path is one of complete disassembly of the attachments of ego. One of the tremendous problems these days is that many people, Westerners and Easterners, become teachers and think that they have the authority to forcibly mind the student's business. But it doesn't work that way. That is unlawful and dangerous. Yes, the disciple gives the master permission to mind their business, but before the teacher is willing to accept that gesture, the student has to be tested to prove their trustworthiness, reliability and integrity. So everybody wants to know these days, 'How can I trust the teacher, is the teacher genuine?'

"What the genuine teacher wants to know is, 'Can I trust the student?' Once we are tested then we are given the tantric initiation, which is a ritual in which in part we give the teacher permission to mind our business. This is a very important element of the path: to what degree do we give the teacher permission to interfere in our business, literally? So we come to the teacher and say, 'Crush my ego, I'm ready for it!' The teacher has an amazing ability to go right to the area we weren't thinking about when we said that.

"So we think, 'Oh, I'm going to give my life to the guru,' but we don't think of vanity. What if the guru said to some woman, 'I want you to stop wearing earrings! Oh my God—not that!' " The women in particular laughed at this. "I've literally had that reaction. 'Stop wearing lipstick.' 'Oh no, not that! Ask me to walk naked through the marketplace, but not that!' " More laughter. "Under any circumstances, the teacher's intersection in our lives is a crucial element to success on the path because the teacher will push us in ways that we will not push ourselves."

At this point one of the ashram cats, everybody's favorite of the three (that is, of those who like the cats)—a white cat named Pebbles who has had many interactions with Lee the past two summers—now jumped up on the sill of the open window. She had already been taken out once. Lee permits cats on the ashram to keep the mouse population down; they are not allowed in the house because there are individuals who have allergies who would not be able to come in the house if the cats were there. This has been a standard policy on Lee's ashrams with regard to animals in general for years.

Now Lee shook his head back and forth and said, 'Ah, ah, ah!' to the cat, indicating with his hands that she could sit on the sill and watch, or 'listen' so to speak, but she *could not* come into the house. He pointed his finger at her as if she understood perfectly what he meant. Then he mimicked throwing her out the window and missing, so that the cat would splat against the wall. All of this was done wordlessly in theatrical mime. A number of people burst out laughing, along with Lee. At first it seemed like she would obey Lee's "instructions," but then she persisted in trying to come into the room through the window. Finally Michael picked her up and put her on his shoulder to take her out of the room. She looked over his shoulder at the room as Michael walked through the door with her.

"She's so *pretty* . . ." Lee said, voice oozing with sentiment. This is the same cat who, last summer, jumped up on the dais with him on several different occasions and was allowed to settle in and stay there with him during darshan and meditation. He was making the same teaching point that he has made on numerous occasions over the years: our relationship to pets is sentimental, puerile and full of projections.

The cat out of the room, he now continued with his discourse. "Okay, any questions?" No one moved or said anything. "Seminars here at La Ferme de Jutreau are really tough. Everywhere else I go people have questions! I never have to think of anything to say!

"So this idea of having the guru minding your business—it doesn't mean that you should write the teacher long letters confessing everything. The disposition is, 'Now that I've come to the path, and now that I'm in your company, you may guide me in any way necessary.' It doesn't mean that you have to testify to all of your secret hells. Please spare the teacher that."

A woman raised her hand and asked, "What are the laws of the path for the couple?"

"There are no laws of the path for the couple," Lee said. "All of the laws are between the guru and the student. Certainly we make recommendations to couples, and considering the tradition of this school, which is the Baul tradition, relationship begins with physical desire. Physical, sexual union is a metaphor, a symbol for union with God. So both the man and woman are trained in sexual yoga, but the impersonal use of the yoga comes way, way later in the relationship. In the beginning it is physical.

"So there are two elements of relationship. There is the machine, the physical biology of it. The other aspect is the whole personal relationship. Can we accept one another's eccentricities? What do we repress? What are we willing to say? Sometimes some thing about our partner upsets us but we don't want to say it. It goes on for months or years and it becomes this gigantic barrier between us. It could be something very dumb. Maybe it's that every time the man has sex he passes loud gas and says, 'Oh, that was great.' "

Lee was building up steam now. He smiled devilishly and launched into a comedy routine. "Men are so *proud* of their gas! They let a good one rip and look around at their wives as if they've done something really significant, substantial, when all they've done is stink up the kitchen!" Raucous laughter broke out from some, while others sat mute, as if in disbelief. Lee proceeded to go off on a monologue about letting off gas, how women do it, how men do it. "I think women have permanent control over the sphincter muscle! They just go *poooh* and men go *braaakkkk!*"

Lee's sound effects were hilarious. The room dissolved into embarrassed giggles and loud guffaws. But after all, the subject matter of the weekend was 'God Does Not Live In the Sky,' one of the fundamental precepts of Lee's teaching. His ongoing demonstrations of our level of contraction or relaxation in relationship to the basic functions of the body were not just the adolescent ravings of a fool but were aimed very directly at an important target. How can we get the teaching in the body if we are frozen stiff from the waist down? If we suppress every bodily function out of fear of censure and shame? How can we even consider sacred sex if the basic functions of the human body, where sex takes place, are considered taboo?

He continued, "We just toured Germany and when you're in Germany you eat a lot of pig. It just *rots* when it gets in there, it takes so long to digest pork! Talk about bad gas— oh, it's terrible! But it's a good way to get seats on the bus!" More raucous laughter from the group.

"So you have to stay in physical contact with your partner, even just looking one another in the eye. And you should maintain committed monogamous relationship. Committed means that you do the best you can to work out any difficulties in the relationship. You don't pretend they don't exist. So to be able to do that we have to have a tremendous amount of acceptance of each other, because we will always have similarities and differences with our partners. Part of the health of the relationship is the allowing of differences to be healthy. Sometimes we want our partner to change in ways that, were they actually to change, they would lose the attraction that they have for us.

"Essentially it's important that partners be friends. Just enjoy one another's company. Be able to laugh together—a very important quality. Every time one partner laughs if the other partner says, 'What did I do—why are you laughing at me?' that's kind of paranoid. So those are just some thoughts off the top of my head. But primarily most of it is not in the domain of a teacher's input but in the domain of basic human common sense."

Lee brought the space to a close with a reminder that in an hour he would be sitting in the salon having tea with anyone who chose to join him. He said smiling, "So, there will be tea at nine-thirty in this room, mint tea with no honey . . . Jai Guru!" As he walked out, people were laughing.

An hour later the group slowly gathered in the salon for tea. Each new person coming in chose a place on the other end of the room from where Lee was sitting in his leather chair by the fireplace. As more people sat down the room became so lopsided in the seating arrangement that it was funny. With each new person who came in and chose a seat as far away from Lee as he or she could get, the whole room burst into laughter. It was a pregnant space, veering along the edge of hilarity just beneath the respectful surface hush. When Marie Françoise came in having just arrived from the train at Chatellerault, she took a seat near the edge of the group rather than one of the many empty seats closer to Lee. Everyone laughed.

Lee said, "Better a little too far from the master than too close." Then he mimicked a future time, pretending to be shocked and horrified at people sitting right around and up next to his chair. "Some day," he shrugged and smiled slightly. All of this went on in an atmosphere of relaxed enjoyment, and included everyone in the space. It was difficult for the guests who didn't speak English to follow, but Lee's communication of all-inclusiveness seemed to be the foundation of the mood that he was creating in this informal space.

The evening tea spaces frequently have a Mahayana flavor to them. "There's room for everyone," Judith Lief once said at a talk on the Mahayana vehicle of Buddhism at Lee's ashram in Arizona. There is a tremendous extension of friendship, warmth, intimacy and enjoyment that is immediately available to everyone who comes in—that is, everyone who is willing to meet that offer with the same. For many people this space can be tense and uncomfortable because of the close proximity to the spiritual master, and yet Lee offers everyone who comes to the seminar the opportunity to come close to him—at tea, at dinner, in the close quarters of the living room dharma talks.

Again Lee inquired about when the Lewises were coming in. Andrea gave him another update. Then he turned his attention toward Guedeh, who had just walked into the room, having arrived a few minutes before from Montpellier. "It's nice to see you. Are all the girls here?" Guedeh shyly said, "Thank you, yes." She gestured outside where her three daughters were having evening snacks with all the other children and teenagers under the maple tree in the courtyard. Lee said, "I saw two of them—they're getting more beautiful every year." He smiled kindly.

Chris came in and mentioned that there was a whole Boston cream pie left from dinner—maybe the guests who just arrived would like some with their tea, since everyone else had the dessert at dinner? Lee turned to Guy, Guedeh, Marie Françoise and a few other guests who had just arrived and asked, "*Gâteau?*" Yes, most of them answered. The Boston cream pie—two layers of vanilla cake with a filling of custard in the middle, lavished with a rich, thick and extremely sweet layer of chocolate on top, was brought out and served to the new arrivals. They sat and ate in silence. Just before she took her last bite Marie Françoise looked up at Lee and said with a little smile, "It's good!"

"English!" Lee said, smiling warmly at her, since Marie Françoise speaks very little English. Sitting by the bookcase Susanne said, "It *was* incredibly delicious . . ." speaking from her experience of having eaten it at dinner. Lee turned toward her and said with a smile, "Just like practice—that pie just reminded me of meditation!" He laughed. Chris said, "Yeah, we were all meditating when we ate that pie tonight—meditating on desire."

Lee looked at the small vase of fresh flowers on the table next to his chair and said with a droll innocence that could only hide a sly and rather dry sense of humor, "It's nice to see flowers that are alive. Most of the flowers in my spaces are dead." He looked around brightly and laughed. Brindavan, the ashram manager who had just returned from being away for a week and who usually puts the flowers on Lee's desk, turned red and shook her head. There is nothing she hates more than some detail around Lee not being handled well, and now she was berating herself for not leaving a note to someone to change the flowers.

Noticing her reaction Lee protested, "Really, it's okay, I kind of like it that way." By now everyone was laughing with him as he said, "It's a good shock for people—they come up to the spiritual master's desk and see dead flowers sticking up . . ." He laughed again, adding his sly chuckles to the growing mayhem.

Suddenly Lee changed the subject, saying "It's a perfect time for a fax!"

Brinda said, "Yes, they usually start coming in about this time," it being early afternoon in the American Southwest.

Lee turned to Valerie and said, "No trip to Brussels this year! Everyone from the seminar last year was from Paris." A conversation began about the first talk Lee gave in Brussels, two summers ago, when one hundred fifty people came and seventy-five of them walked out during the first hour of the talk. The talk was one of those outrageous, provocative and completely ecstatic events that Lee creates with no obvious effort on his part. He was just being himself. People were so offended by his bawdy antics that one of the women who was hosting Lee and his party had said, "Is he *trying* to turn people off?"

The answer was probably yes to that question, but it would have been impossible to put that into the context in which it belonged in the moment as Lee was working the space over. The room was buzzing with shakti. The presence of Yogi Ramsuratkumar was so powerful that everyone was being blasted with heat and light. People had one of two reactions: either allow the mind to be stopped and fall into bliss and open-eyed ecstasy, or contraction and recoil. After half of the people had left, Lee gave the rest of the talk to a group that was in a state of ecstatic intoxication from the subtle wine that flowed for the rest of the night. It was one of those strange nights when no recording equipment had been set up, but the talk turned out to be so extraordinary that it has found a place in the oral tradition of the Hohm Community.

Michael added, "I tried to get a conference there in Brussels to give a talk about Yogi Ramsuratkumar, but they said that if I had a flyer that said Lee Lozowick was my spiritual master, no one would come!" Another wave of laughter passed through the group and subsided.

Even with the discomfort of guests and students who were not sure of the protocol of the space, or how to interact with the guru under these circumstances, Lee had managed to weave everyone in the room into relationship with him through his skillful use of humor, give-and-take conversation and just simply revealing himself to be quite human and ordinary. In the midst of all this, constant small and large teaching communications were offered if one chose to observe at that level. More than anything it seemed that Lee just wanted people to relax and enjoy the good company of friends gathered for the purpose of the path. Not long after that, about ten-thirty, Lee got up from his chair and said goodnight. Lee's parting shot as he walked out the door was, "Quick—send a fax!"

August 7, 1999
La Ferme de Jutreau

Lee began his talk this morning, the second day of the seminar, speaking about the phrase he commonly uses, "Jai Guru." He explained that in India the terms *namasté* and *namaskar* are commonly used, which means, "The oneness in me honors the oneness in you." But the Bauls use the phrase "Jai Guru," which means "Victory to the guru," as a greeting and as a closure to spaces.

"The guru works with us from the human level because he understands our hopes, our dreams and wishes. So he works with us at the human level instead of in some ethereal way. The Bauls say, 'Victory to the guru!' because the guru has only one aim—to serve the realization of the Truth in the disciple. If the guru is victorious, the disciple has realized the Truth."

Halfway through the talk Lee answered a question about enlightenment. He began a discourse that lasted for the rest of the meeting. He said, "In the field of awakening or enlightenment there are no relatives. Somebody is either awake or asleep. They're either enlightened or they're not. They're either self-realized or they're self-centered. It's one or the other, there's no kind of graduation. At the same time, once somebody is enlightened or awake or self-realized, once it is a fact, once it's done, finished, accomplished, then there is a tremendous relativity within that particular context. But no teacher represents it that way. Most teachers are completely idealistic: '*This* is what you have to do, no less will do.'

"Take the Tibetan Buddhists, for example: Let's say there are twenty Tibetan Buddhists in the world who are supposed to be enlightened. Who knows? If you put them all in the same place there is going to be a vast—I mean *vast*—diversity between their manifestations.

"Before the state of awakening occurs everything is subjective. It's all sleep. We have to move from the context of sleep to the context of awakening. But once the context of awakening is stabilized then the whole thing is subjective again. If you look at people who are supposed to be enlightened, everybody disagrees. Every enlightened person in the world disagrees about who else is enlightened. That's very confusing for us poor seekers! How are we supposed to decide anything? Can't these people get together and come up with some reliable criteria or something? I mean, like 'Anybody who's had this many affairs can't be enlightened!' or whatever. Can't we decide these things?" Lee chuckled.

"This is one of the very paradoxical aspects of the spiritual path. Gurdjieff said that unless we master the machine completely, unless there are no autonomous 'I's' but just one unified 'I,' we can't work. Whenever an 'I' manifests, we have to be absolutely conscious. Relatively speaking, that's an ideal that is impossible to achieve. And yet, that's the demand.

"So whatever teacher and whatever path we approach, the demand is impossible. The expectation is impossible. And yet, we have to meet the demand in order to invoke the full effect of the help and blessing of the lineage. But here's a secret—a great, esoteric secret. You only have to do it for a moment. Phew! What a relief! Once you're on the other side then it's a whole different story. Then what do you do with the machine? Who cares! Let the machine do whatever the hell it wants. So, you have to do the impossible to realize, but once you have realized, you don't have to keep doing the impossible anymore. But once you've realized, you still have to function in a way that maintains that realization. You have to keep practicing, and you have to live lawfully in relationship to the laws of Reality. But the machine becomes a tool to be used when necessary.

"So, let's talk about psychological neuroses. If you look at any spiritual master—I have to except my spiritual Master—and study them from a psychological perspective, regardless of how brilliant they are, you may say, 'This person needs help. He (she) is not sane.' One of my former woman students was a therapist. When I would be doing something she used to look at me very lovingly, but she'd be thinking, 'If only Lee would enter into therapy with me I could really fix him. Really get him straight!' " Lee chuckled. "She actually offered me that possibility, but I declined!"

The laughter had begun to build in sporadic bursts of chuckles as Lee continued, "And then I did a terrible thing—I *laughed*, because it was so funny. Then she *really* got furious! She was yelling!" Lee laughed again. "That was all I had to say! And then she finally said, as women will do, 'Hah! You're impossible!' and she walked off." Lee was laughing hard at this point, grabbing his sides and bending over.

"It's still funny! Fortunately, every once in a while I can enjoy my students this way." Still laughing, Lee wiped his eyes and slowly his chuckles died down. "I still remember the look on her face, like it was a personal insult. Oh, boy! She was fit to be tied!"

"So every teacher, if you look at them on a psychological basis, is just as neurotic as anybody else. Maybe not quite as neurotic as everybody else, but still neurotic. There was a very famous Indian guru who had a big ashram in southern India. He had these pets. He had a dog, a pony, and an elephant. They would bring the dog in and the guru would throw the ball. The dog would run and chase the ball and bring the ball back, and the guru would throw the ball again. It was a big, black dog—the kind that really has a body. Maybe it was a Rottweiler. It was big though, you know, one of those big dogs with a body that could stop a truck!

"So he'd take the ball, and . . . you know, if you're raised in America and you play baseball you learn how to throw, but the guy never learned how to throw. So he'd take this ball and he'd kind of . . ." Lee gestured an oddball pitch of the ball to demonstrate, "and the ball would just fly somewhere into the audience, hit somebody in the head!" More laughter as Lee graphically painted the picture.

"There were three, four hundred people there, and the dog would just *take off*, knocking people over as he chased the ball! The guru would, 'Hhhheehh-hhhheehh-hhhheehh,' he'd laugh, you know, watching people get knocked over. The dog would step on people. He thought this was a riot. Is that neurotic or what? But wait! It gets better. We were there in 1976 and I hadn't met Yogi Ramsuratkumar yet, so He hadn't started to work on my so-called enlightened ego. I was very arrogant and irreverent in 1976. It's embarrassing actually. Now, of course, I would never be so irreverent . . ." Lee chuckled.

"So, one time this guy threw the ball and it went right to one of my students. He looked at me and I said, 'Hide it!' The poor dog! The dog went in the direction of the ball and then started looking around." Lee started making noises and looking around as if he was the dog.

"The dog started whining. Everybody else there was a devotee, so when they'd get the ball, they'd give it to the dog so he could run back to the guru, knock over some more people, so the guru could throw it again, and he could knock over some more people. We weren't devotees, we were just tourists visiting the ashram.

"So when he was finished with the dog, the pony came out. The pony was supposed to be some kind of special animal. You know how it is in India when a spiritual master has some kind of animal around him. They always have this myth about how the animal is a devotee from a past life or is going to be a devotee in the next life. So it's very important that the animal act a certain way, because if the animal doesn't act a certain way, then the devotees might lose their faith in the master. They might become disillusioned about the extraordinary blessing aura of the teacher. The objective criterion for such things is someone like Saint Francis. In India, because the life of Saint Francis is so well known, the Western devotees will say, 'Oh, so and so is *just like* Saint Francis. The animals just come and have no fear . . .' So it's very important for the animals to act a certain way." Lee chuckled.

"So they bring out the pony, and the pony is trained. The guru has a piece of sugar and when he offers the pony the sugar, the pony does a little trick. It gets down on its knees and it puts its head to the ground. All the devotees go, 'Aaaaaahhhhhhh!' A collective sigh rises from the devotees, 'Look! The pony is spontaneously demonstrating its devotion to our master.' "

People were laughing hysterically at Lee's theatrical rendering of the tale, falling over their pillows onto the floor. Through the laughter Lee had gotten the room worked up to a point of relaxation and abandon that brought the group attention directly into the moment. Everyone was included in the fun. Nobody was stuck in seriousness or offended by Lee's off-color humor and provocative statements. Self-importance had flown out the window.

"We were there one morning and the guru forgot the sugar. The pony came out—it's just an animal, the poor thing! It looks for the sugar, but he doesn't have the sugar. The guru looks at the pony like, 'You've done this, you do this every morning. Come on! Bow anyway!' The pony doesn't bow without the sugar. The trainer sees the pony isn't bowing. He's got one of those little sticks and he whacks the front shins of the pony, so the pony—*phunmph!*—goes down on its knees because its front legs were whacked. And everybody in the audience goes 'Ooohhhhhhhh!' as if the pony were *pranaming* out of love. Is that neurotic or what? The guru looks at the pony and smiles like, 'My devotee.'

"So, the pony finishes and they bring the elephant out." Everyone laughed. "God forbid that the elephant should have to go to the bathroom while he's with the guru. Or if the elephant had gas! All the devotees are supposed to be mature; they are there with their spiritual master, worshipping their spiritual master. But you know, if the elephant had gas it would be the funniest thing half the people in the space had ever seen in their lives. Instead of laughing naturally, they'd have to keep it together for the master!

"When I was about thirteen years old and I was still very immature, I went with my mother to the Grand Canyon in America. You can look at it and see how beautiful it is, but you can also hire donkeys or a mule and they take you down this very narrow path into the canyon. It takes a whole day to go down into the canyon. You have a terrible little lunch they've put into a cardboard box—a horrible sandwich on dried-out white bread and a piece of limp lettuce—and then you ride back up. Maybe this is a routine, I only did it once, so I don't know, but I was halfway down and all the mules start having this tremendous gas attack at the same time.

"I thought it was the funniest thing I'd ever heard in my life. I was hysterical. All the adults were," Lee's words were inaudible over the loud and rowdy uproar as another fit of laughter took over the group. He continued, "The adults weren't letting themselves laugh, but it was really funny. The thing is all the donkeys go down the path nose to ass. There is no room in between them. It's a line of donkeys. Not only are they making noise, but the person behind them is getting this hurricane-like donkey gas." More laughter. "So, I'm hysterical. I'm practically falling off my donkey laughing and I look at my mother and her eyes are full of tears but . . ." Any shred of order and decorum left in the room now dissolved in unbridled laughter. Lee was laughing too, wiping his eyes, his shoulders shaking with laughter.

"So, you may be asking, 'What does all this have to do with the unitive I?' Ah! More than you might imagine. Are there any questions so far?"

Lee started telling the story of how his teaching work began in 1975 when he was still teaching Silva Mind Control. "So I was walking down the streets of New York City with a friend after having just seen some spiritual teacher, some Sufi or some yogi, I don't remember. We were having this passionate discussion, my friend and I, and he made a statement that was really brilliant. I had this epiphany based on what he said. I said 'Wow! That's great! Who said that?' He turned to me and said, "You did. Just last month." I said, 'I said that? That was pretty good.' Then he said, 'You should be teaching.' I said, 'Maybe I should.' That's how it all started.

"So of course I started teaching, and I was teaching in the form of the guru and disciple. My first book, *Spiritual Slavery*, which is not available anymore, really put me out as a role model. In the book I kept saying things like, 'I did it, you can do it, all you have to do is do like me.' I really fixated on myself.

"All my students kept saying I was enlightened. It's very important for students to feel that their teacher is enlightened!" Lee chuckled. "So as time has gone on, the whole issue of enlightenment has become more and more problematical to me. Why, only today actually I realized why it was so problematical. Not until I started talking this morning about the subjectivity within the domain of enlightenment did I realize, 'Oh, that's why it's problematical.' Right. Never knew that. So as time has gone on this whole idea of how the master is enlightened has become an issue I don't like. I don't like the way we have to define the whole thing—he's this, he's that. After the first year I was teaching I stopped saying things like that about myself. 'I'm enlightened, I'm the greatest teacher the history of the world has ever seen,' and things like that. How embarrassing! How immature!

"Every time somebody has one of these shifts of context, it feels like they are the only one that this has ever happened to. It's like when we have a fabulous sexual experience, and we're thinking to ourselves, 'Only I understand this.' We look at our parents and we don't stop to think, 'Ah, they've been doing that shit for years.' " Lee laughed.

"We look into the gaping chasm of our partner's vagina and we think the Universe is in there! We have this revelation and we think, 'Only someone as sensitive as I could realize such majestic splendor . . .' We don't stop to think that every drunk lying in the gutter has felt the same thing. We think, 'If I could get my head in there, my life would be complete!' With some embarrassment I have to tell you I've tried, and it doesn't work!"

Throughout this monologue people were laughing nonstop, with Lee's words interspersed with his own chuckles. His spontaneity in this craziness was amazing. "Oh, you know, I just got it. Maybe I should try the top first." More laughter. "Maybe it would work then . . ." His words became inaudible again as the volume of the group's laughter reached another peak. " . . . bottom first, no wonder it never worked! Sure, if you could fit the point in first, then maybe you could kind of stretch it out . . . Once you've see that baby come out, you know, it's like, *wow*! That thing can really stretch. Sometimes it doesn't stretch, sometimes it rips. Oooooo!" Lee grimaced as if in pain.

"Or in the hospital, they just take a scalpel. Tchhew!" He shook his head, "Slice it up to make it easy. Then somebody else has to sew you up, so you get to pay another thousand dollars. Why not just have a midwife—any woman who knows how to sew, who's ever sewed a sock—to sew you up. What do you need to pay a hospital technician a thousand

497

dollars to put a couple of stitches in you for? Just get some housewife—tchk, tchk, tchk—to sew you up fine. Take the cat, hang it up, pull out some gut . . ." Lee seemed out of control, hanging on to reason by a slender thread, and it appeared that he was enjoying it immensely. It was crazy, and yet it was a craziness that felt good, while at the same time underlying his monologue was a serious commentary on the downside of life in the Western world. Finally the laughter began to subside.

"Anyway . . . We all think we're so special. 'Oh, I am so sensitive to have perceived this mystical wonder!' You take your girlfriend home—this is only for the men—you take your girlfriend home and you come out of the bedroom having just had this *revelation*. You walk into the living room and there's your father, sitting there with a beer can and his big fat belly, farting and smelling and watching the television. You look at your father with contempt, 'Look at this *slob*! After what *I* have just felt and experienced with my girlfriend—the *wonders of mystical union*—and look at this pig!'

"Your father is sitting there and he looks at you and—you know, he's had a thousand experiences that would make your little epiphany look like nothing. You look at him and think, 'Ugh, if only he understood.' " Lee chuckled.

"There's your mother in the kitchen, cooking away. 'Hi honey!' You think, 'Oh, God! My mother is so droll. So unenlightened. I bet she's never even had an orgasm,' while your mother's been hanging from the ceiling for years, screaming and wailing! Having seen the universe open and galaxies created. We think we're just so," Lee laughed, "exclusive." He kept laughing at how ridiculous the delusions of vanity and self-importance appear to him.

"We smoke a joint and have sex and we think this is the greatest thing. Back in the fifties, when things were innocent, our fathers had visions like that based on our mother's pot roast." The group laughter had been ecstatic for almost an hour during Lee's foolishness. It was jubilant, whole body laughter, unfettered, loose and free. It was a feast for the moving center. Who can say what the long-term effects of this kind of transmission are? Certainly there are potential transformational effects. These experiences also often have a purificatory feeling to them: Lee is working over the first two chakras, where so much psychological garbage is stuck in Westerners. Birth, death, sex, food and shit.

But the immediate felt result is clarity, a feeling of wholeness, a grounded and integral euphoria that comes out of these sessions. One feels revitalized and vivified in an extraordinary way. In all this crazy laughing Lee gives one a taste of the Primacy of Natural Ecstasy and the real life of the body, which is free of the constraints of the mind. Lee transports his audience into these rare experiences by radical means; Bauls are natural rebels and iconoclasts; they travel the *ulta* path—in other words, they go in the opposite direction of mainstream culture.

Lee continued, careening through the labyrinth down which he was leading us, "They didn't need LSD, they didn't need drugs! They'd go to bed and say, 'Honey, I'm so high from that meatloaf you made me for dinner.' That's it! They were into it. Right? We think, 'Oh! If only my parents could have seen this. They *did*, you know?" Lee threw his head back and laughed. "You'd be surprised at the things your parents did making you. Shocked! 'Oh God, no—not my mother!' We do things with our partners and we think nothing of it. And then we look at our mothers and just the thought that our mothers could have done something like that is horrible. They did worse!" More laughter.

"Believe me, when you're locked in your room with your boyfriend or girlfriend, your parents know what you're doing. We bring our girlfriends home from college—maybe they don't do this in France, but in America they do—and we say to our girlfriend, 'Don't make any noise because my parents are right next door.' Our girlfriend's leg accidentally smacks into the wall and we say, 'Woah!' As if our parents don't know what's going on! As if they're saying, 'Oh, isn't that sweet, they're just studying in there!' For biology, you know.

"So you might be saying *again*, what does all this have to do with the unitive 'I' of Gurdjieff? Well, isn't it obvious? It's very important. Students always think their teachers have to be enlightened. I have to keep pretending in between enlightenments, because periodically I have these awakenings, but in between time," he chuckled, "I have to leave it to my dream body. People are always giving me these *fantastic* dreams they have. Wow! Great dreams. I read them. I say, 'Huh, where was I?' because I'm not there. I'm biding time until the next awakening experience, treading water. I'm saying, 'Oh, I hope nobody finds out.' Fortunately they come frequently enough! People say, 'Oh! The guru is really on today.' I say, '*Phew*! I made it through another month!'

"So fortunately for all of us, Yogi Ramsuratkumar never sleeps. He's always on. He often visits my students looking like me. But, you know, it's really Him. He has to look like me to help build the Lee Lozowick myth. And maybe someday, I'll be like Him. Probably not, but one never can say . . . ."

Comments like "I have to keep pretending between enlightenments" are exactly the kind of enigmatic statements that draw criticism toward Lee from those who want their dharma pre-digested. It also drives some of his students crazy as well. The mind interferes with its litany of complaint, "I wish he would just say things clearly," or "I wish he would explain what he means," or "I can't understand him when he's like this" or "I hate it when he talks like he's not enlightened." But it is a teaching style that generates tremendous insight for the student who is willing to burn with a question until it is answered organically, from within the recesses of his or her own innate wisdom and personal experience. The value of this kind of learning is beyond measure.

After a simple but substantial meal of salad and baked potatoes, thirty-five people were gathered in the salon while many others finished hand-washing all the dishes for over fifty people. Lee sat again in the leather chair in front of the fireplace for the evening talk. Marie Françoise talked about using anger to protect one of her children, and she said that her experience was that rage had value at times. Lee began to speak to this issue.

"Ordinarily we are slaves to our primal emotions. Things happen to us and we make decisions based on that. 'I'm bad, I'm talented, I'm stupid,' like that, and for the rest of our lives we function in a way that confirms that original decision.

"I was just reading about anorexia, and how a fair number of Christian saints in the Middle Ages were actually anorexic, because the definition of sanctity included a complete hatred of the body. It was a perfect circumstance to be considered very saintly instead of being considered very sick. The basis of anorexia, according to this book, is a feeling of never being good enough. That gets translated into never being thin enough. This is a decision that is made as an infant based on some stimuli in the environment. Maybe our father says to us, 'I hate fat women; there's nothing worse than fat women,' and we're three years old and something clicks. We spend the rest of our lives, no matter what our objective body image is, wanting our father to love us. We don't feel that he does, so we get thinner and thinner. It's a standard scenario based on a primal decision.

"We can try to change those primal imperatives by efforts of will, and occasionally we can be successful at that, but ordinarily we won't be. Our unconscious will always find some way of sabotaging the change. We have a failure mechanism and we take a positive thinking course. We decide we're going to buckle down and think hard and make more money. And we actually start making more money, but some disaster always happens that takes all our financial reserves. We sabotage ourselves—our house burns down, we wreck our car. Something always happens.

"Often primal decisions have to do with our emotional state, which is much subtler. The psychological cramp isn't just formed around positive states, but also around negative or painful states. Unconsciously we say, 'I'm only going to be happy (or unhappy) when these conditions are met,' or 'I'm only going to be full of pride or vanity when these conditions are met.' It makes no sense. I'm sure you've all seen a man with a really grossly obvious, cheap hairpiece looking in the mirror like no one can see him being completely vain, when actually the hairpiece makes him look like a clown. Or a sixty-five-year-old woman who is dressing like a sixteen-year-old, walking along looking in the mirror, imagining that she actually looks like a sixteen-year-old. Anyone looking at that from the outside wonders, 'How can that person not see?'

"The point is that our manifestations are not spontaneous, and part of the transformational process, which is accepting ourselves as we are, doesn't eliminate those qualities. They don't go away; they become qualities that serve our lives but don't define our lives. If rage can protect our children, instead of saying, 'Rage is bad and I shouldn't manifest rage, I should have equanimity,' there it is and it gets used.

"So when we accept what is as it is, without judgement, without opinion, it alters the mechanism of the fear, anger or happiness. The body in its total complexity—not separated into psychology, personality, mind, emotion, the astral body, the etheral body and all this business—begins to function holistically when we accept what is. The body naturally and instinctually produces what is of value in any given circumstance; what is not of value the body doesn't animate. If fear is valuable, fear arises. If fear isn't valuable, fear doesn't arise."

Someone asked the question, "Would you talk more about Gurdjieff and the separate 'I's'?"

Lee responded, "I guess we got distracted by other considerations, of our college girlfriends. Or at least my college girlfriend." He laughed then continued. "Gurdjieff said that as long as these multiple 'I's' are at war with one another we can never function consciously, because any stimuli can trigger one of the 'I's' that we're not aware of in any moment. Some of you have probably had the experience of going to see a movie or a theatre piece and your conscious mind is responding to it. But you leave the theatre and you are feeling something very different than what your conscious mind says you should be feeling. Often we can't trace where that feeling is coming from. It could be that somebody in the movie looked like somebody from our past, or anything really . . .

"The unitive 'I' is not like a white canvas. It's like a tapestry. It doesn't have an image, but for the sake of conversation we can give it one. So the idea is, in the Gurdjieff work, that when one unifies one's 'I's' that one gains control over one's manifestations, so one is not a slave to personality or psychology. When we are moving through life doing whatever we do—in relationship with friends, lovers, families, business associates—the more free we are in terms of our manifestations the more real our relationships are with our world, whether it be with people, animals, money, nature.

"So the primary principle is to be able to relate with our world objectively for who we are as an entire complex of moods, emotions and talents, and to be at the effect of the need of the moment, or the circumstance. The main point is to be able to relate to our world from a position of Reality as it is, not as we think it is, not as we imagine it to be, not as we wish it was, but *as it is*. If we have a unitive 'I' then we can do what is wanted and needed in any given moment, and we won't be dissuaded by competing 'I's' because there aren't any competing 'I's'.

"When we have a unitive 'I' we are very clear about whatever is most useful for the Work under any given circumstance. Fascinations and seductions may wave at us, but they have no force, they can't move us. Whereas when we have multiple 'I's' each one has a tremendous amount of its own power. When that power is linked with an ally in the environment, it banishes all the other 'I's'. When the 'I' is unitive the circumstances that trigger our psychology have no force because there is no alliance to be formed.

"In principle, this is the theory of the unitive 'I' versus the multiple 'I's'—to be able to practice in every moment in a way that serves that moment effectively, creatively. Whatever serves the moment effectively or creatively is that which takes the entire environment into regard. Theoretically, according to the Work, the only way to develop this unitive 'I' is to give up self-centeredness. As long as we are self-centered we cannot have a unitive 'I'. When we are functioning unitively, we will automatically consider the environment, which includes other people in the environment, the room or space we are in. And we will naturally function in a way that respects the needs or the protocol of the environment. That's one purpose for working toward a unitive 'I'."

August 8, 1999
La Ferme de Jutreau

After meditation the morning talk of the seminar began at eight-thirty. Lee started out by asking, "Any questions, wiggled up from your unconscious?" He chuckled.

Louis said, "In the last darshan you said that the work goes on twenty-four hours a day in a tantric school—in this school. So after I went home, I thought what can I do? I thought about prayer, but I have no material."

Lee responded, "Part of the ongoing process of becoming a student here is getting 'material.' So the word 'prayer' is a good word to use, and there is formal prayer and informal prayer. Formal prayers we could call mantras, or we have a meal prayer—we don't say it out loud in the hall, but people who know it say it to themselves. But informal prayer is like an ongoing question, which can take a very specific form like 'What is God?' or 'How can I work, how can I practice?' or 'How can I pray?' That in itself is a prayer, or a kind of unarticulated question. It can be the mood of desire to serve, or desire to move ahead on the path. It can be that simple.

"Often we think that if we have something concrete that we can wrap our minds around then we are doing something, but not necessarily. If we are going to practice twenty-four hours a day, the mind will get exhausted at some point. No matter how willful we are no one can practice with mental awareness twenty-four hours a day. A lot of the practice is about invoking Presence, in which case whatever we are doing—even day-dreaming or doing nothing—is actually practice.

"I mention this as a formality, not because everybody in this room will become students, and some of you already have teachers: as people progress as students, and the more deeply one wishes to become a student of this school, the more exclusivity I look for. By exclusivity I don't mean that we stop reading other books or going to classical music concerts, or that if we go to see another blues concert besides Shri that we're having an affair or something like that." Everyone laughed. "Although I do expect all students to have all of the music of all of the bands that we have produced. It's just a sign of willingness to support the community in whatever way we can. But as we become more involved in wanting to be a student of this school, I expect to see more exclusivity. That means if you were a *sannyasin*, a student of Osho Rajneesh, but you're not anymore and you're looking for a new teacher, sooner or later, I want the *mala*!" Sporadic laughter sprang from those who knew that all Rajneesh *sannyasins* had a *mala* with Osho's picture on it.

"I was in Quebec at Eric's ashram, Mangalam, a few months ago. There was a woman there who had a *mala* from Siddha Yoga, Muktananda's organization, and a bracelet from Ammachi. She came up to me during one of the breaks and said, 'Can I have a mantra?' I said, 'Absolutely not! For you it's just another souvenir, like you buy at the circus.' So to get materials, or formal practices, I have to see a certain kind of sincerity, which, Louis, you've indicated. Then people have to *ask* for it. Sometimes they get it, sometimes they don't. But I don't give anything away unasked for. All the people who have *malas* that you see, I never gave any of those without having been *asked*. Does that address the question?" Louis nodded yes.

"To take up time until ten-thirty—which is time to *eat*! I don't know how some of you French women stay so thin in this country. We come over here and in four months we go back to America." Lee imitated being fat, spread his arms out as if over a huge belly and puffed his cheeks out. Once again he was poking fun at another form of body hatred—the fear of fat. "You don't *eat*—that's how you do it! I watch you take one tomato and a little piece of goat cheese, one little slice of sausage, one thin slice of bread. People sit there and watch us!" His eyes got big as if in shock at seeing such a sight.

"A couple of years ago we were being hosted and it was salmon season; our hosts served these beautiful little slices of raw salmon with lemon. In America when we eat fish we eat these frozen white fish—terrible stuff! It comes out of the ocean, so we call it fish! You can imagine, raw salmon is really a treat. So we walked in and saw it. It was just an appetizer to the meal—we were supposed to just take one or two slices—but Lee and the gang came in and everybody looked at the raw salmon, then they looked at me like, 'Raw salmon! What should we do?' I wanted to make sure there was a little left for the French, so I only took six pieces, just to start with! That was the go-ahead for the Americans, so that the salmon plates were decimated—they looked like a war area! You know, the hostess was very polite, she came out and looked at the salmon, you could just see the pupils of her eyes dilate. She was very sweet and polite.

"But I always wonder when we go to these houses and they serve these mountains of food—weeks worth of food! I wonder what they do with all of it, because I know people like to go shopping and buy fresh food everyday. I feel responsible to do my part and finish it off! So if any of you ever host us, remember!" Lee chuckled before he said the next sentence. "If you want anything leftover, don't serve it!" Everyone was laughing hard at this point. Lee wiped tears out of his eyes from laughing so hard. "Okay—I'm not sure how we got into that, but . . . I'm not exaggerating, by the way."

Lee began to tell the story of how he realized that Yogi Ramsuratkumar was his teacher. By 1980 and 1981 Lee had started to send Yogi Ramsuratkumar letters and poems of devotion. He then told the whole story of the 1986 trip to India with twenty-one people, who he took to meet his master, Yogi Ramsuratkumar.

"So we got to India in 1986, and when we got there Yogi Ramsuratkumar didn't recognize me. I'd been writing to Him for six years, and when I was there in 1979 I had already dedicated a book to Him. That story is the most miraculous of all, but I won't tell that this morning—perhaps at the next seminar! But seriously folks, I had the book with me in 1979 and He saw it and saw the dedication to Him and He praised the book over and over. So I figured He knew who I was. But in 1986 He didn't remember me—really! This was kind of disturbing, to put it mildly . . . ."

"So we went back to the States, the Work continued to go on, and two years later I got an invitation from one of his devotees, somebody I didn't know in southern India, inviting me to Yogi Ramsuratkumar's birthday celebration in Nagercoil. He wouldn't be there because He never leaves Tiruvannamalai. I didn't know how this man had gotten my address in America, it was all very strange, but somehow significant. I wrote back and said that I would come. I found out when I got there that not only was I supposed to be the keynote speaker at the Jayanthi Celebration, but the way that he had gotten my address was very interesting.

"Yogi Ramsuratkumar in His years on the streets collected many things. He had these big burlap bags, about a cubic meter, full of garbage and strings and rubber bands and newspapers and all kinds of things. He gave this man in southern India one of these big bags and said, 'Don't open this for seven days, and then you can do what you want with it.' After seven days he opened it up and he couldn't find anything in the bag of any significance to him except a bunch of envelopes with my name on them. He went back to Yogi Ramsuratkumar and said, 'I don't know why you gave me the bag—this is all I found.' And Yogi Ramsuratkumar said, 'Invite this man to your celebration and he will come.'

"When I got there and found that out I was pleased, of course. I went back to see Yogi Ramsuratkumar in Tiruvannamalai, and there was a recognition that occurred. Since then I've been returning to India on a regular basis to see Him, and I keep hoping every year that He'll continue to remember me!" Lee laughed. "So whenever I have a personal interaction with Yogi Ramsuratkumar, I don't consciously analyze it and try to figure it all out, but elements of it continue to surface into consciousness to reveal different levels of transmission, of meaning. The pivotal point of this whole story, at least this morning, is when He said, 'I know what you want, Lee. Go find a guru, go find a master. There are lots of them in India. This Beggar is not a guru.' Of course in my own informal use of language I call Yogi Ramsuratkumar my Master, my Guru, my Teacher. I use lots of words to refer to Him. But at the same time this interaction with Him has caused a very searching look at what distinctions there are between a saint, a guru, a master, and Yogi Ramsuratkumar, who calls Himself a Beggar and a Madman.

"It always seems to me that one of my functions is as a revealer of information and a communicator of knowledge, information, data. For those of you who have looked on the book table in the back there is book after book, the Study Manuals—all of this is the transmission of information. In the East there is a several thousand-year-old tradition of guru/disciple relationship, or of master/apprentice relationship. Not just in India, but in China, of course, which has a very ancient culture, and in other Eastern cultures. But in the West we are still very young in the wisdom and laws and protocol of the guru/disciple process. This is true even though many of us have an intuitive response to it—obviously, from the literally hundreds of thousands of Westerners who have gone to

India or Japan with a very instinctual sense of what they would find and the value of that. So I've always seen part of my role as an educator.

"Another aspect of this function is that I am a representative of Yogi Ramsuratkumar in the West. I'm not one of these gurus who loves everybody. Actually people are sort of maddening to me—they're inappropriate and loud and aggressive and needy and intrusive. They are extremely indiscreet. As a representative of Yogi Ramsuratkumar, it is not my function to invite Westerners to visit Him—God forbid! Many do, of course. Many Europeans have visited Yogi Ramsuratkumar because they've been to one of my seminars, but that isn't my purpose or desire. It's to bring His Influence, His Blessing Power, His Presence to the West.

"He said once to one of his closest devotees, 'This Beggar will betray you.' What He was saying was that if you look to the physical body of the master, if you mistake the body of the master for the source of the Influence, the Blessing Power, the Presence, then you will be betrayed because the body of the master is mortal and the body will die at one point. So you have to resort to the teaching as it is represented by the master's physical presence, but not to identify the master's body with the teaching. This is a very important issue. The degree to which Lee Lozowick is transparent to, or surrendered to, Yogi Ramsuratkumar—or maybe we could say resonant to or empathetic with Yogi Ramsuratkumar—the more fully I represent His Presence wherever I go. If I am seventy percent in resonance with Him, then I represent His Presence seventy percent. Obviously the aim is to be one hundred percent.

"In this process of considering what my function is as a teacher, the form that has been given of guru and disciple is very absolute. I've really struggled with it for years and this is what's been given, this is what is. It is the reflection of the lineage; it has an objective value and it gets brought to the West. At the same time, what are the functions associated with this form? Educator, creator of circumstance in which people can experience Reality, and representative of Yogi Ramsuratkumar. Conduit for His Blessing Force, His influence, His wisdom. And how do all those things relate to who He is? The Divine Beggar, the Madman?

"It's clear that His function and my function are very different. Yogi Ramsuratkumar doesn't educate. He doesn't write, He doesn't discourse and discuss. He does communicate *brilliantly*, but He doesn't explain His communications in a linear way. He may have many functions, but essentially He is a Beggar. It's clear to me that amongst my many functions, that's not my primary function. Whether it ever will be or not, who knows? That's academic. I really have no idea. But as things stand now, that's His function, not mine. I don't have the being for it—He does. Whatever my students attribute to me, positively," Lee chuckled self-deprecatingly, "in the same way they attribute things to me negatively. My impracticality and so on my students view as a fault of mine, particularly those who are especially practical. But in any event, the divine qualities that are attributed to me are Him, coming through me. To whatever degree this creature has being," Lee touched his chest, "is the result of my association with Yogi Ramsuratkumar. It is building over time. But it's nowhere near the Being of Yogi Ramsuratkumar, nowhere near.

"So it seems like in the function of a Beggar, or the other name He calls Himself, Madman, there is a tremendous tradition. In the field of Sufism, for example, there is the tradition of the divine madman, which would be interesting to discuss at some point. In the Middle Ages there was a group of Christians called the Fools for God. They weren't mad, but they acted mad as a way to call the righteous Christian to a vision of Reality and to see their hypocrisy. They would sit on the steps of the church naked while services were going on. They were often stoned and beaten and thrown away from the church. But the message was, 'Bring your soul to church, not your greed, vanity, pride or material possessions.'

"The divine Beggar has a very particular function, which is to beg of God for us, to intercede with God. That's what the Beggar does: intercede. This is a very refined function, we could say. This is different than praying to God. All of us can pray to God for another person, when someone is sick or suffering. We may all pray for that person in one form or another. But to represent that person to God is an entirely different function and it requires a Being of extremely refined essence and presence to be able to function in that way. Most gurus don't have a Being of that rarity and quality. Of course I would think that way about my own Master!"

In the span of the past two or three years Lee has started having some of his senior students take on an informal teaching function in that he schedules them to speak at seminars along with him. Usually that means that during a three-day seminar he may have one or two of the two-hour talks be given by one of his students. As he has said, it is tremendously valuable to hear the teaching from someone who is in the midst of it—it presents, in certain ways, a different perspective than that of the teacher because the speaker is in the throes of sadhana. The practitioner has the advantage of speaking from inside the struggle, and can offer the wisdom of experience to his or her peers on the path. At the same time, students are often in a position to represent and articulate the teaching in a more comprehensive and coherent fashion. This is partly true because the teacher *is* the teaching; the teacher is the living embodiment and demonstration of the teaching. In Lee's case this is especially true because Lee's teaching is often obscure and hidden. That Lee feels confident to ask some of his students to take on this kind of responsibility is a sign of the maturation of the sangha at large. Today Rick L., the leader of the Vancouver bordello, gave the talk:

"What I'm wanting to describe is the way into Lee's heart. In order to begin a discussion of that there are some foundation ideas that need to be shared. The path is paradoxical. In order to be successful on the path there are aspects of this paradox that it helps to keep an awareness of. Ninety-nine percent of success on the path is due to miracles, magic and grace. Ninety-nine percent of the work is done by something other than you. The one percent that is left is the part that you are responsible for on the spiritual path. It's only one percent of the whole thing, but it is a *huge* responsibility, a gigantic task. It requires tremendous vigilance, intention and persistence. One percent is what we call the Work and it is a *lot* of work. Ninety-nine percent is somebody else's work, and our great blessing and joy. The ninety-nine percent cannot put itself into play unless you do your one percent. That one percent is *kaya sadhana*.

"We have to understand certain things about ourselves as human beings before we can even begin that one percent of work that is ours. We have to come to grips with the reality of the fact that we do not have a relationship to ourselves. The reason we do not have a relationship to ourselves is because of the first betrayal we experienced at the hands of our parents or caretakers.

"No one I've ever met came out of childhood with a perfect sense of okay-ness. This is very important to understand, and to observe in ourselves over a period of time, because all our efforts to achieve are based on the perceived lack of love we received as children. Everything we do, all our attention, is dedicated to one thing—to finding love *out there*, externally, and devising ways through our behavior, strategies and posture, to try to get that love for ourselves. This chronic activity of looking for love creates a split, a division, a dissociation of ourselves from our *being*. We leave ourselves behind when we go searching for love. We abandon who we are in the hopes of getting it. *Kaya sadhana* is about the reclamation of who we are as simply natural, embodied human beings.

"This seems simple, but there are difficulties, because when we were being the natural innocence we were as children, we were not loved. In this state of profound innocence, when we were not being acknowledged, seen or received, we made a decision. The decision we made was to abandon who we really were because it wasn't working. So now, just the idea of going back to that original innocence will provoke a terror linked to this experience of being unloved. Everything we do is turned toward needing something from others. What is most apparent in looking at people, what is right there is fear—fear that we're not going to be loved by the other. Unless we understand that, we are doing this all the time. Then this invisible, unconscious activity becomes the basis upon which we relate to the guru. Only it's much worse . . .

"This one percent work—not the magic, miracle, grace part, but the *work* part—is a science. It's tremendously precise and exacting. It's clear and it's possible for a human being to follow its dictates. If we try to develop a relationship to the miracle, magic, grace part of the path, we will fail because it is unmappable, uncontainable, and has no feature that we can grab onto with our human senses. This one percent that is a science is very clearly laid out in the Western Baul Tradition. It involves the body of practices that have been clearly described, through which we can develop a body of practice designed to create a super-association between our living body and ourselves. It's designed to root us and ground us in one place.

"Have you ever been lost in one of those huge shopping malls, and you're with another person and you get separated and you're both looking for each other? You just go around and around, missing each other because you're both looking. It's like that. The Divine is the one who does the looking—not you. *Kaya sadhana* is the science of how to stand in one place in the shopping center after you get lost. It's the science of becoming rooted in, tethered to, anchored in being where you are supposed to be when the Divine comes to look for you. We think because of this habit—the search—we should be going all over the place. We're searching, weeping, wailing and gnashing our teeth and God has been to our house fifty times in the last ten minutes, but we weren't there because we were out looking everywhere else for Him! This is *exactly* what we are doing! Our attention being elsewhere and not in the body makes it impossible for the Divine to find us.

"The science of *kaya sadhana*, if we practice it vigilantly, trains us to be able to be sitting there, even while we are doing something. This science is composed of the principles of practice: the dietary recommendations, daily meditation, exercise, study, monogamous sexual relationship, right livelihood. If the practices are practiced properly and with devotion, then we gain *nothing*. We just get an ordinary life, a life in which we are not running around all the time and engaging a thousand forms of dissociation. The practices are very simple, basic, sane practices. So simple, so basic, so sane that we wonder why when just to carry them out causes such stark terror. If you attempt to practice, you will discover that the resistance we have to a simple, sane life is very great. That resistance is because we believe if we stop our search, we will die.

"What the practices create are the only life that is available to a human being, which is an intimate relationship to ourselves in our simplicity. If we stop eating sugar and junk food, for example, our thinking processes become less volatile. All these practices are designed for us to get very close to life. Most people's search for God is based on a life they are running from that happened to them as children.

"What we're asking for or agreeing to on this path is to develop an intimate relationship with life as it is. There is one possible outcome of such a thing, and that is suffering. So when we agree to this intimacy with who we are as human beings, it requires that we go back to all circumstances and relationships and experiences that we've been trying to avoid all our lives. And that's cause for celebration! What we are asking for is really insane. If we actually know what we are doing or what it's about we would probably never chose it at the beginning of the path. It's only because we got hooked in by our illusions that we got into it to begin with. We have to come to our senses in the middle of this unconscious thing that we've done before we can progress. That is not a pretty or comfortable realization.

"The beauty of the whole path is that we don't have to understand any of the grace and magic part of it—all we have to do is the practices, and that keeps us at home. The Divine is making Its rounds, and if It just knocked on our door before we started our practices, while we were out, then we may have to wait awhile before the Divine comes back around again. But It will come back. It's the nature of the Divine that It has to call at our homes.

"All of our practices—diet, meditation, study, exercise, monogamy, right livelihood—are just the appetizers, or the main course, but this particular meal called *kaya sadhana* has a thousand desserts! Those desserts are many other forms of practice which come to us in various ways. Many are given directly to us by Lee to use in daily life, and others we may become instinctively aware of while practicing the main practices."

Rick was touching upon an important aspect of *kaya sadhana:* when the body becomes attuned and aligned to the subtle electrical flow of divine influence or the blessing power of the lineage, it becomes capable of spontaneously revealing esoteric practices which augment, amplify and rest upon the foundation of core practices given by Lee, and which may—or may not—be unique to the individual. The phrase "the body knows" has been used by Lee to point toward the inherent wisdom of the body, which by birthright contains the blueprint for such wisdom. In the guru's company, through diligent practice, obedience and intention, this blueprint is brought to life.

These practices by no means obviate the ongoing need for foundation-level practice, but arise spontaneously as further evolutions springing from the matrix of established practice, and may appear as an aspect of the fruition of mature practice. Similarly, they could be considered some of the secret practices of the school, and are in effect a direct revelation given to the practitioner from the guru that occurs at a subtle level. Obviously any such practices that may arise must be confirmed by Lee, so as to avoid the pitfalls of ego's attempt at co-opting the higher possibility of practice.

Rick continued: "The whole path is one of having to invest in loss. Lee often says, 'Get out if you can!' partly because we get a great big loan from the teacher up-front on the path. It's like someone has handed you ten thousand dollars, but because we have no idea what the path is, we spend it right away, immediately, without even shopping around. Once you spend the money, you owe something, and once you owe something, it's all over and your life isn't yours anymore. What that looks like is investing in loss. You get the lump sum up-front—the promise of communion in the Heart of the Divine—then payment is in the form of a thousand or million small sacrifices. Every sacrifice is, to some small extent, choosing a life of practice over a life of unconsciousness and seeking. You have to make these small but incessant offerings, gestures back to God or to the teacher, and you make these payments over a long period of time to pay back the up-front loan you got.

"Spiritual life is making the purchase of something you always wanted, then having to pay it off over time. Most of the excitement is at first, then there are years and years of toil and labor to get to keep it. But something happens after years of toil and effort—you begin to develop an ability to see what each little payment is actually giving you in return. Then relationship to sacrifice and work slowly begins to change. Each moment of practice may not be so comfortable, but it's not as bad as it was.

"Then you glimpse a perverse joy that you start to get out of moments of sacrifice. This perversity starts to grow and there are areas in which you find yourself wanting to suffer the loss of your previous life—your recent past. Then something very strange starts happening. After decades of conditioning that we had bred into us, that convinced us that what truly feels good we don't want and what feels bad we do want, we get a direct experience of some form of suffering bringing us close to the thing we've really always wanted. We begin to discover the doorway of conscious suffering.

"As our practice matures and we remain devoted to practice, we begin to see that every single way the ordinary world has trained us to look for love, life, all of that, has sent us in the opposite direction of true love and true life. As our appreciation for conscious suffering or *tapas* grows, there comes a point, at least in some areas, where we *want* to suffer. We want what it is that suffering can bring us. It doesn't bring us the thing itself, but it opens the door. Lee is saying, 'Get out before you *want* to suffer,' because if you stay on the path there will be a time when you will be dedicated to finding the suffering that is offered by the teacher. This is not in any way a pretty sight.

"In the 'Guru Gita' there is a stanza that says, 'It is the only mantra that rescues one from the ocean of the world.' The 'ocean of the world' is everything we've ever been told about where to find happiness. The 'Guru Gita' says, 'It is the mantra that puts an end to privations, miseries and the disease of mundane existence.' Who didn't feel that mundane existence? The opportunity to feel the extent of our mundane existence is to me the greatest necessity, and provides the greatest motive to work on the path. That mundane quality of our existence is a structure that is made up of all belief systems of our culture, which supposedly have told us what the good life is.

"You have to be asking a real question of Lee in order to be able to hear a real response from him. If you're not looking beyond the appearances of things you will never get any of Lee's profound communications because all of his profound communications are below the level of appearances. If you're willing to be looking for a real answer, you will get a real answer and save yourself a lot of time and energy. When we practice we develop a resonance, an intelligence in the body, which is capable of making a distinction between a real gift and a baby rattle. Lee offers up many baby toys; it's up to us to have the discretionary capability of choosing the gifts, while everyone else takes their toys that they can't hurt themselves with into the corner. One of Lee's functions as a teacher is to keep us from harming ourselves until we practice at a level that our practice is *insured* by our maturity, discrimination and reliability.

"Dasya talked yesterday about working with discomfort. When we build a body of practice one thing we do is to build a capability to hold discomfort, but also we must become accustomed to holding profound joy, intimacy and communion. Developing an intimate relationship with life through practice, we have to build a strong enough matrix in the body to hold all types of feeling, sensation and phenomena, not just suffering and discomfort. The whole basis of building the capacity to turn to the teacher's true essence and relate to that depends on our ability to be with ourselves as we are. That is the starting point of our work. Then we can be with everything as it is as a profound level of feeling-attention, to the point that whatever we perceive, internal to the body or external to the body, the body of practice is strong enough to let ourselves feel whatever it is and not go away from it. Whatever it is. This being with whatever is, as a practice of *kaya sadhana,* is the only thing that gives us access to who and what the teacher actually is, beyond his body and personality. It is only revealed through this profound feeling-attention that we open to who and what he is. This is part of our function as students. What we are here to do is to feed the teacher and feed the Divine; the way we do this is by using our feeling-attention, directing it toward, or opening it to, what is. By the very fact of our willingness to be with what is in his name, the thing our attention is on is divinized by him, and feeds him.

"So the Heart of Divine Communion is like this raging furnace. It is brilliant, white hot. It's so hot that it radiates out of the Heart of the Divine the possibility of all life in its sphere. But in order for it to exist and keep burning, it must be fed. When we enter the path and step into the lineage, like this one where Lee is the teacher, we are agreeing to a very specific use of our feeling-attention. Feeling-attention is like a shovel. Anything that exists in the world is like coal—an organic substance that has energy bound up in its structure. So when we practice we are using our feeling-attention to go and get the 'coal' and put it in the 'furnace.' This process in which we are continuously turning our attention, alternately and in every moment, back and forth between the world and the Divine, is how we feed the Divine.

"Enlightened Duality is Lee's phrase. It has to do with the particular function that we are meant to serve in this school. This function is to have a facility in both domains of existence. We're able to be in the world and at the same time keep our feeling attention on the 'furnace,' the Heart of Communion, and through our activity use what exists in the world to serve the needs of the Divine."

Today we are riding the peak of the wave that is this particular seminar—a celebration of the dharma. By teatime tonight we will have had over eight hours of dharma streaming into our senses. Lee began his afternoon talk only fifteen minutes after Rick's talk ended. He had taken notes during Rick's discourse and seemed fired up and inspired by it. Lee began by highly praising Rick's talk. He said that it was the best articulation of "Assertion," one of the core practices of the school—and one which people are constantly asking Lee to clarify—that he had ever heard. At first, Lee said, he thought that everyone should hear the tape of Rick's talk, then he thought that he would just keep it for those who were here. Then he began to talk about suffering and accepting what is:

"We imagine that spiritual phenomena has substance; that pleasure has substance and displeasure has substance. The mind says, 'If I suffer, that means I'm going to suffer forever.' The corollary to accepting what is as it is, is to accept what is here and now, because in the next moment, in the next instant, *what is* is different than *what was.* So when our practice is mature we aren't confused by the insubstantiality of phenomena. As our practice matures, part of our experience is that whatever the experience of the moment is is only in that moment, and we don't have to be burdened by that experience for the rest of our lives. Illusion tells us, psychology tells us, that if we experience suffering, we are going to have that experience for the rest of our lives. So of course we do anything we can to avoid the experience of suffering or discomfort. Of course we seek experiences of pleasure.

"The pyramids in Egypt stayed the way they are for thousands of years, but all it took was one shift in human society—the industrial revolution—and acid rain started eating away even the pyramids. Two hundred years, and the Sphinx and pyramids are almost beyond repair. As our practice matures we begin to understand the insubstantiality of phenomena. What is pleasurable is circumstantially pleasurable, and what is unpleasant is also circumstantially unpleasant. So we begin to desire what is permanent, which is what is real—which is what is, as it is, here and now—rather than what holds the promise of something in the future or nostalgia for the past.

"As our practice matures, we begin to want what is true here and now, in each moment, recognizing that each moment is different. As we all know, one minute you're running to the door to greet your lover, and you're so consumed with the vision of your beloved that you don't notice the big rock. In the next moment, where is your lover? Nowhere! All there is is your stubbed toe!" Everyone laughed. "Just like that! Instantly, reality changes. So as our practice matures we come to understand that each moment is unique to itself. We want what is most valuable in the moment, even if it is painful or unpleasant, because the only thing that is substantial is what is real. All phenomena is empty of substance.

"In Buddhism they say, 'Form is emptiness, emptiness is form.' Or, 'Nirvana is samsara, samsara is nirvana.' That means 'heaven is the world and the world is heaven.' The Buddhists had this down two thousand years ago. Now physicists are discovering unified field theory and the law of chaos and all that—the theory of morphogenetic fields. Everyone's all excited—what a breakthrough! And the Buddhists had it two thousand years ago. All the truth is in the traditions. What is, is, here and now. When we find that out, when we do our one percent of the work, the other ninety-nine is right there, accessible.

"The other ninety-nine percent—which is miracle, magic, grace—requires nothing to comprehend. No study. No effort. All we have to do is master the one percent. It's not confusing, it's not paradoxical, it's perfectly obvious. This whole vast unknown, indescribable brilliance—and we don't have to do anything! As Rick was saying, we've got it completely reversed in our minds. We think, 'Oh the one percent—I get that. I know all about that. It's this ninety-nine percent I've got to search for, I've got to march on it, I've got to go out and figure it out. I have to renounce my life, go sit in a cave for twenty-five years so I can understand the ninety-nine percent. It's exactly the opposite. That ninety-nine percent is already taken care of—God's got it covered. It's on pause, just waiting!" More laughter.

"All you have to do is get the one percent. All we have to do is look at ourselves clearly, as we are, and accept ourselves as we are. We don't know that. We think we know all about that, but all we know is what it looks like, not what it *is*. So all of practice is designed to show us what it *is*. As our practice matures, we begin to want what is Real. That sums up that part.

"So we get this loan, up-front, when we come to the path, and it's fabulous. All of a sudden we've got all this wealth, all these resources, money in our pocket. Immediately what we do is go out and spend it. I used to be in business, and I wasn't in business to serve my customers; I was in business to serve myself! That's what happens to us. We come to the guru off the streets and he throws this gold in our laps! He says, 'You know this is a loan.' We say, 'No problem, just give me the money!' We get this loan and say, 'Wow! I'm rich!' What do we spend it on? Disobedience, blindness, naivete, thinking we know. Wow, that is expensive! Thinking we know better than the teacher—that costs! Half the loan, right there! Abuses of practice, arrogance! Taking the gift that we've been given for granted. All those things eat up the loan, quickly, and before we know it, we're sitting with no money and no credit, and we can't get out, because our practice has matured to the point where we are willing to suffer, consciously. And God sends the collectors around, knocking on the door.

"It's amazing that we don't seek the counsel of our equals, because they do know. We see someone who has managed the loan well, and we could say, 'Okay, how should I manage it?' If we did that we would save a tremendous amount of unnecessary suffering. In life there is pain, pleasure, beauty, awe, wonder, disappointment, frustration. Inherent in life is suffering. There is birth, maintenance and death. Destruction is part of the trinity of creation, maintenance and destruction. There is our own death and the death of those we love. That's part of life, there is no way to avoid that. But there is a tremendous amount of suffering that we create by our actions that is not inherent in life. We superimpose it on life as it is. And it feels just the same, it's just as painful, just as miserable as the suffering that is inherent in life, but it's completely avoidable if we seek wise counsel and follow that counsel.

"So in the beginning the advice that we get is going to create a tremendous conflict if we follow it because our habitual psychological tendencies—the ones that want to run into the first store and spend the loan—are going to be in a struggle with the advice that says, 'Don't be impulsive, don't rush into anything. Just look at what's really needed and what's a necessity, and invest wisely.'

"In the beginning there is definitely some tension. But as any mature practitioner of any path or system will tell you, it's worth putting up with the initial discomfort for the benefits that come once you are beyond the initial tension, once you've resolved the crisis, the conflict. What resolves the crisis? Practice. Once you've decided to be a vegetarian, you realize that all of the struggle—taking years sneaking a piece of meat here or there—was totally unnecessary. Once you get beyond the crisis you realize in retrospect that to have indulged and lengthened the crisis would have been totally ridiculous, self-destructive, useless. In English there is a phrase, 'Cutting off your nose to spite your face.' It makes it much worse, but you don't think that in the beginning. You're presumptuous and you act impulsively.

"So if we commit ourselves to the path and then we don't practice we're just cutting our noses off to spite our faces. With no disrespect meant to the French people who have asked to be students, people come to a seminar and they get inspired and ask to be a student. I say, 'These are the recommended conditions. Vegetarian diet, daily meditation, exercise, study, monogamous relationship, Enquiry. Oh, and by the way, vegetarian diet is very specific. It minimizes dairy products, meaning cheese after every meal is definitely out. And oh, by the way, the other dietary recommendation of this school is no tobacco or caffeine. That means no coffee.' They say, 'No coffee!' 'Okay, this is Europe, we'll make some slight exceptions. Oh, I forgot to mention—no alcohol! Not even good wine: okay, this is Europe, we'll make some exceptions. But coffee after every meal, wine with every meal—out!'

" 'I want to be a student?' they say. 'What for?' 'I really connected with what you said, you've really touched me, you've opened my heart!' *Meditation, study, diet, exercise, monogamy!* Europe or not, this is the price for my attention.

"Let's be honest: anyone who wants to call himself or herself a student of mine can if they want to. I don't care. You can even tell everybody I'm your teacher. But if you want the benefit of both my skills as a teacher, and the possibility of that ninety-nine percent . . . because let me tell you something about that ninety-nine percent: it's right here in my pocket!" Lee smiled, everyone laughed. "I have control over it. I bought it, I paid for it, it stays right there. So if you want those things—and not just to feel good when you come from a seminar—from whoever your teacher is, the price for my attention is twofold. One is your—I hate to use this word—love. It really grates on me to use that word, but I can't think of any other way to say it. Love, devotion, dedication, an open heart. But that's not enough. That will only get my sympathy.

"But if you want my Help, if you want me to pull that ninety-nine percent out and lay it on you, you have to practice. You have to meditate, follow the diet—relatively. Some of you are here without the help of your families; I can appreciate that. Maybe your wife and kids or husband and kids think you're crazy. So okay, I'm willing to give you a little space, a little wiggle room. I'm not going to be zealous here. Okay, you don't have to do all the practices right in front of their faces and really get them upset. Nevertheless, the recommendation is daily meditation, exercise, study, vegetarian diet, monogamy, Enquiry and so on. And generosity with resources toward the school! How could I have forgotten that? Most people are very generous, but this is what is expected to be a student. You have to practice and I'm willing to make concessions—for parents who have children and jobs and all that—but at the same time I expect you to practice. Maybe not to spend three hours a day in formal practices, but I expect you to take practice seriously and to be diligent.

"Last year eight or nine or ten people asked to be students. Basically I just said, 'Start with the literature and see how it goes.' When you read in the literature about practice, one of the signs is to take that seriously. You come back a year later and say you read all the books. That's not the right answer. The right answer is, 'I read all the books and I'm meditating and eating on the diet, and—oh! I gave up smoking.' That's the right answer. You come back a year later and I say how are you doing and you say, 'I've left my wife because she's holding my spiritual life back,' bad answer!

"Socrates realized that in order to work effectively you could never get lazy. So he looked for the worst shrew he could find and married her. When we say, 'I can't practice because my husband, my wife, won't let me,' it's not an excuse. It's not that every relationship works because sometimes they don't, of course. But a lot of us don't try very hard. It's infinitely easier to just go find someone else—another honeymoon for the first few months, walking on air. But to stay with it and love the person for five years, ten years, twenty years, that requires something. So that's the point about how we spend the loan."

After a day of feasting with sumptuous meals at brunch and dinner and three dharma talks everyone gathered again for darshan in the meditation hall in the barn. The space was full and active with about fifty people present. Lee had three of his poems to Yogi Ramsuratkumar sung, then after *kirtan* (chanting) he started his discourse by asking for questions.

After a brief pause Lee began, "Perhaps we should, in the context of this formal space, consider the context of the seminar. When I'm in America I don't do seminars like this one. I may give a one-day program or something for one of my students, but basically I don't give seminars. So people in America who don't know how it is in Europe assume that I'm a traditional spiritual master—and traditional spiritual masters don't give seminars. When people find out, they are shocked. They want to get in on it, of course. But the question many people may have is, 'Why give seminars if you've transcended all separation and live in a state of God-realization?' I don't say those things about myself, but other people do. Like, 'And your mere glance is sacred enough to enlighten anyone who looks you in the eye, and knocks over cows fifty feet away!' "

Lee and everyone else in the room started laughing. There was a sparkle in his eyes as he played with this train of thought. He continued. " 'With such shakti force! You just look at a cow and *boom*! Why . . . what do you have to give seminars for?' " More laughter.

"The thing is that the circumstance dictates the manifestation. I suppose I could get away with being a big fancy guru in Europe and not give seminars, but Europeans are confused enough as it is. Go watch Europeans with any other guru and see the confusion! Not that Americans are less confused—they're just confused in a different way. So circumstance dictates form. It's important that we educate ourselves in relationship to people we view as enlightened.

"The seminar form is designed for two purposes: One, as a format in which a lot of information can be passed along in the usual way. Two things went on this weekend. A lot of information was passed along and also some experiential spaces were created in which information was passed along in a non-linear way. Gurdjieff said that man, untransformed, is at the effect of dissonance between his or her three centers: the thinking center, moving center or instinctual feeling center—which includes emotions, sentiment, romanticism." Lee stopped in mid-thought and imitated a seeker in a tone dripping with sarcasm but at the same time animating a gushing and cloying sentimentality. " 'Look! That guru is *enlightened*! Oh, Oh, Oh! Every gesture he makes is so elegant!' Pure romanticism, while the guru is sitting there, scratching his ass!

"All three centers are involved in the educational process during seminars, and not just touched arbitrarily. This is scientific and exact. But Lee Lozowick does not establish the circumstances. The Influence of Yogi Ramsuratkumar through Lee Lozowick and whoever Lee is in relationship with in the space creates the circumstance through which the education of the three centers can take place. It's very specific and very intentional. Otherwise the seminar is a failure, because if all three centers aren't touched the center that is left out will find a way to poison the education received by the other two centers.

"What really goes on during the seminars is just an excuse to get people in what we call an alchemical chamber and keep them there long enough for the education to get passed on, and to give it the possibility of taking root. What's really going on is that we are living for three days in a culture that is defined by Yogi Ramsuratkumar. The linearity of the teaching is just a way of keeping our attention busy while the Work gets done. In a traditional setting, people would come to the ashram with an understanding—already educated—of what is available through the teacher. In a group as we are now there are varying degrees of that education. So a lot of what goes on is entertainment because it

513

keeps us in our seat—keeps us busy, occupied. If the mind is busy it won't disturb the transmission.

"I want to suggest, to be my own apologist, that this seminar is completely different than any other seminar you will go to. Gurus don't give seminars, except in one place! If a guru gives a seminar they call it something like 'Enlightenment Weekend,' and if you say, 'Great seminar!' they say, 'It's not a seminar! It's an Enlightenment Weekend!' Gurus are too rigid, too orthodox to give seminars, too stuck in their guru trip. Guru business! Posing for pictures, taking up the flower and smelling it and going into ecstasy." Lee stopped to demonstrate, pretending that he was picking up a flower and smelling it. His head fell back and his eyes rolled up dramatically. A blissful smile spread across his face while everyone laughed. "It's de rigeur!" he quipped. More laughter erupted in the space.

The translator didn't understand Lee's French and turned around to look at him questioningly. More peals of laughter rang out. Several French guests repeated the French words for her and she laughed, finally registering his meaning. "My translators never understand my French! It happens all the time," he laughed.

"The guru has to be manifesting ecstasy smelling the flowers even if they don't have any smell! You know most flowers we buy don't have any smell any more! But it goes with the job. It's part of the guru thing, part of the guru theatre! Look at their devotees' children with tears in their eyes . . .

" 'It's all a big test!' That's another complaint I have. Everybody thinks that every thing the guru does is a test. Listen, ladies and gentlemen—life is a test and most of you are failing! The guru doesn't have to do anything but sit there and watch you go down the drain. And throw you a life jacket. The guru doesn't have to test anybody. Anyone who tests people is either insecure or just power tripping. When I give somebody a task—writing a book, being in a band, building a better mousetrap—it's not a test. You don't need to be tested. It's obvious to me who you are and where you are, when you're ready for work and what work you're ready for, and your potential for success in that work. When I give a task, it is a *task*, not a test. The guru can see you, as you are. You don't have to pass all the courses to get a degree—just make it until you die! Just keep on practicing! There is no graduation. You never graduate—even if you get enlightenment! And that's going back to kindergarten, starting all over again. You'd be better off not getting enlightenment!"

Lee told the story of being in a school play when he was a little boy. He was given the lead part of the eagle, but he didn't know his lines so they made him one of the crows. "When I first got into this Work, I thought I was going to be an eagle, now here I am again, one of the crows! Enlightenment—you have no face, but you lose it! You don't have pride, but your pride gets hurt. It sucks! I was an interesting person before! I loved to travel, go to the theatre. I had lots of interests, found everything unusual and interesting and exciting. Before this shift of context, life was this unending, marvelous mystery. Then, *this happened!* Now I'm not interested in anything. Well . . . selling books." More laughter. Lee smiled and continued, "I'm a totally boring character. Life isn't mysterious—it's *obvious*, and it ain't pretty! Well, innocent children are pretty. But I used to be interested in people. Now, who could care?"

People were laughing as if they were intimate conspirators with Lee in the playful mood that had permeated most of the weekend. It was clear that nobody in the room believed that he didn't care. The laughter was building again to another high peak. Lee became so hilariously funny that it was impossible to capture it taking notes. He went into another comedy schtick until finally the laughter and high-spirited silliness subsided and Lee returned to his train of thought, which was basically warning away new students and dispelling illusions about spiritual life.

"Once you get this, life isn't mysterious anymore. You meditate and start levitating or gold pours out of your hand and you look at it and say, 'When's lunch?' Maybe it would be better if you stopped looking for enlightenment. I'd rather be a devotee than be a spiritual master. Yogi Ramsuratkumar didn't have to reveal Himself to me; He could have stayed invisible to me like He was for the beginning of this Work. Purely by His Grace did He reveal Himself to me so I could be a devotee. So stop searching for spiritual accomplishments. Enough comes to you anyway, if you're practicing correctly. Just have an ordinary life, enjoy others, and enjoy life."

August 9, 1999
La Ferme de Jutreau

After meditation this morning the atmosphere on the ashram was still vibrating with the high celebratory mood of the seminar. Most of the guests had left, and at breakfast the usual group was gathered. Chris commented that last night she had mentioned the leftover coffee to the person who was making the tea and treats that would be served after darshan. Usually any leftover coffee is used up by making it into mocha, a favorite Hohm Community hot beverage. Her suggestion drew the response, "Mocha has caffeine in it. People complain about getting a buzz that late at night. I'm going to make chai instead." Now this morning the leftover coffee hadn't been served for breakfast either; there were three insulated thermos carafes of coffee sitting on the kitchen windowsill. Lee made a short comment, "The coffee should have been used last night," and the topic was dropped.

After dinner it was discovered that the leftover coffee had been thrown out after lunch. Lee shook his head in disbelief. In a tone of extreme exasperation, he said, "It's a complete desecration of my teaching." One thing like this after a flawless and high-spirited seminar has been known to be enough to cast an unpleasant light on the whole affair for Lee. His disappointment settled on his devotees like a post-seminar blues.

Why would something like throwing out a few liters of coffee—something that happens daily in restaurants and homes all over the world—upset Lee enough to make such a strong statement? The most obvious reason seemed to be that in tantric work nothing is *wasted*. Lee demonstrates this constantly in his attention to leftover food in the kitchen, in his use of resources, time and energy. There is no end to the teaching lessons and communications that he makes in this regard: basically there is no food or beverage that should ever get thrown out unless it is rotten or inedible. Lee has made it clear that he always wants the leftovers stored with care and then served and eaten before fresh food is made. To waste food is to waste energy, and the conservation of energy in all forms is a fundamental aspect of tantric practice.

The conservation of energy is akin to the law of sacrifice. When one takes on a food substance, one becomes responsible for it. In buying the coffee beans one becomes responsible for the life of the plant that sacrificed itself. If the plants that were sacrificed to make the coffee are not respected by consuming the coffee and therefore making it possible for that substance to be part of the transformational process of evolution higher on the chain of being, then the Great Process of Divine Evolution has not been honored. Sounds esoteric—it is. But the tantric path has many such obligations woven into it.

There is another consideration involved in all this. Underlying the decision to not serve the coffee as mocha when it should have been done, which resulted in the throwing away of the coffee the next day, was a rigid and dogmatic mindset. It is form of blind following. It is the mindset that says, "Coffee is not on the diet; coffee has caffeine in it, it's bad for you, we shouldn't drink it," even when it came from Lee's hands. Whatever food is served during seminars is blessed food, Lee's gift of *prasad* to his students. To use the recommended conditions of the school to rationalize one's own self-righteousness or survival strategy is one of the ways that the teaching is made into orthodoxy, or a dogma to which one must adhere.

Lee will sometimes refer to the *pusti* elements of the Western Baul path. This *pusti* flavor is particularly felt when he is lavishing his students with rich food (like during seminars and celebrations or while traveling), movies, pizza and dessert outings. Lee often puts his students into situations in which the senses are drawn into various forms of egoic revelry: for example, with the music and dance of the bands; in underworld excursions into bars and clubs; performing with the Baul Theatre Company; in the writing and publishing of books where critical acclaim and personal acknowledgement may come into play. In tantric practice all this is used as fuel for practice, but it is ultimately Grace that transforms it into that which can become useful in a life of God-reference rather than a life of self-reference.

Given the specific subject matter of Lee's discourse in darshan at the very same time that the coffee was rejected on Sunday night, the teaching lesson was particularly powerful, and came into focus looking back on the gathering after darshan for tea. Coffee is a treat that Lee offers his students sparingly, but intentionally. The sweet, potent mocha with its mind- and body-altering, therefore mood-altering, caffeine seems to contribute to the mood of hearty good humor and gay joviality that Lee has been creating all summer in the evening gathering. The laughter in these gatherings, which has always felt empowered in Lee's company, takes on a more profound possibility if his teaching that the moving center is worked with during laughter is taken seriously. But further, there is the sense that in this mood there is the opportunity to experience a particular facet of relationship with the Divine.

One never knows when one's decisions that are in dissonance to the teacher's context for right living will have a serious effect on the teacher's work—or play, which is also work, depending on how one looks at it. Interestingly, at tea last night—when freshly-made chai was served and the leftover coffee sat unused on the window sill—Lee talked sparingly and quietly with a few people who were sitting on the floor near him. Although other people talked and chattered in an animated way, Lee was predominantly quiet, and when he did speak, it was difficult to hear anything he said. For some reason the chai that night fell short of its usual delicious sweet flavor and potency. Lee left early, shortly after ten o'clock.

August 10, 1999
La Ferme de Jutreau

Sitting at the dining table in the barn after announcements at the end of dinner Lee said, "The After Dinner Talk will start at six forty-five in the salon. Bring your spiritual questions—the doctor will be in! Bring your *soul* questions, that is."

In the salon Lee began to read from the English translation of "Guru and Disciple" from *L'Ami Spirituel* by Arnaud Desjardins, stopping frequently to comment. Now he continued on a theme he had begun during the previous weekend's seminar. "People ask to be students here every year in Europe and it never enters their mind that they will have to *practice*. They have no idea what it means to be a student. They say, 'Lee is in my heart and I dream about Lee,' and they think that's it. I was saying that during the seminar and some of them were crying. There they were, walking along thinking that they've been embraced as students, when they don't practice, don't follow the diet, don't meditate. They don't do anything.

"What distinguishes the good disciple, in Arnaud's language, from the dilettante devotee is that the devotee is always smiling and ecstatic, believes the teacher loves them, sees the teacher's face in the clouds, gets caught in the rain and thinks it's the teacher's tears bathing them. They would never think of engaging hard practice to evoke the direct personal influence from the teacher. To evoke the teacher's influence you have to be *practicing*.

"Maybe you've brought a serious question to an After Dinner Talk and the answer to that question is Enquiry. People look at me with this blank look, as if to say, 'What's that?' Even serious students of ten or fifteen years! Surely you've all read *Laughter of the Stones*. (Lee Lozowick, 1978.) Surely you know that the practice of Enquiry is one of the core practices of the school. There are the recommended conditions—meditation, exercise, study, diet and so on—then there are the core practices. Those core practices are Enquiry, Assertion and the Heart Breath, and any specific practices I've given to individuals over the years."

Picking up "Guru and Disciple" again Lee said, "Quote: 'The test is whether or not the person is conscientiously putting into practice the teaching you receive from the guru.' " (p. 26)

Lee commented, "To do that in this school is to wrestle with the core practices, to have a completely organic intention to practice the core practices and to integrate the conditions into your life. And for the sake of others, don't floss your teeth in public or eat too much garlic!" Lee laughed as he veered rapidly into a humorous bent. "When your sweat starts smelling like garlic, you know you've eaten too much! We should go on a garlic fast some day, just to give the garlic heads a taste of their own medicine!" Everyone was laughing, thinking of the people in the sangha who are so zealous about their health that they often reek from eating raw garlic. Lee picked up the book and read again from "Guru and Disciple," then commented further.

"As Arnaud says, we think, 'The guru is going to do it to me.' But the guru cannot make us change. Depending upon the degree of our willingness (not just sincerity, because we're all goodhearted and sincere) to do what is necessary to mature on the path, the guru will say and do what is needed to create a magnification of our resistance. When asked how many disciples he had, Swami Prajnanpad said, 'I have no disciples!' Arnaud was shocked. Arnaud thought he was a disciple, and so it created in him the question, 'What is a disciple?' and created a clarity in him about his own presumptuousness."

Lee continued reading from Arnaud's book. " 'The most important thing is not what takes place in the presence of the Yogi or the Sage; on the contrary, it is what takes place when you are away from him.' (p. 26) Another one of the elements that defines a disciple is not how you feel when you are in the presence of the teacher, but how you act when you are not in the presence of the teacher.

"When people go with me to see Yogi Ramsuratkumar they feel very elevated in His presence. That's well and good, but the criterion for the value of their trip is not how they felt in His presence. In fact that's academic. What occurs in India will in some way effect the way we act when we are not in India. It doesn't matter how elevated we felt in the presence of Yogi Ramsuratkumar if we don't practice when we get home."

Lee continued to read from Arnaud Desjardins' book:

> Actually, it is only very rarely that [the Guru-disciple relationship] is genuinely established. It is a fact that it is a very rare relationship indeed. All those who approach a Teacher, listen to him, come back again and again to see him, have interviews with him, may imagine that they are his disciples. In point of fact, disciples are rare, very rare. If a true Guru-disciple relationship has been established, it can never in any circumstances be broken. If it is broken, that simply shows that it has never really had any deep roots. (pp. 29-30)

He commented, "So, we know we've got a true relationship to the guru if we've been tested and found that things that can be difficult yet can't drive us away. If there is no possibility of leaving the guru then we're committed through whatever struggles arise. Under no conditions can the relationship be broken. I think most of you in this room have had enough glimpses of the ebb and flow of your enthusiasm to have seen that at play. At some point you say, 'What am I doing here? Is Lee really my teacher?' And by investigating that you get to see that certain elements of your relationship to me just had the *appearance* of clarity, but were not clear at all.

"Whenever there is a transference, a projection—trusted friend, father figure, whatever—we may imagine ourselves to be completely committed, we may be making progress in human terms, but when we see this transference, the shock of that can create in us a question, 'Is any of this real? If I'm just looking at Lee as the good father I never had, is *any* of it real?' You clear away the clouds of illusion and then what is left is real. As you spend more time practicing, then more and more illusions get dissolved."

Lee continued reading a passage from Arnaud Desjardins about repressed infantile emotions dominating one's relationship with the teacher. He dropped the book and started off on a tangent. "Oh yeah—I just read a joke today. This businessman hires a secretary; she's sexy and he wants to get something going and she's amenable to it. So one night he calls his wife and makes an excuse, and he takes the secretary out to dinner. Afterward they make wild love, but when he gets ready to go home he notices he's got this bite on his neck. So he gets an idea: he buys a steak and puts it on his neck and when he goes home the dog comes running up and jumps up on his neck. He calls to his wife who comes running and he says, 'Look what the dog did to me!' pointing to the bite. Then she rips open her blouse and says, 'Yeah, well look what the dog did to my tits!' "

He forged ahead through the scattered bits of laughter. "Have you heard the joke about the ultra-sensitive condom? After the man goes home it stays around and talks to the woman!" Now full-on guffaws broke out. The women in the room especially thought this one was funny. The pointed dig at our repressed, infantile emotions was hard to miss.

August 11, 1999
La Ferme de Jutreau

Last night at tea, and off and on during the last three days, there was much talk about the solar eclipse that would be visible this morning at eleven-thirty in France. Someone mentioned how the Mayans and other shamanistic cultures must have used the solar eclipse as a doorway into intergalatic voyaging. Others had been reading about and reporting on the parties and occult circles that were happening on the Continent and in Britain for this event. There was a rock concert happening in a hemp and cornfield in Hungary, for example, where people were gathering to trip out on the energy of the eclipse. It seemed the excitement was growing in metaphysical and New Age circles because it has been two hundred years since a total solar eclipse was visible from Europe.

This morning at the end of breakfast when Lee asked for announcements, after the usual "Jai Guru . . ." he said in a mildly facetious tone, "on this special day of the solar eclipse!" in a playful reminder that his students were exhibiting a totally self-referenced degree of fascination about the whole thing.

Only fifteen minutes before Lee had been rubbing his neck and shoulders and grimacing as if he was in pain. When he was asked if a massage would be useful he said shortly, "It won't help." Now still sitting at the breakfast table he dove headfirst into one of those spontaneous rants that happen randomly in his company. These diatribes are almost impossible to describe. Even if it had been taped it would be difficult to communicate what he was doing, because the nature of it was like quicksilver, or a wildfire that runs out of control, leaping from one place of dry tinder to the next and catching on, leaving behind blazes or smoldering leaves that will combust minutes later.

He looked at Brinda, who was sitting at the end of the table, and started making acerbic comments about people bucking her authority as ashram manager. During the past four years that Lee has had the ashram in France there has been a history of the ashram residents giving Clint and Brinda, but Brinda in particular, a hard time over their authority. This has shown up specifically around Brinda's demands for a certain level of attention and impeccability in how things are done. Lee made it clear over the years that he has been very pleased with the results of Brinda's management of the ashram; he has continuously empowered and supported Brinda, while at the same time given her strong feedback about her tendency to control with an authoritarian strong arm.

"Fuck 'em!" Lee shouted. "This school isn't a democracy, it's a hierarchy, and people get to the top of the hierarchy for a reason. People who are empowered in the hierarchy aren't perfect, but they are where they are for a reason. If you stop doing what you do, we won't have an ashram anymore. So Anja escaped living under your thumb." Anja sat directly across the table from Brinda. She had lived at La Ferme de Jutreau for almost three years, and now lives at the ashram in Arizona. She was currently at La Ferme de Jutreau on a visit.

Lee continued with taking little sideswipes at people sitting at the table. "And Susanne is getting out," he barged ahead. Susanne has also lived at the ashram for almost four years and is moving back to Germany. She stood nearby listening. Still looking at Brinda, he said, "Maybe *nobody* will want to live with you! Fine—you and Clint can just come back to America if that happens and we'll have no ashram here!" He gave a smug smile and shrugged as if to say, "How would you all like that?"

He continued in the same muckraking tone, "Lack of discipline is the whole problem! People want to be able to throw away food and ruin two hundred jars of canned fruit, so the whole harvest of the orchard is destroyed and say to you, 'Okay, I did that, but I don't like the way you talk to me!' You know what I mean?" He looked piercingly at Brinda and she nodded. He was describing an incident that had actually happened last summer.

"Fuck them! They can leave the ashram as far as I'm concerned if they don't want to do what *you* tell them to do exactly the way you tell them to do it."

Lee was in a fury, but at the same time there was a strange mildness about him. He was fierce and adamant in tone, and yet he seemed completely unattached to anything he was saying. It was impossible to tell exactly what he was doing. On the one hand, he was criticizing the residents of the ashram for being unwilling to follow the ashram manager's direction, while in the bigger picture, he was addressing principles that apply to everyone having to do both with the need for and function of natural hierarchy within the organization of the sangha, and the need for discipline in sadhana. At the same time he was also giving Brinda a big piece of feedback and help in her own efforts to create space for change in her tendencies, to temper her manifestations with greater kindness, generosity and compassion. Woven into all of Lee's comments was his intimate knowledge of everyone's cramp. No one was being let "off the hook" by his remarks, but all seemed visibly moved under the onslaught of his razor-sharp attention.

Brinda asked what she should do about feedback that she gets that she is too harsh and rigid with people. He said, "Well, you do what you can about the feedback, but you don't stop managing the ashram." A fast-paced conversation ensued in which Lee spoke rapid-fire with several of the fifteen or so students who were present.

Now Lee spoke passionately about something he read in *Ruff Times,* the newsletter of ultra-conservative Mormon right-wing financial advisor and social and political commentator, Howard Ruff. It was an article written by an eighteen-year-old girl who said that the whole problem behind the recurring tragic outbreaks of violence with students and guns in American schools was entirely a function of lack of discipline in American society across the board. Lee's flamboyant style continued as he ranted against the permissiveness in American society. He said that Americans were terrified of disciplining their children, and that permissiveness was at the root of the decay of American culture today. Lee spoke in a very loud voice, attacking all liberal political activities as being permissive, even going so far as to attack with disgust "all those marches on Washington" as being aggressive and violent at the core.

He was provoking Jan, who sat nearby listening. She immediately rose to the bait. Her eyes flared as she challenged Lee, "Are you saying that the First Amendment of the United States Constitution is part of the problem of violence? How can you say such a thing? Because the First Amendment of the constitution is about the freedom to gather and express one's opinion . . ."

Before she could finish her objection Lee almost yelled, "All those people who march on Washington—*all of them*—are violent. The First Amendment is not about marching on Washington, it's about the freedom to write and make music and art and . . ." Jan and Lee were suddenly in a hot debate about the difference between societal violence and permissiveness and the First Amendment. Jan's position was that *violence* is the core problem, not permissiveness. She held her ground and the debate was fierce. It was quite a tussle, not unlike watching a sword fight between two people who are equally masterful at the art of fencing.

Jan was dumbfounded that Lee could insinuate that Martin Luther King's marches on Washington were violent. There must have been a number of people in the space who agreed with her side of the debate to some degree, but having the opportunity to watch Lee in action in this incredible display of skillful means one could see that he was not attached to anything he was saying, but was *working* with Jan and the space as a whole.

Lee said, "All these people who march on Washington in the name of peace, if they were on the other side of the fence, if they were the ones with the power and the clubs in their hands, they'd be beating people down. They are exactly like the people they are protesting against!" This statement rang with the truth.

Jan launched a new attack, "What about Alice Miller? Are you saying that Alice Miller is wrong? She says that violence in society is not because of permissiveness but because people are violent and rigid and abusive and repressive with their children . . ."

At this point Lee began to laugh and said, making a *namaskar* with his hands, "I bow and kiss Alice Miller's feet!" He turned to Jan and said, "We agree!"

Jan retorted, highly animated, serious and yet with a smile on her face, "No we *don't* agree . . ."

Lee parried, "Then *I* agree with you!" He bent almost double laughing at this. Jan was stopped dead in her tracks by this tai chi tactic. Abruptly she said, "Okay!"

At this point Lee began to laugh so hard that he was wiping tears from his eyes as he said, "Look at Jan! She's practically channeling. You can see her go from being clear, and then it's as if a dark cloud comes over her face as she rises to the challenge and starts to defend her position!"

Jan was alternately debating aggressively with Lee and laughing along with him. He was pushing her buttons and getting exactly the mechanical response he expected, based on years of working with her as a student, but at the same time Jan was a willing participant in this demonstration of the mechanical nature of our opinions and dearly held beliefs, ideals and moral positions. She chuckled now as Lee dealt the last blow, the blow of his total capitulation to her, a capitulation that came out of pure nonattachment. It was a grand move of nonresistance.

One of the things that was most striking about this was how tremendously animated and passionate and fluid Lee was. He kept everyone captivated at the empty table for almost an hour after breakfast was finished, working people over, making teaching lessons. There were sparks flying off of him, and when he got up to leave he said, "It's been fun!" Then walking out he said, in a quieter voice, "I just love sounding like a right-wing conservative . . ." It was a self-mocking remark, as if he didn't find it particularly agreeable to animate the right-wing conservative point of view.

But the thing is that he is not identified with any particular political stand. Next week or tomorrow he will give a beautiful articulation in favor of the position of the liberal left. It always seems that the bottom line is that Lee is life positive. Whatever supports life, or the ultimate designs of the Work, which could more formally be called the Great Process of Divine Evolution, is what Lee is naturally aligned with. But he will appear to stand behind something that pushes his students' buttons just to give one the opportunity to observe mechanicality and illusion at work in one's self and others.

The morning moved along very peacefully, the solar eclipse started around eleven-thirty and then peaked during lunch. As we sat down at the table in the rather dark barn Lee said to Andrea, "Turn the lights on so we don't have to have the eclipse in here." The children all ate outside so they could continue to watch the eclipse as they watched the sun shine through a small hole in a piece of paper onto another piece of paper that reflected the progress of the moon across the sun.

At the peak of the eclipse there were enough clouds in the sky that Lee and several people went outside to look up in the sky at the eclipse, which came and went, just another simple event of everyday life on the ashram.

August 12, 1999
La Ferme de Jutreau

Tonight Lee and the group gathered in the salon for the After Dinner Talk. He began by asking for questions. Someone asked, "Is it possible for a human being to move out of self-deception?"

Lee answered, "The possibility of moving out of self-deception will seem distant until you've moved out of it. One minute it will seem impossible and the next minute you will have moved out of it. It happens that fast. Even if you are a hairsbreadth away from being free of self-deception, it will still seem impossible. You never know when something will be triggered in the ongoing process that will produce some kind of shift. Some people you can look at and see that things have changed for them—you knew them ten years ago and you know they are different now. Some people you don't see any change. Others just get out of the car to pee one day and they are struck with a shift of context."

The questioner began to cry now. Outside the green countryside was peaceful, the trees moved in a gentle breeze and the children ran and played in a joyful mood of happy content. For some reason the mood inside in the After Dinner Talk was sad and pensive tonight. She continued, "I feel an immense pressure to penetrate self-deception."

Lee responded, "Well, a little bit at a time. If you practice ardently in the exact time and space that is unique to you and your destiny, you will dispel self-deception as quickly as possible ... Better tiny inroads than not at all. It can't hurt enough yet or you would be self-observing in a penetrating way. It's a very direct formula. If it hurts enough you'll do it because you know how to do it, the blueprint is there, the program is laid out; all you have to do is have enough fuel. You have to run toward the pain. You can't *motivate* yourself to run toward anything like that; you just *do* it. Psychotics do it, but of course they can't use it."

"Would you say something about prayer?" someone else asked.

Lee quipped, "I don't know anything about prayer."

"But you said in your poem to Yogi Ramsuratkumar that praying is begging."

"I did?" Lee's eyes were wide and innocent. He started singing to the tune of an old blues song, with his hands clasped in a theatrical gesture of begging. " 'Baby, please, please, please don't go!' When times get tough, the tough pray!"

The questioner persevered, "Is the desire to pray enough?"

"The irritation of desire unfulfilled creates a need to pray," Lee said, "a willingness to pray. It doesn't matter what the motive is, genuine prayer has the same effect regardless of motive. Maybe we're praying all the time! Why not? Give it a highfalutin' name and see if it flies! Call your path tantric and maybe it will be fast! Who knows! Anything else, while we're waxing eloquent about secrets of esoteric spirituality? Before we start waning gross as opposed to waxing eloquently?"

August 15, 1999
La Ferme de Jutreau

Every morning at breakfast after meditation the morning sun comes streaming into the barn dining room through the huge old wooden doors that remain open to this space all day long. The sun happens to hit exactly the spot where Lee sits each morning, in the middle of the big table with his back to the rock wall, above which is an extraordinarily striking two-foot by three-foot color photograph of Yogi Ramsuratkumar and Lee holding hands and looking into each other's eyes. This photograph was taken in India in Yogi Ramsuratkumar's darshan three years ago, and now presides over all the activities of this space.

This morning at breakfast the sun was, once again, shining in Lee's eyes. He was squinting and frowning and looking very uncomfortable. Someone got up to close the huge old barn door through which the shafts of glaring bright light came streaming. Lee stopped her, saying, "In just a minute or two the sun will be higher up, above the door, and out of my eyes," he frowned and added, "I've had eighteen people ask me if they can close the door." Almost every morning at breakfast someone has asked Lee if they could close the door so he wouldn't appear so uncomfortable. Now he continued in a rather irritated tone, "The morning sun is very healthy for the eyes. It's so good for you . . . but people are such slaves to comfort they can't bear even the slightest discomfort, even for a few minutes!"

Chris said, "Speaking of discomfort, pass me the yarrow tea!" The strong yarrow tea has been a source of many breakfast jokes, started by Lee, because it is rather medicinal to the taste. Although many people who live on the ashram have grown to like it very much, it still requires some adjusting to as a breakfast tea. Most people are habituated to taste treats like coffee or black tea with steamed milk, cream, honey or sugar, or at least some perky, invigorating (and currently popular) green tea for their morning repast.

Lee smiled mischievously and countered, "Yeah, speaking of discomfort, eat a bowl of prunes . . . !" He cracked up and launched into a series of scatological one-liners about the cleansing effects of prunes in a fast repartee with several of his students. For probably ten minutes his spontaneous, ribald and sometimes stinging wit was the force at play with a small number of people who sat near him around the table.

Lee often revels in a scatological sense of humor, which at times like this gives his students one of two choices—either to jump on the bandwagon with him and be reduced to laughing hysterically at inane and even stupid jokes about shit, genitals, farts and other bodily functions at the mentality of a prepubescent twelve-year-old, or to sit with arms folded, so to speak (and perhaps invisibly, but the effect is the same), like a disapproving school marm with a Victorian sense of propriety. Neither of these choices is particularly attractive.

This kind of behavior, which is typically and conventionally viewed as puerile and adolescent if not disgusting, forces one to look deeper when it comes from the teacher. First there are the incredulous thoughts: "Surely he's not really like this!" Then the mind might say rebelliously, "Maybe he's just an asshole." The line of thought might continue, "It must be me. Is he trying to push my buttons and make me work?" Then the dharma takes over: "What's the purpose of this activity—is it a teaching lesson about how immature we really are? How we are stuck at the level of the first three chakras?"

There is another option to the conundrum of our reaction to Lee's behavior, which is Enquiry, which cuts through the endless processes and projections of the mind to reveal one's primal discomfort for what it is. Interestingly, our unwillingness to endure the slightest discomfort was the subject that Lee had brought up before his antics began.

The fact is that human beings do shit and piss and fart, emit odors and exude sweat and act completely mad when sexual desire has them in its grip. If we are cut, we bleed, and if the wound doesn't heal and infection occurs, there is pus. If one can't come to terms with the grossest levels of the reality of incarnation in the physical body, then one cannot have a clear perception of the subtle levels of reality within incarnation. Heaven can be as illusory, as completely manufactured by the mind, as hell. How does one tell the difference? By being grounded in the solid earth of reality, and the reality is that we are incarnated beings who live in a body. When one is grounded in *what is*, then the high voltage energies and experiences of the spiritual path can be understood and integrated in a way that is useful in the process of transformation.

This morning many people had just gotten up and left to go about their day, probably feeling this was within protocol since Lee had already asked for announcements and had closed the space with a "Jai Guru!" even though he was clearly still holding forth in the space. And yet the feeling of discomfort with what Lee was manifesting seemed to be a factor for some. It is a complicated teaching circumstance; it is often painful to see Lee sacrificing or deprecating himself in these ways because of our lack of clarity. But then, even the most enlightened of Lee's own peers are sometimes nonplussed by the lengths to which he will go to make a teaching point or to reveal his own humanity and thus urge his students toward greater clarity in relationship to themselves and him.

Lee's eyes had a strange, rather delirious look in them along with tears of laughter as he suddenly changed the subject and slipped into another wave of silliness as he started singing, "I'm a musk deer, I'm a musk deer, sniff my butt!" while doing Jimi Hendrix style guitar licks in the air.

"The musk glands are in the region of the butt of the deer," Lee now quipped with a slightly prissy mannerism. He paused and then continued, "The spiritual master likes things to be accurate! Like, 'The spiritual master was full of gas this morning!' If anyone is going to do an autobiography on me *that* will have to be in there. No one is going to write an *authorized* biography of me unless they totally deconstruct me! Of course, keeping it within the mythology."

The idea of an authorized biography seemed to have captured Lee's attention. Sitting across the table watching him one could almost see the facetious comments working their way up to the surface. Now he burst out sarcastically, "The authorized biography: 'If I read one more time where one of his devotees said, *He had such a good voice,* I'm going to throw up!' " He grabbed his sides and bent over double laughing. Sitting up and wiping his eyes, he looked at the students sitting around him for a minute with wide, tranquil eyes, then said, "Reading the authorized biography: 'His scholarly devotees would sit in talks and cringe at the dramatic bastardization of facts when he was telling stories!' "

Discomfort is the point. Sometimes it seems inescapable that one will stew in one's own juices over Lee's gross exaggerations, outright distortions and infantile sense of humor until the discomfort becomes so great that one has to go underneath his behavior to penetrate into what is real about his communication in those moments. Lee will attack whatever one is attached to, no matter how sacred and beautiful, how moral, how factual in the linear, black-and-white demands of the Cartesian worldview, if it is an obstacle to liberation, to ultimate clarity and infinite possibility. We can thank Descartes to a large degree for the prison of the rational mind. He gave the West a rigid worldview that completely denies and represses the innate human ability to apprehend and rejoice in pure magic, the miraculous, the awe-inspiring, the mysterious. It seems that Lee is often attempting to push us into this mystery—out of our minds and into the infinite impossible.

After breakfast the Sunday morning teaching meeting was held in the salon, led by

Dasya. Lee sat in a chair on the side of the room and listened while Dasya regaled his small audience with hilarious anecdotes and observations of life on the path in Lee's company. Speaking out of twenty-four years of practice in Lee's company, Dasya lead the group into a twenty minute paroxysm of mad laughter over the absurdity of the human situation and the degree of ruin in which one finds oneself as a serious (if at times recalcitrant) practitioner of sadhana.

Ruin is a powerful word to use in this sense. What Dasya was referring to in the use of this word is being ruined to the world of status, separative identity, self-gratification in the domains of money, sex, food or power, worldly attainment and desire. It's not that worldly and egoic pleasures aren't desired anymore once one is firmly established on the path, but that the fulfillment of self-centered desires is found to be so completely devoid of meaning or substance that to constantly seek to get something that will make us feel good—in the sense of permanently fixing our problems or solving our felt dilemmas—is hopeless. Because the context of our relationship to desire is egoic, the voidness or emptiness of the very fulfillment that we seek casts us back upon the illusion of separation and the existential pain of the primal cramp in a way that is indescribable. To continually batter one's head against such illusions is hellish. That is one way of describing being ruined to the glittering array of what the world has to offer in various dimensions of egoic gratification.

In the renunciation to which many of Lee's students are called, particularly in order to live on the ashram, one has to give up having control over the circumstances of one's life to such a degree that would be considered outrageous by conventional standards. Some of Lee's students choose to live in a cold, damp barn out in the countryside of central France for four months out of the year; others give up secure jobs to move to Prescott or one of the ashrams, or make big sacrifices to travel around the world with Lee. Others throw themselves into bands, books and other demanding, whirlwind projects—given by Lee—under circumstances and with inherent pressures that make success or failure such an alchemcial conundrum, a friction and inescapable heat, that one casts back and forth, looking for the fine small window to freedom. By most standards it is an unusual way to live, and one looking at it from the outside would most likely say it is insane. But from the perspective of the tantric path it is the fast path, which is straight and narrow and sometimes treacherous; paradoxically it is also a circuitous and winding road that travels in spirals through the myriad appearances and phenomena of the show we call life. It's easy to get lost on that path without a fierce and uncompromising guide.

The theme of discomfort that started at breakfast followed through into Dasya's talk. At one point Lee told a story about Purna giving a talk, along with another person, to five hundred people in Germany a few days ago. Paula C. had told Lee that Purna said he was so nervous at the talk that he abandoned his well-thought-out plan and notes and simply sat there talking about Lee and Yogi Ramsuratkumar. At one point someone asked him what had motivated him to stay on the path all these years in relationship with his teacher, Lee Lozowick. Purna shrugged and said, "I looked at Lee as my father." This was after his co-speaker had answered the same question in very refined, etheral and philosophical terms about the path. Purna went on to talk about being in the grip of transference. His answer had been such a starkly real and raw response that people were shocked by the reflections that Purna's self-honesty caused in them. Many were experiencing discomfort and some even came up to him after the talk and said, "What you said made me very uncomfortable, but some of your talk was good!" Lee used this as an example of how completely adverse to discomfort we are, and how we expect the path to placate and console us, rather than to confront us into clarity about reality.

August 17, 1999
La Ferme de Jutreau

The days at La Ferme de Jutreau have been characterized by a rolling, steady pace of practice, work, enjoyment, laughter, quiet moments, outings with the children. All this takes place within the context of sadhana, and may be punctuated at times with fierce internal struggle in various individuals. On the outside life appears benevolent and easeful. Practice is the fabric of life, and Lee's presence here ties it all together.

Tomorrow morning Lee will leave with two vans and a car full of twenty-five people who are accompanying him on a twelve-day trip to Germany, Switzerland and eastern France where he will be giving public talks and seminars. Tonight the vans are already packed, and are especially heavy because of the many boxes of books, CDs, cassettes and *vigrahas* that Lee will arrange for sale on book tables everywhere he speaks. All last-minute luggage and bags will be packed into the vehicles at six-thirty, before meditation tomorrow morning, because Lee expects to leave immediately after meditation and *arati*, the *puja* or worship ceremony of a traditional chant, waving of lights (using a brass lamp filled with ghee or clarified butter) and passing out of prasad that is done at the end of meditation. It's a very important ritual in the school that takes place every morning on the two ashrams.

After five-thirty chanting and dinner at six o'clock, everyone gathered in the salon for Lee's talk tonight. The excitement of his imminent departure seemed to permeate the walls of the room as he picked up *Sufi* magazine (Summer 1999) and began to read from an article by Llewellyn Vaughan-Lee titled, "The Invisible Center."

Lee began: "From the section titled, 'Forgetting Our Faults.' Quote: 'Gradually the focus of our journey shifts from the inner work of "polishing the mirror of the heart" to the simplicity of living a daily life with a heart that belongs to God.' "(p. 30)

Lee commented, "In terms of 'polishing the mirror,' when we initially come to the path—whether we've read spiritual literature or we're just struck by something, the teacher or the community—our early experiences are completely related to the mystical side of things. Our attention is on enlightenment or transformation, so all the practices in the beginning are channeled into what he calls 'polishing the heart.' We fall into a very profound faith and devotion in relationship to the teacher. We study and understand the principles of the Work, we recognize a certain truth of the reality of nonduality.

"All that happens in the beginning. Then as the Work deepens and we polish the heart, whatever is hidden comes to light and darkness is revealed. Psychological obstacles become glaring; they leap up and grab us by the throat. We've done our initial sadhana and established equanimity in relationship to the teacher and the path, and all of a sudden we find our psychological difficulties staring us in the face.

"One of my students once said, 'The more you surrender to the guru, the less attention he gives you,' but what she wouldn't embrace was that getting attention from the guru is no longer the issue; you become so consumed with the Divine you don't care who gives you attention, because it is you giving attention to God that is consuming—that is the point. If Jesus Christ himself appeared in front of you and said, 'Darling,' you'd be like, 'I've got dishes to do. I've got to go be with the children.' You would be so consumed with the radiance of God pouring *out* of you that you couldn't be bothered with who was paying attention *to* you.

"Essentially Llewellyn Vaughan-Lee says that we come to a stage where our inherence in the path is so presumed that we are committed to the Work; we're not searching, our illusions have been if not shattered at least muted, and the initial bursts of mystical experiences have been digested. What we have left is ordinary life. Part of ordinary life is our habits, neuroses and so on."

Lee continued reading. " 'The self no longer seems to change or develop. Although we may have integrated some of our shadow, we still find some of our neuroses and anxieties present.' (p. 30)

"Most of the people in the this room are beyond the, 'Do I really want this?' part of the path. Also, the initial buzz, 'I'm going to be enlightened in a year!' is gone. We've sacrificed our desire to be the next Nijinsky, the next Martin Luther King, Jr., to write the next great American novel . . . We've settled into what looks like just ordinary life, and at this point we may question, 'Aren't things supposed to get more and more intense, more and more exciting?' But we've hit this ebb, we're sitting at the bottom of the wave wondering when the next peak is going to hit us." He picked up the magazine again and continued reading:

> We still may have conflicts in our relationships, difficulties in our job. We have not become a 'perfect spiritual person,' but an ordinary human being, and this can be disappointing. Western spiritual conditioning suggests some image of spiritual perfection, and does not prepare us for our ordinary self. Psychological work is never over—there is always inner housekeeping, and our dreams and reactions can still help us, keeping us aware of our shadow and daily psychological shifts. But more and more we have to learn to live with our own inadequacies and problems. Too much attention to inner work can become counterproductive, can be too ego-oriented. (p. 30)

"If we fixate on inner practices it can be counterproductive. It can become twisted. Too much exclusive attention that creates a repulsion for ordinary life creates something like an anti-neurosis, and you become turned off to ordinary pleasures, sorrows or responsibilities of life. If you are repulsed by someone eating meat or smoking a cigarette, or the thought of someone naked or wrinkled and old makes you sick to your stomach, you have become hypersensitive. You become psychologically fixated on something you think is going to allow you to escape from dealing with yourself, but you justify it in the name of sadhana." Lee read again:

> This is a delicate balance, as on the other hand, our shadow can easily convince us that it is not worth bothering about at all. But the wayfarer knows that the purpose of the journey is not to become perfect, because only He is perfect, but to become His servant. As long as our inadequacies do not interfere with our work as His servant, why should we bother to try to change them? (p. 30)

Lee commented, "We've been saying for many years that it is our job to serve the Work; that may mean a position of glory, or just washing dishes for the rest of your life, or working on vehicles. Our job is to serve the Work, and in serving the Work, that doesn't mean you're on stage all the time. Most of your life is spent living an ordinary life. Purna just gave a talk in Freiburg to five hundred people; sometimes you get a shot of glory, and the rest of the time you're just slogging along day to day. Somebody isn't taking care of the children the way they should, someone left the freezer door open and all the food defrosted. What does the guru do when he has finished his screaming fit? Clean up the mess. Even the guru's van runs out of gas—but not anymore!"

Lee referred humorously to the fact that last summer his van ran out of gas two times on two different road trips when he was driving and refused to stop to get gas, but tried to make it further down the road in his obsessed enthusiasm to get to the next seminar. This summer the ashram has equipped each van with gas cans, so even if the guru decides to keep driving on empty instead of stopping for gas (as he has been known to do), he'll be covered. Of course, this summer he has functioned quite differently. Lee continued to read:

> This shift away from our self is illustrated in the stages of repentance in Sarraj's Book of Flashes. The work on the shadow can be equated with the first stage of repentance, which Sahl describes as "to never forget your fault." Becoming conscious of our faults is similar to confronting our darkness, except that shadow work demands that we accept our darkness, rather than turning away from it towards the light. But the next stage of repentance, as defined by great tenth-century Sufi Junyad, is "forgetting your fault," the heart being so occupied with the remembrance of God that there is no concern for repentance. Neither our self nor our faults have any significance. The lover turns away from everything except Him; Sarraj quotes Nuri, who, asked about repentance, said, "It is turning away from everything except God Most High." (p. 30)

"That's pretty obvious, and some of you may have come to some mature sense of that, once you have seen that the Work is about service. E.J. Gold says the purpose of the Work is to share the suffering of Almighty God, or the Absolute. When you've come to the conclusion to serve the Work, that is where your attention goes, whether it is to contribute to the resource base of the ashram, to make the teaching available through talking or writing or art or whatever it might be, or simply to serve your family, to smile at the person behind the register in the market.

"Perhaps serving the Work is simply demonstrating kindness and compassion to others in ordinary life. Whatever the specific is in serving the Work is academic because each one of us has our own destiny and role in the Work. But the purpose is to serve the Work, not to live in some kind of exclusive mystical vacuum. When we realize this, life becomes very ordinary, maybe even boring. When the Beloved wants attention, or service, then the Beloved rings the bell and we walk through the door, but the opportunity doesn't present itself every day. We may go for long periods of time just living an ordinary life, practicing the principles of our work on the outside, while consumed with our Beloved within.

"Once we have glimpsed that Beauty that we have come to adore and long for, that breaks our heart, we turn away from everything that is ours, because we are obsessed with only that which is His. What's ours? Personality, neurosis, psychology. If you don't know your neurosis, you can't turn away from it. In the acceptance of it, it loses power over you. We are only dominated by that which we don't know. Self-knowledge defangs that which is always biting us, that which has us in its jaws, but once we know what that is, it can't manipulate us anymore. If we've seen our demons, if we know our underworld, when it arises we can let it run its course and do its thing or not. We hold the power of awareness—not the thing itself. First we have to see ourselves as we really are. Then comes the Beloved, and turning away from everything else for That. We've already nullified the grip that our undiscovered personality and psychological qualities have had on us in the past."

Lee continued with the reading. " 'But once the lover has been embraced by the presence of her Beloved, she turns away from everything that belongs to her. She knows that all that matters is her Beloved, and that her attention should remain only with Him.' " (p. 30)

He commented, "We know that our attention should be only on the Beloved, but then things happen in our lives—difficulties, frustrations, disappointments. When we handle those things without the unconscious assumption that those things define our lives, it shines a completely different light on things. But we fight with our partners and we believe that fight defines our whole lives. Our response is highly emotional and we are identified with those emotions.

"We understand that the Divine is the center of our lives and our primary focus. If there is a crisis or disturbance you just handle it as it needs to be handled. But some primal element of our psychology says, 'If I don't fix this thing I'm going to die!' When we know that the Divine is really the magnetic center of our lives, then whatever comes up doesn't distract us from this certainty, this knowing. We handle it elegantly, sensibly, but we don't become consumed with the dramas that have nothing to do with what is important in our lives."

Turning back to the magazine, Lee read, " 'Everything that focuses on our self is an obstacle—Ansari when discussing repentance warns against giving too much attention to our spiritual state.' (p. 30) Even when we are in ecstasy the Divine is still the core of our lives—not our ecstasy, our absorption. The only thing that is worth repentance is when we forget God for a moment. Even the greatest saint has got some darkness somewhere, as Yogi Ramsuratkumar has said. I'm sure you've seen how some people carry around their goodness—they are full of pride about how good they are. They say, 'I never lie.' Or you may have grown up in a family that was very proud that they never accepted help from anyone. 'I've never accepted money from the government,' or 'I never lie, I never cheat.' If we become prideful about our pious deeds it poisons the deeds themselves. We have to put our full attention on the Beloved; we have to drop not just our neurosis, but our prideful righteousness in our good qualities, our creativity, our genius, whatever it is. 'I can really cook! When I steam string beans—no one can steam string beans like me!' It's absurd! So we have to turn away from everything that belongs to us to focus exclusively on the Beloved—not just the things we aren't proud of, but our accomplishments."

Lee read again from the magazine: " 'It can be very difficult to realize that the very qualities and attitude that took us through a certain stage have to be left behind once that stage is passed.' (p. 30) In the beginning what gets us to practice is often the attitude, 'I'm going to be a good devotee, I'm going to do it right, so the guru will love, admire, regard, acknowledge me!' That may have gotten us through difficulties, that may have gotten us a foundation on which to stand, but now it has got to go.

Picking the magazine back up, Lee continued with the reading:

> Inner work, attention to our faults and shadow qualities, are such an important part of our first years on the path. They are the tools, the rope and axe, that helped us up the mountain. To leave these qualities behind, to step into the vulnerabilty of the next stage, that of looking

only to Him, can seem like deserting our own aspiration and commitment to the path. Surrendering the qualities that helped to heal and make us whole requires great trust and faith. (pp. 30-31)

Lee put the magazine down and commented. "I hope everybody here has read *Joy of Sacrifice* by E.J. Gold. In that book there is a section in which he talks about the eighteen sacrifices. He says that in the beginning we have to make the sacrifices intentionally because we don't have a mature enough work body for those sacrifices to be made *for* us. Once we make the sacrifices intentionally, the result of that process is that we develop a tremendous amount of skill and power. When you make those eighteen sacrifices out of your own struggle to work and to learn to work, the result of that is a phenomenal force of intention; but once you have finished the eighteen sacrifices, the final sacrifice is your force of will. You have to give up the strength and will you have gotten from making the sacrifices and you have to go through them all again, but having them made *for* you this time.

"The first one is the sacrifice of comfort. The first one, the most insignificant one, the first rung on the ladder, is the sacrifice of comfort. The idea is to make the sacrifice of comfort intentionally—to go without a pillow when you're sitting on the floor and your tailbone hurts. Your butt really hurts and someone offers you a pillow, and you know that in thirty minutes your butt will hurt even more but you decline the pillow. Or you sit in a hot car without asking for the window to be rolled down. You leave the table still a little bit hungry. In many traditions it's a recommended practice to leave the table hungry. That's making the sacrifice of comfort at every meal. Maybe the sacrifice of comfort is to not wear clothes that match in color, top and bottom. 'Oh no! Oh *God* no—anything but that!' Even to the theatre! Okay, you'll do it around the ashram because the spiritual master suggested it, but what about when you're going to the theatre? Wearing a top and bottom that actually clash! 'Oh *God*! Anything but that!' " Lots of laughter broke out in the group as this bit of humor hit its target, especially to the tastefully stylish French.

"So you decide you're going to work with this idea of the sacrifice of comfort and you develop some facility with it. I don't mean to break an arm off or something ridiculous like that, but to get to the point where you can be in an uncomfortable circumstance with some equanimity. You make all the sacrifices intentionally and build up personal power, then you have to sacrifice that personal power. Then you go through the sacrifices again. When you go through them the first time *your* will dominates the process; the second time they get done *for* you. Comfort gets taken from you, in small ways or in big ways, and you have to be with that with equanimity and acceptance."

Lee picked up the magazine and re-read the last line from Llewellyn Vaughan-Lee again for emphasis. " 'Surrendering the qualities that helped to heal and make us whole requires great trust and faith.'

"Gurdjieff writes in *Life is only real then, when 'I am'* about being wounded and lying under a tree and reviewing his life. At the time he was a great magician; he had great facility with his machine and with many occult skills. He was an incredible hypnotist. What he saw as he lay wounded and feverish under a tree was that all of that which he had worked to develop, that he assumed was becoming a man of knowledge, was simply just keeping control. He realized that he had to trust the Work, and he made a personal vow that he would never again use any of those skills to create a personal advantage for himself. So he surrendered all the things that kept him in a position of being an extraordinary man—the things that gave him personal power, that made him attractive to others. He became reliant on the Work. He endured incredible pain that he could have alleviated in himself, but he didn't because it provided fuel for his work.

"Others may consider us to be someone who is really evolved on the path, and then all of those things that are considered extraordinary is what we have to give up our attachment to. We have to give up having anything to do with those things. Then we get to find out if we are willfully doing those things ourselves, or if—when we surrender them— the Work holds them in place for us. We surrender who we are completely so that our entire attention is riveted on the Beloved, the Divine; then we get to see if those things continue unefforted.

"We start out seeking and gathering—skills, wisdom, knowledge. But at a certain point it is this sacrifice of all that becomes the natural progressive stage. It's not going backward. 'Oh I had all these skills, now I'll be nothing without them.' That is going forward. If we do it too soon we delude ourselves; if we wait too long we build obstacles that alter the alchemy of the process. Timing is of the essence; we have to engage the process at the time when the value of that stage is important. If not, it can become dangerous, counterproductive. That's why you work with a teacher, because the teacher knows when you start to animate the signs of a certain stage, whether you are actually able to enter into that stage at all. As Llewellyn Vaughan-Lee says, it requires great trust and faith.

"It's not like we stop using the power we have built for practice, but we throw ourselves on the mercy of the Work. There is a sign on the highway not far from here that I always look at—a little village called Merci Dieu, the mercy of God. You throw yourself on the mercy of God. If we have work the way we have imagined that we have work, then the Work will support us, we will float on the ocean of the Work, and if not, then it's a great sign that we weren't where we thought we were."

Lee returned to the reading:

> As we walk along the path, daily life will continue to present us with the difficulties we have to learn from, challenges we have to confront. However, more and more our inner attention is absorbed somewhere else, but somewhere so different it leaves only a fine residue in our everyday consciousness. Outer life can become quite mundane, even boring, and our inner life may lack the psychological dramas that accompanied the time of intense inner work. (p. 31)

Lee commented, "In the beginning the inner work that takes place is a kind of unveiling and purification of our neurosis—qualities of pride, shame, greed, vanity. In the beginning our inner work is with dreams, visions, self-observation, which is not just about the grossest, outer level of our lives, but also about the emotions and feelings that are present in any given moment. So we sit down and look at our partners and we notice ourselves enjoying our partners' company. We notice their hair, their eyes, how attractive they look in their birthday suit!" Everyone laughed. "As our conscious awareness is noticing that, there are attendant emotions and feelings inside. On the inside we might also be feeling some revulsion or frustration because we are waiting for them to do something, to lean over and kiss us. The longer we sit there and they don't meet our expectation, the more the outer response to them is complicated by inner feelings. We start to become a little annoyed, and before we know it, five minutes after we were in the swoon of love for our partners, we've got this list of faults and we're going over them one by one, ready to kick them out!" More laughter.

"What are my feelings and emotions doing while my mind—that which I'm most clearly in touch with—is going on? What's going on inside? That's the first level of inner work because we discover tremendous amounts of mountains and waves, rhythms that we weren't in touch with before—some wonderful, some terrible. But after a certain point all that psychological work ceases to be necessary, but we've become attached to it. It's very dramatic. As long as this intense personal work is going on we can assume we're making progress on the path. We're sweating out this self-awareness, 'I'm being ruthlessly self-honest, and it hurts! I'm biting the bullet.' That drama can become tremendously addictive, euphoric.

"Then at some point all that is handled. We've had all these mystical delights, visions, swoons, and we've integrated and digested it all, and then what? Nothing. The Beloved just is. He doesn't have to smack us over the head to get our attention. What if you just love your partner and there aren't fireworks? Can you be full of love without there being intense fireworks, dramatic ups and downs?" Lee picked up the magazine and re-read a sentence to make his point. " 'However, more and more our inner attention is absorbed somewhere else, but somewhere so different it leaves only a fine residue in our everyday consciousness.' (p. 31)

"In the gross organism we've got to have a certain level of intensity even to notice anything. Where the Beloved lives the domain is so fine, so subtle, so refined, that when we are moving in that domain there aren't fireworks. The subtleties of love are so delicate and sensitive, it's not this gigantic, indulgent drama. It's like the difference between being jumped on by a tiger and being brushed by the wings of a butterfly. We think being jumped on by the tiger means something is going on, but the Beloved doesn't live in that domain.

"The Beloved doesn't kick you in the ass, the Beloved comes and blows a slight breeze in your face. If we have associated drama with love or success on the path and we actually are successful on the path, we aren't going to be finding the drama anymore. Then the mind comes in and says maybe you've lost it, maybe the teacher is withholding blessings from you. When the domain that our maturity on the path has allowed us to enter is one of subtlety and refinement, it isn't going to give us the same kind of signs that the gross domains will give us. The domain of the Beloved is not going to show up with the signs of the gross domain, 'I have to deal with my neurosis,' or 'Am I loved?'

"You're lying in bed at night and you think, 'Is that incense I smell?' Just for a fraction of an instant the Beloved comes through the room and you smell roses, or there is a breeze but the window is closed. You hear a whisper, a sound . . . you wonder where it's coming from. If we turn those signs into some kind of badge we wear, we have relegated those signs to the gross domain and we cut ourselves off from the communication of the subtle domain. You can't live in the subtle domain in the way you live in the gross domain. You are living an ordinary, matter-of-fact life, but your attention is on the Beloved. Your body of habits is carrying you. The subtle domain is where your stage of work lies now; you've glimpsed the Beloved, and you'll never be the same—you cannot be.

"If we relate to our bliss the same way we relate to our anger—dramatize it, talk about it, write about it like we do our anger, pride and vanity—we will essentially be closing the door on the Beloved. We will be denying that which is trying to impress itself on us. That's why you have to give it all up. You've had all these visions and dreams, but once you *know*, you don't need those things. You've gotten the message. Rather than stop the progress of our work with doubt, we have to read the signs in relationship to the domain those signs are in. The Sufis say there are seven stages . . . The refinements that dealt with the previous stage have to be given up when you enter the next stage of work."

August 18, 1999
Freiburg

Lee and his large entourage left on time, immediately after meditation and *arati*, and arrived nine hours later in Freiburg. As the vans drove up to the apartment where Lee would be staying and where many of the sangha meals and activities of the next week and a half would be happening, the members of the Freiburg sangha hung over the balcony. They waved and smiled and called out to Lee. He came bounding up the stairs of the apartment building, greeting and embracing his students, and without any further ado, said, "Let's eat!" In the kitchen an impressive salad bar buffet was laid out. The word was there was a surprise dessert hidden away in the refrigerator. After the feast of the salad bar the dessert was brought out. It was an excellent tiramisu.

Well fortified by the spirit of the reunion feast, the dishes were cleared away and taken to the kitchen to be washed. There were ten or twelve children running through the house, playing and calling out to each other. The small apartment was brimming with life and a cacophony of sound, all of it seeming to revolve around the serene, unobtrusive, gray-haired man who sat quietly on the couch, just waiting. If approached, Lee smiled and talked to people. Otherwise he just sat in silence with an unmistakable composure.

Lee had brought over twenty people with him on this trip. Hosting Lee and his traveling party involves a tremendous amount of hard work. The bordello in Freiburg was responsible for hosting everyone—that meant providing for all the lodging, food and logistics for everyone, adults and children. Preparing beds and linens, cooking and cleaning schedules, medicinal or health needs, transportation, washing clothes and kitchen laundry for fifty or sixty people—all this and more would come into play, requiring constant attention. Lee and his family would stay in the apartment (which had been given up by the two families that live here for the duration of Lee's stay), but others were staying in various locations around town that the sangha had arranged. A mood of celebratory anticipation and excitement about being in the spiritual master's company again permeated the German sangha. The schedule for the next week was packed with events: a public talk and seminar in Freiburg; a visit to the Dürckheim Center where Lee would give a talk; three trips into nearby Switzerland for evening public talks in Zurich, Basel and Geneva. Ten days from now Lee would drive to Le Rozet in the Jura Mountains of eastern France for a three-day seminar at a remote center run by two of Arnaud Desjardins' disciples.

The students who were traveling with Lee mingled with the Freiburg bordello group, which had expanded since last year, with several families having recently moved to Freiburg from other parts of Germany. The tremendous possibility of this large group crackled in the air tonight as twenty-five or thirty adults gathered in the small living room of the apartment to hear Lee speak after dinner. His discourse centered around instruction for the Freiburg bordello (study) group which will be involved in outreach work in southern Germany.

Lee began by remembering the public talk he gave last year in Freiburg. He laughed and said that he was not on good behavior last year at the talk when he made the offhand comment, "This work is not for everyone." But in reality, everyone needs this work because everyone is suffering. He continued, "The difficulty arises in the fact that in order to do this Work we have to come to it with a certain openness and capacity for it, and then we have to build a foundation upon which this Work can stand strongly. Most people either do not come in the right mood or are not willing to build the necessary foundation. If we come with an impure motive—for power, or for some psychological need, or to relieve our suffering—it doesn't matter because the motive gets purified in the process. Practice itself generates more appropriate motives for continuing.

"People have to build a foundation upon which more serious work can stand, so they can hold up under stress. A lot of that foundation work happens in the chemistry of our first two or three or five years—it doesn't happen in weeks and months, it happens over time. But as long as we stay around and play the game, transformation happens, at least up to a point, at which time we must begin to actively participate.

"One of the things public talks are designed for is my own enjoyment. Of course my students want to bring people to the Work, but public talks are also for research on the psychology of crowds, the psychology of people—for my research and for the research of those who organized the talk here in Freiburg, who came up with the poster, who know the scene. The public talks are for your research, because the clearer the situation of the human condition is to you, the clearer you can be about yourself. 'Would I act like that under the same circumstances? Do I have just as big a blind spot?' And so on.

"Last year's talk was very strong, it was very provocative. There were some strong responses; people either liked the talk very much or disliked the talk very much. I was joking around today and saying I'd better be on good behavior so people will come to the seminar. I always say I'm going to be on good behavior, but then when I get in the talk, whatever lets loose . . ." Lee shrugged and smiled as if to say he had no control over what would happen.

"We are in this vise because we invite friends or work associates and we want people, particularly friends of ours, to share our passions. We have an investment in the talk, especially if we promote the talk and we've spent a lot of time and energy on it. We want it to work, not just for the teacher and the school, but also so that our time and energy has not been wasted. So we have an investment. But as time goes on we get to see that everyone needs this Work and yet the entry requirements are very high. It might cost ten or fifteen D-marks to get into the talk, but the price to get into the Work is very high.

"Before one really gets into the Work they will often start out very enthusiastically. A year, six months go by and some find that their initial practice deepens, they go through a few bubbles of resistance bursting. Others, at the first sign of resistance, justify it in some way, and then you never see them again. Instead of looking at themselves and being honest, they justify their negativity by putting it on the group.

"This Work is very deep. At the beginning people are expected to commit financially at least by buying all the books and CDs and music and all that, but as they become responsible they are expected to enter into household community living. Then participation happens at a whole different level. Given the depth of this Work, when we invite people to a public talk it's like test marketing. In test marketing they aren't sure how something is going to sell, so instead of spending all the money to advertise nationally, they pick a couple of towns and test market it on a few thousand people. Public talks are sort of like that; we go in and give people a glimpse of what the Work is going to look like three or four or five years down the line.

"In most schools there is what we would call the honeymoon period—a time in which you don't experience a lot of stress. Everything is beautiful; the people are beautiful; the teacher is beautiful; the work is fascinating and profound. But two or three or five years into it and you start to discover the layers of psychological denial that are common to everyone. You start to see yourself more clearly and there is a whole different level of stress, of resistance, fear, terror—the terror of obliteration.

"When ego starts to even *smell* its own transcendence, it goes totally crazy. So one of the things we do with public talks is rather than invite people into the Work by showing them what the honeymoon period is going to look like, we show them what its going to look like three or four or five years down the line. What kind of stress they are going to have to manage to be able to work effectively. People are either exhilarated by that or they recoil completely from it.

"When the community first started I said, 'I've woken up, you can too. All you need to do is just do it.' It's embarrassing now! We had Sunday evening *satsangs* with a hundred to one hundred and fifty people every night. I would give this wild talk and people would cheer. Everybody was on the inside of the joke; I would rant and rave about the world, and people would burst into cheers. It was a wild scene. There were no dietary conditions, there was nothing to do, we didn't chant—nothing.

"After awhile, I said to myself, which wasn't really my thought but Yogi Ramsuratkumar's thought, 'We should become vegetarians.' So I came in on Sunday night for *satsang* and said, 'Sooner or later we should talk about becoming vegetarians, maybe calm down and do a little sadhana.' At just the suggestion of sadhana, starting the very next Sunday the crowds were down to sixty people. All the spoiled babies, who just wanted to hang out with an enlightened master and have fun, left.

"I never looked at it this way before, but public talks are about giving people a glimpse of their machine under stress. The people who can't bear the stress leave. Some have very negative responses, but are inexorably drawn back again and again. I gave a talk in Brussels three years ago. It was in the worst possible location. I asked Alain de Rosenbo, who hosted the talk, how he advertised it, how many people he expected. He didn't seem to know. He said, 'Probably nobody will come.' We showed up with no expectations and one hundred and fifty people came. By the time the talk was over seventy-five people had left. At one point thirty people got up and stormed out of that room—all at the same time! It was a fabulous talk—which is usually the case when we don't record them. But we expected nothing.

"The next year one of Arnaud Desjardins students promoted the talk and seminar. She originally said she could get hundreds of people there. When I came to give the seminar she said, 'Everybody that I told about the seminar who was at the talk last year said to me, 'Lee Lozowick? I wouldn't come to a seminar of his if you paid me!' So those people got a very clear object lesson about what kind of stress the machine would have to endure later on, not in the honeymoon stage, but during the foundation stages.

"Once you have passed through the preliminary stages, you're out of kindergarten and you have to start to work, like a child having to learn to read, to learn language. Once we've fulfilled the foundation level stages then we enter into a whole new domain of work. In the beginning we *think* we're under stress: people come to the ashram and think, how can you bear this for more than a weekend? They feel that this is very stressful, but in the beginning stages we are *not* put under stress or undue tensions. We are given lots of room to develop a foundation; but once we move beyond the foundations stage, we've got to deal with our underworld, not just with our intelligence and power and skill, but who we are as people of vanity and cruelty and pride and shame and greed. There is tremendous stress in all that, and we are not given release valves.

"If you are a religious Catholic and you go to confession, that acts as a relief valve. Say a few 'Our Fathers' and you are redeemed. Well, there is no redemption in our school. It's like this: You've sinned? Okay, just accept yourself as you are. You can't make up for it. If you want to be saved you have to save yourself through your own efforts. There is Grace and Benediction, and so there is Help, big Help, but we are not given those kinds of release valves. We have to deal with our sins straight on.

"You get no redemption, but there is cleansing, so what we have held to be dirty becomes clean, and we stop repeating the same old negatives. You don't have to continue to be redeemed for sins that you have stopped doing. In stopping doing the sin, it is literally cleansed. Every moment is eternal. Eternal means not just forward in time, but backward in time, so in any moment eternity exists. That is why they say enlightenment is sudden. It severs the chains that bind you to the wheel of samsara because the moment of true freedom is eternal. It cleanses the past and frees the future. You are finished."

About thirty minutes after the talk was finished tea was served. While everyone sat around with cups of hot, sweet chai, Lee announced more details about going to the Dürckheim Center tomorrow. He would spend most of the day with the people who run the center and then give a public talk that night. He had room for fourteen people and there were twenty people who wanted to go. He seemed to be going out of his way to be considerate of those who wanted to go but wouldn't be given the opportunity.

He said, "There are going to be three more talks next week that everyone will have the opportunity to go to. If you miss tomorrow it will probably be the least exciting of all the talks that are coming up!" As he sat on the couch looking over the list it seemed like a difficult decision, as if he was truly concerned that he might cause some sadness or some difficulty for one of his students. He continued to speak in a tone that was tender and intimate, obviously considering his students who wouldn't go tomorrow. "Whoever doesn't get to go and hasn't been to Freiburg before, there's a beautiful square, cafés . . ." He smiled. A number of people laughed. Someone asked if the trip to the Europa amusement park on Friday with the children was open to everyone. Lee's mood shifted on the spot. He said in a rather acerbic tone, "Anybody can go as long as they don't follow me around!" People covered this comment with a layer of jokes about slinking around the park and pretending that they were just getting a hot dog if they ran into Lee, but the comment was very strong, and the ripple effect of it could be observed many times in the days to come.

August 19, 1999
Freiburg

With two cars following behind him Lee drove his van up through the mountains of the Black Forest, through lush hamlets and beautiful green mountain landscapes and down narrow roads, through wooded copses and past orderly, large two-story traditional German country houses with flowers spilling out of every window. None of this seemed to faze Lee, who drove, as usual, with a concentrated intensity. His ferocity behind the wheel often creates some kind of internal work for people who are attempting to follow in vehicles behind him, or for those who are not adjusted to the vicissitudes (or pleasures, depending on one's disposition) of riding in Lee's van.

After an hour and a half of the winding country roads and charming mountain vistas of rural Germany, we finally arrived in the scenic hamlet of Tutmose and the Dürckheim center, founded by Karlfried von Dürckheim and his wife. They had lived there for many years with a number of students. Standing outside the vans under tall green trees we noticed a sign on the building that said, "Rutte, a center for existential psychology." Lee was greeted by Thomas, one of the "co-workers" who staff the center. He showed Lee and the group around the grounds, which included several houses located along a tree-lined lane in the village.

Lee stood quietly listening in the library of the main house, a fabulous old place with a rich history, while his students plied Thomas with questions that he very graciously answered. He explained that Dürckheim lived in Japan from 1937 through 1947, where he studied Zen Buddhism, which he brought back to Germany and attempted to combine with mystical Christianity. This blend of traditions became the basis of his teaching work. Thomas said that today Rutte accommodates eight hundred to one thousand guests a year who stay for a few days or a few weeks at a time. Dürckheim's wife, now ninety years old, is still alive and lives on the property.

Today the work at Rutte focuses on providing one-on-one therapy for guests who come for a healing experience that will support the process of individuation, and also offers Zen meditation from seven to eight o'clock in the morning and again from six-thirty to seven-thirty in the evening. Guests who come to stay have the option to participate in meditation or not, or to participate in the movement groups that are offered every morning. They are also given special tasks in which they may work, whether cooking or gardening, in a way that focuses them in the present moment. It is this quality of being in the moment, Thomas said, whether cutting potatoes or cleaning the floor, that is the purpose of tasks. Guests are also given free time in which they can walk or reflect upon the daily therapy sessions.

In answer to a question about the movement groups Thomas said, "The sacred dances are taught by three female co-workers who each have their own formulations of the dance. These are not traditional Japanese dances. It's important to begin with a structure in which people can start the day. Some people prefer to start the day not in meditation but in the movement groups. Our structures are not dogmatic, so that people have to do this or that. We give a framework for many different people to find a contact to themselves. Rutte is a living process, and is not set in stone, but one that keeps evolving and living."

Thomas explained to us that the co-workers who make up the teaching staff of Rutte were certified by Dürckheim and his wife as facilitators. When someone asked him about their relationship to Dürckheim as a teacher he said, "We can't continue Dürckheim's work in a fixed way, but the principles and assertions are there. Dürckheim was a charismatic person. We can't do what he did. But everybody is asked to build up that quality out of which Dürckheim lived and worked."

We moved to an upstairs room in another building that had been set up with chairs situated in a large circle around the room. Several of the co-workers waited for us there. The idea was that the two groups would get together and talk about their respective work. A lengthy presentation about the art therapy that is done in the center was given, and a discussion ensued. The lines of difference between the two groups were clearly present within the exchange. These differences seemed to converge around the issue of whether one trusted in an "inner guru" or an "outer guru" in the form of another person. Lee said nothing, but left it to his students to engage their hosts, who explained that the path of the co-workers of Rutte—that they called, using a word coined by Carl Jung, the "individuation" process—focuses on the "inner guru."

As the conversation unfolded there was some degree of negative reaction to the guru-centered path of Lee's students, which relies heavily on the benediction and Grace of the guru's lineage. The one point of commonality seemed to be the fact of human suffering. As one of the co-workers said, Dürckheim often spoke about "absolute conscience"—a critical element of the path as everyone in the room understood it. Lee continued to be silent. One got the feeling that he was biding his time until the talk that night. At six-fifteen we went to the dojo for the evening meditation before dinner.

After a very pleasant, delicious dinner of soup, salad and bread, Lee gave a talk in the small library of the three hundred-year-old main house. At least fifty people were packed tightly into the warm room. The mellow lighting softly accentuated the antique quality of the room with its rich, dark wood wainscot walls. Through the old-fashioned windows one could see the pastoral green beauty of the surrounding countryside disappearing into the dusk as Lee began to talk, drawing the attention of the room immediately and briskly into the here and now.

"I'd like to establish context for this talk tonight. There are probably some doctrinal differences between your path and our path; a lot of people go to war over doctrinal differences and that's absurd because what is true is true. So I'm suggesting that you could put the differences in abeyance tonight, and learn whatever you can learn. Tomorrow morning I'll be gone.

"Everybody is suffering. There are two kinds of suffering—or three maybe, if we put physical pain in its own category. The first kind of suffering is fixated on ourselves. When we suffer because of fixation on self we could care less about the children starving in Africa or the bloodshed in Kosovo. Some of you will disagree with that, but if you do you're just blind. My style—insulting and provoking the audience and despairing that anyone in the audience might ever discover Reality—might be new to you, so I apologize ahead of time if anyone is insulted. It's not personal. You as an audience are no more asleep, unconscious, or psychologically aberrant than any other audience.

"In talking with some of the staff today, and from what little I know of Graf Dürckheim's work, it seems that the work offered here is very liberal. Many opportunities are made available, but not a lot of rules or demands are placed on anyone, so it's a very permissive scene in that sense. At the same time, Dürckheim was no fool, and the way he worked was—from what I can understand from those who worked with him—to offer many opportunities to people and give them a chance to participate. But if they didn't participate, then the level of how he worked with them personally was very small. The direct and personal work, that is. If you willingly took the opportunity he offered, it was a sign he could work with you personally. Then once you had his interest, you got something from him that others didn't get. That's one of the laws of the tantric path. Life is full of opportunities for transformation, liberation and so on. Every day has infinite opportunities within it. If we take them, then Life gives us its treasures, and if we don't take the opportunities, Life doesn't give us its treasures. It's very simple and direct.

"There are opportunities here—morning and evening meditation, whatever work that you get to do. You can go out to work in the garden and pretend you're learning something, or you can *work*! You can go to meditation or not go—your choice. Jacques

538

Castermane, a friend of mine, told me that when he first came here to visit Graf Dürckheim there was daily meditation. One morning he didn't go to meditation, and later he had an appointment with Dürckheim who said, 'Where were you this morning? Why weren't you here for meditation?' Jacques said, 'Oh, I was busy this morning, I had this thing to do and that thing to do.' Dürckheim said, 'If you don't take what is offered here seriously, then go live somewhere else and just here come to visit.'

"So you come up to this exquisitely beautiful mountain hamlet—the air is beautiful and clean, the water is beautiful and clean. You work with a staff that is devoted to your personal integrity. If you want you can wander around the hills and contemplate the sky all day. The staff will let you do that, but that's not what I mean by taking the opportunity. That's forgetting there is such a thing as Reality. The degree to which you take the opportunity is the degree to which Life reveals its treasures to you. The degree to which you don't take the opportunity is the degree to which you are *dreaming*!

"For example, for those of you who have children, you know that they grow up and it's all over. Your child comes running up to you with his or her arms wide open saying, 'Mamma, Mamma, Mamma!' and you say, 'Not now, honey,' and you will never have that opportunity again. It's the same thing with your partner. You may look at your partner and appreciate their beauty and wonderful qualities, but if you don't take the moment and reach out, you have lost the opportunity. Your personal transformation depends on every moment when you move into communion with your partner, your child— or away from communion.

"So the first type of suffering is self-centered, and is also often self-created, as many of you know. It is completely self-created when you blame someone else for your anger or frustration or discomfort when it is really your lack of clarity or kindness that is the cause of your anger and frustration.

"The second type of suffering is a type of resonance to the suffering of others. Not romantic sentimentality, like saying, 'Oh, that poor person,' " Lee exaggerated this with his facial expressions, "to someone whose child has just died, because when you have that reaction you couldn't care less about that person. You are thinking only of how *you* would feel if your child was killed." A perceptible rustle of discomfort went through the crowd. This example seemed particularly raw and touchy. One woman near the front sat with her hand over her mouth and a drawn and sour expression on her face. Others were nodding occasionally in agreement, leaning forward receptively.

"I mean the kind of suffering that overwhelms you with its *inviolability*, with the fact that it couldn't be any other way. The kind of suffering in which you suffer the pain of the suffering of humankind. The kind of suffering of saints. The uncommon saints, like Jesus and Buddha, and the common saints who are hidden away in kitchens and farm houses but have come to realize suffering undeniably.

"Suffering is a fact of life. We come to the Work suffering, but our suffering is transformed from self-obsessed to other-referenced. Part of what could be considered success in your personal work is that you leave your own suffering behind and become cognizant of Universal suffering, and devoted to serving by helping to relieve that suffering in any way you can.

"The first law of the Buddha is that all life is suffering. *All* life is suffering. That is an absolute statement. Often when we come to the Work our motive is to be relieved of suffering. The saints always appear to be happy; they are happy because they are able to accept Reality as it is, not because they aren't suffering.

"I have a Master in India. His name is Yogi Ramsuratkumar. In the Indian tradition there are many testimonies of the extraordinary suffering of saints and sages. On the outside they are happy and serene because they are not resisting Reality. Resisting or reacting to Reality is what causes suffering, not just on a superficial level, but to the depths of our being.

"All of us are made up of pretty things and ugly things. I'd bet money in fact that more than fifty percent of the people in this room were abused sexually in some way. Somewhere in there is very serious rage based on the abuse you suffered. As any of you know who have ever uncovered your rage, it's pretty ugly! We all want to think of ourselves as good people—kind, truthful. You want to imagine yourself to be the sort of person who, if it was World War II, would hide the Jews in your attic. But most of us wouldn't. We don't have the power, the force. So many of your parents were traumatized by what they did during the war, but they were decent people. They just didn't have the power to resist. After the war was over their conflict was so great that they closed over what they were feeling. We all do that to some degree. We all love our fathers; even if they forced us as a three-year-old to have sex. Because we love them we have to justify their behavior or relegate it to the unconscious."

The atmosphere seemed to coalesce into a raw stream of feeling as Lee kept digging into the group psyche. He continued to hit on very raw nerves in his frank and blunt way, and yet there was also a timbre of tenderness, of compassion, in his voice that carried his ruthlessness into the heart, not the mind, as he exposed the undercurrents within the group. This particular nerve—the great shame and remorse of the racial karma or group psyche of Germany—vibrated in the room now like a tuning fork.

"When we say Reality is what is, we mean in every domain, on every level, from the most subtle and divine essence, to the grossest level of our underworld—our repressed rage and frustration, the cruelties that come out anyway. Some of you have seen yourselves fairly clearly. You know how you manipulate your partner so that it doesn't look like manipulation. It's not an accident that you forgot to call home to let your partner know you'll be late, for example. Ego doesn't make mistakes. It runs things with an iron grip. You're never free of it, not even when you sleep. Every now and then we have a mystical revelation that slices through illusion like a sword, but it closes up again. And what do you do with that? Nothing. After a few weeks you wonder if you ever even had it.

"So *what is* is the level of our denial. But we can change. *Things* don't change, but *we* can change. Things don't change, life doesn't change, but we start living in a different domain that is more about creativity and pleasure instead of self-doubt and self-hatred. To begin with when we find the path, the first order of business is, who are we? We want Reality, God, transformation, freedom, but we don't want to look at our tendencies toward greed, pride, vanity, self-hatred and violence. But we have to. If we want to move on to more elevated concerns, we have to start with where we are.

"Some of you may be curious about my tradition, but there isn't a lot of value to discussing that here. If I had a wish for this evening—besides selling my books!—it would be to leave each of you with something about this evening's presentation that won't leave you alone. Something that irritates you, because human beings are really comfort seeking creatures. We come here because we are suffering and we want what's here to help us deal with that suffering in order to be more comfortable. Most people who are here are looking for something very superficial, but discover something much deeper that draws them forward. The kind of irritation I would wish to leave you with is the irritation to discover something about yourself that would help you in your ongoing process. So if you ask a social question, or about the practices in my school, it's not the kind of question that will *serve* you. I'd answer politely—well, maybe not so politely!" Lee chuckled and a few people joined in the laughter with him. "But that's just an idea of what might be helpful in the space.

"In a group like this there is a gestalt, so that someone can ask a question that serves everyone in the room in some way, even if they are served by how angry they get at the stupid questions that are asked. If we look at our lack of generosity something useful can come of it. Any questions?" The room sat still and silent. People seemed stunned by Lee's talk. After a pause he smiled and spoke again. "Okay, ask a curiosity question just to get things started!" He laughed.

A woman raised her hand and said, "I didn't understand the point."

Lee answered, "The point is that we all live under illusion and we all want the truth, so there is a conflict between those two things. We can't have Reality as long as we live in illusion. In order to pierce illusion we have to learn to work in a way most people resist. But we cloak our resistances in justifiable forms and pretend we're not resisting. We can spend lifetimes passionately seeking the truth and never take the first step toward Reality. That should be encouragement for everyone here to be willing to look at ourselves with ruthless self-honesty, because if we don't we will not see ourselves. I just don't want you to waste any more time than usual. That wasn't so bad, was it?" He said this with humor and charm as he smiled at the group, as if holding out a hand to help them cross over a bridge, or like bringing someone out of shock with a small warm sip of whiskey. He turned his gaze on the next person who raised her hand. "This is going to be a good question! I can tell!" he smiled.

She asked, "What is it that is in the books that I can't find somewhere else?"

Lee's voice boomed out, "I'm in the books, and believe me, you can't find that anywhere else! Actually, the Blessing Force and Presence of my Master is in the books. *That* is what makes them of value. That's the secret medicine."

Another person asked, "What is the extraordinary thing about having a master?"

"It's my opinion of course," Lee began. "There are many levels of teachers, from university professors to teachers who teach crafts, woodworking, sculpture, painting. If you study with a woodworking teacher you learn in a different way than if you learn from the professor. The teacher who guides you in your path is different from either of those. Fritz Perls said, 'I'm half God, half son of a bitch!' The half that was God was brilliant at reading what the human being has and needs, and the half that was son of a bitch bullied them onto the path. When you work with someone like him, the person is like a mother in a way. She has a strong hand but cares only for your good. There are a lot of charlatan gurus—people who have no skill, who just wield power. They have no refinement in that kind of teaching; it's gross, ugly, violent. But someone who has the skill to recognize the specific needs in human beings and guide them is a great blessing. Then there are teachers who aren't very skilled but they have very powerful prayers and can pray for you.

"Then there are Masters, at the ultimate level, who have such an intimate relationship with the Divine, or Reality, that they can actually intercede for you, represent you to God. Their blessing is so extraordinary that one word from them and you are saved. Jesus was one of those, I suppose. He stirred up enough trouble! And my Master is one of those. His relationship to God is so intimate, He's not just free, awake, enlightened, He's way beyond all that! Anyone who is awake, free, has an intimate relationship with Reality, but my Master's level of intimacy with Reality is almost unique in all the world. I have to believe that because I have no second to Him and that Influence!" Lee smiled.

"To whatever degree that Influence permeates me and everything I write—the degree of resonance that I have with Him—is the degree to which His Influence moves through me. If I was completely resonant to Him, we wouldn't be sitting here talking, taping and videotaping and all that; we'd just be being together. But my way of bringing His Influence to people, given my small resonance to Him, is through the books, the music."

A man sitting on the front row asked, "Have you found the answer to the question of the purpose of life?"

"Yes, I have! Any other questions?" People laughed at Lee's implication. The room seemed to have relaxed significantly now that Lee was talking about Yogi Ramsuratkumar. He turned back to the person who asked the question about the purpose of life. "As far as I've been able to discover, in general terms, the purpose of life is to serve the Evolution of Life itself, through the ongoing Process of Life. That's good news and bad news. It has nothing to do with art!

"Bach's music transmits something—it's Real. The point of that art is not that we sit, listen and enjoy. That's not the way Bach composed the music. He composed the music to *disturb* us. You listen and find yourself weeping, and you don't know why. It hasn't just dug into your heart and dug out a piece of it, it hasn't just communicated Beauty. You have to find out why you have been so deeply touched. But most artists think their art is the most important thing in the world.

"So to serve this ongoing Process of Life itself means to serve the ongoing increase of clarity in relationship to Reality on a broader and deeper basis, which doesn't mean you become a spiritual teacher or a therapist—there are too many of those already! To serve the Process of Life itself is to be more in relationship with your partner, your children and all the rest of it. In the Zen and Sufi traditions, the profundity of mystical experience has to be tested in ordinary life. If your clarity of Reality fades when you get back to ordinary life, you didn't really get it anyway.

"In my tradition, the Baul tradition of Bengal, India, finding God is not the point—living Life is the point. The purpose of Life is not in any way personal; it's impersonal. What Carl Jung called the process of individuation is a process in which every person has a specific personal potential or possibility; at the same time that individual is not separate and distinct from the world as we know it. He or she is an integral part of the world. If finding ourselves separates us from the world in any way instead of throwing us further into it, then something is wrong."

Another woman questioned, "What will the irritant be for us tonight?"

"It is different for each person," Lee said. "It may be some disagreement with something that I said that angered you, or something that was said in a way that just gets in between the cracks. Or my favorite: 'How can that son of a bitch *presume* to be a teacher, that asshole!' " People laughed heartily at Lee making himself the butt of the joke, but one was left with an uneasy feeling—was this really funny? Or was it tragic, in the sense that he was compelled by the unconscious contents of the group psyche to make teaching lessons in this way.

"It's expensive to have me as a teacher. People have to have enough *being* to work in a way that most people are categorically unwilling to do. Tonight I was on good behavior. I respect the staff here. But ordinarily my personality is paradoxical, difficult, immature.

People have to be willing to put all their faith and trust in *me*, then deal with it when I act like a total ass half the time—and not even an adult ass! And that's just for starters! Most just are not willing to pay the price."

Then quite abruptly he said, "Now we'll end!" After the talk Lee stayed around the book table for awhile talking with different people. One of the co-workers, Peter, is now a student of Richard Baker Roshi who has a new center up in the mountains near Rutte. Lee seemed to enjoy hearing this news and asked Peter to convey his regards to Richard Baker when he sees him next. As people cleared up the space and returned it to order, Lee and several of his students packed up the books, loaded them in the vans, and were soon heading back down the mountains into Freiburg. It was midnight before we got back.

August 20, 1999
Freiburg

Lee spent all day at the Europa Park—a Disneyland replica an hour's drive from Freiburg—with his family. He returned to the apartment at five-thirty to a simple dinner of salad and potatoes with about forty people packed into the living room on pillows on the floor. Children ran in and out of the room, adding more noise and confusion to the scene. After dinner Lee walked the block and a half to the location where his public talk was scheduled to begin at eight o'clock. By seven-fifteen he was firmly established behind an eight-foot-long book table that lined one wall of the room. People began to flow into the room and take their seats on folding chairs or on pillows on the floor in the front of the room near the speaker's chair. Soon the room was packed with about seventy-five people. As the talk began it seemed that he was continuing in the same straightforward and rather serious manner of the talk the night before. He began by asking people to refrain from asking questions until he had talked for about an hour, then he would open the discussion up for questions.

"Ordinarily I would talk about the psychology of selfishness versus the freedom of Surrender to the Will of God, and give lots of practical examples that people can relate to. That's always fun and makes talks clear so that everybody understands, but we all know all that already. We'll touch on that of course, but essentially you have all studied different traditions and therapies to varying degrees. It doesn't hurt to have the truth that we know about ourselves reinforced, but it may not help so much either. If there is an alchemy I would wish for you tonight it would be that something could happen that would be helpful to your spiritual practice, whatever that is. Whether you follow some practice—Buddhist, Hindu, esoteric Christianity—I desire something to happen tonight that will serve your particular practice.

"We were at the Dürckheim Center last night and a number of the co-workers—although some of them have spiritual teachers—rely on 'the guru within' and feel that an external teacher is unnecessary and dangerous. Those two dynamics tend to be completely polarized to each other. People who feel the external spiritual teacher is necessary to help them along the way look at people who don't have a teacher and think they are under illusions and fooling themselves with greater and greater sophistication. And we feel very superior, of course. 'Inner guru' or inner Christ people feel those with a living human teacher are all just transferring on their teacher, will never come to their own individuation and so on. And of course, they feel superior. So we all feel superior!" The audience laughed at Lee's easy and intimate inclusion of everyone into the human condition in a way that was, in the moment, actually palatable. He continued, "Even those of us who have inferiority complexes feel superior! 'No one is as inferior as me!' So, I would like to establish a context here tonight. Whether you don't have a teacher and don't believe you need one is irrelevant!"

Lee pointed to a large color photograph of Yogi Ramsuratkumar that was placed on the table beside him. "This is my Teacher. I believe a teacher is valuable and what I say is relevant to that belief system, but many things I say don't have anything to do with whether you have a teacher or not, so don't bias your receptivity to what I have to say based on that difference. It doesn't bother me if you disagree with me—just leave it at that. We can still be friends and disagree, right? If you disagree with me there is no need to hold a grudge against me for the rest of your life!" Everyone laughed, but in a way Lee was imploring people to practice kindness and generosity. There have been many occasions when members of his audience have not been willing to be so mature about their reactions to his statements. Tonight he was coming across as very warm and amiable yet at the same time very direct and straight. The crowd was already with him. They laughed again as he continued, "Don't get *angry* with me, just don't agree!

"There is something different about those books over there on that table. There's some new information in there, but lots of it you can find elsewhere, if you pick up a book by Gurdjieff, Osho Rajneesh, Krishnamurti. But there is something that makes the information in those books different from any other books, and not because I've written them because I'm not that great—only in my own mind!" More laughter from the group. He was charming everyone with his self-deprecations.

"We have a saying in English, 'He's a legend in his own mind,' a play on words for the saying, 'A legend in his own time.' What makes those books and that music different in this Guy," Lee pointed again to the picture of Yogi Ramsuratkumar, "Yogi Ramsuratkumar. He is my Master. He's still alive and living in India. He's been my Teacher—that I'm *aware* of—for twenty-four years, but actually for much longer than that. Yogi Ramsuratkumar is His Name, I'll say it again. My relationship to Him is probably like the way you relate to your lover at the best of times, and in my relationship with Him there are no worst of times!" Lee smiled.

"India has been the home of many extraordinary, great realizers. People as powerful and radiant in their tradition as the sixteenth Karmapa was in his tradition. He was not just your average enlightened Tibetan Buddhist tulku or Master. I base that opinion on having spent one day as close to him as from here to there." He pointed perhaps six feet away from where he sat. "Enlightenment, awakening, realization is an interesting milieu or field of expression of Being because there are different levels of it. Just because one is awakened or enlightened doesn't put one at the level of Jesus or Buddha.

"A lot of great teachers have served with integrity and left behind brilliant teachings, and so on, but were not fully enlightened. In the traditions when you realize God in this body, in this life, they say it is your second birth. There is a saying in the occult, 'As above, so below.' You all know there are tremendous changes along the way of growing up. There are big differences between being five years old and ten years old. We also sometimes get stuck at different places in our process of growing up. Therapeutic processes are designed to free you from whatever handicap it is that keeps you locked in certain places, so you can finally grow up at forty-five years of age. There are certain areas in which we are very mature and adult and other areas in which we are not. Enlightenment is exactly the same. You have a second birth, and an infancy and growth process, and some who are enlightened get stuck at infancy or adolescence. They may still be great teachers, just as you may be a great human being even though you may be stuck in one area.

"Yogi Ramsuratkumar is not stuck in any area. He is completely mature, adult, grown up in His enlightenment. This puts Him in a very rarified category of enlightened masters because there are probably not more than one handful of teachers in the world at that level. There are those who are close, and a lot who are far away. I would equate the sixteenth Karmapa with Yogi Ramsuratkumar.

"My work as a teacher is an *affect* of Yogi Ramsuratkumar as an enlightened Master. Without Yogi Ramsuratkumar's Influence in my life I would still be a teacher, but I would be completely under illusion instead of relatively under illusion. Without Him, I would have abused the position I'm in—finances, power, all of that. Every time I drive into Freiburg in my Renault traffic van, which on a good day can barely make it up hills, I see a Porsche Carrera and I think, 'Oh boy, would I like one of those!' I've been offered lots of money and I haven't accepted it, but without His Influence I would have bought the car. And *sex*! I've had to turn down lots of offers! I like women! It doesn't matter what you look like! Just the way you flip your hair . . ." Lee sighed as if he found everything about all women simply irresistible. "But I have to turn it down! Without the Influence of Yogi Ramsuratkumar I'd be in big trouble." There was a sense of abandon, a wildness in Lee that the audience seemed to find hysterically funny as he poked fun at himself and his supposed weaknesses. People laughed without restraint.

"So I've done okay in twenty-four years, had some integrity, but only because of Him. He looks over me, blesses me, protects me. The degree to which I am surrendered to His Influence is the degree to which I'm successful as a teacher, and that's what makes everything on that table over there different. It carries His Influence to the degree that I—as His student, disciple, devotee—am surrendered to Him. It's not one hundred percent obviously, or I wouldn't be sitting here talking and giving this seminar this weekend, or making jokes about sex!" Everyone laughed again. People were leaning forward, as if leaning into Lee as he spoke.

Lee proceeded to tell the joke about the old-age home and the woman who says, "Anybody who can guess what I have in my hand can have sex with me tonight!" An old man says sarcastically, "An elephant!" She looks him up and down and says, "That's close enough!" The audience broke into bawdy laughter and guffaws, loving the joke and enjoying Lee, who didn't skip a beat but went immediately into another joke. People shook with laughter.

"So obviously I'm not one hundred percent surrendered to my Master, but after twenty-four years of my physical relationship to Yogi Ramsuratkumar, I've grown up a little bit. I'm twenty-four years old! Still, twenty-four is only twenty-four. It's not forty-five or fifty or fifty-five. Even if we're not on the path, we're just ordinary people struggling to live life, between the ages of twenty-four and fifty-five we learn a lot. We become different human beings. But *okay* . . . I'm a mature twenty-four!" Laughter broke out again in response to Lee's humorous admission.

"My teaching work is not about the glorification of Lee Lozowick. I act the way I do, but it's very intentional. It is done by design because to be in the immediate radiation of this Influence is not for everybody. If we are psychologically in denial about something, we are in denial for a good reason. As children we closed down to our pain because in order to survive we had to. The reasons why the father of a three-year-old girl comes in at night and sticks his fingers between her legs—or worse—is something a three-year-old cannot process. So we close up parts of our lives and keep them closed until it gets opened up as adults in therapy, or when we can handle that energy without being destroyed by it. Different teachers have different levels of radiations. The radiations of Yogi Ramsuratkumar cleanse us and reveal who we are, and if we are not ready to see what we've hidden away, the result can be catastrophic and can handicap our process. So what you are seeing tonight is very different for those of you who were here last year. I thought I'd do a serious talk tonight.

"Ordinarily I act as a buffer to keep people who are not ready for His Radiance from Him by my behavior, by my teaching style. So, the degree to which I am grown up is the degree to which everything on that table is permeated with His Radiance. That is what makes them very different than the books written by professors of Indian studies. Any questions?" The room was still and silent. No one raised a hand.

"Well! Has the talk been that stunning? Thank you! I don't know what to say!" Lee spoke sweetly, with a tinge of humor, but even more so with a disarming vulnerability. It was actually this vulnerability that had stunned the room into silence. This rather intimate glimpse of the spiritual master being vulnerable seems to be something that has been growing as the summer has progressed, as if his comments over breakfast at La Ferme de Jutreau about his own deconstruction were just a hint of what was to come. Tonight he seemed to be demonstrating what that deconstruction might look like.

Someone asked, "Would you talk about the title, 'Accepting What Is'?"

"You know, we just give titles to talks to get people here!" Lee quipped with a smile. People laughed. This was certainly a true statement. "I never prepare for talks! To make it brief, it's like this. We remember the past and project that on the future. We don't live in the present moment as a result. If we stop to look at what our minds and bodies are doing in the present moment, we are either in a state of expectation—waiting for food or sex . . . or waiting for sex to be finished. Sometimes it's a relief for sex to be over!" This brought out another wave of laughter, especially from the men. "Come on, admit it! Admit it, guys! You're trying not to look at the clock . . . you better not let her see you looking at the clock! She sees you looking at the clock and you're like, 'No, baby . . . baby I didn't look at the clock!' Aren't we something? Human beings are just the most amazing creatures!" The men were laughing especially hard now as Lee's animated theatrics added a spice to the common recognition of human weaknesses.

"The mind is always wishing things were different; wishing it was cooler in the room, wishing for a sunny day, wanting a promotion on the job. We can't exactly define enlightenment—words can't capture what it is. We can only imply or talk around it. One definition that applies to this state of consciousness is to live in the present moment. One way to do that is to accept what is, here and now. That doesn't mean that we don't have personal volition, that we don't strive to become closer to our friends, lovers, children. It means that how things are now in this moment can't be any different than they are. That is the physics of things. But in the next moment things can be different. This moment already is—it can't be other than this. To accept what is does not say anything about the future; in the next moment it may be completely different. If in this moment we are not accepting what is, we are either living in the past and our future will not be a function of Reality but of the past, or we are dysfunctional in the moment. To accept what is, as it is, here and now, could be a kind of formula for living an enlightened life—a framework against which to measure ourselves. How awake are we? We're either living in the present moment or not, in which case we are asleep. We're either clear or under illusion. We can't be partly under illusion.

"On any spiritual path the degree of success on the path is the degree to which we live in Reality, not in illusion. Reality exists only in the moment, not in the past. The future hasn't happened yet, so Reality doesn't exist in the future either. When you accept what is in the moment, it doesn't mean that you might not think or wish that it would be sunny tomorrow, but you accept that as a thought, not as something you are identified with. Well, that should give you lots of things to think about. I was hoping not to do that, but it was a sincere question, and I had to answer it."

Another person asked, "Do enlightened people all live in the present?"

Lee laughed, "Is this a test? It's a subjective issue. There are different groups who each think other groups are not enlightened. But there is no absolute criteria. How do you know if someone is enlightened? Because they say so? Ridiculous! When I first started teaching I said I was the greatest master on earth! But things have changed a lot over the years. It's a ridiculous thing to say, even for an infant! It's like a two-year-old saying, 'I'm not leaving,' when his father is pulling him at the door, as if he is stronger than his father.

"So you have to look at the teacher's behavior over time. How do they live their lives? How are their relationships? Kind or cruel? Impatient? Is the teacher attached to qualities, or does he just let them pass through? Speaking of qualities, let's talk about vanity and teachers." Lee went off on a hilarious rant about Western, self-styled divine mothers, their hair and jewelry and stylish silk clothes. This seems to be one of his favorite comedy routines. Audiences either love it or hate it. This one loved it and laughed uproariously.

"So look at the teacher over time. How are they with their students? Imperious and demanding? Or natural with them? How does the teacher apply resources that are available to him or her? A pure Advaita Vedanta nondualist may say that particular criteria has no meaning because everything is illusory anyway. But if you look at a *good* nondualist (and there are good nondualists and bad nondualists) like Nisargadatta Maharaj, who allocated resources by giving it all away, you see something. He could have had a million dollars, but he just lived in his little apartment. His behavior was consistent with someone who understands there is no separation between him and others.

"So, is there a consistent relationship of kindness, generosity, understanding, gratitude between the students and the teacher? A minor point is skillful means—a Buddhist term. As you become more mature in the dharma your ability to communicate becomes more fluid because you have more skill in communicating the dharma. So how skilled at teaching is the teacher? Some are very wise, but are lousy teachers, and some are good teachers but are not very wise. It's a skill to teach—not just that you know something about the Universe, but also about communication, transmission, relationship.

"The fourth thing is, how are the teacher's students? Does the teacher have long-term students who are not blind followers? There are always people who have not outgrown projections on the teacher—they are typically too quick to defend the teacher, too zealous, too quick to defend themselves over meaningless doctrinal points. Don't base your conclusions on the babies, but on the adults.

"And then there is the lineage. A self-appointed teacher may be a genuine teacher and have great value to offer, but without a lineage that the teacher is *accepted* in, it's questionable. The lineage is an important issue."

A long-time friend of the Hohm Community who was in the audience tonight said, "I used to think the criteria of recognizing a teacher was what I feel, what he could do to open my heart and so on. But looking back on my relationship with my old teacher I think he was a lousy teacher but very charismatic. Is this charisma useful at all?"

Lee responded, "Good question. I don't think that's a criteria and I'll tell you why. Many of you know from drug experiences that once you've taken a certain amount of drugs you've patterned your body, so that all you have to do is just stand next to someone who is on the drug and you start tripping. We human beings are very weak in terms of boundaries. The fact that we're getting a 'hit,' a feeling, doesn't mean anything except that the person has some power.

"Often what we call feelings are not feelings but feeling-like sensations that are completely psychologically created and have nothing to do with *what is* feeling-wise. A lot of people who were abused say that they love their father, but really feel rage. They create a feeling that really isn't a feeling. When in the presence of a person of charisma, we are projecting—we see the good father, friend or savior. We interpret what we are actually feeling to justify this transference. That's not a reliable feeling. 'I felt my heart open,' is so often unreliable because we have a big investment to feel that—we *have* to feel that."

As Lee brought the talk to a close he made himself completely available to people, saying, "I'm happy to answer questions informally at the book table as long as people want to stay around and have questions."

All the joking and full-bodied laughter that Lee induced in the audience tonight had opened people up. There was a feeling of being refreshed, alive, vitalized. As he stood at the book table explaining the Shri and liars, gods & beggars CDs and tapes to a couple who smiled into his face and listened intently, about a dozen people clustered around. Many other people congregated in small groups around the room, talking animatedly.

The people talking with Lee were disciples of Arnaud Desjardins; they stayed and talked with Lee for ten minutes. Another man picked up the *vigraha* of Yogi Ramsuratkumar and looked at it for a long time. He seemed to be lost in thought, or in a kind of wistful reverie. He was the same man who was looking at it before the talk began. He picked up several other books and looked through them, the *Yogi Ramsuratkumar Souvenir* book among them. Then he picked up the *vigraha* again. He walked over to his wife and led her to the book table to see the *vigraha*. They spoke together in German, but the conversation was obvious. He was drawn to the statue, and she shook her head no. As she walked away he reluctantly followed her, looking back at the statue of Yogi Ramsuratkumar.

People were lingering and seemed reluctant to leave tonight as Lee continued to talk with many people at the book table. The change in Lee from what he animated during his talk to how he was with people at the book table afterward was noticeable. At the book table he was gentle, almost shy, while at the same time immediately and directly present with each person. As a child and young man Lee was very introverted; it is a quality that seems to show up in his expression as a teacher in the vulnerability he exhibits with people, and in the mood of intimacy that so naturally occurs in his presence. Tonight there was a perceptible glow in the room; it felt like an inviting warmth, a happiness or effervescence that people wanted to bask in. There was a sense of celebration, but what were we celebrating? "Jai guru!" the entire room, the people in it, the air itself seemed to be shouting.

Tom L., a student of Lee's who arrived today from Boulder, Colorado and filmed Lee's talk tonight, stood talking with some of Lee's students. He was remembering a talk on the alchemy of love and sex that Lee gave two years ago in Boulder. People had lingered so late in the rare atmosphere that had been created that, in order to close the building on time, they practically had to pull chairs out from under people.

"Just like tonight," he said. "They don't want to leave." Several of Lee's students were talking together quietly about something different they sensed in Lee tonight. The discussion went toward Lee's recent comments about deconstructing himself. There was a shared feeling that something important seemed to be afoot with Lee, and the general question was, "What's going on?" The guru is a continuing puzzle, a conundrum. Tom said, "I say the only place to find him is in his poetry, and that's where the footprints are leading. What's the ultimate trick of the Master Magician? Making himself disappear."

All this—the lingering guests, the extraordinary mood, the wonder expressed by Lee's students, the shifting kaleidoscope of Lee Lozowick who, in the midst of change, remains miraculously the same steady, composed presence—mingled to heighten the anticipation and excitement for the seminar beginning tomorrow. Around eleven p.m. Lee walked back to the apartment where he was staying. He yawned and smiled, just an ordinary guy.

August 21, 1999
Freiburg

After a breakfast with about fifty people at the apartment at eight-thirty, Lee walked back to the building where the seminar was being held. Now he stood at the book table talking with people as the room filled up. As he began the first talk of the two-day seminar there were about sixty-five or seventy people in the room.

"We're going to start exactly on time! Unlike last night at the public talk, please ask questions anytime you would like. There will be lots of stories about Yogi Ramsuratkumar this weekend . . .

"There are certain specific circumstances in which a level of discomfort is created and sustained. But it will be uncomfortable enough to sit for two hours in the heat without having to create additional discomfort, so please be comfortable. Go to the bathroom if you need to while I am talking, but please use the toilet! The other boundary I would draw is please don't have sex in the room . . . " Lee's timing was perfect with these little jokes. The group was very receptive and laughed along as if on cue.

"There are times in working with a teacher when stress is applied, when we are specifically given times of discomfort. Ego inherently procrastinates. There are times in our process when we don't have time to sit around and be lazy. A certain window opens and we have to go through it now.

"This is a picture of Yogi Ramsuratkumar," Lee pointed to the picture. "He's wearing a wool shawl and shirt and one or two other wool shawls on top of that. In the summer in Tiruvannamalai it can be forty-five, forty-seven or forty-eight degrees (centigrade). He wears that shawl all the time, twenty-four hours a day. He does that for a purpose; because He is committed to that purpose, He doesn't struggle against the discomfort of that."

Someone asked the question, "Where do you draw the line between intentional stress and masochism?"

"That's a good question because some of us are psychologically defined by self-hatred. In the example of the child who is molested, there are two things that typically happen: we close off part of our life energy to protect it, to keep it alive, because sexual abuse to a child feels like the child's soul is being murdered. Secondly, the child sees mother and father as God figures, and can't believe something could be wrong with God, so the mind of the child must be the problem. We come to unconsciously believe that we are bad, dirty, sinful, evil. If we've been trained in the Christian concept of morality we punish ourselves for these sins—always bumping into things, hurting ourselves. Or we hurt ourselves on purpose, like wearing stones in shoes to punish sins, or self-flagellation.

"There is a basic difference between creative stress and masochism. Masochism is psychologically defined and comes from such depths of the unconscious that we can't ordinarily do anything about it. We go through periods of feeling terrible about it and not being able to stop. This is one of the important reasons for practicing this Work with a living teacher, because if we have the tendency toward masochism we are likely to create intentional stress way beyond the body's ability to digest that stress. In different areas we may find that we use spiritual principles to justify our lust for power, to justify greed or pride or vanity. Of course that's not news to anyone.

"There is value in stress, but if you create so much stress that you go into breakdown then you have just created an obstacle. In the way carbon goes from being coal to diamond, when ego is put under stress there are times when it is transformed, but it's a very delicate issue because if you put the wrong element under heat it just breaks down or melts.

"I was visiting Yogi Ramsuratkumar in 1986 with twenty people. We were staying at Ramanashram in Tiruvannamalai. There was a Westerner there who kept staring at our group, so after a few days he came over. He was very outgoing and friendly . . ." Lee then interrupted the beginning of this story of how he came to teach in Europe by giving some background information.

"Years ago, in 1977, Yogi Ramsuratkumar asked me what I wanted. I should've said money and sex! But I didn't. I was very dedicated to my teaching work and my students. The community was very intense at that time and I felt under the pressure of all that. Yogi Ramsuratkumar didn't have a residence then. He just slept wherever He was when night came. He lived on the streets. Every few hours some devotees would find Him and then He would wander away. At the time that way of life looked very attractive to me—just sit by yourself, read good books, every so often someone would come to you and you bless them and send them away!

"Yogi Ramsuratkumar said to me, 'Lee, what do you want?' I said, in a moment of wishfulness, 'I would like to be just like you—to sit in an out-of-the-way place and have people come . . .' Yogi Ramsuratkumar has a way of reading people's futures. He goes into a trance state and He sort of looks at you in this diffuse way. So He looked at me and then looked up for two or three minutes, which seemed like two or three days! He refocused His eyes on me and they were full of tears. And now I know why!" Everyone laughed. " 'No,' He said, 'Lee is going to travel all over the world.' At the time I'd been teaching for one year; I had no concept of traveling. I was living out on a farm in community. I envisioned having a few more students, but that was all.

"So that's what He said. My relationship to Him began to be, and has continued to be, one of not questioning Him. I don't have any questions and if I did I wouldn't ask them. I trust His wisdom that if I have any need, He will offer what I need. When I'm with Him I am in a mood of receptivity. Even a sincere question at the wrong time is aggressive, so I didn't ask what he meant or when that would happen; I just heard it and took it.

"Now we're back to 1986 in Tiruvannamalai. I was talking with this guy from Germany who had been running groups for awhile and had a very large following. He said, 'Will you come to Germany and teach my senior students?' I never assume that the offers people make will be fulfilled. I never thought I would hear from him again. With most people, a week later they've forgotten what they said. But I said, 'Sure, send me a letter in America,' and I gave him my address.

"A month after I got back from India I got a letter with a contract and dates for a seminar. It said 'Please let me know if these dates will work for you' and so on. So I ended up in Germany in May of 1987 and worked with his students—to put it mildly!" Lee chuckled. "That was the beginning. I started coming to Germany every year and really had no intention to travel outside of Germany. I had a very devoted body of students here and I started coming for two to three weeks a year, then four to five weeks a year, then six or seven when France opened up."

Lee then told the story of meeting Yvan Amar in 1988 in Paris. In 1991 Yvan connected Gilles Farcet, a disciple of Arnaud Desjardins, with Lee. He continued, "Gilles was writing a book about Western spiritual masters and Yvan gave him my book, *Living God Blues*, and said, 'You should go meet this man.' Gilles came to our ashram in Arizona and spent a week with us. At one point he said, 'Are you coming to France any time? My teacher would like to meet you.' 'Okay,' I said, so I arranged to visit his teacher while I was in Europe with my German students. It was set up for me to give talks at different places around France, and everywhere I went with Gilles, who was our host, there were crowds of two hundred to two hundred and fifty people. I found out that Gilles was a very well-known author, and that Arnaud Desjardins had spent time with Papa Ramdas, which made Arnaud and Yogi Ramsuratkumar *gurubhais* in a way. Although Swami Prajnanpad is Arnaud's guru, he had a great respect and appreciation for Swami Papa Ramdas. So Arnaud and I made a very deep and immediate connection, as if we had known one another for lifetimes, which is undoubtedly true.

"I don't particularly like to travel, but now here I am traveling all over Europe, and that is what Yogi Ramsuratkumar saw years ago, because that is what the Divine has blessed me with—meaning Him, Yogi Ramsuratkumar. Everything that happens to me is because of His Blessing, His Help. I think Yogi Ramsuratkumar had tears in His eyes when He was reading the future for me because He suffers His devotees' burdens. If His devotee has a burden, He feels it, suffers it personally. He was reading not only my travel in Europe, but many other things as well.

"So, over the weekend we will be sitting here and I'll be talking. We will not be doing any movement exercises or dancing. If you need to dance or express yourself, do it on your own time. There's plenty of good music over there on the book table! The Work is paradoxical. We have two bands in the community. Shri, the blues band, just finished touring Europe this summer. We started out with a rock band about thirteen years ago. We made six or seven tours of Europe, we toured in America. We became a very finely tuned professional group. We put out thirteen albums of original music, each one getting better and better as the musicians became more and more mature as human beings and as musicians, and more proficient in the studio. We just disbanded or broke up the rock band even though as a performing group we were never better. My request to the band was to put out a final album with the new songs that hadn't been recorded. That album is better musically, and the spirit of that album is so far beyond anything we did previously it is like a different band.

"The whole reason for having a band is not for pleasure. It is pleasurable, but that's not the reason we have the bands. The bands are designed as practice for everyone involved. The chamber of the band—the musicians, the road crew, the dancers—is an alchemical laboratory. As the rock band matured we became lazy. But as the music became tighter and better we were unwilling to take risks and look like fools. The way I work as a teacher is to give people a certain opportunity, to create a certain circumstance, then wait for people to take personal responsibility for their part in it. I don't push them. There is no need to.

"The songs that most embarrassed the musicians were the songs I wanted to do most. They were the same songs that the music companies would say, 'That's interesting,' about, but they were a real turn-off to the band. Like 'Sugar Shock.' At the end of the song I would start stuffing candy in my mouth and throwing candy at the audience. If we had a happy audience it was great, but if we had an angry audience, it wasn't so great. I would take handfuls of candy and loop it through the air. Angry people sitting in the audience would take pieces and throw it at someone in the band, as hard as they could. I didn't want to stop doing the song, but it was literally dangerous at times.

"Another one of our theatrical songs was about men's rage toward women. It was about how men say I love you, then the next minute they're hitting. In the bridge between the verses there was a long, wild frenetic interlude—it was dark, threatening, psychedelic—and in the middle of that I would do a spoken rant designed after Jim Morrison and The Doors' 'The End.' It was about child abuse. People in audiences would start to go into spontaneous regressions to childhood. It was very cathartic and provocative. The whole thing was twelve or fifteen minutes long, and people in the band would say, 'Oh, that's kind of gotten old—let's do something new.' 'Sugar Shock' was very popular and people would yell, 'Throw the candy!' So I had an idea of doing a song about the ocean and throwing fish at people, greasy sardines. The composers refused to do it . . . *refused*!" Laughter was interspersed through Lee's words.

"Now we have a new band, Attila the Hunza. Hunzas live to be one hundred and twenty years old up the Caucasus Mountains eating apricots. Who wants to be a hundred and twenty years old? Anyway, Attila the Hunza is a play on words in English. Its members are all young people. I'm not in that band and won't be—I leave that to the kids! And they're fabulous! Eight or nine of them, they sprawl all over the stage so relaxed and loose and spontaneous and creative! Three really strikingly good-looking women up front singing. One of the lead singers is six feet tall, the best of Grace Jones and Madonna. She never sang before in her life. But you can see things in people, you know. When she got up there on that stage and opened her mouth, it was like discovering a treasure. Now she's starting to get a taste of it—the roar of the crowd and all that.

"Nevertheless, we will not be doing any movement exercises in here this weekend. So if you need to shake it out some after lunch, get that cellulite quivering! Yes, the nice thing about cellulite is the way it moves, right? I have plenty of it so I can talk! I don't even look in the mirror anymore.

"So we'll be sitting here talking. There will be a lot of information communicated, but that's secondary. It's good and useful, but the alchemy of the space is what's important. We have the possibility of creating something very useful this weekend. Making gold from lead or iron. Turning this," Lee patted his chest, "into gold; turning the sleeping being into the revealed or awakened being. In the science of alchemy there are two elements that are primarily used—mercury and sulfur. In homeopathic amounts you can take a pill of mercury or sulfur and herbs, but if you put too much mercury in, you will poison yourself. In the Middle Ages many people died from eating mercury.

"We work with an energetic alchemy. Yogi Ramsuratkumar is the mercury and then each of us puts a certain ingredient into the mix—the level of our sincerity, the degree to which we are willing to discover what Reality is. Every seminar I give is an alchemical experiment. We are both the ingredients and the possible result of the experiment. Different people will derive different benefits from this process. We all have different levels of ability to digest, understand, integrate the 'meal' we will be given this weekend. If someone is a heroin user, the body develops the ability to withstand larger and larger doses of heroin. If one gets off the habit and the body is cleaned out and one returns to the habit and the first hit is at the strength they were used to, it kills them. That's what a lot of overdoses are. So a feast will be set before us, thanks to Yogi Ramsuratkumar, and the beauty of this Process is that even if we want to overeat, we won't be able to. We will only be able to take what we can understand, assimilate, digest. So it's lunchtime!"

Grabbing one of the sandwiches that were made for everyone at the seminar off the table, Lee then headed off walking at a fast clip with a few of his students toward the square in old-town Freiburg, where the large daily open-air market was underway. Stopping to buy olives, a roasted chicken, bratwurst smothered in mustard and some other goodies, he headed toward a bench behind the old cathedral and sat down to eat with enthusiasm. On the way back he stopped in for ice cream at one of the shops, making it back in time to start his one-thirty talk. He seemed to be fortifying himself in some way, but also rejoicing or celebrating something.

"As I talked about last night in the introduction, the real advantage of the path is the blessing or the Influence of the lineage. In my case Yogi Ramsuratkumar and Swami Ramdas are the lineage; in some Zen and Tibetan Buddhist lineages there is a history of fifty or sixty teachers, and each of these teachers in the lineage adds an element of magic to the path.

"There is a degree to which we have to work—we have volition, we must have intention. Even God can't do that for us. But the biggest part of the path I use various words for, one being 'magic.' In a traditional religious context we could use the words Grace or Benediction. That aspect of the path is completely mysterious. We can know that it is, we can see the effects of it, but we can't really grab hold of it, in the sense of doing something predictable that we know will bring this quality of mystery or Grace into our lives.

"How we act in relationship is our responsibility; are we kind, are we generous, are we sensitive to the needs of others and so on. If you're kind to someone then they will tend to respond in a certain way. If you're sensitive and understanding of someone, they'll tend to respond in a certain way. But when it comes to Grace there's nothing we can do to guarantee that Grace will be given to us. Some people pray very fervently, and their lives are miserable. Some people don't do anything and their lives are very happy and easeful.

"How to recognize the signs of Grace in one's life is a little bit delicate, a little bit subjective. The signs of Grace in one's life are the demonstration of serving one's personal destiny. So the obvious question is, how do we know what our personal destiny is? Some of us are probably frustrated in certain creative areas of our lives. We think if only we had the time and resources to be an artist, we could really *serve*. We think that we have a skill as a painter that *really* serves humanity; if only we could be taken care of and didn't have to earn a living, the poetry we would write would put Blake to shame!

"How do we know if Grace is active in our lives? It's not always like a lightening bolt that strikes, and it's suddenly obvious because you're levitating and in ecstasy all the time, full of light and beauty! Sometimes you're just the same old slob, but you're a little kinder—like me!" People laughed.

"Grace is a key element in the path. Without Grace we can become better human beings, we can become more mature, we can work hard with integrity, we can serve, but there's some quality of awakened consciousness—of clarity, of the acceptance of what is, of Reality—that, without Grace, doesn't happen.

"Yogi Ramsuratkumar is a Master of magic. He said once that whenever any of His devotees need His help, if they say His Name, even once, with faith, He will be there. His power, blessings, wisdom—literally, as if He was physically there. There are all kinds of miracle stories surrounding Him, as there are surrounding any teacher.

"This quality of magic is something that we can't exactly define because it functions in a domain that has no language, or no spoken language. Every domain has language, but not necessarily a spoken language. The language of the domain of Grace is knowledge. We all think we know a lot of things, but there is knowing, and there's *knowing*. We all think we know things about politics, or things about social action, or things about other people. And yet if we look deeply enough into what we think we know we often find that things are not exactly the way we think they are.

"There's a kind of knowledge based on whatever facts prove the point. Then there is also a kind of intuitive knowledge, which for most of us, if we're honest with ourselves, is not very accurate. Most of us have a lot of intuitions, but they usually turn out to be bogus. Ninety percent of the time our intuition doesn't turn out, but we conveniently forget about that. So there's that kind of knowledge, where we say we know something based on a feeling, and we're so convinced that our feelings are accurate that we just ignore the times when our feelings are inaccurate.

"And then there's knowledge that's absolute knowledge. We know something because we know it, and it's *accurate*, it's real. Obviously that's a very difficult area because whenever we think we know something, we think we know it absolutely. One of the purposes or aims of the path over time is to give us the ability to distinguish between what is actually, objectively real, under all circumstances, and what is simply our subjective opinion, bias or viewpoint. What happens on the path is that this magic, which is the result of the Blessing Power or the Influence of the lineage, in this case of Yogi Ramsuratkumar, slowly transforms our vision from cloudy, illusory and subjective to crystal clear, exact, objective.

"When people become students of this school they'll say things like, 'This is it forever. I've found my path. I'm home.' That kind of commitment is touching, but at the same time we have to keep our eyes open. It took me five or six years after meeting Yogi Ramsuratkumar to realize the overwhelming pervasiveness of His Influence in my life. It wasn't like I took one look at Him and said, 'This is it.' Reality had to prove that out. Even when we have these feelings that after wandering in the desert for years, we've finally found our teacher, it's still very important to take our time and make sure that this sensing is accurate. We do this in two ways: external and internal. On the external level we observe our tendencies: to impulsively jump to conclusions when something looks pretty good, to project on other people, to disregard responsibility and allow someone else to take responsibility.

"As you all know life has its beauties, its joys, its wonders; but it's also hard to live. If

554

there's not heartbreak and stress in our own lives, there certainly is in the world. Here in Freiburg we might not be suffering so much, but in Serbia and in Ethiopia and in Nigeria and Haiti and Cambodia there is a lot of suffering—big suffering. There are two kinds of suffering: personal suffering and universal suffering. When we come to the Work we are absorbed in our own suffering, either a little or a lot. We want the path to be the answer to this suffering, we want the path or the teacher to relieve us of this suffering. Some of this suffering we know about, and some of it we don't know about. Some of it is unconscious.

"The suffering that we know about may be that we're struggling in our relationship and our partner has disappointed and frustrated us. Perhaps they haven't met our expectations and we're in pain over it, or we're simply lonely. Or a parent or a child just died and we don't know how to deal with the pain, and we think the path is going to give us the answer. But as we deepen our maturity on the path our illusions are dispelled, which *is* actually the catalyst for the relief of much of our personal suffering. When someone we love dies there is grief associated with that. At the same time, everybody dies. Our parents have died or will die; we are going to die, our children will die, hopefully after us . . . but everybody dies. Sadness or grief is perfectly normal when someone dies, but to hold onto that person and torture ourselves for years is completely unnecessary and self-created suffering.

"A very well-known teacher in France just died. Many years ago he contracted a kind of parasitic circumstance in his lungs. Over time the ability of the lungs to function properly was handicapped, and so his breathing became more and more labored. This process had gone on for over twenty years until it became very highly exacerbated. His breathing was so labored that he had to be carried everywhere. He couldn't walk anywhere. He was on oxygen all the time; he was in a wheelchair. He died earlier this summer and there was a big funeral for him. Many of his students and many other teachers came to honor him. He was a great man, an extraordinary human being. Everyone who knew him was very deeply touched by his compassion and joy and wisdom.

"When people found out he died they would often say, 'Oh, that's too bad.' They don't mean it's too bad that a presence of such wisdom and compassion can no longer offer that wisdom and compassion in the world. That's not what they mean. What they mean is, 'Isn't it too bad that we don't have this person to hang onto anymore, to rely on anymore!'—without any thought of the tremendous tension and heartbreak that his family went through every single day. For ten years he could have died at any time from his heart stopping or his lungs stopping. People who say, 'Oh, that's too bad,' don't think of his family and their suffering, the children not knowing if they were going to have their father at the end of the day, living in that uncertainty, in that pain, in that struggle, in that heartbreak. No one thinks about that. So, of course his family was deeply grieved at the loss. And they all have their lives. And it's a credit to his teaching that his family's lives have not *stopped* because he's gone physically.

"We are all going to die. Everybody in this room is going to die. Jesus died, Buddha died, Mohammed died, Yogi Ramsuratkumar is going to die. That's incarnation. That's existence. The great architecture, the great buildings of Europe have lasted for hundreds and maybe thousands of years, until the Industrial Revolution. Now it's all being destroyed by acid in the air from large manufacturing plants. Maybe we live a hundred years and we're in perfect health, and it looks like we're going to live forever, and the next day we're dead. It's a terrible thing to believe that when this life ends we go into a kind of annihilation. Any of you who have worked with the dying will see people in such *terrible* suffering; for years they've been in such pain and suffering. They have no lives other than taking medicine and sleeping. And yet, they hold on to life with this iron grip, *terrified* of annihilation.

"As we mature on the path we relieve our personal suffering through the piercing of illusion. But we don't relieve suffering because we begin to suffer in a universal sense— instead of suffering because we didn't have sex last night. Or instead of suffering because we planned this special vacation to the ocean and when we got there, it rained every day. Or suffering because our parents don't understand us.

"When we live in the world of magic, the ordinary world cannot understand what we understand. It's literally impossible. And we shouldn't try to get the ordinary world to understand what we understand. Some communication is possible, but what did Jesus say? Something like, 'Don't cast pearls before swine.' That's a very strong statement. He meant it strongly to make a point. Jesus didn't mean that everybody who lives in the ordinary world is actually a pig. What can a pig do with a pearl? A pearl means nothing to a pig. If we see a beautiful pearl it means something to us. To a pig, if it's not edible, it's useless.

"The teaching of magic, the understanding of magic, is the pearl. The story is a metaphor, right? It's not meant literally. Who would throw a pearl in front of a swine? Maybe Donald Trump or Aristotle Onassis would, just to make a point. Somebody very wealthy that wanted to demonstrate their detachment. 'Look, this means nothing to me. My billions of dollars mean nothing to me. Look, I'm going to take this hundred-dollar pearl and just throw it in front of this pig.'

"The pearl is the teaching, the dharma of the world of Grace, the world of magic. And the ordinary world is like a pig. What Jesus was saying, if I can be so presumptuous as to interpret what he meant, is, 'Don't bother to try and explain these mysteries to people who can't possibly understand them, because it's just a waste of time and energy. All it will do is make them angry, because there's no communication between the two worlds.'

"So, we enter the path, and we're brought from one language and domain to a *completely* different domain. We're transported by Grace from the domain of the ordinary world to the domain of magic. There is a period of time in which we find ourselves not only disoriented, but completely in reaction to the ordinary world. We are completely divorced from the ordinary world and disgusted by it. That's another reason we need a teacher, because it's very easy to get stuck in every one of the stages of the path. What the teacher says is, 'Okay, you're speaking the language of magic very well. Good. You've learned well. Now, to see *how* well you've learned it, go back into the ordinary world and apply it there. Invisibly.'

"When we bring our spiritual maturity into the ordinary world we're instructed to bring it into the ordinary world in an invisible way—not to act superior, and not to make a display, like wearing immense crystals around our necks, or pyramids on our heads, or jeweled headbands with a big diamond over our third eye. Invisibly means to simply serve and to work and to live without having to advertise the fact that you're some fancy spiritual student on the path.

"A lot of my students have these beads, these little finger *malas* or neck *malas*. They're prayer beads. I use my beads when I'm here, not on the airplane or in the supermarket. But there are people who do. There are people who sit in the airport waiting for their plane with their long prayer beads, sitting there like some kind of priest telling the *mala*, looking very spiritual. The idea is to simply integrate the maturity of your wisdom into life so that people don't know that you're different. But you are different.

"Before you set foot on the path you really have to think about it, because once you enter into the domain of magic, *really* enter into it, become rooted in it and start growing in it, you *will* be different than everybody else. You won't be able to come back. You'll look the same, you'll enjoy the same movies and eat in the same restaurants, but you will not be the same, and you will never be able to come back. You'll be some kind of mutant," Lee chuckled, "mutated by Grace.

"When you are in the ordinary world of illusion there is a certain way in which we believe that we can help other people. If someone is sad and they're crying we put our arms around them. We let them cry on our shoulder. Or if someone has a cut we can clean the cut and put a bandage on it. There are ways in which we go to counsel people who are dying or people who are sick; we talk with them and we make suggestions. We help them orient themselves in their lives and we actually think we're helping them. It's very comforting. It makes us feel like our lives are worth something if we can help the people we love. If we can serve people. It's very heart-warming.

"But when you begin to understand the language of Grace and you look at people in the ordinary world, you will see exactly how they create their own suffering and how they refuse to stop creating suffering for themselves. You will see how they refuse to admit that they create their own suffering, so that they always act like victims in the face of it. You'll see this about all the people you love, and you won't be able to do anything about it. Have you ever been helpless in relationship to somebody you love? It's not a very comfortable feeling.

"When you live in the domain of Grace you realize that there is nothing you can do to help the people you love. Not really. You can put Band-Aids on the wound, but you can't stop the bleeding. Only they can do that. You look at their mechanicality and their psychology, and it's nothing but constant suffering. We live in a state of constant suffering. Once in awhile you forget. You get to go to a good movie, like 'Elizabeth.' Have you seen 'Elizabeth?' It's in town. It's really a good movie—you should see it! You'll forget your suffering for two hours, but the minute you walk out of the movie, there it is again! Every time I go to a good movie I always hope that when I walk out of the movie the ordinary world will have disappeared entirely. But it hasn't happened yet." Everyone laughed.

"So, we all want something on the path: God, enlightenment, realization, freedom. You can have it, as long as you're willing to take suffering along with it. *Constant* suffering. *Relentless* suffering. *Unrelievable* suffering. *Eternal* suffering. The fundamentalist Christians say 'Accept Jesus as your Savior and Lord or you will burn in hell forever.' Well obviously they wouldn't know Jesus if he stood in front of them and said, 'Here, put your hand in my wound,' because to really accept Jesus as your Savior and Lord is to be in hell. Except you aren't on fire." Lee chuckled.

"Reality is hell. It's constant suffering. But because it's not *personal* suffering you don't feel victimized by it. If you aren't victimized by it you aren't always reacting to it. The saints look very calm and very peaceful, not because they aren't suffering, but because they're not reacting. It is reactivity that creates tension and anxiousness or uptightness.

"So before you walk very far on the path, think very seriously about it. Maybe you don't need it. Maybe it's not that important to you. Maybe you should just read some books and let it be a hobby. It's a *fascinating* hobby, the path. Go to all the seminars! I'll be gone next week, but all the Western divine mothers will be here soon and you can chant your heart out and float on clouds of bliss. So go to all the seminars and buy all the books, listen to the teachings, take a lot of notes. It's fascinating! You never run out of interesting things to have a fascinating time with." Lee chuckled again. "But don't get too serious. Why bother, you know? What for? Wouldn't you rather just be entertained all your life? Yes, you'll be under illusions, but so what? As long as you're under illusions you can always pretend that some day it's going to get better." Lee doubled over with laughter, then continued, "There will be a short period of time before you die when you'll realize that you made the wrong choice, but . . . it's worth a few minutes of total suffering," a few people chuckled, "for a life of entertainment!

"Somebody asked Suzuki Roshi, 'Can you enlighten me? Can you give me enlightenment?' He said, 'What do you want it for? You might not even like it.' He knew. It's not a great prize. It's just a natural stage in evolution. Somehow people that get deeply into the path wouldn't give it up for anything, wouldn't trade it for anything. They're very committed to it, myself included. I don't know why—it's insanity. So before you learn the language of Grace, be careful. Because once you learn it, you won't be able to go back."

After the talk while Lee was busy at the book table, one of Lee's newer European students, Danielle, spoke with Jane. Danielle was obviously deeply moved and perhaps even shaken. She said, "May I speak with you? I am seeing something in Lee these past two days that I have never seen before." She seemed to be at a loss for words. When asked what she was seeing she said that although she didn't feel that she could really articulate it, she would try. "He is so much more vulnerable," she said, tears welling up in her eyes. She seemed to be wrestling with the paradox of the guru in a whole new way—the guru as human being. She went on, "When I watch him talking I feel I am seeing God crying. I sense there is a big change coming, and I feel he is preparing us for something—perhaps for the death of Yogi Ramsuratkumar?"

The imminent possibility of the death of Lee's master seems to permeate much of his constant stories of Yogi Ramsuratkumar, and also of Lee's self-exposure in story after story in which he reveals himself to be a very human and very heartbroken devotee. Later tonight in the last session he said, "The sword of Yogi Ramsuratkumar is cutting away all that is left of Lee." There is no question that the death of his master, Yogi Ramsuratkumar, will mark an irrevocable change for Lee Lozowick. He seems like a man who is dealing a final hand of cards before he is swept out of the current game altogether and into a new level of playing. The new game may be the end of Lee as his students know him. It's as if he is saying, "Here, this is how I want to be remembered."

August 22, 1999
Freiburg

Lee started his talk this morning by saying, "I'd like to talk about the essence of the teaching and my relationship to Yogi Ramsuratkumar. The essence of the teaching is there is only God, and God is continuous. Everything that exists does so within a common field. Things look separate, but energetically there is continuity between all things. The dharma, practice and the path is about dismantling our illusions so we see clearly what is always already true. Whether we call this truth God or the Universe or Reality doesn't matter, just as long as we practice with clarity. You think your dogs and cats understand you . . . Let me enlighten you! They are only dogs and cats!" The audience laughed. "Even your pets will not be spared in the teaching, so be careful how deeply you get involved in the Work. You may lose that inner connection between you and your dog!" More laughter. "I, of course, am a cat man! I've never liked dogs. I always had cats, but my friends had dogs . . . Cats are conscious beings, you know! I'm kidding, of course." Lee went off on a comedy routine about cats versus dogs that had people shaking with laughter.

"There is only God. Within that Reality is Creation, or existence. There is only God and manifest Reality functions according to the laws of physics. Within all of created existence is a polarity, positive and negative, which in the organic world of plants and animals is the masculine and feminine. Even in single-celled creatures like amoebas there is still a polarity at work. So you have two choices: to give your power to this Work, or to ego. If you chose against the Work, you should pray to be reborn as an amoeba, because then you're only in relationship with yourself—perfect! On the other hand, 'As above, so below' applies because all of Reality is like one big amoeba!" The crowd seemed primed and laughed readily with Lee this morning.

"The essence of the teaching is there is only God and within Creation there is polarity, and it's our job to deal with that polarity—to function lawfully within it. Every level of existence has its own laws. At the densest level—of ego and illusion—there are social laws. Social laws are the laws of the gross domain, so every country has its own laws. Then there are natural laws. If it rains or snows, the social laws are still laws but weather doesn't respect social laws. The whole dance of natural laws—gravity, weather, the cycles of the seasons and so on—are higher than social laws. Nature predominates. Then there are the laws of the miraculous—levitation and so on. The law of gravity is absolute in the domain in which it is lawful, in the domain of nature, but levitation goes against gravity. Levitation happens not because you are so light that you float, but because you are so ecstatic that your being transcends the laws of nature. It's a function of a higher law and it doesn't capitulate to lower laws.

"There are lots of critics who say this is just a trick, but they're not willing to research the subject matter. For example, Satya Sai Baba has been materializing objects for years, like holy ash. But he also makes gold rings, candy, statues of deities. It all goes against the natural laws. All these manifestations function according to the laws of a higher domain.

"The literal fact that God is everything—or more accurately, there is only God— functions lawfully in the way that everything that happens in the energetic field affects everything else in the field. If something happens over here in the field, the results can show up over there, but the path between them can be completely invisible. You may have had headaches or moods of great exaltation then found out that your brother or sister was experiencing the same thing at the same time. That's especially true of brothers and sisters who are close to each other. This is not a comforting piece of information.

"Anything that happens within a field—and the field includes all of Creation—affects everything else in the field. Bummer! But there is one important point: certain individuals function in relationship to this principle the way a lightning rod functions in relationship to electricity. When lightning hits it doesn't hit everything at once, but is drawn to certain points that take the electricity and ground it.

"There is a popular Christian phrase, 'Jesus died for our sins.' This idea is very misunderstood. What it means is that Jesus was one of those characters who took the heat, took the lightning for everyone. There are those like Yogi Ramsuratkumar who basically protect us from being at the effect of the lightning. What's the lightning? Clairvoyance to suffering, pain. Some of you know that when something happens that is difficult to accept—the death of a loved one, our house burns down with all of our family heirlooms and treasures in it, our partner has an affair—your mind is going mad with the thing. You can't turn your mind off. That is only one person, one mind, one event, but look at the difficulty, the tension and crisis it creates in life. Imagine if you took all the deaths from cruelty, the personal tragedies, the betrayals . . .

"Imagine an energetic field, and in that field anything that happens in any part of the field affects the whole field to some degree. The human body is a field. The communication channels of that field are the nervous system, the circulatory system, the muscular system. Anything that affects one part of the field affects all of it. If you eat something toxic, even a little toxic, whether it's LSD or bleach, the entire field is dramatically affected. One little tablespoon of bleach affects the entire field dramatically. If you stub your little toe, the entire field is affected. If someone you love dies, whatever perception you have of that affects the entire field. The mind may be the specific that is full of pain and grief, but it affects the entire field. You can't eat or sleep, the body shakes and weeps.

"Every impression you take in—every movie, article you read, advertisement you see—affects all of the field. If the kind of information you take in is full of violence and pornography, then your entire field is going to be affected by that. Imagine the entire world, every act of cruelty and violence, every love affair, every earthquake or tidal wave: if we as individuals were openly sensitive to that entire field of which we are lawfully a part, we personally would feel all of that. We can't even handle *stau* without getting angry." Lee used the popular German word for large traffic jams that occur frequently on the *autobahn* in Germany.

"So people like Jesus and Yogi Ramsuratkumar are the lightning rods that take all that and ground it for us so we don't have to feel it. They take all this upon themselves, the sins of the world, and ground that energy. But they can't help being affected by it in some way. There is a difference internally in the structure of a lightning rod. Jesus died in his thirties at the height of health and authority. Yogi Ramsuratkumar will be eighty-two years old in December and is showing the wear and tear of having been a lightning rod for eighty-two years. This is the lawfulness of Reality.

"Everything that happens within the field affects everything in that field, and there is a particular function within the field that keeps the field healthy, like digestion in the body. If we didn't shit we would become poisoned, so the digestive system has a very important function within the field. The kidneys, the digestive system and so on keep the body healthy. The same is true in the field of humanity. John the Baptist served one particular function, Jesus served another function. Both served to keep the field healthy. With Swami Papa Ramdas and Mother Krishnabai, she had one function and he had another, though their purpose was the same—to keep the field of humanity healthy.

"God's consciousness is masculine and God's body is feminine—Creation. Being feminine in essence, we are all part of the body of God. When we realize the mind of God, which is called union or enlightenment, we have become complete. That's why people like sex so much. We're drawn to sexual union because it is symbolic of our instinctual desire for the ultimate union of oneness. It's why we eat too much, why we take drugs, why we want to make money, have power, jump out of airplanes. It's all about our instinctual drive for oneness, which is to unite our consciousness with the consciousness of God. Creation is the body of God—'as above, so below'—meaning that our human drive is to unite the human body with human consciousness. It's the first step of sadhana on any path—Buddhism, Hinduism or other.

"In Communion the wafer represents the body of Christ and the wine represents the blood of Christ. Jesus was someone who was complete—the complete man. That completeness permeates the wafer and wine, that's why they call it the 'Host.' If you eat the Host and sip the wine you are taking the completeness of Jesus in an energetic seed form into your body. Your body is a sympathetic host for Jesus' completeness, because both you and Jesus are human beings.

"All rituals of the Church actually have objective sources. All liturgies, at least those in Latin, have traditional objective sources out of which they have arisen. If we change them enough, we destroy the possibility of transformation, which is what the Church suffers from today—loss of the roots and heart.

"Beings like Yogi Ramsuratkumar act as human lightning rods. They take on the suffering of mankind, metaphorically and literally, so we don't have to be at the effect of the whole mass of suffering in the world. Yogi Ramsuratkumar feels it, all of it, but He feels it in a way that grounds it; otherwise He would just explode—literally, physically.

"When we intersect with energy that is beyond our ability to manage, some form of breakdown occurs, from headaches, exhaustion or nervous tension to complete obliteration. You may have heard of those rare cases where people just spontaneously combust. They disappear in a burst of flame. It's a rare phenomenon, but it happens. The path is designed to build energetic tenacity over time, so that as we progress on the path we are able to carry more and more and more energy through this vehicle." Lee touched his chest to indicate the body. "Various kinds of healers differ in just how much energy they can handle in their circuitry. To be successful at prayer, you have to have a lot of energy. All the formative stages of the path are about creating a matrix that can hold or handle more and more energy.

"Because Yogi Ramsuratkumar exists means that we do not have to suffer the effects of everything that arises in the field of existence, or Creation. With every breath He takes for our sins, He dies. Whether there is more than one person at the top of the pyramid at any given time doesn't matter.

"The lightning rod can never take a vacation from being a lightning rod. Yogi Ramsuratkumar can never rest. It's a very big sacrifice. He didn't choose the sacrifice—it was given to Him. *We* can always take a vacation. If things get too intense for us we can always take a break—contemplate our genitals or something. At least they're still there!" The comic relief of the laughter that ensued seemed like a necessary respite within the burning intensity of Lee's discourse. There had been a poignant hush hovering over the entire audience. People were quite literally sitting on the edges of their seats, absorbing the magnitude and sanctity of the kind of sacrifice that Lee was describing. In naming the sacrifice of Yogi Ramsuratkumar so clearly it became a reality and palpable presence that permeated the room. There was something so heartrending in Lee's words that feelings were aroused from a domain completely beyond emotional reaction. Perhaps these "feelings" could be named awe, gratitude, humility. What could move an individual to enter into such a sacrifice, motivated entirely toward the benefit of others? To bear the suffering of the entire world in the way Lee described was unimaginable and unthinkable, and yet his quiet and intense speech vibrated with the truth of what he was saying.

"Yogi Ramsuratkumar can't even find five minutes alone. That's a great sacrifice. His humanness happens to be the sacrifice God made. When we find someone who is living that kind of sacrifice it makes sense we would be grateful that they are doing it instead of us—so grateful that we would do anything. And out of our gratitude, the least we would do is offer honor and respect to such a person with a *pranam*, a bow. We are submitting ourselves out of honor and respect at the most superficial level. The gesture is simply a

561

function of gratitude, respect and honor. It brings dignity to our lives. At the greatest level the gesture of submission is not only a sign of gratitude, but a message saying to the Pole of Grace, 'Here is my gratitude to you. Because your sacrifice is so great, if there is anything I can do to serve you, or to participate in your sacrifice, I am submitted to your sacrifice.' But you don't get to make that decision. Yogi Ramsuratkumar makes that decision.

"People say you are just giving your power away to bow to another human being, but you cannot give your power away. You can act in a way that appears to put people of power in domination over you, but that's not really your power. That's merely psychological. You don't have to worry about getting involved in this over your head because God makes that decision. We cannot give our power away—lots of people want it, but they can't take it! Only God can take your power. So when we offer our *pranam*—our bow to the guru—in this way to honor the sacrifice of the master, it is the dignified way to be. And as you all know, to be in the presence of someone who has no dignity is distasteful.

"We are creatures who have the capacity to live lives of elegance and dignity. Anything else is disrespectful. When we offer ourselves to the master in submission—if we are willing to prove our integrity to the master—slowly over time our gesture of submission goes from being one of respect and honor for the master's sacrifice to a request for the master to give us a way to serve him or her. Every act of service relieves the master of one little bit of suffering. The more pure the service, the more suffering you relieve the master of. The ultimate service which relieves the master entirely of suffering is to duplicate the master's function—to become a lineage holder. Insane! Totally insane! But we don't make that decision; only the master makes that decision.

"As we continue to offer ourselves to the master with dignity, he offers us ways to serve him." Lee paused here and proceeded to tell an irreverent and funny version of the story of Jesus and Peter. Laughter took over the room as Lee deadpanned a camp version of Peter's Jewish mother calling Peter to come in and eat dinner.

"So Peter couldn't have followed Jesus in a million years if Jesus hadn't *called* him to him. Thousands of people were at the Sermon on the Mount. How many *followed* Jesus? Thirty, forty, fifty? What it must have been like! Wow! The Sermon on the Mount! But most of the people there just wanted fish and bread!" More laughter broke out. "Just like, 'Wow! That was a great seminar!' And then off they went to fight with their families.

"Only the master gets to choose who serves, and every bit of service relieves the master of unimaginable suffering. I'm talking about Yogi Ramsuratkumar. If it was two thousand years ago I would be talking about Jesus. Yogi Ramsuratkumar asks many people to serve in small, unobtrusive ways. The way the master decides who has integrity in service is by proving first your integrity and trustworthiness. We prove our integrity and reliability and then we get to serve the master in larger and larger ways. But there is only one master and lots of disciples. Everyone can't serve in the same way. The master gives directions to disciples through establishing a certain mood of practice. Everyone can't be the master's personal attendant. But if you want to submit honor, respect and gratitude to the master through service, then charity begins at home. A lot of people think they can serve others, but ignore and neglect their family."

The afternoon session began with questions. "Did your teacher pick you or did you pick your teacher?"

Lee responded, "In the traditions they say that when the student is ready for the teacher, it is the teacher who calls the student to him. In one sense both the teacher and the student participate in that. Sometimes we meet and everything is clear right away, but with others it becomes clear over time that we are moving toward this teacher, this path.

"When I first met Yogi Ramsuratkumar I'd been traveling around India meeting yogis, masters, gurus. Yogi Ramsuratkumar was only one of many impressive people, but there was something about Him. The interactions we had with Him were very powerful and I thought if I came back to India I wanted to see Him again. I had no concept that He was my Teacher at the beginning. He had given me a significant amount of attention compared to the others who were with me, and I liked that. So three years later I went back to India and planned to meet Him again. The same thing happened; He gave me a lot of attention. But He didn't make any indication that He was my Teacher or imply anything. I just recognized His obvious spiritual maturity, and I felt I could learn something from Him.

"We came back to America and one year later I found Yogi Ramsuratkumar was very important to me. I was thinking of Him a lot and He was taking on a very specific function for me. I began to write to Him. I like to read mystical poetry and I featured myself somewhat of a mystical poet, and I began to send poetry to Him. It was pretty bad poetry, but it had some heart to it. So as I wrote to Him it became clear to me that He was my Teacher. It was a very big shock to everyone in the community because my approach had been that you don't need a teacher, just realize God. My students all thought once they realized God they wouldn't need me anymore!" Lee laughed. "Well, I was only three years old!

"So after that meeting with Yogi Ramsuratkumar I was reviewing my history on the path and I began to see amazing synchronicities. I saw that before I met Him physically, Yogi Ramsuratkumar was guiding my path from the beginning. I made an announcement to my students and everyone was shocked, but they got over it quickly. In 1986 we took a big group trip to India and showed up at His door. I'd made this extraordinary, exciting discovery—He was *my* Teacher! I thought He'd be *thrilled*!" The group laughed with Lee at his confession of pride. "I was this great American guru and so on. But He didn't even recognize me! Before, on earlier trips, He had rolled out the red carpet: He invited us in, spent time with us, gave us tea. This time He was standing there blocking the door! I'd already told my students how it would work—He would invite us in, tea would be served, He'd talk with us, et cetera."

As Lee told this story again—and he has probably told it a hundred times over the past thirteen years—he skewered himself with an amazing combination of subtle innuendo and sophisticated humor that came through the innocent tone of voice he used to describe the whole scenario. The room laughed along with him, but the laughter was warm, intimate and kind. He rendered himself and his experience into such perfectly human terms that everyone could relate with his predicament in a very direct and immediate way. The storytelling continued, liberally spiced with shared laughter.

"Yogi Ramsuratkumar speaks excellent English, is ordinarily very polite and well-spoken. So He looked at us and said, 'What do you want?' He had had Westerners visiting Him for years. He knew what we wanted! I was completely at a loss for words at this point. He looked at me again, rolled His eyes, sighed like, 'Oh boy, do I have to do this?' I had seven people with me. I thought I would take a few and come back later with some of the others. In 1976 and 1979 we sat with him two or three hours at a time. Now we sat there for half an hour and brusquely He said, 'That's enough—you can leave now!' Okay.

We got up to leave. Americans always act like our heads are up our asses, like we don't know what to do. People were sort of standing there, bumping into one another. I said, 'There are more people with us—can I bring them?'

" 'No, you've seen me. The others don't need to see me,' He said. Oh no! People had sold their cars, begged money from their parents to come meet my Master. I didn't know what to do! So I did something really stupid—I decided to bring people back anyway and hide around the corner and watch, as if He couldn't tell they were with me! So that's what I did. They knocked on the door. A big smile came to His face. He opened up His arms and said, 'Come in!' So I was a little disturbed. *I* was the great student! He was *my* Master! *I* had been writing Him for five years. After an hour they came out all smiling, full of light. I was disturbed, and I thought, 'Well, I'm going to have to remedy this!'

"The way Yogi Ramsuratkumar works is by example, through symbol and metaphor. My pride was burning—and it was *all* pride! So I went up to His door and knocked. He opened the door and said, 'Yes? I already told you I didn't want to see you again. So, what?' I poured out my troubles, said, 'I came all the way here to see You, I've been writing to You.' He'd already said to me, 'You know this Beggar?' Yes. 'Couldn't be!' He said. So I was pouring my heart out to Him. He said, 'Lee, I know what you want. You just want a guru, a saint. India is full of gurus. Go away, don't come back.'

"So I thought, 'He's still my Teacher, this doesn't change His Benediction. I'll keep my relationship with Him on the subtle planes.' But I was heartbroken. 'Absence makes the heart grow fonder,' you know. All the years since I'd last seen Him I'd been sending Him letters and poetry and I had this tremendous expectation and excitation, like when you are away from your lover for a long time. You know, I ran up to his door, and then He didn't remember me. He really didn't remember me. He wasn't acting. I would've recognized that because I was highly trained. Then when He sent me away, saying, 'Go find a guru'—oh, what an insult! I'd even dedicated a book to Him in 1979 and He had seen it, had it read to Him. All this longing was dashed on the rocks of despair. I thought to myself, 'I'm never going to see Him again.' There was heartbreak in that. I would never come back to India again.

"We were going to be in Tiruvannamalai for another five or six days, so I decided I would *burn* His image into my mind; I would sit out in the street and see Him when He opened His door for other devotees. It was thirty-two or thirty-three degrees, sunny with no shade. I sat in the sun where I could see His door clearly—no hat. It was like being in an oven; sweat was pouring down my body. I crossed my legs, went into a meditation posture and stared at His door. I was about one hundred and fifty meters down the street from His house, not close, but close enough for Him to see me if He opened the door and looked down the street. He saw me sitting there at two o'clock in the afternoon sun. He invited an Indian man in, let him out, looked at me. This went on for over four hours. Once an hour He would come to the door and look, and there I was just sitting there in a yoga posture—the last heroic thing I've done!

"I told my students to go elsewhere, to stay off the street where I was. I said, 'It's my business. You stay out of it.' Finally He looked out. I was still there, and He called me over and said, 'How long are you going to be here?' Six days, I said. 'Alright, you can come see this Beggar once in a while.' That was His concession. I went away very happy, feeling I had bullied Him into giving me attention, but I was too ignorant at the time to know that *nobody* bullies Him. So I decided not to go every day. I had been pushy enough. Once He had given me a concession I became all dignified. When I'd seen Him before He'd held my hand and done all these rituals with me. This time there was none of that. He sat me across from Him and talked about the most superficial things—the landscape, American politics, sports. I *hate* sports! He wanted to know how American football teams were doing! He didn't ask me anything personal—not a thing.

"So I continued to send Him poetry after that. It got much better—now it was *real*! All the early poetry I was just trying to be Rumi. There was no heartbreak in it, though it had the right form. After 1986 it started to get very real. Two years later, in 1988, I got a letter from one of His devotees who I'd never met, inviting me to the Jayanthi Celebration, the celebration of His birthday in Nagercoil, southern India. Yogi Ramsuratkumar had told this devotee, 'Invite this man and he will come.' I didn't know what to think but I decided to go, and took some of my men students with me. I added on three days at the end of the trip in Tiruvannamalai, just in the hope that He was willing to see me.

"At the end of the trip we got to Tiruvannamalai and I knocked on His door very tentatively, very lightly. He came running out of His house as if He'd been waiting, and He swung open the gate and said, 'Lee!' " Lee held his arms out wide, showing the physical gesture of embrace that Yogi Ramsuratkumar gave to him then. Lee's storytelling had been so captivating and animated that it was as if the scene was unfolding right before our eyes.

"The poetry I was sending began to increase. In 1986 I sent seventy-five poems to Him. In 1993 He had one of his devotees publish the poetry. He had the book come out just as I got there, and He was having the poetry read to Him over and over again all day long. He said, 'This Beggar always wanted someone to write about him, but this poetry is it. Now no one has to write anything else about this Beggar.' The definitive statement on Yogi Ramsuratkumar. He said, 'This Beggar threw out all the early poetry you sent—this Beggar just didn't know what it was.'

"Not only did it take some time for me to recognize Him, but it took some time for Him to recognize me, to recognize that I wasn't going to be just another Westerner to disappoint Him. He has had Westerners disappoint Him before. He's given His heart and soul to some and they've sold it in the marketplace. It's very hard for Him.

"One of the things about the relationship with the teacher is that you can't fool around if you really want the teacher to take you seriously. If you want your teacher to take you seriously you must have one teacher and one teacher only. You won't get very much from your teacher otherwise. So sometimes it takes time on both sides for the master and the student to recognize each other."

Lee paused then asked, "Any other questions?"

"How could you be in the influence of Yogi Ramsuratkumar without meeting him?" someone asked.

"All existence is encapsulated in each moment," Lee began. "Yogi Ramsuratkumar's body lives in time. He's grown older, He's not healthy now, but that's just the body. His consciousness does not live in time. Past, present, future—He can be in any of these. He was my Teacher before I met Him because He knew I was going to be His student in the future, not in the conscious mind, but in that which makes Him the lightning rod.

"It took His conscious mind time to realize what His Body of Benediction had been doing all along. He said to His Indian disciples that we have been together in past lives in India. I have that perception about some of my students. I've never told them, and I don't talk about it, but it's real. I know what we have done and have yet to do in the future. At first I may not know that. I may see some aspects of them, like how sick they are!" Lee chuckled. "Some students come around for years before it's clear they belong here. It's like a karmic *thang*."

Another person from the audience said, "I didn't come here looking for a spiritual teacher but this has been the theme yesterday and today. It's really shaking me up . . . I thought I was in a state that I wouldn't need a spiritual teacher in this life. Yesterday you spoke about love with a partner or children, that this love could be exclusive and keep others out. This was my fear when I had a teacher who was a human being, that my love for him would be so strong that I would exclude others."

Lee answered, "First of all, it's true in my community and in all other schools that there are people who use the dharma and put their attention on the spiritual master in order to avoid relationship and/or responsibility. The way I work is not to attack such things head-on: 'You're in denial; I'm not your father!' I could do that for each student, but people tend not to learn that way. I don't teach through the direct approach because I have found that to be ineffective. When people realize something from within their experience, then they've got something.

"What I would call a genuine teacher—like Yogi Ramsuratkumar, Ramana Maharshi, Anandamayi Ma, Jesus—is God in human form. We are all God in human form, but the Master is someone who has become so conscious of Reality, of existence, that they are able to function as a reference point for That in the world. They transmit that Reality. How can we give our love to something that is completely abstract? If we try to concretize God, all we get is our own image based on training, education and so on, and that is not God. The spiritual master is literally God incarnate—no more than any other human being, but different in context.

"When we ask to be the student of a teacher, we've got a concrete form on which to focus. Not only does the master test the student, but the student tests the master. A good student capitalizes on the revelatory presence of the master. A good student is someone who can be lost in their love for the master without mistaking that focus as disregarding their life as it is. For a good student, their love of the master will be completely exclusive and radiant, and the effect of that love will be clear attention on every aspect of their lives—deeper relationship, deeper intimacy with others.

"In my community there are people who allow their love for me to create separation with life, but it's a sign of immaturity. It doesn't mean they aren't good students; they just aren't grown up yet. The process of becoming grown-up students is often a matter of many years because it takes awhile to get the lessons."

"Do you think having a teacher is the only possibility for loving God?" someone asked.

Lee laughed. "Of course there are exceptions to the rule, but we tend to assume that *we* are the exceptions! There are people who quietly and invisibly love God, but that is a true exception to the rule. Most people will not have the maturity to love God without the teacher. Under extreme conditions the heat and intensity of those conditions can create exceptions. There are unheralded saints who have come out of Russian or German concentration camps, for example. Ordinarily we would never find ourselves in situations of that intensity, even if we are working with the dying. The situation is typically not extreme enough to push us into the mood of loving God.

"There is the ultimate field of existence—there is only God—and there is the organic field of the body, and the field of the teaching and the sangha. When I talk about something when I'm in America or Europe, my students who are not with me are talking about the same things. Every year when I come to Europe there is a theme to the seminars that year, and I find out that other teachers are talking about the same themes at the same time. I often say to my students, 'You never miss anything.' Even though our creature attention is not reveling in the eloquence of the master, we don't miss anything.

"The conscious mind doesn't have it, but the being has it because it is hooked into the field. They are part of the nervous system. That might not be satisfying because we may be disappointed—'Oh, I missed a great seminar, or a great time at a café with Lee!' But you really never miss anything. Your maturity is not based on how many gigs, seminars and so on you've been to. Your maturity has to do with serenity, with how you *use* the opportunity of wherever you are.

"So, what makes a seminar good is not just my inspiration, but the alchemy of the whole group. I think there were some good things, and some great things, said here this weekend. The great things come out because of who you are on the path. Every once in a while we have a seminar where people put their money in the machine and all they want is a pack of cigarettes and a Coca-Cola—one of the few things American culture has contributed to world culture, to go down in history!" The group laughed. "But, whatever has come out has been a response to you, because I'm not doing this alone. Some of the concepts that came out this weekend I've never talked about before—they literally just came out here! Revelation! That's what we were sitting with here this weekend, but you were the catalyst. The Bauls, whose tradition I am part of, have a saying, 'Jai Guru.' It means victory to the guru, because the guru only wants the clarity and maturity of his disciples. So that's what we'll end with. Jai Guru!"

After a crowded dinner for fifty people in the apartment, the eight o'clock darshan began in the same place where the seminar was given. Lee walked over in the mild summer evening air from the apartment carrying a cardboard box with the *prasad* he would give to those who offered him *prasad*. He unceremoniously breezed in, taking his seat in the room which had been transformed into a formal ritual space, and was now packed with about sixty-five people—most of them his students and some of them guests or friends of the community who had attended the seminar. Darshan began with forty minutes of chanting while Lee sat on his chair surrounded by flowers and the large color picture of Yogi Ramsuratkumar that had been by his side all weekend. Candles burned on either side of him. The mood was somber and reverent.

The chanting swelled and filled the place and *prasad* was exchanged between Lee and the participants. At one point two people, a man and a woman, came up together to *pranam*. Each one carried a rather ratty-looking black crow feather. The woman handed Lee her feather and he gave her *prasad*—a small package of hard candy—then he stuck the feather in his hair on top of one side of his head. A wave of soft laughter passed through the crowd. Then man then handed Lee his feather, and as he was receiving his *prasad*, Lee stuck the second black feather in the top of his head on the other side, somehow spontaneously placing them exactly so that he now had two black, raggedy "horns" sticking out of the top of his head. People laughed in earnest and Lee grinned. It seemed to be his definitive statement on any projections or false ideas of holiness—our *own*, based on the fact of proximity to him—that might be coming his way. As soon as everyone had given *prasad* he gestured for the chanting to stop and began his discourse by asking for questions, the feathers still prominently in his hair.

Someone asked, "Would you say more about accepting what is?"

Lee answered, "*What is* in any given moment includes everything that goes into making up that moment. That includes one's karma, tendencies, aberrant psychology, illusion—all of that. Those things are inclusive in what is in the moment. One of the things that dissolves the grip of those things on us is accepting them exactly as they are. When we react to something we are actually giving it power over us. The complete acceptance of those things as they are alters them. If we have some tendency from the past and we accept it completely as it is, it stops its ability to manipulate us, literally. Even karmas are changed, though that is a complex issue. If we look at things in a temporal framework, there may be contradictions, but if we look outside the temporal framework, we see holistically. To accept what is, as it is, is a holistic statement. When we project on the future and we don't realize it, those projections are keeping us stuck within our expectations, but if we realize that and stop projecting, things can change."

A German woman who has been a student of Lee's for many years said, "I feel that my practice has become empty. I have no inspiration right now. What should I do?"

Lee's response was mild and kind. He said, "It's just a stage, and the answer is to keep practicing. We could go into a long explanation, but it doesn't matter. Pretty soon it will be gone and you'll be in another phase, so just keep practicing. It's not a sign of any problem."

Forgoing more questions at this point, Lee turned to address the whole group. "For those of you who didn't understand the chants, they are all in Sanskrit and basically say 'Surrender everything to the guru and be happy with whatever you get back, even if it is pain and suffering.' Once you commit to the Work it is irrevocable. You can easily say, 'Yeah, I've committed myself to the Work and it's nothing but suffering from now on, *ha ha ha* . . . I have nothing now, *ha ha ha* . . . I gave it all away and I'm just a renunciate living on the ashram, but it's great, *ha ha ha* . . .'" Lee kept repeating this almost maniacal laughter, *ha ha ha*, with an intonation that was hilarious but oddly piercing in its insinuation of the hopelessness that ego will sooner or later encounter on the path. There was madness, almost wrecklessness, in that laugh—the kind of madness that will be produced on the path of annihilation and ruin. Everyone in the room was laughing along with Lee, then the laughter subsided as Lee continued and the mood went suddenly very deep.

"The Sufis call it *ruin*. They only pray so they can be ruined to all but the Beloved. To ego it's bizarre! But once you get bitten, you don't want anything else. You throw yourself on the floor and cry, 'Break my heart! Oh God! Make me long for you!' You have to become totally crazy to be doing this, but it's a sweet kind of insanity. To the world it is insanity, but to the Beloved's lovers it is the only true sanity. Here we are, intelligent adults sitting in this room, courting ruin and heartbreak! Yogi Ramsuratkumar says about Papa Ramdas, 'My Master murdered this Beggar in 1952.' That's when Yogi Ramsuratkumar shifted context. He says, 'There was no Beggar anymore.'

"At the beginning of the community my students would look at me and say, 'There's nobody home!' We'd all laugh. Now a couple of them have experienced what it's like to not be there—what on earth would anyone want to do this for? But after a certain point you can't turn back—so if you can get out, get out now. At a certain point you aren't laughing anymore. It's like washing clothes. The clothes think, 'Oh boy, I'm gonna get washed! I was all dirty, now I'm going to be sparkling clean!' But it's only fun before the clothes know what's going to happen to them. They can't remember what it's like to be in the washing machine. They're in the middle of it and the water is steaming hot, they're drenched and they can't breathe. They're being pulled this way and pushed that way!"

568

Lee demonstrated being tossed and torn and splashed while people laughed, getting the metaphor. "They're being ripped apart! Five minutes later they're screaming, 'I'm drowning!' Then finally they come out and get pressed and starched and they are all sparkling and look beautiful. It's the same for us. Before and after we're laughing, but in the middle—oh boy!

"The difference between us and the clothes is that you can't get the clothes out of the process of getting washed any sooner than the machine takes to do its thing. Human beings can speed up the process of transformation. This is a very important secret. The way to minimize the difficulty of transformation is to run toward it as fast as you can. Don't look to the left, don't look to the right, never mind what's behind you, just run as fast as you can toward transformation.

"So when you're looking at transformation, faith, surrender, love, most people hesitate, try to figure it out, get some kind of advantage, or take a few steps back, thinking it will look different somehow. If you want to minimize the degree of conflict, run toward it as fast as you can. That's my advice," Lee chuckled mischievously, "for the evening. Any questions?" He started playing with the feathers that were still sticking out of his hair throughout this solemn discourse on the nature of ruin, then he muttered almost to himself, "French ticklers . . . German ticklers." Once again the group was laughing.

"What does it look like to run toward transformation?"

Lee answered, "What does it look like to run toward it? Sort of like *Butch Cassidy and the Sundance Kid*." Lee began to tell the story of the movie in which two outlaws defy the law in stunning feats of bravery and bravado. They are very sympathetic characters, sort of Robin Hood archetypes who rob from the rich and give to the poor, this being enhanced by the very sympathetic actors who played them, Paul Newman and Robert Redford. At the end of a series of miraculous escapades in which they persevere against all odds, there is a long chase by the law in which they end up in a house down in Mexico, surrounded by an army. There is no way out, and their situation is hopeless.

Lee continued, "So one of them turns to the other and says, 'What are we going to do?' The other replies, 'What we always do.' They run out shooting madly, hoping for a miraculous escape against all odds, and the movie ends there, freeze-framed, with them in the midst of the dust and bullets and chaos . . ."

The quiet, absorptive listening to Lee's voice telling this story was so strong in the room that you couldn't even hear people breathing. The metaphor was perfect and struck home resoundingly. "So if you are successful metaphysically speaking, who you were before you started this process will be *dead*—gone!

"I'm reaching my limit of students. We have about one hundred and fifty students now in the school. I sometimes name the children, give them some Indian or Tibetan name, and if I don't see them for two years, I can't remember their names! When I can't remember names anymore . . . that's enough!

"I'm happy for people to stay asleep—*really*!—because this Work entails an agony. There's also ecstasy, but there is agony as well. Who wants to see people in agony? Oh, it's ugly! At first we're only given a taste. We're not shown the whole panorama—'Here, have all the suffering in the world!' So we just get a taste and then it closes up again. But if we stay on the path we get more and more, and finally we get the whole mango—all ripe and juicy and dripping with nectar. The agony and the ecstasy, all of it at the same time. Who cares about the lightning rod before then anyway? Some say they do, but that's just vanity."

"What would happen if nobody had this function of the lightning rod?" someone asked.

"There's never been such a thing," Lee answered. "It would make an interesting novel, though. We'd better hope when Yogi Ramsuratkumar dies there is someone who holds that function, or we might get to see what happens."

Lee started loading up the gifts of *prasad* he had received tonight into the cardboard box he brought. An awed silence filled the room. He looked around at everyone and started to rant in a soft and amiable tone of voice.

"I have this personal preference. When I go to see a spiritual teacher and they just sit there in silence, I'm saying, 'Somebody say something! Make a joke—something.' Whenever there is silence I'm really uncomfortable! I hate to be alone. I might have to look at myself, and that would be terrible! Who knows what I would discover! What a scary thought." Lee was grinning broadly. He had completely changed the tone, mood and subject. He was up to some kind of mischief.

"So if no one says anything I have to just keep rambling on. It doesn't matter if it doesn't make sense. Then you'll say, 'There! That's the kind of teacher these students have!' People wonder if I'm kidding or serious—I'm serious! I can bear about five or six seconds of silence. They say God speaks loudest in silence—but what if God says something you don't like!"

Lee's grin deepened into a sly half-smile as he loaded up all the chocolate bars and candy near him. He looked rather like a fox who had just outsmarted the farmer and was just about to get in the chicken coop. "I'm almost done!" he said, piling the last of his *prasad* into the box just exactly so. He looked out at everyone's open faces and slowly took the feathers out of his hair, caressed them, straightened out their ragged edges and smiled as he put them into his box with the rest of the *prasad*.

"I'm so insecure! I'm dragging my heels because I'm afraid if I go out that door everything will end. I'll go to Ute and Volker's apartment and ring the bell, they'll say, 'Who is it?' I'll say, 'Lee,' and they'll say, 'Lee who?' " A few people were laughing while others, especially the new students and guests, listened in disbelief or confusion. It seemed like Lee was very intentionally covering his tracks, which had led into such deep terrain as Grace and ruin. Now he returned to the same mood that had been threaded throughout the seminar. He was, once again, deconstructing his own mythology and the projected image of the guru, and he was doing it right before our very eyes.

Still smiling, he continued, "You must be thinking, 'God, he's so neurotic! He needs therapy!' Most of my students are psychotherapists, so maybe I can get a discount!" Everyone in the room laughed. Lee got up from his chair and shouted, "Jai Guru!" to a thundering response of "Jai Guru!" from the group.

August 23, 1999
Freiburg

This morning brunch was at the apartment of Thomas and Helma, two of Lee's students who live in a small village near Freiburg. Lee played bridge then drove back into Freiburg for a three o'clock appointment. He planned to meet with a wholesale dealer of artifacts from India, Nepal and Tibet who sells out of his home. He had a one-hour appointment because he planned to leave at four-thirty for Zurich, where he would give the first of four talks in Switzerland this week. One of Lee's students had made the connection with this dealer, knowing that Lee was interested in looking at and possibly obtaining some more sacred statuary.

Lee drove his van full of people while another carload of people followed behind. Before he left the apartment several people had approached Lee wanting to know if they could go with him. At the time it seemed that he just acquiesced to their request, and on the way to the appointment he made a sarcastic comment about how he had ended up taking many more people with him than he wanted to. When asked why he didn't just say no to people who asked to come—with his voice dripping with what? Irony, perhaps?—he said, "I can't say no to my loving devotees."

During these ten days in Freiburg, where there were many people crowded into small spaces, it seemed to be a recurring theme—people following Lee everywhere he went and Lee making comments about how he just wanted to be alone with his family or with the small, hand-picked group that he invited to accompany him to certain events. Asking to go when one wasn't invited was an innocent faux pas, but at the same time, a serious breach of spiritual protocol between student and teacher.

Lee drove through the orderly suburbs of Freiburg where townhouses and apartment buildings and private homes were interspersed with many green trees and lush gardens. He pulled up to the house and about twelve people piled out of the vehicles and walked to the door behind Lee. Just as he rang the doorbell and the dealer opened his door a glass jar suddenly fell to the floor inside the house. It hit with a loud crash, as if it was announcing something, and shattered glass across the floor. Standing behind the man at the door were two women and some children in a kitchen and living area. The place looked like a hippie den inside.

There were artifacts everywhere, and the walls were covered with many paintings and drawings of nude women, landscapes and nature scenes. One wall had two large, very nice aquariums built into the wood. They were full of exotic fish. The room was sandwiched between the kitchen and a tiled-floored glassed-in porch that led outside to a small, overrun wild garden. Scattered all around the room on various shelves and counters, as well as on the floor, were many different deities in bronze, copper or iron ranging from one inch to one meter high.

The dealer was very friendly and relaxed with the large group, allowing people to wander freely in order to look at things. As soon as we walked in Lee noticed a bronze deity that had a swathe of cotton taped around its eyes. "Who is this?" Lee asked the dealer. He explained, "This is Manjushri, the bodhisattva of compassion. Some of the Buddhas have their eyes closed and some have their eyes open. His are open, and out of his open eyes come blessings. Because Manjushri's eyes are open the artisans who made this covered his eyes until he gets to where he will be enshrined, where he will be blessing. Some Manjushri faces are benign—this Manjusrhi's face is fierce and horrific. But if you see the heart of Manjushri, it is benign and beautiful." This statue was obviously the most powerful piece that was in the upstairs room. Lee's gaze lingered on it. The dealer explained further, "He holds a sword to cut the knot of illusion, and a rope to bind you to wisdom."

Below the shelves that held the Manjushri was a three-foot high ancient feminine deity, some kind of tribal piece. She was stylized in clay-dusted, light iron, with a naked torso and eroticized breasts. Around her head was a halo or corona indicating sanctity and shakti power. Her hands, which were extended out in front of her body, held highly stylized herbs, flowers or perhaps grain. She was clothed from the waist to her upper thighs in a curved wrap that hung down between her legs, which were spread apart and bent at angles outward at the knee. Her feet were firmly planted on a decorative rectangular platform. She was adorned with a simple headdress, earrings and nose ring. Her chest and stomach seemed tattooed with intricate designs. Her eyes were flared and open, and seemed to be staring intently into reality, or the void. Her face communicated a strong congress with the primal forces of life.

"Who is this?" one of the women asked the dealer. He said, "She is one of the thirteen original Primal Mothers of the universe, made by a nomadic tribal people in central India." He proceeded to explain the process by which the statue was cast. Inside it is hollow, he said, and made of clay.

When the dealer showed Lee the basement room downstairs everyone followed him down. It was filled with all kinds of bronze deities at very reasonable prices. People began to set aside things they would buy. Lee looked carefully at everything, commented on pieces that people brought to him for his opinion, but remained noncommittal. Back upstairs perhaps thirty minutes later he began to set aside pieces, beginning with Manjushri and going on to a small Garuda, Ganesha and two crawling Gopalas. He also set aside a beautiful Durga killing the buffalo demon, a seated Parvati, an unusual dancing Shiva Nataraj and two lingam stones. These all seemed to be marked as gifts for others, with the possible exception of the Manjushri.

The dealer brought out a case of jewelry that captured the women's attention. Suddenly it was discovered that there were deep drawers containing many trays of very inexpensive silver jewelry concealed within a step in the wooden floor of the room. The women gathered around the jewelry and began to pull out more and more cases of rings, bracelets and earrings in silver and assorted semi-precious stones—lapis lazuli, amethyst, onyx, carnelian. It was an interesting scene in which many different elements came into play, and bore some similarities to the situation that arose at the Mehta brother's silk factory in India nine months prior. A kind of frenzy began to take over as the time to go loomed closer, and the jewelry had only just been discovered. Decisions had to be made quickly as to what to buy. The women tried on this and that piece, exclaimed over the cheap prices, puzzled over what to buy.

Once again, desire became a ruling force to be reckoned with. At the same time, it wasn't that not buying—that is, abstinence—was the correct way to handle the situation. Rather it was an opportunity to make judicious choices and work with desire in a way that was measured and included some degree of forbearance and balance, while at the same time being generous to the extreme in giving others space to do what they do and be however they are.

But while neuroses and greed came rushing to the foreground in the melee of forgetfulness for some people, others sat back and coldly watched their companions with frowning, judgmental faces. The tension created by this judgmental attitude cast a pall over the space and added another dimension in which to practice—the question became how to stand apart, if one is choosing not to participate, in a mood of kindness, generosity and compassion, while others choose to throw themselves into the fray with abandon? Group sadhana in Lee's company is constantly putting the burn of this kind of challenge in one's face. Magnanimity, or generosity, extended toward others becomes a higher practice in almost all situations, so that we are assuming the best of those with whom we share the process of sadhana, even if we find their behavior in the moment distasteful. It is a Mahayana aspect of the path, in which one extends good will and friendship, even in the midst of perceived differences or indiscretions. Clarity is a reconciling factor in these circumstances; if one is truly clear about one's own practice, there is simply no judgement or contempt for others.

Both approaches to tantric practice—restraint and abandon—in such a situation may be valuable to sadhana if done with intention. On the one hand, practicing restraint and taking a conservative approach is a function of discipline and force of will applied in relationship to desire and greed when it arises, and may be the appropriate response. At the same time, to abandon one's self, to allow one's neurosis to reveal itself may provide an opportunity to observe the real nature of the survival strategy in a way that makes a lasting impact on the practitioner. In either case seeing oneself *clearly* is the necessary demand. When one sees oneself clearly, the suffering that is revealed within the grasping and desperate emptiness of greed and unconstrained desire is shockingly undeniable. Similarly, when one sees oneself clearly, the grasping and suffering of separation that underlies pride, superiority and self-righteousness also becomes undeniable. The possible pitfall in the approach of applying sheer discipline toward restraint in such situations is that one can hide one's real greed and unconscious desire behind pride of practice for a long time, which does not serve sadhana. The possible pitfall of throwing oneself in with abandon is that if one fails to see oneself clearly, it becomes nothing but a spree of self-indulgence.

In the end everyone bought something, and some bought quite a number of items, both bronze deities and jewelry. The purchases of the group as a whole added up to a large amount. Lee was spacious and generous through all of this as he gave advice when asked for it and patiently waited for everyone to shop. He concluded his own buying, added many pieces of jewelry to his pile of deities and lingam stones, paid the dealer, thanked him very kindly, and left carrying a number of packages with the group in tow. We had almost cleaned the man out, and had certainly taken almost all of the more appreciable pieces in his inventory.

Lee got back to the apartment at four-fifteen. Fifteen minutes later he tore off in the van down the street with a second van full of people behind him. Hitting the highway he headed south toward the Swiss border, only a few miles away. He has taken to wearing a crocheted Rasta hat that was given to him—it seems to be the most effective method of protecting his eyes from the wind that comes in through the windows and whips tendrils of hair into his face while he drives.

Arriving in Zurich Lee drove immediately to the building where his public talk would begin at seven-thirty. Parking in back, Lee and several of his students began to carry the many boxes of books, CDs and tapes he takes everywhere with him into the room. Setting up the book table is always the first order of business in the spiritual master's traveling dharma caravan. It was very interesting to observe the bustle and work that ensued. Five or six people threw themselves into carrying the ten or twelve heavy boxes downstairs, where they set them down. Lee began to unpack and arrange his book table, as usual, with the utmost attention to detail and care.

It doesn't matter to Lee how much hassle or time it takes to enact this whole process of heaving and hefting boxes up and down stairs, through hallways, from parking lots or across high traffic streets. Often the talk space may be five long flights up with no elevator or lift, so that the boxes have to be carried. Sometimes there are only one or two people to help. If there is no one there to help, Lee will carry all the boxes himself without muttering a word of complaint. One would think that the spiritual master would manage the whole thing more economically: he could easily take three or four copies of each book, a few of each CD or tape, and then make up two or three boxes that would cover his inventory needs for the evening. In fact, managing the current boxes of inventory to be sold at talks could easily be a job delegated to one of his students. Instead he does it all himself and carries volumes of product along on each excursion. His students dive into this repetitive and time-consuming activity with enthusiasm, appreciating the opportunity to serve him, no matter how impractical or arbitrary it may seem.

The space for the talk tonight seemed to be a combination New Age and yoga center, a beautiful place with hardwood floors, very nice zafus and floor cushions, plants and Turkish carpets. A gorgeous, full bouquet of fresh flowers adorned the front of the room by Lee's chair. As soon as the book table and space were set up, Lee suggested that we go to a nearby café and get something to eat or drink. He very generously suggested that people could order dinner if they liked, but as we sat down at the wooden table at the café a few blocks away, he declined having any food. Instead he ordered a small coffee with milk, having eaten one or two pieces of fruit and a few handfuls of roasted pumpkinseeds (with the shells on, *prasad* that was given to him by one of his students) in the van on the way down. This is a very common practice for Lee—he will have a piece of fruit and then say, "No thank you, I'm stuffed!" when his devotees ask him if he would like dinner.

As soon as the orders were placed Lee surveyed the two tables of people and said, "Who's missing?" As it turned out four people who had driven down with Lee were not with us. It seemed that they had somehow not kept up with him when he left the building where his talk would be held. He moves very fast when he is in this mode of traveling and teaching; one of the basic demands of traveling with Lee is to pay attention and keep up. A crucial element of the master's momentum is that the pace he sets, which is very intentional, should not be dragged down by his students' failure to pay attention. This is something he has talked about time and time again, but it is still a bone of contention because he frequently has to wait unnecessarily for people.

Now he invited Tom to sit at his table with a few other people. Lee began to talk about buying the bronze deities today. He described the place and the dealer to Tom and Thomas, who was also sitting at his table. He talked about how excellent the bronzes were by and large, and how good the prices were. He spoke about how hard it is to find artifacts of that quality in India anymore, and how disappointed he had been in Banaras and Rishikesh last year when looking for bronze deities. He seemed to be encouraging Tom and Thomas, along with Dasya, to get an appointment to go back the next day and look for themselves. Tom said, "Oh, I'm sorry I missed it today! I didn't know the trip to the art dealer was that open!"

Lee replied, "It wasn't open, but people kept asking if they could come . . ." Then he added, "Once the jewelry came out it was just like Banaras!" He laughed affably. He was in a noticeably benign and jubilant mood. He then began to tell Tom about the tribal deity, one of the thirteen Primal Mothers, that the group had seen. He spoke about what a fine and unusual piece it was. He also talked about a small Kali figurine that he had seen which he thought Tom might be interested in.

As Tom's potatoes and tea came, Lee looked at the large cup for the tea and said cryptically, "That's a big glass! You might need to put in two packages of sugar!" Tom looked down at the tea.

Lee immediately went back to the original subject. He spoke about a bronze cast lizard he had seen at the dealer's house that Tom might like to get for his youngest son. He seemed to be lavishing Tom, who had flown all the way from Colorado to be with him for just one week, with affectionate regard.

Back behind the book table by seven o'clock, Lee was there to greet the first people who came in for the talk. The place began to fill up and hum with excitement. The title of the talk was, as advertised, "God Does Not Live In the Sky." There were about forty people there including Lee's group of students.

Lee began, "This is my first talk in Switzerland this lifetime. I used to give talks in Switzerland two hundred years ago, but they were a little too radical so I got chased out of the country! Ended up in Spain . . .

"So a couple of things can happen tonight. My aim for the talk is to provide a learning situation. I don't just mean that you learn something with your mind that you can get from a book or a college professor. Besides, I don't have much knowledge of facts, so I couldn't tell you much of anything you don't already know. The possibility is to learn something holistically—to actually learn something experientially. The problem is, of course, that to really learn something *valuable* experientially you have to be disturbed. If you're just pleased then the experience will be considered by the mind to be entertainment and the mind will not allow the body to learn anything from it.

"I don't know what I'm going to speak about tonight. I don't prepare talks ahead of time, I don't know what's going to happen—although I had some coffee just a few minutes ago up the street, so probably I won't fall asleep! Although, no guarantees. Whatever happens, whether the talk is very linear and very clear, very understandable, or whether it's very obscure and paradoxical, even bizarre, I have no idea ahead of time. The way it works is that I just start talking and by the end of the talk, something has happened. But the intention is always to create some disturbance, some irritation, because I want people to go up to the book table after the talk and buy big stacks of books and videos and tapes and cassettes!" Lee was speaking in a rapid-fire style. His tone at this last remark took on a humorous hue, but no one laughed. The room was silent and still except for Lee's words.

"If the experience you have in the moment is irritating or disturbing then usually when the talk is over you just walk out—quickly. That's bad for me, because you don't take any books home. Usually after a day or a couple of days or a week or two weeks, the irritation you walked out with begins to trickle up to consciousness and you begin to realize experientially what a gift you've been given. But in a week I'll be back in France and it will be too late to buy books, so even if you're disturbed tonight, don't leave without buying a few books—which we have in French, German and English, so we've come prepared!

"So, a question might be, 'Well, what is there to learn? What are we supposed to learn from being irritated?' It's a long, interesting story, but I'll make it very short for the purpose of the talk. In principle it's like this: We are born in a condition of innocence and receptivity. Our parents, as well meaning and intelligent as they are, are assholes. They have no idea how to treat children. So in one form or another they condition us, through subtle or overt abuse, to withdraw from life and begin living in a dream. And as we grow older, we forget our original experience of withdrawal, and the dream becomes reality to us.

"The average adult is living in a dream. Sometimes it's a very pleasant dream; sometimes it's a very unpleasant dream. Sometimes it's a dream with a lot of pain and suffering in it; sometimes it's a dream that is fairly well buffered from the pain and suffering that exists in our lives. So when you come to the path, or when you become interested in some kind of spiritual work or personal transformation, in effect what you are saying is, 'I would like to know what Reality is. I'd like to wake up from the dream.' Then the obvious question becomes, 'Okay great, we want to wake up from the dream—how?' Well, that's not so easy because our unconscious believes the dream to be reality, and our unconscious is much stronger and more powerful than our conscious. The conscious mind says, 'I want to wake up from the dream; I want to see Reality,' and the unconscious mind completely ignores that wish or that intention. In this metaphor the unconscious mind is like a fortress, and it's very well defended. Any frontal attack will be repulsed very easily. So the only way to get into the unconscious—to begin to have a real possibility of shifting the assumption of dream as reality—is to either sneak in somehow through the back of the fortress or make a crack in the wall. If you sneak in, get in through the servants' entrance, you have to disguise yourself so if anybody sees you, they'll think that you belong there. This is a metaphor, by the way, just in case any of you weren't following it. You look like a pretty intelligent bunch of people; nonetheless, as most of you know, intelligent people can be pretty deaf and blind sometimes.

"The unconscious is like a fortress and it defends us against perceiving reality. We either sneak in or we create a crack in the wall; it's one of the two. How we disguise ourselves so we can get in the servants' entrance and not be discovered is by doing one thing while pretending it's something else. What it looks like I'm doing right now is giving a public talk in Zurich. But that's actually not what's happening—that's all a veneer, a pretense. What's really happening is that I am creating a circumstance in which your unconscious is going to become accessible. And as long as you stay in this room until the end of the talk there is nothing you can do about it—not a single thing. You can think you can protect yourself, you can listen to every word I'm saying clearly, you can put a hex on me, you can cover yourself in a gold psychic shield—nothing will keep your unconscious inaccessible tonight. So if you don't want your unconscious to be vulnerable, then you should leave now, before it's too late.

"Thank you for your sense of humor, by the way. I'll try not to share my opinion of the cultural dynamic of the Swiss people with you. But . . . lighten up people! Smile once in awhile so I know I'm not going to get stoned before the talk is over tonight!" A few people in the somber crowd chuckled. "Oh, thank you!" Lee smiled.

"So then the question is, if the unconscious is accessible, what's going to get in? I call it Divine Influence. It's not me! I don't want to know anything about your unconscious. I want to stay as far away from your unconscious as possible! But I've got a job. I'm an agent, a representative, and I represent a big company. The CEO is God Himself. So I'm just a tool. I have no personal will in this matter, so if some disturbance arises, don't blame me—I'm just doing my job. I'm just the messenger. If you don't like the message, don't blame the messenger. That's not very intelligent. The poor messenger listens to the boss and the boss says, 'Go into this kingdom of my enemies and give the king my ultimatum. Either he surrenders to my army or I'm going to burn down his city!' The messenger goes in, gives the message and the king kills the messenger. What did the poor messenger do?! Nothing! He's just following orders!" People chuckled a little. There were still a large number of stony faces staring back at Lee from the crowd.

"So it's like this. Creation, all of Creation functions based on a primal impulse. We could call that impulse evolution. Nothing that happens in Creation is devolutionary. Everything that happens in Creation is evolutionary. So the phrase I use for this impulse of evolution is Divine Influence. As human beings we have a particular aspect that can actually interfere with, even stop, this impulse from having any effect in our lives, and that is free will.

"The average human being imagines free will to be the greatest thing about his or her life. And it could be, if we used it properly. But the thing is, by the time we are adults we are so conditioned by our psychology that even when we think we are making a free choice, we're not. We are making a choice that has been decided for us a long time ago. People like to think that they are their own person. If you say to them, 'Why do you like this kind of food? Why do you like this kind of music? Why do you like this kind of environment?' they will often give you very clear, articulate, intelligent responses. But if they were to really look closely at their parents, they would be shocked to see that most of what they think are their own personal likes and dislikes are actually the likes and dislikes of one of their parents. If most of you look really closely at your partners—I'm sure some of you have already seen this—they start to look exactly like your parent of that sex. I don't mean physically, I mean psychologically. We tend to marry our parents because of psychological transference.

"When the unconscious becomes accessible or vulnerable it becomes open to entry by this impulse of evolution. The first order of business is to deal with free will, because in actuality, if our will is not truly free, we cannot evolve. We can become smarter and learn more facts, earn more money, have great sex—even better when we're fifty than when we were twenty-five!—but that's not evolution. That's change within the dream. As some of you know from remembering your dreams under ordinary circumstances, all kinds of dramatic changes can happen in dreams. But when you wake up you see that all those changes were completely empty and insubstantial. In fact, who you were when you went to sleep and who you are when you woke up was exactly the same person. So no matter what happens in the dream, you don't change. For you to change, you have to work consciously while awake.

"So the first order of business is to create accessibility in the unconscious. Unless we realize that our will is not free it is impossible to have free will. We have to see that we are completely conditioned and programmed. If we can recognize that and accept the reality of it, then we can begin to activate free will as it actually is. We have no choice; we can't just start having choice, because everything that we think is choice is just another conditioning. First we have to see clearly that we have no choice, and that free will exists in us but it's not active. What is active is our fantasy of free will, which is defined by and run by our psychological disposition. Our psychological disposition is based on our retreat from life as children. Of course there are also elements of our psychological disposition that are based on an entry into life rather than our retreat from life. We have certain enthusiasms for art or for relationship or whatever, that are functions of life-positive decisions we made as children. But before we make positive psychological decisions, we make the negative ones that are a retreat from life and that define the context for relationship with existence or life. So even the positive decisions are somehow based contextually in the negative decisions. Yes?"

A woman sitting on a pillow on the floor in the front of the room had raised her hand. She said, "Is this necessary that we have these negative decisions and why is this happening?"

Lee answered, "It's not necessary, academically, but it just happens for everybody." She began to argue with Lee about karma being the root cause of problems and not childhood abuse. She was explaining karma to him as if he probably hadn't taken it into consideration, using the example of children who are raised in very positive environments. It seemed that Lee's intention to irritate was already taking effect in her case as her tone was rather adversarial and challenging.

Lee responded, "I understand, but the way I approach these things is that they all have their inception in this lifetime. It's not that I don't believe in karma. It's that for the purposes of our personal work on ourselves, it's healthier if we assume that what we have to work on started here and can be worked on here. So that we don't justify our lack of work on principles that are bigger than us. Clear?"

It couldn't have been clearer, but she doggedly continued. "I believe that a child can continue living positively if the influences from the parents are not being negative. Is that true?"

Lee was very patient and kind in his answer. He said, "I hadn't finished answering your first question, so I was going to get to that. Obviously the parents are the pivotal force for conditioning in the child's life. A completely benign and positive and non-abusive child-raising environment will produce a predominantly life-positive, psychologically healthy adult. And of course that happens sometimes, but . . ."

She interrupted again, "Okay, I just asked if it's *possible*."

Lee said, "Absolutely. Okay, I won't cover the 'but'—unless somebody asks another question later."

Another woman broke in, saying, "I would like to hear that."

Lee said, "Okay. *But*, the average adult, being unaware of the effect of their own manifestations and believing, out of love for their child, they are serving their child well, may actually be abusing the child in some way, which is what creates the retreat from life. They could be completely unconscious of their abuse. Let me give you an example: most parents love their children as far as they know what love is and as much as they can. Still, at the same time, we have our own lives. When children start to develop language skills they become tremendously curious about everything. As any parent knows, if you haven't forced your child into a silent mode by making them be quiet before they have language, once they have language they will have hundreds, thousands of questions a day. Most adults don't have the patience to answer each and every one of those questions calmly and with complete attention to the child. Maybe we just want to go to the bathroom without the child running into the bathroom, 'Mommy, Mommy, why this? Why that? Why this?' What we often do when we as adults have answered enough questions for the day is unconsciously tune out the child's voice. In the morning the child says, 'Mommy?' and you turn around and say, 'Yes, sweetheart?' But by five o'clock in the evening, if you've spent all day with your child and by now they are saying, 'Mommy? Mommy? Mommy? Mommy!' " Lee's voice got louder and louder and more high pitched, more frantic as he demonstrated the child's desperation.

"And then you finally say, 'Yes! What is it!?' " He snapped this out in an impatient tone. "Or maybe when you *finally* hear them you say, 'Yes?' calmly and cooly, but that mood of relationship is perceived by the child as neglect. It is a very subtle form of abuse to the child. Under reasonable adult circumstances everybody loses their patience once in awhile. Everybody needs a breather once in a while. But to the *child* it's perceived as, 'My mother doesn't listen to me. She's not paying attention to me.' So, that's the 'but' that I was referring to.

"Under ordinary circumstances the average adult loses their patience sometimes, gets angry at their child sometimes. Even the best parents, every once in a while. Here's another example: Shit smells bad. Especially a lot of children's shit. I don't know what they do to that stuff in there, but man, when it comes out—whoa! To the child, shit is very interesting stuff. It's part of their body. If any of you have left your children alone long enough with shit in their diapers, by the time you come in, if it's not all over the walls, if they haven't drawn some beautiful pictures with it to please you, you're very lucky. The child shits in his diapers, he's a year old, you go to change the diaper, and what's your reaction to the shit? 'Oohh! Whew!' Particularly fathers. They say, 'God! Honey! Honey! Could you change the diaper!' What the child gets from this is, 'I stink.' Not, 'My shit stinks,' but 'I stink,' because a one-year-old child hasn't made those distinctions yet. That's why children should not be toilet trained sooner than they are naturally ready to be toilet trained. If you train them too soon because it's more convenient for *you* as an adult if they are toilet trained, it's very damaging to their psyche.

"What it is that is disturbing or irritating to the unconscious is the divine impulse of evolution because psychologically speaking, the last thing in the world that we want is transformation. Ego is terrified of transformation because to ego, transformation means death. As long as will is not free, ego effectively obstructs the divine impulse of evolution. When will is free and we can actually make a choice based on Reality rather than on the dream—meaning when we can actually make a choice based on clarity, not based on psychological manipulation—then we can deal with ego. But if we are not able to make a choice like that, then ego deals with us, however it wants. So, this is the intention of our being together this evening—to allow some trickle of Divine Influence into your unconscious."

Another woman asked, "How do we recognize if our free will is free or not?"

"That's a very good question," Lee answered. "There is only one way to recognize whether our will is free or not. Probably everybody in this room thinks their will is free or relatively okay. We have to observe our manifestations, starting with our physical manifestations—literally, how we walk, how we sit, how we read, how we act, how we gesture in relationship to other people. That will lead to being able to observe our subtle manifestations, inner manifestations, emotions and thoughts.

"When we begin observing ourselves we see that certain gestures we have always taken for granted as being spontaneous are actually motivated by something that is not spontaneous. When we walk into the Chinese restaurant we think it's just because we've always liked Chinese food. If we really have the intention to see if our will is free or not and we start to pay attention, we may begin to have memory flashes of something having to do with a Chinese restaurant when we were a child. Maybe whenever our parents took us to a Chinese restaurant it was always on a very special occasion. We start to realize that our appreciation of Chinese food and our decision to go to the Chinese restaurant has nothing to do with free will. Nothing. It's all a wish to revivify the good feelings of childhood. And so on and so on and so on about *every* choice that we make.

"Let's get personal. What turns us on sexually? Don't answer! It's a rhetorical question. We probably think we are attracted to someone and we're turned on. If we really start to pay attention, under most circumstances, not all, we will find that there is a trigger mechanism that creates physical, sexual desire. If we pay attention even more closely, we begin to find the source of that trigger mechanism. That doesn't mean once you discover that even sex is completely conditioned that it will ruin sex forever. 'Oh no! I'll never enjoy it again!' It means, in fact, that you'll finally be able to begin enjoying sex freely for the first time in your life because the difference between functioning at the effect of psychological conditioning and functioning freely is the difference between night and day. It's the difference between a photograph of a juicy, ripe mango and eating a juicy, ripe mango. Until you know the experience of freedom, you can't imagine what it is, because a lot of our experience in the dream is not so bad. Like sex, for example. Sex can be pretty good in the dream, but it is actually pale compared to sex in reality, in freedom. But we're certainly not going to prove that tonight! At least not in this room . . ." Lee chuckled. It seemed that he was making a reference to how often people in his seminars exhibit absolutely blatant and ugly sexual groping of one another.

"If we are paying attention to ourselves with intention, things will become clear that have never been clear before. It's as if we are staring at the cloudy sky and all of a sudden the clouds start to disperse and there is the beautiful, blue, sunny sky. It's like that. Before I was doing the work I'm doing now—and I've been doing this work for twenty-five years—I was doing occult work. I don't mean I was a bad witch or warlock, but I was doing magic. People who do magic basically learn how to manipulate energy. I used to do it in positive ways, healing and things like that, but there were some tricks we learned. One day I was with my son, he was about nine or ten years old, and I was talking with some other adults about this magic. He said, 'Teach me something.' So I took him outside, and it was a cloudy day. I said, 'Watch. You see where my finger is pointing?' He said, 'Yes.' All of a sudden a big hole opened up in the clouds, and it got bigger and bigger and bigger. He went crazy, 'Wow! Teach me how to do that!' So I did, and he used it to impress his friends, many times.

"But the clearing of the clouds in our psyche is not something that we can do by manipulation of energy or force. We do it by simply observing ourselves as we are, and then as we continue to observe, the clouds just disappear. We see things that we've never seen before. So that's the actual first practical step that we take. Maybe in the past there have not only been clouds, but also good experiences. So I think that children also have this experience of free will and when later on they remember this free will, this is not a bad thing. These are not always bad conditions."

He turned to her and said, "Are you trying to convince yourself of that, or are you asking me a question? Which one?"

She said, "No, I believe in that."

"So you are trying to convince yourself of that. Or am I putting words in your mouth?"

"This answer is putting words in my mouth," she answered.

"Okay. If you believe that, and it sounds like I'm saying something different, and you want to know whether your beliefs are true or my beliefs are true—the fact is that most people don't really want to know which is true. Most people assume their beliefs are true, and they couldn't care less about the other person's beliefs. Like the Muslims versus the Christians, right? They don't care about what is *true*; they are willing to live with their beliefs with complete disregard for reality. But if it means anything to you to find out whose beliefs are true—your beliefs or my beliefs—if you start paying attention to yourself, exactly in the way we just talked about, then you will find out over time. You will either confirm your beliefs as true, or you will find out that there is something about your beliefs that you didn't take into consideration in forming those beliefs. That observation will either be interesting and inspire you to dig deeper, to go further, or will be terrifying and create a complete turning away from your investigation. That's where it stands. I'm not going to tell you that your beliefs are not true because I have beliefs, like everybody else.

"I have a spiritual Teacher. He's alive and he lives in India. His name is Yogi Ramsuratkumar. He's in his eighties, so He's not real young at this point. I first met Him about a year after I began teaching. I'd been teaching in the occult field for five years, but a year after I'd been teaching this spiritual stuff," Lee chuckled, "I went to India. I had a tremendous arrogance about my clarity of truth. I traveled through India and visited many saints and many yogis, and I was very critical, very cynical, because I felt I knew better than they knew. The only person I didn't feel that way about was Yogi Ramsuratkumar.

"So, I believed I was perfect—finished, totally enlightened! Done! Awakened! Realized! And Yogi Ramsuratkumar had a different belief. We got along very well—we liked one another. But His belief was something like, 'This guy Lee is really under some illusions, and perhaps I could help him pierce some of those illusions.' My first interaction with Yogi Ramsuratkumar made it very clear to me that there was something about Him that was bigger than my beliefs, beyond my beliefs. I could have done one of two things. I could have said, 'Well, I'm a teacher, I've got my students. I live in America, I've got my little kingdom—to hell with it!' I could have turned my back and gone on as I was, functioning according to my beliefs.

"I really believed I was finished, and I wanted to bring integrity to that. So if I was not finished, if I had not come to the end of the path, then I couldn't very well bring integrity to my work if I knew that. When it became clear that Yogi Ramsuratkumar had something bigger, higher, the only response that had integrity was to enter into relationship to that and to submit myself to it—to test my beliefs against His beliefs. At that point, to me He wasn't my teacher; He was just another Indian saint, one of many that I had visited on that trip. But He was the only one who provoked this response in me, so I entered into relationship with Him, and it took a number of years to be accepted by him. I accepted Him as my teacher right away but He didn't accept me as His disciple right away. It took eleven years for Him to accept me as His disciple. As time and experience have proven, His belief was accurate; my belief system was inaccurate. But as a teacher, I have never wanted to represent myself as something that I am not. My students might want to, but what can you do with students?

"I personally want to bring as much integrity as I can to my teaching work. Yogi Ramsuratkumar's belief system was the accurate belief system; mine was not. So I submitted myself to whatever degree I was able to His Influence and direction. In the twelve years since I have been accepted as His disciple—twenty-four years since I first met Him— He has continued to refine my belief system. He has continued to chip away whatever remnants of illusion are left. He has continued to dispel them, dissolve them. And He continues to do that, to this day.

"This whole issue of belief systems is a very important one because we all have our belief systems. Nobody's belief system is one hundred percent wrong and nobody's belief system is one hundred percent right."

"I would like to know what enlightenment is," someone from the audience asked.

Lee chuckled, "Wow, that's a hard question to answer. I don't know if I can give an exact definition, but I would say that enlightenment is a process, an ongoing process that I would equate with the term Surrender to the Will of God. We can't define what the Will of God is, because in every moment the Will of God is unique and specific to each circumstance. But we could say that enlightenment is complete resonance to this impulse of evolution, this divine impulse of evolution. If we don't like the use of the words 'God' or 'the Divine,' we could say enlightenment is something like being completely one with the natural and spontaneous life force as it manifests unobstructed, unblocked, in our case. Something like that. Thank you."

The next question was, "When you start realizing your illusion and there is something left—love of God—is this another illusion?"

Lee answered, "The way you find out is by applying the same process. Whatever experience arises you apply the same process of observation. If something is real, observation does not create any dissolution of that experience. There are no clouds, so nothing dissolves. And if it's not real it will dissolve just like the previous illusion.

"It's very inspiring and meaningful to feel that we love God. Probably all of us would wish that, but often what we call love is designed to comfort us. Krishnamurti said, 'Love has no questions.' Love is completely radiant. The mystical Sufis say that love in its true form knows only the object of its attention: the lover loses the sense of 'I' in the Beloved. So if we are getting some pay-off from the feelings that love is generating, then it means that that love is relative, not absolute."

"I didn't understand," the questioner interjected.

Lee continued to explain, "Okay. For example, we may be getting some personal benefit from what we believe our love to be. If we find ourselves sitting there one day looking at our partner thinking, 'He or she is really better looking and smarter than most other people's partners, then what we call love may actually be pride for ourselves. Real love has no personal motive. It is simply radiance, and one becomes lost in the Beloved."

A woman said in a very irritated tone of voice, "The first thing I saw in the hand-out paper about the talk was something about God, so I had trust and I was happy. And then I saw in the newspaper that the title was 'Love, Sex and Death,' and then I was happy again."

Lee chuckled, "The best of both worlds!"

She continued, "And I'm finally being a little impatient and I'm excusing myself because other people probably have questions too, but my question is very burning, about love and sexuality. Even more about sexuality."

"Okay, what's the question?" Lee asked mildly.

"In the Indian tradition or in the Christian tradition monogamous relationship has a meaning. I would like to know more about polygamy and how to realize this or how to put this into practice."

Lee looked at her intently for a moment then responded, "Mohammed was supposed to have had ten wives. Of course he was asked about that and he said that as long as someone can bring integrity to their relationship with each person in the system, then the system can work. First of all, leave Christianity out of it because it's a relatively new system compared to the Indian system which is five, six, seven thousand years old. The Chinese system is five, six, seven thousand years old, and so on. In the most ancient of the traditions the issue of multiple partners was dealt with in an entirely different way. When the context of one's life was the realization of and the ongoing demonstration of truth or reality, then sex and love were simply a part of that context. Under the right conditions or circumstances, if more than one partner would serve that process or context—the realization of and the ongoing demonstration of truth—then it was a completely acceptable form of life. As time went on, and humanity became more feminine negative and more patriarchal, political and social laws began to be forms of domination and manipulation and control. Society and culture lost the spirit of truth and reality.

"The culture that exists in the world today is sex-negative. America is full of sexual perversion, child abuse, sexual frustration, and a legal system that is totally sex-negative. Switzerland is probably full of it. The culture is repressive and sex-negative in the name of protecting people. In this day and age, after a couple of thousand years of cultural conditioning, the average person is so far away from what is essentially organically true that any attempt to experiment with anything other than monogamy usually ends disastrously, with lots of pain, emotional crisis and so on. Does that answer your question?" She nodded. "Thank you."

Lee began to answer a question about evolution. He said, "For evolution to progress unhindered, or naturally, it requires the participation of all the systems—the conscious mind, unconscious mind, astral body, subtle body, physical body, the whole thing. If any one of those systems is in some way handicapped, then it can slow down the process, interfere with the process, or stop the process completely. These systems don't all move at the same speed. Often when the evolutionary impulse is active in us, one system is moving at a different rate than another system. One system moves faster, another moves slower. Sometimes it looks like evolution is happening without, or in spite of, one system—like the unconscious—because we are looking at the one that is moving fast. But in fact all the systems are involved; it's a holistic process that takes place over time."

After a few more brief interchanges with the audience Lee said, "I'd like to thank you for staying, those of you that stayed." He chuckled. Several people had gotten up and left earlier in the talk. "And I'll be at the book table for a few minutes if any of you have questions that you did not get to ask. You can come and ask them back there, informally. And obviously, any of you who would like to buy books and take them home, we'd be more than willing to accommodate you! Thank you very much."

Lee's talk had been so pristine in its clarity and so captivating that the two hours flew past very quickly. It seemed like we had hardly sat down to listen, and then it was suddenly time to end. It was like getting on a magic carpet and being transported somewhere, only to wake up back at the original point of departure, but sensing that you've been somewhere extraordinary. Something felt different, but it was an indefinable rawness, a fire that was burning deep under the surface of things.

During the talk perhaps six or seven people had gotten up and left. There were a number of people who seemed very contracted and disturbed, and others who sat radiantly and quietly listening. It was amazing to see people react negatively to this talk because Lee's presentation was so gentle, so crystalline, so rational that it was a surprise departure from the usual crazy antics and hilarity he creates. For example, he didn't tell a single joke. Now several people gathered around the book table, which stayed busy for the next thirty minutes, while Lee's students talked among themselves.

The general consensus among Lee's students was the striking way in which Lee's talk had been revelatory—not just the clear and precise articulation of Lee's teaching, especially with regard to the primal cramp and survival strategy, but the statement he had made, for the first time ever, that it took Yogi Ramsuratkumar eleven years to accept him as a disciple. Somehow this re-writing of his own history was having the effect of making Lee ever more transparent to the Influence of Yogi Ramsuratkumar. This transparency had the palpable effect of permeating the space with Yogi Ramsuratkumar's presence on this evening, and a number of people commented on it. When I asked Dasya what he thought of the talk, he said, "I look at Lee and I see him dissolving."

As Yogi Ramsuratkumar became the topic of conversation among a few of Lee's students who were standing together talking, Mariana told a story I had never heard before. She had lived in Tiruvannamalai for some months over five years ago, and during that time there a woman who was usually at Yogi Ramsuratkumar's darshan, and who Yogi Ramsuratkumar treated with a particular kindness. As the story went, when Yogi Ramsuratkumar was living on the streets of Tiruvannamalai he used to beg for coffee or tea from some of the tea stalls. In the course of his begging he was at times abused or treated harshly. This woman's husband had gone around to all of the tea stalls in Tiruvannamalai and paid each one every month, saying, "This money is for Yogi Ramsuratkumar. If he comes here wanting tea or coffee, that's what this money is for." In that way Yogi Ramsuratkumar was provided for. After this devotee died his wife used to come regularly to see Yogi Ramsuratkumar, who always remembered the kindness of her husband, and treated her with the utmost regard and respect.

As Mariana finished the story Lee began to pack up the book table. Within ten minutes everything was packed and back in the vans, which were parked and waiting just outside the door. The twenty or so people in Lee's party moved quickly as he whisked out of the place. Soon he was driving back through the streets of Zurich toward the highway. It was about eleven o'clock at night.

Lee seemed highly enthused, and talked in an animated way with Tom and Thomas, who sat in the front seat with him as he drove. They were asking him questions and got into a conversation about Gurdjieff's idea that one has to build a soul in the Work. Then someone asked Lee if tonight was the first time he had thought of speaking of his relationship with Yogi Ramsuratkumar in the way that he did, referring to Lee's statement that it took Yogi Ramsuratkumar eleven years to accept him as a disciple. Lee answered, "Yes, sure—why not! It makes it exciting for first time participants, and for those who know it's happening."

Later Lee commented, "Boy! That was a tough crowd! As soon as I said they needed to loosen up, you could just see people getting ready to get up and leave. There were some really sour faces out there!" Lee laughed and kept driving.

August 24, 1999
Freiburg

Before brunch this morning at ten-thirty Tom, Thomas and Dasya returned from their appointment with the artifact dealer. Tom stood in the entryway of the apartment holding a long, large bundle wrapped in cotton cloth. It was obviously heavy, and he held it as if it was very precious. He presented it to Lee, saying, "This is a gift to you from Colette and I." It was the meter-high iron Primal Mother that Lee had admired at the dealer's house; he had told Tom about it last night in Zurich.

Taking the artifact into his hands, Lee said, "Thank you." He hefted its weight slightly. "This thing is heavy—in more ways than one!"

He put the statue away in his room and went in to brunch in the living room, which was crammed with about fifty-five people. The food was being set out in a buffet in the kitchen while adults milled around talking, taking care of business, arranging schedules, transportation and other group logistics. Children ran about yelling and scrapping with each other happily but noisily, to a large degree unheeded by their parents. Lee threaded his way through all this and took his seat on the couch. "It's a madhouse," he said, sitting down on the couch and looking around.

After brunch the group reorganized for the trip to Basel, Switzerland today. Lee had planned an outing with his family at the zoo in Basel before his public talk tonight. After the zoo he would go to dinner at a pizzeria, and then drive over to the space where his talk was scheduled to begin at eight o'clock. Somehow this was another situation in which the list of people accompanying him had grown so out of proportion that he ended up with thirty-five or forty people in tow. He made one comment: "Just don't follow me around the zoo." At noon, as soon as the brunch dishes were cleared away and washed, he took off in the van with the second van and four or five cars following behind him.

After five long hours at the zoo, the bulky group settled in with Lee around five-thirty at two long adjoining tables in a very nice pizzeria and Italian restaurant. The ensuing confusion and cacophony was deafening as the Germans and Americans attempted to read the menu, talk to each other and their children, and place their orders with the waitress who appeared to speak only French. It quickly became clear that the waitress, who had difficulty with the chaos around our large group from the beginning, couldn't deal with the large group. Volker, who speaks German, French and English, got up and took orders to help ease the tension of the situation. He became the liaison between the group and the waitress.

Lee grimaced slightly at the general pandemonium. Chris commented that she thought he had originally just wanted a small gathering tonight for dinner. He shrugged. Jan asked, "Is this what *you* wanted?" Lee shrugged again and said in an irritated tone of voice, "Having all these people here having to order is about as close to hell as it gets for me." When pressed further about why he didn't just say no when people asked if they could come along, he said, "It's just a community thing—it's *my* problem. I have to get used to it." He smiled innocently, "We don't want anyone to feel left out!" When asked why he didn't let someone else handle it when people were swamping him with requests to come along, he shrugged and said, "Why give somebody else the headache?"

At Lee's invitation Tom was seated across the table from him. Lee began to talk about how extraordinary Tom's gift, the Primal Mother, was. Tom had a copy of *The Beloved* by Rajneesh in his hands, and was telling Lee more about the deity itself. As it turned out the particular nomadic tribe that made the deity is written about in the book, which Tom—rather amazingly—happened to be reading at the time that all this occurred. Tom said that the artisans came from the nomadic Kont tribe of Bastar, a primitive part of Madhya Pradesh in central India. He described the method of casting in detail from the book and said that the deity was dressed similarly to the women of the tribe—naked to the waist with a draped cloth skirt, along with jewelry adornments.

Suddenly Lee broke in and said to Tom, "Don't take this personally, Tom. Don't add this to your already heavy burden of shame and guilt."

Tom interjected, "I've worked through the guilt thing, really, it's okay . . ."

"Really?" Lee said, fixing Tom with a piercing look. If there was any shred of guilt or shame in Tom in that moment, he would have to know about it. Tom smiled and blushed, taking it with a good-natured affability. He was raised in the Catholic Church, and has heard plenty of this kind of feedback from Lee, who now continued, "This isn't meant for *you*, of course, but one word out of my mouth and people leap to fantastic assumptions and bizarre projections. I can't even make a social comment without having people go and change their entire house or something because of what I've said! Really, it's maddening."

Tom listened, taking it in. Of course yesterday Lee had just mentioned how fine and unusual the Primal Mother piece was, and Tom had immediately bought it for him as a gift, so it would be difficult not to take the feedback as being meant personally for him. At the same time, it was entirely possible that Lee meant it exactly as he said it—it wasn't for Tom, but a general statement Lee was making in principle. Something, most likely a combination of things, seemed to have Lee in an irascible mood. The large, unwieldy group scene wasn't helping. Tom said, "I'm learning while I'm burning . . ."

Lee said, "Well, that's the way the learning is *effective*. You don't learn without a burn."

I asked Lee if he had heard any other details about the thirteen Primal Mothers from the artifact dealer. He snapped, "What the hell do I care! If it feels good, stick it where it will radiate its sanctity and forget about the rest!" In other words, don't let your mind get in the way! The talk turned back to the day before at the dealer's house.

Lee said, "I didn't think it was going to be like Banaras until the jewelry came out." Tom chuckled, remembering the scene at the Mehta brother's silk factory from last December. This morning Tom had also bought two other pieces that Lee had recommended to him, and Thomas and Dasya had made purchases as well. Lee said, "I don't think the dealer has another nice piece left—I think we cleaned him out of everything."

Lee and Sylvan began to pore over the bill for dinner for almost forty people, concentrating on the confusing task of having to figure out what each person needed to contribute financially for the meal. Lee accounted for his family and paid for several other people, including Andrea, an ashram renunciate, and Tom. Lee will at times very specifically offer to pay for one of his students when eating out in a restaurant. There is always a lawful element to this that can be sensed, although there is not an obvious rational or linear purpose behind it. One is reminded of the story of Lee going to a restaurant in Tiruvannamalai with Yogi Ramsuratkumar and ten of his men students about ten years ago. They sat down to eat together, and when the meal was over the men began to get their rupees out to pay their part. Yogi Ramsuratkumar interrupted and said emphatically, "No! *Lee* pays. Lee pays for all."

During dinner Lee made several comments about the adults not paying attention to the children. He seemed generally irritated by the whole scene throughout the meal. Afterward, as the group made their way out of the restaurant to the street, Lee asked if anyone wanted dessert. He seemed rather unenthusiastic about it, and no one jumped on the offer. "What about after the talk?" someone suggested as an alternative dessert plan. Lee said that might be a possibility. All the children were riding the train back to Freiburg and would have dessert or ice cream when they arrived there.

After the children and mothers in the traveling party had taken off, Lee's irritation seemed to deepen in the general confusion and mayhem that surrounded the evening. Refusing to drive in the van the four or five blocks to the talk space, he stalked off down the street leaving some of his students sitting in the van wondering what had happened amidst a general mood of grumbling and breakdown. When we caught up with him he was already unpacking books.

The location for the talk was a beautiful old building. The room had an executive feeling to it, with about fifteen rows of very nice chairs neatly lined up in an almost mathematical orderliness. Lee stood behind the book table as people came in, the fifteen boxes of books stored under the table. Books and CDs were neatly laid out on top of the table, the *vigraha* sitting serenely in the midst of it all. Gradually about fifty people filled the space. Lee's talk proceeded in a way that is very uncharacteristic of him—although there were good points that were made, it seemed that his words didn't carry the kind of power and potency that most of his talks transmit.

He started out commenting on the talk he'd given the night before, saying, "Last night I gave a talk in Zurich to a very different crowd than we have here tonight. I can't say what was different, but I would like to talk about what happened. I was commenting on the crystallized rigidity of the faces in the room. I was being very funny, but their faces didn't crack a smile. Nothing! As two people left they told someone, 'That man's talk is so disrespectful to the space that we're going to have to come back here later and clear the space out!' "

He went on to the basic subject of the talk for the evening, which was that there are two dimensions of created existence—personal reality and universal reality. "The first order of business when we enter the path is to deal ruthlessly and self-honestly with ourselves. So the people who walked out of the talk last night in Zurich left not out of boredom, but out of anger and recoil as evidenced by their facial masks and mood. The reason they walked out was that they didn't want to deal with their personal reality. They didn't want to see that they were abused as children and probably abuse their own children now—it's a hell realm to really see that. To admit that we're sadistic is very difficult because we feel it's so bad. But when a shift of context occurs, when we begin to live from the universal reality, then we can't be sadistic because we'd be doing it to ourselves, and we couldn't be masochistic because we'd be doing it to others! Before we can begin to revel in the fact that we are divine beings and children of God—the universal reality—we first have to deal with the fact that, because we have free will, we also have the ability to block or stop Divine Influence in our lives. Unless we deal with who we are *now*—the ugliness, the cruelty, the beauty—we won't make that shift of context. We may look and talk like we have, but we haven't."

One quote from Lee stood out in it all, coming in response to a question about the title of the talk, which was "Love, Sex and Death." Lee quipped, "Love—most people, when they're getting it, don't trust it or believe it! Sex—when they're getting it, most people want to get it more, or in some other way! And death—happens to everybody! Now I feel like I can go on with integrity!" After about an hour several people walked out, the last of them slamming the door. All in all it had been a very strange evening. But the last question seemed to perk him up. Someone asked, "Are you all the time happy?"

"Me? No way! I wish! Great question! Thank you, time to end." He chuckled as he got up and walked over to the book table. A few people came over and browsed, but very shortly it was completely dismantled and Lee was ready to go.

As he walked out of the building he said to some of his students, "Do you want to go get dessert?" He was referring to the plan he'd made at dinner to get dessert after the talk, but his tone of voice was so flat, and he looked so tired and weary, that the only answer could be, "If you want to, but otherwise, it's fine to go home right away."

Lee said, "Then I think we'll skip it and go back to Freiburg."

Very quickly Lee was back in his van, pulling on the crocheted Rasta hat and driving the hour back to Freiburg. As he drove he commented on how the talk was the worst talk of the summer. He said, "That's what I get for trying to talk about something I was considering earlier today, instead of just going in there and winging it." When asked to elaborate on what he meant, he said, "I had this fabulous consideration this morning about personal reality and universal reality, and I thought I would try to recreate it tonight. But it was gone. It was complete this morning when it came up, but tonight it was empty, finished. I won't do that again."

August 25, 1999
On the road

After brunch the whole group packed everything up and loaded the two vans and two cars to head out to Le Rozet, a center run by two students of Arnaud Desjardins where Lee and company would stay for the next five nights just across the border in France and only a few kilometers from Switzerland. After arriving at Le Rozet, Lee would leave almost immediately for Geneva, where his public talk was scheduled for eight o'clock.

The trip to Le Rozet took almost four hours. Passing through a beautiful French town, La Chaux de Fonds, where Lee would be giving a public talk the next night, one of Lee's students, referring to the fiasco of the night before, said jokingly to Lee, "Look at that lovely ski museum and all those restaurants! How about an afternoon at the ski museum and lunch for twenty-five in this beautiful little hamlet? Sound good to you?" Everyone in the van laughed. Lee gave a short chuckle and said facetiously, "Oh yeah, that sounds very inviting . . . anything for the sake of the book!"

As it turned out last night, Volker and Sylvan, who had been responsible for gathering all the money for dinner from the thirty-five people who were there, had come up twenty-five dollars short. Most of the group had already left the restaurant by the time the money was organized for the waitress. Volker ended up paying the twenty-five dollars out of his own pocket. He could be reimbursed later out of the Freiburg sangha funds, but that is not the way Lee typically wants such situations handled. When Lee found out as he sat at the book table waiting for the talk to start, he said, "I do *not* want the Freiburg sangha paying—people should pay for what they personally ate."

It was a symptom of the kind of shabby group dynamics that create murkiness in spaces where Lee is attempting to establish a texture of clarity, responsibility and crispness. It is this clarity that makes room for the many moods of delight that spontaneously arise in Lee's company. When the clarity is seriously compromised as it was during the whole day of the Basel excursion, the delight typically does not show up. It seemed that this mood was reflected in Lee's public talk as well.

Traveling in a large group with some degree of facility and finesse is not an easy thing to do. The group around Lee almost always includes numbers of new students or those who haven't traveled much with Lee and aren't used to the rigors of travel sadhana. Handling the logistics, communications and food for many different people and interfacing with hosts is a very complex situation. This pressure cooker of sadhana is complicated further by the fact that Lee chooses to travel gypsy style and never first class. While he usually does not delegate formal authority to any one person to organize the traveling party, Lee expects someone to rise to the occasion, assume responsibility for what needs to get done, and carry it out efficiently, and he expects his students to learn to function with elegance in all these situations. On the road one has the opportunity to learn the art of living in a way that is rooted in a truly tantric relationship to the world.

These opportunities for learning are constantly arising, and the next opportunity was on the horizon as we arrived at Le Rozet, a renovated old stone farmhouse located deep in the green, pastoral Jura mountains. The house has been converted into living quarters and a center for the teaching of Arnaud Desjardins, run by Jean Pierre and Josette Mongeot.

As Lee got out of his van Josette came walking up to greet him. Quickly the backpacks and boxes and suitcases and duffel bags were hauled out of the vans. Lee went inside, settled into his room and then came down for tea. The plans for the evening in Geneva were extremely vague. I asked Lee, "What is the plan for dinner?" No one had eaten anything since brunch at ten-thirty that morning. People had only had tea and apple juice, and now with another three-hour drive ahead, we were beginning to wonder what the food situation would be. Stop and get something? Go to a café? It didn't seem like there would be time for any of that.

Lee answered, "No plan. We are at the mercy of our hosts!" His eyes gleamed in that challenging way that seemed to say, "Surely you can go without food for a few hours!" It was certainly a clue for how to practice for the rest of the day.

Immediately afterward, at three-thirty, Lee was ready to go. He stood waiting on the country road beside the vehicles in the parking area just down from the house. He had been saying since brunch that we would have to leave promptly at three-thirty in order to make it to Geneva on time. He wanted, as usual, to leave *exactly* on time, not one or two or five or ten minutes later. Jean Pierre had just gotten home from work and planned to accompany Lee and three of Lee's students in the small car that Lee would drive for the evening. Dasya was driving one of the vans full of people, and another car was also full and would join the caravan. This meant that Lee was basically waiting for about twenty people to get organized and on the road.

Finally the group was settled in the vehicles, which were now parked outside the front of the house. Josette had prepared some picnic fare—cookies, crackers, apples, bananas and bottled water—to send along, and Debbie was bringing large brown paper sacks full of these various items out from the kitchen to Lee, who sat behind the wheel of the small car. Jean Pierre sat at his right side in the front passenger seat. With each sack that came toward him Lee said, "Take that to the van," or "Give that one to me."

There was much confusion and the mood of chaos and incoherent disarray from the night before seemed to prevail again. Most of the people traveling with Lee were staying in another house about a kilometer away from the seminar house. One of Lee's students, Martin, had to take the train back to Berlin from Geneva after Lee's talk. His luggage had been inadvertently taken into the other house along with everyone else's luggage and left in a pile, so that once the caravan started rolling, we had to make yet another stop almost immediately. For some unknown reason it took about ten minutes at this stop before Lee could get back on the road. His patience was wearing very thin at this point as people ran back and forth from the vehicles to the house with their last minute things to do. Sitting at the wheel of the car, which was now parked in front of the second house and once again waiting, Lee sighed and said with deep frustration, "People cannot move fast in this community to save their lives! If the S.S. was coming for us now, we'd all be dead." Jean Pierre sat listening silently.

The food was also problematical. Lee wanted an apple, but the paper bag with the apples in it had been whisked off to another vehicle. When someone in the backseat of his car offered to get the bag of apples, which would involve getting out of the car and walking to the car that was parked behind Lee's, he snapped, "No. Forget it." He paused and said, "It's one thing to have one person with their head up their ass, but when you get six people in one gang . . ." He shook his head and said, "Just be grateful that everybody's healthy." He sighed again and added, "Of course, I'm sure if I was the one responsible I'd make more mistakes than anyone."

Another five minutes passed and Lee gestured to Claire, who was driving the car behind Lee's where the apples had been passed. She jumped out and came up to his window. Lee asked her for an apple. She said, "We have no apples, we only have nectarines." Lee sighed. "Okay. Never mind." She walked back to her car and within thirty seconds was back with the bag of apples that she had located in her car. Lee took one and passed them to the backseat, offering them to those of us sitting there. They were delicious, fresh farm apples, crisp, sweet and tart. Lee finished his apple and took another one.

Finally we were on the road, with Lee driving like a bat out of hell. In about thirty minutes he stopped, caravan in tow, to get gas. Lee came back to his car and said to us with a tone of incredulity, "I tried to get you some of the crackers from the van to eat, but they're all gone!" Fortunately we had kept a box of cookies from one of the paper bags that had been handed to us in the back seat but was then taken away to the van. Ann showed them to Lee. He said, "Go on and open them if you want to." The cookies were shared among the passengers, everyone eating some of them but Lee, who declined. "No, thank you," he said, "the apples were good for me." His mood was now mild and sweet, with no trace of the frustration of the earlier scenario.

We arrived in the international and cosmopolitan city of Geneva around six forty-five in the evening. The van and car behind us seemed to have disappeared in traffic. Maybe they were looking for a parking place, we theorized. Lee pulled the small car up to the curb in front of the six-story building where the talk would be held. It was a busy metropolitan corner, with cars going past, much honking of horns, people walking their dogs.

"Get out, quick, quick, quick! Just get the boxes unloaded—hurry!" he yelled at the three backseat occupants. The boxes were stacked on the concrete sidewalk, quickly, as Lee zoomed off with Jean Pierre to find parking. The talk space was six floors up—a yoga center on the top floor. The boxes, this time about eight or nine of them, were hauled into the building and stacked on the floor in the hallway foyer. Then they had to be re-stacked in the elevator, which was done with the help of a very fresh-faced young French woman who appeared as if out of nowhere, saying that she had come for Lee's talk. Soon Lee appeared walking briskly down the street with Jean Pierre and began hoofing it up the stairs with his students while one person took the small elevator up with the books.

The woman who ran the yoga center—a disciple of Arnaud Desjardins—greeted Lee warmly and gave him a quick tour of the place. The room was a renovated attic with skylights and exposed, thick old wood beams. The low dais was set up with flowers, a *zabuton* and zafu for Lee. A large picture of Yogi Ramsuratkumar, which had been brought from Freiburg, was placed on the dais right away. The room had been set up so that the audience had a choice between chairs in the back and zafus on the floor in front of Lee.

Lee immediately got to work on the book table, the arrangement of which must have happened in some kind of record time. It seemed like only seconds later he was scouting out the place and pointing out the sandwiches that were waiting for us in a back room of the center. A large round loaf of fresh bread had been carved out, and nestled down in its ample bowl and kept fresh by the top of the bread, which was used like a lid, were probably three dozen half-sandwiches. These were filled with an assortment of salmon, pate, black olive spread, cheese—each one delicious. Lee ate four or five of them very rapidly, then polished off a fresh grapefruit that had been brought for him from the Freiburg apartment kitchen. So this was what being "at the mercy of our hosts" meant, I thought. The provisions were very satisfying and the *lila* of it all quite delightful. When one goes empty-handed and open-minded into new situations with Lee, this is usually the result—the Universe, as Lee might say, or the blessing of Yogi Ramsuratkumar, is bountiful in giving what is needed. But where was everyone else?

Lee's other students, who had been following behind in the van and second car, finally arrived. They came in and looked at the sandwiches with crestfallen faces. No one ate anything. When asked if they wanted to eat, Mariana said, "We stopped and ate something on the way here, so we're not hungry." She had a baleful look on her face as she continued, "As soon as I saw those sandwiches, my heart dropped. Immediately, without even thinking about it, my lack of trust was so obvious. I knew we'd made a big mistake." She shrugged, "We missed it! I should have known better."

She described how the van had just arrived in Geneva and someone said, "Let's go to the sandwich shop." She said she had a strong feeling that she should go up to the yoga center instead, but because someone who was a senior practitioner had suggested it, she allowed herself to be pulled along with the group, saying to herself, "Oh well, I guess he's probably right." Two other people mentioned that they were having misgivings about getting something to eat, but shrugged it off as well. It's not that the senior practitioner was to blame, it was a case of blind following—deferring to an idea of "seniority" without thinking for one's self. As she said, "All of it just happened so fast and so unconsciously."

It was one of those opportunities to travel the way Lee travels—like a beggar. He regularly casts his fate to Divine Influence, which is what he was hinting at when he said, "We are at the mercy of our hosts." He does not like to ask for special things, extra food, more blankets, nice pillows, or anything else. Every time one of his students makes special requests of their hosts, Lee visibly cringes. It goes against his practice, his sensibility and sensitivity to the Law of Hospitality. But beyond the Law of Hospitality—what it means to be a good guest or a good host—there is the consideration of beggary, an obscure principle of practice in the Western Baul Way, and yet one which Lee is constantly making teaching lessons in regard to. In fact these teaching lessons have been made over and over again, and will continue to be made. Part of the regret Lee's students were experiencing when they saw the sandwiches was that when one is given food as a gift, it is blessed. For the Bauls of Bengal, begging, or *madhukari*, is a sacred practice. Any food or gift that is given becomes *prasad*, and not only is the one who is begging blessed by partaking of such a thing, but the giver also receives blessings.

Lee began the talk, as usual, exactly on time. The entire room was packed with people who sat on pillows on the floor or on chairs and stools. Some of them leaned against the walls or perched on any spare surface they could find. There were about ninety people, a mixed and interesting crowd of all ages that seemed very willing to pack into the space that grew hotter by the moment in the sultry August evening. Most looked wizened or well experienced in some way, or as if they were living an unconventional life somehow. Lee was sparkling, obviously in high spirits, as he sat down on his zafu and began to speak.

"*Vous m'excusez, je parle anglais ce soir,*" Lee said, then paused with a smile. "Nobody understands my French!" Everyone laughed heartily. We were off to a good start.

"Usually we give a public talk a particular title to bring people to the talk, but I never talk about the subject matter! I thought I'd break with tradition tonight and actually talk about the subject matter listed on the flyer, which I think is the first time in the history of my teaching work that I've actually done that!

"The title is 'Love, Sex and Transformation.'" Lee laughed. "First I should say that this picture is of my Master. His name is Yogi Ramsuratkumar. He is still alive and lives in

India. He never travels. Actually He never travels out of His small town in India; He's been there for about forty years and that is where He stays.

"I'm very pleased to be here tonight. It's my first time in Geneva. I hope that as an audience, you prove to be more French than Swiss." There were some loose chuckles scattered around the room at this. "Or perhaps each town is a little different. I've been in Zurich and Basel so far . . .

"So, 'Love, Sex and Transformation!' " Lee paused again and looked over his audience, then with the timing of a seasoned comedian, plunged into the joke about the man who tells his wife he's been attached by a dog. A number of people laughed loudly.

"Have you heard about the brand new, ultra-sensitive condom? After the man is finished, it stays around and talks to the woman." Another burst of laughter, from the audience and Lee. It was clear he wouldn't have to do much to establish rapport with this crowd. They were already attuned to his style.

"In the Baul tradition human sex is considered to be a symbol of union with God. I should say before I go on that I might use the word 'tantra' tonight, but you can be pretty sure that what I mean by it and what all these workshops that are given on tantra and tantric sex mean by it are totally and completely different. Anyone who gives a workshop and calls it 'tantric sex' is a liar and a thief and a charlatan, without question. There is no one who gives a workshop on tantric sex who is actually teaching tantra. No one. So, in case I use that word, please don't associate my use of that word with all of that shit out there. And if any of you in this room teach those workshops, I apologize for insulting you. I'm sure, not having gone to your workshop, that *you* are probably the exception to the rule!" This last comment was dripping with sarcasm. The audience laughed again. They were loving it. Lee launched into another joke.

"This couple decides to go on vacation to St. Tropez. They are lying out on the beach naked, when all of a sudden a wasp flies in between the woman's legs and up inside her vagina. So, of course, they are a little worried. Very carefully they get up and get dressed and go to a doctor. They explain the situation to the doctor and he says, 'Wow, I've never seen such a thing. This is an unusual situation. Well, look, come in the back, I think I have an idea. I think I have a solution.' This is such an unusual situation that the doctor calls all his nurses into the room. He says to the man, 'This is what we're going to do. You get undressed and we're going cover your sex with honey and you just stick it in your wife and the wasp will come to the honey and very slowly you pull it out. No problem.' Okay. So the woman gets undressed, the man gets undressed. She lies on the table. But the doctor is watching, the nurses are watching. The husband can't get an erection. Wouldn't you guys be embarrassed under such a circumstance?" Lee looked at a dark-haired, bulky hunk of a man who was sitting on the front row smiling broadly. He pointed toward him and said, "Well, *he* wouldn't!" Everyone laughed loudly, including and maybe especially the man.

"The husband looks at the doctor and says, 'What am I gonna do?' The doctor says, 'Well, look. It's a very unusual circumstance. In my professional capacity as a doctor, you understand, perhaps I could do the thing.' The husband is a little unsure, but he's worried about his wife, and she's extremely worried. She doesn't want to get stung. So the man says to the doctor, 'Okay, let's try it.' Of course, the doctor—he's *French*—he has no problem getting an erection!" Another wave of laughter at Lee's insinuations. "So he covers himself with honey. I think they have to test French doctors for that before they give them their diploma!" More laughter.

"So the doctor slips it in and they are just lying there for a minute. And slowly the woman starts to move a little bit and the doctor starts to move a little bit and the woman starts to move a little more and the doctor starts to move a little more. And before you know it the woman is gasping and moaning and the doctor's panting and," Lee made heavy panting and breathing noises to demonstrate, "the husband says, 'Hey! Hey! What's going on?' The doctor looks up for minute and says, 'First plan didn't work. I'm going to plan B. We're gonna drown the little fucker!' " Loud guffaws of laughter came from certain members of the audience, while others laughed along with Lee, chuckled to themselves or sat with smiles on their faces.

"So," Lee was still laughing, seeming to enjoy the audience, which was still laughing with him, "thank you all for laughing! One time I told all these jokes and no one laughed. It wasn't in France, of course . . . it was in Quebec.

"In the Baul tradition—I know I said this before, but I want to say it again in case we've forgotten—union between man and woman is symbolic for union between the human being and God. The Bauls are a group of yogic practitioners from Bengal, India. Rather than renouncing any aspect of life, their philosophy is to embrace all natural forms of life—sex and eating and song and dance and enjoyment of life. This is essentially traditional tantricism. There are different specific sects of tantra—Buddhist tantra and Hindu tantra and Shakti tantra and yoga tantra—but basically the essential thread of similarity between them is that all things that are created are Divine. To reject any aspect of life as if it were sinful is actually to reject an aspect of God. In paths of orthodox renunciation, money is considered to be the root of all evil, sex is considered to be sinful, eating meat, drinking wine—all that is considered to be sinful, meaning against God.

"There are two approaches with the practice of sex between a man and a woman as a symbol for union between a human being and God. One is the approach of the freeing-up of passion, the release of expression; the other is the approach of the containment of passion, using the containing of that energy as alchemical fuel. Both paths work with conservation of orgasm in the male partner and release of orgasm in the woman partner. Either of those two dynamics can be successful—the criteria for success being resonance with the Divine, or Reality, not great sex. Great sex may be a secondary effect of the process, but that's not the aim.

"Every one of us, whether we know it or not, has been drawn to the path—whatever your particular path is—whether you have a teacher or don't have a teacher. We are all seeking union, and really in the actual sense of things we already are one with God. So, when I use the phrase 'union with God,' I don't mean we as a separate entity enter union with a bigger, separate entity. Union with God is a phrase used in the context of the path of adoration that signifies the realization of truth. So don't be mislead by the implication of the language. It's just a phrase that is used within a particular context. It may sound separative, but it isn't. It means the realization of truth, here and now, as we are, because God is not somewhere else. God is not in the past. God is not in the future. God is not in some other dimension. God is here and now, as we are. Since most of us desire sex in one form or another, hopefully in fairly healthy forms . . . although looking around the room I can tell there are a few perverts here and there!" Delighted laughter filled the room. Lee smiled, obviously enjoying himself. For some reason, the crowd tonight, in contrast to the audiences in Basel and Zurich, was on his wavelength.

"I was having to look away so I wouldn't be staring at anyone . . ." More laughter from Lee and the crowd as he teased everyone. "Don't worry! I won't expose your cover. Your secret is safe with me!

"When we find the path we all have to begin transformation somewhere. We can only begin where we are. We can't start in some advanced state. If we are in the grip of some neurosis, as we all are in some way, that means that our lives are not our own. The neurosis defines our thoughts, our speech, our actions, our likes and dislikes and so on. That is true to varying degrees for all of us, myself included. If it wasn't true of me, I'd be where He is—and I'm not." Lee gestured to the photograph of Yogi Ramsuratkumar.

"To begin practice with some very high and refined esoteric technology is useless because all refined esoteric technology is designed to be applied after we have dealt with the grip of neurosis. If we have not resolved this dominance, if we are still under it, to use this refined technology will create something twisted. It will not create what the technology is designed to produce. Most people who call themselves a guru or a master are completely deluded. The charlatans who take advantage of and abuse people who are naive enough to become their disciples often begin with very genuine intentions. They have the same intentions most of us have; they want to see humanity be healthier and more in balance. They want to serve God. They want to help heal individuals and the planet. But somewhere in their process, in their practice, they begin to use very highly refined esoteric technology—Hindu yogic or Buddhist yogic technology. Much of it is described in fairly accurate books that are commonly available to anyone these days. Although, that bullshit you learn in tantric workshops is just about total self-indulgence. It's not really esoteric technology.

"What happens is that this technology works with an energetic field that is not yet prepared for the actual power of the technology. Two things happen simultaneously: the technology produces a state of consciousness that looks and feels like a genuine state of higher consciousness, of clarity, of awakening, of realization. The other thing it does simultaneously is push all the energy into aspects of neurosis that have not been dealt with consciously. If you fill a balloon with air and the balloon has a weak spot in it, that is where the balloon will break as soon as there is too much air in it. There is a saying in English: 'A chain is only as strong as its weakest link.' This refined technology accesses far, far greater sources of energy than an individual human has been prone to use for our ordinary daily lives. And all of that energy goes into undealt with areas of neurosis; instead of dissolving the neurosis it exaggerates and dramatizes it.

"So, if someone who hasn't dealt with abusive tendencies or abusive sexuality in themselves becomes a teacher, and all of a sudden there are trusting disciples sitting in front of them worshipping every word out of their mouth and trusting every action they make, their neurosis takes advantage of the circumstance. Their neurosis may move them in the direction of sexual abuse—having sex with men, women and children with complete disregard for the suffering that it creates, the harm that it causes and the disillusionment that it produces in people who don't realize what's actually going on. Or their neurosis may show up in abuses of power and money."

For years Lee has criticized teachers who claim degrees of realization they don't have. The dangers of prematurely assuming the role of teacher has been demonstrated many times, in particular in the past two decades in the Western world. In the past few years there has been a virtual explosion of new "spiritual teachers" making outrageous claims and offers of instant or quick enlightenment, bliss, liberation. The kind of self-delusion that generates such deception is something Lee rails out against often. It seems to be one of the reasons he goes to such lengths to continually deconstruct the myth that grows around him; he does this in part by demonstrating his ordinary humanity and his commitment to a life of discipline, practice and integrity, and in part by acting the fool, the rascal, the gutter-mouthed provocateur.

Lee is a teacher who has been thrust into the guru function by the power of his own surrender to the Will of God as a result of his relationship with Yogi Ramsuratkumar, and yet he maintains a fierce and fastidious relationship to practice. When he could, even lawfully, place himself "beyond" it all, he adheres religiously to the rhythm and discipline of daily practice—most obviously vegetarian diet and meditation, but by observation his practice extends into every domain of action and relationship. The rigor of his dietary practice alone—predominantly raw food—requires daunting discipline, but he maintains it with what appears to be simple ease. Although he often says, "Don't use me as an example," and "Do as I say, not as I do," he provides a stellar example in the domain of discipline, commitment to practice and integrity in relationship with his family, friends, peers and students. In fact, Lee's advocacy for conscious child raising is legion, and he is a living example of what he teaches in this regard.

At the same time Lee walks a very fine line in his criticisms of others. In his book, *Holy Madness*, Georg Feuerstein used Lee Lozowick as an example of the crazy-wise teacher as divine fool. The path of the divine fool is completely intertwined with paradoxes, and is particularly misunderstood in postmodern times, when there is very little understanding of crazy wisdom, much less the specific manifestation of crazy wisdom that appears in the divine fool. Lee's antics provoke everyone, and in the process he actually creates a ground of work for himself in which he is dancing through the projections, outrage, disgust and false ideas of who he is and what he is doing.

His crazy behavior in public talks and seminars, for example, do not support our ideas of the holy man, or even begin to approach our projections and expectations of a self-realized human being. One might observe Lee superficially in these situations and react with fear and dismay, or charge, "You are hardly in any position to criticize these other teachers—look at how *you* are!" The smoke screen of divine foolishness serves many purposes; primarily it is a teaching device found in many traditions—the Fools for Christ, the Native American *heyoka* or contrary, the shamanistic clown. Lee's cheeky clowning around actually dismembers us and discombobulates the mind; the strange combination of foolishness and wisdom marks the paradox of his character as a divine fool and is a coincidence of opposites that strikes a deadly blow to the prison of the diehard, linear mind. But the clowning fool of the theatrical tradition has always worn a different face just below the surface of smiles and guffaws, and it is out of this depth of feeling and awareness that the cream pie in the face becomes more succinct than all the philosophy in the world.

Undeterred by the power of the prevailing conventional flatworld view or the praise or blame of his critics and supporters, Lee continues to speak loudly to critical issues of spiritual life in his inimitable way. Now he turned his talk toward the need to remain ordinary: "So, we have to start where we are. Before we can start where we are, we have to *see* where we are. Very basic, very obvious, very ordinary. We don't begin with dealing with our neuroses; we begin with looking at ourselves and we continue to observe ourselves until we can see ourselves exactly as we are and accept that. Seeing ourselves is the first step; accepting ourselves as we are is the second step, because some of the things you find will be wonderful, and some of the things you find will be not so wonderful.

"What you want is truth or reality—not just an appearance of things that is very different than your habitual appearance. Most people presume if they're doing some kind of spiritual practice and the form of their life changes that the practice is being successful because they associate a change in form with actual change. When there is actual change the form might change, but the two are not equated. Many people who we would consider to be great masters look exactly the same as masters as they did when they were just completely unconscious individuals.

"Then the question is, 'What is the difference?' Context! One minute we're under illusion and the next minute we are in Reality. Of course, when you're living in the context of Reality the perceived or recognizable or felt difference is like the difference between night and day. But it doesn't necessarily look any different.

"We see a Tibetan and we think that just because they are Tibetan they've got to be some kind of spiritual giant. We are bowing to them when they are nobody, and we don't know the difference. All we see is the difference in form and right away we're running after them, 'Give me an initiation, bless me, oh great master!' "

Speaking to the disciples of Arnaud Desjardins who were in the audience, he added, "This is why most of you take Arnaud for granted—because he looks just like you! Maybe he's more elegant, more refined, and maybe he's a little wiser. But if you really understood who Arnaud was you wouldn't be running after every divine mother because she's been born in India, and every Tibetan and every la de da de da. You would understand that Arnaud can give you everything they can give you, and more. If only you knew how to get it! It's not that if you accidentally run into one of these divine mothers on the street you wouldn't greet her with the utmost honor and respect. But it's the running after people and the taking of initiations in paths that are not your own that is problematical. When you mess around with large energies that are not the energies of your chosen path, all you can do is get into difficulty. Not only do you insult your teacher and your path, but you mix energies that can produce very toxic results.

"That principle is a principle of the tantric path also. You have one master, one path. You may respect teachings from many sources, of course. But you do not take initiation or get involved in other esoteric practices because that energy will disrupt and interfere with the delicate matrix that your teacher and your path is building in you. In this case, more is not necessarily better. When you work with a teacher, that teacher builds a foundation in you upon which the teaching can take root and thrive. While that foundation is being constructed—and the building of that foundation can take many years, depending upon whether we are receptive to that construction or resisting it and interrupting it—it's a very delicate process. Only your teacher understands the delicacy of it and is able to complete the construction effectively. If you take the delicate foundation that your teacher is building in you to another master on another path—a master who would like nothing better than to have you as their student regardless of your teacher, who couldn't care less about respecting and honoring your work with your teacher—it's like taking a car that's missing some of its vital parts out on the highway and driving at a hundred and ninety kilometers an hour. Something is going to happen and it's not pleasant.

"I'd like to spend the rest of the time tonight answering questions rather than just continuing to talk. I realize that I've barely scratched the surface of the subject matter, but another hour wouldn't change that. Love, sex and transformation is a subject matter that ideally we would have twenty or thirty hours together to cover. Even that would be only a foundation."

A man asked the first question. "I have a question about what's happening nowadays in the media, on television, about sexuality. How can we deal with all that overwhelming baggage of pictures, in every sense? Ads on the wall, films on TV, violence and sexual excess."

Lee nodded and said, "Good question."

The man continued, "My question is, could it be that in ten years or twenty years people would get fed up with it and find some other solution? Is it possible? What's your vision about that?"

"So, first of all, to establish a context, Gurdjieff said that human beings eat three levels of food: gross food, or the food we eat when we sit down for dinner or lunch; subtle food which comes to us through breathing, which is much more than the physical elements of the air like oxygen and hydrogen; and the third level of food, which applies to this question, is impression food, or everything that we take in through the physical senses. Everything we hear, see, taste is all impression food, plus the sixth sense; everything we take in psychically is impression food. Impression food effects us the same way physical food effects us. You all know what happens to your body when you eat too much, or eat the wrong combination, or eat food that is bad. There are foods that are poisoned by some kind of virus or parasite. If you've ever traveled through a third world country and had dysentery you know how strongly you can be affected by a parasite that happens to ride along with the gross food that you eat.

"The sexual impressions that we receive, many of which imply or actually represent violence and sex together, are constantly on television. You can't open a magazine without seeing these same impressions. The advertisements on billboards, on the covers on books—it's everywhere. This is impression food. It can't help but affect you. When you are not conscious about its effects, the effects are toxic. You begin to become more perverse about your sexuality. You begin to make unconscious assumptions about sex that can actually destroy your life. So, I agree with you that it's a very unhealthy circumstance, and I think things are getting worse.

"If things get bad enough it will start to turn around, but I don't think we've seen the worst of it yet. You said in ten or twenty years, but maybe in thirty or forty, unfortunately. I think things are bad now, very bad, but we are completely unconscious, both about how bad things are, and about why they are as bad as they are. 'We' meaning humanity. Not the few people who understand.

"There are two intelligent responses to the situation as it is. We can't necessarily stop it. It's too pervasive. And in fact, it's controlled by economic and political and social forces that are way beyond us. But every individual has a personal responsibility. The first aspect of your personal responsibility is to learn about impression food, how it works, what it does, what it is. If you know it when you perceive it, it will not have the same effect. It has the effect it has because it goes into your unconscious. If you can keep it conscious, it will not have the same effect.

"Another thing you can begin to do, any time, even starting tomorrow morning, is to start to bring discrimination to the impression food that you ingest. If you're riding on the Metro in Paris, you're going to see the ads on the sides of the walls. So, there is a certain amount of impression food that, no matter what you do, you will take in. But you don't have to go after it and gorge yourself on it.

"If you are driving down the highway and you are going to buy a magazine, you could buy 'Geo,' or you could buy one of those magazines with all the naked women in provocative poses with gigantic breasts leaping off the pages. Now, you might be provoked and titillated by the magazine with naked women. But you have no idea what that impression food is doing to your worldview, to your perception of life. We like the things that keep us enslaved to our neuroses. We're attracted to them. We desire them. We enjoy them. They feel good. And they are *killing* us, and our children and our grandchildren. So you can begin to discriminate in your personal life about what impression food you spend your time eating.

"If you go to Paris and you have three hours to kill—excuse me, I don't know Geneva, so I'm talking about something I know—you can go to the Louvre or you can go to a sex shop in Place Pigalle. If you go to the Louvre, you'll get one kind of impression. If you go to a sex shop and watch a video, or a dance show, you'll have another kind of impression food. One will be healthy, one will be unhealthy. The thing about unhealthy food is that it doesn't get to you right away. You can eat McDonald's food for thirty or forty years before you have your heart attack, and until you have your heart attack it feels like you're perfectly healthy. But that food is building up weakness in you. It is poisoning you, slowly, so you don't notice it until the poison becomes great enough to have its effect. The same is true of negative impression food. When you read your pornographic magazines, and you say, 'This isn't hurting anything, this is not hurting anybody, I don't rape anybody, I don't beat anybody up, I enjoy healthy sex,' it's still poisoning you and you won't notice it until the poison gets to a large enough volume to have its effect."

A woman sitting on a chair in one of the back rows raised her hand. She said, "What is the advice you would give to someone who is attracted by pornography?"

Lee answered, "To discover what is underlying that attraction. To try to withdraw, cold turkey . . . Do you know what cold turkey is, in English? Cold turkey means when you stop a drug addiction without any chemical help, like with heroine. You just stop and that's it. To try and stop an addiction cold turkey rarely works; to fight against something gives it more force.

"Instead of running away from it, run toward it as fast as you can run. But that doesn't mean do more of it; it means gain clarity. You ask yourself, 'What is this? Why am I so attracted, where did it come from, what's the payoff? What do I get from it?' Essentially I would suggest self-investigation. Simply look into the matter, clearly. Self-investigation but no self-judgement. Not, 'Oh, this is bad. I shouldn't enjoy it. I feel so guilty.' That burden only makes the situation unworkable. So don't look at it as a problem, but as simply something that you don't know as much as you could about, and you want to find out everything that you can about it. You observe yourself the way you would observe anything you were curious about. You know, if you were curious about the esoteric symbolism of the stained glass windows at Chartres, you'd get large pictures of the windows and you'd study them in every detail, in a mood of receptivity and openness, so the symbols could reveal themselves to you. That is the way you study yourself—no guilt, no blame, no judgement. Just with an innocent curiosity to know, to discover."

"In the society in which we live," she continued, "where guilt and so on are so strong around this issue, what tools would you give to a person to help them unglue themselves from that, so they can observe it rather than be impacted by it each time?"

Lee responded, "I wouldn't give anyone any tools; I would recommend a certain attitude—the attitude of intention. The strength of your intention will generate within you the necessary antidotes to guilt, fear, shame and self-hatred. If you want to pierce this knot, to untie this knot badly enough, *intention* is what generates the means. But you have to want to untie the knot badly enough, because every one of us has all the tools inside us. If tools are superimposed upon what we already have, they may have some effect in the short run, but in the long run they will tend to be counterproductive.

"Secondly, there is no substitute in the universe for the regard or the Blessing Force of the genuine spiritual master. That quality of what we could call Grace is totally mysterious, irrational, untraceable. In itself, it is completely intangible. The reality of it is seen in the experience of those in its path. I don't know if you have a teacher or have had one or are looking for one, or don't want one. Or if you are one yourself. Why not? I think that covers all the options. But there is a quality of help in that relationship of master and disciple that we can't get anywhere else—not in therapy, not from our family, not from love. It is a quality that is unique to human relationship. That relationship adds a divine possibility to the human intention that we give the situation. God working alone has a certain power; human beings working alone have a certain power. Put them together and the power is exponentially increased."

A man sitting on the floor halfway toward the back of the room spoke. "Hearing what you say about the teacher and the importance of that relationship I come to my question, of course, with Yvan and his passing away. I'd like to hear you speak about this for his pupils."

"At Yvan's funeral," Lee began, "Arnaud said something very important. It's a principle of relationship with masters that when they die, their external death is their internal birth within their disciples. There are one of two things which are possible, and which of those two things will be most effective depends on the disciple. A good disciple may find another teacher—but not to replace their teacher, simply to give them a circumstance in which to apply what it is that their teacher is still giving them. A lot of good disciples feel their master within them when the master is alive, but there really is a difference.

"Irina Tweedie just died, by the way, two days ago on August 23, for those of you who know about Irina Tweedie. She once said that until her master died, she had no idea what he had given her, because as long as he was alive she never gave him a chance to really blossom in her. A good disciple will allow the blossoming of that with receptivity and attention.

"When we are raising a child, the child will tell us what it needs. All we have to do is be receptive to the child's messages. The same is true of the birth of our guru within us. If we think we know it all, we aren't hearing the messages. We aren't going to perceive the messages the guru in us is giving us. But if we allow this birth to grow and mature, then we'll continue to get a steady stream of help, communication, revelation . . . all of it. As long as we don't start thinking it's *us*. But a good disciple wouldn't think such a thing.

"An immature disciple may find it actually necessary to find another teacher because of their inability to allow the birth of their master within them to blossom and mature as he or she inevitably will. So one might still need an external source of feedback."

The next question was, "What is devotion?"

"Devotion is dedication to the path. Dedication can show up in several different moods: a feeling mood, an emotional mood, a thinking mood. So, people are one of three organic types. It has nothing to do with psychology, nothing to do with astrology, nothing to do with karma. Very briefly, we are one of three types: hot, cold or indifferent. The hot type of dedication is passionate. We swear to give our life for our master, throw ourselves at their feet whenever we see them. The cool type of dedication is very matter-of-fact; we make a decision, 'This is my teacher. I'm going to practice and serve the path.' And we do that without fanfare, without drama. We just simply go and do it. And then there is the indifferent type of devotion, in which one just sort of sits there, metaphorically speaking. We're just sitting there loving the master, like a bump on a log. In the Indian tradition they call these three tendencies *sattvic, rajasic,* and *tamasic. Tamasic* is indifferent, *rajasic* is hot and *sattvic* is cool. If you see a spiritual master who is a *sattvic* type, they are very serene, very peaceful. Nothing bothers them. They are always observing everything impartially. The *rajasic* type of spiritual master is yelling, doing things, jumping around, grabbing their disciples and throwing them against the wall. The *tamasic* type of spiritual master is like Shiva Bala Yogi. He sat in the same place for fourteen years without moving, and he got to be eight hundred pounds! He never cut his hair, so his hair was about four meters long. He was a big, fat, gigantic guy; he just sat on the bed like a big hunk of meat, with Blessing Force pouring out of him. But the body was totally indifferent.

"Okay! If there are other questions that did not get asked, I will be at the book table as long as people are back there looking and buying. I'd be very happy to speak to any of you informally; ask your questions there and I'll continue to blather on. There are books and music from our community bands and some cassette tape sets of seminars that I've given in France and Quebec, which are in French and English. It's quite warm up here, so thank you very much for sitting in this room for two hours and paying attention and being patient."

Lee turned to his hostess and said, "And thank you very much for letting us use this space. It's a very beautiful space." He turned to Claire, the translator and said humorously, "And thank *you* very much for the translation!" To the audience, which was laughing hard and clapping enthusiastically, he said, "And thank you very much for the talk. *Thank you!*" Lee laughed, got up from the dais and threaded his way very slowly through the thick crowd, stopping to talk with different people, slapping them gently on the back and smiling.

When he got to the book table where a crowd was already gathered, he wrote in magic marker on the magnetic board on the wall behind it, "*Les livres, cassettes et CDs sont incroyables, magnifiques et fantastiques!*" He laughed and smiled, turning to the people who were already flooding up to ask questions. For an hour he signed books and talked with each person who waited patiently for an opportunity to speak with him. He had two or three of his students helping him take money and chat with people. The mood of the whole space was heightened and lively, warm and generous. People looked brightened and invigorated. While Lee worked the swarming book table, his students were involved in numerous conversations that sprung up around the room with people who lingered for almost an hour.

The woman who managed the yoga center and her husband, both of whom had met Lee before at Hauteville, were bright-eyed and happy. It had been a good night. One got the distinct feeling that Lee would be coming back to Geneva again next year to give another talk. As he walked away from the book table he came up to some of his students and said, "I've redeemed myself!" referring to the glum talk of the night before.

"Do you want to get ice cream?" Lee asked a few of us enthusiastically, his eyes sparkling. Sure, was the reply. He instructed us to gather with everybody downstairs on the sidewalk and let people know that we would go get ice cream as soon as the books were packed up and brought down.

Moments later down on the street in the night lights of the city, Lee started making a plan for ice cream. "I want an ice cream *parlor*," Lee said clearly and precisely, "Would you find out where there might be one?" He turned to asked Claire. She ran back upstairs to ask Lee's hosts and in moments returned with one of them, who joked around with us about Americans liking ice cream. He instructed, "Walk a few blocks that way toward the lake and you will find lots of ice cream places, and Häagen-Dazs—you like Häagen-Dazs?" Yes, several people replied.

Lee said definitively, "I'm looking for an ice cream *parlor*, not an ice cream stand."

"Yes, yes, go that way and you'll find lots of places along the lake," the man insisted.

Lee and his entire entourage headed down a dark side street and in two or three blocks came to the vast lake, glittering with reflected light from the farther shore. About seventy-five meters away was a brightly lit kiosk with a counter for ordering and picnic tables set in an orderly fashion under a festive canopy strung with lights. Overhead were leafy trees by the lake where sailboats were docked. It looked fairly inviting. Lee and three others ran over to it. It had possibility, but Lee took one look at it—it did have Häagen-Dazs ice cream—and said, "No, that's not what I'm looking for." Disappointed, we walked back and rejoined the group. Clearly there were other ice cream stands like this one, but no ice cream *parlors* anywhere up or down the darkened lake.

As he rejoined the rest of the group Lee called to Claire, who had translated his talk into French tonight, and who often finds herself in the position of being a liaison for Lee with the French-speaking world. "Claire!" he yelled. She came running up. He seemed to be instructing everyone, and making it clear she should pay particular attention, about a specific principle of how he works.

"If it's not an ice cream *parlor*, I don't want it!" his voice penetrated the atmosphere. "It's no good. I don't want an ice cream stand. Claire, ambiance is *everything*—you know what I mean?" Claire nodded, listening intently.

The whole group, about fifteen people, stood clustered around him on the empty street corner by the lake in the rather sultry night as he held forth. "I *never* want ice cream, or sausage, or coffee, or hamburgers, or whatever, unless the ambiance is right! Why would I want to eat another one thousand calories of pure fat unless there is a purpose? The *ambiance* has to be right." He took off walking as fast as he could back toward where the cars were parked. Jean Pierre walked beside him, seeming to soak up the opportunity to be so close to the man who has such an extraordinary relationship with his own teacher, Arnaud Desjardins.

The intense feeling of pure focus that radiated off of Lee's back as he stalked up the street could be construed as frustration, but looking more closely it was clear that was only my projection. No, it was something else, some unfathomable sense of purpose, timing, necessity, obligation. Every detail seemed to be strung by fine wire from this immense sense of purpose, and if the detail did not resonate with that purpose, the wire was unsentimentally snapped in two. We walked fast to keep up with Lee to get to the car, which was uphill from the lake. Lee directed the rest of the crowd to the van and second car and said, "We'll see if we can find something on the way out of town."

Back in the car as we suggested various café or restaurant possibilities, Lee said, "I really want ice cream and not just dessert." We drove along the lake toward the main boulevard of the city, the lights glimmering about a half mile away. Overhead the full moon glowed behind black vaporous patches of cloud. The van and second car drove along behind him. It seemed like he was going all out for this *soirée*. Usually if it's this much trouble he abandons the idea, but tonight it seemed he was in pursuit of something. Turning onto one of the main streets along the other side of the lake there were a few restaurants open along the now well-lit streets, but nothing that even vaguely resembled an ice cream parlor. Cruising along and looking while he drove, he finally gave into what seemed to be the inevitable and said, "Nope—that's it. We'll do without it!" and zoomed off into the night.

August 26, 1999
Le Rozet

This morning before breakfast, as we stood waiting in the room where meals would be held during the seminar over the weekend, Lee explained to his traveling party what the set-up would be. "I'll be sitting here with my family and Josette and Jean Pierre," he indicated the table that was set now for breakfast, "and there will be a buffet table set up there," he pointed toward the breakfast buffet set up along one wall on the other side of the room. "The way it works is that there will be a lot of people here for the weekend, and the deal is," his eyes flickered briefly with a devilish gleam, *whoever gets in the food line first gets the most food!* Lee's students stood in a slightly embarrassed silence, taking this in. It was obviously a teaching communication that seemed to go along with so many he'd made over the summer, about his students being pigs and having no manners, eating everything in sight and so on. There also seemed to be a hint about last night's food wars, having to do with the level of scarcity that most people have in relationship to food. No one said a word, but looked at Lee solemnly. Then Dasya laughed and started making pig noises. "Pigs to the trough!" he laughed, as others joined in.

It was a quiet day for a change, a welcomed break from the hectic pace Lee had been keeping. He played bridge most of the afternoon, and after dinner the whole group took off for his public talk in La Chaux de Fonds, about forty-five minutes away by car. Driving the van on the way to the talk Lee veered slightly off the road when he couldn't make the curve at the speed he was going. He commented, "A little too enthusiastic—just a little too enthusiastic." Jean Pierre sat in the front seat again, directing Lee through the French countryside with wordless, efficient, simple, clear gestures, right or left. He didn't try to engage Lee in idle conversation, but kept his attention focused and on the road ahead. He never flinched at any of Lee's driving quirks, and carried a presence of dignity and crisp attention. He struck me as the best navigator I'd seen with Lee so far.

Lee arrived at the building and we went through the usual ritual—carry heavy boxes upstairs, down hallways and into the room, watch Lee set up the book table, check out the room. After the table was set up Lee came over and said, "You want to go check out ice cream parlors?" Of course! Something nearby, he said, and he emphasized that he wanted an ice cream *parlor*, not an ice cream stand. "Or someplace that might work, where we can sit down and they serve a variety of ice cream." Three of us took off and scoured the streets, running into Sylvan and Mariana who were already out on the streets, on the look-out for ice cream parlors—just in case the spiritual master wanted to have ice cream after the talk. Finally a small restaurant three blocks away from the talk space was zeroed in on. Paula C. spoke in French to the waiter who affirmed, yes, they would be open late and a large group for dessert only was fine. The ice cream menu looked adequate, and they had a back room that could be used. Reporting the details back to Lee, he frowned and said, "We'll see."

The talk was in another executive conference room, with orderly rows of chairs, some of which had little fold-down or upright desktops for taking notes. An upstairs balcony with seats ran around four sides of the room; with the balcony included, the room could accommodate perhaps one hundred fifty people. As the space began to fill up, Lee stood in the balcony and danced, hanging on a pole and swinging his hips back and forth in a parody of the kind of burlesque dance that topless dancers do in the U.S. He grinned as he danced, looking down on the audience of about fifty, which was unaware of him, with the exception of a few of his students. A few moments later he appeared suddenly in his chair, ready to start the talk.

Lee began, "Welcome to the talk this evening. I'll talk a few minutes, then answer questions. If, as the talk goes on, you find yourself believing you know more than me, you should get up and leave immediately! I don't want to waste your time or my time. You don't want to listen to someone who knows less than you.

"Let's assume for a moment that I know more about the spiritual path than you. There are lots of things many of you in this room know more about than I do—politics, cooking, biology. I only have one area of expertise—I'm completely stupid in every other area but that of the spiritual path. I have no credentials, but I've been teaching for thirty years. I'll bet you don't believe it—I don't look a year over thirty-five!" Lee chucked and some hesitant laughter popped up around the room.

"I've been teaching for thirty years and I've learned some tricks. I've developed some skill based on those years of practice, but none of that is what's important tonight. I don't know what I know for any reason. Nobody taught me anything in this field; I didn't get it from books, I've had no spiritual experience, no visions, no mystical revelations, no kundalini rising. None. I know what I know only because I know. Even though I have no credibility, there are many masters—Tibetans, yogis, nondualist masters, Zen masters— who accept me as an equal. But then, others think those are idiots!

"In the spiritual field there is no agreement about the equality of teachers. I have no credibility in the ordinary sense of things. I know what I know only because I know what I know. I'm completely stupid about everything that doesn't have to do with transforma- tion! Ask my ex-wives! Why, I've destroyed more cooking pots and peed on more bath- room floors than you can imagine!"

Lee went into a lewd description of how men seem unable to aim correctly at the urinal or toilet bowl. "It doesn't matter whether they piss standing up or sitting down— it's a good thing men aren't using guns in there! Men can't aim!" Lee laughed at his derisive commentary, but no one else was laughing. Lee's tone had been raw and acidic up to this point.

"I have a living teacher, Yogi Ramsuratkumar. He lives in India, in the same city where He has lived for forty-six years . . ." He pointed to the color picture of Yogi Ramsuratkumar that was on the table at his side.

"There is one criteria for proving that I know what I know—that criteria rests in you. How you feel based on being in this space tonight would be a clear indication for whether I know what I know, or if I'm just bullshitting everybody. Though I've been doing this for thirty years, there are lots of charlatans who have been teaching a lot longer, so the ability of Westerners to discriminate is pretty low! Many end up with genuine masters like Arnaud Desjardins just because they're lucky. Human beings are so lacking in the ability to discriminate that we find the right master just by coincidence, by sheer luck! I should also say, by the way—before the questions begin—that under ordinary circumstances if a human being has the ability to discriminate accurately, the only criteria for deciding if the master is genuine is how you *feel* in relationship with that person. You can't believe the testimony of your friends—look at the idiots your friends have thought were great masters! Like Sun Myung Moon. Scientology. Imagine how little discrimination someone must have to believe in that!

"All of us will have some feeling response to this evening. Some will enjoy it and feel good; some will be bored and feel it's a waste of time; some will leave feeling aggressive and angry. We do not have an accurate understanding of what our feelings are. Gurdjieff was a spiritual genius whose behavior was intentionally provocative and designed to avoid the trap of having lots of stupid followers. If you study Gurdjieff you come to realize that mind can create what appears to be real feeling, but are only mental models of feeling. When most of us say, 'I feel happy, angry, sad, bored,' we have no idea what we are talking about because we don't know who we are. When I give a seminar that's one of the primary things we consider. But the point is, let's assume you came here tonight to learn something, not that I'm your teacher or that you even think I'm a genuine teacher. Maybe the notoriety of my reputation has proceeded me. Or perhaps you're reading one of my books and wanted to see what the author was like in person. Let's assume though that you came to learn something. If you really want to learn something you should know that just because somebody knows something doesn't mean he or she is a good teacher. What makes a good teacher is the ability to transmit or communicate what one knows.

"If you go to someone to learn something, you don't tell them how to give it to you; you take it however it's given. What's gone on tonight is a very effective form of communication. I would bet my fortune—which is very small! I spent most of it on my students!—that there are people here who are already thinking, 'I wish he would do things differently. Why is he insulting the audience? Why doesn't he say something useful?' I suggest that what is going on is, in my opinion, actually in my knowledge, the most effective way to communicate. You may want something besides what I want to communicate—something superficial, not challenging; something academic or scholarly, but something that will in no way compromise your illusions about who you are. I'm not *interested* in communicating that—if I was I'd be a professor of comparative religions in some university somewhere.

"If you really *heard* what I just said, you would be completely free of discomforting emotions right now. Your mind would be serene, relaxed, attentive, your body relaxed and receptive; your emotions would be still. But I am relatively sure that most of you don't meet those conditions. When I give a seminar there is something I want to communicate. Some of you have different paths, teachers, psychological conditions. Maybe many of you are more concerned with getting laid tonight when you get home than with learning something here. You're just here because the person you are with wanted to come— you just wanted to be humping, sweating, screaming," Lee demonstrated in gross terms, huffing and heaving his body. "Right? You don't just pop the old babe with equanimity, then roll over and have a cigarette, do you? You get *into* it, right? If you don't get into it, why take the chance of getting pregnant, staining the furniture, all that . . . I mean, sex is a risk—you could knock the lamp off the wall if you get too wild!"

People were dumbfounded. There were a few scant chuckles coming from Lee's students, but everyone else sat stony-faced, with the exception of a few who were smiling. "Or your red high heels that turn your man on so much could go through the window, broken glass falls three floors down and hits somebody walking along the street! All kinds of trouble! Not to mention somebody could be pregnant. You don't have any contraceptive, but you just can't control yourself, 'No, no, I need you *now!*' " Lee laughed sardonically. " 'I won't come inside you, I promise, I won't come inside you!' Fifteen minutes later—oops!"

In a high, hysterical voice, still acting out the scenario he was painting, Lee almost shrieked, " 'You said you wouldn't come in me!' "

Three people got up and left with disgust written all over their faces. The room was tense with a heavy silence broken only by Lee's antics. He watched the three people leave with an ironic smile on his face and then he deadpanned, "And I hadn't even gotten started yet on eliminatory functions!"

The fury seemed spent as Lee's tone changed to one of a man who is simply telling the truth. "All of you who have seen many of my talks know the truth of this: this rambling soliloquy on the provocative side of sex is very intentional. I want to assure you I have thirty years of experience in creating circumstances and exact situations to optimize a certain transmission I have to make. Some of my best disciples first came to a talk like this and left furious, swearing they'd never come close to me again, and found later that they had *seen* something about themselves that was so revelatory they couldn't attribute it to anything but the talk. So I assure you I know what I'm doing—that doesn't mean it's for everybody. In Zurich twenty percent of the crowd left, in Basel only ten percent, and last night we only lost two or three out of a good-sized crowd. But some people always leave because they are too psychologically defended to be able to look at themselves in a way other than their habitual way. I assure you what I am doing tonight is going to create self-reflection in you that you could never create for yourself.

"When we step onto the path, we make a certain commitment, consciously or unconsciously, to see ourselves as we are, here and now, in every moment. No progress on the path is possible without the foundation of seeing oneself with such ruthless self-honesty that there is no aspect left unseen. We enter the path our conscious aim might be realization, liberation, illumination—that's perfectly reasonable. Everyone deserves such a state of consciousness. If we want to realize that goal we have to enter into a certain relationship with our being. We are holistic creatures: mind, body, emotions, aura, etheric body, astral body—all of it together. If the mind gets enlightened and the body doesn't, you could end up in a mental institution. If the body gets enlightened and the mind doesn't, you could kill yourself with excess.

"So we begin by seeing who we are and accepting who we are here and now. Without this, any progress we make is illusory, or we are stuck. We have made this commitment to ourselves as we are, here and now. To be interested in high, esoteric technology is well and good, but first things first. I want to assure you that what I've said tonight is not arbitrary—it's very scientifically designed and the Scientist is God! Most of us think we know better than God. Sooner or later we have to find out that we don't. Well, you can start tonight.

"Okay, I've talked for an hour. I said one or two things that might be useful—if you were listening. Any questions? Yes, sir."

Lee's tone of voice had changed dramatically since several people had walked out of the talk. Although he was still direct and confrontive, his tone was now benign and kind, and he was smiling rather than smirking or scowling.

"What is spiritual transformation?" a man asked.

Lee answered, "A process, a living process that clarifies all misperceptions and illusion in consciousness. The body may not change, or it may. Spiritual transformation has nothing to do with physical health. Habits may change, or they may not, because spiritual transformation has nothing to do with psychology. Our politics may stay the same, unfortunately.

"So spiritual transformation is about clarifying illusions and misperceptions. I use the word God and say it has to do with the human being becoming divinized, but you don't have to use the word God. You can say the Universe, Reality, Truth. God is just a human word for Truth because it comforts us to imagine a greater Being taking care of us. Spiritual transformation has nothing to do with miracles, altered states of consciousness and all that."

Another man asked, "Does the repression of sexuality in monogamous relationship block spiritual growth?"

Lee responded, "Sex has nothing to do with spiritual transformation. There is such a thing as the transformational use of sexual energy, but it doesn't have to do with sex because lots of great masters were celibate and yet had extraordinary sexuality and transformation in their lives. We think if we can't fuck anyone we want to whenever we want to then we're repressed . . . so we blame monogamy. Sex has no relationship to spiritual transformation—sexual energy does have something to do with spiritual transformation. The external form of sex has nothing to do with whether we are using sexual energy transformationally or not."

"About the teaching of Yogi Ramsuratkumar . . ." one man began his question.

"Good—I'd love to talk about that!" Lee interjected with a smile.

"What are the main points?" the questioner concluded.

"I wouldn't call Him a Teacher although He does teach by the power of His presence," Lee said. "He never discourses, but He teaches by example. For instance, in 1979 I was visiting Him with some of my students." Lee then told the story of Yogi Ramsuratkumar asking each of Lee's students what their name was. Each one had been given a Sanskrit name that was the same as one of the characters in the Krishna tales. Each time Yogi Ramsuratkumar heard the name of the person, he would say, "Oohhhh," and nod his head, looking very impressed. Finally he turned to Lee and said, "And what is your name— Krishna?" and burst into peals of laughter, his whole body shaking with mirth.

Lee continued the story, "For the next two hours, every ten minutes or so He would turn and look at me and start laughing so hard that His body was quivering.

"He doesn't explain anything. Whatever is occurring is the circumstance He has created for that time and place. If I want to make use of what He has to offer I have to Pay Attention. He was saying to me that I had to be pretty presumptuous to give American people those names. I'm not yet who I am implying I am—or if ever! I had to look at something very closely when I realized what He was saying to me. So, He's not a teacher, but He teaches in the flow of things—lessons get made. He has one essential teaching— or at the heart of His communication there is one essential concept, which is that God is one, unitive, not separate. He goes into ecstatic swoons in which He will say, 'Father in Heaven is one, all, indivisible!' He will go on like that for five or ten minutes.

"There is a big difference between saying 'God is one' and having an ongoing, unbroken experience that God is one. Most people in this room have had some experience of that oneness; a lot of us have read books by Nisargadatta Maharaj or some other great Advaita Vedantist, and it resonates with us and we say 'yes.'

"Yogi Ramsuratkumar's Master was Swami Papa Ramdas. He lived in southwest India in Kerala state. He attributed his realization to repetition of a mantra. In the early 1950s when Yogi Ramsuratkumar was with Ramdas, He asked for initiation into the mantra and Ramdas gave it to Him. Yogi Ramsuratkumar did it heroically, like a warrior. It made Him mad—mad in God—but everybody thought He was just insane. That created some small difficulties for Him, but after wandering for some years He ended up in Tiruvannamalai, where He begged for food and lived on the streets. Some shopkeepers fed Him and after seventeen years on the streets, He allowed some of His disciples to get Him a house. After another seventeen years He allowed His disciples to put up the money and build an ashram. He'd never given initiations, but when He got the ashram He began telling people they could repeat His Name, Yogi Ramsuratkumar, but not to get enlightened; He offered His Name for Grace and blessings.

"Of course I interpret His Name as mantra, and if repeated with enough attention and consistency, it can produce the same state of consciousness He is in. If it could be said that a practice has been given by Yogi Ramsuratkumar, repeating His Name is it. He doesn't initiate people in it, but says, 'This can be done.' He is such a high Master He doesn't have to *initiate* anyone. But everyone should feel their Master is the highest, the most beautiful! I've known Him physically for twenty-three years. I've seen a lot of interactions between Him and others."

At this point the mood in the room had completely changed. People were relaxed, some of them were smiling. The space seemed to be flowing instead of discordant. It seemed to have been completely turned around and now a deep rapport was established. People listened intently as Lee spoke about Yogi Ramsuratkumar.

"Yogi Ramsuratkumar treats people with kindness and generosity. Several years ago He presided over an inter-caste marriage at His ashram temple. He believes love is more important than empty formality. He is a strict vegetarian—not that everyone should copy Him, but there is something there to learn from. When Yogi Ramsuratkumar gives public darshan He doesn't allow people to come up and bow and give gifts, or *prasad*, to Him. Only a select few are allowed to come up and do that. 'You don't need to *pranam* to this Beggar,' He says. He hasn't set Himself up as a king. I've seen lots of those kinds of things in Him over the years. He has preferences for how He would like to see people live, but He hasn't made a law out of it. There is only God—that is the basic teaching, and to say His Name is a way to realize this, over and against simply having the rhetoric. When people come to see Him, He says, 'My Father blesses you.'

"To say it in my language, when one contacts the presence of Yogi Ramsuratkumar— and one does not have to be in His physical presence to do that, His Name is enough— the contact with His presence initiates Grace in one's life. I would call Grace the regard of God. Often what is best for us is not what we want. We want what's comfortable and satisfies our desires, but not necessarily what's best in the long run. Grace is the force that, when we invoke it, begins to orient our lives to get what we need, not what we want. This is a key element of who Yogi Ramsuratkumar is. When He says, 'My Father blesses you,' He backs it up with His relationship to God. He is really giving everyone He says that to an opportunity to receive Grace. Some receive His Grace, some repel it. Many come to Him soliciting blessings for their sick children or relatives. Sometimes His blessings may mean that it is best for the person to die more quickly. But Westerners think that if His blessings don't turn out the way they want them to and think they should, then the blessings are no good. They turn to psychology instead of turning to the higher context of what is best for us, in terms of the ultimate evolution of Life in our case."

"My personal relationship to Yogi Ramsuratkumar is one of obedience, because my experience has shown me that I can't *do* anything else. I can obey Him out of will power, out of effort. I can do it. I can't make myself feel devotion for Him. I used to teach meta-physics—the manipulation of the mind/body unit. So I used to know a lot of technology. I could get someone all cranked up and believing they were feeling devotion, but if you take away the crutch of the technology, they wouldn't be feeling devotion because it wasn't real.

"Sometimes I feel moved devotionally in relationship to Yogi Ramsuratkumar, but most times I'm just thinking about something else—ice cream, or good looking women in the audience." The audience was loose enough to actually laugh together at Lee's im-promptu jokes at this point. "So faith, devotion, surrender, I can't do, but obedience is something I can do to be receptive to the *Grace* that gives surrender, faith, devotion. There are no guarantees—nothing can guarantee surrender.

"Well, that's a good place to end! I'll be out at the book table to answer any informal questions you have. Thank you for your questions."

A woman sitting on the back row raised her hand. Even though he had formally closed the space, Lee asked her if she had a question. As soon as she began to speak it was clear that she hadn't really been present in the space for the last hour. She said, "I came here tonight to hear about the title of the talk, which was Shiva and Shakti. I feel very angry because I didn't get what I came here to get, and I came because I have a friend who wanted to come but couldn't, so I came for her. I don't know what I'm going to tell her now."

"Hmm! I've been talking about Shiva and Shakti all night!" Lee gave a little laugh. "But obviously my presentation was too obscure. I'm very sorry you're disappointed. Just tell your friend that the speaker was an idiot and a pig, and if he ever comes here again, don't go!" That seemed to enflame her further. She said, "You said that, I didn't, and I won't tell her that."

"Well, thank you!" Lee gave her a small bow of his head. "I'll be out there at the book table, drinking water from a bottle!" The audience burst into loud applause as Lee got up and walked out to the foyer where the book table was set up.

At the book table after the talk Lee was surrounded with people. A familiar woman came walking up. Some of Lee's students recognized her—she was Tina Singh, the French wife of the tabla player from Banaras, Lacchu Maharaj, who had played for Lee at the Mehta brother's silk factory. By an interesting coincidence, she lived in La Chaux de Fonds part of the year with her daughter. She had seen the ad in the paper and lived only a few blocks away from the building where Lee was speaking. She walked over to Lee and spoke with him briefly. "It's a pleasure to see you again," he said, giving her a comple-mentary copy of his new book, *N'essayez Pas—Vivez!*. "Please give your husband my fond-est regards." She shook Lee's hand and smiled, then left to go back to her young daughter.

After about thirty minutes the crowd thinned out. When the books were packed up and back in the vans Lee headed down the street toward the little restaurant, only three blocks away, to check it out for a possible ice cream fest. Walking into the back room of the restaurant, Lee looked around and, seeming to capitulate, said, "It will do." The tables had to be rearranged to allow the group to sit together, and everyone pitched in to rear-range the room while the waiter stood by watching. Ice cream was ordered and eaten with numerous misunderstandings between the American and German group and the French waiter, who seemed happy in the end.

It was an uneventful gathering, there was no sense of a teaching circumstance having been created, and certainly the ambiance was not right. As Lee said later, "Nothing happened. It was the wrong place, another example of misperception. You don't go to an Italian restaurant when you want to order ice cream."

August 27, 1999
Le Rozet

The seminar started this morning with a thirty-minute meditation. After the bell rang Lee immediately plunged into his discourse. This is the second year that Lee has given a seminar at Le Rozet, where almost all of the participants are students of Arnaud Desjardins. As he does at Hauteville and other centers for the teaching of Arnaud Desjardins, Lee will couch much of his discourse in the particular language that Arnaud uses, and the context of his work with people will be aimed directly at turning Arnaud's disciples toward their teacher. Lee's desire to turn disciples toward their teacher and his profound regard and respect for Arnaud is often reflected in Lee's outpouring of unstinted and heartfelt praise of Arnaud as a teacher.

Both years that Lee has given seminars at Le Rozet the schedule has been particularly intense, with four dharma talks every day, two meditations and two meals. Tea would be served between two-thirty and three o'clock during a short break between the two afternoon dharma sessions, each of them two-and-a-half hours long. The days would begin with meditation and end with meditation. Overall the schedule amounts to over nine hours a day sitting in the meeting or meditation hall of the center, with almost no personal or private time to walk or smoke or whatever one might do to blow off some of the pressure of the pounding influence of the dharma.

Lee began: "I recognize a lot of you from last year. So, if the schedule is uncomfortable for you, don't blame it on Jean Pierre or Josette—it's my design. Your day will just have a little different flavor than usual. We have four talks today and tomorrow, and three talks on Sunday, and very little free time.

"I tend to be a very lazy character. If I allowed myself to be motivated by that laziness we'd have two talks a day, time to sit around and take walks. Part of the schedule is designed for you and part of it is designed for me. Someone asked me a week ago if I didn't think it would be better to push myself less and live longer, and therefore have more time to make the teaching available, instead of pushing myself hard now and perhaps ruining my health and living a shorter life. The answer was, 'There is no question about it: push myself to the point of exhaustion, because there is no time to relax—not for myself, and not for the people I work with.'

"You have two opportunities to learn from the teacher. One is to learn from obvious instructions that you are given, and the other is to learn from how the teacher himself or herself lives in relationship to the teaching. I've found for my own students that learning in the second way is almost negligible. I've been doing this for twenty-five years and many of the people who have been with me for twenty-five years haven't learned a single thing from how I live. If the people who want me to rest really wanted me to rest, they would start learning something from how I live in relationship to the teaching, and demonstrate that they have learned something. Perhaps then I could rest. The manifestation of the teaching impresses me, but the sentimental care for my being—I couldn't care less. But don't follow me to the bathroom, hoping you'll learn something! The way I go to the bathroom has nothing to do with the teaching. People take things so literally I wouldn't be surprised if someone didn't try it!" The laughter that came from the group provided a momentary respite from the intense power that seemed to bear down on the audience from Lee's strong presence this morning. It was like being in an invisible vice, so that impurities were being squeezed out of the body by virtue of sitting in the room with him—an experience that isn't particularly comfortable.

"So this weekend is very heavily scheduled. To be in this room for nine hours is a very intense process, but one of the implications of that is that there's no time to lose, no time to waste. Each of us has a certain appreciation, a certain practical ability in the teaching. There are some mature practitioners in this room; at the same time whatever undiscovered or unresolved elements of our lives exist could completely undermine or sabotage, under the right circumstances, what we've already done. So there's no time to waste, to close our eyes and take a little nap.

"The schedule is the way it is because I'm lazy, and if I don't push myself, nobody else will. Everyone who comes to this seminar gets to benefit from the intensity of my pushing myself, because by Sunday afternoon I'll be feeling the tension myself! I'll be pretty . . . full! But there's only two times to stop: when a session is over, no matter what's going on, it's time to stop. I may be in a sublime revelation of the teaching, but at ten-thirty it's time for brunch, and we stop, no matter what is going on. If someone is in catharsis, crying and screaming on the floor, and the breakthrough of their lives in on the line, at ten-thirty we stop! It doesn't matter, because if we aren't breaking through *now*, another thirty minutes won't make any difference. The other time to stop is when to go on would actually crush what we've just received.

"Years ago we saw an exhibit of Maori art. It was incredible, and made a very strong communication of sanctity and relationship to the Divine. When we came out of the exhibit there was the possibility of going to a concert of Maori music, but the delicacy of the influence the exhibit had had was just perfect. So even though the concert would have been wonderful in its own right, to put that on top of what we'd already received would have been counterproductive.

"The language I use is designed to create a certain effect. But even when we're discussing something very articulately, and our minds can follow the discussion, there is always something else going on. That something else that is going on while we're having a conversation is what is most important. Last night in the talk a man was smiling, laughing at jokes. His face was open and clear. The jokes were a little bit crude, I admit. But then when he stood up to speak he said he was angry. He was smiling and looking very happy, but he said how angry he was, and how unhappy he was at how the talk was going. Yet his appearance didn't indicate what he said his experience was. It was a great example of this Influence that affects us above and beyond the language. And then there is what the mind does with that language. It was clear that his body was being touched by something that was creating a brightness and radiance in him, but his mind was reacting to my linear presentation. There is great benefit in that because the body is superior to the mind, and so he went home with something of great value from the talk. But it's probable that he won't be able to capitalize on the gift unless his mind gets in sync.

"So I share this with you to help optimize what can be exchanged between you and me this weekend. What goes on this weekend is reciprocal—it goes both ways. It's advisable to have all your perceptions aligned, so the mind and body are in the same mood of receptivity. That optimizes the situation. There can still be great benefit if the mind and body are fighting. If the mind is fighting, how can you get it to be receptive? There is a rhyme in English that children use when they are calling each other names. 'Sticks and stones may break my bones, but words will never hurt me.' So if the mind is fighting because of some language I've used or some concept I've discussed, the way you can relax the mind is to say, 'Well, it's only words. What *else* is going on?'

"Gurdjieff taught the concept of multiple 'I's' and a singular 'I'. We each have many 'I's' within us, each one with its own purpose, aim and autonomy. When any one 'I' is dominant, it believes itself to be unitive—the only one. Even the 'I's' are separate—we are actually shattered, like a bottle that falls to the floor. But each little piece of glass still thinks it's the whole bottle because it's still glass. One way we get a clear object lesson about this concept is to be given the experience of the dramatic difference between one or more of the 'I's'. If we have enough clarity of self-observation to see the mind, emotions and body all doing different things—if we can really see that clearly—it clarifies this point of the separate 'I's'. It creates a question in us. 'If this is the way it is now, how is it when I'm not separate?'

"Ordinarily we take our state of consciousness for granted. We assume that what appears on the surface is what is going on in the entire system. What's on the surface? What's on the inside? What's at the deepest levels of being? Most of us don't do that. We don't investigate what is at levels we are not aware of, but that's how the process is effective.

"If you study martial arts, you find that you can't relax your attention. If for one instant your attention goes anywhere other than in the immediate conflict, you're lost. In the dojo it's not that big a deal if your attention slips, but if you're in a conflict out on the streets, you could die. Your attention on the path has to be that intense."

In the afternoon session today Lee told a long version of the story of Shakyamuni Buddha, using it to spin off many different dharma points. Tonight after dinner he began the session answering questions.

A woman asked, "My question is about trust; sometimes there is anger or fear that gets in the way of trust."

"It's only ego that is afraid," Lee answered. "Fear never disappears, but fear of fear disappears. When fear appears we view it as a problem. But in one sense the path is about annihilation, so of course there should be fear. Our deepest consciousness knows what the path is about. If we are successful on the path, everything we believe, all our assumptions, will be shattered, so it's very sensible to have fear. The master may look very sensible, pleasant, peaceful, but like a samurai, at any second the master's sword could come out and slash right through us. So fear is natural. The body itself functions under survival messages, and anything that threatens survival creates fear. That's very healthy because if we didn't have instinctual fear we'd walk off cliffs and jump in fires. The world would be a nicer place! All those people gone!" Lee chuckled.

"So it's healthy to have fear, but hold it in its appropriate context. Do not be afraid of fear or assume it is a weakness or an obstacle. The relationship with the master is in one sense about extinction—not of consciousness, but of illusion and trying to live out of the past. Any level of extinction is naturally greeted with fear. It's a natural protective mechanism, so it's not a problem. There is fear—see it as it is. It is not a handicap, not an obstacle. Only when we make it something other than what it is does it become a problem."

August 28, 1999
Le Rozet

After lunch Tom gave the talk. He talked about the bulky and immense *Hohm Sahaj Mandir Study Manual* as a "living thing"—not just a text but a living description of practice and states of experience or consciousness on the path that one can access in the body. He spoke at length about Lee's poetry. He said, "When the poetry first came out in 1993 I read it and I thought it was really bad poetry. I didn't get it. I kept reading it until one morning one of the poems opened up to me, literally. After several years of being immune to it, the poem came alive, and I had a bodily response to the poetry after that. Several more poems opened up to me and I became aware of the mood of the poems.

"In *Sahaj Mandir,* the Study Manual, I came across a key element of the Baul tradition that helps explain one principle that is active in Lee's poetry: the principle of *rupa* and *svarupa,* which is about finding the extraordinary in the ordinary. Where can a master put, for all time, the treasures of his teaching? In a place where they cannot be destroyed. In a sacred architecture, or inside devotees. *Rupa / svarupa* is about hiding the treasures in the most obvious place. Baul philosophy says the God decided to hide the treasure in the universe, in the human body. A core principle of Baul sadhana is that the principles of the universe are operant in the human body. The same principle operates with Lee's poetry; the principles of his teaching are accessible in the poetry, on many levels, from energetic to intellectual.

"Saying this does not give you access to it, however. What you get is only through intention and attention to the poetry, and what you need to get when it shows up. You could read Lee's poetry and have enjoyment of it, and you can read them in a personal search for the teaching, which becomes available as you develop the intent and attention to hold that poetry in a sacred regard. That sounds esoteric, but it can be as ordinary as reading the poetry and opening up to what is available. I'm not suggesting you look at Lee's poetry like a graduate student in English Literature, although I'm sure in the near future people will be looking at his poetry as a literary device. But that won't give them access. It has to be realized, it has to be approached from a certain level of consciousness.

"Another aspect equally important is the hidden teaching in Lee's poetry that is found in the history of the evolution of his relationship with Yogi Ramsuratkumar. Any student of the path can look at this poetry and receive something about how a master approaches his master—this in and of itself is probably the greatest teaching. There are many facets and moods in Lee's poetry that express his relationship with Yogi Ramsuratkumar. Studying this poetry one gets the very clear impression of what it takes to be obedient and to surrender, and the implications of that. The medium for this message is his poetry. It goes straight to the heart, so there is an alchemical effect in the poetry. What I get from all this is that the teaching has to come alive in the body."

In the late afternoon session Lee began by talking about what it means to be a good disciple. He said, "What's the difference between a good disciple and a disciple? There are a lot of specifics, but something general that we could say without going into the whole psychological background, which most of you are probably more than familiar with anyway, is that the average person is satisfied to live in illusion. They have no interest in who they are. Even if they get a glimpse that they are not who they think they are, they have no interest whatsoever in finding out more—none. As in the story about

Shakyamuni Buddha, the average person doesn't have the slightest interest in discovering a resolve to the great problems of life. So then we could say on the positive side that the disciple is interested in discovering reality and is completely antagonistic to remaining in illusion. Essentially, that may be the primary difference.

"So many ordinary people in the world could be said to be disciples, but not disciples of a spiritual master. Disciple of a politician, disciple of Princess Di, or a movie star, or some football star. That kind of disciple is very common in France, Germany, England, and Brazil," Lee chuckled, "because their attention is on a particular person and they have a tremendous amount of devotion to that person. Devotion of a sort—I mean obsession. That kind of devotion or obsession is a quality of discipleship also. Our attention is on the master. We want to know about the master, about his or her life, who they're sleeping with," Lee chuckled, "especially if it is not us. It's a perverse curiosity.

"But seriously, when the master has a certain wish, the good disciple will want to align himself or herself with that wish. Often we don't do that; often in relationship to the master we assert what we imagine is our independence. In fact that is not independence at all—it's complete slavery. What we are assuming is independence is really a function of our habits, our psychological script, our neurosis. Often we will do things our way, assuming that the master will be pleased with the end result, but in many cases the end result is irrelevant. What is relevant is that we are resonant to the master's wish.

"In every group of students of every master, there are people who are very practical. Whenever they set out to accomplish something, they always set out to accomplish it the most efficient way, with the least use of resources, and get it done as professionally and as quickly as possible. But that often is not the point. The point is resonance to the master. It is more important to me that my students be resonant to my wish; I appreciate efficiency, but not when the efficiency is at the cost of resonance to me.

"Yogi Ramsuratkumar is an Indian, steeped in Eastern culture, and I'm a Westerner. Naturally I would often do some mundane things very differently than He would under ordinary circumstances. I only see Him about two weeks a year—probably very similar to some of you and Arnaud. Maybe some of you see Arnaud more often because Hauteville is closer to where you live than India is to America. But even if India were closer I wouldn't go that much more because my responsibility is to Yogi Ramsuratkumar's Work first—the Work He has given me to do. My heart belongs to Yogi Ramsuratkumar, but my responsibility is to His work. He can do whatever He wants with me. Sometimes what He does is not very comfortable, but it's His business. And sometimes it's not so bad, and maybe even great! The rest of the time it's fighting for crumbs. Yes, with all the other disciples, just like pigeons in the park!" Lee laughed and the audience joined in with him. "It's a great image, and very accurate.

"You know how sometimes you see people with their dogs, and when they've been with their dogs long enough you can't tell who is the person and who is the dog? They look so much alike! I can tell by the haircuts on some of the women what kind of dogs they have!" Everyone laughed. "It's a very accurate system of psychological articulation. Disciples all get to look like pigeons after a while. Fat pigeons, getting stale bread. Every once in a while the master comes out and throws a little cake, you know, 'Oh!' and all the pigeons go crazy for the crumbs of cake." Lee chuckled.

"Never mind everything I just said—it was irreverent. So, whenever I go to visit Yogi Ramsuratkumar, I always try to do things the way He wants them done. If we want to know what the master's wish is all we have to do is pay attention. The master will communicate his wishes or her wishes very clearly if we simply pay attention. In Arnaud's case all of his instructions are very clearly in his books," Lee chuckled.

"Somebody came downstairs to the book table to ask about the poetry book. She asked if there was a poem in English she could read to see if she could understand the English. She read a poem and she said, 'Well the English is clear, but I have no idea what the poem means.' My writing tends to be that way. If you read my writing it's like, 'What on earth does this mean?' It's totally obscure. But Arnaud's writing is breathtaking in its clarity and articulation. So as a foundation, if anybody wants to know how to serve Arnaud, it should be very obvious because there are no cryptic messages. He is very clear in what he expects in practice, and very clear in what he expects in terms of people's relationship to him as their master.

"So one of the qualities of a good disciple is that we study the master to find out what the master wishes, and then we define our activity, our behavior in relationship to the master, to be in resonance with those wishes. The master always wants us to work a little bit. I was with Yogi Ramsuratkumar a few years ago and He asked me if I would look up a couple of people in America. They were Americans who I'd heard about from the early seventies, who had been around Yogi Ramsuratkumar. I knew their names but I didn't know where they were; I knew one was in New York, but the other one I had no idea about. I said, 'Okay, I'll try.' Yogi Ramsuratkumar said, 'You won't try, you will do it.'

"As fortune would have it, it wasn't terribly difficult to get the addresses of both of these men. I happened to have the right sources, and I made the right guesses, so it came very easily. I went to see both people and I did what He asked me to do. It turned out that one of these people writes to Yogi Ramsuratkumar every couple of months. Yogi Ramsuratkumar could have given me his address and his phone number, but He didn't. He wanted me to do the work. Often the master will expect the disciple to do a little research, just to prove that they are really interested. So, a quality of a good disciple is that the path, or the relationship to the master, means enough to us that we are really willing to go out of our way, even suffer some discomfort, to please the master—to resonate with the master's wish.

"Another quality of a good disciple is psychic sensitivity to the master. There is such a thing as too much of a good thing. I'll tell you a funny story, with no disrespect to the incredible dessert we had last night, so please don't anybody be insulted." Lee chuckled. "Years ago we were in Paris and somebody made me a perfect tiramisu. Perfect! Unequalled. Unexcelled. Unparalleled. Whenever you eat something that is perfect, you know, it's one of those pivotal moments in your life. Most tiramisu is great, but this tiramisu was *perfect*. So somehow I got into talking about it at a seminar early this summer, and I was going on and on about the perfect tiramisu, sort of like guys after their first experience with sex. They can't stop talking about it, bragging about it! So I was going on and on about this perfect tiramisu and all of my students were," Lee gestured as if he was scribbling frantically, "writing it down in their books!" Lee chuckled and the group laughed, especially since Lee's students were the only people in the room who were attempting to catch every word of Lee's discourse in their sometimes overwrought rapid note-taking—scratch, scratch, scratch, and the turning of pages throughout the day.

"So the summer went on and we went to the next seminar. Something really funny was going on. I was walking around, people were coming out of the kitchen, kind of looking at me with looks of anticipation. I'm thinking, 'Is my shirt stained? Do I have a pimple? What's going on?' My students start throwing out little hints, 'Wait until you see the dessert tonight!' The dessert came out and it's, of course, tiramisu. I was very happy, it was very good. It wasn't perfect, but it was very good, because perfection just doesn't happen that often. But it was good. Last night's was better than good, it was very good. I ate too much! I was lying in bed saying, 'Oh my God! I'm stuffed.' because I have absolutely no discipline when it comes to good food. I've been stuffing myself to the point of pain for twenty years and every time I do it I say, 'I'm not going to do this again,' but I always do it again. Just being enigmatic!" Lee laughed at himself.

"So the tiramisu was very good, it was very nice, it was great. The next place I went, what comes out for dessert? Tiramisu." Lee chuckled. "And the host came and smiled. The perfect tiramisu. It's like a grapevine. Everybody got on the phone, 'Lee's coming! He likes . . .' People told the story of the perfect tiramisu over and over. I haven't had enough yet, *but* I can just see next summer. I can see it coming. An avalanche of tiramisu. Every night. Every where we go! *More! More!*" Everyone was laughing while Lee's amused chuckles interspersed his storytelling. He proceeded to go into a long diatribe about Charles Bukowski, telling many bizarre and humorous anecdotes about his life, in the process churning the group up into a frenzy of laughter.

"Bukowski's poetry is so real you don't even want to read it!" More laughter. "You say, 'What do I need this for? Can't I keep some of my illusions?' It took awhile for him to get popular because his poetry was so different—radical, revolutionary.

"Bukowski was a professional alcoholic. In a magazine interview the interviewer once said to him, 'Don't you think that glorifying your alcoholism is a bad example? Other alcoholics who have quit alcoholism and dried out, they're upset by this.' Bukowski said to the interviewer, 'None of those people are real alcoholics!' Meaning if they were critical of him they couldn't possibly understand him.

"All of his early poetry and his early novels are about getting drunk and having sex. He brings sex down to the barest gut-level, gutter reality that it is. Oh boy! All romance does is ruin the damn stuff!" Lee chuckled. "If you're too romantic about it and your partner forgets her feminine deodorant spray, all of a sudden you can't have sex because you don't like the way something smells. Bad vibes, man.

"When you read about sex like that you have one of two reactions. You either say, 'Oh this is disgusting!' That's what all priests say on the pulpit, then they run back to their rooms after the sermon and they pull out their Bukowski!" Lee threw his head back and laughed. "Tom knows, because he's walked into a couple of nuns reading Henry Miller!" More laughter. Lee was stirring things up. The group was very loose at this point, enjoying Lee and beginning the descent, or ascent, depending on how one looked at it, into a kind of bacchanalian hilarity. He continued with a smile, "*Tropic of Capricorn* . . . drooling on the pages! You get so wrapped up in what you're reading you forget to swallow!" The laughter kept building on itself.

"So you have one of two reactions to somebody like Bukowski. You either get turned off or you get turned on. At one time in his life when he got popular he was inundated with college girls who wanted to have sex with him. He was fifty-plus years old and all these fresh, innocent nineteen-year-olds were knocking on his door with a bottle of whiskey in their hand. 'Hi! I'm Marge!' " Lee quipped this in a high pitched voice and then chuckled. "Well at first, you know, it was kind of nice, because he was used to sixty-year-old women who had been alcoholics for forty-five years! So here are these nineteen-year-olds—fresh, young, untouched—and they had been having sex for eight years, but they were untouched, if you know what I mean. All the women know what I mean and the men are going, 'No, what do you mean?' " Lee made a gesture as if he was totally puzzled.

"How did we get on this subject?" He asked with mock innocence while wiping tears of laughter from his eyes. The women were laughing and nodding their heads in the affirmative. The men, with a few exceptions, seemed generally as confused as Lee said they were. "How could we possibly go through a whole seminar without getting on this subject? Oh yes—too much of a good thing." Lee laughed again.

"So at first every time one of these girls would come through his door he'd have her come in and stay for a day or two, then send her home and make room for the next one. But the thing is, is he couldn't be himself anymore. They couldn't keep up with him drinking-wise, and when they weren't drunk, all they did was follow him around—you know, the great *'poet.'* Some of you are writers, right? You're sitting at your computer keyboard. You look up, and there's your beloved wife or girlfriend and she says, 'What are you writing?' I mean, that kills an inspirational and spontaneous mood like a large turd in bed!"

More unrestrained laughter came spilling out of the group. Lee's translator, Claire, looked dumbfounded. Lee laughed and turned to her, saying, "I only said that for you! Can you imagine? You have a hot date and your girlfriend—maybe to you it means nothing, but to the men it means a lot—says, 'Come up to my apartment.' Oh boy! Your skin is tingling with anticipation and you go up to the apartment and she says, 'Let me go get more comfortable,' and she goes into the bathroom and you *whip* the covers off the bed and there's a big piece of shit just sitting on the sheet, staring up at you. *Gawd!* Would that kill the mood! Not for some men. Some men would say, 'Wow! Boy, is this going to be a night! Ahhhhhh!' " People were doubled over with laughter. Lee too was laughing as if he was listening to someone else's comedy routine. He grabbed his sides and threw his head back. It took a minute or so for things to calm down long enough for him to go on.

At one point Lee took a piece of tissue and blew his nose loudly over the microphone. He looked up and said, "Excuse me." With a grin he rubbed the tissue over the microphone, making a loud rumbling noise that would, of course, be recorded on the tape. "I love it when one of my disciples is listening to one of my tapes and all of a sudden, 'Ooooowwwww! Oooooo! Oooooo, what was that?!' " Lee covered his ears as he yelped in pain. "That will teach them to use earphones!" Everyone was laughing. Lee rubbed the microphone again with the tissue, saying, "Excuse me," as the laughter continued to resound in the room. Finally he resumed the story.

"But after a while Bukowski couldn't work, and if he couldn't work, it was death. If he couldn't work it was worse than no alcohol, worse than no sex, worse than anything; if he couldn't write it was death. People would come to see him, and because he was so famous they wouldn't leave. They had no sense of dignity, no sense of elegance. He was like the original hippie—just come and crash and do your own thing. He had real difficulty kicking people out. But after a while, even the most beautiful woman had to go. It was too much of a good thing.

"So, I can just see next year. Gosh, I'd hate my taste for tiramisu to be destroyed by too much tiramisu. Not too much at one time that is; too much at one time is okay!" More laughter. "Oh, we're having fun this afternoon—some of us! We'll get profound later. But you know, we need variety, because if every session was profound, by the last session we'd be asleep. We'd be ignoring it. How's *that* for profundity? If something is always on, then it becomes boring. Even God becomes boring—when you're always in the midst of the realization of God. That's why God created Creation. So we go through periods where our practice is tremendously invigorating and we're passionate about our practice and then we come to a point where we can't even seem to sit on the meditation pillow.

"It's the physics of life—ebb and flow, ebb and flow." Lee chuckled. "Everything in life is cyclical, including our realization of God. Sometimes we're standing right in the heart of God. Everything is bright, everything is glorious, we're ecstatic. We have endless patience, we are kind to every living creature. And then sometimes we look around, and we wonder, where did it go? We're at the depth of despair, of hopelessness. That's life.

"The teaching of accepting what is *as it is* is not about achieving a particular definitive state that never changes. It's a context, because states always change. You can look at any spiritual master and if you look closely enough, you'll see their states change. Not their context, but their state. Nobody is happy *all* the time, but someone can be accepting of what is as it is all the time because that is a context out of which life is lived. It's not a rigid form that we have to conform to.

"Because we're not able to accept what is, very understandably, we want what's pleasant. We don't want what's unpleasant. Based on our heartful response to the teaching and to the master, we make a psychological projection—we assume that if we said yes to life and accepted what is as it is here and now, in every moment, that there would never be down periods. Sorrow is not so bad. Hopelessness, frustration, despair, terror, and so on. We assume there is something wrong with us when we feel these things because we're feeling what we consider to be negative feelings, but life is not one-sided. Life is a tapestry of a vast variety of expressions; some are very pleasant, some are very unpleasant. But when we live in context, then we understand that life is not one-sided, so when we happen to hit a cycle that is not beautiful and pleasant, if we accept it as it is, it doesn't create the same effect in us as if we resist it. That is Arnaud's gift to everyone—the gift of context. Rather than complicating matters by specifying a lot of different forms, Arnaud's gift is very straightforward and direct. Just like Arnaud. Accept what is *as it is*. Context.

"My teaching is very obscure and convoluted, because that's the way I am. I'm not simple and direct. Somebody asked before about life on our ashram, and Tom was talking about our practices. We have formal meditation, then we have specific meditations that I've given to individuals who are ready to go beyond the formal meditation. And then there is study. There are dietary recommendations. There is a practice we call Enquiry that is similar to Ramana Maharishi's description of enquiry. There is a practice that we call Assertion. Then there is a whole body of technical yogas. All of these things are kind of a maze, a labyrinth that we have to find our way through to get to the heart of the teaching. That's my style, my culture, my tradition.

"Arnaud doesn't bother with any of that. He just gives you the core, the essence of the teaching, with no fancy frills. Accept what is *as it is*. That's context. Life has a tremendous amount of texture that is all singular in the sense that there is continuity between every aspect of Creation. In the Eastern traditions the phrase is 'God is One.' God is everything, all is One. That's true and at the same time, within Creation—within the creative reality of things—there are an infinite number of changes, moods, ups, downs, highs, lows, rough, smooth—everything." Outside the sky was bright gray over the dark green firs of the mountains. The light from behind the clouds illuminated Lee's face as he sat in the darkening afternoon light and the mood in the room struck a deeper vein.

"The essence of the teaching is context. We can't control life, we can't control the future. We can't make what comes to us be just exactly what we want and how we want it. To some degree we can, but that is a very artificial and illusory way of living. Our aim is not to define life in our own terms. It's to be able to resonate, ultimately, to the Will of God. We don't create life, God creates life. Or if you don't reference things in a theistic way, you could say that Life creates itself. In any event, we don't create Life. We just live in right relationship with Life.

"Our aim is to live in a context that is accepting and acknowledging, rather than a context that is demanding and exclusive. That is the gift Arnaud gives us: *context*. In one phrase—very clear, very simple. Realizing it may require some effort, but you don't have to be confused by a dozen different practices. You don't have to be following your breath and counting beads, which is another practice my students do—prayer beads. You don't have to be doing this yoga and that yoga. It's very simple, but the end result is the same. It's just very straightforward and direct instead of very labyrinthine. My students have to take a very labyrinthine path to get to the same place. But again that's life. Every master is not the same. Every real master is the same in context, but not in form. Okay? Thank you."

August 29, 1999
Le Rozet

After a long, full day of dharma talks in the formal sitting hall and a feast at dinner, Lee gathered in the evening for a final, informal session in the kitchen with about fifteen people who are associated with Le Rozet, including Josette and Jean Pierre. All day Lee had been sitting up on the dais in the hall elucidating the teaching while ruminating, telling stories, making people laugh, cranking up the energy, raising us up and then taking us down into labyrinths of new insights. The exchanges had been strong between Lee and the practitioners who were present.

Slowly darkness fell outside now as Lee began to answer questions in the smaller group. Someone said, "You spoke about how E.J. Gold would 'open the space.' What does that mean?"

"When people get together who are of the ordinary mindset the space is defined by illusion and is closed. If the Ku Klux Klan got together in America there would be no room for someone to say, 'Racism is unjust.' It's a closed space. When spiritual students get together everyone has projections and expectations of enlightenment and what they are looking for in the space. Some want miracles; some want healing. Everyone is looking for something different. The Divine has no way into a space when everybody has an already established idea of what they want. To open the space one must get all the energy in the space moving toward a common aim, and then with the energy united, create a crack in the shield of illusion through which the Divine can manifest. This is called 'opening the space.'

"That is done in a number of ways. One way is to bring one person's conflict up to the front so everyone is focused on that person. E.J. Gold used to give discourses on a regular basis to students, and at one point he stopped and said that each student could ask one question on their birthday every year and no others at any time. So it was a big thing on that day. If you asked the wrong question, that was it for a year! The energy in those spaces was always very receptive out of necessity. People came to the space ready because they weren't lost in their own subjectivity."

"Why did he leave when the space was open?" the questioner continued.

"Because he already knows how to make use of God—how to make use of Reality—and his students don't," Lee answered. "He would open the space and then leave them to discover how to use that space because they had to learn by experience, not by verbal instruction. So he would invoke the Divine and throw the gift in his students' laps. Sometimes someone would take over and close everything down, so the training was also about teamwork.

" 'As above, so below.' To learn to work as a group is a symbol of the reigning body of the Universe, the ruling body of the Universe. That is the other reason E.J. left the space. He knew how to do group work. He and I would work together as a team. If you want the sublime gifts this space has to offer you have to be able to work together, or the space closes down and you miss the nectar. If his students could work together as a team in those circumstances, then they would learn something that would profit them greatly.

"You said that Arnaud's gift to us is context. Would you explain further?" another person asked.

"Context is the essential space out of which everything arises, out of which Creation comes—an unending spring of existence, eternal and unchanging. Content is about everything. Context is not about things. 'What is, is' is a constant matter. 'What is' changes from moment to moment, but 'what is, is' always is. You have to be in context to know what context is. Otherwise we are thinking from content, so the drop can't see the ocean."

September 2, 1999
La Ferme de Jutreau

Lee returned from Germany last night, two days after his students who were with him on the trip. He had stayed behind to take care of some personal business in Salzburg, Austria. Everyone else drove back from Le Rozet the day after the seminar was over.

This morning over breakfast he talked about installing the Primal Mother in the salon today. He made an announcement, saying, "There will be a new artifact installed in the salon to the right of the fireplace beneath the light. Please be careful not to touch it, not to knock it over. When Clint gets home I'll ask him to build a case for her, but until then, *please* be careful and pay attention when you walk past there. It is a gift to the sangha from Tom and Colette, so we have them to thank."

Lingering over the breakfast table he was animated and giving instructions to someone to call Dave, one of his students who lives in England. Lee had purchased a Shiva Nataraj for Dave while he was in Germany, and wanted to get it to him as soon as possible. Lee said, "Call him and tell him I've got something for him and to call me back at six-thirty tonight." He turned to Michael, who also likes to collect bronzes, and said, "It's a really unusual Nataraj—I've never seen one like it. He told me to get a bronze for him if I ever ran across something I thought would be good for him, but the more I look at it, the more I like it! Maybe I should just keep it for myself!" he teased.

Breakfast had ended and people were beginning to clear the dishes away, but now stopped to listen. Without raising his voice or doing anything at all to call attention to himself, Lee had gathered the attention of the everyone in the dining room. It is an amazing phenomena that happens very frequently. Lee can be speaking in a quiet voice and a busy, cacophonous room will suddenly hush as all attention goes to the spiritual master. Another variation on this theme is that Lee often makes it extremely difficult for anyone beyond the person to his immediate left and right and one or two directly across the table to hear him without straining to listen. This can add an element of irritation at times for those who really want to hear him when he is sitting only four feet away, but he refuses to speak in a forthright tone of voice. In this way Lee seems to be saying, "Pay attention." Now he laughed and got up to leave. "Jai Guru!" he yelled.

Just before lunch he brought the meter-high iron and clay Primal Mother down from his room and installed her by the fireplace, to the right of his leather chair. As he placed her on the floor he knelt down beside her and gazed intently at the deity for a while. Several people stood behind him, watching. After about thirty seconds that seemed to encapsulate an infinite and unchartable period of time, Lee leaned back and started with the wise cracks. It's typical of Lee to mask something he is doing on a subtle level with sarcasm and humorous comments. He has said on many occasions that it is one of the ways he protects the Work, but it seems that it also provides a certain goad for his students. He gives nothing away for free. He expects people to pay, because when one pays for the Work, the benefits are much greater. To get through Lee's style one has to pay attention, to work much harder to get the teaching, or the transmission, that he is making in the moment. If you are spacing out or distracted or self-absorbed in negativity, you miss the moment and the opportunity.

Almost immediately the word spread around the ashram that Lee was installing the deity. People began to flood into the room. With each new arrival there was an exclamation and a series of questions, each time the same questions—what is she, where did she come from, how was she made?—which Lee answered very kindly and patiently each time, until the whole thing became funny. It was like an instant replay or déja vu that kept happening.

As a group gathered around him in front of the statue, he said, "Well . . . that should add something to the women's groups around here! Maybe things will be different now."

The women's group at La Ferme de Jutreau has had a history of conflict and discord and lack of unity. His comment seemed very serious. At breakfast he had said that the gift of the statue was to the sangha, but the gift was actually given to Lee, who chose to use it to bless the ashram in France.

The children came running in from their class to look at the statue, exclaiming and freshly happy, then ran back out again. As Lee walked out of the salon he said with a quiet appreciation, "Her hair is really beautiful in the back, too . . ." And indeed, the back of the deity's head was honeycombed with a delicate pattern in the clay-dusted metal.

September 4, 1999
La Ferme de Jutreau

"Hello . . . this is room 201. The people in room 200 would like you to stop banging your partner's head against the wall—it's keeping them awake!" Lee camped it up in a falsetto voice in the office to Andrea, who had just answered the telephone, saying, "Bonjour, Association Ramji." The spiritual master was back at work behind his large, cluttered desk, which fills most of the very small office at the ashram—along with five other desks, four computers, a fax machine and telephone. It's an intimate workspace from which Lee manages his humble empire.

His desk seems to be holding tremendous weight, from the subtle point of view. On it are three *vigrahas*—the fourteen-inch-high bronze statues of Yogi Ramsuratkumar—an eight-inch-high carved stone Ganesha, a rather garish contemporary Kali done in metal by one of Lee's students, a nine-inch-high carved wooden laughing Buddha. Most of these are gifts that grace his immediate viewing area along with other miscellaneous gifts—artwork and such—given by friends or students. In addition are many piles of notes, letters, papers, tapes, a bird's nest, a flying plastic Superman and other unidentifiable objects. Beneath his desk is a Fellowes Powershredder—an electric shredding machine made for office use. He uses it to shred letters that come in from his students, or private mail that he has read. At times he seems to particularly relish feeding letters into its jaws.

Above his desk is the Vajrakilaya that Marcus painted recently and another large painting, also by Marcus, of Yogi Ramsuratkumar. A dried *mala* of roses and marigolds, given to Lee when he first arrived at La Ferme de Jutreau this summer by Brindavan, hangs from an electrical plug on the wall. Two pictures of Lee's oldest son posed with E.J. Gold taken in early 1999 are propped up against the wall. At different times there are also piles of manuscripts that Lee will read for Hohm Press.

It is a working guru's desk. There is none of the affected purity and effete ambiance so easily affected by many teachers who would like to believe that they are beyond the hustle and grit and stress of everyday life—who remove themselves from life. There is absolutely no trace of the decadence of someone who believes he or she has gone beyond the need to be humble—gone beyond the necessity to keep working, to practice, to be ordinary, to demonstrate the teaching in every moment of life. It is a working guru's desk.

September 5, 1999
La Ferme de Jutreau

The devotional aspect of Baul sadhana is one of the dimensions of Lee's multifaceted relationship with his students. Traditional darshan is held every Sunday night on Lee's ashrams in Arizona and in France, as well as at households where bordello is held in Vancouver, San Francisco, Boulder or Freiburg. In essence it doesn't matter whether Lee is physically present or not. The guru's physical presence is always treasured, but Lee has consistently instructed that the subtle power of Divine Influence, benediction and the transmission of the "clan essence" of the lineage is the foundation potency of darshan. Still, there is no replacement for being in the presence of the physical form of the guru for periods of time in one's sadhana.

Tonight Lee came into the hall in the barn and took his seat for darshan. He was wearing a thin cotton white robe, a gift from a Sufi friend from Morocco, his head wrapped with a light red cloth. The transparency of his appearance cast him in a radiance that seemed to flood his body and face. Tonight his face in particular seemed very ancient and sculpted, a living mystery, softened and fierce at the same time. His eyes were burning and dispassionate, and as he settled into his seat they rested on one person after another, each glance lifting the recipient, for the moment, into the guru's world. There was a pervasive peace and serenity in him, and yet he was not passive, but active in the most true sense, in that he appeared to be deeply in relationship with every single person in the room simultaneously, and at many different levels of being. He looked almost mythological, as if he had just stepped out of a dream—Vishnu's world-sustaining dream, the conscious dream of a Krishna or a Rama, not the dream of the sleeping world.

Tonight the darshan of Lee Lozowick, a self-confessed "bad poet" and son of Yogi Ramsuratkumar, was compelling. The powerful emanations of light, beatitude, even bliss that poured from Lee gave me pause to consider, once again, why this man—sanctified through the surrender to the Will of God which his Father Yogi Ramsuratkumar enacted in him twenty-four years ago—intently creates the opposite appearance as much as he can. As someone once wrote of Gurdjieff, it seems to be the mask that Lee is obliged to wear. He hides his sanctity and compassion behind the mundane, the crude, the appearance of belligerence, insults or arrogance. If he didn't, perhaps his own students would be lost in a morass of spiritual materialism, or of the particular romantic self-delusion that characterizes many devotional schools.

As soon as the chanting was finished Lee plunged in, working off of the consideration he had been having with his students during recent After Dinner Talks of Llewellyn Vaughan-Lee's article in *Sufi Magazine*, as well as the discussion of the morning's teaching committee meeting. He referred specifically to two statements that Dasya had brought to the meeting for consideration: "Union with the Divine is irrevocable," and "One needs to continue to guard one's work, or one's work could be lost."

Lee began, "After union with God, one's relationship with the Beloved would remain the essential mechanism or motivation for the rest of one's life, in contrast to the need to protect one's work. Not even the teacher can rest on his or her laurels, as if one's work is guaranteed. If you stop working, you could lose everything. We ask ourselves, if one is in union with the Divine, then how could one's work be lost? Great confusion reigned this morning at the meeting. People were unsatisfied, which is good because it leaves people hungry. Some were articulate and accurate as far as they went, but nobody went far enough with the consideration. Given the depth of the dharma that we have been given—the Study Manual, the poetry book, After Dinner Talks—and the depth and strength of our experience in this school, we should have a greater understanding of such a question.

"We enjoy the dharma, we are passionate about it—and we should be. But there is still the tendency to make some unconscious assumptions in relationship to the dharma. Generally speaking, we still believe that this Process can be figured out with the mind—this Great Process of Divine Evolution, Grace, alchemy, transformation. We think that if we study hard enough and think hard enough, we can wrap the mind around it. But our progress depends upon direct perception, not understanding with the mind.

"Once we find complete union—or we become fully awakened, with the emphasis on fully, because we may have reached a platform of maturity, but it is not full awakening—that union is irrevocable. At certain points and at certain stages along the path we may look like we're awakened. We may have clarity, be full of mystical phenomena, have successful meditations. We may look enlightened, but as practice matures we may find that whatever occurs is just a passing state.

"If one is completely awake, one cannot fall asleep again. Enlightenment is the knowledge that all experience is transitory, including enlightenment. Direct perception is not experience, it is knowledge. Thought can point at direct perception, but if thought tries to be part of direct perception, it always obliterates direct perception.

"So this morning we were trying to take two statements and put them together. There was no workable resolve because the two statements seemed to contradict, and yet the master said both of them. These statements may appear to be contradictory but each means what it means within its own context. If we try to wrap the mind around the dharma, we will find conflicts of context that cannot be woven into one another. We have to recognize that at some point, 'What is, is' is not in relationship to something else that could be or is somewhere else. The phrase that defines Assertion is 'Just This.' It means not 'Just This and,' but 'Just This.' 'Just This' is that we have to protect our work. 'Just This' is also that true union with the Divine is irrevocable. There is no conflict between the fact that we have to protect our work once we have entered into full awakening or union, even though we cannot fall out of union. But if we look at this from the platform of the mind, then there is conflict between those two statements.

"Essentially we have to come to the point where we use the mind, not the mind uses us, so that we are not identified with the mind stream, whatever it is doing. We can use it for necessary purposes—to process dualistically. But direct perception is about the transcendence of all illusions of duality. There comes a point at which we need to function nondualistically as a platform from which the Gifts of God can be received. At one point in this school nondualism was our dharma—that was all there was. Then we developed this sophisticated tantric dharma, but the trap is that we leave behind the core foundation of the realization of nonduality, and the understanding of the mind, the function of which is to perceive dualistically.

"You don't move into Enlightened Duality from duality; you move into Enlightened Duality from nonduality. This is what the meeting could have been useful for today—for us to see clearly how easily our minds are drawn into confusion and how easily we forget the higher demand, which is the realization of nonduality. Those two statements were said at two different times in different contexts—there was no conflict. To take the statements out of context has no value except to produce confusion.

"Trying to use our minds to solve problems that only direct perception can resolve can only create frustration. Llewellyn Vaughan-Lee says that we function a certain way up to a certain point, but then we must leave that way of functioning behind and function in a new way. We deal with our psychology up to a point, and when we have a deep enough and mature enough relationship to the Beloved that we begin to work in a different way. We may not root out every psychological tendency; if some of our tendencies are not antagonistic to the Work, then it doesn't matter.

"In Buddhism they sometimes speak of 'entering the stream.' When we become a stream enterer we still have to work, but the stream carries us. The current is only moving in one direction. If we don't swim, we can sink and drown, so we still have to work in relationship to the current that is carrying us along. We still have to do our part.

"You can't think your way into awakening. You have to disidentify. The mind will not give up its grip on your throat. The needs of the mind are devotion and obedience. The needs of the Divine are devotion and obedience. You cannot give devotion and obedience to both at the same time; it's one or the other. We start out all mind, no Divine. When you reach fifty-one percent, you should stop being devoted and obedient to the mind and start being devoted and obedient to the Divine. It is literally that simple."

September 7, 1999
La Ferme de Jutreau

This morning about three minutes after the bell rang to begin meditation Lee started writing poetry. The sound of his pen skipping and scratching across the paper punctuated the absolute silence in the meditation hall in the barn—a vast old stone structure with a soaring ceiling and gnarled old wooden beams spanning its roof and sides. Outside a heavy white mist lay over the land under a gray sky that was quickly brightening to silver. The mist seemed to add to the quality of an enclosed silence, a shroud of soundlessness out of which the poetry appeared, spun from nothing onto the white paper of the big hardbound notebook that lay open across Lee's lap. Pushing back the edges of the heavy wool plaid blanket, a gift from a disciple which Lee wears draped around his frame during meditation on chilly mornings, Lee sat holding the notebook and writing continuously for forty-five minutes.

Just as the sound of his pen disappeared back into a background silence so alive it seemed to pulsate with hidden sound, one could hear the ashram cat, Pebbles, meowing. She had gotten in the barn, probably looking for mice, and had made a beeline for Lee's dais. She jumped up on the divan with him and nuzzled her way underneath his blanket, purring. Lee reached out his hand and began to very lightly stroke her fur, and as she settled in beside him with her head and paws on his knee, he played with her a little, wagging his finger and tempting her to play. When the *pujari* rang the bell, Lee picked up the cat and left with her.

The barn has no heat or insulation, and is really, literally an old barn with open spaces where the rock walls meet the roof. The floor is concrete and has been covered with white carpets. The shrine with its *vigraha* of Yogi Ramsuratkumar and Lee's dais are flanked by large arrangements of fresh flowers and candles to create a beautiful meditation space. It is one of those enigmas of life on Lee's ashram in France: that which seems crazy or irritating or half-baked becomes imbued with grace, a kind of poetry, and becomes in fact a matrix for the transmission of presence. The barn doors have many cracks and chinks in them, and although one is sheltered from rain inside it, there are ways in which meditating in the barn is not unlike meditating outside. The sounds of birds (and sometimes morning symphonies of birds) or rain, for example, are exquisitely piercing in their beauty in the silence of the barn, and seem to echo off the three-hundred-year-old stone walls.

There is something tremendously innocent and refreshing about meditating in a place that sheltered cows and goats and horses for hundreds of years, that protected the harvests of hay, corn and wheat in the winter weather. Where sacks of potatoes and apples and hanks of cured meat were kept out of the weather, where the musty, rank yet curiously clean smell of dung and hay and dirt and animal hair proliferated and permeated everything. Those smells are gone now. The meditation hall is quite pristine and airy, with an occasional whiff of incense drifting on the air while the pujari performs the morning *arati puja* to the lineage. But the barn still carries something of that wholesome natural life. Once one gets used to the condition of being cold, slightly damp or bitten by mosquitoes and other insects while meditating, this quality of earthiness, space and simplicity becomes very exhilarating—a reminding factor of Organic Innocence, the foundation of all manifest life.

That the sangha has the opportunity to meditate with Lee every morning is a gift of great generosity on the part of the teacher. These morning meditation "darshans" are a time of silent transmission, the value of which is inestimable. The barn, with all of its ambiance, lends itself beautifully to this communication. Lee is perfectly ordinary as he sits writing poetry to his Father, but at the same time one can't help but be impacted by the magnanimity of his actions—the fact that he shares these moments openly with his students.

These days of being on the ashram are some of the best times of the summer with Lee in France. At times it is as if the poetry that Lee writes in the morning meditation hour is reflected everywhere one goes on the grounds. Walking in the vegetable garden the change of the season—the imminent process of death, making way for rebirth—is seen everywhere. Tomatoes, green beans, rich pale orange winter squash and immense pumpkins hang heavy on old green and brown vines, beginning their ritual decay back into the earth but still abundantly giving. The peach trees are heavily laden with a harvest of small, sweet peaches, and the flower gardens are dotted with bursts of color. The fruit harvest is ample this year at La Ferme de Jutreau; the apple and plum and persimmon trees hang with fruit, and breakfasts are warmed with bowls of naturally sweet, hot fruit compote. These ambrosial essences of life on a country ashram—where the focus is on the teaching, on practice, raising children and growing food—all become reflections of Divine Influence.

Even the rickety and rusty old bicycles, donated by friends of the community, used for exercising have a certain spirit to them. It seems fitting that Lee's ashram has these old bicycles that no one else wants, and would in fact be considered fit for the garbage dump by most people. It is a small testimony to renunciation and beggary.

At breakfast Lee talked with Brindavan about his upcoming seminar at Maison Raphael in Paris that is scheduled for the last weekend he will be in France. He instructed her in handling the logistics for his last few weeks in France. More and more he begins to wrap up his business in France for the year as he turns his attention toward America. In less than four weeks Lee will be returning to Arizona, to the core body of the sangha that awaits his return. They are the ones who have worked diligently to keep the Arizona ashram thriving. There the focus is on practice within the nitty-gritty work world of running Hohm Community's two business—Hohm Press and the glass case business—plus two bands and a theatre company, as well as Hohm Sahaj Mandir, the church itself, with its community, publishing and educational concerns.

The foundation that has been forged over almost twenty years in the Arizona ashram provides the matrix out of which the more contemplative ashram in Europe, with its focus on providing hospitality to guests and the transmission of dharma, or the teaching, has been able to blossom. The sangha has grown now to the point that there are members of the American and European sangha who have never met each other. As the network of the Hohm Community extends to include many friends of the community and people who participate every summer in Europe by coming to Lee's seminars at La Ferme de Jutreau, the number of people who are woven into the shawl of Yogi Ramsuratkumar, even on the fringe, so to speak, is bigger than Lee's conservative estimate of one hundred fifty.

Coming back into the salon in the *grande maison* after breakfast, Lee hung a newly framed, very large charcoal pencil drawing of Yogi Ramsuratkumar's face that was given to him by an artist, a friend of the community who comes to Lee's seminars. In this way Lee continually brings the ashram to life with the all consuming presence of his Father. The drawing captures something about Yogi Ramsuratkumar, especially around the eyes, but at the same time makes him look almost like a Sufi, with a turban-like head wrap as opposed to the humble green wrap Yogi Ramsuratkumar wears around his head, which sometimes falls off, he has so little care of it. Then he will absently re-wrap it, with his long hair falling through the gaps that he, in his total lack of self-consciousness, leaves in the weave of the wrap.

Later in the office, Lee was reading a letter from Dean, his student who leads the bordello in New York City. Lee laughed and said, "Andrew Cohen said recently in a talk in New York City, 'Enquiry is more important than the practice of meditation.'" Lee smiled. He seemed to find great enjoyment in this piece of news. Andrew's statement was very similar to what Lee himself had said about Enquiry earlier in the summer. Not long ago Lee commented that it wasn't uncommon to discover that different teachers he knows are talking about or addressing the same issues at the same time. The fact of these kinds of synchronicity was again bearing itself out.

September 8, 1999
La Ferme de Jutreau

Michelle arrived today from Boulder. After dinner as the group sat around the table with Lee she mentioned that Tom had just gotten back from France and had regaled them with stories of his time here with Lee.

"What stories did he tell?" Lee asked.

"He told a story about you yelling at him, standing just three inches away from his face." Everyone listened closely as she continued, "He said, 'You know, the way Lee's tone can be dripping with disgust.' Tom said Lee was screaming at him like that . . ."

Lee looked around incredulously. "Does anyone remember me yelling at Tom?" A number of people said no emphatically. Remembering the scene at the restaurant, Jane asked Michelle, "Are you talking about when Lee talked to Tom at the restaurant in Basel about buying the statue? Lee wasn't yelling at Tom at all, he was actually speaking very quietly." The story as people remembered it was relayed to Michelle. She chuckled. The scenario remembered by everyone else was completely different than Tom's experience of it as he relayed it to the sangha in Boulder.

Lee laughed as if in disbelief and said, "Yes, people often remember things very differently than the way they really happened." Then he began to talk about the teaching point that he was making in the conversation in Basel that night. He said, "All I said to Tom was that the statue was a nice piece. He asked me if he could go back to the guy and look for himself. I said, 'Sure.' I'd already ended up taking half the sangha, when I really just wanted to go alone. As it turned out all these people ended up buying the same piece of jewelry that I had bought. The nerve of it! But the point I was making in Basel was that I can't say anything—this thing is nice, that is pleasant, such and such is attractive—without people projecting on me that I want the thing and running out and buying it for me. If I want people to project like that on me I won't be cryptic and drop hints. I should just ask for things outright like most spiritual teachers do!" Lee paused for a moment, then yelled, "Bridge, *dans le salon*! Jai Guru!" Then he abruptly pretended to fall, face forward, into his plate.

"One spade!" Lee shouted into the space. There were four bridge games going in the salon. Now people stopped their low-key talk and looked up at Lee, who sat at the bridge table in his leather chair in front of the fireplace. "Sorry!" He looked around at the people playing bridge. "I'm over here with the deaf people!" He smiled apologetically. "Somehow I always end up with the deaf people. If I had a dollar for every time someone said, 'What?' after a bid, we'd have a new ashram already!" It was a perfect delivery of an ongoing criticism of the lack of mindfulness at the bridge table, especially glaring since the purpose of playing bridge is to work with paying attention and self-observation. Just before this the people at Lee's table had gotten caught up in a discussion about Y2K, and the fact that tomorrow is 9.9.99—a date that is supposed to create possible major glitches in computers all over the world.

The conversation continued as Michelle, who was Lee's partner, told everyone about some of the relatively minor glitches that had been reported so far, like one in England where a huge amount of food was thrown away because the computer said it was three hundred years old. Lee said almost deadpan, "Regardless of what happens tomorrow, we will have lunch."

Then he added with mild sarcasm, "We *will* have an After Dinner Talk, regardless of what happens tomorrow . . . one heart!" He yelled out his bid in a penetrating tone that was an unmistakable call to attention. The bridge game carried on.

Lee had spent a good deal of the After Dinner Talk the night before talking about the fears about Y2K that came up for a number of Lee's students when the information about the computer bug had hit the mainstream press. A number of his students were reading articles at that time about the possibility of widespread breakdown in the computerized infrastructure of the technologically driven Western world. Now Lee commented again on this, saying, "People were hit by the possibility of going without electricity for a month as if they were facing their death. The possibility of a little discomfort and people fall apart! It was unbelievable, the level of recoil and fear that came up over this thing, even for long-time practitioners who should know better." All along Lee has continued to make it clear that the scare over Y2K seemed overblown and highly unlikely; but if anything should happen, the possibility of breakdown in the usual comforts we take for granted should be considered an excellent opportunity for one's work. That is the context of the practitioner.

September 9, 1999
La Ferme de Jutreau

The white cat was back in Lee's lap this morning for meditation. After a while she settled down on Lee's leg, curled her tail around her body, yawned and stared out at everyone, then closed her eyes. Lee petted her for a few minutes, then with the cat dozing on his lap, he seemed to sink more deeply into meditation until the bell rang, when he got up and carried her outside.

At breakfast Lee regaled his students with hilarious anecdotes from various movies, like "Dumb and Dumber," "Romy and Michelle's High School Reunion," or "Austin Powers"—the kind of movies that require one to get down on the level of the banal to join in the fun. These movies seem to provide Lee with a kind of entertainment, a comic relief that he appreciates. He said to Michelle, "Have you seen "Dumb and Dumber?" You've got to see "Dumb and Dumber!" It's the lowest kind of humor—the best kind!" He was playfully pushing on Michelle's attachment to refined tastes in art of all kinds. He pulled a folded red napkin out of the pocket of his red corduroy shirt, tore it in half and proceeded to blow his nose with one of the scraps. The red napkin looked suspiciously like something he'd been saving from the Shri tour to use as needed. Someone said, "Oh! It's 9.9.99, and it's nine o'clock!"

Lee chimed in, "Yeah, I can't wait to hear from America about what's happening over there." Clint, who just returned from the U.S., said, "Well, my watch is still working, that's a good sign."

Lee shot back a dry remark, "Yes, if it's the end of the world it's good to know what time it is!" As he finished blowing his nose, he tossed the rolled up, used napkin into a bowl with prune pits that would be cleared away with the breakfast dishes, and then carefully folded the other half of the napkin and put it in his pocket. Referring to Lee's constant example of conserving energy and resources in many practical ways, Chris said, "When you die we're going to throw a whole box of brand new tissues in the grave with you!" Lee laughed.

Putting the napkin in his pocket, he discovered a toothpick and pulled it out with an exaggerated look of surprise. "Ahhh! A treasure!" He immediately put it in his mouth. Everyone at the table was laughing along with him. Lee said, "Do me a favor—don't take this as a sign that I want toothpicks for *prasad*!" This spawned more laughter and jokes about Lee getting jewel-encrusted toothpicks in gold toothpick holders engraved "Baba," one of the names Lee's students sometimes call him.

The laughter had just begun to subside when he got up to leave and looked down on the floor. With a melodramatic "Oh!" as if he'd just uncovered another treasure, he bent down and picked up an unused paper napkin that had dropped to the floor. "Ahhh!" he said with a satisfied smile at his discovery—another paper product that would have been thrown away preemptively and injudiciously and that would now be made full use of.

He folded the napkin and tucked it away with the other in his pocket, then got up and sauntered out of the dining hall.

Everyone sat at the table laughing. It was another one of the guru's comedy routines, in which he engaged his students in a kind of foolishness and crazy banter and playing around that often results in both the lifting of spirits and the producing of somber considerations. In this particular mood one often leaves with something to chew on, while at the same time resentments that tend to accumulate in the hotbed of sadhana melt away, people relax and enjoy each other's company. According to Lee, there are more esoteric benefits to laughter, having to do with working the moving or instinctual center of the body. But one can only make use of this particular form of teaching circumstance, which Lee has been creating almost every morning over breakfast at La Ferme de Jutreau, if chronic self-importance is dropped. We have to learn to take ourselves much less seriously. It's also one of the values—for sadhana—of watching movies of the genre that Lee was describing.

Back at his desk in the office Lee's attention turned to Jan, who has started a new book project given to her by Lee. "Can you meet a deadline? You've never met a deadline yet," he said looking at her penetratingly.

"I'll do my best," she answered.

"If you write twenty pages a day for three weeks the book will be done . . ." he paused to observe the look of absolute shock and disbelief on her face, then continued with, "but okay, we'll give you a break." Her concern for whether Lee was actually serious that he wanted a completed book in three weeks relaxed, and he went on, "Have it finished by the end of the year. That's too much time, but . . ." he shrugged, as if to say, what else could he do with people's resistance.

Brindavan walked in. "Excuse me, Lee," she began.

"Anytime! You can barge right in and just rip things apart anytime," he smiled sweetly, but his tone was ambiguous and almost impossible to decipher. This ambiguity is one of the most potent skillful means that Lee uses with his students. He will make a statement that either appears totally innocent, but is, by nature of its content, completely loaded with innuendoes about the student's cramp or habitual tendencies, or he will couch a teaching communication in hilarity, foolishness, or bawdy or inane humor. We are left with the feeling that the rug has just been pulled out from under us, and we are left standing on nothing but our own ability to self-observe. It is a tremendously useful tool, very similar in impact to Lee's famous chuckles, snickers and outright guffaws, which also often leave one nonplussed, vaguely uncomfortable and wondering.

"Never mind," Brinda laughed.

"No, really, I'm serious," Lee insisted innocently, nodding and encouraging Brinda to continue.

"I wanted to know if you had given Susanne instructions about when to leave," she said. Susanne stood in the doorway. She has lived on the ashram for the past four years as a renunciate, and has been asked by Lee to move back to Germany. He gave the date— next Monday—and discussed the travel details of how she would get to Freiburg.

"So next Monday," he said, looking at her intently. "It won't be put off—right? That's the final date?" She had already changed her plans three or four times, and Lee doesn't like to have plans changed due to personal attachments. "Do you need some money?"

"Yes," she nodded, "I can borrow it from Ramji Association."

"No. You don't borrow it from the ashram. I'll give it to you." She registered this with a rather shocked look on her face. "It's yours!" he continued, "It's a *loan*. You can pay me back next year in Freiburg. By then you'll be a working stiff—because when you get a job in the sleeping world you're dead. That's why they call them a working stiff—a corpse, you know?" This warning reverberated around the room for a second before Lee continued, "Then you'll have money and freedom and everything. Great!" He was looking steadily at Susanne, who quietly took this in. "Works for you? Okay."

The deal was concluded. Lee had, once again, made sure that he is the responsible party. In this gesture he said many things. It was a gesture of support and confidence—he had asked this person to leave the ashram and go back to Germany to live, but at the same time he was making it possible for her to make the transition through his personal financial support. At a more esoteric level, it was a statement of the lawful relationship between guru and disciple: the guru takes on the disciple's karma.

Susanne said, "Yes, I'm ready. Thank you." She and Brinda left the office and Lee went back to the work at his desk. A little later he picked up two newspaper advertisements that had been cut out and sent to him by a woman student whose therapist had recommended that she go to some tantric workshops.

Lee read the copy out loud, " 'Sacred sexuality . . . Private sessions for individuals and couples . . . Specializing in sexuality and spirituality, tantric practices, orgasmic expansion, personal transformation, emotional release.' Wow, that sounds awful!" He threw the ads in the trashcan. I fished them out to get the exact wording of the copy. The photograph of the workshop leader grinned garishly out at me. She was pictured leaning against a tree with a lascivious smile on her face that said, 'I've got a naughty secret and I'm going to let you in on it.' The photograph communicated a complete travesty of tantric principles and sadhana. Lee said, "These people are all successful. They've all got scads of clients, they're rolling in money. It's disgraceful." I threw the ad back in the trash.

Over the summer at La Ferme de Jutreau there has been a perpetual flow of the teaching and transmission that goes from space to space with Lee—from meditation to the breakfast gatherings to the work in the office where Lee sits at his desk and holds court, to lunch, back to the office, to After Dinner Talks or bridge. There is a subtle current that seems to weave the whole day into a realm that is beyond what we conceive of as ordinary life, so that everything is imbued with the living presence of the Divine, or what traditional dharma might call being, consciousness, bliss—*sat, chit, ananda*. It is this very quality of the conscious matrix and ground of all life, interacting with itself, that is brought from background to foreground in Lee's company. All this is experienced within the flux and flow of a daily life that would appear not just modest but uneventful and boring to the eye that is chained to worldly excitements.

It is through Lee that the influence of Yogi Ramsuratkumar has come to such a steady blaze here on this small, humble ashram hidden away in the French countryside, where an invisible burning presence is felt right away, as soon as one enters the ashram grounds. And as Brindavan said, when she and Clint and their daughters first came here in October four years ago, Yogi Ramsuratkumar was already here, waiting for them. But over the past ten days, particularly since returning from the last trip, there have been many people who have had a heightened experience of the presence and benediction of Yogi Ramsuratkumar at La Ferme de Jutreau. There are periods of time in which his presence seems to become even more acutely real, to the point that the emanation of his physical image is seen in moments.

Tomorrow morning Lee and company leave immediately after meditation in the two vans for Lee's weekend seminar in Bordeaux. He will give a public talk tomorrow night at the Centre Equestre Equilibrethe—a *gite*, or hostelry, that the group who is hosting Lee has rented for the weekend.

September 10, 1999
Joué near Bordeaux

After the usual picnic on the road on the way down, Lee had planned to spend most of the day at the beach on the Atlantic Ocean near Bordeaux before he went to the *gite* where the group would stay for the weekend and where the seminar would begin at eight o'clock tonight. It was a beautiful sunny day as the two vans were parked under tall pine trees and the group trudged through the low sandy dunes to the gleaming wide white beach. In the distance the blue of the sky met the hazy green-blue of the sea at the edge of the world, giving the immediate impression of vastness. Gulls wheeled and turned up above. Breakers curled in gentle sprays of white foam at the shore, and overhead the sky was clear except for a few hazy clouds that drifted at the horizons. It was a blissful sight, and archetypal in its awesome power to communicate at an essential level. The ponderous, unfathomable power and presence of the ocean—a living divine mother—was immediately overwhelming to the senses. Although the waves were gentle at this time of day, here was an undeniable, impersonal force of Nature—one with which there is no bargaining, only submission and respect. She could be gentle, rock us in her arms, or she could annihilate us with complete ruthlessness. Encountering such an entity gives one pause to consider the reality of one's smallness.

The children immediately ran to the water, and Lee accompanied them for a brief bit of swimming and floating and gentle play chest-high in the water. Then he moved to the wet sand just at the edge of the waves and built sandcastles with them for awhile. Covered with wet sand and dripping a little, Lee came back up to the spot where a number of his students were either sitting or lying in the sun on thick sheets or towels that had been laid out. He lowered himself to a place on the sand under one of the umbrellas. When she saw Lee sitting on the sand instead of on the readily available towels, Ann said to him, "Would you like a towel?" He shook his head no and she asked in disbelief, "Do you like the sand?"

"No," Lee smiled. It was reminiscent of when, three years ago at the beach, Lee had made numerous teaching lessons to the adults who accompanied him. For example, in three days at the beach he had been the only person out of about twenty people who never showered, or even rinsed the salt and sand off in the cold water shower outside the bungalow. He had been down in the sand and surf with the children just like everyone else, but everyone else rinsed off or headed as quickly as possible for the only hot shower in the cottage. Lee had come back and sat down to read in a chair, completely outside of and unmoved by all this rush to get comfortable.

After an hour or so, while Lee was playing bridge with some of the adults and the children played around the edges of the water, the surf was noticeably changing. Now it was quickly becoming rough and wild, whereas before it was gentle. The waves were much higher, and rolled in with resounding booms and crashes. Looking at the ocean Jane said, "Now is the time to be out there in the water!" The incoming waves were four or five times higher than they had been only minutes earlier. They were gathering force in swells that surged and grew much further out, past the breakers, to climb to small mountains that peaked for a fleeting moment of perfection in form, then surrendered themselves into the next moment, when they became roaring freight trains of froth and foam that pounded into the shore in a churning paroxysm of sand and water.

Lee looked up, seeming interested. It's not the sort of thing that he would normally respond to. Usually he would just say, "Hmmm," with eyebrows raised, as if to say, "That's vaguely interesting, but what does that have to do with practice?" Now he did something totally uncharacteristic. He got up and said with a smile, "Okay, I'm going to go get rocked in the waves!" He chuckled a little at the incredulity on the face of one of his students. Rewording it for some reason, as if he was adding an important piece to the communication, he said a second time, "I'm going to go get pounded by the waves!"

He walked across the hard packed sand and without hesitation directly into the water, going in deep as strong waves came billowing toward him. About twenty-five feet out into the water a huge wave came gathered force and built momentum. He caught the wave and rode it into the surf. He floated the wave in a way that appeared effortless, even in the turbulence near the shore. Swimming and wading back out again, he caught another wave. His mood was infectious, and several of us joined him in the ocean. After about five minutes of this he said, "That was great! That's it for me," and walked up toward the beach umbrellas.

The ocean continued to get wilder and more tumultuous. The French lifeguards set up red flags to indicate where people should swim if they were going out into the flux of the surf so that they could be within the watch. Every ten minutes or so the lifeguards called out over loud speakers, warning people of the dangerous undertow that ran in swift currents under the high surf. The waves were running higher and higher up onto shore. Five or six times our towels and beach umbrellas had to be quickly moved to avoid getting completely inundated by a wave as it ran up.

While the drama of the living ocean unfolded, asserting its right to claim the earth, Lee left with the children to get ice cream. But it was as if he had opened a doorway for an object lesson for the four or five of us who stayed in the water and were thrown into a state of abandon as we rode the waves and the surf, getting seriously and even dangerously pummeled at times by wave after crashing wave of seething water and sand. The whole experience became a striking metaphor for the felt experience of the force of Grace. The object lesson couldn't have been more direct.

What we discovered was that if one didn't maintain a high degree of intention, the fierce riptide took one swiftly out to sea—a very risky thing, because of course it meant almost certain danger or possibly death. Perhaps one could be saved by the shore patrol, but in an undercurrent that swift, it would be unlikely. It took a good deal of physical strength and effort to meet the power of the ocean; it was impossible to play in the surf at this point unless one was an excellent swimmer.

Simultaneously and paradoxically there was a very high degree of relaxation and surrender that was necessary. If we attempted to outrun the sheer weight and volume of the next wave, or to avoid it by forcefully standing our ground against it, we were immediately thrown down by the immense, overpowering force of the water—a living thing against which we had no power whatsoever—and ended up fiercely tumbled with the sand and shells and rocks in the chaos of the wave breaking on the shore. If we resisted the wave, bringing tension to the relationship of human body to living water, then the wave would take the body, now completely out of control, and thrash it soundly underneath pounding water and sand. If we got caught in the surf the body was inundated by wave after wave, sometimes not able to get a breath, and tumbled and whirled about in the continuing onslaught of the ocean.

On the other hand, when we dove directly into the wave just as it peaked and began its relentless descent, then we would glide through the center of chaos and destruction at the core of the wave, passing through unscathed to the other side, to come out wet and gleaming and enlivened. This was a function of having perfect timing, and the only way to have perfect timing was to be one with the wave. Timing, as Lee has discussed it many times over the years, is everything; perfect timing only comes from essence attention, or the instinctual attention of the body aligned with the other centers of thinking and feeling.

The whole experience was a direct metaphor for how to live in the annihilating flood of Grace. In sadhana one has to find the courage to dive into the tremendous force of Grace, against which we have no power and no control. No matter how many times we get pounded (which is often perceived as failure—"I'm *still* full of greed, anger, sloth, selfishness," and so on), we must keep throwing ourselves back into the tide. If one stays in the tides of Grace long enough, sooner or later (lifetimes later) one will be surrendered to its waves, and like Lee, ride without effort. But you have to be a good swimmer, which means you must have the well-developed muscles of practice in order to enter into the swift flow of it. There is a physical, tensile strength with correlates in the subtle dimension that is necessary to meet the force of Grace as it assaults the human body. This is especially true in Lee's company.

After forty-five minutes of throwing ourselves intentionally into the maelstrom of the surf, we came out dripping and gritty with sand and salt, but also giddy and intoxicated. It was a joyful experience. The loss of ego control as one was swept into the unrestrained force of the ocean was exhilarating, ecstatic. This crazy game became more than a symbolic act; it was a gesture toward Grace—"Come get me, I'm willing to play."

This kind of experience—working directly with the raw powers of nature—is a learning circumstance that Lee almost never orchestrates for his students. One can say "almost never" because on this particular day it seemed that Lee opened the window for this experience, more or less offering it with his own physical gesture, then went to get ice cream with the children, leaving the rest to the devices of his students. Would we walk through the open window? Would we even notice that it was open?

Around four-thirty the group packed up and walked back to the vans. Lee changed from his bathing suit back into the gray sweatpants and tie-dyed violet shirt he'd been wearing on the way down. After another hour on the road the group landed at the *gite*, an equestrian center as well as hostel. The place itself was a cluster of low bungalows and horse stables with a central gathering room and two kitchens, one of them bigger and equipped to serve larger groups of people. The whitewashed bungalows had tiled roofs the color of fired clay, darkened by the green moss that grew rampant on the roofs, the trees, the grounds. Less than an hour away from the ocean, the whole place had the look of many places in southern Louisiana, with its humid, salty air, and moss and ivy encrusted oak trees towering over wide green yards. This feeling of the deep south was oddly combined with a sort of northern California guest ranch ambiance, all of it extremely run-down and unkempt.

Looking into the main room where Lee's public talk tonight and the seminar Saturday and Sunday would be given, the horse motif continued and expanded into variations on the theme. Old kerosene lamps hung all around the walls, which were populated with paintings of different varieties of horses, many of which hung crooked on the walls from which plaster peeled. One cupboard near the front door was stuffed full of silver cups and prize ribbons for winning horses. The walls were also decorated with green plastic lattices—the function of which was hard to guess, or perhaps they were just there to add to the aesthetics of the place.

Before dinner everyone went off to their rooms to shower—except Lee, who, after setting up his book table across the back of the main room, sat in his room reading a book. He went to dinner, then directly over to the book table wearing the same gray sweatpants and tie-dyed T-shirt, and yet somehow appearing fresh. As people began to come into the space he sat so quietly and invisibly in the back by the books that if one didn't know who he was, it would be a shock to find out that he was the "tantric teacher" who would speak tonight. The space was set up with very uncomfortable plastic chairs in three rows just beyond a dirty Oriental rug placed below the small couch at the front of the room where Lee would sit. A hastily thrown together meager bouquet of yellow sunflowers on long thin stems and overblown pink roses had been moved to the front of the room to a table beside Lee's couch. Along the sides of the room were more of the small couches—crude iron frames with foam pads covered in dingy orange broadcloth. Along the backs of the couches were foam pillows covered in an orange, brown and yellow print of the same material. In the back were three low wooden benches with some pillows piled precariously on them. They looked incredibly uninviting.

As the room filled up with people it got stuffier and hotter, in spite of the fact that the front door and the back door were open. Both of these doors opened onto the grounds, allowing the two large, furry, filthy ranch dogs that hung around the front door easy and frequent access to the room. One of them was part sheep dog, its hair matted and stinking. It trailed leaves and burrs and sandy dirt everywhere it went—and it went everywhere, walking in and out of the room, under people's feet, threading its way through the crowd, back and forth, in and out. The other dog was bigger and black with brown markings, and looked a little like a Irish Setter with some black Labrador retriever mixed in. It was huge and smelly as well. Both dogs seemed to claim the room in which Lee would speak as their personal space, over which they would periodically square off in fierce growls and moans. In addition to the dogs, the room was plagued with flies, which swarmed in the air and lit on every available surface, especially human surfaces.

The crowd was a strange mix of people. There was a huge, gruff, bear of a man who came in looking fierce even though he was smiling. He was immense and rather crude in appearance, and he ambled over to greet a number of people, then found a seat on a plastic chair in the back. There were a number of fresh-faced, very bright and handsome young people who had all gone to Michael's talk on Yogi Ramsuratkumar in Bordeaux some months ago. They sat across the front row. Several couples walked in, eight or nine students of Arnaud Desjardins and a woman wearing a glittering *bindi* dot from India on her third eye. Another woman, a former disciple of Osho Rajneesh, had been at the Guru Purnima Celebration at La Ferme de Jutreau earlier this summer. She looked happy to be back among Lee and his gang. The woman with the *bindi* dot was her friend, also a disciple of Rajneesh. An older woman came in and, putting a thin foam pad on the floor, laid down in the front of the room to the left of where Lee would sit. She obviously had some problem with her back.

It was in this scenario that Lee came walking to the front of the now crowded room

634

and took his seat, sitting cross-legged. He started in a blast, his voice acidic and dripping with irony.

"Some of you are here for the weekend and some of you just for tonight. I'm pretty sure my style is something most of you have never seen before—most speakers who give seminars are interested in establishing a continuing relationship, but I'd be just as happy to never see most of you for the rest of eternity. Tonight and this weekend the book table is the center, the focal point of everything. I'd be happy never to see you again, but I want you to buy my books!

"I'm only interested in the teaching. I'm not interested in being friends, not interested in socializing, not interested in your precious feelings not getting hurt. If you are looking for a seminar that will give you peace and happiness, you've come to the wrong place. In order to know the teaching you have to know yourself, and you don't come to know yourself by having your illusions capitulated to. That's what the average seminar leader does—stroke your illusions! I look out at you all, and although some of you may look attractive on the surface, it's what's underneath that counts. Look at the people in this room! Pah!" Lee spit this out with seeming disgust. "*Ugly*! Uuuuhhh-gly! You're all full of illusion, pride, greed, vanity. Ugly!!" Lee laughed derisively. "Unfortunately, it's the truth. I wish I was just trying to get a rise out of you, to provoke you, but it's the truth! On the other hand, you found your way here tonight, so you must sense there is some value in looking at yourself with more clarity, honesty, greater vulnerability.

"My seminars aren't about peace and feeling good. My seminars are about war—a war that exposes reality. If you aren't at war with your illusions then my seminars are about starting that war. My wars are not aggressive or violent, like Christian wars. They are sacred and compassionate. I'm interested in the kind of war that has no winner and no loser. It's not a competition. There is no enemy. This war is about exposing reality, and when Truth is the victor there is *no* loser."

Lee was ruthlessly and relentlessly tearing into the thick maze of illusion, penetrating the space with his stinging wit and *vajra*-like delivery. His mood seemed to have the effect of whipping the group psyche into a state that would either force the attention into the felt sense of the body, or repel one from the room. At the same time as he continued he became hilariously funny. Flies were buzzing around everyone's head as the big, shaggy sheep dog wound his way through, between people's legs, under chairs, stalking the room and establishing his territory. Just as Lee began to tell one of his favorite jokes that has a dog in the punch line, the sheep dog squared off near the door with the Irish Setter, who wanted to come back into the room from outside. Low growls began, and by the time Lee had reached the point in his joke when he says, "Honey, honey, look what the dog did to my neck!" the two big dogs began to fight and scuffle at the door, rearing up on each other and snarling until someone shooed them out the door. It was a crazy synchronicity—the theatre of the absurd, manifesting itself in the room in concert with Lee's wild mood. The dog fight quelled, he went into another comedic monologue then he veered back into the dharma, giving people straightforward information about how to decode his teaching style.

Lee had a big grin on his face, people were smiling and laughing in camaraderie—we were all in it together now with the dogs, the flies, the crude dirty jokes, the insults and the guru sitting before us. Lee was like Shiva's wild and uncontrollable consort, Kali, the destroyer of illusion. It seemed that she was having a little tea party tonight with some unsuspecting beings who thought they had come to hear about love and sex and magic.

Lee was pure enigma with a gleam in his eye. Sometimes his head was thrown back in wild peals of laughter as he regaled the crowd with stories, metaphors, bad jokes, funny jokes. Sometimes he was sober and deadly. I couldn't help but reflect: which one of his peers would be willing to drive to this hole in the wall—this funky, run-down mess of a place, so far off the beaten trail—to make the teaching available? None of them, and each for his or her own reason, one might assume. Undoubtedly E.J. Gold could appreciate the satiric edge, the cutting paradoxes of such a situation, and yet he never leaves his cloistered stronghold, but lives in relative seclusion.

Lee, on the other hand, came driving up with two vans full of people, kids, a ragtag crew sunburned and salty, trailing sand but bright-eyed. Lee's hosts—two very nice couples who have only recently formed this association—greeted him warmly, if a little uncertainly, and now here he was.

Outside the windows that spanned the upper half of the back wall the sky was a deep periwinkle blue streaked with coral and lavender swaths of color. Tall black oaks and distant pines stood in stark silhouette to the sky. This grand display spilled in through the windows as night fell and Lee talked. People were listening intently, laughing; many had taken their shoes off and leaned back in their chairs, or with an arm around their partner. So much is lost in putting Lee's words on paper because his subtle theatrics, his flair for melodrama and his intonations and gestures so richly nuance and spice his talks. The body language, tone and facial expressions of Lee as raconteur are compelling, fascinating to watch. Just as you begin to feel repulsed by the absurdities, the insults, the crude innuendoes which Lee throws out on his audience, suddenly, before you know what has happened, you find yourself so magnetically drawn in that you can't turn away. You are captivated, and smiling foolishly, laughing at things you never thought you would find yourself laughing at. On this occasion, Lee was at his strongest. All this, which flows so naturally from a person who is by born tendency shy and retiring, is a powerful lesson in itself. Lee keeps telling us that however he is animated is purely a function of what is most needed to communicate the teaching for the people who are present in his company at any given time. Underneath the madness of this scene hummed a palpable fiery force of transmission—the blessing power of Yogi Ramsuratkumar.

Holding his sides in gales of laughter Lee wiped the tears from his eyes and said, "Well! I was enjoying the talk so much I forgot what the speaker was talking about!" He laughed heartily. "What *was* he talking about?!" He laughed again at his own joke—a thinly veiled comment about what was really going on.

In a conversation before dinner someone had said laughingly, "I wonder if our hosts will make enough food for all of us? That is, not knowing how much we can eat." As it turned out a rich lasagna was served in huge portions. After dinner Lee had commented, "Well, they've read my books; let's see how they respond to me in person."

"Do you think your reputation precedes you here?" I asked.

"Yes, some of the people who will come are Arnaud's students, some are not," Lee had answered.

Now he was saying, "I introduce you to *knowledge* . . ." The smell in the room was permeated by the rank scent of wet filthy dog fur. Some people looked insulted now, as if they were barely hanging on. Some had deeply pained looks on their faces. One yawned. Some looked disturbed and upset as Lee careened through the underworld labyrinth nonstop, pushing buttons and getting the predictable responses.

"The mind is not all that important. It doesn't eat. It doesn't have sex. The problem with most people's diet and most people's sex is that they are letting the mind do it. The way I teach is to circumvent the mind. The way I teach is to provoke emotions and feelings. The domains I provoke are often atrophied, so having them stimulated is often uncomfortable. Our muscles of Truth and Reality are atrophied. We've forgotten what it is to be real or true. In one way I am like a spiritual physical therapist, and it's not always pleasant for the client.

"I create circumstances where revelation is possible. This is not linear teaching. If I say something that makes sense to you and you assume that you know it because it makes sense to you, that is just one more illusion that will have to be dispelled. But if I am able to create an experience that will allow knowledge to spontaneously arise within you, then you *will* know it.

"Yogi Ramsuratkumar is an accessible point of Grace. Two things are necessary for the transmission of Grace to occur. The sender must have It and the recipient must know how to receive It. You get to learn the language of receptivity to Grace when I'm around." The sheep dog stood at the door about six feet away from Lee and made a low growling, groaning sound. "Hi! Hi!" Lee waved to the dog. "Dogs!" he added brightly.

As he brought the evening to a close he became somber and respectful, even grateful. "Thank you for coming, thank you for staying and participating tonight," he said seriously, obviously meaning it. He had put people through a very intense process—a skirmish in the war he had talked about. Now people looked much brighter, cleaner and saner than they had when they first arrived.

Lee walked back to the book table and talked with a number of people. A tall man walked up and spoke with Lee at length. It seemed that he had a Sufi teacher. "Who is your teacher?" Lee asked. Lee smiled as he recognized the name. He listened to the man, looking up into his face, then answered his question, "If he means as much to you as he seems to, the practice will come back to you, just naturally. One day you will just find it there." The man walked away and more people came up to ask about Lee's tapes from a seminar last year. The man with the Sufi teacher came back and asked some more questions, while a group of about six people stood not six feet away from Lee, smoking cigarettes in the doorway. The smoke drifted inside and across the book table. The scene was incredibly loose and casual.

On a shelf behind the book table Lee had set up an issue of *Tawagoto*, the Hohm Community journal. It was the issue on sex that was published in the fall of 1998, with a red cover. On the cover Lee had written in black magic marker SEX. "It will make them sell better," he said when asked about it. Now it stood out under a small lamp, the shade of which harbored the bodies of many moths and assorted flying insects that had apparently been dead for years and left to rot by whomever "cared" for this space. Those same shelves were covered with a melange of *brocante*—brick-a-brac and cheesy junk. A man walked away with a CD, a video of Yogi Ramsuratkumar and two books in his hand. The woman with the *bindi* dot came up and asked Lee if she could come to the seminar for the weekend. Lee said yes. Slowly the crowd thinned out and Lee was ready to leave. His only comment was, "Well, that was a first for the summer—no one walked out during the talk."

September 11, 1999
Joué

The dog sat outside the door like a shaggy, smelly sentinel as people came in just before nine o'clock, when the first session was to begin. Most of the people from the night before were back again, with some notable exceptions. The older woman took her place, lying back on the floor again on a foam pad. At five till nine Lee walked in and went straight to the book table. Promptly at nine o'clock he took his seat and began. After about fifteen minutes the woman with the *bindi* dot—only this time without it—arrived.

"You're late!" Lee yelled at her as she picked her way through the crowd to find a seat. She almost jumped out of her skin.

"You must not have wanted to be here too badly!" He paused for effect as she searched for a seat, looking up at him apprehensively. "Just kidding! I'm just offended that some-one would come late to *my* seminar! The spiritual master's poor ego is pricked!" A few people chuckled at this. Others just sat in confusion. Without skipping a beat he continued.

"But fortunately we haven't gotten to the point yet . . . what *is* the point? I can't remember!" Lee grinned. He had been talking about two dimensions of the path—infinity and divinity—and laying the contextual groundwork for the next two days in a discussion of the realization of nonduality. He had just begun to talk about how the Earth is reacting to being poisoned by human beings and their technological culture of nuclear wastes, war, pollution. He was making outrageous statements about the Earth killing off millions of people like lice in floods, earthquakes, volcanoes. He predicted a general increase in natural disasters. As his attention turned back to the group at large a challenger to his premise stepped to the fore, saying, "Why do you talk about the Earth, about storms and earthquakes, when those things have been happening on the Earth long before there were human beings?"

Lee said, "Afraid of death, eh? Don't want your family to die? We're *all* gonna die—your mother will die, your father will die, your brother will die, your sister will die, all your friends will die, your lovers will die, your mistresses will die, your misters will die . . ." People laughed. "We're all going to die," Lee continued, "and yes of course, there were natural disasters long before there were human beings. But in the next fifty years, in my opinion, we will see a frequency of natural disasters that are not a function of the Earth's natural expansion or settling in. Mother Gaia is angry and we're going to get a spanking!" He laughed. "It's just an opinion. My other opinion is, let's get going!

"There is a law of action and reaction called karma in the Eastern traditions. It was well known to Jesus, but it wasn't easily manipulated by the early church fathers, so they cut it out of the doctrine. In the first few centuries of Christianity karma was an important part of the teaching. We tend to think that what we do has no reaction beyond this life-time, but Reality is a function of polarities, and there is no separation between us and everything else. So every action one makes produces a karmic reaction in other domains. Our actions affect the natural world in this way; it's not just that we do something negative and we get something negative back in a personal way, but also impersonally.

"Life is about infinity and divinity. It's about realizing the teaching in context—infinity—and acting in a way that serves the creative evolution of existence—divinity. How we *live* is as important as what we *know*. To know what is true without *living* on the basis of what we know to be true is just half of what the path has to give. So the teaching is designed one hundred percent to serve the creative evolution of Life."

Lee introduced the audience to his Master, Yogi Ramsuratkumar. He talked about his sadhana and divine madness and the great Mahayana statement of Yogi Ramsuratkumar: "I do not seek for happiness. I only want to do my Father's Work. If even one being has benefited from my life, that is enough. It has been worthwhile. And if this body dies, the soul that may remain, may it be born again to do my Father's Work." He touched on very fundamental precepts of his own particular teaching: the fact of no separation, or "There is only God"; the Bodhisattva ideal of serving all sentient beings; Surrender to the Will of God; the Baul tenet of the master as divinized human being, *ishta devata* or chosen deity. He was skipping over the basics and laying groundwork in rapid-fire fashion. People were either keeping up or they weren't. He wasn't waiting for anyone.

He told the audience that two of his students would be presenting two sessions of the teaching—one on Saturday and one on Sunday—during this seminar. "The success of the teaching is not in the teacher. It shows up in the lives of the students. Because of that I like people to get a look at the maturity—or lack of it, as the case may be—of my students. I don't give seminars to get students. I gave up a very lucrative business to teach! I'd be making millions of dollars now if I'd stayed in that . . ." Pausing for effect he quipped, "Oh my God! What have I done?" putting his hand to his face in mock horror with a smile. "Now here I am a beggar, living in poverty—relatively speaking. Not like in India, of course. So I have an investment in giving seminars. I want what I have to communicate to be *used*. That's my primary investment. So if my students impress people with their maturity, it helps you use that communication. If not, then that's the risk we take.

"My work is not designed to be done with novices or beginners—people who haven't at least moved into the wisdom to be able to see more deeply beyond the appearance of things. I'm not a world teacher—I'm too low class. I'll never be a world teacher. I'm too lacking in sophistication or refinement for that, but if the appearance of things contradicts what you feel, that is a good thing to question. Time for brunch!"

During the early afternoon session Michelline, the older woman who was lying on the floor on a thin foam pad, obviously for a health reason, asked Lee a question about the difference between psychotherapy and spiritual work. She said that she had been in analysis for ten years with a very fine therapist, and she had never understood the distinction. Lee's answer was crystal clear, concluding with, "The difference between psychotherapy and spiritual work is context. Psychotherapy takes 'the dream' to be real. Manipulating the dream is the basic, bottom-line idea of therapy. A disturbance in the dream that can be redesigned to not be disturbing fixes the problem from the point of view of therapy. The unspoken assumption is that a healthy psychology is the Truth. Psychology is about coming to a healthy, sane balance, a harmonious balance within the illusion, and can be a good preliminary stage to the path, but psychotherapy can only take us so far because it functions under the context of illusion, not the context of spiritual life, of the reality of no separation.

"There are two contexts: ego and Truth. When we live in the context of ego, Truth can arise. But the experience arises and subsides back into the context of illusion. When we live in the context of Truth, an experience of ego can arise. But it arises and subsides back into the context of Truth. The path shifts context from ego to Truth. Our experience may remain the same in form, but not in essence. One of the things the Work does is turn difficult elements of our psychology into useful forces or tools on the path."

Afterward Michelline thanked Lee, saying that it was the first time she had understood the difference. She had an unusually innocent and pure face. She seemed like some-one who had managed to live a relatively long life without creating a trace of bitterness or anger in her features.

Between two-thirty and three o'clock there was a thirty-minute break. Juice and fruit were served on a table outside. Several people walked around the grounds smoking ciga-rettes after they had eaten a piece of fruit. At the book table Lee was inundated with well-meaning but inappropriate questions. One woman stood directly in front of Lee and very close to his body for about ten minutes, weeping and crying about a love affair that had gone wrong. Lee was quiet, kind, compassionate. His body communicated a deep seren-ity and quietude—the opposite of the wild and seemingly reckless personality he often animated during the talks. He was saying very little and mostly listening to her as she sobbed over the knowledge that she had just repeated a painful pattern in her life.

It was another example of misusing the spiritual master, however well-meant and sincere the seeker may have been. The guru is not a psychotherapist or counselor, and yet Lee was willing to answer her in the same context as that from which the question was asked—from the psychological domain. But this was just one of many such interactions that lacked the dignity of protocol that should be shown to the guru. For a teacher of Lee's caliber to make himself vulnerable to the unconscious abuses of protocol in relation to his person, and the rampant flood of projections and assumptions that must bombard his senses constantly, is sometimes shocking to observe.

Lee would never ask for or demand the basic courtesy and respect that should be extended to the teacher—or allow his students to ask or insist on these courtesies for him. He takes whatever is given to him with equanimity. But who knows what opportunity is lost, however, when the teacher is not extended the gratitude and dignity of the kind of elegant protocol that comes naturally in the presence of one whose only care is for the liberation of others from illusion. Despite all the seminars and dispensing of dharma over the summer, at times like this the feeling is that nobody gets it. The spiritual master gets approached like a cheap therapist and the treasure and gold of his presence and wisdom is left unmined. Overall this weekend was proving to be particularly challeng-ing in this respect.

Clint gave the three o'clock talk. The general mood seemed to be one of truculence, as one person after another challenged Clint, who spoke a great deal about responsibility and reliability on the path. The woman wearing the *bindi* dot on the first night raised her hand. She said that she was very angry with the way things were going, that she had come here to get something and she wasn't getting it. "Nothing is happening," she said, the muscles in her jaw working, her eyes dilated and wide. "We are just talking, talking, talking. There is nothing going on, nothing moving me." No matter what Clint did, she was clinched in her position. Eventually, after about ten minutes of dialogue with her, Clint moved on. Very shortly a man raised his hand and spoke about his discomfort with what was going on also. He said that he didn't trust Clint, that Clint seemed like a war-rior and he couldn't find those qualities in himself.

At one point Lee intervened in the dialogue, saying in a loud tone of voice from a couch on the side of the room where he sat and listened, "I hope I get some of that action! Clint is getting all the action here today! I'm itching for action! It's like the difference between *kata* and sparring."

Kata are the memorized, specific moves that are done in martial art forms, the pur-pose of which are to train one in all the variety of moves. Each move is designed to be a response to a set attack. Sometimes there is even *kata* work with a partner in which the attack and the defense are predesigned. It exhaustively trains the body in the moves, and then when one has the moves, one can begin to be spontaneous in applying them in actual sparring. Much of Lee's discourses during the day seemed like he was going through the paces—passing through the basics, just doing *kata*, with no "partners" in the audience who were willing or able to spar with him. One got the sense that to "spar" with Lee might mean to be available to create a possibility of real opening in the space, in the way that Lee has described.

As Lee took the floor back for the evening talk, he began to speak about how everyone just wanted to be entertained. He seemed to be addressing the woman who was angry. In between talks she had spoken with one of Lee's students and asked a lot of questions about the community bands, about how the women interact in bars with the opposite sex, about the music. It seemed that she was frustrated, having expected a more "loose" approach from a tantric master with a blues band and rock & roll music. Such a thing sounds potentially very entertaining, especially to a *sannyasin* who is used to Osho's free-wheeling, free love style. Instead she had found a very serious and fierce call to context, practice and discipline.

Tonight Lee touched on many important aspects of the path, giving very freely and magnanimously to the group. The flies and the dogs had only increased their activity in the room during the day. The dogs lay under couches or walked through the room brushing up against people's legs and trying to lie down on their feet. The flies continued to buzz annoyingly in a last moment frenzy before the frost would kill them all, probably in the next few weeks. Lee continued to cast out gems that a real practitioner would recognize as a treasure, but to the spiritual dilettante would probably be irritating in their stark confrontation to a self-indulgent ego.

Despite the few inspired moments, Lee seemed tired and drained at the end of the day on Saturday. It was very much like what mariners call the "doldrums" at sea—when there is no wind, no current, nothing happening, and the boat is just sitting in the water. This can go on for days at a time at sea, and is not one of the sailor's favorite phases of the journey. After the evening Lee commented that he was having to work very hard to make the teaching spaces "useful" to himself.

September 12, 1999
Joué

Lee came in briskly, rather like a top executive taking over his desk with total confidence and a "let's get down to business" attitude. He seemed to be finished with the doldrums of the day before. He immediately began to delineate the alchemy of love and sex—the title of the seminar—with vivid clarity and simplicity.

"I'd like to talk this morning about what alchemy means in relationship to love and sex. Love and sex are two different things. Sometimes love includes sex, sometimes not, and sometimes sex includes love, sometimes not. To most people sex is nothing more than an itch that has to be scratched, but you can't really reach it, so you scratch and scratch. Of course you can just consider that opinion the ravings of a maniac, and maintain your own opinions at all costs this weekend.

"There are also two distinct domains: sex and sexual energy. Sex is just two bodies meeting and doing whatever they do." Lee switched into a theatrical mode, speaking for the woman's side of things. " 'Does he have to do the same thing every night? He unbuttons my blouse the *same* way, takes off my pants the *same* way, lays me down on the bed the *same* way!' " Lee exaggerated the word *same* throughout this sentence in a singsong voice, getting his point across while people laughed at the truth of what he was saying.

" 'Can't we do it in the kitchen tonight?' she asks. 'The *kitchen!*' he says sarcastically, then knows he's made a mistake and covers it up, saying cloyingly, 'Oh honey, the kitchen floor is so hard, I don't want you to hurt your sweet little behind!' I'm sure when the women in France say they want it in the kitchen, the men sweep their women off their feet and say, 'Now baby! Right now!' " He growled this for effect. The men in particular were shaking with laughter. "In fact, when we reprint *The Alchemy of Love and Sex* remind me to add a chapter called, 'In the Kitchen.'

"So most sex is nothing more than two bodies scratching an itch. The intelligent use of sexual energy may have sex as its starting point, and may not. Many people in both Eastern and Western traditions are celibate, and are tremendously vital and juicy individuals. That results from the intelligent use of sexual energy. There are two domains of sex itself: physical sex, which is almost always debilitating, believe it or not, and sex that is energetically creative, or subtle sex. That's where the alchemy comes in.

"Every individual human being could be considered an energy generator. There is life as we know it, in which there is a certain amount of energy—money, resources or subtle energy. We feel alive or feel exhausted. But there tends to be a limited amount of energy, so the alchemy of sex and love is geared toward generating more energy.

"Human beings can serve many functions on Earth. We can actually help create a world of greater peace, harmony, health and beauty—not that we can make war stop, but if enough people were using energy creatively, the result would be the end of war and violence and cruelty. Personally, I'm cynical—I think that human beings are unwilling to do anything that doesn't serve themselves, so I don't think we'll see that in our lifetimes. However, every little bit helps.

"This energy can be used completely selfishly or more generously, more selflessly. Most of the occult, metaphysics and of course black magic are all about using this energy selfishly. If someone is giving a fancy lecture on love but is thinking about how the success of this lecture is going to make them famous, then it is done for selfish reasons. So sexual energy is a doorway to extraordinarily subtle, refined and higher forms of energy, but we have to use it properly.

"The metaphysical journey of the human being is a constant cycle from the most refined and subtle realms to the grossest realms," Lee slapped his chest for emphasis. "There are two options: we can continue to function in that cyclical pattern over and over but nothing ever changes, or we can enter into a cyclical pattern that is like a spiral, so every time we enter the cycle at a different or higher level. That's what the path is about.

"We're already as gross as we are going to get, physically. When our attitude is self-centered rather than other-centered, that's as gross as our attitude gets. Some people are more inhuman in their behavior than others, but the psychology is the same. The difference between a killer and a healer, or a professor, is our childhood psychology, but the context is no different. We are manipulated by unconscious forces in the psyche; we have no choice in anything. Doctors and nurses have chosen their profession because of childhood experiences, not out of conscience. If you want more about this I suggest you read Alice Miller, but read with an open mind because what she has to say is shattering.

"Human beings are essentially at the bottom of a cycle: energy has descended, become matter and ego, and we are stabilized in this position. From here we have the opportunity to begin the process of ascension. Sex happens at the base of the trunk of the body. In the Eastern tradition there is the concept of the chakras—seven of them—with the highest at the peak of the head and the lowest at the base of the spine. The way the subtle energy is blueprinted in the subtle body follows the physiological system of brain and spinal cord. It starts in the head, goes down the front of the body to the base of the spine, turns around and goes back up the spinal line to the head. There are a lot of technical specifics to this, but I'm being very brief because the specifics are not the point this morning.

"Physical sex happens with the genitals, down at the bottom of the cycle, so the descending energy flows down . . ." At this point a woman walked in looking totally out of place. She took a seat up front on the couch to Lee's left and sat down. Her face was pinched and wary; she looked very hassled, as if she was sitting on a volcano. Lee immediately turned to her and spoke in a brusque tone of voice.

"Are you supposed to be here? This is a seminar, we're talking about sex. Is that okay with you?" She stared at Lee nonplussed, seeming to not comprehend his challenging tone. She was clearly put on the defensive. She looked around hesitantly. A flush of anger colored her face and the muscle in her jaw flexed involuntarily. Lee pursued it further.

"Are you here for the seminar?" She nodded yes as the translator put Lee's words into French and understanding began to dawn in her. "Okay," he relented. He explained further that because this *gite* was a public place, he did not want someone stumbling into a seminar on the alchemy of love and sex who did not belong there and who could cause problems for everyone. She settled nervously into a seat and he continued with the discourse.

"When energy comes to rest at the bottom of the body, we have two choices: to let it run out of the body because that's the momentum and direction in which it is going, or to turn it around and encourage it to ascend. All forms of yoga—hatha yoga, *kriya* yoga— are designed to take the current of descending energy and turn it around, allowing it to be used in subtle domains of energy we could call ascent.

"There are three primary forms of energy leakage in the body: 1) Serious physical illness. When we get sick, we just get sick—there's not much we can do about it but take care of ourselves and heal. 2) Negativity, like gossip, criticisms of others, focusing on violence, or passionate discussions of war and cruelty. Emotional outbursts—anger, rage, vindictiveness. All these are forms of energy leakage in the body that lead to weakness and degeneration. And, 3) the usual forms of sex.

"Sooner or later what we want to do is to begin to work with alchemical sexuality, or the transformation of sexual energy. There are two ways in which that can happen: unconsciously and consciously. My work could be called transformational work or tantric work. In my work this energy is worked with consciously, technically. But there are many spiritual schools in which the practices—if engaged properly and practiced with integrity—alter one's relationship to sex, and this process happens unconsciously. If we are working with principles of kindness, generosity and integrity in relationship without dealing specifically with sex, automatically sex—as one of the most intense aspects of relationship—begins to enter into transformational possibility.

"The more energy we have, the more energy we conserve, the more energy we are able to generate—which means we can better serve the evolution, harmony and health of the world. The more energy we have, the more powerfully our acts of kindness and generosity communicate to others, and the more power our prayers have . . ."

Lee continued to elucidate the psychology of the need for release of tension, based in childhood suffering and abuse, and the psychological motivation for sex. He said, "The psychological motive that drives us toward sex is not the urge for pleasure or beauty; it's the urge for the release of tension, or to control, manipulate or dominate the other, or just the biological urge to procreate. If we look at our sexual activity and take the last ten times we had sex—with ourselves or with a partner, it doesn't matter—we should consider how many of those ten times we were motivated by pleasure, love, beauty, or by those neurotic needs. Are we motivated by the drive to get something for ourselves, for our own pleasure, or are we motivated by the desire to serve others? For sex to be alchemical," he concluded, "or transformational, we have to turn the flow from down and out to up. This is the natural evolution of sexual energy from youth to old age, or sexuality for nuns and monks and practitioners of all traditions . . .

"We've really just scratched the surface of this subject. We really didn't get to the heart of the matter, but have only laid a preliminary foundation, and we probably won't return to it unless there are specific questions. Time for brunch!"

After brunch the group reconvened for Dasya's talk. The mood was completely different now. Lee sat on the couch to Dasya's left and listened with his eyes closed much of the time. The mood in the room was extremely intimate and tender, which manifested itself in the vulnerability that many people exhibited in their questions and willingness to talk about their personal situation. One woman spoke about feeling drained and that she had lost a great deal of energy. She felt that she needed to move faster, to make more progress on the spiritual path, but she has no energy. After a lengthy interchange in which she seemed to be dodging the crux of the situation as Dasya asked her questions in an attempt to help her, he finally asked her how her marriage was. She said that her marriage was wonderful and her husband cared very much for her and gave her a lot of attention. He said, "You're very lucky then. But you strike me as a very sad person."

She looked genuinely perplexed and shook her head no at first, then the truth came out. She revealed that she had been married for seventeen years. For the first ten years of that time it had been an open marriage, so that she and her husband had multiple partners. As she revealed the situation in a conversation with Dasya the pathos in this situation was a palpable force in the room as everyone seemed to feel into her pain. Dasya said, "When you get in touch with your feelings about what you went through, it's going to be very intense. It's so sad I'm barely keeping it together—I'm about to burst into tears for you." He said that with such honesty that the entire room shifted. People were visibly moved by what was occurring. She was being given a gift, a rare opportunity, to move on—which was actually what she asked for. But it is often the case that when one has a real necessity for some kind of catalyst or change, the catalyst or change comes in unexpected packages. Ego can never second-guess the process of its own undoing.

Several people asked self-revelatory questions. The woman who had been angry during Clint's presentation the day before spoke now. She began by saying that when she was angry yesterday she had spoken because it helped her to speak. Now she was no longer angry and didn't really know why she was so angry yesterday. Dasya interrupted her and said, "You don't need to make excuses for being angry. It seems like you are trying to justify or excuse your behavior. You were angry, and that's all. What is your name?" She answered, "Prema." She listened as Dasya spoke about being responsible for one's feelings. It seemed like she was being carried along on a wave that was beyond her control. She had called a kind of feedback to herself that was giving her direct glimpses into a totally different perspective on herself and her motives than she had ever seen before.

A student of Arnaud Desjardins raised his hand and said that he had made an appointment to ask Arnaud a question, but that now he would like to hear what Dasya had to say about it. Dasya replied, "If you've already made a request to ask Arnaud, why would you want to ask me? He's your teacher! Look, I have all my eggs in one basket. Any progress I've ever made to any degree is because I have all my eggs in one basket. You lose a tremendous amount of energy if you ask your question here and get another opinion. If your attention is focused on your teacher, you can throw yourself into the answer once you get it. If you sit with your question and give it more energy, it will become more real to you. The more real it becomes to you, the more your teacher can give to you. I can put myself in a position of receiving, but ultimately my teacher is the one who will advance me to the next level." The man nodded his head, indicating that he understood.

A woman made a very friendly challenge to Dasya, saying, "My path is to find my own way without a teacher. I find my own answer in myself—sometimes through trial and error. Referring to somebody else, for me, I wouldn't find easy because I want to find out for myself."

Dasya answered, "I feel the same way. There is a part of me that would love not to have a spiritual master, a part that would love to go off and do what I want to do. And every time I do that I end up in big trouble! Ego just wants gratification and stimulation and power. I might be tremendously sincere in those moments, but the result of those times always bring me great pain. They tend to accumulate and become an obstacle to that which nurtures and sustains me. I don't have the energy to waste. Even if my teacher is bogus, if he was a false guru, I'm in it to find out for me. Until that is answered it doesn't make a difference because I don't see my master for who he is anyway—I just see me, with a big 'M'! I have to accept that as a part of the dharma. It's true—I'm only out there for *me*.

"I've had a lot of spiritual experiences. I've been plugged into the spiritual battery of the universe and had my brains blown out. But you still have to get up the next morning! I've overcome psychological obstacles that have plagued me for forty years, and it turned out to be an insignificant victory. Only because of what my teacher has allowed me to glimpse have I realized how hollow the pursuit of a personal life is. Still it comes up. If left to my own devices, I'd be sitting outside that Coke machine," he gestured toward the vending machine in front of the building next door, "popping change in and drinking Cokes every two hours!

"The desire to do what I want to do doesn't go away. My experience is that my desire to not take orders and help has over time indicated to me how much help I need. I've relaxed into it incrementally over a long period of time. I'm just an average student, just a regular student. There are people here who are much more intelligent than me, but I'm stubborn! Really stubborn! Just ask my teacher, he'll tell you.

"So having the freedom to run your own life—I don't want that anymore. I've screwed it up enough to know. I have a wife and a family, I'm somewhat responsible and so on, but that's not it—that doesn't make a difference in the long run. The truth of the matter is there is just this hunger, this desire, to know the truth and try to live it. It's staggeringly simply, but I can't get away from it. Most of the people here can't get away from it. I've made a commitment. Everybody still struggles with that commitment—that doesn't go away. But I've made a commitment . . . I'm on the train and I'm not going to get off until the end."

Dasya's talk was a powerful testimony to years of work on self in the company of a teacher. The whole room was softened by the felt impact of it. The group took a short break for tea after his talk, then Lee gave the last session of the seminar.

Shortly after Lee began, the dogs started growling and barking. Their constant presence, along with that of the flies, had been an inescapable element of irritation and discomfort for everyone in the space. Now Lee was answering questions and discussing the difference between catharsis and cathexis—an important follow up to his discussion of containing energy in sex from the morning session. It was an important piece of information, especially for those who had great difficulty with the form of the seminar, and wanted more action—movement, dance, a catharsis of some kind.

Lee said, "Catharsis is about expending energy to relieve tension. Then we feel good, more balanced, more harmonious, but we haven't learned anything. We can always apply catharsis again, but we still haven't learned anything. Cathexis is not about suppressing, but about staying with the energy and not blowing it off. If we stay with the energy it forces us into a different kind of harmony because the body naturally seeks harmony. If we don't take the usual route to harmony—the expenditure of energy through a release of tension—we find knowledge. But cathexis is very uncomfortable because the tension remains until it is relieved, and that can take awhile depending on who we are and how we deal with it. Conserving energy is about recycling energy in the body.

"To bring the body out of tension with hard exercise makes us feel better, but we've used up all the energy bound up in tension—another energy expenditure. When we try to stay with the energy it may feel like we absolutely *cannot*. It feels like we are going to explode, but no one has exploded yet. No matter how much anyone has sat with intense amounts of tension, no one has exploded. So what we call an explosion is that we'll scream at someone or break something—another form of catharsis. My recommendation is to stay with the tension. Chögyam Trungpa Rinpoche—a great Tibetan Buddhist teacher who died about ten years ago—was giving a seminar and talking about the mythological hell realms as metaphors for states we experience in our lives. One student asked, 'What do you do when you find yourself in hell?' Trungpa Rinpoche answered, 'I try to stay there.' I'll leave you with that consideration."

A woman asked a question that would have weighed the space down completely with considerations that should be addressed in a psychotherapy session. Lee said, "Oh well darling, I'm not a psychotherapist, and we've only got two hours left." He went on to call on Prema, who had been angry yesterday during Clint's talk and had gotten further feedback from Dasya, and now had her hand raised.

"So about the anger I had yesterday," Prema said in a very quiet and subdued tone of voice, "would it have been better to sit with it?"

Lee answered, "Yes, and see what it reveals to you. Were you really angry because you came here for something you weren't getting, or were you angry about something else? The whole recommendation to sit with something presumes we are asking the question to allow us to see ourselves more clearly. It's not recommended for everybody—it's not for your mothers and fathers and sisters and brothers, but for those who have an intention to progress on the path."

Prema began to respond to him in the same tone when he interrupted her, saying, "I'll tell you one thing . . . you were a very different person yesterday when you were angry than you are right now!" She nodded yes. "So maybe being in touch with who that was—to discover who that person is, in essence—would be of great value to you. If you *express* the anger it is unlikely you will get to know that person. That person is more interesting, but more interesting in *essence* than in expression. That's the value of sitting with something because you can discover something hidden that wouldn't be available any other way."

She seemed to be deeply absorbing what Lee said. With a smile that communicated her dawning understanding of his words, she said, "She was very alive, yes?"

Lee responded, "Yes. If aliveness is wasted in anger, then the other expressions of aliveness don't get to be expressed." It was a very big piece of teaching for her and everyone in the room, and took the consideration of conserving the energy that is usually wasted through the expression of negative emotions into very practical and immediate terms. It was an exact object lesson for the whole group, who had witnessed and in fact traveled along with Prema over the course of the seminar. It was a classic example of how one person's vulnerability and willingness to be worked with by the teacher can benefit everyone in the space. What she was learning about herself and fundamental principles of tantric practice was invaluable to everyone, even to those who have been attempting to practice such a thing as containing energy, or cathexis, for years.

The large bear of a man, Simon, who had been asking very articulate questions all weekend in between walking to the doorway and smoking cigarettes, now confronted Lee about his constant advertisements for his books and other products. Lee gave him a scathingly clear response, concluding with, "If there is something between the lines that can be read, I expect you to read it. I expect you all to be *adults*. If you can learn to tell the difference between a false master and a real master this weekend, then it will have been worth a million dollars to you.

"The way I work is like setting up a treasure hunt for children. I hide different clues, but all the clues are hidden and they are obscure. If you find enough clues, you get the treasure, which is . . . Swiss chocolate!" Everyone laughed. "No. You have to pick up the clues, sometimes by accident, stumbling upon them. When I say 'I', I mean the way the Universe sets itself up to help you find the answer to your existence. I'm speaking identified with the Universe, for the time being. It's pretentious, I agree, but it will serve the purpose for a moment. If you have ever set up a treasure hunt for children with obscure clues, you find out that if you get a bunch of children together in a group they will figure it out quickly, whereas one child alone may not.

"So the treasure is the Self. Since the treasure is so great, to just throw it into your lap would be uninteresting to God. You have to pay for it, go the distance, with intention, commitment. Every once in a while you get another clue. Trying to figure it out in a group is easier than trying to figure it out alone."

Just then the sheep dog came walking up through the audience from the back of the room to the front of the room. His shaggy, matted body bumped into the people who were sitting on the floor in front of Lee. They tried to push him away unsuccessfully. He stopped in the center of the floor four feet away from Lee's feet and started rolling around, scratching, biting and shaking his whole body. As people laughed the four women sitting on the floor, who were getting covered with dog hair, laughed and made faces at the grossness of the dog and its manifestations. Several times it rolled around, changing

647

positions to get to another place that itched, so its hind leg could thump away, scratching. With each scratch hair and dirt flew into the air, the filth of the dog permeating the whole front part of the room.

People were laughing hysterically, including Lee. It was a grand moment, rather epitomizing something about the weekend in a totally irrational but highly effective way. Only fifteen minutes before Lee had said that there were *devas* that irritated dogs to upset people, and here was the dog, obliging him with a demonstration. Finally, after what seemed like ten minutes but was probably more like a long five-minute interlude of this farcical nonsense—which couldn't have been more perfectly orchestrated if it had been planned in advance—the dog got up and shook one last ferocious whole body shake from head to tail. Hair, dirt, sticks, burrs went flying, and then the dog headed out the front door of the room. The group was practically woozy from laughing.

The fun finally died down. About five minutes after Lee resumed his discourse, Michelline, who was still lying on her pad on the floor, raised her hand. She said, "I want to thank you, because although nothing has provoked me all weekend, now I see that all of my questions have been answered."

Lee said, "Well, we'll see if you use it. Sometimes people say, 'Oh I'm too old now to do anything . . .' "

She said, "Oh yes, if I had known all this when I was twenty years old it would have changed my life."

Lee said, "It's never too late to make progress on the path. It doesn't matter how much you do, but that you do the best you can. How old are you Michelline—if you don't mind me asking?"

She said that she had turned seventy-one yesterday. Lee then told her the story of Irina Tweedie, who didn't meet her teacher until she was fifty-four years old. He talked about how Mrs. Tweedie had given all her money, all her security—a small monthly pension—over to her teacher, and about the tremendous vicissitudes she had endured to get the transmission from Bhai Sahib. The entire room seemed to be feasting on the sweetness in the air that was palpable in this exchange between Lee and Michelline. He didn't in any way express sentimentality about the fact that she was growing old and obviously struggling with health problems. Instead he called her to integrity with herself—an act that demonstrated his tremendous respect and regard for her.

"So if I see you next year, Michelline, I don't want to hear you whining about this. I want to hear you say, 'I have done the best I can.' Okay?"

She smiled. "Okay."

September 14, 1999
La Ferme de Jutreau

Tonight Lee has a celebratory meal planned for the ashram residents and guests who are here, about twenty-six people including the children and teenagers. The menu will be roasted chicken from the *charcuterie* in La Roche Posay, salad and fresh bread. Wine will be served, and Lee asked Ann to come up with an idea for dessert. She planned a lavish chocolate mousse cake with lush mocha icing to be served with coffee. As he discussed some of the particulars of the evening's plans over breakfast he said, "If it's balmy, we'll eat outside tonight in the courtyard. If not, we'll eat in here," indicating the barn dining room. After two rainy days and a misty, overcast morning today, it was unlikely that eating outside under the red maple tree would be an option, but it's typical of Lee to hold the possibility that anything could happen between breakfast and dinner.

Lee was lingering over breakfast again this morning. As the summer has progressed the breakfast gathering has become more and more extended, sometimes lasting until nine-thirty while Lee commands the space, working with this person or that. Everyone gets the benefit of whoever happens to be in the limelight, or on the hot seat, at any given time. When he isn't working directly with someone, he is often making teaching lessons or expounding the dharma in cloaked terms, using the metaphors of everyday life to make his point.

Now as the talk about the evening meal came around to the young teenagers wanting to have glasses of wine along with the adults, Chris mentioned that the teenagers are frequently given wine in the homes of their French friends. One of them had been given three glasses of wine in one meal, and she heroically tried to act like it hadn't affected her.

"That's a lot of wine," Jane commented.

Chris said, "If I drank that much wine my head would be on the pillow." A number of people shook their heads and voiced agreement that three glasses of wine would be far too much for most of the practitioners now, after so many years of abstinence or very small amounts of wine at special dinners.

Once again bursting the bubble of self-delusion—in terms of one's supposed sensitivity and the delicate level of one's practice—Lee interrupted in an irascible tone. "Hah! More like you'd be talking *really* loud and laughing at people's bad jokes," he demonstrated with an irritating and crude "hah, hah, hah, hah," like that of a sloppy drunk, "and yelling, 'I got a story to tell—hey y'all, I got a story to tell!' " He mawkishly mimicked the shoddy world of the false personality exaggerated even further by the effects of alcohol. It was a sobering scenario that sank in around the table. He couldn't have said it more clearly: Observe yourself and don't be deluded about where you are in your sadhana.

Moving on very quickly Lee looked around and said, "What's the theme for the seminar this weekend?"

Paula answered, "Accepting What Is."

Lee said, "That's a great title for a seminar, a great consideration. Now that's the seminar to do naked! Start with what's real—'Look at your legs, now at your thighs, at your stomach!' " Lee laughed rather sardonically, as he perfectly mimicked a New Age seminar leader doing a guided meditation. Another direct hit at the illusions that we labor under, including the illusion that we've transcended in any way the worldly perspective of vanity.

Laura began to tell stories of the famed "Six Day" program of Werner Erhard and Associates, a follow-up to the est or Forum courses. Each person would have to stand in their bathing suits and talk about their bodies in front of the whole group—what they didn't like, what they wanted to change. People would shake and cry or sometimes even faint, it was so emotionally intense.

Lee began to talk about how much the est course had meant to him twenty-five years ago when he took it. He was the State Director of Silva Mind Control in New Jersey, and when he took the est course Silva Mind Control faded in comparison. It was a shock to him. Lee began to talk about Werner Erhard. Lee has been a constant supporter and apologist for Werner Erhard over the years and has great respect for his work as a teacher. It was a reminder of something Lee had said last night in the After Dinner Talk. He was laughing about his own reputation and the way some people respond to his style—the foolishness, the jokes, the crude references to genitals, sex and eliminatory functions.

He said, "When they say to us, 'After twenty-five years on the path haven't you built some integrity?' we'll say, 'No, I've lost all my integrity. I've lost everything!' " He paused, then continued, "There is power and protection in idiocy . . . it's good to be an idiot! People don't bother idiots. No one is interested in you if you are an idiot. Nobody *shoots* idiots. They only shoot important people."

Back at breakfast, Lee announced the special meal that would happen tonight. When someone asked, "What's the reason, the occasion for the meal?" Lee shrugged and said, "Nothing in particular." The breakfast darshan, as some of Lee's students have begun to call these morning gatherings which have turned into teaching spaces, was soon over. Lee walked across the courtyard to his desk in the office.

Shortly after that Lee left to drive alone to Chauvigny to buy the bread for the meal tonight—an activity which he often chooses to take care of himself and which seems to bring him a good deal of pleasure. An hour later he was walking across the grassy courtyard where Dasya and Michelle were raking leaves in the misty early autumn air. He had a huge bag full of crusty fresh loaves in his arms and a smile on his face.

The meal was a lovely affair. The tables in the barn were set with white tablecloths, goblets and beautiful flower arrangements of dahlias, nasturtiums, lavender and small sunflowers from the ashram gardens. When the bell was rung people took their seats, with the children at a separate table of their own next to the adult table. About halfway into the roasted chicken and salad people were engaged in soft but animated conversations around the table. Lee tapped his wineglass with his spoon to get everyone's attention. All faces turned toward him expectantly and he said, "Today Purna signed the papers on an ashram for his group, so let's use this opportunity to toast their success." Wineglasses clinked around the table as people exclaimed quietly. The new ashram would be in Bozeman, Montana, Lee said, to a chorus of comments about the many famous people and movie stars who live in Bozeman.

"Yes, he'll be rubbing shoulders with the stars up there," Lee said, referring to Purna with a laugh of enjoyment, his high spirit infectious.

Clint said, "The work that Purna is doing in the prisons is really breakthrough work." Lee nodded his head in agreement and said that Purna would be going to a major conference on prison reform this fall with a number of other people in the spiritual network, mostly Buddhists, who are also involved in working inside the prison system in the U.S. He said with a smile, "It's good that Purna can have such high visibility, so we can hide!"

On the one hand it could have seemed like a strange remark, but on the other hand it pointed directly toward a basic principle of tantric work that Lee had made many times over the summer—tantric work is not for everybody, and in fact is for very few. The nature of authentic tantric work is that it will never be understood, and will always be a threat to the status quo. Radical transformation is something that very few are interested in engaging because it involves the total dissolution of the personality and the entire complex of the flat worldview of illusion. It seemed like the same thing Lee was referring to when he joked last night, saying, "I've lost all my integrity. I've lost everything!" On the tantric path, one loses it all. The sacrifices are immense, and one cannot really grasp that this is so until it is too late to turn back, which is why Lee so often warns people at his seminars. His warnings, cloaked in clowning around and insults to the audience, are full of compassion.

Often the success of a celebratory meal can be gauged in one way by how long Lee lingers at the table. Tonight the meal went on for over an hour and half, and after dessert over coffee Lee regaled the table of twenty-four adults with stories of other teachers he'd known, met or heard speak over the years. He talked for quite a while about Richard Baker Roshi, and the ordeal he underwent with the San Francisco Zen Center, where he left amidst scandals involving money and sex. Now Baker Roshi has a zendo in the Rocky Mountains at Crestone, Colorado and a zendo in the Black Forest mountains near Freiburg, only a few miles away from Rutte, the Dürckheim Center. It seems that he is focused on working with smaller groups of serious practitioners. Lee talked about the last time he saw Baker Roshi, when he gave a talk at the Sorbonne in Paris, and how brilliant the talk had been.

Tonight Chris remembered reading in *The Crooked Cucumber*, the biography of Suzuki Roshi, the teacher of Richard Baker, that when Suzuki Roshi gave Baker the empowerment to teach, he said, "I'm so sorry for what I'm about to do to you." The implication was that the responsibility and obligation that a teacher takes on is a burden that is so heavy one who has never been there simply cannot really understand it.

Lee also talked about seeing Richard Baker and Joan Halifax speak together many years ago in San Francisco. When they were challenged by a woman in the crowd who thought the ten dollar entry fee for the talk was elitist and exclusive, Richard Baker had given a very articulate and considered answer. But Joan Halifax had blasted her, talking about her years in Central America with the shamans, and how people who came to the shamans for their wisdom or healing power came bearing substantial gifts, sometimes all they could possibly afford, to pay respects and offer gratitude for the shaman's wisdom. Joan Halifax was someone Lee Lozowick could relate to; someone who did not suffer fools gladly, and was willing to stand for the principles of the Work uncompromisingly.

Lee then began to talk about Stephen Gaskin, whom he has always spoken of with great regard and respect. He talked about The Farm, the huge commune in Tennessee that Stephen Gaskin founded, and where a tremendous amount of important work happened in the early 1970s in particular, though it lasted as an experiment in spiritual community for many years. The Farm was responsible for the enlivening of the whole movement of home birthing in the U.S., and produced an important and uniquely extraordinary book, *Spiritual Midwifery*. The emphasis of Stephen Gaskin's work turned toward social action and the political arena years ago. Lee said, "I saw him speak in the seventies. He came to the podium with his long hair and dressed like a hippie, but as soon as he opened his mouth you couldn't help but sit up and listen. He was tremendously charismatic and powerful."

When Lee shares memories of his friendships, his interchanges, meetings or his general knowledge of the work of other teachers at many different levels and domains of spiritual life, it seems immensely empowered. This network of those who are involved in teaching is something he speaks about frequently. As he talks about various individuals— many of whom are close personal friends, like E.J. Gold, Andrew Cohen and Arnaud Desjardins—there is an underlying feeling of a tremendous gratitude which Lee bears for their work in the world. Lee is an ongoing advocate and apologist for spiritual teachers of many kinds and at many diverse levels of realization. He is especially supportive of the black sheep or crazy wisdom teachers who he feels have gotten a raw deal from the conservative, narrow-minded and ego-threatened moral majority that exists within the contemporary spiritual scene in the West, particularly in the U.S. and even Europe.

Through the course of the day on this occasion, he had talked about Werner Erhard (at breakfast), Stephen Gaskin, Joan Halifax, Richard Baker and Purna Steinitz, who just started his own community a year and a half ago with Lee's blessings. It seemed no accident that these conversations were occurring, interwoven within the day and the auspices of the celebratory meal, which as it turned out, Lee dedicated to the inception of a new ashram, where work would go on that could only benefit all sentient beings.

September 15, 1999
La Ferme de Jutreau

After lunch Lee asked for announcements. There were none and he gaily said, "Jai Guru!" but continued to sit with his students, talking about a book he is currently reading, a biography of Sir Richard Burton. There was a general discussion of how Richard Burton's wife had burned part of his manuscripts after his death, and about the tremendous legacy that he left behind in his many translations of various esoteric texts, the twenty-two volume *One Thousand and One Nights* being a notable example. The discussion was lively and interesting with many people participating in it. Lee listened attentively to his each of his students speak as they added to the conversation and kept it going long after the last person had completely finished eating.

Suddenly Lee leaned forward with his hands on the table and looked around at the faces that looked back at him, waiting for the words that were obviously lurking behind his sly smile. Poised on the edge of his seat as if he would get up at any moment he said, "Now, has everyone been acknowledged?" If there had been any reaction around the table to his spontaneous acknowledgements of various individuals during the lunch meal, he was pointing them out now. He chuckled and the group burst into laughter as he got up and walked out.

Dasya said, "He's done that several times this summer. He'll say something like, 'Did you want to be acknowledged too?' Or 'Is everybody okay?' and then laugh, as if to say, 'You people are just sitting here talking so you can be heard.' It's like when he said at La Bertais, 'I'm surrounded by students who talk. I'm sitting there not saying a word and they're just chirping away—chirp, chirp, chirp!' "

Later over bridge with Lee the group was talking about the seminar this weekend, "Accepting What Is." I asked Lee why he didn't use his own language to title the seminar and instead had used Arnaud Desjardins' language. "Because I don't write up my own advertisements," he snapped, "that's why!" It was a reference to his students' lack of attention to their own unique dharma language.

September 16, 1999
La Ferme de Jutreau

Every morning now in meditation the white cat comes in and usually sits on the divan with Lee. Sometimes she curls up and sleeps between Lee's crossed legs for the entire meditation period. Sometimes she just jumps up and meows, sniffs around, gets scratched for a minute or played with (by Lee), then jumps back down and resumes her mouse patrol of the barn. This morning she came in and jumped up on the dais to Lee, who was writing poems in his large book. She sniffed around a moment then jumped down. Forty minutes later, just before the bell rang, strange sounds began to fill the hall. The cat began to growl like a dog as pitiful shrieks rended the air. Lee sat up on the dais with a curious smile on his face as he calmly watched the drama that was unfolding just behind the men and women on the back row. The cat had a mole, and was playing with it, taking it up in its mouth, then dropping it down. The mole would try to move away in a confused fashion, but the cat had total control over the situation, and would pounce on it, snatching it back up in its mouth while the mole squealed piteously. Lee was smiling broadly, as Marcus got up and took the cat, with the mole in its mouth, out of the hall. Within a minute or two, the bell rang and Lee left, still looking rather amused.

Of course, over breakfast the cat and mole situation was one of the topics of conversation. Dasya commented to Lee, "You were smiling . . ."

"I was feeling into the reaction of the people in the room, who were very uncomfortable with the suffering of the *poor* little animal!" Lee smiled devilishly as he emphasized the word poor.

"That thing was really terrified. I've never heard a mouse make that much noise while it's being killed by a cat," Lee laughed with a kind of glee that could only be taken seriously. There were a number of directions one could go in from his comments. The shrieking of the terrified mole—which was being ruthlessly played with in a way that amounted to torture from the humanistic perspective—was getting to a number of people in the hall. The meditation was completely distracted by the sound of the mole's cries. It seemed on the one hand that Lee was saying, what kind of practice is that? Certainly not fierce practice, but sentimental practice, shoddy practice, romantic practice, cowardly practice perhaps. But not the practice of a strong practitioner. What was it really that was so disturbing? Death. The raw terror of animal death. The impersonal ruthlessness of the processes of Nature which every organic being faces sooner or later. As Gurdjieff said, most people will die unconsciously, like a dog. Or a mouse. Or a small dark mole, screaming in terror. And there it was, being demonstrated right in front of our faces.

Marcus said, "I just didn't want there to be blood all over the rug." The artist's perspective on the situation.

As people sat finishing their fruit compote, oats and almonds in a brief moment of silence, Lee chuckled. As his students looked at him questioningly, he leaned back in his chair and said, "I'm imagining you all just waiting for your piece of attention." Lee threw his head back and laughed. A few people chimed in with, "Yeah, our piece of the action, our piece of the magic."

Laura said, tongue in cheek, "Could I have my piece of acknowledgement right now, so I can feel good all day, instead of tonight? Because then I'll only feel good tonight."

Jumping into the play Lee patronized theatrically, "Very *good* Laura, that's the kind of question a *good* devotee would ask!"

Laura said, playing her role to the hilt, "Thank you, I feel much better now."

This little bit of badinage was very playful and light, but the point of it was aimed at a very painful aspect of the shadow side of relationship between student and teacher. It was the third or fourth time in the past month or so, including yesterday at lunch, that Lee had made a facetious remark about the degree of clutching or grasping toward his physical attention that he perceives coming from his students.

When our self-worth and sense of dignity and wholeness becomes dependent on whether the teacher is smiling at us or not, we are actually in the grips of very profound suffering, although many of us cover this drive for acknowledgement and empowerment from the teacher with our illusions. It is difficult for ego to perceive pride, vanity and egoic posturing as suffering because the mechanism is such that one believes oneself to actually be special—as set apart from others—and therefore worthy of attracting more of the guru's attention than anyone else. We can only imagine what it must be like for the spiritual master to sit at breakfast every morning looking around at the hopeful and expectant or brooding and angry faces, or to feel the tendrils of subtle demands constantly pulling on his attention. "Me, me, look over here!" Or, "You'd *better* look over here or I'm going to make life hell for you today." We may think that we are containing all this, or that our manifestations are subtle, when for anyone with much sensitivity we are broadcasting on a high-beam frequency. We are actually blasting the space and everyone in it.

Much of the time we really have no idea that this is going on, or that the manifestations of ego, which are glaringly apparent to the guru, are what he is greeted with on a constant basis. Every now and then there is a free moment, when ego has relaxed its vise-like grip, but for the most part the day is tangled up with a constant stream of unconscious motivations, projections, expectations and assumptions. The guru bears all of this, much of it focused on himself, and much more. It is at its worst, as Lee has said on many occasions, when the drive for his attention becomes so overriding that one begins to compete viciously with one's sangha mates for every little shred of the guru's time and attention. When one begins to face this dynamic in oneself, it becomes painfully and sorrowfully obvious that the spiritual master has no sanctuary in which he can rest.

Now asking for announcements, Lee said, "Tonight the seminar begins with an After Dinner Talk, so we have chanting, right here where we are sitting right now, at five-thirty. Jai Guru!"

After breakfast in the library or salon of the *grande maison* Lee spent the next thirty minutes talking to Marcus in front of the Primal Mother. Lee sat in his leather chair and Marcus sat on the floor, looking at the large bronze figure of the goddess. Walking past one could hear Lee telling the story of buying bronzes in Freiburg, "We cleared the dealer out of all his finest pieces." As they sat there together for the next twenty minutes or so talking, a subtle exchange was going on. Lee continues to support Marcus in his apprenticeship to the Tibetan *thangka* painter, an example of how frequently Lee plays the role of champion for his devotees, affirming and promoting the best qualities in those whose spiritual evolution is in his care. It is an expression of regard and even love in the objective and impersonal sense of the word. Too often this form of his teaching goes unnoticed, while his wilder, more brash behavior—in which love takes the rakish form of criticism or blunt reminders and unpleasant calls to mindfulness, or the trickster who shocks us from the condition of sleep—is remarked upon again and again. But at a deeper and more important level, these kinds of simple interactions and moments of communion or friendship between Lee and any one of his students seem to carry, hidden within them, the potent seeds of spiritual empowerment or initiation. The Tibetans use the Sanskrit word *abhisheka* (consecration) for this empowerment from guru to disciple. Hidden within an ordinary exchange, a subtle substance, or the guru's *jyoti* (light) is transferred, and for the moment the disciple is transported into the guru's world. The guru is encoding the body of the disciple in this way by fact of close proximity to his own body.

Sitting at the table after lunch, Brinda had just made an announcement about using extra hot water for washing dishes tonight because a cold was going around the community. A number of people were talking about the seminar in Bordeaux the past weekend. Lee said, "That is the seminar that *was*; tonight begins the seminar that *is*. Tonight all *those* people will be coming to our ashram with their dirty habits . . . so be sure to wash those dishes, and wash away all those germs!"

He was referring to the three-day seminar, the last event of the summer to be held at La Ferme de Jutreau, that would begin tomorrow, titled, "Accepting What Is." He seemed to be baiting the small group that sat around him. But in what way?

"But you use all that for transformation, right?" Jan smiled, biting the hook. Michelle chimed in, "Whose transformation—yours or ours?"

"The hell with transformation," Lee barked, "I use it to get money for the ashram! Francs, dollars, Deutsch marks, soon to be Euros—I'll take it! Bring those white sheep in here and I'll shear 'em!" He went through the motions, pretending to pick up a sheep by its hind legs and flopping it down and running the shears up the length of its imaginary flank. "Have you ever seen those professional sheep shearers? They can do a sheep in fifteen seconds! Of course they cut them once in awhile. But they don't mind."

"You don't mind if you cut them either, do you?" Jan laughed.

"No, I don't care! Get those white sheep in here—I'll use them to pay our bills, to support this ashram. Bring 'em on." Listening to Lee's scathing statements it struck me again that he is constantly speaking in veiled language that is pure metaphor or symbolic speech. Everything he says has at least one underlying communication and usually several. There are no casual conversations with Lee, and now it seemed that everything he was saying about white sheep he was also saying about his own students. He was talking about *everyone's* dirty habits—the degree to which we live by the standards of the world and not by the standards of the Work.

While on one level he was making a true statement about the ashram which needs money to carry on the Work, and the fact that it is lawful for him to receive that money, at another level he was feeding his student's sense of superiority. "They are white sheep, we are black sheep; we have different sensitivities." This feeding of egoic presumptions puts one off guard, and in the moment of being off-guard Lee makes a direct teaching hit, like a fist right into the solar plexus, while one is vulnerable by virtue of the fact of being off guard, or having lost one's vigilance. In the midst of that vulnerability, he made a communication about the dirty habits of his students, and the ways in which his students themselves may be like white sheep. It seemed linked to any fears we might harbor of contamination as well— "They are sick and they might make me sick as well." It pointed out the tendency to divide things into "us" and "them"—all of which springs from the mood of separation and fear.

Just before the chanting started at five-thirty Lee was playing a card game in the living room with one of the children. Regina, the editor of Hohm Press, called from the ashram in Arizona. When Lee found out it was Regina on the phone he jumped up and stalked briskly into the office. Taking the phone in hand, he began without a greeting or any formality, "Regina! Don't be talking on the phone with Dasya for forty-five minutes, going on and on like you all did last night. If Dasya is talking and going on and on, just get off. I don't care what business has to be taken care of for Hohm Press. It shouldn't take that long. There's a phone bill to consider here. Okay? Great, thank you very much." End of conversation. As soon as he returned to the living room one of the children asked why he was talking to Regina like that. Lee answered mildly in a benign and instructive voice, "Because Regina wants to be a better student, and I was giving her a lesson in crispness and conservation of energy."

Shortly afterward Marcus came in with a book of pictures of Tibetan Buddhist iconography. He showed it to Lee to pick out his next project. Lee looked at one of the pictures Marcus was considering. "Oh, I don't like that one so much," he commented, "I don't mind the fierce face, but that particular face I don't like so much." He turned some pages and came to another one. "This one is good." Marcus smiled as Lee handed the book back to him and walked away.

Mariana arrived back at La Ferme de Jutreau after a short visit at Hauteville where she was interviewing Arnaud Desjardins and his teaching assistants for a new book on spiritual authority. Over dinner she was reporting to Lee about her time at Hauteville. She had been especially surprised at how accessible Arnaud was to his students. Because he has over one thousand students, she expected Arnaud to be rather removed from it all. Instead what she found was that Arnaud was deeply involved in the daily flow of the ashram, presiding over the formal silent lunch meal in the main dining room and giving talks in the Ramdas Room every day.

Lee listened, quietly absorbing what Mariana was saying and not commenting other than to nod his head as if none of this was news to him. She went on to talk about how she wasn't aware until this visit how much the presence of Papa Ramdas is alive at Hauteville, and what an important influence Ramdas had on Arnaud in the years of his sadhana. She said that because of the presence of Ramdas that she experienced at Hauteville, she became more curious about him as part of her own teacher's lineage. She felt more attuned to understanding something about the communication of Swami Papa Ramdas that she hadn't before. Part of this was because Arnaud mentioned Papa Ramdas many, many times a day. In the interview she did with Arnaud for her book he mentioned Papa Ramdas second only to his guru, Swami Prajnanpad, and Anandamayi Ma. Arnaud has often spoken of Papa Ramdas and Anandamayi Ma as two of his *upa* gurus—helpers on the path, in addition to, but not in replacement of, one's *satguru* or root guru. In this way Anandamayi Ma and Papa Ramdas were very strong influences for Arnaud, who now passes that influence on to his students in his teaching.

Last week in the Ramdas Room at Hauteville, where a *vigraha* of Yogi Ramsuratkumar is enshrined, Arnaud came walking in with one of the permanent ashram residents who accompanied him as his escort for the session. When people raised their hands to ask questions Arnaud said, "We are in the Ramdas room, so here we can just speak," indicating that in the Ramdas room people didn't have to raise their hands and be formal. Arnaud was charismatic, enormously powerful and animated, even theatrical, Mariana said. This is a different Arnaud than Lee's students see when Lee is there because Arnaud steps aside and gives his ashram over to Lee. As Arnaud has said on more than one occasion when Lee has come to visit him, "This week, this is Lee's ashram!"

Several people arrived for the seminar before chanting at five-thirty and joined the group for dinner. As Lee began his discourse of the After Dinner Talk at ten till seven, nine people had joined us. Lee picked up the new issue of *Shambhala Sun* (September 1999) and resumed reading from an article by Sherab Chodzin Kohn titled, "Ouch! Hooray!" that he had read from last week at the After Dinner Talk. He read, " 'You, the student, hang on for dear life to your habitual reference points. The guru undermines these same reference points by playing with you, by maneuvering, or just by the way he is. Ouch! Hooray!' " (p. 52)

Lee commented, "The guru undermines your habitual reference points by undermining you—not like a cat playing with a mouse—but like playing cards, or bridge. Even within this playing we have very exactly defined reference points for how we think it should be. So even when the guru is playing with you it is different than how you think it should be. 'It's unfair,' you say. 'Why doesn't he play the way he's supposed to?'

"The guru undermines your reference points by maneuvering—by getting you into a position of possibility and blowing your mind with it. If you look at any disciples who are in business and have a sense of the magic of the guru, they always make incredible things happen. The guru maneuvers us to where we have to bend time or space, or else fail, because our habitual reference points have no value in the guru's world. There's no magic, no mystery in our habitual reference points. They are all about what's not possible, whereas the guru's reference points are about possibility.

"If the guru gives us any warning of when or how he is going to breach the defense system of ego, ego will attempt to outsmart him, so the guru has to maneuver until there is an opening. Once there is an opening then the benediction of the lineage can get in. And, the guru undermines our habitual reference points 'just by the way he is.' That's my specialty, because I'm not so good at maneuvering, but I'm very good at just being the way I am. That I can do! You say, 'How can a guru be like that?'

" 'Ouch! Hooray!' Because the unspoken agreement is that we want our habitual reference points to be undermined. If we want to live in Reality, our habitual reference points must be undermined. The basis of our habitual reference points is separation, so we are always at war within ourselves and at war, in one way, shape or form, with the other, whoever it is—lover, friend or stranger.

"The guru is an enigma in the world, meaning that the guru is God and man at the same time. *Who* he is is God; *how* he is is man. Just the way he is is the way we are, and yet the guru is God. So the guru trips, he stumbles, he runs into things and in his graceful way through life dispenses blessings. The guru doesn't eat the way we expect him to eat, he doesn't dress the way we expect him to dress, he doesn't act the way we expect him to act. Just the way the guru is undermines our habitual reference points. At the same time, hurray! Because that's what we 'pay' the guru to do. That's why we bought a ticket to this show. We come to the guru and accept the guru, then we start putting the guru's humanness in the way of Grace. Isn't that ridiculous? The past Shankaracharya of Kanchipuram said that actually you are better off with a bad guru, then you don't have to worry about developing pride in your guru.

"The guru is always ready, waiting for the opportunity to undermine our habitual reference points. He's maneuvering, and then when the opening is there, Divine Influence that has pierced our defense system is literally like a shaft of light entering a dark space. Under ideal circumstances we would open further to let more light in, but what we tend to do is immediately close up to defend against the light with the logic of doubt. 'How can the guru say the things he says? How can he have set me up in this relationship? Couldn't he have foreseen the difficulties? Why isn't the guru more compassionate? He had no feeling for that poor little mole that got dragged into the meditation hall screaming and crying—right in the middle of meditation!' "

Lee laughed, catalyzing a round of laughter in the room for the people who were in the meditation hall or at breakfast that morning for the discussion. He was getting a lot of mileage out of the cat killing the mole. He continued, speaking the part of the student in doubt, " 'That poor thing was screaming, the cat was throwing it around and jumping on it. Why, the spiritual master was smiling! How could he do such a thing? Why didn't he rescue the poor thing? Why, my heart was just going out to it . . .' " His voice had become fatuous and insipidly sentimental as he animated the character to drive home the point. He changed back to his normal voice and said, "That's the way we start to think! All of our logic comes up—the logic of doubt, the logic of hope. 'Why doesn't the guru appreciate me? He's always working with the women and never with the men. I work my fingers to the bone and he never compliments me. Brinda? Brinda could serve a turd on a silver platter and he would say, 'Brinda, that was a wonderful dinner! You are such a good cook!' And me, I work my fingers to the bone, hidden in the kitchen cooking lovely meals, and he never even notices me!' " Lee threw his head back and laughed loudly to a silent audience.

Someone asked a question, "What does the guru pay for our resistance?"

He answered, "He pays in suffering because his work with us is slowed down and handicapped. He has no other wish than our success on the path. If the suffering gets through to the human side of the guru, then the guru gets depressed and withdrawn. My devotees say to me, 'You're going away.' People say, 'I can't feel you,' because they are trying to feel the human being, not the Divine."

September 17, 1999
La Ferme de Jutreau

Thirty minutes after meditation Lee sat in the big leather chair barefoot, with one leg folded up underneath him. He looked fresh and bright, like he was poised to celebrate something. There were about eighteen people sitting on the floor on cushions or in chairs around the edges of the salon. More people would be arriving later in the day. Lee had the doors taken off the antique armoire and shelves put inside. Now the shelves were stocked with books, CDs, videos and two *vigrahas* of Yogi Ramsuratkumar. Looking around, Lee seemed to be taking stock of the situation as people got settled. At eight-thirty on the dot he began the first session of the seminar:

"Well . . . for brunch this morning we're having American pancakes—they're like big fat thick crepes. Instead of folding delicious things into them you pile everything on top!"

Just then someone came in and called Ken out of the room to help with some task. He had just arrived from Arizona the day before, and will be staying for six months to help on the ashram after Lee leaves for the U.S. Now Lee asked someone to get up and go into the kitchen. "Tell them I want Ken in here all weekend, for the entire seminar. I'm leaving in two weeks and they'll have Ken here to bust his butt for them! I want to make sure that he gets to be here in the room during all of the talks." In a moment or two, Ken walked back in and took a seat.

Lee continued, "So, 'Accepting What Is—the Foundation of Tantric Practice.' I'm going to break tradition and actually talk about the subject of the seminar. I'm going to give the best talk first, so all the people coming tomorrow will be anxious and upset that they missed it, and next time they'll be on time.

"What is tantric practice? The phrase we use for tantric practice is Enlightened Duality. In the East there are very old and deep, profound traditions of tantra in Buddhism and Hinduism, as well as in pre-Buddhist and pre-Hindu cultures. That statue over there," he pointed toward the Primal Mother to his left, "is from a contemporary family of artists who continue to produce art in the ancient style. The ancient cultures could all be considered to be tantric cultures. There are many levels of prayers, ceremonies of worship, offerings to gods and goddesses. Particularly in Vajrayana Buddhism there are exceptionally detailed visualizations for the purpose of invocation. There are ritual practices in relationship to eating, sex, breathing, handling money, relating with the world in every way.

"As the tantric tradition becomes alive in the West it's very important that the roots, the source, the essence of the tradition not be compromised. However, to import the exact letter of the law—in addition to the spirit of the law—might be counterproductive in the West. We can learn the details of ritual ceremony, of Sanskrit, and many Western scholars have. But generally speaking, such extensive and exclusive memorization might be counterproductive for the average Westerner on the path. Speaking as a Westerner and a tantric teacher, we want to impart the *spirit* of the law, or the true essence of tantra, without having to demand the extensive years of study to learn the ancient rituals in their exact, archaic, cultural forms.

"To give a particular example: we bought this statue in Germany. We cleaned the guy out, actually! Unfortunately I had to drag students along with me who begged to come, which obstructed my relationship with this dealer. But, he had a statue of Manjushri, gold-plated with one-thousandth of an inch of gold—but gold, nonetheless! Manjushri in his fierce aspect—sword in one hand, *dorje* in another, and with a cloth wrapped around his eyes. The dealer said that the family who makes these deities are very religious and makes the statues according to ancient guidelines with all the rituals and prayers. They say that the statue is empowered as a sacred representation of Manjushri, and that the eyes are the focal point of the transmission of blessings. Wherever the eyes are first uncovered will be the location where blessings will pour out and integrate with the environment.

"This is one small example of the kind of ritual that completely pervades all traditional tantric work and practice. In principle, it's a very important aspect of guarding our work, protecting our work, and discrimination. We use the word 'discrimination' in a very particular technical way. Obviously the word means to be able to recognize differences between things. We use the word to refer to the utilization of making distinctions of what is Work useful and what is not Work useful, or Work toxic. We use the word 'work' in the sense that Gurdjieff used it, which we could also equate with the higher meanings of the word 'practice' in our school—or, that which facilitates transformation in a shift of context from self-reference to God-reference, or from the reference of illusion to the reference of Reality, which by its definition serves the Great Process of Divine Evolution. E.J. Gold, a friend of mine, might say, to allow one to share in the suffering of the Absolute.

"This principle which is highly ritualized in the East—of guarding and protecting one's work—is totally integrated into the training which we receive in this work in the West. The invocation of the Divine is totally integrated into the training that we participate in. The invocation of the Divine in specific forms of worship have their time and place. The Sufis, particularly—not the wandering dervishes, but ordinary Sufis—are businesspeople and craftspeople. They go to their shop in the morning like everyone else. They are unrecognized as anything other than businesspeople, craftsmen, artisans. They have families, homes, and they go home after work and have dinner with their families, play with their children. Then at the end of the day and into the night they do their esoteric prayers and rituals. The Sufis filmed by Arnaud Desjardins performed the *dzikr*, or ritual circle of prayer, in the middle of the night.

"One of the laws of the Work is that through the practice of discrimination as we have defined it very generally—to protect one's work from toxicity and degeneration—there will be demands made upon us. Unfortunately in most of our cases illness doesn't stop us, but ego does. We allow our resistance to others—what Gurdjieff called personality clash or friction—to keep us from self-honesty. This can handicap our work for years, or a lifetime. Every time we allow our work to become toxified by damaging physical food, subtle food or impression food, there is a recovery period required. During any recuperation you may be able to do some things, but your vitality and health have not fully returned because you are recuperating. It is likewise if our work suffers some setback or 'illness.'

"This is all tantric nonsense. You won't hear this anywhere else! I know many of you," Lee laughed. He made a plug for grounding the information he was dispensing in the reality of the body. He is always returning his audience toward a possibility of living from the wisdom of the body, which cannot occur unless we are accepting and realistic about the necessities and truths of basic human experience. He does this, in his inimitable way, by joking around. "I assume you've all come back to get another dose of whatever it is you get when you see me—the clap!" People laughed; there was some discussion of what the clap is. "It's gonorrhea," Lee insisted, as some people argued over the definition.

It struck me as another of Lee's metaphors using the language of the streets and sex. How does one get the clap? By sleeping with whores, an appellation Lee has used for himself on numerous occasions. It's consistent with the fact that Lee calls the community outreach groups "bordellos." If Lee is the whore, then who is the Pimp? And what would "the clap" be? A heat and an irritation, a process that burns and ferments internally. An illness for which there is only one cure and only one Doctor.

"So, *discrimination*—which is protecting our work. We're either progressing in our work, stagnant with our work, or we're being bled dry, so that our work is seeping out. It's very important to make the distinction when I speak of transformation or progress on the path that I'm not talking about it from the illusion of separation. When we talk about being 'in process' it's clear that there is no place to go on the path, nothing to transform into, and no movement, except within the context of Enlightened Duality. So please do not assume in your cultured expertise of nonduality that the language we are using somehow defines this work as inferior to the work of nonduality, Advaita Vedanta, or Mahayana Buddhism; in fact, it is far superior. But we have to advance one step at a time. You can't do geometry and algebra unless you learn to add and subtract first. So we start at the beginning and methodically work up from the foundation stages to more subtle and refined and esoteric practice.

"Transformation is a function of becoming more and more useful to God. In one sense just being alive is useful to God, like dry wood is useful to fire. But as those of you who are familiar with fire know, there are different kinds of dry wood. Soft dry wood burns quickly with a low heat, and hard, solid, dense wood burns slowly with a high heat. Green wood hardly burns at all. If you are in a cabin in the middle of the winter and you need a fire to keep from freezing, then obviously different types of wood will either be more useful or less useful to your purpose.

"If the purpose of existence is to serve God, then there is a difference between being less useful and more useful. All work is useful to the Divine in this lifetime and possibly beyond. Gurdjieff talked about building a soul that would make us useful to God beyond this lifetime. If you take this consideration in a nondual way it will make no sense, but if you take it from the tantric perspective, it makes perfect sense—not necessarily to the mind, but to the heart and to the body. It is what attracts us essentially to this Work. A teacher can be extraordinarily charismatic, sublime in his or her exposition of the teaching, talented in many areas of life, a great artist, but none of that is what essentially draws us to the Work. If it is what draws us, we need a wake-up call, and we will get one sooner or later.

"We all want to be more utile, more useful, like Jesus or Yogi Ramsuratkumar, who are not just useful, but of rare value. All transformation is about usefulness to the Divine. Transformation is not about becoming something we are not, but about being able to manifest who we really are—not just in the human sense of healthy, successful, talented and so on, but in the ultimate sense . . .

"If we don't protect our work, various forces, entities, beings will come in and steal what we are gathering; whatever resources we have put aside for future use will be stripped, so we must protect the construction of what Gurdjieff called a 'soul' or it will never happen. If we want to insure that the project we have begun will go through to completion we have to protect our resource base, which is the guru, sangha, dharma, or the teacher, community and teaching. As we begin to work we enter into a whole different level of resources of energy and subtle forces. Very much like in the world of human beings, where there are people who are trustworthy and those who aren't, likewise it is the same in the subtle world, except they are forces of various kinds rather than human beings.

"I've been reading the biography of Sir Richard Burton who translated *One Thousand and One Arabian Nights*. It is filled with stories of jinns, or genies. Some are helpful, some are mischievous. These are not simply fantasies, but real aspects of life. There are very real forces that will use up your resources.

"Let's take sex—many people's favorite subject! I know this is France, and I'm just an uncultured, uptight American with Victorian attitudes . . . it's just my opinion and you can ignore it if you want . . ." Another outbreak of laughter filled the room. During the past hour while Lee talked six more people came into the room and threaded their way through to find small open places on the floor where they could sit. Lee was getting brighter by the moment; he seemed to be doing what he calls "entertaining" himself.

"So, when someone has sex with no ongoing emotional and relational intimacy, not only is that sex enervating in the moment, even if you feel fabulous—like you've had a great adventure and you're hungry as a bear the next morning and you just want to lie around languorously, going over every detail of those twenty minutes . . ." More laughter. "Even so, you want to take hours to get dressed, to feel your clothing brush sensuously against your tender ravaged skin . . . you can't wait to get to see your girlfriend or boyfriend again to show them your wounds . . . teeth marks! Even so, it's still enervating in the moment and has the long-term effect of deterioration, both subtle and physiological, but predominantly subtle. There is only one counteracting force, which is a relationship on the subtle level that can re-infuse, protect and rebuild the damaged matrix.

"This is why some great teachers have chosen celibacy. In the Christian monastic tradition and in the East you find the tradition completely steeped in body-negative attitudes and denial of the senses, as if any physical intimacy is sinful, but in fact the real saints who are celibate are not celibate because they are body negative. Like Saint Teresa of Avila, whose poetry is of a great intimacy, ecstasy and joy in the body, not a rejection of the body. Their celibacy was chosen in empathy with the system that they were working within.

"There are two branches of tantric practice—right-hand tantra and left-hand tantra. Left-hand tantra is the experiential physical use of ritual and right-hand tantra is the imaginal use of ritual. In left-hand tantra one has sex with a partner and as the sexual relationship of physicality and intimacy and emotional bondedness deepens, then one's partner becomes infused with the deity. So physical sex becomes an invocation and the union of man and woman becomes the union of god and goddess, the result of which is a very useful contribution to the Divine.

"In right-hand tantra one does not have physical sex to achieve that aim, but imagines having sex with the deity, and one is drawn up into the subtle realms. In left-hand tantra the deity is drawn down, into our world. In either case, sex is used to feed the Divine. When the Divine is fed, It shits, and the shit of the Divine is energy. So when we feed the Divine we get energy. When we have sex for no reason but to conquer, manipulate, dominate the other person or satisfy our own crude desires, not only is our energy completely wasted, even if our partner loves us for the rest of our lives, but we've entered into a karmic bond that will bring nothing but suffering. So the only answer to our wild and savage youth is entering into a relationship that can rebuild that foundation and protect us from deterioration."

Lee closed the space and everyone moved over to the barn dining room for a celebratory and immense brunch of homemade pancakes, wild blackberry conserve, honey butter and mocha. During the meal Gerard, a friend who drew the picture of Yogi Ramsuratkumar that Lee recently hung in the salon, was sitting across from Lee. Jane asked him if drawing the picture had had any particular effect on him. He said yes, nodding his head enthusiastically, and then with a slight pause his eyes widened and he said, "Oh yes."

He began to describe his experience, speaking in French with Michelle translating, "There is such radiance and light that comes from Yogi Ramsuratkumar," he said, "it goes out to the sky. It is vast. Even the sleeve of his robe, the folds of his robe, the fabric," he looked up at the picture of Yogi Ramsuratkumar and Lee that hung above Lee's head as he spoke, "everything is so tender. The feet are so tender and solid on the earth." He shrugged and smiled at Lee's students who were listening intently, then he added, "*You know.*"

"He is vast, and yet the center is very concentrated and very intense," and he made the motion of an explosion, indicating that as vast as Yogi Ramsuratkumar's being is, it is also very concentrated with power. He went on, "There is such vastness of love, like the sky, it overwhelms everything, overflows everything. It is ineffable—*you* know. There are no words—one becomes very silent. When I paint or draw I have to become silent; it is so vast and so tender, such love. We are very lucky," he said. He looked directly at Lee's students and said, "You are the luckiest people on earth. I try to bring that into what I draw." He said that he had started a new drawing, one of Yogi Ramsuratkumar wearing a red shawl from a photograph in the book, *Yogi Ramsuratkumar Souvenir.*

Gerard was freely showing his own tenderness and awe as he spoke. He was shameless and yet discreet in what he was saying. There was no showiness in it at all. Lee was listening quietly but obviously paying close attention to what Gerard was saying. He seemed to be absorbing Gerard's words, understanding the French effortlessly and sometimes translating for Jane. One of Lee's senior students threw out a casual compliment to

Marcus, who was sitting beside Gerard listening to the conversation, saying, "Marcus knows what Gerard is talking about!" Marcus blushed deeply and seemed disconcerted and uncomfortable with the praise, or perhaps not sure how to take the person's nonchalant remark. Lee immediately took his attention away from what Gerard was saying and began to engage Marcus in a conversation about his work with the *thangkas*. The discomfort passed right away, and as the conversation went on Lee unexpectedly mentioned that he would like to come to London next year and give some talks. It has been five or six years since Lee has been to London.

After brunch the group dispersed for three hours to participate in various activities of guru *seva*. At three o'clock Lee started his afternoon talk in the salon to a packed room. A new picture of Swami Papa Ramdas, taken by Arnaud Desjardins and given to Lee as a gift, had been framed and sat on the floor next to Lee's chair on his right. Now as people looked at Lee sitting at the head of the room, they would also be looking at Papa Ramdas and the large picture of Yogi Ramsuratkumar which graces the fireplace mantle above Lee's head. It was a powerful tableau.

After the sober talk of the morning Lee cracked a few extemporaneous jokes about all the heavy food planned for the weekend. "We should have some partying here, some drinking, but I'm so conservative—all we do is *eat*! Just wait until tonight. We're having a huge Indian feast, then we'll be back here, sitting in this room burping and farting and groaning!" People chuckled, some laughed loudly. "And tomorrow night we're having turkey! We practically had to kill them ourselves, they were so hard to find . . ."

He then began to discuss accepting what is as it is. He began, "So, Surrender to the Will of God. The phrase 'what is, is' is about the reality of our situations on all levels," then he stopped in mid-stream. Maybe we needed to laugh some more, to become more receptive, because he started talking about the support groups in his community, lampooning his students and using them as the foil for his antics, which generated plenty of laughter.

From there he began to plow into the dark soil of the group psyche, heaving his shovel directly into the child abuse that the vast majority of people have endured. He was particularly penetrating in his references to the sexual abuse of children—"A crude description of an all too common reality," he said. He liberally interspersed his discussion with direct hits on the denial of psychological wounds that many bear, at the same time talking about how behavioral modification through the process of psychological work on self may produce some changes, but not the kind of radical change of spiritual transformation. "We learn from our mistakes as we grow older," he said, "but essentially the psychological motivation that keeps us animating pride, greed, shame, vanity, anger or fear doesn't change, no matter what we do. But our psychological motivation can change, if we accept it *as it is*. But it is necessary to feel the pain the child felt . . ."

As Lee went more deeply into this subject that is so familiar to his students, a woman who had come to hear Lee speak for the first time sat with tears streaming down her face. She seemed strangely both at peace and deeply moved into sorrow and grief, the paradox held within the mood of profound acceptance that Lee was creating and sustaining in the space. While he spoke about accepting what is as it is, he was giving the felt experience of it in the subtle atmosphere, so that the group could be imprinted with the teaching not just in the thinking center, but in the feeling and instinctual centers as well. This felt experience of total acceptance was tremendously healing and affirming; as the woman cried silently, she expressed what many were experiencing more internally. Outside the sun was shining, giving a brief respite from the cloudy early autumn chill. It shone into the salon through the tall French windows and made a beautiful dappled shadow play on the floor.

"We are handicapped in our relationship to the brilliance of the Divine to the degree we do not allow those old relationships of abuse and pain to fall away. It is literally a matter of dropping them, but first we have to see them and accept the pain of them." A strong receptive listening could be felt in the room, and a mood of contemplation. Some were pondering what Lee was saying with their heads down. One woman covered her mouth. Some took notes. Others sat with very sober faces. The woman still cried silently. The room seemed unified within a field of compassion that was unfathomable, and somehow the *murtis* (sacred images) of Swami Ramdas, Yogi Ramsuratkumar and their living representative, Lee Lozowick, were the source of that compassion—a benediction at work so far beyond the mind's understanding that one could only wonder at it.

Lee continued: "So change is constantly pushing against the restrictions our psyche has imposed upon us. If we remove those restrictions, change will happen naturally by itself because the nature of existence is natural evolution. We can't change ourselves, except within the restrictions. We may become more relaxed, more sophisticated, we may be relieved of some of our prejudices. But to actually change at the core level of what motivates us to act—*we* can't do that. But change is built into the organism as what Chögyam Trungpa Rinpoche called basic goodness. We have to allow our basic goodness to actually be expressed. All therapeutic processes are about removing the obstacles to basic goodness. To accept *what is* is to see things as they are in the moment—good, bad, like, dislike. There are many things in each of us that are likeable, and there are many things in each of us that are not likeable. But all of that is also subjective.

"One of the aims of tantric work is to accept what is as a context for living, not as a method of change. As a context, accepting *what is* allows the Divine to manifest, with the individual being the submitted vehicle for that manifestation, so that one is acting as the Divine would act were we not manifesting the free will of neurosis. If all restrictions are removed—expectations, wishes, dreams, projections—then the Divine has the opportunity to freely experience Itself through us. But as long as all that is the function of our psychology, then we obstruct the Divine in its urge. Free will is a great gift, but it has a high price, which is that we can, unknowingly, obstruct the flow of natural life.

"We have to surrender our identification. We are identified with our dreams. 'Some day I'm going to be rich, be a great writer,' or whatever. We're identified with it, but year after year we fail to achieve our dreams. Life keeps kicking us, 'Hey! Hey!' trying to get our attention, but we just keep going on because we're identified with our dreams. It's the identification that keeps us from being the very thing we want to be. It's all projection of the mind! Who are we? Nobody! In the Sufi tradition, the only way one can get into the Tavern of Ruin is, when they ask who it is knocking at the door, the Sufi says, 'Tell them it is nobody, son of nobody.'

"So who are we? Nobody. We keep trying to make ourselves somebody because the mind can't accept being nobody. It keeps trying to identify as this 'somebody.' Then we come to the path and hear the philosophy that we have created this whole persona from childhood trauma, but we are nobody, and ah! We've found the Truth! So we take on a new identity—nobody!" Lee chuckled.

"We start writing all our letters in the third person. 'That's me—nobody!' But we're still identified. This is what the mind does. It's a matter of making distinctions. We have to be under no illusions about our illusions. We have to accept the dream as a dream, not the wish of a somebody. What or who is it that can accept what is? Consciousness itself— or you can call it Life, the Universe, God, Mother."

The translator, Michelle, inserted the word "great" before Mother in French. Lee corrected her, as he often does with his translators when they have made a slight change in what he said. He said with a deliberate smile, "No, not 'Great Mother,' just Mother!" Michelle changed the translation and, satisfied, Lee continued.

"Consciousness only exists in the here and now—not in the past or future. As far as consciousness is concerned there is no past or future, except in the mind of duality. When we are accepting what is we are identified with consciousness, which has no definition, no limitation, no boundary. That is where the statement 'I am God' comes from, when one is speaking from consciousness, not from the individual."

Lee began to crank up the room with little one liners—funny, spontaneous quips. He told a joke and got almost no response from the group. Undaunted, he then plunged immediately into a another joke, with still no response other than a couple of half-smiles. Staring back at the audience who sat staring at him, Lee said, "Wow—this is a tough crowd!" Everyone burst into laughter. Lee turned back to the dharma.

"The path is about an ongoing progression of the realization of the reality of nothing-ness and nobody-ness, out of a context of somebody-ness, until the weight of revelation has become so dominant that it pushes us into the other context—the context of nobody-ness. There are only two contexts: nobody-ness and somebody-ness; nothing and something; consciousness and definition. Consciousness has no definition, and defini-tion cannot accept what is as it is. You cannot have both at the same time. Enlightenment, illumination, awakening all refer to life lived from the context of consciousness. Consciousness is nonduality; definition is duality. To accept what is as it is begins as a formula. It is like getting a mantra—as you repeat the mantra more and more the Name of God is invoked by the technology or methodology of using the mantra."

Leigh Goldstein's watch alarm went off. He quickly turned it off, but it had captured Lee's attention. Looking at Leigh he said, "Time to call your mother! We never want to forget when it's time to call *Mother*!" Once again, "Mother" was coming up. Which "Mother" was he referring to? It was one of those comments that could be taken in many different ways. The Primal Mother stood sentinel at Lee's side with a large orange red dahlia placed as an offering at her feet. She communicated the epitome of Organic Innocence. Her som-ber yet somehow awestruck face exuded power and strength as did the pose of her body. At times her eyes seemed quite alive, but it was hard to tell what quality was coming through them as they constantly changed. At times they seemed objectively sorrowful, like the Pietà, or Mother of Jesus, grieving over the dead body of her Son. At other times the deity's eyes seemed to gleam with pure ecstasy, the whole body taut and surging with shakti force. Reaching his hand down to touch the framed photograph of Swami Papa Ramdas to his right, Lee forged ahead.

"So this is a picture of Swami Papa Ramdas. It's a very rare picture, taken by Arnaud Desjardins. Swami Papa Ramdas was initiated into the mantra, 'Om Sri Ram Jai Ram Jai Jai Ram.' It means 'Victory to Ram, Victory to God,' because if God is victorious, who benefits? We do. We benefit from the Grace of God. So Ramdas began to say the mantra more and more until he became possessed by the passion to realize God."

Lee's talk seemed to be building to the crest of a wave that was carrying everyone along. His fervor was infectious, and the mood of sanctity in the space was a still, burning presence. He could not disguise this burning presence with his jokes and randy sense of humor or self-deprecations, and it seemed as if the new *murti*, or sacred image, of Swami Papa Ramdas had added an important element to the presence that now permeated everything.

"Over time the formula of the mantra begins to take on a life of its own. Then that which the formula is defining becomes the reality. You start with an empty ritual and end up with the thing itself. If you practice with the appropriate vigor, this is realizable. You start out with the phrase, 'Accept what is, here and now, as it is.'

"If you practice using the phrase with diligence and integrity, what happens is that consciousness, in its desire not to be misrepresented by ego, begins to accept what is as it is, here and now, which is an experience of such distinction from ego accepting what is that it is experienced as bliss or ecstasy. It is an experience of revelation, or vision. It is such a strong experience that one can believe that it is a permanent enlightenment—the belief in which is a big mistake . . ."

Someone came in from the kitchen to tell Lee that the five-thirty meal would be ready a few minutes early. "So! Be prepared to eat! Tonight we have a feast cooked by one of our Indian chefs. There is dessert, so when you're pigging out, save room. If anyone is interested in books, take what you want, then you can see Andrea later and pay her. Dinner in five minutes! Oh boy—early!" He jumped up enthusiastically and headed over to the barn.

After dinner, before the evening talk was to begin, Ann came into the office and told Lee that the fresh turkeys, which had just been delivered after a long search for a place to buy them, still had their heads on. They were to be cooked for the meal tomorrow night. Lee said, "Clint can cut the heads off."

"I'll do it," Ann offered.

"That's right, you're an old farm girl," Lee laughed.

She left to do the deed, but within a minute or two Lee stepped out of the office and into the room where the turkeys were lined up on a table for de-heading. He watched Ann hacking away at a tough, thick, rubbery turkey neck. After a few moments of little progress he said, "I'll do it." He took the large hatchet into his hands and in one resounding thud chopped through the thick neck of the first turkey, completely and cleanly severing the neck from the body. The irrevocable force with which he chopped reverberated around the room. One or two people winced involuntary at the sharp thud of the hatchet into the cutting board beneath the turkey neck. Then he chopped again, cutting another head from the neck, and stood back while Ann put the turkey into a plastic bag and pulled out the next turkey. This continued until Lee had made clean cuts on three turkeys while the small group watched his movements.

Dasya, who had come in and stood watching, laughed and said, "Is this where the turkeys line up?"

Jane said, "Yeah, we'll all waiting to get our heads cut off." While some grimaced, others chuckled or just stood and watched soberly. Someone said, "Look at the jugular vein on that one—that's how they killed the turkeys, they slit their throats!"

Lee said, "I'm trying not to look! I wouldn't make a very good surgeon," he laughed, then joked, with his hand over his eyes like a squeamish doctor, "Where am I supposed to cut, nurse? Up here or down there?" Lee handed the hatchet to Debbie and turned to walk out, the job done.

After a dinner of dahl, coconut rice, vegetable *sabji* and halvah Lee gave a talk from seven to nine o'clock. He fielded a number of questions, and at around eight-fifteen the questions from guests and French students subsided. He asked if there were other questions. Suddenly the room went into a momentary lull. The mood shifted as Lee became focused inwardly, his attention no longer on the group but elsewhere. There was a slight smile hovering on his face, and he looked as if he was gazing at something in a completely different domain. After thirty seconds that had the surreal quality of expanding time into infinity, Lee looked up and said smiling, "What's going on? Where are we? Who are all you people?" He laughed. The group laughed with him, a little hesitantly. Whatever was going on was beyond anyone's ken.

He began to answer other questions, particularly from a woman who said she was considering becoming a student of Lee's. Her question now was how could it work for her to have a different guru than her husband, who is a disciple of Amritanandamayi. Lee entered into a lively discussion with her. As he tore into the exchange in a sarcastic tone he was like a wild *heruka* brandishing an invisible lightning bolt.

"How can your husband have a hard time with it when my advice to married women is to honor your husband, serve him in everything, put your family first, be invisible in your work? You know, lots of teachers don't support couples in having sex. Like Amma. To be close to her, to be getting her attention, you have to be celibate. I'm not saying that she splits up couples, but she has thousands of disciples, and she takes the celibates more seriously."

Lee began to joke around irreverently about divine mothers. He made some outrageous and highly provocative comments about Amritanandamayi, as if he knew her personally. At this point a man in the audience, who had seemed full of fear and had been very aggressive with Lee and many other people since he had arrived on the ashram the day before, took offense at Lee's words about Ammachi. As Lee continued to speak the man started talking loudly and attempting to "defend" Amritanandamayi. Lee bantered with him for a few moments, then kept going with his discourse. Frustrated by Lee's antics, unable to get another word in as Lee kept going, his anger obviously mounted. Finally he got up and walked out of the room, heading for the men's dorm in the barn where he had stayed last night.

Lee glanced at the man as he walked out the door and kept talking. The living presence of the Primal Mother stood guard by Lee's left hand. The man had to walk past her and Lee to get out of the space. The rest of the group seemed very content to keep their attention on Lee. But still, this piece of theatre gave everyone an opportunity to consider. There was a question hanging in the air: Was Lee really being disrespectful to Ammachi, or was something deeper and more profound going on under the guise of provocation? Each person had to answer this by feeling into Lee's intention.

If one puts the pieces of his teaching together, Lee's relationship to the Divine Feminine comes into focus. It is a relationship of adoration, deeply truthful and invocative. Observing him over years he has often appeared as a one-man renaissance in which the Feminine is brought back into its rightful place in the scheme of all things—from the cosmic to the most earthy and mundane. His presence has the sometimes unnerving effect of bringing the Feminine back into its native radiance and power. In this regard Lee is often like the Pied Piper. Most of the men and women who are drawn to Lee are those who have a natural resonance to the Feminine dimensions, sometimes through more earthy means of pure instinct, the body, the feeling life, and sometimes through direct perception or radical insight. Now as the scruffy, angry man snatched up his bag and walked swiftly to the parking lot and roared off down the long driveway to escape the clutches of the tantric master, upstairs in Lee's room Vajrayogini danced and laughed, and across the ocean in the darshan hall in Arizona, twenty-one Taras glowed in their oceans of worlds, emanations of compassion, of vividness and emptiness at play.

One gets the sense that Lee speaks of Amritanandamayi because it is somehow lawful; his relationship to her has nothing to do with the fact that he has never met her, but is beyond time and space. In his mentions of Amritanandamayi there is no sentiment, no paternal nonsense, and actually no arrogance. He treats her like an equal who is perfectly capable of taking strong force or energy from her peers. Years ago Lee passed a videotape around his community; it was a recording of Osho Rajneesh talking about Lee Lozowick, whom he had never met. One of Lee's former students who had become a student of Rajneesh had given Rajneesh a letter in which she said that she still loved Lee and was confused as to whether she should go back to Lee or stay with Rajneesh. Rajneesh responded with a playful repartee that, although on the surface appeared highly critical of Lee, was part of Rajneesh's whimsical style. On another occasion Rajneesh had said that Lee Lozowick was an enlightened master, but on this day he said Lee was a charlatan who would lead her astray. Lee had his students watch this tape and then commented on it. He said that he didn't care what another teacher said about him, as long as they talked about him. He considered it all *energy* that contained power and blessing—the form it took didn't matter in the least to him. It was a completely impersonal and contrary view of things—contrary to the view of the world, which weighs everything in terms of superficial appearances.

Viewing Lee's playful pokes at Amritanandamayi from the tantric perspective, and remembering having heard him speak of her many years ago with tremendous regard, his comments now were cast in a very different light for me. But most people have to sense into Lee's meaning without the benefit of having observed over time how he works. Of course it is possible to have known Lee for years or heard him teach many times and still not get what he is doing because sooner or later, to get to the jewels of Lee Lozowick's communication, one must bypass the mind completely and listen directly through the gut and heart.

Watching through the window as the man walked toward the parking lot with his bag in hand, Lee reflected, "Well, we got rid of another person who doesn't belong here." Now switching tactics, Lee turned back to the woman and said, "You know about Andrew Cohen? He's great—why don't you and your husband go see him? Maybe you'll both like him, then your problem will be solved! Andrew and I are good friends, and we can make a deal! Maybe your husband will like him." He had a huge grin on his face.

"In fact, he'll be in Paris in . . . wait, I've got it right in here . . ." He got up and almost ran, dodging and threading his way through the crowded room and into the office, where he rummaged around on his desk and called out, "I found it!" He whirled back into the room, like a witch stirring a pot. "Here it is!" Everyone was laughing except the woman Lee was talking to. She looked disturbed by Lee's rakish sense of humor and the fact that he was handling her consideration about having Lee as a guru so casually. Now he tossed the brochure to her and said, "Andrew will be in Paris in November. Here, you can have that. Show it to your husband. You and your husband should go. Okay?" She nodded and took the brochure. He was rather like an unstoppable train coming full speed down the tracks as he continued. "I was just using Ammachi as a foil! You know what a foil is?

She's a great old dame—or a young dame. But man, people are sure attached to those bracelets she sells! People swear by them. You have to cut their hands off to get them!" He laughed again then said sweetly, "I'm just fishin'—seeing if I can get a rise out of anybody."

He asked if there were more questions. One of his American students asked Lee if he would put the consideration of accepting what is as it is into his own language, which is the practice of Assertion, or "Just This." There was a general and very confusing discussion and debate with Lee in which a number of other American students asked questions about the nature of consciousness, accepting what is and the use of mantra. After throwing out a few scattered jewels like, "Organic Innocence is the isness of each thing," and "The mantra becomes worshipful rather than methodological, and when it becomes worshipful, then it becomes attractive to the Divine," Lee seemed to give his students space to ramble in their comments and questions. Finally he said, "The confusion you've seen here tonight in my students is the result of not discussing our own dharma for twenty-four years. You throw a couple of diamonds on the ground and don't explain them, then you just wait for somebody to find them and figure it out. Whoever finds them gets rich. Everybody else walks by them and says, 'Oh, that's a pretty stone,' and throws them in the basket with the quartz crystals."

Paula asked, "Is the practice of 'Just This' still relevant?"

Lee snapped, "Sure—why not?" He paused and then went into a scathing indictment of his students who had participated in the questions about the formal language of his teaching. He said, "I tell my students, my American students, not to ever ask questions at seminars and now you can see why—*and I hope it is crystal clear to them as well*—because of the incredible confusion that was demonstrated here tonight!" His words were penetrating. His students' questions and comments had completely changed the mood of the space on this evening.

Gerard made a comment that it seemed an important translating distinction that the word was Assertion, not insertion. Lee laughed and said, "See what I mean? All it does is cause more confusion. Yes, very important. Insertion is definitely something else!" he added, his voice brimming with innuendo. Everyone laughed. He concluded, "Language is only a means to an end. It's nice that we can resolve our language differences peacefully."

Immediately after the talk was over Lee walked into the office and instructed Andrea to send the check for the seminar paid by the man who left back to him immediately with a polite note. Lee said, "Tell him the dinner was on me."

September 18, 1999
La Ferme de Jutreau

This morning the mood in the salon as people gathered for the talk was very sober. It was chilly and overcast again outside, and people bundled up in sweaters, jackets or shawls. The summer was over and fall had arrived. The sobriety was in part that people had just come out of meditation and directly into the session; a rather contemplative mood permeated everything as a result. Lee opened his discourse talking about Yogi Ramsuratkumar and the Shankaracharya. Very quickly he noticed Marcus, who was sitting in a chair completely wrapped in a big white wool shawl. He looked quite ill.

"Marcus, is it allergies?" Lee queried.

"No, it's a virus," Marcus answered.

"Oh, okay. I was going to put the cats in bottles for the rest of the seminar if it was allergies . . ." Lee laughed, "for the rest of the time you were here!" He doubled over with laughter, holding his hands up and demonstrating, "Can't you just see it, the cats in bottles! Those of you who got here today missed it because the cat brought a mouse into meditation yesterday and ate it right there in front of everyone. It was so inspiring!" He cracked himself up again with just the mention of it. After another volley of chuckles and cackles from Lee, he continued in a poetic, playfully wistful tone, "Ahhh, the wild, unrestrained wonders of Nature! Combined with my reading of Sir Richard Burton's biography, I want to go to Africa and watch the lions chew up gazelles!" He threw his head back and laughed wildly. He seemed to enjoy putting the raw facts of nature, life and death into direct contrast with the fear of death and dismemberment that so completely dominates the egoic mind.

Lee moved into a mode of buffoonery that seemed designed to loosen up the mood of the group. He talked about his peers in the Work as a bunch of rakes, rascals and libertines, leapt skillfully from one mountain peak of dharma to another—one moment expounding on the guru/disciple relationship, the next moment reeling off on another hilarious tangent. At the end of the session he began another exhortation to the group to rethink their relationship to the Work. Then he was off to the barn dining room for a satisfying breakfast of scrambled eggs and toast.

Smells of the baking turkeys wafted into the room. The meal promised to be incredible. The menu was typical American holiday fare—turkey, stuffing, gravy, mashed potatoes, peas and carrots, apple crisp. You'd think it was Thanksgiving, but of course it was not. It is not uncommon for Lee to have this particular meal—a favorite of many Americans and quite loaded with memories, both pleasant and unpleasant, and sentimental emotional states—served at completely different times of the year than when it is typically served by American tradition. It gives the Americans an opportunity to work at different levels, whether it is on the tendency toward sentimental nostalgia, pure greed or scarcity which causes overeating, or resistance to the reality of having given up control over when one gets to have one's Thanksgiving dinner—on the guru's timetable, which is September or April, or on ego's time table, which is in sync with the rest of the conventional world. Everything in tantric work goes against the grain of the conventional mindset, and even something as simple as a "Thanksgiving" dinner on a rainy evening in September in France can be a vehicle for that rub. This particular meal was inspired by the massive amount of leftover bread that Lee had been given by the hosts at Joué near Bordeaux after the seminar. Looking for a way to use the free bread, Lee had said, "Let's make some stuffing," an favorite American side dish usually served with turkey. From there the idea expanded into turkey and stuffing, or dressing as some call it.

The group reconvened for Lee's afternoon talk after three hours of guru *seva*—hard work with shovels and picks, or with trowels and rakes in the garden. As Lee spoke many people were taking notes on his answer to Annette, a psychiatric nurse who deals with very ill and psychotic people, some of them murderers. She said that she was able to stay positive with them during the day to the extent that she would not draw their violence and negativity toward herself, as many of the nurses and doctors do. But when she came home at night she realized that she was carrying the negativity and poison of the situation. She asked Lee for his advice.

He spent the next hour talking essentially about how to "Be that which nothing can take root in," a dharmic phrase that Lee gave to his students at his first talk in France in 1988. He did not use this phrase during his talk today, but described it in many different ways instead. By not using this phrase it is as if he was hammering in the point that his students have drifted farther and farther from using the language of their own teacher and school. And yet at the same time he had just the day before castigated his students for bringing questions about this very thing to the group.

The phrase, "Be that which nothing can take root in," as it was given by Lee serves as a reminding factor of a mood or attitude of disidentification. "Being that which nothing can take root in" is a cornerstone of the tantric path, in which no aspect of life is rejected, but is entered into without the prison of identification. Being "that which nothing can take root in" frees *all this* to be used, to be distilled into its essential energetic viability for the transformational process.

Today in answer to Annette's question, Lee talked about "the eternal, stainless, pristine essence of being," which is beyond characteristics but in which qualities arise and subside. "The practice is to not identify with what arises," Lee said, "but with that which is stainless, pure and eternal. If you can see that pure, eternal essence in your patients at the hospital, then they will see that in themselves in some way, and in you, and trust you for it. The core of the practice of not identifying is, 'This is arising, that is arising, but it is not me.' "

Much of what Lee offered to people this afternoon focused on the art of relationship. He has spoken in years past about "objective relationship," saying that his vision for the community is that at some point the focus for the core group of his students would be on practice and the embodiment of objective relationship, so that one's life becomes an artifact of the Work. This vision shows up in the emphasis he often places on the practical aspects of how to forge the underpinnings of such an ultimate human possibility. Today he spoke about how necessary it is to not project one's assumptions and expectations on others while at the same time seeing one's own tendencies and habits with clarity. All these forms of internal awareness are part of basic psychological wholeness, and lay the foundation for the possibility of relating with the world at large with kindness, generosity and compassion.

Throughout this afternoon session Lee provided concrete help to his audience. Everyone in the room could relate to Annette's question, the principles applying to all relationships. Lee was not throwing cold, impersonal dharmic platitudes at people, but reaching into the heart of their experience and working with them there, where they live. It was practical, grounded help, and it was an exact demonstration of what he had talked about yesterday when he spoke of bringing the living principles of tantra into the West in a way that the tradition stays authentically alive. In his ability to translate the dharma he offered refuge—how to live according to cosmic law—into the terms of peoples' lives.

At the same time, the touch of his attention was such that it seeded within the being of the receptive questioner a thirst for more: more of what this refuge is, this feeling of rightness, of basic goodness, of Organic Innocence. The taste of the Primacy of Natural Ecstasy arises in many spaces when Lee conducts its occupants into states of receptivity, delight and bodily wonder, either through laughter or through sometimes exquisite renderings of perennial truth into the language of our times. Today Lee did exactly that in a discourse in which he used a question posed by one of his French students, of whom there were several in the room.

Marie Françoise, who has been a student for two years, raised her hand. "What I experienced before in dreams I experience now during the day, frequently. I am not managing it well, fear takes over, and it is very painful. What should I do?"

Lee answered, "I have described the process you are in as a process of purification, from subtle realms to gross realms. Not as in subtle energy, but purification from the superficial level to profound levels. Because the purification is deepening it's with you now in your waking state. You deal with it exactly the same way as with your dreams. Eventually the idea is that we have purified every level. You keep taking refuge in the guru, the dharma, the sangha.

"The important thing is, don't give up in the middle of the process of purification. Your connection to me is very strong and has been from the beginning, so don't give up, and don't identify with the fear or dramatize it. Is that helpful?" She nodded yes, the radiance of her face unmasked by the tears in her eyes as she listened attentively. He turned from her toward the whole group, using the tenderness of the moment to step off into what would turn out to be not only an empowerment of the new French students in the room, but also a clarion call to take the next step in commitment on the path.

"Perhaps we can consider devotion to the guru versus practice. Generally speaking, there are two elements of relationship with the teacher. Both have personal and impersonal dimensions. Often when we meet our teacher there is a strong sense of recognition. Sometimes it is obvious that the teacher is our teacher, sometimes it is subtler and takes time. Sometimes we feel knocked off our feet from the initial connection with the guru. It's immediate and powerful.

"So whether it is fast or slow, when we start to get involved with the teacher we develop a certain bonding with him or her. The underlying bond is the eternal bond of reciprocity, but it tends to take on a personal quality—love, devotion, trust, gratitude and veneration. Over time it can become deeper and more meaningful to us than anything else. Sometimes because of the strength of this we assume that this mood of relationship is enough to see us through to the end of the path, and we ignore the domain of practice, because practice doesn't make us feel how we feel when we contemplate the master. When we contemplate the master we feel comforted, loved . . . unappreciated . . . oh no—that comes later!" Lee slid off into irony. He and several of his students who have been with him for ten or more years laughed together.

"So we want to contemplate the master—we feel such compassion, love, understanding as we look at his photo. Then we contemplate practice. 'I have to get up at six-thirty to meditate? Oh no! Then I have to sing that dumb Sanskrit song . . . I don't even know what it means!' Then there is the diet—oh, the diet! You go down to breakfast, you make your family a delicious breakfast of eggs, bacon, toast, and you sit down with your warm oatmeal and unsweetened herbal tea! 'This sucks!' you say. 'It's terrible! What does this have to do with love, compassion . . . or sex?' " The whole group was laughing now. Lee had definitely struck a chord of common understanding. This is indeed what most of the French students are dealing with—many of them are women whose husbands are not interested in the Work, and who must somehow juggle the difficult and delicate terrain of serving their families, putting their families first as Lee instructs, and following the recommended conditions and practices of the school at the same time.

"So the master is not separate from the practices that he or she recommends. We have a saying in English. 'Love me, love my dog.' So that's exactly the way it is with the guru and his practices. We fall in love and want to move in with our new beloved, but they have a dog!" The room had gotten very bright and warm as people sat smiling and enjoying Lee's playful way of giving them the bad news, as he continued talking about one of E.J. Gold's maxims, " 'You can't change what is, but you can learn to like it.' So there are two things you can't change—the master, and how the master is."

Lee went into a comedy routine that could have been written by a team of comedy experts about his own quirks and eccentricities—wearing secondhand clothes, for example, or having his ashrams filled with donated and mismatched furniture. "It's not that I don't have taste, it's that no one puts those kinds of clothes in the giveaway box! And if you think this ashram is full of ugly furniture that doesn't match, you should see the American ashram! It's a museum of junk!" Laughter filled the room. He was using the commonality of the people in the room as the jumping off point for bringing them into a chamber in which spiritual principles could be transmitted and clearly laid out. People were disarmed by such unself-conscious laughter, which shook the whole frame of the body and caused tears of pleasure to well up in the eyes. The group waited to hear what outrageously funny thing he would say next. How far would he go? He tore into a diatribe now that had people practically rolling on the floor as he went into an almost burlesque send-up of his own penchant for mismatched clothes, his bad jokes, his sexist comments and so on and so on. Finally everyone sobered up as Lee turned back toward the teaching point he was making.

"In some schools there are virtually no practices given. In this school there are practices upon practices—meditation, vegetarian diet, study, exercise, breath practices, mantra practice, monetary practices. So, 'You can't change what is, but you can learn to like it.' You can actually come to look forward to meditation in the morning, or to a big plate of salad for dinner. In that sentence, 'You can't change what is, but you can learn to like it,' the key word is 'learn.'

"Loving the master is wonderful; bonding deeply with the master is wonderful. That has to do with the eternal world, but we don't live in the eternal world, we live in the relative world. If you love the master but are miserable in your daily life, you may be 'saved' in heaven (though it really doesn't work that way), but you're still miserable in this world and spreading misery all around you. You have to ask yourself, are you happy, successful, creative? Are you a force for transmission of the teaching in the world? Are you in communion with your teacher? Being in communion with the teacher is not the same thing as loving the teacher. Those questions have to do with *practice*. Learning is a process that occurs in time. We don't always just immediately love something. We have a practice called Enquiry. Lots of my students love meditation or using mantra, but hate Enquiry or the diet. You can learn to like the practice, but you have to *do* it to learn to like it. You have to do the practice in spite of resistance, distaste, lack of understanding. So what if you don't understand the practice? Do it anyway.

"The core practices of this school are about the esoteric side of the school, but not at the beginning. The recommended conditions—meditation, study, exercise, vegetarian diet, monogamous relationship—are about defining the dream, aligning the dream, priming the dream. The core practices are about a shift in context. The core conditions and the practices are blessed by the nature of their revelatory appearance. The important thing to understand is that each of the practices and conditions of this school were revelatory. I didn't establish them because I liked them, but because they were given to me. They intruded their way into this Work; they penetrated our lives.

"To practice any of those things without investing in studentship in the school produces positive effects, but without a connection to the teacher, they don't produce the result that they are designed to produce. The idea is for people to enter into a committed relationship with a school, and then practice where they are, with their families, in ordinary life—not necessarily on some ashram."

This afternoon's talk seemed centered around a strong empowerment of the growing French sangha to go on to the next step in their sadhana. He was calling them toward the path in a way that made the medicine quite palatable—by joking and entering into their world completely, by extending his understanding of just how difficult it can be to make the necessary life changes to engage a life of disciplined practice. The daunting array of practices in the school have driven some people away. But tonight he was making a call to his French students who have made it through the first of many gargoyles or difficulties that must be pierced to enter fully into the Western Baul path. The next step would be coming into a relationship with the practices as Names of God, in which one realizes that it is only through practice that the delicate but strong connection with the guru is nourished and brought to greater and deeper fulfillment. His call for the next step in practice was a compliment to their work, depth of their commitment and dedication to the path.

September 19, 1999
La Ferme de Jutreau

At brunch a newcomer, Evelyne, sat across from Lee. She is a Frenchwoman who has lived in London since her childhood, and since coming to the seminar has made a very strong connection with Lee and his teaching. Out of the blue she said, "I'd like to bring you to London next summer." It was a bold statement from someone who had no idea what that would entail, since Lee usually brings anywhere from ten to twenty people with him wherever he goes, and he does nothing by standard rules. Whoever hosts Lee is in for a very fast and fiery ride of one kind or another.

She had been very visibly and genuinely moved during Lee's discourses, crying a number of times, and now was expressing her gratitude. She seemed very smitten with Lee, and watching him buttering his bread there were tears gathering in her eyes again. She burst out, "You are so adorably crazy!"

Visibly unmoved, Lee said dryly, "In a conservative sort of way."

She said, "What's on your bread?"

He shrugged, "Butter."

She continued, "You look at it as if it was something incredibly rare!"

"It is," he laughed.

Chris added, "It is for him—he hardly ever eats butter."

Looking at Lee affectionately, Evelyne smiled and said, in relation to her gushing emotionality, "I know you're going to kick my butt! I just know you are . . ."

Noticeably unaffected by the gush of compliments and looking at the baguette he was holding in his hand and had just buttered, he said in a matter-of-fact and cool tone, "You have to bend down first!"

She laughed and said, "Yes, but I am resistant!" He shrugged again very slightly, totally unimpressed by any declarations of awe. Lee's students often comment on how deeply they have been moved by the transmission they experience coming from him. Lee's almost constant rejoinder to this is, "We'll see," referring to the fact that nothing is trustworthy in one's sadhana until it has been put into practice with such diligence that it becomes completely reliable. Shortly Lee tapped his glass with his spoon and asked for announcements, then ended brunch with a "Jai Guru" and walked out.

During the afternoon on Sunday, the last day of the seminar, Lee had Dasya give one talk and Clint give another. At the beginning of Clint's talk someone asked a question, "Could you speak about the role of community in your school, and how it is possible for people to live in community when the teacher lives so far away most of the year in America."

Clint started to answer. In each sentence there were five or six concepts woven in. It was complex and difficult to follow, and the translator, Michelle, began to falter. She seemed suddenly unable to process what Clint was saying. He began to talk about how the disciple thinks that because the guru is here in the room the guru is *here*, but actually there is nobody there. There is nobody in the body of the guru because ego, the sense of somebody-ness, has been completely subsumed in surrender to the Will of God. At that point, Michelle blanked out completely and began to cry. Clint said one more rather long sentence, and she turned to him and said to him through her tears, "Clint, you need to speak less words at a time, I can't follow this." She was clearly overwhelmed and started to cry more until she was choking in her attempts to translate what he was saying into French. When he said that we want the teacher to be here with us—we don't want the teacher to leave, we are fixated on believing that if the guru is with us physically, then we are in the guru's presence—Michelle began to cry hard. It was obviously impossible for her to translate. Evelyne started translating for her, but it was also clear that she was not ready to take over either, so Michelle drank some water and forced herself, still sobbing, to breathe deeply and translate. She translated two sentences, her voice was deep and throaty.

Clint continued, "The guru is not in his body, and in fact there is nobody there in the body of the guru. Still we say to the guru, 'Stay here, don't leave.' " The more Clint talked the harder Michelle cried until she started crying uncontrollably. From his leather chair on the side of the room Lee called out like a referee, "Object lesson—this is great! The guru is three feet away from her and the guru is not there! Object lesson! Get it?" He looked at Michelle and said, "Do you get that?" With a look of incomprehension, she answered, "No, I don't get it." She was totally disoriented; although she seemed to realize that she was somehow illustrating Clint's point, manifesting what he was talking about, she didn't get the lesson.

Clint continued speaking, reiterating his point. He was basically saying that we have to realize that the relationship with the guru is impersonal. Whether we like it or not, there is "nobody there" in the person of the guru no matter where he is, while at the same time, the Influence of the guru is everywhere, regardless of the location of his physical body. What Michelle was demonstrating was that, even though Lee was sitting only a few feet away from her, she was gripped with grief and the pain of separation as soon as Clint started speaking passionately about the subject.

Lee said softly to Michelle, "Do you want to take a break?"

"Yes," she answered, without looking at Lee. She sat on one of the armchairs and waited while Claire was called in from the kitchen to translate. Lee turned to Michelle and said, "You deserve a break anyway. It's your break time." The talk ended forty-five minutes later. Michelle had fallen asleep in the chair, and at the end of the talk Lee walked past her as she talked now with Ann about what had happened. He beamed at her, "I love these object lessons! This was the best thing of the entire seminar! Those kinds of things have more impact than a down-loading of information." Then he said in a hip street dialect, "You the star, girl!"

After dinner—a very rich, cheesy spinach lasagna, salad and apple pie for dessert—the group gathered for the last event of the seminar, which was the formal Sunday night darshan in the meditation hall. Lee came in and took his place on the dais, wearing the same white robe and head wrap he'd worn all summer in darshan at La Ferme de Jutreau. After the singing of several of Lee's poems to Yogi Ramsuratkumar, chanting and the giving and receiving of *prasad*, Lee motioned to the person who was leading the chant to end quickly so he could begin his discourse. He clearly had something very specific on his mind.

"This afternoon in Dasya's talk Laurent said, 'You make this sound so difficult. Why?' and Dasya responded, 'I don't want to give anyone a false impression.' So, there are two things that go on here: seminars, and what you are participating in here tonight with us. What you are participating in here tonight is the core and essence of the relationship my students have to me. I never give seminars in America. I've been offered many opportunities and significant resources to give seminars in America, but I turn them down because that is not what my work is about. People come to seminars, rub shoulders with the community and experience something of the depth and sanctity of what we are doing, and they think, 'Oh, this is kind of attractive!' Certainly there is a kind of passion associated with it, but we don't want to lead anybody on or give false impressions.

"This Work is hard because what it stands for is in one hundred and eighty degree opposition and conflict with what everybody in the world stands for. I know those of you who have been around here some have heard this, but I suggest you look again, deeply and seriously, into the foundation of this Work before becoming naively and enthusiastically attracted to it.

"This Work is hard first of all because it deals with the absolute authoritarian domination of ego on every individual in the world. If you take the Work seriously it doesn't mean you'll have to give up family, career, good wine," he chuckled, "but you'll have to give up your relationship to those things. Your romanticism, your sentimentality, your illusions. In other words, *you*! We are called to see things as they are in this Work—that means human nature. Your illusions must be confronted directly and without compromise. Socrates said 'Know thyself.' If we know ourselves then we will know others because we all have the same tendencies. To know our own ego is to know the world.

"This Work is radical, heretical to everything ego stands for, so it is hard work. We don't want to encourage you irresponsibly. It's very important to be clear about the degree to which you are willing to have your illusions shattered. So when you look into your heart deeply, what do you find? Are you going to follow the path at all costs, or when things get hard and your illusions begin to crumble, are you going to run for a place where your illusions will be protected, like some New Age temple with 'God is love' written on the walls? Most of my students—as much as they love me and are dedicated to this Work—will not do the work necessary to get what the heart of this path has to offer.

"It's not that my students won't make tremendous sacrifices to travel all around the world with me and be heroic in many ways, but as Dasya said, 'A secret life will betray you in ways you can't imagine.' It's not our conscious willingness to work that is pivotal, but our inner willingness to surrender our projections and illusions. Most of us are willing to be heroic at the level of action, which may be asked for, but there is also a requirement

676

to be heroic internally, and one can't have an internal secret life. Our internal secret lives are even more devious than our external secret lives, and much harder to root out. So, forewarned is forearmed."

The mood in the darshan hall had struck a deep vein of sadness in the truth of what Lee was saying. The timbre of his voice was profoundly sobering and measured.

"Ego doesn't care how much misery and destruction results from its authority. What enables you to do the inner work? Take it one step at a time. Opportunities are offered all the time to make the small gestures that lead to the big gestures. But if we want to pierce the core of this Work, we will have to pierce our illusions.

"In this school you will be expected to practice, and to do many practices. The longer you are around, the more you'll be expected to practice. So you may want to consider another teacher. There might be an easier place to do sadhana, where if you want to take on some Indian affectations, you can!" Lee laughed. The space seemed to need the brief bit of levity, and several people responded with chuckles.

"The closer you get here, the more you will be expected to practice because what you get here is in direct relationship to your practice—not the romantic level, where Lee likes you and you come and get a big hug and the ashram becomes your second home and blah, blah, blah. That's the romantic level of things. Lee's face brightens up and his eyes sparkle when he sees you and you think, 'He loves me!' But at the level that Lee doesn't mean anything, Lee doesn't exist and the blessings of Yogi Ramsuratkumar are pouring out and flooding into you like being hit by a freight train—the TGV! Lee means nothing. Lee is just a sheer veil covering the inner sanctum, the treasure house.

"At the personal level Lee knows your children's names, and that won't change, but that's a pleasant consequence of this Work. At the heart of the transmission of the Benediction of Yogi Ramsuratkumar, Lee has no meaning whatsoever. This delightful human relationship is as ripe for sacrifice as the illusion of separation. So you should think seriously about getting more involved on this path. I have to talk like this a couple of times a year to remind people that there's more to this Work than what's on the surface. So the really good students make the guru work! The guru can't say no to a good student. He's got to serve them.

"This ritual that we performed in darshan here tonight is at the heart of our tradition. We're offering ourselves up, completely, everything—not just our resources, minds, bodies, but everything. *Prasad* is a metaphor for the exchange, a metaphor for consciousness. When you offer *prasad* it represents the submission to Grace which makes this exchange. You can maintain protocol for years and never really touch the esoteric level of this path. That is, you can keep from getting into trouble. But once you get serious, God starts to get serious. So you have to be very sober about taking that one step because pretty soon you'll be stepping more quickly but God will be running full speed toward you! Be careful about that first caress—you could get pregnant! That's what it's like when God takes over—there's labor and childbirth! But then, one of my students laughed all the way through her second labor.

"So this Work is hard because you have to consciously experience the transition phase, like in childbirth, because the transformational process is not easy. It's hard because we are taking a long and lonely path. We have each other—there is some comfort in that. But even among each other we don't know who is going to turn on us until it happens—we don't know what's going to do it. So this is a long path and a lonely path. Even though we have each other, this path is not about living in a vacuum. My students who live on the ashrams, their lives are more insular, but that's not the idea of this school. The school has doubled in numbers in the last fifteen years. But the idea is not to live in a vacuum but to have a job, to work, to travel, to have a family, to be in relationship with the world—with the exception of a few people whose lives become more singular and insular, more exclusive in terms of function. But for most of us the idea is not to come to live on the ashram. The ashrams are like training institutes—we come and get training and then go out and practice it. Then we come back for more training.

"To live in the world without sentimentality, romanticism, projections, expectations is very hard because you will see people all around you suffering and there is nothing you can do about it. You know that they don't have to be suffering, but there is no way they will take the medicine that will keep them from suffering. The more you see, the more you feel. The more you feel, the more ecstasy and joy and pleasure and also the more pain. So this Work is hard. Not around the edges of the Work, but the closer you get to the Heart of it, the harder it is. It's not that you can't have friends outside of the sangha, but you will know that you are irrevocably different than they are, and you will never be like them again—your family, your mother, father, brothers, sisters. And it's painful, when you see the illusions that they are suffering under, and there is nothing you can do about it. It's hard to see that and bear that. You are as different from your friends and family members as they are from a cow or turtle, and they will never understand it."

It felt as if the whole room could burst into tears at any moment. Lee's voice was unbearably kind. Every word was heavy with compassion. For many of Lee's students in the room who have traveled down the path with him some distance, what he was speaking about was completely real. The loss of one's connection to the human family is bittersweet.

At one point in the evening Lee spoke about his elderly mother—her pain, denial and fear of death—taking the audience into the tender heart of human feeling for the other, but also into a confrontation with the reality of death. The fact that even the guru is helpless to change his mother's suffering the illusion of separation was a stark reminder that we are each responsible to forge a relationship with that which is eternal. There is no other refuge.

Lee's words sank into very deep places in each person in the room. The reality he described was that most of us would never make it far enough in this Work to realize the kind of faith, the kind of unshakable cellular knowledge of the Divine, that would allow us to have refuge in the end. If there was a way to somehow inspire what is real in each of us, to vivify the call of the path, Lee had tapped into it in this discourse. He continued:

"Most of my students will never reach this point. Maybe a few have, but most won't. It's too close, too intimate, too hard. But consider seriously before you enter into this, just to make sure that you won't be one of the ones who won't make it.

"Michelle asked me how many French students I have now. I said twelve or fifteen. Wow! It surprised me when I counted them. That's a lot of people. Too many! A couple of people every year would be enough, but now we're picking up steam. Four, five, six people asking to be students every year. *Oh God!*" Lee smiled a wan little smile.

"I'm talking like this because I mean it to be sobering. On the other hand, I could just be bullshitting. The whole thing could just be a big piece of theater. And on that note . . . Jai Guru!" He got up and walked out. Tears were falling on faces, and outside the rain poured down.

September 20, 1999
La Ferme de Jutreau

Brindavan decided last night to make the elderberry tonic for breakfast. It's a potent elixir steamed from the fresh, wild berries by a special machine so that the juice is uncooked and very concentrated and pure. It's a particularly healing tonic, and many people had contracted colds or flu-like symptoms with the wet and cold weather over the weekend. It seemed like a good time to serve the elderberry tonic. It is extremely tart and slightly bitter, so honey is always added. She had asked Lee the night before if he would like some of the elderberry tonic served at breakfast and his sharp reply was, "I don't care! Don't ask me—I'm not the cook!"

This morning Lee went into breakfast and took a small glass of the tonic and sat down to eat his almonds and sunflower seeds soaked overnight in pineapple juice, which he spooned into his bowl with a small amount of homemade yogurt on top. As soon as he tasted the elderberry tonic he made a face and said, "This is too sweet! Somebody poured a lot of sugar into this!"

Lee saw Brinda sitting at the next table and craned his neck to catch her eye. "This elderberry juice is far too sweet," he said. There was an almost inaudible rumble around the table, as those who did not think it was too sweet squirmed in their seats. "Maybe it's just my taste," he capitulated immediately, "You should make it the way everybody else likes it. But I think it's too sweet." Brindavan had a strange look on her face—the look she usually has when something has gone awry for the spiritual master that she feels she should have handled properly but somehow did not.

After breakfast Michael mentioned to Brinda that he in fact remembered hearing her tell Claire, who had heated the elderberry tonic this morning and added the honey on Brinda's request, that the tonic was sweet enough and that Lee didn't like it very sweet. As it turned out, when Brinda had asked Claire to make the tonic, she put a jar of honey on the counter that didn't have a lot of honey in it. She said, "Use this honey first, and if you need more I can get it." She tasted the tonic after the first amount of honey was added by Claire and said, "That's enough honey. Lee doesn't really like it very sweet."

The story got more complicated. Claire had received instructions from Lee over the weekend concerning the elderberry *blossom* syrup, a bottled, sugar-sweetened product from England that gets added to sparkling water and served sometimes as a beverage at evening tea time. He had said that the elderberry blossom drink wasn't strong enough and he wanted more of the sweet elderberry blossom syrup added. Somehow having that in her mind, Claire did not hear Brinda say, "That's enough honey." Instead, she imagined Brinda saying, "Put a little bit more in."

Later that day, Brinda was talking with Claire on the phone in the office. Lee heard them and interjected, "Tell Claire she's got a new name—Honey Jar!" Brinda relayed the message. She said that Claire laughed and laughed. Later, when Claire returned to the ashram and saw Lee in the office, he said, "Do you know why you put too much honey in the elderberry?"

"Yes," Claire answered.

Lee smiled, "So your new name is a reminder to Pay Attention."

Lee has increased his input and feedback to most of the residents of the ashram, and to Brinda and Claire in particular. It seems he is preparing everyone for the long autumn, winter and spring months when he will be in Arizona. It's as if he is stoking their work fires, giving them plenty of coal and wood to burn until he returns.

September 22, 1999
La Ferme de Jutreau

Brinda was on the phone in the office talking to Sylvie Peytel of Maison Raphael in Boulogne, a suburb of Paris. Lee had been sitting at his desk reading, but his attention had been pricked by the conversation, which was getting more convoluted as the moments ticked by. There seemed to be some general mayhem with regard to organizing Lee's upcoming seminar at Maison Raphael. Brinda's attempts to clarify for Sylvie which of Lee's students would be accompanying him to Paris for the seminar was getting more confusing as she spoke about one of Lee's French students in particular.

Lee intervened in a loud voice. "Brinda," he said, trying to get her attention from the phone conversation. "Brinda!" he yelled. She looked up at him, the phone cradled on her shoulder. Referring to this student, Lee said, "It's not your job to take care of that for her!" His voice deepened, gathering force. "Trying to clarify her confusion is like trying to map deep space, baby. It's deep space! Let me talk to Sylvie!" He was standing behind his desk, and suddenly appeared, almost without any appearance of having moved, at Brinda's side now to take the phone from her hand.

"Sylvie, if she shows up, she shows up. If she doesn't, she doesn't, okay?" he barked. Being used to Lee's style from years of hosting him at Maison Raphael, Sylvie just said, "Yes, okay." The potential misunderstanding now clarified to Lee's satisfaction, he hung the phone up unceremoniously, then turned back to Brinda. He was still talking about this student.

"Trying to put ourselves on the line for everyone's personal jazz with people like Sylvie who are sources of trust and confidence with us is just too much! You should not be trying to represent that chick. Let her manage her own life. I don't want you involved in it." As he turned back to the papers he was reading at his desk, his rant subsided as suddenly as it had arisen.

"Lee?" Brinda's voice rang softly into the quiet space that was left after the brief storm.

"Yes, Madame Ashram Manager?" he looked up smiling.

"Muriel would like you to come for dinner on Sunday night after the seminar in Paris, but she only has room for you and your family in her small apartment. She says she can't possibly fit more than nine people. Thursday night is not an option because she has to work," Brinda explained. Lee has known Muriel Maisl, a disciple of Arnaud's, for years. She was one of the people who helped organize some of Lee's early teaching visits in France, and she was there when Lee met Arnaud for the first time. She had invited Lee for dinner, but it would only work for Lee to come on Thursday night, when he would have a free evening. If it had to be on Sunday night, he would have to bring a much larger number of people with him—all of his students who will be in Paris to see him off to Arizona.

He answered Brinda. "Okay. Well, please tell her that I would love to come to her house. I wish she was free on Thursday night, but I will have to decline because Sunday night is the last night I'll be in France for eight months, and it would mean abandoning the European sangha who will be in Paris to see me off, after everything they've done for me this summer. I just can't do it. I'd love to see her, but . . ." It was another case of "love me, love my dog." In this case the dog is the twenty or more people who will accompany Lee to Maison Raphael, wanting to be with him as much as possible until the moment he boards his plane for the U.S.A. on Monday morning, October 4. Lee's way of working is that we can make any space, no matter how small or uncomfortable, work so that more people can be included, but most people only think in conventional terms—"Oh, my apartment is small; I couldn't possibly have more than nine people."

The conversation turned to the "Honey Jar" event. Both Brinda and Claire, who were in the office, were laughing with Lee about it. When someone asked what the buzz was about Lee said, "I can tell you the whole story, but I've only heard Brinda's version of it," Lee said. "Maybe I should hear Claire's version—get some fuel for the next women's meeting." Having just moved to France from Germany, Claire is one of the new additions to the women's group at La Ferme de Jutreau. It seemed like Lee was baiting Brinda and Claire. "Just fishing," as he said recently, "to see if I can get a rise out of anybody!"

Brinda said to Lee, "Claire told me today that it would take a lot to get her mad and then if she gets mad, I can't brush her off."

Lee looked at Claire in disbelief. "Oh? That's not what the German women told me about you, Claire—that it takes a lot to get you mad."

Claire said, "It takes a lot to get me mad . . ." But as she began her explanation Lee interrupted her sarcastically. It seemed that if he could push her buttons, make something rise to the surface that he suspected was lurking under the cool façade, he would do it before he left France.

"Yeah, I believe in cool vengeance too. An eye for an eye, a tooth for a tooth, eh Claire? But that's all history now because you're here in France and part of this women's group! And Brinda will be very happy if you don't get angry with her because Susanne got really mad at her, red-hot anger . . ." He trailed off for a second, long enough for Claire to launch her justification.

"Actually I didn't say I don't get mad easily to Brinda, I said it takes a lot to lose my friendship—to lose my friendship you have to really do a lot."

Brinda came to Claire's defense, laughing a little as she said, "That's right, we were speaking about liking and not liking, and the tendency to need to have people like us."

Claire laughed and said, "Perhaps I will be sometimes bad, but I hope I won't be." But Lee's attention had already gone on to something else. He was up and out of the room to pack his books for the seminar this weekend.

Tomorrow morning Lee leaves with twenty people and the two vans packed with books, bags, suitcases and picnic fare for Touzac in southwest France, not far from Spain. There he will give a three-day seminar at La Source Bleue, the four-star hotel owned and run by Sian and Jean Pierre Bouyou, both disciples of Arnaud Desjardins.

September 23, 1999
Touzac, La Source Bleue

Over six hours on the road, the usual road picnic, and Lee and the gang arrived around four o'clock at La Source Bleue. Jumping out of the van, Lee gave Sian a warm embrace. She greeted him with the deepest respect and affection, explaining that Jean Pierre was at work and would be back shortly. Turning to greet the rest of Lee's party, she said wonderingly, her voice soft with its classic Welsh undertones, "You brought the sun with you! It was storming all day—thunder, lightning, rain. Really," she smiled, "the sun came out only an hour ago!" Indeed, the weather was perfection. The sky was bright blue and the sun sparkled on the freshly washed trees and lush gardens of La Source Bleue.

Turning back to Lee, Sian waited to see what he wanted to do first, which was to unpack the vans. Fifteen minutes later Lee was setting up his book table in the large upper room of the eight hundred-year-old building where his talks of the next three days would be held. The walls of the room were beautiful ancient stonework. Equally ancient rough-hewn timbers held the ceiling up. The room had been carefully prepared for Lee's arrival. A large bouquet of fresh flowers was placed up front near the speaker's chair, and a deep pink flowering hibiscus with glossy rich dark leaves sat on the table by the chair, a gift for Lee from Sian's daughter. It was exactly like some of the hibiscus shrubs that grow on Yogi Ramsuratkumar's ashram. Pillows and chairs were arranged on Persian rugs in deep jewel tones of red, blue and burnt orange. These were set out on the light gray carpet in a striking contrast of color, the whole effect creating a sense of richness. On the stone wall behind the speaker's chairs that were set up for Lee and a translator was a picture of Yogi Ramsuratkumar with his hand raised in blessing.

Someone had put on a tape, and the evocative sounds of a sitar accompanying a lilting Indian voice flooded the room. Suddenly Yogi Ramsuratkumar's name could be heard reverberating in the verses of the *bhajan* and then repeated many times in a refrain. As the music drifted in the air the sound of Yogi Ramsuratkumar's name had the effect of melding the room into a seamless whole—Lee arranging the books, the *vigraha*, the chanting, the plaintive sitar all became one singular expression of benediction.

This is the fourth year that Lee has given three days of teachings here in this extraordinarily beautiful place. The land and buildings have been in Jean Pierre's family for five hundred years, but many of the ivy-covered rambling stone buildings on the property are much older; next to the seminar house is the oldest structure, a one-thousand-year-old mill house located twenty feet away from the wide, smooth river that appears placid on the surface but runs swiftly through the hotel grounds. Its banks are lined with lush bamboo forests and stately rows of tall chestnut trees.

Behind the seminar building rushes the stream of *la source*—a magnificent blue spring that pours out hundreds of thousands of gallons of water every day from beneath a fifteen-foot-high limestone ledge, carved out by slow transformation through water over the millennia into a semi-circle of pale gray rock that contains one side of the wide blue-green pool. The pool of the spring is thirty feet in diameter, and is surrounded by the lush growth of many kinds of native ferns, grass and wildflowers, above which grow palm trees, cedars and groves of thirty-foot-high bamboo. On the water float delicate water plants, lacy algae and watercress. It is a stunningly beautiful and benevolent place, the kind of place the Druids and ancient Celts would have considered highly sacred and auspicious—a natural temple and place of worship.

With the arrival of Lee Lozowick, the living, felt presence of nature mingled now with the influence of Yogi Ramsuratkumar, which began to coalesce in a concentrated beam of divine influence that would come to permeate this place for the next three days. Outside the high bamboo rustled in the wind; sun glinted through the willow trees by the river and shimmered on the moving water. Upstairs in the seminar room Lee was putting out copies of his books, *N'essayez Pas—Vivez,* then *Le chemin divin pour devenir humain,* and *l'Alchiemie de l'amour et de la sexualite.* The book table grew in weight and dimension with each placement. *Death of a Dishonest Man* had been given a prominent place in the center of the table next to the *vigraha* of Yogi Ramsuratkumar and the *Yogi Ramsuratkumar*

Souvenir Book. High stacks of audiocassettes balanced out one end, and another table was set up nearby with all the LGB and Shri CDs, cassettes and T-shirts. Satisfied with his work, Lee left the books.

He immediately went to the wooden deck overlooking the pool of the spring. The deck is an extension of the small reception area and hotel restaurant; it spans the gushing spring water that cascades musically over a rocky streambed and winds around to converge with the river, only a hundred feet away. There he ensconced himself at one of the round, cedar tables to play bridge until dinner. The air was misty with the churning waters of the spring and the silent emanations of the pool. Clouds massed overhead and a light rain pattered gently on the immense white canvas umbrellas above the tables where Lee sat. Beauty pulsed all around as nature became revealed in the master's presence as the living garment of God.

Sian came out and stood beside Lee smiling. She was the epitome of the gentle and elegant hostess. "Would you like something to drink?" she asked. "Juice, Cokes, water? We have grape, pineapple, apple juice . . ."

Lee said, "I'll take a Coke. Others will probably drink juice." Lee was well into the first rubber of bridge when she returned with the drinks, mostly juice and two Cokes—one in a bottle and one in a can—for Lee. Not long after that she arrived again bearing trays of a variety of cakes which were cut into small finger portions: little bite-sized cakes, some chocolate, some vanilla, with whipped cream or mousse toppings, some with a bit of a raspberry sugar glaze on top, or perhaps a thin strip of shaved or powdered dark chocolate. At first Lee declined, saying that he was waiting for the special dinner which Sian had planned for later in the evening. Then he looked more closely at the cakes on their silver trays and said, "How can I refuse these?" Each one was a delicious, delicate confection—a world of sweet perfection. He ate three of them with relish, offered them around the table to the people playing bridge with him and then passed the platters to his four students who were playing bridge at the table next to him. After everyone had had some, he sent the rest to the children and adults who were at the swimming pool.

Lee seemed very pleased to be back here again. The mood around him was calm, peaceful, serene. Sian returned with copies of the invitation she had sent out for this weekend. They were written in French. She gave some copies to Lee. He picked one up and read it aloud. "Mr. Lee will be with us for three days at the end of the month. The theme that we propose is to consider the central question, 'What do you want?' Ostad Elahi writes," Lee paraphrased as he translated the French for us, " 'We wish to find a love which lasts forever. That which knows no decline, a flower which never fades. We wish to find a pleasure that knows no misery, a love that knows no separation, a glory that does not decline. Our only Beloved, who is the one that we adore, is only He. Is it not He who is eternal, while all the rest are fleeting? It is this love of Him that we are always aware of and we always go toward. Is not this love the love that we know to be true and the Truth?' What do you want, what do you really want?' "

When he finished the translation Lee looked up at Sian and said, "It's a good question." Then he looked over the schedule that Jean Pierre had brought in and said, "Perfect." The days would be packed with dharma talks, two meals each day and an evening talk as well. In simple interchanges, in the sound of Yogi Ramsuratkumar's name commingling with the surrounding natural beauty and the enjoyment of friendship, of friends coming back together with the purpose of praising God, the mood for the weekend seemed to have been already established. After a very lovely rich dinner of pasta with salmon, baked tomatoes and strawberry pastries for dessert, Lee visited for awhile with everyone and then retired early to spend time with his family.

September 24, 1999
La Source Bleue

Lee played bridge for awhile before brunch at eleven o'clock. Sian served simple egg omelets, pan fried and rolled like crepes, bacon, croissants, baguette and tea for breakfast. A large bowl of gooseberries in *fromage blanc* sat on the serving table along with muesli and milk. The tables were laden with extras—homemade strawberry, plum and fig jams and jellies, grapefruit juice, butter. By Lee's place was a basket full of grapefruits and a small, sharp knife, just like at La Ferme de Jutreau.

Sian, Anne and Kathleen sat with Lee and some of his students at brunch. They told Lee that a woman who had come to one of Lee's seminars at La Source Bleue a few years ago and had helped with translating had recently died. Although her health had always been rather frail, they said, it was unexpected. Lee's response was almost celebratory. Lee began to talk resolutely about his mother. He said that her attachment and fear had kept her from moving to Arizona when her health would have permitted it, and now that she was too frail to travel she was regretting her decision to stay on the East Coast. He shrugged as if to say, "That's the human condition in spades, isn't it?"

Taking Lee's words in and chewing on them, Sian asked, "So we are totally responsible for all of our decisions, for everything that happens to us?"

Lee said, "We are more or less, but there's also outside circumstances that occur and karma. The big things—like finding our teacher—are decided for us. Staying with the teacher is usually up to us." Jan began to talk about how she met Lee. She said that there were circumstances in her life that would have allowed her to meet him sooner, but she had made decisions that seemed to delay that meeting. She said, "I was driven to do what I did . . ."

"Driven by the great whip of God!" Lee quipped in a cheerful tone. "Yes, if you are stubborn enough you could put off meeting the teacher for a long time," he added.

Sian asked, "What is the karma if one leaves the teacher?"

"You have to come back and do it all over again under worse circumstances," Lee answered.

"It's relentless," she said reflectively.

"Yes," he agreed. Lee looked around the table at the small group. The rest of his students who were sitting at a long table about eight feet away had now stopped talking among themselves and were all turned toward Lee, listening intently to his words. He continued speaking, answering another question about how often one needed to see the teacher. "It depends on how far along the path you are. If you've walked far enough along the path you don't have to see the teacher all the time, but if not . . . If you haven't really established yourself on the path with the teacher, and you go to another teacher, all you get is confusion."

Kathleen then asked Lee a question, this time about how Arnaud so freely allows his students to go to other teachers for teachings. Lee was building up steam as he tore into this subject matter, very close to his heart. "Some teachers are very spacious about those kinds of things, like Arnaud. Arnaud isn't forcing teachings on anyone. If people want what he has to give, he's there completely, but he's not pushing. Me—I keep 'em till they *die*!" His voice began to rise in volume and his eyes took on that blue glint of something that might be enthusiasm but is probably closer to madness. Pagala Lee, he called himself once in a poem to Yogi Ramsuratkumar. Mad Lee, driven by the "Great Whip of God." Driven to dispel illusions wherever he goes—and he never stops. No rest for the weary, as he often says. He went on, "That's the only way they get out with me—in a *coffin*!" He grinned devilishly at Kathleen. "That's why Arnaud is so relaxed and I'm so nervous. I keep beating dead horses, *wake up, wake up, wake up!*

"Arnaud is complete. He is a rare teacher. His students don't need anything but him—they think variety is the spice of life, but Arnaud is the mother, the father of compassion. His students don't need other teachers. To go to another master who wants your soul when you have a master like Arnaud is like having a fine gourmet meal and pouring ketchup all over it. You get the analogy?" His eyes bored into Kathleen's. She nodded yes.

He began to talk about how Yogi Ramsuratkumar had sent away some of his devotees who had asked him to take medicine or pills to make him better, "As if the body meant something!" Lee blazed. Without notice the small restaurant with its antiques and chintz and lace doilies and ancestral portraits hanging on the old stone walls had metamorphosed into an charged chamber in which the radiations of the guru were suddenly a burning force.

Just then Jean Pierre walked in with a letter that had arrived in the post for Lee. Visibly surprised, Lee took the letter and looked at the return address. Noting who it was from—one of his students—he shook his head and laughed. "I can't get away from her, even in heaven! When I get to heaven God's going to bring me a letter and it's going to be from her." He read the letter and sighed, "Poor thing." He tore the stamp off and handed it to Brinda, saying, "Give it to me when we get back to La Ferme." He would add it to the stamps he collects and sends to children in India.

At one o'clock Lee began his first talk of the weekend. There were about twenty-five people in the room, eleven of them the students who were traveling with Lee. By tomorrow morning the number will have increased significantly, as many people were coming only for Saturday and Sunday. Lee took his seat beside the flowering hibiscus and started.

"The schedule this weekend is not Jean Pierre's or Sian's fault. It is my schedule and it is very deliberate. So if you don't like it, don't blame them—blame me! Here we are in this beautiful place, we'll be eating great food all weekend. The average person uses beauty, pleasures and comfort to distract themselves from the Divine rather than to show them the Divine which is inherent in those things. Everything—sex, natural beauty, good food—could reveal God to us, but usually doesn't because we don't let it.

"This space that we will share together for the weekend is a chamber—an alchemical laboratory. Something can happen here that will transform you in terms of your perspective or attitude. Everything is a matter of context.

"The assumption is that everyone who walks into this room functions from the psychological perspective. Most of you have a teacher; you've read lots of spiritual books and are familiar with the rhetoric of the path. But one way our psychology tricks us is by convincing us that we are free of it by assuming a spiritual veneer that is only psychological.

"This space is a chamber for transformation even though I'm just going to be talking; there won't be any exciting group participation exercises like in a New Age workshop. The union we will be talking about is the union of the Bauls. In the Baul tradition it begins with sexual union—it's a great tradition to be part of!" Everyone laughed, and Lee most

685

of all. He was laughing so much in fact that he was wiping tears from his eyes. This is something that usually happens later in a seminar, or after he has been on a roll, making people laugh for thirty minutes. "God, I don't know why I'm having such a good time!" He kept wiping the tears from his eyes, shaking his head. "I hope the rest of the people who come don't ruin it!"

As the talk progressed Lee sat very matter-of-factly in his chair, his bare feet on the floor, hands in his lap, or sometimes with his arms draped around the back of the chair. By all appearances it looked like nothing special was going on. Lee was being humorous and funny, but underneath that and at the level of what one could perceive directly he was working an invisible magic. The whole space was coming to life in a bombardment of vivid impressions on the senses, both physical and subtle. The deep jewel-like burgundies, reds and blues of the carpets at Lee's feet offset the white of the stone walls behind him. The abundance of beauty in nature all around seemed to breathe life into the space. The clear cold water of the spring, which rushed along in the channel of its fern-studded banks just below the open windows, was a faint background music that permeated the room as Lee talked.

The magic of the environment and the enchantment Lee cast in the "chamber" he just described combined in this way until the room seemed to grow and swell, to lift or rise. It seemed as if the whole gestalt of the space was being transported to another domain as Lee opened a certain window through which the power of Grace flowed steadily. A mysterious divine presence drifted in this subtle air, impossible to capture or describe, but alive and interacting with the human world. It beckoned us into other domains and yet remained elusive and tenuous, like a wisp of smoke, while at the same time it was immanently real. One can only perceive this mystery burning on the edges of consciousness, and then it is gone again. The Bauls say the Beloved, or the "Man of the Heart," is ungraspable, unknowable and always elusive; it is their joy to endlessly yearn for that sublime touch again and again. This life of longing is what creates the Baul mystique, and causes the Bauls to wander restlessly, to beg and sing.

The lingering effects of this *rasa* or mood left me open to images, impressions or memories that seemed lodged and dormant within the stone walls and in the grounds themselves. These impressions rose effortlessly to the surface as the melody of the spring spoke of times past, when its flowing waters mingled with the muddy brown of the river five hundred, six hundred, a thousand years ago. Just outside the seminar room, not fifty feet away, was an old stone quay by the river where one thousand-year-old stone steps lead up the embankment of the river by a row of tall chestnut trees.

This part of France so close to Spain has the feel of the gypsies—like Saintes Maries de la Mer, where *Sarah la Kali*, or Sarah the Black, the patron saint of the gypsies, is enshrined in the crypt of a thousand-year-old church. Every year the gypsies make a pilgrimage in May and again in August to Saintes Maries de la Mer to carry Sarah the Black to the sea, where she is ritually submerged in the warm waters of the Mediterranean. The gypsies must have also passed through places like this for hundreds of years and perhaps worshipped at the natural shrine of the spring, or soaked in the sheer beauty as fuel for their longing for the Divine.

The Bauls are close kin to the gypsies, not only historically, in their common roots in Mother India, but spiritually. Both are wanderers—*rawinda*, the Persians say—and beggars, people of the earth, singers and musicians. They live on the margins of so-called civilized culture, refusing to be tamed and forced into the soul-deadening molds of the social ethic. They have woven their life of longing into the culture and fabric of their lifestyle—music, dance, begging and always moving on, moving on. Restlessness is their metaphor for the mystical truth that there is no home other than the Heart of God. The gypsies choose to live without an earthly home because it is a constant reminder that imbues their way of life with a grand passion. This homelessness is precious to them, far more precious than the security and status of normalcy by *giorgio* (non-Gypsy) standards.

In response to one of his student's question about the constant traveling in his company, Lee once said, "What is realization but homelessness anyway? The only home is the Heart of God." It is a quintessential Baul statement, and reflects also the gypsy point of view, from which they carve a life of wandering and longing for the unattainable reality of the personal Beloved. It was this divine mood that Lee invoked with his audience this afternoon.

Continuing his introduction to the seminar, Lee talked about the necessity of building a matrix, a precondition for the shift of context that is enlightenment. This matrix is very delicate, he said, because we are defined by twenty, thirty, forty years of selfishness, by patterns of habitual thought and action.

"What it is that we are building in this room this weekend is very delicate and needs to be protected. If we leave this room and take the energy we've gotten here and throw it away, even in pleasure, then when we walk back into the room we have to start all over again, building. As the weekend goes on we are building something vital, something important, block by block. If every time you walk out you knock a block out of the bottom of your foundation, then you weaken the subtle structure. I'm not suggesting you walk out and withdraw or isolate. You should be with everyone, do what you do, enjoy the wonderful food, the beauty of nature. But you do all of that with *consciousness*. If you interact with everything you encounter over the weekend with clarity, it will reinforce what we are building in this room. If you don't, your habitual patterns will take over and undermine what we are doing.

"When you are in relationship with the Divine you don't need a savings account because God takes care of everything. But in the relative sense, it's like building a saving account. In the relative world we need to protect this fragile structure we're building. Ordinarily ego finds ways to vent the energy, to create an opening so the energy flows out. Too much talking, too much eating, too much sex—and in many other ways. So when dinner is served tonight, don't eat too much because that's a way of buffering ourselves from Reality. Of course, when we've eaten too much, the reality is that we've eaten too much—but that's in another context!"

Lee dropped that comment into the room; it was ripe with obscure meanings, but before there was time to reflect on what he might have meant he quickly went on to talk about how the seminar would be formatted. He urged everyone to ask questions at any time, even to feel free to interrupt him.

"So . . . as the weekend goes on, we will be building something. This room is the alchemical laboratory in which definitions of the experiment we'll be doing are created. Even walking out of the room you can stay in the chamber with what is being created. To walk out of this room and walk out of the chamber—into the beautiful scenery, beautiful weather, beautiful food—is to take your attention away from what is happening here. It's a matter of attention and what you focus on.

"Someone who is enlightened like my Master, Yogi Ramsuratkumar, doesn't have to place His attention with any degree of awareness. On the other hand, *we* have to.

Yogi Ramsuratkumar doesn't have to make any effort; there is no effort needed because there is no separation between His attention and the Divine. So what is the end of the path? No effort. This weekend this room is the inner sanctum. But the whole space, wherever we are on this property, is the temple. You should consider everything you do to be part of your worship, and bring sensitivity and respect to it."

After the talk there was a short break, during which Lee wrote *dédicace* in books that he sold. He made change, counting it out in French to one man, who exclaimed, *"Vous parlez français!"* Lee smiled and shrugged, *"Un petit peu."* He speaks quite a lot more French than he ever lets on or admits to speaking. It will come spilling out of him when the need is present, for example if someone cannot speak English and has a need involving Lee. It is often a surprise to hear him suddenly speaking French, as if it appeared out of nowhere.

As he started the three o'clock session he dove into telling stories of his relationship with Yogi Ramsuratkumar, beginning with talking about his early teaching work. He was continuing the theme of the summer, which from one perspective was Lee deconstructing himself, or one could say retelling a story with a new interpretation. Lee Lozowick reinventing himself. There is something else that happens whenever Lee talks about Yogi Ramsuratkumar. Invariably the experience becomes one of delight and joy, often deepening into *rasa*. Lee talked about his Father, and the window of Grace opened a little wider.

"I thought I was fully enlightened and didn't really need any help," Lee said candidly. "Wow—was that an illusion! But it didn't seem like an illusion to me or to those who came to me to be students. When I first came to Yogi Ramsuratkumar in 1976, He separated me from my five students. I thought it was an acknowledgement! It took me five years to figure out not only was Yogi Ramsuratkumar my Master, but He had been guiding me since long before this shift of context took place. And it became obvious that the reason He separated me from my students was than I needed more help than they did! And He gave me a lot of help.

"He gives help in a way that you have to figure out what He is doing. Here is an example of something He did that made me feel very important. He had each one of us, starting with my students, come up and sit in front of Him. Then He asked each person to light a cigarette for Him. He would smoke and look at the person, do things with His face. Each person did this with no problem. It was a calm day, no wind. Finally He got to me. He gave me a pack of matches, put the cigarette in His mouth, but when I lit the match, it went out! He looked surprised. There was no wind, everybody else did it with no problem. He indicated the matches and I lit another match. It too went out. He looked more surprised, and dramatized it like it was a big thing. Then the third, fourth, fifth, sixth matches—same thing. Each time He would shield the match, and each time it went out he would make a more dramatic gesture of surprise.

"The seventh match was also the last match in the pack. He looked at it and made some big thing like, 'It's the last match and don't mess this up,' as if it was my fault. I was very nervous, as you can understand! Finally the match burned, I lit the cigarette, and He relaxed. Of course this event immediately became mythologized among my students— seven matches, seven chakras and all that—so that each match that went out was symbolic that it was unnecessary to purify my lower chakras. It was significant, but not in the way that I thought. With anything like that, Yogi Ramsuratkumar never explains Himself. If you ask Him a question He just laughs. He never discourses, gives talks or explains anything. You either get it, or you don't.

"So at the time I'd been teaching a year and a half with tremendous arrogance. Some things have changed, but that hasn't!" Lee laughed uproariously at that. The group was hanging on every word of the story, which was being told with great relish and enjoyment by Lee.

"What Yogi Ramsuratkumar was showing me was that I still needed help. Not so much that I was doing anything wrong, but simply that I was very immature. I could have grown up drawing my own conclusions from the environment . . . What he was indicating by distinguishing me from my students was that in my position it was very important that I not mislead other people, and that I still needed lots of fine-tuning. It was very wise counsel.

"In the trip to India in 1979 Yogi Ramsuratkumar had already taken root in me. The things He demonstrated when we were with Him were very much burning in me when I returned. Similar things happened this time. For example, I'd written this little thirty or forty page pamphlet called *For the Love of God*. I dedicated it to Yogi Ramsuratkumar. I sent them out to some friends, sold a few, distributed a few hundred of them. So we got to Tiruvannamalai in Yogi Ramsuratkumar's company, and there was another Westerner with Him. We were all sitting there and Yogi Ramsuratkumar talked to this American man. Yogi Ramsuratkumar said, 'How do you like India?' The man said, 'Oh, very much, but some things are difficult. It's my first trip. If it wasn't for this little book I have that I read every day, that gives me strength, I wouldn't be able to handle it.'

"Yogi Ramsuratkumar said, 'What little book is that?' The man pulled out my book, *For the Love of God,* and said, 'This book.' My students were going, 'Oh my God! It's Lee's book!' I was totally convinced that Yogi Ramsuratkumar had planned this whole thing in advance, that it was a setup." Laughter broke out in the group. The story was compelling; it was as if Lee had transported the whole room back in time, to India with him.

"But Yogi Ramsuratkumar said in total innocence, 'Who wrote this little book?' The man said, 'Lee Lozowick.' Yogi Ramsuratkumar turned to me and said, 'Have you ever heard of this man?' I said, 'Yes,' trying to be humble." More laughter. The portrait Lee painted of himself as being very human with his own master was drawing people closer to him. The feeling of rapport was thick in the air.

"Yogi Ramsuratkumar said, 'Who is he?' I was looking at the ground, you know. I said, 'It's me.' His whole face went into awe. '*You* wrote this book!?' 'Yes,' I said. 'Ohhhh,' He said, as if he was meeting Jesus or something. He said to the other man, 'Can this Beggar see this book?' He opened it up and there on the first page was the dedication to Him. He read it, then He gave me the book and said, 'Read this,' pointing to the dedication. I read it out loud and He said, 'Is that to this Beggar?' As if there could be more than one person with that name! 'Yes,' I said. He sighed, as if it was the greatest honor in the universe. He said, 'This Beggar would like to hear you read this book.'

"The book is about being annihilated in love for God, and it's written in very nondualistic language. After God, there is no you, and so on. It's a nice little piece, very inspired. I started reading and got a page or two into it. He was listening very intently with tears in His eyes. 'Is this true?' He asked me." Lee stopped talking and laughed his characteristic heh, heh, heh. You could hear a pin drop in the room it was so quiet as everyone waited to hear what Lee's answer to Yogi Ramsuratkumar had been.

"I said, 'Yes.' Yogi Ramsuratkumar said, 'This can really happen to somebody?' I answered yes. He didn't ask if it had happened to me. He spared me that embarrassment.

But it was obvious that He was telling me to look at myself—to measure myself against the words that I had written. But this is how He works. He puts you in a situation and you either get it or you don't. He's detached! Not like me . . . I run after my students, 'Hey, hey—you didn't get it!' I'm very attached . . .

"Yogi Ramsuratkumar throws out the gem and if you get it, great; if not, He just goes on. The power of His Influence is such that it demands more than a superficial engagement. I kept going over that exchange—the way I acted in His presence versus what was going on in my mind, which was very different. My mind was going, 'That's *my* book, I wrote it—pretty good, huh?!' So, I needed help and He knew I needed help and He was offering it—in a very detached way. It took a long time, eleven years, for Him to accept me as a devotee . . ."

As Lee walked across the grass from the seminar building to the area where dinner would be served, he checked out the scene. The food was being set up buffet style about twenty-five feet from the river's edge just outside the old stone mill house. Woven straw mats had been laid out on the ground for a picnic-style seating arrangement a few feet away. He walked into the open doorway of the old mill house where meals had often been served in past years when Lee had given seminars here. The room was musty, unswept, with five or six dining tables scattered around the edges of the room and a few miscellaneous chairs here and there. Lee's hosts obviously hadn't planned on anyone eating in there for this evening's meal. Surveying this scene, he turned to Jane and said, "Go ask Sian if I can eat in here."

Sian and Jean Pierre were walking down the gentle slope toward the buffet tables. Jane went to them and said, "Lee would like to know if he can eat in the mill house." Jean Pierre said, "Of course!" Sian's eyes widened slightly in alarm that Lee wanted something she did not have prepared for him in a way that she considered acceptable. She said, "It's not set up . . ." Within seconds, as if out of nowhere, they produced two table cloths and whisked them on two of the tables just moments before Lee sat down with his plate. Lee, his family, Jean Pierre and two other intrepid guests came in and joined Lee. Everyone else ate outside on the straw mats in the gorgeous early evening weather. It was warm and bright, the sun just above the horizon, the spring splashing along in trills of sound. The slanting light was beautiful on the big weeping willow, the cedars and the vast overgrowth of Virginia creeper, just beginning to turn red from the chilly nights, that covered the stone walls of the seminar building.

When asked why he chose to sit inside the slightly dank and shadowy mill house instead of outside, Lee said, "With a meal like this, the meatballs and sauce, I don't want to have to juggle my plate. When we're in India I like to eat like the Indians, but here in the West, I prefer tables and chairs for this kind of meal." It was an interesting comment, especially considering that Lee eats many meals seated on the floor in the crowded greenhouse of the Arizona ashram, where he has eaten everything from spaghetti and marinara sauce, soup, vegetable stews, to just about anything you might think of. It's the same wherever he travels, like at the households of sangha members in Freiburg, in Boulder, Colorado, or at Maison Raphael where the meals are taken on the floor.

It was more of the unexpected from the guru, who keeps everyone guessing. These kinds of interactions can be seen as a compliment to one's practice. They may seem minor or insignificant, but the stronger one's desire to work, the more one will draw the guru's help in terms of paying attention to details and never taking anything for granted. Maybe he was also demonstrating the teaching of the day, in which he had exhorted the seminar guests to maintain attention to the "temple" of the dharma chamber even when they left the room, to not get distracted by the food, the beauty of nature, or by interactions with others.

After the meal Lee went immediately back upstairs to the seminar room, where he sat at the book table, balanced on the stone ledge of the window and leaning back. All was quiet, almost meditative in the room while a handful of people sat around waiting for the talk to begin. He sat alone, and no one came forward to engage him. Promptly at eight o'clock, he started the evening talk.

"We were talking earlier today about this room being the inner sanctum for the weekend. In a temple the inner sanctum is where the deity actually resides. Even though the Divine is everywhere, in this room this weekend, this is where the Divine is most interested in displaying Itself. The Divine displays Itself in a variety of ways, but predominantly in the clarity of individuals. So how we see what we see is relevant. Do we see through our biases and buffers, or do we see things clearly, as they are?

"There are many things going on at any given time. We're all in this room, we may be warm or cool, thinking certain things, feeling certain things. There are also lots of subtle things going on at the same time. Every time you breathe in several things happen: you take in chemical components of air—nitrogen and oxygen—but also you take in *prana*, shakti energy, or *chi*. That could be called life force also. The physical body is sustained because of the chemical breath; the subtle body is sustained because of *prana*. There are also all kinds of things going on that are not visible to ordinary sight. We look around and see the wooden beams and walls and photographs and plants and one another, but there are also subtle beings in the room with us. The whole room is choked with *devas*, gods and goddesses, heavenly dancers. If you walk outside this place is full of invisible beings, fairies, but we don't see them with these physical eyes.

"Each of those elements, subtle and gross, have an effect on consciousness. Some of you are familiar with Findhorn in Scotland where they propitiate the *devas* and get cabbages this big!" Lee demonstrated, holding his arms up at a width of three feet. "If the *devas* can do that to a cabbage, imagine what they can do to you at a subtle level! All of our senses are cataloguing the input of all this which produces thoughts, feelings, emotions; plus the subtle food we are eating affects our consciousness at subtle levels. All of this is going on at the same time.

"The Influence of Yogi Ramsuratkumar is here in this space this weekend, through His picture, through the *vigraha*, through me," Lee tapped his chest and it echoed through the microphone that was clipped to his shirt. He kept doing it, playfully making the noise again and again while he laughed. "Wow! That was trippy!

"So, because Yogi Ramsuratkumar's Influence—you could say His blessings, His attention—is here, many subtle beings come here to feed. His blessings are food for such beings, and they have come here to feast! The happier these creatures are, the more we benefit. This may sound strange to some of you, but bear with me. It works like this. We all make the seminar together. Whatever invocation gets made here we do it together, whether I'm talking or you're talking." Lee yawned and laughed. "The sleep *devas* must be dancing around here!

"Yogi Ramsuratkumar said some years ago that if even one being has benefited by His life on Earth, then He would be willing to return, to reincarnate again and again and again to serve God. What does it mean to benefit? Any of you who have been to India around a master know that masters get a lot of people who come and ask for help and blessings. Most of them want some small worldly accomplishment: they want their child to be healthy, their wives or families blessed for this or that. Rarely does anyone ask for Truth or Reality.

"I'll give you my insight: there is a hierarchy of importance to the teacher, to the master. At the bottom of the spectrum are material wishes—money, cars, houses. Physical healing is in the middle of the spectrum because there is genuine suffering involved. To ask to be healed, or for someone else to be healed, is a higher request. At the top of the hierarchy is something we could call Surrender to the Will of God.

"When we are in the divine presence of a teacher like Yogi Ramsuratkumar or Anandamayi Ma or Ramana Maharshi, just to be around them creates spontaneous phenomena. Similarly, the closer you get to a fire, the more the fire has an effect on you because it is the nature of fire. Depending on your level of combustibility, you could burst into flame. If you put green wood to flame, it won't burn; it has to be dry. If you put dry thin paper near the fire, it doesn't even have to be close to burst into flame. The presence of a great teacher is like that; it has an automatic effect if you get close enough to it, which could include spontaneous healings, betterment of life and circumstances—money falls out of the sky and things like that. If we're like wet wood, then nothing happens, but if we're like dry paper, all kinds of things start to happen."

Lee paused then said, "Time for a joke," and tore off into a joke that fell like a lead brick into the middle of the room. One or two intrepid people chuckled. He plunged into a second joke and got a little more laughter. "Where were we? Oh yeah . . . inner sanctum," he laughed easily, totally unencumbered.

"So, we all make the invocation together. I could make it very easy for everybody here, get you all chanting and dancing—you'd all get high and think you saw God face to face. That's too easy! We'll try to go a little deeper than that. Yogi Ramsuratkumar's blessings are here. That's a given. There is no question about it. So what we do with those blessings is up to us as a group, to some degree. The more sophisticated we are, the greater our understanding, but what really matters is how *real* we are.

"The question is, 'What do you really want?' We've come here in this room, we're discussing exalted matters, but what we really want may just be more money, or to look different. In the sixties all I wanted was straight hair!" Now people started laughing while Lee went off on a comedy routine about having curly, kinky hair. He was wearing a T-shirt with a huge yellow Tweetie Bird standing on a black and white checked background. Underneath Tweetie Bird were the words, 'High Performance.'

"But what do we want at heart?" he continued. "If we are honest, the blessings of the Divine respond to us because the blessings of the Divine respond to self-honesty. If we really just want more sex or more money and we're here because we like to talk about God as a hobby—some people are interested in biology or football, some people are interested in spiritual life—then still you get His Influence, just in being here. You can get a picture of Yogi Ramsuratkumar and get His blessings.

"But if you really want God, Yogi Ramsuratkumar has said that anyone who calls His Name with faith, He will be there to help them. No restrictions. All that is required is to think of Him with faith and His full blessing is there. It's true of Yogi Ramsuratkumar, Anandamayi Ma, Arnaud Desjardins—it's not just true of Eastern teachers, but of Western teachers as well!" Lee chuckled.

"The kind of flash experience we could have here this weekend is easy to create, but

692

I'd rather go more deeply into the question, 'What do I really want?' I'd like to get us to be honest with ourselves. Do we really want what the path has to offer? In the depth of our being, what do we really want? Because the path has its benefits, but it also will crush everything in us that is an obstacle to our realization. The Sufis talk about annihilation of ego—that's not like bliss, beauty, wonder, awe. Annihilation is as bad as it sounds, until you are annihilated. Then it's great, because there is no one left. But while you are in the process there can be periods of great difficulty. You can go through them quickly, but you do have to go through them.

"There are many different forms that enlightenment can take. Some are attractive, some are not so attractive. Superficially we might say, 'I want enlightenment from the path,' but what each of us might find on the path is an unknown because each of us is different. We all want to be free, but my view of enlightenment is not freedom, but slavery! My first book was called *Spiritual Slavery*. The idea of that was and still is that when God takes us, everything we call choice—personal likes and dislikes, what we find beautiful or not beautiful, who we like and who we don't like, where we live or don't live—is no longer a choice. In my case we ended up with ashrams in environments that are very beautiful and pleasant. I was just lucky.

"So what do we really want? If we really want to love God there are consequences. Rumi's poetry, for example, came out of heartbreak. Rumi's master, who he loved profoundly, disappeared. Most scholars say he was murdered. Rumi went mad with longing. We read his poetry and are inspired by it; we presume that Rumi was in bliss when he wrote it, but he was in an agony of longing. We can never *have* God; we can only love God. We can be one with God, be in union with God, but we can't have God like a parent and child, or a lover, like someone who is there for us. The process of loving God is a process of love in separation because if you find union with God, then there is no you, and no God, anymore.

"As long as we are in this process it is very bittersweet. It is sweet but painful because the heart is open, but what it is open to in one sense, for ego, does not exist. It exists in Reality, but not in the realm of ego. Ego is trying to realize what it can't realize, so there is pain. When we enter the path most of us are very sincere and dedicated as far as we understand things. We are genuine, but naive. Freedom from the tyranny of ego is freedom, but ego is a very complex adversary. We have no idea the length that we will have to go to actually trick ego into some kind of surrender."

Despite the bad news Lee was delivering to hopeful spiritual aspirants, the room was vibrant and the air thick with energy and presence. In the midst of this sat Lee, who was so transparent that he seemed like nothing more than a passing phenomenon, a concrete emanation of something far beyond my ability to perceive.

At nine-thirty Lee ended for the night, spent awhile at the book table talking with people, joined the group for tea and cookies, then retired.

September 25, 1999
La Source Bleue

Lee began his talk this morning with questions. The first question was about trust between husband and wife. As the man spoke it became clear that his wife was sitting beside him. He said, "I feel that my wife doesn't trust me completely. I can't seem to touch her." Lee asked his wife if this was true. She answered that, although she didn't mind being touched physically, part of her has difficulty letting go inside.

Lee said, "What woman in this room doesn't have trouble letting go totally?" He paused and looked around the room. "No one. No woman here is totally free." Turning his attention back to the man, Lee continued, "Maybe you wouldn't really want a woman to be totally free. Talk about a love monster! You'd be thinking differently as she sucked the marrow from your bones, crunched like a cat eating a mouse . . .

"There is something a woman has inside that is very sacred and valuable that she wants to protect. So if a man wants that, be warned! I wasn't joking around before—you'll be devoured. It will be wonderful, but it will take everything.

"In India there are fierce female deities like Kali and Durga. When you see Kali she's ugly, with blood dripping from her fangs, a necklace of skulls and a skirt of severed arms hanging down. She's naked, depending on the image, and if she is young she has full vibrant breasts, beautiful hips, and she stands on Shiva who is her husband. There are certain tantric rituals in which you are supposed to go out and spend all night meditating on a corpse. You have to prepare carefully because the first glimpse of Kali can be devastating. The purpose of the meditation is to allow Kali to devour everything in you that is dark and terrifying so that what is left is beautiful. When you can sit through an evening of meditation with Kali devouring you, what you are left with in the morning is an image of Kali that is extraordinarily beautiful.

"It's a fine metaphor and fairly accurate for contemporary woman. Women guard the treasure within themselves with fierceness and ugliness. If you are able to understand more deeply what appears on the surface and allow yourself to enter into union with that, then the woman will reveal herself completely, freely. But that revelation is blinding and overwhelming.

"You are in the same position every man is in. Your wife is a lovely woman, and there is this thing she's protecting inside. The worst thing you could do is become dissatisfied with your wife under the assumption that you could get it by leaving your wife and find it with another woman.

"E.J. Gold once said something like, 'The real woman, objective woman, has to be invoked by masculinity.' Not her own, unfortunately. Many women try to invoke the real Feminine with their own masculinity; it's disastrous and ugly besides! But that's another issue. It's our responsibility as men to invoke in a woman enough trust and passion that she becomes willing to open up that closed place. The exposure of real Femininity demands to be met by real Masculinity. If we want to be real men, we have to invoke real woman. Then if we don't die of fright or exhaustion trying to outrun them, it will be great!

"So the responsibility is ours—men's—because in the last three or four thousand years with the exception of certain cultural pockets, certain tribal societies or sects in India or Tibet, women have needed to guard this secret place. That is because this secret place is so terrifying to weak masculinity that patriarchal cultures have attempted to destroy it. So we find our partners, our lovers, conditioned by thousands of years of patriarchal domination. The gates that guard this treasure in women is where it becomes very complex, because this is where we meet the confusion of childhood psychological protection that has been created from either physical, sexual, emotional or psychic abuse. This abuse has driven little girls to take the deepest part of themselves, which is completely trusting, and wall it off from abuse by fathers, grandfathers, uncles, brothers and other predators.

"That psychological protection is all wrapped up with the instinctual protection of that which is the true Feminine, which is protected, even genetically, based on thousands of years of attack. As you all know, in the Middle Ages women who used herbs for healing and knew the ways of childbirth were killed as witches, which was an attempt to destroy this Feminine. A woman's being is like a labyrinth; the path to a man's being is far more direct. The path to the Feminine is extremely complex—it is a maze. We have to be extremely patient, diligent, disciplined, gentle. Any violence from the man—real or implied or threatened—and the vault slams shut.

"So we have to, over time, be willing to draw out the trust our lovers have in us. Understand, it is terrifying for a woman to open that place because it is the Heart of Life in woman. Understand, a woman is tentative in revealing that because if that gets hurt, that's it for her. You are a doctor; this is very much like a delicate surgery at the subtle level. The point is to get deeply enough into a woman's psyche that she will trust you with the treasure. It requires time, attention and delicacy.

"On the other hand, when this part of a woman is closed off, inactive, it also creates a kind of dissatisfaction in the woman. Women want this part of themselves to be opened and touched, to be loved and honored. They are willing to help us, and maybe they are even a little desperate. At twenty or twenty-five years of age, what does a woman want to get open for? All she wants, typically, is to get laid and have some fun. Most women are too blinded by addictions to even know that part of themselves exists at that age: addicted to satisfying themselves with pleasure, with drugs, sex, entertainment, clothing, and one of the most popular forms of addiction—*power*! But that's just a veneer. Underneath that they are scared, lonely and desperate, a little too anxious for that secret part to be discovered. Which makes them willing victims to every seducer, every man who just wants to shoot another tiger, another rhinoceros, another elephant—except their gun is their genitals. Hot and vibrating, a throbbing shaft of steel, of manhood!" Lee threw his head back and laughed with derision. His voice was dripping with sarcasm as he continued, "We men whisper to it at night, 'You rule, baby, you rule!' "

He bent over double laughing and holding his sides. His laughing fit subsided and he continued, still chuckling. There were a few quiet chuckles in the room, but overall people were taking this answer very seriously. Lee admitted, "It is serious subject matter, but also funny! We have to be able to see ourselves and our desperation in a humorous light—men and women—or we're in trouble.

"So, the older we get, usually the wiser. Sometimes we just get more desperate. We realize that we're not getting any younger, and our chances for discovery of this secret as women is getting less and less. So women become more hungry, when she may have been satisfied all her life. All of a sudden something starts bubbling up from this secret part, saying, 'Hey, don't forget about me!'

"You two look to be the perfect age to begin this journey, because when we are in our twenties, we're just not ready. Too many mountains to climb, races to win. But as we get older our attention drifts to deeper subject matter, like who we are as men and women. Your question is a very real question, a very scary question to ask, but probably shared by everybody in the room.

"When asked why he got into the Work, E.J. Gold said, 'I had nothing left to live for.' It's almost easier to work with people who come to the path in middle age, having been successful with a career and love lives, having already gotten over alcoholism. They've done everything and nothing has been satisfying. They have nothing left to live for. But when we're young we still have fame and success to tease us. We look for things outside ourselves to satisfy us, but no amount of fame and success or external stimulation will touch that sacred place inside.

"Marriage is really a partnership. To be trusted—and all women understand trust—requires work on both people's parts. Trust is a key element in love, so we want to feel trusted and we want to trust our partner. But especially we want to feel trusted. One of the most damaging psychological characteristics we bring to marriage is to mistake the trust we want to feel for the superficial niceties of social interactions. If we forget our anniversary, our wives will feel, 'I can't trust you.' Or if we burn the dinner or urinate all over the bathroom floor—one of men's favorite tricks—our wives will say, 'I can't trust you.' It's dangerous to equate trust with those surface things because trust is deep and profound. In successful, working relationships people respond at levels of depth and are willing to overlook day-to-day clashes of preference. That's all neurosis. What really satisfies us in relationship deepens over five years, ten years, fifteen years, twenty years. If we don't just get resigned to the way things are, if we're going to keep being in love, then we need to seek communion at deeper levels. That kind of communion is rare in the world, but it is the only thing that satisfies us in our wisdom."

During this session the space became very deeply tender. Lee seemed to be speaking to each person individually, as if each person was sitting face to face with him by a fire over tea, listening to and absorbing the wisdom of a revered elder. His answer affirmed and bore witness to that which is profoundly human and yet also divine in the hearts of men and women. He spoke to a dimension of human possibility, the dimension that the Bauls consider the jumping-off point for the relationship between human and Divine. This jumping-off point is love between woman and man, in which the primal passions are tempered in the alchemical fire of sadhana and gross desire is transmuted into transcendent love. In the *Bhagavata Purana,* in which the mythos of Krishna in his love play with the *gopis* is expounded, it is called *sarvatmabhava,* or total love (*prema*)—complete, selfless, stainless, primordial, sublime in its divine innocence.

While sitting at the book table after the session Lee looked out the window to see Michael, one of his long-time students, sitting on a bench in the grass down below with a woman. They were talking passionately. Michael had been giving talks around France about Yogi Ramsuratkumar, and had attracted a bit of a following, mostly women. Lee quipped sarcastically as he watched, "If we ever have too many men in this school we'll just send Michael out to give more talks . . ."

Now the woman was crying on Michael's shoulder, who listened very intently and comforted her. His posture with her was compassionate and attentive. He said something that made her laugh through her tears. Lee laughed as he watched this scene, saying facetiously, "Now she's laughing, now she's crying, now she's laughing, now she's crying!" He watched for a moment then moved away from the window. "I used to do that, thirty years ago. I'd go to the Unity retreats and pick out the best looking, most tortured babe, and then act the sensitive man!" Lee gave a capricious little laugh.

Just then a couple came in to present their new adopted child, a one-year-old baby, to Lee. They had attended Lee's seminar at La Source Bleue last year also. The child was from southeast Asia, and looked very happy. Lee looked at the couple and the baby. "Very beautiful," he smiled.

After brunch Lee played bridge upstairs in the seminar space. He sat cross-legged on the floor by the window overlooking the spring. After fifteen minutes of playing, Lee had won two, seven-hundred rubbers in a row, bidding three no-trump. The other people were just bit players, props for his victories. While this was going on Lee was serene but active.

"Six no-trump!" Lee shouted in response to his partner's bid of one diamond. He was bidding outrageously with a hand that defied any rationale for such a bid. He often plays bridge along this kind of sharp edge. Now, as his opponents laughed at his chutzpah, he shrugged and said, "Well, you've gotta just go with it when you're on a roll."

There are times when Lee loses at bridge. This he also manages with aplomb. After a series of routings by his opponents, he will often say humorously to his partner, "We got 'em on the run now!" Even when he complains of getting bad hands, or not enough points to bid for many hands in a row, his sense of humor and perspective make it less of a complaint and more of a statement of his enjoyment of all the nuances of the game— including the enjoyment of losing.

Bridge is an excellent metaphor for life. It is a dance of opposites—in this case, winning and losing. The fact of duality is that if there is no losing, then there can be no winning, and without the interplay of these two, there is no game. To play within such a milieu from the nondual perspective is to be the same in relationship to both. A master of enlightened duality, Lee constantly demonstrates the warrior's ability to roll with the punches. But even more, he demonstrates that there is enjoyment or appreciation or equanimity within all aspects of experience.

Now he swept the board clean, racking up all the tricks and playing the hand in less than one minute flat. He threw his last three cards down in victory—two aces and one queen. "Okay," he laughed, "you can have the queen. Six no-trump!" He picked up the score sheet, which always sits to his right while he plays, and wrote in the score, then he went back to the window by the book table and sat on the stone ledge with one leg up, knee bent.

People kept drifting in and out, passing by, stopping and looking, talking with Lee, browsing. Outside the spring rushed by playing its endless music, a trill of notes over glistening mossy stones. A lull passed over the space while one person quietly browsed the books. Lee's face became noticeably soft and radiant, his eyes interiorized, as if he was looking at something no one else could see. Whatever was passing through him communicated itself to the environment in a *bhava* that seemed to come out of nowhere and was indescribable in its expression of the sublime within this ordinary moment. It was a fleeting moment in which in the human form, the man himself, was only a transparent medium for the objective life of the soul. Mariana picked up the camera and attempted to catch the moment on film, but before she could adjust the camera Sian came up and began to talk with Lee. Like a chameleon changing the color of its skin, he immediately shifted into a different mood.

At one o'clock Lee started the afternoon session. The mood that had been building for two days carried over from one session to another, like pearls on a string that connected them into a necklace.

He began: "In the Baul tradition sexual union is a symbol or metaphor for union with God. The Bauls practice a form of technical couple yoga and have yogic techniques for single people also. The assumption is that if one can be in a couple, one will do that. Sometimes when we're single and wanting to be in relationship we're also very critical in terms of our choice of partner. Sometimes we save ourselves for Mr. or Mrs. Right so long that we end up with only ourselves.

"In the West, tantric workshops often instruct people to see their partners as the god or goddess. Sometimes they suggest you get a picture of a divine couple and imagine having sex using that imagery. At the level of understanding at which that is recommended people might as well imagine themselves having sex with movie stars! Michelle Pfeiffer or Brad Pitt! It's all a function of people's vanity. With consciousness-raising groups we've gotten this idea that the woman is the goddess and the man is the god. It's completely a function of self-reference. When women say in frustration, 'My husband doesn't see the goddess in me!' like we would talk about Marilyn Monroe as a goddess, we've forgotten God in this god/goddess, male/female tantric nonsense!

"In tantric workshops, the implication is that seeing God will make you superman or superwoman. Anything but! When you walk through the door to the Divine you find nothing! You become nobody, no person, no 'I', no man, no woman. Union with God doesn't reinforce and justify our egocentricity, but that is the message of contemporary tantric workshops in the West: your egocentricity will be empowered. If you really confront the terror of the situation, you will find annihilation.

"If you associate viewing your partner as god or goddess with self-aggrandizing personal factors, you will get into trouble. If we say 'I'm going to view my wife as the goddess and worship her,' and in our mind we are thinking of Marilyn Monroe, and we expect our wives to smell, look and act like Marilyn Monroe, we are going to be disappointed. To view our partner as god or goddess is to accept their humanity *completely*. They look the way they look, dress the way they dress, the bathroom smells when they are done in there. They are picky, manipulative, domineering, and also patient, strong, understanding. But if you think, 'The goddess wouldn't ask me to take out the trash, the real goddess would just be radiant and submissive all the time!' then you are missing the point. We have to get out of this mindset of psychologizing the Divine. To personalize the Divine is one thing; to psychologize the Divine is another. God is personal, intimate, immediate—but not psychological. When the Bauls say that your partner is the doorway to the Divine they are not under any illusions that your partner has to be psychologically, or in any other way, perfect.

"To walk through the doorway of union is to lose yourself—not to become psychologically healthy. We assume that success on the path means if we are awakened, we will be psychologically healthy. Not necessarily. You look at the Western divine mothers and gurus—these people are not psychologically healthy! If they have realized God—and I put a big *if* on that, including myself, although my students think I'm enlightened. Some of them fall in love with me, then they take a good look at me and wonder how they got hooked up with such a loser!" Everyone laughed. The levity was a needed ingredient at this point in the intensity of the talk, the mood continuing to run deep from the morning session, like strong water wearing out channels in soft soil.

Lee continued, "So, being psychologically healthy is not indicative of anything except psychological work on self. Some people, the most interesting thing about them is their sickness! Then they get all healed and you don't even want to know them anymore!" People laughed again. Lee warmed the group up with a diatribe about how neurotic artists are. It is one of his favorite subjects to joke around about—the immense egos of artists who are terrible artists but think they are God's gift to the world of fine art.

"Enough insults flung at the audience," he laughed. "That treasure of woman is not psychological. It's primal, essential. It is the tangent point in woman between human and divine. When that element is revealed—is open, is vulnerable and trusting—then the doorway to the Divine is open and there are no obstacles. All we have to do is walk through the door and we're in heaven. The way we walk through the door is to be in communion with that. Sex can either relax our guards or make our guards stronger. If our experience with our partner is that they are respectful and sensitive to us, the guards will relax. If not, if our partner is insensitive and disrespectful, then the guards get stronger.

"If we are going to approach this whole subject of men and women, it starts with respect, sensitivity, understanding. If we want our partners to be vulnerable, we have to figure out a way to deal with our own psychological reactivity. It can't be a situation of 'I loved you yesterday, but today you don't count. It's *my* turn to be loved!' "

Lee went into a piercingly accurate commentary on men and women and the respective cramp that tends to be animated on each side in relationship to the other. It was a powerful reminder that, although he was throwing diamonds and pearls out to his audience in this sublime talk of the human possibility, the psychological reality of men and women in the West is a dire situation in which each is mired in deep illusion in relationship to the other.

"We have got to be able to put our psychological worldview on the line if we are going to discover this secret of Masculine and Feminine because when we get in there with our partners and it's life or death to ego, every one of our critical faculties will be on red alert. Ego is going to say 'You've got to keep control—dominate the situation!' We've got to be able to see that and say, 'Not now—later, not now.' When a couple is approaching this essential vulnerability they've got to put everything nonessential out of the space—all of their expectations, projections, opinions, biases. When we're approaching this space of vulnerability we are more or less able to be in that chamber. One thing that allows us to be more rather than less in the chamber is our *intention*.

"When you really have the intention to meet your partner with communion, you don't let ego get in the way. Save your arguments and opinions for the morning, not for the chamber of communion. There are moments of profound communion and moments of disappointment. One of the ideas is the more we have moments of communion, the more we build momentum for communion rather than for frustration and disappointment.

We're all human; we're not going to hit it every time, but create the intention. 'This is what I want. I want trust.' What is trust? To be in communion with the deep, deep part of our partner. We can use the word 'trust' or the word 'love,' but what we're really saying beneath our psychological needs is 'God.' We want God, Reality, Truth."

At three o'clock Dasya gave a talk. He started out saying, "Lee speaks from revelation, directly from what is needed and wanted in the moment, and that is very rare." After answering some questions Dasya talked about the form of Lee's teaching in seminars. He said, "Lee doesn't give seminars in America. Here in Europe in his seminars he lets people see what relationship with him is like in very tiny little pieces. He shows us our romanticism. Our romanticism is a veil, a drug to the reality of the situation. He's really killing romanticism, putting a big stake through its heart, once again. To ego, the relationship with the spiritual master is about as romantic as taking your walk down death row to your execution! There should be a warning with these seminars—'Don't try this stuff without a teacher!' We really don't have any idea how to get from one point to another on the path without the teacher's help.

"When Lee talks about Gurdjieff, Lee is making an analogy, talking about himself. For the spiritual master born in the West, his experience is so foreign to our cultural biases that we can't imagine it." Lee sat listening from his spot on the floor a few feet away from Dasya where he leaned against the rock wall. Dasya's voice penetrated the room softly.

"There is no such thing as a safe place. Real life is not safe, for any of us. Whatever we think is secure is not real. The Universe changes in every moment. Anything could happen. The teacher is proof of that, and yet—look! This person exists. The teacher exists. The teacher is a constant sacrifice of safety. He is always unsafe, always on constantly shifting ground. He is always going on for us, sacrificing his life, bit by bit." The mood of Dasya's talk was aligned perfectly with the sublime mood that had continued to build and grow in force during the seminar.

After the talk Lee went to the book table and talked with some people. Very shortly Lee called out, "Let's play bridge!" to some of his students who were standing nearby. As he sat down he said happily, "Enough material for three sessions!" He was referring to Dasya's talk, and was obviously pleased that it had gone so well. His mood was buoyant. Three people sat down with him on the floor by the window and Lee quickly dealt out a hand. Picking up his cards and putting them in order, Lee said emphatically after a swift scrutiny of his points, "Three no-trump!" It was another wild bid that started and finished the bidding, skipping the formalities of normal bidding and going directly to game. Scooping up tricks, he looked at his hand and pretended not to know what to play next. "Dawg!" he exclaimed humorously. Another foursome gathered and played bridge next to Lee's group.

The bridge game proceeded for forty-five minutes. The bidding for another hand came up. There were three passes to Lee. He said victoriously, shutting out any and all other bidding possibilities, "Three no-trump! Only fifteen minutes till dinner . . . let's kick some butt!" He made the three no-trump—his specialty—in another one-minute hand, got up and walked out to go to dinner.

Dinner was served in the old mill house, which had been arranged with tables, chairs, white tablecloths. Sian served succulent Moroccan chicken cooked with lemons, olives and onion, couscous, eggplant, tomato and zucchini ratatouille. The wine was a dark red local wine from Cahors—very delicious. Dessert was fresh pears cooked in spiced sweet wine, a traditional dessert of France that Sian had served once to Arnaud. She said that he had liked the dessert so well that he had her heat the leftover spiced liquid, the sweetened pear and wine nectar, to serve as a nightcap.

The extraordinary meal lent itself to the divine mood that lay just below the surface of gentle and easy conversation that hummed around the room. When someone mentioned the unusual mood of the whole seminar, Sian talked about how smoothly things were going in the kitchen as well. There were no conflicts, there was lots of help, nothing got dropped or forgotten, people were enjoying each other's company. The mood in the kitchen for the cooks had been the same as the mood in the seminar talks, and it was all reflected in the communion that was present over the food tonight.

At eight o'clock everyone was settled in his or her seat as Lee walked up to the front and took his place. "Thank you for indulging us, those of you who were up here listening to the music in here after dinner. That is the last album of our rock band, which played for thirteen years. The music is very close to our hearts; it means a lot to my students. One of my students once said that if anyone wanted all the esoteric teaching on relationship he should just get all the music and listen to it over and over again." As he had several times over the summer, Lee reflected on the end of the band, how the band had stopped being willing to take risks, even though they started out from nothing. He said, "In the Work what matters is possibility, not talent. Once the band was not willing to take artistic risks anymore, the transformational possibility got smaller and smaller.

"I don't like to give seminars," Lee changed his train of thought. "It's nice to meet people and make jokes and make new friends and all that, but I really don't like to give seminars. I do it because the transformational possibilities created in seminars, particularly for my students and secondarily for guests, is profitable. Everything is about profit. When something starts losing profitability, it gets the guillotine, like the band. Everything the teacher does is for the teacher's students. The teacher doesn't need anything else . . . When we are in relationship with the teacher we see that the teacher treats people differently. That is because different people need different things.

"The student transforms himself with the help of God, but the master is the deal maker. The master can fix it for the disciple as long as the disciple becomes the good disciple, as in reliable, not submissive. The further we go on the path, the more powerless we are—that's the point! The more powerless we are in Reality, the more God is running things for us. Someone said to me, 'The deeper I go, the more I feel powerless.' Great! Deeper, deeper, deeper, *deeper*! Until you find *real* powerlessness. We don't language it that way—we say we want to be free. But if we actually get those things we say we want, we will be powerless. God moves—we move. God breathes—we breathe. God stops breathing . . . !"

Lee commented on some of the points Dasya made in his talk and then answered questions. Near the end of the evening the man from Martinique raised his hand. He asked about the secret in the heart of a woman. "You say that when a woman opens up she devours. Does the masculine disappear altogether?"

Lee answered, "It's exactly the opposite. Actually what gets devoured is our aggression, violence, tendencies to manipulate and dominate others. What gets left after all that gets devoured is the pure Masculine. To be devoured in that way exposes the Masculine and frees it."

The man asked, "You said only the real Masculine can evoke this part of woman. Is it a gradual back and forth process or . . ."

Lee said, "It works back and forth. Plus, we want to get laid!" Everyone in the room burst into laughter at the blunt truth of Lee's statement. He had a big smile on his face. He seemed to be feasting on the rapport that he had with this group.

"There's the whole neurotic part of it—we want the woman to be satisfied so we can feel good about our sexual prowess and all that. As we are Paying Attention, all of a sudden we will notice something is being evoked in the woman at the same time that neurosis is active. The more we notice that evocation, the more we will be attracting that. The final shift of context happens like that," Lee snapped his fingers to indicate that it happens instantaneously, "but the building up comes first."

Lee spent the rest of the evening in dialogue with different people who had been at his seminars at La Source Bleue for the past three or four years. Outside the moon was almost full. Its silver rays shone down through heavy banks of fast-moving rain clouds and melted the landscape, casting the temple of this place into pure magic. The evening passed before our eyes, as if we were riding on a magic carpet through unknown and exotic lands. Soon the talk was over, tea was served and around ten o'clock Lee walked up the driveway through the dark, rainy night under the towering chestnut trees to the house where he was staying.

September 26, 1999
La Source Bleue

The air turned chilly this morning, and the mood seemed to turn deep and sad in some unknowable way. Lee started his morning session in a fierce, implacable mood. He seemed depressed, upset. The moods of the master are inexplicable at best and completely confounding much of the time. One could only guess at what must have precipitated his mood, but any attempt to do so is typically a useless occupation. The best one could do this morning was stay in place, take the acid bath he flung out at the room, trust the blessing power underlying all of his communications.

He was wearing the Tweetie Bird, "High Performance" T-shirt. His eyes blazed as he said, "It's the last day of the seminar. If only it was the *last day* . . ." Did he really want to die? He had made frequent comments during the summer in which he welcomed death to come at any time. These comments often seem to be the symptom of a particular frustration with the level of practice demonstrated by his senior students—a frustration that periodically peaks in outbursts. But it is more than frustration that Lee communicates: it is the pain, especially the sorrow, of the burden that he bears. The guru suffers with his devotees. He is not outside of their struggle, but in the midst of it, at the core of it.

He continued, "I hate to give you the bad news but, from what I've been able to understand about life, the more conscious you are, the more pain you feel. What I've found out so far about life is that if you're going to have an open heart, you're going to be in pain—every day. People you love will shoot you," he raised his arms and took aim as if he was holding a rifle, "but they're not even a good shot. They don't just hit you in the heart and be done with it—boom! Instead they take off an arm, a leg, a piece of shoulder. No, they don't just shoot you in the heart and get it over with. But somehow you love each other anyway . . ." His tone was horrible, grating, unbearably acidic. He was using himself like a battering ram on the hard barriers of the heart. Then he was off on a diatribe about the dark side of the path—the weight and burden of the illusion of separation.

After awhile Sian asked a question. She began by saying that lately, this morning in particular, she was in touch with the barriers that keep her from being truly alive. She said that she felt hopeless and stuck in the labyrinth of her life. Her question seemed to resonate deeply with the mood of the space.

Lee said, "This morning I'm right where you are! When someone matures enough on the path to explore the underworld, at first it is hell. In every myth, exclusively, the thing that allows people to survive the underworld and come back is making friends with the demons there, because if you don't have friends to fill you in on the secrets of survival, you never come back . . . ." As Lee spoke his mood began to soften, and the deep undertones of the mood rose to the surface like sunlight glittering on the vast ocean.

"Sooner or later we have to map the underworld, to undertake the journey of dismemberment, and then we have to be resurrected. As long as there is duality—hope for salvation—there is also the other side of that: despair, hopelessness. When we are feeling hopeless, we have to really be hopeless, one hundred percent. When we are hopeless one hundred percent, everything changes because then hopelessness is not provoked by the desire for transformation, peace, et cetera. Then there is equanimity in hopelessness. So we are back to being where we are, one hundred percent. Even if we are there ninety-nine percent, it's hell. Three percent is hell, twenty percent is hell and ninety percent is hell. It's just if it's three percent or twenty percent, then we can pretend it's not hell. Instead of facing where we are, we seek comfort in our children, or imagine that we will see our teacher next month."

Sian said, "I feel like a fool . . ."

"We're all fools on a ship of fools," Lee said. "If changes are to happen, they will happen organically. It's not that you'll never be able to do things differently. Everything is a matter of timing. If we try to do the right thing at the wrong time, it's disastrous. So you hold intention without attachment as much as possible. When you have intention you are giving notice to the Universe, then the Universe decides. If the Universe sees it is right, the Universe will open doors in a way that allows your dream to manifest. If not, it's not your fault. People don't think that their prayers are heard when they don't get action right away, but our prayers are heard . . . When we are too emotionally invested in something, rather than calling it to us, we actually push it away."

Jean Pierre asked, "Will you go deeper into this matter of prayer?"

"Well," Lee laughed and paused. "When we are living here and now, when we are accepting what is, then every thought and every gesture is a prayer. The way I define prayer it would be worship, or an expression of gratitude in praise of God, wonderful and holy, magnificent, rather than some kind of request—'Something for me, to make my life better,' or even to make other people's lives better. That's supplication. When we understand that whatever arises in the moment is the Gift of God, then we can praise God for whatever is given. Life is the Gift of God, but we don't know that, because we keep trying to mold it in our image. And even that is something to be accepted as it is."

At this point Kathleen, who was translating, started crying. Tears were rolling uncontrollably down her face, to her own dismay it seemed, as if something had just welled up inside her and taken over.

Lee looked at her and said gently, "It's okay to cry." Her tears seemed like a manifestation of everyone in the room; they were not her tears alone, but everyone's. After long hours of sitting together and traveling through the inner landscape that was revealed by Lee's words and presence, the increased charge of the chamber had everyone poised on an edge of raw vulnerability. People had been broken open to feel at a level that was usually not available to them. Kathleen tried to translate through her tears until someone offered to translate for a few moments until the tears passed. Lee continued.

"So when we recognize that, there is a sense of gratitude. And that may manifest as praise, as service, or as complaint—as strange as that seems. But it's all prayer, because it rests in the context of the recognition of what is as it is. The Universe is absolute, so in the recognition of absoluteness, there is gratitude. We don't have to say the words, 'Thank you, God.' All we have to do is *live* here and now. Whatever action is here and now as it is, is prayer."

Many people walked out of this talk with wet eyes. It seemed like the seminar had peaked in a kind of collective breakthrough at the level of the feeling heart. When asked on the way to brunch about the morning session, Lee commented seriously, "People are *pondering*—the way Gurdjieff used the word. They are going into deep contemplation." A few minutes later he said, "We got them in touch with their pain and then . . ." His voice trailed off as someone came up and asked him a question.

Lee spent the remaining two sessions of the day returning to the question, "What do you really want?" beginning with his usual call to practice. Not just a little practice, but fierce, dedicated practice.

"What all this business boils down to is the question, 'What do I want?' We all mean it when we say that we want clarity, but we all have big lives. Sooner or later it comes down to, 'How badly do you want it?' We are all willing perhaps to sacrifice time, money, material things. But as we begin to deepen in our practice we are called to sacrifice non-material things. Greed. Vanity. Pride. Lust. Guilt. Are you willing to sacrifice those things? Because that's what it's going to come down to—sacrificing your self-hatred," Lee chuckled. "Self-hatred is miserable; it's so full of suffering! We think, 'Oh yes, I'd love to sacrifice self-hatred,' but when the teacher is standing in front of us and says, 'Okay, your self-hatred, give it to me!' we say, 'Oh no, it's so familiar! Who will I be if I'm not hating myself?' Are we willing to sacrifice the things *dear* to us—our psychological viewpoints about ourselves?

"Arnaud's statement 'Accept what is' is a statement of Reality, but to accept what is you have to see what is. Are you willing to sacrifice opinions, projections, your love of the past? 'Oh my relationship with my mother is so sacred, so precious. I just can't see it without judgement. I can't sacrifice my attachment to my mother—it means too much to me!' So the real question is not, 'What do you want?' but, 'How badly do you want it?' If we don't want it badly enough, we won't do the work necessary. We'll stay philosophers."

The afternoon had become golden with the sun shining on the green trees and water, making a luminous haze in the air. And yet the space where we sat inside with Lee, the alchemical chamber of the inner sanctum, still carried a quality of the bleeding heart, like the bleeding heart of Jesus. There was a poignant and piercing quality in the air. All the falling rain of the past thirty-six hours, the *rasa*, the battering and softening of the defenses and barriers had opened the heart. As Jakusho Kwong Roshi had said many months ago, the relative and the universal are one. A window in the back of the room suddenly swung open by itself, letting the golden, brisk cool of the afternoon come rushing into the room. The constant music of rustling leaves, the whisper of the moving water, the river so close, the extraordinary quality of the afternoon light—all this flooded in and mingled with the atmosphere of the room. Lee answered many questions in the peak of this mood. There was easy laughter, and he was gentle with everyone, a tenderness left from the breaking open of the morning.

A disciple of Arnaud Desjardins raised his hand and said, "I am trying to develop a more impersonal relationship with Arnaud so that I will feel Arnaud is with me more and more. But the child in me needs Arnaud's recognition. I try to just go on . . ."

Lee responded, "That's the answer. Just go on." He smiled gently. "Your commitment to practice to have Arnaud with you more and more is the correct approach. To view the master as an impulse to Truth rather than as a human being with a personality and all that is the right approach. The more you do that the more you will see. The more you find Arnaud in you, the more you will have no illusions about yourself because Arnaud has no illusions about himself. The more self-clarity you have, the more you will act with integrity.

"If we don't know that we are seeking the master's approval like a child with a parent, then when we are with the master we have no choice but to act that way—demanding his attention and so on. But if the adult in us sees the child in us, then we can decide that we don't want to relate to the master that way. It's the adult who sees the child, and once the adult has seen that, it's the adult who has the control. If we don't see it, then the child is in control. So it sounds like you are right on target. We have to grow into that, more and more. We're all very impatient. We have experienced a clarity and we want to be living in that right away. Just keep going forward."

The last talk came to a close. A feeling of fullness, of satiation, of deep nourishment was the momentum now as Lee returned to his post at the book table and people began to gather themselves together to leave. It did not feel like an end, but a seeding of possibility, as if every person left with something precious that would grow over time.

A woman walked up to the book table to give a donation for the Prison Library Project which Lee had "begged" for at the beginning of the last talk. People waited in line to see Lee at the table. A second donation for the Prison Library Project was offered. *"Pour livre,"* she said smiling, meaning the books that are sent free to prisoners all over the United States through the project. Many people walked past and caught Lee's eye to *pranam* or touch their hearts. Devadatta, a sannyasin from Martinique, asked if he could come visit Lee in Arizona. "Yes," Lee said, "just call ahead before you come and ask for me."

A woman walked up and stood shyly in front of the book table. "I want to thank you," she smiled. "I have been very quiet this weekend, but I have been very deeply touched." A young French man came up and asked Devadatta to translate for him. He said, "He thanks you . . . he would like to see you again." Lee smiled and said, "Next year." Another donation for the Prison Library Project was offered to Lee. People cleared out of the room while Lee's students carried the chairs downstairs for the evening meal.

Mariana said to Lee, "It was a really, exceptionally good seminar."

Lee answered simply, "I thought so." He was even, steady, as self-contained as always. As soon as the room was cleared out he started playing bridge again. His opponents won two games and made a rubber. He said playfully, with a joyous smile on his face, "We run home with our tails between our legs!" He whined like a dog, making everyone laugh. He seemed to be enjoying everyone's company immensely. Losing at bridge is never a problem for him—he plays straight on, full in the game, win or lose. But when he corrected his partner's playing after she had just made a very poor play, he barked, "Your partner likes to *win*! First rule: Pay Attention. Second rule: Learn the rules. You said you wanted to learn how to play better, right? Okay!"

It didn't matter that the weekend had been sublime, extraordinary, one of the peaks of the summer. Lee was tending to business, as usual. The next morning after a rich brunch with Sian and Jean Pierre, Lee and company loaded the books and bags and packs and people back into the two vans and drove back to La Ferme de Jutreau, gypsy business as usual, practically jingling all the way.

September 27, 1999
La Ferme de Jutreau

Lee pulled into La Ferme de Jutreau around three-fifteen in the afternoon. Jumping out of the van he strode into the house and into the office to check his mail. He immediately found out that the mail hadn't been brought from Saint Pierre de Maillé yet, so he jumped in the car and drove into the post office to get the mail himself.

Around five o'clock he walked downstairs carrying his bright red corduroy long-sleeved shirt which he wears almost every day as a light jacket over T-shirts. Andrea, who was putting all the books away downstairs, looked up and saw him walk up holding the red shirt out. "Do you want this?" he asked mildly.

"It's yours," she said, hesitating.

"Yes . . . do you want it?" he pressed her for an answer.

"Sure!" she replied enthusiastically. He handed her the shirt and walked out.

After dinner Lee was playing bridge in the salon. Several other foursomes gathered around and started playing on the floor near Lee's table. Claire was Lee's partner. She and Volkmar had invited Lee and his family to tea the next day to bless their new apartment in Angles sur l'Anglin, a nearby village. It is a common practice in the Hohm Community to invite the spiritual master to a new household or home of sangha members as a gesture of offering him hospitality, inviting his presence into the house, and to ask for his blessing on the home.

Brindavan came and knelt at the side of Lee's chair. She had a number of questions to ask him about details of Lee's schedule for the next week. As he reviewed some of the details of the Paris schedule, he talked about the next two days at La Ferme de Jutreau. It would be his last two days on the ashram this year. "The girls can make their dessert," he said to Brinda. "They can make whatever they like. Just serve it Wednesday night after dinner, or tomorrow night."

Brinda said, "But tomorrow you'll be going to Claire's for tea, so it might not be the best time to have dessert . . ."

He interrupted fiercely, "That's okay. It's not a problem."

"I didn't know if you wanted two sweets in one day," she continued.

"And besides," Lee said scathingly, "if Claire serves me anything sweet I'm never going back to her house again! This isn't Austria where people get together and have fancy cake at teatime! Of course my family would *love* to go there and eat all that stuff. I'll go to Claire's for tea and have to eat whatever 'treats' she serves and come home to the *sacred* food served here for dinner stuffed like a pig with a shiny red apple in my mouth. Then I won't be able to eat the sacred food that is here because I'll be stuffed!"

He looked across the table at Claire and continued in the same fierce tone. "But don't change what you were going to do, because then the people coming with me are going to chew up my ass on the way home." He started speaking in a high-pitched voice in a caricature of a bitchy woman, " 'Claire had this great plan and *you* had to go and ruin it, you bastard!' They're gonna be chewing up my ass like army ants. Do you know what army ants are?" Claire shook her head no. He said, "They're those ants that start moving and devour everything in their path."

There were three bridge games going in the salon at this point and several other people sitting in chairs around Lee's table to watch. Claire was practically sizzling in her chair. Obviously she had planned to serve sweets for the tea. He looked at her and said, "Now Claire is all upset because I've ruined her plans."

She said, "No, I want to serve what you would like to eat."

His eyes blazing, he answered her in a loud voice. "If you wanted me to eat, you should have invited me to lunch or to dinner, not to *tea*. I'm not into tea. Everybody thinks I'm a normal person who they can invite to *tea* and I'll come over and everything will be so nice . . . just like some ordinary guy. But I'm not a normal person." He was white-hot. Even though his voice was loud and even shocking, Lee had the uncanny ability to be simultaneously even and moderate, even mild. It was a total contradiction to the senses which perceived both of these simultaneously—the loud, piercing voice that seemed to penetrate all the way to Arizona, and the even, tempered voice of equanimity. All activity in the house had come to a stop as everyone listened or was drawn into the room to hear Lee's rant. He seemed tremendously irritated. The bridge game kept going, but time was suspended. Every now and then, just to keep the game going, Lee would toss in his bid when it was his turn, or a new hand would get dealt in the midst of the interchange. In this way he continued to play cards while he spoke.

Claire asked, "What would you like to eat?"

"You don't *want* to know what I want. Nobody would want to know what I want. If people knew what I *really* wanted they'd turn green and shit in their pants." This statement reverberated around the room and into the ethers. He wasn't kidding. His fervor made it seem like we were seeing the real Lee Lozowick—uncensored, unleashed, uncompromised by anybody's reactivity or rational demands. "But I have to capitulate to my devotees. I have to . . ." he paused for emphasis, "*make concessions . . .*" He smiled as if, from his point of view, the irony of the situation was so far beyond anything comprehensible to the people sitting with him in the room right now that it was just indescribable.

"I'm a boring character, Claire. I'm a totally boring character. I want everything to be the same, day after day, exactly the same. I'm such a boring character. I like lunch at noon and dinner at six, and no changes. I'd be perfectly happy eating one meal a day, having everything the same. I dislike variation. But I have to eat two meals a day because everybody wants me to be a normal human being. I'm not a normal human being."

Brinda came back to the table with a fax that had just arrived from Arizona and some questions. "What time do you want dinner for the return feast in Arizona? They are thinking six o'clock," she said.

Lee snapped, "Six o'clock? What do I want to wait till six o'clock to do it for?"

Jan said, "You're the one who decided you wanted it that late so that people who have to work can come."

Lee was irascible. Untamed. Nobody was going to stop him or get in his way now. He raved on, "What do I want to wait for those people for? People think they can be in the Work and have a normal life." He looked around the room, scanning as if looking for something, and continued, "Is there anybody in this room who has a normal life? Do you see anybody here who has a normal life?"

There was definitely no one in the room who had a normal life. He was right. He charged ahead, "People living in Prescott don't come to clean cases on the ashram. They come for feasts, but to work? No. They move to Prescott from Colorado or California, and then they don't come to Celebrations because they can't afford it!" He paused, then added, "They don't come to Celebrations and they don't help out on the ashram and I'm supposed to wait dinner for them? Why does anybody want to be a student of mine anyway? I'm such a critical parent, a patriarchal bastard! Listen to me ranting and raving!"

Jan said, "Well, you're the one who said you wanted to wait so there would be people there to hear the stories. You can make it any time you want."

Ignoring her comment, he went on, "People think they can have a normal life and be in this Work. Don't tell this to anybody in Arizona. If you repeat it to anybody in Arizona the people who need to hear it won't listen, and the people who don't need to hear it don't need to hear it." He paused. Brinda sat waiting at his side. He turned and said fiercely, "Make it six o'clock."

Every eye in the room was turned on him. His statements rang out in the space and then settled into a burning silence. After a few moments Jan took up the banner again and pursued him, asking, "People want to invite you to their houses to have their houses blessed. Is it that you don't have to be physically present to bless the house, you can bless it from a distance?"

As if the most obvious thing in the world had just been stated Lee snapped, "You got it. I don't have to *be* there to bless their house! Why would I want to go to somebody's house when I'm living on the ashram? On the ashram there is sanctuary; if I'm traveling I go to my students' houses because that is sanctuary when I'm on the road. But why would I want to leave the ashram to go to my students' houses?"

Pursuing further Jan said, "But shouldn't people ask anyway? Isn't it better to ask and say, you know, 'I'd like to invite you to my new house and if you prefer not to come it's really okay, but if you'd like to come . . .' "

Lee interrupted before she could finish her thought. "No, they shouldn't do that because when someone like Claire, who has done so much for the Work, invites me I *have* to say yes. If someone mentions it at all it's obvious they want me to come and then I have to say yes."

Jan asked, "Then how can your students best get your blessing?"

Lee fired out, "*Leave me alone.* Leave me alone. Leave me alone. Leave me alone." He repeated the phrase, "Leave me alone," emphatically in a powerfully measured and serious tone that seemed to strike a deeper note each time. He continued without pause, "*Until I make a gesture to you*, leave me alone! If I never make a gesture to you in fifty years and you live your whole life simply with your attention fully on me, you'll be incredibly blessed. Is that clear?"

He turned to me and said, "Put that in your book! Not that anybody is going to read it anyway! Who wants to read about all the stupid things I do? Can you imagine 'Yoga Journal' reviewing this stuff?" He snorted. "Ha! If they didn't throw up they'd call Hohm Press and say, 'Now you've really lost it! There's no way we're going to review this book. Have you lost your mind over there?' "

The whole room was shocked into silence. Lee kept playing cards as if nothing had happened. After a few minutes he looked directly into Claire's stunned face. "So, Claire . . . you just go ahead and serve whatever you were planning to serve. Your spiritual master has given you instructions to do that. You understand?"

She met his penetrating gaze, listened to every word and said, "Yes, I understand."

Jan played the last bridge hand. "Well played!" Lee smiled at her.

She said laughing, "You're just trying to make me feel better because you've just said to leave you alone and you don't want any of us in the same room with you for the next fifty years!"

He protested with a smile, his voice dripping with charm, "I didn't mean *you* all . . ." He stretched his arms out as if to embrace the three people sitting at the bridge table with him, then brought his arms in toward his body and looked around the room. It was as if he had gathered everybody into himself. "I didn't mean the people at this table, I didn't mean all of you in this room . . . I didn't mean my *devotees* . . ." He hugged himself as if in rapture at the thought of his devoted and loving students. His tone was light and bantering, tinged with humor, and yet it was also innocent. Did he really mean what he had just said, or was he being completely facetious? Based on everything that had just happened, he couldn't possibly mean what he was saying, but at the same time there was a complete truthfulness in his mood from moment to moment. There was irony and innocence in these two true statements that couldn't fit together but that coexisted simultaneously somehow. Clearly he does want the company of his devotees, and he clearly wants to be left alone. One could take the nondualist approach and say that if one were really his devotee—a true disciple—then one would have such resonance with him that he would, in effect, be alone. But that was too much of a linear approach—an error of rationality. He seemed to be doing something much more powerful, more out of control. He was applying alchemical principles, mixing explosive ingredients, speaking in dangerous riddles.

After another two hands of bridge he left the room. The energetic impact of his paradoxical tirade had left me shaking and fully disarmed. What was he doing? It was impossible to say what he was doing on subtle levels. The challenge was to stay psychologically free of any reactivity and keep the mind out of it. The devastating power of clarity in his statement, "Leave me alone," seemed like a strange kind of epiphany of the past five days with the guru. Any misplaced and mistaken romantic ideas about the path that may have taken root during the "lovefest" at La Source Bleue were now burned away.

Tonight he appeared as a dancing *heruka*, a wild wisdom being, and had given everyone in the room an opportunity in those moments to enter into a relationship with him that was beyond the mind, beyond doubt, beyond illusion and romance, beyond rational and circumscribed behaviors. With the mind disarmed and reduced to its essence of emptiness, the heart could feel into what he was doing. It was like driving a car very fast to blow the carbon off the engine. It actually felt good in the body—in the wise innocence of the body, unencumbered or interfered with or polluted by the mind. The result was that he had made some room, some space, some clarity, where before there was a residue of psychic sludge.

September 28, 1999
La Ferme de Jutreau

Brinda and Clint sat down at the breakfast across the table from Lee. Brinda had a clipboard with several lists of things she was working on for Lee. She asked, "There are some projects we're considering for this winter. Is there anything in particular that you would like to see done this year?"

Lee shook his head no and answered, "No . . . just the case for the Primal Mother." Clint nodded.

After a few minutes of reviewing the list with Lee, Brinda asked, "Is it okay to do this now?" Lee laughed and said, "Taking care of practical business is the only thing I can do with my students with any equanimity!" He seemed to be referring to his wild outburst over bridge the night before. While everyone else sat eating and listening, Brinda and Lee covered several items on the list until Lee starting joking around with Brinda about making concrete paths around the property, one to the outhouses, one here, one there. The farcical scenario he painted of these "yellow brick roads" sounded incredibly awful. What if it got implemented just because he said it in a moment of incomprehensible fooling around? People shifted nervously in their seats. The beautiful ashram would be made into a carnival sideshow if such a thing was done. Lee wouldn't hesitate to do that if it would bring his students to clarity. He laughed and concluded the conversation saying to Brinda and Clint, "I leave it all to you!"

He was smiling as he went on to work with one person or another sitting at the table, and then joked mercilessly about himself. Someone brought up his comments from last night over bridge. "I didn't mean any of you," he said, once again in the charming tone, "you're all my *darling* children!" He paused, "But I'm a nineteenth century guru!" He laughed and slipped easily into character, pretending to wield an invisible ruler and hitting hands. "That's why Alrun likes me so much, I'm just like her father." Alrun, who was sitting across from Lee, turned red and laughed. " 'No, children, you cannot do that!' " Lee poked fun at our projections on him as he spoke this like a patriarch, in a stiff, cold, forbidding German accent. Then he dropped the posture and laughed lightly.

This morning Lee was continually referring to last night's episode in the salon over bridge. His joking at breakfast seemed rather like a healing balm, but at the same time he was continuing in the half-kidding, half-serious tone, drawing everyone in and making them part of the play, while at the same time leaving heads spinning and questioning the underlying meaning of his throwaway, theatrical schtick. For the past three days a number of people have been walking around with eyes swollen from crying. The *rasa* that had been felt by everyone at La Source Bleue had dissolved some of the hard and encrusted places, but the devastating effects of the alchemy that Lee had created and sustained with his devotees during the summer was coming to a peak. It is a necessary and purposeful devastation—that is, the dissolution of the false personality and the forging of gold from lead. It involves high heat, the churning, breaking down and combining of elements, the salt and sulfur and mercurial change, the unsettling and disarming quicksilver of a delicate and sometimes agonizing inner alchemy. Lee does all this in actions that are often unfathomable.

After breakfast Brinda and Clint brought a gorgeous black and gold silk sari into the office to show Lee. It was a gift to the ashram from Marcus. Lee instructed Brinda to make the solid black part with gold peacock brocade trim a cover to drape the front of the armoire which is now Lee's permanent book display in the salon of the main house. A more ornate piece of the sari, black with many rows of golden rectangles—peacocks woven into delicate brocade designs—Lee wanted made into a hanging curtain to cover the *thangka* of Vajrakilaya that hangs above his desk. It will be covered for the next nine months while Lee is in Arizona. Brinda and Clint took in the details of his instructions and left to begin their tasks.

At lunch Jane asked Lee if he was going to rest after lunch. "Yes," he said, taking a bite of the copious green salad piled high on his plate. He added in a dry tone of voice, "I have to rest up for *tea* this afternoon!"

"Oh I'm sure Claire will probably just serve a little tea and something light," someone said.

Jane countered, turning to Lee, "I don't know—you told her to go ahead with whatever she had planned to do. She'll do what you told her to do."

Lee looked at Brinda and said, "Will she do what I told her to do? Nobody does what I tell them to do except Brinda!" Brinda turned slightly pink. Lee went on, "Look at Brinda—she can't stand to get a compliment! Everybody else is just dying for a compliment. They're hanging under my window, scratching their nails on the walls, crying, 'Give me a compliment, give me a compliment!' Not Brinda." He looked at her and smiled.

She smiled back at him, somewhere between embarrassed and self-revealed. He'd been relentlessly working with her all summer, giving her many compliments and empowerments and at the same time a lot of feedback, practically watching every move she made.

"I'm just really confused, I don't know what to do or say or think," she laughed.

Lee rejoined playfully, "Your *ego* doesn't need to know what to do, say or think—*you* will know."

Brinda's face was tired but radiant. The stress of the summer showed in visible ways, but it seemed like an enhancement of her being and her physical person, rather than a downward pull. Lee had created a circumstance that had placed tremendous demands on everyone, and particularly on those who were willing and able to take on greater responsibilities in relationship to his work.

Now he tapped his glass to get everyone's attention. "Any announcements?" he queried, going through the daily ritual. "After Dinner Talk tonight and tomorrow night, chanting here at five-thirty tonight and tomorrow night. And no tea. Jai Guru!"

At three-fifteen Lee left with a small entourage to go to tea at the apartment of Claire and Volkmar in the nearby village of Angles. Even though Lee had made it clear that it was not his preference to do this kind of thing anymore, during the visit he was placid and kind—the perfect guest. He partook of the refreshments of cakes and tea, talked quietly with Volkmar and Claire, and stayed for an hour and a half. At five o'clock he said very elegantly, "If you'll excuse us, we have to get back to the ashram for chanting."

Walking out to the van I asked Claire what her reaction had been to Lee's teaching of the night before about this tea event. She said, "Oh, at first I was devastated, really devastated. But then . . ." she smiled and shrugged as if to indicate that she had gone through some process of assimilating or deeply considering the whole thing. "I just feel gratitude."

September 29, 1999
La Ferme de Jutreau

It was another chilly gray morning on the ashram. As we walked across the grass on the way to breakfast the gardens were particularly alive and vivid. It had rained during the night again, and the grass and flowers were spun with silver drops scattered in perfect symmetry. They shook like small round mirrors when the breeze lilted through.

Lee was at his desk reading under the small lamp after breakfast. Therese, who had come in last night from Bretagne (Brittany) just for the last two days before Lee leaves, walked in and asked if she could talk with him. She was hoping that she could somehow be squeezed into the seminar in Paris at Maison Raphael, but there have been some difficulties. There was no place for another person to stay because Lee was already taking over twenty people to Maison Raphael. Every year he brings more and more, and his hosts kindly stretch to accommodate him. But there is, at some point, a physical limit for even the most magnanimous hosts. He looked up at Therese and said, "Yes?"

"Can you see anything about my right eye?" she asked, referring to the health problems she has been having.

"That's not one of my jobs," Lee said. It was a simple statement. No embellishments or explanations. It should have been obvious—it was to him.

"Yes but I thought you might . . ." her voice trailed off as she took this in. She stood looking at Lee. There was another question working its way to the surface.

"About Jeanne?" She asked about a woman she knows who thinks she is a student of Lee's, but in fact is not and has been asked not to come to the ashram. This woman, Jeanne, had been at the recent seminar at La Source Bleue.

Lee answered in a voice so sober that as he spoke every syllable in each word seemed to dig into the ground. "There is nothing I can do to help Jeanne. Jesus Christ couldn't help her. She is stubborn, she is closed. It's impossible to help her. She needs serious psychotherapy. She's a very sick woman. She doesn't belong on the path; she's totally unprepared. She has no capacity to work." Lee was being crystal clear—there could be no question about his meaning. Therese nodded in comprehension.

"So if she phones me?" she asked. It was the most practical and possibly the most important question she had asked so far.

"Tell her she is not my student. I am *not* her teacher. I am not, and I will not be. She is not my student and she never will be, not in this lifetime, period. *Fini. Pas d'espoir. De rien. Jeanne est morte* to me." He pounded the desk with his fist lightly but firmly and slowly in time with his words for emphasis.

Therese said, "Thank you."

"Anytime," Lee responded mildly.

"Any time?" she asked, not understanding the English idiom.

He explained, " 'Thank you,' you said, and I said, 'Anytime.' "

About five minutes after Therese walked out Lee said, "She's probably having difficulty with her right eye because of me. It's the right side of her body . . . a man she can't see. I'm the man she can't see." He shook his head and went back to his book. He was speaking about how the body always demonstrates in its symptoms and processes the state of the soul—the right side of the body is traditionally considered the masculine side, the left side of the body is the feminine side. His comment was exactly the piece of information she was asking for in her question to him. It seemed to be something that he intended for her to find out for herself.

But it also seemed to me that in the act of voicing it, of putting it to words and speaking it out loud, Lee had directly given her the help she had asked for. It would be up to her now to find it within herself, where it was all along but was now vibrating and alive with the guru's attention. All she had to do was go inside and ask for clarity, but in a mood of total self-honesty. To find something like that out for oneself, through the arduous work of self-reflection, of digging in deep within the soil of one's own psyche and seeing the motivations, the projections and expectations of the psychological labyrinth, has a possibility of making a lasting impact. It has the possibility of being a piece of transformational work for the student, whereas if the guru handed the information out like a piece of candy, it would mean virtually nothing.

So often this is true in relationship with the guru. Ego wants to be appeased with these little things—another form of self-gratification. "Just give me the answer," or "Give me the recognition, the compliment," or whatever it might be that one craves from the guru. So often the guru must say no. Usually Lee says nothing. He is a master of forbearance and tolerance. He just sits and gazes at the questioner, turns them away artfully, or casts them back upon themselves, as he did with Therese. But these are acts of compassion. It forces one to do the necessary work that will ignite the fires of real transformation. Otherwise, it is just another fleeting moment of self-gratification, another transitory pleasure; once the momentary sweetness is sucked from it, it is gone as if it had never existed.

Around ten-thirty he cleaned his desk off and covered the *thangka*, Vajrakilaya, with its new black and gold brocade silk covering that Brinda made yesterday from the sari. As he placed the few pieces that would remain on his mostly empty desk during the winter Mariana looked at the plaster headless Jesus. She said, "Where did you get that?"

Lee answered, "It was a gift. An amazing piece of bad taste."

Lee quickly and efficiently put his desk into order, most of it packed away in the drawers or thrown away in preparation for his imminent departure. A little later Therese came back into the room. Lee looked up at her and smiled. "See my desk, Therese?"

"Yes . . ." she said, more a question than an answer as she gazed at the empty expanse of Lee's usually cluttered desk.

"It's all cleaned off. That means I'm leaving Europe," he said gently. She gave him a wistful smile. It was a moment of rapport between them; it seemed like Lee was acknowledging the sadness she was so obviously feeling at his departure, the reason why she had driven all the way to the ashram for such a short visit.

The air was thick with the bittersweet flavor of endings. Outside the office windows the red maple tree was beginning to lose its leaves. Many of them lay scattered across the green grass, curled and brown with a tinge of yellow gold here and there. The autumn wind tossed the branches of the tree under the cloudy gray weight of the sky. The ashram seemed to ache with beauty. The flower gardens were having a last furious fit of blossoming before the frosts would start to come. Bits of color glowed vividly all around the courtyard in the damp air as the beautiful dahlias burst out again in concert like stars and mandalas in their perfect symmetry—red, orange, yellow, violet, white and maroon.

Somehow the cloudy day seemed to conspire with the burning presence of the ashram and the sure knowledge of winter coming on to bring nature into a vibrancy that was startling and at the same time poignant. The tall autumn sunflowers still bloomed in profusion, and in the terraced vegetable garden the copious cayenne peppers in their mulched straw beds hung heavy from green bending stalks. Their deep red glossy splendor was the first thing one could see walking into the garden from the stone passageway between the two houses. The pumpkins and winter squashes—orange and gold and brown—dotted the ground here and there, while flame-red nasturtium blossoms glowed jewel-like, nestled in the lively round green leaves that grew in hummocks to mark the white limestone borders of the garden terraces. The garden itself transmitted the teaching: the most sublime beauty we experience in this earthly realm is transitory. The fact that such beauty appears and disappears causes the heart to be pierced, broken open, devastated with longing for that which is beyond appearances, beyond the processes of birth and death.

The garden crew had spent the morning gathering apples from the orchard, and now the cellar pantry was filled with a half-dozen large buckets and another dozen crates of crisp red and yellow apples. In the barn dining room there were large bowls full of walnuts, just fallen from the orchard trees and waiting to dry and be cracked and eaten fresh during the winter. The harvest was in, and in many different ways, on different levels. The harvest of the Work that had been done over the summer was being gathered, and would be brought with Lee back to Arizona, to his students there. But the effects of that gathering and harvesting, then the preparing, cooking, eating, digesting, assimilating of all this life would go on and have much further reverberations and ripple effects, imagined and unimaginable in many realms.

Everyone walked around in warm wool sweaters. Last-minute preparations for leaving for Paris in the morning were being made. At lunch the group of about twenty-five people gathered in the barn. Alrun served a beautiful repast of chickpeas in a thick tomato curry sauce, brown rice, steamed spinach, cucumber and yogurt *raita* with toasted black mustard seeds, green salad from the garden.

Lee joked lightly with people over lunch. His mood was tranquil and smooth. There were no fireworks, no grand teaching lessons. He just seemed to be enjoying the moments as they flowed past. After announcements he said, "Chanting, at five-thirty, here. After Dinner Talk tonight. Jai Guru!" He got up and left, stopping by the buffet table to survey the leftover food, as he usually does. Then he was out the door.

Tomorrow morning Lee will leave with thirteen people in one of the vans and a car for Paris. A number of people will drive to Paris the day after that in the second van to meet Lee for the last seminar of the summer. The next five days will be spent in Paris at Maison Raphael, a center for psychotherapy and "lyings" run by Christophe Massin and Sylvie Peytel, disciples of Arnaud Desjardins, and Bernard Pernel, a friend of Lee's and the community. For the past two days people had been packing up their belongings and preparing for the trip back to Arizona. While many last-minute details of Lee's departure were being attended to the ashram was very peaceful. A natural and easy transition was underway.

September 30, 1999
On the road

The group was scheduled to leave with Lee at seven o'clock in the morning. He had said to have the baggage ready to pack in the van by six forty-five. At six-thirty he sent someone around the ashram with a message: he wanted all the duffel bags and luggage downstairs pronto! Lee often decides at the last minute that he wants to leave ten or fifteen minutes earlier than he originally indicated, so one learns—usually the hard way, over time—to be prepared for anything. He was downstairs in the predawn dark, hauling heavy bags around and directing the loading into the two vehicles that were pulled up to the front door. It was slightly misty and threatening to rain as the vehicles were loaded. All the ashram residents were up, either helping Lee carry the heavy bags and load them into the van or waiting for the opportunity to say goodbye until next year.

At six forty-five the van and car drove off. As Lee maneuvered the van from the yard onto the driveway, he looked at the gas tank. "No gas," he commented dryly. It is one of his pet peeves to get in the van to start out on the road and find the gas tank low or on empty, which forces him to have to stop right away and get gas. Usually someone makes sure that the gas tanks of the vehicles are full whenever Lee is scheduled to head out on a trip, a task that had been overlooked for this trip.

Pulling out onto the road the rain started pouring. It was still pitch black. Lee said, "That was a blessing—it waited to rain until we got the van loaded." Thirty minutes later Lee was buying bread for the picnic brunch at the *confiserie* in Chatellerault. Luckily the rain had stopped as he came out carrying bags of round loaves and warm and fragrant baguettes. Settling back into the driver's seat, he steered the van toward the *autoroute*. As the van sped down the highway at a steady clip I asked, "Are you looking forward to being back in Arizona?"

"Yes," Lee said. At first it seemed like that was all he was going to say, then he added, "Wherever the ashram is—that's where I want to be and look forward to being. And the band. Wherever there is work going on." He seemed to be mulling the question over further, and continued, "It would be nice to be out of America at some point. I've been looking for a bigger ashram, but nothing has shown up yet, so I've been considering that it may mean we're not supposed to be in America. Time will tell."

I said, "Sometimes its hard to imagine Shri still performing, you know, ten years from now. It's even harder to imagine you at seventy, coming out onstage and doing the blues thing, like many old blues singers do. Do you think Western Baul music will continue after Shri—that there will continue to be more bands, like Attila the Hunza?"

Lee said, "I'm sure once Shri is finished I'll completely lose interest in it, ten years from now. Maybe Shri will last another ten years. But at seventy—no, I don't see myself being with the band and performing onstage. Then I'll be giving small seminars to select groups, giving talks, writing books, publishing articles. Maybe I'll get inspired and do some more writing at that point. I'm so lazy though, I can't imagine it," he shrugged, "but who knows? Maybe I'll get inspired . . . You know, Sir Richard Burton wrote two, three-volume books in two months *by hand*." He glanced over at me piercingly. My laptop was snuggled in its padded leather case on the floor in the back of the van.

He went on, "We're all just *whiners*. That's how much we've lost with computers. It's a huge loss. In the next fifty years we'll have no racial memory left, nothing." It was a dire and depressing statement, but it seemed to melt into the miles as the van sped along.

The night had given way to a glorious morning as the pouring rain stopped. The eastern sky was now full of stratocumulus clouds that glowed with morning light, a lambent ivory with wisps of pale gray riding over them. A wide blue sky stretched out directly overhead, but at the northern horizon there were heavy bands of dark blue-gray rain clouds. Lee pulled over to get gas.

As Lee drove the van out of the parking lot of the gas station he said, "We'll stop for brunch in about an hour." Fifteen minutes later, eyeing the menacing storm clouds on the horizon in the direction in which we were traveling, Lee pulled into a rest stop with a picnic area. It was eight-thirty. "Let's eat!" he enthused. We had a windy, very chilly early brunch of egg salad, tuna salad, raw vegetables, fresh bread. It was the only meal we would have until dinner, around six o'clock.

After a stop at Fountainbleau to visit the grave of Gurdjieff, Lee pulled into Paris around one-thirty in the afternoon. He drove to the Montparnasse area, found a place to park and walked along with his troup past theatres and sex shops and restaurants to the Café La Liberté on the corner of Rue de la Gaite. There he planned to meet Muriel Maisl, a disciple of Arnaud Desjardins, and Philippe Coupey, an American Zen Buddhist, meditation teacher and long-time disciple of Taisen Deshimaru who has lived in France for over twenty-five years.

Taking a table near the street corner, Lee sat down to wait. Philippe arrived very shortly and embraced Lee. They have known each other for several years, their connection beginning with Hohm Press publishing *Sit—Zen Teachings of Master Taisen Deshimaru*, translated and edited by Philippe. The book was a labor of love for Philippe, who knew and practiced closely with Deshimaru for ten years, from 1972 to 1982 when Deshimaru died.

The day was overcast and gray with occasional drops of rain. A magazine kiosk on the busy corner near the café tables drew a number of passersby on the Rue de la Gaite. The street was lined with chestnut trees; their leaves were turning brown, and mingled with the green and flowering acacia trees. Pigeons flew down the boulevard and landed nearby to hunt and peck. As they sat down to talk Lee ordered Perrier and Philippe ordered coffee.

Philippe turned to Lee, "So how is it in Jutreau?"

"Very good," Lee answered. "We had a number of people here this summer. We're starting to get seminars going year-round there, and we have a solid group of people who live there." Philippe mentioned that his group has a new center in Paris and about thirty people living at Gendarniere, the country zendo of Deshimaru where his *samadhi* site is located. Philippe laughed and said, "We're always busy, busy, busy with construction at Gendarniere. Always making improvements. Once it's perfect—then what?" He laughed and shrugged.

The conversation went on to Buddhism in the West, about Japanese Zen masters supporting the Nazi sentiment during WWII and anti-Semitism in Buddhism. Philippe said, "The Americans are very apologetic. 'Oh, we're so sorry our master did this or that. We hang our heads in shame!' " He was referring to the scandal that accuses Yasutani, a well-known Japanese Zen master, of being a pro-Nazi, pro-Emperor and anti-Semitic and racist. He said, "It's very upsetting for Zen Buddhists in America because their line comes from Yasutani, and many of the American Buddhists are Jews, like Bernie Glassman. I like the way *he* talks about it, but I find it very spineless of the Americans in general."

I asked, "How would Deshimaru have responded to the whole thing?"

Philippe threw his head back and laughed. "Deshimaru! Deshimaru would have just . . ." he waved his hand as if to dismiss the whole thing as totally ludicrous. Then he shrugged. "Deshimaru just happened to have been very clear of all that kind of thing, but . . . We're not looking to do good like all the Americans. We still have the tip on the point of the spear. They've taken the tip off the point of the spear in America. They've abolished other use of the stick."

Lee said, "The American Buddhists are terrified of anything they consider to be abuse. There is all the political rhetoric, and the essence of the tradition is getting farther and farther away."

Philippe reflected, "I think the Deshimaru line will become more accepted in the years ahead in the States because our practice is more strict. We will become more popular because of that, sooner or later, as the pendulum swings."

Lee asked, "Do you know of Sasaki Roshi?"

Philippe said, "Yes, of course, the master of Leonard Cohen. They are Rinzai Zen, but they sit for twenty-five hours out of twenty-four! Incredible! Their practice is just unbelievable. Everything I've read about Leonard Cohen is so interesting."

Lee continued, "Yes, he's refreshing. Most of the Zen Buddhists are following the party line now, the political rhetoric, but he is really his own person."

Jan asked, "Even though they have a long sitting practice, would you say that your school is more rigorous?"

Philippe answered, "In the Soto school we are very rigorous. We consider our practice a lifelong practice. What other schools call 'lay disciples' we don't even have. We don't make a difference between monks and people who live a 'normal' life. A new direction is being created by us—we're not making that separation at all. We don't have those terms, 'I'm a monk,' or the idea of a social world being separate from practice. Who isn't in the social world? We all consider ourselves to be true monks. In ancient times there were no monasteries, just dojos.

"No, our *real* problem—to use the words of the Buddha or Deshimaru—our problem is, are we really *living* this teaching? Our word is 'No object.' We don't practice to gain power. The question is, are we really living up to what we preach? This is to me the problem."

Muriel arrived and Lee stopped to greet her as she joined the group. Philippe asked how Andrew Cohen was doing. Lee answered, "Andrew is very well, traveling a great deal and teaching. He's very successful at what he is doing. And yes, he is very strict. People don't like him because he criticizes other teachers so fiercely. Some people are hoping there will be a scandal around him because of his strong moral stance. It's terrible."

Philippe continued, "Deshimaru didn't hesitate to criticize other schools, other groups—the Yasutani line, the Tibetans. I didn't censor that in [*Sit*], and I could have. This is one of the reasons why it rubs the Americans the wrong way. In France I had to take out some of what Deshimaru said about psychology. Maybe in fifteen or twenty years this criticism will be more acceptable.

"They put these Zen masters on a pedestal and don't want them to make any mistakes. Lots of scandals come up in the States, but we've never had any scandals. We have problems over personalities, over character . . . One of the first three [empowered disciples] of Deshimaru claimed to be the only master after Deshimaru died. The group threw him out. We'd be singing the Heart Sutra and he'd start singing a communist liberation song! He split with his disciples . . ."

Lee laughed, "I'll bet his disciples thought that was great!"

Philippe smiled, "Oh yes. You know, they were looking at him like, 'There is the most enlightened person in the world!' " They both laughed at the absurdity of it. Philippe continued, "So, are there interesting things happening in the States?"

"There's nothing exciting going on in the States," Lee answered. "Scandals over sex, sometimes money, those things are happening, but nobody really exciting has come on the scene as a spiritual teacher."

Philippe said, "You once talked to me about a roshi who you sent a copy of *Sit* to— Kwong Roshi? How is he?"

"He's great. I just saw him last winter. He was accused of some scandal last year, some ridiculous thing. It's hard to believe—someone as kind and with as much integrity as him." Lee shook his head in disbelief.

Philippe nodded and said, "That's the problem with democracy!" He talked about a new book that has come out called *Ambivalent Zen,* a contradiction in terms. That seemed to symbolize the crux of the problem.

"The faith that just comes, thanks to God—people just don't seem to have it," Phillipe went on. "Without that faith you got no motor. And Arnaud Desjardins? How is he?"

"Arnaud is great!" Lee answered enthusiastically. "He is doing really well. I was at Hauteville with him this summer for a week. It was fantastic." The conversation moved on to Lee's new book in French, *N'essayez Pas—Vivez.*"

Sparking on the title, which translates as *Don't Try—Just Live,* Phillipe laughed, "Just the opposite of ambivalent!" They talked awhile longer, exchanging news, talking about their respective schedules, about Lee's seminars in Europe and the *sesshins* Phillipe would be leading. The visit came to a close, they embraced goodbye and Lee took off for dinner at a nearby pizzeria with his entourage.

October 1, 1999
Paris

After a private meeting during the morning, Lee met with some of his students and François Fronty in Montmartre for lunch at Deben Bhattacharya's home on the Rue de Lepic. As gracious and elegant as ever, Deben greeted everyone with refreshments and Sufi music he had just recorded in Banaras in January, 1999. The lyrics were in Urdu, and Deben kept exclaiming over the beauty of the poetry.

"Incredible lyrics," he said, obviously moved by the music, "things like, 'They put me under the earth / and no one came to see / This is how my end came.' Beautiful poetry! I recorded it one night in Banaras. They were going to record at the tomb of a Sufi sage, their teacher, but there was a storm so strong it was impossible. So I brought them to my family home in the old part of the city. The storm was raging outside!" His eyes glowed as he remembered the scene. His passion for his work was highly infectious, and the music that flooded the small living room was immediately mesmerizing. It lifted the whole space into a realm of mystery and longing.

He continued the story, saying, "The Sufis had asked for five thousand rupees for the recording. I came to Banaras and met them and made the arrangements; I got all the rupees plus some more because I understood that the tradition was to offer money whenever the music was particularly inspired. When the musicians would hit a peak, one would reach over and place a few rupees, an offering, on the floor." Deben gestured in a way to indicate that the offering of money should be given very discreetly and elegantly.

"We had a wonderful evening. Afterward I offered the five thousand they had asked for to begin with and they said no! They wouldn't take it! They said, 'No, it has been such a lovely evening with you that we can't take the money.' Finally they took fifteen hundred rupees." Deben sat back and looked around at his guests to emphasize his message. It was a story that demonstrated the integrity the Sufis had as musicians representing their tradition of sacred music. Suddenly Deben turned to Lee, who sat cross-legged and barefoot in the middle of the couch. "I'd like to do a Sufi record for you like the Bauls. Are you interested?"

Without a second of hesitation Lee answered firmly, "Yes." No qualifications, no questions.

Deben said, "Let me know when you would like to have it."

Lee smiled, "I want it as soon as you can have it!" Everyone laughed, Deben perhaps especially so. He leaned back on the padded ottoman where he sat next to Lee and laughed, his chuckles trailing off. He explained that he would be going back to India in January 2000 and there were several groups he had lined up to record at that time.

He said, "It's a deal then!" Lee leaned toward Deben with his hand outstretched and they shook on it. Deben got up to check on lunch and then went to answer a phone call. Jane gave Lee a message that had come in to Maison Raphael that morning from Japan. Two of Lee's students had called the ashram. There had been a nuclear accident only fifty kilometers away from their home. They were concerned and wanted Lee to know the details. Jane commented to François that Lee had talked a number of times over the summer about the increase of earthquakes, nuclear accidents and natural catastrophes as part of the Earth ridding herself of the parasitic elements of human culture. In the last few weeks there had been terrible earthquakes in Turkey and in Mexico. François asked Lee, "Do you think it's just beginning?"

Lee answered, "Yes, it's just beginning. But people will die in earthquakes still typing away on their computers, getting their last moment of time in on the Internet, totally lost in the subjectivity of their illusions!" Lee's pronouncements sliced across the atmosphere like a scimitar, something one could easily imagine hanging on the walls of this room, along with the many musical instruments. The floor was covered with colorful hand-woven Bedouin carpets; Rajasthani prints hung on the walls. The sublime mood of the Sufi music suffused the atmosphere.

Deben returned and sat down. He looked at Lee and said, "You come from the States and you bring the States with you! It was a phone call from someone there." Deben began to talk about the few true Bauls who are left in Bengal. He said that their children are very smart, wear Western trousers and want money, fame. The whole tradition is degenerating, he said sadly.

I asked, "So is it the end of a five hundred-year-old tradition?"

Deben looked at me with surprise. "Oh no! In a country where reincarnation is a fact, nothing ends like that! Whether reincarnation is true or not doesn't matter—it's in your mind." He shook his head, "Oh no, it will show up again somewhere. Who would have known two generations ago that you would be calling yourself an American Baul?" He turned to Lee and smiled. "Someone once told me a definition of a Baul—someone who is affected by the wind, who is mad, completely mad. I've never forgotten that description. How did you get involved with the Bauls?" he asked Lee.

Lee answered, "I'd been working with my students for years and certain practices started spontaneously arising. Then I read a book by Das Gupta called *Obscure Religious Cults*. He wrote about the Bauls and when I read it I said, 'This is exactly what we are doing!' So in 1986 some of my students went to Calcutta looking for Bauls and they met Sanatan Das. Then five years later we set up a tour for Sanatan Das and his sons in the U.S. We arranged everything for them; we set things up with colleges, different cultural centers and so on. So they came to America and we became very close. I traveled with Sanatan Das on tour as much as I could. He came into our office and picked up a tape of liars, gods & beggars, our rock band, and said, 'American Baul music!' That was it. "

Jane asked Deben about how the music of the Bauls was composed. He said, "Different groups have their own style. This is how music is developed in living traditions: one is humming a tune, then suddenly someone is accompanying, a drum here, an instrument there. It grows without effort. For weddings and things the musicians are invited to play, they earn a little money."

Lee said, "When Sanatan came and we toured with him, there was never a request for money. He only received that which was offered as gifts."

Deben began to talk about Purna Das, a famous Baul who has performed a great deal in the West, and his father Nabanidas. "I have seen Nabanidas sing in the public park in Calcutta in front of two thousand people, with Purna Das standing nearby, maybe fifteen years old, playing the *gugubi*. The entire crowd was absolutely enchanted and held under the grip of that broken voice of his . . ." He went on to describe the rough, gritty and soulful quality of Nabanidas' voice, and how compelling it was.

"That was in 1954 at the All Bengali Music Festival. It was my first recording of Nabanidas," Deben continued. "Then Nabanidas said, 'Come to my village, I will sing for you, I will give all my songs to you.' His village was just two straw huts. We were there ten, twelve days. We were working on a shoestring budget, we had no money. Nabanidas had been going out every morning singing and begging to feed us. So we scraped together twenty rupees and Richard [the photographer] took it to Nabanidas. Richard came back saying, 'I've done something to offend Nabanidas—you should go talk to him, Deben.' So I went to him and Nabanidas said to me, 'How long have you been in England?' I said, 'Four years.' 'You've become an Englishman!' he said. 'I am a beggar, but I don't run a hotel. I can't take money for this poor rice and dahl you have eaten here!' "

We were all sitting on the edge of our seats absorbing Deben's story. He had transported us to the Bengali village of Nabanidas, and now we wanted to hear what happened next. His eyes were wide as he continued, the memory completely alive and powerful for him, "I felt I had been slapped! I said, 'I'm sorry!' "

It reminded me very much of the story he had told earlier about the Sufis he'd just recorded; Nabanidas too reflected the principles of his tradition with integrity. Bauls consider their begging to be a sacred act, and have a deep relationship to the Laws of Hospitality. Nabanidas was offended because his integrity had been put in question. But more importantly, he made a fantastic teaching lesson for his guests.

Deben turned to Lee and said, "Come to Banaras when I am there one time! Of course, it doesn't have the same atmosphere anymore. It's not the same as it was then . . ."

Lee said, "That would be great. I won't be traveling in India this year, I'll just go to Tiruvannamalai, but perhaps some time in the future I will be back in Banaras. We've seen a very big change in India, between 1976 and now. There has been a big change between 1986 and 1998. All the hippies and dope addicts and people who think they are sadhus in Banaras—but they're aren't sadhus, they're just dirty Westerners. It's become very commercial."

A delicious lunch of Indian food was served by a young woman, a close friend of Deben's daughter, a member of the Bhattacharya's extended family. Lingering after lunch over coffee and dessert, several people in Lee's party began to ply Deben with questions about his unique and quite incredible life. He was born and raised in Banaras, and he laughed wonderingly as he said, "I've never been to school anywhere in my life. At thirteen, fourteen, fifteen, I used to run away from home! My only schooling was the alphabet. How I got this wandering spirit from this traditional Brahmanic upbringing, I don't know! I would just get on the train and go until the conductor came and pulled me by the ear and threw me off. I spent several years like that.

"When I landed in England I had eighteen shillings in my pocket and a friend. He is still a friend, a professor emeritus in England. He was my connection to Europe, and out of India. When I first met him I was fighting the English with guns! I was working as a journalist in Banaras and had learned some English. A friend of mine wanted me to meet this man and I said, 'Why do you dump this Englishman on my head?' He was a captain in the English army! But he was a decent man, and my friend convinced me to meet him.

"My father was an Ayurvedic doctor, and all my uncles were Sanskrit scholars. I would have stayed a Brahmin Sanskrit scholar in Banaras, but I met the English poet, Louis Thompson there. Just through a series of coincidences I began recording music. No one had recorded the gypsies until I did. They were my first recording here in France. It was 1955 when I first recorded the gypsy guitar player, Maneta De Platé. He sued the record company, said I had stolen his music, recorded without permission! But a friend of mine had taken a photograph while he was playing with the microphone right there in front of the guitar and Maneta De Platé looking at me. Obviously I was recording with his permission. But it was the last time I recorded him!" Deben chuckled.

Deben described how he had followed the gypsies from France to India in his quest to answer many questions about the origins of the gypsies and their culture. For example, why did the European gypsies (Gitan) become blacksmiths?

He talked about his time traveling and recording musicians in Afghanistan, "Always on a shoe-string budget," he laughed. "Every ten kilometers we'd have a tire puncture, in Afghanistan, in the Middle East. But everywhere we went people helped us. You had real friendship in those days, in 1954-55." He recounted many things about his time in the Middle East and laughed about eating the grilled eyeballs and testicles of camels. It was one thing that he couldn't quite embrace. He spoke with deep sorrow and anger about the repression of women in modern Afghanistan and the political situation there.

While Deben was talking he had passed around a number of things for everyone to look at, one of which was a recently published, hardbound coffee table photojournal, *Benaras Seen From Within,* by his old friend and photographer, Richard Lannoy. In the back of this beautiful book were some fragments of poems written by Lewis Thompson, which a number of people noticed. When asked, Deben spoke again of his friend, Lewis Thompson, who lived in Deben's family home in Banaras for seven or eight years. He was forty years old when he died of sunstroke; it was 1956. A natural mystic, he had a deep rapport with the Indian people and in fact lived off charity all the last years of his life. Deben brought out a copy of Thompson's only published work, titled *Mirror to the Light—Reflections on Consciousness and Experience.*

Someone asked for the second time today, "So how did you get into these incredible situations, how did you get the traditional tribal people to allow you to record their music?" The first time the question was asked Deben had smiled and said, "That's *my* secret!" Now his eyes beamed as he said, "I'll tell you my secret. The secret is, be a fool, be a Baul. If you submit yourself, then people will open up to you."

The book of Lewis Thompson's writings had been passed over to Lee. He had been listening to Deben and looking through the book at the same time. Now he said, "Listen to this," and started reading a quote from Lewis Thompson: " 'Need of love is the demand for ratification by others of feebleness, laziness, lack of authority. It is the betrayal of love by unconscious egoism.'" (p. 151) Lee looked up at his students and said, "That's fabulous! There's a man I can relate to."

Deben said, "Lee, if only you had met that man! There was an electric quality to that mind!" Lee commented that Thompson's comments in the book on innocence and sex sounded a lot like Wilhelm Reich, the radical psychologist who died in prison for his revolutionary ideas concerning the human body, sexuality and spirituality.

The afternoon came to a close and Lee got up to leave. It had been an extraordinary time with a remarkable man, whose contribution to world spiritual culture was inestimable. Deben Bhattacharya told us that he would turn eighty next year, in the millennium. He has produced one hundred and twenty-eight albums of folk, classical and sacred music, recorded in nearly thirty countries of Asia and Europe. It was a tremendous honor to visit him, to have the opportunity to sit with him and gather stories. Lee's whole party was tremendously moved by the experience of meeting him.

Standing in the room near the hallway that led to the front door to the apartment, Lee said to his students, "It's time to go." People stood around, smiling, bumping into each other, saying goodbye to Deben, lingering and dragging things out. Lee repeated, "It's time to go." Still no movement toward the door. Finally he shouted in pure frustration, "Let's go!" A couple of people made a beeline for the door and slowly the rest of the train began to follow, finally leaving Lee some space to say goodbye to his friend and host.

Lee took the Metro (subway) across Paris to Maison Raphael in the suburb of Boulogne, where he was greeted by Christophe, Sylvie and Bernard before rejoining the rest of his traveling party in the downstairs *grande salle* (main room) where the seminar would be held. The room would also double as a dining room for all of the meals during the weekend. Immediately Lee began to set up his book table in a small adjoining room, then returned to the *grande salle* and perched on a low chair. Some of his students, along with FrançoisFronty and a few of the Parisian guests, gathered around him on the floor. Alain René arrived and greeted Lee; he would be translating for the weekend.

Paula Z. walked in and sat down. She had been at the afternoon visit with Deben Bhattacharya and now had some questions for Lee about her participation in that event. She said, "My tendency is to just sit back and be quiet, to let other people do all the talking or asking questions. You invite us to participate in things like that, and I wonder if just being silent is the right thing. How can one be useful in those circumstances?"

Lee spoke sharply, "I don't bring people anywhere to be *useful,*" his tone turned slightly scornful on the word useful. "I bring people to places to *learn* something. You think I bring people to meet my peers to be *useful*?" He laughed.

"If you have a genuine question, then ask it, but if you just want to make a social comment, then often you end up looking dumb. If you have a sincere question, it's fine to speak. Thomas and Claus were very useful at the Dürckheim Center in Germany because they spoke the language and were familiar with the psychological technology used there. But generally speaking, if I wanted people to be useful then I would send them and I would stay home!" Lee laughed again.

More of Lee's students and friends from Paris arrived and began to gather around Lee. As he talked quietly with a few people he mentioned that Brinda and Ann, who went to park Brinda's car, had been gone for over thirty minutes. When Clint, Brinda's husband, arrived Lee called him over and said forcefully, "Clint! Brinda's been gone four hundred times longer than she should have been gone to get a parking place. There were plenty of places right outside on the street. Go out and see if you can find her!" Clint walked out and Lee continued in a mild rant, "Oh ye of little faith! We always just assume things aren't going to work out, so we don't even look for parking places right on the street where we want to be. The street was loaded with parking places! We should write on the door of the ashram, 'Oh ye of little faith—welcome!' Everybody will say, 'What does that mean?' And then ten years later . . ." His voice trailed off as he rolled up his sleeves. Maybe in ten years someone would finally get it, but it would take ten years just to get something as obvious as that, he seemed to be saying. He concluded, "We make life difficult for ourselves and then we suffer under the burden."

Lee turned his attention to a list of sayings by Daniel Morin in French that François Fronty was translating into English. François conferred with Lee over the translation for a moment, their heads close together. As the time for dinner drew closer, several large tablecloths were laid out on the floor and set for about thirty-five people. At seven-thirty everyone gathered and sat down. It was a long, leisurely dinner of quiche and salad with many delicacies on the side, and the ubiquitous baguettes. There was much enjoyment and lively conversation as Christophe, Sylvie, Bernard and Marie-Noelle crowded in to sit around Lee.

Lee smiled at Sylvie and Christophe. "We should have a hot weekend!" he said. They smiled and translated Lee's metaphor into French, *"Très forte!"*

"Yes—strong, fiery," Lee added. "That's unusual!" he said with a chuckle.

On the wall behind where Lee sat on the floor were a series of photographs: a Tibetan rinpoche, Swami Prajnanpad, Amritanandamayi, Arnaud Desjardins, Lee Lozowick. Up high on the wall to Lee's right was a photograph of Anandamayi Ma; on the wall to his left was a Japanese brush painting. One of Lee's students asked him who the Tibetan rinpoche was. He said, "I'm not sure. He looks pretty enlightened, doesn't he? And that's Swami Prajnanpad," he pointed to the picture and then pointed across the room to the Japanese brush painting, "and that's bamboo. Very highly enlightened!" Everyone laughed, then Sylvie told Lee that in fact the painting was done by Graf Dürckheim. "Oh yes, it's very nice," he responded, looking at it closely. "I gave a talk this summer at the Dürckheim Center in Germany. It was a great talk . . . but they'll never have me back again!"

Sylvie asked, "Were they upset?"

"They weren't upset," Lee answered, "they were angry. They must have had some great group sessions after we left!" Lee laughed. He turned to Christophe to explain further. "On the outside it was calm and nice there, but on the inside very intense . . ." Just then the upstairs toilet was flushed and could be heard swishing and gurgling down the pipes that ran inside the walls of the house. Everyone laughed and Lee said, "There goes another ego!"

Alain René said, "If only it were that simple!"

Lee responded, "It could be."

Sylvie reminisced, "The first year you came here there was a flood! Do you remember?" Lee has been giving seminars at Maison Raphael every summer since its inception five years ago. Lee had first met Bernard and Christophe eight years ago on the visit to France in which he first met Arnaud Desjardins at Font d'Isière.

Lee changed the subject now, asking, "Is Andrew Cohen coming back this year?" Andrew had given a seminar at Maison Raphael last year, and three or four years ago Andrew and Lee had given an evening talk together there in the *grande salle*, which had been packed far beyond its capacity with about seventy-five people. Alain René said, "They cancelled Andrew's tour in Paris because he's too busy."

Lee threw his head back and laughed. "Maybe I'm not busy enough! Too bad, because I just gave someone his brochure for his November talk in Paris. Now maybe we'll see her back at our place. You can't get rid of them—send them to Andrew and he cancels his tour!" He laughed again as if he was enjoying the irony of the situation.

The group fell into a quiet spell—a long contemplative silence in which the moments were stretched out. Everyone sat unmoving around Lee, the remnants of the meal left in bowls—a little fruit salad, a larger portion of vegetable salad, some cheese and baguette scattered on the big, rectangular tablecloth.

Finally Lee slapped his hands on his thighs and bounced a little on his knees. He said, "Okay, everybody go home!" Everyone laughed, getting the message. "I don't know any polite way to say it," he laughed, got up and walked out, still chuckling.

October 2, 1999
Paris

The next morning Lee started his first talk of the weekend with about fifty people sitting on zafus on the floor of the *grande salle*. Beside his chair he had placed the *vigraha* of Yogi Ramsuratkumar. "I heard recently from someone that a friend had a goal of being enlightened," he began. "What a stupid goal! We should just want to be human! So this weekend is not going to be about enlightenment. Enlightenment is about being responsible. How many of you want to be responsible? Because being enlightened is being responsible for the entire world! You don't want to be responsible. You want to go eat when you want to, you want to have sex when you want to. Enlightenment is about responsibility, about being responsible for the entire world and about your personal wants being last on any list of responsibilities. Do you want to be responsible for everyone in this room, let alone the entire world? Look around you. You don't even want to be *sitting* next to some of these people, so never mind enlightenment. It sucks . . .

"Let's talk instead about becoming human and having some small degree of dignity. To be a human being, to have some honor, some dignity—that should be our goal. But look at the people you see on the streets of Paris. Paris is very dark, psychically dark. People are crazy, insane. People are driven mad by their unwillingness to just be human. When I was thirty-five years old I just said, 'Get enlightened!' to my students. I would shake them, throw them down! But after thirty years of students who swear they want to get enlightened but metaphorically cannot even wipe their asses, dignity and kindness are the name of the game—just some dignity and kindness.

"So if we can give a theme to the weekend it would probably be 'becoming human.' In order to follow the divine path to becoming human, you have to follow the human path to the Divine. It is how we *live* that makes us divine or not, and then from the viewpoint of the Divine you can finally become human at last. If we can define enlightenment then— which we can't—it could be 'ultimate humanness.' Ultimate humanness is not about escaping from the world. If you are honest with yourselves, for most of you the search is not about serving the world but about escaping from your responsibilities and from your suffering. None of us wants to suffer. There was just an earthquake in Mexico, one in Turkey, a nuclear accident in Japan; even if your life is perfect, if you have any dignity in you, you suffer for those whose homes are destroyed, those who are burned and mutated. You've got to suffer for those people. Suffering is part of life, and the more enlightened you are, the more you've got to suffer.

"If any of my students get enlightened it's going to break my heart. Liberation is such a weight I would wish it on my enemies, not on my friends. Becoming human is a result of enlightenment. We should not be under the illusion that enlightenment means we are free. Gurdjieff says you are literally a slave of identification or you are a slave of that Unity we call God. You are either a slave to suffering or a slave to responsibility. If we're here this weekend hoping to be enlightened I've got bad news. First of all I'm not the agent of anybody's enlightenment. I'm just a bookseller and a critic—a spiritual critic!

"I love people who criticize me. Not *you*, but other teachers! Rajneesh once spent an hour and a half criticizing me at one of his darshans. I have the tape of it!" Everyone laughed, as Lee said this with a child-like enthusiasm, as if he could prove his claims with the tape. He continued, "One of my spies sent it to me." More laughter. "I have spies everywhere! So be careful! I wrote Rajneesh a letter thanking him. I got a personal letter back inviting me to tea. Unfortunately, he died before I could get back to his ashram in India.

"I'm not sure I would have wanted to go to his ashram in Oregon—all those uzi's . . . scary! But the only thing scarier than the guns was who was holding them. They were all just like you and me—adolescents in adult bodies! Just think how you would be if you had absolute authority and your passion was fueled with paranoid fantasies about how the world was out to get you, and then they gave you a brand-new machine gun with all the ammunition you could want. Imagine *you* in that position. Would you be responsible? Would you care for your fellow human beings—those pigs, sheep, slugs, those *escargot*?" Everyone laughed again, the comedic moment a relief from the level of confrontation and brutal self-honesty that Lee was challenging the audience to embrace. His words were searing into the fabric of whatever denial had been carried into the room by each person there. Now he went on relentlessly, "Maybe not. Maybe your ideals—kindness, respect, dignity—would go out the window. Gone! You'd be standing there with nobody to contradict your authority—imagine that!

"So, enlightenment. What good is it? Besides which it just makes you ultimately responsible for everything and everyone. Better to just be human. Be kind to everyone you meet, even to Parisian waiters! Even to New York waiters, who would treat you worse than a dog once they realized you weren't a New Yorker. Even to treat them kindly, with patience. To bring dignity to your life—now *that* would be something!"

Lee described the selfishness that people exhibited last year on his trip to India. He described the discomforts of India and said that people reacted to the level of discomfort with panic to such a degree that the unconscious took over. He said, "Just a cup of coffee was something to fight over. People destroyed their partners to get their morning cup of coffee.

"My personal teaching work has taken a major shift from the beginning, from enlightenment, enlightenment, enlightenment to kindness, dignity, responsibility. I would much rather have a disciple who is reliable in their responsibility than one who is enlightened, because what is enlightenment? Who knows? Enlightenment is like love: it means whatever anybody thinks it means. You take fifty different people and ask them what love is and you get fifty different answers. To some it is sacrifice, to give and give to the other; to others love is submission, submerging yourself completely in the other; to another it's 'Remember my birthday!' "

Everyone laughed. Lee delivered this almost deadpan, with a little smile hiding around the corners of his mouth. At the same time he was deadly serious, almost deadpan. There were many smiling faces looking at Lee, listening intently. A number of people here have known him for five, six, eight years. He continued, "It's the same with enlightenment. But dignity, kindness—everybody knows those things. They are the same to everyone. When someone treats us with kindness, we all feel it in the same way. Yes, some of us are suspicious when someone treats us with kindness, but that's why we do therapy, because your parents were never kind to you unless they wanted something. But beyond that, if we are honest with ourselves, the feeling is the same."

In this way he set the tone for the weekend. After the talk he was at the book table. An American man, David, who has lived in France for many years, came up to Lee, who was sitting in a wicker chair a few feet away from the books. David had been at Lee's seminar at La Bertais at the beginning of the summer, and at the Guru Purnima Celebration at La Ferme de Jutreau. Now he approached and said, "I'm reading the Study Manual, a chapter a month as you suggested. It's great. It's incredibly well written. It fits in perfectly with what's happening for me." He walked to the book table and looked over the books, saying, "Is there anything new?" Lee answered no, and David commented that he had already bought everything on the table. A few moments later David walked back over with a stack of old journals of the Hohm Community, *Divine Slave Gita,* in his hands. He looked up at Lee and said, "These are all the old ones?"

"Yes," Lee replied.

Standing about three feet away from Lee and holding the journals in his hands, David asked with a straightforward simplicity, "Would you accept me as a student?"

Looking up at David from his chair Lee said, "Keep doing what you're doing, reading all the literature. What you have should keep you busy through the winter. And then ask me next year when I come back. If you ask me again next year I'm sure I'll say yes." David smiled and said thank you, then walked back to the book table to look around more. He seemed satisfied with Lee's answer.

A very lovely woman walked up to Lee with a book and asked for a *dédicace.* Lee asked for her name then started writing, paused to say to David, who was still standing nearby, "You should write me also. Once a month or so."

David nodded and said, "One thing I read in *Tawagoto* was about calling out your name. That's been a real lifesaver for me this year."

A woman with a ravaged face, unkempt brown hair and bleary hazel brown eyes came in and looked around. She seemed very melancholy and disoriented. There was a vapor of sadness and confusion around her. Suddenly she was kneeling in front of Lee and talking about how terrible her life has been, how bad things are for her. She asked if she could be Lee's student.

Lee gently said no to her request and then added, "You can't just find a master. You have to be ready for a master. You have to prepare yourself. You have to keep trying, making yourself strong." He was giving her all he could—kindness, honesty, and the encouragement to try and heal further against overwhelming odds. Her suffering was vibrating like a wire in the room. Tears started rolling down her face as she said, "Life is getting harder and harder. What can you tell me?" She implored.

Lee answered softly, "We'll see what I may say over the weekend that will help you. What's you name again?" Francis, she told him, and he wrote the *dédicace* she had asked for. She sat in front of him, her posture utterly hopeless and forlorn. Suffering seemed permanently stamped across her face. She sat crying, wiping the tears from her eyes. As Lee handed her the book she had bought, she said, "Thank you. Thank you." She moved closer to Lee.

"It's very important. It's *very* important. *Something* must happen," she mumbled. She was almost incoherent, her speech unnaturally slow, as if she was operating under the effects of drugs or alcohol. She turned around so that her back was an inch away from Lee's knees. Her suffering was palpable, her face falling apart in spasms of pain. She had bought Lee's books, *The Yoga of Enlightenment* and *The Only Grace Is Loving God*. She wore a bracelet from Amritananda Mayi. She turned back to Lee, mustered a smile and pointed questioningly to the "Jai Guru" on the *dédicace.*

"Jai Guru—means victory to the guru," Lee said.

"I understand," she smiled, and rose shakily. "Thank you," she said and left the room.

Marcus came in with a letter for Lee, who sat reading it. Valerie had been sitting quietly and got up to leave. Lee looked up and said, "You know you can always stay for the meal." Lunch was going to be served in about fifteen minutes.

She smiled, "Thank you, but they didn't count me in."

Lee chuckled, "I don't care. I always add some people in—they know that. Now you're counted in!"

Valerie sat back down laughing and said, "Okay."

Lee continued to read Marcus' letter, and as Alain René came in he looked back up and said, "Well, that was a great first session." He and Alain René began to talk about various things—today's translation, Espace Harmonie in Paris. Alain René asked Lee about his plans for next year.

Lee said, "I may be here for five months next year, depending on the Shri tour. I'd rather do festivals than clubs, but September and October is when the club scene is really busy and active. But, the festivals are really great . . ."

Alain René asked, "What about LGB?"

Lee said, "They're finished!"

Alain René was surprised; he had not heard the news yet. "That's your decision?" he asked. Lee nodded.

"Detachment on all levels!" Alain René quipped with a laugh.

Lee said, "We have a new band already. Attila the Hunza. They're all young people. LGB had gotten lazy. They weren't willing to sacrifice, take risks, so what good was it? But it was hard to let go. The music was better than ever, but . . ." he shrugged. Lee had explained this so many times over the summer, talked about it at length in many seminars. The very situation was itself a teaching lesson worth repeating many times, but now it had become part of the oral tradition of the Hohm Community.

Lunch was ready and, as people began to gather, it was clear that the table was short about ten plates. Lee's students began to hastily set up more places for people to eat; it was going to be a very cramped seating situation, but that's the way Lee likes it—pack as many people in as possible so everyone who wants to can have the opportunity to spend time in his company. Lee went to the head of the table and took his seat.

Back at the book table after lunch François approached Lee and presented him with a gift. It was a small stone carving from Colombia, a representation of a shaman from the Kogui tribe in some kind of jade or jasper. "I have brought this for you from Colombia," François said as he put the paper-wrapped stone form in Lee's hand. "I hope it's not too heavy."

Lee unwrapped it and hefted it in the palm of his hand. It probably weighed about a pound. "Not at all," Lee said. It was about five inches long and highly stylized. "Very nice. Thank you," Lee smiled up at François.

At the beginning of the afternoon session Francis, the troubled woman who had approached Lee at the book table and asked to be a student, asked a question. Her voice quavering, she said, "I feel the anguish and fear in the streets, every day, in the enterprises, everywhere. Everywhere there is fear . . . I thought it was my problem, but I see that it's not . . ."

Lee said, "You are either part of the solution or part of the problem. I think this mood you are describing is pervasive in every Western city and country. It's easy to feel overburdened by it, but you have to take the view, 'I'm either part of the problem or part of the solution.' You fight it one day at a time."

She continued to talk about her desperation, the melancholy and the loneliness. She said that she was out of work; her depression filled the space. Lee continued, "Well, we all have to start where we are. At least you're here this weekend trying to get some advice and help. One thing you could do would be every morning at eight o'clock you could say to yourself, 'For the next ten minutes I'm going to pray or meditate or read poetry—I'm not going to be overwhelmed with negativity.' Then make it twenty minutes, then one hour. As you build a habit of not giving into negativity, you increase the time. Obviously it's easier when you are at home alone." Lee laughed and began to banter with the crowd, attempting to lift Francis up in the interchange. He was being funny but at the same time he was giving Francis something to hold on to, like throwing a lifeline to a drowning person. She sat in the front row and drew the exchange out as long as she could.

Lee went into a social commentary, a discussion of societal ills and problems, the educational systems in the West, medicine, politics. As if she hadn't understood a word he said, she interrupted him and repeated again, "But what is happening? I have a feeling something terrible is happening . . ."

Lee broke into song at that point, singing a few lines from the Bob Dylan song "Thin Man" from one of Dylan's early albums, a searing commentary on the human condition. He has often recommended that people sing show tunes when they are depressed. His choice today was not show tunes but Bob Dylan, one of his all time favorite artists.

"All we can do," he continued, "is to live a life of integrity, and if enough individuals live a life of integrity it gathers force. We read in *Newsweek* about GM shipping genetically engineered food into France and people protesting, refusing to eat it. The French are reacting—I think it's fantastic, because Americans have been lazy. They've quit complaining and just take it. It's destroying everything. It's not food, it's some kind of fantastic science fiction creation. The percent of oxygen in the breathable air is one third less than it was twenty-five years ago! The destruction of our oxygen is happening at an exponential rate. But we would rather have a diesel engine car and burn less gas and more oxygen because we're all lazy. So raise your children to be radical! To fight for what's right—but without guns, because violence in the name of peace only creates more violence, not peace."

Lee started a series of interchanges with women in the audience, flirting, cajoling, then applying small shocks to their belief systems. Before long he had everyone bouncing with laughter on their zafus. Some people knew Lee very well, and were continuing with questions they had been asking for years. Other questions were naive or mundane, but very sincere. A lot of the questions were psychologically based, as if the guru was a psychotherapist or family counselor. Lee answered many questions about family matters, work, children. He made it all useful. In this way it seemed that he was spinning gold from straw, and it was somehow tangled up in the laughter that shook the whole space. It felt like the molecules of the air were jiggling, dancing, and we were breathing in the laughter, the golden ions and particles and subatomic particles that are the physical carriers of the influence of Yogi Ramsuratkumar. It was an immersion in Yogi Ramsuratkumar, cloaked within the ludicrous, the serious, the ordinary, even the convoluted and murky questions. Outside it rained and water dripped from the thirty-five foot high cherry tree that was just beyond the window. Through all this Lee sat casually in his chair wearing the same gray sweatpants and blue-green flannel shirt that he'd had on for a week or more. Around his waist was a leather fanny pack; in his ear a diamond earring twinkled surreptitiously.

"What confuses us when we come to the path gets cleared away, then another level of confusion appears. People go from thinking observation of their neuroses, to emotional observation, to feeling observation. This is moving from illusion to Reality. If we look at that process superficially it looks like nothing has changed, but the confusion is at a much deeper level. The deeper we go, the less the thinking mind can articulate what is happening, so it might even feel like we are going backward. When we can't understand with the thinking mind, we feel out of control, but it's actually a sign of success on the path."

One questioner said, "I have a feeling that simple observation is not enough, that all this is just engendering more and more fear."

Lee answered, "Self-observation is a means to an end. Self-observation leads one to *see*. To *see*, the way Swami Prajnanpad used the word."

Suddenly Lee held up the *vigraha*. "This is Yogi Ramsuratkumar. My favorite Master!" He turned the *vigraha* upside down, bounced it around with a gleeful smile on his face. "He likes to play; He's very child-like!"

Lee began to tell stories of Yogi Ramsuratkumar. He told the story of meeting Yogi Ramsuratkumar in 1976 and again in 1979, when Yogi Ramsuratkumar had said, "Oh, you must be Krishna!" and laughed. Again Lee told everyone, "Twenty years later I realized, 'Oh! How embarrassing!' because He was saying, 'You know, I think you're taking this a little too seriously.' " Then Lee launched into another story of Yogi Ramsuratkumar.

"Some years ago I wanted to do a book that would make Yogi Ramsuratkumar more well-known in the West. I thought the best way to do that would be to put Him in a book with famous masters—Ramana Maharshi, Nityananda and so on. It was to be called *Facets of the Diamond*. So I wrote to Yogi Ramsuratkumar for permission to do the book. I got this call from His ashram in India. He said, 'If Lee is not in the book, there is no reason to do the book.'

" 'Oh, boy,' I thought, 'what are all my Western guru friends gonna think when they see all these famous Eastern masters and *me*? Oh boy! I'm not in their category!" Everyone laughed with Lee at his dilemma. "As a Westerner I'm not bad, but . . . So we did the book and Yogi Ramsuratkumar started calling me an Indian saint. A few years later we were in India, and one of my students had written to ask Him if He would give me an Indian name. You know, something like *Salaud-ananda* or *Tapette-ananda*!" People burst into laughter. Lee was using the French terms for bastard (*salaud*) and effete male prostitute (*tapette*).

"So we were there and He was reading the letter. His attendant, Devaki, who is sort of the mother of the ashram—He's fierce and demanding and she is soft and embracing—saw Him reading the letter and said, 'Bhagavan, why don't you give Lee an Indian name?' Whenever anyone wants to get something from Yogi Ramsuratkumar, they ask Devaki.

"He turned around and said, 'No! This Beggar has said that Lee Lozowick is an Indian saint, therefore Lee Lozowick is an Indian name!' Then I thought of all the Indian names I'd given to other people. Oh boy! He was saying, 'You guys are Westerners. You don't have to be pretentious. Just relax and be who you are instead of trying to be somebody else.'

"We wear Indian clothes when we are in India. Last year He said to me, 'Do all your disciples wear Indian clothes all the time?' No, I answered, only in India. He just wanted to make sure we weren't totally affected. So He was very happy! He's still got to watch out for me because I'm still a little mischievous. Every year He asks me one or two questions, just to make sure I'm not out of line."

Lee began to tell the story of going to see Yogi Ramsuratkumar in 1986, when he brought twenty of his students with him and Yogi Ramsuratkumar didn't remember him at all. "He looked at me like I was some suspicious character, some *salesman*, then He embraced my students with this big smile. Kicked me out after thirty minutes, while the second group of my students got to see him for an hour and a half!

"Whoever I was in 1986, I wasn't Lee anymore, or Krishna; He really *didn't* recognize me. The one who was there in 1976 and 1979 was not His disciple but a treasure hunter, a mercenary. But the 'me' who went in 1986 had already entered into a very deep apprenticeship to Him. So He didn't recognize me because it wasn't the same one. When I was there in 1986 I was seeking His approval. You know how it is—I was groveling on the ground!" Lee smiled at the memory.

Everything about his relationship with Yogi Ramsuratkumar seems to bring him great pleasure, especially those things that are associated with his own unraveling—the undoing of Lee Lozowick. He always seems to be using these stories not just as teaching lessons for everyone, but also as leverage to praise and exalt Yogi Ramsuratkumar. The more Lee is revealed and humbled in his shortcomings, the more glory Yogi Ramsuratkumar receives. In this way the telling and retelling of these stories throughout the summer has brought Lee to life each time. Now he continued:

"Yogi Ramsuratkumar has a very acute understanding of Western psychology. He's never studied it, but he is a genuine wise man. He *knows*. He couldn't have missed my posture, which was tremendously small, submissive, grasping. It must have broken His heart. Years later when He had the poetry I had written to Him published by His devotees, we were talking and He said, 'You sent this Beggar a lot of poetry and he threw it out.' Yogi Ramsuratkumar started *crying*. He said, 'This Beggar didn't know what they were.' It must have really broken His heart to see His disciple groveling and grasping for His attention, but He would not compromise or capitulate the teaching lesson for anything. I had to handle my reaction—that's part of the training of the disciple. If every time your child whines you give them what they want, they'll be spoiled, not strong."

Outside a chilly rain was pouring down again. It dripped through the Virginia creeper that grew on the side of the building and fell through the leaves of the cherry tree as the wind blew its branches. The mood had once again gone soft and deep. Lee's words penetrated through layers of hard and viscous buffers and struck the heart. Everyone sat extremely still, their eyes riveted on Lee, who spoke with natural candor and ease. It was a powerful teaching lesson to see the spiritual master undressed and vulnerable, because in that vulnerability was tremendous strength and power and dignity. His stories revealed many different facets of the relationship between guru and disciple, the most obvious one being that Lee was willing to submit, to accept fully and even embrace joyfully, Yogi Ramsuratkumar's wisdom in however he chose to work with Lee as disciple. As Lee has said in his poetry, he "runs willingly" to the fire of Yogi Ramsuratkumar's Grace.

He continued: "The master can't capitulate, no matter how much his heart is breaking for the disciple. When the master makes a communication he or she has to stand behind that communication, and Yogi Ramsuratkumar did. A good actor is always in his role whenever he is onstage. In the same way the master has to maintain his communication. I saw Yogi Ramsuratkumar three more times the following week and He did not break His role. I was there for two hours one time, and He did not give me any sign of recognition. *None*. Not a word of anything spiritual, of importance, *nothing*. When I left there was no sign of any kind of recognition—none. But I thought, He was my Master before this, and He is still my Master now.

"It all turned out very differently, but at that time He was making a forceful communication, and if it had been otherwise it would have ruined it for me. It's very important to understand this quality of the master: all he cares about is the success of the disciple. That is why I always sign books 'Jai Guru'—victory to the guru.

"So this is the way that Yogi Ramsuratkumar teaches. He gives you the input, then He goes on. He doesn't stop to see if you took it; He is *moving*. When He throws you a lesson you have to take it because He's fast, and by the time you've gotten it, He is on about something else."

October 3, 1999
Paris

The morning session seemed to drag along. The space was packed—there were more people here today than yesterday. The questions were to a large degree self-centered and once again more related to psychotherapy or family counseling than to spiritual life and sadhana. Lee somehow got traction in all that slippery stuff and took off, but meanwhile there were moments in the group alchemy when it seemed that time dragged on and the group as a whole was bogged down, like carrying a heavy weight uphill. Many of Lee's devotees sat in the back of the room. As the questions dragged out some of them were sporadically taking notes, yawning, shifting around on the uncomfortable floor or just sleeping.

A woman, Isabel, began to talk with Lee about her situation at work, where she has a great deal of responsibility and often has people getting angry with her. In the course of their dialogue she told Lee that a woman who works for her has three children and a four-hour commute to work, and her husband beats her. The woman was often not able to finish her work, and was generally a problem. Lee answered:

"I would finish her work for her. No, it's not fair, but in life we have to be bigger than a circumstance that is not fair. If you asked any of my students in this room if I was fair as a teacher they would say definitely not. The men say, 'How did I end up in such an unfair situation? If I had tits he would look at me! He just gives me more work to do—"Do this, do that!" '

"Once a month I can count on some man saying, 'Why do you work so differently with women than with men?' What they mean is, 'I want attention.' The people who are bad at everything get to sit on their ass all day while the people who are good at everything work hard. Those who are bad at everything say, 'Remember the story of Mary and Martha!' "

Lee went into one of his favorite humorous diatribes—the unparalleled laziness of his American students, as opposed to the hard-working Europeans. Several of the French guests turned around and grinned at Lee's students, who were all awake now and paying attention. After about five minutes Lee returned to his train of thought.

"So life is really not fair. The jungle is full of lions and gazelles. Lions eat the gazelles. The woman you were talking about would have been eaten by a lion a long time ago if she was in the jungle. Human beings have created a society that is completely unfair—it's totally arbitrary and unjust. The trade union you talked about is a good idea, but it functions within a system that is not reliable, not mature, not fair. If we are women, we live in a world that is even less fair. And they're getting back at men now! 'Vengeance is mine,' sayeth *la femme*! It's in the Old Testament, with the patriarchal judging God.

"Somehow you have a position of responsibility and authority and you have a high standard for the job being done properly, but you live in a highly imperfect system. So you have to be extremely creative, because the system is not going to function according to your high standards. Somebody has to stand for integrity. You have to figure out how not to be dragged down by these things—how not to get hooked—which is a function of not being identified. Give the poor woman a break—her life is hard enough as it is."

Charlotte, a woman who had asked lots of questions in earlier sessions of the seminar began to talk about a conflict she had with Isabel. She said, "I have a problem with Isabel and I never told her about it."

Lee laughed and said, "I'm sure you're going to tell her now, aren't you?" referring to the total predictability of human psychology. He turned to Isabel and quipped, "Never cross an artist, Isabel—oohhhh!" Everyone laughed at Lee's theatrics. Charlotte started pouring out a long, tedious story. After a few minutes Lee laughed and said to Isabel, "Wait, I haven't heard the whole story yet—I might be on her side!" Charlotte went on, speaking rapidly, obviously upset. Isabel sat quietly listening.

As the two women sat almost side by side directly in front of Lee, it was easy to imagine King Solomon meting out wisdom to the two women who both claimed the same baby. As the women argued over the baby Solomon said, "Then cut the baby in half and give one half to one woman and one half to the other." Immediately the real mother of the child said, "No, no, give the child to her!" to save her baby, and in this way Solomon got to the truth of which woman the baby belonged to.

Now Lee spoke, saying, "It's very simple. It's a misunderstanding of communication." He very patiently explained again in detail to Charlotte the point he was making. He said again, "It's very simple. If she wants you to work for her again you say I'm happy to do the job but we need a more concrete understanding, more time, less rush, and if she says okay, then you have a job."

His tone was one of extreme reason and grounded sanity. Charlotte began to equivocate again, arguing with Lee. Clearly she was attached to being angry and didn't want to let go. He interrupted her, saying, "Are you happy being full of rage like this at people? Obviously it's not just her, it's a lot of people. You know it feels very good when we have that kind of rage toward someone. It's very satisfying—they are wrong, we are right. We're Joan of Arc, fighting for justice, and the other person has walked all over us, made us promise our Sunday afternoon and then didn't call!" Lee started stating the facts of Charlotte's complaint against Isabel in a tone of voice that was a combination of wounded pride and righteous outrage couched within a childish pout. "Even if a friend calls and wants to go for a walk, no, no! I have to stay here! I would have just said, 'Well, no message.' Why get angry?

"So, are you happy being angry at so many people?" She stared blankly at Lee. He said forcefully, "Yes or no!"

She said, "No. I have the impression that it makes me more vibrant."

Lee laughed sardonically and then looked at her, considering. "Do you have a partner?" he asked.

She answered, "I'm in the mood to have a partner. But everyone just goes away when I fly into a rage. I'm fed up with it."

Lee chimed in, "Oh good! Because we really don't change until we're fed up with it. So what are you going to do about it? Maybe Valium would be a good idea!" Everyone cracked up laughing. It was something this therapy-oriented crowd could relate to. Lee qualified his comment by telling a story of Llewellyn Vaughan-Lee and Irina Tweedie. When he had first come to Mrs. Tweedie as a young man he was very nervous and stressed-out, and Mrs. Tweedie's recommendation was to just take Valium. He was shocked at first but then he realized that she was just being very practical.

Lee continued, "So what is it that you need right now in this moment? You're not going to change right now, so just chill! Then when you're relaxed, you can see what the next thing to do is. I'm not making a recommendation about the Valium, I'm just telling a story. So who is it you are really angry with? Your mother, your father? We are a sick bunch of people. The whole human race, except the tribal people, are each one sicker than the next." Lee laughed, and his laughter had an edge of madness in it, a wild freedom. The laughter seemed to ring on and on, leaving everyone else in the room in the dust.

After awhile his laughter subsided and he continued, "It doesn't stop us from bowing and scraping." He laughed some more. His laughter was ironic, mysterious but contagious, and although no one else knew what he was laughing about other than him, some began to laugh along with him, just shaking and moving with laughter. His thoughts, which he began to voice as stream of consciousness, bounced from one to another, although it was clear that for him they were all perfectly connected to some large picture which one could ascertain perhaps through a kind of skip-step reasoning. He seemed to be laughing at the absurdity of the whole situation. He broke down into serious belly laughs, held his side and rocked back and forth, wiping the tears from his eyes. "Oh boy! Two hours till lunch! I don't know if I'll make it!"

Slowly Lee's fit of maniacal laughter died down. Francis asked the next question. She said, "Sometimes things like that can close your heart. That's what happened to me. Yesterday was a very good day for me. I felt a connection to something greater, bigger, maybe to God . . ."

Lee said, "Wow! Okay, so?"

"Well, I came home and some friends called and I couldn't discuss those things with them . . ." she said in her broken, halting voice.

"You're lucky you have friends!" Lee interjected.

She continued, "Suddenly all was gone. *Suddenly, all was gone.* I woke up this morning and there was nothing. Nothing! How can I keep feeling? How can I go on?"

Lee answered, "But that's the way it goes. These things come and go. The way you keep that feeling is to realize that things come and go. Otherwise when it comes we are high, and when it goes we are down. If we can accept the fact that it comes and goes, when it comes we are grateful and when it goes we realize, 'This is the way it is, and it will come back.' "

Francis continued, "But when it goes I feel all is crazy, all is craziness . . ."

Lee laughed, "That's what all the cult people say! There are only sixty people in this room and everyone out there," Lee pointed outside the building "thinks this is completely crazy. We have to understand that what we are doing is not acceptable to mainstream neurosis. We are alone. Most of the people in this room cannot talk to friends or families or co-workers about this. There are people in our community who have been in it for ten years and their parents still don't know what they are doing. 'What's that you do?' they ask. We give them some answer and they say, 'Oh, philosophy.' "

Everyone laughed at this, but Francis went on as if the cloud of doom was hanging over her head. She was a tragic reminding factor of the human condition, the deep woundedness that human beings bear. Now she mumbled incoherently, "It's gone, *gone.*"

Lee said patiently, "That's right. It will come back. The community has these bands. We used to have a rock band. It's gone. Now I sing—sort of bellow—in the blues band. Sometimes when we do a lot of performing I get up and say, 'Oh great! We perform tonight,' and other times I get up and say, 'Is this ever going to end? Another performance tonight is the worst thing imaginable!' If there is a gig when I'm in that mood, I just do it. Nothing ever stays the same, you have to understand."

Like a broken record she repeated agonizingly, "Yes, but it's gone, it's really gone . . ." as if Lee hadn't said any of the things he'd just said. She seemed unable to register his meaning; it had no place in her psychological worldview. Lee's forbearance and compassion through all this was incredible.

Now he said, "Yes, of course you don't feel it now because it is *really* gone! And when it comes back, it will *really* be here! Nobody's happy, sad or full of joy all the time. What you can be all the time is fully present with whatever is here. In being one with *what is* then there is serenity, equanimity. But that doesn't mean the state you are in is serene. It may be quite disturbed."

She was on the verge of tears again as she said, "It makes me suffer a lot."

Lee said, "You suffer a lot because you don't accept, you don't have faith." Lee picked up the *vigraha* of Yogi Ramsuratkumar and held it in his hands, sort of bouncing it a little again. "This Guy, in His human form, says that we can't make faith happen. Faith is given to us by God. There are things we can do and can't do. Either there is faith, or there isn't. But we can seek the company of friends, inspiring impressions, certain music, literature, visual arts. Take a hot bath. Spend all morning making special forbidden treats for yourself—like tiramisu. Or napoleons! You don't have a teacher, so your circumstance is different, but for people who do have a teacher, my relationship to my Teacher is one of obedience. It's my responsibility to be obedient. What we can do is practice in a way that has been blessed by the lineage and path."

His discourse expanded to take everyone into its scope as he began to talk about practice, the need of the teacher to have the freedom to teach. He talked about his French students needing to embrace practice if they wanted to have access to what he has to offer. He ended the session and went to the book table. Two of his French student came up to ask questions.

Sitting near the book table I watched as one after another of the seminar participants came up, sometimes reaching out to shake Lee's hand, sometimes just standing. "I'm glad to tell you that you really touched me. It's the first time I've met you, and I was really touched, really . . ." and "I wanted to thank you. I read your book. Thank you for what you did for me." Lee took all of this in without any visible response other than kindness and generosity. It was as if no one was sitting there, even though he looked into each person's face and smiled warmly or responded with simple answers to questions.

Gilles Farcet arrived to have lunch with Lee and the group. He embraced Lee and sat by the book table with Lee to visit. His hair had been buzzed off and was about a quarter of an inch long. Gilles said that he had just felt moved to do it, and that Arnaud was very pleased with it when he saw it. "The new Gilles!" Arnaud had said with a smile.

Another man, Michael from Brussels, came up and asked Lee if he would give him some feedback that might be helpful to him. Lee said, "Ask me some question in the afternoon session—maybe something will come up."

A steady stream of people came and went while Lee sat in his chair and visited with

734

Gilles and Alain René. About twenty minutes before lunch Sylvie came in and asked Lee, "How many people can I invite for lunch?"

Lee said, "As many as you like! It's your house."

Sylvie countered, "No, it's your house!"

Lee repeated with a gentle smile to Sylvie, "Really, invite whoever you would like to invite."

In the afternoon session Lee called on Michael, who began to talk about his fear and his failures in relationship with women. He blamed himself for these failures and seemed to be struggling with a deep lack of self-esteem.

Lee said brusquely, "Not necessarily! Don't let those bitches get off that easily!" Everyone laughed. The room was bright and easy, people were relaxed and trusting in Lee's company. There was a love affair going on between Lee and his audience that allowed a great deal of room for Lee to work with each individual in very different ways.

Michael shared confidences and went further into his feelings of guilt and inadequacy. Then he offered on a different train of thought, "I try to eat consciously."

Lee laughed and said, "With what? Your mind?"

"Yes, my mind. So I want to be vigilant but in fact I am trying to be in control," he said.

Lee said, "Just like everybody else." Laughter shook the room again.

"I don't feel I'm in connection. I feel separate from God, angry at God!" Michael said.

Lee smiled, "Angry at God is a good step. What is your anger at God about?"

"Because nothing on Earth makes any sense," Michael answered.

Lee looked at him and responded lightly, "That's not God's fault. You're angry at the wrong Guy! God just hangs out doing nothing, contemplating Himself, and we're down here cursing Him. 'What'd I do wrong?' God says. 'Okay, I created human beings—everybody makes a mistake now and then!' If you have to be angry at God, be angry because Häagen-Dazs ice cream is so expensive." This wisecrack brought on more laughter. "So what are you doing about it?"

Michael responded, "I try to do the best I can at my profession." As it turned out he was in the civil service. Lee commiserated with him, listened to his story, then he began to answer in earnest: "Everybody starts as neurotic, groveling, greedy territorial creatures—like animals! We don't start on the path as saints. You want to control everything? Great! It's a great place to start. It's even better if you are vigilant about how you want to control everything. You observe yourself—the good, the bad, the ugly.

"So what do you want? Oral sex every day? Not to give it but just to get it?" People were falling off their seats laughing at this. Michael was laughing and smiling along with everyone. Lee continued, "No really—what do you really want, essentially? The thing is that you have to be willing to pay. You want Perrier at the movies, you have to put the twenty francs in the machine. You can push the button all you want, but until you put the twenty francs in the machine, you won't get the Perrier. So what do you want?"

Michael answered, "A mate, a more fulfilling job and social situation. I'd like to work in environmental protection."

Lee asked him if he had ever tried to get the job he wanted and Michael said no. Lee said, "Just go and get the job. What's stopping you?"

Everyone laughed along with Lee and Michael. The sheer delight of laughing fostered a fluidity of feeling, a willingness to go with Lee wherever he steered the boat. The combination of Lee's direct confrontation to the rigid attitudes of the psychological strategy, his sense of humor and pure empowerment of Michael were masterful in creating an opportunity for everyone in the space. Michael was obviously a gentle, retiring and probably rather shy person; Lee was empowering him with every interaction. Now Lee began to push him a little, to tease him about his relationship with his mother.

"Just don't move back in with your mother!" Lee warned with a laugh. He encouraged Michael to approach women, to be in relationship. He said, "Go to the market and see which women have wedding rings on. If they have a wedding ring on, don't approach them. If not, go up and say, 'I'm really helpless—can you tell me if this melon is ripe or not?' But don't look at their breasts when you say it!" Gales of laughter passed over the crowd and continued off and on throughout Lee's monologue. "Or go to group therapy, and then you can just ask outright, 'Who's single?' Then you can find somebody who is also guilty, just like you!"

Michael explained that his ex-companion was still clinging to him even though she had another boyfriend. Lee exploded humorously, "Oh, so she doesn't want you, but she doesn't want you to have anyone else either? I told you, you're being too soft on those bitches!" More laughter.

Even though he had been laughing along with everyone else, Michael now said, "I really don't laugh much."

Lee answered, "Maybe nothing's funny! I was in Brussels a few years ago—I didn't see much that was funny there!"

After another round of playful repartee and hilarious laughter, Lee got serious: "It's fun to joke around, but the bottom line is that either your fear and guilt are stronger, or your desire is stronger. Consciously you want a partner, a different job, but unconsciously you are holding on to the guilt and fear. You are getting a payoff from it. You have two choices: go ahead anyway, no matter what, or engage in some process, therapy or something, that gets you in touch with your unconscious so you can deal with it at that level. Either way is going to be effective for you, both approaches have a positive and negative side, but the point is that you need to *move*. Don't stay paralyzed. The first step is to accept yourself as you are, full of guilt, full of fear, wanting to control. That's pretty much everybody, to some degree. The point is acceptance. To accept everything about yourself is to put yourself in a position where anything is possible.

"Or maybe you just don't want to leave your mother!" More laughter, as Lee started digging deeper, pushing a little harder on Michael's weak spots, giving him the opportunity to confront himself at a deeper level. Lee had spent almost an hour talking with this man. Although he was approaching middle age, Michael had a quality of youthfulness about him. He was boyish and had a certain innocence; it was this innocence and vulnerability that seemed to attract Lee's attention. Throughout the interaction Lee was sending out a strong message: "I'm on your side." It was probably the most healing interaction Michael had ever had with another man, especially an older man who represents authority.

Lee is at times willing to work at this level with people, to enter into the psychological realm and work directly with human suffering from that perspective. Watching him operate masterfully in such a way it becomes clear that many dimensions of spiritual help are given and received in these circumstances. The rest of the session was spent wrestling with the various psychological problems of individual people; to each of them Lee gave the same kind of understanding, sometimes providing a mild shock, but always nudging them toward a higher context for life.

Lee opened the last session of the seminar by answering a question, which he turned toward a consideration of the necessity for having a teacher and a consideration of the relationship with the teacher:

"It helps to rub up against a person who is awakened. Just being in the proximity of such a person is enough. So when the disciple is ready, the teacher appears. It's nice to have a dialogue with your teacher, have your teacher know your name, but really the transmission happens completely beyond the personality level of relationship. When one is ready for the teaching, the teaching just flows to him or her.

"On the other hand, when we have the opportunity to relate with the teacher and have a dialogue, it does create a certain mood. But if someone develops a more lasting relationship with the teacher, then the question is, what is it that pleases the teacher? On a very human level, to do what pleases the teacher makes one vulnerable to what the teacher is transmitting beyond the personal level.

"The best we can do is spend time in the company of saints. True, and beyond that, if we want a more objective relationship with a saint, we have to put into practice what the saint says to practice. Yogi Ramsuratkumar is very high, consciously. He typically doesn't ask people to do anything except to remember Him, to use His Name, Yogi Ramsuratkumar, to chant, to use a picture of Him or something more dynamic, like the *vigraha*. But He doesn't tell people to meditate or anything. He also has said that what pleases Him is praise. He says when His disciples criticize one another it hurts Him personally. So we praise Yogi Ramsuratkumar in whatever ways we can.

"There is a difference between transmission and awakening. In fact there is no one to transmit and no one to transmit to. In that sense it all happens outside of time and space, outside of duality. Transmission is a spark catching fire, when really that fire is in each of us."

Marie-Noelle asked, "I understand from speaking with people who are committed with you . . ."

Lee interrupted, "Let's see what fantastic theories my students have come up with!" He chuckled.

She continued, ". . . that their commitment came from an inner certitude that it was you, as their teacher, and nobody else. And this brings with it devotion to you."

He answered, "Yes, it does have to be me and nobody else with my students. There are many forms of devotion. There is the expressive form of loving devotion where the disciples sit and stare at the master and their eyes glaze over; there's a funny look on their face. All they want to do is throw themselves down at the master's feet and dance through heaven with the master! Fred Astaire and Ginger Rogers! It's ecstatic. Then there is devotion that takes the ordinary form of responsibility, in which the disciple says, 'What can I do for you?' Some say, 'All these people are in love with you—I don't know about that, but can I fix the sink or something?' Yes! Someone has to tune-up the car.

"In Vaishnavism there are five categories of relationship to the master. There is lover to beloved, which is lush and opulent in its response to the master. It is rich and thick and often has the quality of eroticism and sensuality, which disturbs disciples of the same sex as the master. Then there is the relationship of parent to child, in which the guru is the child and the disciple is the parent. The disciple wants to take care of the guru, to take lint off his shirt and brush his hair. There is also the relationship in which the disciple is the child and the master is the parent; this one can look unhealthy, full of dependency and so on, but it has a pure form also. Servant to master is another form of relationship with the guru, in which the servant will do whatever is necessary, will handle practical needs, cover the details. The fifth form of relationship with the guru is friend to friend, where there is a kind of camaraderie, joking around, a personal level of relationship—for example when I travel with the band, especially as I used to with the rock band. Within each of those forms there is devotion, but they look totally different on the surface, although the level of commitment is the same in all of them.

"But we think that if someone throws themselves at the master's feet it's more devoted somehow. We are helplessly in love, practically swooning when the master enters the room. We can only wish! I'm not like that with my Master. I walk in the room and look around to see how many crazy people I'll have to contend with! I'm like, 'It's cold in here. The floor is hard.' That kind of adoring devotion looks more committed than the one who says, 'Do you need something taken to the post office today?' but the commitment is the same.

"I want exclusivity. It may take some time. I'm willing to be patient. But sooner or later I always get the *mala*! You know, the Rajneesh devotees always have this *mala*, and all the special pictures of him. But sooner or later I get it all and it all goes into the fire. I'm willing to be patient.

"Many people are good friends of the community; there are many who are committed in their own way. I'm not so stubborn that I refuse those gestures. But there is a difference in my mind between a lovely person who I'm happy to see every year and a committed student. There is a difference. I assume that's the same for every teacher . . ."

Marie-Noelle said, "I heard what you said. When I spoke about the devotion I felt in your disciples for you, I didn't speak about the level you talk about, but a more profound level of devotion. I would like to talk about myself. Each request you have made of me, everything you have asked of me I have said yes . . ."

Lee interrupted, "Be careful, because I haven't asked for much yet!" Everyone laughed along with Marie-Noelle and Lee.

She said, "I always consider your requests a big honor and I have a feeling that through the request you ask of me, I am relating to the sacred, and it's pretty strong for me. It's direct, through action. If you are speaking of the Beloved, I don't feel that."

Lee interjected, "Be careful . . ."

Marie-Noelle said, "It's my level . . ."

"It's not your level but where you're at right now," Lee charged ahead of her. "The Sufis call this thing ruin—annihilation! Wow! That doesn't sound very pleasant! What they mean is that once you really know the level of sanctity you are dealing with you are ruined for anything less. You know what ruin means?" Marie-Noelle nodded.

"When you are in touch deeply enough, you can't forget. You can kill the machine, but you can't forget. It puts everything else in life in which you cannot find the sacred in another category. It makes it all less important, which is devastating because you can't find that level of the sacred in a job, in friends, in mothers, fathers . . . Most people can still find it with their children, but not with other adults except those who share the same level of having been touched. It makes life difficult because we love our parents, family, professions, and yet all of that becomes empty, so we are ruined. Most people can have a good day easily, but not us, because none of that means anything to us anymore. It's pleasant, it's nice, but we're ruined. So, you were saying about devotion?" He smiled.

. "When I am near your disciples," she continued, "I have the feeling I am missing something. I'm not missing that in my daily life, but when I'm with them I feel that I am missing."

Lee answered, "My disciples haven't become sophisticated enough yet to make people who are not at an equal level of exclusivity feel included. Were they that sophisticated, you would begin to feel what they feel, even without that exclusivity. So what comes first, commitment or feeling? The answer is always feeling. A lot of people make the commitment without feeling, but their commitment is not reliable. It's tentative. They mean it, they're sincere, but they don't know themselves, they don't know how dominated they are by their own neuroses.

"Feeling always comes first; sometimes that leads to commitment, sometimes not. My students, as mature as they are and as much as I love them, are exclusive like me, and they protect their exclusivity. Even with people like you—you are always welcome any time, you can come around as much as you want, participate as much as you want—they exclude you. If they didn't you would feel what they feel. It's a good thing they are exclusive, because they have very little discrimination, meaning they would include people who shouldn't be included. It's crazy!"

Bernard asked the next question. He said, "Also about devotion and commitment—is it possible that one encounters the master and the devotion that comes up is so deep and profound and ego is so terrified that paradoxically the devotion is an obstacle to commitment?"

Lee said, "That happens."

Bernard qualified, "Generally speaking; I'm not talking about me." The whole crowd burst out in raucous laughter. The questions went on for awhile until Francis started questioning Lee again.

"I was listening to Michael when he spoke of being angry against God. I'm angry against God," she began in a gloomy voice.

"Oh! That's what you said last year!" he wisecracked.

"Then there is the longing for God . . . I don't have anyone I can talk to about this, I'm alone . . ." her watery voice trailed off. The pathos in the room was thick.

"Life's a mess for me too, except it's a pretty mess!" Lee said.

Her voice droned on darkly. She was even more despondent, if possible, than she had been the first day of the seminar as she mumbled, "Completely contradictory . . ."

"Great!" Lee shouted, "An insight a day! We have to break the pattern, the habits of pessimism!" He paused and looked at her, his voice changing back to a tone of extreme kindness and patience, but at the same time he was ruthlessly honest with her. "If you haven't found the thing that breaks the pattern, keep looking. You have to keep looking until you find the thing that will do it for you—that will break the pattern. I keep sending people to Andrew Cohen because he's a good pattern-breaker. Irina Tweedie looked for four years for her teacher. I'm not the one who can break the chains for you, who can provide that certain thing that you need."

He gave her a penetrating look then told the story of E.J. Gold saying that life is like a game of cards: sometimes you get an ace, sometimes a king or a queen, and sometimes you get a two or a three, or anything in between. He said, "So you got a four or a five in this lifetime. You're alone. Accept it completely. Stop wishing and dreaming and hoping for change—to have someone to talk to about these ideas. Accept it completely, then maybe something can change for you. In acceptance there is peace; in nonacceptance there is struggle. You aren't the only person who is alone. Some have no one to talk to about *anything*. At least you have somebody to talk to about the news, the earthquakes, but maybe not about spiritual life.

"True acceptance has no implications. If it has any implications it isn't true acceptance. But psychologically speaking, the way we ordinarily function is that our future is already defined by the past. We work hard and we struggle . . . To accept what is as it is brings everything to the present moment, where there is no past, no future. When that happens the future is not predictable anymore. Anything could happen, including dramatic change. But the only way we free the future is to completely accept what is, here and now. Any small degree of holdout is still defining the future. Acceptance brings the whole of Reality into the present moment. There is no past, no mechanically predictable future. It's very simple, but not so easy to do."

Lee's statement to Francis was a tremendously forthright thing to say: "Yes, you got a four or a five this lifetime." He was speaking to that part of her who was capable of knowing the truth and bearing it, because it was only from that position of radical self-honesty that she would be able to heal herself. Lee's strong words settled into the space. With each person that he worked with Lee offered something to the group as a whole, so that one could find a kernel of meaning, of truth and relevance in each person's situation. Who hasn't felt alone and inadequate? Who hasn't struggled with anger, or how to wield authority with compassion? Who hasn't been mired down with attachments within a dysfunctional family? Who hasn't realized that he or she is controlling, lost, full of illusions? I found myself being impatient at times during the weekend, wanting the questions to turn toward considerations of dharma and practice, but reflecting further I came to the conclusion that really we are all in the same boat.

Bernard raised his hand again. "Something says that to commit oneself completely to the spiritual path one must be mad, and I'm afraid to be mad."

Lee said, "That's why feeling comes before commitment. By the time you commit totally to the path, you're already mad."

Bernard said, "I'm not kidding."

Lee answered lightly, "Me either!"

Bernard stopped for a moment and looked at Lee. He plunged ahead, "Every time I come near you I feel you are mad in some way, but mad in an attractive way, and I need you to help me accept to become mad."

Lee said, "You have to stop defining madness before you can become mad. You define it as a loss of control or something. We can't accept that. We have to be able to use the word 'mad' in the divine sense, knowing that it is attractive and yet has no definition, and there may be fear in relationship to it. As long as we give it definition we won't be able to accept it because the definition will always be wrong, even if it is positive. So we have to accept it as it is, not as we imagine it to be. The task is to come into relationship with this madness that may have fear related to it, but that has no definition."

Bernard said, "So I have the tendency to think too much about what might happen."

Lee said, "You have to be more introduced to *this* Guy." He picked up the *vigraha* of Yogi Ramsuratkumar and waved it around in the air. Lee was exuberant. He smiled recklessly and jostled the *vigraha* about as if he was playing a game with it. "You think *I'm* mad? *He's* off the scale! This Guy is so mad He redefines the word!"

Bernard watched Lee with a serious face. He said, "You never say things like that. I would like to know what it means to be introduced more to Yogi Ramsuratkumar."

Lee's smile was infectious. He said to Bernard, "You have to have more commitment to *me*!"

Bernard said, "It's the same thing."

Lee laughed. "I'm the doorway to That! Like it or not, that's the way it is. People go to India; they don't even know what's going on. Westerners have to go through me—not the

Indians. For the Indians I just get in the way. But the Westerners have to go through me. It's a dirty job, it's a horror, a misery, a disaster, a catastrophe! But I got the job!" Lee gave Bernard a dazzling smile. "So, you're in the right place and the right time, and you're moving in the right direction."

Bernard resumed, "One time you said, 'I am on a train of fast speed—get on or off, but I won't be back for millions of years!'"

Lee asked innocently, "I said that?"

Marie-Noelle jumped in, "At Jutreau, three years ago!"

Lee smiled, "Wow! That's heavy. Pretty poetic. That's big shoes to get in!" He chuckled a little. "There is time, but you shouldn't hesitate too much. It's like pole-vaulting. You take the pole, but the timing has to be perfect. If you hesitate, the jump doesn't go well. If you hesitate a fraction of a second too long, you miss the train. There's a time for everything, so you want to catch the window when it is open . . . ."

Lee began to bring the seminar to a close. "Thank you for your attention, your presence, your generosity . . ." and then began to beg for donations for the Prison Library Project that is run by Rick M., one of his students in Claremont, California. He explained the value of the project and ended saying "Thank you for indulging my begging for money. Perhaps we'll meet again."

At the book table immediately after the end of this final session—the last session of this seminar, the last session of the summer—Bernard, Christophe and Sylvie gathered around Lee in the small room while people looked over the books and made final selections. They were talking with Lee about obtaining a *vigraha* for Maison Raphael. Lee instructed them in the daily ritual that is performed to the *vigraha*—a specific ritual done every morning "to invoke His regard, His blessings for the day," Lee said. After explaining the details of the *puja* and the care of the *vigraha*, Lee said, "When I go to India this year I'll tell Yogi Ramsuratkumar that you have one and He'll be very happy." He held the statue out to them; they took it together in their hands and went out of the room to place it on the shrine in the small meditation room next door.

Many people came in and gave generous donations to the Prison Library Project. The mood before dinner was very high and celebratory. The *vigraha* sat in the meditation room, waiting to be consecrated by Lee after dinner. The table was set and about forty people packed in around it to feast. Christophe, his wife Muriel and their children, Sylvie, Bernard and Marie-Noelle, and Patrice and Veronique, old friends of Lee's from Paris, sat together on either side of Lee. Their faces were bright and animated and happy.

After dinner Lee went into the meditation room with them and showed them the ritual ceremony associated with the *vigraha* while some of his students chanted the name of Yogi Ramsuratkumar. The ceremony took less than two minutes to perform, and yet the effect was striking. The room was filled with the presence of Yogi Ramsuratkumar to such a degree that if one walked past the room and looked in at the *vigraha*, it seemed to be the living form of Yogi Ramsuratkumar sitting there. Numerous people remarked on it, and one by one people went in and paid their respects to the shrine. After a short while Lee, modest and unpretentious as usual, said his good-byes. He would be leaving with his American students who were returning to Arizona with him the next morning at five-thirty.

October 5, 1999
Prescott, Arizona

Lee and his traveling party arrived at the Arizona ashram last night at nine forty-five amidst a flurry of embraces and greetings and the final hoisting of luggage and seventy-pound duffel bags from the vans through the dark air into the ashram greenhouse. After twenty-four hours of traveling, three different plane changes and two hours by van—with a stop at Fuddrucker's in Phoenix for hamburgers before the drive through the desert mountains—there was no downtime, no stopping to regroup or rest. Just straight-ahead and carry on. At seven o'clock this morning Lee and those who traveled with him were sitting in meditation in the meditation hall with the sangha.

Walking into the meditation hall at seven a.m. for meditation to a room full of people sitting on zafus, the sanctity of the space came rolling over like a warm wave. Being away for over four months one gets to see with new eyes. The first perception of the meditation hall was that this place is suffused with the power of Grace. The visual impact alone was very strong. Lee's dais is surrounded by artifacts—the large Shiva lingam given to him by Yvan Amar, the *thangka* of twenty-one Taras given by Arnaud Desjardins, the two foot-high heavy brass Hanuman given to Lee by his student Purna. The Hanuman seemed especially powerful this morning. The deity has a human body with a monkey face and tail. He wears a warrior's helmet and balances a large mace over his left shoulder. His right hand is raised, palm open in the blessing *mudra*. His eyes are sublime, very beautiful and alive as he gazes straight ahead and slightly down. Hanuman the archetypal devotee stands like a sentinel, a peaceful warrior of the heart, appropriately beneath and in front of his Ram, the most powerful artifact in the hall—the *vigraha* of Yogi Ramsuratkumar. The smallest of all the artifacts, Yogi Ramsuratkumar sits smoking his cigarette. On this morning the palpable sense of blessing power that emanated from this small statue was indescribable. Like the *vigraha* at La Ferme de Jutreau, it was alive and drew one's attention like a magnet; the living image of Yogi Ramsuratkumar seemed to laugh and dance in three-dimensional color around its solid metal form. On the high wall eight feet above Lee's seat are large framed color photographs of Papa Ramdas and Yogi Ramsuratkumar. The space is a temple with correspondences in other realms, consecrated by Lee and empowered through years of meditation, prayer, worship and the transmission of dharma. It draws the heart to rest, sometimes to wrestle and burn, but always toward the living God. It is a powerful sanctuary.

By nine o'clock Lee was back at his desk, where people approached him one by one to greet him, ask questions or pass on information. As Lee conducted general business, on the wall behind his desk hung a *thangka* painted by Marcus—Mahakala standing in a corona of leaping red flames. The deity glared out in a fierce grimace, his four arms holding various sacred objects—a necklace of skulls, a skull cup filled with boiling blood, a sharp ritual implement for cutting off heads. The office was buzzing and snapping with energy. A dozen people were busy at work at the ten or twelve desks—on phones, on computers, in small huddles—or just walking through. Upstairs in the kitchen several people bustled around, working on the "Return Feast," which would start tonight at five-thirty. People would be flying into Phoenix today from around the country to greet Lee and participate in the feast and storytelling tonight.

Later in the afternoon the activity in the office and greenhouse increased while the energy built toward dinner and the evening's gathering. Devi arrived from Texas, Rick L.

from Vancouver. Purna and his student Rick N. had arrived the night before and met Lee at the airport, and now mingled with people in the office. The "table" was being set—strips of cloth running the length of the long narrow "greenhouse" room that is much like an enclosed, ground floor verandah. Smells of lasagna came wafting down from the kitchen upstairs. The mood was highly celebratory as many of Lee's students who haven't seen him for months approached him. Outside it was extremely warm and green from the monsoon rains that fell heavily in Arizona during the summer. The cottonwood trees were still leafy and green, and the children ran and played joyfully, happy to be back. Chanting would start at five o'clock, dinner at five-thirty and the stories would begin in the meditation hall at six-thirty.

The feast turned out to be substantial—spinach lasagna, salad, crème brulée, coffee—and the stories were enjoyable, with lots of scattered laughter, especially when stories of the Bordeaux seminar—the dog and fly seminar, as it was called—were recounted. Lee sat on his dais and listened while his students reported. For two hours people sat listening raptly to the stories, asking questions here or there. Lee occasionally added something now and then. During the storytelling someone was recounting Lee's antics at one of the seminars. Lee interjected, "People come in the room with me and something is going to happen. I'm like an idiot savant. The only thing I know anything about is spirituality."

October 6, 1999
Arizona Ashram

Today autumn is in the air. It's cooler than yesterday and very bright. The sky is blinding and vast after the soft blues of the sky over Europe. In the high desert everything is kissed with biting sun and sky and wind. Outside the main house of the ashram there is a big wind blowing around the big sky, tossing the cottonwoods fitfully. Their leaves are green and silver, and they rustle musically in the wind. The mood of practice permeates the atmosphere of the ashram like a faint, inaudible hum beneath the solid foundation of ordinary daily life. Despite the major transition of Lee's return, here at the mother ashram, almost twenty years old since its inception in 1980, life goes on without skipping a beat. This is a working ashram, meaning that there is a very strong focus on work and taking care of business.

Less than forty-eight hours after Lee returned it already felt like he never left—as if he had always been here. Everything seemed extremely ordinary and grounded, a mood that emanates from Lee and settles everything and everyone in. As a result, there was very little fascination or hoo-hah about Lee's return. People were happy to see him, enthusiastic, but still going about their many tasks and jobs. Many of Lee's students here are long-time practitioners for whom the ecstasies of living in the spiritual master's company have metamorphosed over time, carving out a bedrock foundation of practice within ordinary life. These are seasoned practitioners who have carried heavy loads of responsibility for many years.

Yesterday and today Lee is hosting Purna, Rick N., and their friend Dennis, a highly disciplined personal body trainer who flew out from Little Rock. At lunch Dennis told Lee and the others about the racial workshops he is involved in, attempting to bridge the gap between whites and African Americans in the South. People are resistant, he commented.

Changing the subject, Dennis asked, "So, how is it to live here?"

Purna said, "It's wonderful to live here." When Dennis looked surprised to hear this, Purna said, "Really, it is very wonderful to be here."

"It's sanctuary," Chris added.

Looking not entirely convinced Dennis laughed and said, "Everyone else is keeping their mouths shut."

Jane commented, "Well, it's heaven but it's also hell, because the level of self-confrontation is demanding." She talked about the burn of confronting levels of pride, greed, selfishness, the unwillingness or failure to truly serve others. "It can be very painful to confront those levels of the drive to control, to power, to the manipulation of others, even in the most mundane circumstances."

Dennis looked skeptical and said, "Where I come from that's an indulgence of white people, doing that kind of self-reflecting . . ." He briefly commented on how African Americans have a necessity in their circumstance that places them beyond such luxuries. It was an interesting momentary interface between spiritual life and the platform of social reform. Lee sat listening quietly. He seemed to have a natural, unspoken rapport with Dennis, and invited him to give a talk to the sangha after dinner.

Later about seventy people gathered in the greenhouse for chanting and dinner, which Lee made for his students—a choice between a thick and chunky raw green salad—lettuce and other vegetables from the ashram garden—or fruit salad. Lee's salads are always a unique experience. One never knows what will show up in them, from walnuts to pasta to cheese or olives or anything that is leftover, sometimes just rice or barley or baked potatoes cut into square chunks and thrown in the mix. They brim over with shakti and life force. Eating these guru salads is like getting a hit of pure fire in the veins. There is nothing consoling about these salads; instead they are a confrontation to ego. Guests often sit wonderingly with the huge plates of salad and nothing else at Lee's After Dinner Talk table. It is simplicity itself, and yet there is nothing sparse about it. As Dennis ate his salad at dinner he laughed and said, "You guys may need to work on exercise, but you've got the diet thing together!"

October 8, 1999
Bullhead City, Arizona

Lee left the ashram with seven people in the mini-van at four-thirty to drive the three hours to Bullhead City for his reunion gig tonight with Shri. His mood was quiet and inward as he drove the van up through the scraggly scrub brush and tumbleweeds of Chino Valley to Interstate 40, where he headed west toward Kingman. The landscape gave way to evergreen shrubs set in red dry earth. These odd shrubs, low and pear-shaped, dotted the ground and spread out toward the low hills that flanked higher mountains which rose in progressive waves to crest and peak many miles away. Pale green grass and desert sage covered the lower ground, complement to scattered round boulders and interspersed with scruffy junipers, chaparral and the ever-present wind-warped and twisted cedar trees. Along the arroyos dense cottonwood thickets grew beneath craggy outcroppings of rock as the land rose up dramatically. The mountains were a brooding green-black silhouette of goat's horns, devilish against the pale orange sky of the horizon. Sunset was just beginning to come on and would offer up a constantly changing view of natural wonder as day changed to night over the next two hours.

The land seemed like the broken bones of the earth, protruding in the hills and bluffs, the looming mountains growing higher as we wound our way through this chiseled scene of incomparable beauty. Lee drove in silence, answering a few questions here and there, his eyes on the road. The mountains seemed to reflect his mood: solitary, alone, complete in and of themselves. Following the seemingly endless ribbon of road into the western sky, the mountains became a massive wall of purple rock set against a faint golden light that bled into the pearl gray sky. Even higher peaks in the distance seemed to be leading us on, as Lee answered a question about the difference between the France ashram and the Arizona ashram. There seems to be a difference between the two ashrams, not only in the physical circumstances, but in the mood of the sangha itself. The sangha in Arizona seems more set in their ways, someone commented, more stolidly ensconced in the status quo, less open to possibility and even cynical, while the European sangha seems more fluid, more ecstatic, more grateful.

The Arizona sangha has very deep roots in the Work, in practice. The Arizona ashram is the backbone, the foundation of the Hohm Community. There is a tremendous maturity and dedication in Lee's American sangha, but having years in the master's company is both a blessing and a curse in some ways. It is a blessing because one has worked through a tremendous amount of obstacles over time, as the guru literally empowers and initiates the disciple through various means—from subtle, energetic and ethereal to gross, physical, concrete—to the point that the body becomes encoded with the teaching. Over time in the master's company, if one is engaging the practices fully, the student becomes a living artifact of the Work, or of the teacher's transmission, despite tenacious areas of weakness that must be continually fed as fuel into the fire of sadhana.

On the other hand, having years in the master's company can be a curse because the psychological tendency of human beings is to become more and more crystallized. The visionary idealism and zealousness for the path that carries one along for years can erode into cynicism and disillusionment as one's false notions of the path block the way of deeper understandings and abiding insight. The very fact of one's helplessness to transform oneself is a barrier, and the truth of this hopelessness becomes brutally apparent over time. Paradoxically, it is this very hopelessness—when grounded in the context of the path—that is the doorway to transformation. When the context of hopelessness is the understanding that nothing but the realization of God will satisfy our longing, then hopelessness as a state of mind becomes tremendously freeing, as Chögyam Trungpa Rinpoche so eloquently described from the nontheistic perspective. To be truly hopeless is to end the search for self-gratification, for consolation, for salvation. To be truly hopeless is to realize that nothing in the temporal realm will satisfy our ultimate desire, which is for that which transcends all desire, or the stainless, primordial and impossible world of the guru.

Sitting behind the wheel dispassionately Lee answered the question about the two ashrams, saying, "It's all the same to me." It was a definitive statement. It's all the illusion of separation, regardless of appearances, until one is surrendered to the Will of God. We may appear ecstatic or cynical, happy or sad, but the underlying cramp is, at core, the same thing—we live and labor under the illusion that we are separate from God. When pressed further, he said, "There are differences in form of course, and because of the laws in France we have to work differently in practical terms. If it weren't for that, we'd have the same kind of work load," he said, meaning the businesses, the bands and so on, "that we have in Arizona. But to me, it's all the same."

Lee fell silent again. It was warm in the van with all the windows closed, and with Lee at the wheel it seemed like we were on some kind of fantastic voyage through space and time as we zoomed past the surreal scene outside. The emanations of Lee's silence drew the drama of the desert twilight into the thick chamber of the van as it sped down the road. Dusk turned mountains, trees, rocks and shrubs to fantastic, magnificent or grotesque black contours and forms set against pale gold, which changed to a burnished gold and then luminous copper as the sun dropped more deeply behind the mountains. The distant northern mountains became ancient massive beings, elements of mineral life, bathed now in mauve and rose, then muted into shadows. Some of them resembled waves of the ocean, frozen in form at the peak of the wave. The signs on the highway flashed by—"$5.39, Steak & Eggs" in neon—along with truck stops, gas stations, cheap food, fast food, Indian jewelry, junk. Heading west on Interstate 40, zooming through the Mohave Desert, we were back in America on the road with Lee, headed to some other remote outpost to play Baul music.

There was a terribly lonely feeling to everything in this twilight crack between the worlds—the juxtaposition of the desert with its fierce communication of raw life so real, set against distant clusters of city lights that populated the oncoming night. Telephone poles stretched out into the distance, black against the sunset, wires humming with the play of maya—hours spent in idle gossip and meaningless chitchat to relieve the ennui of the day. They seemed to epitomize the opposite of Lee's pristine silence, which was completely free of any noise or static.

Lee's silence is often experienced as disconcerting or disturbing because there is nothing going on under the surface. His silence reveals everything around it, and there are only two possibilities: illusion or Reality. His silence resounds with radiant emptiness, *shunyata*, and was in this moment a teaching communication in itself in striking contrast to the noisy chatter of the mind. Some people are silent and quiet, but their silences are noisy or screaming, even violent, with the active underworld elements of the psyche churning and bubbling just below the surface. These silences have the power to dominate and control the environment, to manipulate through their freezing or burning effect. Lee was pure freedom within the silence he emanated. He was a vast space driving into vast space, and yet he was there, a man driving toward the Western horizon, now burned into luminous orange behind the heavy black mountains. In these moments nothing else existed but driving through the desert on the way to the gig. Just This.

"Rattlesnake Wash," the sign said, just before Kingman, where Lee turned the mini-van up out of the desert floor into a maze of wild mountain peaks. Driving into Bullhead City, Arizona and its twin, Laughlin, Nevada, the immense lights of the casinos—a mini Las Vegas—reflected in bright streaks of silver, gold, blue and red in the slick, glittering water of the Colorado River. Scraggly palm trees and eucalyptus trees lined the water. Riverfront property is worth a fortune here in this desert oasis, and commerce thrives along the river's shore. We drove past pawn shops, fast food joints, car dealerships and palm readers while Rakini, the drummer for Shri, talked about a new gig they'd just gotten, playing in one of the casinos. "Good pay and all you can eat off the buffet tables, but boring audiences," she said.

Lee commented, "That's great! We should get as many of those gigs as we can. A few weekends of those kind of gigs could help pay for our Europe tour next summer. I'd rather play to boring audiences and make good money than play to exciting audiences for three hundred dollars a night!"

Lee pulled into the parking lot—half-vacant, half-full of cars and gleaming Harley Davidson motorcycles—in front of the bar. The Store, it was called, partner to the restaurant, El Rey, on the second floor of the square, box-like hunk of a building. Lee walked in and looked around. He'd been here before with Shri.

Bullhead City is also the scene of another bar, the Riviera Roadhouse, where Lee played with liars, gods & beggars several times in years past. At the Riviera Roadhouse the local people literally adored liars, gods & beggars. A motley mix of bikers and friendly working-class people, the "regulars" of the establishment were, as Lee once said, perhaps the only real, lasting fan base LGB ever had. As soon as the band arrived people started would walk over and talk to Lee, shaking his hand, buying any new CDs the band might have, asking for autographs. Like one man in particular, who spoke of losing his wife in a divorce. He was about sixty-five years old, with a two-day growth of gray beard on his haggard face. "I don't have anybody to talk to now," he said to Lee one night, "I'm all alone. Nobody understands."

Being at the Riviera Roadhouse one was constantly reminded that all life is suffering. It was populated with many interesting characters who, although often warm, friendly and accepting, were obvious societal outcasts. It was the place where a very unusual reciprocal relationship between local folks and Lee's Baul band had just sprung up out of nowhere in a seedy little neighborhood bar. Liars, gods & beggars traveled the long miles to Bullhead City on many nights to play for these good people. Although The Store (or Senor Shrimp, as tonight's venue used to be called) had some similarities—in that it was also a working-class bar—it almost instantly it showed itself to be very different than the Riviera Roadhouse.

Walking into the bar the senses were immediately assaulted with the flamboyant, overdone décor of the bar. The walls were festooned with Halloween motif cutouts, pumpkins, skeletons, ghosts. These mingled with the neon beer signs, the chrome and wood of the bar, all of it reflected in the long mirror behind the bar itself. As we took our seats at a table in the back of the bar, we looked above our heads to see what had to be the most immense plastic chandelier in the world. It rotated slowly, trailing a white plastic ghost and a blow-up plastic racecar that said, "Betty's car" on the side.

A few people populated the bar, but mostly it seemed empty. Several bikers sat nearby at the bar. They yelled and slapped each other on the back, laughing in their bellicose way. All along the bar people were sitting and drinking, most of them "regulars" of the place because of their familiarity with each other and the bartender. The owner, a man with silver hair and a craggy face, came walking through now and then.

The band went into its first song and about halfway into it the shrieking scream of electronic feedback blasted through the room. It was painfully loud and took longer than usual to get under control. The bikers at the other end of the bar started yelling at the band. "You suck!" one of them shouted. He was a big, muscle-bound guy with brown hair and ruddy cheeks, probably thirty-five years old. His buddy echoed, "Yeah—suck!" The barmaid, who really likes Shri, came down to their end of the bar and said, "That was really rude. That wasn't nice at all." Another woman who was sitting at the bar halfway down toward the band with a drink in her hand leaned over and yelled at the men, "*You* suck!" She continued to glare at them. In the meantime the band kept going, Deborah making some joke to cover the awkwardness of the moment. The man who had yelled out first walked down to the woman at the bar and talked to her. She frowned and reprimanded him in a loud voice, shaking her head angrily. She was obviously giving him hell for being so rude to the band. After about a minute of that exchange the burley biker went stalking up to the band. He stood in front of Lee like a little boy, hung his head and said, "I'm sorry, man. You guys are okay, you're really good." Lee smiled and nodded his hand and gave him a friendly slap on the shoulder, saying, "It's no problem. It's okay." The man shook hands with other members of the band who smiled at him, the interaction erasing the tension.

The place was set up so that the band was completely separated from the rest of the bar. In between the band and the tables where people sat was a pool table with an immense rectangular beer sign light hanging down low over it. An older woman dressed in a mini-skirt danced provocatively around it to the music as she played game after game of pool. It served as an effective barrier between the few tables of people who were listening and the band. Even the music seemed somehow muted in the back of the room. The tables themselves were on top of a disco-style dance floor, but no one danced. There were three or four televisions going all the time, including one on the wall behind the band. It was not a good situation for band and audience rapport, and as it turned out, the whole night was dominated by a kind of psychic barrier that could be felt in the space, with the pool table as a concrete manifestation of that.

One of the band members commented that the ground along the back wall of the building, where they had unloaded their equipment and carried it through the door into the bar, smelled of urine and vomit. The men's bathroom had just been remodeled because two men had a fight in it recently and destroyed it. Tonight was a good night—no violence—but overall it was a rather painful gig after experiencing Shri in the festivals and beer gardens of Europe. Everett commented on the place, "It's a bardo transit station." All around the top of the cheesy plastic chandelier, which turned around and around, were written the words "Señor Shrimp" in large red letters. At one point in the slow turning only the "Shri" was visible. It was one of those quirky little details of a place that adds an element of the absurd to the situation, bringing the surreal bardo atmosphere eerily into focus.

There had been some hopeful expectations about Lee's reunion with Shri tonight. Naturally everyone wanted the first gig back together with the spiritual master to be inspiring, but one thing about band sadhana in Lee's company is that it is always real—a reflection of reality. Reality is not going to be inspiring all the time; on the contrary, it is going to be communicating every possible expression or quality of the Divine, from splendor, beauty and mercy to raw power, boredom, severity or ferocity.

In this way circumstances seem to conspire with the influence that guides Lee's work with his students to create situations in which constant learning is the opportunity. No amount of bravado or musical skill could penetrate the deadening elements of this place tonight. It would take powerful magic to blast that place open, and that is something Lee never manipulates in any way. If divine influence orchestrates an opening at times like this, it is all a function of the blessings of Yogi Ramsuratkumar. If not, then it is just what is.

The Baul bands have experienced this kind of bardo many times over the years of performing. Like LGB before them, Shri is heroic in the face of these kinds of obstacles. They played on this night like champions, staying light and laughing a lot among themselves, even though there were many difficulties with the sound onstage in addition to the general weirdness of the place. Talking later about the difficulties of the gig, Steve B., the keyboard player, said, "We were just playing for Lee, playing for the 'other audience,' playing for each other to have fun."

The "other audience"—the unseen dimensions of higher beings, the *devas* and *devis*, the angelic forces that congregate wherever the influence of Yogi Ramsuratkumar is present in the form of his son Lee—seemed to be at work behind the scenes. It's not uncommon when these doldrums occur that something useful will end up coming out of it—a certain connection, an opportunity, a meeting between the band and one or two people that makes itself noticed. Despite the impasse of the denying force at work, in the middle of the evening a big guy walked in and introduced himself to the band. "My name is Rick *Love*," he smiled and made a play on words with his last name. He handed a card to Tina, "I book bands. Give me a call—you guys are *really* great!"

October 9, 1999
Arizona Ashram

At eight-thirty this morning Lee watched out the kitchen window of Arrakis, his house on the ashram, as the white mini-van, a recent addition to the ashram vehicle pool, trundled off down the dirt road from the office toward the ashram gate. Since Lee has gotten back to Arizona he has made numerous comments about how ashram residents were consistently and unnecessarily using the mini-van for errands instead of taking the older and smaller Toyota that had been driven for four years and is run-down and funky. Time and again over the past week he has watched out the kitchen window as the mini-van left with only one person in it. Each time he shook his head in exasperation.

His eyes were on the mini-van now as it stopped at the gate. Looking more closely, he asked, "Who is that?" He paused and said, "It's Brother Juniper," answering his own question. Someone said, "Probably on his way into town to sell glass cases."

Lee grumbled, "People are so predictable! Everyone is using the mini-van just because they think it's a 'nicer' car. It's all vanity and greed. It's disgusting from people who are supposed to be practitioners. The mini-van will be trashed in no time if this keeps going on." He walked swiftly out of the kitchen and downstairs to the office, going through the greenhouse and the front door to stand outside on the flagstones by the garden. Brother Juniper was now closing the gate about one hundred yards away. "Hey!" Lee shouted to him, gesturing with his arms to come back. As soon as it was clear that Brother Juniper had seen him and was turning back, Lee went back inside.

Kyla, the ashram office manager, was just walking up. Seeing Lee calling Brother Juniper back, she hurried into the office and to the blackboard where cars are signed out and the keys to vehicles are hung. As she said later, "It was one of those rare moments when you know what he needs and you can perhaps facilitate it."

Walking to the vehicle sign-out board, Lee turned to Kyla and said, "Is there another vehicle available?"

"Yes, the Toyota," she answered, but it was available for twenty-five minutes less than the time that Brother Juniper had signed out the mini-van for. Lee said very politely and graciously, "Kyla, would you ask Brother Juniper when he gets here, if it is at all possible would he please take the Toyota? Tell him I apologize for the time difference; if it won't work for him he can go on and take the mini-van, but if it is at *all* possible, it would be better for him to take the Toyota." He walked back upstairs and left Kyla to deliver the message.

Kyla met Brother Juniper at the door to the greenhouse and relayed Lee's message.

Brother Juniper had several appointments in town and had taken the mini-van because the Toyota was signed out almost all day in a crazy criss-crossing of notes and names on the vehicle sign-out board. He listened to Kyla's message and immediately said, "Sure!" Kyla handed him the keys and off he went. As it turned out, because he had to get the car back to the ashram twenty-five minutes earlier than he'd planned, he missed a few appointments for Baul Theatre Company business—selling ads for a program for *The Elephant Man*—which the theatre company planned to perform in November. When asked about it he said, "It didn't matter because what Lee wanted was what was important."

Within hours everyone on the ashram had heard about Lee "running out to catch" Brother Juniper. Some heard that Lee had run down the road to get him; others knew he stood outside the door and called to him. Exaggeration being a common tendency of devotional schools, it is one of the traits that shows up in Lee's students, and in this case it was a little comical as the story gained the momentum of added embellishments. Some groused about how the Toyota was known to leak exhaust fumes into the car; others said that wasn't true, or that it had been repaired and was now fine. Reactivity and fascinations aside, the point was made and the mini-van sat unused in the parking lot.

Other than the vanity and desire to "look good" driving a newer car, or having the comfort of sitting in a newer car, it seemed that there was another aspect to what Lee was pointing toward, which has to do with restraint and conservation of resources. Resources are forms of energy, whether they are financial resources, human resources, or material objects like cars, equipment, food—all of which cost money. In tantric practice it is crucial that one learn to observe and work with how one manages the domains of money, food and sex—which covers everything in one way or another. Money is a metaphor for power and energy; food is a metaphor for everything we eat, from gross physical food, to air, to subtle impressions; and sex is a metaphor for the entire spectrum of relationship. If we cannot or do not apply tantric principles of discrimination, forbearance and beggary to our everyday actions, we are not embodying the teaching. If there is a new car available and we are compelled to use the new car instead of continuing to make do with the still perfectly good old one that we used to use, we are probably acting from the unconscious motivations of a grasping ego.

As it turned out there was also a shiny new stainless steel industrial stove with a convection oven sitting in the kitchen in Arrakis when Lee got back to Arizona. It had been bought to replace one of the two stoves that had been in the kitchen for fifteen years or more. Lee made a similar teaching lesson about new stove. When he found out that it should not be cleaned with anything abrasive, he practically shouted at Jaya, the ashram cook, "Only one or two people should be allowed to clean the new stove! If you want the stove to be cared for properly, you're going to have to do it yourself!" He also made the point that the other stove, which had been in the Arrakis kitchen for years, should still be used as much as possible, rather than turning to the new stove for every kettle of water or leftover pot of soup that needed to be heated.

The "stove teachings" continued. Yesterday Lee was walking across the ashram property when he noticed that the old kitchen stove was sitting on the rough ground in the weeds by one of the storage sheds. There was junk piled on top of the stove—lumber and boxes. If it rained, the stove would be ruined. Lee stopped, looked at the stove and muttered, "Unbelievable." Someone said that there wasn't room in the storage shed when the stove was removed, but there was a plan to put the it inside the shed as soon as the shed was cleaned out and reorganized. It was a big project involving locating more storage options for some of the contents of the shed—something that has become more and more problematical in the over-crowded Arizona ashram. Lee shook his head in disbelief and said, "That's not good enough. It's a perfectly good stove and it's going to get ruined sitting out there on the ground."

Thirty minutes later when Steve B. walked into the office Lee called him over to his desk. "I want the old stove moved into the storage shed *today*," Lee said briskly. "If the stove isn't stored somewhere safely, where it won't get rained on, *by this afternoon*—and I don't care where that is, as long as the stove is taken care of—then I want it put in *my bedroom*." Steve looked at Lee incredulously. The whole office was quiet, everyone listening to this conversation.

"What about the porch of Ladala?" Steve asked.

"I don't care what you do," Lee responded tersely, "as long as the stove is properly stored out of the weather and off of the ground. If it's not stored somewhere else this afternoon, I want it in my bedroom." Lee wasn't kidding; on the contrary, he was totally serious. If the stove ended up in Lee's bedroom, it could very easily stay there for the next ten years, just to make a point to his students. A point perhaps related to the eyesore of the old toilet that adorns the rock garden outside the meditation hall. Lee had the toilet installed there when it was taken from one of the buildings on the ashram property five years ago. Every time we walk into the meditation hall—every morning for meditation, on Sunday evenings for darshan, on Tuesday and Thursday nights for After Dinner Talks— we pass the white porcelain toilet set against a cottonwood tree. Now it has honeysuckle growing stubbornly out of its bowl, which is filled with dirt.

Steve nodded in assent and left to make the arrangements. He immediately drove his van down to the shed and put the stove in it, which was where it stayed for a few days until it landed on the porch of one of the buildings on the ashram.

On the way out the ashram gate to a rush hour movie later in the day Lee greeted a new visitor, a woman from San Diego who had met Lee at a public talk he had given there last spring. She smiled when she saw that it was him stopping to talk at the gate. "I'll be back later this evening—we're going to a movie," he smiled, welcoming her. "Just go up to the main building ahead of you there," he pointed toward Arrakis, "and there will be people in the office who can show you around."

After the movie later that night in the evening gathering over tea, Lee talked with her again. "Be careful what you do around here," he laughed dangerously, "because a lot of the people here are zealots. If you breach protocol they'll give you hell." He laughed again. She looked at him with surprise on her face.

Someone asked the guest, Christine, how she had heard about Lee. She said that her chiropractor, Dr. Michael, who hosted Lee in San Diego last spring, had shown her the flyer for the public talk. It said, "The Divine Jester." She said "I looked at the picture of Lee and said to myself, 'I want to see that man. That is someone I can relate to.' She seemed very happy to be sitting having tea now with Lee and his companions.

She began to tell Lee a dream that she had in which she was sitting across the table from Lee. Between them was placed a plate of chocolate. He gestured to her to eat it. She ate it and it tasted like air; it wasn't sweet, but at the same time it was delicious. She said that she felt wonderful when she woke up. "What does that mean?" she asked, smiling.

"I don't know anything about dreams," he said. "I used to interpret my students' dreams, but I would tell them what I thought and they would just look at me like, 'That's interesting.' So I quit doing it because all they wanted was a reinforcement of their own interpretation. If I was a therapist I'd charge $125 an hour!" Lee paused, then said, "My students *think* they pay me," Lee laughed and continued with a trace of irony in his voice, "but I pay my students, by the hour, eternally."

There was a slight lull in the conversation while this comment was absorbed in silence by the small group that sat around Lee. The talk turned to the movie Lee had gone to see, "American Beauty." He said forcefully, "So many of my students recommended that movie to me when I got home. After all the rave reviews I got from my students and then seeing it tonight, it makes me want to pack up my bags and go to California—leave it all! I can't believe that my students have so little discrimination!"

Lee's movie habits have changed over the years. He used to go see everything. Now, and for the past several years, he goes to movies that are either uplifting, entertaining, funny and light-hearted, or children's movies. He avoids the heavy doses of the bitter reality of human suffering. The best actors, like Kevin Spacey in "American Beauty," can invoke that reality to such a powerful degree that the images of the movie and the feelings that are invoked have a deep impact on the psyche. For Lee, it seems to be a matter of making judicious choices about what kind of impression food he will eat.

Now he explained, "We should already be so deeply in touch with the reality of suffering, it should be such a *cellular* knowledge for us, that we hardly need to go to a movie to remind us of it. That stuff is too real to me—it's too much like my daily life. I want to go to movies to be entertained, to laugh." To Erica, visiting from San Francisco, he said, "Did you like it?"

She laughed and said truthfully, "I loved it." Lee smiled at her. There was not even the thinnest thread of judgement, disapproval or pressure to be different. As much as Lee may rail against something in principle, or even against a particular individual's actions, the underlying mood of his relationship with his students remains one of total acceptance and positive regard, if we are able to see it through our filters.

Mariana began to talk about the interviews for a new book she is writing. During one interview the person she was interviewing got fifty e-mails in ten minutes. The people sitting around the circle who don't use e-mail for various reasons were shocked. The conversation turned again to the insidious effects of computers on human life, including the loss of privacy and the intrusiveness of e-mail. Lee said, "Everyone I know who is an intelligent, thinking person thinks that computers are deadly. They are ruining human culture. They're killing us. But we carry on about them, can't live without them. We *revel* in them in fact," he said with disgust, "and that's what's so horrible about it—we are reveling in our own downfall."

October 10, 1999
Arizona Ashram

Lee came into darshan at seven-twenty. He had just rushed back to the ashram from a Shri gig at a local restaurant. It was a patio gig, with a happy, attentive audience sitting out on the Southwest-style adobe terrace. About thirty-five members of the community were there, having dinner and watching the band, mingling in the crowd with the local clientele—a real family scene. Lee left after the first set and came back to give darshan. Now he sat down, carrying his cardboard box of *prasad*. He was wrapped in a large gray-blue wool shawl given to him by Yogi Ramsuratkumar. Around his head was a green cloth wrap.

After the chanting Lee asked for more stories from the summer in France. In the middle of the stories Laura had been commenting on how much she liked the meals in the barn, and the kinds of teaching spaces that Lee had created during those group meals, when someone brought up the differences between the Arizona ashram and the France ashram.

Lee snorted, "Yes, my students romantically started calling those spaces 'darshan.' It was more like . . ." he grappled momentarily for the right description, found it and continued, *"gripe sessions!* Even the spiritual master needs someone to complain to. If we were meant to return to that kind of process over meals here in Arizona, everybody in town would start coming out here for meals. As it is, we only participate when we want to here in Arizona. We come to special meals, to feasts, but not to the Sunday afternoon period of *seva* (work). If there was more participation under ordinary circumstances it might provoke something more, but now there is too much of a discrepancy between participation when there is a reward—a flash of some kind—and participation when all you have to do is work or serve.

"The dharma says that everything associated with this Work carries the Influence of Yogi Ramsuratkumar. Whenever I go to India to visit Yogi Ramsuratkumar I don't expect Him to be available to me; I'm very grateful when He comes to darshan while I'm there. I am fully prepared to only see Him at the temple and then to spend the rest of the time chanting in darshan without Him—sitting and listening to my students while they lead the chants, as difficult as that would be! People come to Yogi Ramsuratkumar and they want a personal task, but it's obvious that anything we do for Him has His Blessing. If we pick up a piece of paper on the ashram ground, we have His Blessings!

"So something like more participation from the sangha here could provoke something more from me. When we were looking for a new ashram we were planning a more adequate dining situation, but the timing isn't right yet for a new ashram. For that to happen, our relationship to what is already offered would have to change . . ."

The rest of the evening was given over to storytelling and lots of laughter at the foibles of Lee's students, with Lee listening and occasionally interrupting with, "Let me tell my side of the story!"

October 17, 1999
Phoenix

It was Sunday morning and a group of about ten people drove one of the ashram vans down through the mountains into the Sonoran desert toward Phoenix, where they would meet up with Lee, Shri and Attila the Hunza. Lee had spent the night before in Tucson performing at a street festival with Shri. They were driving up from Tucson to Phoenix this morning to hook up with Attila the Hunza, where both bands would play the AIDS Walk Arizona—a benefit street corner concert for the large crowd of local people who would march this morning to raise money for AIDS. Many local businesses, newspapers, radio stations, public utilities and so on would put up money for every person who walked. There would be local television stations filming the short performances—only thirty minutes for each band, with Hunza starting and then Shri coming on after them. Shri would play until the last of the crowd walked past. The fundraisers expected twenty thousand people to walk. The organizers had eight or ten bands playing on street corners throughout the fourteen-block route of the march to entertain the crowd and create a celebratory atmosphere. Word was that Sista Blue, a popular Arizona blues band, was also playing for the march.

The streets were empty as we walked the two blocks from where the van was parked to the corner of Third Avenue and Washington Street in downtown Phoenix. The police had barricaded the whole area for the march today; the deserted streets and the huge vacant buildings, half constructed with chain-link fences around the construction sites, added to the feeling of strangeness as we walked past. Elyse, who had booked this gig, laughed and said, "It's like a scene out of 'Planet of the Apes.'" Very soon we heard music drifting on the air. Someone said, "Oh that must be some other band," but as we got closer we saw that it was Attila the Hunza doing their sound check. They sounded fantastic.

Lee was standing on the street corner by the portable stage where the two bands would play. He walked across the street to greet his students who had just arrived for the performance. While Hunza finished their sound check most of the members of Shri and their road crew came over and joined their friends. Lee, Jim C., Tina and Deborah started talking about the gig in Tucson the night before. Lee's take on it was rather different from the reports that were coming in from some of the band members. It was a street fair gig, with the band set up in a parking lot. About seventy-five people gathered around the band, while a couple of hundred milled around the area. Some of the band members described it as a great gig; one of those outdoor gigs in which nature combines with the music to create some magic, but Lee kept insisting, "It was okay, nothing special."

There was a rather angry drunk who kept coming up onstage last night. He was trying to harass members of the band. While others talked about Lee's interactions with the drunk, saying that the drunk was hanging on Lee, talking and embracing him, Lee said, "That's what I'm for in Shri—to keep the drunks away from the rest of the band."

This morning in Phoenix with Shri and Attila the Hunza the weather was gorgeous in that dazzling way of the desert, with its blinding sunlight and immensity of sky. It was getting hotter by the moment, and the trees planted along the streets—feathery palo verde, olive trees and Japanese pines—stood quietly in the still, warm air. We stood in the bit of shade provided by the trees the city had planted in small, square concrete gardens along with aloes, century plants and other succulents or cacti that can survive one hundred and twenty degree heat for several months out of the year. Cops drove by in pairs on motor-cycles, checking out the empty streets. Three blocks away one could see an immense crowd amassing as the march began to wind, snake-like, through the city streets. It would take another fifteen or twenty minutes for them to get within hearing distance of our corner, when Attila the Hunza would start playing.

A street person walked up, his skin dark and leathery from living outside. His clothes were disheveled and dirty and hung loosely on his body. He looked at Lee and said enthusiastically, "When's the band going to start playing? Let's go! Get those drums going!" He exchanged a look with Lee, smiled a huge, lopsided friendly smile and walked on. While Lee stood on the sidewalk he talked with some of the men, Bandhu and Jim C. and Sylvan. More street people wandered past in filthy, ragged clothes. Their faces were smudged with dirt and they carried brown paper bags rolled down around bottles of liquor. As the group waited for the march to reach our outpost Elyse talked about how they were having a prayer vigil and Unitarian Church service where the march began, several blocks away. They were praying for those with AIDS, and for those who have already died. Lee snapped, "Yes well, they shouldn't have created it if they didn't want people to die from it." It was one of those radical social commentaries that Lee will make at times.

"How long do you play?" Bandhu asked Lee, referring to Shri.

"We're gonna play until the last straggler, the last policeman, the last person walks by . . ." Lee answered with a grim enthusiasm. Thirty-minute performances are famously frustrating for the bands. They hardly get started and have to stop again, feeling unfinished. It is an unsatisfying situation, but Lee has always encouraged the bands to do benefit concerts like this regardless of the circumstance.

The earliest marchers begin to walk past in short spurts of people—two or three or four or five at a time. Still the main part of the crowd was not visible yet. As soon as they got within hearing distance, Attila the Hunza would begin. Lee's group stood in the now burning hot sun and waited. Another ten or twelve joggers came by with a dog on a leash wearing a T-shirt that said "AIDS Walk Arizona" on it. Finally around eleven o'clock the beginning of the marching throng appeared and Hunza struck into their first song. Dressed in black, in miniskirts and high boots with black feathers or thin, lacquered sticks arranged wildly in their hair, with eyes painted in iridescent blues or browns, Kate and Clelia jumped up onstage and started dancing and bantering to the audience. They were glamorous and hip and chic and loose in a way that Lee's bands have never been before. They glittered with mystery in the midday sun of this very middleworld downtown gig. Right away the television cameraman who had been floating around the scene tuned into them and started filming. Clelia said over the microphone, "We are an interplanetary exploratory vehicle, a voyaging machine. Get ready to depart!"

The first song was a Lee Lozowick/Everett Jaime original called "Everywhere You Turn," sung by Kate. It was a fabulous song with lyrics that go beyond social protest to probe the existential suffering of humankind and the illusion of separation. The melody, beautifully rendered in Kate's rich and evocative voice, takes one into a feeling of collective heartbreak—a shared sadness at the way things are.

Everywhere you turn
You see another violent war
Outside's a reflection
It would pay to know the score
We'll never find the peace
That we are looking for
If we don't stop the certain death
Our minds have got in store

(Chorus)
Everywhere you turn, you turn
The story's just the same
The question that is burning us
Can we re-write the game
Everywhere you turn, you turn
A losing proposition
Are you willing to stand out
To be in opposition

Look at other people
Feeling sorry about their pains

Ignore our gaping wounds
And our fevered brains
We're never going to dry
While standing in the rain
Hell's around the corner
Not upon some distant plain

(Chorus)

Everywhere you turn
It seems that things they are failing
It only gets more difficult
When we consider bailing
Where we go that's where we are
It's trite yet it is true
It's not over there upon some distant star
It's right inside of you

Clelia came in with Kate on harmonies, their voices mingling and soaring through the air while scores of young, attractive people walked briskly by, many of them looking up at the band, waving or smiling or just listening intently as they walked. Lee stood across the street on the opposite side of the stage with his students and Shri, watching every move of Hunza. After the last chords of the song died away Everett yelled out, "You guys *rock!*" Lots of cheers and whoops of appreciation greeted the band. This was only their seventh performance.

The crowd was a river of people of all colors—Mexican and African and European and Hispanic Americans—flowing through the streets. It was made up of mostly young adults and couples, gay, lesbian and heterosexual, some holding hands, but also some middle-aged folks and now and then an older person. Many of them had their dogs with them on leashes.

The band went into a Bob Dylan number, "All Along the Watchtower," with Kate singing and then an Iggy Pop song that Clelia sang. The two women's voices blended in harmonies that lent a shimmering edge to the bright colors of the day. Kate called out to the crowd, "Hey, you guys are *great*—you're walking for a really great cause!" Throngs of people swept by in shorts, T-shirts, hats. There were babies in backpacks on Mom's or Dad's back, toddlers in strollers, water bottles and dogs.

Attila the Hunza's thirty-minute set was going by fast as they went into one of their more provocative numbers, "Submission," by the Sex Pistols. In this song Clelia and Kate went into a slightly toned-down version of the sadomasochistic theatre they do during this song. Many people in the crowd watched the band as they walked past, their faces turned toward the performance until they had to turn the corner and walk away down Washington Street. A gay pride contingent walked past waving a rainbow banner. They were riveted on the outrageous theatre during "Submission." They hooted and yelled out, "Right on!" while Clelia wielded an invisible whip over Kate's submissive and bent head and the music crashed straight ahead. Clelia pointed toward the crowd, pulling them into her words in a magnetic and compelling delivery of the song. The cameraman rolled on, honing in for a closer shot.

Hunza had done this same piece of theatre at a restaurant gig in Prescott during the summer. Although the owner of the club had loved the band and rocked-out all night with them, two of his customers complained about the S&M theater at the end of the night. The band was not invited back to the club again. When Lee had heard about it in France he said, "It's just some old Christians getting bent out of shape. If they're uptight about sex, it's their problem. If the manager wants to cater to that kind of mentality, let him. If that's the clientele he wants at his restaurant, fine. I want the band to do whatever theatre they want to do—*within reason.*"

He watched them now quietly, soaking it up. The band's rough and raw edges as inexperienced musicians were easily reconciled by their enthusiasm and flair for the theatrical. They were far from being perfect or great as musicians in the technical sense—time, practice and experience would upscale all that and smooth over the rough edges for them. But it was the lack of guile, the lack of the pretensions and affectations of the "artist," that in part made their performance so fresh and enlivening for the audience.

Clelia and Kate went into a riveting and slightly menacing version of "One Way or Another," by Blondie. In the meantime the ordinary, mundane affair of the march went rolling past. A two-year-old boy rode past in a red wagon, his mother pulling him along. More dogs of all kinds, shapes and sizes trotted past with their masters. Some of them were four feet high while others were tiny Chihuahuas. It was funny to watch them with their owners, all of them on leashes.

The band brought Justin Hitson, the former drummer of liars, gods & beggars and a very talented musician, onstage to sing and play lead guitar on their last song, "Play That Funky Music, White Boy." It was the first time they'd ever performed it. When Justin played with LGB they used to call him Justin "Big Funk" Hitson because he has a natural soulful quality as a musician. Today he *was* the white boy playing that funky music, delivering a stinging guitar solo backed up by Andrew on rhythm guitar and the bass, played by Zachary, which thrummed in a funky bottom line, laying down the rhythm section with Steve S. on the drums. The women's back-up vocals were sassy and sexy. The cameraman had been moving from one position to another in front of the stage, capturing the band at different angles. He seemed very enamored with the band, and indeed they were visually awesome with the two women up front dancing like sirens—strutting, playing tambourine, playfully dancing around each of the musicians.

A group of graduate students carrying a banner that said, "Thunderbird—The American Graduate School of International Management," stopped to listen for awhile. They were buzzing among themselves, and when Hunza came off the stage one of them approached Kate. They wanted to book the band for their graduation gig in Phoenix. Kate turned them to Atilla the Hunza's booking agent, Elyse, who took their card and promised to call. It was all very exciting for a group of young people, most of whom had never even thought about singing in a band or playing an instrument before a little over a year ago.

Attila the Hunza, the peaceful warrior, and Shri, the secret in the heart of a woman, literally traded places after thirty minutes. Shri took the stage while Attila the Hunza settled in across the street with the rest of the group to listen. There was an exhilaration riding high in the air as Shri struck up the first chord and Deborah went into "Walkin' Blues." Instantly the band was there with a complete communication—their combined years of experience and talent and dedication was like a full-on assault that flooded the senses. They were in sync, tight, and came across like a fine, aged wine after the youthful electricity of Attila the Hunza. The two bands complimented each other beautifully—partly a testimony to the friendship and camaraderie and strong fiber of common purpose that binds the members of the bands.

By now the incandescent midday sun was bearing down on the scene. The march kept parading past, dogs and people. There was a water station a few feet away from the stage where bottled water, dog biscuits and banana slices were available to walkers in case anyone needed reinforcements. The water boys who manned the station danced in the streets. It was no joke that there were dog biscuits at the water station. The crowd was full of dogs. As Shri took over the stage two huge sheep dogs came by with bows in their hair. It was an incongruous sight.

Lee sang the next song, "I Seen," and as soon as his voice rang out over the mike a lovely, brisk breeze sprang up, much welcomed in the strong sun. It blew steadily for the rest of the gig.

Before his next number Lee picked up the mike and said, "Like wow . . . Like, cool man. Wow . . . wow . . . wow . . ." He sounded spaced-out, like a 1950s beatnik, or maybe just a timeless cosmic junkie. "Wow, man . . ." he said dreamily one last time, then as if he'd just woken up, he said crisply, "Okay!" We looked at each other. What was he doing? It added a touch of the surreal to their performance and seemed to change the mood as he went into another rousing version of "Smokestack Lightnin', " one of his signature songs. It is a song that carries its listeners into a kind of ecstatic absorption, and as Ed went into the guitar solo in the middle of the song, Lee started talking to the rapidly thinning crowd that trickled past now as the march came to an end.

"I just have one question," he rapped in a husky, low voice, "do you get more money if you bring your *dawg* on the walk? It's an *important* question, an earth-shaking question, a *universal* question . . . I'm gonna start a magazine that asks the question, 'Do you get more money if you bring your dawg on the walk?' If I don't find out, I'm not gonna be able to sleep tonight. Somebody help me! Help me, please . . . aawwwww!" It was pure satire and social commentary. This is what Americans have been reduced to—caring more about their dogs than anything else in life. Two or three police cars were parked on the corner, the officers standing around listening. Lee sang the last verse of the song, then picked his rap back up, saying, "Oh don't mind me, I'm just entertaining my friends. We are Shri, getting ready to end, thank you . . ."

About ten thousand people—a midsection of Phoenix—had walked through this "Baul battery," as Steve B. described it, with the band, either Hunza or Shri, on one side of the street and the rest of Lee's group of students standing and listening on the other side. Finally a marching phalanx of Marines came through, signaling the very end of the affair. Within minutes of leaving the stage Lee was ready to leave. Jumping in the van behind the driver's seat, he headed back toward Prescott. When asked what he thought of his new band, Attila the Hunza, he said, "I thought they were great. Fabulous! A real party band!"

October 21, 1999
Phoenix

The two big vans and several cars departed from the ashram at three-thirty on this Friday afternoon. The group would meet Lee in Phoenix for a talk to be given by William Patrick Patterson, the author of several books about G.I. Gurdjieff, including *Ladies of the*

Rope and *The Struggle of the Magicians*. Almost everyone in the American sangha of the Hohm Community had read both of these books. Having a passionate appreciation for the teaching of Gurdjieff, Lee has used many books on the life and teachings of Gurdjieff as teaching material for his After Dinner Talks, including these two.

Lee had been away on personal business and would be flying into Phoenix from Florida earlier in the day. He had asked Chris to bring two apples from the old apple tree on the ashram in front of Arrakis for him for his dinner, which he would eat when he met the group at six o'clock, an hour before the talk would begin.

Last night after dinner most of the Prescott sangha and ashram residents were gathered in the greenhouse when Steve B. made an announcement about the trip down to Phoenix today. He said that the caravan would leave at three-thirty and that the ashram residents were taking sandwiches to eat since Lee wasn't planning a restaurant outing. Lee's dinner plan, Steve said, was two apples. There seemed to be a subtle reaction when the news hit that there wouldn't be an opportunity to go out to eat before the talk. Trips to Phoenix are made often for errands, business appointments or just for pleasure, like going to certain movies that don't make it to the little town of Prescott. Going out to eat is often part of these Phoenix outings for the Prescott sangha—a "treat" that is not uncommonly indulged.

Dasya stepped in at this point and made a suggestion that people might consider just eating two apples for dinner also. He laughed and said, "God forbid that we should miss a meal!" There was the slightest touch of scorn or irony in his laughter. He looked surprised at himself, and then said with a laugh to the people sitting next to him, "Am I channeling someone?" referring to Lee. Around the two long "tables"—long rectangles of red cloth where people sat on the floor to eat—a moment of heavy silence prevailed. People frowned or shifted in their seats in irritation. It was a call to practice from Dasya, and some of his sangha mates didn't like it at all.

Immediately after dinner the group gathered in the darshan hall for the talk, given by Dasya. He began to talk about the recoil around the food issue. Several people argued with him, saying that people really were not in survival about food and that apples would be fine, but essentially that it was the *way* he had said what he said. One person said that his tone was "shaming." Others felt that he was trying to act like Lee. He listened and then finally shrugged and began to talk about his own relationship to food, and how he sees consistently that he is in survival about food. At every meal there is an opportunity to observe just how primal the contraction in relationship to food actually is, he said. Then another person said that Dasya had been away for five months and they didn't want to hear him talk about the food issue, they wanted to hear about what he had absorbed, what his experience had been in France with Lee. But in his comments about food Dasya was in fact sharing a part of what he had gotten during his summer in France. He acquiesced and started telling stories in a more linear vein and things settled down.

What people wanted was to be inspired and uplifted by stories—to get a little "hit" of juice, of power—but not to be called to the kind of practice that Lee's ferocious momentum in France demands from his traveling party. Lee's summers in France are about the fiery demand to practice, about the joy of practice. That might mean missing meals—or eating apples, for example—but more than anything it means doing things Lee's way rather than ego's way. "Lee's way" on the Friday night excursion into Phoenix was to take two apples, or the equivalent of two apples in one's own case.

It's typical in virtually every sangha or spiritual community that people have great difficulty hearing the teaching or being called to practice by one of their sangha mates. We may able to smile and laugh or appear to be serious or charmed or inspired when the guru says the same thing, but if one of our peers makes a radical comment, we are quick to persecute that person. As Matthew wrote about this exchange between Dasya and the sangha members who were involved:

> What is it in us that allows Lee (well, sort of) to remind us, to call us to practice in exactly the same fashion that Dasya did, but not someone whom we consider a peer? Actually it seemed to me that the vocal resistance against Dasya's intrusion into our comfort was an externalization of the same inner dialogue that goes on when Lee does exactly the same thing. But since it wasn't Lee (or was it?) ego decides that we are perfectly justified in voicing our particular point of view, rather than feeling into what Dasya is attempting to communicate. God bless us.

Tonight as the group met with Lee on the sidewalk in front of Changing Hands Bookstore where the talk would be held, he said, "Are you all hungry?" It seemed like he had something in mind. "We've got sandwiches that we brought for everyone from the ashram," someone said. "Jaya and Debbie are bringing them from the car."

Lee said, "Oh, you have sandwiches?"

Jan asked, "Would you like to eat?" There was a natural foods restaurant right next to the bookstore, with tables outside on the sidewalk. We were standing right outside its front door. He said, "Yes, I would have ordered something, but since you already have food I won't." The reality of this statement fell like a heavy stone cutting through water. It landed on the muddy bottom with a dull thud, bounced once or twice while the murk settled in around it. Slowly the water cleared again.

"Would you like a sandwich?" someone else asked Lee.

"What kind?" he asked. When tuna was the answer he said, "No, not since it's tuna." He sat down at a table with some of his students, then in a few minutes went in and got a cold unleavened flatbread with jalapenos, herbs and tomatoes baked on top of it. He brought it back out and sat eating, pulling pieces of the chewy, tough bread with his teeth and then exclaiming over how good it was. The tuna sandwiches were passed around to the twenty-five people who gathered at the empty tables around Lee. Lee's apples were there also, and a couple of grapefruits that had been brought in case he wanted one. There was much laughing and joking about the sandwiches now as a number of people went in and ordered additional food—bagels and cream cheese, Greek salads, pecan pie. Even though people got food from the restaurant, sitting and eating with Lee seemed like a rather perfunctory thing. It was just a bunch of people grabbing something hastily. Dasya laughed and said, "This is the best tuna sandwich I've ever had! I'm eating my words now!"

But there was no need for him to eat his words because actually if everyone had done what Dasya suggested—which was to take two apples to Phoenix—it's very likely there would have been a different scenario. The group could have gotten to Phoenix and when Lee said, "Are you hungry?" someone could have said, "We've got some apples, and yes we're hungry!" Given Lee's moods and comments when he met his students, it's likely that the group would have then gone with Lee together into the restaurant, sat down at the tables and ordered, and it could have easily turned into one of those occasions of delight in the guru's company when he creates a spontaneous opportunity to celebrate with him around food. But those kinds of things only occur when his students are relaxed and free of grasping and survival about food and there is a mood of surrender, of alignment to Lee, a true willingness to go with whatever he has in mind. Everyone had missed the boat, in more ways than one.

At ten minutes till seven Lee went into the bookstore and made his way to the small room in the back where the talk would be held. He took a seat near the back of the room. As his entourage of twenty-five drifted into the room in groups of twos and threes, the chairs in the room began to fill up. In the next ten minutes another fifteen or twenty people came in, until there were no chairs left. The room was small and enclosed with no windows. In one corner was a book table with Patterson's books and his new video on Gurdjieff in Egypt, some flyers for his seminar tomorrow and other information.

A woman representing Changing Hands Bookstore came in and introduced William Patrick Patterson. She seemed extremely concerned about whether or not people would be too hot. She said in a softly faded British accent, "I don't want you to be uncomfortable. We can turn on the air conditioner, bring in fans and place them around the room if you are uncomfortable." Maybe she wasn't used to the room being so packed with people. Every chair was taken and one or two people stood in the back. An old man, probably seventy or eighty years old, sitting on the front row raised his hand and said fearfully, "Is there going to be enough air to breathe in this room? I have a breathing problem." She was so accommodating, so placating and people were so expressive of their concern with the discomfort that the whole conversation took on a quality of the absurd. It struck me as so totally antithetical to the teachings of Gurdjieff, which everyone had ostensibly come to hear about, that it was almost comical. The old man moved to a chair by the door, trading with one of Lee's students who offered her seat to him.

Finally everyone was settled, the woman had finished her introductions and William Patrick Patterson came walking slowly in. He was a tall, elegant man in his sixties, dressed in black jeans and a charcoal gray sports shirt. He brought a noticeable electric charge into the room with him. He took his seat and silently looked over the audience with his light blue eyes. A ripple of real discomfort now passed across the placid surface of the room.

He began, "Thank you for coming. I assume you're all interested in the Fourth Way. What is interest? *Attention*." He began to talk about the quality of attention, and how important it is to know where one's attention is and where it is not. He said, "Don't give your attention to me; give it to yourself. If you give it to me, I'll keep giving it back to you; otherwise you'll just be hypnotized. See where your attention is right now. What part of the body? Locate your attention. Accept that. There is nothing right or wrong about it; now redirect your attention to your left foot. Before I said that, did you have a left foot? Without having attention in the body, we are just a thought, a body uninhabited, unattended. We don't live anywhere; in fact, we don't exist at all!" He smiled and looked out at everyone, very at ease and masterful as a public speaker.

He said that when we begin to see how we are with our attention, we can begin to realize that we don't give ourselves the attention we need. We have to begin with giving attention to ourselves. "I suspect I don't give myself attention," he said, speaking for the average person, "so I come to you needy and neurotic. But if I give myself attention, then I'm not so needy, so suggestible." He said, "Now anchor your attention in your left foot." He began to work with the group to get people grounded and present in the body.

He reiterated, "In terms of actualizing the body, we have to have our attention here, in the body, or we aren't here at all. We are only a thought in our minds, and what is the mind? Until we incarnate our attention in the body, we don't really exist. We are isolated, alienated, and in this need to isolate ourselves all of our attention gets eaten up. Gurdjieff said that unless the wisdom of the East and the energy of the West was harnessed and used harmoniously, the world would destroy itself. He said the civilization we live in is aberrant, psychologized and maleficent. That was in the 1920s—but wouldn't we all like to return to that time? Or was it just the same as now, only now it's more obvious?"

Incredibly knowledgeable about Gurdjieff and fluidly quoting him verbatim, William Patterson spoke in a very hypnotic, evenly paced and soft voice. Lee sat listening, absorbing and watching raptly. He leaned forward almost imperceptibly in his seat. He appeared completely invisible in his gray sweat pants and T-shirt with a green singing lizard on it. When Mr. Patterson began to talk about Gurdjieff in Egypt his tone of voice changed from the hypnotic style to that of a lecturing professor. His knowledge of esoteric traditions was enjoyable and impressive. He talked about the Sarmoung Brotherhood, maps of pre-sand Egypt, the Sphinx as the "pre-eminent symbol of esoteric knowledge," which some experts believe is at least ten thousand years old. He spoke about Atlantis, the "island inhabited by the primeval ones which sank, and who came to Egypt to found a new civilization based on the esoteric myth of Osiris and Isis." He spoke about Gurdjieff's great classics, *Beelzebub's Tales to His Grandson,* and *Meetings With Remarkable Men*. He said, "The essence of the ancient religion of Egypt was changelessness, or immortality, which equals *being*." He talked about how he had put together the symbolism of the Egyptian myths and connected them with the teachings of Gurdjieff.

In all this he seemed to be constructing a platform for talking about the building of a soul, or a body of immortality in Gurdjieff's work. He gave a captivating talk skipping all around the Fourth Way tradition, from P.D. Ouspensky to Gurdjieff's travels in Egypt, to the building of a soul, the subduing of the lower nature of man by the higher nature of man, the need for secrecy in esoteric initiation. He said, "Why not give esoteric secrets to the uninitiated? Because esoteric secrets corrupt themselves and become power if they become commonly known, as we have seen in Europe and America today."

He mentioned his teacher, Lord Pentland, who studied for a time with Gurdjieff toward the end of Gurdjieff's life. Lord Pentland once said to Patterson, "One day you will write a book about the Fourth Way." Mr. Patterson said, "It was like putting a sword in my stomach." Eventually he began to write, "emptying himself out" to find the right direction every step of way. At one point, when he was writing his first book on the Fourth Way, *Eating the I,* he began to remember events holistically, rather than from the standpoint of his own egotism. He began to see what a raging egotist he had been over the years and, "As you can imagine, a lot of tears were shed over that typewriter."

In his research he was lead to read the first draft of Ouspensky's *In Search of the Miraculous* and eventually found Solita Solano's private papers. She was Gurdjieff's secretary for four years and the author of four novels. She took extensive notes from all their meetings, and she was extraordinarily beautiful. Although his expertise as a researcher and scholar of the tradition was obvious, what shone out in his words more importantly was his obvious years of practice within the tradition. This came through loud and clear as he kept bringing his audience back to grounding the work in the body.

"There's nothing wrong with ego," he said, "most of us need more ego. Most of our egos are shrunken. We don't have enough self-esteem. Is your attention still in your left foot?" He smiled. He began to direct the audience back toward the idea of using attention in a way to ground oneself in the present reality of the body. "So you've made the attempt to come out of the automaton. Nobody asked you to be perfect. We ask you to observe, simply observe. It's only the mind, you're still in the mind." He was answering a woman's question about not having enough attention and self-esteem. "The peace spoken of in the Bible is beyond the mind. What would it be like to not have your mind chattering all the time? You can know that by coming into the body and actualizing the body. You have to be actualized *in* time and space. You have to come into the body," he returned to one of his main points. "If not, you're just a thought, a thought in the mind. You don't exist anywhere.

"We go into some excess, some inebriation, just to get to feel something. We take drugs to increase our rate of vibration. Then we hear things and see things. The world is speaking to you, but what are you speaking to it with? Just your thoughts, your projections. If you believe in the devil, you get the devil back from the world! All your half-formed thoughts are just imagination . . . ."

He spoke with a warmth and friendliness that doesn't come through in his books. He was immediately likeable, but at the same time he seemed to be a man of great constraint and discipline, with a certain circumspect quality. His blue eyes crinkled up in frequent smiles as the audience laughed at his impromptu jokes while he hawked his books. Lee laughed and smiled along too. He seemed to be enjoying the talk very much. His attention had stayed quite riveted to Mr. Patterson, who was obviously a man of authority and power, and yet he seemed also gentle and kind.

Skipping over another question about ego he laughed and said, "All these people who are in love, who think they are in love! Love is not *personal*!" He was passionate on this subject, smiling and picking up speed, "All this tripe about love between people who *aren't even there*!" He threw his head back slightly and laughed, his face blushing red. "Love is *Divine*, not personal!"

He smiled at his audience, very relaxed and charming now. He was answering a question about what he meant when he said that Ouspensky reported Gurdjieff saying that without the Work there is no reincarnation, but one will "die like a dog." He said, "It all happens through the body, but if I own the body in an egotistical way—the *kundabuffer* Gurdjieff talked about—then we get into what the great Tibetan master Chögyam Trungpa Rinpoche called 'spiritual materialism.' If you look in *Search* in the index for reincarnation you won't find a single entry, but if you look under immortality you will find many entries. Gurdjieff said we basically live like dogs—a dog is a two-centered being with no possibility of becoming a three-centered being." He went on to say that we have to create a soul, to build *being* in order to have a disembodied afterlife. Otherwise what little being we have will be drained away by our addictions and obsessions in the moments after we die. He talked about desire, and said we should think about how much we desire just an ice cream cone. We have tremendous anguish over something like an ice cream cone. He continued, "In the Bible they say 'dust to dust.' Anguish in the disembodied state will melt down what little being I have; so it is dust to dust, food for the moon. So, we have to pay attention to ourselves in a genuine way, not in an egotistical way."

After touching on many important Fourth Way precepts, he answered another question from Jim C., who asked, "Would you talk about your teacher, Lord Pentland?"

Mr. Patterson nodded and said, "Yes, he was my teacher. Well, I wrote about all that in *Eating the I* and I recommend the book to you."

Jim countered, "I was hoping you would talk about him now."

Mr. Patterson smiled broadly, "Oh come on—give me that $19.95, will you!" Everyone laughed. He was quite a salesman. He said, "In the Gurdjieff Work, we are material—in the *real* sense of the word!" Lee had a big smile on his face at this little quip. Mr. Patterson also smiled, enjoying his audience, then continued to answer Jim's question, saying, "It became apparent to me that what I wanted was Lord Pentland's attention. When that was realized, the question became, 'Should I say this?' In a group session, with my heart thumping so hard that I thought all I was was heart, I said to him, 'I want *all* your attention!' It was a tremendous connection between he and I. Through work on myself I am able to realize what is true in this moment. As you connect with the teacher you discover them as human beings, not just as gods. When that happens with your spiritual teacher it's a chance to realize something important. You come to have a real language that is born out of your own suffered truth."

After answering a few more questions he began to conclude his talk. He said, "The great thing about the Gurdjieff Work is that it is practical, imminently practical in life. We have been given this tremendous opportunity to evolve, and yet we live as two centered animals. We say we want freedom, but what we want is the freedom to live out our instinctive impulses, to do what we damn well please. We misconstrue what freedom is. A life unlived is a 'vale of tears.' So don't give your attention to me. I give it back to you."

He thanked the group and invited people to participate in his seminar the next day. After a short applause, he stood up and a number of people got up to shake his hand and talk with him. Lee got up and walked out quietly, heading straight for his car and the two-hour drive back to the ashram. Regina, Jim C. and Steve B. stayed and spoke with Mr. Patterson. They gave him two CDs, one of liars, gods & beggars and one of Shri, and conversed with him for awhile. When he found out who their teacher was he said, "Oh yes, Lee Lozowick. I know of him. He hangs out with Andrew Cohen and E.J. Gold." Whether he knew that Lee was in his audience that night or not was left to the unknown.

October 26, 1999
Arizona Ashram

At the After Dinner Talk tonight Lee asked Mariana and Sylvan if they had any stories from their trip to California from which they had just returned this afternoon. They were interviewing different people involved in spiritual life and the path for Mariana's next book. Some of them were teachers and some of them well-known authors, transpersonal psychologists or serious practitioners of various traditions.

She had met with many different people—John Welwood, Georg Feuerstein, George Leonard, Charles Tart and Sam Keen. When each one asked how her flight was to California—naturally assuming she had flown—she just said, "Oh, it was fine," not really wanting to get into the fact that, on Lee's recommendation, she had taken the Greyhound bus to California.

The interviews all went very well, it was a tremendously productive trip. She was particularly looking forward to interviewing Llewellyn Vaughan-Lee, whom she had interviewed for her last book, *Halfway Up the Mountain*. The interview with Llewellyn for that book had been particularly noteworthy, and Mariana had reported that there was a tremendous sense of divine presence and communion that was invoked in his company. She had been ecstatic for a couple of days after the interview.

When she first arrived at his home Llewellyn cordially asked if she had driven to California from Arizona. "No," she smiled, then making a sudden decision to let him in on the story, she added, "Lee wanted us to take the Greyhound bus." Llewellyn immediately started laughing. "Well, how was it? Did it take a long time?"

Mariana said, "It took fifteen hours, and it was long and exhausting." Llewellyn's students who were listening exclaimed over this hardship. Llewellyn just chuckled to himself. He seemed amused and at the same time impressed.

Relaying the story now to the group that sat in the meditation hall with Lee, Mariana said, "Toward the end of our time with Llewellyn, as things were winding down, he turned to Sylvan and I and asked when we would be leaving. We answered either in the middle of the night or very early the next morning. He laughed and said, 'Maybe tomorrow morning would be a little easier!' Llewellyn pointed to us and said to his students, 'Oh it doesn't matter. In their school, they're a bunch of *yogis*. They have all kinds of practices. Their master makes them ride the Greyhound bus to California!' Then he laughed."

Sylvan picked up the story, going back to the interview. He said, "At one point I said to Llewellyn, 'In our school Lee has spoken of three different ways to relate to the guru. First, you wait until the guru asks you to do something and then you do it; second, you ask the guru what is needed before he has to ask you, then you do it; or third, you intuit or already know what is wanted and needed without the guru having to ask you or you having to ask the guru, and you do that. You seem to only be speaking about the third possibility.'" Sylvan was referring to the fact that throughout the interview he and Mariana had been asking Llewellyn to comment about people's resistance to the authority of the spiritual teacher and psychological issues in relationship with spiritual authority in general, but Llewellyn seemed genuinely confused by the whole issue. Finally he clarified his perspective, saying, "I have a very limited perspective. I have no experience of these things. Resistance and authority—it's all very simple to me! I have no experience of resistance. I met Mrs. Tweedie when I was nineteen. I knew she was my teacher and that was it. I immediately accepted her as an authority, and ten years later I moved to California to teach."

At this point Lee interjected, "I don't have *any* resistance to my Teacher. I don't have any idea what that's about either."

Mariana said, "But you get down in that with us . . ."

Lee countered her rather sharply, "That's because resistance is what I'm given to work with! But I don't know *anything* about it personally."

Picking up a stack of stapled papers he waved them in the air and said, "I really want to read this, so let's go on. Regina got this off the Internet today. It was written by C. who was in the community in the very beginning, between 1975-1977. Some of you who were there will know right away who wrote it. It's a scathing critique of me and the community, and whatever he felt betrayed by. He was one of the editors of *In the Fire*. It should be very interesting!"

He plunged into reading. It was a very well written and evocative memoir of the early months and years in Lee's company. About fifty people sat in the hall listening as Lee read, often laughing hysterically at the descriptions of people like Bala, Dasya, Brother Juniper and others. There were many things about the writing that was quite moving, especially some of the descriptions of Lee, the darshans or *satsangs*, his interactions with devotees. As the story unfolded from the perspective of C., the source of his conflict became more and more apparent.

At one point in the reading Lee stopped and commented on one of the author's key disappointments; he had made the stated assumption that Lee's style in his first book, *Spiritual Slavery,* was deliberate. Lee said, "That was his basic mistake. The primary mistake everybody makes who comes to the guru is that they assume what the guru is doing is deliberate, but it's not deliberate. Acting deliberately is an act of ego. He assumed that what I wrote in *Spiritual Slavery* was stylized, when in fact it was not.

"This is what Yogi Ramsuratkumar meant when he said, 'This Beggar will betray you.' If we think the guru acts deliberately, we will feel betrayed and lied to. It's as reliable as the sunrise! Everyone has to come to resolve in this regard. If you go to Yogi Ramsuratkumar's darshan and you see someone who thinks Yogi Ramsuratkumar's acts are deliberate, you would laugh! It's absurd—beyond absurdity! So you have to come to clarity in that regard."

The manuscript was quite long—thirty-three pages grouped into eight chapters. As Lee read through the first three or four chapters he kept saying, "Gosh, I wish we'd get to the betrayal! This is interesting, but I want to get to the good part, the part that precipitated this serendipitous little occurrence." He talked about what a fine poet C. had been when he knew him, in the style of Rumi. Every now and then Lee would read something from the manuscript and say, "How embarrassing!" and put his hand to the side of his face with a little laugh. There was a lot of laughter, sometimes shrieks and belly laughs over certain descriptions that were obviously right on, but the machinations of the mind and all the ways in which it undermines the truth of what the body feels and knows to be true were clear in C.'s description of his own process. The entire reading brought the After Dinner Talk space to life and generated a lively discussion. Unable to finish the reading in one night, Lee promised he would save the rest of it until the Thursday night After Dinner Talk.

It is Lee's style to take criticisms that are leveled against either himself or the community and make them readily and openly available for everyone's consideration. He never blanches or runs from any of this, but meets it all head-on, finding use in even the worst of it. In this case it was amazing that someone had described with such intimate detail the scene around Lee in those early years, a time which Lee finds embarrassing now, and frequently refers to as such.

October 30, 1999
Arizona Ashram

Once a month the Arizona ashram has a Work Weekend. This is a time when Saturday and Sunday are set aside for Lee's students who live in town or the surrounding area to come and spend the weekend participating through guru *seva*, or service to the guru, which usually involves the care and upkeep of the ashram in some way. The schedule is meditation at seven a.m., a talk by Lee at eight-thirty, ten o'clock brunch, a work period from ten-thirty to five o'clock when chanting begins, and dinner at five-thirty. Usually Lee plays bridge on the Saturday nights of a Work Weekend unless there is a gig.

This morning after meditation the group gathered in the hall for Lee's talk, but he decided to show a video instead. The video that he chose was William Patrick Patterson's "Part I, Gurdjieff in Egypt." It was very interesting, with stunning scenes from many holy sites in Egypt including Karnak, Thebes, the Temple of Luxor and the "objective art" of these places—sculptures, hieroglyphs, immense columns, sacred architecture. Watching Mr. Patterson connect the dots between the gods and goddesses of ancient Egypt and the work of G.I. Gurdjieff was stimulating and easily captured one's attention.

After the video Lee turned to the group and said, "Any questions?" After a short pause he snapped, "Well, are you all ready to go to Egypt?" He laughed sarcastically and said, "I'm not!"

A couple of people seemed to jump on what they perceived to be "Lee's bandwagon" with lightly cynical remarks. A few questions were asked about the video, about the nature of the struggle between Horus and Set, the two primal opposites of the affirming and the denying forces according to William Patrick Patterson. Then Karl brought the teaching into focus with a question. He said, "It seemed like we were being derogatory toward the video, and I really didn't get it. What was that about?"

Lee proceeded to state that he loved the video and in fact thought it was excellent study material. Then he said, "But maybe I'm handicapped as compared to the average person because to me none of that means anything. Everything, all that, is just so completely obvious to me that ancient cultures don't hold the key to anything, religions don't hold the key to anything, sacred artifacts don't hold the key to anything. Nothing holds the key to anything for me but the immediate experience of what is already completely obvious. Tough for the people who travel with me because they don't get the benefit of getting to tour through all these museums and see all the sacred artifacts and be shown the beauty of all that objective art!

"We have to *realize* without help from the external world, outside of the obvious reflection of our lives as they are, uncomplicated by desperate searches for entertainment and *meaning*." He threw out the last word in a challenging tone. He continued, "The teaching, the rituals we do, everything is just a matter of tenderizing the meat. Everything we do is to produce a circumstance of possibility. It has no inherent meaning, no ability to create anything.

"Everything depicted so beautifully on the video is completely obvious to me. It's so obvious to me that all the museums, the sacred art, the culture, all of it is totally boring to me. That's the source of my sarcasm. I *loved* the video, but I want to indicate that I wouldn't love it if we, as individuals or as a group, are *fascinated* by it and sentimental in our response to it."

The dharmic principle of what Lee calls "already present enlightenment" says that there is nothing to attain, nowhere to go, nothing to get, and in fact the constant seeking for gratification, for the end of suffering or even for enlightenment, is precisely that which keeps one from resting in the reality of "already present enlightenment," or the "disposition of enlightenment," which is the natural state. Even though we may have deeply and profoundly heard and registered this truth, we are typically and habitually still seeking, searching for something—even if for more esoteric knowledge, more artifacts, more momentary distraction from *what is*. Our desire to travel and touch sacred culture becomes ego's endless search for romance, for gratification and consolation. Lee keeps bringing his students back to the fact that there is no consolation; there is only Just This.

In other words, it can all be found right here in one's own backyard, and yet it is ego's design to ignore what is and keep looking somewhere else. Why? Because to acknowledge what is here and available now is a confrontation with the demand to take full responsibility for that. Okay, now that you have it all, what are you going to do about it? The search is over; now there is the Work: a life of practice, sacrifice, discipline and service. Unavoidable, relentless, ever present, endless and infinite. It is the end of ego's "freedom" and the beginning of slavery, Spiritual Slavery. Even long-time students who are ardent practitioners forget that ego is always looking for a back door, a way out, and if the back door can be couched in spiritual terms, it can be easily justified by the mind and included in practice, when in fact it drains away vital work energy.

Someone asked why Lee's students spend time investigating their roots in the spiritual traditions. He answered, "We're not so much investigating our roots as establishing a matrix. Study is valuable only in that it affirms what we already know. It reminds us that we know things that we aren't taking responsibility for. A lot of us would prefer a more reverent approach than mine."

Shukyo said, "You say that, but at the same time I've traveled around India with you and been to many temples and holy places and shrines. I've seen your devotion . . ."

Lee raised his eyebrows in mock surprise. "Gosh! What can I say? I've been exposed!"

Karl asked, "I have a question then. It would seem like it is better to wash the dishes from all three centers, if that's possible, than to do a puja, for example, all spaced-out. Is that true, or is there something in the puja that . . ."

Lee answered, "Both. I would say that to wash dishes in a unified state is more valuable than to do a puja in a distracted state. But at the same time there is an inherent transmission that is embodied in certain artifacts, spaces or actions. To not engage those is to miss that opportunity."

It was a weekend of gigs. Last night Lee drove to Sedona with a vanload of people to watch Attila the Hunza perform at the Oak Creek Brewing Company. Tonight he performed with Shri at a fashionable local restaurant in Prescott where Shri has become a regular act, and where they would play again tomorrow night. About thirty-five of Lee's students came for dessert after the early dinner prepared by Lee of vegetable soup and salad served at the ashram. It being Halloween weekend—what used to be Samhain of the old Celts or the Feast of the Dead—the members of the band were dressed in costume. Each one had on a blue choir robe with his or her face painted in various styles, some gruesome, some psychedelic. Deborah wore a vintage sequined hat from the 1940s. Lee was the only one without the robe. Instead he was dressed as the Phantom of the Opera, in a floor-length, swirling black Dracula cape and a black felt bowler hat pulled down over a white clay "phantom" mask that covered half of his face.

All the waiters were in costume, as were many of the clientele. At a front table sat two couples in costume. One of these couples has been coming to every Shri gig for the past couple of months. They literally follow Shri around Arizona, and have plans to drive all the way to Laughlin, Nevada when Shri plays the casino there in late November. The couple with them had an interesting story to tell members of the band during the break between sets. The woman, who was dressed as a black cat, had seen an interview with Shri on an Arizona television station and loved the band and their music. She wanted to go see them perform live, but in her excitement she had forgotten to catch the name of the band. That weekend her friends—the other couple—had invited her and her husband to come out to dinner and listen to their favorite band, Shri. When they got to the restaurant the black cat woman recognized the band from the television interview. "It's them!" she exclaimed when she recognized Deborah. They stayed for the entire performance—three hours—and left when the band did.

During the first set the band sounded great, very professional as usual, but the audience was focused on ordering and eating food. It was a middleworld scene where people were generally staid and circumspect, even though the ambiance of the restaurant had

768

possibility. The motif of the place is a warm Southwestern adobe, with copper walls and pots hanging in the open kitchen, pinion fires burning in a brick oven. The grills sizzle and pop, and the heat and juice and activity of the kitchen spills over into the dining room. The ceiling is a burnished copper and the wooden tables and chairs are very comfortable. Lots of windows open onto the patio and live plants thrive in the corners of the room.

While steaming plates of food were served to waiting patrons who sat over mixed drinks, wine or beer, Lee whirled his black cloak around and made little comments over the mike. "It's Halloween weekend! I hope you're having a good time. You all should get a little wild! Take your clothes off when you get home, get naked, get loose on this Eve of the Eve of All Souls' Day . . ." People seemed fairly oblivious with the exception of Lee's students and the two couples at the front table, who were having a wonderful time.

Things began to pick up when Lee and Deborah sang "Left My Baby Standing" and they both began to snake their way through the tables, singing to the audience. Doug and Ed followed with their guitars, the four of them winding through the seated audience like a soul train. There was a glimmer of magic, of mystery that was sparked in that interaction. Lee bent down and shook hands with people as he passed by, looking every bit the preternatural being in his long black cloak.

At the end of the first set the band went into "Smokestack Lightnin'." That was when the mojo really started working. The band hit a groove during the instrumental solo on this song that built to a sustained height of pleasure. Lee stood whirling his cape, his strange refrain, "Hoo hoo . . . Hoo hoo," going out like a mystic call, seeping like a mist through the crack between the worlds. This song was written by Howlin' Wolf, one of the greatest black shamans of the blues tradition. It has an amazing effect on audiences and lends itself to Lee's particular voodoo with an uncanny perfection. It carries a rhythmic and melodic power akin to the mood-altering effect of repetitive African chants; it induces a trance-like state, and in the elixir of that mood, one is transported into a completely different perspective. The song steals up like a thief, the only evidence of its powerful subtle effects being a certain heat and happiness that begin to pervade consciousness, until the listener becomes one with the music. One minute you are sitting and listening, the next minute you feel better, so much better that you are maybe even compelled to dance. It's like medicine in that way—exactly the way the old blues shamans of African American culture in the South cured the soul of its malady—the malady of suffering. What are we suffering? The illusion of separation from God.

When the band came back onstage after their break it was almost nine o'clock. The late diners who had just arrived at their tables were more of a party crowd. Right away they began to cheer and pay close attention to the band. They were drinking more heartily, and in the spirit of the weekend. The band came back on with an undeniable force. They were warmed up and jazzed by the music and the crescendo of "Smokestack Lightnin'." They were having fun with each other and with the audience. Lee and Deborah called up the members of Attila the Hunza who were there to play "All Along the Watch Tower" with Kate on vocals. It is an instantly recognizable Bob Dylan song that always pleases a crowd. The song was woven into a guitar solo by Ed, and at the end there was a round of loud cheers and enthusiasm from the crowd.

Three songs into the set Lee said into the mike, "You all can get up and dance, you know! We'd love to see you dance!" His comment seemed to break the spell of conventionality. Suddenly about ten people were up and dancing. For the rest of the night, until ten o'clock when the gig was over, clusters of dancers stood squeezed between the tables, big smiles spread over their faces as the danced. Slowly but surely people began to do what Lee had asked them to do earlier in the night—to get into their bodies and feel. The manager stood at the far edge of the room, watching with a look of curiosity, wonder and perhaps doubt, as if he had seen his diners break into dancing outside on the patio to Shri or Attila the Hunza, but he'd never seen them dance in the more staid dining room. He stood with his arms folded across his chest, smiling and watching, clearly affected by the music too.

The whole scene began to teeter on the edge of the bacchanalian as the band and dancers hovered on the threshold while the veils between the worlds were parted. Perhaps it stirred some archaic memory of the Feast of the Dead for us all—the day when the unseen comes into view, when the marginal and liminal side of life takes over and the underworld is close at hand. In olden times spirits moved through the land, the ancestors blessed or cursed, and great magical potencies were brought to life. Despite our modern cynicism, the fact is that magic *is*. The understanding of that fact exists in our cellular memories as the primal reality of every indigenous people of the Earth. The world's earliest religion was, after all, shamanism, and it was a purely tantric perspective of life in all its glory and misery.

As the music worked its magic, it got inside the bones and muscles and buzzed around until some ancient merriment crept through the body, seeping through old protests, dissolving the knots, now pressing its owner to move and move some more. You could almost hear the conversation between "yes" and "no" that ricocheted around the room. The body says, "Yes, it feels too good not to move." The mind is circumspect, wants to know, "Are you sure all this ecstasy is okay? This isn't a nightclub, it's a restaurant! Besides, I don't want to look foolish." The soul says, "Doesn't matter—it's divine! Got to move. Here we go . . ."

The people at the table in the back of the room were up on the floor, the black cat woman danced beside Lee's students. Deborah looked happy, Rakini was on the drums with her painted zombie face, arms pumping the beat, smashing into the cymbals. Steve pounded the keyboards and Nachama wailed away on mouth harp while Ed went careening into the psychedelic landscape of "Voodoo Chile," dropping to his knees on the carpeted floor. Doug's guitar was the perfect complement to Ed's wild ride; Everett was grooving on the bass, cutting loose visibly in a way he hadn't since the death of LGB. All this and the guru, shaking his tambourine and dancing around the floor with his mask off, watching the audience, his face inscrutable and sublime.

October 31, 1999
Arizona Ashram

In darshan tonight while Shri played their Halloween gig at the same restaurant where they had performed the night before, Lee asked for questions. Sylvan said that at the After Dinner Talk last week Lee had talked about how the guru never does anything deliberate, and yet it seemed to him that the guru's actions were quite deliberate.

Lee answered, "Everything the guru does is deliberate, but it's not deliberated by the guru. It is deliberated by the Divine." He began to talk about how karma is involved with everything the guru does. Because the guru is working from a very broad and vast perspective or overview, what appears unreasonable or incomprehensible may in fact be working in our favor from a karmic point of view. He said, "In this Work, when we become somewhat conscious we realize that we can pay off a lot more karma than can be paid off with the natural progression of things. We can pay off two, three, four, five lifetimes of karma—if the timing is right. If the timing is not right, then we can go through a lot of stress and not pay off any karma at all. It may be a great idea to work off some karma, but if the time isn't right it just backfires. The higher the perspective we have, the less confusion and paradox there is in day-to-day things for us. There are reasons for why things are turning out the way they are."

Lee commented on Mariana's recent interview with Georg Feuerstein, who had said that obedience to the guru doesn't necessarily mean that you take everything the guru says literally and do it. Lee continued on the subject of obedience. "Often things the spiritual master will say are metaphorical. If we imply something literal from what the guru says, then we may be missing the point. Many of us, myself included, are poor communicators. Often we misread what the guru is saying—to the extent that what we think we've heard is the complete opposite of what the guru is saying to us."

Lee mentioned that he had been reading Llewellyn Vaughan-Lee's most recent book, *Circle of Love.* He said, "Llewellyn Vaughan-Lee says that we meet the Beloved by being the same as the teacher. You surrender to the *shaikh*, not as a person, but for the purpose of becoming the same as the master so that you stand beside the master—not beneath or behind, but beside the master—and you are both in relationship with the Beloved. Through obedience you get to be the same, or in a similar state, as the guru. All the rules of obedience are to help you become the same as the master, not to keep the master in a position of dominance.

"There is a quality of softness that is necessary for this. Bandhu, for example, has to hold a certain context, a certain focus to blow glass, but at the same time he has to be flexible, or the piece won't turn out. In the same way, to be resonant to the master we have to be soft, not hard. Whatever in us is hard—pride, shame, vanity, guilt—must be softened. Resonance can only happen when there is softness, vulnerability, not rigidity. We have to be contemplative and allow other viewpoints to be what they are. Often our rigidity, our belief in our own intelligence will bias us against the very things that could help us grow. So that quality of softness is a primary quality on the path."

Elyse had asked a question about obsession earlier in the weekend. Now Lee returned to the subject. He said, "Obsession can look bad on the surface to us, but in reality can be the best thing for our sadhana. It scares us because we think that we are out of relationship with others. Often when my support is there and people don't know it, they are critical of someone who is out there doing something unusual, but I can see that the person is building a clarity and passion in what he is doing. That's part of the softness and lack of rigidity on our part.

"There are people whose work is integral in a practical way, whose function is fundamental to the ashram, and who benefit the sangha tremendously. Then there are others who create great value for the sangha in what they are doing, or in some other, less tangible, way. Without those people we would be perhaps malnourished in some way. Our vision has to be broad enough to take in all these things that nourish the Work. But don't mistake workaholism for obsession—they aren't necessarily the same thing."

November 4, 1999
Arizona Ashram

Lee plays bridge almost every Monday and Wednesday night at his kitchen table. It is an open space, meaning that everyone is invited to come and either sit, watch and participate in the conversation, or start a second or third bridge game. In years past, and especially in the early years of the Arizona ashram, there were sometimes as many as three or four bridge games going upstairs in Lee's kitchen and dining room.

Tonight Lee played bridge for an hour and a half. It was a mellow and uneventful evening; only Paula Z. came up to sit and watch. After sitting quietly for a long time, making occasional mild comments while the game rolled along, Lee suddenly said, "I'll give you an example for all these people who talk about these 'breakfast and lunch darshans' in France. People used to come to these bridge spaces in the early years, but now nobody comes. There is an open invitation for people to come here and participate, and who shows up? Even when there is an open invitation, no one makes use of this space, and it is available to people every week. All this romanticism about France is just an unwillingness to work. People don't want to have to create work for themselves; they all want to be carried like a baby."

After a few moments of silence Paula said, "But coming back to Arizona from France it seems like the pace of life on the ashram here is insane. People are working really hard—we are all over-committed and have tons of different jobs to do. There are the bands, the community businesses, the Baul Theatre Company, families . . ."

Lee said, "I wish it was that way at the ashram in France! If I have my way about it, it will be someday. It's not now only because the laws in France stop us from doing the same kind of business that we do here." He paused and finished playing out a hand, then continued, "I'm constantly going out of my way to offer various teaching opportunities to people and they aren't taking what's available now. So why should I go out of my way to offer them these teaching chambers they are dying to get into?"

Paula continued, "One of the things I've realized is that I can only handle the pace of life here if I manage my energy carefully, and one way to do that is to exercise. So I'm finding myself exercising about an hour a day and feeling guilty about it."

Lee responded, "Well, exercise is one of the practices of this school, and sooner or later people are going to have to make a stand for practice. If they don't, at the end of the day, at the end of their lifetimes, the 150 people in this school are not going to be satisfied with the progress they've made. Sooner or later we have to take our stand at the OK Corral . . ."

November 7, 1999
Arizona Ashram

Lee returned from Phoenix an hour before darshan. He had driven down to perform with Shri at the Arizona Blues Showdown at the Rhythm Room, a popular blues club, in a contest sponsored by the Arizona Blues Society. The winner would have the opportunity to go to a national blues contest in Memphis, Tennessee and have a shot at a record deal. If Shri made it into the Arizona finals, they would go back next Sunday, November 14, and compete again in the play-offs for the ticket to Memphis.

An hour later he came into darshan wearing the pleated tuxedo shirt he'd had on for the Shri gig underneath the voluminous gray wool shawl from Yogi Ramsuratkumar. The shawl enveloped his whole body as he sat on the dais, leaving only a shoulder exposed. After chanting and having some of his poems to Yogi Ramsuratkumar sung, Lee asked for questions.

Nachama asked, "Why is adoration so important in our school, and what is it about sex that can be a doorway to that?"

Lee chuckled a little then began to speak. "Adoration happens to be what is given in this path; it's the aim of this Work. Adoration tends to imply a romanticism. People imagine movie heroines or covers to romance novels where the man has the woman by the waist and she gazes into his eyes. In fact, adoration is annihilation. There is nothing romantic about it. In the ultimate sense, although there is pleasure involved, there is no one there to experience those pleasures that are associated with it. There is no one to pat on the back for having experienced such a thing.

"Enlightened Duality is about love in separation. The ostensibly awakened seeker cries to the Beloved not to take the sense of separation away. The Hindu poetess and saint Mirabai felt herself to be wedded to Krishna, but the physical Krishna would never show up, so she spent her life in union with Krishna but longing for Krishna at the same time. So longing is the hallmark of this path. Liberation happens along the way, and adoration stands upon liberation. Once we've tasted the sweetness of longing, we don't want to sacrifice that for the peace of union, even though there may be suffering. Longing is not a suffering we would petition God to relieve us of. Some scholars would disagree with me, but I would say that in tantric work adoration is the aim. Even in the higher stages of Vajrayana Buddhism all forms are considered insubstantial and there is a clear focus that all phenomena is insubstantial, but at the same time there is also a substantial and refined invocation of the deity.

"We don't want to function in relationship to the word 'adoration' without knowledge of what it is. In years past we've had a very strong consideration of the language that is used in *The Only Grace Is Loving God* (Lee Lozowick, 1982). We dissected the language of that consideration so that our concept was not naive and sophomoric. What is adoration? It's necessary to have a sense of this so we are working under correct assumptions.

"One reason sex can be a powerful and obsessive doorway to the experiential domain of adoration is that it involves the primal core energy of the human being. Since we are driven to procreate, sex is the most primal urge in the body. Biology aside, all the associated desires and feelings and associations we have with sex make us unlike animals. Maybe monkeys really like it, but I've watched monkeys and I think male monkeys do it to establish dominance, and the female monkeys do it to ingratiate themselves with the power structure, with safety. Human beings have a complex set of associations with sex beyond procreation, which is powerful enough. That energy gets turned inward toward the path. When that powerful energy is turned to the path, we have extraordinary insights and epiphanies. These point us toward the doorway to what sex is about, and we can study these experiences. But when the door opens a crack and we get a little glimpse of adoration, it blows away all previous illusory ideas of what adoration is."

He continued, "Essentially it's straightforward and has to do with energy. We think it's about worshipping the other, but that's not at the core of it. At the core of it is the connection between existence and nonexistence. The energy of procreation is about maintaining existence—if we don't use the energy toward that, then it becomes about falling into nonexistence.

"A person may symbolize the Divine for us. In the historical Mirabai's case, Krishna—the image of the sublime young man with the long dark hair and beautiful eyes—symbolized the Divine. So we focus on a person, when in fact the energy and momentum that longing creates is not personal. Actually it's about the Divine without any anthropomorphized image.

"In the Sufi framework annihilation is used because when we describe the impersonal nature of adoration it doesn't change the personal flavor of it. We understand it is impersonal, but it remains personal, which continues the urge to surrender to adoration itself. It's impersonal, but it wears a personal face; the face of your partner."

Nachama asked, "Could that be a trap?"

"If you're careful, and you have some sensitivity, you don't confuse your partner with that. If you look at your partner as the doorway, your relationship to your partner can become possessive and exclusive, and you can forget what you are doing—that all this process is the result of the blessings of the path. You can get lost and lose the value of it. As long as you remember, acknowledge that you are remembering your work, it can intensify and deepen the whole process. The key is not to make the satisfaction of longing the payoff. In personifying adoration, we tend to qualify it. If we give it personality then we can get lost. We start wanting more time with our partner. We don't want to go to sleep right after we've made love. We want two hours of foreplay. We want our partner to wear their hair differently; we want them to get contact lenses, and so on and on.

"If we give it personality, essentially we've put obstacles on the path that are immense, gigantic, and can confuse us to the degree that we lose the thread of connection. We don't want satisfaction to depend on personality factors. Those kinds of demands can handicap or bind the process so that the occasion fails to arise; the Divine stops giving the offerings of such things."

Bala asked, "It sounds like an expanded or additional opportunity to experience the guru, so that the relationship with one's mate is an opportunity to be at the effect of that transformational energy."

Lee answered, "Well, it is another facet of the guru as manifest Divine, not the guru as a person. We have to see from a less rigid perspective. When we trust the space of knowing—what we knew in that moment when we saw what was Real—then doubts and confusion are literally like flies buzzing around us. We just brush them away. Faith is being able to take the guru's transmission without demanding a linear explanation. Faith comes from the willingness to own our moments of knowing. It's almost like a déjà vu—it is elusive and comes and goes like that. But faith is built in that way, in moments of knowing. The more faith we have, the more we are accessible to the guru's Benediction. The less faith we have, the more walls and defenses we have around us."

In the evening gathering after darshan Lee and a number of members of Shri began to talk about the Arizona Blues Showdown they performed in earlier today. Nachama, Steve and Rakini were relaying a story about how a photographer had walked up to Lee after their thirty-minute spot at the Rhythm Room and said, "Shri—is that the same as Sri Chinmoy?"

"It comes from the same root," Lee answered. "Do you know Sri Chinmoy?" he asked the man.

"I don't know him," the man answered, "but I love him." Just as he started to walk away, the man turned to Lee and said, "Jai Guru!"

Listening to Nachama and Rakini tell the story, Lee now said, "Yes, I was so surprised that I just stood there for a moment sort of dumbfounded. Then I said, 'Jai Guru to you too!' Then another man came up to me after the gig and said, 'You're with Shri, aren't you?' I said yes and then he said, 'I recognized you from the morning show the other day!' "

Shri had been interviewed and performed a few songs on "Good Morning Arizona," an independently produced morning talk show that is the most popular independent morning show in the country, and is even bigger than "Good Morning, America" within the state of Arizona. The funny thing about this interchange was that Lee hadn't been there. The band had left at five-thirty in the morning to drive down to Phoenix for the interview and performance, and Lee had stayed at the ashram.

After the interview every member of the band had reported people stopping them in grocery stores, gas stations, virtually everywhere they went, saying, "I saw you on TV this morning—you guys were great!" It had been a very exhilarating event, the show opening with a shot of the news helicopter flying into the sunrise to the strains of "Dreamin' About Dreamin' " by Shri. It had seemed that doors were opening all over the place, with the Blues Showdown just around the corner.

Now over tea Lee and the members of Shri talked about how many people had come up to them at the Rhythm Room after they played this afternoon. They were showered with thanks and praise and appreciation. People wanted to know about their European tours, and where they would be playing next. Steve said that people were literally riveted during "Smokestack Lightnin'," and Ed's guitar solos drew loud, long rounds of applause, hoots and shouts of appreciation. Afterward a man had walked up to Nachama and said, "You guys were fantastic! I really liked your harmonica playing. It's great to see a woman up onstage playing harp. You know, most harp players are men."

Nachama nodded and said, "Were you sitting in the audience?"

He answered lightly, "I'm the owner of the club. I'm a harp player myself," he smiled. "You guys are really good." A little later he approached Tina, the band manager, and said, "Your music was really great! You know, you guys did really well."

Tina said, "Thanks! Can I give you a call about booking us here?" Tina had been talking on the phone with him recently about playing a gig at the Rhythm Room. He had said to wait until Shri came down to play at the Arizona Blues Showdown, when they could speak in person. Now in answer to her question he said, "Oh, you'll probably be here next week for the finals, let's talk then," just assuming, like everyone did, that Shri would make it into the finals. It seemed to be the most obvious thing that Shri was one of the better bands that performed.

As it turned out, Shri did not make it into the finals. The talk in the evening gathering turned to general commiserating between Lee and the members of Shri. It was hard to believe, but certainly not uncommon. The music business, even at the most local, amateur level, is incredibly insular. It is basically a closed system; for the most part, whether a group makes it or not depends on who they know and how well. Still, spirits were high. Rakini laughed and said, "Oh well—now we'll just play next Sunday in Prescott, and all our friends will be there!"

Lee shrugged it off. He's been going through this for over twelve years with LGB and now with Shri. Nothing seems to stop him, and it makes one wonder about all his protests that he basically wants the bands to be commercially successful. Lee's students have said for years that the fact that the bands haven't succeeded in commercial terms is a result of the "denying force," using the Gurdjieff model of the Law of Three. The bands represent the "affirming force," the "denying force" is the big "no" that seems to stand at the door to commercial success for the Baul bands and the "reconciling force" is the influence of the lineage, of Yogi Ramsuratkumar. From this point of view it is time alone that will tell the ultimate success of the band, which more accurately lies in keeping the teaching alive over generations, not in some kind of financial gauge of albums sold and playing time on the air.

Lee's ongoing admonition that it is commercial success he is interested in has always been hard to take at surface value because there is the pervasive sense that there are much greater forces and purposes at work behind the scenes, in the invisible worlds. From this perspective one could say that the guru is the affirming force, the sleeping world is the denying force and the music itself is the reconciling force precisely because the music will live on.

In the legacy of the Western Baul path there is a tremendous wealth of dharma transmission that has been given through Lee's music, lyrics and poetry. These offerings are much less threatening than the guru himself, and have already touched many people who would have never been in contact with Lee Lozowick, or who would not have been moved in the same way through contact with the teacher. There have been countless nights with LGB when the dharma has been victorious; on one particularly memorable night students from five different spiritual schools converged to dance wildly to the music in a little bar called the Trade Winds in Cotati, California. But most of the time it is ordinary, hard-working people who are suffering ordinary separation in lives of ordinary drudgery and hopelessness who are touched by the music. Now Shri has stepped up to carry this torch. The primary underlying purpose of the music and the bands, despite Lee's protestations that its "just rock & roll," or "just the blues," has always seemed to be the safeguarding of the Work, and the insurance that the teaching will go on in perpetuity as a beacon of truth in a darkening world.

November 11, 1999
Arizona Ashram

This morning Lee got a phone call from the translator for Garchen Triptrul Rinpoche, a Tibetan tulku who has recently moved to the Prescott area where he is establishing a center for Tibetan Buddhism. Lee spoke on the phone at length with Ari, the American translator, to clarify the details of the invitation that had been extended for Garchen Rinpoche to come and speak at the Appearance Day Celebration next week. In answer to her questions Lee began to describe the ashram and community. His humility in these situations is a striking contrast to the brash, arrogant and foolish rascal he would have the public believe him to be. He spoke very simply and respectfully, saying, "One of the principles of our teaching is Assertion, which is the use of the phrase, 'Just This' as a definition of Reality in every moment. We are a theistic school. The aim of the work is worship of the personal Beloved, very similar to the relationship to deities in Vajrayana Buddhism. We have a phrase, 'God does not live in the sky,' which is rooted in the understanding of the insubstantiality of all phenomena but brings the understanding into the body here and now.

"We aren't scholars of course, but we have studied the tradition of Vajrayana Buddhism. I hope this doesn't turn you off, but I have the greatest respect for Chögyam Trungpa Rinpoche, and we have studied his teachings extensively." He paused and listened as she responded, then he smiled and said, "Great! Then that gives us a strong foundation together." Later Lee said that she had said that Garchen Rinpoche had only the greatest reverence for Chögyam Trungpa Rinpoche as one of the most enlightened vajra masters of Tibetan Buddhism. This alone seemed to strike Lee as enough common ground for a rapport between Garchen Rinpoche and the Hohm Community.

"We're not strict vegetarians, but our diet is primarily vegetarian. At certain sacred feasts we eat meat, but whatever Rinpoche needs in terms of diet we can provide. Does he eat meat? Sugar? Honey? Yes, okay, that's not a problem at all." He scribbled her answers down on a piece of paper as he continued speaking.

"The theme of our celebration is 'Roots'—going back to the starting point which is also the end point—so it's in perfect resonance with what you have been saying." He paused often throughout the phone call and listened as the translator spoke. As the conversation concluded he said, "Yes, so let's leave it open and let Rinpoche see who is here and sense out the group. We would be most happy with whatever he decides to offer to us." They discussed the schedule of the two days that Rinpoche would come, Thursday and Friday of the Celebration, and ended with Lee giving her directions to the ashram. The last thing he said was, "Thank you very much—that's very generous of you."

November 14, 1999
Arizona Ashram

Lee was gone most of the day today. He and a small group of his men students had driven to Yuma, Arizona yesterday afternoon for the Shri gig last night. A formal work day was held today to get the big tent put up on the tennis court and clean spaces in preparation for the Appearance Day Celebration which will begin in a few days.

In darshan tonight Lee started out saying, "I wasn't here today, but I want to thank everybody for getting the tent up and for all the preparations for the *grande fête* coming up." He paused then continued, "I want to read from my notes, some things that I wrote in meditation last week. I was thinking earlier about how in the early days of the community I used to feel that I had to *do* something to make work for people . . ."

Lee and a couple of his long-time students began to tell funny and offbeat stories of the early years of Lee's teaching work in New Jersey, but even funnier was the idea that Lee *used* to "make work" for people—as in, that was only in the past. Then Lee began to make a distinction.

"Work doesn't have to be created, it just is. Whatever life brings us has the potential to create transformation. I don't have to do anything—the sangha has proved itself to the point that the Universe has taken over and provides opportunities automatically. The Universe has taken over the reigns of opportunity and possibility. It is all the Blessing Force; I don't have to do anything but be in relationship with Yogi Ramsuratkumar and be transparent to Him. Having proved ourselves as a sangha, our personal transformation is a side effect of the process. There is an impersonal side to transformation. We just get to be the spark plugs, the cams, the pistons, the engine itself or the brakes in the vehicle that we are for the Work of the Universe. Life, or the Universe, structures the whole thing and gives us the opportunities, creates the circumstances.

"In the process of transformation shocks are necessary, but if the shocks, to use Gurdjieff's language, are out of the natural order of the octave, then great damage can be done. So the shocks have to be provided in the right order at the right time. This is the danger of a false teacher; everybody thinks they can apply shocks for others, but the Universe is the expert at this. So we're very lucky for the Universe to be pulling the strings. For those of us who are in a hurry, this may be difficult because the Universe is not in a hurry. A lot of our work is just learning to wait while nothing much is going on. But we have to wait with *intention*.

"In order to make optimal, or even minimal for that matter, use of the gift of the Universe, which may be to open a window for a minute and give us a glimpse of something, we must have intention. Intention is the key. If we can maintain intention over time with strength—intention that is purely motivated, or even relatively purely motivated—we will be given the necessary discipline and attention. So, I could be creating more stress for people. I could be driving crazy, hitting dogs on the road—nice German Shepherd dogs and beautiful Collie dogs!" Lee laughed at this bizarre thought along with a number of people. "Think of what a shock that would provide for the bleeding-heart romantics riding in the car! I'm always thinking things like that. But literally everything we need is provided by the Universe. That cuts out a lot of excitement and heroism on the path!

"The Universe creates situations for us. Like when someone is betrayed by a family member over a will . . ." Lee described a situation with one of his students who was cut out of her mother's will and had to make a decision as to whether to call her stepfather to integrity, or to surrender to his plan, knowing that to surrender would be letting that person off the hook. In this case calling the person to integrity meant taking legal measures against the person or "accepting the pittance that was being thrown her way to try to get her to go along with the situation."

He continued, "We have earned the great gift of having the Universe minding our business, so the human being of the guru doesn't have to mind our business, as expert and skillful as the human being may be. Every human being makes mistakes, sooner or later, so it's a great gift to have the Universe minding our business.

"So, as a school we are stable. We're not a fly-by-night community, we haven't fallen into the trap of rainbows and unicorns, we aren't switching partners every week, the guru isn't vacationing in Hawaii at five-star resorts on his loving devotees' money. We have integrity. We've earned the right to have the Universe create situations for us that serve our transformation."

Changing the subject after a while Lee talked about how to receive feedback from others. He said, "After we've heard something a few times, it's very easy to capitulate to a view of ourselves that others are trying to convince us is so, but with which we essentially disagree. We may seem as if we are vulnerable and self-honest when someone is giving us feedback. But once you've been on the hot seat, what else are people going to say to you? They are going to tell you the same thing you've heard before, over and over again, using different metaphors and examples and situations. We hear this feedback a few times and we know what's coming down the pipe. Ego says, 'Hey, get with the program! Admit it!' "

Lee described how this becomes just another strategy of ego to maintain its position of dominance. "Yes, yes," we say, "I know I'm full of pride," or vanity or shame or avarice. Saying that does not mean that one is being vulnerable or self-observing—in fact, it can be the opposite of that.

Jane asked, "So if you find yourself in that situation in which someone is giving you feedback about yourself and you've heard it before—you know what they are talking about—what is the best way to be vulnerable in that situation?"

Lee answered, "Don't say or do anything. Don't defend yourself or say, 'You're right.' Just listen and let the heat of that work on you."

November 16, 1999
Arizona Ashram

Tonight at the After Dinner Talk Lee asked if there were any questions.

Steve B. said, "I have a question about the phenomena that seems to happen with regularity here around Celebration times, which we could probably call breakdown." Everyone laughed, knowing what Steve was talking about. With the demands of many projects, the Baul Theatre Company performance of "The Elephant Man" scheduled for tomorrow night involving many members of the community, band gigs over the weekend and many preparations for guests for the upcoming Appearance Day Celebration, a number of people were experiencing added stress. But at the same time before and during Celebrations there is an upsurge in the energetic current around Lee and in the sangha. All these combined factors are often associated with the unusual degree of physical or emotional "breakdown"—minor illnesses, stress and emotional reactivity that occur within the sangha at these times. Someone jokingly called it "PCS—PreCelebration Syndrome."

Lee laughed, "Oh, that!"

"It seems like it's a regular thing that goes on for various people and couples, and I was wondering if you would comment on it. It doesn't seem like we're growing out of it or growing necessarily bigger than that kind of phenomena," Steve continued.

"Well, we should be," Lee answered. "I was reading a martial arts book on aikido. There were pictures of a sixty-seven-year-old martial artist who has a ninth-degree black belt. In fact he was the youngest man to ever earn a ninth degree. You know, as one rises in the art form the tests get harder and harder, not easier and easier. Imagine the kind of energy someone has to have at sixty-seven or seventy to get a ninth-degree black belt. There is a very one-pointed intention to build *chi* or *ki* and to keep becoming more and more capable of channeling *ki*. It stands to reason that as someone gets older, they have more and not less chi even if in some instances certain parts of the body would function a little more slowly.

"In one sense, ideally that should be happening for us naturally, based on our practice and our attention. Essentially the breakdown is a function of energy leakage. It's like throwing a breaker off when there's too much juice coming through the lines. In principle it is the same thing—we can't hold the energy so it short-circuits in various ways. Over time we should be growing out of that. Maybe it's because new people keep coming and so breakdown keeps sparking through them. But over time we should be able to recognize that the tension that wants to produce breakdown is just a function of the build up of energy and we should be able to handle the energy. I don't think it's as big as it used to be. It's nothing like it was five years ago. So, some progress is being made, definitely."

"Maybe it just seems bigger when it's personal," Steve commented dryly. Everyone laughed.

The conversation turned to the meditation form that Lee has recommended for his students as Jane said, "Some years ago you gave a talk about meditation that was reprinted in *Tawagoto*. In the peak of that discussion you talked about the transformational potential of the mind. You said that a certain kind of relaxation and receptivity within the meditation form was necessary to get into that state. So it seems that what would be the correct form in another school might be too harsh an approach to the meditation form for us. In other words, in our practice the same approach as, say Zen Buddhism, could thwart or cut off the receptivity and relaxation you described.

"So, is that an accurate view of what it is we're working with, and is our aim—if one could even say that there is an aim in meditation—this transformational possibility of the mind? And is there something that's slightly different about that than, say, the aim of Vipassana or something like that?"

Lee responded, "I haven't studied it that closely, but I would say the aim is different in various forms of meditation. Many of the Vajrayana texts say the aim is different. We could say that we have three categories of purpose: worshipping the personal Beloved, which we could call adoration; secondly, realizing nonduality, which we could say is ultimately about annihilation, or surrender of the self into emptiness, *shunyata*, the void; and the third aim would be alchemical or transformational work. In Gurdjieffian terms that would be uniting the three centers through developing the singular 'I,' the 'I' of the Work, at least at the foundation stages."

"The first step is realizing nonduality because without realizing nonduality we can't possibly hold transformational work or adoration in the proper context. We're trying to hold adoration or transformational work in the proper context, but we're under the illusion of separation and therefore we can't. Intellectually we can have the right answers, we can say the right things, but we can't possibly hold transformation or adoration in the appropriate context unless we're standing on the foundation of the realization of nonduality.

"From the realization of nonduality, Enlightened Duality is not paradoxical or enigmatic. It makes perfect sense, and the law of chaos is clear, it's not chaotic. There is no confusion or doubt about the apparent chaos in the universe. So, that's the first thing, and while we're working on that, there is transformational work going on. Obviously people are very moved devotionally and go into states of adoration and wonder and awe and gratitude for the great sacred mystery of this life in the company of the lineage of Yogi Ramsuratkumar.

"Ego can only hold this in the context in which ego is the object of adoration and the beneficiary of transformation. And obviously ego is only the object of adoration within duality, because in nonduality there is no ego. Likewise ego cannot be the beneficiary of transformational work, for that is completely contradictory to the true aim of the Work. So that's the trap.

Jane commented, "It seems like from that description our practice of meditation really applies to all three of those domains, and some practices may lend themselves to the realization of nonduality, like Assertion, but that our practice of meditation is really dealing with all three of those."

Lee responded, "Well of course. Meditation more than any of the other practices is a base out of which many of the other practices are refined and clarified."

Dasya continued the conversation, saying, "This is not the first time you've explained about the fact that nonduality is the basis of adoration and transformational work, but overall we don't actually address that on a regular basis. We tend to talk about the guru and disciple relationship. It seems like you salt and pepper it enough so that it comes up, but I was wondering if we were to think more about that and discuss it more . . ."

Lee clarified, "There's a system to transformational work and there's a clear framework for adoration, but the realization of nonduality, as we discussed extensively in the early days and probably all through *Spiritual Slavery* and *Beyond Release*, does not rest on any linear process. There are things we can do to engage transformational work and there are forms that we can engage to actualize a field out of which adoration can rightly arise, but none of that applies to the realization of nonduality. The realization of nonduality is deeply coded into our Work, but one of the reasons we don't focus on it is because of the fact that the more we try to grasp it, the bigger a net we build, the more of a morass we get ourselves into. When some realization of nonduality happens, whether it's temporary or permanent, which has been true of most people in the school, it's always a surprise. We never see it coming, but we also have a sense of what it is. So there's enough data on the realization of nonduality that the understanding is there when we need it. That is a good note to end on!"

November 17, 1999
Arizona Ashram

This morning Lee said, "I won't be going back to Yuma anymore with Shri. The owner of the restaurant doesn't like me. She told the band that if they bring 'that guy' back with them, she won't book them anymore." He said this as if he was reporting on the weather. His eyes were wide and blue in the bright morning light. His words had such an inflection of detachment that he could have been talking about someone else.

The Yuma gig is exactly the kind of gig that Lee has encouraged Shri to get. It's a very nice, upscale supper club with valet parking, a large stage and dancing area. It pays the band extremely well. The owner wants to bring in more blues and jazz acts, and even though there haven't been very big crowds when Shri has played there before, she still really enjoys the band and continues to have them back. Although they have played there several times in the past few months, last Saturday night was the first time Lee had gone with the band. As one of the band members said, "Every time we play there we pay the plane ticket for one band member to go to Europe next summer."

Later in the morning Tina filled in the details of the story. She said, "I didn't want to have to tell Lee. I hated it. Of course we'd rather not go than play without Lee." It is a dilemma that liars, gods & beggars used to encounter on the road with Lee also—certain people in some clubs have a gut level response to the threat to ego that Lee poses without doing anything at all. It's a miracle that more people don't sniff him out. Over the years the comments that have been made by club owners or local clientele have ranged across a wide spectrum, but almost always there is some response, positive or negative, to the unusual atmosphere that permeates everything around Lee Lozowick. "Who is *that* guy?" has probably been the most common question. That is a question that can mean many things. Sometimes it means they were struck by Lee's style as a blues singer and/or his presence onstage in an inexplicable and positive way. Sometimes it means they are uncomfortable with something unusual they sense around him.

Tina continued, "When I told Lee that the owner had said, 'Why is that man singing with your band? Don't bring that man back anymore with you,' I said, 'We don't have to play there anymore. We don't want to play there without you—you're the only reason we're playing anyway!' Lee said, 'How much do they pay you?' When I told him, he said, 'Oh yes, you should play there. Absolutely! I don't care how they feel about me—who cares?' "

Lee's comments were like a vajra sword cutting though the sentimental illusions we project on the "man" who is the guru, which can run rampant in moments like this. Who is it in Lee that we think we need to protect from someone's negative comments or criticisms? The answer is no one. He continually demonstrates what it is to be free of self-reference, free of the vanity and pride that is pricked in praise or blame, criticism or acknowledgement. The band project is designed by Lee for one purpose only—to serve the Work—and this was another instance in which the project provided the backdrop for his teaching communication.

The energy has been steadily building toward the Appearance Day Celebration that begins tomorrow with Lee's *jayanthi*, or birthday. It is traditional in India to celebrate the day the guru appeared in the manifest world, or his *jayanthi* day, and each year the November Celebration on Lee's ashrams in Arizona and France is called the Appearance Day Celebration. This year the theme is 'Roots'—a return to the basic dharma as it has been given by Lee to his students.

A hundred details and preparations were being handled today in the ashram office as guests and students from out of town began to arrive. The final organizational chaos—trips to the airport in Phoenix, the logistics of where everyone will sleep (some on the ashram in sleeping bags on the floor, some in community households in town) menus, special food needs, childcare schedules, clean-up and serving crews—were being finalized. Large amounts of food had been bought and came flowing in through the office to the large refrigerator in the laundry room downstairs, or to various storage areas.

There are many new people coming to this Celebration, the first of whom arrived last night and yesterday. A steady wind has been blowing, but the weather has remained unseasonably warm and dry for late November. The grounds are covered with scattered brown and yellow cottonwood leaves, some of them raked up in big piles. The trees are bare now against the blue sky and the signs of winter are everywhere. Lee leaves for India in a week, and nature seems to reflect his mood: like summer sap now sunken deep in a tender brooding upon that which is the root of all things, Lee's attention is turned more than ever toward Tiruvannamalai. Within this turning inward, in which it seems that Lee is preparing for the imminent visit with Yogi Ramsuratkumar, Lee's mood has seemed mild. He is often smiling gently, even though he is animated or raises his voice to make a point. But the wild *bhavas* and crazy storms of the summer seem cloistered in some way within him now—not that they aren't present, but they seem contained and gestating.

This morning on the phone he talked almost nonstop to people who called to connect with him. He would pick up the phone and, depending on the moment and the recipient on the other end of the line, say "Hello!" in any one of a number of tones that seem to transmit a mild shock. Sometimes he happily shouted this greeting with a brightness and noticeable enthusiasm. At other times it seemed to be an extension of some irritation he was exhibiting in the moment. Sometimes it arrived as a challenge to ego, as if he was saying, "And who are you?" Even when it is a simple "Hello," it is never a simple "Hello." It reverberates with some cryptic communication that seems tailored for the person on the other end.

This morning he quipped to one person over the phone, "How are you?" After a brief pause, during which one could imagine that the other person had just returned with, "Fine, how are you?" Lee answered laconically, "I'm the same. I'm always the same as *you!*" A quiet moment rippled through the office, as if on the other end of the conversation Lee's student gathered his wits about him and attempted to continue with the business at hand.

It was a literal statement, a teaching communication of what is. Lee is always the same as each and every one of his students, a byproduct of his surrender to the Will of God. He is the same as whomever he is talking to, whoever is in front of him at any given time by virtue of the fact of no separation. Paradoxically he is always the same, and exists fundamentally as pure context, or Just This. This is one of the most disconcerting qualities of the guru—the fact that he is not really there at all in the personal sense. He is an amalgam of mysterious forces that are incomprehensible at best and perplexing, even stupefying, in many moments. Those forces somehow provide his students with exactly the alchemy that is needed in any given moment, whether the student is receptive in the moment or not. Simultaneously the company of the guru is the most sublime experience of total relationship, intimate kinship and the true bond of the heart.

Tonight Lee and members of the Hohm Community and their guests drove twenty miles to Prescott Valley to watch the Baul Theatre Company performance of "The Elephant Man," a play based on the life of John Merrick, who lived in late nineteenth century London. He was afflicted with an extremely rare genetic disorder, neurofibrometosis, in which bone mass grew wildly in grotesque formations over his body. He was malodorous and had sacks of cauliflower-like skin than hung off of his body. His head was enormous, totally misshapen, and so heavy that he could not lay it down without restricting the flow of air into his windpipe to the extent that he would asphyxiate if his body was prone. He was a tiny man, but his body was inflated beyond proportion; his face was expressionless because of the disfiguration of his facial skeleton. He suffered from constant severe pain, and yet the doctor was quoted as having said that he never knew John Merrick to once complain about his condition, or to speak ill of the extreme mistreatment he received in his life.

The action of the play centered around John Merrick and his doctor, Frederick Treves, whose worldview was shaken in his relationship with Merrick. Treves was forced to confront his assumptions, morals and values as he witnessed the nature of human suffering and the nobility of the spirit that can come of it. The play communicated a powerful message: if John Merrick could forge a being of such innocence, integrity and dignity under those conditions, there is no excuse for the average human being to indulge in bitterness, cynicism or self-pity for one's misfortunes. There have been individuals like John Merrick throughout history who are potent reminding factors that one's relationship to God is the only place to take refuge. He not only endured the cruelty and unconscionable treatment of others, but he was known to often comfort others who felt pity and shame and sorrow over how he was treated. He was a source of compassion, understanding and kindess for those who knew him.

About three hundred people attended the performance, some of them high school students who came with their drama class. The entire audience was deeply moved by the performances that were delivered, and when we walked out during the intermission there were tears on many faces. At the end of the second act there was a spontaneous standing ovation.

The Baul Theatre Company had been working feverishly for two months to make this performance happen. They had flown Sean Hoy, a professional actor and friend of the Hohm Community, down from Canada for two weeks to direct the play and perform in the role of Treves, the protagonist opposite the character of John Merrick, played powerfully by Everett Jaime. It had taken a tremendous amount of time and energy to pull the whole event off, but the rewards were great.

Afterward in the evening gathering back at the ashram someone asked Lee how the play was. He said, "It was excellent." He looked at his student Elyse, who has participated in the Baul Theatre Company since its inception in 1986, and added, "But I think it's time for a comedy."

November 18, 1999
Arizona Ashram

About forty people sat in the meditation hall this morning with Lee for the first meditation of the Appearance Day Celebration. The hall was full with flowers in honor of Lee's birthday—lilies and roses and large yellow chrysanthemums banked in green. Ten minutes before meditation was over Tina opened the door slightly and signaled to Lee that Garchen Rinpoche had just arrived with his translator and attendant. Lee got up from the dais where he sat meditating and walked out. At eight-twenty about fifty people convened in the meditation hall for the first of four talks to be given by Garchen Rinpoche that were scheduled for the next two days.

Lee had had his divan removed and two wooden seats set up side by side on the raised dais. There were two *zabutons* covered in black silk laid out on the wooden seats, and Lee put both in one seat for Rinpoche. He put a small pillow on the second wooden seat on the dais for Rinpoche's translator, and prepared a place for himself to sit on the floor against the wall on the men's side of the room. When he escorted Rinpoche into the room, as soon as Rinpoche saw the seating arrangement he picked up the second *zabuton* and put it in the other wooden seat. Turning to Lee he gestured for Lee to sit beside him. Lee indicated that his seat was by the wall, but Rinpoche insisted. With a smile that could melt icebergs and a slight inclination of his head, Rinpoche gestured unmistakably, "Here, please take this seat."

They sat down together with Ari, the translator, who sat on a pillow on the floor below the dais at Garchen Rinpoche's feet. Rinpoche began the session with a series of traditional prayers in Tibetan. A silver and copper prayer wheel turned in his right hand almost nonstop and continued all morning. He began to speak, stopping for his assistant to translate.

"Thank you for your invitation to give teachings here this week," Ari began translating for Rinpoche. "All teachings have the same purpose, so we can consider ourselves to be dharma friends. So, I wish auspicious good fortune to all of you. All spiritual traditions have the same purpose that unites us all in our endeavors.

"Without exception, all sentient beings experience suffering. Our purpose in practicing dharma is to find methods that will alleviate suffering. Only dharma practice will alleviate suffering of sentient beings. In this worldly realm there are two ways of conduct: the way of the worldly being and the way of one who practices dharma. All are still seeking to alleviate the root cause of suffering, but only through the practice of dharma can we alleviate suffering when we realize that one's mind is dharma. Mind is the principle cause of attaining enlightenment—realizing the Buddha. We take refuge in the Buddha, but we are actually taking refuge in the true nature of our own minds. The dharma comes from the Buddha and the sangha comes from the dharma, so these three jewels of refuge are actually complete in the enlightened Buddha.

"There are two paths of practicing the dharma: one is a more scholarly, intellectual approach and the other is the approach of practice. I was in prison during the Communist revolution for twenty years, and I haven't had the opportunity to develop the scholarly and intellectual path in this life. I do have changeless faith and changeless belief, and on the basis of this I have done a little practice toward the path of realization in the tradition of Buddha and dharma.

"Buddha taught that one should avoid all negative conduct, should cultivate positive conduct, and should discipline and transform your own mind. The view that suffering will be immediately alleviated once we have heard the teaching is a false view, and can lead us to turn away from the dharma."

As Rinpoche went on to describe the concept of karma, the prayer wheel continued to turn in his hand. "As a result of my former actions, I have come to my present situation, which is the fruition of former actions. If we realize this we become free of hope and fear, which is itself a cause for happiness." His frequent smiles and gracious gestures were disarming expressions of a deep authenticity. He began to elucidate the basic precepts of Buddhism: the insubstantiality of all phenomena; the fact that all life is suffering; that when we rest in the true essential selflessness of the mind as Buddha nature, we are free from fear or happiness. He talked about the importance of, through years of practice, gaining a "meditative stabilization" in which we see that all thought forms are without basis, without substance.

A precept that he returned to again and again was the importance of cultivating *bodhicitta*, which he described as the "precious mind of enlightenment" that is also characterized by "loving-kindness or compassion." This cultivation of *bodhicitta* is done for the benefit of all beings. In this effort we abandon negative emotions, actions, self-clinging and self-cherishing. He said, "Of primary importance is this love for all sentient beings, which becomes the cause for happiness in this and all future lives. We must cultivate the love that a mother has for her son for all sentient beings; if we only cultivate it for those near and dear to us, then it will not benefit all beings. *Bodhicitta* is no different than love; its brilliance is said to be greater than one hundred thousand suns. The more we cultivate loving-kindness, the stronger it becomes, so we cultivate a sense of compassion which will cause the great tree of loving-kindness to grow."

Rinpoche began to talk about the strongest emotions—anger and hate—and the non-virtues of the mind: avarice, jealousy, wishing harm on others, hatred and perverted views, which are not in accordance with the dharma teachings. Lies, harsh speech, divisive speech, meaningless speech or idle chatter all fell into the category of non-virtuous action.

After an hour and a half Rinpoche suggested that we take a break and stretch a bit. He, however, continued to sit in his chair, never moving at all. He exuded innocence and purity. Even though the language barrier was total, there was a feeling of continuity and connectedness, of friendship and warmth that flowed from him to each person. The dharma was pristine and detailed as he continued laying out Buddhist precepts.

Toward the end of the morning session he spoke about taking refuge: "At the beginning of the path we take the vow of refuge in the Buddha. The Buddha will protect us by virtue of having given the dharma, so we take refuge in the Buddha, the dharma and the sangha. The Buddha is the wish-fulfilling jewel. Realizing that the Buddha has given us all this, we become joyful, and we cultivate gratitude to our parents, to the government and laws of the country, to our teachers, and especially to our guru. In this way we begin to purify our obscurations. If we properly revere our spiritual guide, we will see the Buddha-nature in him. All spiritual guides have not developed all qualities, but the mind of the spiritual guide is still one with the Buddha-nature. As we reach fruition in one path, we find that we are reaching fruition in all paths . . . ."

At brunch, one of the two meals of the day, the menu was extremely simple—hard and soft-boiled eggs, sliced rye bread and apple butter, mint tea. Salt, pepper, cayenne, Tabasco and butter were available as condiments. During the meal Garchen Rinpoche, his attendant and his translator sat directly across the table from Lee. Garchen Rinpoche does not speak a word of English. He simply sat and ate. In between bites of food his lips moved in a silent mantra. As soon as he finished eating Rinpoche began twirling the prayer wheel again. He and Lee regarded each other with slow smiles. There was a mood of graciousness between them. Rinpoche listened to all the announcements at the end of the meal with a smile, as if he recognized the dynamics of human community. Afterward the group dispersed for two hours of guru *seva*.

At the beginning of the afternoon session Rinpoche answered a question in relationship to the Tara *thangka* in the meditation hall. After telling the story of Atisha, a great yogi who traveled to Tibet and Sri Lanka and whose devotional practice was to Tara, Rinpoche then began to speak about the impartial love and compassion of Tara for all beings. He said, "If we lack faith and devotion, there is no connection with Tara. We cannot receive her blessings. But if we have faith and devotion, but we find that compassion does not arise spontaneously in our mind-stream, we can pray to Tara that compassion and love will arise in us and she will give it to you. All things that are pleasurable to the senses—flowers and fruit and food offerings are made to Tara. Even if you see a beautiful flower on the road, you can offer it to Tara without picking it. But before practicing devotion to Tara you must take refuge in the three jewels, then cultivate loving-kindness, compassion and *bodhicitta*. To accumulate blessings only for oneself is not satisfactory. Rather we do this practice of devotions to Tara to have the power and means to benefit all beings. We visualize Tara inside ourselves—her ornaments and silk clothes and so on. Then we also practice her mantra. Over many years, signs of accomplishments will arise, such as dreams.

"The precious *bodhicitta*, or generating the mind of loving-kindness, is essential for engaging any practice. Once we have accomplished *bodhicitta* then it becomes effortless to realize the qualities of any deity. Without *bodhicitta*, we will not see the signs of authentic or real realization of the qualities of any deity whom we propitiate or practice for.

"When we habituate the mind to deity worship the image of ourselves falls away and we begin to see and visualize ourselves as deity. Through the use of mantra we will no longer engage ordinary speech, but only the speech of the deity. Our mind becomes the enlightened mind of the deity. If we have practiced this form of meditation well, at the time of death in the intermediate stage we do not arise in our old form, but in the form of the deity. Then wherever we are becomes the realm of the deity. When we have the motivation of leading all beings to liberation, we meditate as the deity for the means to achieve this, and we become skillful in methods that will bring enlightenment to ourselves and others. We become the body of the deity, the sangha; the speech of the deity, the dharma; and the mind of the deity, or Buddha, which is meditative stabilization.

"We begin on the path by attaining our own liberation, which is the lesser vehicle, Hinayana. The moment we cultivate *bodhicitta*, loving-kindness, we enter the Mahayana or greater vehicle. The approach to the deity is really taking the three vows: the first vow of refuge in the three jewels of Buddha, dharma, sangha; on the basis of the that, we take the second vow, the vow of the bodhisattva; and on that basis, we take the vow of the secret mantra in which we realize our own mind as the mind of the Buddha, and our own body as the body of the Buddha. Then we realize the deity as ourselves.

"The practice of Tara is very easy to realize because through the force of the Tara's blessing it will be easy for *bodhicitta* to arise for those beings who have faith and devotion. Even after twelve months we will find some accomplishments in our practice. First you contemplate the meaning of the three jewels, then the vow of the bodhisattva, then the vow of the secret mantra. But the vow of the secret mantra is undertaken only when the first two vows are stabilized. When we take Tara as a guide we make a commitment, called *samaya*.

"We have habitual tendencies or ingrained habits or propensities. Many of these are negative in nature and bind us to cyclical existence. We have to practice mindfulness to recognize when we are engaging in negative forms of conduct. Eventually it will be easier to practice virtuous actions. Whenever we take the vows of refuge, of the bodhisattva, we should take these very seriously and work to develop new patterns of behavior. The mind of compassion is linked with our own Buddha nature. The single most effective is the cultivation of loving-kindness to embody the three jewels in one's own body, speech and mind.

"There are three types of faith. The first one is developed when we realize that whatever path people follow brings benefits to all beings and are all the Buddha himself. We should develop impartial faith in all spiritual guides and traditions. The second type of faith is longing faith, which occurs when we see the suffering of ourselves and others and we develop a heartfelt longing to save ourselves and others from the ocean of suffering. The third type of faith is a belief or trust when we come to a place of total assurance, of unshakable faith that enlightened Buddhas are totally omniscient, and we have no doubt of the teachings that have been given to us by sublime beings.

"Doubt comes from ignorance. This third type of faith comes when there are no more doubts, and faith is unshakable. So it is important to read great stories, liberation stories, of saints like Milarepa. In doing this we will see what it really takes to realize our own Buddha nature. Because of the efforts of such a one as Milarepa, it is easier for us today in this lifetime. This is the blessing of the dharma, and it is *real*. We should look at Milarepa and take inspiration, not feel that it is impossible for us."

In the course of answering other questions that were posed to him Rinpoche said that he has been reading the life story of Milarepa for sixty years, over and over again, and each time he reads it he gains something for his own meditation practice. He said, "All of you have accumulated merit in past lives to find an authentic spiritual path and an authentic spiritual guide in this life. We have to hold on, even if we do not realize in this life. We will continue to purify the mind's obscurations and lifetime after lifetime, we will be able to find the precious teachings again. Sooner or later the mind will be revealed, and we will continue to purify even the subtlest of the mind's obscurations."

Someone asked about their work with emotionally troubled, often aggressive, institutionalized teenage girls. Rinpoche answered, "When we have taken on the bodhisattva vow we take on the commitment to save all sentient beings, regardless of their mind state. Regardless of how someone acts the first step is to love that person. There is no question that it is a difficult climate in which to love. When we have faith in the Buddha and the teachings, then we have the foundation. When we see others who do not have that, we feel sad and cannot sustain joy. All we can do is practice and find the means to help them find the teachings. In these situations we focus on their lack of faith, or their suffering, not on ourselves. When we see their pain, our problems fall away."

Another question was about anger. Rinpoche said, "About anger. There is ordinary anger and then there is the wrath of a deity. With ordinary anger we must distinguish in our own minds why we are engaging such conduct . . . Ordinary anger will create karma, whereas a wrathful deity or guru manifests anger only because beings cannot receive the teachings in any other way. They manifest wrath while having a mind of great compassion, like a mother who disciplines her child. In order to benefit all different kinds of beings, deities or gurus manifest in different ways. Peaceful qualities are to slowly pacify the negativity of beings; increasing qualities are to increase wealth, joy, blessings and the happiness of beings; powerful qualities are used when beings have gone astray and through certain activities are led to the proper path of action.

"As a result of clinging to the idea of a self, the dualistic extremes of aversion and attachment arise. Aversion can take the form of something we'd prefer not to deal with, like illness, or hatred. The basic nature of mind is obscured, and from that obscuration comes the dualistic notion of self. If we express anger in words, our speech will be 'dirty' and we will create negative karma. At the moment we recognize anger arising we hold back and engage a strong, firm meditation and turn the mind back in upon itself; then we can see where the anger arose from. When we find that the anger or negative emotion becomes empty or dissipates—in that instant we have liberated that emotion. Perhaps if we then speak, anger will arise again, so instead we sit further, a few minutes longer . . .

"Anger is without essence; it is like a wind that arises, a wind energy that arises in the subtle body. Like the wind, it is gone in a moment if you turn the mind in on itself. When we start to practice in this way we start to realize that anger is like a cloud floating through vast space. We realize, 'My mind is the clear sky.' The anger itself is the object of where we direct our energy, not the individual to whom the anger is directed. In tantric practice if we turn the mind in upon itself, we recognize the dissipation of the emotion and what is left is the mirror-like wisdom of the mind, untainted, vast. If once we are able to cut through a negative emotion, then each time it will be easier and easier. By conquering our negative emotions, eventually we will be able to conquer all of our negativities. This is the result of our practice of meditation."

Toward the end of the afternoon session the children came in with some questions for Rinpoche, which he seemed to take great delight in. They asked Garchen Rinpoche how he became a rinpoche. He smiled very broadly, his eyes emanating joy. He responded, "Yes, in fact I am a rinpoche. It's really not such a great thing to be!" He laughed, his deep eyes shining with kindness. He began the story of how he was found as a child by his lineage. When the lamas were looking for the next incarnation of the Garchen Rinpoche, he said, they got his father's name and his mother's name through divination. His father was a very strong yogi and meditation practitioner and his mother was also a strong practitioner of dharma. The lamas began to look for his mother and father, but they lived in a very different area than central Tibet, where the monastery of his lineage was. When he was seven years old, they found him and took him to the monastery. He said, "Ever since then I haven't had any freedom whatsoever." His eyes sparkled. "Since I was seven years old I have only served the monastery." His uncomplicated and radiant smile lent volumes of meaning to the truth of what he had just said.

After the talk Garchen Rinpoche and his students returned to their home about an hour south of Prescott. At five-thirty dinner was served in the big tent. It was another very simple affair of steamed broccoli and cauliflower, white rice, miso soup with tofu chunks and chopped scallions, and a lemon tahini dip. Afterward a large, three-layer birthday cake with chocolate icing was brought out. There was one single candle burning on the top of the cake. When Debbie asked Lee if he would blow the candle out, he laughed as if in surprise, "You want *me* to blow it out?" He stood up and almost fell over in extricating himself from his seat at the table while everyone chanted *Om Sri Ram Jai Ram Jai Jai Ram*. He was still chuckling as he sat back down and waited for the cake and Häagen-Dazs ice cream.

Shortly after dinner Lee gave a talk. Someone asked if Lee would talk about the three main practices that he had called the "core practices" of the school earlier this year—Enquiry, Assertion and the heart breath. Lee answered, "The Buddhists call it *tonglen*, or the bodhisattva breath. We use the term 'the heart breath,' and the practice is about each of us being able to purify the world. The way we do it is significantly different from the bodhisattva breath of the Buddhists, even though it is, paradoxically, exactly the same thing, and even though we do it as bodhisattvas. The heart breath came from revelation, like all of our practices.

"Garchen Rinpoche said that since he was seven years old he has had no freedom; in this school no one has a private life. If you do, you haven't understood this path yet. As long as you have a private life you've missed something of the teaching. So, one of the distinctions I made last summer was that I divided practice into two domains: the recommended conditions, and core and secondary practices. The core practices were Assertion, or the use of the phrase 'Just This' to define Reality in every moment, Enquiry, or the use of the phrase 'Who am I kidding?' and the heart breath. My first book, *Spiritual Slavery*, is about Assertion. Spiritual Slavery is a phrase that defines you as a slave to Spirit. Whatever Spirit wants of you is what you animate. What Spirit wanted animated in Jesus' case was death, crucifixion and resurrection in a very dramatic act of symbolism. Whatever Spirit wants to animate in each of us has a specific destiny. The primary, unique core of this school is Spiritual Slavery. The root of all root practices is Spiritual Slavery. When we Surrender to the Will of God certain practices arise for us—the heart breath, Enquiry, Assertion."

Lee talked about the detailed visualization that is necessary in the deity meditation of the Vajrayana path. Every single thing must be recreated through the meditative visualization, from the jewels and clothes and adornments to the minute aspects of the artist's rendering of sacred objects, sky, water and other symbolism. His eyes sparkled mischievously as he added, "On the other hand, with guru yoga all you have to remember is the color of your guru's eyes—really!"

Another student commented on how pristine and orderly the teachings of Tibetan Buddhism are in comparison to the dharma of this school. "Our practices and the teaching seem so hidden, so confusing," she said.

Lee answered, "Today and tomorrow we are receiving instruction in our path in the language of Tibetan Buddhism. It's true this school can look like an immense rambling mess because we don't have the formal structure and a thousand years of sacred culture, but everything that you hear is there."

Occasionally one of Lee's students will comment that the teaching as Lee has given it is unclear, or that he is not giving definitive instruction in the more esoteric or advanced practices. And yet if one listens carefully with open ears, the hints and teaching instructions are liberally threaded throughout his discourses. The unorthodox form of Lee's teaching, as he said many times during the past summer, is intentional: the Bauls go to great lengths to keep their esoteric teachings from becoming crystallized in formal scripture. They shun all forms of dogma and orthodoxy, and do not believe in codifying their teaching in any way other than in the music and poetry.

Today as Garchen Rinpoche spoke the parallels between the "secret mantra" aspect of Tibetan Buddhism—the tantric vehicle or Vajrayana—and certain practices which Lee has given were striking and clear. Lee continued to speak to the question, saying that actually there should be no confusion if we are practicing properly, because the practices are revelatory and reveal themselves to us.

He began to talk about what he wants from his students. He said, "I'm not interested in the pushy, loud, aggressive approach. Elegance and dignity have become very important in this school. Elegance and dignity are looming gigantic in my perspective. I want spaces to begin on time and end on time. The longer I go in this Work and the deeper my relationship to Yogi Ramsuratkumar is, the more I realize that Divine Influence is handling everything. I don't have to do anything—the Influence covers it all. You go into Yogi Ramsuratkumar's Darshan and you sit down. That's it. You don't give *prasad*, you don't *pranam* at His feet. Divine Influence does it all—but we think we have to do it. If we are practicing properly and aligning ourselves to the teaching, Divine Influence sort of surfs through our veils and the mind to effect or communicate to us."

He spoke again about Garchen Rinpoche's years in prison, and came back to the point that Rinpoche had had no freedom since he was seven years old; since that time, all he has done is serve his monastery. Lee ended on this note: "In this school, our prison is longing."

November 19, 1999
Arizona Ashram

This morning Garchen Rinpoche resumed his discourse on the dharma. He began by saying that our enemies should be placed first and foremost in our cultivation of *bodhicitta*. "Our enemies are absolutely necessary for the generation of *bodhicitta*. We need to understand that our own anger is the primary cause of our taking rebirth in the three lower realms. Our enemies provide us with the opportunity to practice, so in this way our enemies benefit us.

"If Milarepa had not had so many difficulties in his sadhana posed by his enemies, his aunt and uncle, he could not have realized. Our enemies are actually like a wish-fulfilling jewel that brings us closer to enlightenment. We have the opportunity to eliminate negative karma in this way. Also, those who speak badly of us—this is helpful to eliminate pride in us. When people are harmful to us through speech this gives us the opportunity to see our own shortcomings and weaknesses. When we see the benefit our enemies are to our practice of dharma, we cannot wish them harm. We cultivate *bodhicitta* for the benefit of all beings, not just for one lifetime, but for many lifetimes, until enlightenment."

He spent the morning elucidating the six perfections, focusing for a long time on generosity. He spoke about generosity as a practice of making offerings: "The first of the six perfections is generosity. We make offerings with the intention to bring no harm. Many will make offerings to gain comfort and so on for the future, but this too is a tainted offering. We make offerings solely for the benefit of all beings—then our offerings can be said to be pure. When we make offerings or accumulate virtue the state of our mind is what is important. If our aspiration when accumulating virtue is great for the benefit of all beings, then the fruits of that offering will be correspondingly great. We make a prayer that our offering will be medicine for all, then the merit of that offering increases a million-fold.

"There is also the offering to the three jewels. We should make offerings without any hope of positive karmic result for self. When we set up an altar, for example, we imagine that all three of the jewels are present. If we truly perceive the spiritual master as the embodiment of the three jewels when we make the offerings, then the offerings become bigger. When we see beautiful things when shopping, we don't have to possess those things in order to offer them up to the spiritual master. There are many benefits of making offerings, or generosity; there is also a corresponding degree of harm when we withhold offerings because of self-clinging, a dualistic sense of 'I'. There is attachment and clinging because we see that we want to possess that object for ourselves.

"With the offering of protection or fearlessness we are protecting life. Offering a place to stay, protecting insects, offerings of dharma or giving teachings—these all accumulate merit. But even more important is the practice of meditative stabilization, or calm abiding. This benefits all beings. If we cultivate the power of meditative stabilization we can bring benefit to many beings. Marpa had many disciples, the greatest of which was Milarepa. His practice was like the life force, and he had many difficulties; many demons came forth, and so the blessings of Milarepa are like the sun.

"If we think, or we have the mindset, that everything we do is for all sentient beings then our practice of *bodhicitta* will increase. Lack of avarice *is* the practice of generosity. When we freely give offerings, give away, then that possession is truly ours because the fruition of that offering is positive karma. The accumulation of good karma is like having money in the bank—it draws interest and accumulates. The purification of all avarice and greed and self-clinging results from the cultivation of *bodhicitta*. Loving-kindness and compassion are the essence of all virtue and merit; they are like a great jewel that brings joy and bliss to the mind. We will lose this body, but the mind is beyond death. There are those of us who have a great love of the teachings—this too is the result of many lifetimes of rejoicing in the teachings. It is another example of the mind existing beyond death."

After the morning talk brunch was served. Once again the food was a choice between hard or soft-boiled eggs, rye bread, apple butter and mint tea—simple, basic, to the point. A pattern was beginning to make itself known, and one could guess that Lee had planned that every brunch and dinner during the four-day Celebration would be exactly the same fare. When I asked him what the symbolism of the food was he said, "It's just food." He might as well have turned to me and said, "Just This." The food was a direct communication about perceiving the simple bare bone of reality in any given moment. As Arnaud Desjardins would say, "What is, is." While the eggs and bread were passed up and down the table, Rinpoche sat across from Lee and smiled as he ate, all the while turning the prayer wheel in his hand.

After a period of guru *seva*, Garchen Rinpoche gave the last of four, three-hour talks to the sangha. When he came in and sat down he slipped a colorful, laminated card into the basket in front of the *thangka*. When asked what it was he answered, "The card [depicts] a collection of the most auspicious offerings, which I have offered to the goddess Tara."

He continued his discussion of the six perfections. He said, "With regard to morality and ethics we abandon all conduct that brings harm to others, however subtle that conduct may be. Even if it is something as simple as slamming doors in the house, the slamming of the door may cause suffering to another. Avarice arises out of desire. If the object we desire goes to another, then we feel jealousy.

"We maintain virtue of body by protecting the vows we have made. Helping establish or maintain a dharma center is also an accumulation of virtue of the body. We may think that we are not the responsible party, that someone else should clean up, but having taken the bodhisattva vow, we go ahead and clean up because it may benefit others— someone else gets a rest. Particularly for those who are involved in running a dharma center, it is a grave nonvirtue if the center becomes so divisive and disharmonious that someone cannot stay and leaves. About the temple in the community—where four or more are gathered, we have a sangha. Whatever we do to make offerings or accumulate virtue with our bodies has great merit. Every time we say the mantra of the deity, the physical form of the deity emanates out into the world.

"We devote body, speech and mind to the benefit of beings through the dharma center. We must have patience and perseverance. And yet, day-to-day difficulties will arise; we have jealousy, we gossip and there may be anger toward each other. All this can ultimately effect the dharma center. Those who encounter difficulty must turn to the teachings. The minute a difficult person has arrived at the dharma center, we say, 'Oh, a wish-fulfilling person has come into our presence!' If you can bear it, this person will become your own best friend in your spiritual development. Even if someone comes only for one day and receives help from the dharma teachings, the merit of that will not be exhausted even for lifetimes. If even for a single day someone receives benefits the merit of that will go on for lifetimes. If a very difficult person comes who is so needy and so difficult and they end up leaving, this is bad for us and for them. So we practice all the virtues—patience and generosity are all in place.

"The third of the six perfections is patience. We cultivate being satisfied with whatever we have. If we desire a lot of different kinds of foods it can cause problems, for example. We should eat for the benefit of the body, not just for taste, attachment or aversion. We think we have to have all these vitamins and such things. For twenty years in prison I was consistently fed a diet of filthy food, and I found that not only did I not die, but I am fine today!"

Rinpoche's gentle and benevolent smile graced the room once again. It was a simple statement given with a humility that made it that much more powerful and drove home Lee's seemingly constant admonitions about the absurdity of the desperate consumption of gross volumes of "nutritional supplements" in the community. From Lee's point of view our attachment to health and almost superstitious belief in the efficacy of nutritional supplements has reached such a point of absurdity that he has joked that, despite his pointed comments, some of his students have developed an addiction to digestive enzymes that is not unlike an addiction to heroin.

Rinpoche continued, "When difficult people come we have to have patience and reign in our emotions, but not suppress them. What does more harm to me—this person, or the anger that I generate inside? This person cannot throw me into the hell realms, but my anger has the power to throw me into hell realms and create karmic debts. The root of taking rebirth in hell itself is the emotion of anger. That which preserves life force is patience. Patience is the antidote to anger.

"Anger arises in subtle ways, especially in family circumstances. We need to make efforts to purify even the subtlest anger as it arises in our mind-stream. If we look too closely at our partner we will begin to see faults and have a perverted view. If I see faults in another they are only my own faults I see there. So if I don't look too closely it will be the cause of harmony for many years in my household."

Rinpoche offered to answer questions for awhile. His translator, Ari, had a small pile of hand-written questions from the group that she posed to Rinpoche. The first one was about cultivating loving-kindness and compassion in children. He said, "Whether or not children will have respect for others depends on their own merit. Parents should teach generosity and patience to their children. We give the foundation and education for respect and love of others, and the inherent value of such things. But whether or not a child will make use of it is due to their own accumulation of merit and karma. Love and consistency is the foundation of the education we offer to children."

The translator read the next question: "Is illness always related to karma, and can one interfere with karma or help purify the karma of others by helping them heal from illnesses?"

Rinpoche responded, "All illnesses are due to past negative actions. With confession and purification of negativities, it is possible that illness can be cleared away. But the karma may be such that a person must experience the fruition of karma in an illness in this lifetime, maybe for the entire lifetime. In both Tibetan medicine and Ayurveda, illnesses are in three categories: wind energies or illnesses, which come from desire; bile illnesses, which come from anger; illnesses related to phlegm, which come from ignorance.

"If we generate enough *bodhicitta* we can effect or purify others. This is part of the training of a doctor. Through the arising of *bodhicitta* we can do something . . . As much as we cultivate meditative stabilization we can influence the healing process through subtle means. If we practice the healing arts we also practice "sending and receiving" or *tonglen*, the bodhisattva breath, then the benefits to others will be greater. The patient must have a receptive mind and accept that this is an opportunity to purify past actions and negative emotions. They must have an understanding of karmic causality, and then this can be an effective way of eliminating their own and other's suffering."

Rinpoche spoke about perfect enlightenment as the sixth of the six perfections. He said, "All compounded phenomena are impermanent; this is the teaching. The guru's form is the sangha, the guru's mind is the Buddha. We should focus on the guru's mind, not on his form. When our meditation is stabilized we will be free from thoughts and there will be no difference between our mind and the mind of the guru. That is ultimate *bodhicitta*, in which the mind is free of any extremes. This is the way we should practice now and in all lifetimes. If we practice in this way whether the guru is near or far or embodied or passed away, we will be one with the guru."

Another question was read, this time about cultivating the form of the guru within. Rinpoche became very animated, as if this was a subject that carried a certain enthusiasm for him. He said, "Cultivating is anything that we make efforts toward. In the practice of the deity Tara we have to cultivate this through consistent effort, by applying the method daily. The ground, root and basis of all practice we do is having love and compassion for all beings. It is like sunlight that shines on all beings. If we have that *bodhicitta*, then it is not difficult to [become one with] Tara. So we have to begin with generating *bodhicitta*. First we look at the picture of the deity; we look at it again and again, until when we close our eyes the picture is there. We look at it again and then close our eyes. We go back and forth between the picture and our meditation and in this way we habituate our minds to the image of the deity.

"Tara is the embodiment of omniscient wisdom. Her love is like that of a mother to her son. She sends countless millions of emanations to beings. Having internalized the image of the deity and practiced daily to emanate as that deity, we become able to carry that off of our meditation cushion and into our daily work, so that all of our activities become the enlightened activities of the goddess Tara. But all this begins with *bodhicitta*, then we can habituate ourselves to the form of the deity, and become that form. Without compassion we cannot realize this practice in any way. The root of this practice is compassion."

The translator read the next question, which asked Rinpoche to address the comment made by Chögyam Trungpa Rinpoche, who, when asked what he did when he found himself in hell, said, "I try to stay there."

Rinpoche answered, "Whenever we take the vows of the bodhisattva we cultivate certain attitudes of a warrior, a courageous being, a hero or heroine. The bodhisattva is not afraid of the suffering of others. First it is necessary to realize the wisdom of the three lower and three upper realms. If we are able to uproot anger in our own minds then we are not afraid of hell realms. If we lack pure view, we cannot benefit even if we are in a god realm, but if we have pure view, we can descend to any realm and bring benefits to others. This is a very profound topic; it is hard to realize but easy to talk about. Until we have some degree of meditative stabilization we will always want to run away. If we practice daily, we will grow in our ability to stay in hell."

At the beginning of the questions Lee had handed a written question to the translator and said, "After everyone else's questions are answered, if there is still time, here is my question." Now she picked it up and said that she had not been able to translate the whole question, which was almost a page long. "But," she said, "Rinpoche in his omniscience manages to grasp the question anyway." She read the question aloud in English. It was essentially a question about whether Lee, in his position of authority, should warn a seeker who is approaching a teacher whom Lee knows to be a false teacher, who has unethical sexual relations with his students and so on. Or, on the other hand, should he remain silent on the subject and not interfere with the karmic situation at all.

Rinpoche responded, "With regard to spiritual guides, it is the karma of a disciple to be attracted to one teacher over another. Many beings, because of karma, are attracted to teachers who may not be pure practitioners. Pure view is the issue; if the disciple has pure view, then the disciple has the opportunity to realize great enlightenment. Even if we are in a position of authority, it is not our responsibility to influence with regard to guides. We cannot know the full influences [of what goes on between masters and disciples]. Likewise we cannot comprehend the activities of a great master. Many masters have appeared in many different ways for the purpose of benefiting others. Therefore we should allow people to go their own way. If we interfere, we can incur karma. We should keep the faults of other teachers to ourselves and allow other beings to go the way of their own karma."

After Rinpoche gave his answer Lee nodded his head once and said thank you. Rinpoche finished the last part of his teaching by talking about transcendent wisdom or awareness. He said, "The mind itself is enlightened potential, Buddha nature. At the beginning we have to make efforts to realize this. We have to push on toward meditative stabilization. If we follow thoughts they can harm us, but if we leave them behind, we see that they are no different than the nature of the mind itself. However many thoughts may arise in the mind, if we don't follow them then they don't have the power to harm us. The thoughts we have are habits that have accumulated over lifetimes—karmic habits.

"By making efforts in this way we recognize the gap between thoughts; then we can be in the gap between the thoughts, which is the enlightened potential of all beings. When that becomes habituated we can remain in that state for long periods of time and experience joy. This too is a thought form and it must be let go. Once we are in calm abiding, if thoughts arise it is no fault of our meditative practice. Vigilant mindful awareness is the practice of calm abiding, which becomes the basis of cultivating wisdom. Within the practice of calm abiding there is the recognition that thoughts arise, and there is a nonengagement and dissipation of thoughts.

"The nature of mind is empty of any inherent self-existence. It is clear and luminous, vast like the sky. This is *Mahamudra*, ultimate *bodhicitta*. That mind is completely naked, free of any identification. Like a son and mother recognizing each other—this is how one's own mind recognizes that is it one with the mind of the Buddha. This practice takes many years to realize.

"Tilopa said, 'Not seeing is the supreme insight.' What this means is that when we see the naked, empty essence of mind, there is nothing there to see, therefore the realization of the mind's nature is totally beyond description. Look outside at the sky and at the same time we look inside at the mind—there is a recognition there. All Buddha mind has one cause—enlightened potential. The nature of water is the same everywhere, and it is the same with the essential nature of all beings—the same everywhere.

"So what are the benefits of meditating in this way? Whenever we experience suffering and gross thoughts, negative emotions arise. Through this kind of meditation we realize they are illusive in nature. The mind is as vast as the sky and has no trace or stain. Thoughts are only like clouds in the sky."

The translator concluded, "Rinpoche's instruction to you is to remain in that nature and see that negative thoughts have no existence. At the time of death when consciousness separates from the body we enter into the intermediate state; then we will sense and see things as if we still had form. We will still be at the effect of habits. But if we have practiced there will not be the propensity toward those habits. Milarepa is the principle guide of the Kagyu line; we call on Milarepa for cutting through in times of difficulty. But whoever we have faith in, we should call upon that person in difficulty."

Rinpoche beamed at everyone and slowly said, "Thank you," in English with a broad smile. He turned to Lee and bowed, then ended the teaching with Tibetan prayers.

He stayed for dinner, which was the same as the night before—white rice, steamed broccoli and cauliflower, miso soup with chunks of tofu and chopped scallions, a lemon and tahini sauce. A very simple dessert of whole-wheat honey gingerbread was served with whipped cream. Everyone ate enthusiastically and with relish, and yet the mood was much quieter than usual celebration meals where elaborate feasts are served. These meals can often be frenetic and tense with scarcity. "Will I get enough of the treats? The meat, the gravy, the coffee, cake or pie?"

During the meal Rinpoche's translator spoke with Lee about coming to visit the Rinpoche at the temple they are building on the land that was donated to establish a Tibetan center in Arizona. It is about an hour's drive from Lee's ashram. After the meal Rinpoche, his translator and his attendant said goodbye to Lee and left with absolutely no fanfare or hoo-hah. In much the same way that Lee does things, when it was time to go Rinpoche just got up and walked out of the tent, which was bustling with the activities of clean-up, and into the dark night.

At six-thirty Lee's talk started in the meditation hall. Lee walked in briskly and took his seat on the divan, which had been placed back on the dais. He seemed revved up, as if he was brandishing an invisible warrior's mace. With a slightly bellicose edge to his voice he snapped, "Well, I thought what Rinpoche had to say was fantastic! He offered to give everyone refuge, but I declined. I think many of us should not be mixing paths or practices because we are not mature enough . . ." He paused, perhaps to let that sink in and to gauge everyone's reaction to this small provocation. It seemed as if he was testing the water to see if his students were responding to Garchen Rinpoche's presence with any degree of romanticism.

He continued, "But it was a fantastic gift to us, and I think we should practice what he has talked about. Even so, we will still attribute our psychological knot to our *parents*, not to karma . . ." He threw this out with a challenging tone, as if he was daring anyone to take the bait and argue with him.

On many occasions Lee has voiced his frustration at seeing his students lose perspective after hearing dharma teachings from other paths. The Bauls are naturally eclectic in one way—they take what is useful from many traditions and incorporate it into their practice and way of life, the Baul relationship with the Sufis of northern India being an example of this. But at the same time the Baul path has a very specific integrity of its own that is adhered to fiercely. One of the four basic tenets of the Baul path is radical reliance on the guru, which may take the form of guru yoga. A practitioner can lose invaluable momentum by becoming distracted by another teaching or the practices of another path, or by the glamour of another teacher. In this regard Lee is quite fierce and protective of his students, at times seeming even seeming jealous and possessive.

With the comment about karma Lee was making an important distinction about what he considers to be the best approach for Westerners. On many occasions Lee has talked about the reality of the laws of karma in one's life, and yet he has found that Westerners typically do not have the matrix of understanding to embrace the concept of karma without using it as an excuse to avoid taking personal responsibility for our negative tendencies, abuses of others and outright selfishness. He emphasizes dealing with psychological tendencies from the point of view of this one lifetime alone—that is, from early childhood trauma and familial relationships, particularly those with mother and father—as the root cause of the psychological cramp and survival strategy.

Although there is no fundamental difference between his teaching and that of Tibetan Buddhism in the regard of karma, or causality, or the other principles of dharma articulated by Garchen Rinpoche, Lee went on to discuss the very fine point differences in practical application between the Tibetan Buddhist path and the Baul path. Then he laughed and said, "Listening to Rinpoche I was thinking, 'Oh no! Am I going to have to let everybody into the school who wants in? What about the people who have left over the years! We're in trouble!' I still won't be letting everyone into this school who thinks they want in . . ."

In one way it seemed like a basic difference between the Mahayana stream of Buddhism with its expansive focus on generosity—"there is room for everyone"—and the more ancient, mother-teaching of Hinduism. There is a wild and radical element that exists in Hinduism that has its roots in pre-Vedic India, and which gives rise to marginal tantric sects like the Nath Siddhas, the Sahajiyas, and the Bauls of Bengal. It is not that the Bauls turn anyone away because of their caste or creed, sex or color of skin; on the contrary, the Bauls welcome everyone. It is more that the very nature of the wildness of the path itself—the infliction of divine madness, in which one becomes mad for God, afflicted by the wind (*vatula*)—is an unrealistic pursuit for most people. It is actually a form of compassion to turn away those for whom the path would not prove to be beneficial because of its radical nature.

As the talk went on it became clear from the interchange between Lee and his students that the mood was not one of romanticism and distraction, but one of a sober consideration of the teachings that had been given. Lee's gruff attitude melted away and he became rather tender and mother-like. He continued, "Any invocational practice that calls God to us is going to have two sides: benign and fierce. All the qualities are objective qualities. In this kind of practice we have to learn to deal with objective qualities of anger, jealousy, greed and so on, so that the fierce aspect of the deity is something we have to deal with in ourselves. We have to know that we can deal with raw anger without killing somebody, but typically we are afraid of it and recoil from it, seek to repress it. We worry, 'What kind of monster would I be if this passion was let free to rage?' There is tremendous force and power in rage. It has an objective side. When we invoke the deity both aspects are accessible, so that whatever is needed to become manifest will manifest. In Tibetan Buddhism you don't get the technology of invocation of the deity until you are ready for it, until you have *earned* it."

Lee used the enneagram of the Fourth Way and the five Buddha families of Tibetan Buddhism as examples of systems in which the qualities of the passions are depicted in their objective and subjective expressions. With his comments about invoking the Divine it was as if he had opened Pandora's box when he spoke of the necessity for handling the objective qualities or passions of a deity without subjectivizing or psychologizing them. The unspoken but obvious correlate was that in guru yoga one works to duplicate the state or condition of the guru, exactly as in the practice of becoming the deity. He had mentioned that one would need to be able to handle raw anger or rage for example, but he had not given any suggestions as to how one might do that. Perhaps he felt it was totally unnecessary to say more since Garchen Rinpoche had more than adequately covered that. If one was paying attention, the answers were all there.

As in his talk the night before, Lee left the group almost abruptly, dropping a small, humble gem. Just before he walked out to get ready for the Shri gig he said in answer to a last question, *"Waiting* is a way of embracing this path in its entirety. We could wait all our lives, just doing the practice we've been given to do and nothing else, and be perfectly happy with that."

Fifteen minutes later everyone stood waiting in the dark parking lot by the vans to drive into town for the Shri gig at a local bar where the band has played many times over the years. Lee took off driving the teal green van, racing through the gate and down the dirt road under cold bright stars that twinkled between the bare branches of the tall cottonwood trees.

Walking into the bar the cacophony and warmth of a packed room immediately impressed itself on the senses. The bar itself is in an old building that reflects the time period in which it was built—the turn of the twentieth century. The floor is covered with a rather worn dark carpet, making dancing a difficult procedure that was nonetheless engaged full-on for the next four hours. The dark gray walls were decorated with neon beer signs and tiny multi-colored Christmas lights. The local folks were drinking and partying like there was no tomorrow, while Lee's crowd drank nonalcoholic beer, cranberry juice and club soda as usual.

Even though there were many more of Lee's students than the Prescott celebrants, the two groups mingled easily. The band delivered a first set that was designed to get everyone up and dancing, so that the dance floor was packed with a mix of practitioners and local people who threw themselves into the stew of music and revelry. The dancing was so enthusiastic and the music so incendiary and exciting that people walked in the back door of the bar dancing. They would then make their way across the crowded and hot dance floor, dancing along with everyone, snapping their fingers and bobbing up and down to the beat as they headed toward the bar—a carved, heavy oak counter reminiscent of the old-time Western saloons, behind which rows and rows of liquor bottles sat reflected in the mirror that covered an entire wall.

Around nine o'clock Ging and Raymond Martinez arrived and sat in two folding chairs that had been placed below the stage and to the right near the wall. They sat there for the rest of the night listening and watching. During the second set Raymond got up and played drums on two songs. I talked with Ging for awhile. She laughed as she watched Raymond getting helped up onstage by two of the men. She said, "You know, the last time we heard Shri, Ray went up to play and a man standing near me said, 'You've got to be kidding—that old guy is going to play the drums? He can barely walk, much less hold the drumsticks!' When Ray started playing the guy just stood there with his mouth open. He clapped and yelled after the songs. Then when Ray came back across the stage after he played he wasn't just walking, he was dancing! I guess that showed him!"

She looked up at Lee, who was singing at the moment. She inclined her head toward Lee and said, "He's my soul buddy. He's a pro. You know honey, he is really *serious*." She smiled again. She said, "We wouldn't miss being here for anything. We always look forward to it."

After sitting on the floor in the meditation hall for nine hours a day for the past two days to receive the dharma teachings of Garchen Rinpoche and Lee, the dancing was driven in part by the sheer need to move. Absorbing this transmission of dharma at many different levels leaves the body glutted with energy and the influx of something difficult to define, but which Lee might call blessing force. In this exchange there is an actual substance that is given from teacher to student. As subtle and energetic as this substance is, it has a weight, gravity and potency that the physical and subtle bodies must digest and assimilate.

Too often this kind of communication or empowerment given from teacher to student is taken for granted by Westerners, or missed completely. We do not realize the potency of the spaces that we enter into with our teachers, and we easily blow off the transmission of such subtle states or energies. This blowing off of energy can take any one of a number of forms, but is always related to an inappropriate relationship to money, food or sex. Sometimes we leak away this precious accumulated force by immediately returning to bad habits—eating too much, indulging in addictive substances like alcohol, coffee or cigarettes, engaging sexual relations for the wrong reasons, talking too much, gossiping, manipulating and controlling others and so on.

In one way dancing to Lee's music could be called an antidote to such casual but consequential actions. Working the body in this way causes the energy to be digested and metabolized for further and deeper use by the interrelated physical and subtle bodies. It has the potential to bring the three centers—thinking, feeling and moving—into simultaneous aliveness and unity. Tonight the music and movement served this process of integration, while at the same time the whole evening seemed to be a celebration of the sangha. The mandala of the band—eight people onstage including Lee, plus the dancers and onlookers—easily hooked together in an extraordinary weave in which the night became a long paean in praise of the miracle of the Buddha, the dharma and the sangha arising in the West. At one o'clock the gig was over. Lee quickly left the stage, picked up his coat and walked out into the icy night air and drove the van full of people back to the ashram.

November 20, 1999
Arizona Ashram

This morning after meditation the Celebration continued with a talk on the core practice of Enquiry given by Dasya in the greenhouse. As the morning progressed, the sun streamed in through the glass walls and baked everyone who sat listening in the long, narrow room. During the talk Lee sat at his desk, or at times in a chair in an unobtrusive corner of the greenhouse, listening quietly. He was wearing an oversized pale yellow corduroy shirt and sweatpants, his dreadlocks pulled back into a ponytail. Once again he seemed far away, even though his eyes were quick to smile when someone caught his glance. There was a mood of deep benevolence and quietude around him as he walked through spaces or sat listening to his students give talks. At times he simply sat at his desk in the dark corner of the office, not bothering to turn the light on, while the talk continued on the other side of the sliding glass door that leads from the office to the greenhouse.

Dasya worked off the teachings given by Garchen Rinpoche by commenting, "As twenty-first century Westerners we take refuge in shopping, in new cars, in new clothes—in money, food and sex. We've already taken refuge in these things, and now we have to uproot that to make room for taking refuge in the Buddha, the dharma, the sangha. Reactional Enquiry is a way to do that.

"Reactional Enquiry will lead us to remorse, or compassion for one's self. We can only have false compassion for others until we have compassion for ourselves. When will we see how much pain we have created for those around us and ourselves? Haven't we done enough damage?"

At brunch the mood was somber as over a hundred people gathered in the cool tent for boiled eggs, rye bread, apple butter and mint tea. Afterward people scattered around the grounds to various tasks during the two-hour period of guru *seva*. Everyone reconvened in the early afternoon for a talk on Enquiry and Assertion given by Rick L. It was a brilliant dissertation on the core practices of the school, flavored with Rick's particular brand of earthy mysticism, liberally sprinkled with a warm sense of humor. He spoke about Enquiry—the use of the phrase "Who am I kidding?"—as a movement of attention.

He said, "We use the words, 'Who am I kidding?' to catalyze the movement of attention until we no longer need the words. It culminates in its most radical and ruthless state as 'Just This.' 'Just This' is the *nature* of attention; 'Who am I kidding?' is the *movement* of attention. The point at which we usually stop Enquiry is exactly the point when the survival strategy interrupts the practice by asserting itself as true over and above discovering Truth.

"The mind fixates constantly. Enquiry is not the process by which we determine what is valuable to fixate upon; it is the process by which we abandon fixation as our primary relationship to reality. Enquiry is how we habituate the mind to 'Just This' and root it in the body."

Rick used Raymond Martinez as an example of having a bodily relationship to music that is very similar to the full-body, felt awareness that is necessary in transformational spiritual work. He said, "These two extraordinary people, Ging and Raymond, have an amazing reciprocal rapport with Lee and the band. You see Raymond and you think, 'That guy can't play the drums—he can't even walk!' Then he gets up onstage and he just drops into the seat behind the drums. Nothing in his body resists rhythm as it exists in the universe. Every cell in his body is an integral expression of rhythm."

Commenting on how Lee demonstrates 'Just This,' Rick said, "You fall in love with all of Lee's self-deprecation because it's just what it is—he is the most *human* human being you have ever met. 'Just This' is when no cell in the body resists where attention naturally goes unprompted by any impurity in the whole nervous system."

Dinner was served again at five-thirty—white rice, steamed broccoli and cauliflower, miso soup and tahini dip with the dry honey bread and whipped cream. The food seemed to be growing in attractiveness with each passing night, partly because one was so hungry, but also because the essence of the food itself became very familiar and real. The temperature was chilly outside now that the sun had set. The serving crew set up propane heaters that blasted warmth into the space. Everyone ate and talked quietly. With the simple, repetitive meals, the partaking of food had been stripped down to its essence. "It's just food," as Lee said. There was no extraneous ballyhoo over the food, no discernable grasping for more, and almost no leftovers. If people were tired of having the same thing for the third night in a row (and clearly we would have the identical meal again tomorrow night as well), no one mentioned it. Instead there was a willingness to jump into the play, to participate with enthusiasm in a way that might reveal Lee's intention in it all.

As the clean-up crew hustled after dinner to get the dishes into the kitchen for all the laborious hand-washing and scrubbing that would go on for the next two hours, everyone else gathered again in the parking lot to zoom off to the Attila the Hunza gig. It was another night of dancing, but this time the location was a rented space near the Prescott airport. The event was only for community members and Celebration guests. The space had a large stage and dance floor with tables set up in the back of the room. About fifty people sat listening as the band started right on time.

Lee sat at one of the front tables and listened. He didn't move from that spot for the next three hours. Occasionally he would comment on something he really liked. "They have a great selection of songs," he said a couple of times, or "Fabulous!" when Kate and Clelia generated fun and laughter onstage while they enacted the lyrics to songs. At one point they staged a mock battle between the two of them and tore up a feather pillow, the feathers flying all over the stage and dance floor. When the children discovered this they came running out onto the dance floor and started a delirious feather fight with Kate and

Clelia, throwing the feathers back up onstage to the delight of the singers. Later they pulled out scissors and snipped the shirts right off the backs of Sylvan and Steve S. in the middle of a song while they played. Lee seemed to be watching his young students with pleasure. "Great theatre," he commented with a smile.

November 21, 1999
Arizona Ashram

Today, the last day of the Celebration, Lee scheduled a *yajna* fire—a sacrificial fire—from eleven-thirty in the morning to one-thirty in the afternoon. This traditional ritual fire is done every few years on the ashram during one of the three yearly celebrations. It is a time when Lee's students are given the opportunity to make offerings of those things which symbolize something in themselves they wish to be purified in the heat of sadhana.

This purification can be represented by the sacrifice of anything from old photographs, childhood memorabilia, letters, journals, mementos of past relationships and lovers, clothing or shoes or various junk that is associated with an aspect of one's life or experience. It could be something as simple as writing a particular intention for one's sadhana on a piece of paper and throwing it into the flames. The most powerful example of the use of the sacrificial fire was demonstrated when Lee burned all the remaining copies of his first book, *Spiritual Slavery*, in a *yajna* fire in 1991.

Or one might choose to sit without making any concrete gesture of offering, watch the fire and interact with the power that is generated by the intention of the group in a subtle way. As with everything in sadhana, intention and effort plays an important role. Grace is the other vital element, but it is completely beyond any human concept or construct of the mind. Who can speak of Grace as if it could be known? To allow oneself to be absorbed into the power of the fire, to be bathed in its heat and smoke, might be enough to find the heart melting, burned to ash. At the same time, what one gets out of sadhana is in exact proportion to what one puts into it, and action counts. To burn every photograph, letter and emblem, for example, from a ten-year marriage to a former partner who might in some way now symbolize one's resistance to sadhana requires serious contemplation and commitment. In one resolute and potent act, the tangible proof of ten years of one's life and personal identity are gone within minutes, maybe even seconds. Once burned, an object is gone forever. The reality of impermanence strikes a deep chord.

For such an act to have power requires not only intention, but faith. One must have faith in the miraculous, in the power of the subtle world, the graceful world of the guru, in the invisible processes of surrender and transformation. Otherwise such an act becomes banal, fatuous, meaningless—an empty gesture, a kind of blind following. This kind of faith is based on certainty born out of one's most primal and cellular experience, not out of an intellectual or romantic fascination with ideas. It is a kind of faith that stands on the courage of the heart, which leads one to go against everything that the conventional mindset says is safe, good, normal. By worldly standards it is madness to stand around a fire with a bunch of people and burn pictures of one's relatives or friends or lovers—or two thousand copies of a book. And it is madness of a certain kind. One must be mad in the most divine sense to cast away all that the world holds valuable in an act of abandon and freedom. It is an act that proclaims, "These pictures, these identities, these attachments—none of this holds any power or meaning for me." Certainty comes in the faith that it is the essential truth of divine life that will now rock the cradle of soul in its newborn state of emptiness and nothingness.

At eleven-thirty about thirty people gathered outside around the small fire that burned merrily in the middle of the dirt road between the garden, now wintered over, the compost piles, the tennis court and the swimming pool. The fire area overlooked the garden, the children's playground and the scruffy woods of thorny scrub oak and tall green pine trees on the other side of the arroyo. The flames leapt up, quickly consuming the neatly stacked wood. It was a small fire, but would end up, after two hours of burning many different things, six feet or more in diameter. People leaned against the rickety wooden fence that borders the swimming pool with bags and boxes and odd collections of things sitting at their feet. Everyone waited quietly for Lee to appear. Doug and Ed had brought their mandolins and waited with Wolfgang, who sat on a log with a *doumbek* in his hands. They would be leading a series of chants, written and composed by either Ed or Doug, for the next two hours. Inside Lee went about in a benevolent mood, collecting things he wanted to burn, going upstairs to his living room and his private quarters, and then downstairs to his desk in the office, gathering as he went. At eleven-thirty he sent word out that people could start making offerings if they wanted to; it would be a few minutes before he could get there. Doug began the chanting, *"Om guru charinam, om guru charinam, Yogi Ramsuratkumar, Om guru charinam."*

The next two hours were permeated with smoke and sky and wind and flames and the name of Yogi Ramsuratkumar. Whole picture albums, dried marigold malas, rose petals, personal items of all kinds—letters, journals, books, checkbooks, file folders full of typed sheets of paper, manuscripts, framed pictures, hand knit ponchos, dresses, shirts, shoes, shawls, boxes of unidentifiable objects, a zafu, sandalwood *malas*—all disappeared into the flames, becoming nothing but infinitesimal bits of ash, their energy released into the void. Lee came out with a box of things, which he placed one by one into the fire, tossing in a handful of sage. People were beginning to come in a steady stream now. The chanting seemed to surge, ebb and swell with many voices singing, buoyant and floating on the light, high strings of the mandolin, which made a slightly plaintive but joyful complement to the complex rhythms of the *doumbek* and the piercing beat of the cymbals.

Above our heads the empyrean arc of the sky was stainless, blue, and curved hopelessly to meet the earth in an impossible union of elements. All around rose the dry wintry mountains, craggy with rocks and splotches of dark green cedar and pine. The boundless deep blue sky was witness to this event. It covered everything, hosted the ephemeral entities of water and air as fluffy white clouds drifted by or sat on the horizon. The sun pervaded all things under the sky, penetrated the air, burned softly like a caress in the mild winter air as one by one people came up and fed the flames.

The flames consumed it all—glossy pages of paper curled into black emptiness, plastic melted down in drops across photographs as they withered in the flames and dripped down into the hot ash. Clothing turned black, melted or caught the flames right away, depending on the fabric. Each item had its own unique way of entering oblivion, first roasting or sizzling or dripping, or simply turning black, then giving over totally to flame. We could have been watching the bones, the feet and stiff arms, the bursting skulls and boiling brains of the *smashan* in Banaras. It was the same burning of *samskaras*. The smells, the wind, the black smoke, the ash and living sparks thrown off by the fire—all of this enveloped the senses. At times the smoke was so intense that the cerulean of the sky became an infinite backdrop behind veils of smoke, the glowing red of the ash flashing briefly as it cooled to gray flakes in the air that lightly pelted our faces and hair.

The chanting kept flowing, like waves from an ocean, unceasing. No one seemed to tire or flag in the constant singing. Many people stayed for the entire two hours while the group as a whole fluctuating from thirty or forty people as some came and went to attend to other tasks for the Celebration. The strum and beat of mandolin and drum designed a musical cohesion that held the group together as well. After the first hour Stan took over on *doumbek* and played for the next hour while Ed and Doug traded off leading chants.

As the group stood in a loose circle around the fire chanting and watching, the mood deepened as we spiraled down into the heart. Introspection was written across faces that contemplated impermanence, death, sacrifice. Who can know the power of the sacrifices that individual people have made to walk this path? The sacrifices on the path never stop; often they are more obvious and concrete at the beginning, but become more internal, subtler and more powerful as time goes on. As Lee said during the summer, the path demands the sacrifice of our pride, shame, vanity, greed, fear, selfishness, anger, self-hatred; these are where the most deeply rooted attachments are entwined. Every sacrifice along the way on the path is called out of us by the lure of the Divine toward the realization of no separation, and yet it is a bittersweet process.

Someone walked up and placed a handful of pictures in the fire; on the top was one of Satya Sai Baba. Looking at the pictures Lee joked, "There go the saints! Sai Baba's hair may not be able to be cut, but it's going to *burn!*"

Jaya and Jere walked up carrying the model church that was used as the prop in the play for the church which John Merrick, the Elephant Man, built in the last years of his life. Jaya asked Lee, "Should we burn it?" Jere and Jim had built the model—it was quite beautiful. Lee looked at Jere and said, "Do you want it?" He answered no. Jaya said, "Assuming we're not going perform the 'The Elephant Man' again, that is."

Lee said, "Well, there are no guarantees. But we won't do it again anytime soon. You might as well go ahead and burn it, unless Jere wants it." They threw it in the fire and walked away. Made of thin, dry wood, it burned very quickly.

An hour into the burning people were still coming forward in a steady flow to offer this or that, piles of papers, boxes of photographs. Some people simply put in scraps of paper with something written on them. As the "bodies" burned, the fire grew bigger, took on more dimensions, and the mood continued to deepen. Now and then someone would walk over to Lee and show him something they intended to burn—childhood pictures, a high school yearbook, a piece of clothing. Usually he looked at the picture or the book and chuckled. Mostly he was silent, like everyone else, except for the chanting. Every now and then he would interject some humorous remark—like when, after an hour of steady burning, he said, "I feel lighter already!" At some point every practitioner on the path has to take the work upon himself or herself, so that the necessity for intentional sacrifice becomes more urgent. The more the disciple can do this work for himself, the more it lightens the guru's load.

Occasionally Lee walked over to the fire and, taking the fire stick from Michael's or Tom's hands, dug it in deep under the burning pile and lifted, turning it over so that air could feed the fire. The blaze brightened when he repeated this several times as he walked around the fire.

When Ed started calling the last chant with the beginning line, *"Jaya guru om,"* a melodic and almost pensive voice came springing out of nowhere. It was Lee, singing along with Ed. Immediately Lee fell back into silence again while everyone else took on the response to the chant. It was as if Lee set the mood for this chant, blending together longing and burning and madness and the freedom of living on the edge of nowhere. After an hour and a half the offerings were still coming. We stood suspended within the chant, buoyed up by the power of Yogi Ramsuratkumar's name. *"Jaya guru om, jaya guru om . . . Yogi Ram, Yogi Ram, Yogi Ram Surata Kumar!"* And then the name of his son, *"Khepa Lee, Khepa Lee, Khepa Lee, Khepa Lee!"*

No one had guessed that the *yajna* fire would penetrate so deeply today. There was the fire, the sky, the earth, the chant, the guru's presence, and a living silence that enfolded it all. At one point in the sustained silence Lee said very quietly, "We should be tossing in sage and feeding the fire ghee." When someone offered to get some sage he said, "I've already put the sage in, but you can get a small bowl of ghee and a spoon." When it arrived he took the ghee and walked over to the fire, spooned small yellow globs of it out over the flames in three or four quick offerings. The sun was still shining like a fine golden haze in the air, the blue of the sky sweeter and stronger than ever, the silent garden laying fallow—all this existed as witness to Lee's acts. He walked back to the spot by the fence where he had stood for almost two hours and turned to gaze at the fire. The blaze sputtered a little, eating the ghee quickly, devouring, taking, destroying, transforming ghee and everything else it consumed into spirit and fine black ash.

That night the meditation hall was packed for darshan with over a hundred people. Everyone was primed, hearts were opened from the previous days and nights of the Celebration, and from today's talks on the heart breath, by Regina, and the principle of beggary, given by Debbie. But most of all, the *yajna* fire had left the mood very deep and inward.

In spite of the late November chill in the air, as soon as one walked inside the hall it was exceptionally warm. By the time ten poems to Yogi Ramsuratkumar had been sung and the *kirtan* (group chanting) started, it was quite hot despite the rapidly dropping temperature outside. One by one people went up to enact the ritual of giving and receiving *prasad* with Lee. He sat wrapped in the gray shawl he usually wears and in an old dhoti that was tied across his chest. The dhoti, still tied in the bulky knot that Yogi Ramsuratkumar often uses to tie the shawls that he wears over his shoulders, was given to Lee several years ago by Yogi Ramsuratkumar. It bears the stains and streaks of dust from having been on Yogi Ramsuratkumar's body for years.

The *prasad* piled up around Lee—volumes of flowers, mounds of fresh fruits and vegetables. The chocolates, books, letters and notes all quickly disappeared into neatly arranged piles at Lee's side. The overflowing brass trays and vases at his feet were like cornucopias of abundance, the brilliant multi-hued roses and lilies making a strong visual impression set against red mangos, succulent grapes, glass pitchers of fresh grapefruit juice, dates, figs, nuts. Music swelled in the room, lifting and carrying everyone along with the rhythm of the bells and drums. The chanting was like a conductive element—a kind of transportation through the doorway of the guru. The Sanskrit words themselves, especially the name of Yogi Ramsuratkumar, are alive with a very specific vibrational power. If one relaxes into the whole effect of the *kirtan*, it can be experienced as a current that sweeps one along with it, like stepping into a swiftly moving river.

As the chanting intensified and mingled with the building heat it seemed that the molecules of the air were stirred and lively, so that the air danced and shimmered with a barely perceptible motion as the candles burned brightly around the shrines and the dais. Everything was vividly apparent, interconnected and interdependent. Sitting on the dais, his head wrapped in a green cloth, the emanations of Lee's being were both remote and immediate. Without doing anything he exuded an aura that made him unfathomable, impersonal, unknowable, and yet intimately real, personal and closer than one's breath. The guru is both near and far, and in fact occupies all space, all time, because the guru principle is nowhere and everywhere. This experience permeates Lee's darshan—the air itself seems to be charged with the transmission of the truth of nonduality. There is only God, and all this is the display, the dance, the appearance of phenomena. Even the physical body of the guru is only a thin veil overlaying the all-inclusive and unitive presence of the Divine.

After the *kirtan* was over Lee asked if there were any questions, particularly from the new people, of whom there were eight or ten. He chuckled, "Although you may be awed by the august company that surrounds you on all sides!" Everyone laughed. "You could always ask questions of some of my students, but, in the name of accuracy, you should probably ask me." More laughter. A young woman who had just met Lee for the first time during this Celebration asked, "How does one pursue this school?"

Lee said, "That's a very good way to phrase it—to 'pursue' this school—because I don't make it easy for people to come in." Lee began to talk about what it means to enter the school. He said that he has consistently tried to keep the school small, and there is a reason for this. The esoteric side of the Work has to be kept to a small and highly prepared and reliable group because of the nature of the Work itself.

He continued, "You should be aware that you are entering a path of esoteric work in which you will have no personal life. If there is any personal life given, if that is what arises in your life, it is purely a gift of the Work. But you must expect nothing; if the Work gives you relationship, children, or vocation, you should embrace it fully, but it must be understood that all this is not your personal property, or something for which you can take credit or grasp toward. Having a personal life is not a problem; it is *grasping* for a personal life that is the problem. The problem arises when one has illusory ideas of what God and love actually are.

"As we move into the esoteric side of the Work, we find that in this school one of the benefits is how small we are. But that is also the downside, because new people don't have anywhere to be 'new' students. New people have to start out swimming at the same speed that everyone else is swimming. There is a very big difference in working at higher levels or at beginning levels. Certain tasks should be saved for people who are practicing at higher levels, but often new people have to work at levels and in ways that are beyond them."

Lee began to talk about the crowds who flock to Yogi Ramsuratkumar now. He said, "It could all change, of course. I've always seen that our school follows the path that Yogi Ramsuratkumar's work has taken, but about twenty years behind Him. The kind of crowds that Yogi Ramsuratkumar gets now—that could be us in twenty years. But who knows? Maybe not."

"So, people get thrown in at a level that in a regular mystery school would normally take years to get to. The Essenes had a system in which it took three years before one could actually enter into the school." He went on to say that many people try to muscle their practice at the beginning because of the high demand, so that in a way they appear to be practicing at a level they haven't really earned yet. "If someone is trying to do something by sheer force of will power, through the use of 'muscle,' they can make a lot of fast progress, but sooner or later it won't work. It's the same with really great tasks—we may be able to do it awhile, but sooner or later it may get to be too big for us."

He told the story of a woman who had come around the school about ten years ago. She made a very deep connection to the heart of the school; she was someone who had touched the mystical core of the school, and had asked to be a student. Lee invited her to come to darshan, and that night he gave a discourse about the nature of sacrifice in this path, about the necessity of having no personal life, other than that which is given as gift by the path. That night she made a very conscious decision not to stay. She withdrew and went back to her busy life. She knew that she was not ready; she wanted self-indulgence, she wanted to do whatever she wished with her life. She was clear that she wanted to taste all the rewards that conventional life would have for ego. She wanted the glittering array of maya.

"So sooner or later we have to factor that in. When we get deeply into the path we have to be clear about how much of a personal life we actually want. If the Work gives you a personal life, then that's what the Work gives you. And, the deeper you get involved, the closer you get to the community, the more you have to deal with the paradox of the guru's humanness. My eccentricities are hard to deal with—my refusal to answer your questions, my filthy personal habits, my quirks and so on. The more deeply you get involved, the more you will have to see me as I am. Sooner or later you will have to deal with me. This isn't 'God direct'! It's like FTD. You want the flowers? I'm the delivery boy!

"The more deeply involved you get, the bigger the shock you will have when you see me as I am in the relative world before you see me in the absolute world. If you go to seminars and hear me making the same old lewd jokes about breasts—but I don't use that word!—and being misogynistic, you will be saying, 'What does he have to do that for? It's so disgusting! It's beside the point . . .' You'll have to deal with my lack of reverence.

"So be warned! The Rinpoche's translator said that many people understand the dharma and speak it fluently, but don't practice. So one thing we look for over time is an integration of the Work within one's daily life. We establish a foundation through the recommended conditions of the school—meditation, vegetarian diet, study, exercise, monogamous relationship. It's like learning a martial art, like *kata*. At the beginning everything is like an orchestrated or choreographed movement, then over time it becomes possible to have spontaneous movement."

As Lee began to gather his things together to leave the room he picked up a leather-bound copy of the Koran in Arabic. One of Lee's students who used to be a Muslim had given it to him as *prasad*. She was going to burn it in the *yajna* fire, but when she asked Lee about it he said, "Don't burn it, give it to me." Now he pulled it out of its ornate leather cover and leafed through the pages.

"Did you read this?" he asked her as she sat in the back of the room against the wall.

"No," she said, "I don't read Arabic."

"That's the right answer . . ." Lee chuckled, "you probably wouldn't want to translate one of my books into Arabic, would you?" She laughed and said no, definitely not.

Precariously balancing his box full of carefully stacked and arranged *prasad* he moved forward on the divan and said, "The guru never asks an innocent question—except when he asks an innocent question. The key is to discriminate when it is innocent and when it's a trap!" He chuckled, "Jai Guru!" and left the room.

November 22, 1999
Arizona Ashram

Due to some minor miracle the unseasonably warm weather had continued throughout the Celebration until last night's darshan. Today the temperature continued to drop steadily as a group gathered at seven p.m. for bridge at Lee's kitchen table. The room was crowded with people who came to play, to sit and watch, to ask questions. Several people who had come for the Celebration and would be leaving in the morning came with questions. Erica had a list, mostly related to some current health concerns. Lee responded, "That I cannot answer for you. You have to decide." The young woman who had asked how to pursue the school in darshan the night before now asked, "Would there be room for me in a household in Boulder?"

Lee said mildly, "I have no idea. You would have to ask them. But you are probably too new to be in a household."

Karl, who was standing nearby, began to ask questions about managing depression with herbs like St. John's Wort. Lee's answers were noncommittal or he else just didn't answer at all. Perhaps he thought Karl already knew the answer and his silence was pointing that out. Maybe his silence was a "no" to the question. His communication was too obscure to read in moments. One had to feel into the space to get anything at all.

The atmosphere was warm and pleasant, but it seemed as if Lee was already on the plane to India. In less than two days he will depart. Each year his attention begins to turn toward Tiruvannamalai in the weeks prior to his departure, leaving his students in a kind of twilight world of in-between. He was physically present, yet he seemed to be elsewhere; he was completely here, he was also somehow there.

At the late evening gathering Lee was quiet. He commented a few times, but mostly listened to the conversation around him. His students began to tell stories of past trips to India with Lee, and *lilas* of times they had spent in Yogi Ramsuratkumar's company. The community has a tremendously rich oral tradition of these *lilas* and stories, and tonight they were being retold again. After a short while of listening, Lee unobtrusively said goodnight and left the space.

November 23, 1999
Arizona Ashram

All day the kitchen has been busy in preparation for the feast tonight that Lee has planned for Christophe and Muriel Massin, the son-in-law and daughter of Arnaud Desjardins who have been visiting Lee for the past three days. Lee's family and a number of his students will be coming. During the day today large bags of food came into the kitchen; interesting mystery desserts appeared wrapped and were stashed in the refrigerator as preparation for the feast began. A candle burned on the *puja* above the stove, and after lunch the narrow dining room and gallery of saints was prepared with long tables set for twenty-one people.

At six o'clock the feast began. It was a delicately spiced seafood gumbo, cajun chicken, cucumbers and tomatoes marinated in vinegar and saffron rice served with a complementary wine. A dessert custard made with mascarpone was served with slices of a dark chocolate tart on the side.

The feast was high spirited and merry, slightly tinged with a wistfulness that pulsed under the surface as Lee's impending trip to India hovered on the periphery of everyone's thoughts. After the dessert and coffee were finished Lee suggested that everyone move into the living room, where the whole group gathered around sitting on the floor or on chairs or couches. Lee sat on the big couch in front of the windows, and in the mellow light of the living room he looked slightly tired but peaceful.

Chris began to remember Andrew Cohen's visit last spring when a similar group was gathered in the living room. One of Andrew's senior students had been offered a chair to sit on and Andrew had said, "She can sit on the floor."

Now Lee commented, "Andrew's students are very well trained toward their practice." He smiled and looked around, then added emphatically, "The more important the student, the more the teacher should be guarding their work!"

Dasya added, "One hundred and ten percent." They were referring to a statement made by Chögyam Trungpa Rinpoche, who said that in the tantric path the guru minds the disciple's business two hundred percent.

Just then Kelly and Ann came around with trays of peach cognac. When everyone was served Lee made the toast. He raised his glass and said, "May everybody who is going to India's *samskaras* be toast!" He smiled over at Kate and Dean, who sat across the room from him, and at Deacon who sat nearby. The three of them would be going to India with Lee tomorrow, along with others.

With Lee leaving the next day the conversation naturally turned toward Tiruvannamalai and Yogi Ramsuratkumar and life on the ashram. Stories began to flow out of various people from visits of years past. Lee talked about the ashram cooking one hundred-gallon pots of rice and serving two thousand people last year during Deepam.

He said to Deacon and Dean, "I'm glad you don't have much to take to India because I've got boxes of poetry books to give to you to carry!" He smiled again, rather mischievously. "We sold twenty-four poetry books last year—this year we're going to have forty books there, in case He is in a selling mood!"

Someone asked Lee if there was any recommendation or comment he would give to his students who would be staying in Arizona while he traveled. He responded simply, "Nothing I haven't already said every day." Hundreds of times, one might add.

Jan said, "My response to you leaving for India seems to have changed since I went to India with you last year. It's like my heart has been pierced in some way. Now there is this longing—I want to go this year too. Even though I went last year, now I want to go again, and I never felt that way before. Is there a way to make use of that?"

Lee answered, "Not to have any 'you' involved. The more 'you' there is the less value; the less 'you' there is, the more value you will get. It's a matter of self-cherishing, as the Rinpoche said. You have to accept the arising of desire simply for what it is. Don't draw conclusions or dramatize it. Just accept it for what it is, and don't blame me for not taking you. In the areas in which it shows up, it does, and in the areas in which it doesn't show up, it doesn't." Lee paused for a moment and asked what time it was—twenty minutes before nine o'clock. He said, "Excuse me, I have to be about other things. I'll see you all shortly. Jai Guru!"

The kitchen crew was still busy cleaning up when Lee walked through on his way downstairs. In the office more people were coming in for the late evening gathering, wanting to sit one last time in Lee's company before he left for India. Noticing the jubilant and sparkling atmosphere as she came in the door Regina said, "It feels like a party in here!"

She was feeling the ripple effects of the evening—the ease and friendship and enjoyment of the convivial company of the guru before his departure to India and the face-to-face encounter with Grace in the physical person of his father, Yogi Ramsuratkumar.

November 24, 1999
Arizona Ashram

It was icy this morning in the high desert. Even the hardy pine trees were subdued in the piercingly cold air. A pale sunlight shone dimly through diaphanous lengths of white clouds that covered the sky, hints of colder weather to come. Autumn had passed overnight, and winter was here. It seemed a fitting backdrop for the journey into the unknown which Lee and his traveling party would embark upon today.

There is a sense of wonder and infinite possibility, of impending change, when Lee reconnects each year with the physical form of his spiritual father, Yogi Ramsuratkumar. The forces of transformation are stirred in the subtle realms, and there is a very palpable condition that arises in which it seems that anything could happen. It is not uncommon for Lee's students to feel the effects of his time with Yogi Ramsuratkumar halfway across the world in tangible ways. Some report that they cannot sleep while Lee is in India. With the twelve hour time difference between Arizona and India, they find themselves wakeful at night and wanting to sleep during the day, as if their bodies fall into the same rhythm as those who sleep and wake in India. The interconnectedness of events and relationships becomes more apparent during these times as the veils between the worlds are thinned by the quickening of Grace, all swept into motion with the inhalation of smoke from Yogi Ramsuratkumar's Charimar.

This morning after meditation Lee's kitchen in Arrakis was still permeated with the aromatic scents of the cajun spices from the feast the night before, as if the spirits of the ashram were still celebrating. Lee would leave at one-thirty today with his small group for the Phoenix airport. Arriving in the city they would go to a movie before their plane departed at seven o'clock tonight for Los Angeles, where they would change planes and head across the Pacific Ocean toward Asia. Landing in Chennai many hours later they would meet up with the rest of Lee's traveling party coming from Europe and then drive to Tiruvannamalai.

Lee spent the morning navigating a thick obstacle course of questions, last minute meetings, details and business at hand with an amazing dexterity of skillful means. A cluster of his students' "personal needs" seemed to hover in a throng and follow him around the building. In a devotional path, this dilemma of attachment to the guru becomes, at some point, an obstacle along the way. Three weeks of physical separation from the object of one's love may seem like an eternity to the worldly lover, but for the practitioner the heart of longing is sweet and unrestrained while, at the same time, it is contained and interiorized.

Today some of this grasping at the guru seemed like a thin disguise for the very real and objective longing that was present in the atmosphere as Lee prepared to leave, while some of it appeared as a clutching at something so unattainable, so completely free of it all, that it was ridiculous. Lee's ease in extricating himself from his students' projections and illusions was effortless, and in his apparent freedom the fact that the guru belongs to everyone and no one came into sharp focus. No one can possess the guru, and yet many will try, each in his or her own way. Ego demands, "Give me one more word, one more moment of attention, one more glance," as if that would make a difference. But there is no amount of the guru's physical attention that will make even the smallest iota of difference, ultimately, in the suffering of the separative one. Only the guru's Grace can heal the wounds of separation.

Being cast in the role of guru is one aspect of Lee Lozowick. As guru he is bound to his students in inexplicable ways. On the other hand, Lee the eternal devotee belongs to no one but Yogi Ramsuratkumar. In Lee as devotee one gets to experience firsthand his longing and broken-heartedness, his humanness, yet still he is elusive. Lee has made it clear in his poetry: he has abandoned all concerns, desires and designs for one thing only—to be nothing but the dust at his Father's feet. The fact that Lee goes to be with Yogi Ramsuratkumar brings all this further into focus as we act as witnesses to the extraordinary nobility of their relationship. In the process of that witnessing we face our own inability to love, completely free of motive, in our faltering attempts at the guru yoga of this path.

Throughout the morning Lee appeared completely ordinary, and yet at the same time he seemed to be getting visibly brighter. Although business was conducted as usual in the office, there was a distinct electric current running in the air as the excitement mounted. Finally around eleven o'clock Lee disappeared into his private quarters to pack his single backpack. It took him about thirty minutes to get ready for the trip. At lunch he ate a large plate of green salad, smiled and talked easily and jovially with everyone. The conversation at the table turned toward Lee's return on the night of December 13. The next day a return feast and evening of stories were planned. People would be coming from around the country and Europe to gather with Lee for the feast. There was already a high anticipation for the tales and *lilas* that would be brought back.

Ten minutes before Lee was scheduled to leave the mini-van was parked and waiting in front of the greenhouse door by the flagstone garden. Lee came down wearing his yoga whites, a long warm shirt and sandals. His *jatta* were freshly washed and hung in thick, matted gray strands. Backpacks and boxes of poetry books, *Death of a Dishonest Man,* were packed in the back of the van and under the seats. A small group of about a dozen devotees stood in the chilly bright air a few feet away from the van to see Lee and his party off.

After embracing his family and saying last good-byes, Lee laughed and jumped into the passenger seat of the van. His beaming face smiled through the window as he held his hand up in a gesture of blessing. The van started rolling along. Dried roses and flower petals pelted the hood and sides of the van as everyone tossed dried flowers and chanted, "*Yogi Ramsuratkumar, Yogi Ramsuratkumar, Yogi Ramsuratkumar, Jaya Guru Raya.*" Then the van was off, small puffs of dust rising behind the wheels as it made the curve past the gate through the cottonwood trees and headed off down the road. The chanting continued until the last sight of the van, as it chugged around the bend and then disappeared into the trees.

BIBLIOGRAPHY

Anirvan, Sri. *Letters from a Baul: Life within Life*. Calcutta: Aurobindo Pathamandir, 1983.

Bowker, John, Editor. *The Oxford Dictionary of World Religions*. Oxford: Oxford University Press, 1997.

Bukowski, Charles. *Living on Luck: Selected Letters, 1960s-1970s*, Volume II. Santa Rosa Calif.: Black Sparrow Press, 1995.

Castaneda, Carlos. *The Wheel of Time*. Los Angeles: L.A. Eidolona Press, 1998.

Das Gupta, Shashibhusan. *Obscure Religious Cults*. Calcutta: Mukhopadhyay, 1969.

Desjardins, Arnaud. "Guru and Disciple," excerpt from *L'Ami Spirituel*; English language translation from unpublished pamphlet by W. P. Halliday.

Flaherty, Ed. "The Crown King Gig." *Tawagoto*, Summer/Fall 1999.

Jung, Carl. *Psychology and Alchemy*. Princeton, N.J.: Princeton University Press, 1968.

Kohn, Sherab Chodzin. "Ouch! Hurray!" *Shambhala Sun,* Volume Eight Number One, 1999.

McDaniel, June. *The Madness of the Saints—Ecstatic Religion in Bengal*. Chicago: The University of Chicago Press, 1989.

Peters, Fritz. *Boyhood With Gurdjieff*. Baltimore, Md.: Penguin Books, 1964.

Taylor, Rogan. *The Death and Resurrection Show*. Great Britain: Anthony Blond, 1985.

Thompson, Lewis. *Mirror to the Light—Reflections on Consciousness and Experience*. London: Coventure, 1984.

Vaughan-Lee, Llewellyn. "The Invisible Center." *Sufi Magazine,* Issue 42, Summer 1999.

BOOKS BY LEE LOZOWICK

THE ALCHEMY OF TRANSFORMATION
by Lee Lozowick
Foreword by: Claudio Naranjo, M.D.

A concise and straightforward overview of the principles of spiritual life as developed and taught by Lee Lozowick for the past twenty years. Subjects of use to seekers and serious students of any spiritual tradition include: A radical, elegant and irreverent approach to the possibility of change from ego-centeredness to God-centeredness—the ultimate human transformation.

Paper, 192 pages, $14.95   ISBN: 0-934252-62-9

• • •

THE ALCHEMY OF LOVE AND SEX
by Lee Lozowick
Foreword by Georg Feuerstein, Ph.D.

Reveals 70 "secrets" about love, sex and relationships. Lozowick recognizes the immense conflict and confusion surrounding love, sex, and tantric spiritual practice. Advocating neither asceticism nor hedonism, he presents a middle path—one grounded in the appreciation of simple human relatedness. Topics include: • what men want from women in sex, and what women want from men • the development of a passionate love affair with life • how to balance the essential masculine and essential feminine • the dangers and possibilities of sexual Tantra • the reality of a genuine, sacred marriage . . . and much more. " . . . attacks Western sexuality with a vengeance." —*Library Journal*.

Paper, 312 pages, $16.95   ISBN: 0-934252-58-0

• • •

CONSCIOUS PARENTING
by Lee Lozowick

Any individual who cares for children needs to attend to the essential message of this book: that the first two years are the most crucial time in a child's education and development, and that children learn to be healthy and "whole" by living with healthy, whole adults. Offers practical guidance and help for anyone who wishes to bring greater consciousness to every aspect of childraising, including: • conception, pregnancy and birth • emotional development • language usage • role modeling: the mother's role, the father's role • the exposure to various influences • establishing workable boundaries • the choices we make on behalf of our children's education . . . and much more.

Paper, 384 pages, $17.95   ISBN: 0-934252-67-X

TO ORDER PLEASE SEE ACCOMPANYING ORDER FORM
OR CALL 1-800-381-2700 TO PLACE YOUR ORDER NOW.

BOOKS BY LEE LOZOWICK

DERISIVE LAUGHTER FROM A BAD POET
Excerpts from the Teaching of An American Baul
by Lee Khépa Baul
Foreword by Claudio Naranjo, M.D.

True to the itinerant spirit of the Baul, Lee Lozowick (Khépa Baul) has been travelling regularly to Europe since 1986. This book grew out of an expressed desire, particularly from his audiences in Germany, to read his words in their own native language. With translations in both French and German, each excerpt opens another window, offering the perceptive reader a glimpse of one of the many moods of this Bad Poet and a vision of the expansive nature of the dharma of this spiritual Master. Topics range from the nature of prayer and the Grace of loving God, to the illness of contemporary culture and the unique challenge of building genuine community as an alternative.

Paper, 80 pages, $8.95   ISBN: 0-934252-36-X

• • •

LIVING GOD BLUES
by Lee Lozowick

This book is the first exposition of a twenty-year experiment in both intentional community-living and spiritual practice that has been going on in the United States and Europe. Focused around the author's teaching work, the Hohm Community has grown from a handful of friends and students to a culture of several hundred men, women and children. Drawing from its roots among the Bauls—or Bards of Bengal—a rag-tag bunch of musicians, ecstatic poets and lovers of God, this community of Western Bauls share an eclectic approach to spiritual life, drawing from all the great religious traditions—Sahajia Buddhism, Vaishnava Hinduism, esoteric Christianity, and others. Introductory sections, written by senior students, describe the spiritual practices of the community and spell out principal tenets of the Master's teaching —such as the idea that "God does not live in the sky."

Paper, 168 pages, $9.95   ISBN:0-934252-09-2

• • •

THE CHEATING BUDDHA
by Lee Lozowick

The necessity for a spirituality grounded in the body and relevant to the times in which we live is the thread that ties together the essays in this book. Lee Lozowick writes here about the nature of human communication/communion; compassion for others, and the fantasies vs. the realities of enlightenment. A book of living words, full of earthy wisdom.

Paper, 144 pages, $7.95   ISBN: 0-934252-03-3

TO ORDER PLEASE SEE ACCOMPANYING ORDER FORM
OR CALL 1-800-381-2700 TO PLACE YOUR ORDER NOW.

BOOKS BY LEE LOZOWICK

THE ONLY GRACE IS LOVING GOD
by Lee Lozowick

Love, God, Loving God, Grace, Divine Will—these subjects have engaged the minds and hearts of theologians throughout the ages, and even caused radical schisms within organized religions. Lee Lozowick dares to address them again, and in a way entirely original. He challenges all conventional definitions of love, and all superficial assumptions about the nature of loving God, and introduces a radical distinction which he calls the "whim of God" to explain why the random and beneficent Grace of loving God is humanity's ultimate possibility. More than just esoteric musings, *The Only Grace is Loving God* is an urgent and practical appeal to every hungry heart.

Paper, 108 pages, $5.95   ISBN: 0-934252-07-6

• • •

LAUGHTER OF THE STONES
by Lee Lozowick

Wise teachers have always used laughter as one effective tool in preparing the student's heart for essential instruction. In this refreshing book, Lee offers his humor, piercing sarcasm, and practical wisdom in a series of classic essays including: "How Not to Act Superior When You Really Are," and "The Divine Path of Growing Old." A necessary book for any *serious*, spiritual student.

Paper, 140 pages, $9.95   ISBN: 0-934252-00-9

• • •

IN THE FIRE
by Lee Lozowick

This book addresses the issues that arise in every student's relationship with a spiritual Master: service, friendship, surrender, obedience, humor, devotion and faith. A clear and readily-usable foundation for practice, *In The Fire* will bring seekers face-to-face with their own questions, resistances and fears. It will also substantiate their heartfulness and longing.

Paper, 264 pages, $9.95   ISBN: 0-89556-02-X

**TO ORDER PLEASE SEE ACCOMPANYING ORDER FORM
OR CALL 1-800-381-2700 TO PLACE YOUR ORDER NOW.**

BOOKS BY LEE LOZOWICK

ACTING GOD
by Lee Lozowick

Can humanity be saved from hunger, fear, its own suicidal tendencies? Is it possible to create a new culture of sanity and enlightenment? An eminently practical book which addresses these questions, offering not only ideas, but definitive means to disentangle our priorities and redirect our focus to the "bottom-line" of spiritual life.

Paper, 64 pages, $5.95   ISBN:0-934252-05-X

• • •

THE YOGA OF ENLIGHTENMENT/ THE BOOK OF UNENLIGHTENMENT
by Lee Lozowick

Enlightenment, contrary to popular misconceptions, is much more than the experience of the "heaven-realm" of bliss and light. To fully grasp the reality of enlightenment is only possible when one is willing to embrace the other side—the not-knowing, the ignorance, and the darkness. The balance and interdependence of paradoxes is the basis of this book.

Paper, 240 pages, $9.95   ISBN: 0-934252-06-8

• • •

AS IT IS
A Year on the Road with a Tantric Teacher
by M. Young

A first-hand account of a one-year journey around the world in the company of a *tantric* teacher. This book catalogues the trials and wonders of day-to-day interactions between a teacher and his students, and presents a broad range of his teachings given in seminars from San Francisco, California to Rishikesh, India. *As It Is* considers the core principles of *tantra*, including non-duality, compassion (the Bodhisattva ideal), service to others, and transformation within daily life. Written as a narrative, this captivating book will appeal to practitioners of *any* spiritual path. Readers interested in a life of clarity, genuine creativity, wisdom and harmony will find this an invaluable resource.

Paper, 840 pages, 24 b&w photos, $29.95   ISBN: 0-934252-99-8

**TO ORDER PLEASE SEE ACCOMPANYING ORDER FORM
OR CALL 1-800-381-2700 TO PLACE YOUR ORDER NOW.**

ADDITIONAL TITLES FROM HOHM PRESS

THE SHADOW ON THE PATH
Clearing the Psychological Blocks to Spiritual Development
by VJ Fedorschak
Foreword by Claudio Naranjo, M.D.

Tracing the development of the human psychological shadow from Freud to the present, this readable analysis presents five contemporary approaches to spiritual psychotherapy for those who find themselves needing help on the spiritual path. Offers insight into the phenomenon of denial and projection. Topics include: the shadow in the work notable therapists; the principles of inner spiritual development in the major world religions; examples of the disowned shadow in contemporary religious movements; and case studies of clients in spiritual groups who have worked with their shadow issues.

Paper, 304 pages, $16.95   ISBN: 0-934252-81-5

• • •

HALFWAY UP THE MOUNTAIN
The Error of Premature Claims to Enlightenment
by Mariana Caplan
Foreword by Fleet Maull

Dozens of first-hand interviews with students, respected spiritual teachers and masters, together with broad research are synthesized here to assist readers in avoiding the pitfalls of the spiritual path. Topics include: mistaking mystical experience for enlightenment; ego inflation, power and corruption among spiritual leaders; the question of the need for a teacher; disillusionment on the path . . . and much more. "Caplan's illuminating book . . . urges seekers to pay the price of traveling the hard road to true enlightenment." —Publisher's Weekly

Paper, 600 pages, $21.95   ISBN: 0-934252-91-2

• • •

THE JUMP INTO LIFE: *Moving Beyond Fear*
by Arnaud Desjardins
Foreword by Richard Moss, M.D.

"Say Yes to life," the author continually invites in this welcome guidebook to the spiritual path. For anyone who has ever felt oppressed by the life-negative seriousness of religion, this book is a timely antidote. In language that translates the complex to the obvious, Desjardins applies his simple teaching of happiness and gratitude to a broad range of weighty topics, including sexuality and intimate relationships, structuring an "inner life," the relief of suffering, and overcoming fear.

Paper, 216 pages, $12.95   ISBN: 0-934252-42-4

**TO ORDER PLEASE SEE ACCOMPANYING ORDER FORM
OR CALL 1-800-381-2700 TO PLACE YOUR ORDER NOW.**

ADDITIONAL TITLES FROM HOHM PRESS

WESTERN SADHUS AND SANNYASINS IN INDIA
by Marcus Allsop

This book contains interviews and stories about a unique group of Westerners who have lived in India for twenty years or more. Now known as *sadhus* and *sannyasins* (traditional Indian holy men or women), they have renounced the materialistic values of their native culture in favor of a life of austerity and spiritual practice. Their exact numbers are unknown—since many of them have chosen a life of anonymity. Marcus Allsop's pilgrimage takes him from Mt. Arunachala in southern India to the source of the Ganges in the foothills of the Himalayas. He stops at age-old shrines and majestic temples, and shares the powerful insights into Indian spiritual culture that he gains along the way.
Paper, 232 pages, 24 photographs, $14.95

ISBN: 0-934252-50-5

• • •

FACETS OF THE DIAMOND: THE WISDOM OF INDIA
by James Capellini

Anyone who has ever felt the pull of India's spiritual heritage will find a treasure in this book. Contains rare photographs, brief biographic sketches and evocative quotes from contemporary spiritual teachers representing India's varied spiritual paths—from pure Advaita Vedanta (non-dualism) to the Hindu Vaisnava (Bhakti) devotional tradition. Highlights such well-known sages as Ramana Maharshi, Nityananda, and Shirdi Sai Baba as well as many renowned saints who are previously unknown in the West.

Text in three languages—English, French and German
Cloth, 224 pages, $39.95, 42 b&w photographs

ISBN: 0-934252-53-X

• • •

THE YOGA TRADITION: *Its History, Literature, Philosophy and Practice*
by Georg Feuerstein, Ph.D.
Foreword by Ken Wilber

A complete overview of the great Yogic traditions of: Raja-Yoga, Hatha-Yoga, Jnana-Yoga, Bhakti-Yoga, Karma-Yoga, Tantra-Yoga, Kundalini-Yoga, Mantra-Yoga and many other lesser known forms. Includes translations of over twenty famous Yoga treatises, like the *Yoga-Sutra* of Patanjali, and a first-time translation of the *Goraksha Paddhati*, an ancient Hatha Yoga text. Covers all aspects of Hindu, Buddhist, Jaina and Sikh Yoga. A necessary resource for all students and scholars of Yoga.
"Without a doubt the finest overall explanation of Yoga. Destined to become a classic." – Ken Wilber

Paper, 708 pages, Over 200 illustrations, $39.95
Cloth, $49.95

ISBN: 0-934252-83-1
ISBN: 0-934252-88-2

TO ORDER PLEASE SEE ACCOMPANYING ORDER FORM
OR CALL 1-800-381-2700 TO PLACE YOUR ORDER NOW.

ADDITIONAL TITLES FROM HOHM PRESS

THE PERFECTION OF NOTHING
Reflections on Spiritual Practice
by Rick Lewis

With remarkable clarity, reminiscent of the early writing of J. Krishnamurti or Alan Watts, Rick Lewis weaves practical considerations about spiritual life with profound mystical understanding. Whether describing the "illusion of unworthiness" that most of us suffer, the challenges of spiritual practice, or his own awe in discovering the majesty of the present moment, this book is full of laser-sharp analogies that make complex philosophical/religious ideas attractive and easy to understand. His nonsectarian approach will be appreciated by seekers and practitioners of any religious tradition—whether they are actively engaged in spiritual work, or approaching it for the first time. His words provide guidance and inspiration for revealing the spiritual in everyday life.

Paper, 180 pages, $14.95   ISBN: 1-890772-02-X

SELECTED MUSIC — *liars, gods and beggars* and *Shri*

STEAVIE BEAVER
liars, gods and beggars

An eclectic combination of hard rockin' and soulful songs from the founding fathers of Western Baul rock music. A must listen for fans and rock connoisseurs alike.   CD, $15.00

• • •

TRANSFESTITE
liars, gods and beggars

Another ecstatic banquet of rock, blues and country sounds. Their last recorded album together, *Transfestite* is a well-crafted farewell from an inspired and prolific band.   CD, $15.00

• • •

HOOKED
Shri

Their most jazzy effort. Features a moving rending of "Can't Find My Way Home," which was selected to appear with Eric Clapton and many others on a blues compilation CD in Europe.   CD, $15.00

• • •

SEE SHRI PLAY THE BLUES
Shri

A double CD set packed with 17 originals and covers from B.B. King, Jimi Hendrix and a host of others. This album gave rise to Shri's reputation as a *blues sensation*.   Two CD set, $27.50

TO ORDER PLEASE SEE ACCOMPANYING ORDER FORM
OR CALL 1-800-381-2700 TO PLACE YOUR ORDER NOW.

RETAIL ORDER FORM FOR HOHM PRESS BOOKS

Name _____ Phone (   ) _____

Street Address or P.O. Box _____

City _____ State _____ Zip Code _____

	QTY	TITLE	ITEM PRICE	TOTAL PRICE
1		ACTING GOD	$5.95	
2		THE ALCHEMY OF LOVE AND SEX	$16.95	
3		THE ALCHEMY OF TRANSFORMATION	$14.95	
4		AS IT IS	$29.95	
5		CHEATING BUDDHA	$7.95	
6		CONSCIOUS PARENTING	$17.95	
7		DERISIVE LAUGHTER FROM A BAD POET	$8.95	
8		FACETS OF THE DIAMOND	$39.95	
9		HALFWAY UP THE MOUNTAIN	$21.95	
10		HOOKED — CD	$15.00	
11		IN THE FIRE	$9.95	
12		THE JUMP INTO LIFE	$12.95	
13		LAUGHTER OF THE STONES	$9.95	
14		LIVING GOD BLUES	$9.95	
15		THE ONLY GRACE IS LOVING GOD	$5.95	
16		THE PERFECTION OF NOTHING	$14.95	
17		SEE SHRI PLAY THE BLUES — TWO CD SET	$27.50	
18		THE SHADOW ON THE PATH	$16.95	
19		STEAVIE BEAVER — CD	$15.00	
20		TOWARD THE FULLNESS OF LIFE	$12.95	
21		TRANSFESTITE — CD	$15.00	
22		WESTERN SADHUS AND SANNYASINS IN INDIA	$14.95	
23		YOGA OF ENLIGHTENMENT/BOOK OF UNENLIGHTENMENT	$9.95	
24		THE YOGA TRADITION — Paper	$39.95	
25		THE YOGA TRADITION — Cloth	$49.95	

SURFACE SHIPPING CHARGES
1st book $4.00
Each additional item $1.00

SUBTOTAL:
SHIPPING: (see below)
TOTAL:

SHIP MY ORDER

☐ Surface U.S. Mail—Priority   ☐ UPS (Mail + $2.00)
☐ 2nd-Day Air (Mail + $5.00)   ☐ Next-Day Air (Mail + $15.00)

METHOD OF PAYMENT:

☐ Check or M.O. Payable to Hohm Press, P.O. Box 2501, Prescott, AZ 86302

☐ Call 1-800-381-2700 to place your credit card order

☐ Or call 1-520-717-1779 to fax your credit card order

☐ Information for Visa/MasterCard/American Express order only:

Card #_____–_____–_____–_____ Expiration Date _____

Visit our Website to view our complete catalog: www.hohmpress.com
ORDER NOW! Call 1-800-381-2700 or fax your order to 1-520-717-1779.
(Remember to include your credit card information.)